STAR WARS

DROIDS & Ewoks

CREDITS

WRITERS
Dave Manak & George Caragonne

PENCILERS
Warren Kremer, John Romita Sr., Mary Wilshire & Ernie Colón

INKERS
Marie Severin, Warren Kremer, Jon D'Agostino, Jacqueline Roettcher, Carlos Garzon, Al Williamson & Joe Sinnott

COLORISTS
Marie Severin & George Roussos

LETTERERS
Grace Kremer & Ed King

ASSISTANT EDITORS
Nancy Brown & Laura Hitchcock

EDITOR
Sid Jacobson

EXECUTIVE EDITOR
Tom DeFalco

COVER & VARIANT COVER COLORIST
Matt Milla

COLLECTION EDITOR: Mark D. Beazley
ASSOCIATE EDITOR: Sarah Brunstad • ASSOCIATE MANAGER, DIGITAL ASSETS: Joe Hochstein
ASSOCIATE MANAGING EDITOR: Alex Starbuck • EDITOR, SPECIAL PROJECTS: Jennifer Grünwald
RESEARCH: Mike Hansen • LAYOUT: Jeph York
VP, PRODUCTION & SPECIAL PROJECTS: Jeff Youngquist • PRODUCTION: ColorTek, Romie Jeffers, Joe Frontirre & Ryan Devall
SVP PRINT, SALES & MARKETING: David Gabriel

EDITOR IN CHIEF: Axel Alonso • CHIEF CREATIVE OFFICER: Joe Quesada
PUBLISHER: Dan Buckley • EXECUTIVE PRODUCER: Alan Fine

Special Thanks to Frank Parisi & Lucasfilm, Bob Almond, Deidre Hansen, Daron Jensen, Rob Kirby, Mark Newbold & Rancho Obi Wan

STAR WARS: DROIDS & EWOKS OMNIBUS. Contains material originally published in magazine form as EWOKS #1-14, DROIDS #1-8 and EWOKS ANNUAL (UK) 1989. First printing 2016. ISBN# 978-1-302-90085-4. Published by MARVEL WORLDWIDE, INC., a subsidiary of MARVEL ENTERTAINMENT, LLC. OFFICE OF PUBLICATION: 135 West 50th Street, New York, NY 10020. STAR WARS and related text and illustrations are trademarks and/or copyrights, in the United States and other countries, of Lucasfilm Ltd. and/or its affiliates. © & TM Lucasfilm Ltd. No similarity between any of the names, characters, persons, and/or institutions in this magazine with those of any living or dead person or institution is intended, and any such similarity which may exist is purely coincidental. Marvel and its logos are TM Marvel Characters, Inc. **Printed in China.** ALAN FINE, President, Marvel Entertainment; DAN BUCKLEY, President, TV, Publishing and Brand Management; JOE QUESADA, Chief Creative Officer; TOM BREVOORT, SVP of Publishing; DAVID BOGART, SVP of Operations & Procurement, Publishing; C.B. CEBULSKI, VP of International Development & Brand Management; DAVID GABRIEL, SVP Print, Sales & Marketing; JIM O'KEEFE, VP of Operations & Logistics; DAN CARR, Executive Director of Publishing Technology; SUSAN CRESPI, Editorial Operations Manager; ALEX MORALES, Publishing Operations Manager; STAN LEE, Chairman Emeritus. For information regarding advertising in Marvel Comics or on Marvel.com, please contact Jonathan Rheingold, VP of Custom Solutions & Ad Sales, at jrheingold@marvel.com. For Marvel subscription inquiries, please call 800-217-9158. **Manufactured between 1/29/2016 and 4/11/2016 by R.R. DONNELLEY ASIA PRINTING SOLUTIONS, CHINA.**

10 9 8 7 6 5 4 3 2 1

CONTENTS

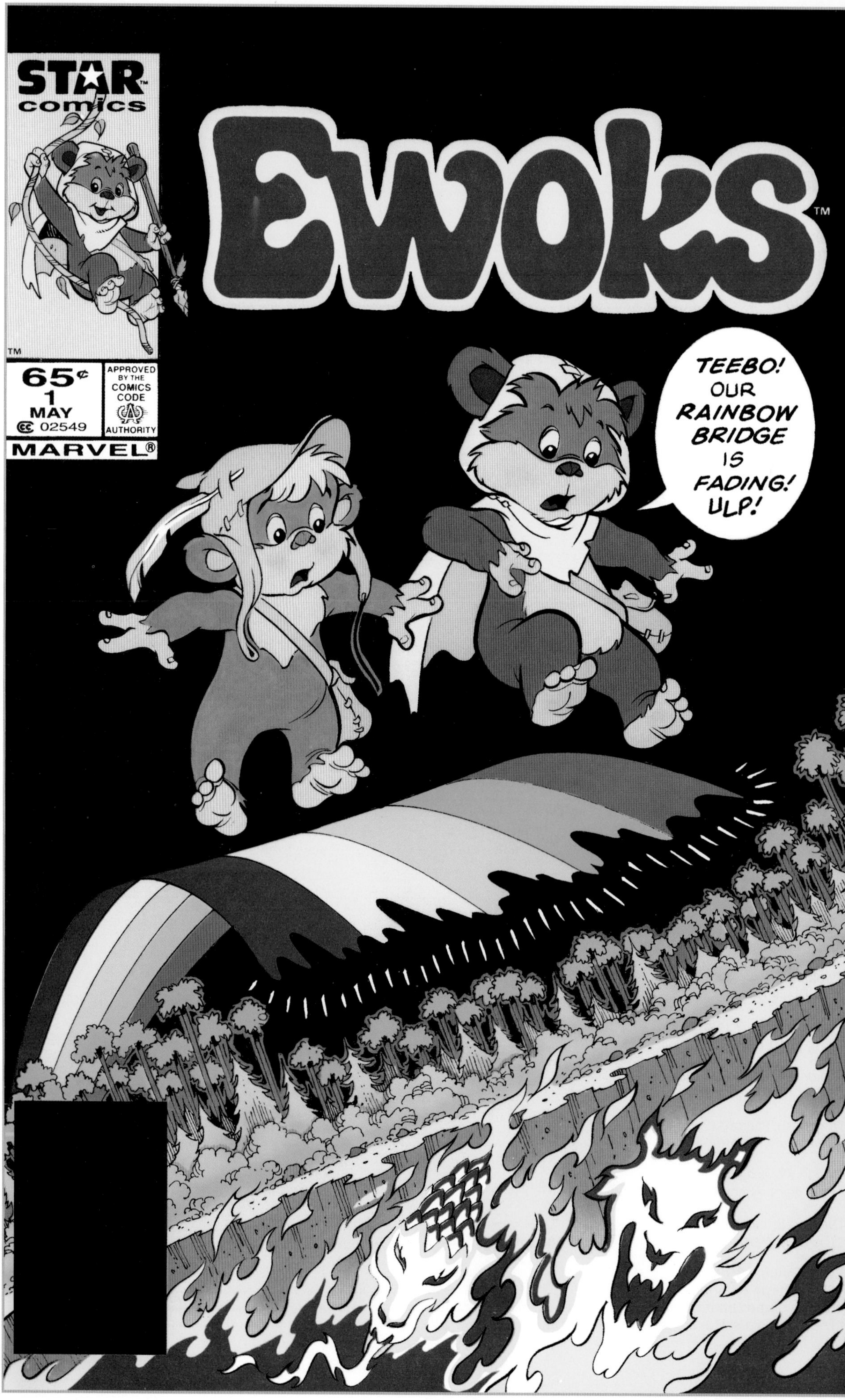
STAR comics
EWOKS™
65¢
1
MAY
02549
APPROVED BY THE COMICS CODE AUTHORITY
MARVEL®
TEEBO! OUR RAINBOW BRIDGE IS FADING! ULP!

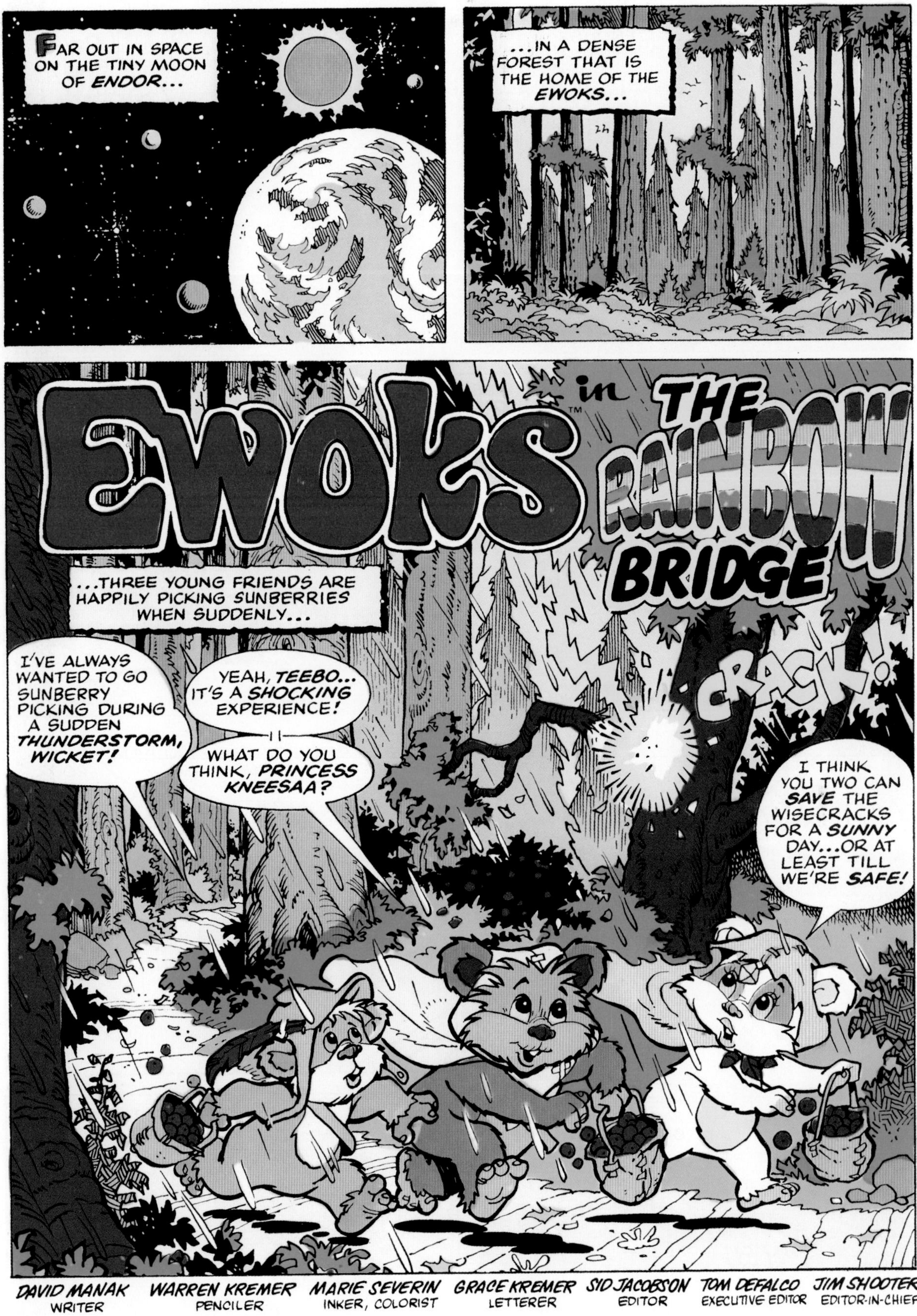
FAR OUT IN SPACE ON THE TINY MOON OF ENDOR...
...IN A DENSE FOREST THAT IS THE HOME OF THE EWOKS...
EWOKS™ in THE RAINBOW BRIDGE
...THREE YOUNG FRIENDS ARE HAPPILY PICKING SUNBERRIES WHEN SUDDENLY...
I'VE ALWAYS WANTED TO GO SUNBERRY PICKING DURING A SUDDEN THUNDERSTORM, WICKET!
YEAH, TEEBO... IT'S A SHOCKING EXPERIENCE!
WHAT DO YOU THINK, PRINCESS KNEESAA?
CRACK!
I THINK YOU TWO CAN SAVE THE WISECRACKS FOR A SUNNY DAY...OR AT LEAST TILL WE'RE SAFE!

DAVID MANAK, WRITER · WARREN KREMER, PENCILER · MARIE SEVERIN, INKER, COLORIST · GRACE KREMER, LETTERER · SID JACOBSON, EDITOR · TOM DEFALCO, EXECUTIVE EDITOR · JIM SHOOTER, EDITOR-IN-CHIEF

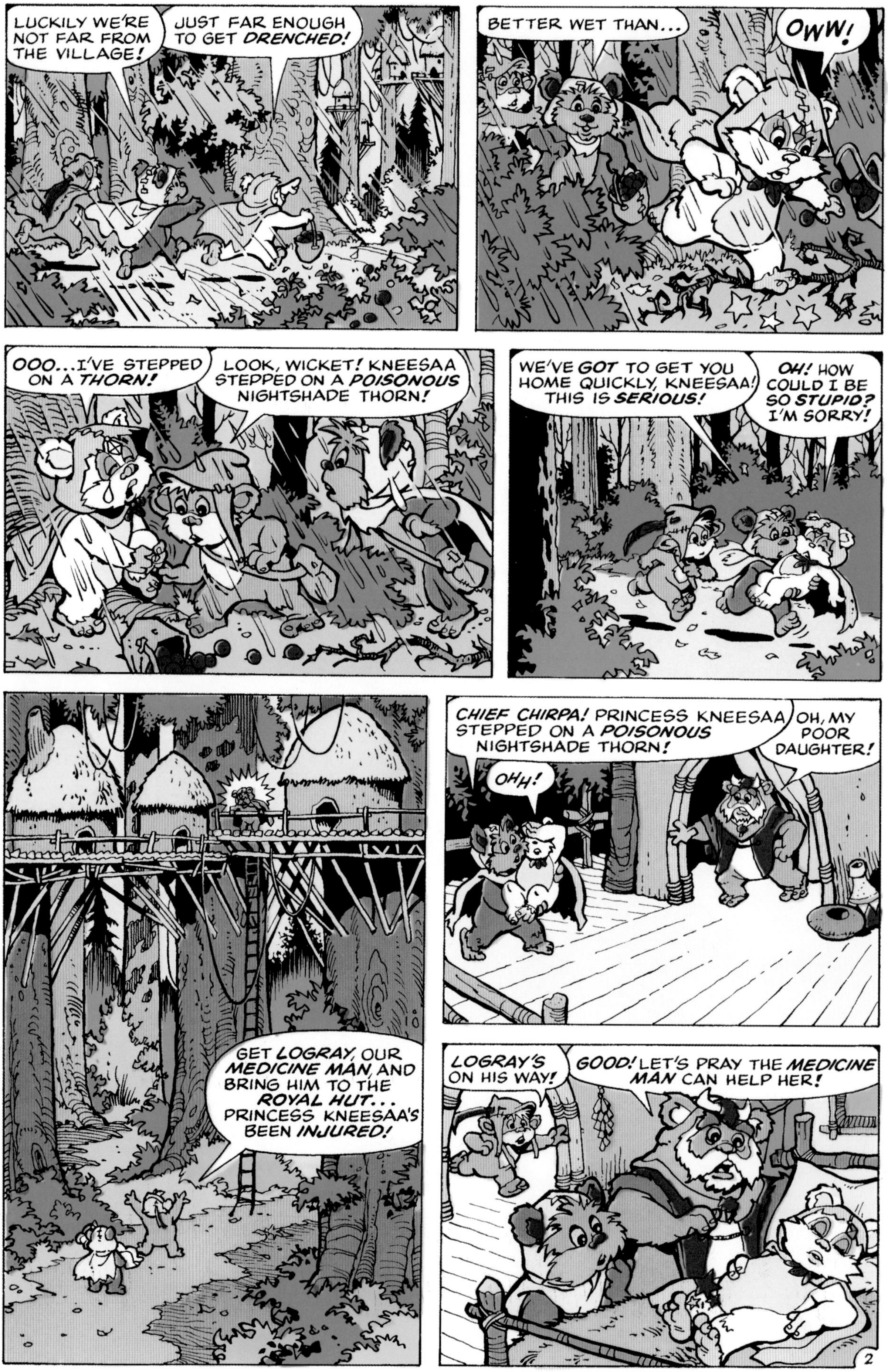
LUCKILY WE'RE NOT FAR FROM THE VILLAGE!
JUST FAR ENOUGH TO GET DRENCHED!
BETTER WET THAN...
OWW!
OOO...I'VE STEPPED ON A THORN!
LOOK, WICKET! KNEESAA STEPPED ON A POISONOUS NIGHTSHADE THORN!
WE'VE GOT TO GET YOU HOME QUICKLY, KNEESAA! THIS IS SERIOUS!
OH! HOW COULD I BE SO STUPID? I'M SORRY!
GET LOGRAY, OUR MEDICINE MAN, AND BRING HIM TO THE ROYAL HUT... PRINCESS KNEESAA'S BEEN INJURED!
CHIEF CHIRPA! PRINCESS KNEESAA STEPPED ON A POISONOUS NIGHTSHADE THORN!
OH, MY POOR DAUGHTER!
OHH!
LOGRAY'S ON HIS WAY!
GOOD! LET'S PRAY THE MEDICINE MAN CAN HELP HER!
2

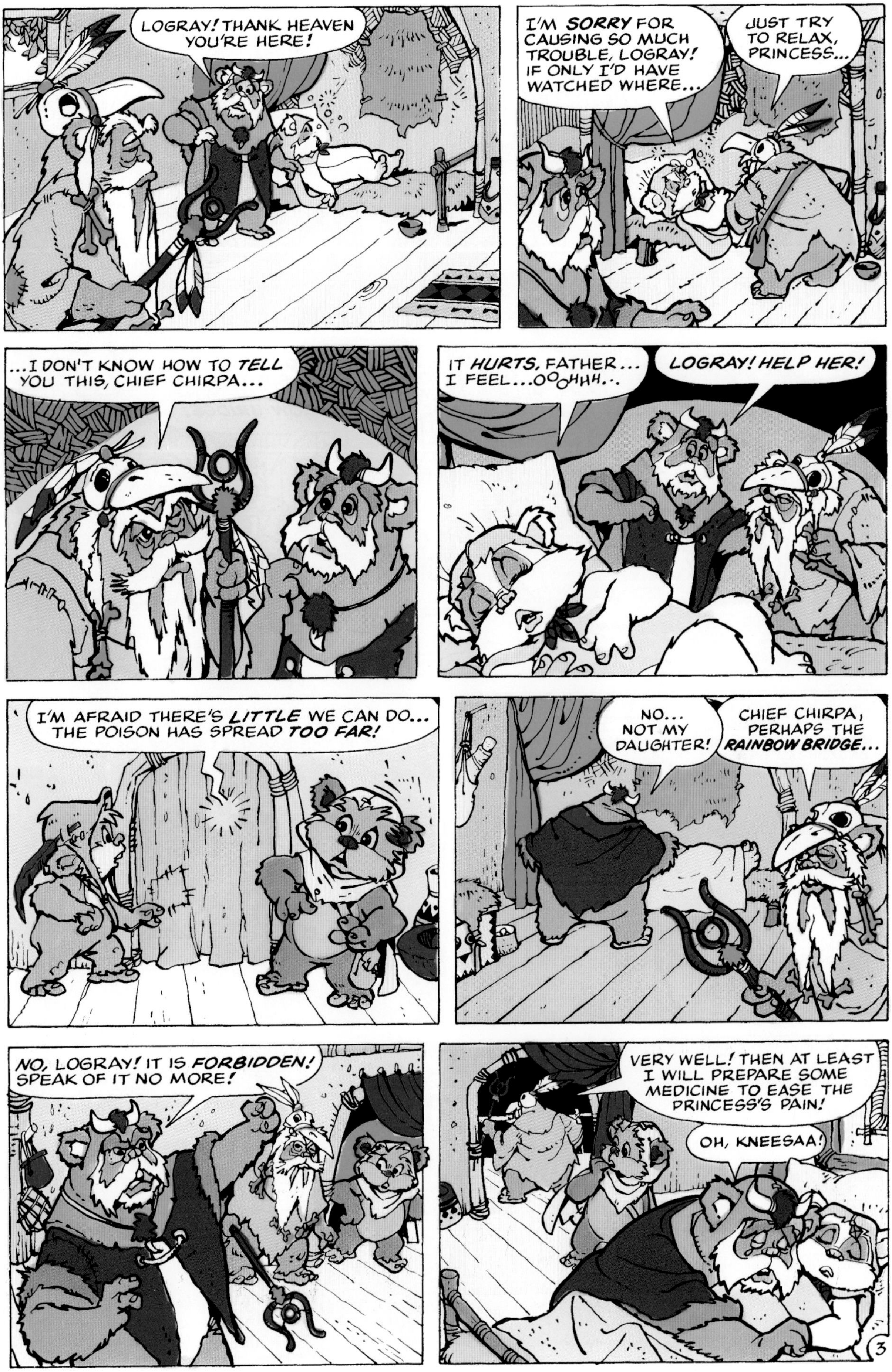
LOGRAY! THANK HEAVEN YOU'RE HERE!
I'M SORRY FOR CAUSING SO MUCH TROUBLE, LOGRAY! IF ONLY I'D HAVE WATCHED WHERE...
JUST TRY TO RELAX, PRINCESS...
...I DON'T KNOW HOW TO TELL YOU THIS, CHIEF CHIRPA...
IT HURTS, FATHER... I FEEL...OOOHHH...
LOGRAY! HELP HER!
I'M AFRAID THERE'S LITTLE WE CAN DO... THE POISON HAS SPREAD TOO FAR!
NO... NOT MY DAUGHTER!
CHIEF CHIRPA, PERHAPS THE RAINBOW BRIDGE...
NO, LOGRAY! IT IS FORBIDDEN! SPEAK OF IT NO MORE!
VERY WELL! THEN AT LEAST I WILL PREPARE SOME MEDICINE TO EASE THE PRINCESS'S PAIN!
OH, KNEESAA!
3

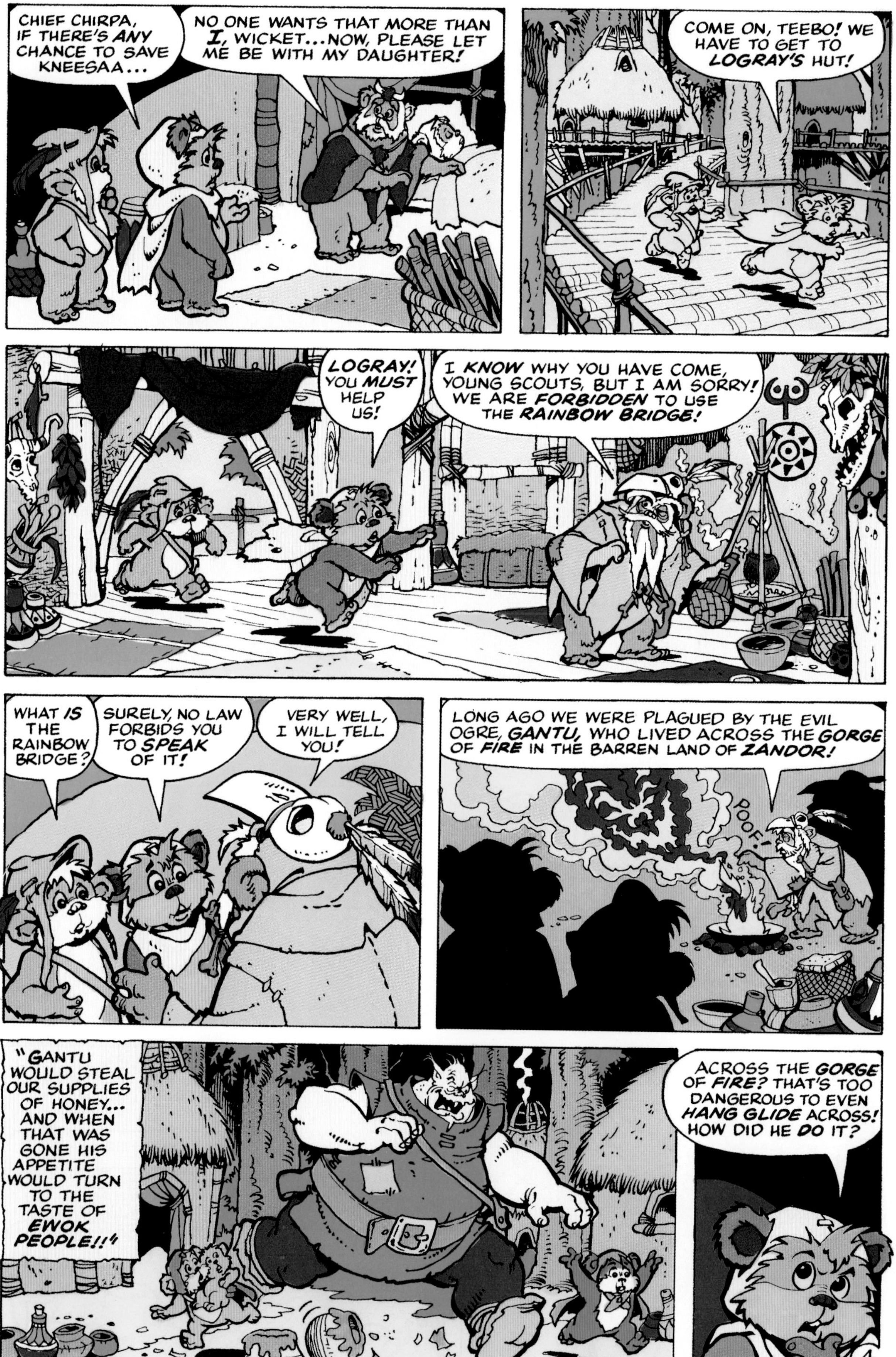
CHIEF CHIRPA, IF THERE'S ANY CHANCE TO SAVE KNEESAA...
NO ONE WANTS THAT MORE THAN I, WICKET... NOW, PLEASE LET ME BE WITH MY DAUGHTER!
COME ON, TEEBO! WE HAVE TO GET TO LOGRAY'S HUT!
LOGRAY! YOU MUST HELP US!
I KNOW WHY YOU HAVE COME, YOUNG SCOUTS, BUT I AM SORRY! WE ARE FORBIDDEN TO USE THE RAINBOW BRIDGE!
WHAT IS THE RAINBOW BRIDGE?
SURELY, NO LAW FORBIDS YOU TO SPEAK OF IT!
VERY WELL, I WILL TELL YOU!
LONG AGO WE WERE PLAGUED BY THE EVIL OGRE, GANTU, WHO LIVED ACROSS THE GORGE OF FIRE IN THE BARREN LAND OF ZANDOR!
POOF!
"GANTU WOULD STEAL OUR SUPPLIES OF HONEY... AND WHEN THAT WAS GONE HIS APPETITE WOULD TURN TO THE TASTE OF EWOK PEOPLE!!"
ACROSS THE GORGE OF FIRE? THAT'S TOO DANGEROUS TO EVEN HANG GLIDE ACROSS! HOW DID HE DO IT?
4

WITH A **CRYSTAL** THAT WHEN HELD TO THE SUN CREATED A WONDROUS **RAINBOW BRIDGE**... LASTING AS LONG AS THE SUN **SHONE** UPON IT!

"ONE DAY, YOUNG **CHIEF CHIRPA** FOLLOWED THE OGRE BACK TO HIS CAVE!

"AND WHILE THE OGRE SLEPT, CHIRPA **TOOK** THE CRYSTAL! BUT BEFORE HE LEFT, HE NOTICED A STRANGE **GLOWING LIQUID** THAT LIT UP THE CAVE LIKE A HANDFUL OF **STARS**!"

ZZZ...HUH?

"CHIRPA **ESCAPED** WITH THE CRYSTAL AND WITH A **JAR** OF THAT **GLOWING LIQUID**! AND GANTU VOWED TO **DESTROY** THE EWOKS IF EVER HE COULD CROSS THE GORGE AGAIN!"

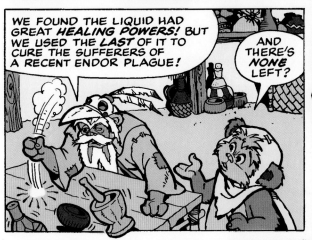

WE FOUND THE LIQUID HAD GREAT **HEALING POWERS**! BUT WE USED THE **LAST** OF IT TO CURE THE SUFFERERS OF A RECENT ENDOR PLAGUE!

AND THERE'S **NONE** LEFT?

I WILL SAY **NO** MORE! LEAVE THIS HUT AT ONCE!

COME, TEEBO, LET'S GO!

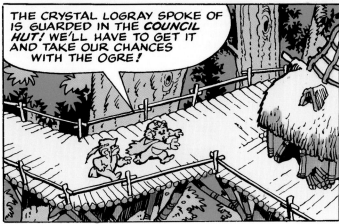

THE CRYSTAL LOGRAY SPOKE OF IS GUARDED IN THE **COUNCIL HUT**! WE'LL HAVE TO GET IT AND TAKE OUR CHANCES WITH THE OGRE!

GOOD LUCK, YOUNG SCOUTS!

5

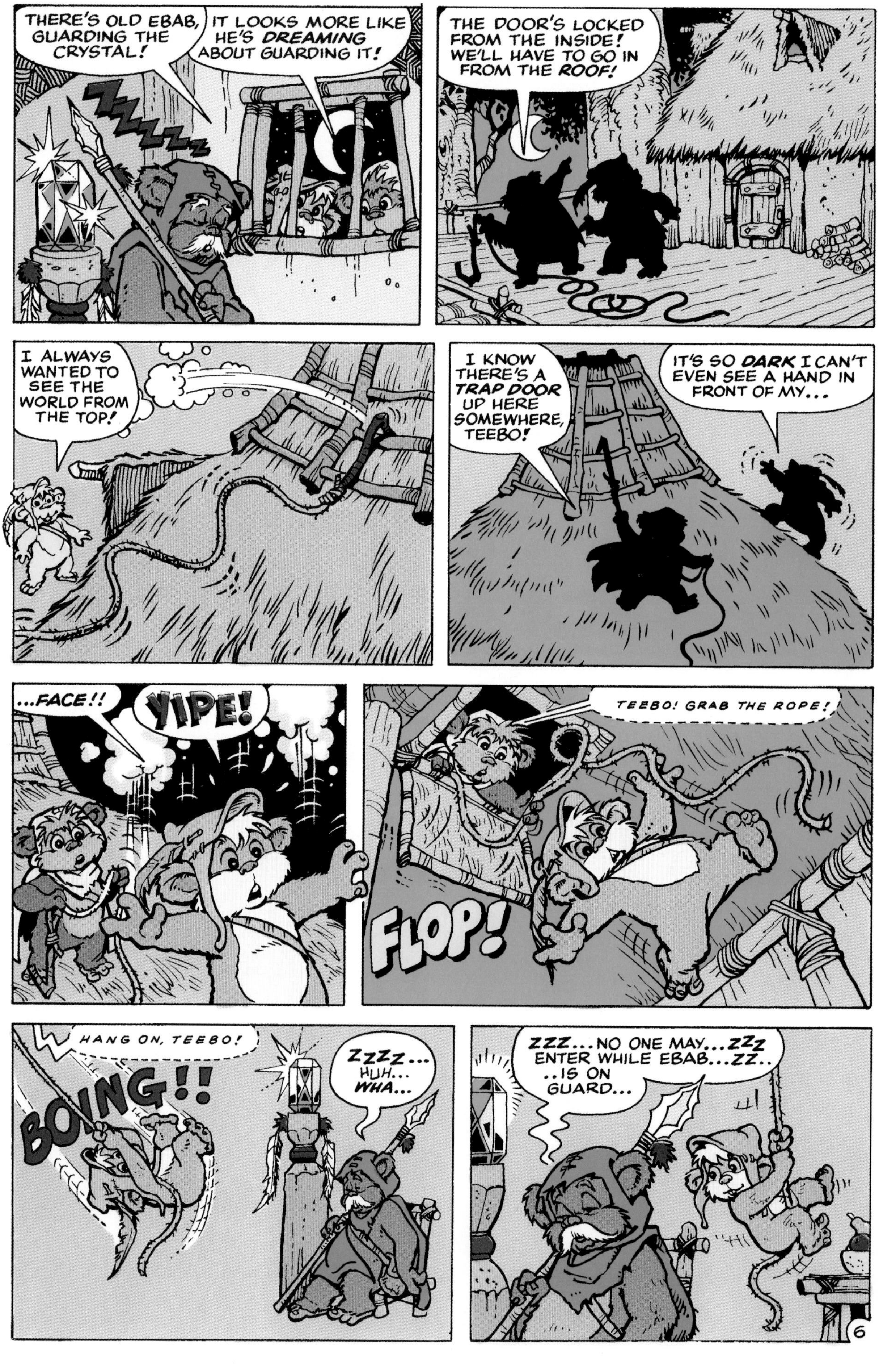
THERE'S OLD EBAB, GUARDING THE CRYSTAL!
IT LOOKS MORE LIKE HE'S DREAMING ABOUT GUARDING IT!
ZZZZZZ
THE DOOR'S LOCKED FROM THE INSIDE! WE'LL HAVE TO GO IN FROM THE ROOF!
I ALWAYS WANTED TO SEE THE WORLD FROM THE TOP!
I KNOW THERE'S A TRAP DOOR UP HERE SOMEWHERE, TEEBO!
IT'S SO DARK I CAN'T EVEN SEE A HAND IN FRONT OF MY...
...FACE!!
YIPE!
TEEBO! GRAB THE ROPE!
FLOP!
HANG ON, TEEBO!
BOING!!
ZzZz... HUH... WHA...
ZZZ...NO ONE MAY...ZZZ ENTER WHILE EBAB...ZZ.. ..IS ON GUARD...
6

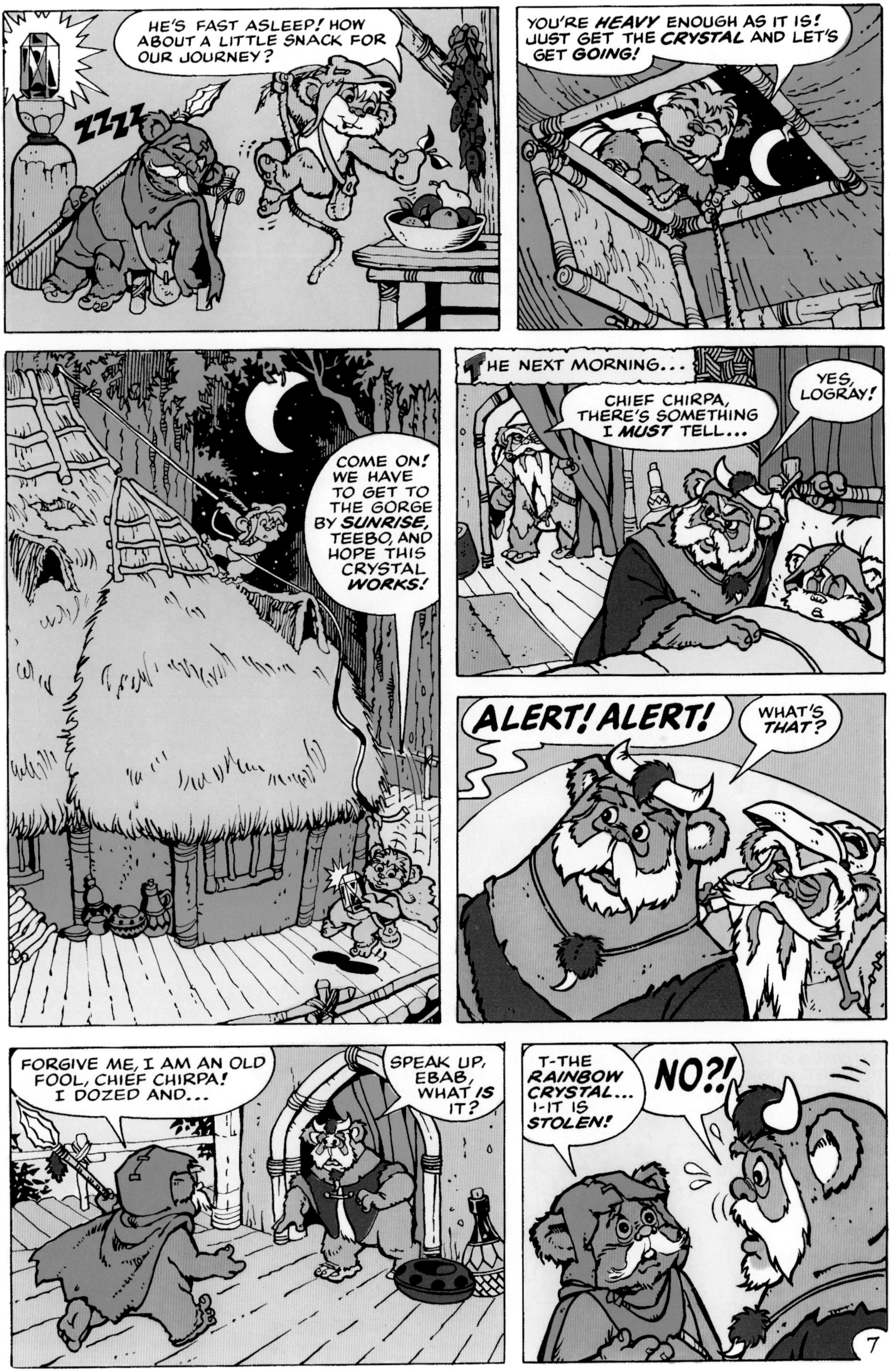
HE'S FAST ASLEEP! HOW ABOUT A LITTLE SNACK FOR OUR JOURNEY?
ZZZZ
YOU'RE HEAVY ENOUGH AS IT IS! JUST GET THE CRYSTAL AND LET'S GET GOING!
COME ON! WE HAVE TO GET TO THE GORGE BY SUNRISE, TEEBO, AND HOPE THIS CRYSTAL WORKS!
THE NEXT MORNING...
CHIEF CHIRPA, THERE'S SOMETHING I MUST TELL...
YES, LOGRAY!
ALERT! ALERT!
WHAT'S THAT?
FORGIVE ME, I AM AN OLD FOOL, CHIEF CHIRPA! I DOZED AND...
SPEAK UP, EBAB, WHAT IS IT?
T-THE RAINBOW CRYSTAL... I-IT IS STOLEN!
NO?!
7

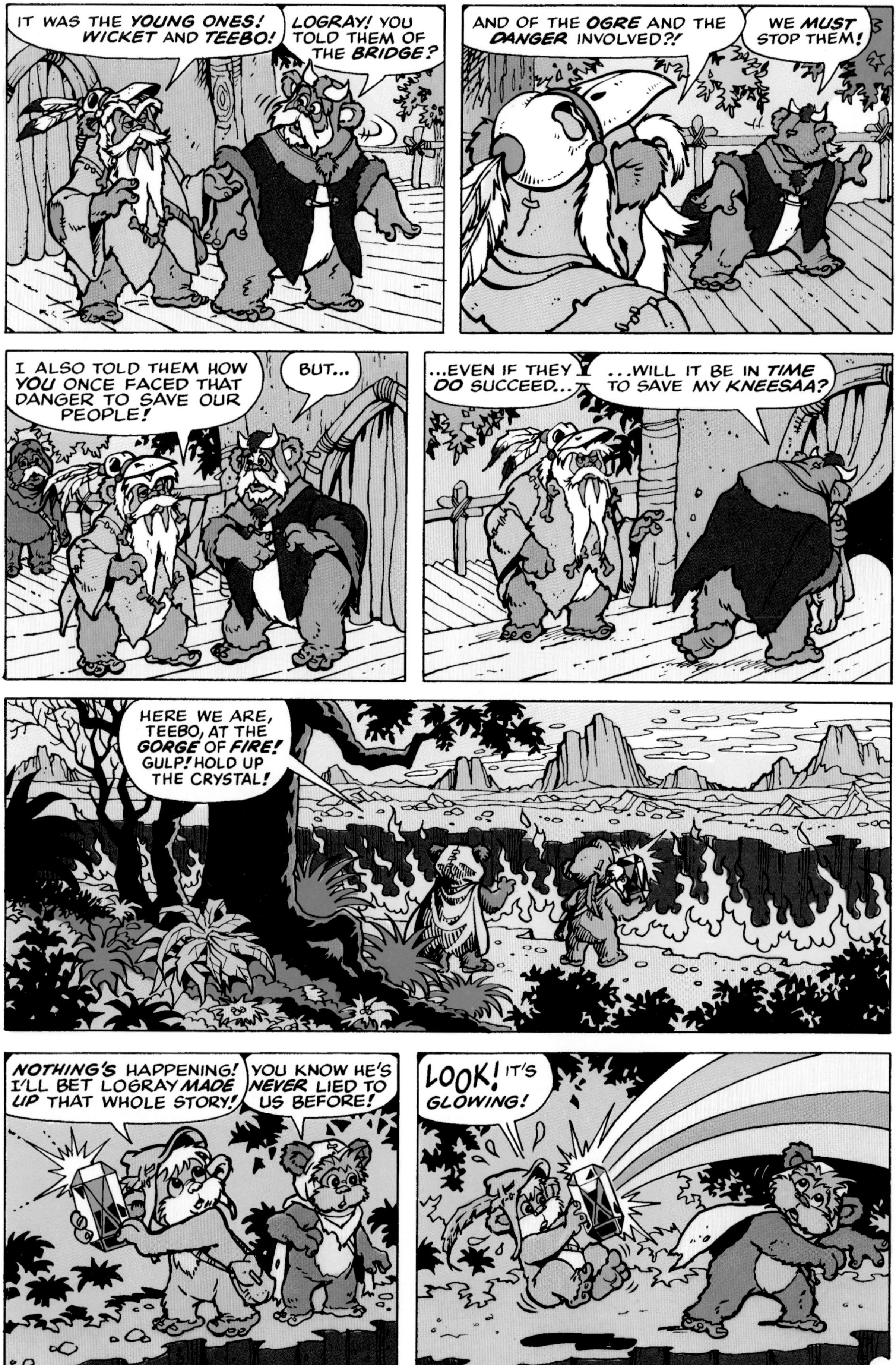
IT WAS THE YOUNG ONES! WICKET AND TEEBO!
LOGRAY! YOU TOLD THEM OF THE BRIDGE?
AND OF THE OGRE AND THE DANGER INVOLVED?!
WE MUST STOP THEM!
I ALSO TOLD THEM HOW YOU ONCE FACED THAT DANGER TO SAVE OUR PEOPLE!
BUT...
...EVEN IF THEY DO SUCCEED...
...WILL IT BE IN TIME TO SAVE MY KNEESAA?
HERE WE ARE, TEEBO, AT THE GORGE OF FIRE! GULP! HOLD UP THE CRYSTAL!
NOTHING'S HAPPENING! I'LL BET LOGRAY MADE UP THAT WHOLE STORY!
YOU KNOW HE'S NEVER LIED TO US BEFORE!
LOOK! IT'S GLOWING!

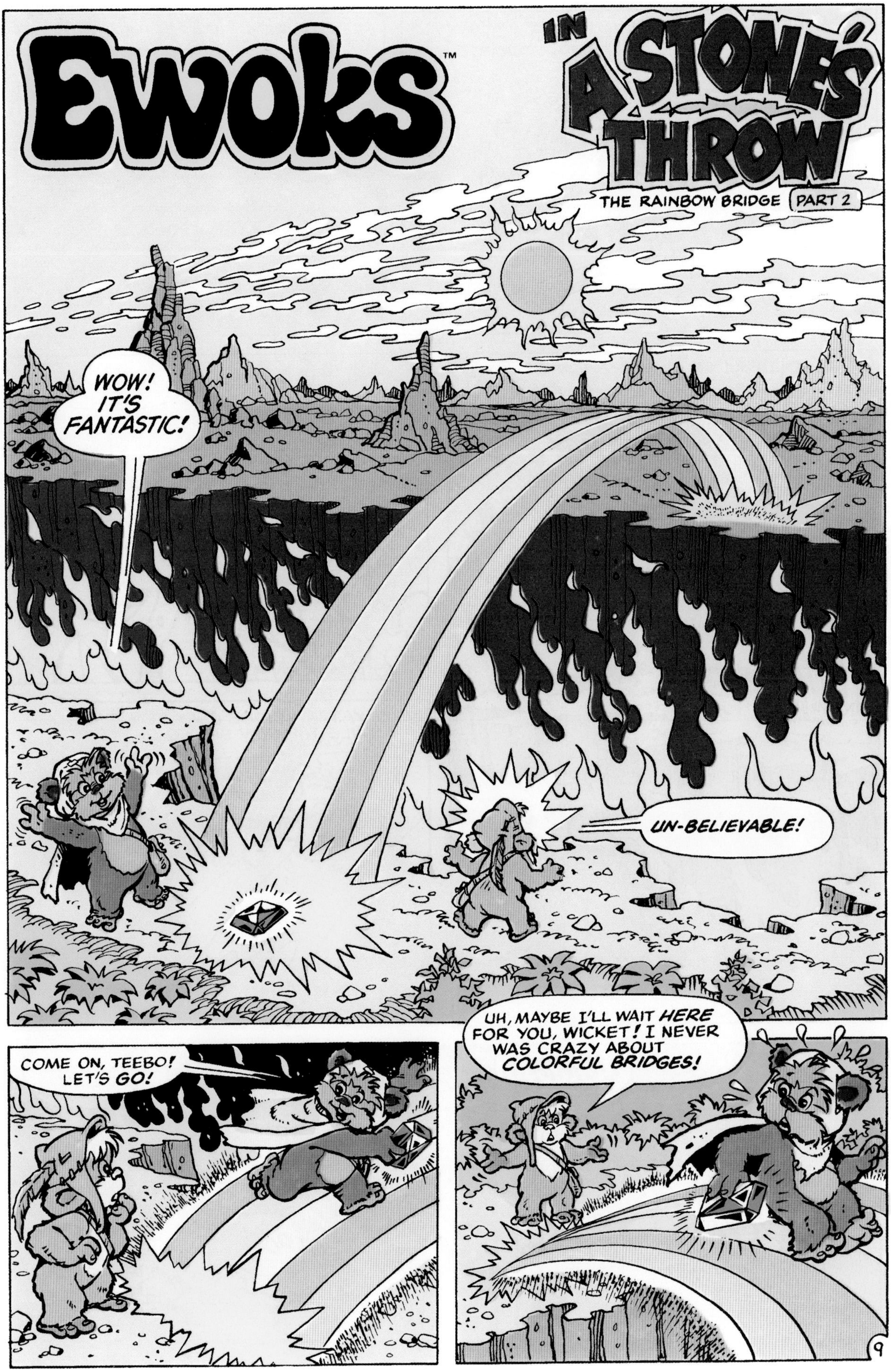
EWOKS™
IN
A STONE'S THROW
THE RAINBOW BRIDGE PART 2
WOW! IT'S FANTASTIC!
UN-BELIEVABLE!
COME ON, TEEBO! LET'S GO!
UH, MAYBE I'LL WAIT HERE FOR YOU, WICKET! I NEVER WAS CRAZY ABOUT COLORFUL BRIDGES!
9

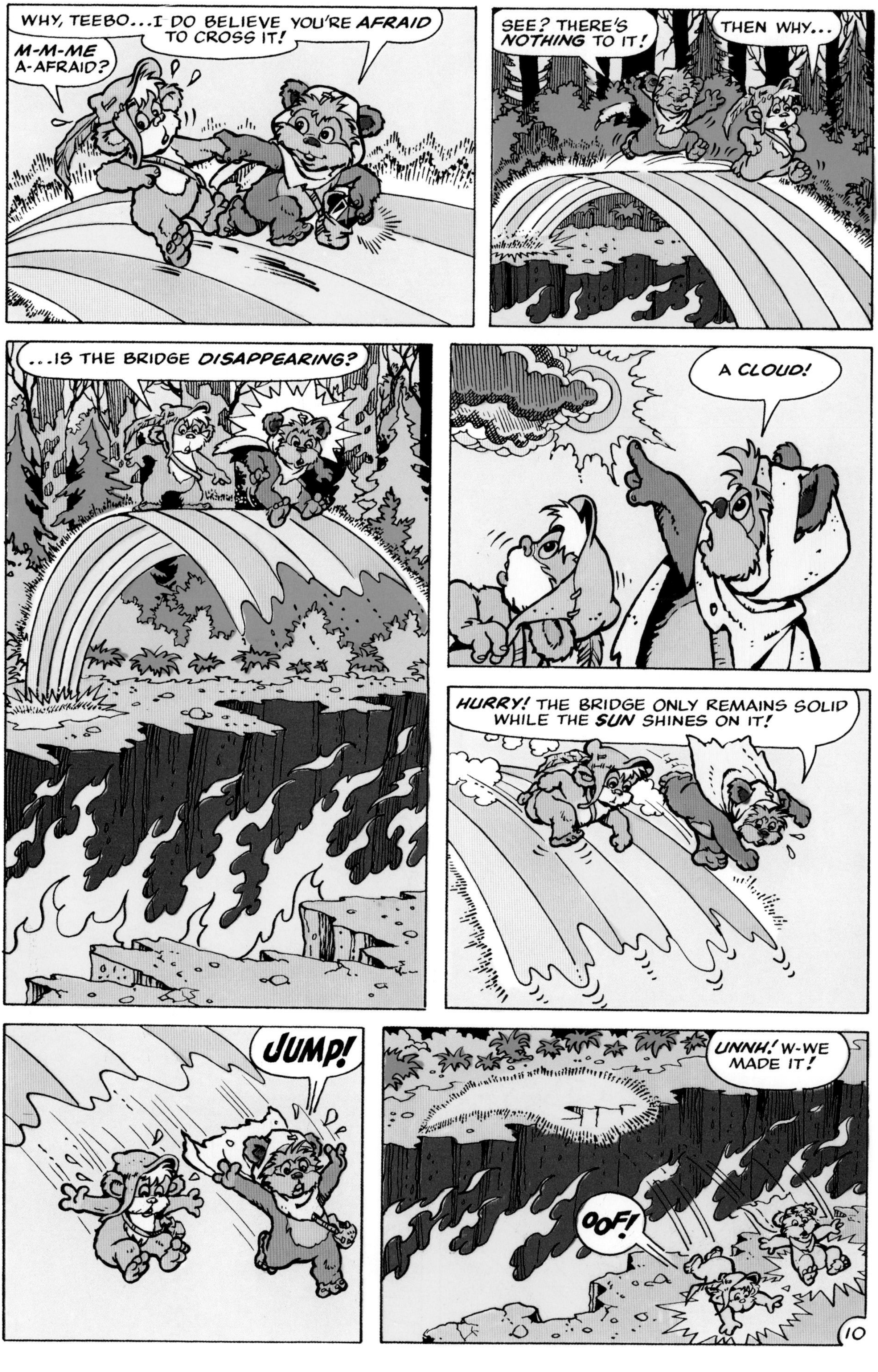
WHY, TEEBO...I DO BELIEVE YOU'RE AFRAID TO CROSS IT!
M-M-ME A-AFRAID?
SEE? THERE'S NOTHING TO IT!
THEN WHY...
...IS THE BRIDGE DISAPPEARING?
A CLOUD!
HURRY! THE BRIDGE ONLY REMAINS SOLID WHILE THE SUN SHINES ON IT!
JUMP!
UNNH! W-WE MADE IT!
OOF!
10

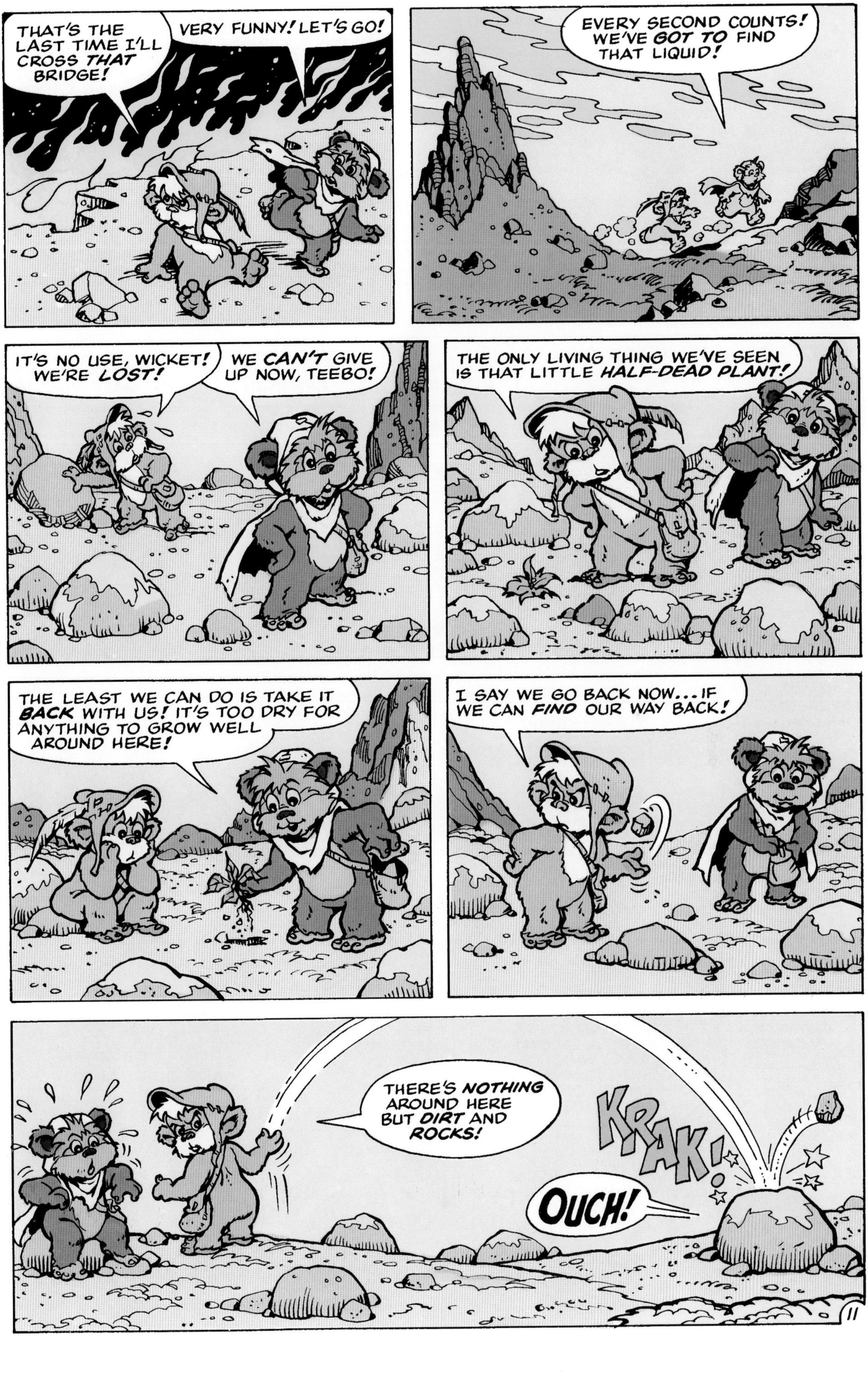
THAT'S THE LAST TIME I'LL CROSS *THAT* BRIDGE!
VERY FUNNY! LET'S GO!
EVERY SECOND COUNTS! WE'VE *GOT TO* FIND THAT LIQUID!
IT'S NO USE, WICKET! WE'RE *LOST!*
WE *CAN'T* GIVE UP NOW, TEEBO!
THE ONLY LIVING THING WE'VE SEEN IS THAT LITTLE *HALF-DEAD PLANT!*
THE LEAST WE CAN DO IS TAKE IT *BACK* WITH US! IT'S TOO DRY FOR ANYTHING TO GROW WELL AROUND HERE!
I SAY WE GO BACK NOW... IF WE CAN *FIND* OUR WAY BACK!
THERE'S *NOTHING* AROUND HERE BUT *DIRT* AND *ROCKS!*
KRAK!
OUCH!
11

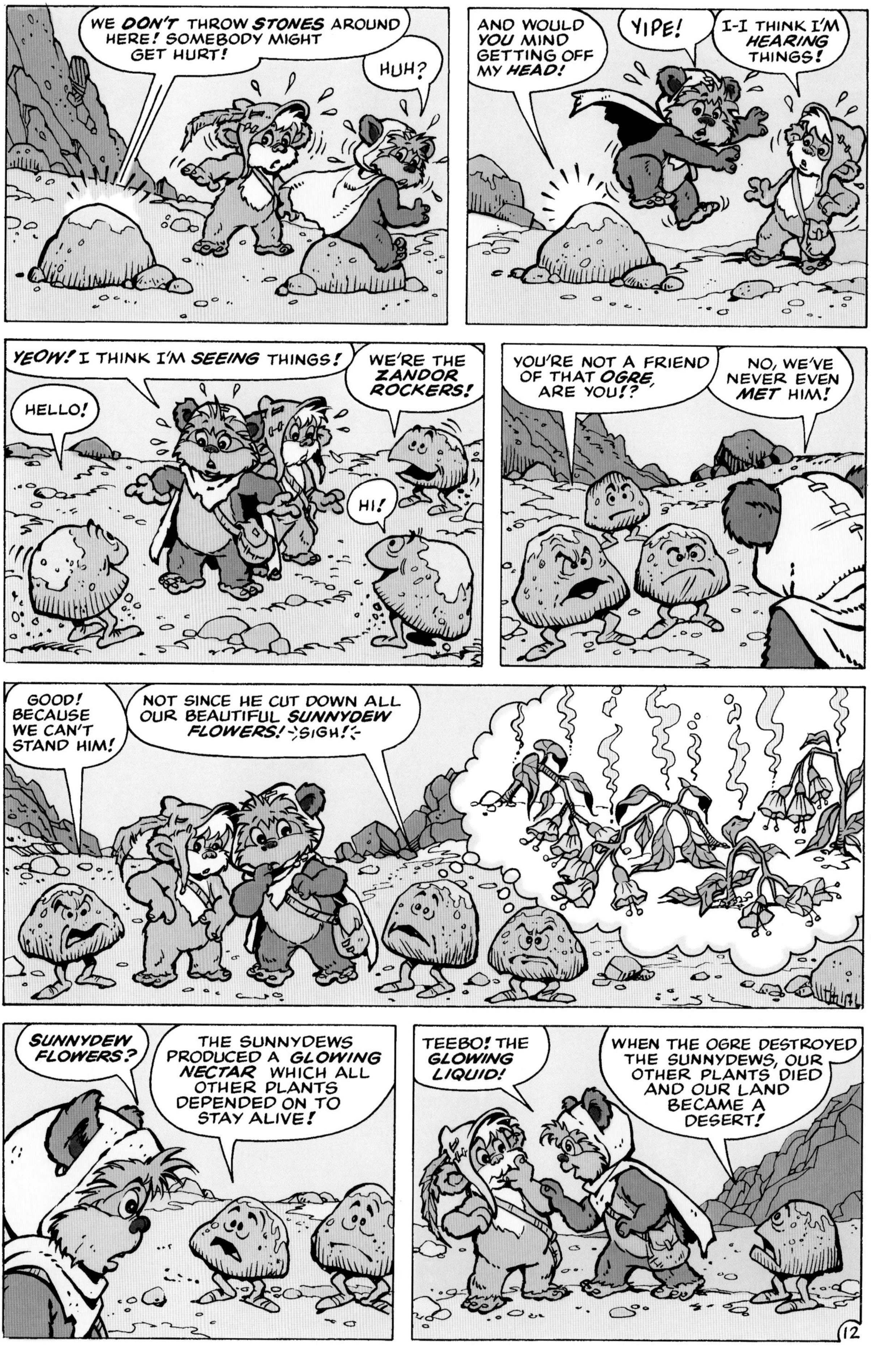
WE DON'T THROW STONES AROUND HERE! SOMEBODY MIGHT GET HURT!
HUH?
AND WOULD YOU MIND GETTING OFF MY HEAD!
YIPE!
I-I THINK I'M HEARING THINGS!
YEOW! I THINK I'M SEEING THINGS!
HELLO!
WE'RE THE ZANDOR ROCKERS!
HI!
YOU'RE NOT A FRIEND OF THAT OGRE, ARE YOU!?
NO, WE'VE NEVER EVEN MET HIM!
GOOD! BECAUSE WE CAN'T STAND HIM!
NOT SINCE HE CUT DOWN ALL OUR BEAUTIFUL SUNNYDEW FLOWERS! SIGH!
SUNNYDEW FLOWERS?
THE SUNNYDEWS PRODUCED A GLOWING NECTAR WHICH ALL OTHER PLANTS DEPENDED ON TO STAY ALIVE!
TEEBO! THE GLOWING LIQUID!
WHEN THE OGRE DESTROYED THE SUNNYDEWS, OUR OTHER PLANTS DIED AND OUR LAND BECAME A DESERT!
12

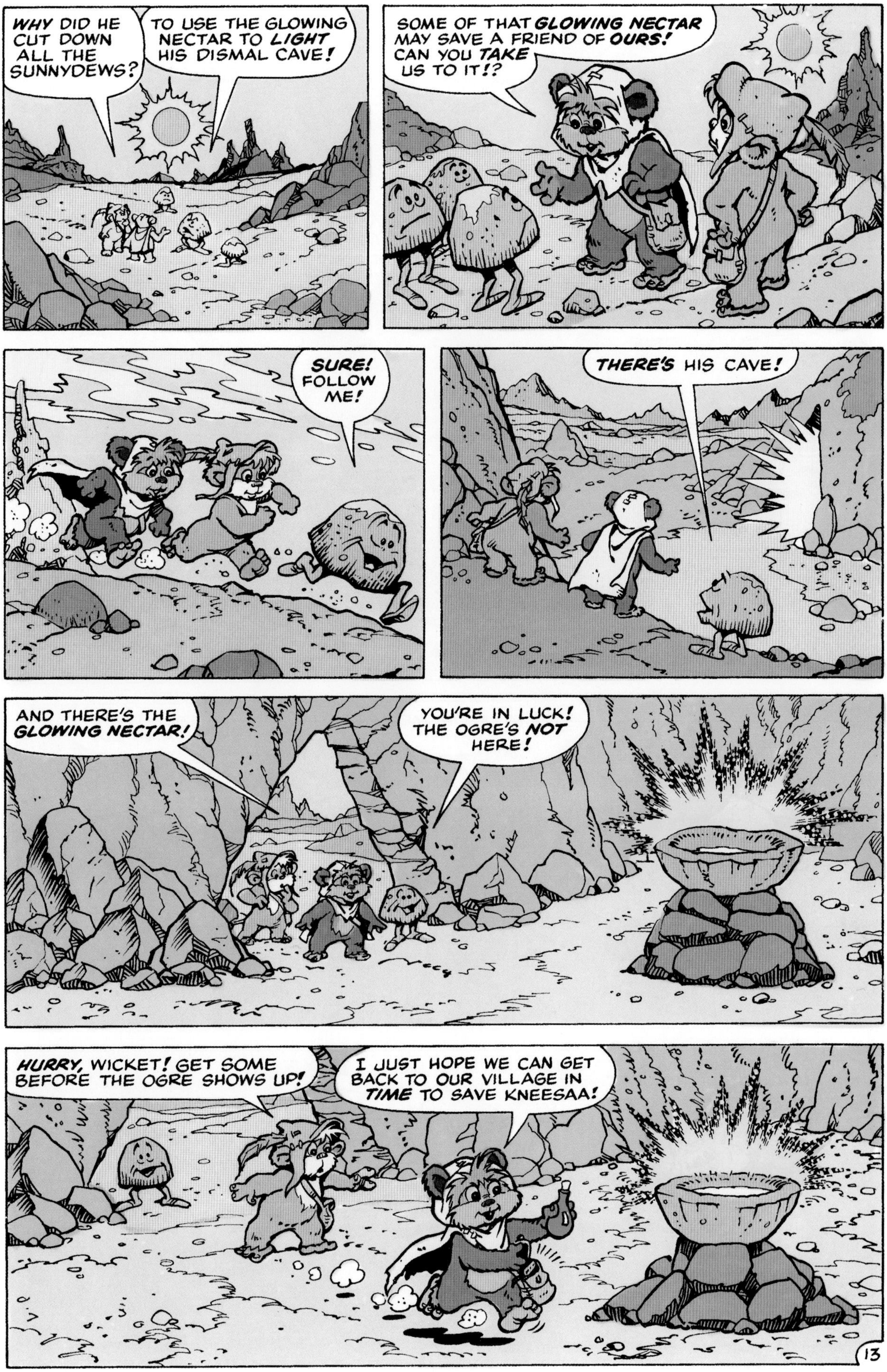
WHY DID HE CUT DOWN ALL THE SUNNYDEWS?
TO USE THE GLOWING NECTAR TO LIGHT HIS DISMAL CAVE!
SOME OF THAT GLOWING NECTAR MAY SAVE A FRIEND OF OURS! CAN YOU TAKE US TO IT!?
SURE! FOLLOW ME!
THERE'S HIS CAVE!
AND THERE'S THE GLOWING NECTAR!
YOU'RE IN LUCK! THE OGRE'S NOT HERE!
HURRY, WICKET! GET SOME BEFORE THE OGRE SHOWS UP!
I JUST HOPE WE CAN GET BACK TO OUR VILLAGE IN TIME TO SAVE KNEESAA!
13

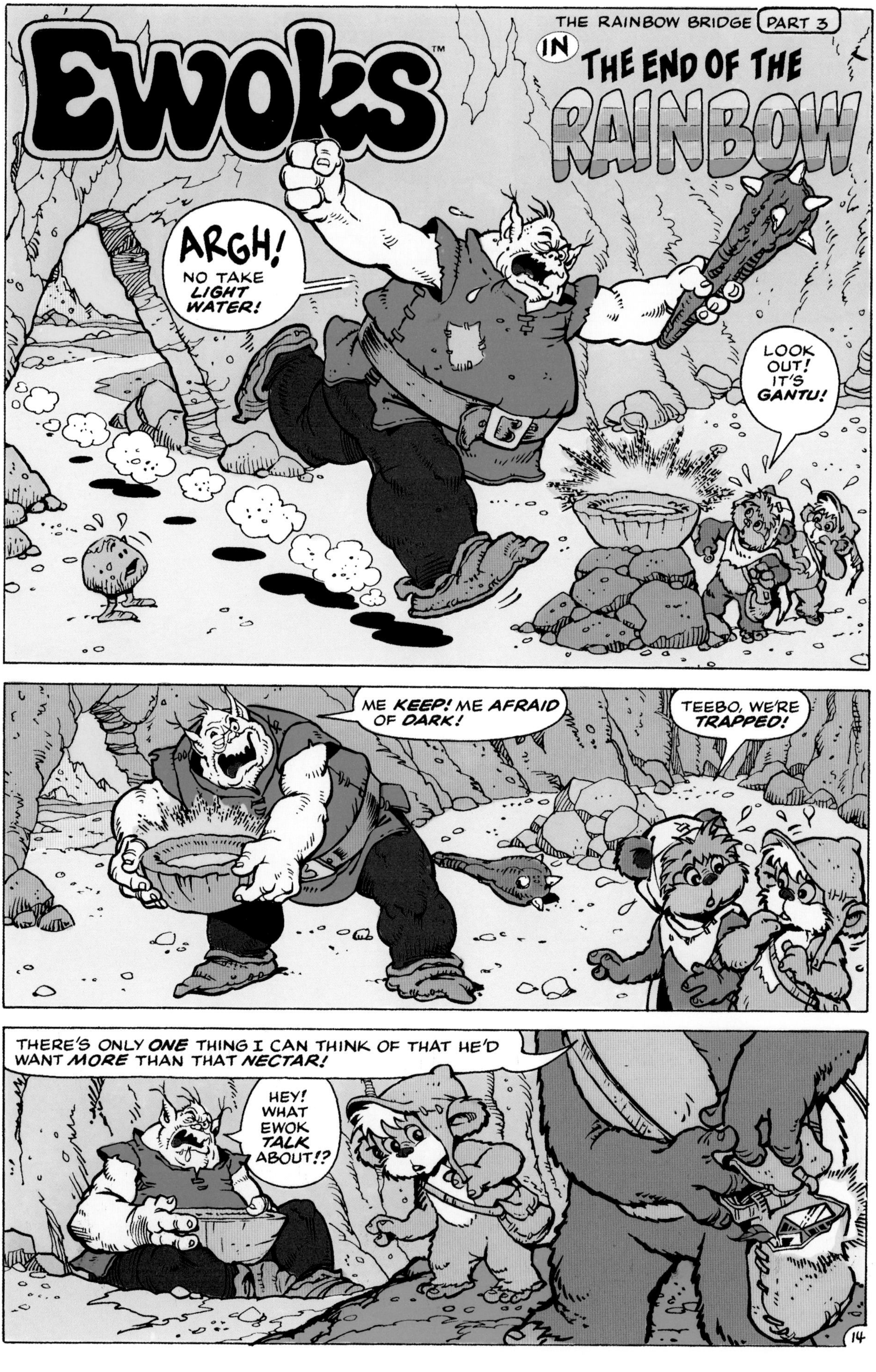
EWOKS™
THE RAINBOW BRIDGE PART 3
IN THE END OF THE RAINBOW
ARGH! NO TAKE LIGHT WATER!
LOOK OUT! IT'S GANTU!
ME KEEP! ME AFRAID OF DARK!
TEEBO, WE'RE TRAPPED!
THERE'S ONLY ONE THING I CAN THINK OF THAT HE'D WANT MORE THAN THAT NECTAR!
HEY! WHAT EWOK TALK ABOUT!?
14

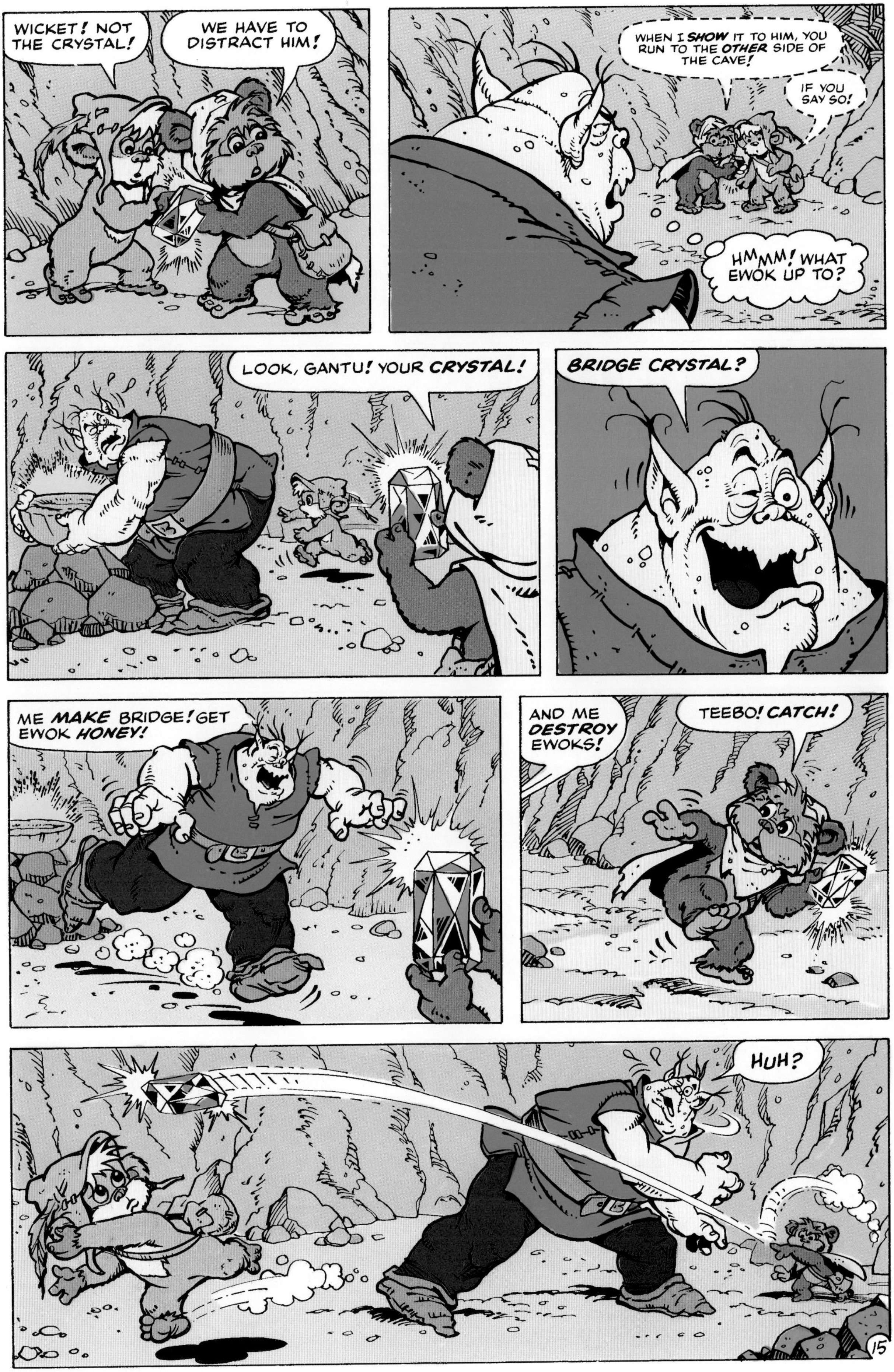
WICKET! NOT THE CRYSTAL!
WE HAVE TO DISTRACT HIM!
WHEN I SHOW IT TO HIM, YOU RUN TO THE OTHER SIDE OF THE CAVE!
IF YOU SAY SO!
HMMM! WHAT EWOK UP TO?
LOOK, GANTU! YOUR CRYSTAL!
BRIDGE CRYSTAL?
ME MAKE BRIDGE! GET EWOK HONEY!
AND ME DESTROY EWOKS!
TEEBO! CATCH!
HUH?
15

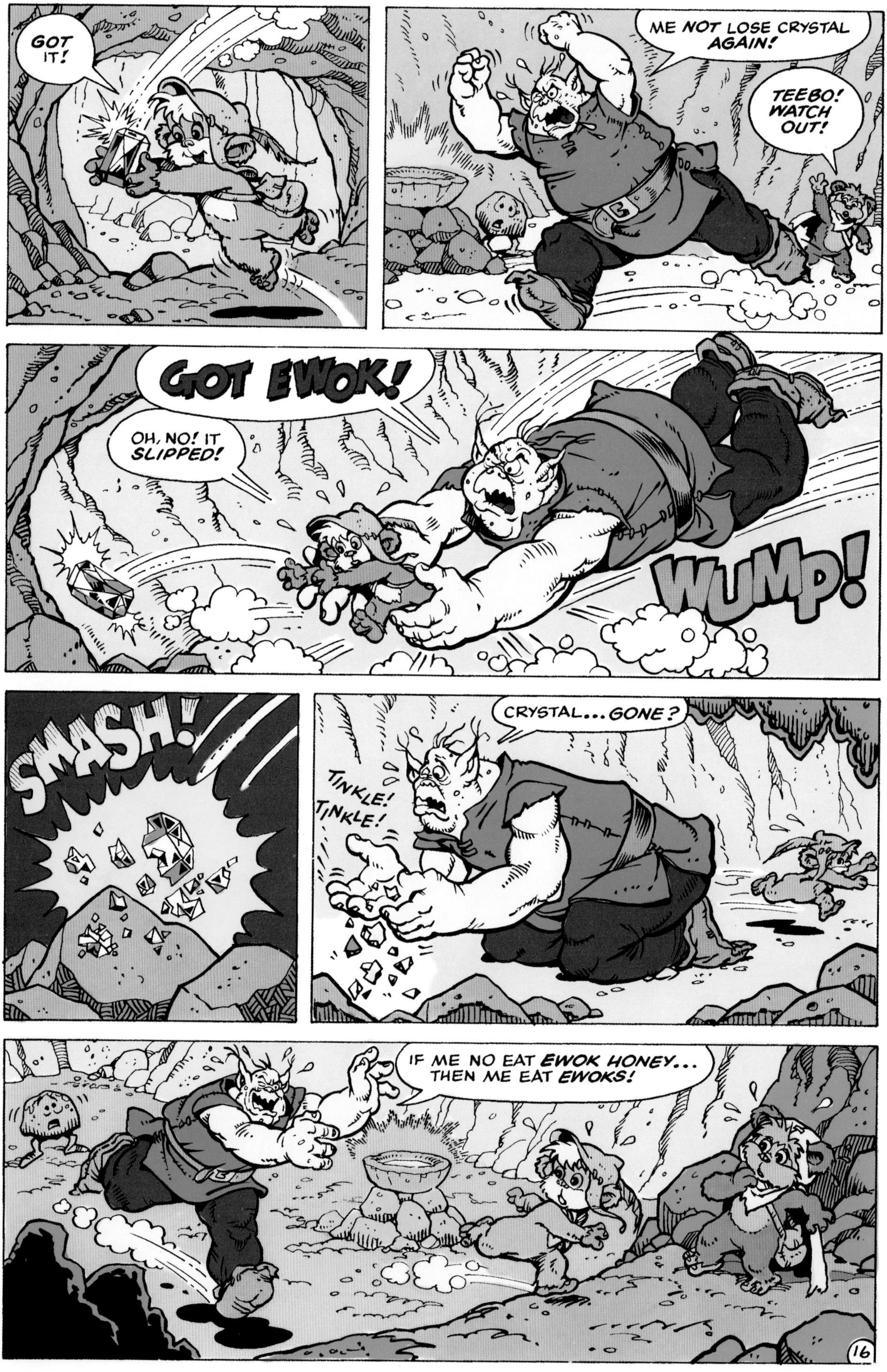
GOT IT!
ME NOT LOSE CRYSTAL AGAIN!
TEEBO! WATCH OUT!
GOT EWOK!
OH, NO! IT SLIPPED!
WUMP!
SMASH!
CRYSTAL... GONE?
TINKLE! TINKLE!
IF ME NO EAT EWOK HONEY... THEN ME EAT EWOKS!
16

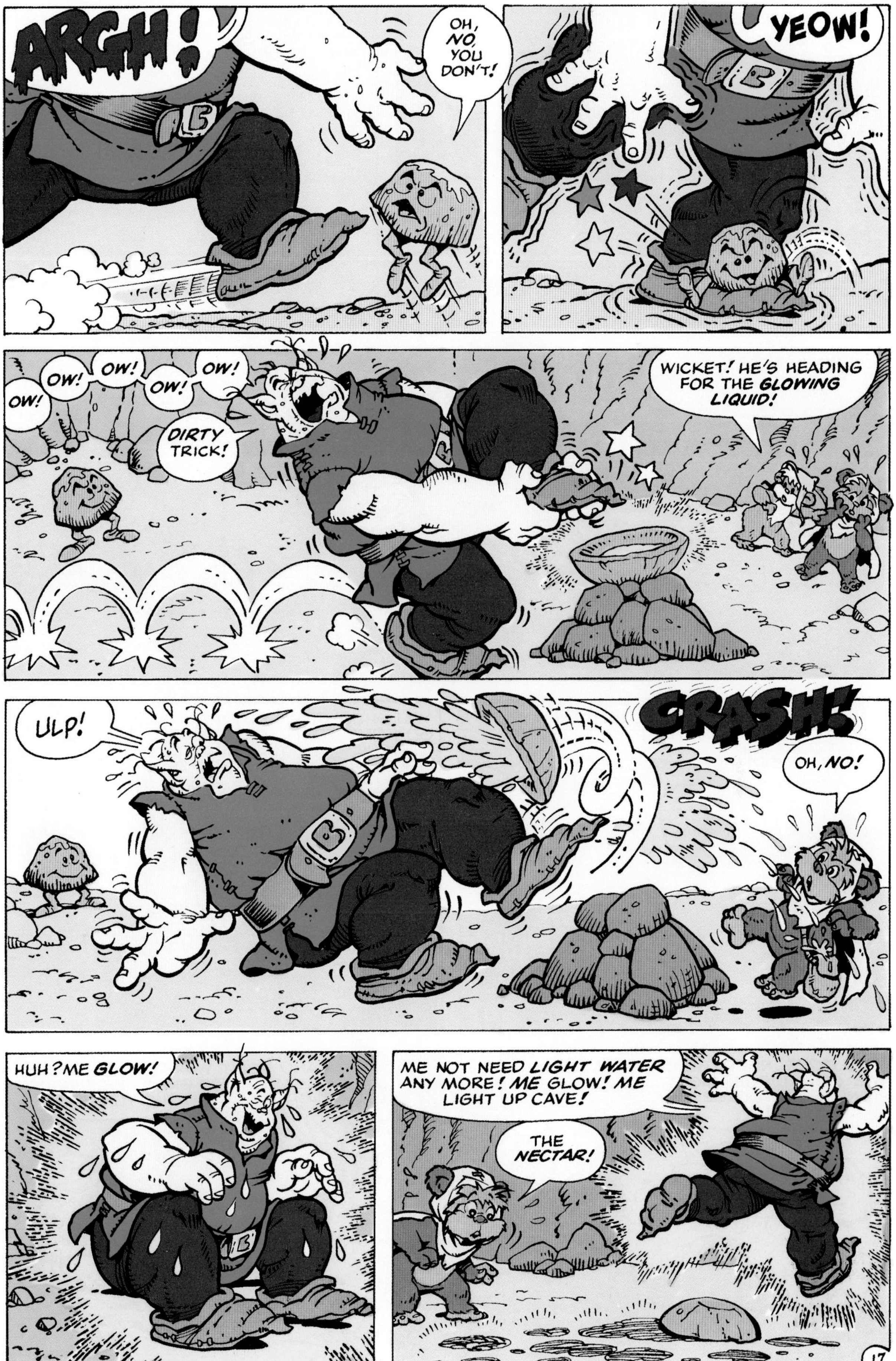
ARGH!
OH, NO, YOU DON'T!
YEOW!
OW!
OW!
OW!
OW!
OW!
DIRTY TRICK!
WICKET! HE'S HEADING FOR THE GLOWING LIQUID!
ULP!
CRASH!
OH, NO!
HUH? ME GLOW!
ME NOT NEED LIGHT WATER ANY MORE! ME GLOW! ME LIGHT UP CAVE!
THE NECTAR!
17

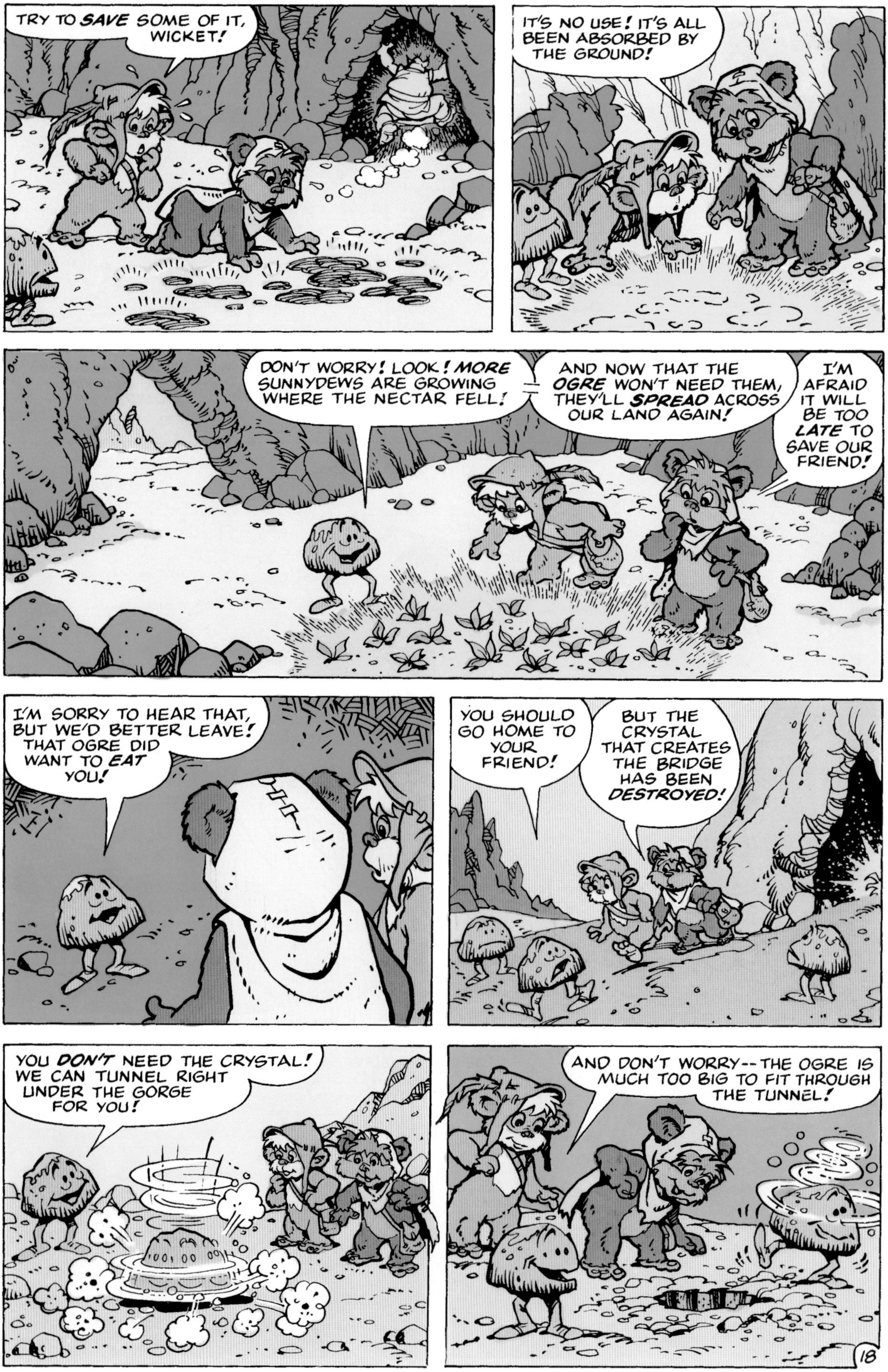
TRY TO SAVE SOME OF IT, WICKET!
IT'S NO USE! IT'S ALL BEEN ABSORBED BY THE GROUND!
DON'T WORRY! LOOK! MORE SUNNYDEWS ARE GROWING WHERE THE NECTAR FELL!
AND NOW THAT THE OGRE WON'T NEED THEM, THEY'LL SPREAD ACROSS OUR LAND AGAIN!
I'M AFRAID IT WILL BE TOO LATE TO SAVE OUR FRIEND!
I'M SORRY TO HEAR THAT, BUT WE'D BETTER LEAVE! THAT OGRE DID WANT TO EAT YOU!
YOU SHOULD GO HOME TO YOUR FRIEND!
BUT THE CRYSTAL THAT CREATES THE BRIDGE HAS BEEN DESTROYED!
YOU DON'T NEED THE CRYSTAL! WE CAN TUNNEL RIGHT UNDER THE GORGE FOR YOU!
AND DON'T WORRY--THE OGRE IS MUCH TOO BIG TO FIT THROUGH THE TUNNEL!
18

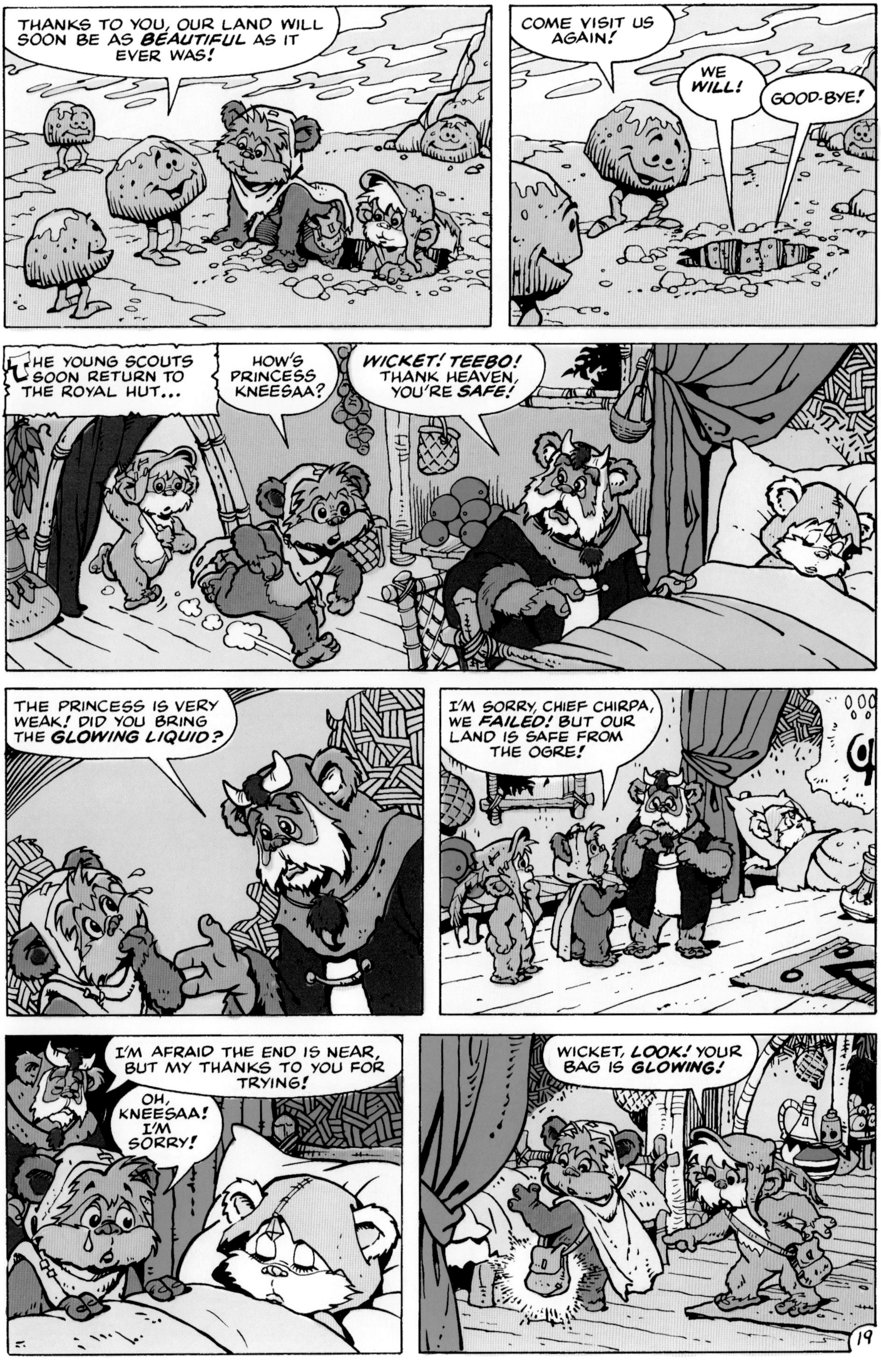
THANKS TO YOU, OUR LAND WILL SOON BE AS BEAUTIFUL AS IT EVER WAS!
COME VISIT US AGAIN!
WE WILL!
GOOD-BYE!
THE YOUNG SCOUTS SOON RETURN TO THE ROYAL HUT...
HOW'S PRINCESS KNEESAA?
WICKET! TEEBO! THANK HEAVEN, YOU'RE SAFE!
THE PRINCESS IS VERY WEAK! DID YOU BRING THE GLOWING LIQUID?
I'M SORRY, CHIEF CHIRPA, WE FAILED! BUT OUR LAND IS SAFE FROM THE OGRE!
I'M AFRAID THE END IS NEAR, BUT MY THANKS TO YOU FOR TRYING!
OH, KNEESAA! I'M SORRY!
WICKET, LOOK! YOUR BAG IS GLOWING!
19

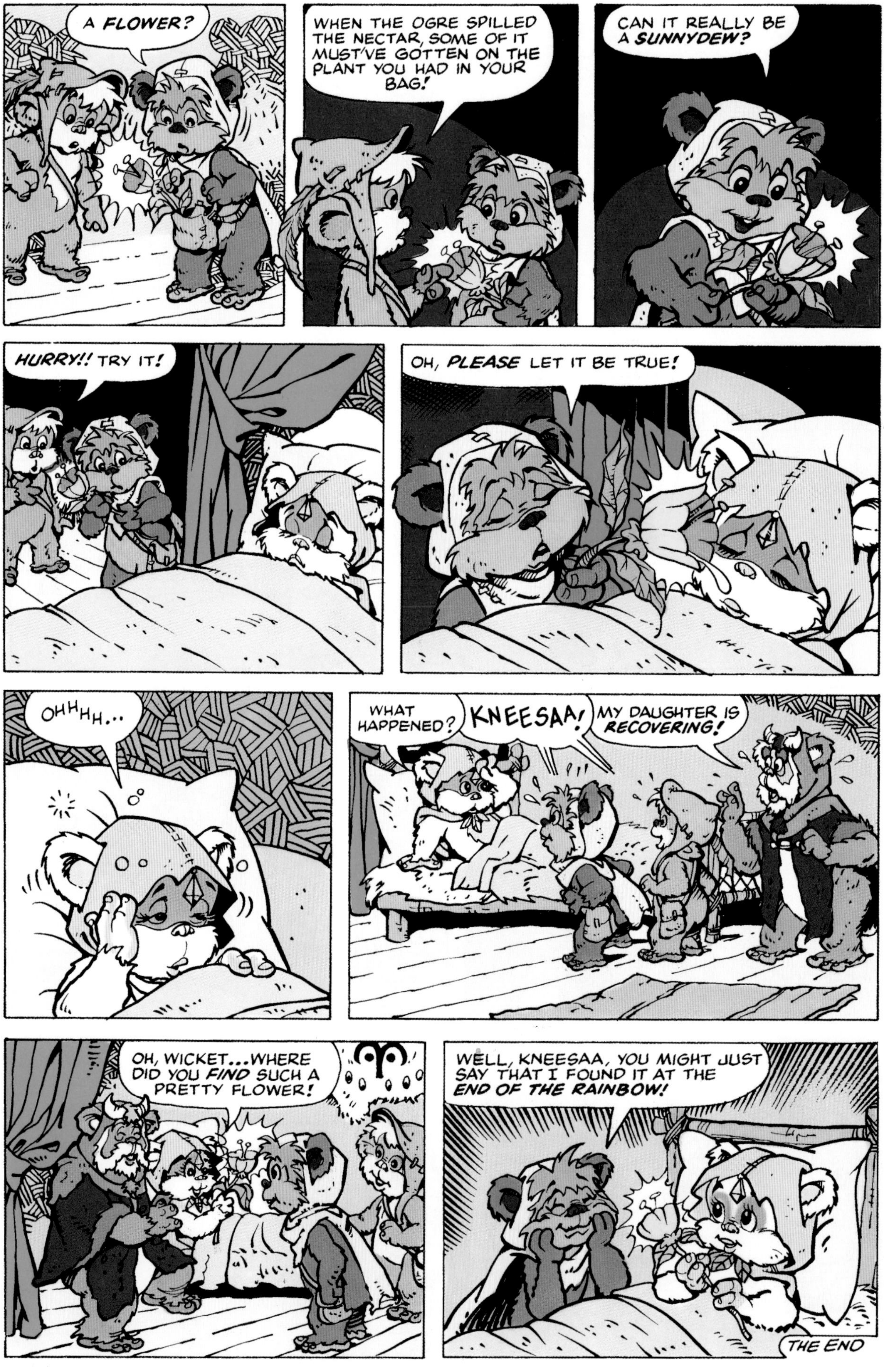
A FLOWER?
WHEN THE OGRE SPILLED THE NECTAR, SOME OF IT MUST'VE GOTTEN ON THE PLANT YOU HAD IN YOUR BAG!
CAN IT REALLY BE A SUNNYDEW?
HURRY!! TRY IT!
OH, PLEASE LET IT BE TRUE!
OHHHH...
WHAT HAPPENED?
KNEESAA!
MY DAUGHTER IS RECOVERING!
OH, WICKET...WHERE DID YOU FIND SUCH A PRETTY FLOWER!
WELL, KNEESAA, YOU MIGHT JUST SAY THAT I FOUND IT AT THE END OF THE RAINBOW!
THE END

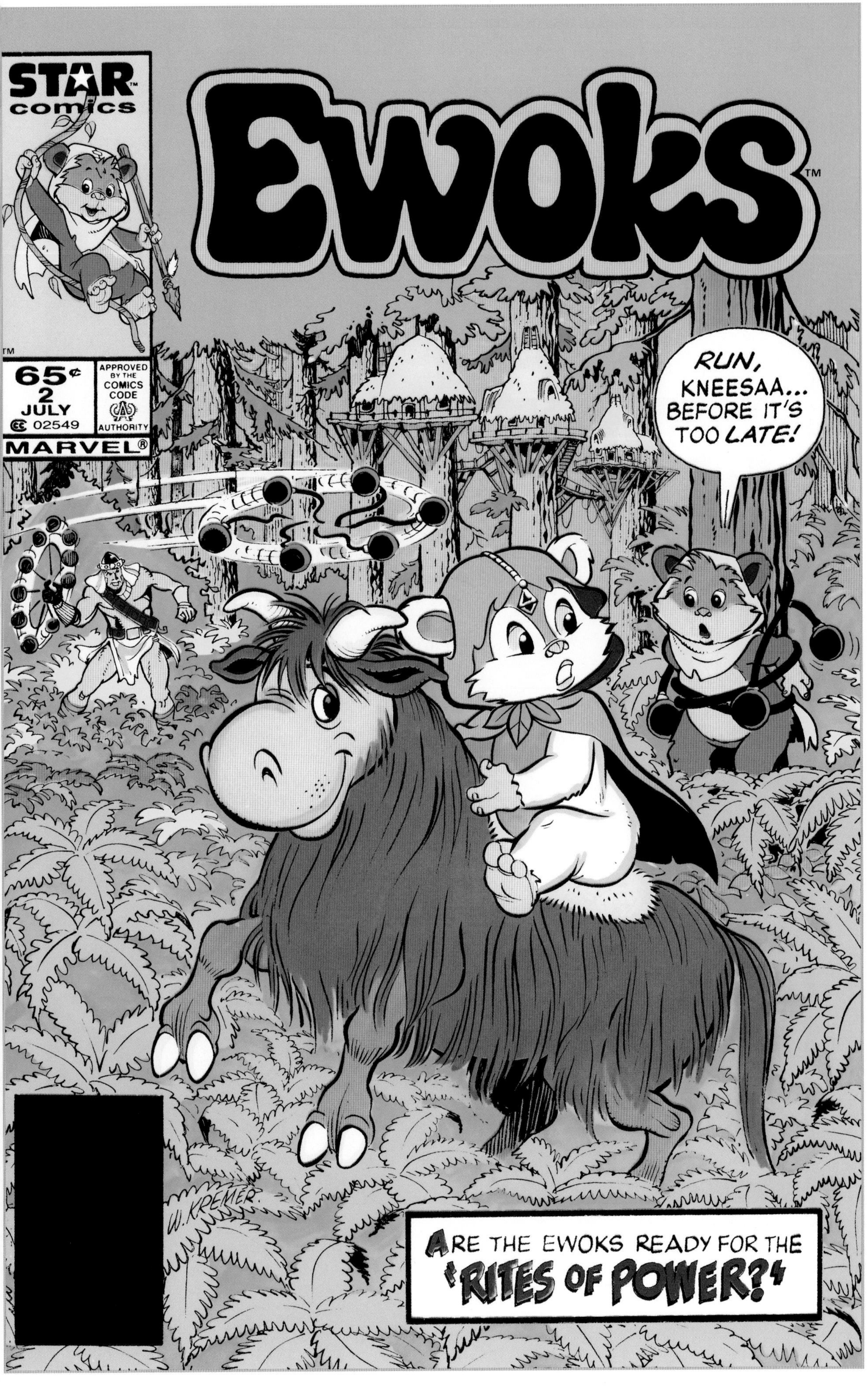
STAR comics
EWOKS
65¢
2
JULY
02549
APPROVED BY THE COMICS CODE AUTHORITY
MARVEL
RUN, KNEESAA... BEFORE IT'S TOO LATE!
W. KREMER
ARE THE EWOKS READY FOR THE 'RITES OF POWER?'

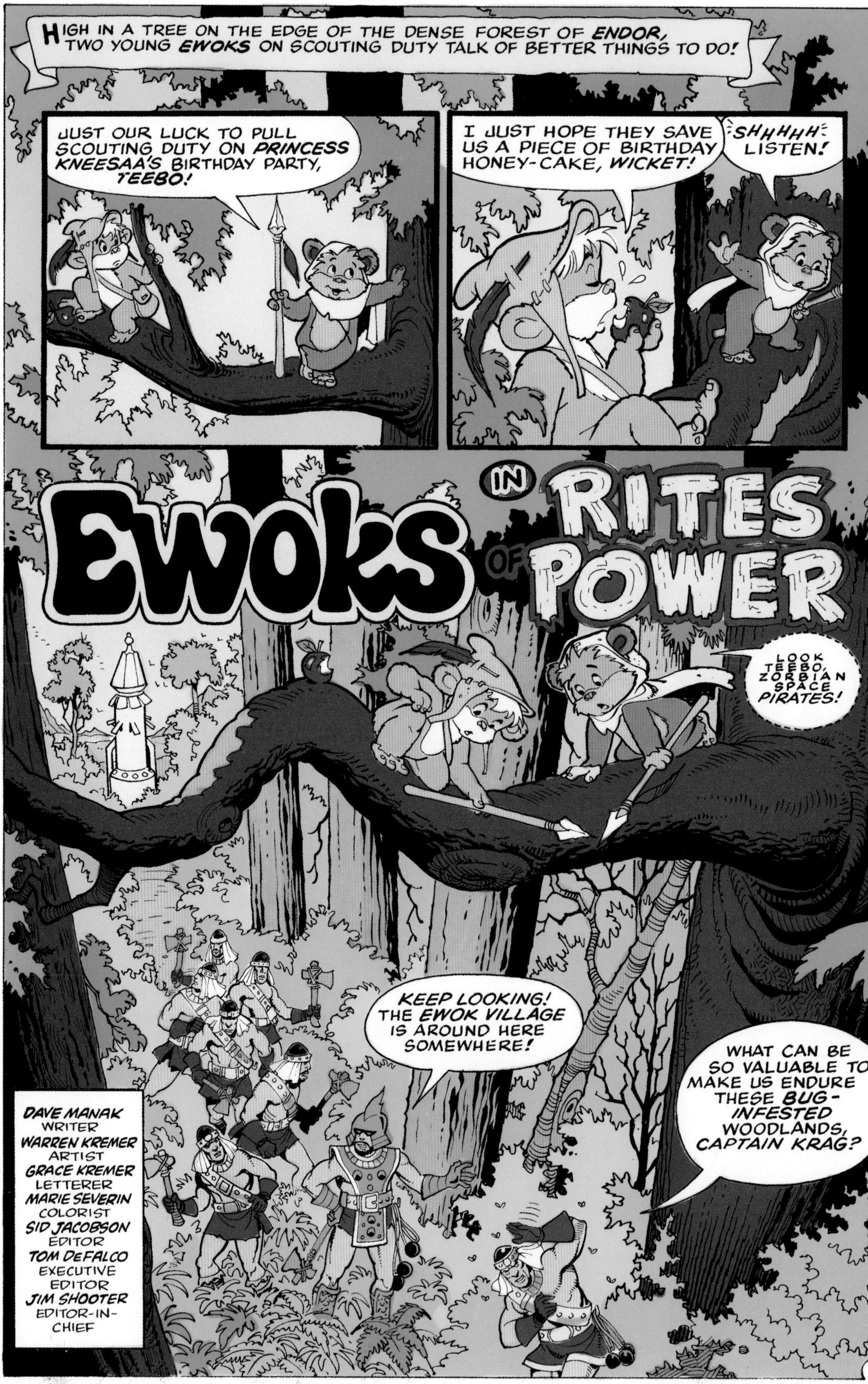
HIGH IN A TREE ON THE EDGE OF THE DENSE FOREST OF ENDOR, TWO YOUNG EWOKS ON SCOUTING DUTY TALK OF BETTER THINGS TO DO!
JUST OUR LUCK TO PULL SCOUTING DUTY ON PRINCESS KNEESAA'S BIRTHDAY PARTY, TEEBO!
I JUST HOPE THEY SAVE US A PIECE OF BIRTHDAY HONEY-CAKE, WICKET!
SHHHHH! LISTEN!
EWOKS IN RITES OF POWER
LOOK TEEBO, ZORBIAN SPACE PIRATES!
KEEP LOOKING! THE EWOK VILLAGE IS AROUND HERE SOMEWHERE!
WHAT CAN BE SO VALUABLE TO MAKE US ENDURE THESE BUG-INFESTED WOODLANDS, CAPTAIN KRAG?
DAVE MANAK WRITER
WARREN KREMER ARTIST
GRACE KREMER LETTERER
MARIE SEVERIN COLORIST
SID JACOBSON EDITOR
TOM DEFALCO EXECUTIVE EDITOR
JIM SHOOTER EDITOR-IN-CHIEF
1

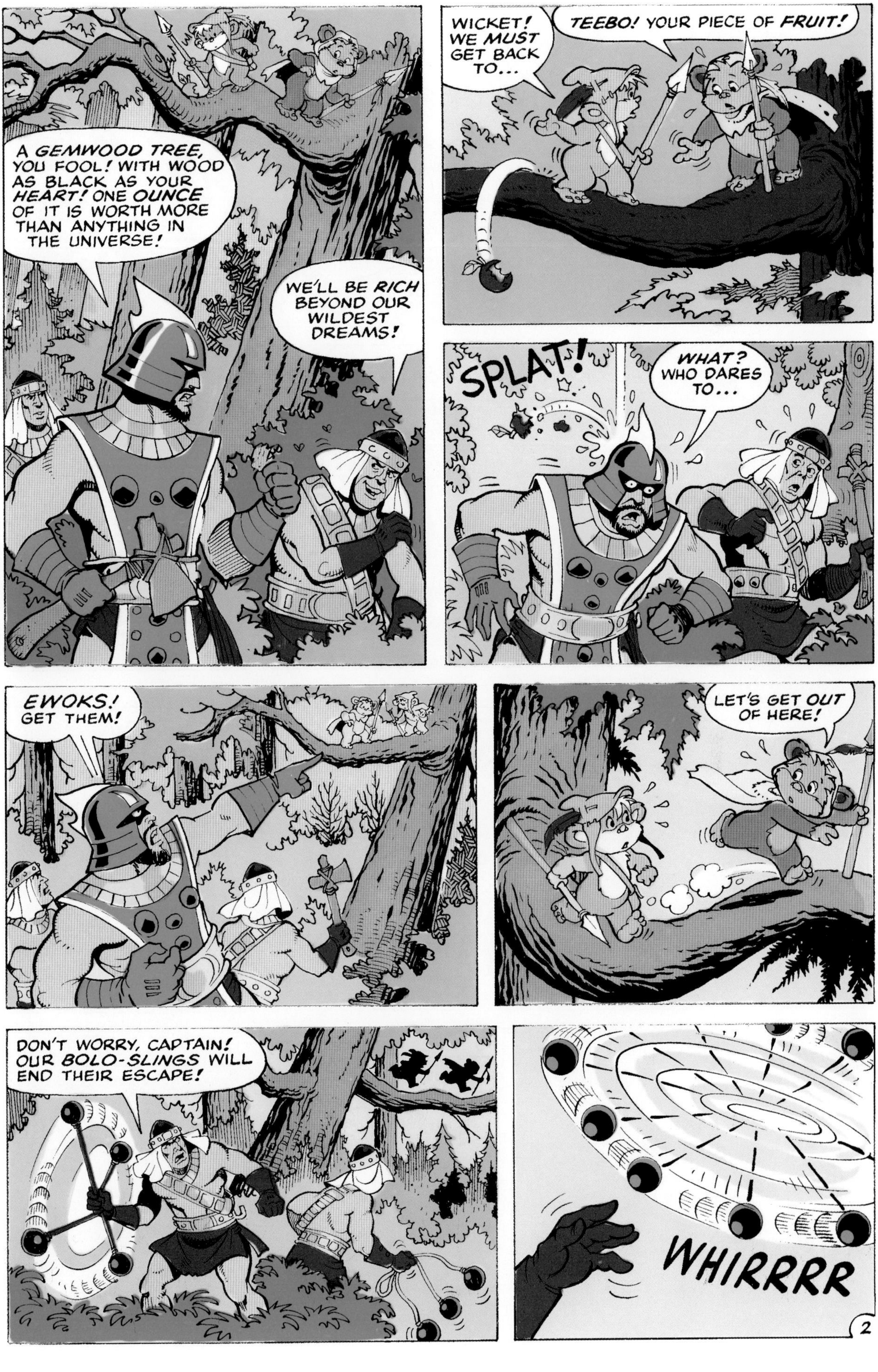
A GEMWOOD TREE, YOU FOOL! WITH WOOD AS BLACK AS YOUR HEART! ONE OUNCE OF IT IS WORTH MORE THAN ANYTHING IN THE UNIVERSE!
WE'LL BE RICH BEYOND OUR WILDEST DREAMS!
WICKET! WE MUST GET BACK TO...
TEEBO! YOUR PIECE OF FRUIT!
SPLAT!
WHAT? WHO DARES TO...
EWOKS! GET THEM!
LET'S GET OUT OF HERE!
DON'T WORRY, CAPTAIN! OUR BOLO-SLINGS WILL END THEIR ESCAPE!
WHIRRRR
2

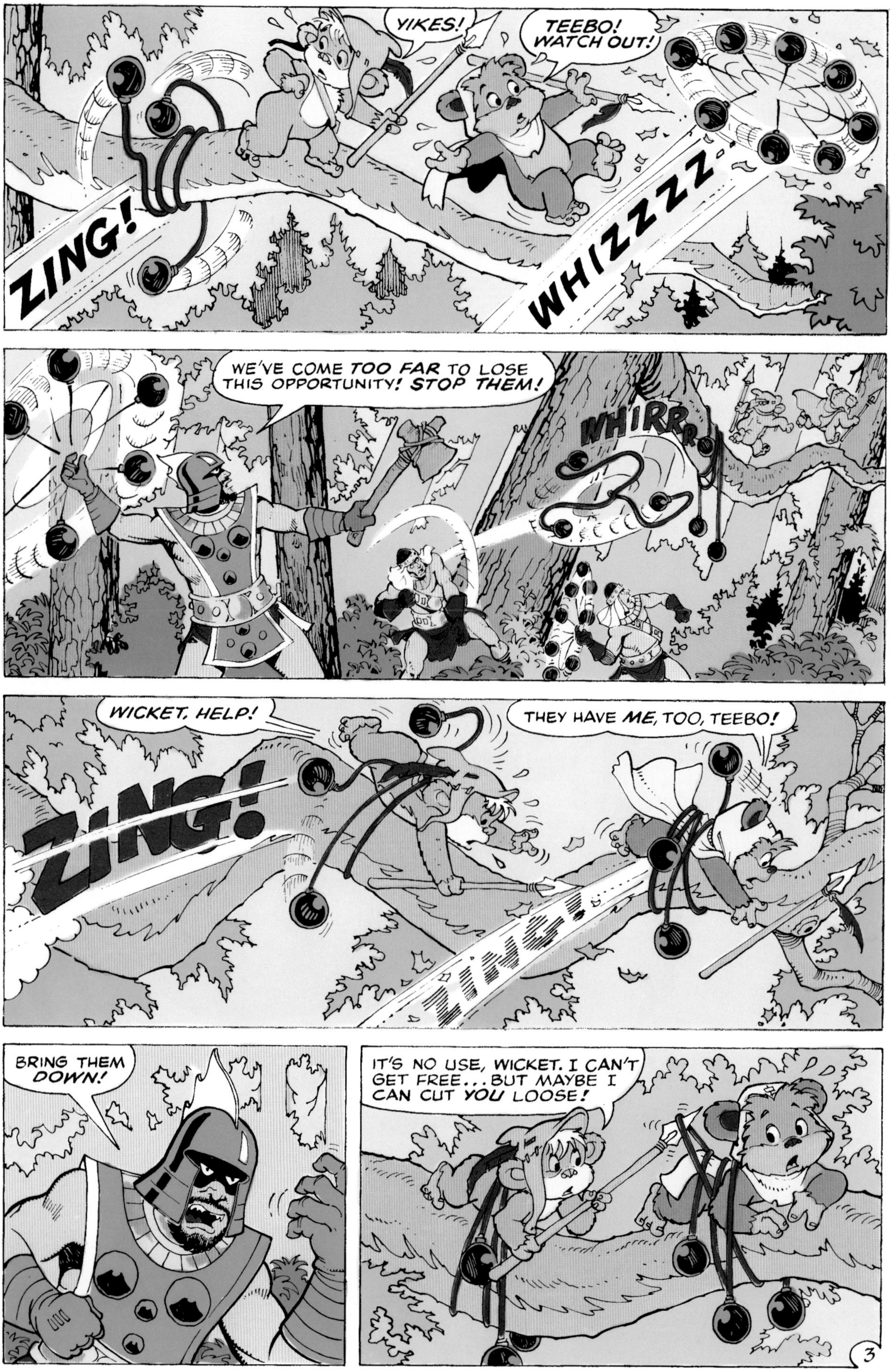
YIKES!
TEEBO! WATCH OUT!
ZING!
WHIZZZZ
WE'VE COME TOO FAR TO LOSE THIS OPPORTUNITY! STOP THEM!
WHIRRR
WICKET, HELP!
THEY HAVE ME, TOO, TEEBO!
ZING!
BRING THEM DOWN!
IT'S NO USE, WICKET. I CAN'T GET FREE... BUT MAYBE I CAN CUT YOU LOOSE!
3

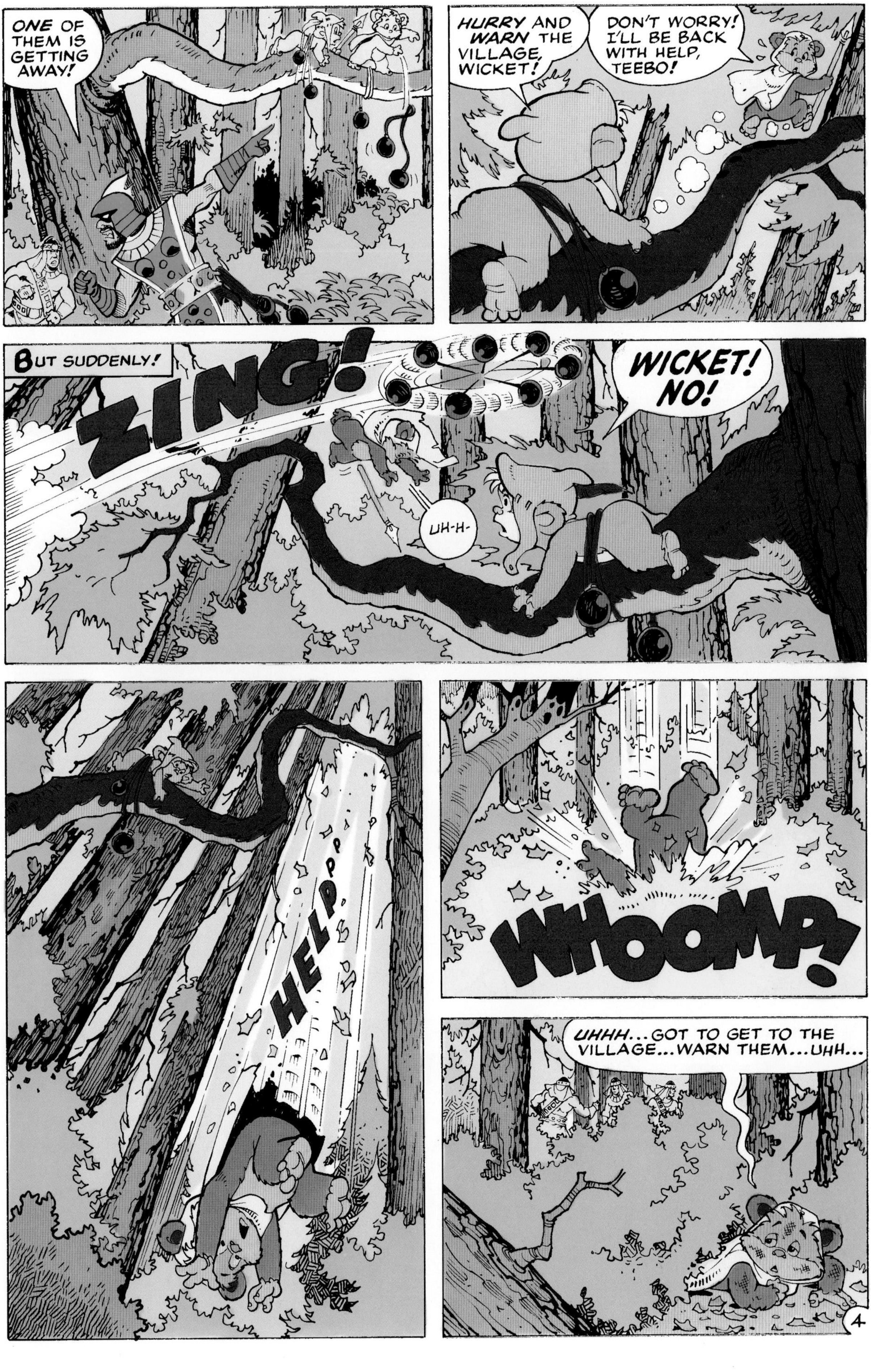
ONE OF THEM IS GETTING AWAY!
HURRY AND WARN THE VILLAGE, WICKET!
DON'T WORRY! I'LL BE BACK WITH HELP, TEEBO!
BUT SUDDENLY!
ZING!
WICKET! NO!
UH-H-
HELPPP
WHOOMP!
UHHH...GOT TO GET TO THE VILLAGE...WARN THEM...UHH...
4

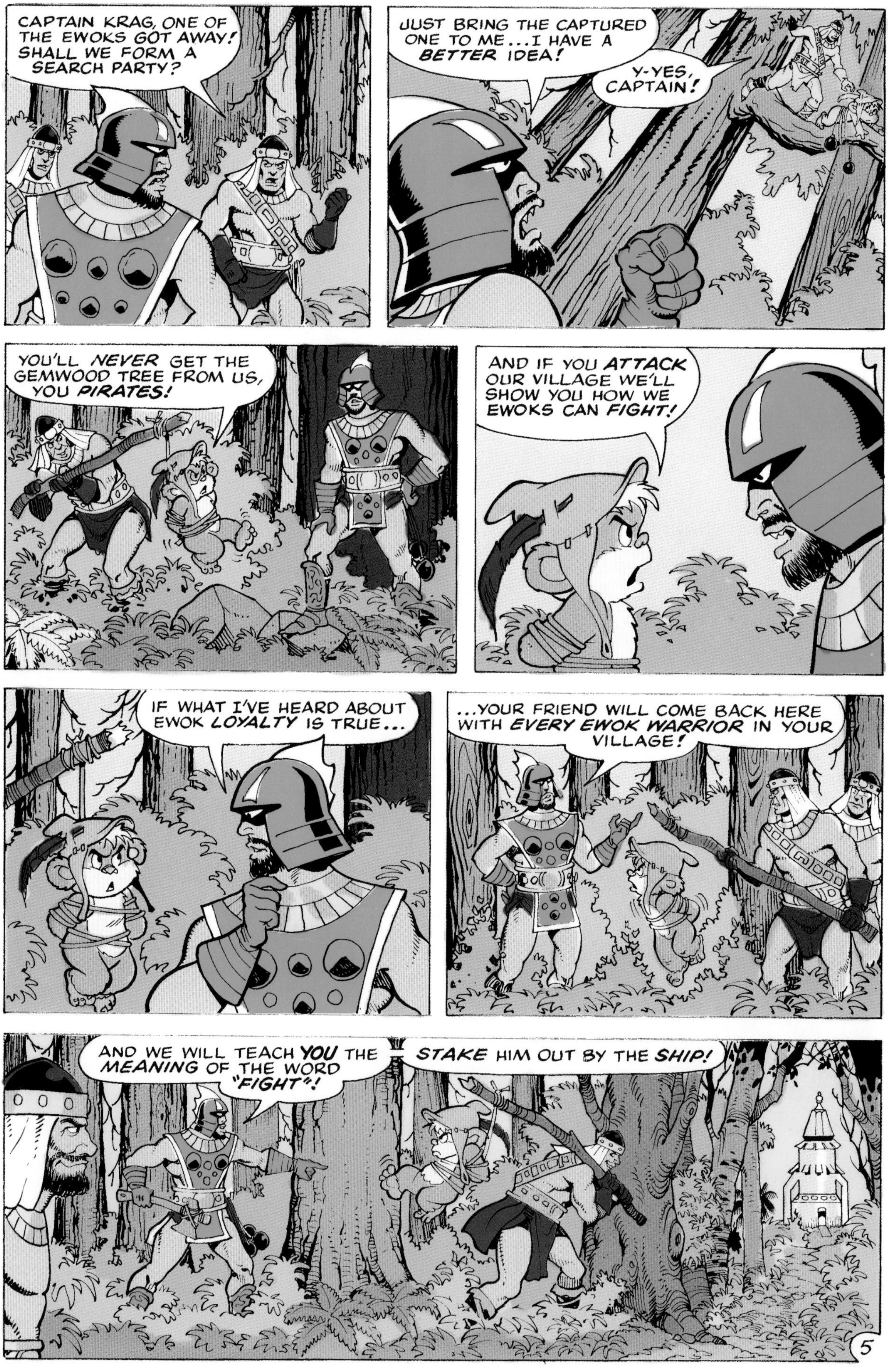
CAPTAIN KRAG, ONE OF THE EWOKS GOT AWAY! SHALL WE FORM A SEARCH PARTY?
JUST BRING THE CAPTURED ONE TO ME... I HAVE A BETTER IDEA!
Y-YES, CAPTAIN!
YOU'LL NEVER GET THE GEMWOOD TREE FROM US, YOU PIRATES!
AND IF YOU ATTACK OUR VILLAGE WE'LL SHOW YOU HOW WE EWOKS CAN FIGHT!
IF WHAT I'VE HEARD ABOUT EWOK LOYALTY IS TRUE...
...YOUR FRIEND WILL COME BACK HERE WITH EVERY EWOK WARRIOR IN YOUR VILLAGE!
AND WE WILL TEACH YOU THE MEANING OF THE WORD "FIGHT"!
STAKE HIM OUT BY THE SHIP!
5

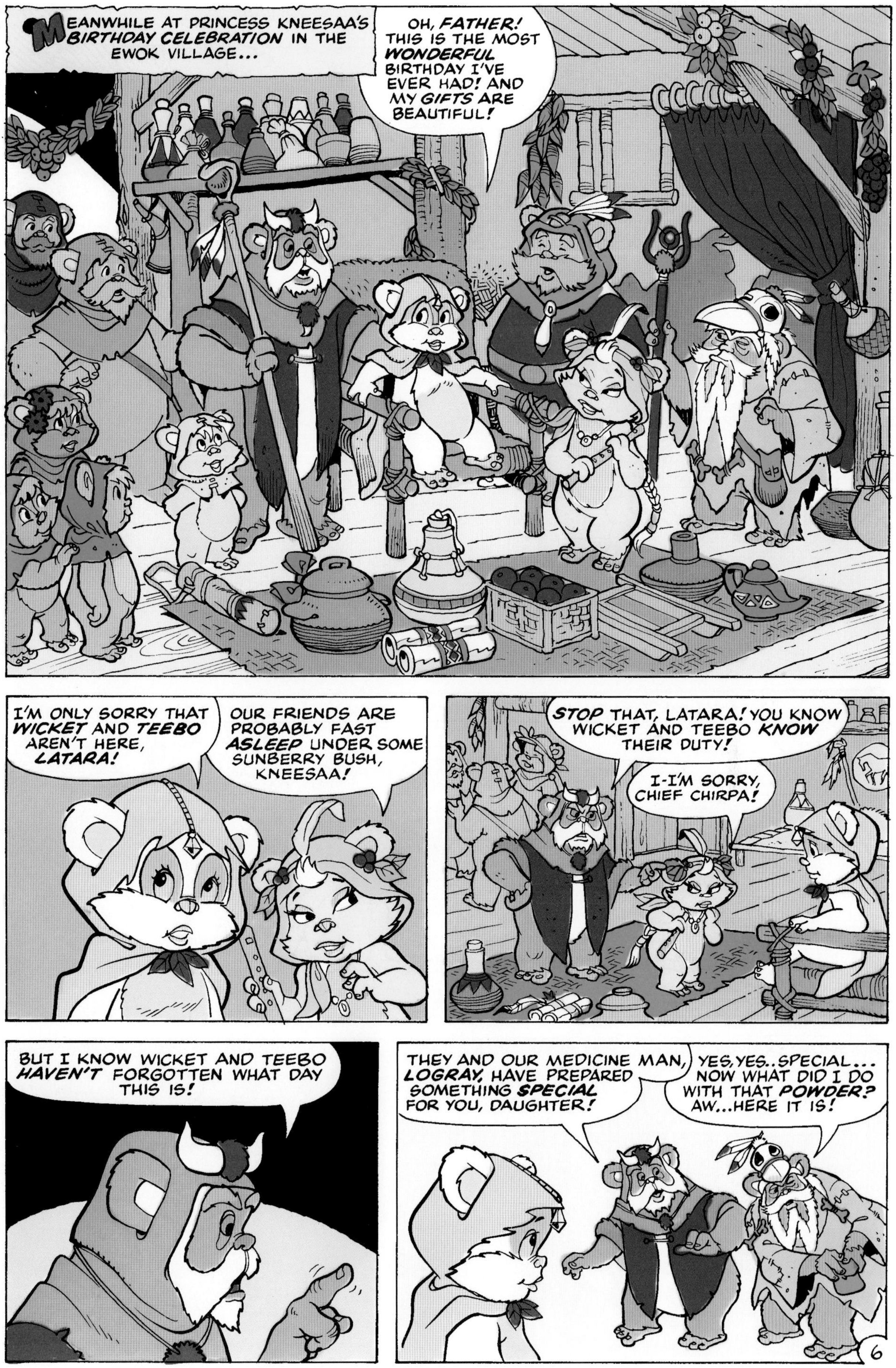
MEANWHILE AT PRINCESS KNEESAA'S BIRTHDAY CELEBRATION IN THE EWOK VILLAGE...
OH, FATHER! THIS IS THE MOST WONDERFUL BIRTHDAY I'VE EVER HAD! AND MY GIFTS ARE BEAUTIFUL!
I'M ONLY SORRY THAT WICKET AND TEEBO AREN'T HERE, LATARA!
OUR FRIENDS ARE PROBABLY FAST ASLEEP UNDER SOME SUNBERRY BUSH, KNEESAA!
STOP THAT, LATARA! YOU KNOW WICKET AND TEEBO KNOW THEIR DUTY!
I-I'M SORRY, CHIEF CHIRPA!
BUT I KNOW WICKET AND TEEBO HAVEN'T FORGOTTEN WHAT DAY THIS IS!
THEY AND OUR MEDICINE MAN, LOGRAY, HAVE PREPARED SOMETHING SPECIAL FOR YOU, DAUGHTER!
YES, YES..SPECIAL... NOW WHAT DID I DO WITH THAT POWDER? AW...HERE IT IS!
6

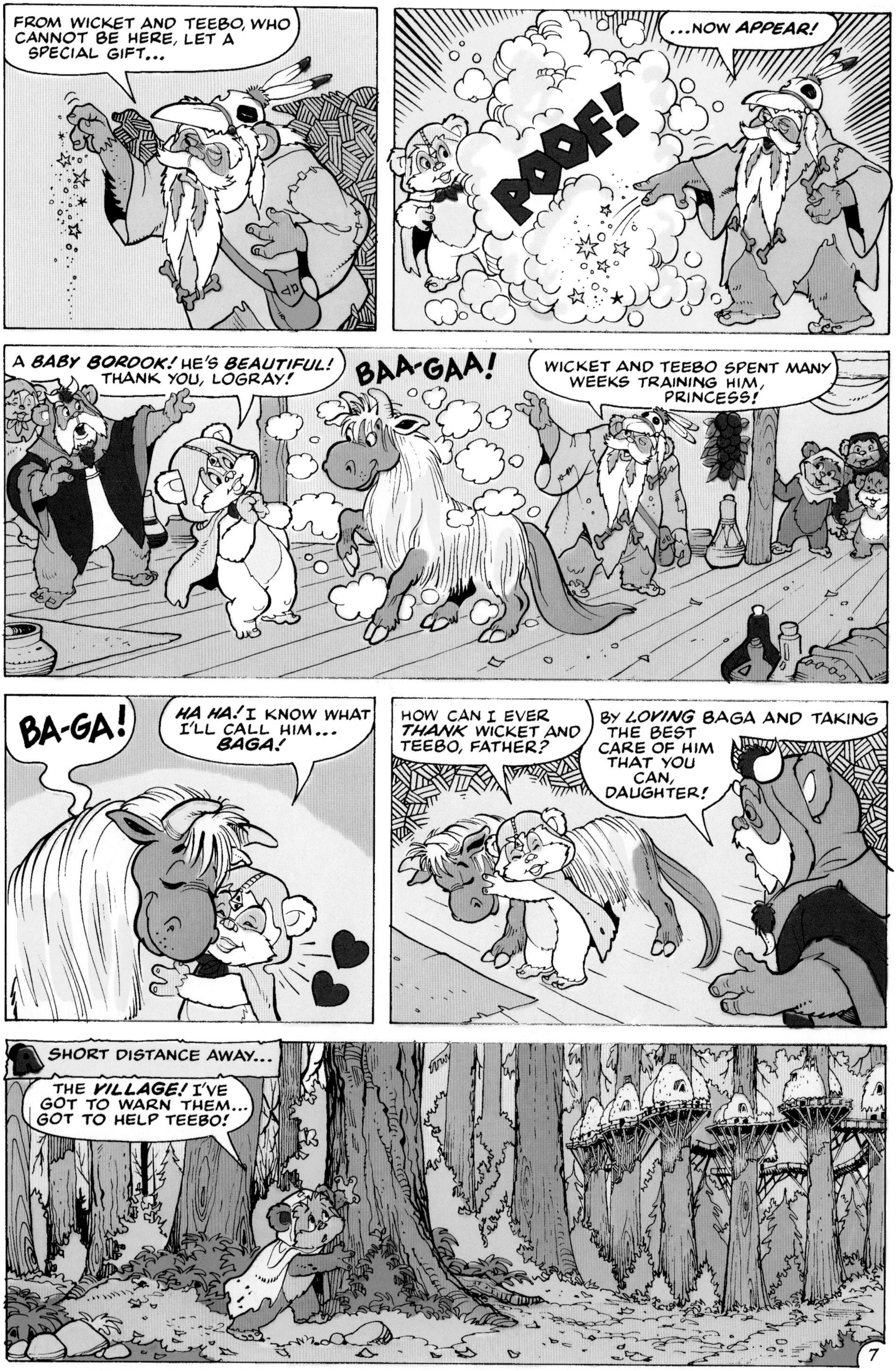
FROM WICKET AND TEEBO, WHO CANNOT BE HERE, LET A SPECIAL GIFT...
...NOW APPEAR!
POOF!
A BABY BORDOK! HE'S BEAUTIFUL! THANK YOU, LOGRAY!
BAA-GAA!
WICKET AND TEEBO SPENT MANY WEEKS TRAINING HIM, PRINCESS!
BA-GA!
HA HA! I KNOW WHAT I'LL CALL HIM... BAGA!
HOW CAN I EVER THANK WICKET AND TEEBO, FATHER?
BY LOVING BAGA AND TAKING THE BEST CARE OF HIM THAT YOU CAN, DAUGHTER!
A SHORT DISTANCE AWAY...
THE VILLAGE! I'VE GOT TO WARN THEM... GOT TO HELP TEEBO!
7

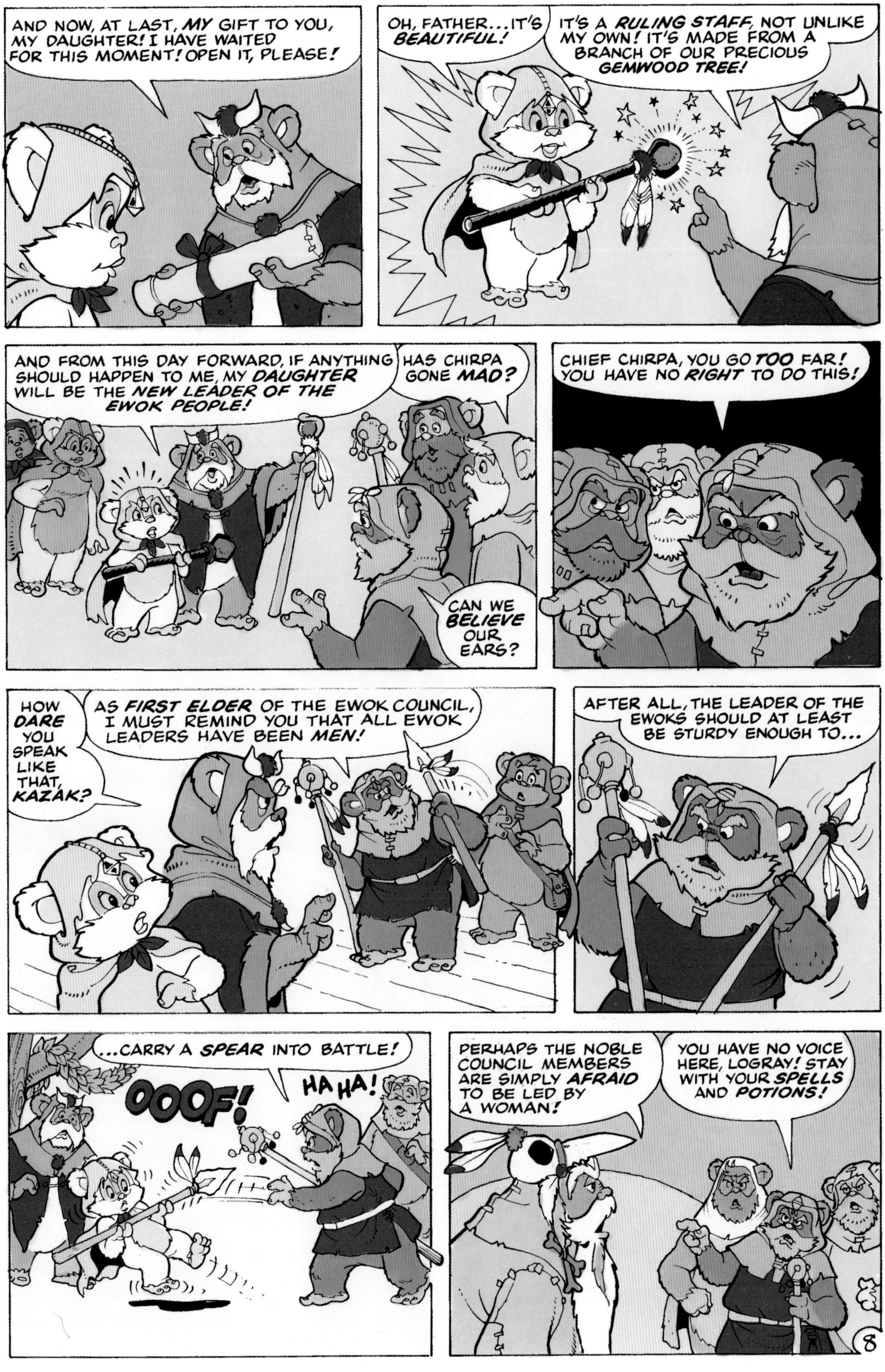
AND NOW, AT LAST, MY GIFT TO YOU, MY DAUGHTER! I HAVE WAITED FOR THIS MOMENT! OPEN IT, PLEASE!
OH, FATHER...IT'S BEAUTIFUL!
IT'S A RULING STAFF, NOT UNLIKE MY OWN! IT'S MADE FROM A BRANCH OF OUR PRECIOUS GEMWOOD TREE!
AND FROM THIS DAY FORWARD, IF ANYTHING SHOULD HAPPEN TO ME, MY DAUGHTER WILL BE THE NEW LEADER OF THE EWOK PEOPLE!
HAS CHIRPA GONE MAD?
CAN WE BELIEVE OUR EARS?
CHIEF CHIRPA, YOU GO TOO FAR! YOU HAVE NO RIGHT TO DO THIS!
HOW DARE YOU SPEAK LIKE THAT, KAZAK?
AS FIRST ELDER OF THE EWOK COUNCIL, I MUST REMIND YOU THAT ALL EWOK LEADERS HAVE BEEN MEN!
AFTER ALL, THE LEADER OF THE EWOKS SHOULD AT LEAST BE STURDY ENOUGH TO...
...CARRY A SPEAR INTO BATTLE!
OOOF!
HA HA!
PERHAPS THE NOBLE COUNCIL MEMBERS ARE SIMPLY AFRAID TO BE LED BY A WOMAN!
YOU HAVE NO VOICE HERE, LOGRAY! STAY WITH YOUR SPELLS AND POTIONS!
8

IT IS MY DAUGHTER'S **BIRTHRIGHT** TO ONE DAY LEAD OUR PEOPLE!

PROTEST ALL YOU WANT, CHIRPA, BUT WE **EWOK ELDERS** WILL CHOOSE A NEW LEADER WHEN THE TIME IS AT HAND!

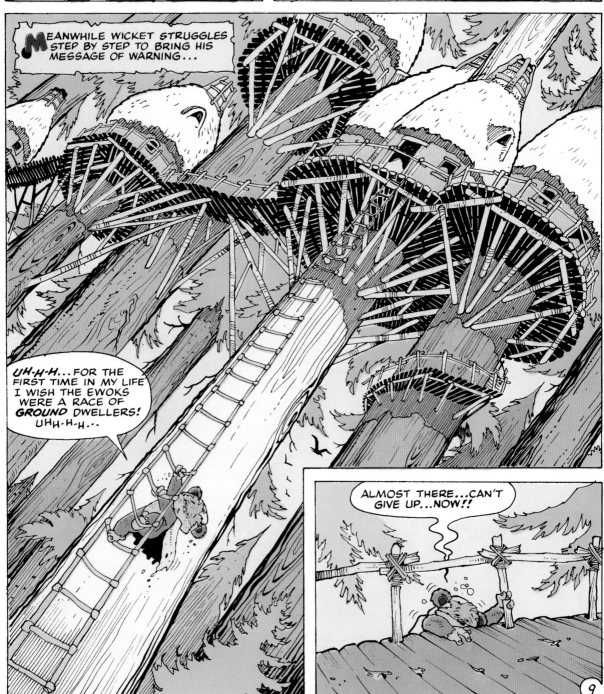

MEANWHILE WICKET STRUGGLES STEP BY STEP TO BRING HIS MESSAGE OF WARNING...

UH-H-H...FOR THE FIRST TIME IN MY LIFE I WISH THE EWOKS WERE A RACE OF **GROUND** DWELLERS! UH-H-H-H...

ALMOST THERE...CAN'T GIVE UP...NOW!!

9

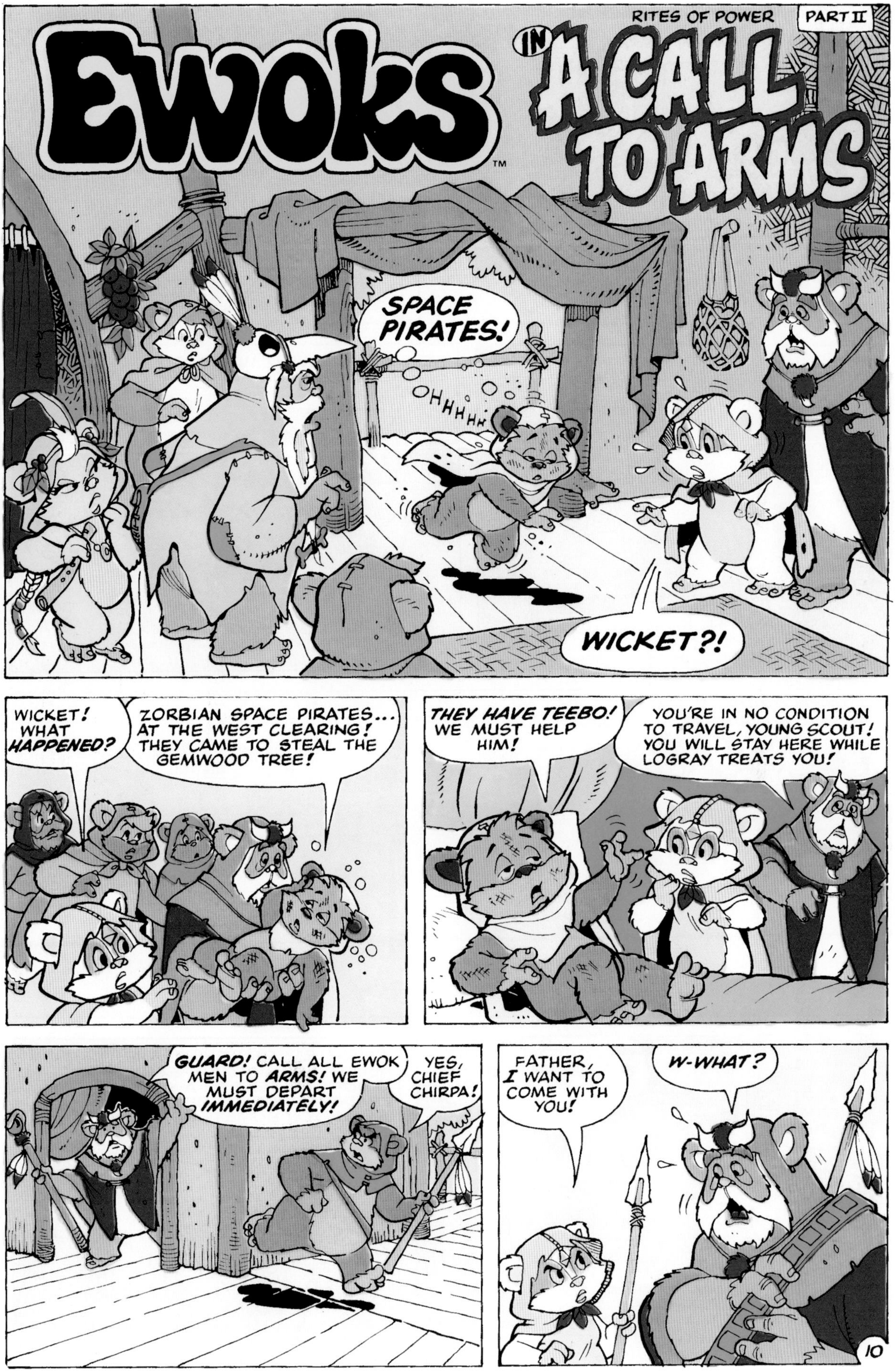

Ewoks™
IN A CALL TO ARMS
RITES OF POWER
PART II
SPACE PIRATES!
OHHHHHH
WICKET?!
WICKET! WHAT HAPPENED?
ZORBIAN SPACE PIRATES... AT THE WEST CLEARING! THEY CAME TO STEAL THE GEMWOOD TREE!
THEY HAVE TEEBO! WE MUST HELP HIM!
YOU'RE IN NO CONDITION TO TRAVEL, YOUNG SCOUT! YOU WILL STAY HERE WHILE LOGRAY TREATS YOU!
GUARD! CALL ALL EWOK MEN TO ARMS! WE MUST DEPART IMMEDIATELY!
YES, CHIEF CHIRPA!
FATHER, I WANT TO COME WITH YOU!
W-WHAT?
10

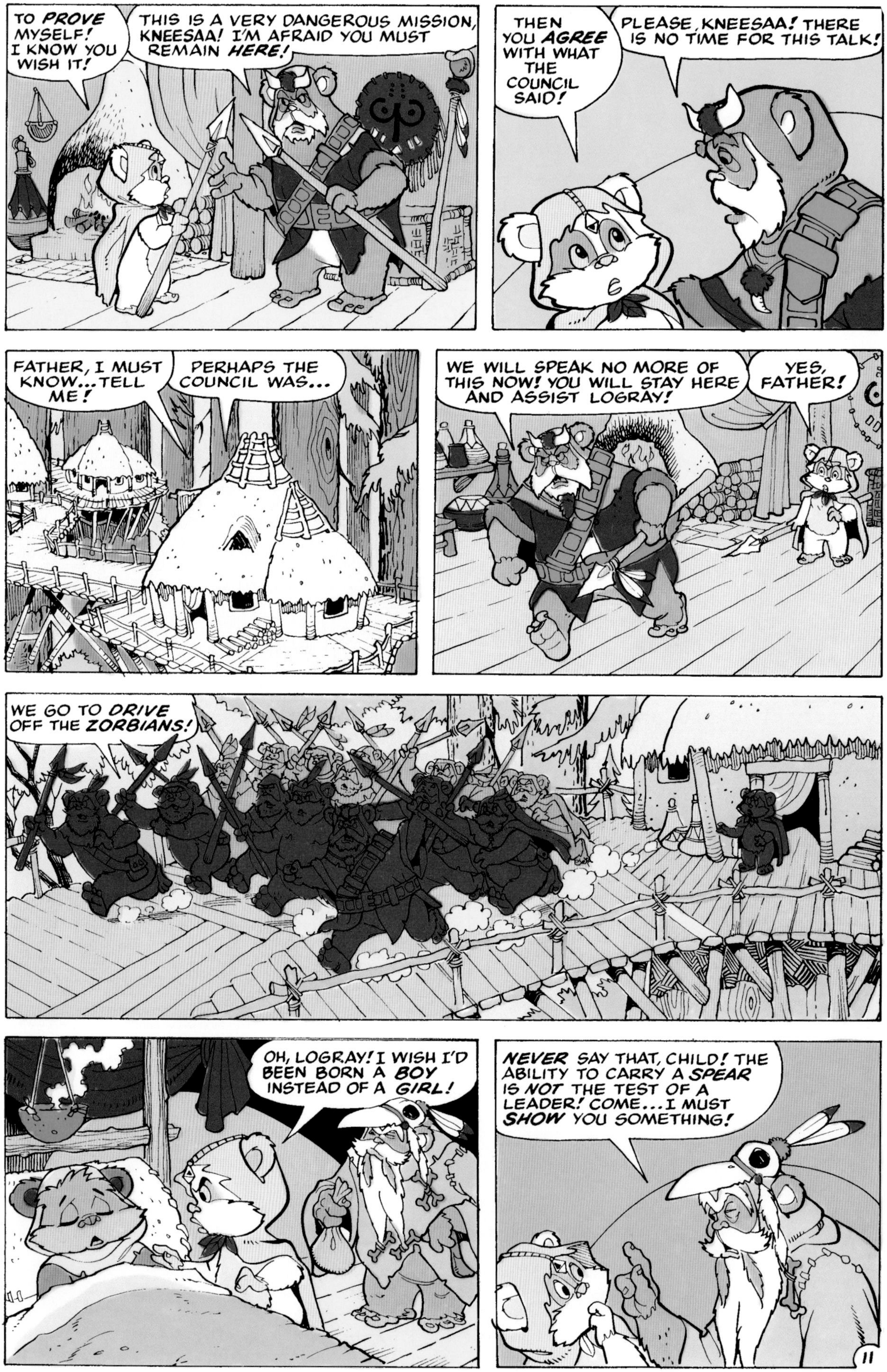
TO PROVE MYSELF! I KNOW YOU WISH IT!
THIS IS A VERY DANGEROUS MISSION, KNEESAA! I'M AFRAID YOU MUST REMAIN HERE!
THEN YOU AGREE WITH WHAT THE COUNCIL SAID!
PLEASE, KNEESAA! THERE IS NO TIME FOR THIS TALK!
FATHER, I MUST KNOW...TELL ME!
PERHAPS THE COUNCIL WAS...
WE WILL SPEAK NO MORE OF THIS NOW! YOU WILL STAY HERE AND ASSIST LOGRAY!
YES, FATHER!
WE GO TO DRIVE OFF THE ZORBIANS!
OH, LOGRAY! I WISH I'D BEEN BORN A BOY INSTEAD OF A GIRL!
NEVER SAY THAT, CHILD! THE ABILITY TO CARRY A SPEAR IS NOT THE TEST OF A LEADER! COME...I MUST SHOW YOU SOMETHING!
11

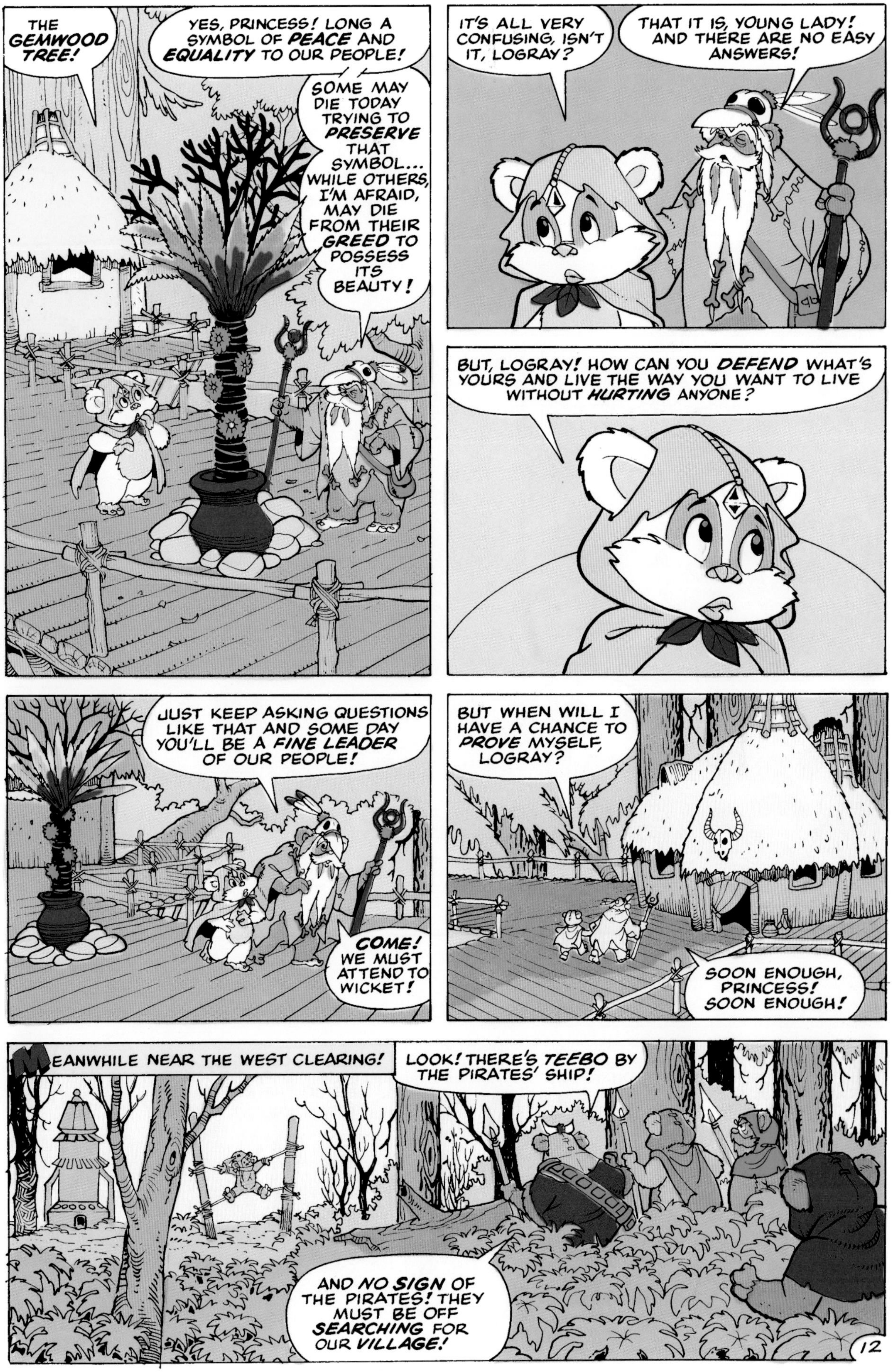
THE GEMWOOD TREE!
YES, PRINCESS! LONG A SYMBOL OF PEACE AND EQUALITY TO OUR PEOPLE!
SOME MAY DIE TODAY TRYING TO PRESERVE THAT SYMBOL... WHILE OTHERS, I'M AFRAID, MAY DIE FROM THEIR GREED TO POSSESS ITS BEAUTY!
IT'S ALL VERY CONFUSING, ISN'T IT, LOGRAY?
THAT IT IS, YOUNG LADY! AND THERE ARE NO EASY ANSWERS!
BUT, LOGRAY! HOW CAN YOU DEFEND WHAT'S YOURS AND LIVE THE WAY YOU WANT TO LIVE WITHOUT HURTING ANYONE?
JUST KEEP ASKING QUESTIONS LIKE THAT AND SOME DAY YOU'LL BE A FINE LEADER OF OUR PEOPLE!
COME! WE MUST ATTEND TO WICKET!
BUT WHEN WILL I HAVE A CHANCE TO PROVE MYSELF, LOGRAY?
SOON ENOUGH, PRINCESS! SOON ENOUGH!
MEANWHILE NEAR THE WEST CLEARING!
LOOK! THERE'S TEEBO BY THE PIRATES' SHIP!
AND NO SIGN OF THE PIRATES! THEY MUST BE OFF SEARCHING FOR OUR VILLAGE!
12

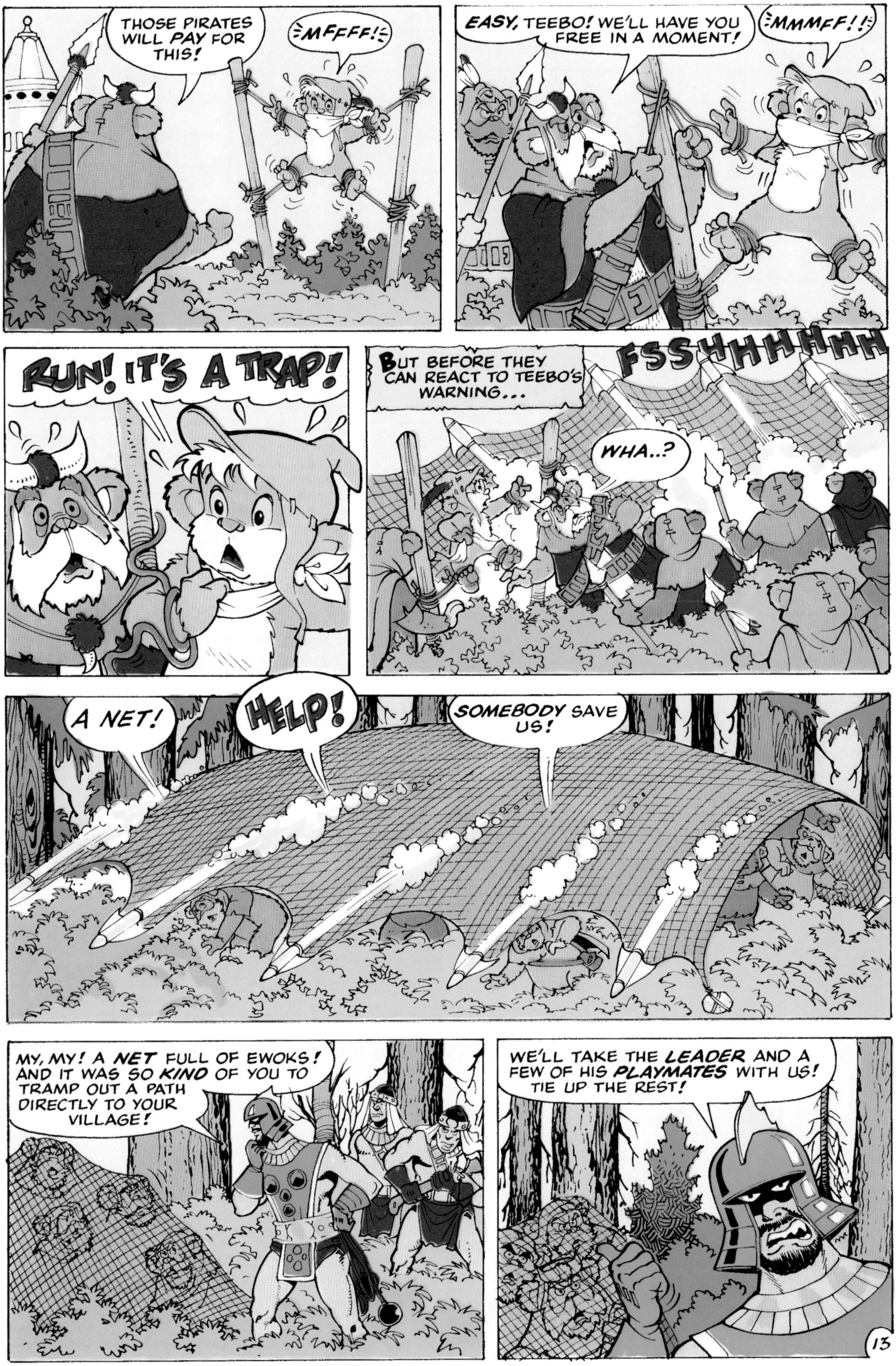
THOSE PIRATES WILL PAY FOR THIS!
MFFFF!
EASY, TEEBO! WE'LL HAVE YOU FREE IN A MOMENT!
MMMFF!!
RUN! IT'S A TRAP!
BUT BEFORE THEY CAN REACT TO TEEBO'S WARNING...
FSSHHHHHH
WHA..?
A NET!
HELP!
SOMEBODY SAVE US!
MY, MY! A NET FULL OF EWOKS! AND IT WAS SO KIND OF YOU TO TRAMP OUT A PATH DIRECTLY TO YOUR VILLAGE!
WE'LL TAKE THE LEADER AND A FEW OF HIS PLAYMATES WITH US! TIE UP THE REST!
13

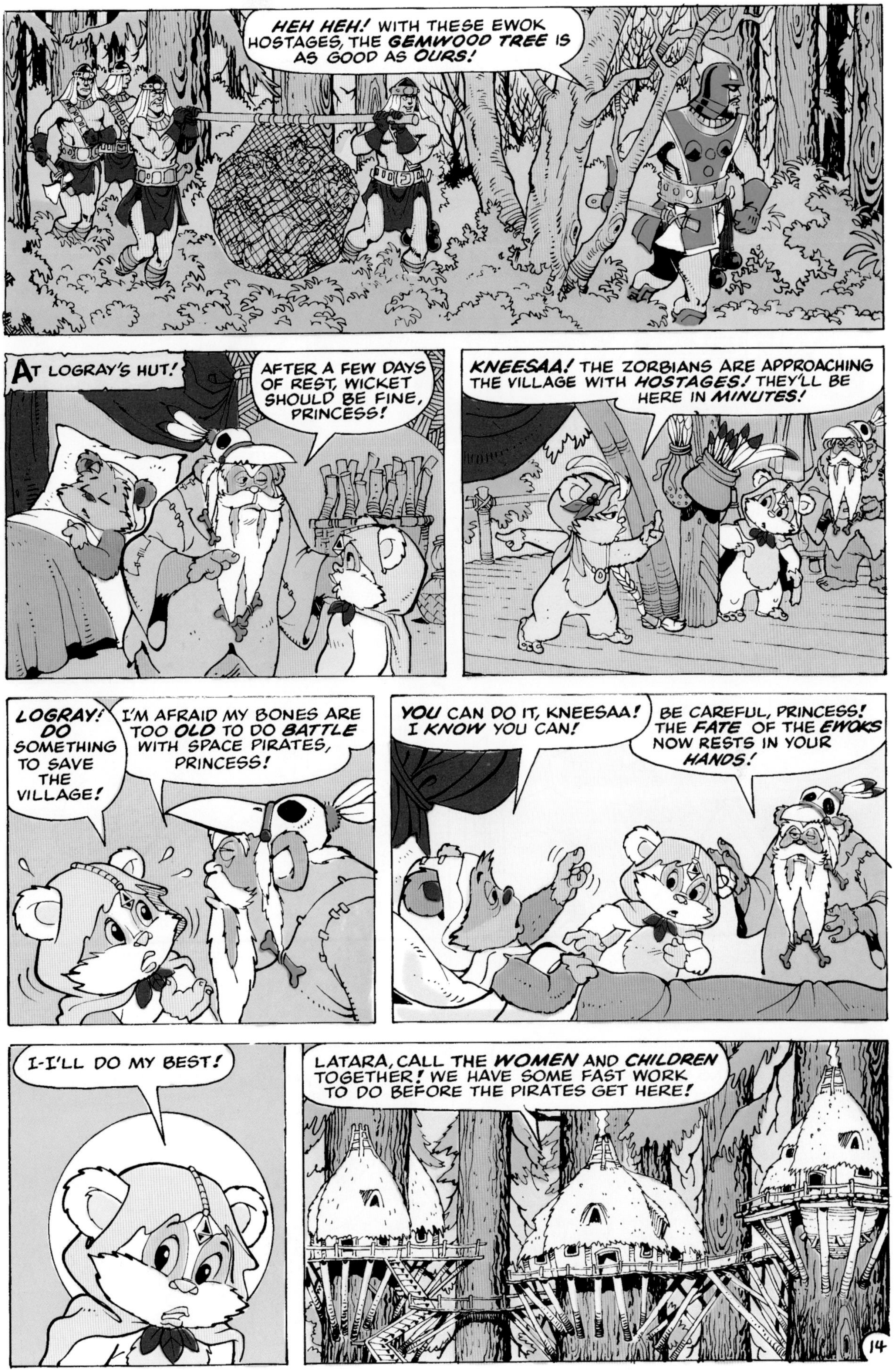
HEH HEH! WITH THESE EWOK HOSTAGES, THE GEMWOOD TREE IS AS GOOD AS OURS!
AT LOGRAY'S HUT!
AFTER A FEW DAYS OF REST, WICKET SHOULD BE FINE, PRINCESS!
KNEESAA! THE ZORBIANS ARE APPROACHING THE VILLAGE WITH HOSTAGES! THEY'LL BE HERE IN MINUTES!
LOGRAY! DO SOMETHING TO SAVE THE VILLAGE!
I'M AFRAID MY BONES ARE TOO OLD TO DO BATTLE WITH SPACE PIRATES, PRINCESS!
YOU CAN DO IT, KNEESAA! I KNOW YOU CAN!
BE CAREFUL, PRINCESS! THE FATE OF THE EWOKS NOW RESTS IN YOUR HANDS!
I-I'LL DO MY BEST!
LATARA, CALL THE WOMEN AND CHILDREN TOGETHER! WE HAVE SOME FAST WORK TO DO BEFORE THE PIRATES GET HERE!
14

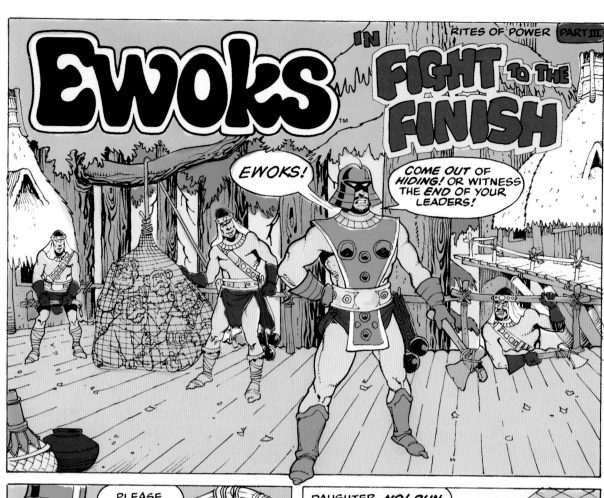

EWOKS

IN FIGHT TO THE FINISH

EWOKS! COME OUT OF *HIDING!* OR WITNESS THE *END* OF YOUR LEADERS!

PLEASE DON'T HURT THEM!

COME OUT, EVERYONE!

DAUGHTER, *NO! RUN* WHILE YOU CAN!

WELL, AT LEAST THERE'S *ONE* AMONG YOU WITH SENSE!

AND SUCH A *PRETTY* ONE AT THAT!

15

40

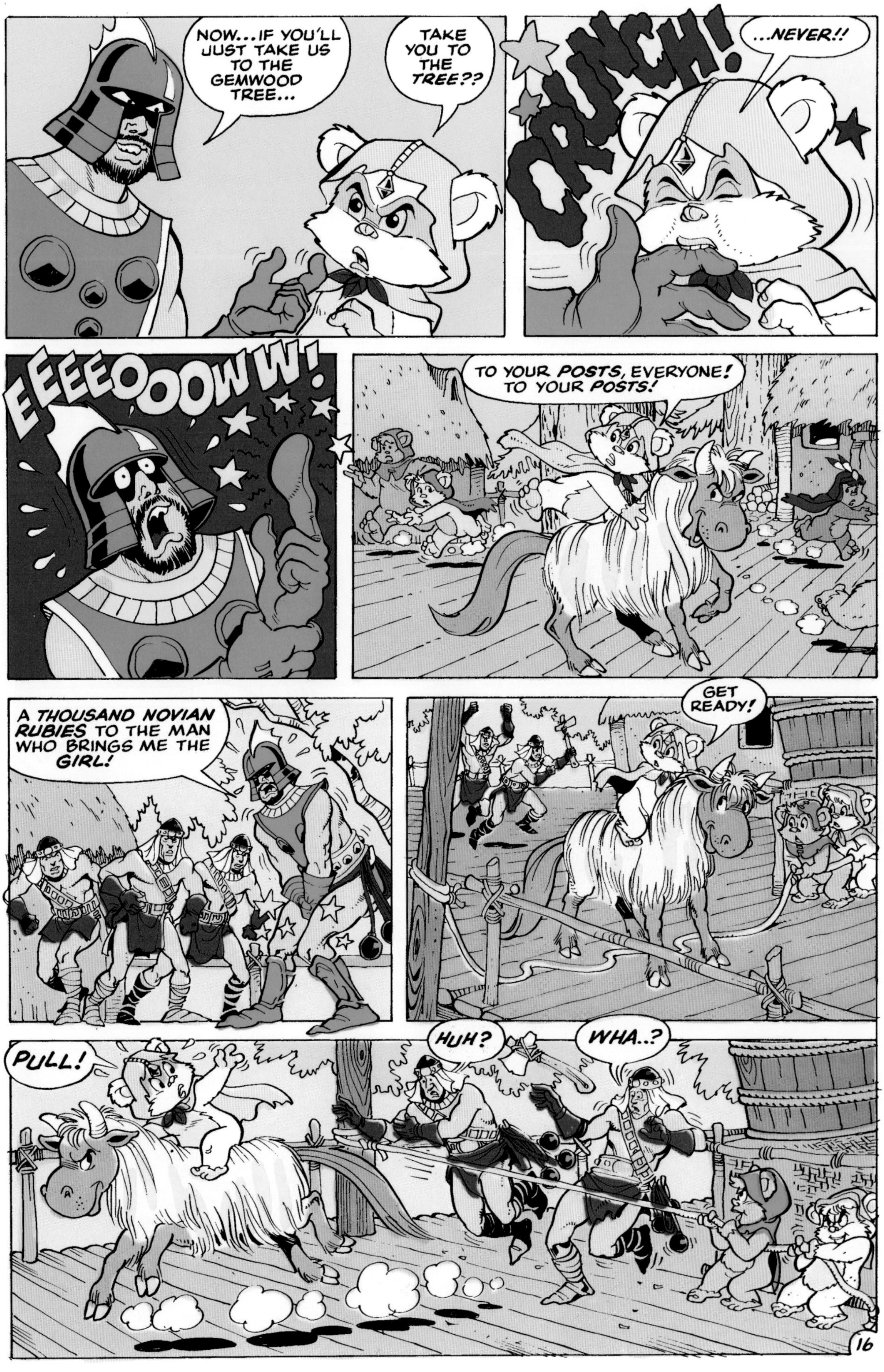
NOW...IF YOU'LL JUST TAKE US TO THE GEMWOOD TREE...
TAKE YOU TO THE TREE??
CRUNCH!
...NEVER!!
EEEEOOOWW!
TO YOUR POSTS, EVERYONE! TO YOUR POSTS!
A THOUSAND NOVIAN RUBIES TO THE MAN WHO BRINGS ME THE GIRL!
GET READY!
PULL!
HUH?
WHA..?
16

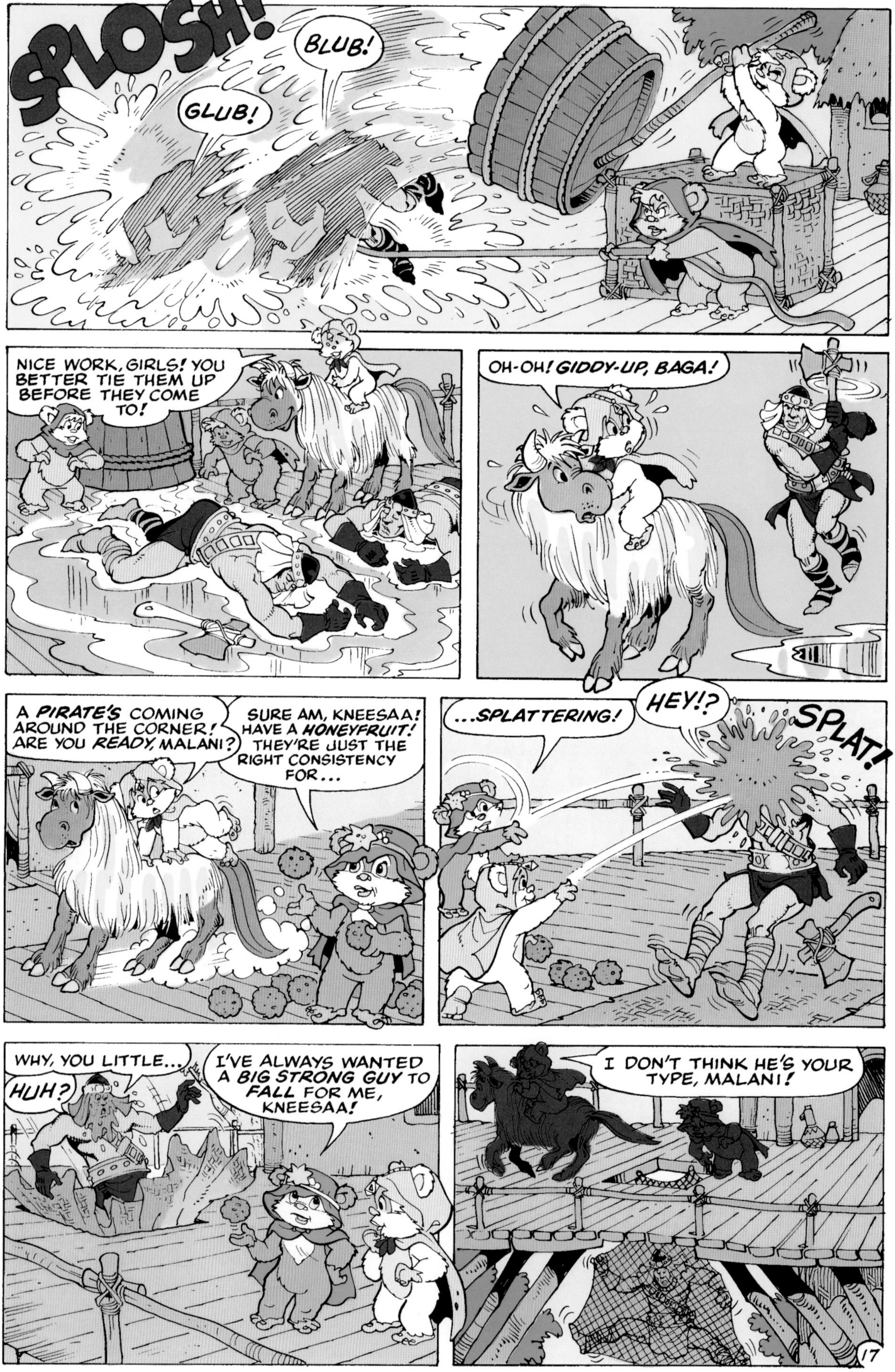
SPLOSH!
GLUB!
BLUB!
NICE WORK, GIRLS! YOU BETTER TIE THEM UP BEFORE THEY COME TO!
OH-OH! GIDDY-UP, BAGA!
A PIRATE'S COMING AROUND THE CORNER! ARE YOU READY, MALANI?
SURE AM, KNEESAA! HAVE A HONEYFRUIT! THEY'RE JUST THE RIGHT CONSISTENCY FOR...
...SPLATTERING!
HEY!?
SPLAT!
WHY, YOU LITTLE...
HUH?
I'VE ALWAYS WANTED A BIG STRONG GUY TO FALL FOR ME, KNEESAA!
I DON'T THINK HE'S YOUR TYPE, MALANI!
17

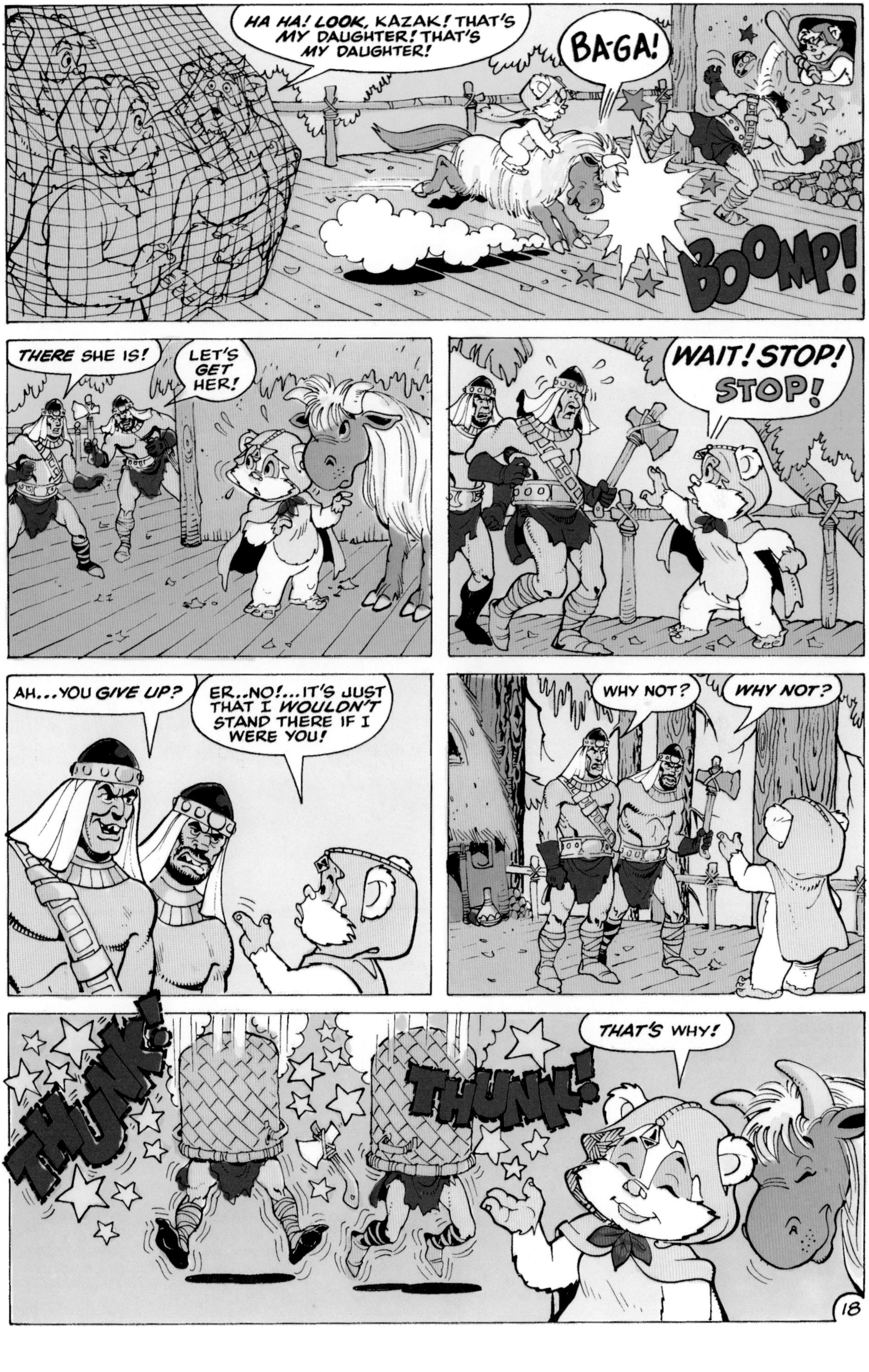
HA HA! LOOK, KAZAK! THAT'S MY DAUGHTER! THAT'S MY DAUGHTER!
BA-GA!
BOOMP!
THERE SHE IS!
LET'S GET HER!
WAIT! STOP! STOP!
AH...YOU GIVE UP?
ER..NO!...IT'S JUST THAT I WOULDN'T STAND THERE IF I WERE YOU!
WHY NOT?
WHY NOT?
THUNK!
THUNK!
THAT'S WHY!
18

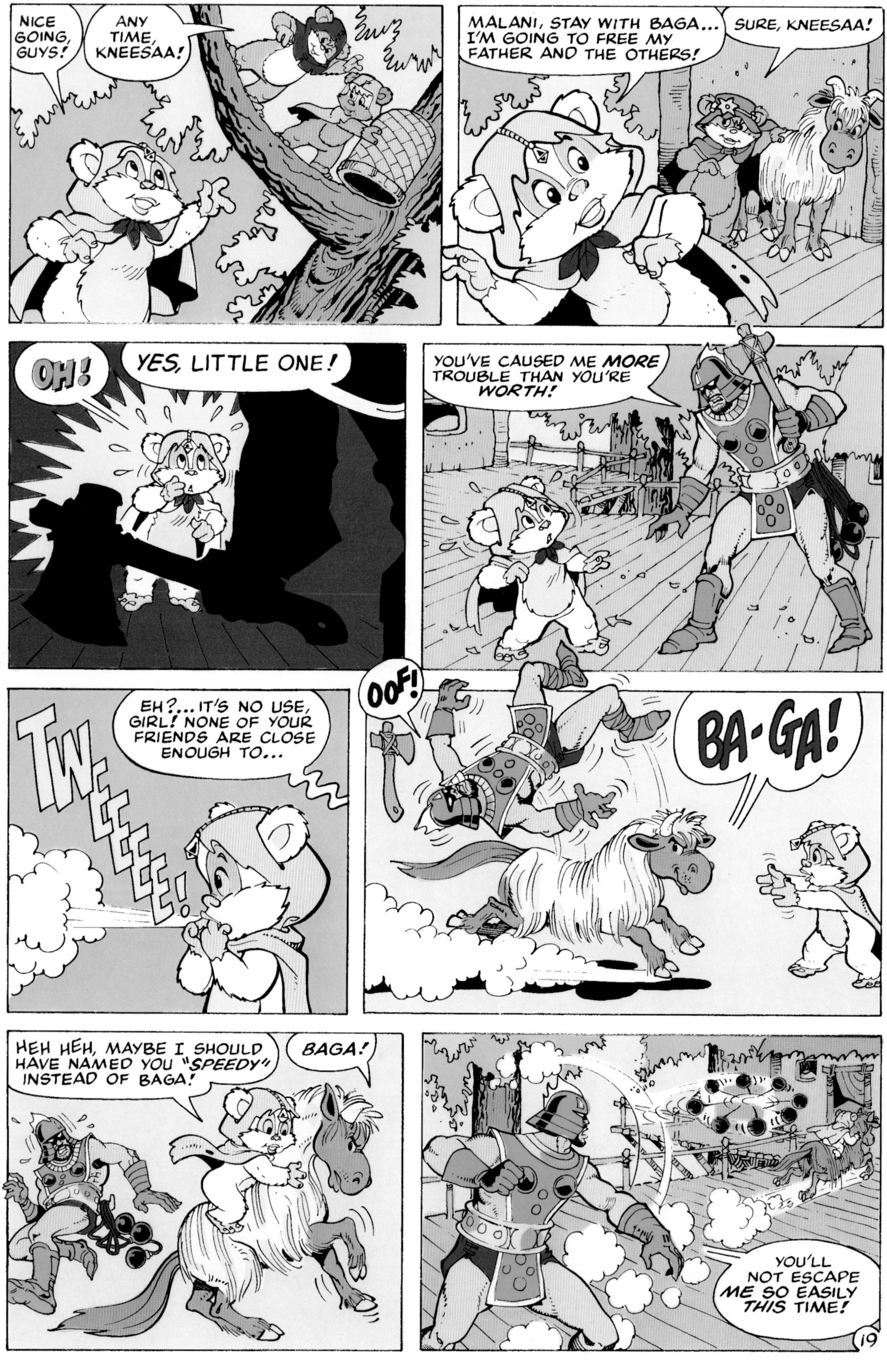
NICE GOING, GUYS!
ANY TIME, KNEESAA!
MALANI, STAY WITH BAGA... I'M GOING TO FREE MY FATHER AND THE OTHERS!
SURE, KNEESAA!
OH!
YES, LITTLE ONE!
YOU'VE CAUSED ME MORE TROUBLE THAN YOU'RE WORTH!
TWEEEEEE!
EH?...IT'S NO USE, GIRL! NONE OF YOUR FRIENDS ARE CLOSE ENOUGH TO...
OOF!
BA-GA!
HEH HEH, MAYBE I SHOULD HAVE NAMED YOU "SPEEDY" INSTEAD OF BAGA!
BAGA!
YOU'LL NOT ESCAPE ME SO EASILY THIS TIME!
19

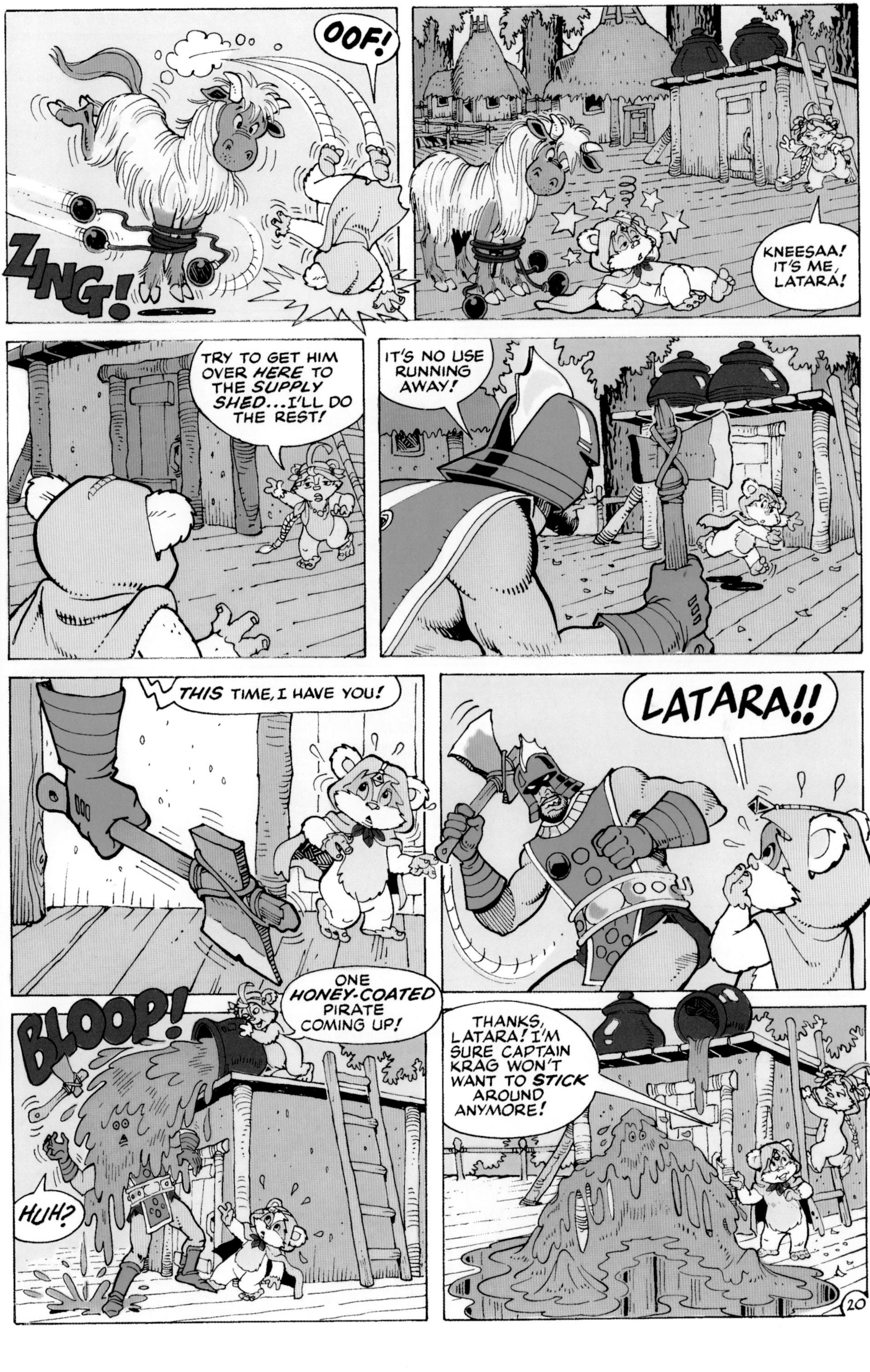
OOF!
ZING!
KNEESAA! IT'S ME, LATARA!
TRY TO GET HIM OVER HERE TO THE SUPPLY SHED...I'LL DO THE REST!
IT'S NO USE RUNNING AWAY!
THIS TIME, I HAVE YOU!
LATARA!!
BLOOP!
ONE HONEY-COATED PIRATE COMING UP!
HUH?
THANKS, LATARA! I'M SURE CAPTAIN KRAG WON'T WANT TO STICK AROUND ANYMORE!
20

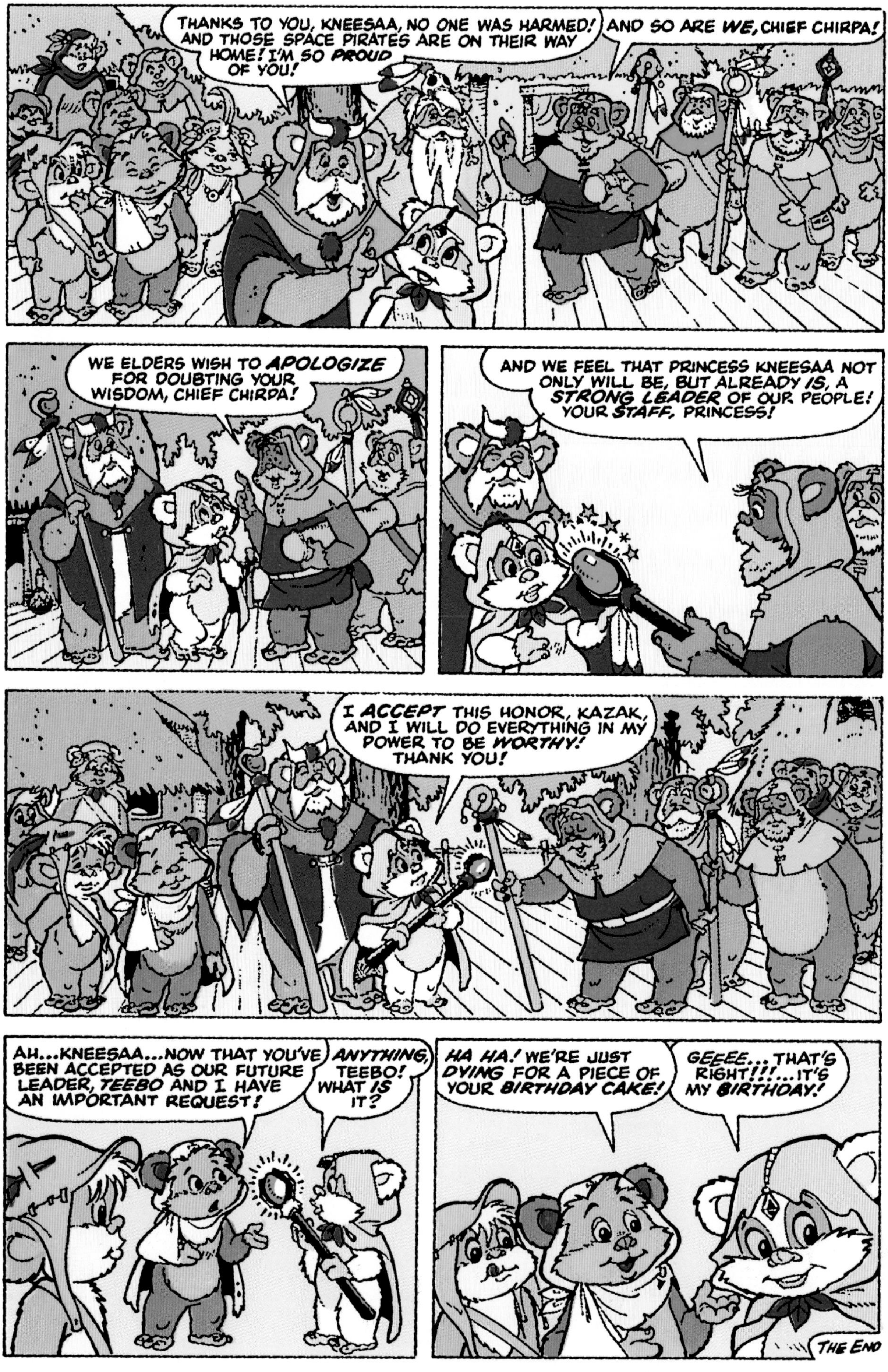
THANKS TO YOU, KNEESAA, NO ONE WAS HARMED! AND THOSE SPACE PIRATES ARE ON THEIR WAY HOME! I'M SO PROUD OF YOU!
AND SO ARE WE, CHIEF CHIRPA!
WE ELDERS WISH TO APOLOGIZE FOR DOUBTING YOUR WISDOM, CHIEF CHIRPA!
AND WE FEEL THAT PRINCESS KNEESAA NOT ONLY WILL BE, BUT ALREADY IS, A STRONG LEADER OF OUR PEOPLE! YOUR STAFF, PRINCESS!
I ACCEPT THIS HONOR, KAZAK, AND I WILL DO EVERYTHING IN MY POWER TO BE WORTHY! THANK YOU!
AH...KNEESAA...NOW THAT YOU'VE BEEN ACCEPTED AS OUR FUTURE LEADER, TEEBO AND I HAVE AN IMPORTANT REQUEST!
ANYTHING, TEEBO! WHAT IS IT?
HA HA! WE'RE JUST DYING FOR A PIECE OF YOUR BIRTHDAY CAKE!
GEEEE... THAT'S RIGHT!!!...IT'S MY BIRTHDAY!
THE END

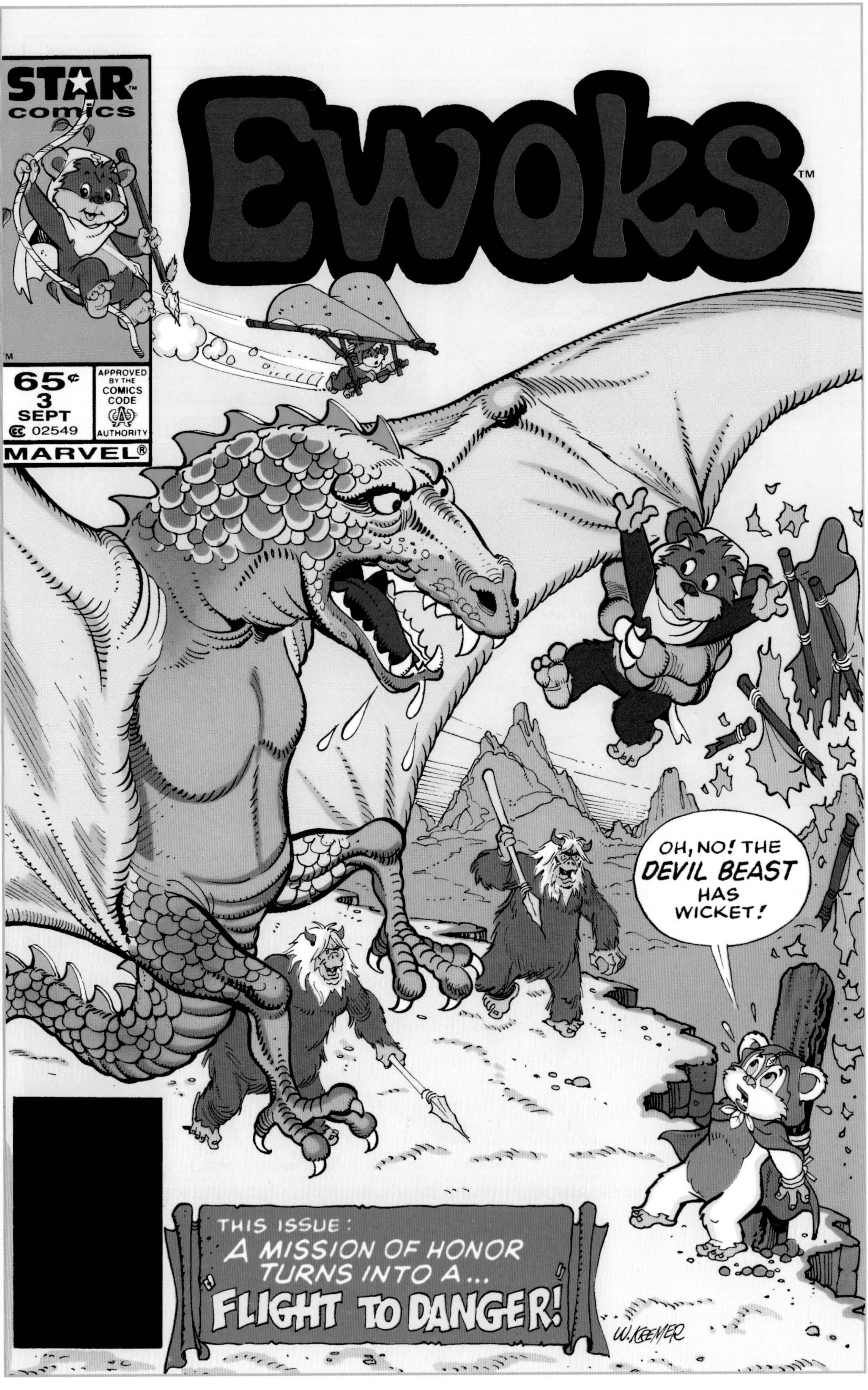
STAR comics
Ewoks™
65¢
3
SEPT
02549
APPROVED BY THE COMICS CODE AUTHORITY
MARVEL®
OH, NO! THE DEVIL BEAST HAS WICKET!
THIS ISSUE:
A MISSION OF HONOR TURNS INTO A...
"FLIGHT TO DANGER!"
W. KREMER

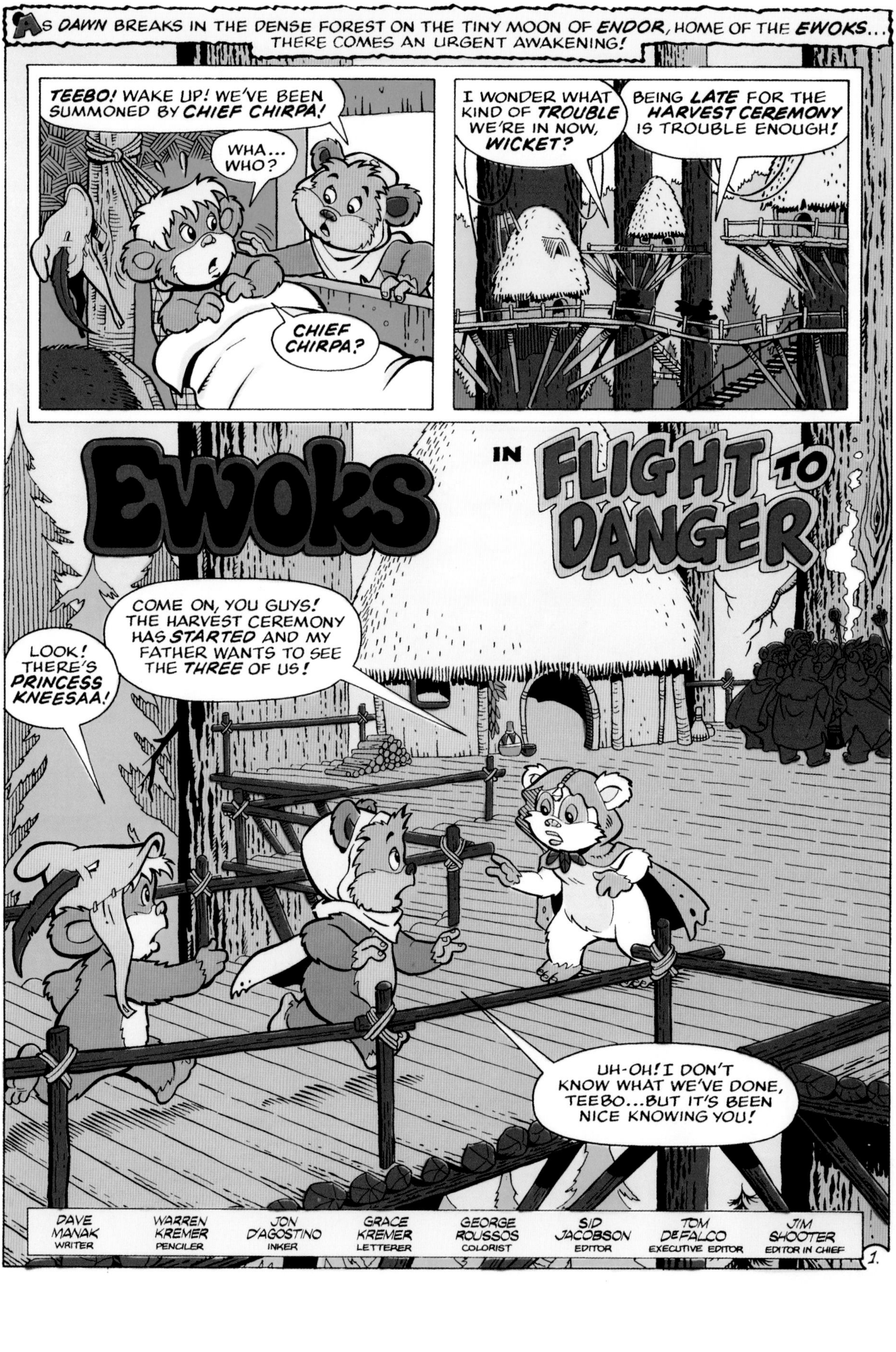
AS DAWN BREAKS IN THE DENSE FOREST ON THE TINY MOON OF ENDOR, HOME OF THE EWOKS... THERE COMES AN URGENT AWAKENING!
TEEBO! WAKE UP! WE'VE BEEN SUMMONED BY CHIEF CHIRPA!
WHA... WHO?
CHIEF CHIRPA?
I WONDER WHAT KIND OF TROUBLE WE'RE IN NOW, WICKET?
BEING LATE FOR THE HARVEST CEREMONY IS TROUBLE ENOUGH!
EWOKS IN FLIGHT TO DANGER
COME ON, YOU GUYS! THE HARVEST CEREMONY HAS STARTED AND MY FATHER WANTS TO SEE THE THREE OF US!
LOOK! THERE'S PRINCESS KNEESAA!
UH-OH! I DON'T KNOW WHAT WE'VE DONE, TEEBO...BUT IT'S BEEN NICE KNOWING YOU!
DAVE MANAK WRITER
WARREN KREMER PENCILER
JON D'AGOSTINO INKER
GRACE KREMER LETTERER
GEORGE ROUSSOS COLORIST
SID JACOBSON EDITOR
TOM DEFALCO EXECUTIVE EDITOR
JIM SHOOTER EDITOR IN CHIEF
1.

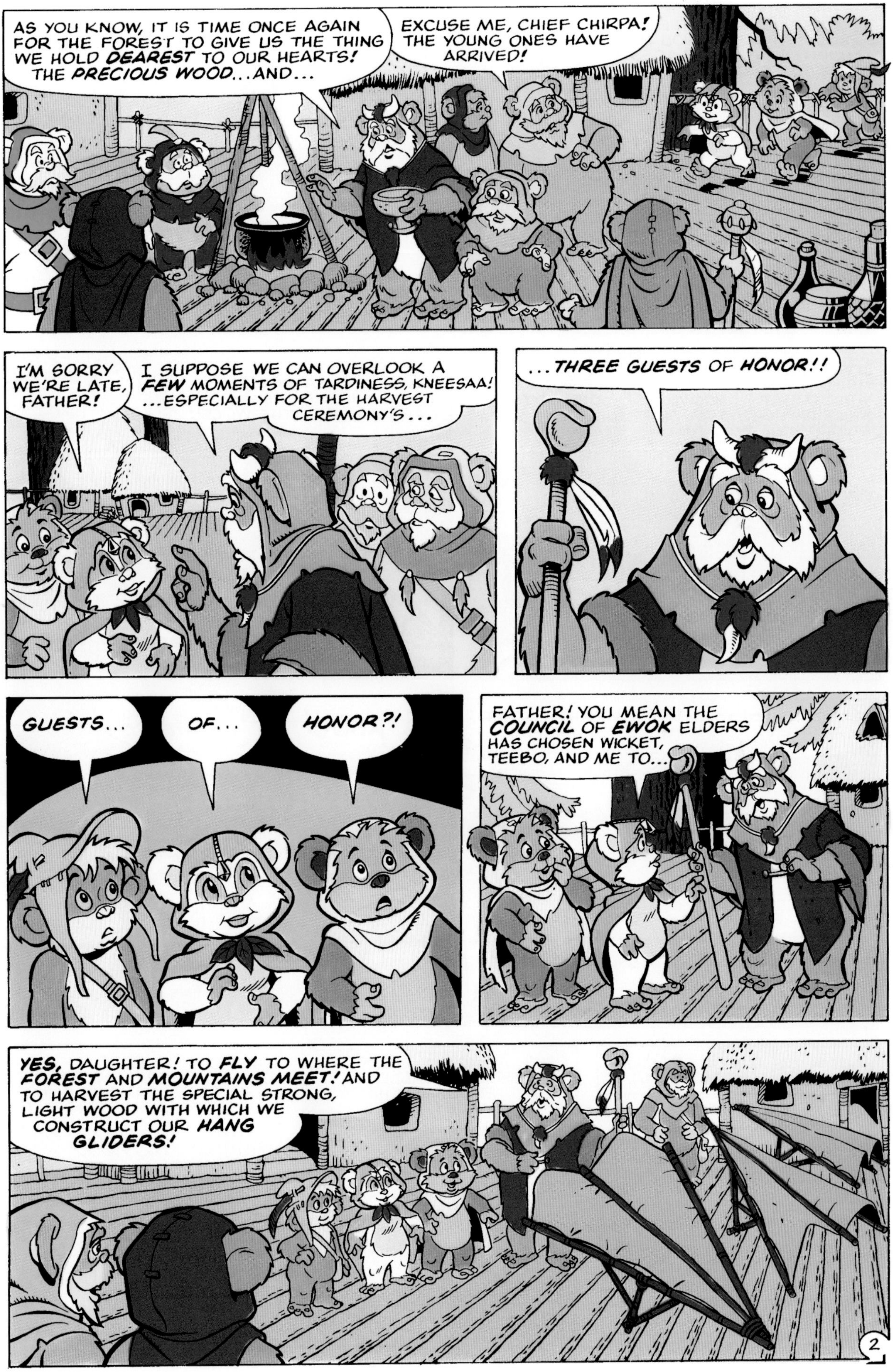
AS YOU KNOW, IT IS TIME ONCE AGAIN FOR THE FOREST TO GIVE US THE THING WE HOLD DEAREST TO OUR HEARTS! THE PRECIOUS WOOD...AND...
EXCUSE ME, CHIEF CHIRPA! THE YOUNG ONES HAVE ARRIVED!
I'M SORRY WE'RE LATE, FATHER!
I SUPPOSE WE CAN OVERLOOK A FEW MOMENTS OF TARDINESS, KNEESAA! ...ESPECIALLY FOR THE HARVEST CEREMONY'S...
...THREE GUESTS OF HONOR!!
GUESTS...
OF...
HONOR?!
FATHER! YOU MEAN THE COUNCIL OF EWOK ELDERS HAS CHOSEN WICKET, TEEBO, AND ME TO...
YES, DAUGHTER! TO FLY TO WHERE THE FOREST AND MOUNTAINS MEET! AND TO HARVEST THE SPECIAL STRONG, LIGHT WOOD WITH WHICH WE CONSTRUCT OUR HANG GLIDERS!
2

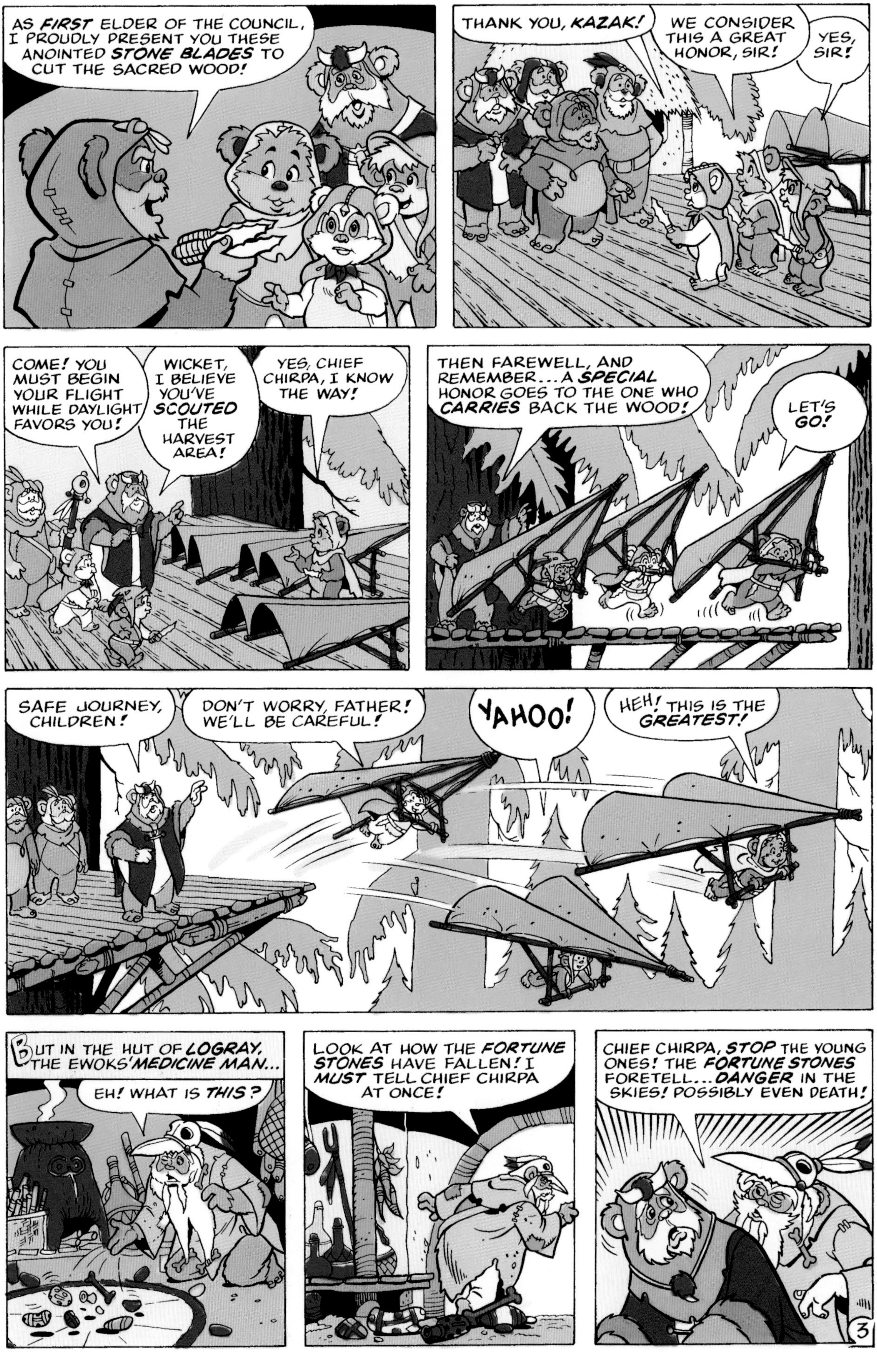
AS FIRST ELDER OF THE COUNCIL, I PROUDLY PRESENT YOU THESE ANOINTED STONE BLADES TO CUT THE SACRED WOOD!
THANK YOU, KAZAK!
WE CONSIDER THIS A GREAT HONOR, SIR!
YES, SIR!
COME! YOU MUST BEGIN YOUR FLIGHT WHILE DAYLIGHT FAVORS YOU!
WICKET, I BELIEVE YOU'VE SCOUTED THE HARVEST AREA!
YES, CHIEF CHIRPA, I KNOW THE WAY!
THEN FAREWELL, AND REMEMBER... A SPECIAL HONOR GOES TO THE ONE WHO CARRIES BACK THE WOOD!
LET'S GO!
SAFE JOURNEY, CHILDREN!
DON'T WORRY, FATHER! WE'LL BE CAREFUL!
YAHOO!
HEH! THIS IS THE GREATEST!
BUT IN THE HUT OF LOGRAY, THE EWOKS' MEDICINE MAN...
EH! WHAT IS THIS?
LOOK AT HOW THE FORTUNE STONES HAVE FALLEN! I MUST TELL CHIEF CHIRPA AT ONCE!
CHIEF CHIRPA, STOP THE YOUNG ONES! THE FORTUNE STONES FORETELL... DANGER IN THE SKIES! POSSIBLY EVEN DEATH!
3

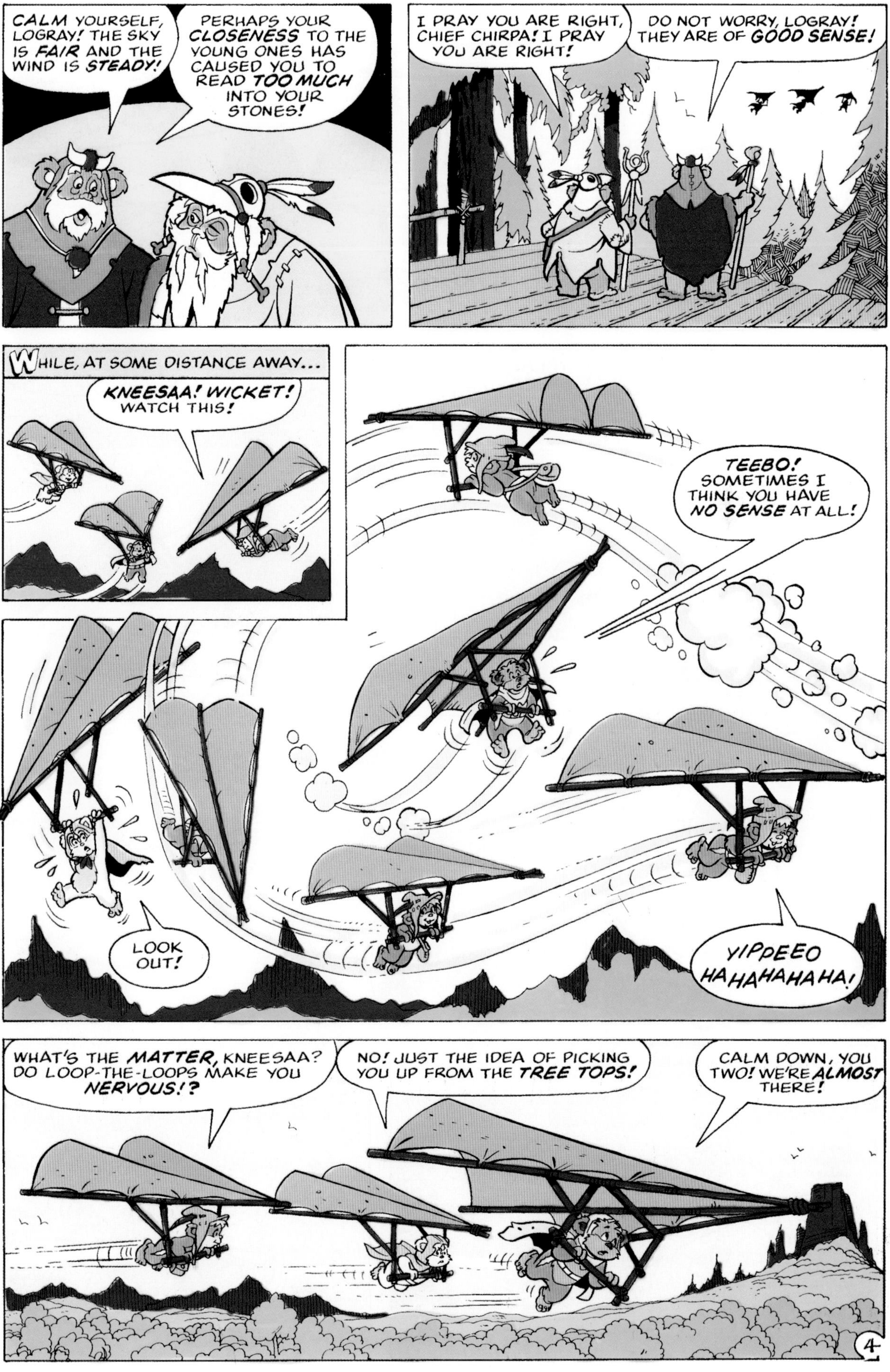
CALM YOURSELF, LOGRAY! THE SKY IS FAIR AND THE WIND IS STEADY!
PERHAPS YOUR CLOSENESS TO THE YOUNG ONES HAS CAUSED YOU TO READ TOO MUCH INTO YOUR STONES!
I PRAY YOU ARE RIGHT, CHIEF CHIRPA! I PRAY YOU ARE RIGHT!
DO NOT WORRY, LOGRAY! THEY ARE OF GOOD SENSE!
WHILE, AT SOME DISTANCE AWAY...
KNEESAA! WICKET! WATCH THIS!
TEEBO! SOMETIMES I THINK YOU HAVE NO SENSE AT ALL!
LOOK OUT!
YIPPEEO HAHAHAHAHA!
WHAT'S THE MATTER, KNEESAA? DO LOOP-THE-LOOPS MAKE YOU NERVOUS!?
NO! JUST THE IDEA OF PICKING YOU UP FROM THE TREE TOPS!
CALM DOWN, YOU TWO! WE'RE ALMOST THERE!
4

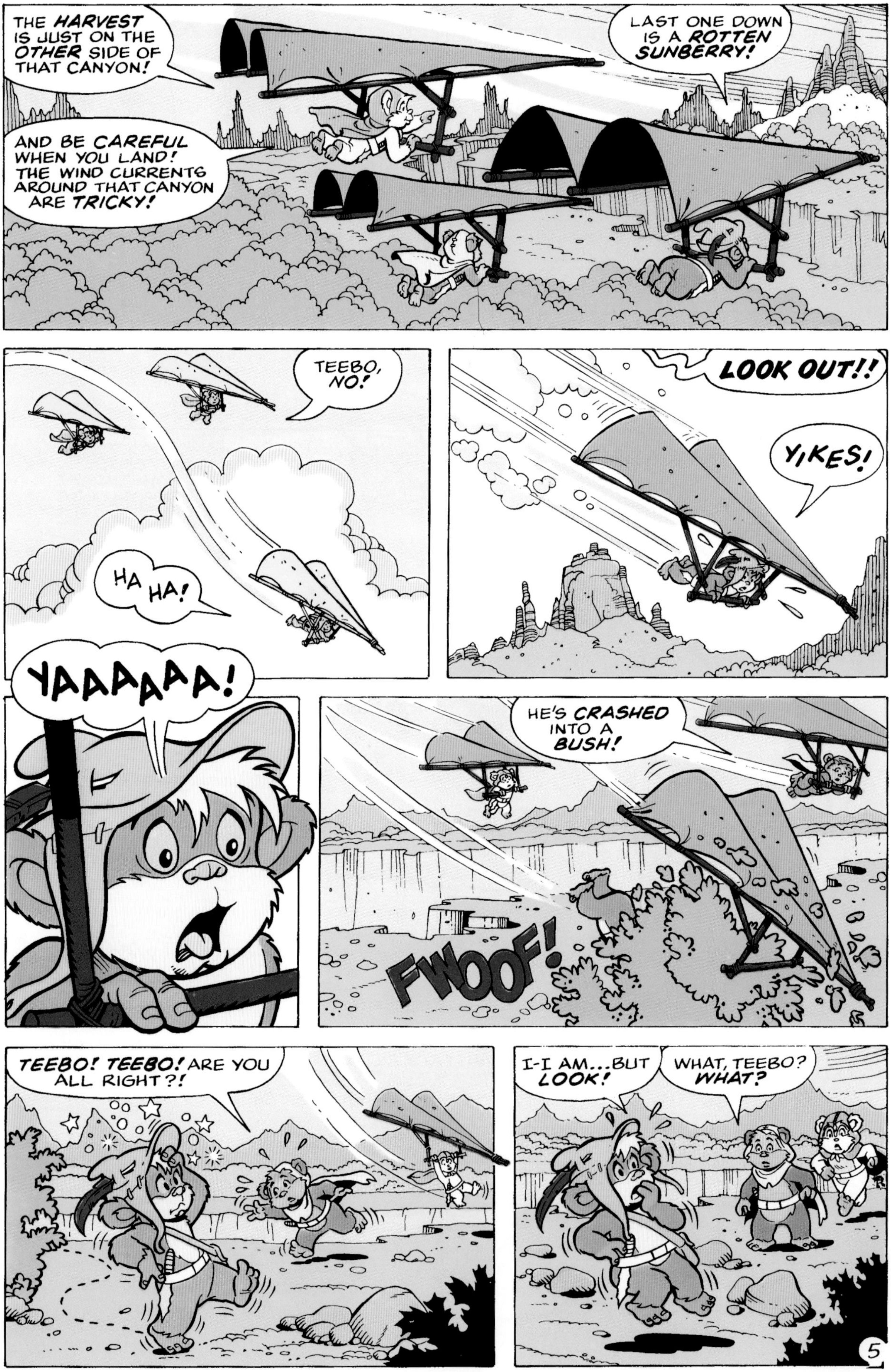
THE HARVEST IS JUST ON THE OTHER SIDE OF THAT CANYON!
AND BE CAREFUL WHEN YOU LAND! THE WIND CURRENTS AROUND THAT CANYON ARE TRICKY!
LAST ONE DOWN IS A ROTTEN SUNBERRY!
TEEBO, NO!
HA HA!
LOOK OUT!!
YIKES!
YAAAAAA!
HE'S CRASHED INTO A BUSH!
FWOOF!
TEEBO! TEEBO! ARE YOU ALL RIGHT?!
I-I AM...BUT LOOK!
WHAT, TEEBO? WHAT?
5

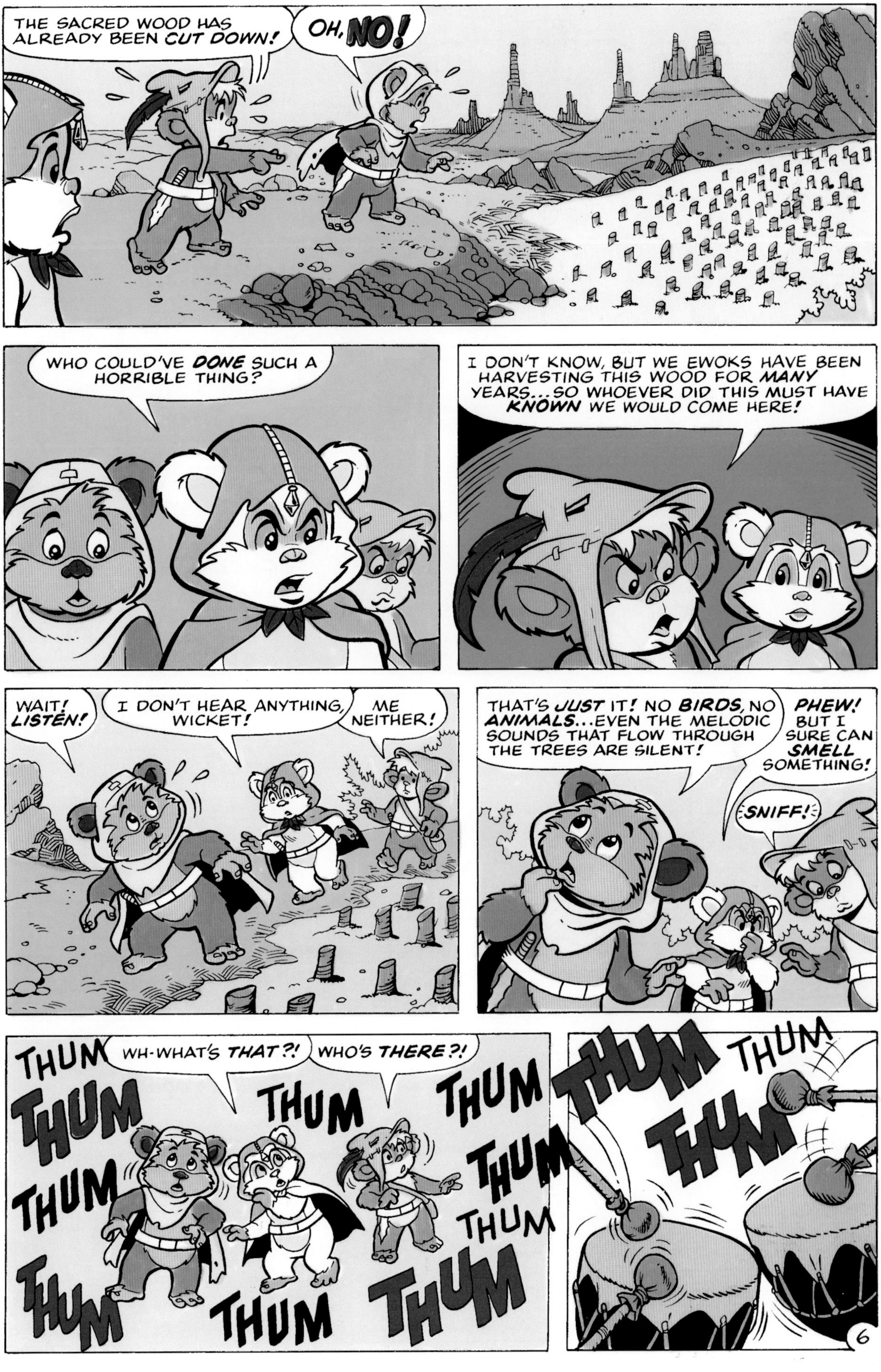
THE SACRED WOOD HAS ALREADY BEEN CUT DOWN!
OH, NO!
WHO COULD'VE DONE SUCH A HORRIBLE THING?
I DON'T KNOW, BUT WE EWOKS HAVE BEEN HARVESTING THIS WOOD FOR MANY YEARS...SO WHOEVER DID THIS MUST HAVE KNOWN WE WOULD COME HERE!
WAIT! LISTEN!
I DON'T HEAR ANYTHING, WICKET!
ME NEITHER!
THAT'S JUST IT! NO BIRDS, NO ANIMALS...EVEN THE MELODIC SOUNDS THAT FLOW THROUGH THE TREES ARE SILENT!
PHEW! BUT I SURE CAN SMELL SOMETHING!
SNIFF!
THUM THUM THUM THUM
WH-WHAT'S THAT?!
WHO'S THERE?!
THUM THUM THUM THUM THUM THUM THUM
THUM THUM THUM
6

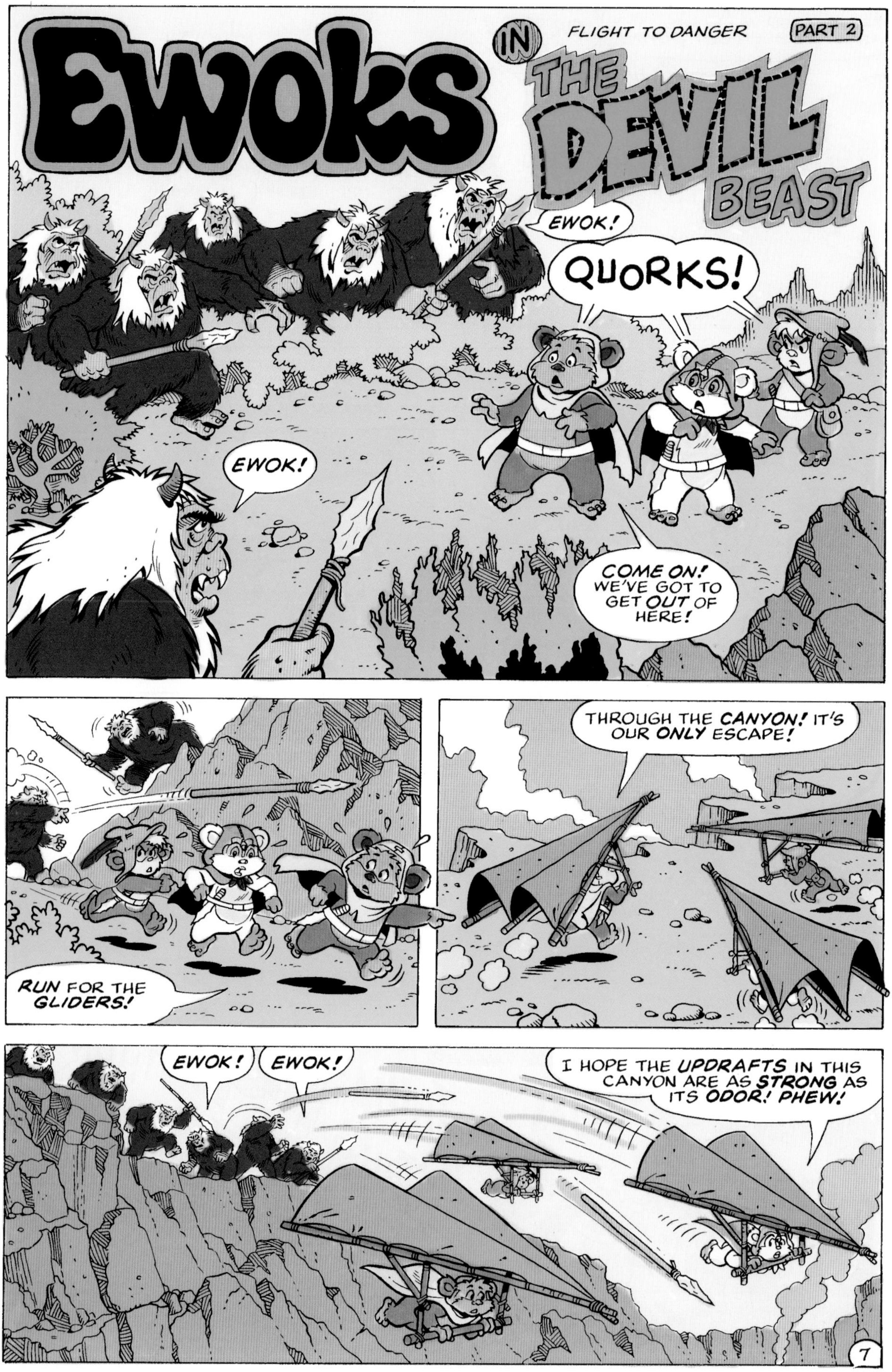
Ewoks
IN
FLIGHT TO DANGER
PART 2
THE DEVIL BEAST
EWOK!
QUORKS!
EWOK!
COME ON! WE'VE GOT TO GET OUT OF HERE!
RUN FOR THE GLIDERS!
THROUGH THE CANYON! IT'S OUR ONLY ESCAPE!
EWOK!
EWOK!
I HOPE THE UPDRAFTS IN THIS CANYON ARE AS STRONG AS ITS ODOR! PHEW!
7

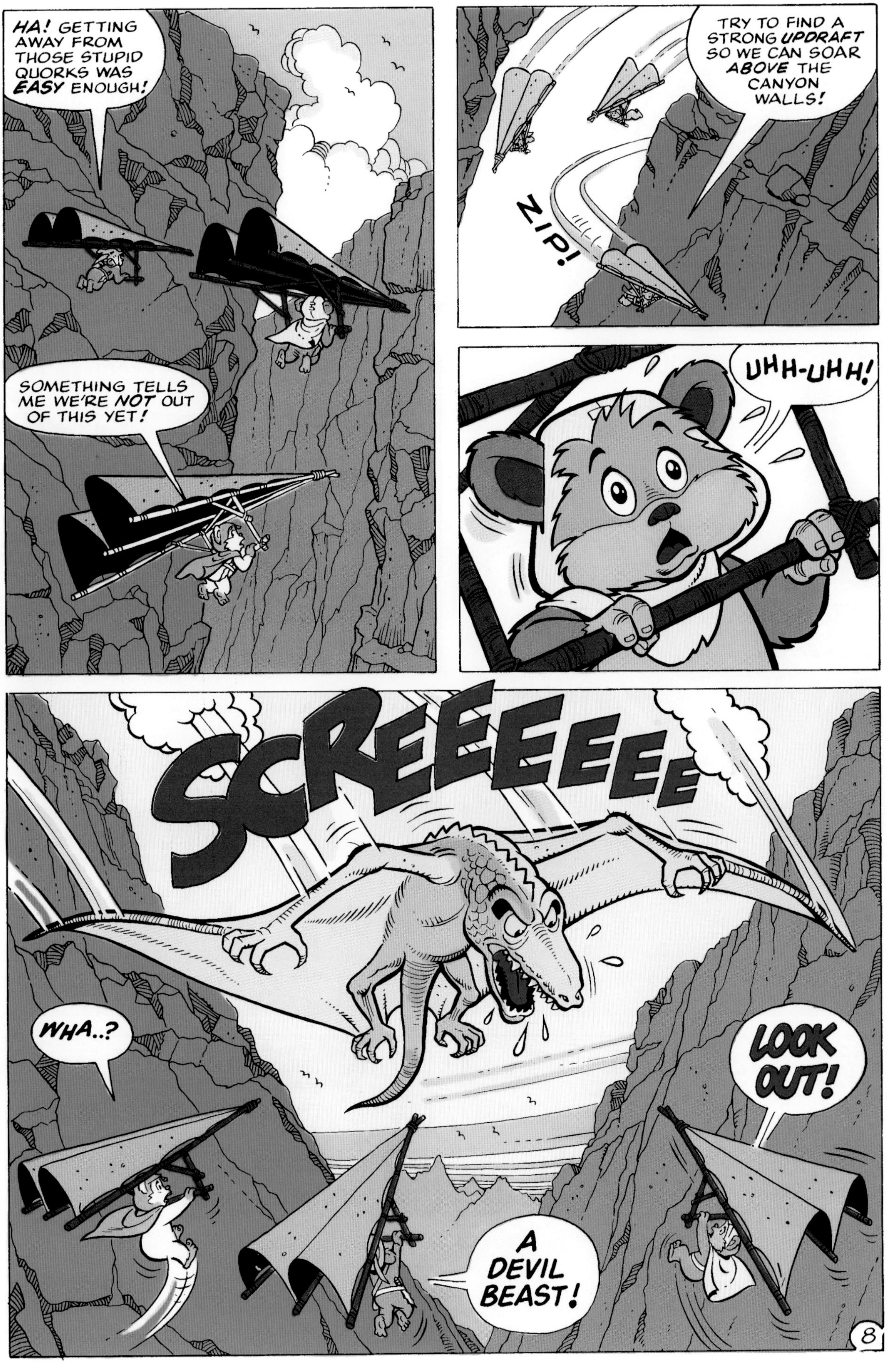
HA! GETTING AWAY FROM THOSE STUPID QUORKS WAS EASY ENOUGH!
SOMETHING TELLS ME WE'RE NOT OUT OF THIS YET!
TRY TO FIND A STRONG UPDRAFT SO WE CAN SOAR ABOVE THE CANYON WALLS!
ZIP!
UHH-UHH!
SCREEEEEEE
WHA..?
LOOK OUT!
A DEVIL BEAST!
8

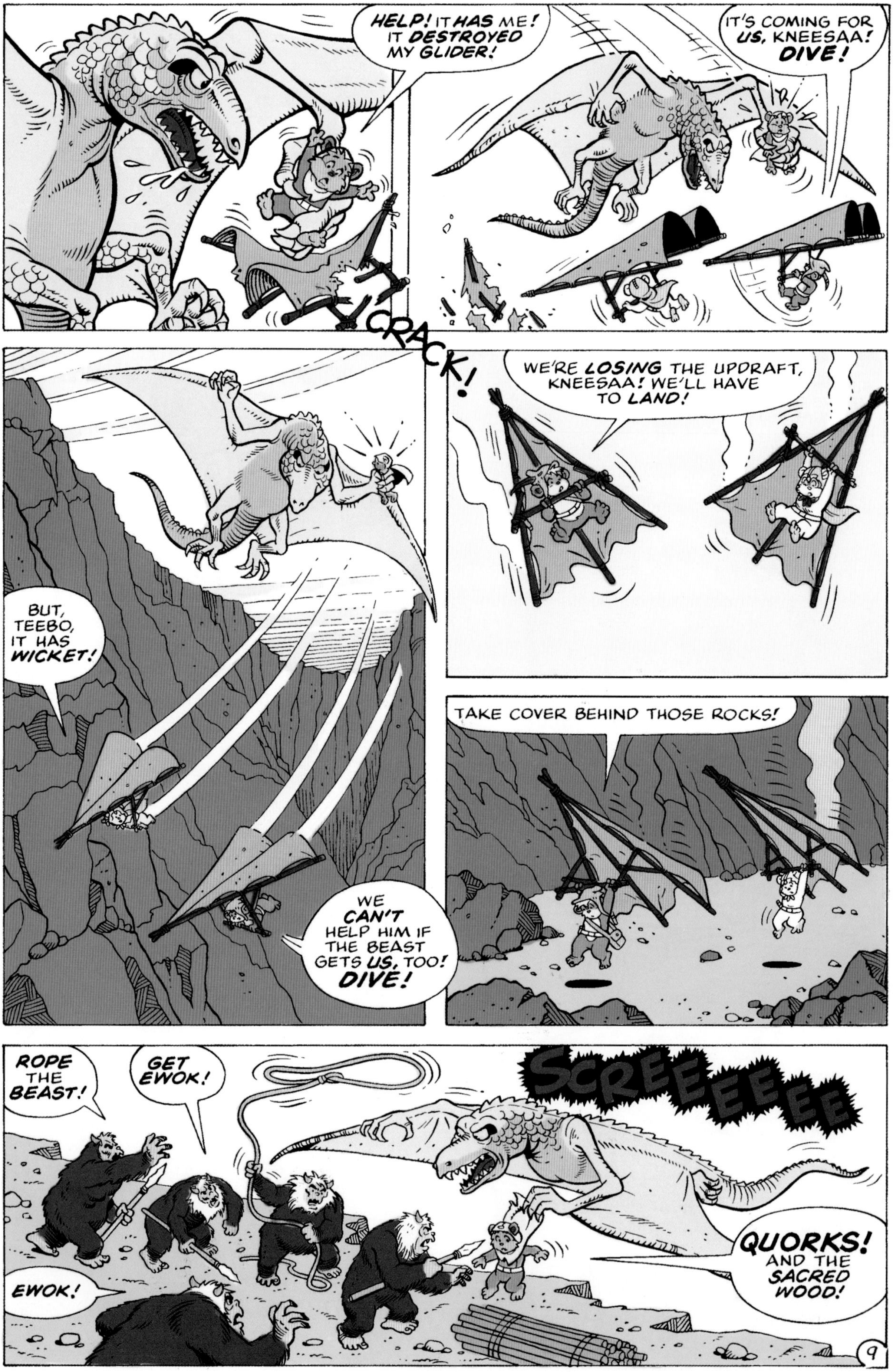
HELP! IT HAS ME! IT DESTROYED MY GLIDER!
IT'S COMING FOR US, KNEESAA! DIVE!
CRACK!
WE'RE LOSING THE UPDRAFT, KNEESAA! WE'LL HAVE TO LAND!
BUT, TEEBO, IT HAS WICKET!
WE CAN'T HELP HIM IF THE BEAST GETS US, TOO! DIVE!
TAKE COVER BEHIND THOSE ROCKS!
ROPE THE BEAST!
GET EWOK!
SCREEEEEEE
EWOK!
QUORKS! AND THE SACRED WOOD!
9

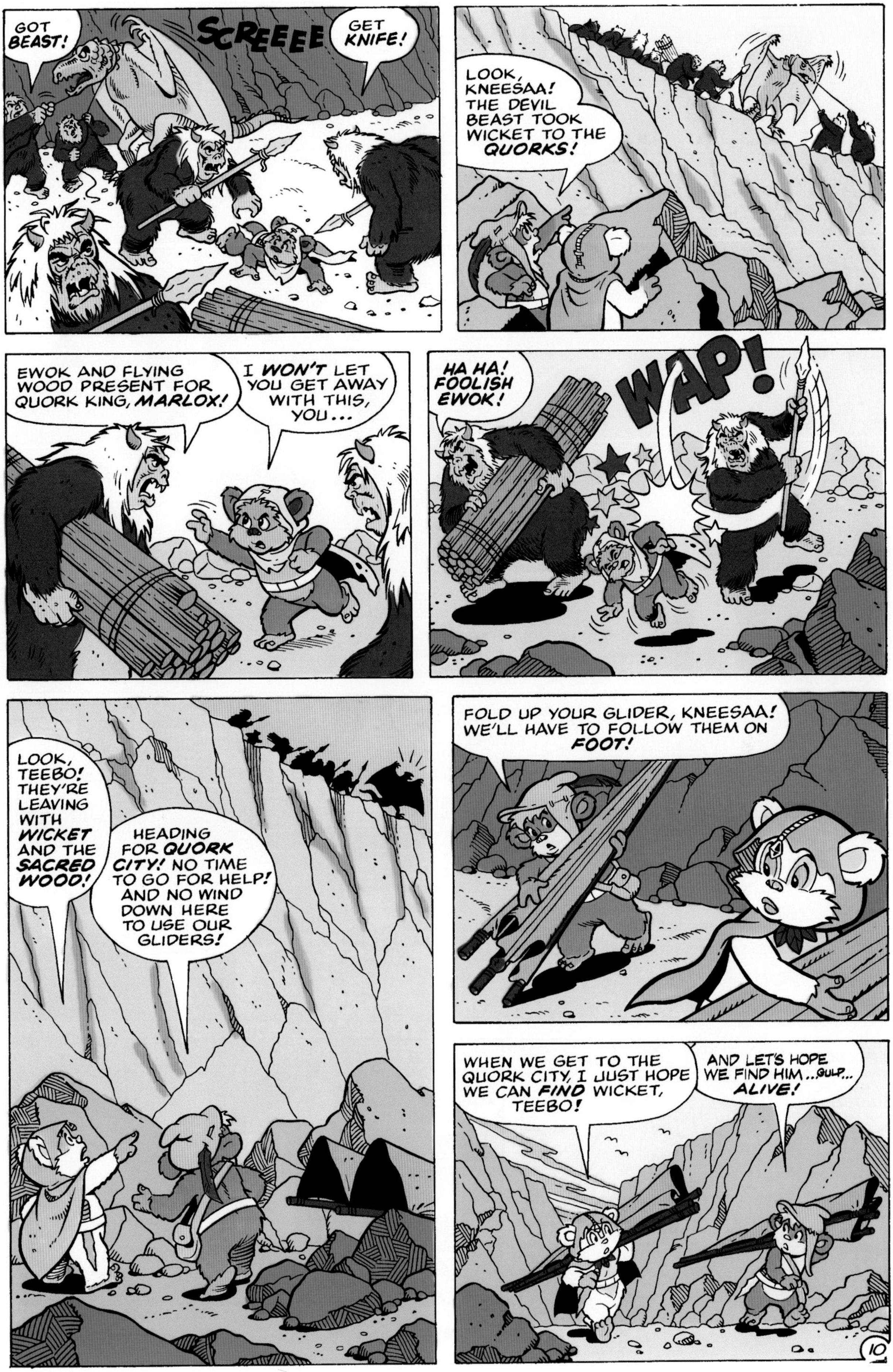
GOT BEAST!
SCREEEEE
GET KNIFE!
LOOK, KNEESAA! THE DEVIL BEAST TOOK WICKET TO THE QUORKS!
EWOK AND FLYING WOOD PRESENT FOR QUORK KING, MARLOX!
I WON'T LET YOU GET AWAY WITH THIS, YOU...
HA HA! FOOLISH EWOK!
WAP!
LOOK, TEEBO! THEY'RE LEAVING WITH WICKET AND THE SACRED WOOD!
HEADING FOR QUORK CITY! NO TIME TO GO FOR HELP! AND NO WIND DOWN HERE TO USE OUR GLIDERS!
FOLD UP YOUR GLIDER, KNEESAA! WE'LL HAVE TO FOLLOW THEM ON FOOT!
WHEN WE GET TO THE QUORK CITY, I JUST HOPE WE CAN FIND WICKET, TEEBO!
AND LET'S HOPE WE FIND HIM...GULP... ALIVE!
10

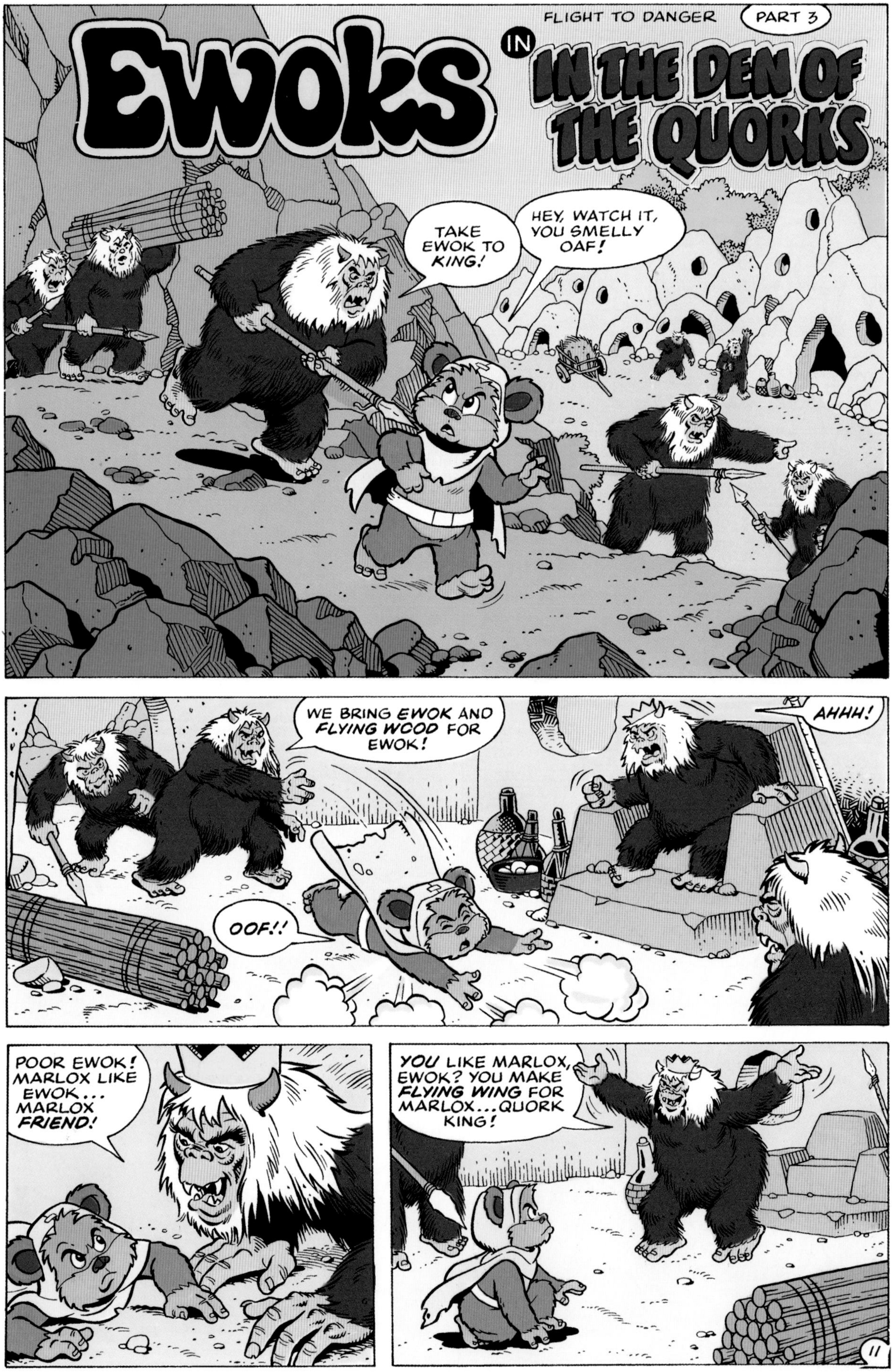
FLIGHT TO DANGER
PART 3
EWOKS
IN
IN THE DEN OF THE QUORKS
TAKE EWOK TO KING!
HEY, WATCH IT, YOU SMELLY OAF!
WE BRING EWOK AND FLYING WOOD FOR EWOK!
AHHH!
OOF!!
POOR EWOK! MARLOX LIKE EWOK... MARLOX FRIEND!
YOU LIKE MARLOX, EWOK? YOU MAKE FLYING WING FOR MARLOX... QUORK KING!
11

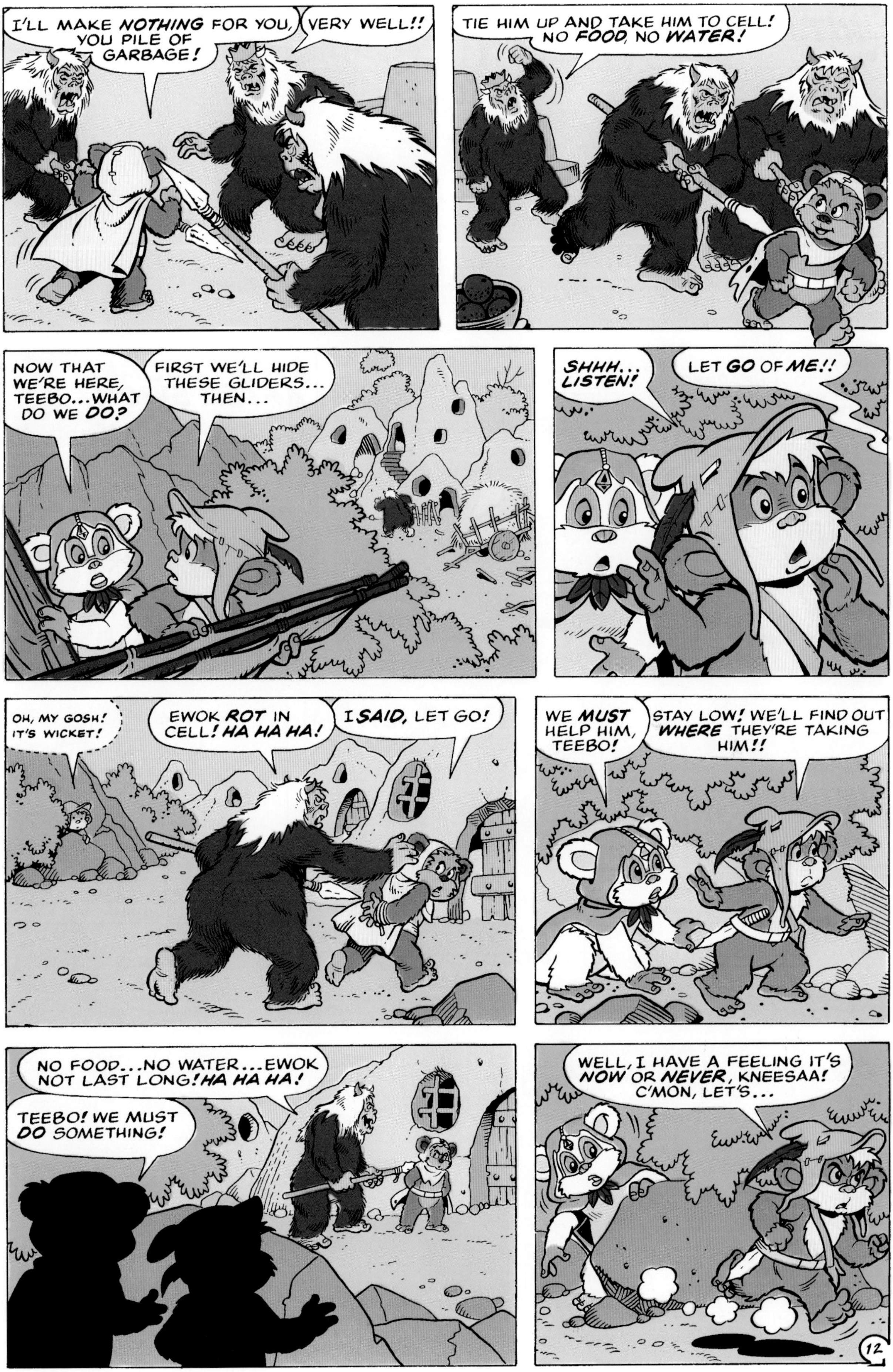
I'LL MAKE NOTHING FOR YOU, YOU PILE OF GARBAGE!
VERY WELL!!
TIE HIM UP AND TAKE HIM TO CELL! NO FOOD, NO WATER!
NOW THAT WE'RE HERE, TEEBO...WHAT DO WE DO?
FIRST WE'LL HIDE THESE GLIDERS... THEN...
SHHH... LISTEN!
LET GO OF ME!!
OH, MY GOSH! IT'S WICKET!
EWOK ROT IN CELL! HA HA HA!
I SAID, LET GO!
WE MUST HELP HIM, TEEBO!
STAY LOW! WE'LL FIND OUT WHERE THEY'RE TAKING HIM!!
NO FOOD...NO WATER...EWOK NOT LAST LONG! HA HA HA!
TEEBO! WE MUST DO SOMETHING!
WELL, I HAVE A FEELING IT'S NOW OR NEVER, KNEESAA! C'MON, LET'S...
12

...HIT HIM!

HUH?

OOF!

KNEESAA! TEEBO!

BOY! AM I GLAD TO SEE YOU TWO!

OUR GLIDERS ARE HIDDEN NEARBY! YOU AND I CAN DOUBLE UP, WICKET!

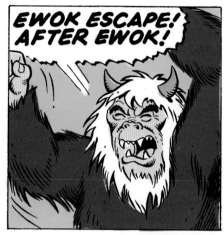

EWOK ESCAPE! AFTER EWOK!

THUNK!

HEY!

I'M PINNED!

HOLD ON, KNEESAA, WE'LL...

YOU STAY!

HUH?

ULP!

AFTER ALL...THREE EWOKS BETTER THAN ONE...YOU GO TO CELL!

13

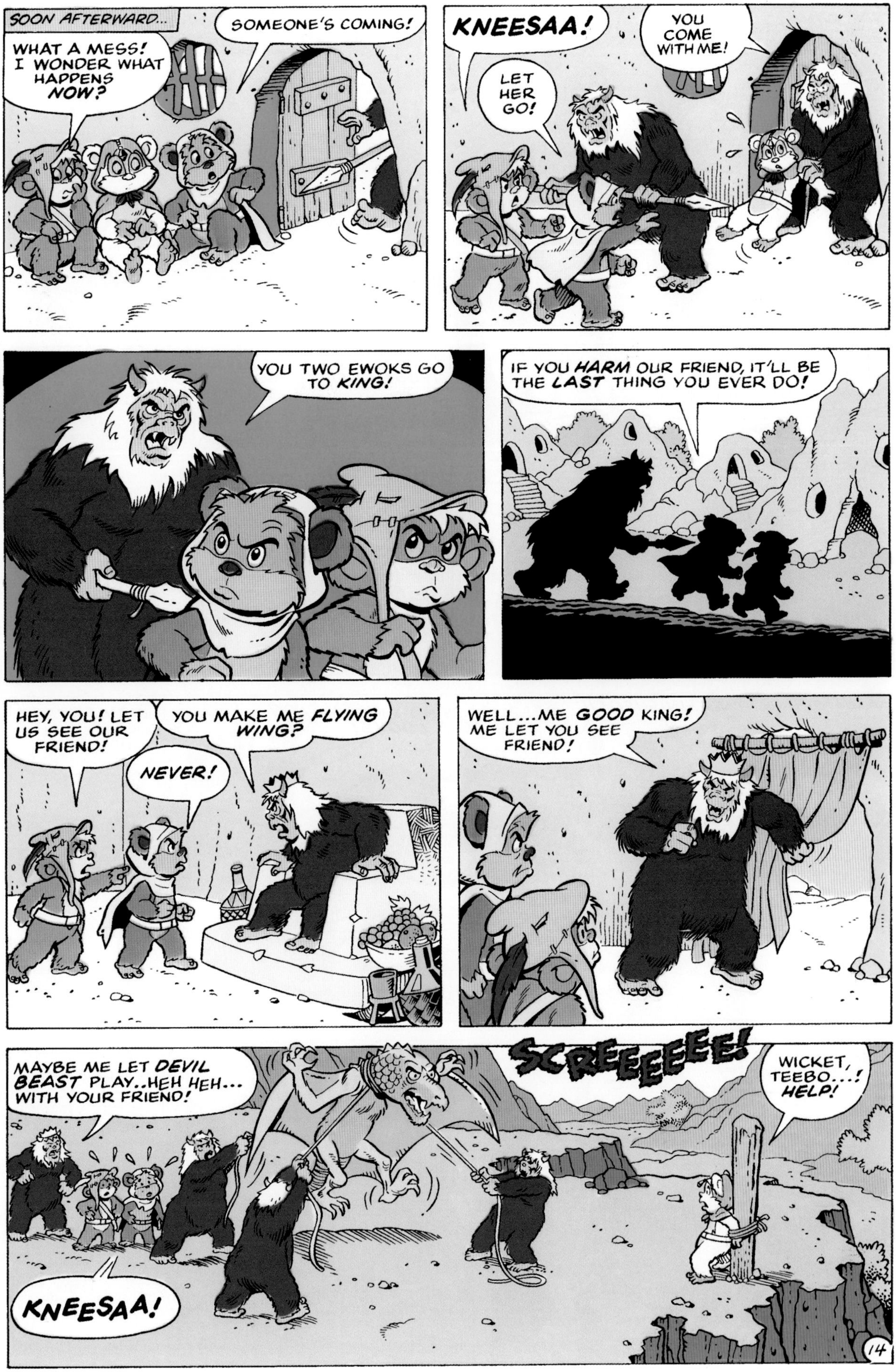
SOON AFTERWARD...
WHAT A MESS! I WONDER WHAT HAPPENS NOW?
SOMEONE'S COMING!
KNEESAA!
YOU COME WITH ME!
LET HER GO!
YOU TWO EWOKS GO TO KING!
IF YOU HARM OUR FRIEND, IT'LL BE THE LAST THING YOU EVER DO!
HEY, YOU! LET US SEE OUR FRIEND!
YOU MAKE ME FLYING WING?
NEVER!
WELL...ME GOOD KING! ME LET YOU SEE FRIEND!
MAYBE ME LET DEVIL BEAST PLAY..HEH HEH... WITH YOUR FRIEND!
SCREEEEEEE!
WICKET, TEEBO...! HELP!
KNEESAA!
14

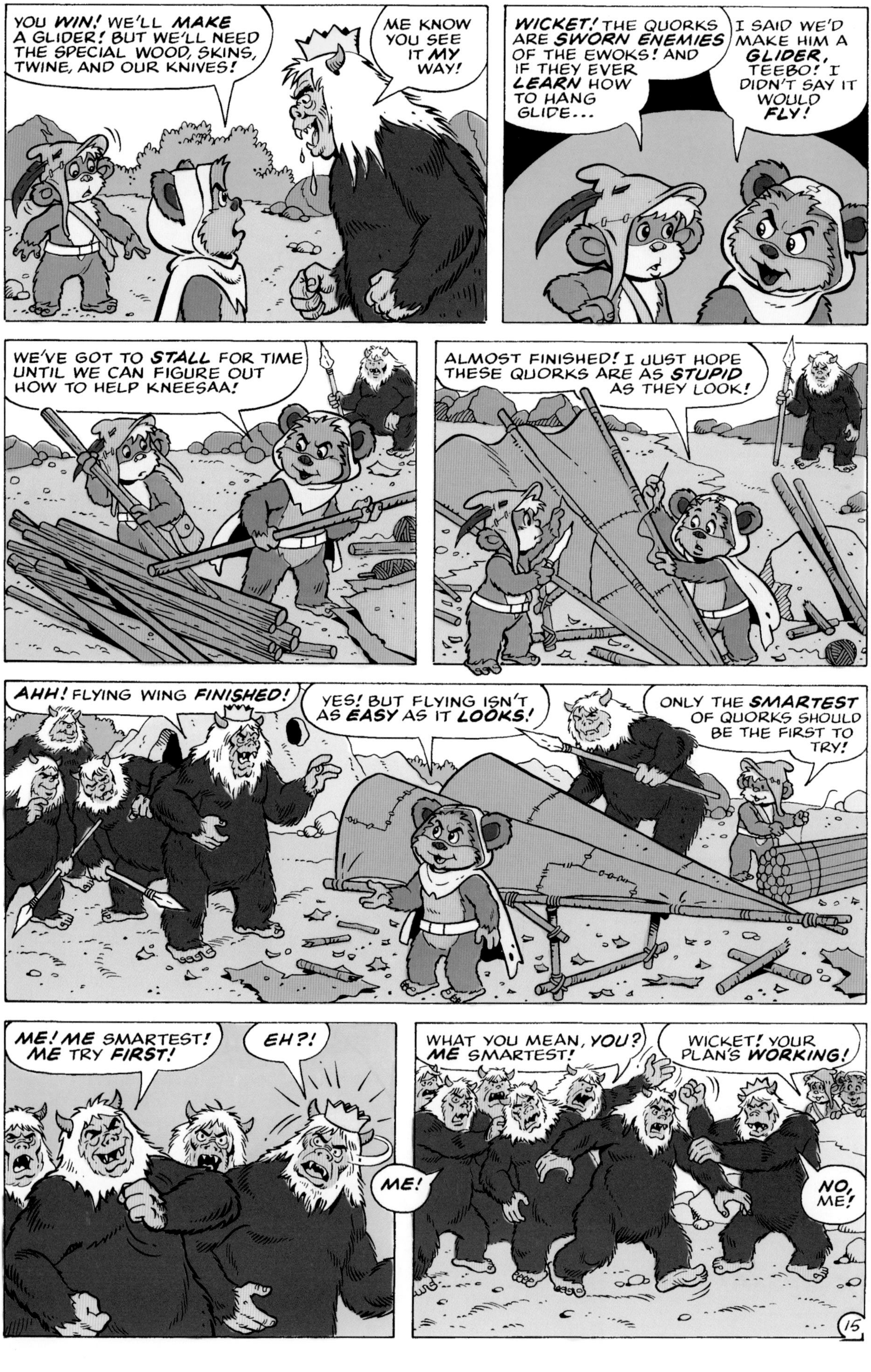
YOU WIN! WE'LL MAKE A GLIDER! BUT WE'LL NEED THE SPECIAL WOOD, SKINS, TWINE, AND OUR KNIVES!
ME KNOW YOU SEE IT MY WAY!
WICKET! THE QUORKS ARE SWORN ENEMIES OF THE EWOKS! AND IF THEY EVER LEARN HOW TO HANG GLIDE...
I SAID WE'D MAKE HIM A GLIDER, TEEBO! I DIDN'T SAY IT WOULD FLY!
WE'VE GOT TO STALL FOR TIME UNTIL WE CAN FIGURE OUT HOW TO HELP KNEESAA!
ALMOST FINISHED! I JUST HOPE THESE QUORKS ARE AS STUPID AS THEY LOOK!
AHH! FLYING WING FINISHED!
YES! BUT FLYING ISN'T AS EASY AS IT LOOKS!
ONLY THE SMARTEST OF QUORKS SHOULD BE THE FIRST TO TRY!
ME! ME SMARTEST! ME TRY FIRST!
EH?!
ME!
WHAT YOU MEAN, YOU? ME SMARTEST!
WICKET! YOUR PLAN'S WORKING!
NO, ME!
15

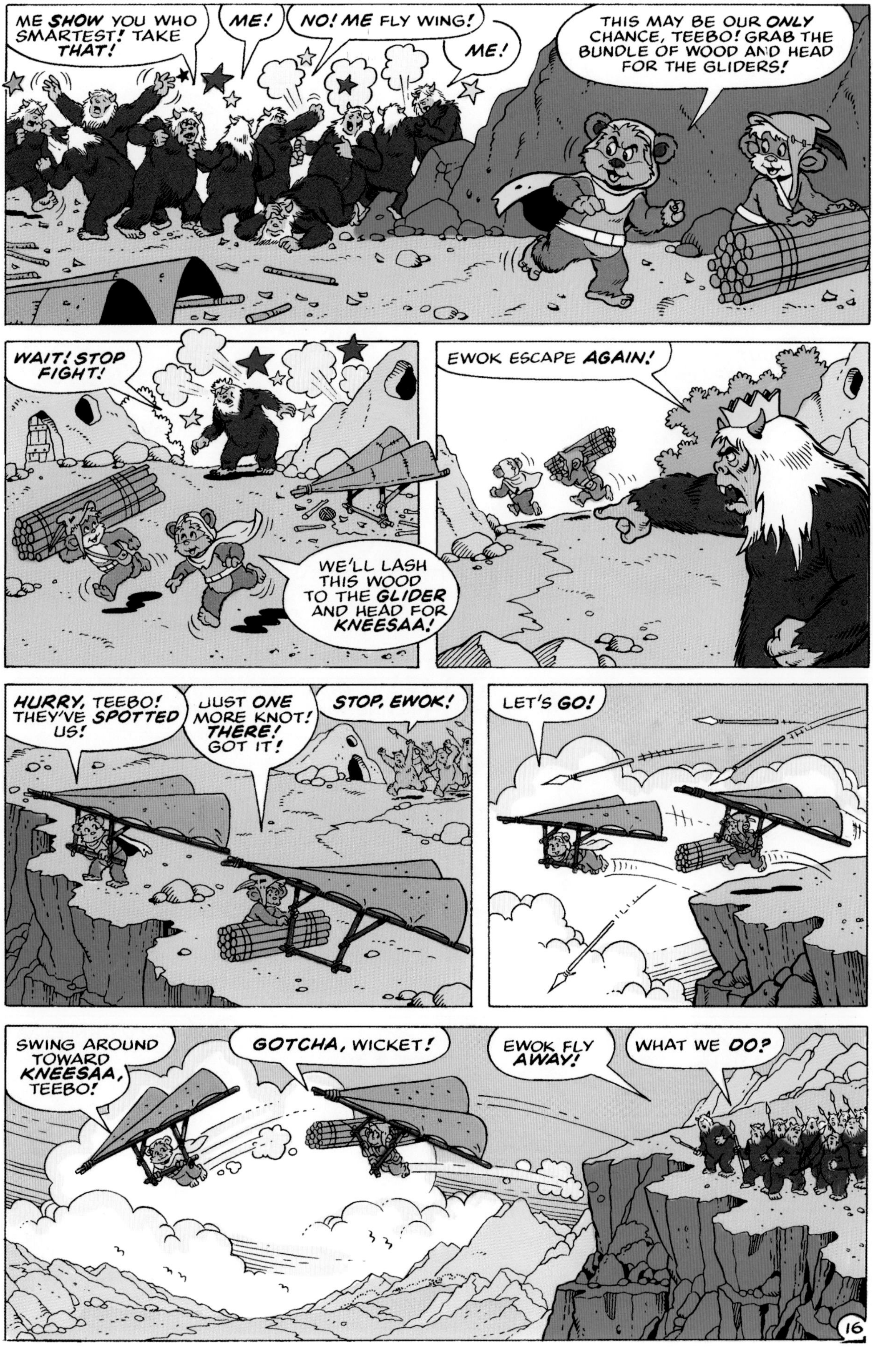
ME SHOW YOU WHO SMARTEST! TAKE THAT!
ME!
NO! ME FLY WING!
ME!
THIS MAY BE OUR ONLY CHANCE, TEEBO! GRAB THE BUNDLE OF WOOD AND HEAD FOR THE GLIDERS!
WAIT! STOP FIGHT!
WE'LL LASH THIS WOOD TO THE GLIDER AND HEAD FOR KNEESAA!
EWOK ESCAPE AGAIN!
HURRY, TEEBO! THEY'VE SPOTTED US!
JUST ONE MORE KNOT! THERE! GOT IT!
STOP, EWOK!
LET'S GO!
SWING AROUND TOWARD KNEESAA, TEEBO!
GOTCHA, WICKET!
EWOK FLY AWAY!
WHAT WE DO?
16

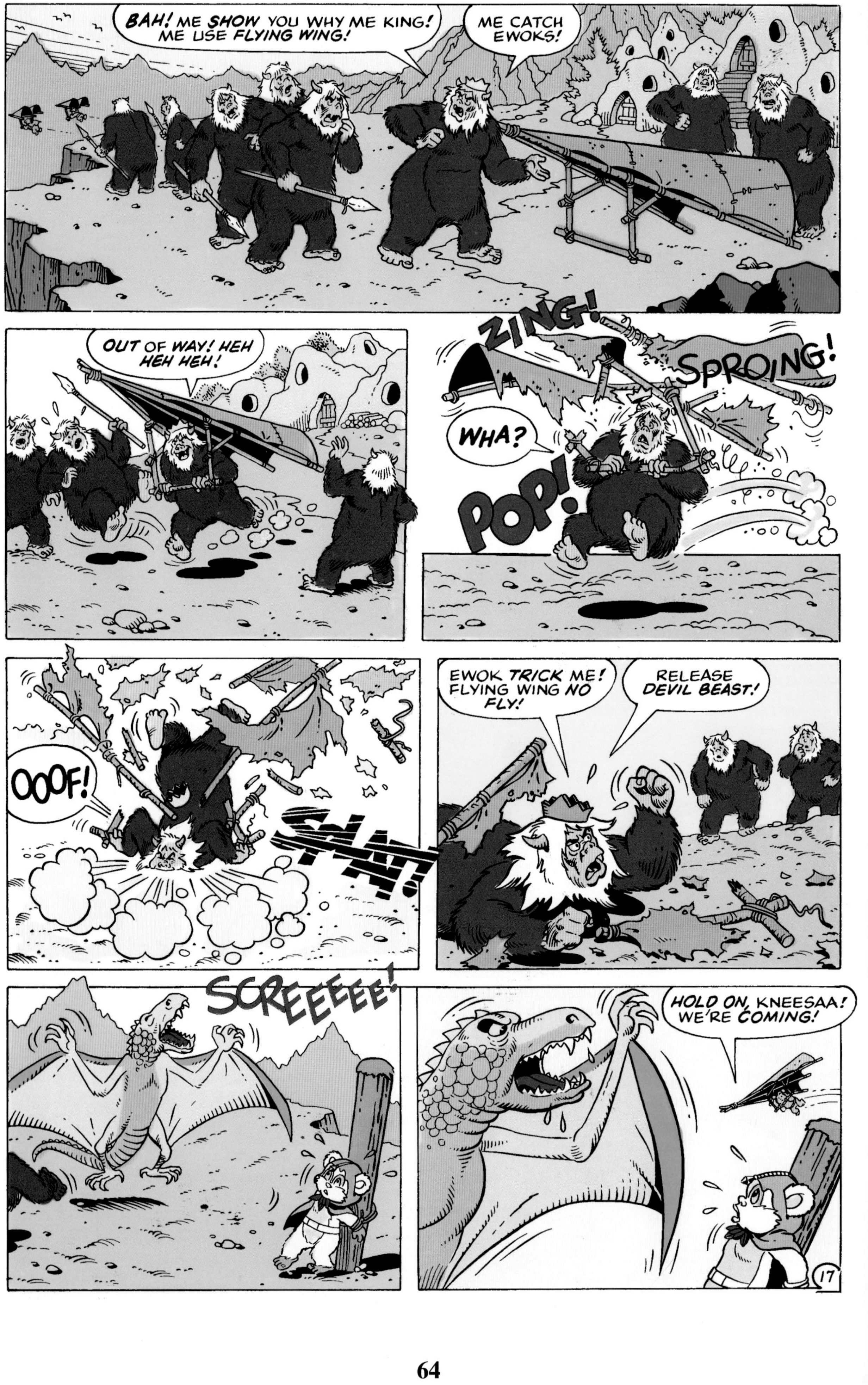
BAH! ME SHOW YOU WHY ME KING! ME USE FLYING WING!
ME CATCH EWOKS!
OUT OF WAY! HEH HEH HEH!
ZING!
SPROING!
WHA?
POP!
OOOF!
SPLAT!
EWOK TRICK ME! FLYING WING NO FLY!
RELEASE DEVIL BEAST!
SCREEEEEE!
HOLD ON, KNEESAA! WE'RE COMING!
17

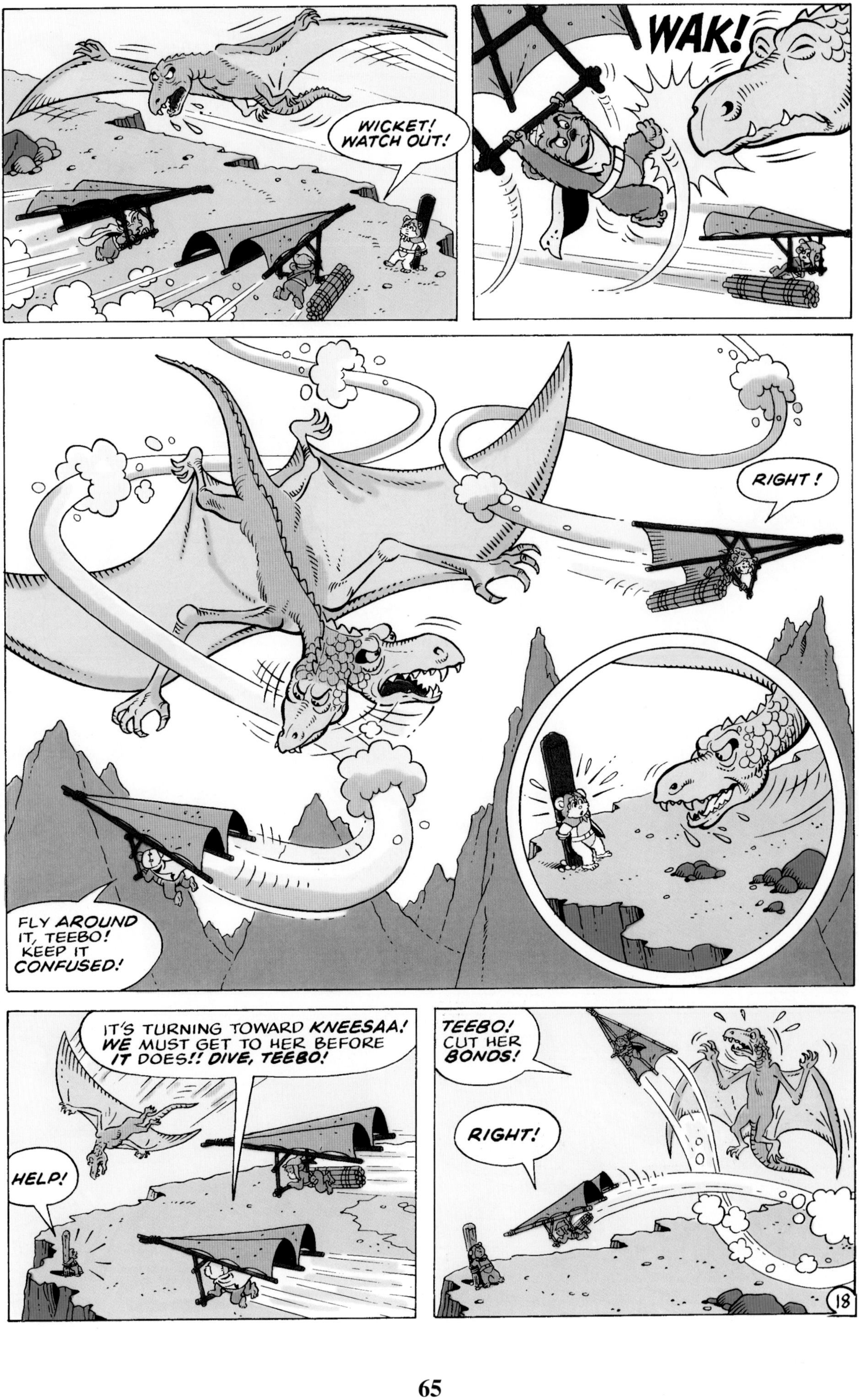
WICKET! WATCH OUT!
WAK!
RIGHT!
FLY AROUND IT, TEEBO! KEEP IT CONFUSED!
IT'S TURNING TOWARD KNEESAA! WE MUST GET TO HER BEFORE IT DOES!! DIVE, TEEBO!
HELP!
TEEBO! CUT HER BONDS!
RIGHT!
18

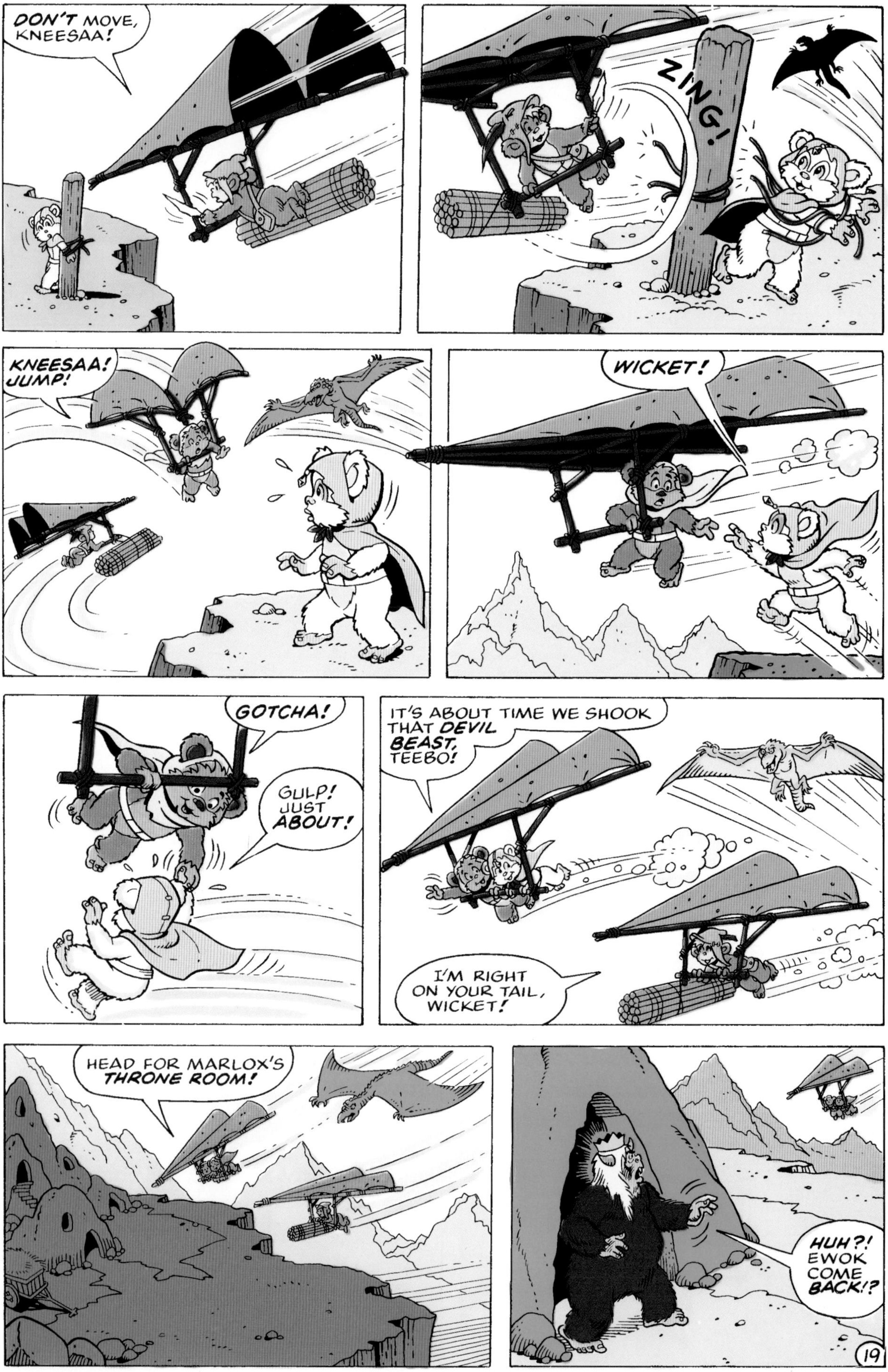
DON'T MOVE, KNEESAA!
ZING!
KNEESAA! JUMP!
WICKET!
GOTCHA!
GULP! JUST ABOUT!
IT'S ABOUT TIME WE SHOOK THAT DEVIL BEAST, TEEBO!
I'M RIGHT ON YOUR TAIL, WICKET!
HEAD FOR MARLOX'S THRONE ROOM!
HUH?! EWOK COME BACK!?
19

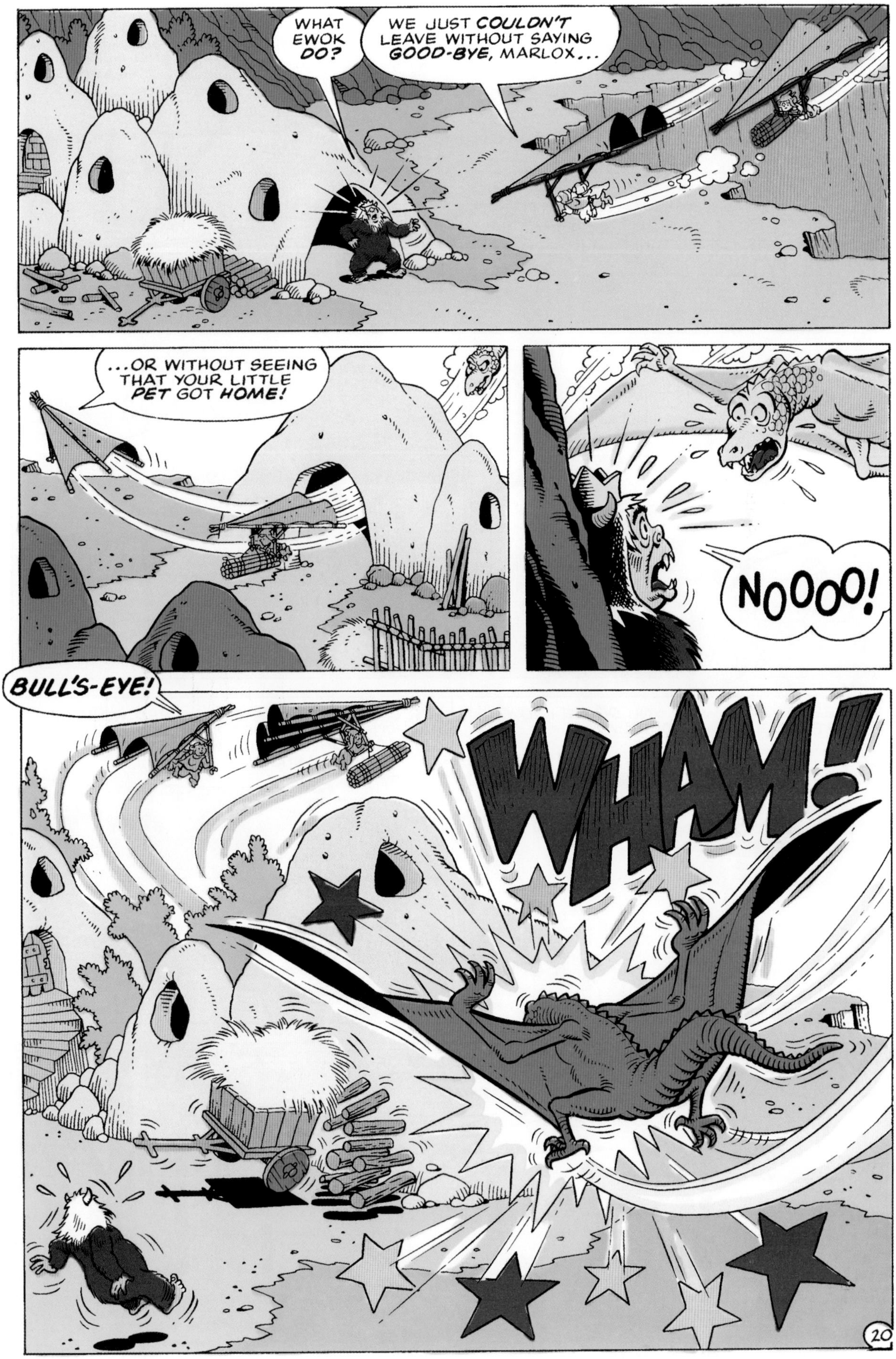
WHAT EWOK DO?
WE JUST COULDN'T LEAVE WITHOUT SAYING GOOD-BYE, MARLOX...
...OR WITHOUT SEEING THAT YOUR LITTLE PET GOT HOME!
NOOOO!
BULL'S-EYE!
WHAM!
20

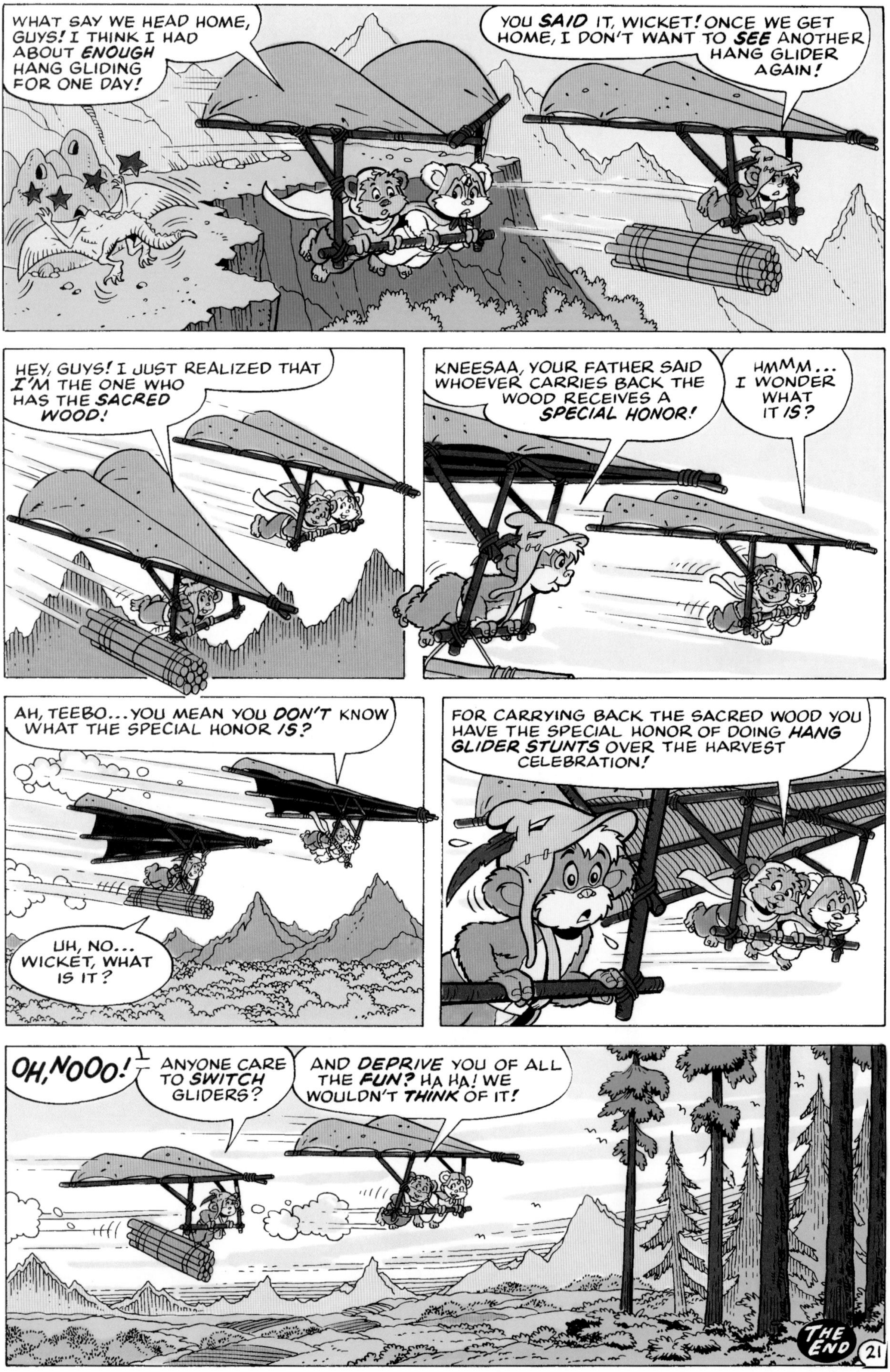
WHAT SAY WE HEAD HOME, GUYS! I THINK I HAD ABOUT ENOUGH HANG GLIDING FOR ONE DAY!
YOU SAID IT, WICKET! ONCE WE GET HOME, I DON'T WANT TO SEE ANOTHER HANG GLIDER AGAIN!
HEY, GUYS! I JUST REALIZED THAT I'M THE ONE WHO HAS THE SACRED WOOD!
KNEESAA, YOUR FATHER SAID WHOEVER CARRIES BACK THE WOOD RECEIVES A SPECIAL HONOR!
HMMM... I WONDER WHAT IT IS?
AH, TEEBO... YOU MEAN YOU DON'T KNOW WHAT THE SPECIAL HONOR IS?
UH, NO... WICKET, WHAT IS IT?
FOR CARRYING BACK THE SACRED WOOD YOU HAVE THE SPECIAL HONOR OF DOING HANG GLIDER STUNTS OVER THE HARVEST CELEBRATION!
OH, NOOO!
ANYONE CARE TO SWITCH GLIDERS?
AND DEPRIVE YOU OF ALL THE FUN? HA HA! WE WOULDN'T THINK OF IT!
THE END
21

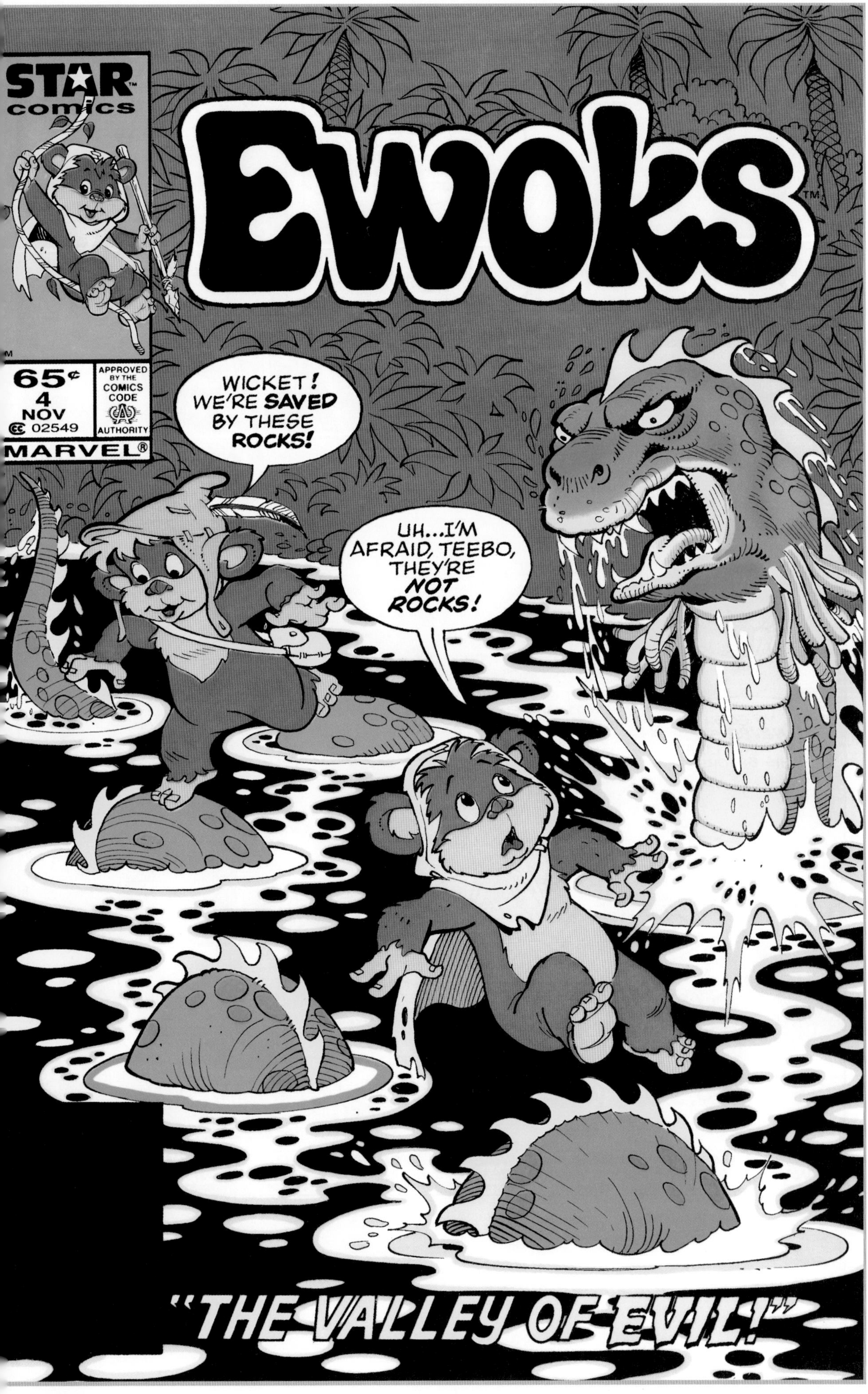
STAR comics
EWOKS
65¢
4
NOV
02549
APPROVED BY THE COMICS CODE AUTHORITY
MARVEL®
WICKET! WE'RE SAVED BY THESE ROCKS!
UH...I'M AFRAID, TEEBO, THEY'RE NOT ROCKS!
"THE VALLEY OF EVIL!"

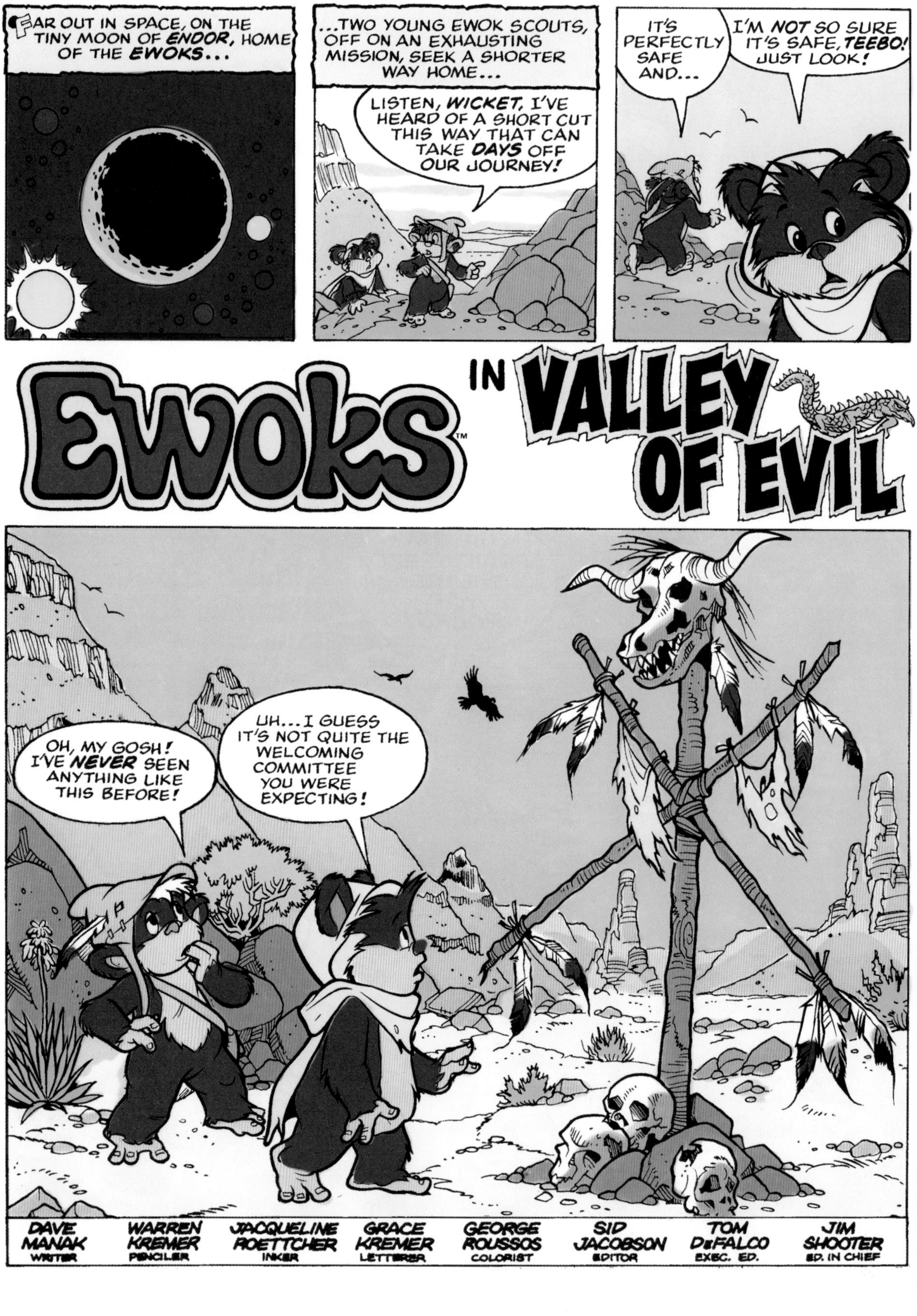

FAR OUT IN SPACE, ON THE TINY MOON OF ENDOR, HOME OF THE EWOKS...
...TWO YOUNG EWOK SCOUTS, OFF ON AN EXHAUSTING MISSION, SEEK A SHORTER WAY HOME...
LISTEN, WICKET, I'VE HEARD OF A SHORT CUT THIS WAY THAT CAN TAKE DAYS OFF OUR JOURNEY!
IT'S PERFECTLY SAFE AND...
I'M NOT SO SURE IT'S SAFE, TEEBO! JUST LOOK!
EWOKS™ IN VALLEY OF EVIL
OH, MY GOSH! I'VE NEVER SEEN ANYTHING LIKE THIS BEFORE!
UH...I GUESS IT'S NOT QUITE THE WELCOMING COMMITTEE YOU WERE EXPECTING!
DAVE MANAK WRITER
WARREN KREMER PENCILER
JACQUELINE ROETTCHER INKER
GRACE KREMER LETTERER
GEORGE ROUSSOS COLORIST
SID JACOBSON EDITOR
TOM DeFALCO EXEC. ED.
JIM SHOOTER ED. IN CHIEF

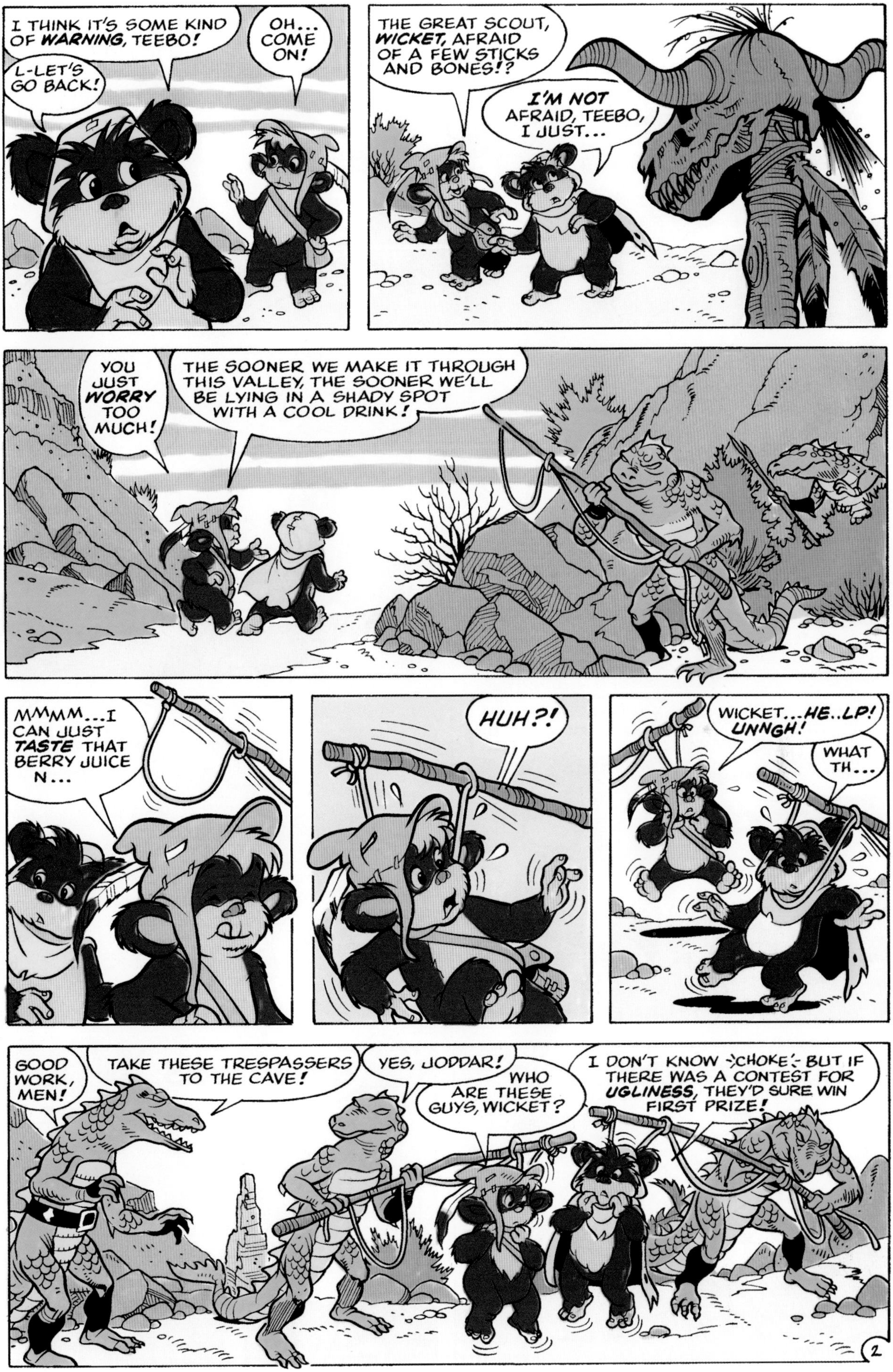
I THINK IT'S SOME KIND OF WARNING, TEEBO!
L-LET'S GO BACK!
OH... COME ON!
THE GREAT SCOUT, WICKET, AFRAID OF A FEW STICKS AND BONES!?
I'M NOT AFRAID, TEEBO, I JUST...
YOU JUST WORRY TOO MUCH!
THE SOONER WE MAKE IT THROUGH THIS VALLEY, THE SOONER WE'LL BE LYING IN A SHADY SPOT WITH A COOL DRINK!
MMMM...I CAN JUST TASTE THAT BERRY JUICE N...
HUH?!
WICKET...HE..LP! UNNGH!
WHAT TH...
GOOD WORK, MEN!
TAKE THESE TRESPASSERS TO THE CAVE!
YES, JODDAR!
WHO ARE THESE GUYS, WICKET?
I DON'T KNOW -CHOKE- BUT IF THERE WAS A CONTEST FOR UGLINESS, THEY'D SURE WIN FIRST PRIZE!
2

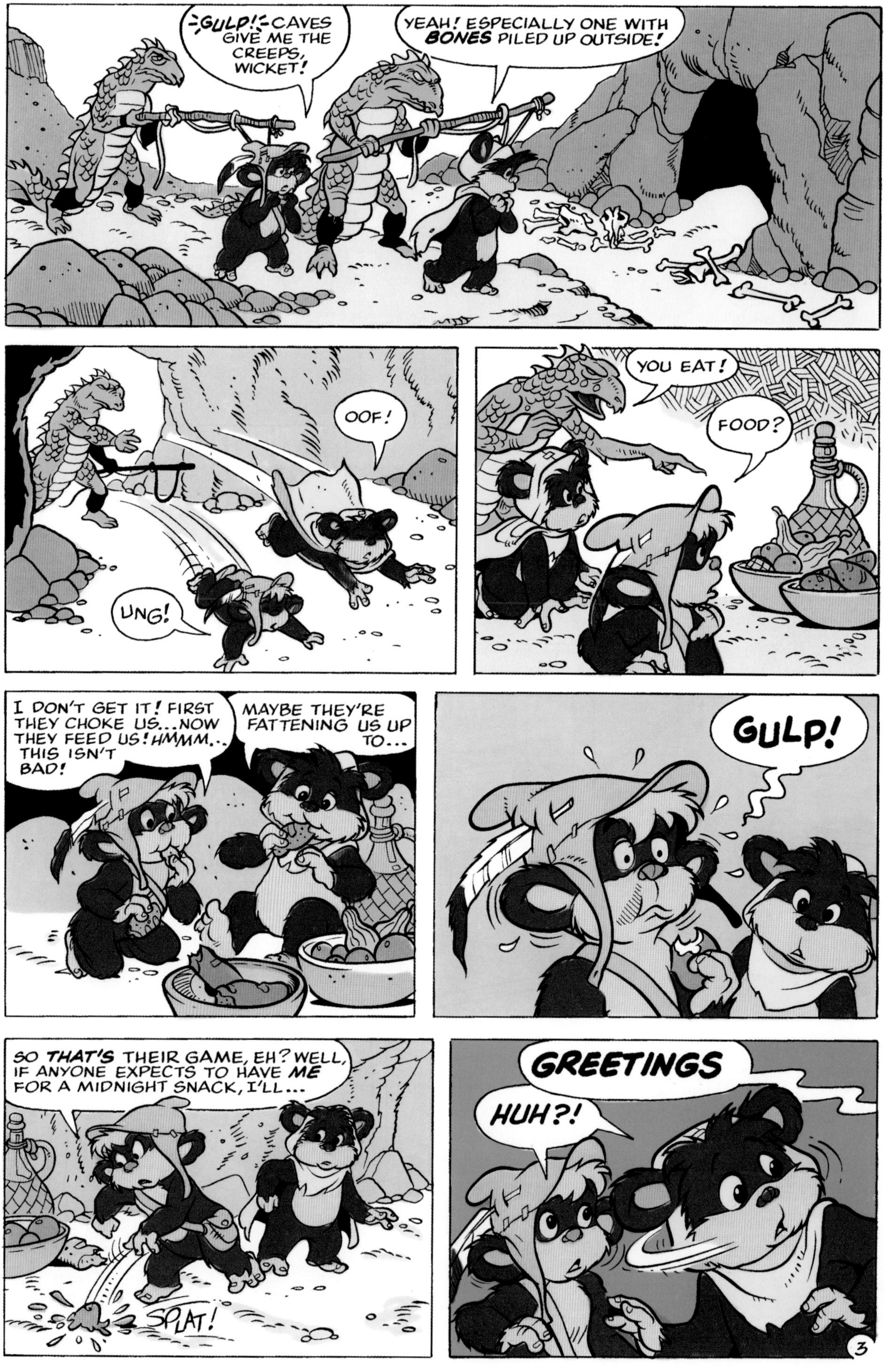
GULP! CAVES GIVE ME THE CREEPS, WICKET!
YEAH! ESPECIALLY ONE WITH BONES PILED UP OUTSIDE!
OOF!
UNG!
YOU EAT!
FOOD?
I DON'T GET IT! FIRST THEY CHOKE US...NOW THEY FEED US! HMMM... THIS ISN'T BAD!
MAYBE THEY'RE FATTENING US UP TO...
GULP!
SO THAT'S THEIR GAME, EH? WELL, IF ANYONE EXPECTS TO HAVE ME FOR A MIDNIGHT SNACK, I'LL...
SPLAT!
GREETINGS
HUH?!
3

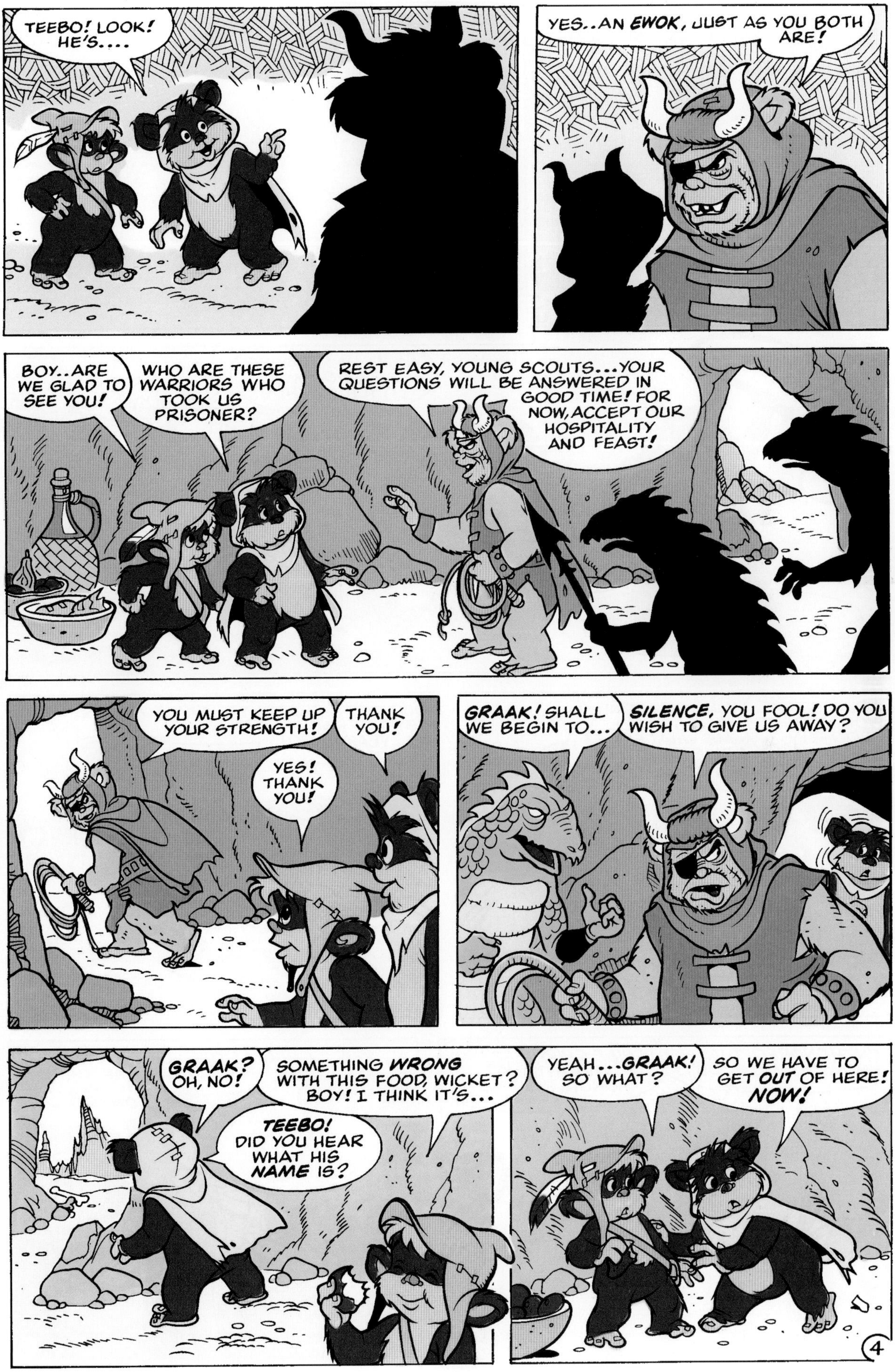
TEEBO! LOOK! HE'S....
YES..AN **EWOK**, JUST AS YOU BOTH ARE!
BOY..ARE WE GLAD TO SEE YOU!
WHO ARE THESE WARRIORS WHO TOOK US PRISONER?
REST EASY, YOUNG SCOUTS...YOUR QUESTIONS WILL BE ANSWERED IN GOOD TIME! FOR NOW, ACCEPT OUR HOSPITALITY AND FEAST!
YOU MUST KEEP UP YOUR STRENGTH!
THANK YOU!
YES! THANK YOU!
GRAAK! SHALL WE BEGIN TO...
SILENCE, YOU FOOL! DO YOU WISH TO GIVE US AWAY?
SOMETHING **WRONG** WITH THIS FOOD, WICKET? BOY! I THINK IT'S...
GRAAK? OH, NO!
TEEBO! DID YOU HEAR WHAT HIS **NAME** IS?
YEAH...**GRAAK!** SO WHAT?
SO WE HAVE TO GET **OUT** OF HERE! **NOW!**
4

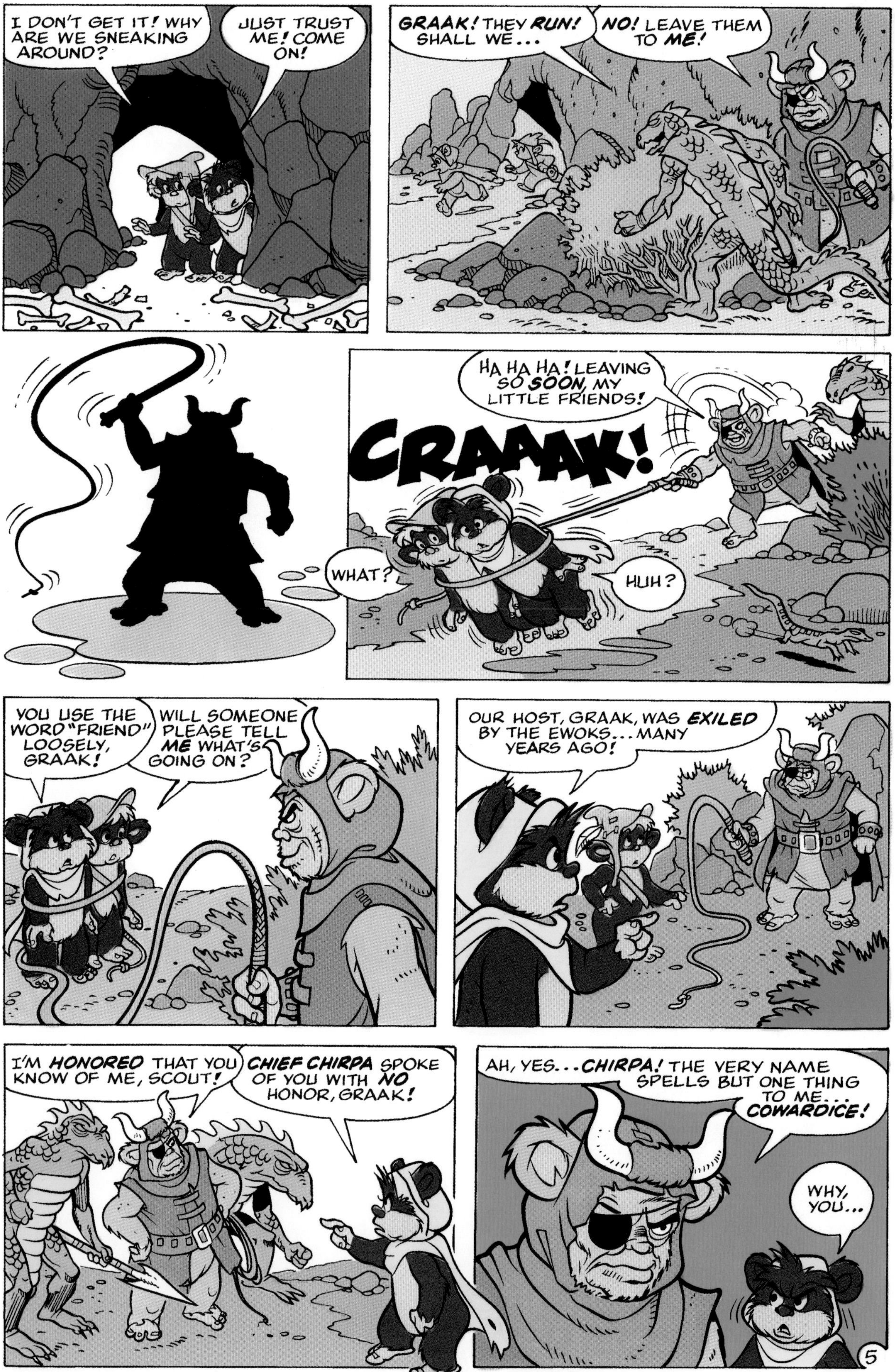
I DON'T GET IT! WHY ARE WE SNEAKING AROUND?
JUST TRUST ME! COME ON!
GRAAK! THEY RUN! SHALL WE...
NO! LEAVE THEM TO ME!
HA HA HA! LEAVING SO SOON, MY LITTLE FRIENDS!
CRAAAK!
WHAT?
HUH?
YOU USE THE WORD "FRIEND" LOOSELY, GRAAK!
WILL SOMEONE PLEASE TELL ME WHAT'S GOING ON?
OUR HOST, GRAAK, WAS EXILED BY THE EWOKS... MANY YEARS AGO!
I'M HONORED THAT YOU KNOW OF ME, SCOUT!
CHIEF CHIRPA SPOKE OF YOU WITH NO HONOR, GRAAK!
AH, YES... CHIRPA! THE VERY NAME SPELLS BUT ONE THING TO ME... COWARDICE!
WHY, YOU...
5

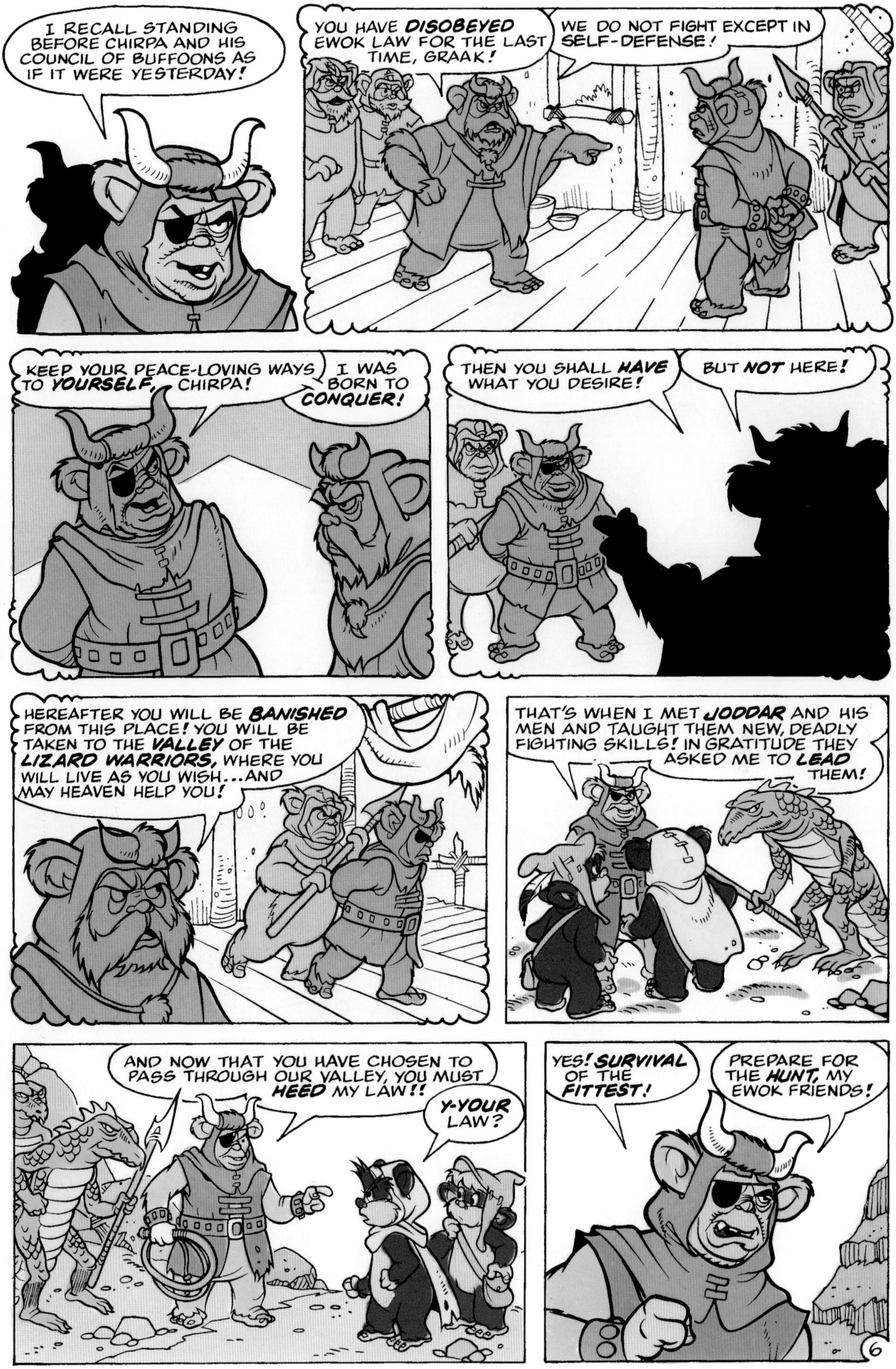
I RECALL STANDING BEFORE CHIRPA AND HIS COUNCIL OF BUFFOONS AS IF IT WERE YESTERDAY!
YOU HAVE DISOBEYED EWOK LAW FOR THE LAST TIME, GRAAK!
WE DO NOT FIGHT EXCEPT IN SELF-DEFENSE!
KEEP YOUR PEACE-LOVING WAYS TO YOURSELF, CHIRPA!
I WAS BORN TO CONQUER!
THEN YOU SHALL HAVE WHAT YOU DESIRE!
BUT NOT HERE!
HEREAFTER YOU WILL BE BANISHED FROM THIS PLACE! YOU WILL BE TAKEN TO THE VALLEY OF THE LIZARD WARRIORS, WHERE YOU WILL LIVE AS YOU WISH...AND MAY HEAVEN HELP YOU!
THAT'S WHEN I MET JODDAR AND HIS MEN AND TAUGHT THEM NEW, DEADLY FIGHTING SKILLS! IN GRATITUDE THEY ASKED ME TO LEAD THEM!
AND NOW THAT YOU HAVE CHOSEN TO PASS THROUGH OUR VALLEY, YOU MUST HEED MY LAW!!
Y-YOUR LAW?
YES! SURVIVAL OF THE FITTEST!
PREPARE FOR THE HUNT, MY EWOK FRIENDS!
6

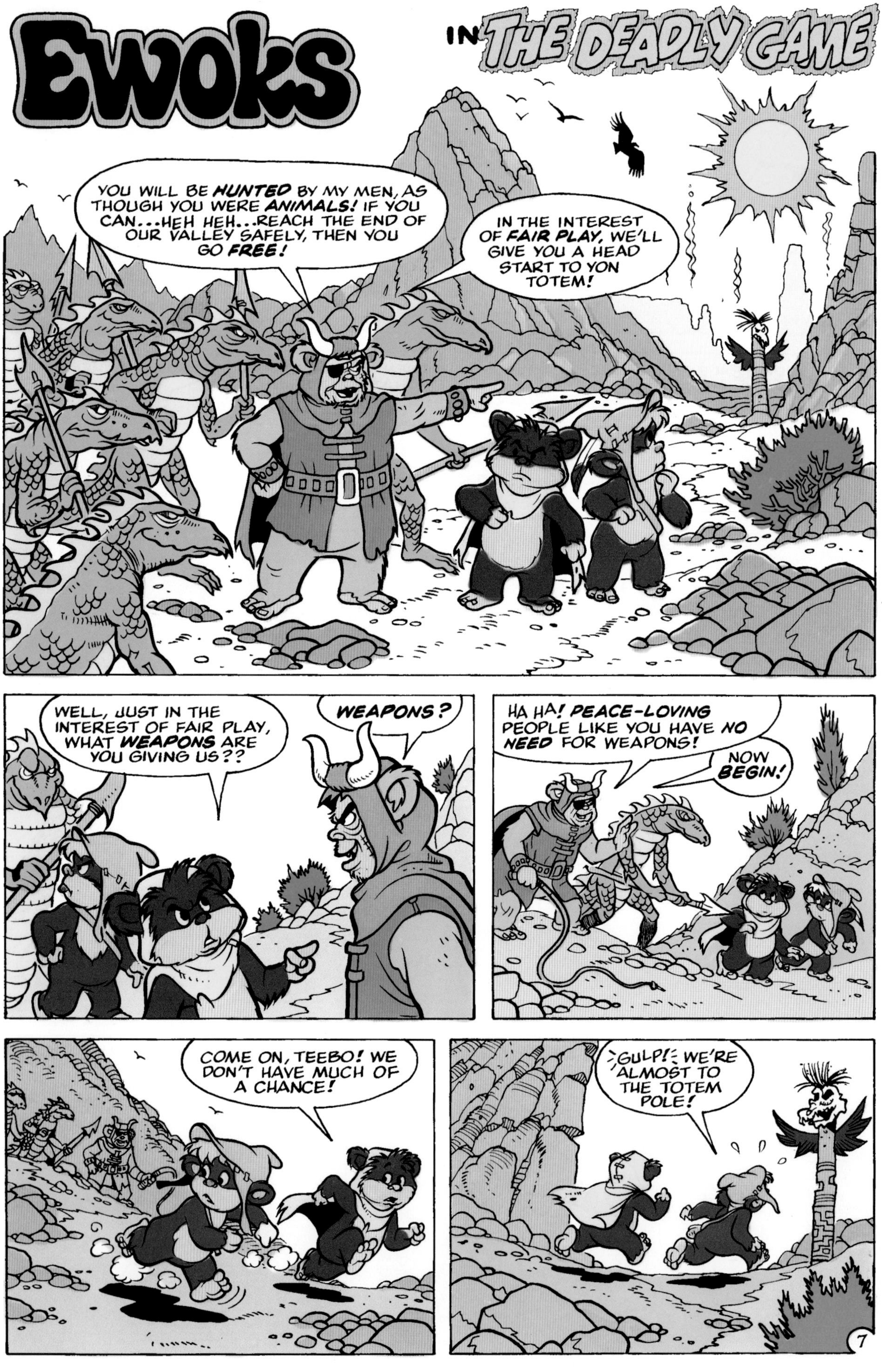

Ewoks in THE DEADLY GAME
YOU WILL BE HUNTED BY MY MEN, AS THOUGH YOU WERE ANIMALS! IF YOU CAN...HEH HEH...REACH THE END OF OUR VALLEY SAFELY, THEN YOU GO FREE!
IN THE INTEREST OF FAIR PLAY, WE'LL GIVE YOU A HEAD START TO YON TOTEM!
WELL, JUST IN THE INTEREST OF FAIR PLAY, WHAT WEAPONS ARE YOU GIVING US??
WEAPONS?
HA HA! PEACE-LOVING PEOPLE LIKE YOU HAVE NO NEED FOR WEAPONS!
NOW BEGIN!
COME ON, TEEBO! WE DON'T HAVE MUCH OF A CHANCE!
GULP! WE'RE ALMOST TO THE TOTEM POLE!
7

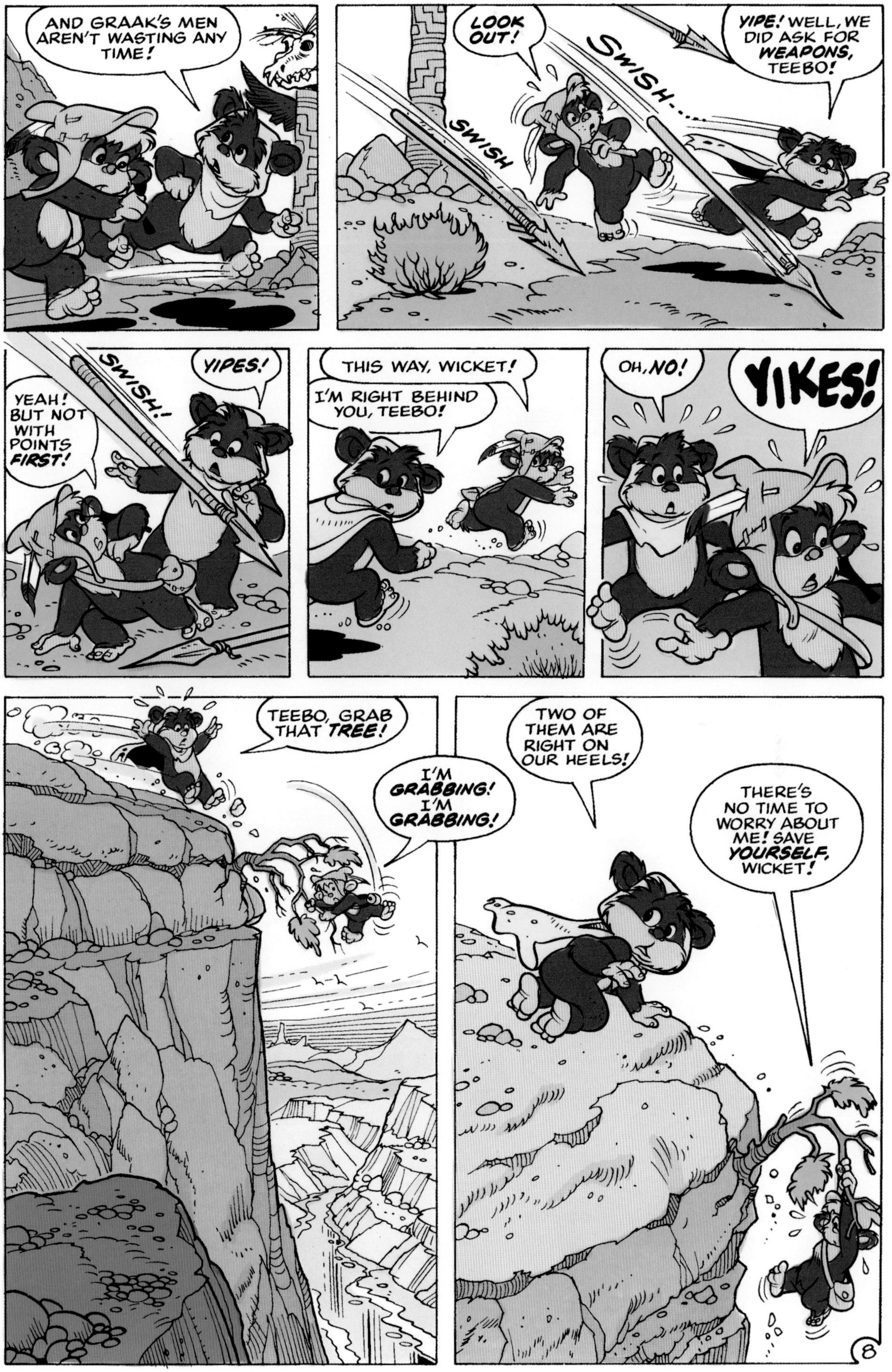
AND GRAAK'S MEN AREN'T WASTING ANY TIME!
LOOK OUT!
SWISH
SWISH...
YIPE! WELL, WE DID ASK FOR WEAPONS, TEEBO!
SWISH!
YIPES!
YEAH! BUT NOT WITH POINTS FIRST!
THIS WAY, WICKET!
I'M RIGHT BEHIND YOU, TEEBO!
OH, NO!
YIKES!
TEEBO, GRAB THAT TREE!
I'M GRABBING! I'M GRABBING!
TWO OF THEM ARE RIGHT ON OUR HEELS!
THERE'S NO TIME TO WORRY ABOUT ME! SAVE YOURSELF, WICKET!
8

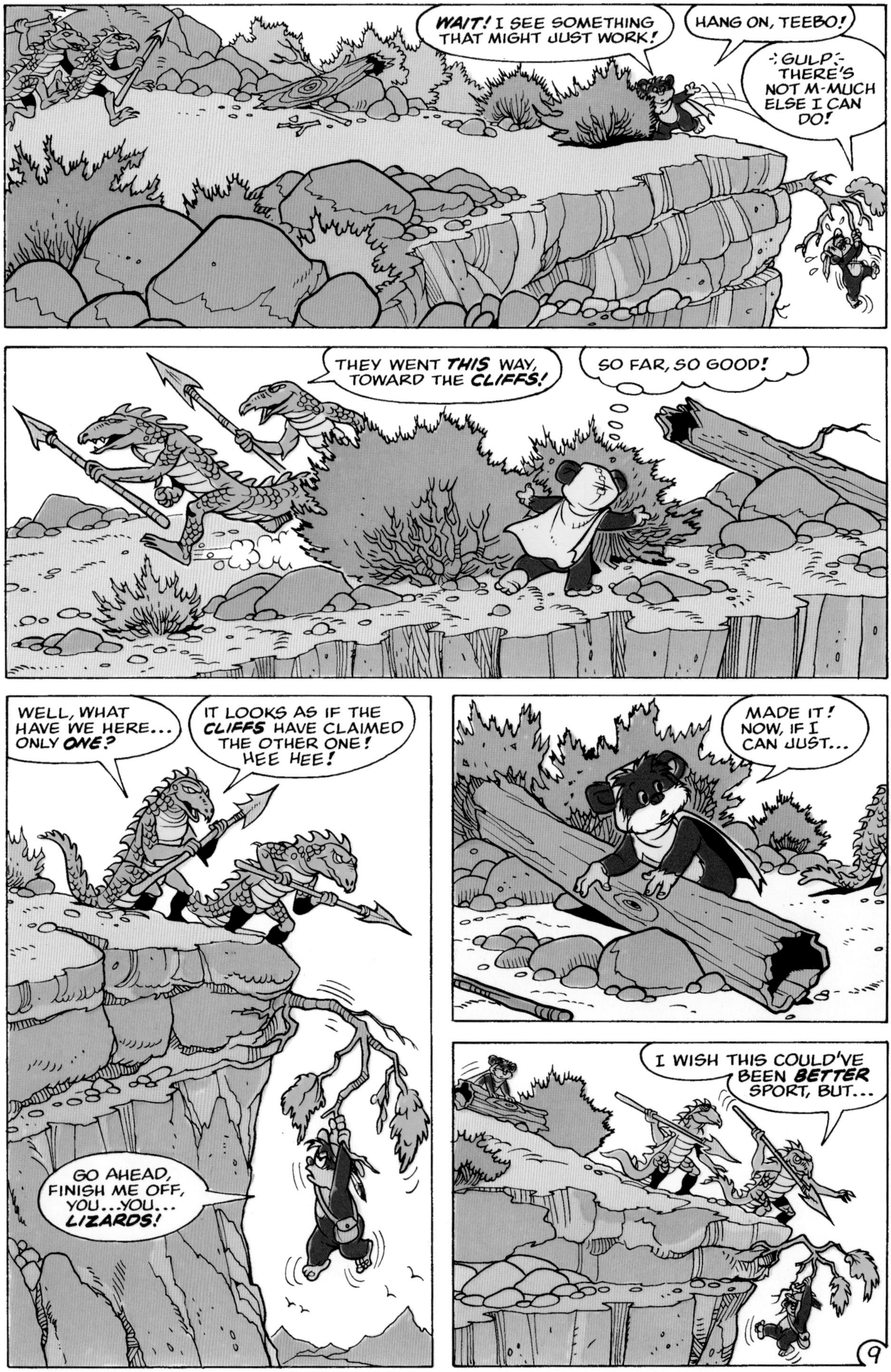
WAIT! I SEE SOMETHING THAT MIGHT JUST WORK!
HANG ON, TEEBO!
GULP THERE'S NOT M-MUCH ELSE I CAN DO!
THEY WENT THIS WAY, TOWARD THE CLIFFS!
SO FAR, SO GOOD!
WELL, WHAT HAVE WE HERE... ONLY ONE?
IT LOOKS AS IF THE CLIFFS HAVE CLAIMED THE OTHER ONE! HEE HEE!
GO AHEAD, FINISH ME OFF, YOU...YOU... LIZARDS!
MADE IT! NOW, IF I CAN JUST...
I WISH THIS COULD'VE BEEN BETTER SPORT, BUT...
9

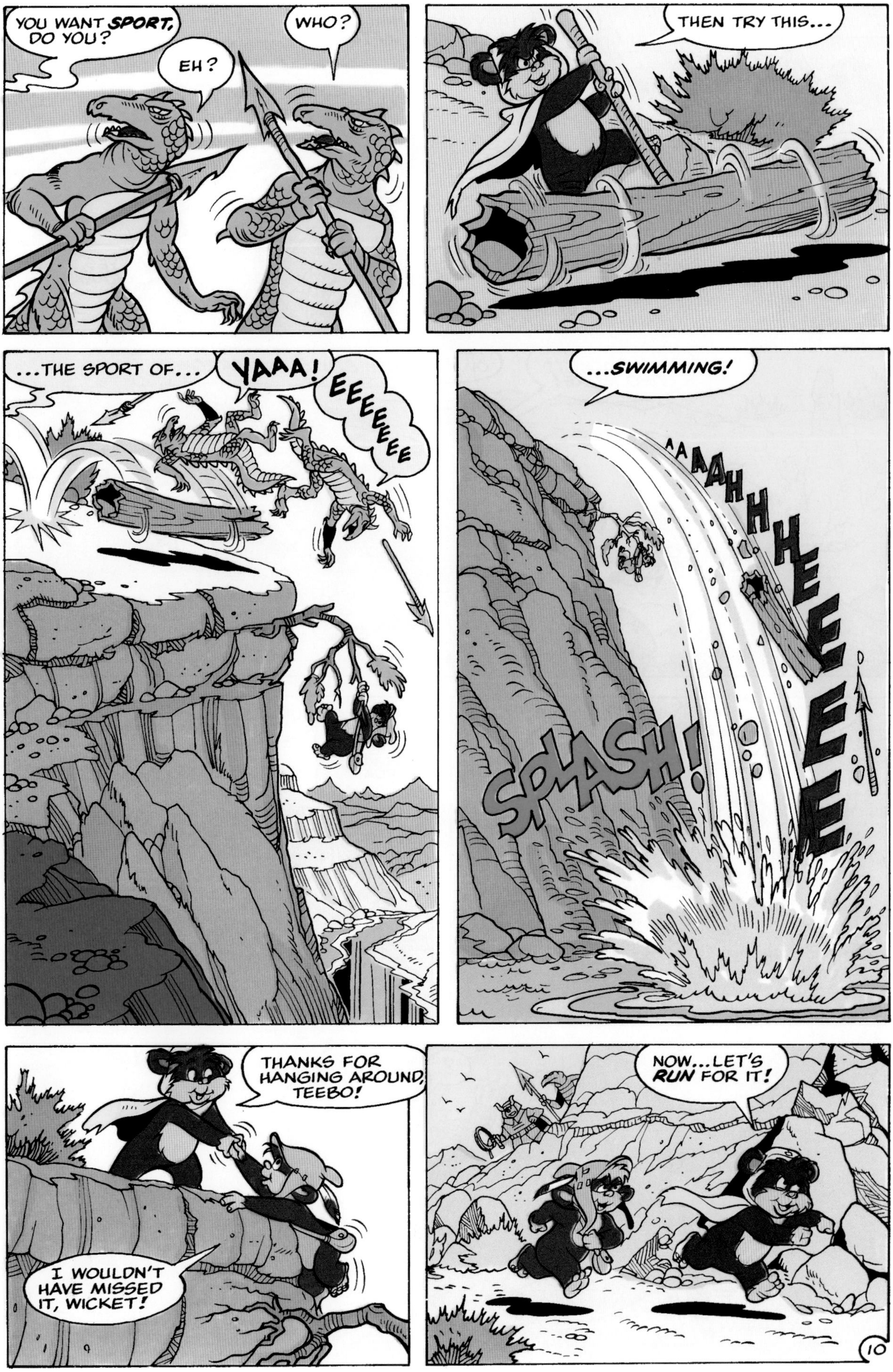
YOU WANT SPORT, DO YOU?
EH?
WHO?
THEN TRY THIS...
...THE SPORT OF...
YAAA!
EEEEEEE
...SWIMMING!
AAAHHHEEEEEE
SPLASH!
THANKS FOR HANGING AROUND, TEEBO!
I WOULDN'T HAVE MISSED IT, WICKET!
NOW...LET'S RUN FOR IT!
10

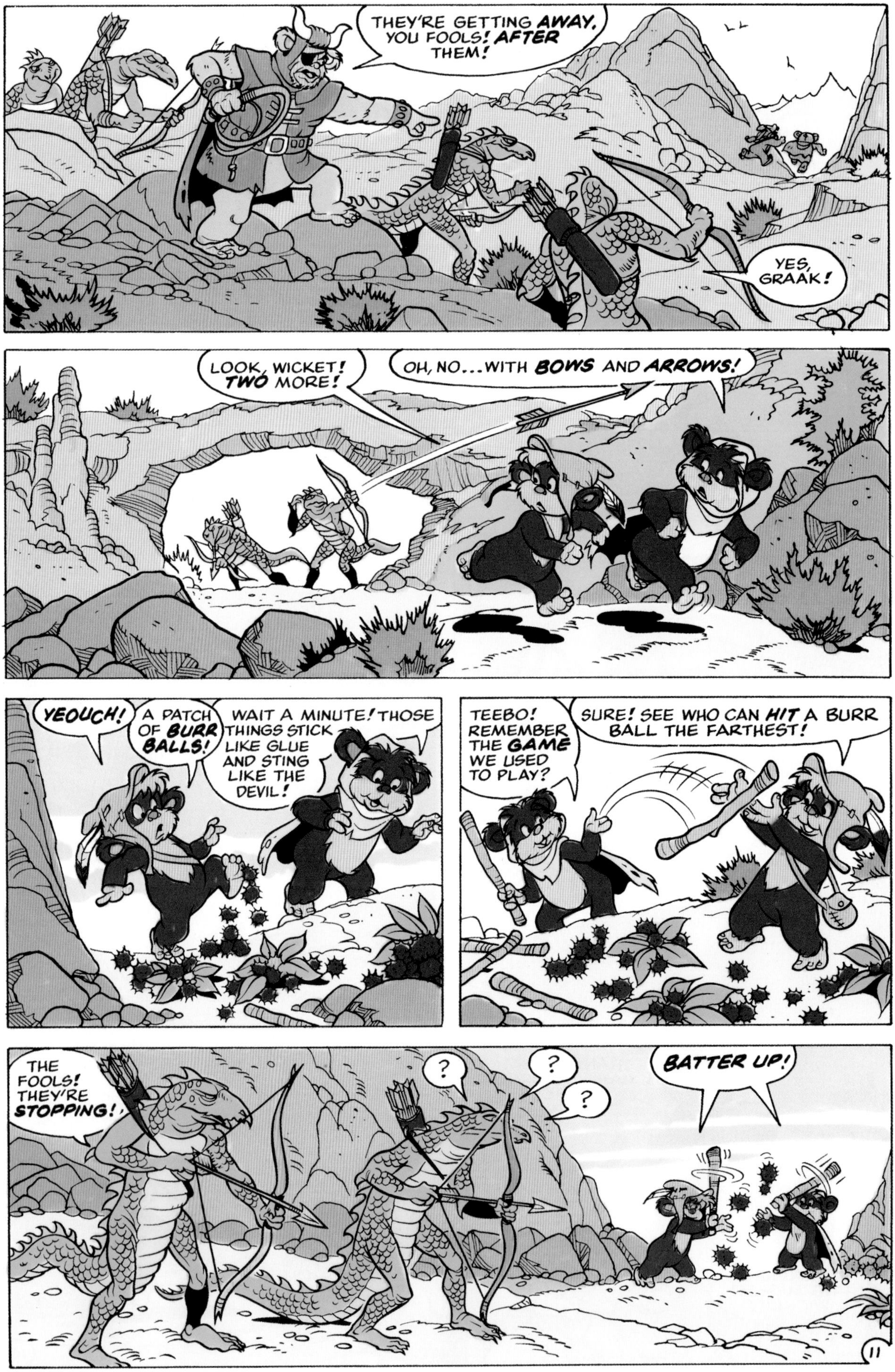
THEY'RE GETTING AWAY, YOU FOOLS! AFTER THEM!
YES, GRAAK!
LOOK, WICKET! TWO MORE!
OH, NO...WITH BOWS AND ARROWS!
YEOUCH!
A PATCH OF BURR BALLS!
WAIT A MINUTE! THOSE THINGS STICK LIKE GLUE AND STING LIKE THE DEVIL!
TEEBO! REMEMBER THE GAME WE USED TO PLAY?
SURE! SEE WHO CAN HIT A BURR BALL THE FARTHEST!
THE FOOLS! THEY'RE STOPPING!
?
?
?
BATTER UP!
11

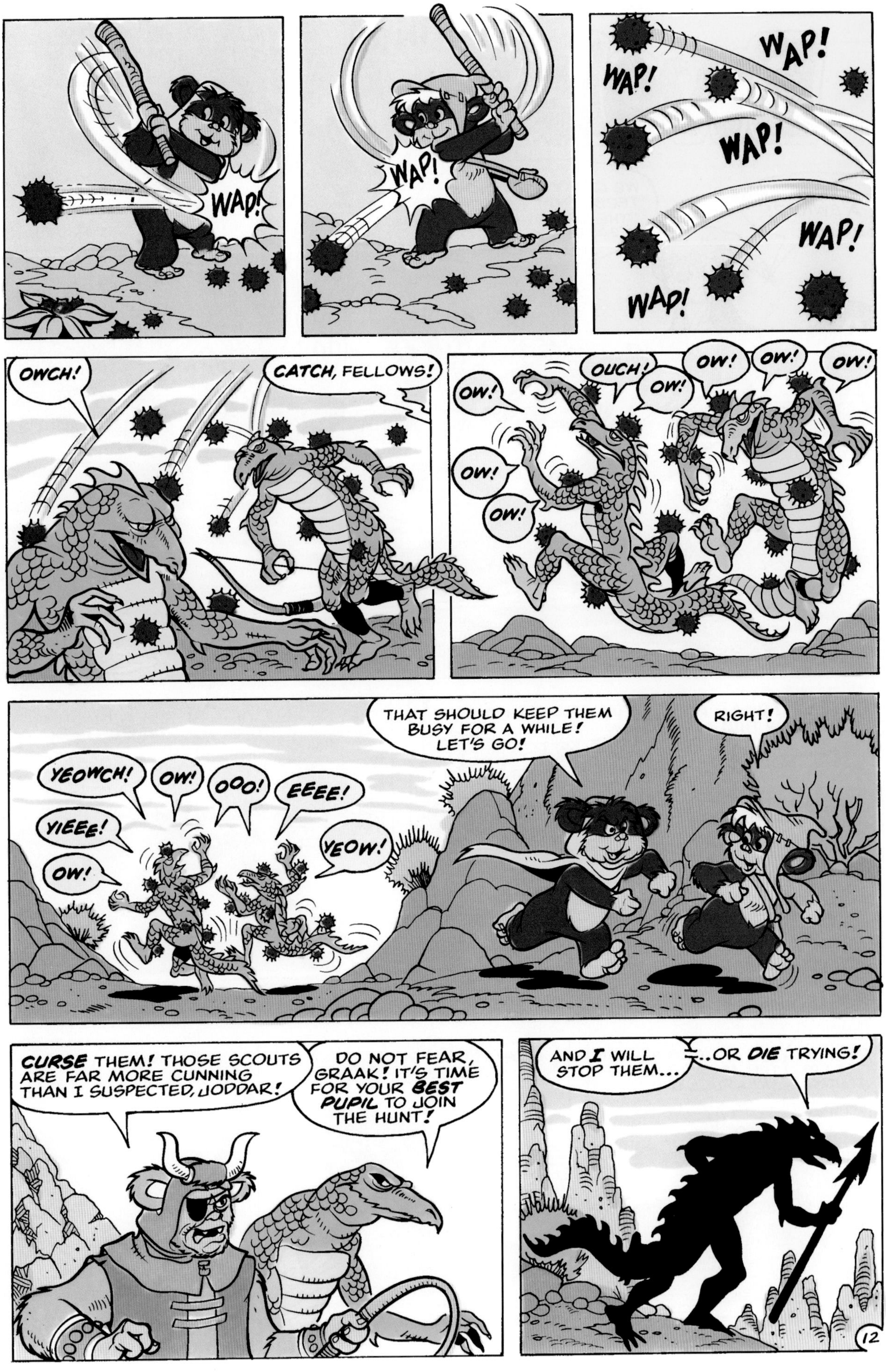
WAP!
WAP!
WAP!
WAP!
WAP!
WAP!
WAP!
OWCH!
CATCH, FELLOWS!
OW!
OUCH!
OW!
OW!
OW!
OW!
OW!
OW!
YEOWCH!
OW!
OOO!
EEEE!
YIEEE!
YEOW!
OW!
THAT SHOULD KEEP THEM BUSY FOR A WHILE! LET'S GO!
RIGHT!
CURSE THEM! THOSE SCOUTS ARE FAR MORE CUNNING THAN I SUSPECTED, JODDAR!
DO NOT FEAR, GRAAK! IT'S TIME FOR YOUR BEST PUPIL TO JOIN THE HUNT!
AND I WILL STOP THEM...
...OR DIE TRYING!
12

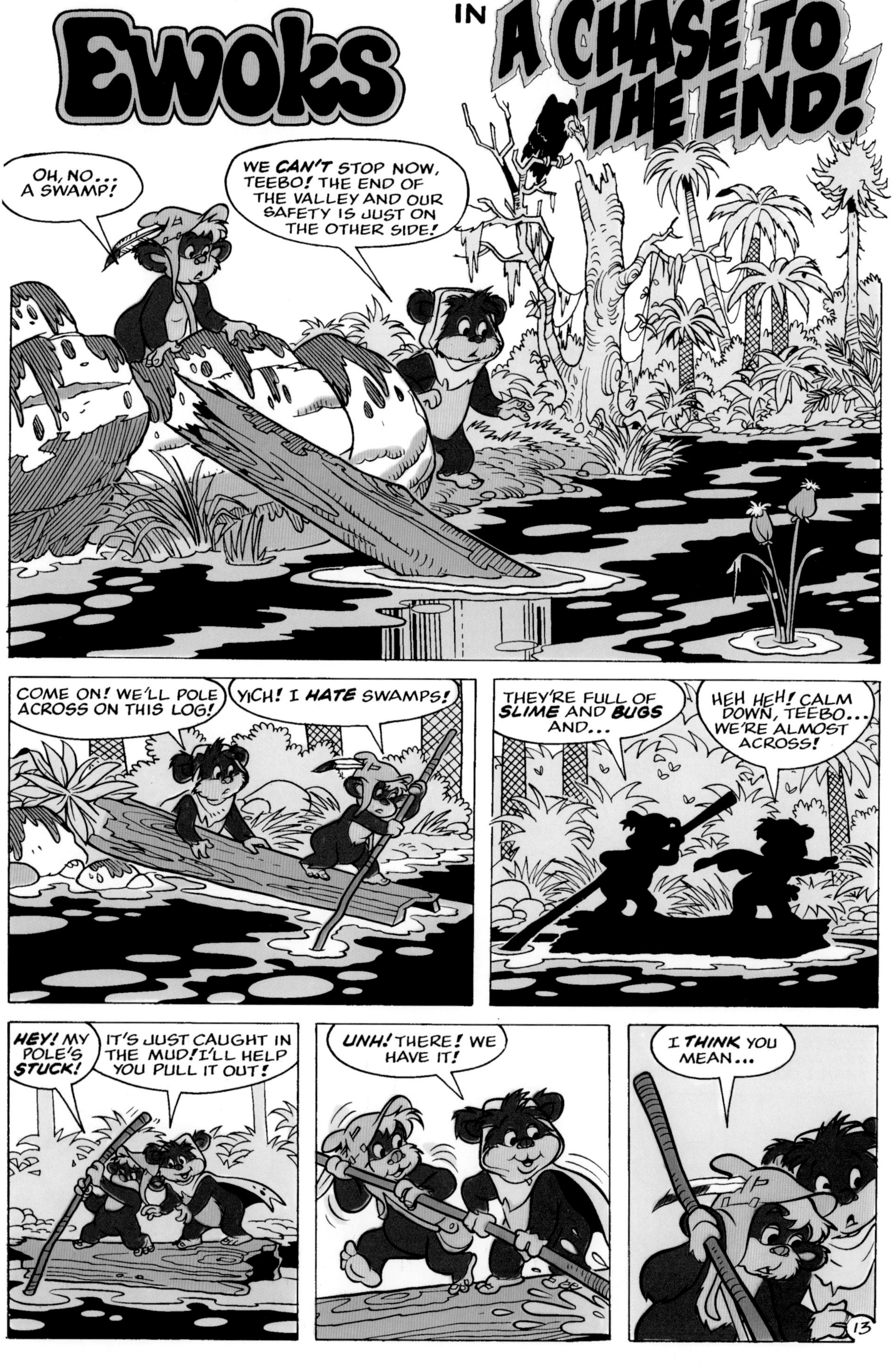

Ewoks
IN
A CHASE TO THE END!
OH, NO... A SWAMP!
WE CAN'T STOP NOW, TEEBO! THE END OF THE VALLEY AND OUR SAFETY IS JUST ON THE OTHER SIDE!
COME ON! WE'LL POLE ACROSS ON THIS LOG!
YICH! I HATE SWAMPS!
THEY'RE FULL OF SLIME AND BUGS AND...
HEH HEH! CALM DOWN, TEEBO... WE'RE ALMOST ACROSS!
HEY! MY POLE'S STUCK!
IT'S JUST CAUGHT IN THE MUD! I'LL HELP YOU PULL IT OUT!
UNH! THERE! WE HAVE IT!
I THINK YOU MEAN...
13

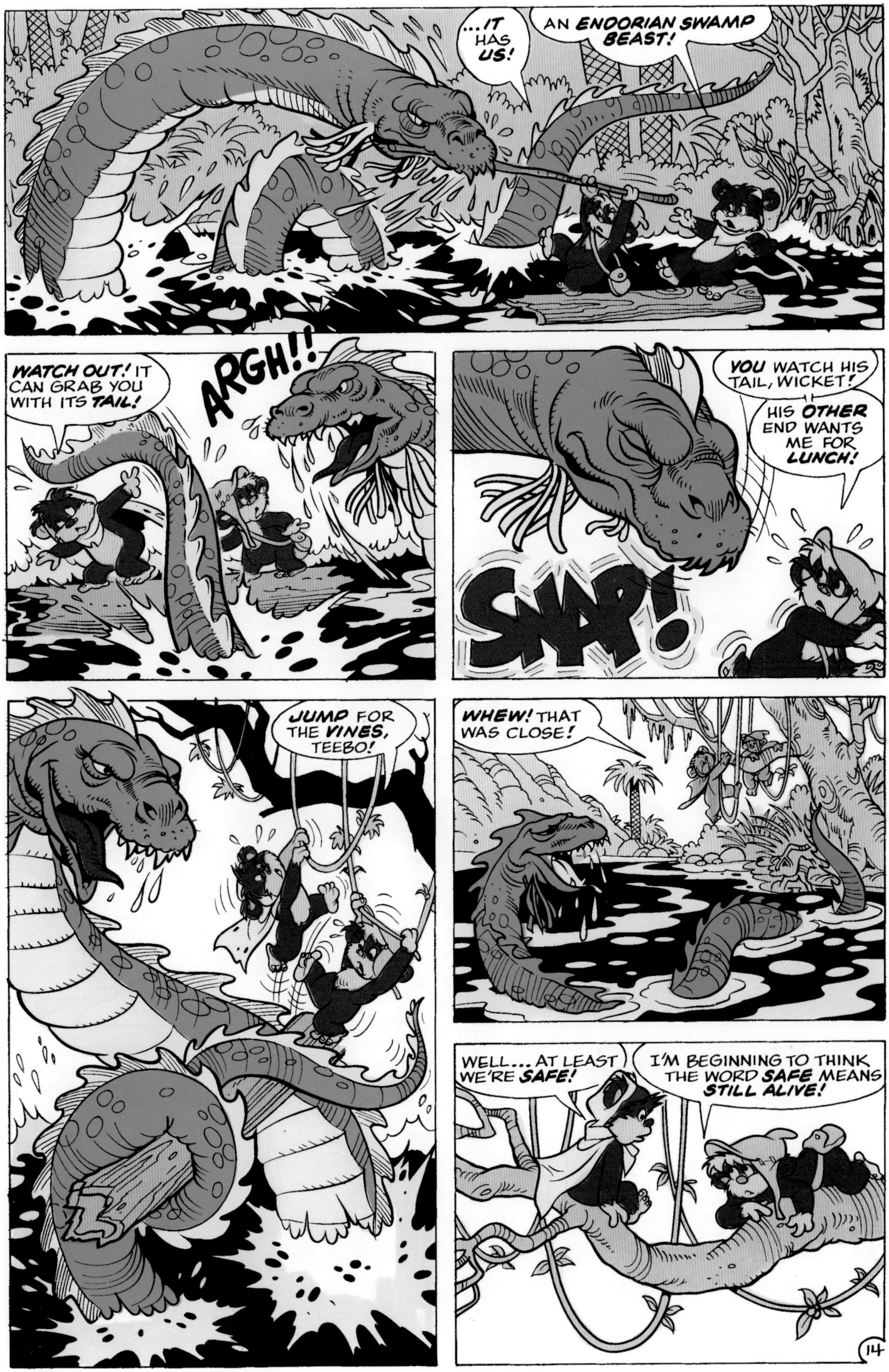
...IT HAS US!
AN ENDORIAN SWAMP BEAST!
WATCH OUT! IT CAN GRAB YOU WITH ITS TAIL!
ARGH!!
YOU WATCH HIS TAIL, WICKET!
HIS OTHER END WANTS ME FOR LUNCH!
SNAP!
JUMP FOR THE VINES, TEEBO!
WHEW! THAT WAS CLOSE!
WELL... AT LEAST WE'RE SAFE!
I'M BEGINNING TO THINK THE WORD SAFE MEANS STILL ALIVE!
14

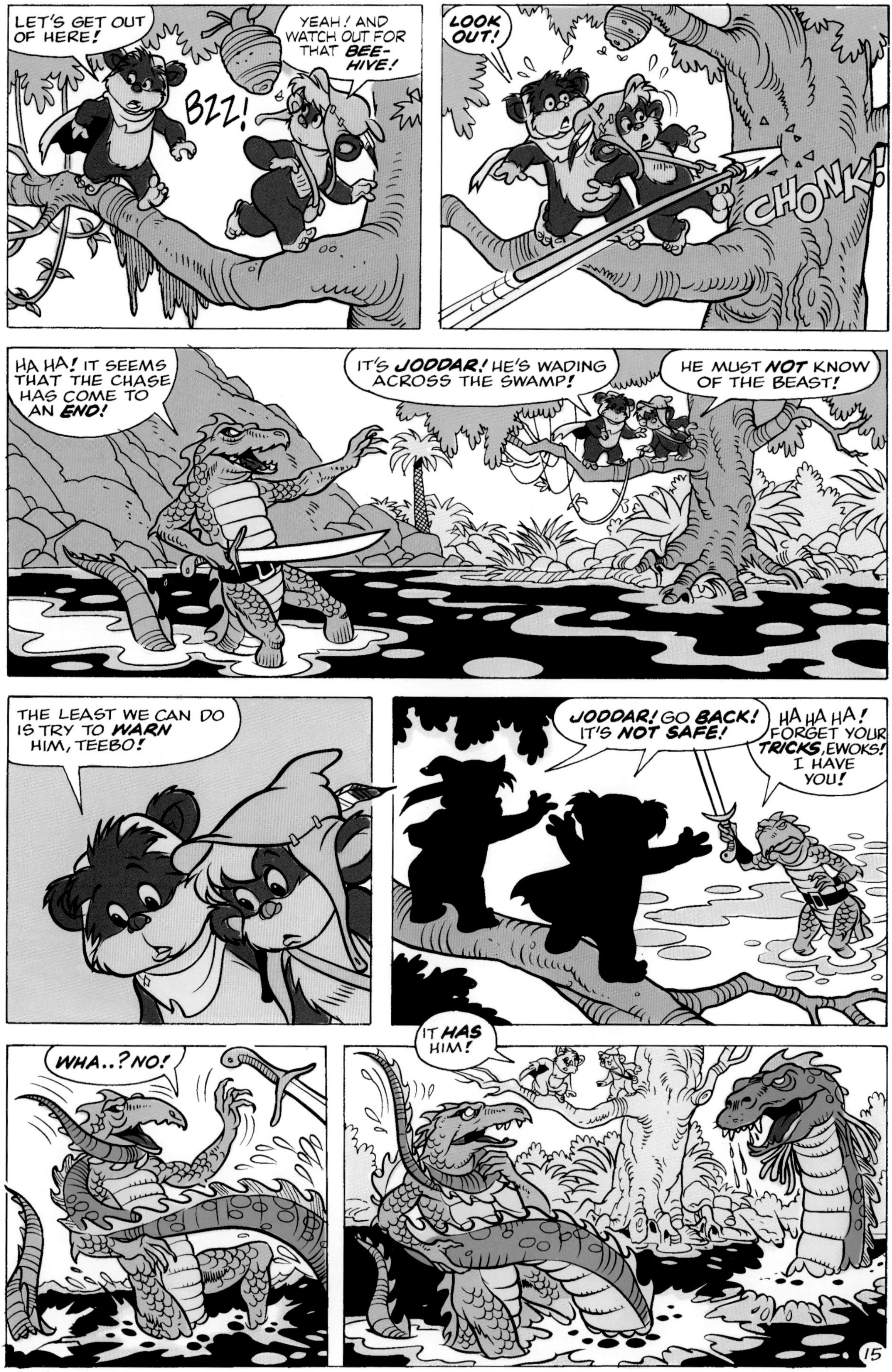
LET'S GET OUT OF HERE!
YEAH! AND WATCH OUT FOR THAT BEE-HIVE!
BZZ!
LOOK OUT!
CHONK!
HA HA! IT SEEMS THAT THE CHASE HAS COME TO AN END!
IT'S JODDAR! HE'S WADING ACROSS THE SWAMP!
HE MUST NOT KNOW OF THE BEAST!
THE LEAST WE CAN DO IS TRY TO WARN HIM, TEEBO!
JODDAR! GO BACK! IT'S NOT SAFE!
HA HA HA! FORGET YOUR TRICKS, EWOKS! I HAVE YOU!
WHA..? NO!
IT HAS HIM!
15

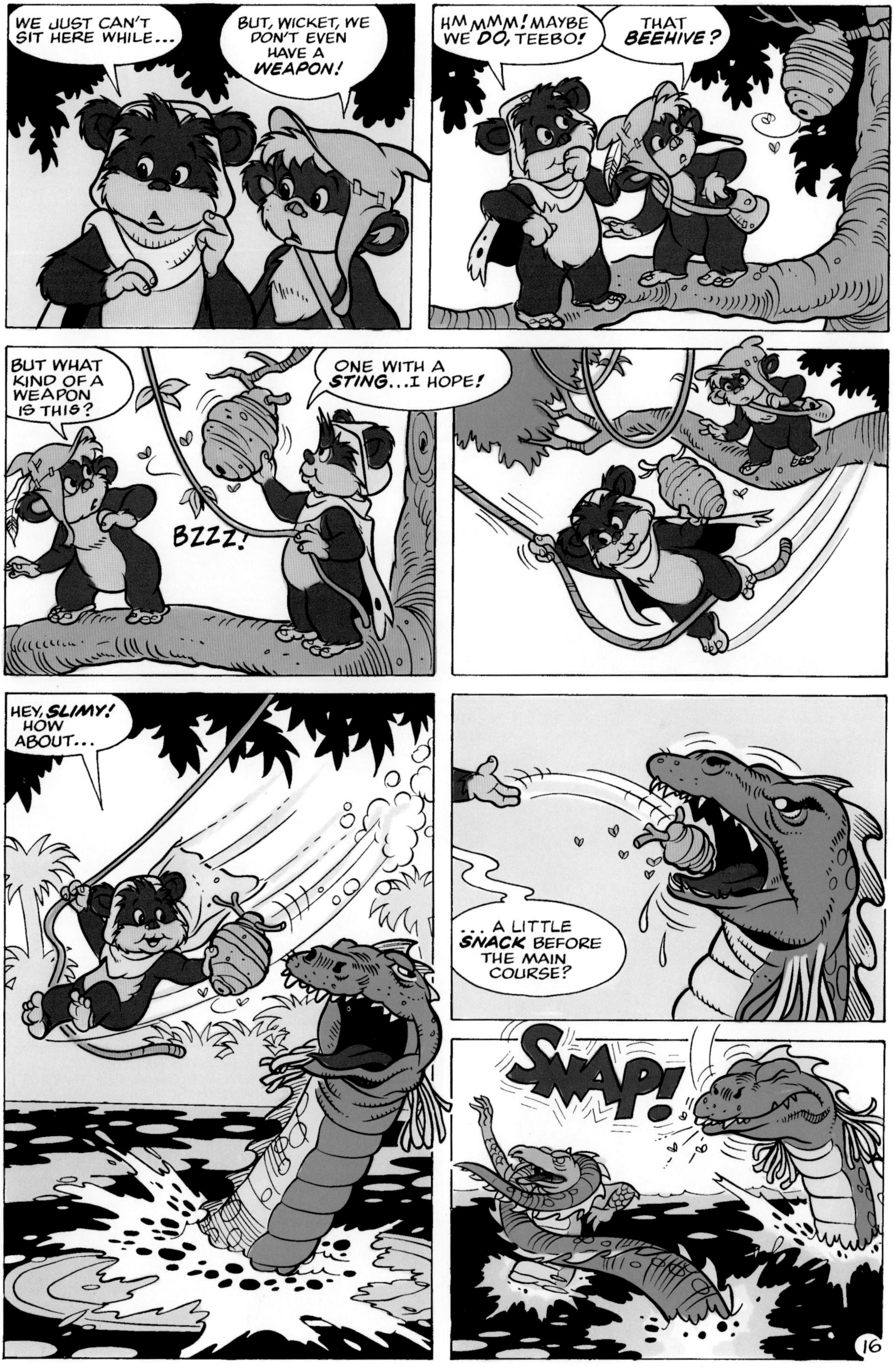
WE JUST CAN'T SIT HERE WHILE...
BUT, WICKET, WE DON'T EVEN HAVE A WEAPON!
HMMMM! MAYBE WE DO, TEEBO!
THAT BEEHIVE?
BUT WHAT KIND OF A WEAPON IS THIS?
ONE WITH A STING...I HOPE!
BZZZ!
HEY, SLIMY! HOW ABOUT...
... A LITTLE SNACK BEFORE THE MAIN COURSE?
SNAP!
16

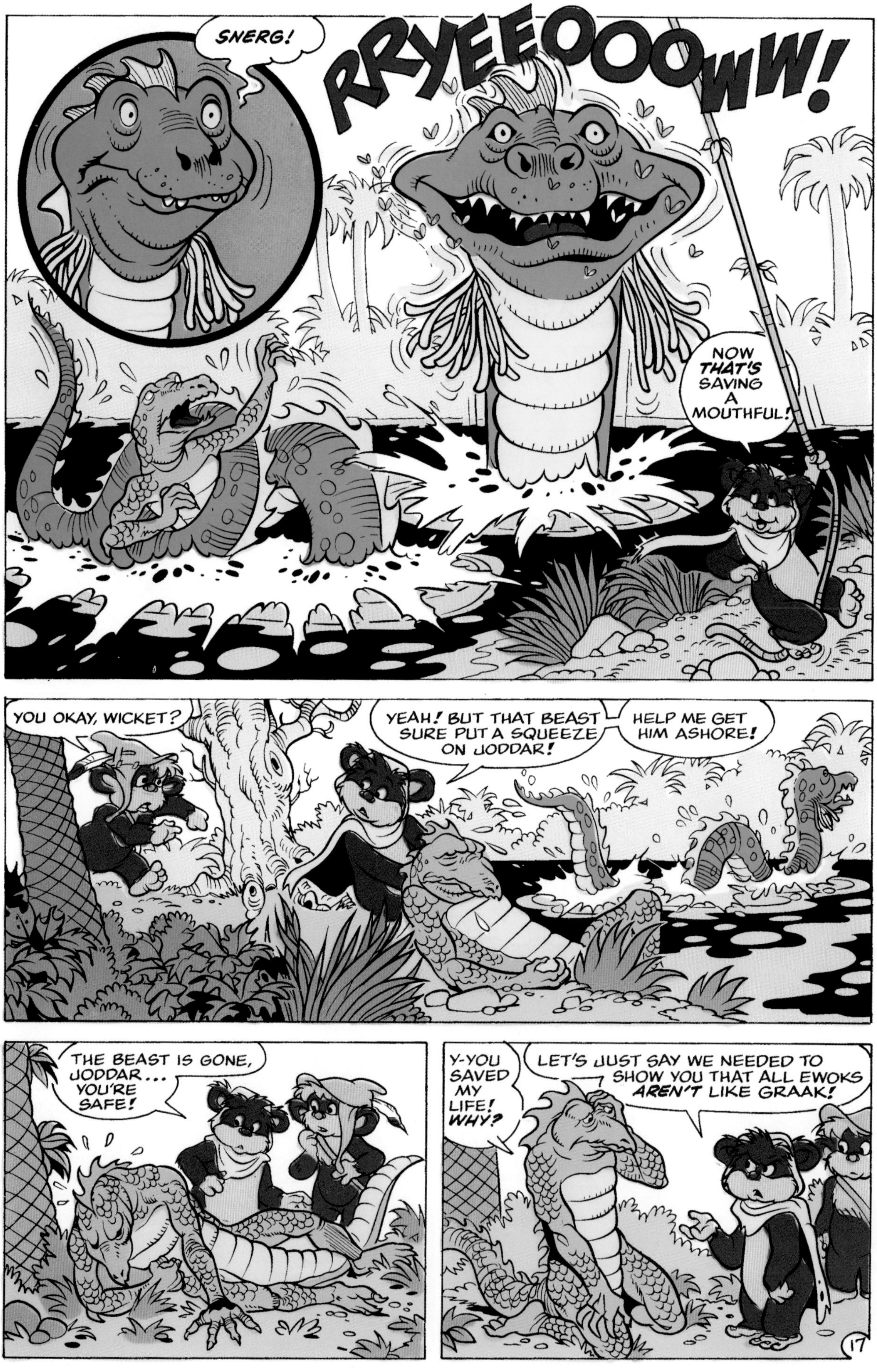
SNERG!
RRYEEOOOOWW!
NOW THAT'S SAVING A MOUTHFUL!
YOU OKAY, WICKET?
YEAH! BUT THAT BEAST SURE PUT A SQUEEZE ON JODDAR!
HELP ME GET HIM ASHORE!
THE BEAST IS GONE, JODDAR... YOU'RE SAFE!
Y-YOU SAVED MY LIFE! WHY?
LET'S JUST SAY WE NEEDED TO SHOW YOU THAT ALL EWOKS AREN'T LIKE GRAAK!
17

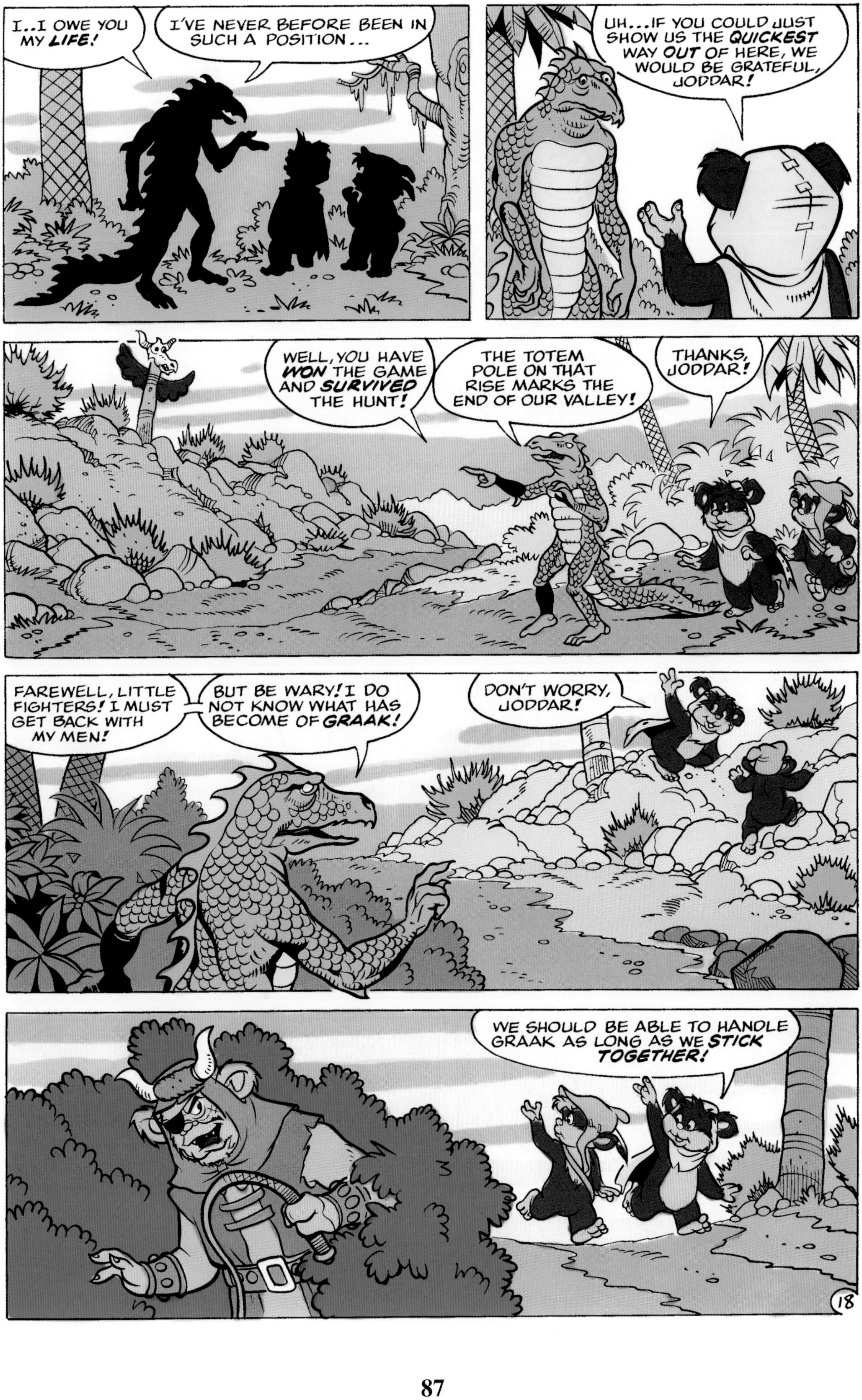
I..I OWE YOU MY LIFE!
I'VE NEVER BEFORE BEEN IN SUCH A POSITION...
UH...IF YOU COULD JUST SHOW US THE QUICKEST WAY OUT OF HERE, WE WOULD BE GRATEFUL, JODDAR!
WELL, YOU HAVE WON THE GAME AND SURVIVED THE HUNT!
THE TOTEM POLE ON THAT RISE MARKS THE END OF OUR VALLEY!
THANKS, JODDAR!
FAREWELL, LITTLE FIGHTERS! I MUST GET BACK WITH MY MEN!
BUT BE WARY! I DO NOT KNOW WHAT HAS BECOME OF GRAAK!
DON'T WORRY, JODDAR!
WE SHOULD BE ABLE TO HANDLE GRAAK AS LONG AS WE STICK TOGETHER!
18

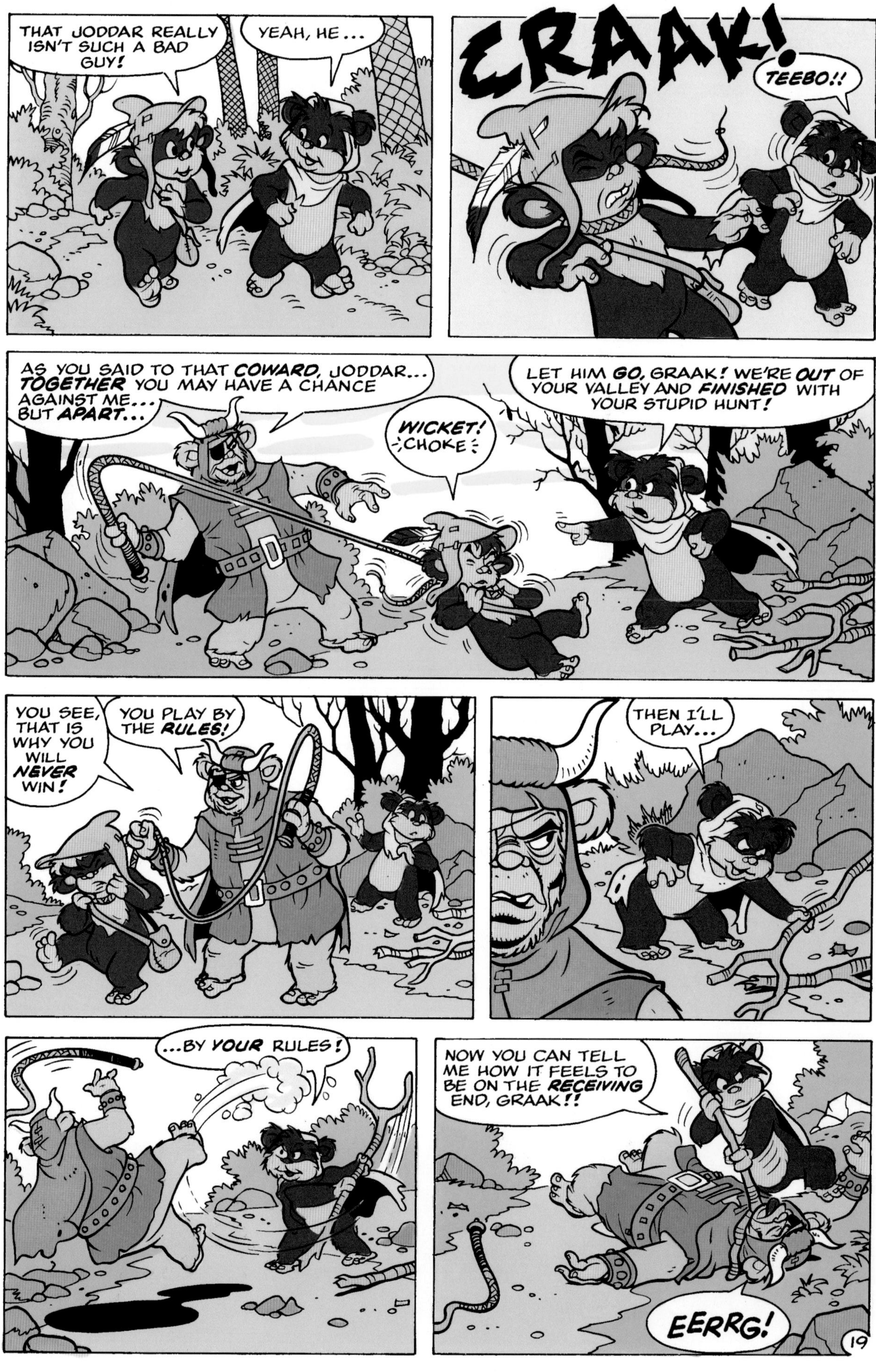
THAT JODDAR REALLY ISN'T SUCH A BAD GUY!
YEAH, HE...
CRAAK!
TEEBO!!
AS YOU SAID TO THAT COWARD, JODDAR... TOGETHER YOU MAY HAVE A CHANCE AGAINST ME... BUT APART...
WICKET! CHOKE
LET HIM GO, GRAAK! WE'RE OUT OF YOUR VALLEY AND FINISHED WITH YOUR STUPID HUNT!
YOU SEE, THAT IS WHY YOU WILL NEVER WIN!
YOU PLAY BY THE RULES!
THEN I'LL PLAY...
...BY YOUR RULES!
NOW YOU CAN TELL ME HOW IT FEELS TO BE ON THE RECEIVING END, GRAAK!!
EERRG!
19

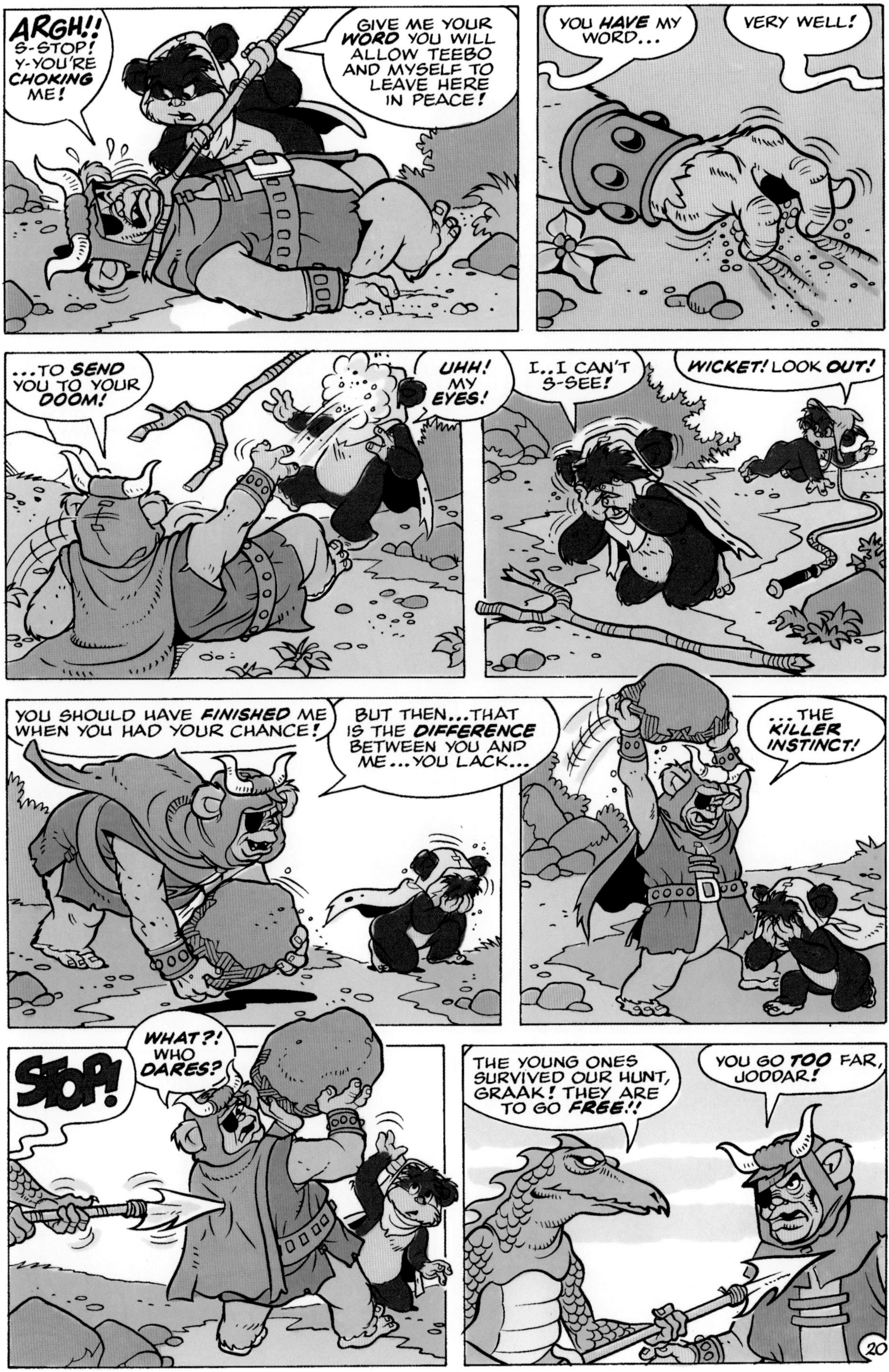
ARGH!! S-STOP! Y-YOU'RE CHOKING ME!
GIVE ME YOUR WORD YOU WILL ALLOW TEEBO AND MYSELF TO LEAVE HERE IN PEACE!
YOU HAVE MY WORD...
VERY WELL!
...TO SEND YOU TO YOUR DOOM!
UHH! MY EYES!
I..I CAN'T S-SEE!
WICKET! LOOK OUT!
YOU SHOULD HAVE FINISHED ME WHEN YOU HAD YOUR CHANCE!
BUT THEN...THAT IS THE DIFFERENCE BETWEEN YOU AND ME...YOU LACK...
...THE KILLER INSTINCT!
STOP!
WHAT?! WHO DARES?
THE YOUNG ONES SURVIVED OUR HUNT, GRAAK! THEY ARE TO GO FREE!!
YOU GO TOO FAR, JODDAR!
20

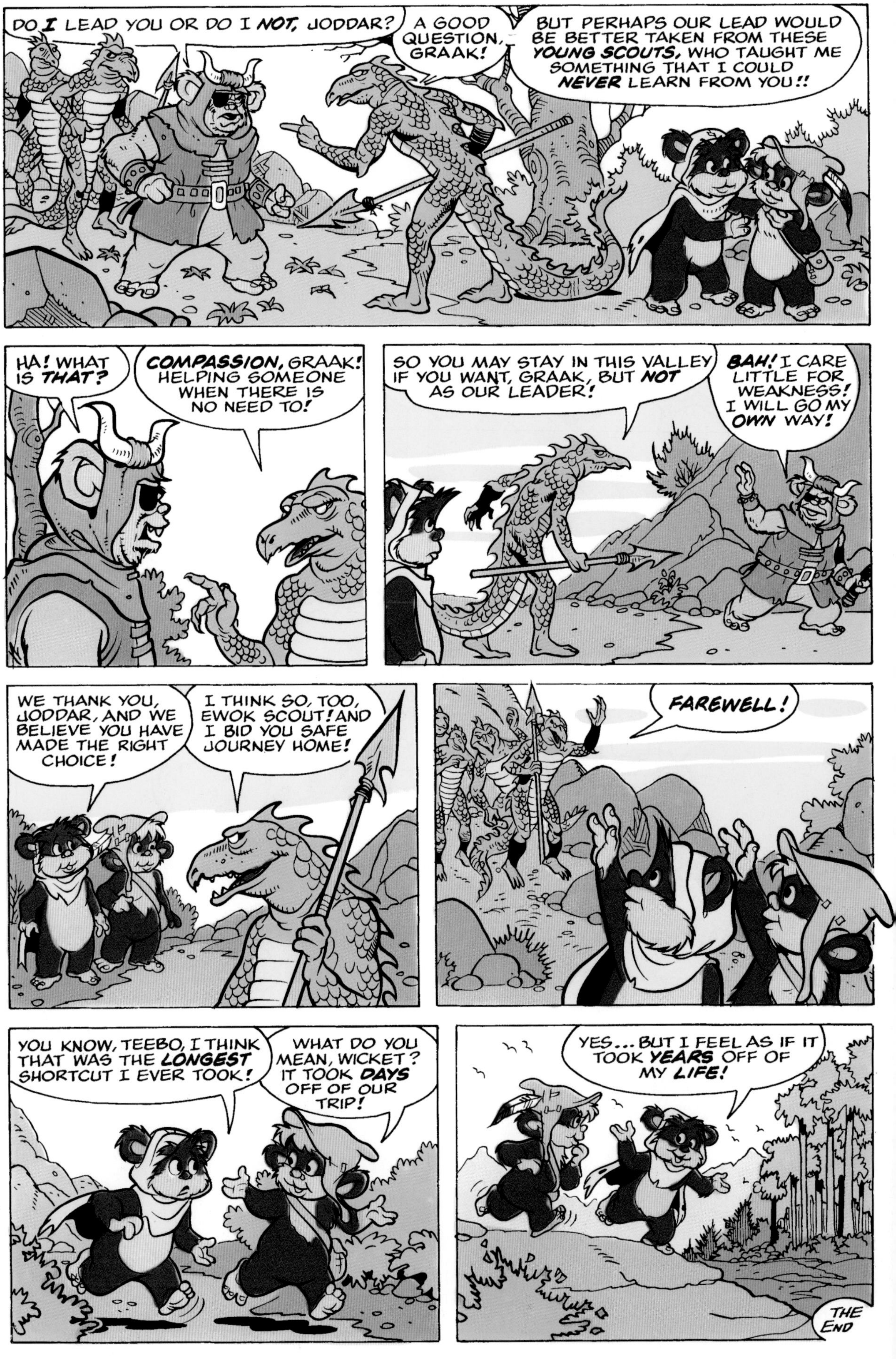
DO I LEAD YOU OR DO I NOT, JODDAR?
A GOOD QUESTION, GRAAK!
BUT PERHAPS OUR LEAD WOULD BE BETTER TAKEN FROM THESE YOUNG SCOUTS, WHO TAUGHT ME SOMETHING THAT I COULD NEVER LEARN FROM YOU!!
HA! WHAT IS THAT?
COMPASSION, GRAAK! HELPING SOMEONE WHEN THERE IS NO NEED TO!
SO YOU MAY STAY IN THIS VALLEY IF YOU WANT, GRAAK, BUT NOT AS OUR LEADER!
BAH! I CARE LITTLE FOR WEAKNESS! I WILL GO MY OWN WAY!
WE THANK YOU, JODDAR, AND WE BELIEVE YOU HAVE MADE THE RIGHT CHOICE!
I THINK SO, TOO, EWOK SCOUT! AND I BID YOU SAFE JOURNEY HOME!
FAREWELL!
YOU KNOW, TEEBO, I THINK THAT WAS THE LONGEST SHORTCUT I EVER TOOK!
WHAT DO YOU MEAN, WICKET? IT TOOK DAYS OFF OF OUR TRIP!
YES... BUT I FEEL AS IF IT TOOK YEARS OFF OF MY LIFE!
THE END

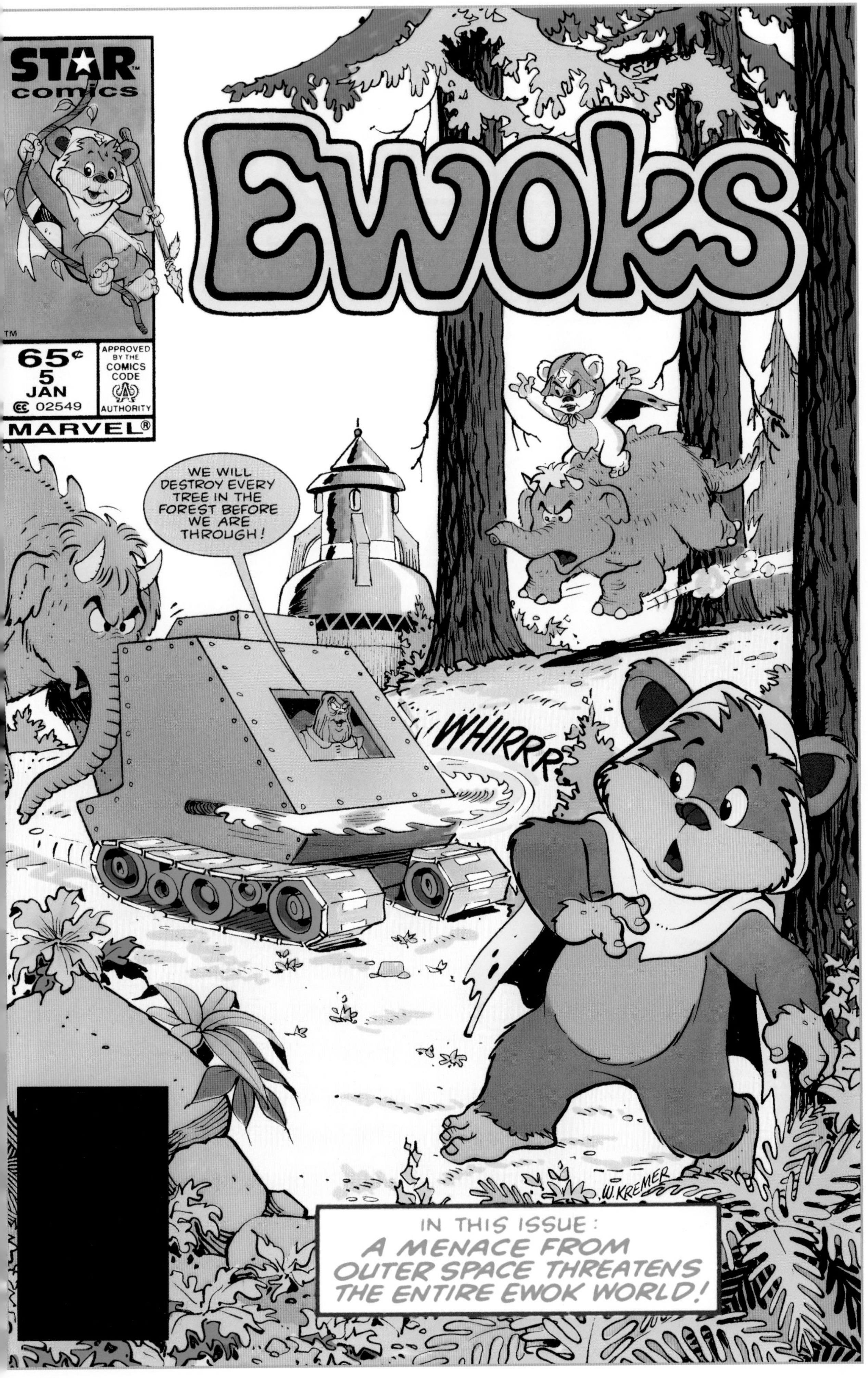
STAR comics
EWOKS
65¢
5
JAN
02549
APPROVED BY THE COMICS CODE AUTHORITY
MARVEL®
WE WILL DESTROY EVERY TREE IN THE FOREST BEFORE WE ARE THROUGH!
WHIRRR
W. KREMER
IN THIS ISSUE:
A MENACE FROM OUTER SPACE THREATENS THE ENTIRE EWOK WORLD!

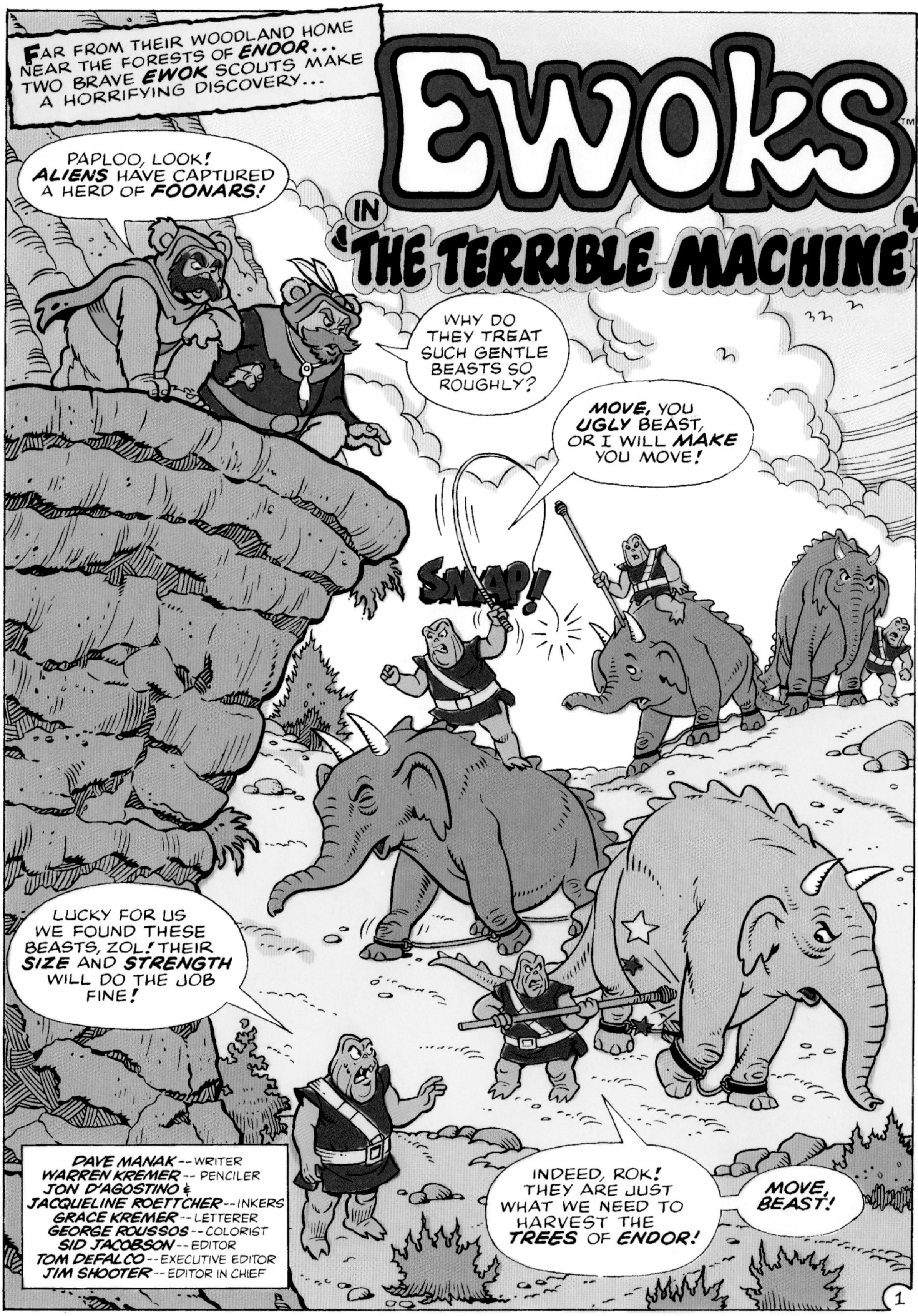
FAR FROM THEIR WOODLAND HOME NEAR THE FORESTS OF ENDOR... TWO BRAVE EWOK SCOUTS MAKE A HORRIFYING DISCOVERY...
EWOKS™
IN "THE TERRIBLE MACHINE"
PAPLOO, LOOK! ALIENS HAVE CAPTURED A HERD OF FOONARS!
WHY DO THEY TREAT SUCH GENTLE BEASTS SO ROUGHLY?
MOVE, YOU UGLY BEAST, OR I WILL MAKE YOU MOVE!
SNAP!
LUCKY FOR US WE FOUND THESE BEASTS, ZOL! THEIR SIZE AND STRENGTH WILL DO THE JOB FINE!
INDEED, ROK! THEY ARE JUST WHAT WE NEED TO HARVEST THE TREES OF ENDOR!
MOVE, BEAST!
DAVE MANAK -- WRITER
WARREN KREMER -- PENCILER
JON D'AGOSTINO &
JACQUELINE ROETTCHER -- INKERS
GRACE KREMER -- LETTERER
GEORGE ROUSSOS -- COLORIST
SID JACOBSON -- EDITOR
TOM DEFALCO -- EXECUTIVE EDITOR
JIM SHOOTER -- EDITOR IN CHIEF
1

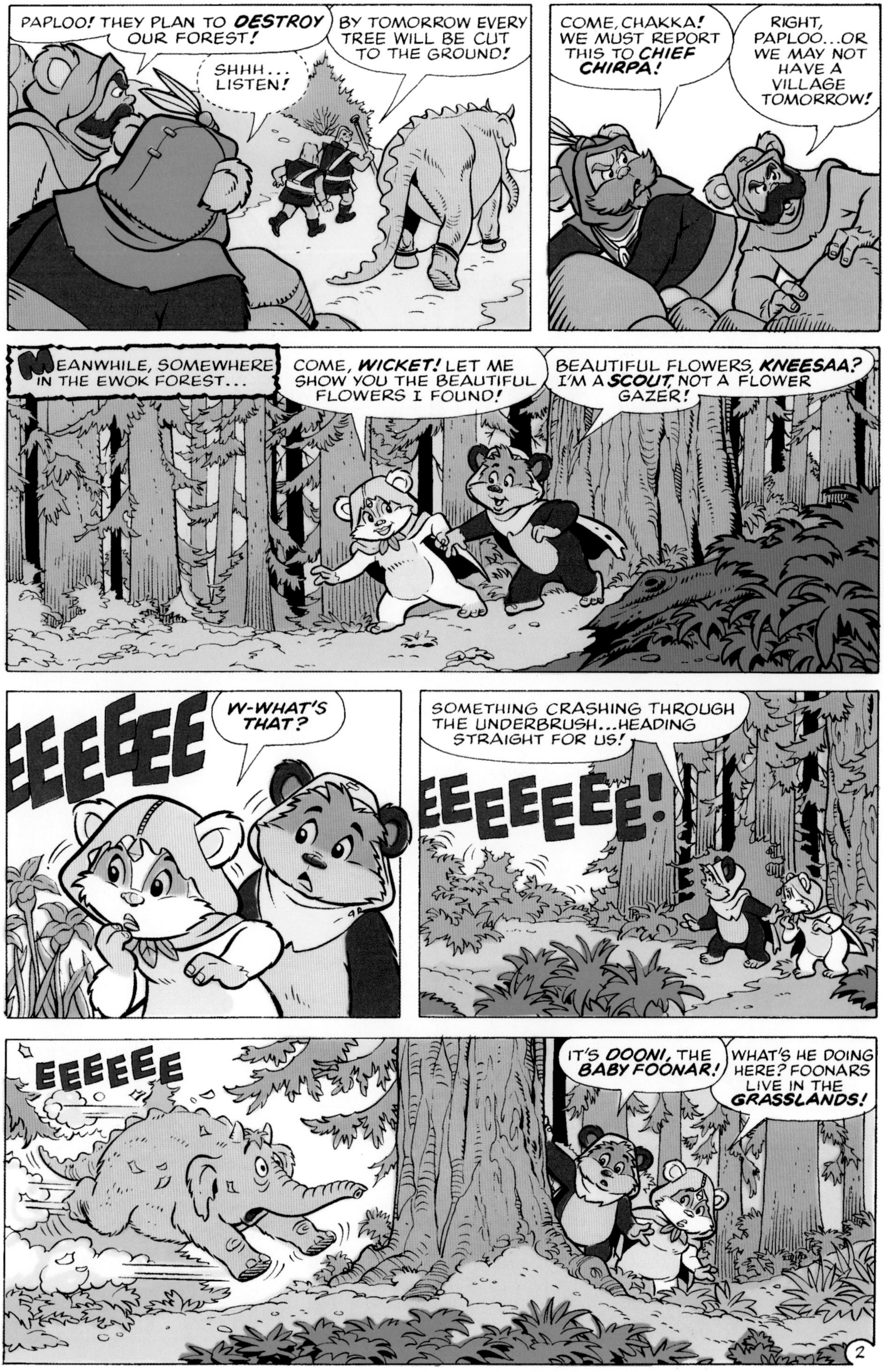
PAPLOO! THEY PLAN TO DESTROY OUR FOREST!
SHHH... LISTEN!
BY TOMORROW EVERY TREE WILL BE CUT TO THE GROUND!
COME, CHAKKA! WE MUST REPORT THIS TO CHIEF CHIRPA!
RIGHT, PAPLOO...OR WE MAY NOT HAVE A VILLAGE TOMORROW!
MEANWHILE, SOMEWHERE IN THE EWOK FOREST...
COME, WICKET! LET ME SHOW YOU THE BEAUTIFUL FLOWERS I FOUND!
BEAUTIFUL FLOWERS, KNEESAA? I'M A SCOUT, NOT A FLOWER GAZER!
EEEEEE
W-WHAT'S THAT?
SOMETHING CRASHING THROUGH THE UNDERBRUSH...HEADING STRAIGHT FOR US!
EEEEEEE!
EEEEEE
IT'S DOONI, THE BABY FOONAR!
WHAT'S HE DOING HERE? FOONARS LIVE IN THE GRASSLANDS!
2

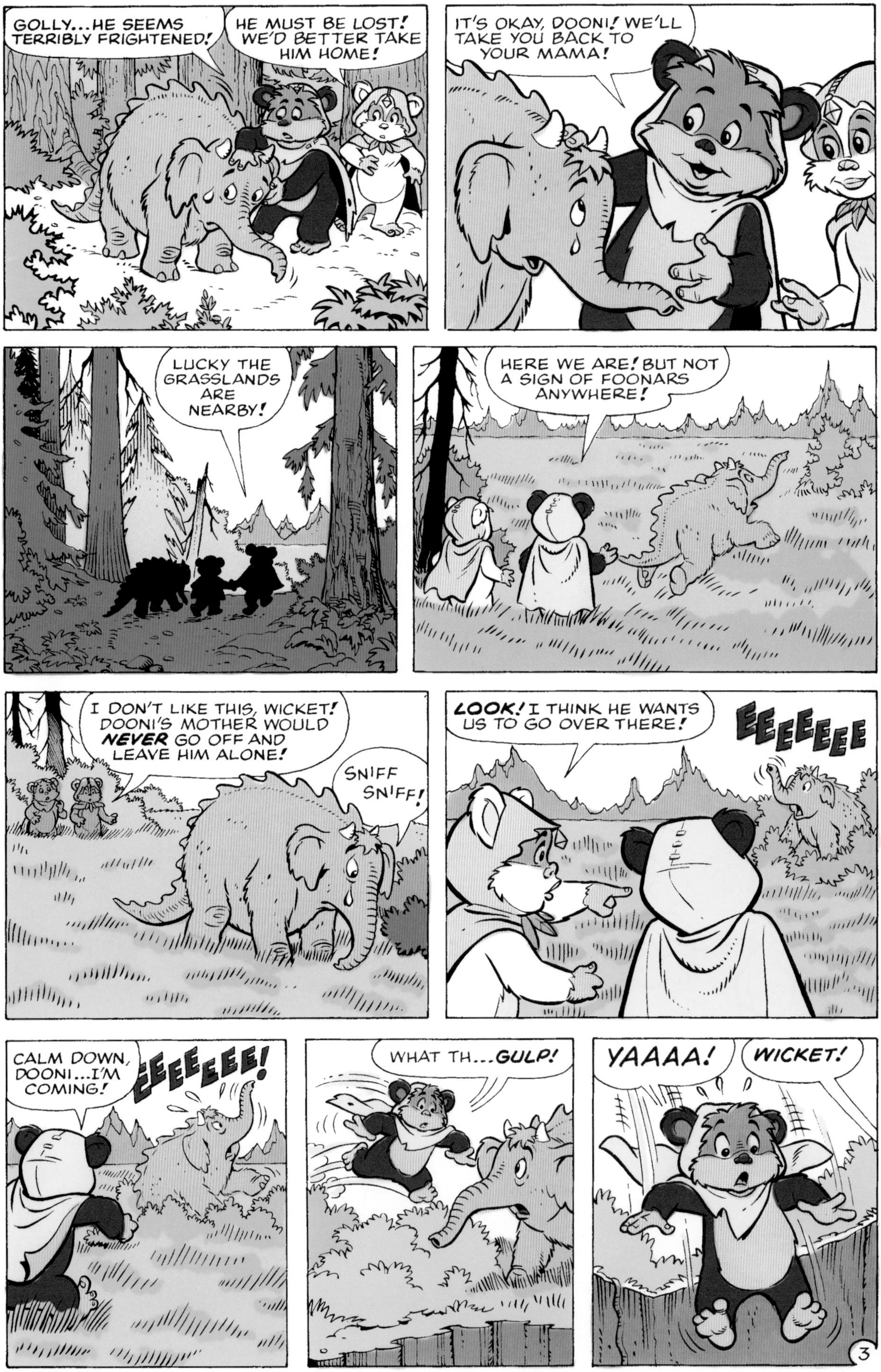
GOLLY...HE SEEMS TERRIBLY FRIGHTENED!
HE MUST BE LOST! WE'D BETTER TAKE HIM HOME!
IT'S OKAY, DOONI! WE'LL TAKE YOU BACK TO YOUR MAMA!
LUCKY THE GRASSLANDS ARE NEARBY!
HERE WE ARE! BUT NOT A SIGN OF FOONARS ANYWHERE!
I DON'T LIKE THIS, WICKET! DOONI'S MOTHER WOULD NEVER GO OFF AND LEAVE HIM ALONE!
SNIFF SNIFF!
LOOK! I THINK HE WANTS US TO GO OVER THERE!
EEEEEEE
CALM DOWN, DOONI...I'M COMING!
EEEEEEE!
WHAT TH...GULP!
YAAAA!
WICKET!
3

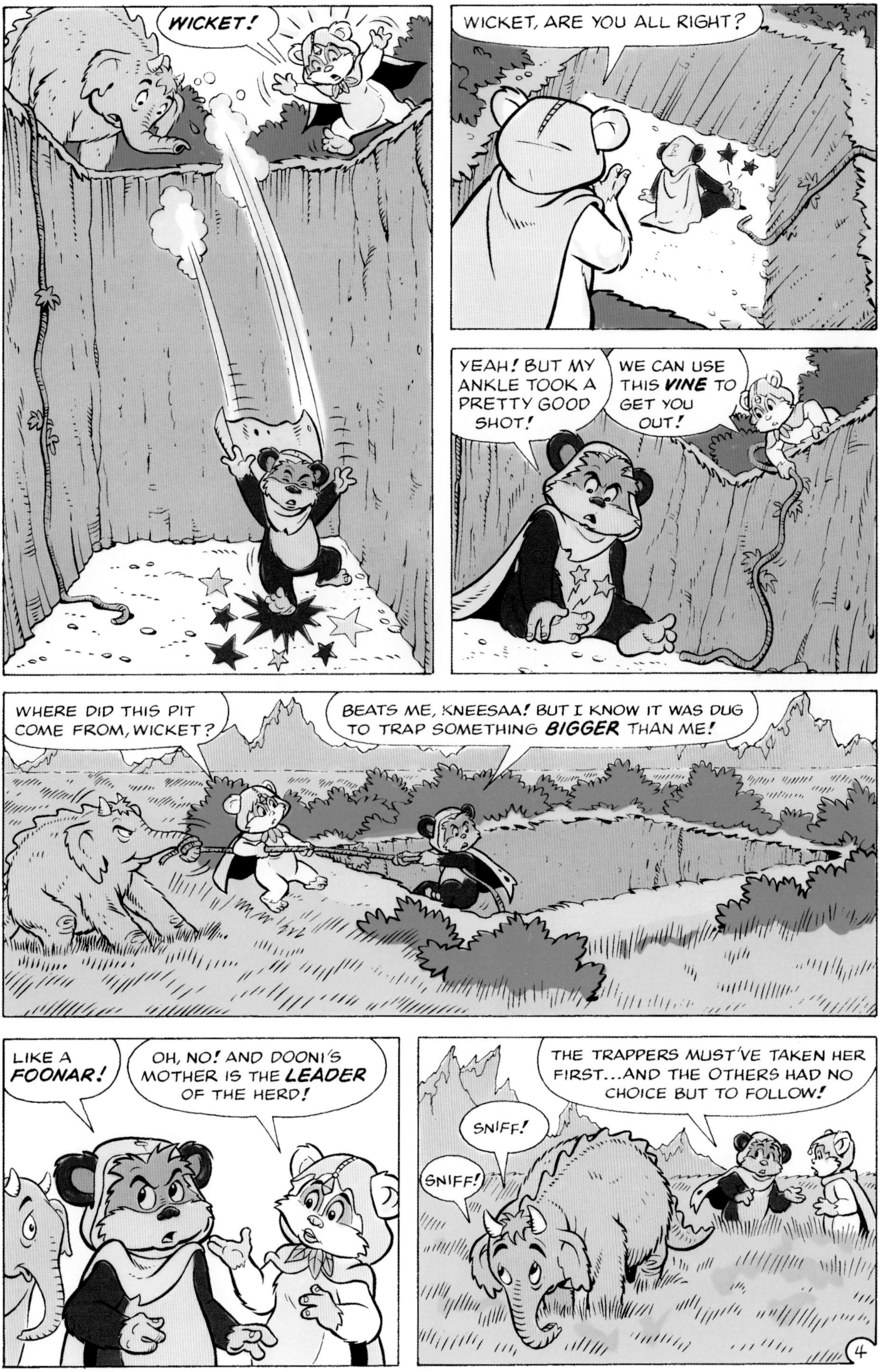
WICKET!
WICKET, ARE YOU ALL RIGHT?
YEAH! BUT MY ANKLE TOOK A PRETTY GOOD SHOT!
WE CAN USE THIS VINE TO GET YOU OUT!
WHERE DID THIS PIT COME FROM, WICKET?
BEATS ME, KNEESAA! BUT I KNOW IT WAS DUG TO TRAP SOMETHING BIGGER THAN ME!
LIKE A FOONAR!
OH, NO! AND DOONI'S MOTHER IS THE LEADER OF THE HERD!
THE TRAPPERS MUST'VE TAKEN HER FIRST...AND THE OTHERS HAD NO CHOICE BUT TO FOLLOW!
SNIFF!
SNIFF!
4

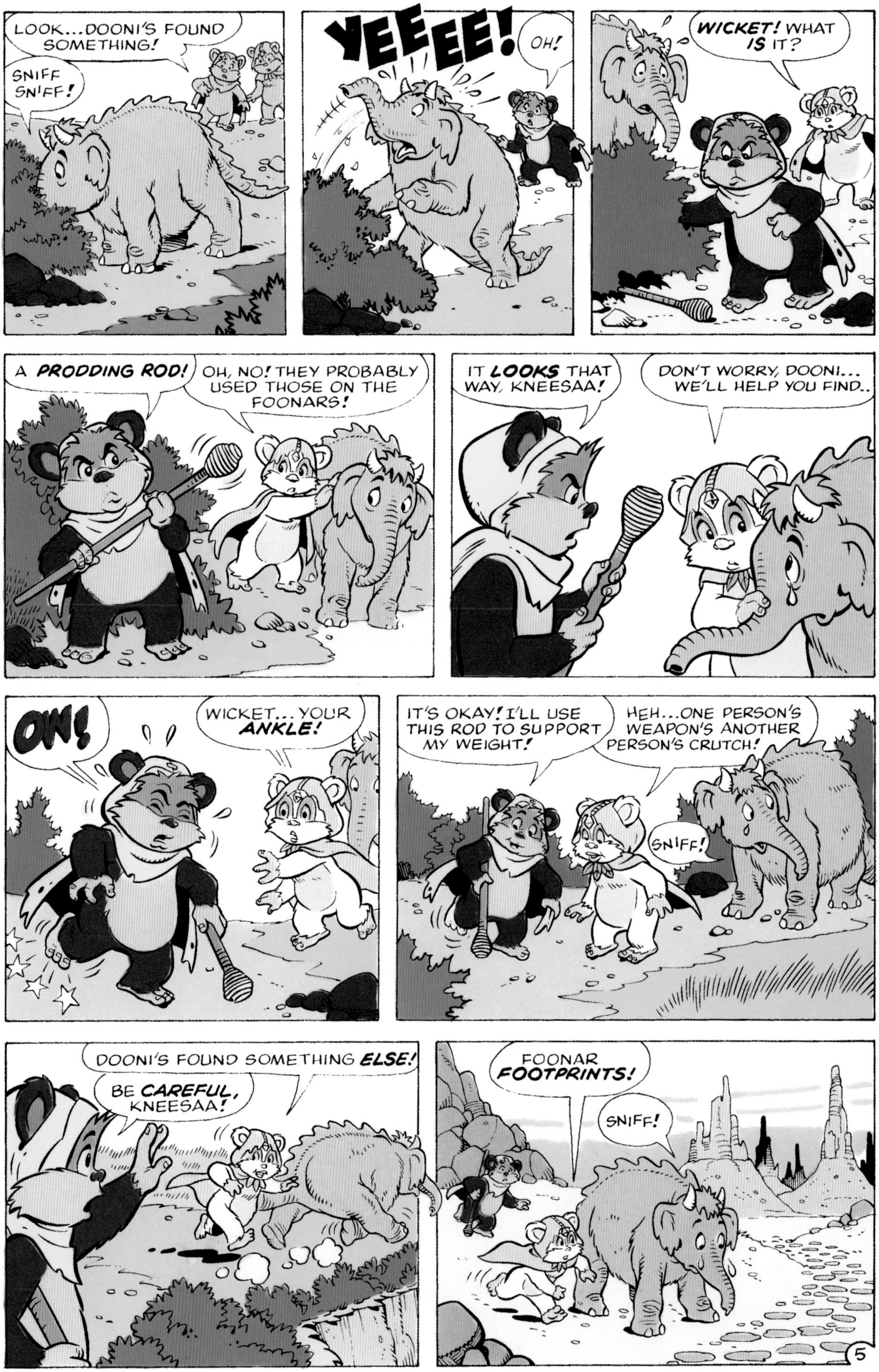
LOOK...DOONI'S FOUND SOMETHING!
SNIFF SNIFF!
YEEEEE!
OH!
WICKET! WHAT IS IT?
A PRODDING ROD!
OH, NO! THEY PROBABLY USED THOSE ON THE FOONARS!
IT LOOKS THAT WAY, KNEESAA!
DON'T WORRY, DOONI... WE'LL HELP YOU FIND..
OW!
WICKET... YOUR ANKLE!
IT'S OKAY! I'LL USE THIS ROD TO SUPPORT MY WEIGHT!
HEH...ONE PERSON'S WEAPON'S ANOTHER PERSON'S CRUTCH!
SNIFF!
DOONI'S FOUND SOMETHING ELSE!
BE CAREFUL, KNEESAA!
FOONAR FOOTPRINTS!
SNIFF!
5

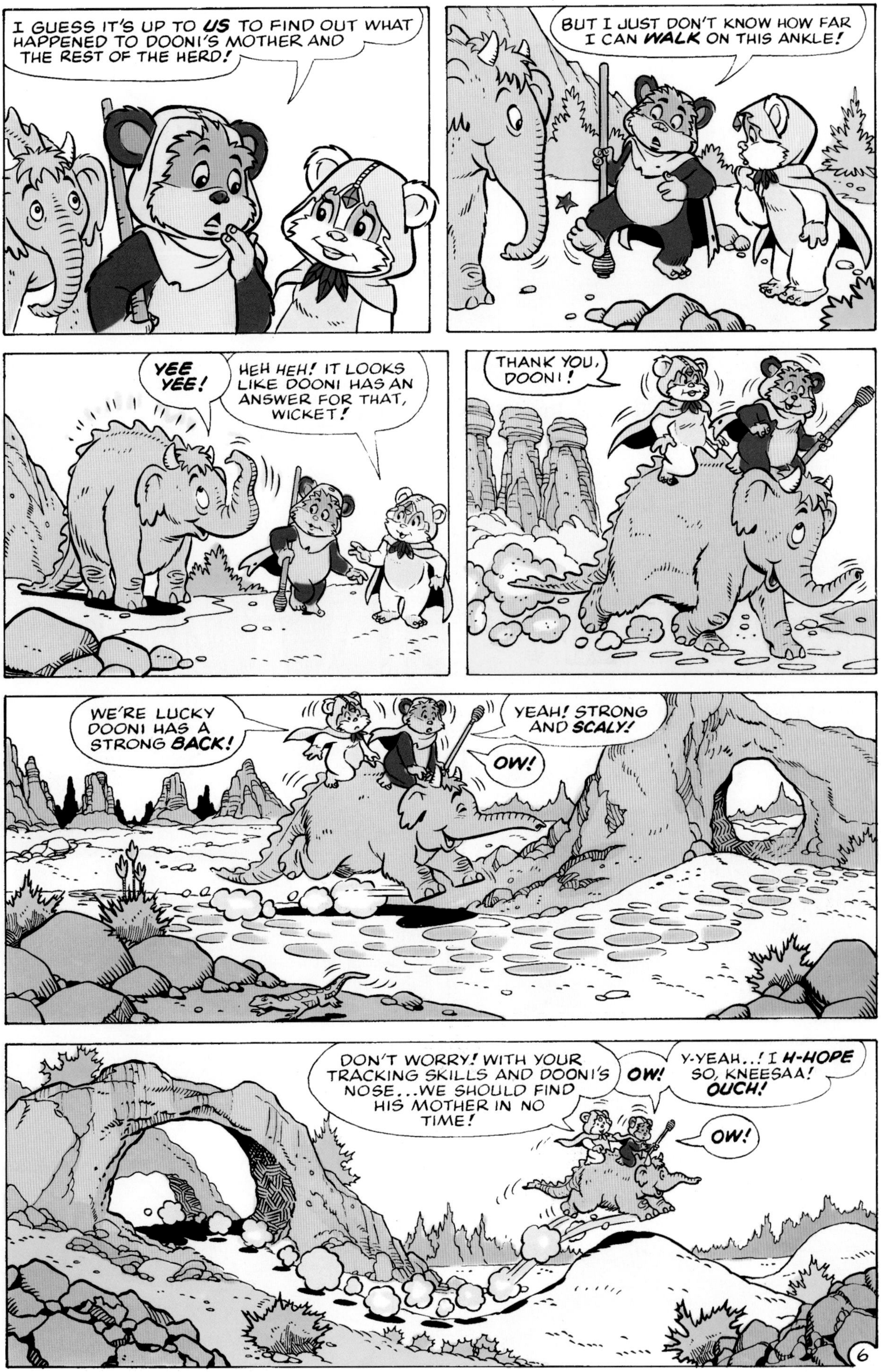
I GUESS IT'S UP TO US TO FIND OUT WHAT HAPPENED TO DOONI'S MOTHER AND THE REST OF THE HERD!
BUT I JUST DON'T KNOW HOW FAR I CAN WALK ON THIS ANKLE!
YEE YEE!
HEH HEH! IT LOOKS LIKE DOONI HAS AN ANSWER FOR THAT, WICKET!
THANK YOU, DOONI!
WE'RE LUCKY DOONI HAS A STRONG BACK!
YEAH! STRONG AND SCALY!
OW!
DON'T WORRY! WITH YOUR TRACKING SKILLS AND DOONI'S NOSE...WE SHOULD FIND HIS MOTHER IN NO TIME!
OW!
Y-YEAH..! I H-HOPE SO, KNEESAA! OUCH!
OW!
6

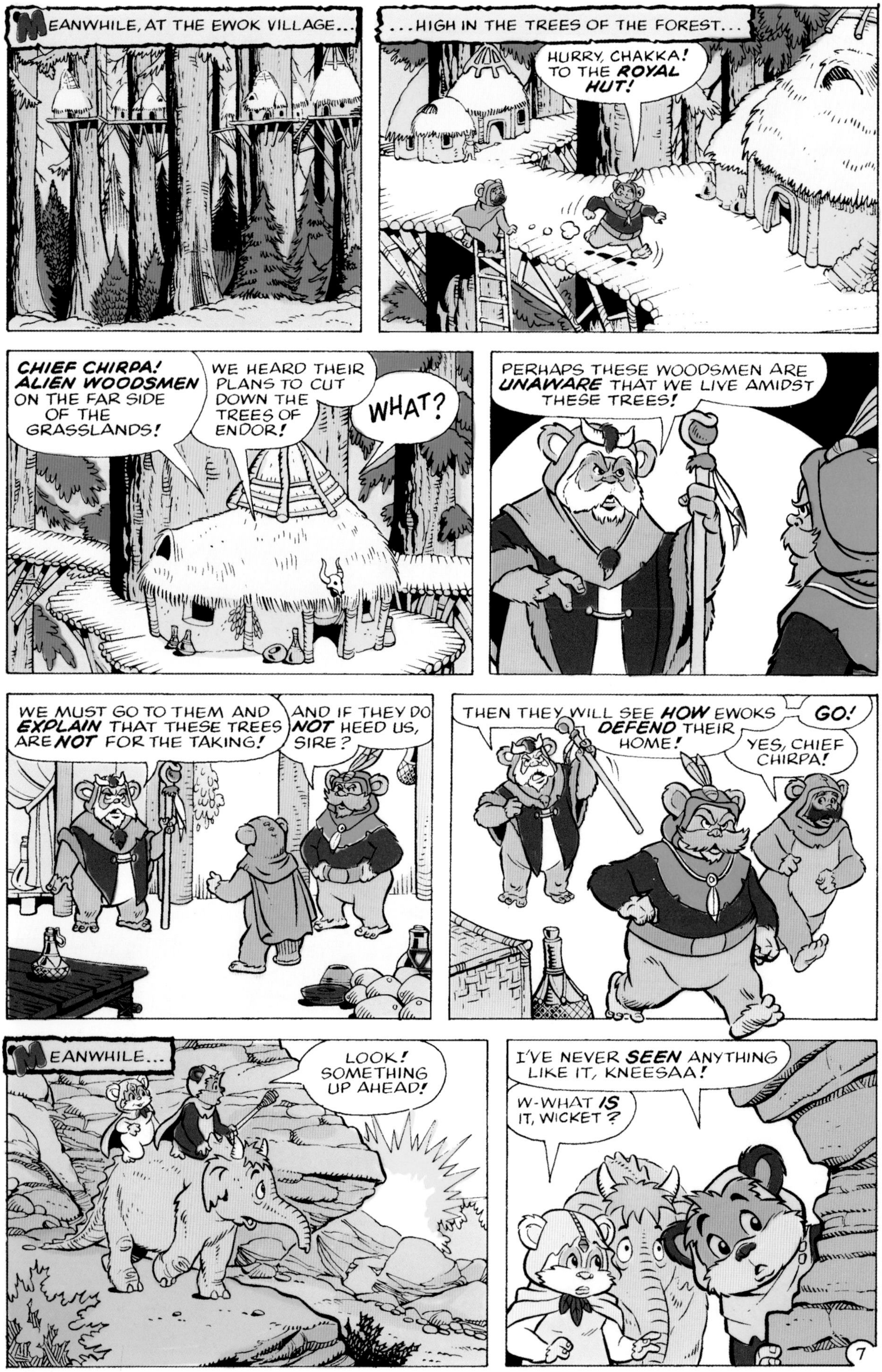
MEANWHILE, AT THE EWOK VILLAGE...
...HIGH IN THE TREES OF THE FOREST...
HURRY, CHAKKA! TO THE ROYAL HUT!
CHIEF CHIRPA! ALIEN WOODSMEN ON THE FAR SIDE OF THE GRASSLANDS!
WE HEARD THEIR PLANS TO CUT DOWN THE TREES OF ENDOR!
WHAT?
PERHAPS THESE WOODSMEN ARE UNAWARE THAT WE LIVE AMIDST THESE TREES!
WE MUST GO TO THEM AND EXPLAIN THAT THESE TREES ARE NOT FOR THE TAKING!
AND IF THEY DO NOT HEED US, SIRE?
THEN THEY WILL SEE HOW EWOKS DEFEND THEIR HOME!
GO!
YES, CHIEF CHIRPA!
MEANWHILE...
LOOK! SOMETHING UP AHEAD!
I'VE NEVER SEEN ANYTHING LIKE IT, KNEESAA!
W-WHAT IS IT, WICKET?
7

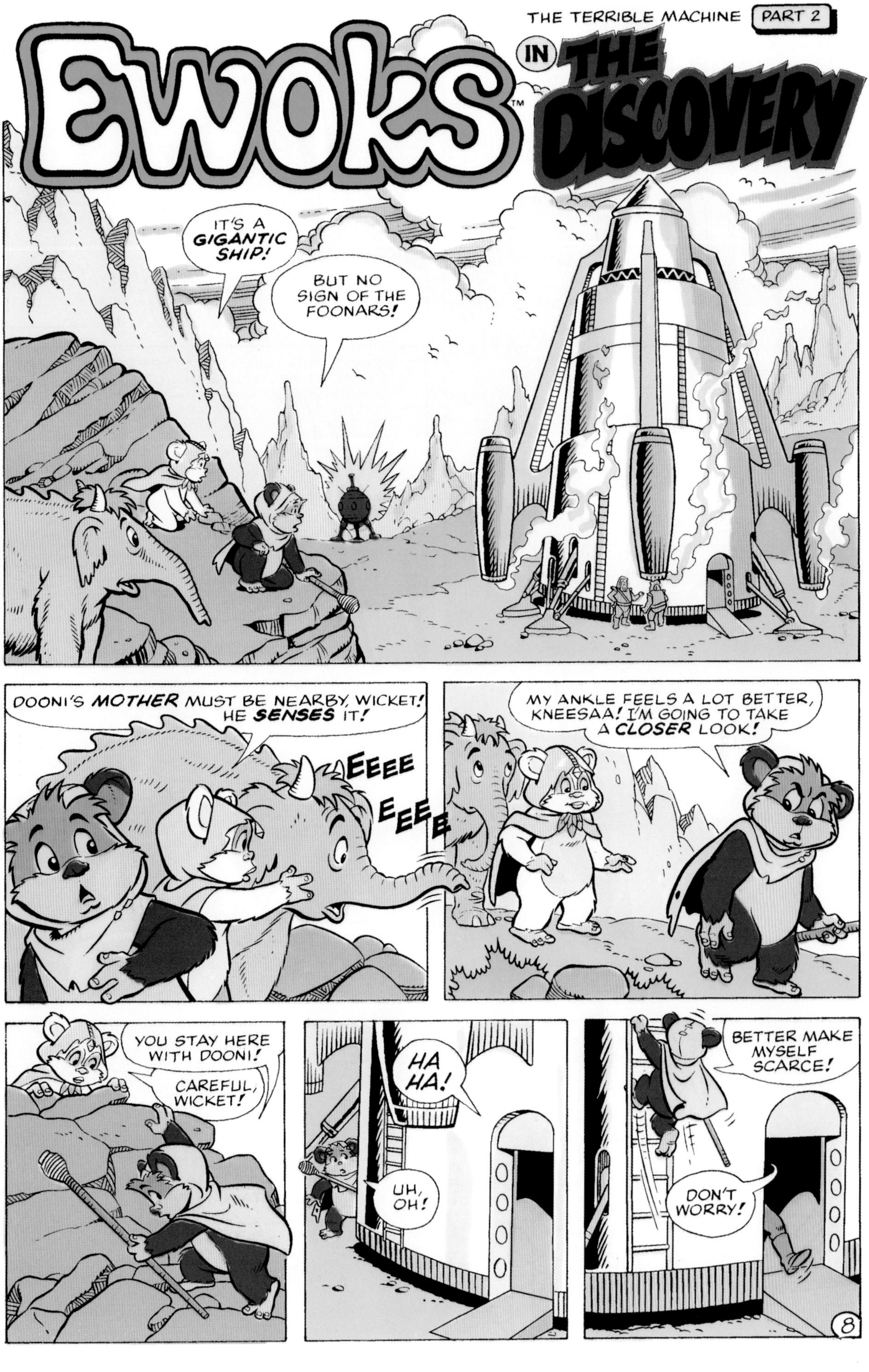
THE TERRIBLE MACHINE PART 2
Ewoks IN THE DISCOVERY
IT'S A GIGANTIC SHIP!
BUT NO SIGN OF THE FOONARS!
DOONI'S MOTHER MUST BE NEARBY, WICKET! HE SENSES IT!
EEEE EEEE
MY ANKLE FEELS A LOT BETTER, KNEESAA! I'M GOING TO TAKE A CLOSER LOOK!
YOU STAY HERE WITH DOONI!
CAREFUL, WICKET!
HA HA!
UH, OH!
BETTER MAKE MYSELF SCARCE!
DON'T WORRY!
8

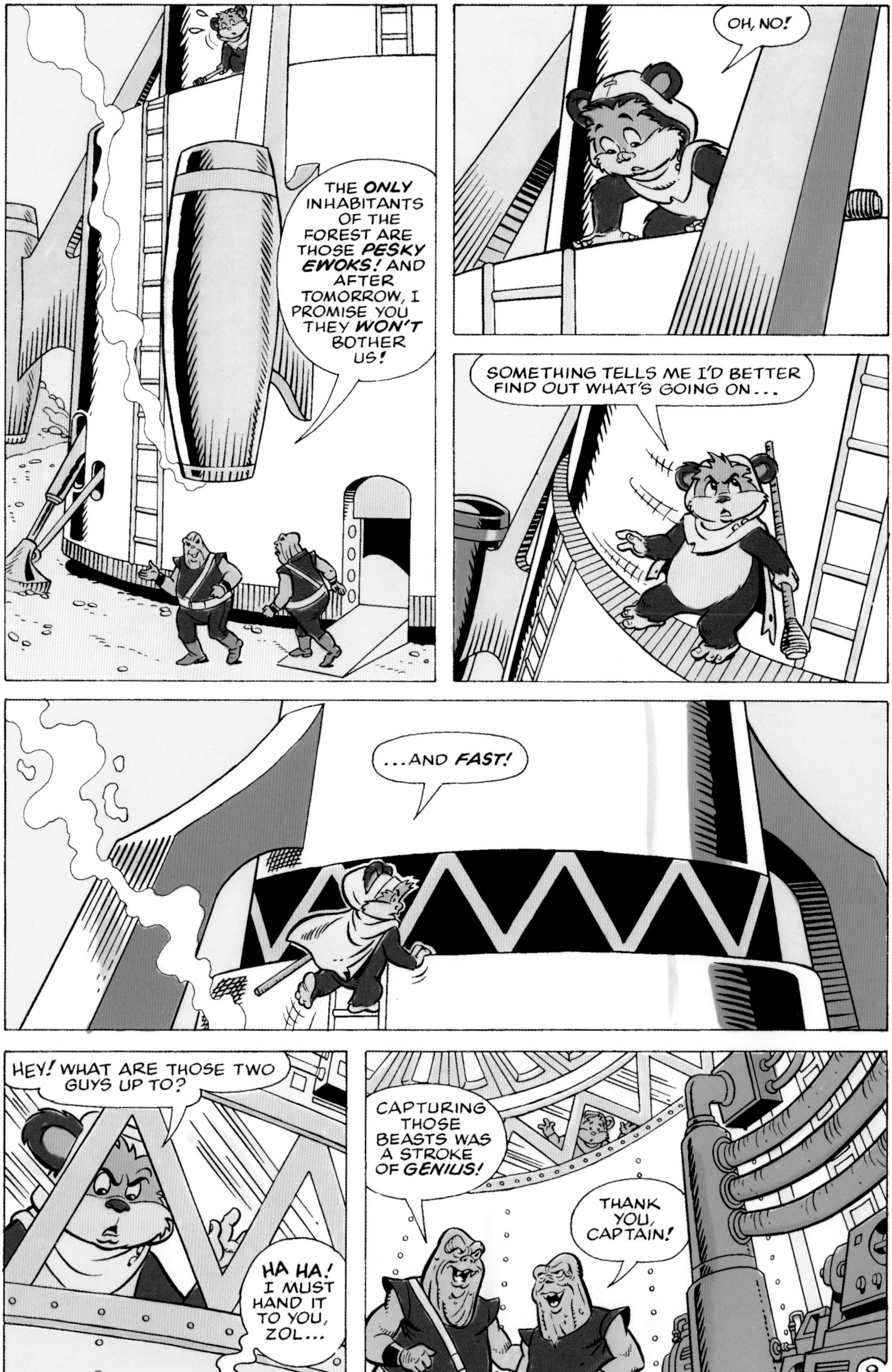
THE ONLY INHABITANTS OF THE FOREST ARE THOSE PESKY EWOKS! AND AFTER TOMORROW, I PROMISE YOU THEY WON'T BOTHER US!
OH, NO!
SOMETHING TELLS ME I'D BETTER FIND OUT WHAT'S GOING ON...
...AND FAST!
HEY! WHAT ARE THOSE TWO GUYS UP TO?
HA HA! I MUST HAND IT TO YOU, ZOL...
CAPTURING THOSE BEASTS WAS A STROKE OF GENIUS!
THANK YOU, CAPTAIN!
9

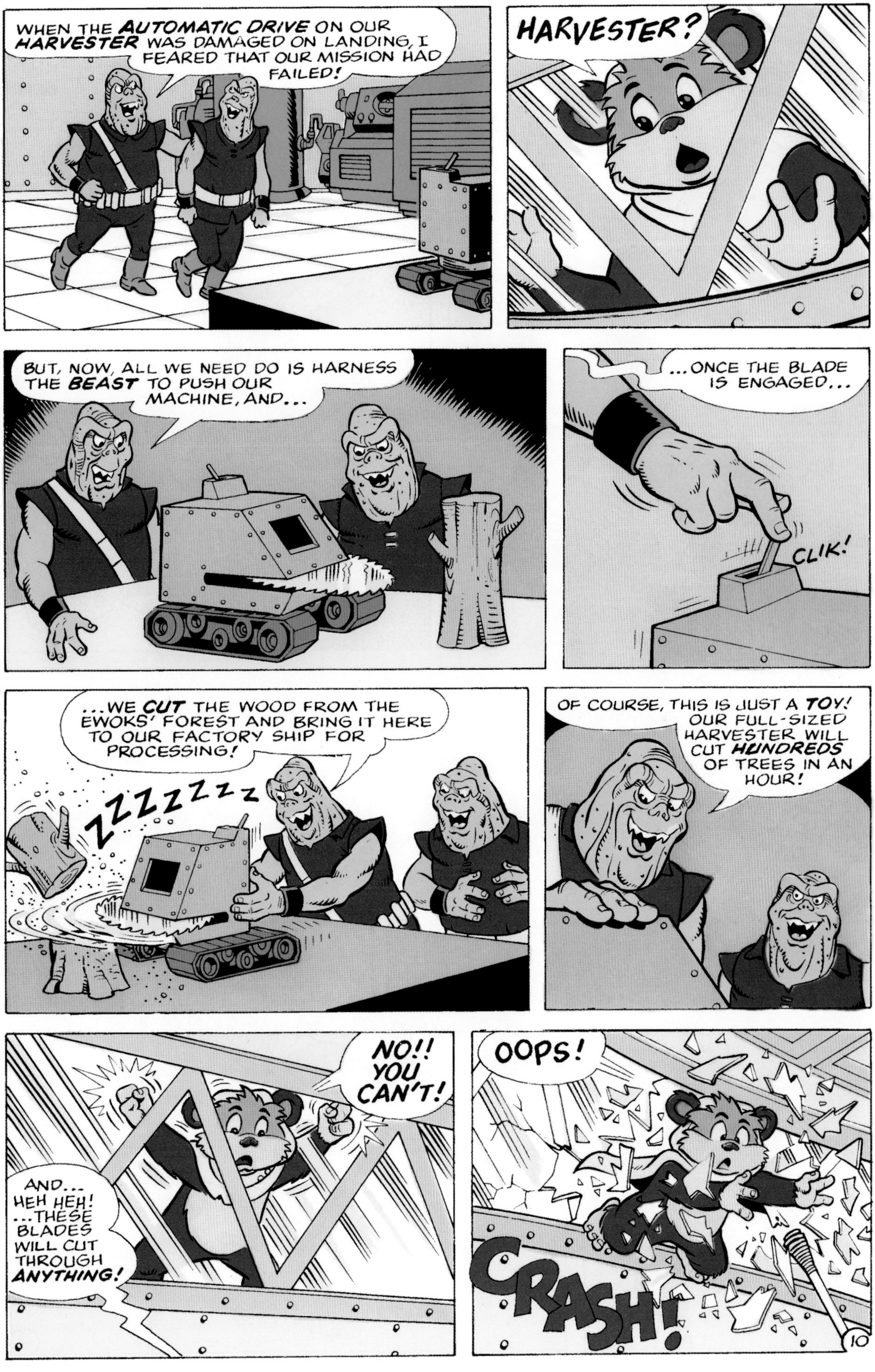
WHEN THE AUTOMATIC DRIVE ON OUR HARVESTER WAS DAMAGED ON LANDING, I FEARED THAT OUR MISSION HAD FAILED!
HARVESTER?
BUT, NOW, ALL WE NEED DO IS HARNESS THE BEAST TO PUSH OUR MACHINE, AND...
...ONCE THE BLADE IS ENGAGED...
CLIK!
...WE CUT THE WOOD FROM THE EWOKS' FOREST AND BRING IT HERE TO OUR FACTORY SHIP FOR PROCESSING!
ZZZZZZZZ
OF COURSE, THIS IS JUST A TOY! OUR FULL-SIZED HARVESTER WILL CUT HUNDREDS OF TREES IN AN HOUR!
NO!! YOU CAN'T!
AND... HEH HEH! ...THESE BLADES WILL CUT THROUGH ANYTHING!
OOPS!
CRASH!
10

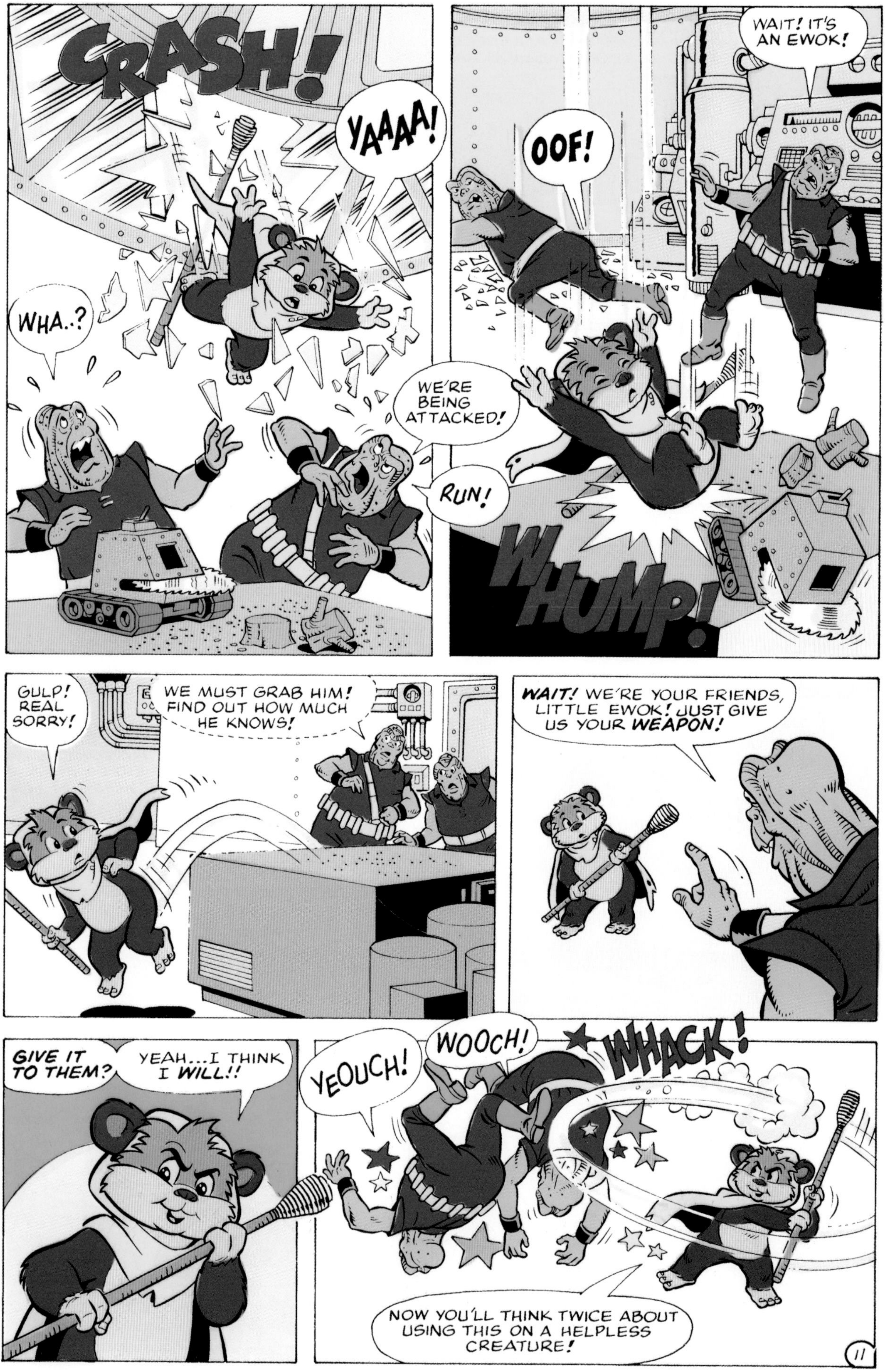
CRASH!
YAAAA!
WHA..?
WE'RE BEING ATTACKED!
RUN!
OOF!
WAIT! IT'S AN EWOK!
WHUMP!
GULP! REAL SORRY!
WE MUST GRAB HIM! FIND OUT HOW MUCH HE KNOWS!
WAIT! WE'RE YOUR FRIENDS, LITTLE EWOK! JUST GIVE US YOUR WEAPON!
GIVE IT TO THEM?
YEAH...I THINK I WILL!!
YEOUCH!
WOOCH!
WHACK!
NOW YOU'LL THINK TWICE ABOUT USING THIS ON A HELPLESS CREATURE!
11

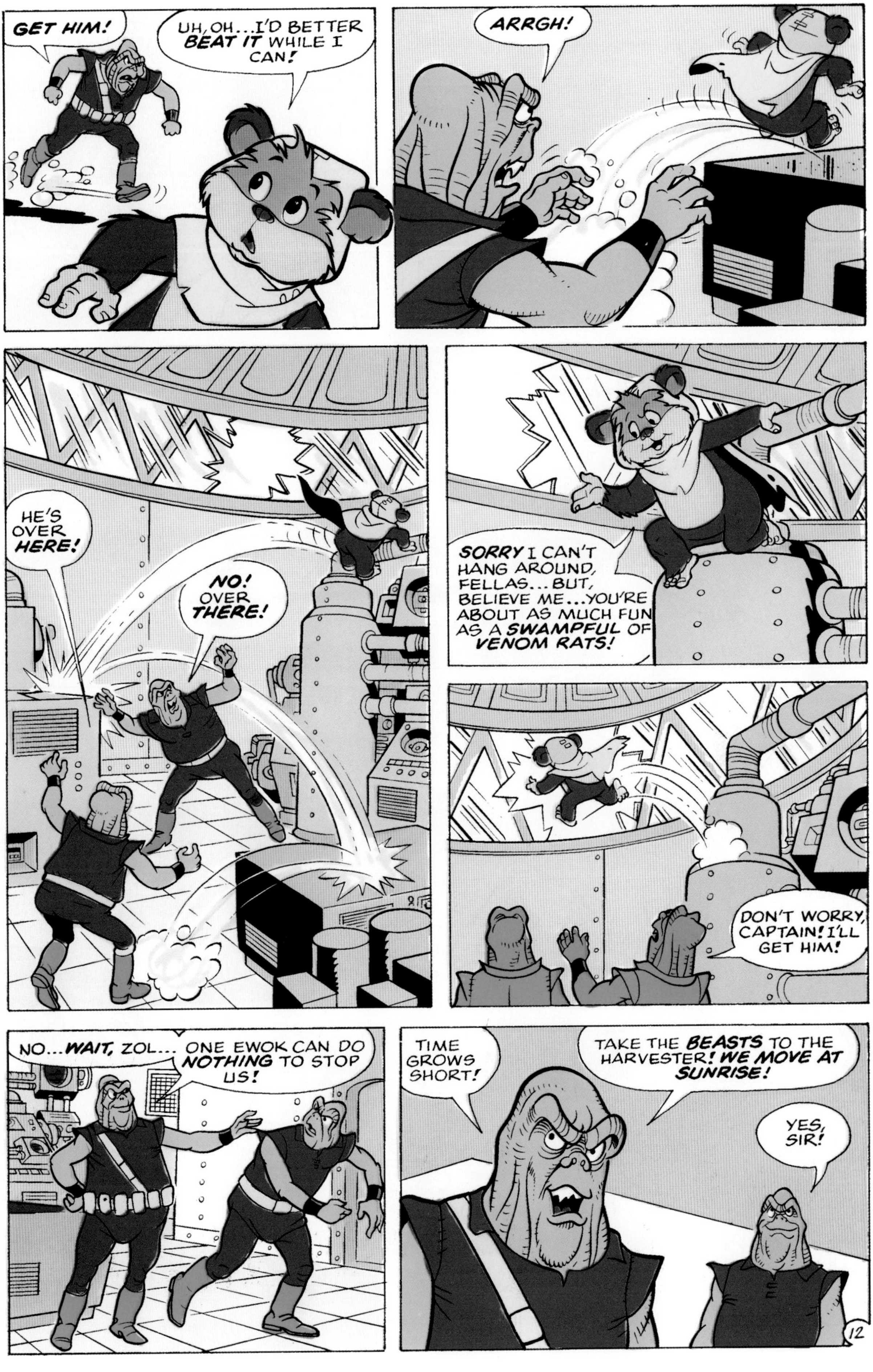

GET HIM!
UH, OH...I'D BETTER BEAT IT WHILE I CAN!
ARRGH!
HE'S OVER HERE!
NO! OVER THERE!
SORRY I CAN'T HANG AROUND, FELLAS...BUT, BELIEVE ME...YOU'RE ABOUT AS MUCH FUN AS A SWAMPFUL OF VENOM RATS!
DON'T WORRY, CAPTAIN! I'LL GET HIM!
NO...WAIT, ZOL...
ONE EWOK CAN DO NOTHING TO STOP US!
TIME GROWS SHORT!
TAKE THE BEASTS TO THE HARVESTER! WE MOVE AT SUNRISE!
YES, SIR!
12

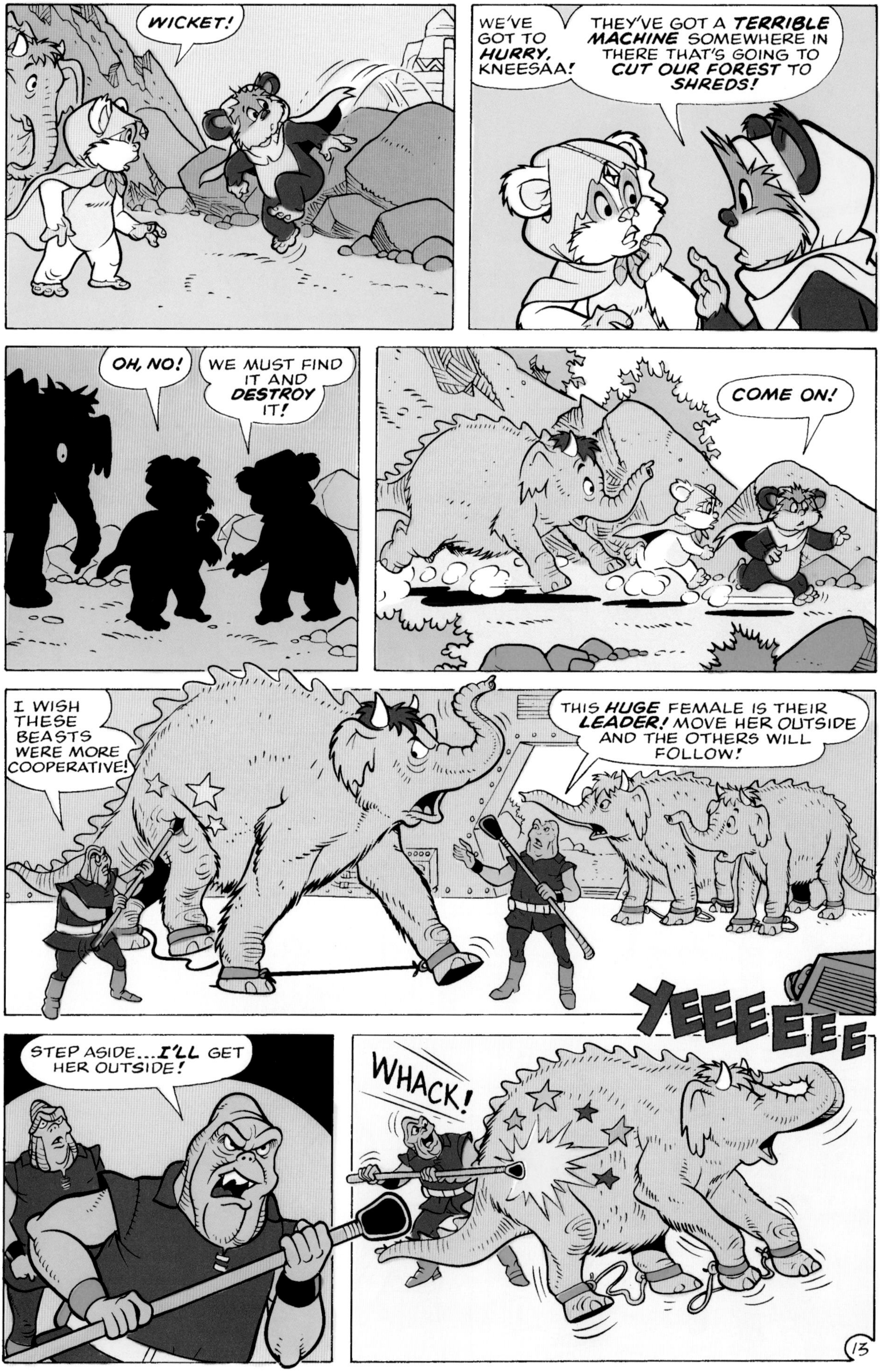
WICKET!
WE'VE GOT TO HURRY, KNEESAA!
THEY'VE GOT A TERRIBLE MACHINE SOMEWHERE IN THERE THAT'S GOING TO CUT OUR FOREST TO SHREDS!
OH, NO!
WE MUST FIND IT AND DESTROY IT!
COME ON!
I WISH THESE BEASTS WERE MORE COOPERATIVE!
THIS HUGE FEMALE IS THEIR LEADER! MOVE HER OUTSIDE AND THE OTHERS WILL FOLLOW!
STEP ASIDE...I'LL GET HER OUTSIDE!
YEEEEEEE
WHACK!
13

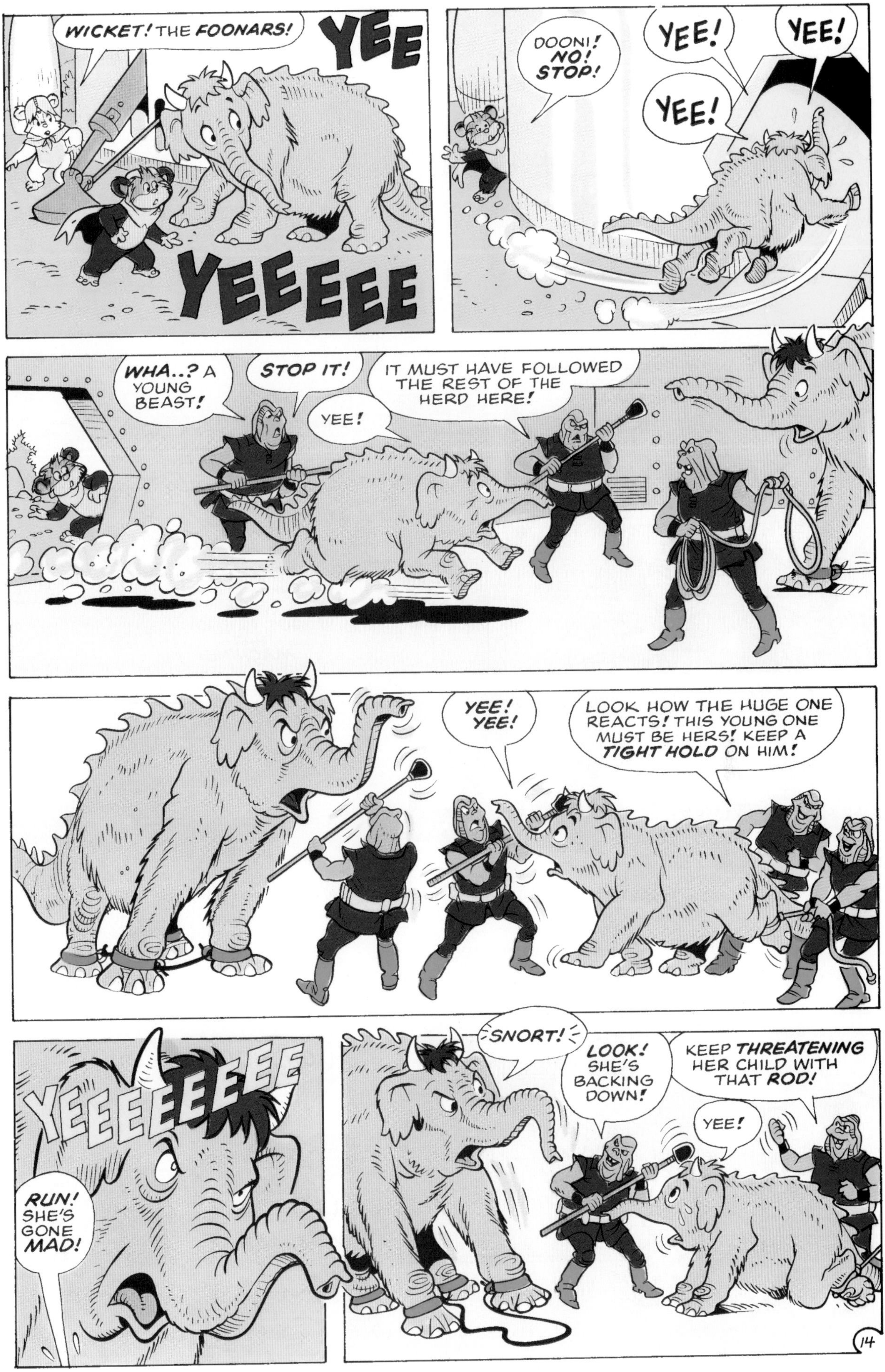
WICKET! THE FOONARS!
YEE
YEEEEE
DOONI! NO! STOP!
YEE!
YEE!
YEE!
WHA..? A YOUNG BEAST!
STOP IT!
IT MUST HAVE FOLLOWED THE REST OF THE HERD HERE!
YEE!
YEE! YEE!
LOOK HOW THE HUGE ONE REACTS! THIS YOUNG ONE MUST BE HERS! KEEP A TIGHT HOLD ON HIM!
YEEEEEEEE
RUN! SHE'S GONE MAD!
SNORT!
LOOK! SHE'S BACKING DOWN!
KEEP THREATENING HER CHILD WITH THAT ROD!
YEE!
14

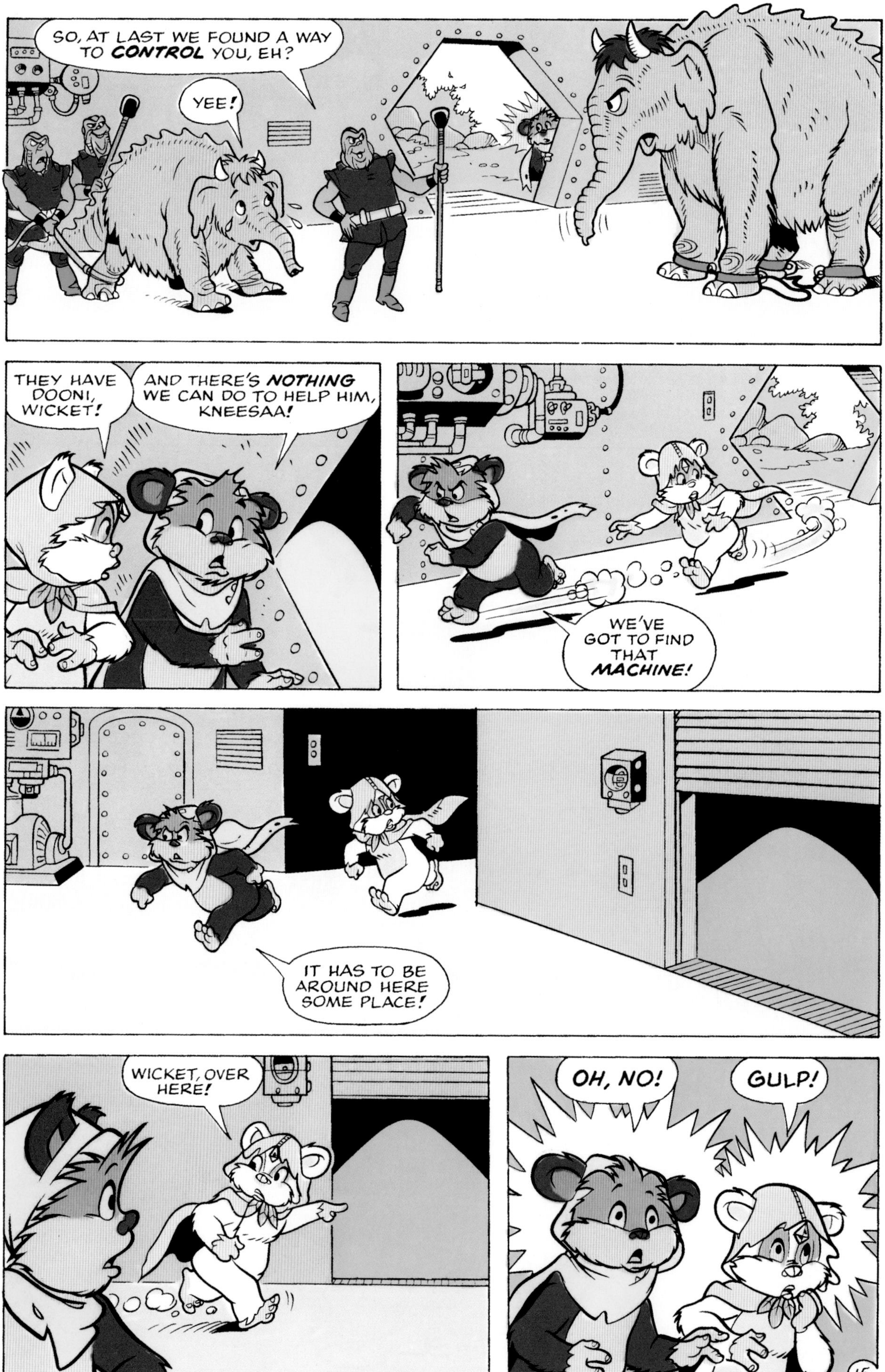
SO, AT LAST WE FOUND A WAY TO CONTROL YOU, EH?
YEE!
THEY HAVE DOONI, WICKET!
AND THERE'S NOTHING WE CAN DO TO HELP HIM, KNEESAA!
WE'VE GOT TO FIND THAT MACHINE!
IT HAS TO BE AROUND HERE SOME PLACE!
WICKET, OVER HERE!
OH, NO!
GULP!
15

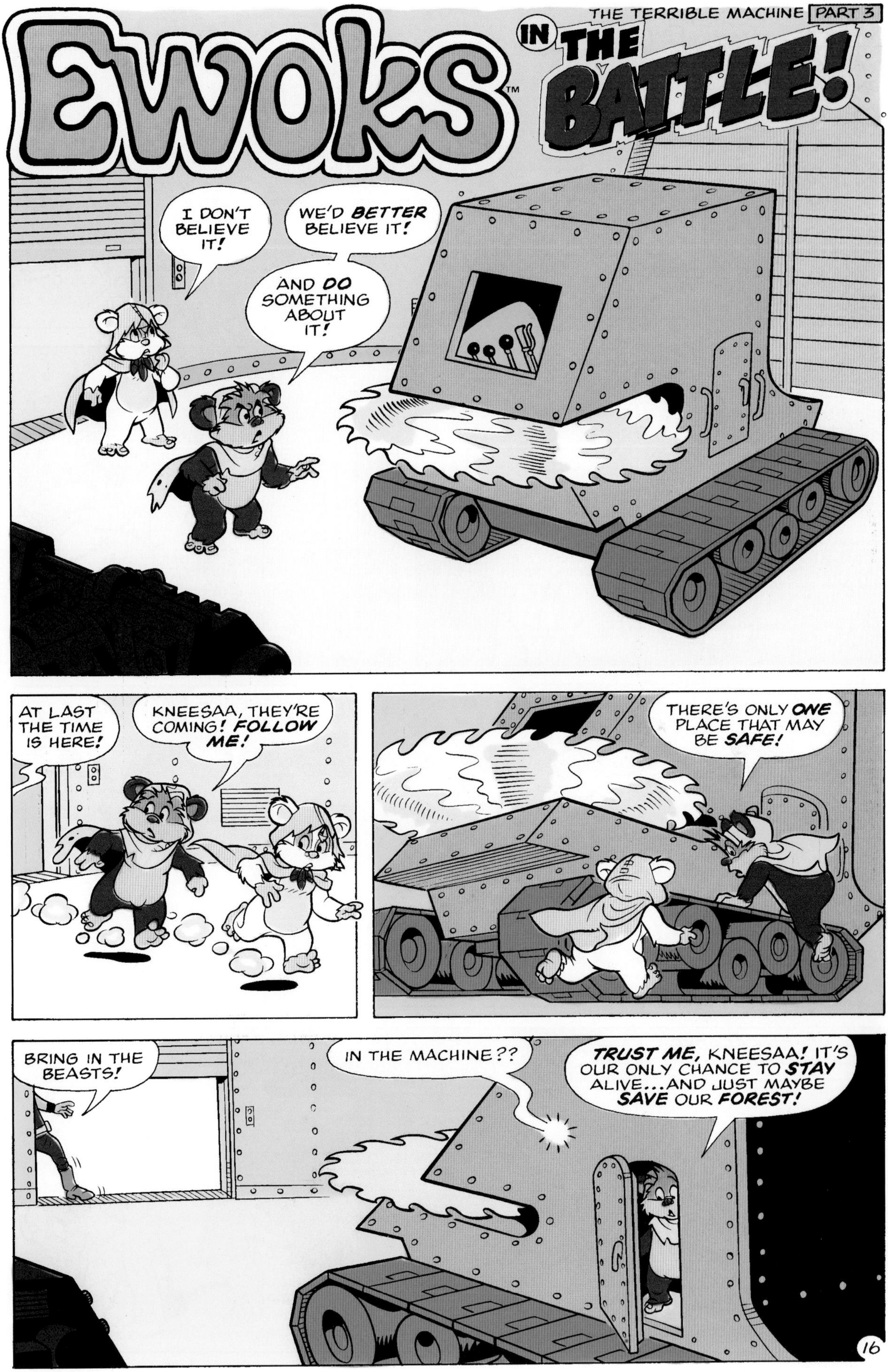
THE TERRIBLE MACHINE PART 3
EWOKS
IN THE BATTLE!
I DON'T BELIEVE IT!
WE'D BETTER BELIEVE IT!
AND DO SOMETHING ABOUT IT!
AT LAST THE TIME IS HERE!
KNEESAA, THEY'RE COMING! FOLLOW ME!
THERE'S ONLY ONE PLACE THAT MAY BE SAFE!
BRING IN THE BEASTS!
IN THE MACHINE??
TRUST ME, KNEESAA! IT'S OUR ONLY CHANCE TO STAY ALIVE...AND JUST MAYBE SAVE OUR FOREST!
16

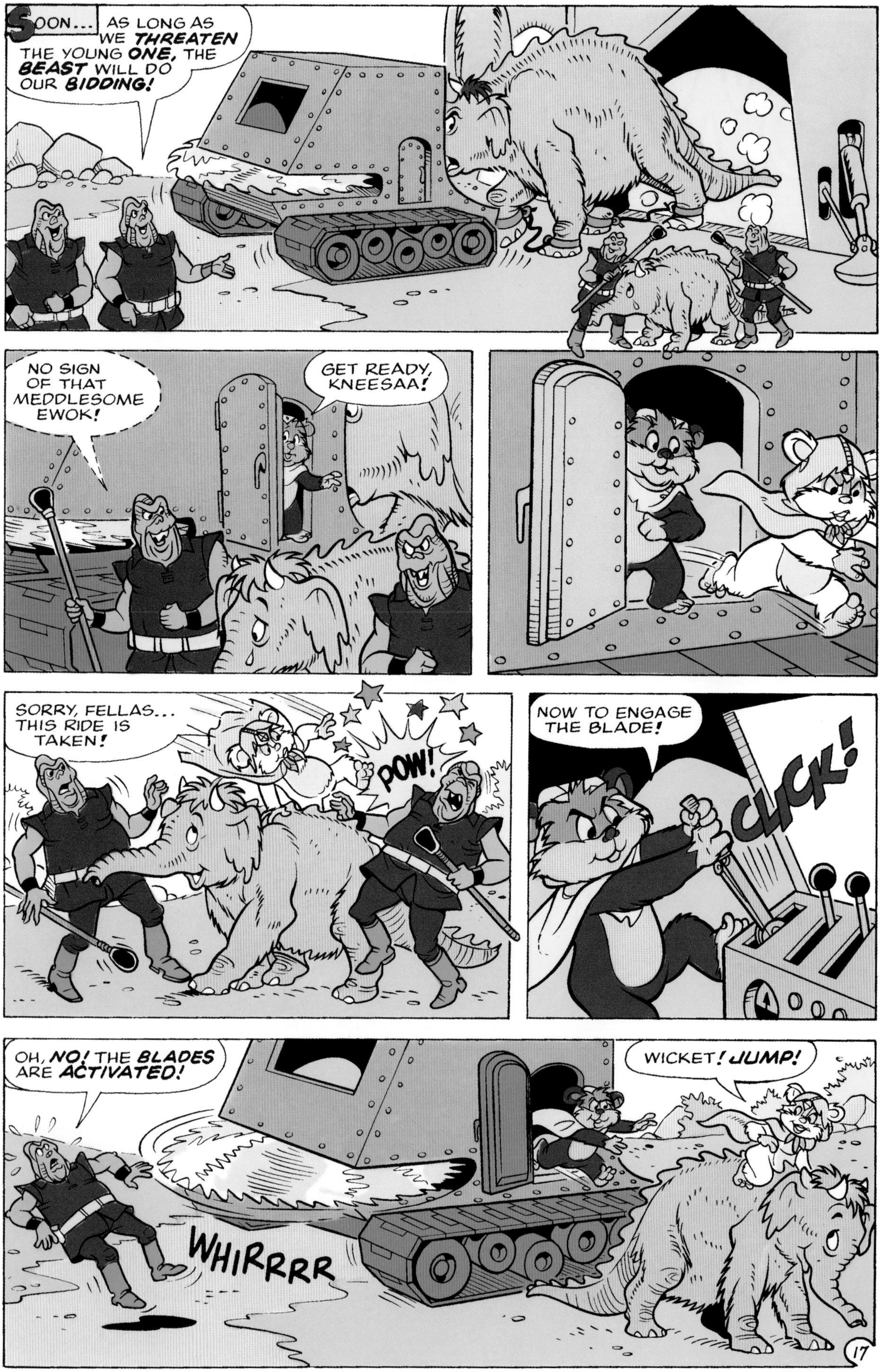
SOON...
AS LONG AS WE THREATEN THE YOUNG ONE, THE BEAST WILL DO OUR BIDDING!
NO SIGN OF THAT MEDDLESOME EWOK!
GET READY, KNEESAA!
SORRY, FELLAS... THIS RIDE IS TAKEN!
POW!
NOW TO ENGAGE THE BLADE!
CLICK!
OH, NO! THE BLADES ARE ACTIVATED!
WICKET! JUMP!
WHIRRRR
17

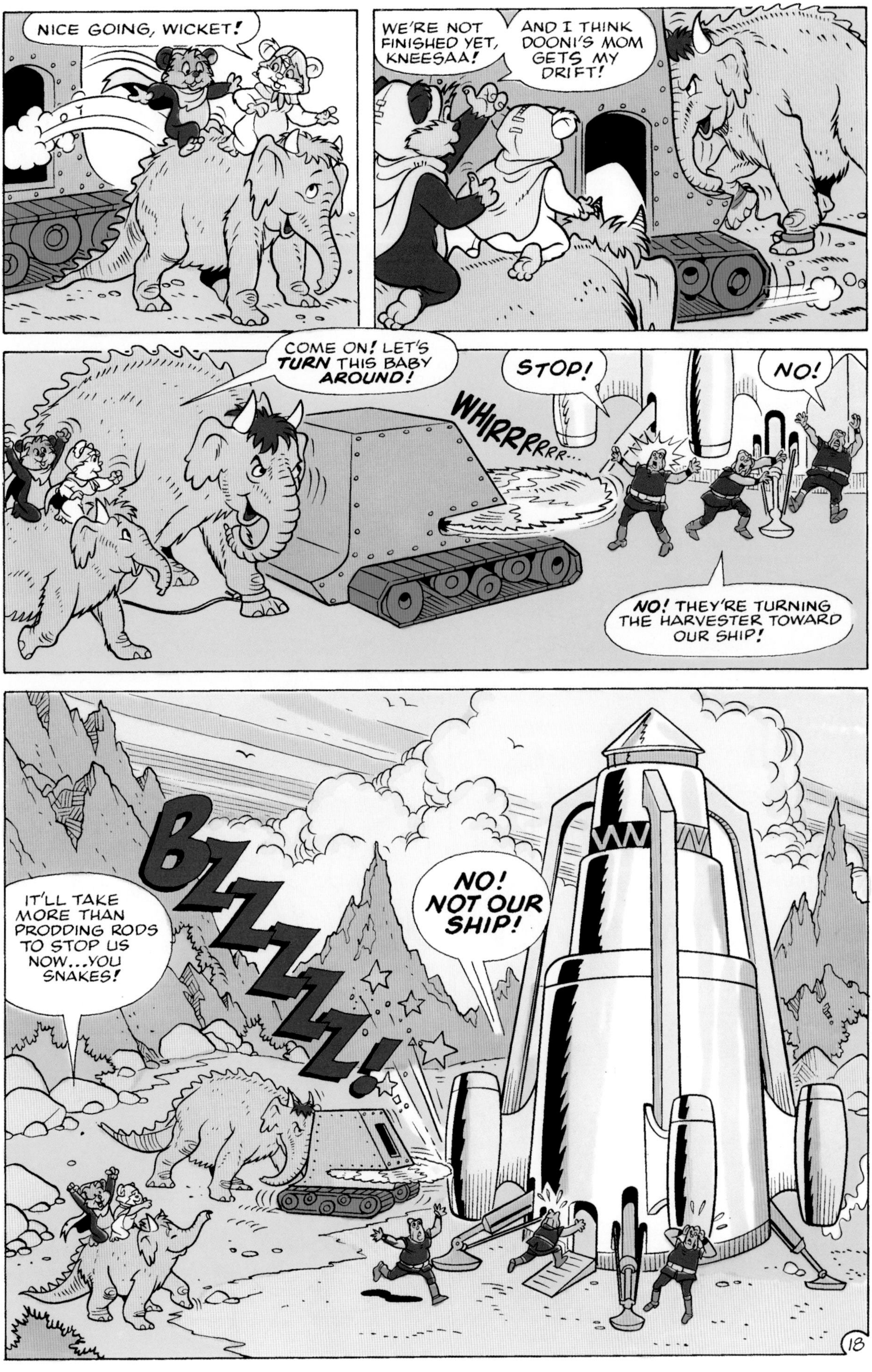
NICE GOING, WICKET!
WE'RE NOT FINISHED YET, KNEESAA!
AND I THINK DOONI'S MOM GETS MY DRIFT!
COME ON! LET'S TURN THIS BABY AROUND!
WHIRRRRRR...
STOP!
NO!
NO! THEY'RE TURNING THE HARVESTER TOWARD OUR SHIP!
BZZZZZZ!
NO! NOT OUR SHIP!
IT'LL TAKE MORE THAN PRODDING RODS TO STOP US NOW...YOU SNAKES!
18

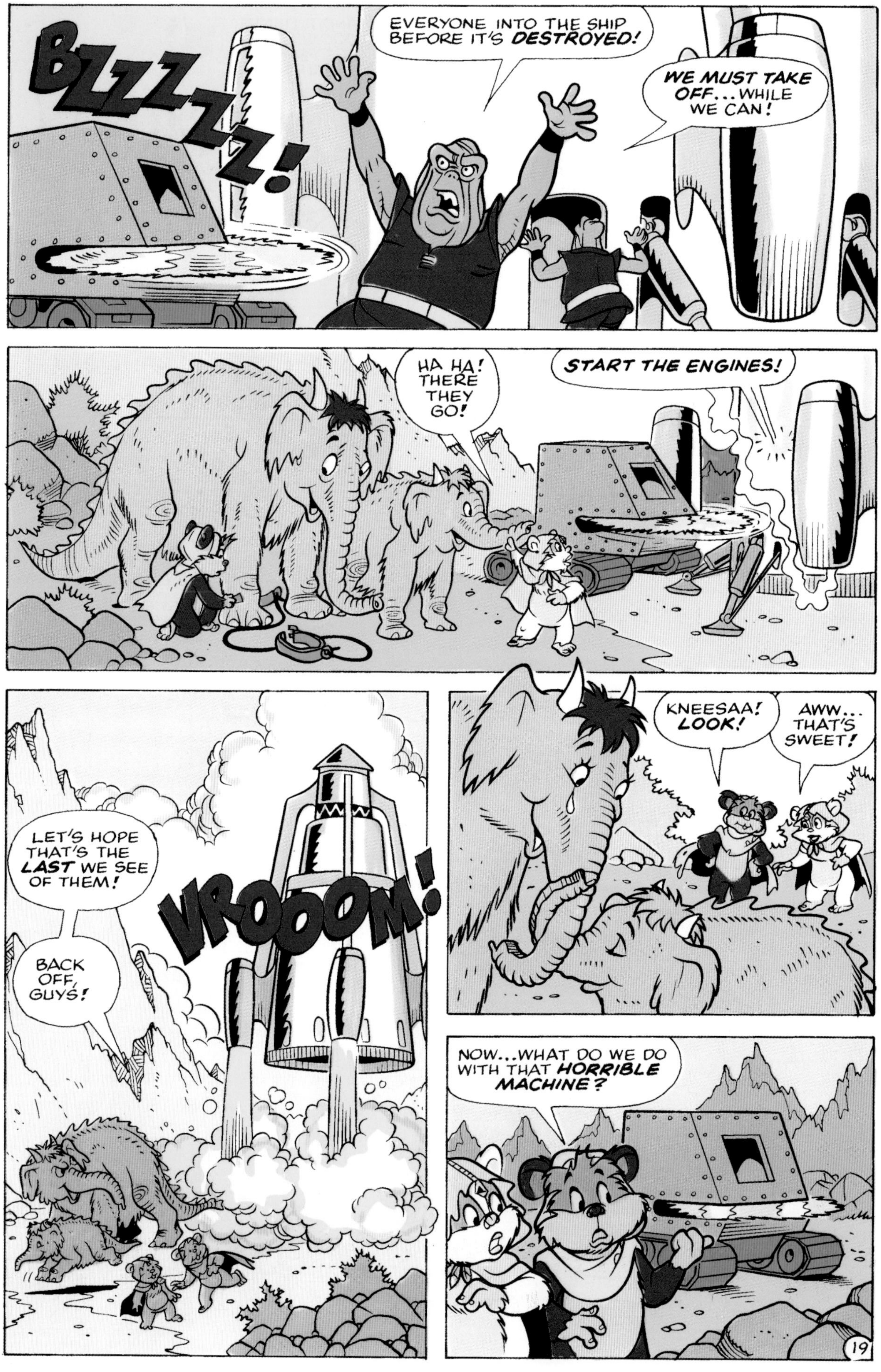
BZZZZZZ!
EVERYONE INTO THE SHIP BEFORE IT'S DESTROYED!
WE MUST TAKE OFF...WHILE WE CAN!
HA HA! THERE THEY GO!
START THE ENGINES!
LET'S HOPE THAT'S THE LAST WE SEE OF THEM!
BACK OFF, GUYS!
VROOOM!
KNEESAA! LOOK!
AWW... THAT'S SWEET!
NOW...WHAT DO WE DO WITH THAT HORRIBLE MACHINE?
19

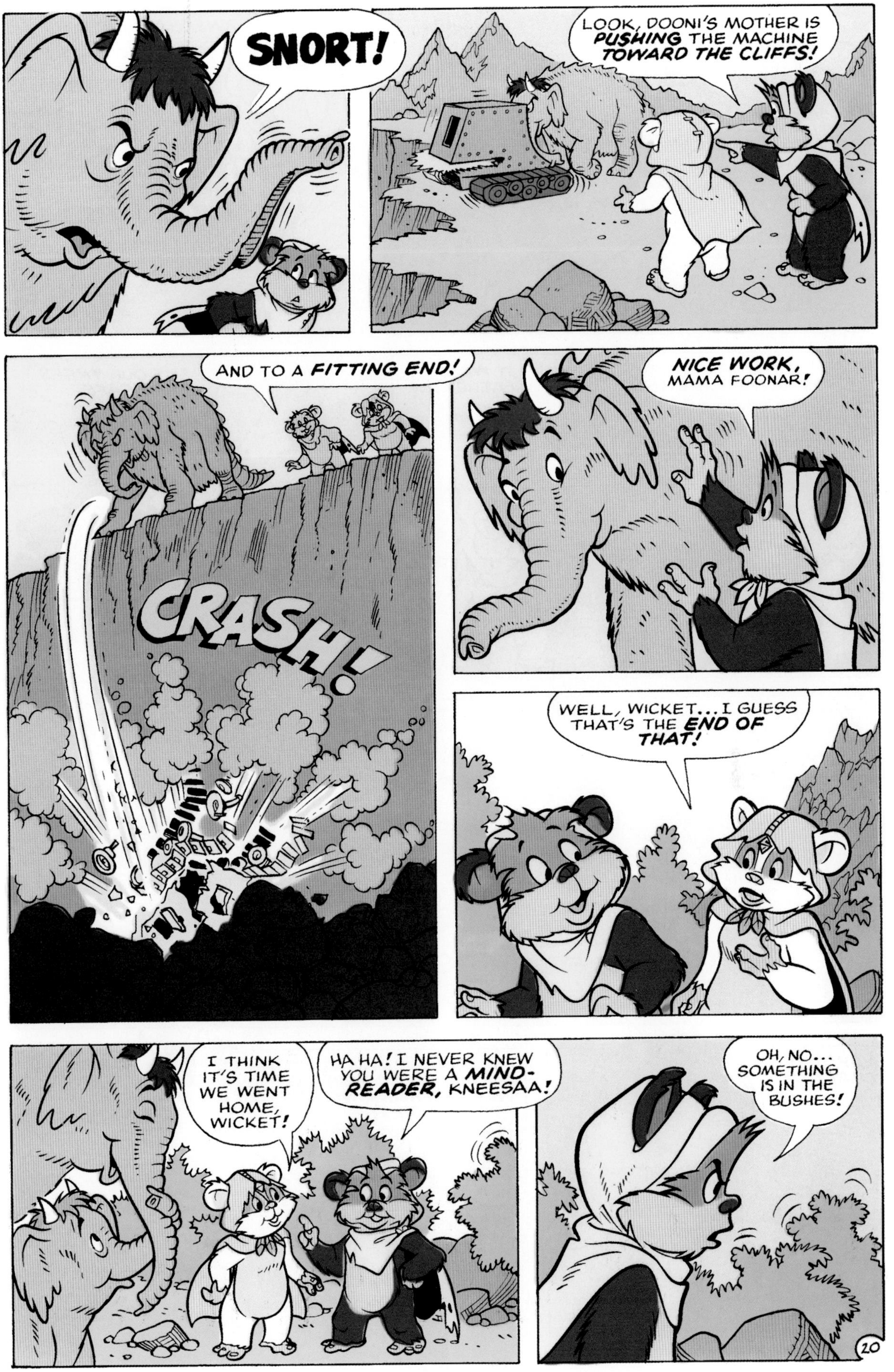
SNORT!
LOOK, DOONI'S MOTHER IS PUSHING THE MACHINE TOWARD THE CLIFFS!
AND TO A FITTING END!
CRASH!
NICE WORK, MAMA FOONAR!
WELL, WICKET... I GUESS THAT'S THE END OF THAT!
I THINK IT'S TIME WE WENT HOME, WICKET!
HA HA! I NEVER KNEW YOU WERE A MIND-READER, KNEESAA!
OH, NO... SOMETHING IS IN THE BUSHES!
20

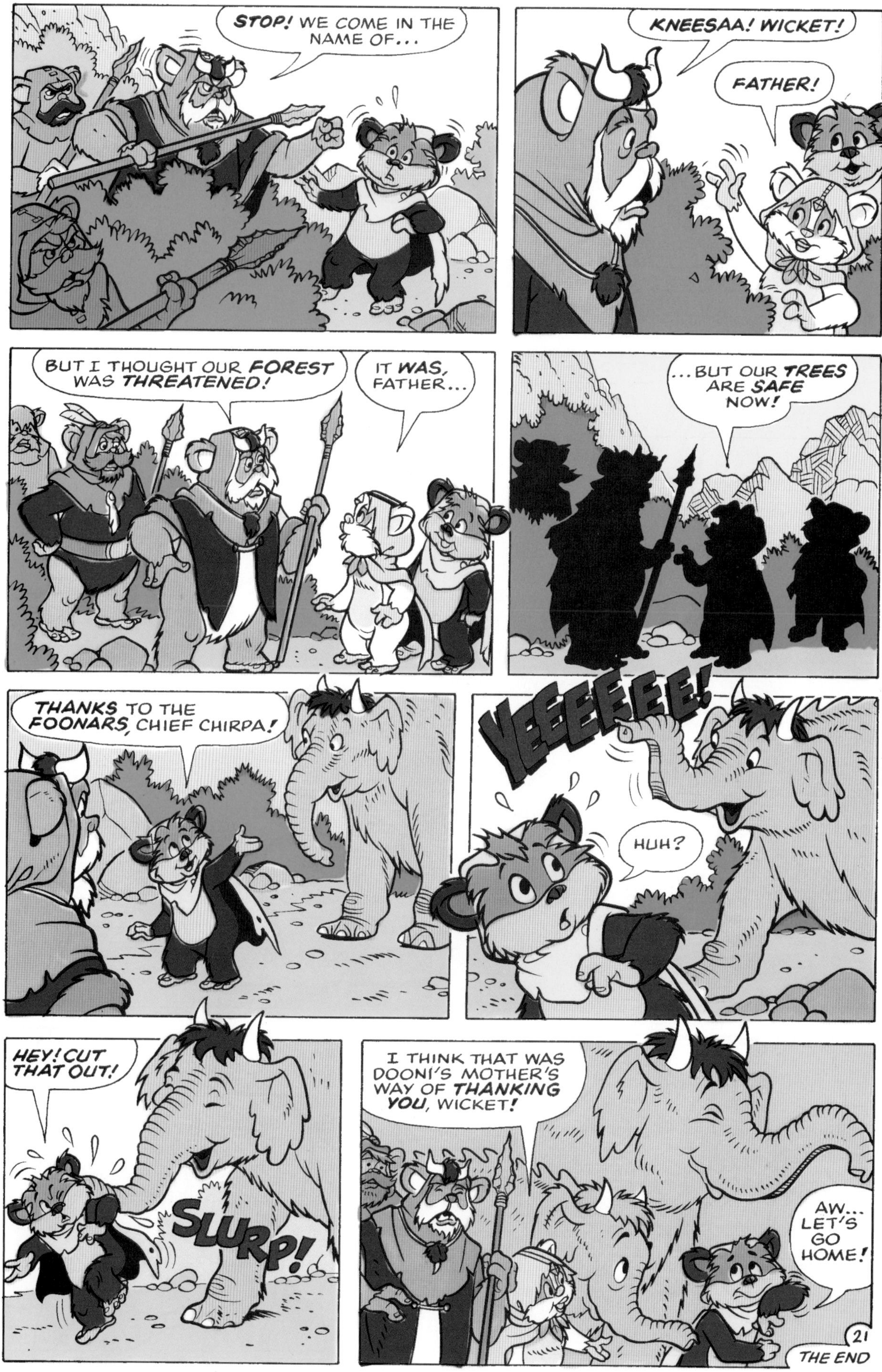
STOP! WE COME IN THE NAME OF...
KNEESAA! WICKET!
FATHER!
BUT I THOUGHT OUR FOREST WAS THREATENED!
IT WAS, FATHER...
...BUT OUR TREES ARE SAFE NOW!
THANKS TO THE FOONARS, CHIEF CHIRPA!
YEEEEEEE!
HUH?
HEY! CUT THAT OUT!
SLURP!
I THINK THAT WAS DOONI'S MOTHER'S WAY OF THANKING YOU, WICKET!
AW... LET'S GO HOME!
21
THE END

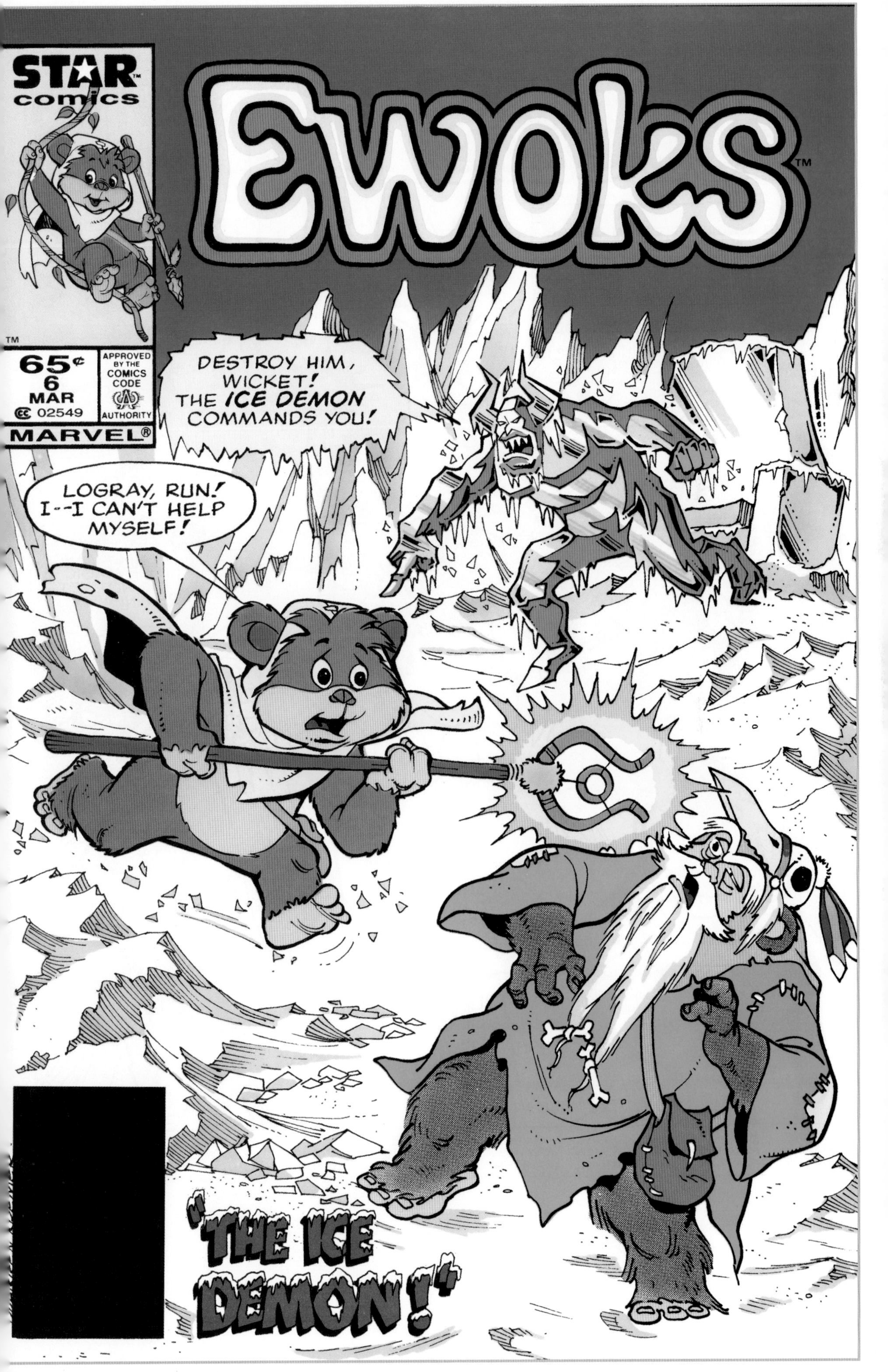
STAR comics
EWOKS
65¢
6
MAR
02549
APPROVED BY THE COMICS CODE AUTHORITY
MARVEL
DESTROY HIM, WICKET! THE ICE DEMON COMMANDS YOU!
LOGRAY, RUN! I--I CAN'T HELP MYSELF!
"THE ICE DEMON!"

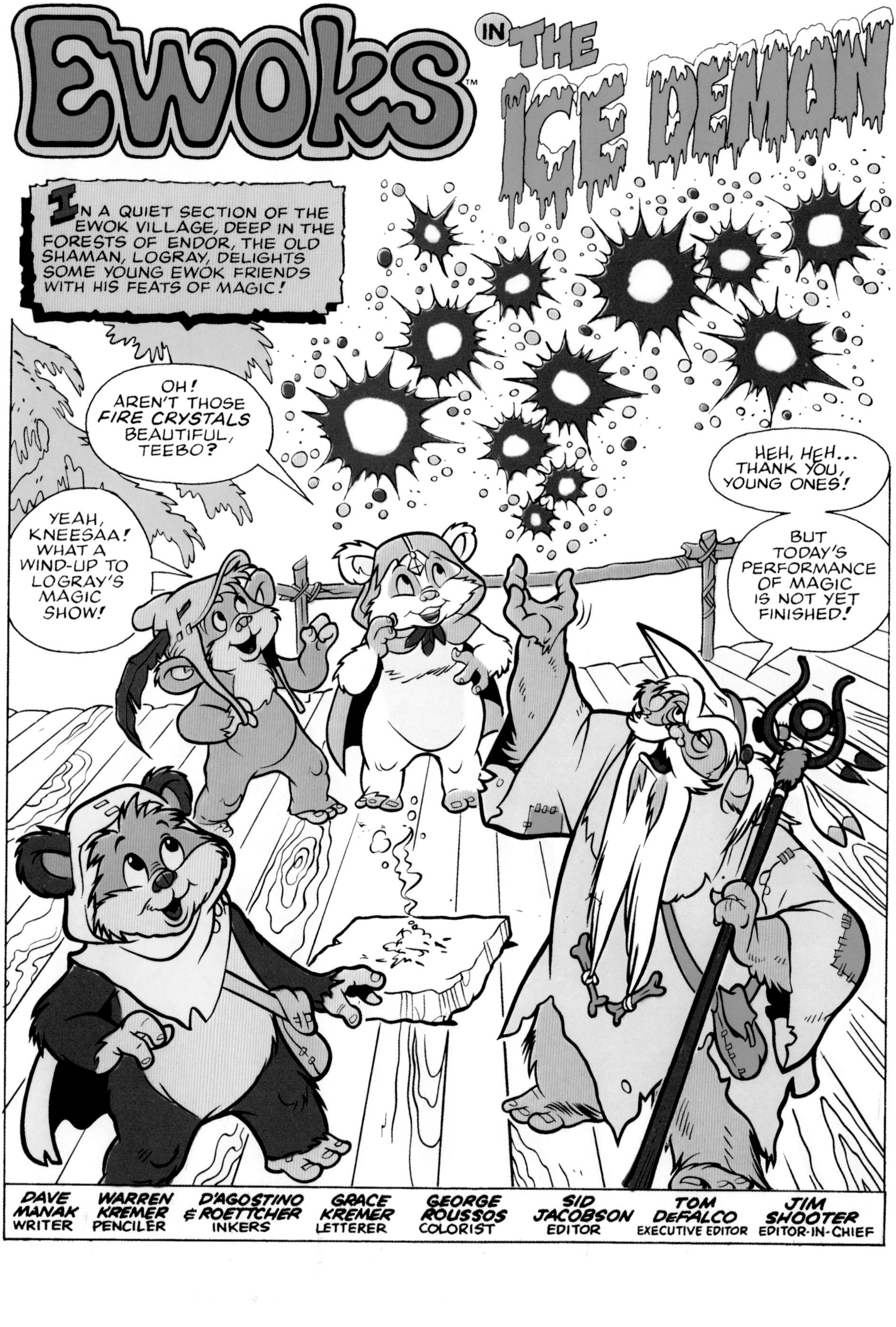
Ewoks™ in The Ice Demon
In a quiet section of the Ewok village, deep in the forests of Endor, the old shaman, Logray, delights some young Ewok friends with his feats of magic!
OH! AREN'T THOSE FIRE CRYSTALS BEAUTIFUL, TEEBO?
YEAH, KNEESAA! WHAT A WIND-UP TO LOGRAY'S MAGIC SHOW!
HEH, HEH... THANK YOU, YOUNG ONES!
BUT TODAY'S PERFORMANCE OF MAGIC IS NOT YET FINISHED!
DAVE MANAK WRITER
WARREN KREMER PENCILER
D'AGOSTINO & ROETTCHER INKERS
GRACE KREMER LETTERER
GEORGE ROUSSOS COLORIST
SID JACOBSON EDITOR
TOM DEFALCO EXECUTIVE EDITOR
JIM SHOOTER EDITOR-IN-CHIEF

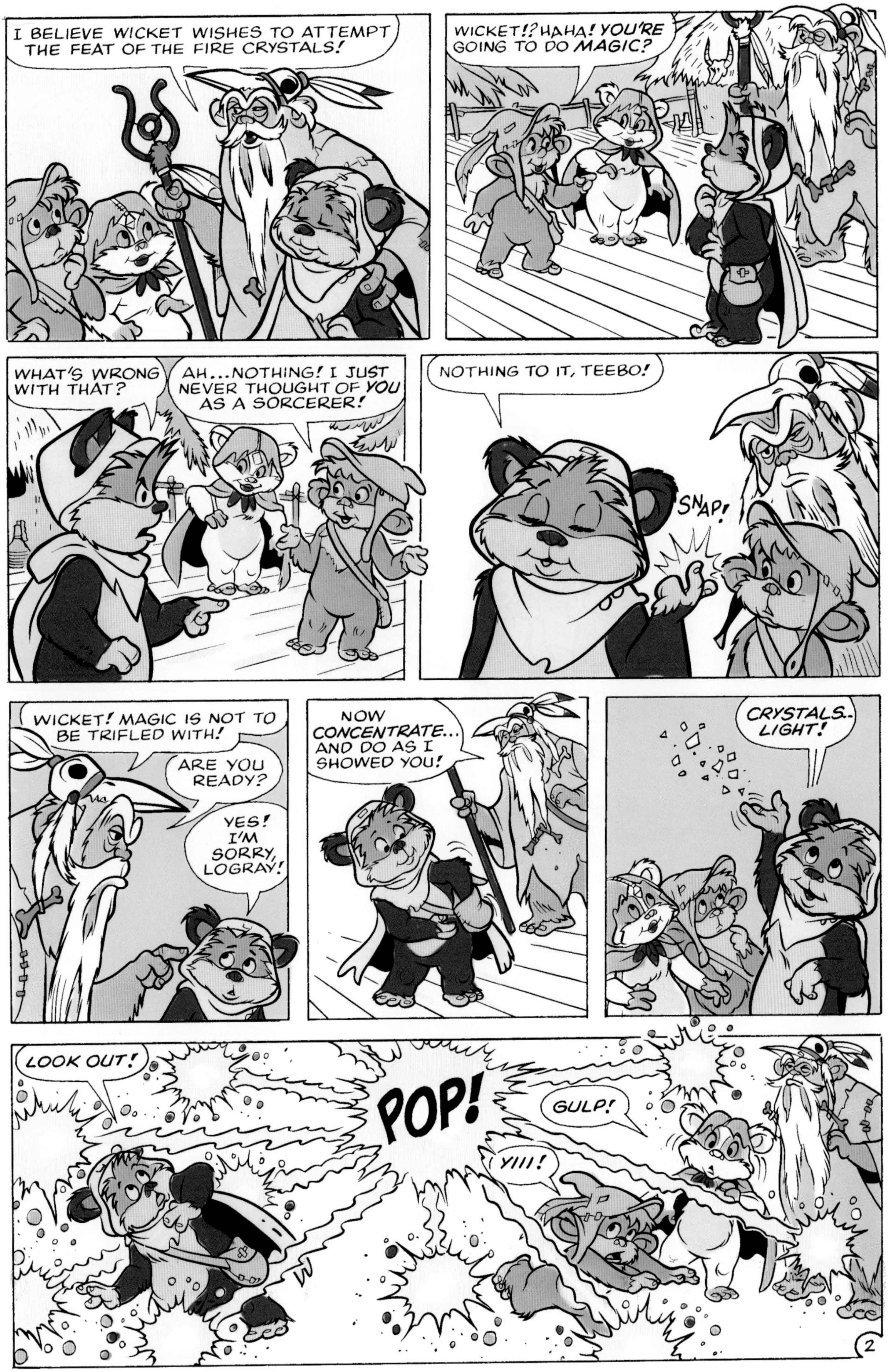
I BELIEVE WICKET WISHES TO ATTEMPT THE FEAT OF THE FIRE CRYSTALS!
WICKET!? HAHA! YOU'RE GOING TO DO MAGIC?
WHAT'S WRONG WITH THAT?
AH...NOTHING! I JUST NEVER THOUGHT OF YOU AS A SORCERER!
NOTHING TO IT, TEEBO!
SNAP!
WICKET! MAGIC IS NOT TO BE TRIFLED WITH!
ARE YOU READY?
YES! I'M SORRY, LOGRAY!
NOW CONCENTRATE... AND DO AS I SHOWED YOU!
CRYSTALS.. LIGHT!
LOOK OUT!
POP!
GULP!
YIII!
2

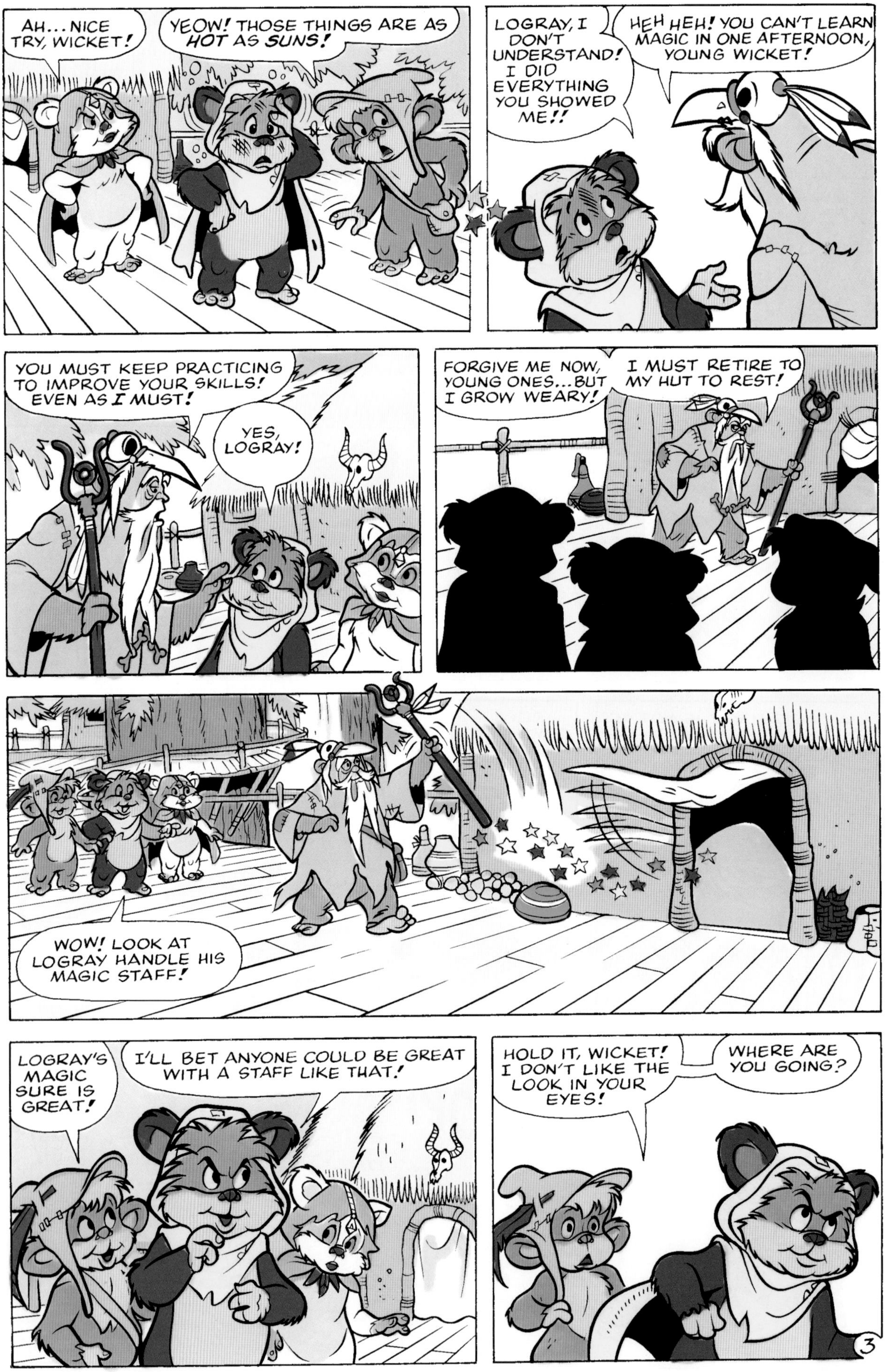
AH... NICE TRY, WICKET!
YEOW! THOSE THINGS ARE AS HOT AS SUNS!
LOGRAY, I DON'T UNDERSTAND! I DID EVERYTHING YOU SHOWED ME!!
HEH HEH! YOU CAN'T LEARN MAGIC IN ONE AFTERNOON, YOUNG WICKET!
YOU MUST KEEP PRACTICING TO IMPROVE YOUR SKILLS! EVEN AS I MUST!
YES, LOGRAY!
FORGIVE ME NOW, YOUNG ONES... BUT I GROW WEARY!
I MUST RETIRE TO MY HUT TO REST!
WOW! LOOK AT LOGRAY HANDLE HIS MAGIC STAFF!
LOGRAY'S MAGIC SURE IS GREAT!
I'LL BET ANYONE COULD BE GREAT WITH A STAFF LIKE THAT!
HOLD IT, WICKET! I DON'T LIKE THE LOOK IN YOUR EYES!
WHERE ARE YOU GOING?
3

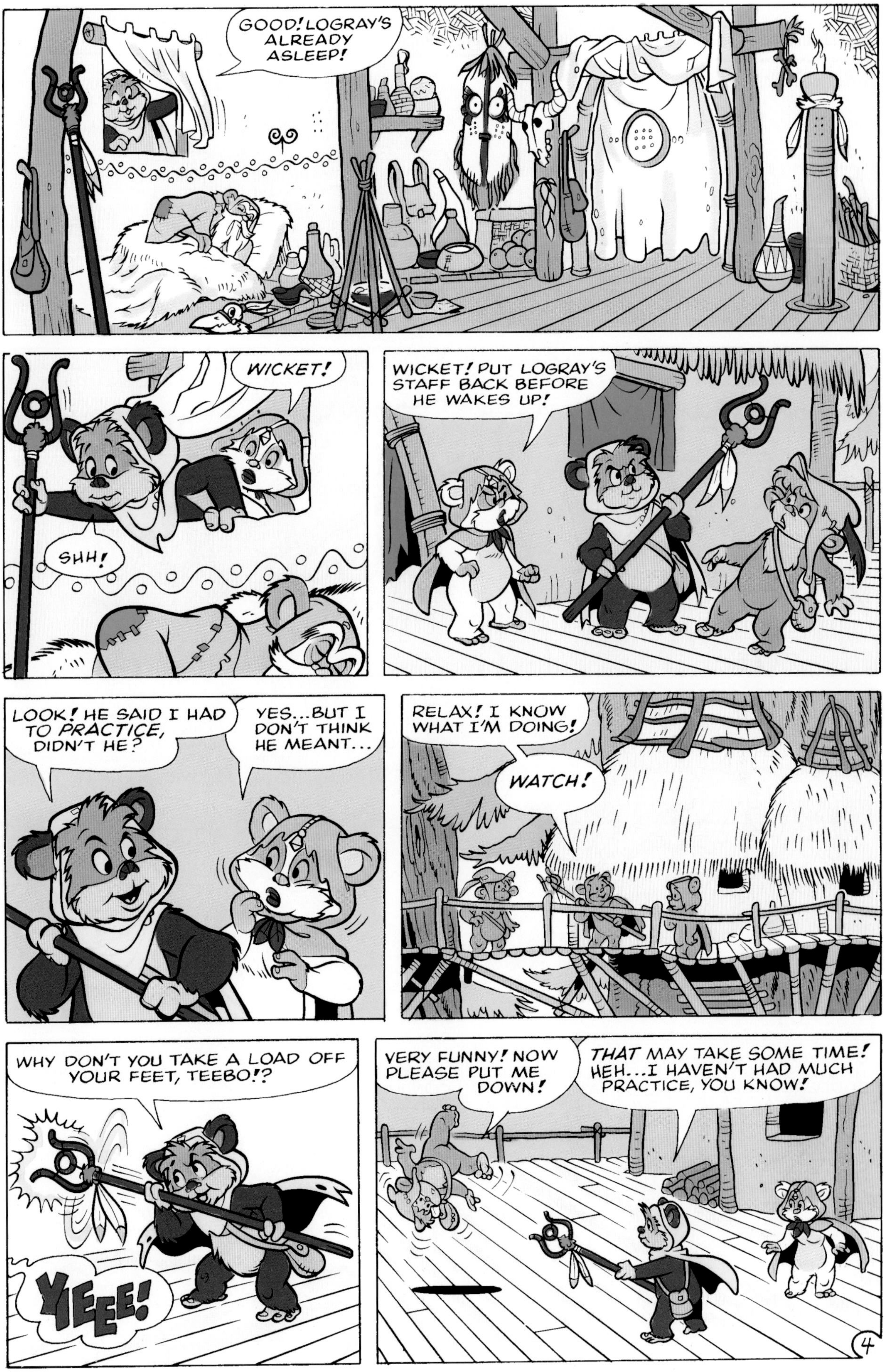
GOOD! LOGRAY'S ALREADY ASLEEP!
WICKET!
SHH!
WICKET! PUT LOGRAY'S STAFF BACK BEFORE HE WAKES UP!
LOOK! HE SAID I HAD TO PRACTICE, DIDN'T HE?
YES...BUT I DON'T THINK HE MEANT...
RELAX! I KNOW WHAT I'M DOING!
WATCH!
WHY DON'T YOU TAKE A LOAD OFF YOUR FEET, TEEBO!?
YIEEE!
VERY FUNNY! NOW PLEASE PUT ME DOWN!
THAT MAY TAKE SOME TIME! HEH...I HAVEN'T HAD MUCH PRACTICE, YOU KNOW!
4

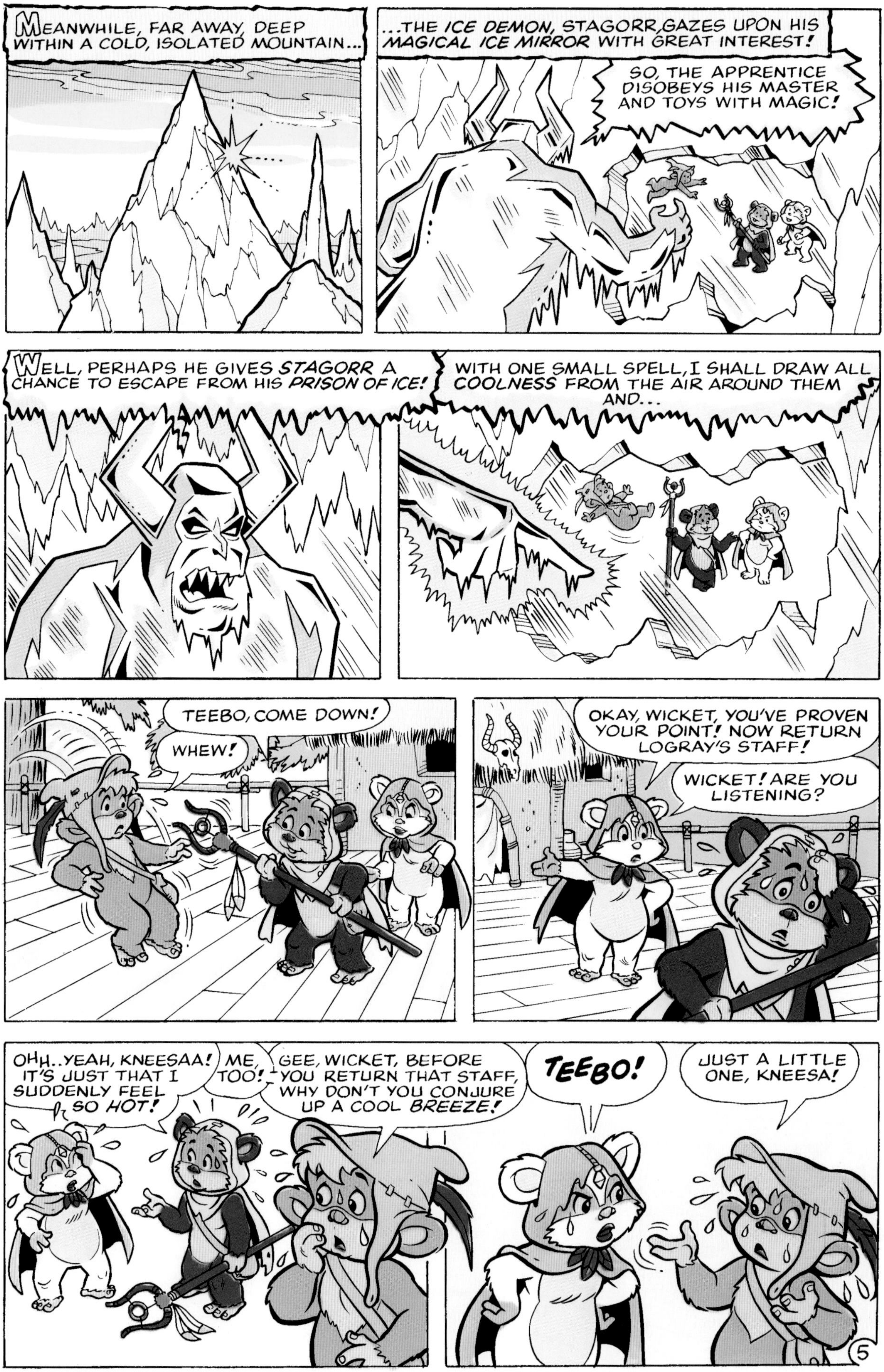
MEANWHILE, FAR AWAY, DEEP WITHIN A COLD, ISOLATED MOUNTAIN...
...THE ICE DEMON, STAGORR, GAZES UPON HIS MAGICAL ICE MIRROR WITH GREAT INTEREST!
SO, THE APPRENTICE DISOBEYS HIS MASTER AND TOYS WITH MAGIC!
WELL, PERHAPS HE GIVES STAGORR A CHANCE TO ESCAPE FROM HIS PRISON OF ICE!
WITH ONE SMALL SPELL, I SHALL DRAW ALL COOLNESS FROM THE AIR AROUND THEM AND...
TEEBO, COME DOWN!
WHEW!
OKAY, WICKET, YOU'VE PROVEN YOUR POINT! NOW RETURN LOGRAY'S STAFF!
WICKET! ARE YOU LISTENING?
OHH..YEAH, KNEESAA! IT'S JUST THAT I SUDDENLY FEEL SO HOT!
ME, TOO!
GEE, WICKET, BEFORE YOU RETURN THAT STAFF, WHY DON'T YOU CONJURE UP A COOL BREEZE!
TEEBO!
JUST A LITTLE ONE, KNEESA!
5

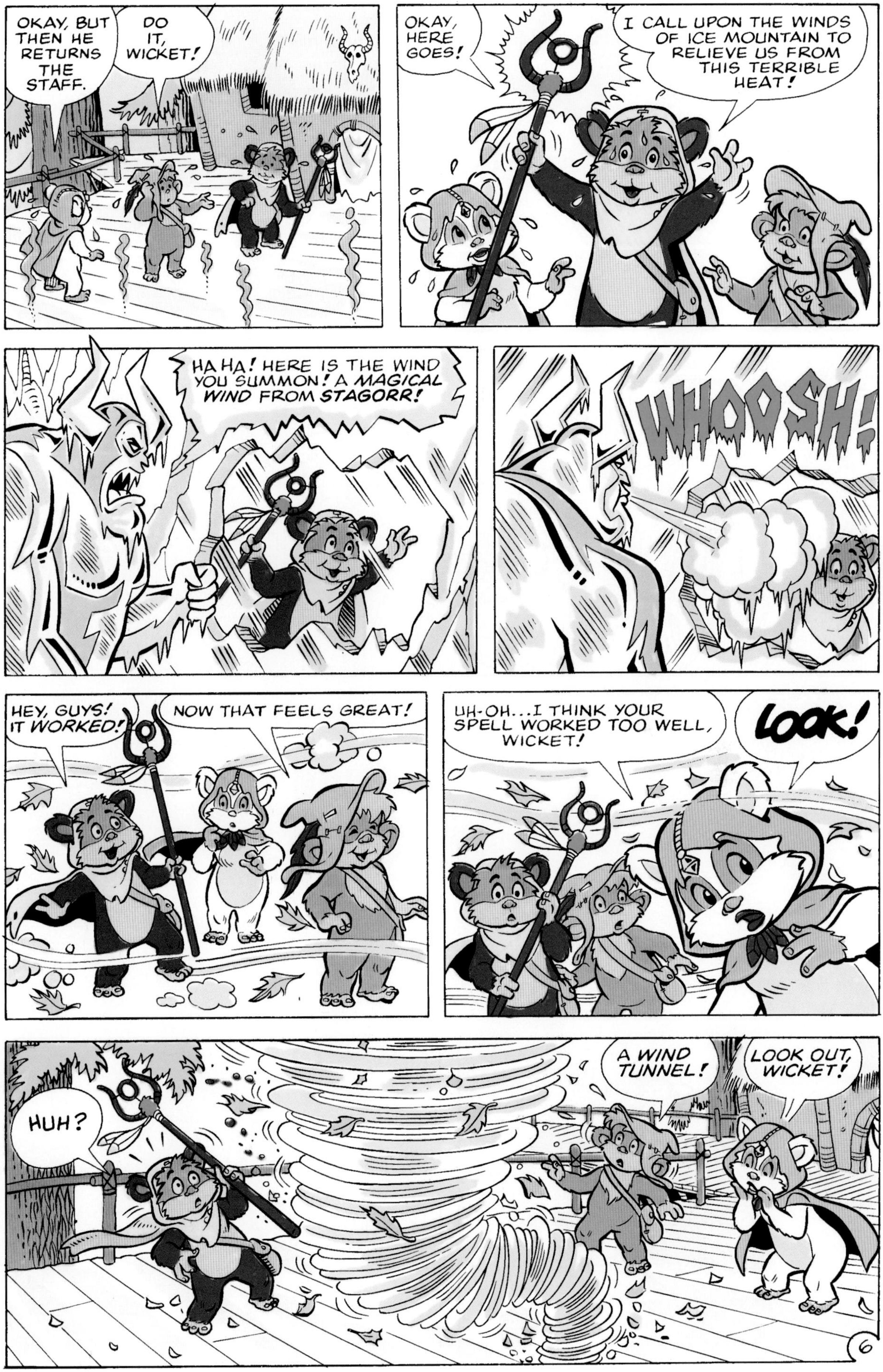

OKAY, BUT THEN HE RETURNS THE STAFF.
DO IT, WICKET!
OKAY, HERE GOES!
I CALL UPON THE WINDS OF ICE MOUNTAIN TO RELIEVE US FROM THIS TERRIBLE HEAT!
HA HA! HERE IS THE WIND YOU SUMMON! A MAGICAL WIND FROM STAGORR!
WHOOSH!
HEY, GUYS! IT WORKED!
NOW THAT FEELS GREAT!
UH-OH...I THINK YOUR SPELL WORKED TOO WELL, WICKET!
LOOK!
HUH?
A WIND TUNNEL!
LOOK OUT, WICKET!
6

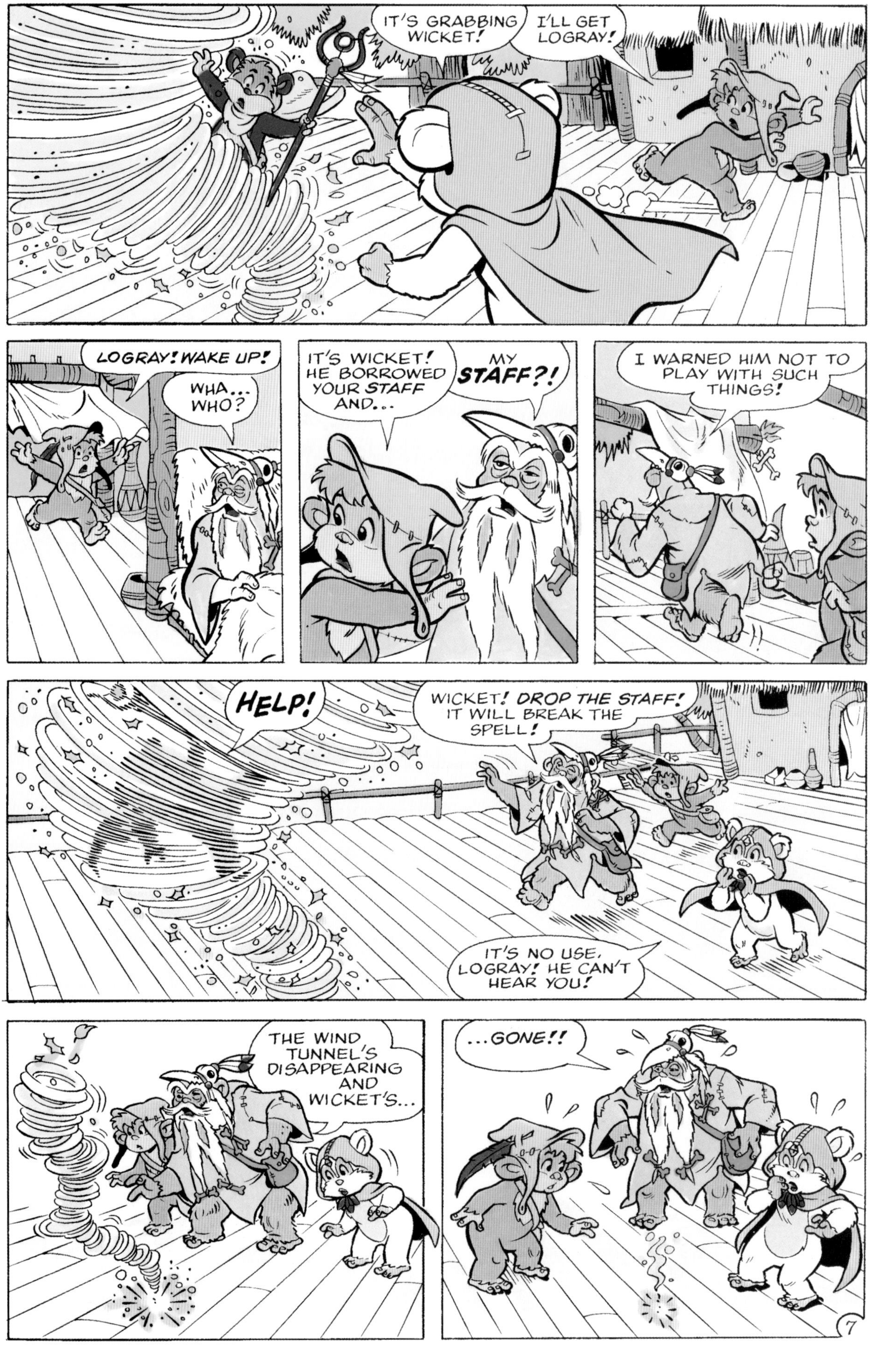
IT'S GRABBING WICKET!
I'LL GET LOGRAY!
LOGRAY! WAKE UP!
WHA... WHO?
IT'S WICKET! HE BORROWED YOUR STAFF AND...
MY STAFF?!
I WARNED HIM NOT TO PLAY WITH SUCH THINGS!
HELP!
WICKET! DROP THE STAFF! IT WILL BREAK THE SPELL!
IT'S NO USE, LOGRAY! HE CAN'T HEAR YOU!
THE WIND TUNNEL'S DISAPPEARING AND WICKET'S...
...GONE!!
7

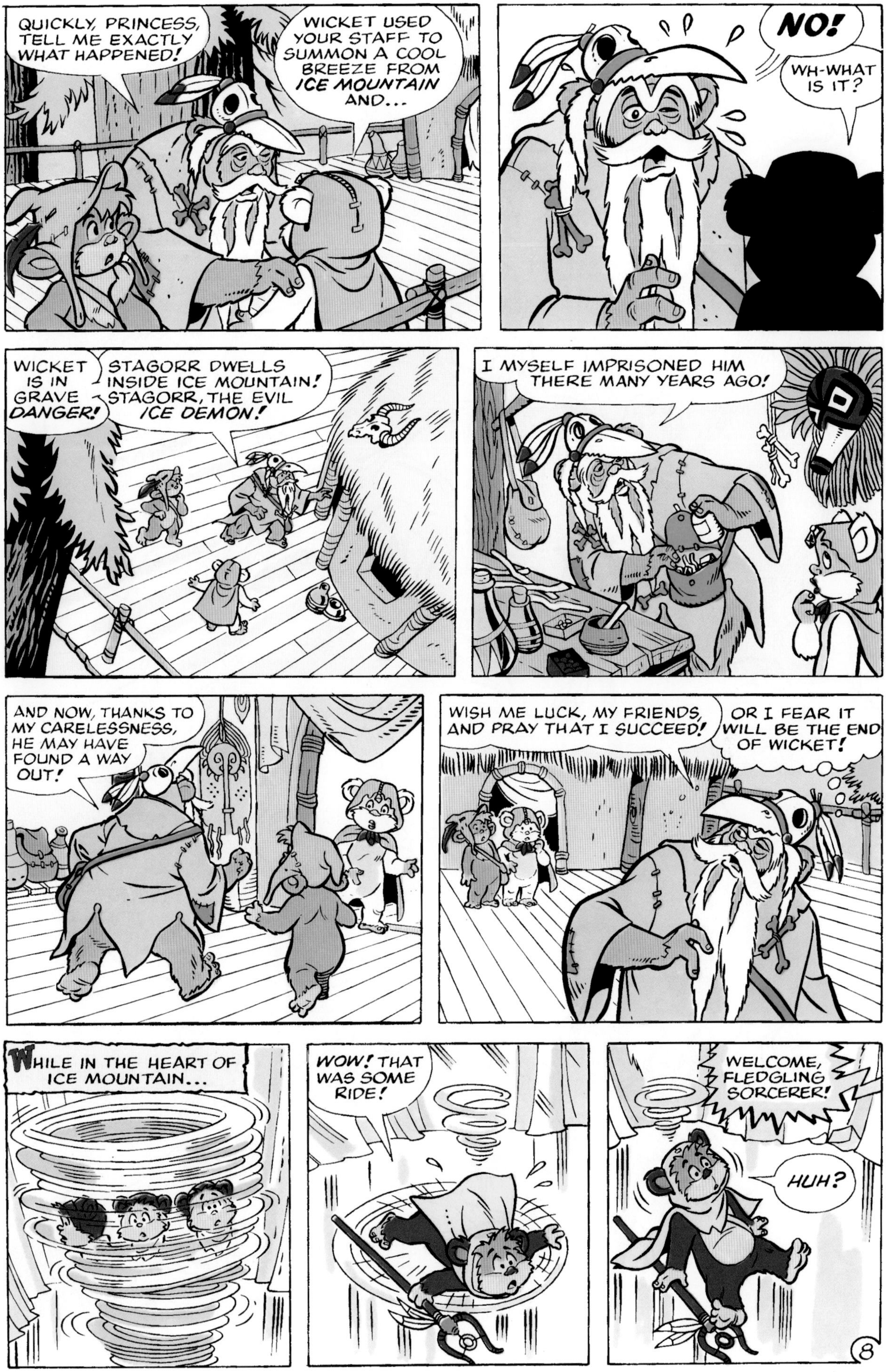
QUICKLY, PRINCESS, TELL ME EXACTLY WHAT HAPPENED!
WICKET USED YOUR STAFF TO SUMMON A COOL BREEZE FROM ICE MOUNTAIN AND...
NO!
WH-WHAT IS IT?
WICKET IS IN GRAVE DANGER!
STAGORR DWELLS INSIDE ICE MOUNTAIN! STAGORR, THE EVIL ICE DEMON!
I MYSELF IMPRISONED HIM THERE MANY YEARS AGO!
AND NOW, THANKS TO MY CARELESSNESS, HE MAY HAVE FOUND A WAY OUT!
WISH ME LUCK, MY FRIENDS, AND PRAY THAT I SUCCEED!
OR I FEAR IT WILL BE THE END OF WICKET!
WHILE IN THE HEART OF ICE MOUNTAIN...
WOW! THAT WAS SOME RIDE!
WELCOME, FLEDGLING SORCERER!
HUH?
8

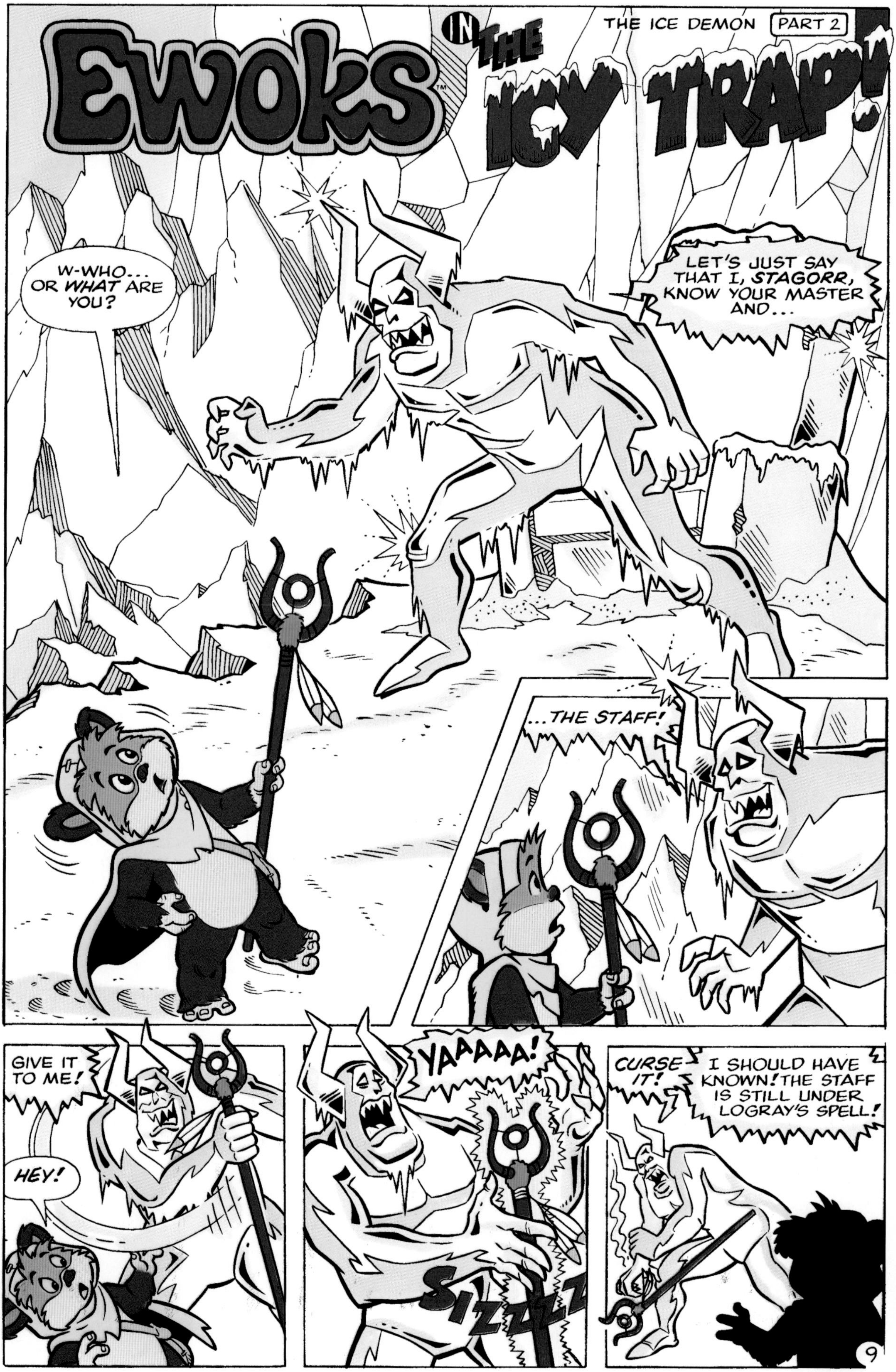
THE ICE DEMON PART 2
Ewoks™ IN THE ICY TRAP!
W-WHO... OR WHAT ARE YOU?
LET'S JUST SAY THAT I, STAGORR, KNOW YOUR MASTER AND...
...THE STAFF!
GIVE IT TO ME!
HEY!
YAAAAA!
SIZZZZ
CURSE IT!
I SHOULD HAVE KNOWN! THE STAFF IS STILL UNDER LOGRAY'S SPELL!
9

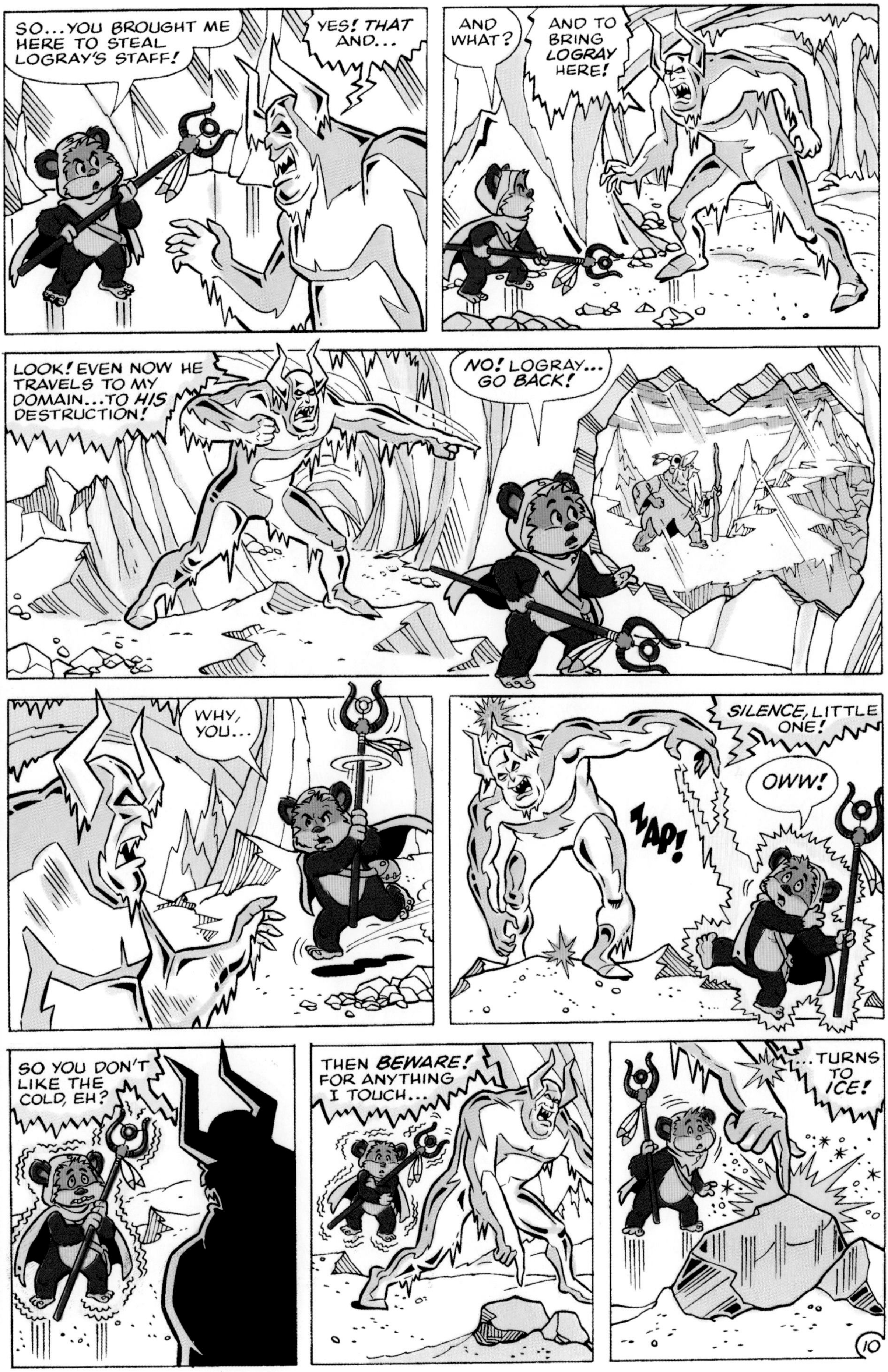
SO...YOU BROUGHT ME HERE TO STEAL LOGRAY'S STAFF!
YES! THAT AND...
AND WHAT?
AND TO BRING LOGRAY HERE!
LOOK! EVEN NOW HE TRAVELS TO MY DOMAIN...TO HIS DESTRUCTION!
NO! LOGRAY... GO BACK!
WHY, YOU...
SILENCE, LITTLE ONE!
ZAP!
OWW!
SO YOU DON'T LIKE THE COLD, EH?
THEN BEWARE! FOR ANYTHING I TOUCH...
...TURNS TO ICE!
10

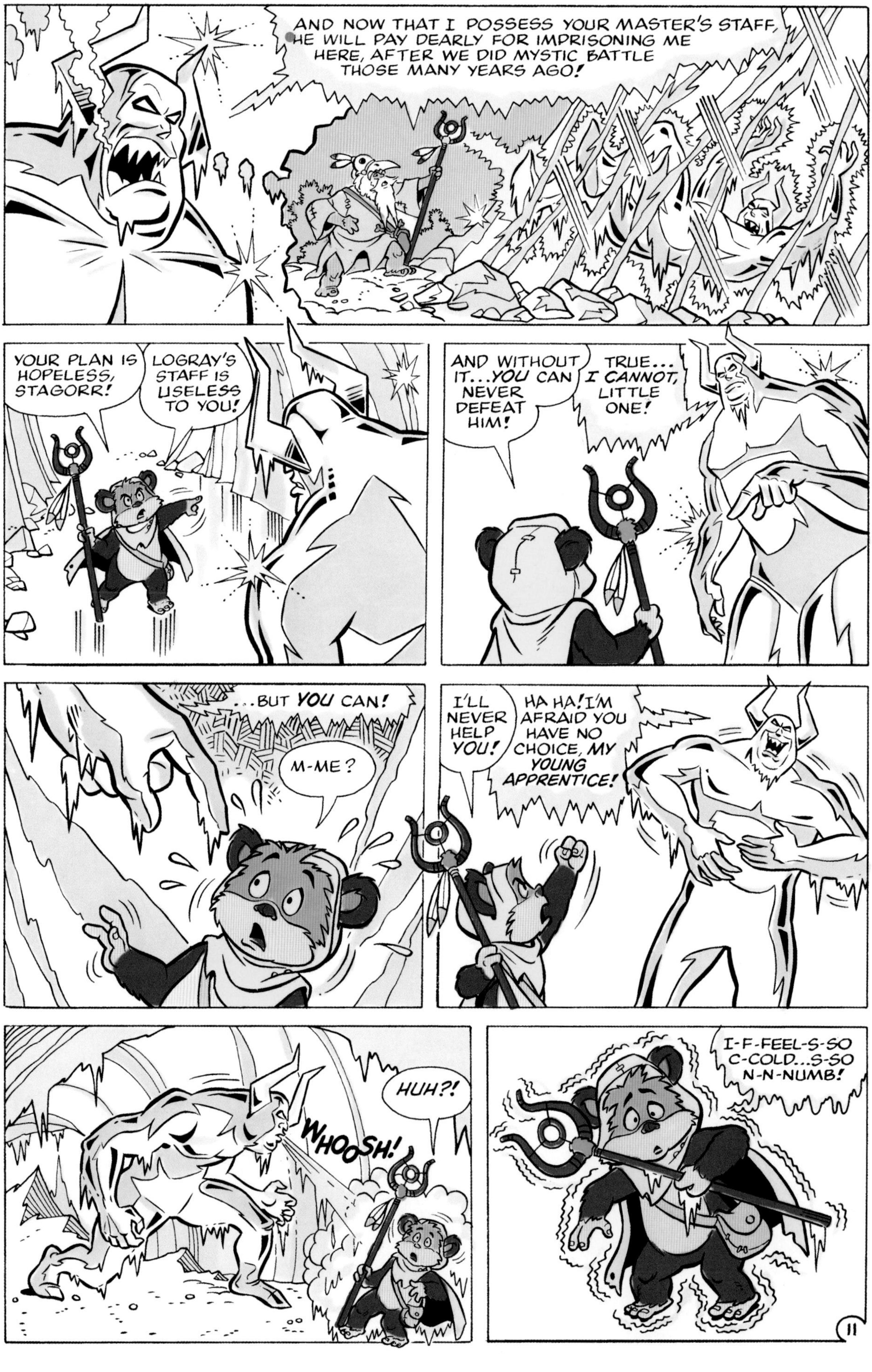
AND NOW THAT I POSSESS YOUR MASTER'S STAFF, HE WILL PAY DEARLY FOR IMPRISONING ME HERE, AFTER WE DID MYSTIC BATTLE THOSE MANY YEARS AGO!
YOUR PLAN IS HOPELESS, STAGORR!
LOGRAY'S STAFF IS USELESS TO YOU!
AND WITHOUT IT... YOU CAN NEVER DEFEAT HIM!
TRUE... I CANNOT, LITTLE ONE!
...BUT YOU CAN!
M-ME?
I'LL NEVER HELP YOU!
HA HA! I'M AFRAID YOU HAVE NO CHOICE, MY YOUNG APPRENTICE!
HUH?!
WHOOSH!
I-F-FEEL-S-SO C-COLD...S-SO N-N-NUMB!
11

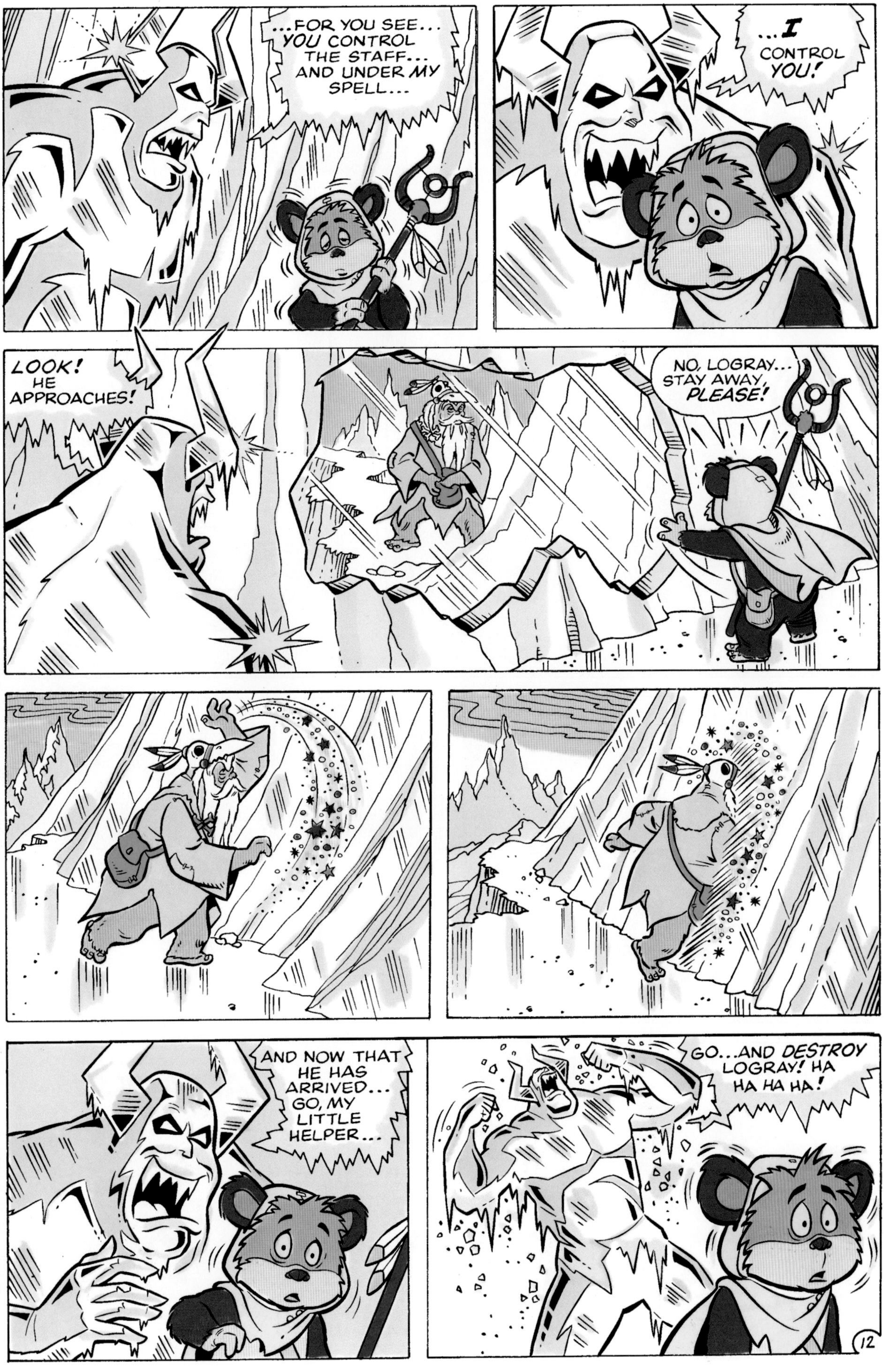
...FOR YOU SEE... YOU CONTROL THE STAFF... AND UNDER MY SPELL...
...I CONTROL YOU!
LOOK! HE APPROACHES!
NO, LOGRAY... STAY AWAY, PLEASE!
AND NOW THAT HE HAS ARRIVED... GO, MY LITTLE HELPER...
GO...AND DESTROY LOGRAY! HA HA HA HA!
12

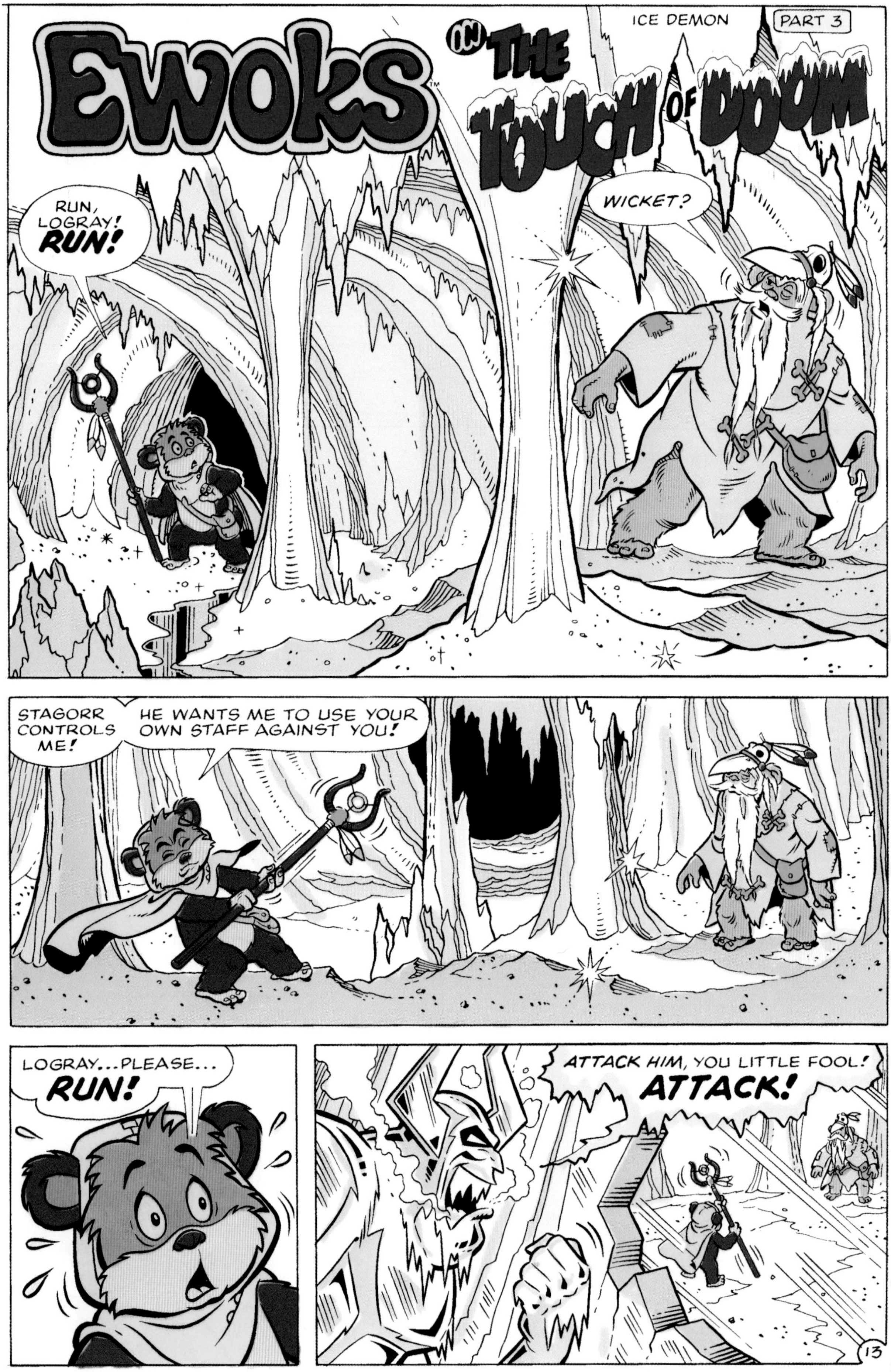
EWOKS
ON THE TOUCH OF DOOM
ICE DEMON
PART 3
RUN, LOGRAY! RUN!
WICKET?
STAGORR CONTROLS ME!
HE WANTS ME TO USE YOUR OWN STAFF AGAINST YOU!
LOGRAY...PLEASE... RUN!
ATTACK HIM, YOU LITTLE FOOL! ATTACK!
13

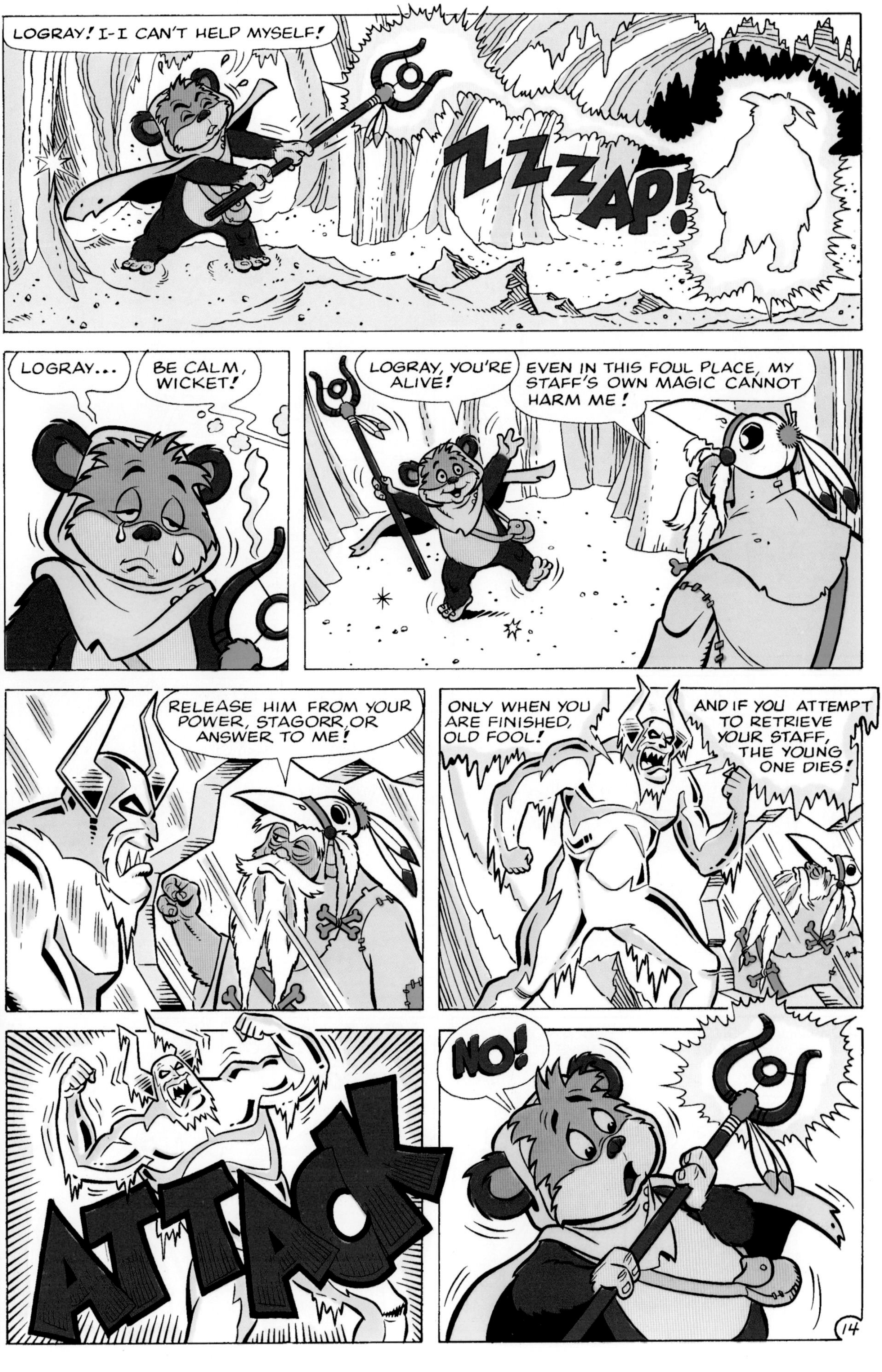
LOGRAY! I-I CAN'T HELP MYSELF!
ZZZZAP!
LOGRAY...
BE CALM, WICKET!
LOGRAY, YOU'RE ALIVE!
EVEN IN THIS FOUL PLACE, MY STAFF'S OWN MAGIC CANNOT HARM ME!
RELEASE HIM FROM YOUR POWER, STAGORR, OR ANSWER TO ME!
ONLY WHEN YOU ARE FINISHED, OLD FOOL!
AND IF YOU ATTEMPT TO RETRIEVE YOUR STAFF, THE YOUNG ONE DIES!
ATTACK
NO!
14

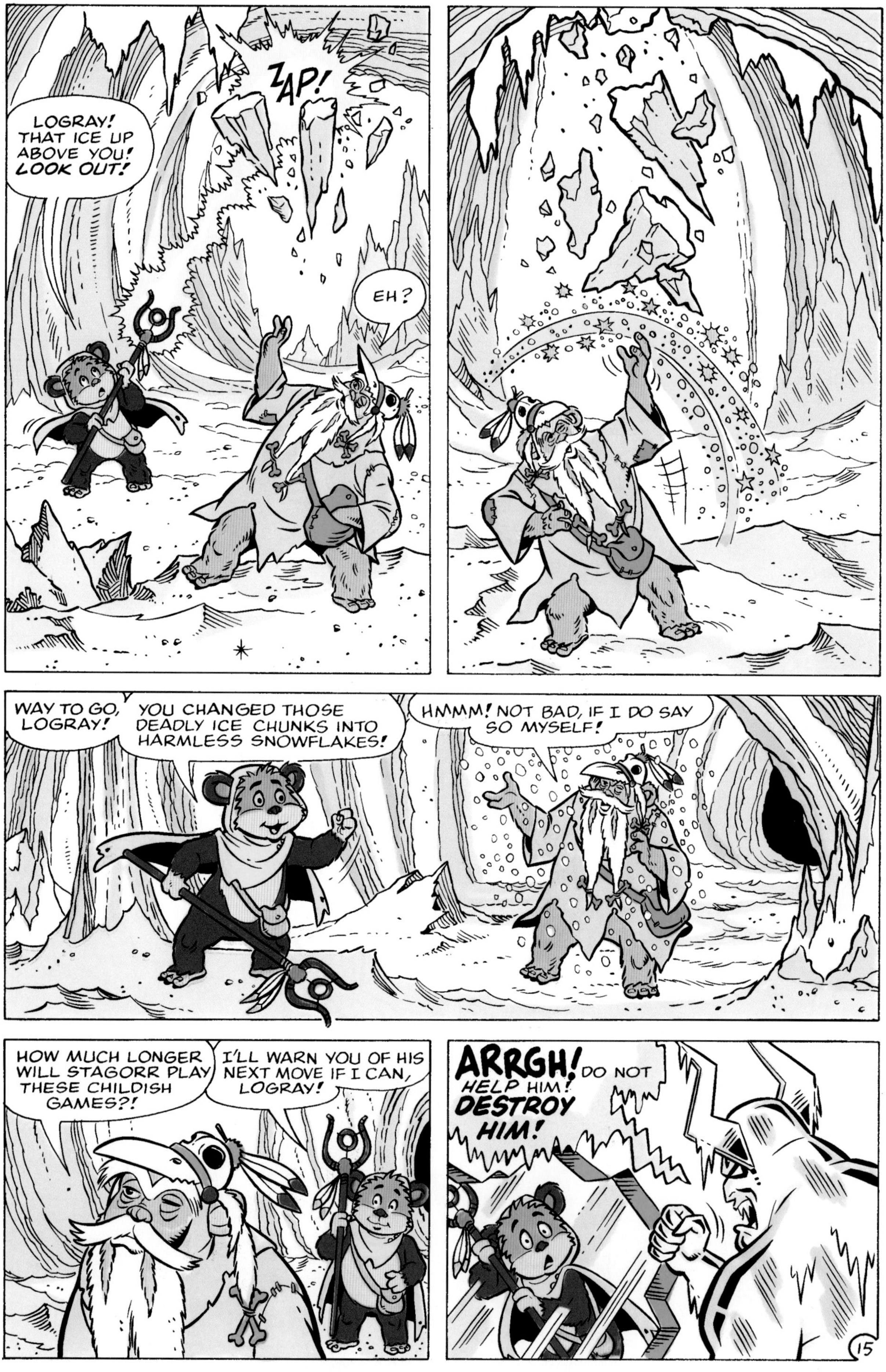
LOGRAY! THAT ICE UP ABOVE YOU! LOOK OUT!
ZAP!
EH?
WAY TO GO, LOGRAY!
YOU CHANGED THOSE DEADLY ICE CHUNKS INTO HARMLESS SNOWFLAKES!
HMMM! NOT BAD, IF I DO SAY SO MYSELF!
HOW MUCH LONGER WILL STAGORR PLAY THESE CHILDISH GAMES?!
I'LL WARN YOU OF HIS NEXT MOVE IF I CAN, LOGRAY!
ARRGH! DO NOT HELP HIM! DESTROY HIM!
15

OH, NO! ICE CREATURES FORMING FROM THE WALLS!

ARRGH!

DO SOMETHING, LOGRAY! DO SOMETHING!

ZAP!

ZAP!

THEY CAN'T KEEP THEIR FEET...

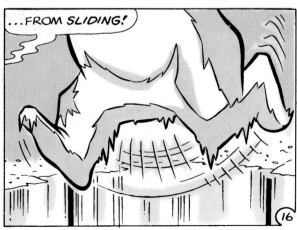

...FROM SLIDING!

16

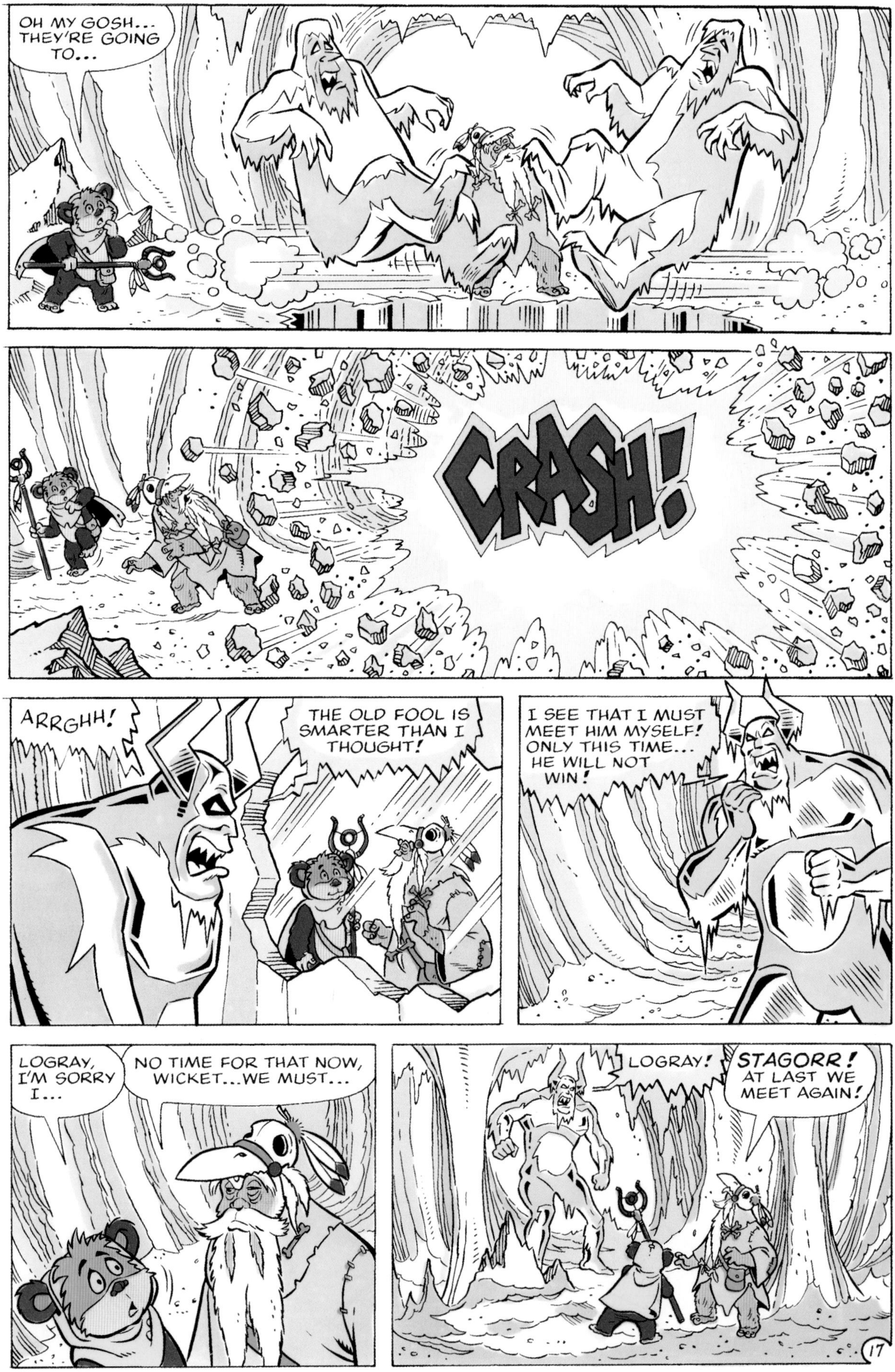
OH MY GOSH... THEY'RE GOING TO...
CRASH!
ARRGHH!
THE OLD FOOL IS SMARTER THAN I THOUGHT!
I SEE THAT I MUST MEET HIM MYSELF! ONLY THIS TIME... HE WILL NOT WIN!
LOGRAY, I'M SORRY I...
NO TIME FOR THAT NOW, WICKET...WE MUST...
LOGRAY!
STAGORR! AT LAST WE MEET AGAIN!
17

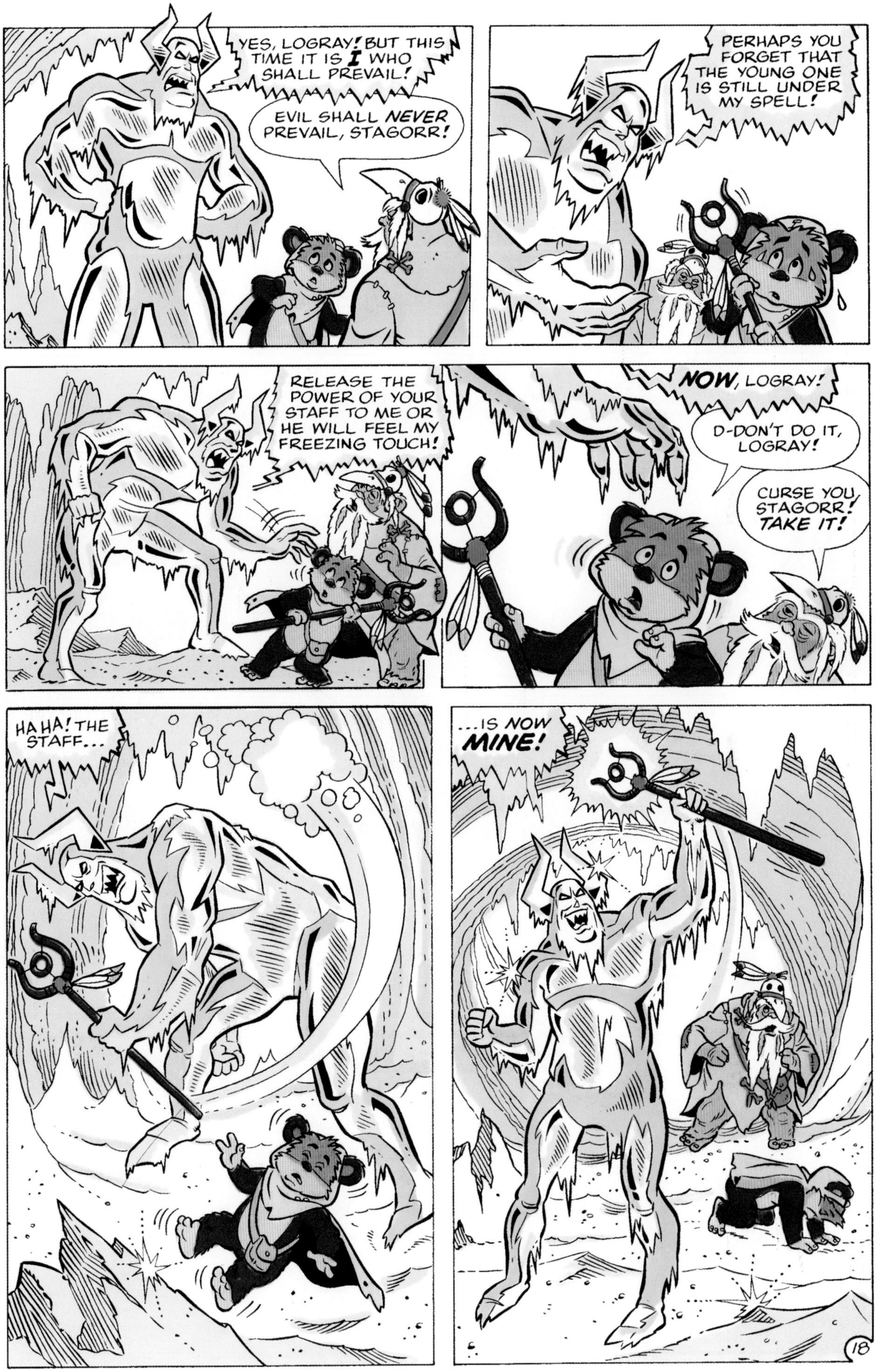
YES, LOGRAY! BUT THIS TIME IT IS I WHO SHALL PREVAIL!
EVIL SHALL NEVER PREVAIL, STAGORR!
PERHAPS YOU FORGET THAT THE YOUNG ONE IS STILL UNDER MY SPELL!
RELEASE THE POWER OF YOUR STAFF TO ME OR HE WILL FEEL MY FREEZING TOUCH!
NOW, LOGRAY!
D-DON'T DO IT, LOGRAY!
CURSE YOU, STAGORR! TAKE IT!
HA HA! THE STAFF...
...IS NOW MINE!
18

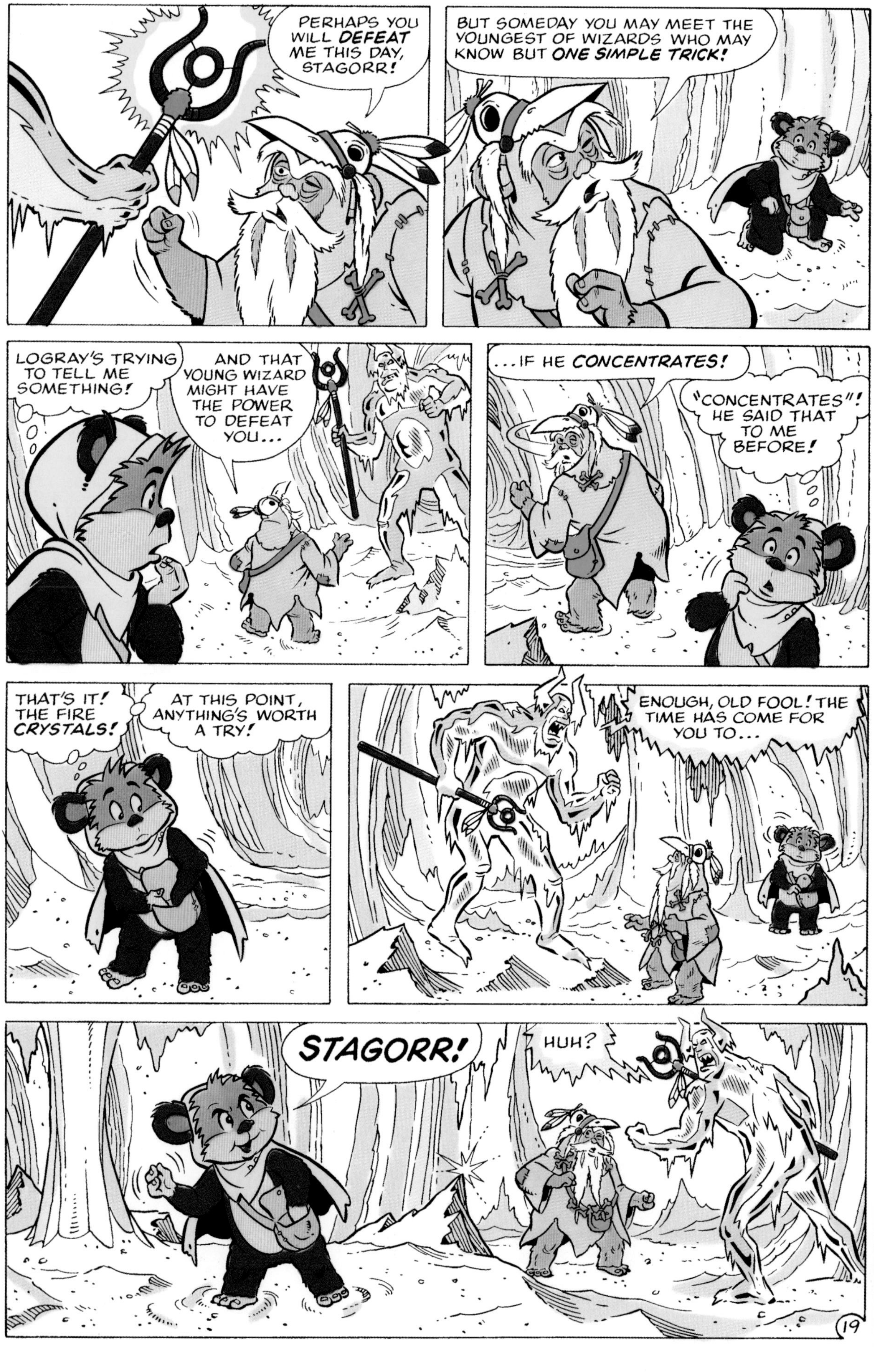
PERHAPS YOU WILL DEFEAT ME THIS DAY, STAGORR!
BUT SOMEDAY YOU MAY MEET THE YOUNGEST OF WIZARDS WHO MAY KNOW BUT ONE SIMPLE TRICK!
LOGRAY'S TRYING TO TELL ME SOMETHING!
AND THAT YOUNG WIZARD MIGHT HAVE THE POWER TO DEFEAT YOU...
...IF HE CONCENTRATES!
"CONCENTRATES"! HE SAID THAT TO ME BEFORE!
THAT'S IT! THE FIRE CRYSTALS!
AT THIS POINT, ANYTHING'S WORTH A TRY!
ENOUGH, OLD FOOL! THE TIME HAS COME FOR YOU TO...
STAGORR!
HUH?
19

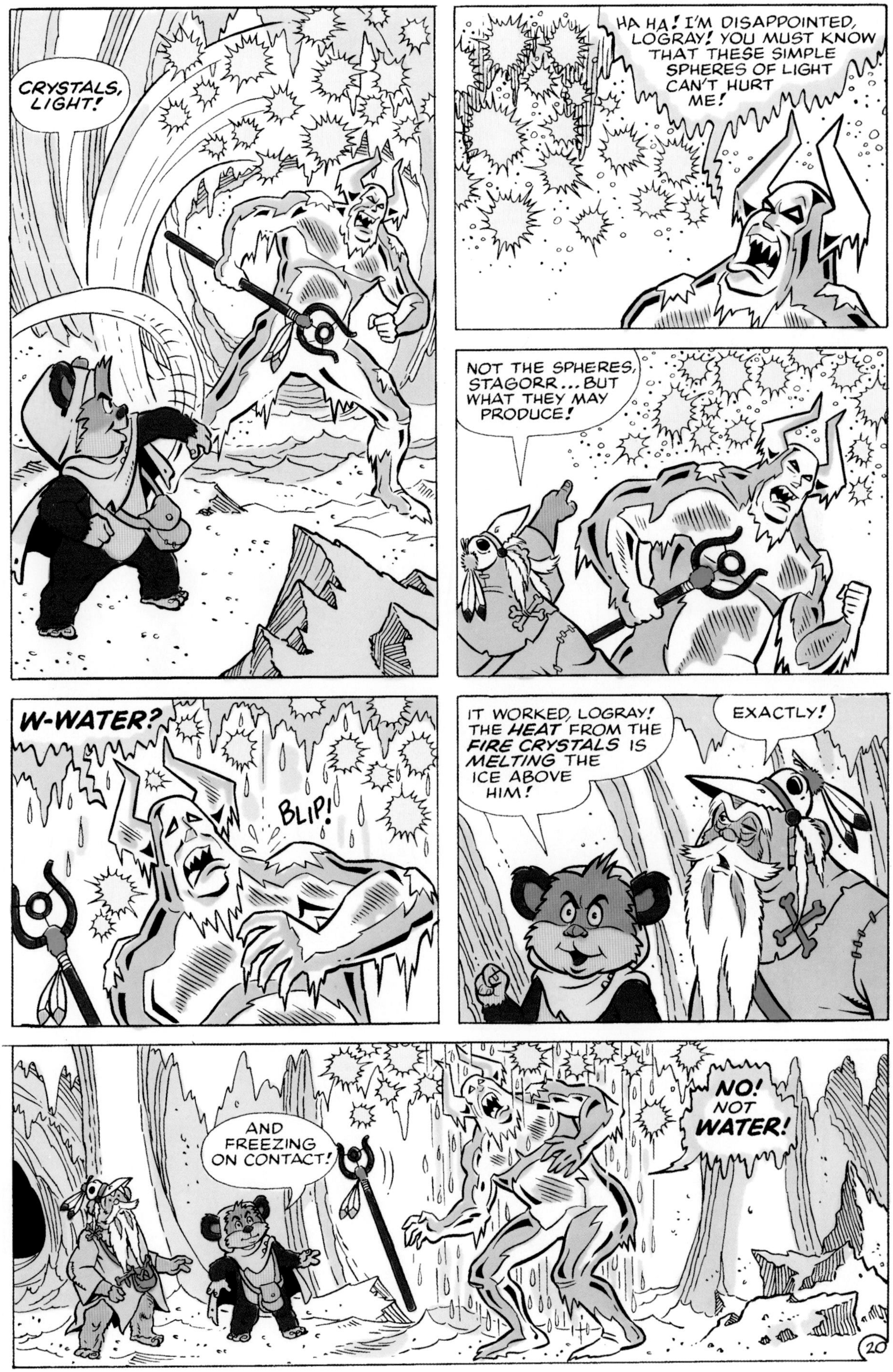
CRYSTALS, LIGHT!
HA HA! I'M DISAPPOINTED, LOGRAY! YOU MUST KNOW THAT THESE SIMPLE SPHERES OF LIGHT CAN'T HURT ME!
NOT THE SPHERES, STAGORR... BUT WHAT THEY MAY PRODUCE!
W-WATER?
BLIP!
IT WORKED, LOGRAY! THE HEAT FROM THE FIRE CRYSTALS IS MELTING THE ICE ABOVE HIM!
EXACTLY!
AND FREEZING ON CONTACT!
NO! NOT WATER!
20

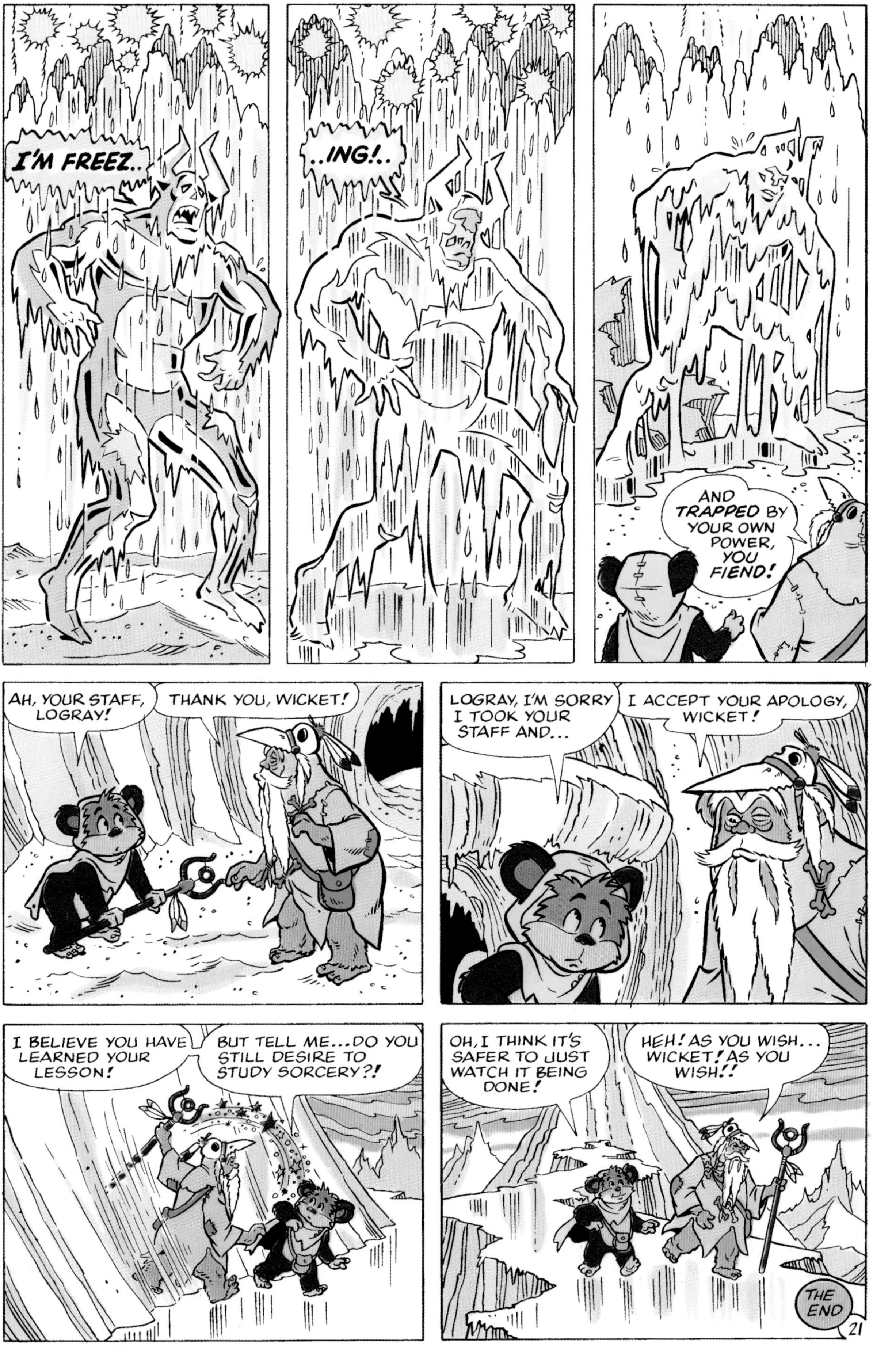
I'M FREEZ..
..ING!..
AND TRAPPED BY YOUR OWN POWER, YOU FIEND!
AH, YOUR STAFF, LOGRAY!
THANK YOU, WICKET!
LOGRAY, I'M SORRY I TOOK YOUR STAFF AND...
I ACCEPT YOUR APOLOGY, WICKET!
I BELIEVE YOU HAVE LEARNED YOUR LESSON!
BUT TELL ME...DO YOU STILL DESIRE TO STUDY SORCERY?!
OH, I THINK IT'S SAFER TO JUST WATCH IT BEING DONE!
HEH! AS YOU WISH... WICKET! AS YOU WISH!!
THE END
21

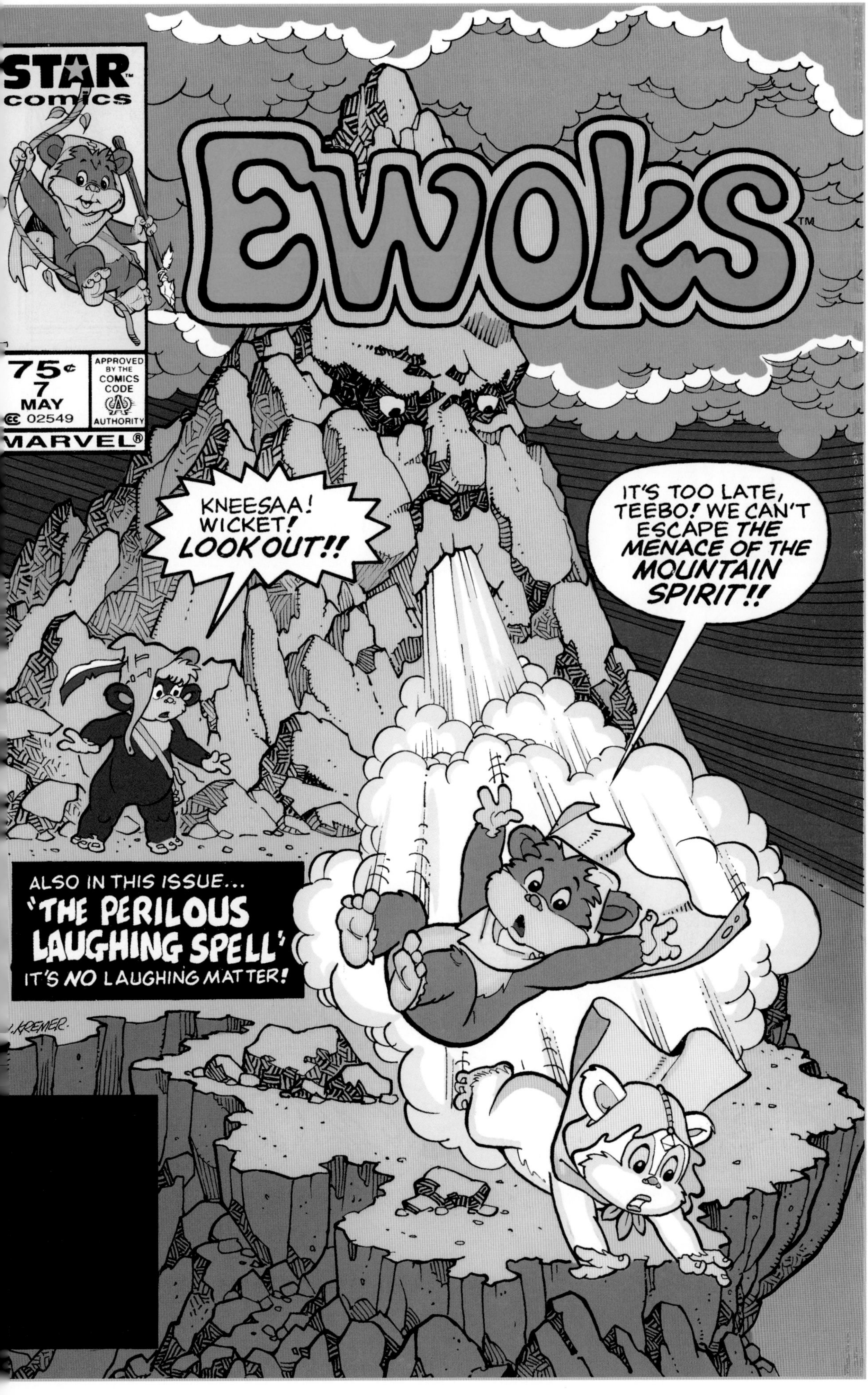
STAR comics
EWOKS
75¢
7
MAY
02549
APPROVED BY THE COMICS CODE AUTHORITY
MARVEL
KNEESAA! WICKET! LOOK OUT!!
IT'S TOO LATE, TEEBO! WE CAN'T ESCAPE THE MENACE OF THE MOUNTAIN SPIRIT!!
ALSO IN THIS ISSUE...
"THE PERILOUS LAUGHING SPELL"
IT'S NO LAUGHING MATTER!

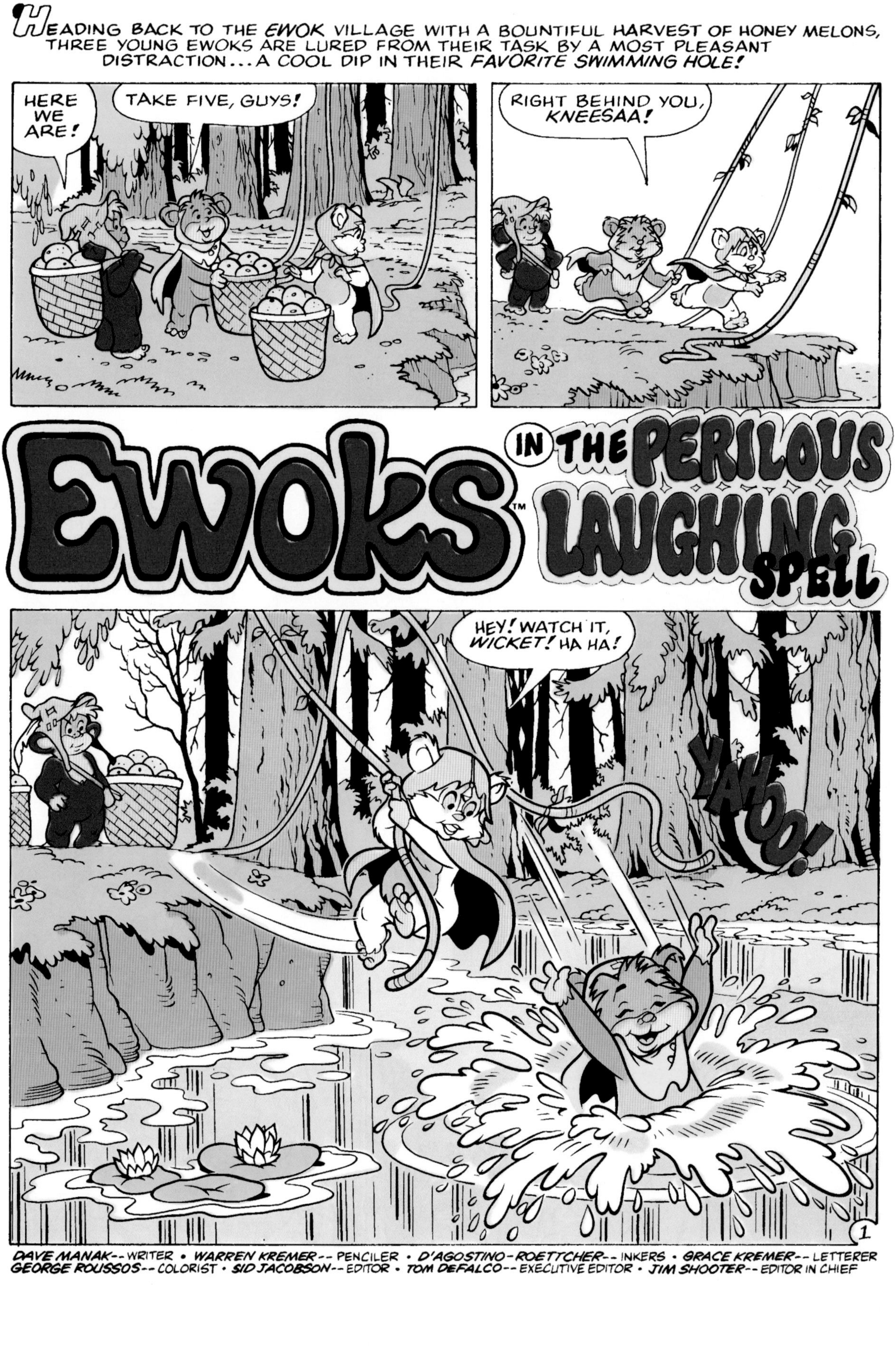
HEADING BACK TO THE EWOK VILLAGE WITH A BOUNTIFUL HARVEST OF HONEY MELONS, THREE YOUNG EWOKS ARE LURED FROM THEIR TASK BY A MOST PLEASANT DISTRACTION... A COOL DIP IN THEIR FAVORITE SWIMMING HOLE!
HERE WE ARE!
TAKE FIVE, GUYS!
RIGHT BEHIND YOU, KNEESAA!
EWOKS™ IN THE PERILOUS LAUGHING SPELL
HEY! WATCH IT, WICKET! HA HA!
YAHOO!
1

DAVE MANAK--WRITER • WARREN KREMER--PENCILER • D'AGOSTINO-ROETTCHER--INKERS • GRACE KREMER--LETTERER
GEORGE ROUSSOS--COLORIST • SID JACOBSON--EDITOR • TOM DEFALCO--EXECUTIVE EDITOR • JIM SHOOTER--EDITOR IN CHIEF

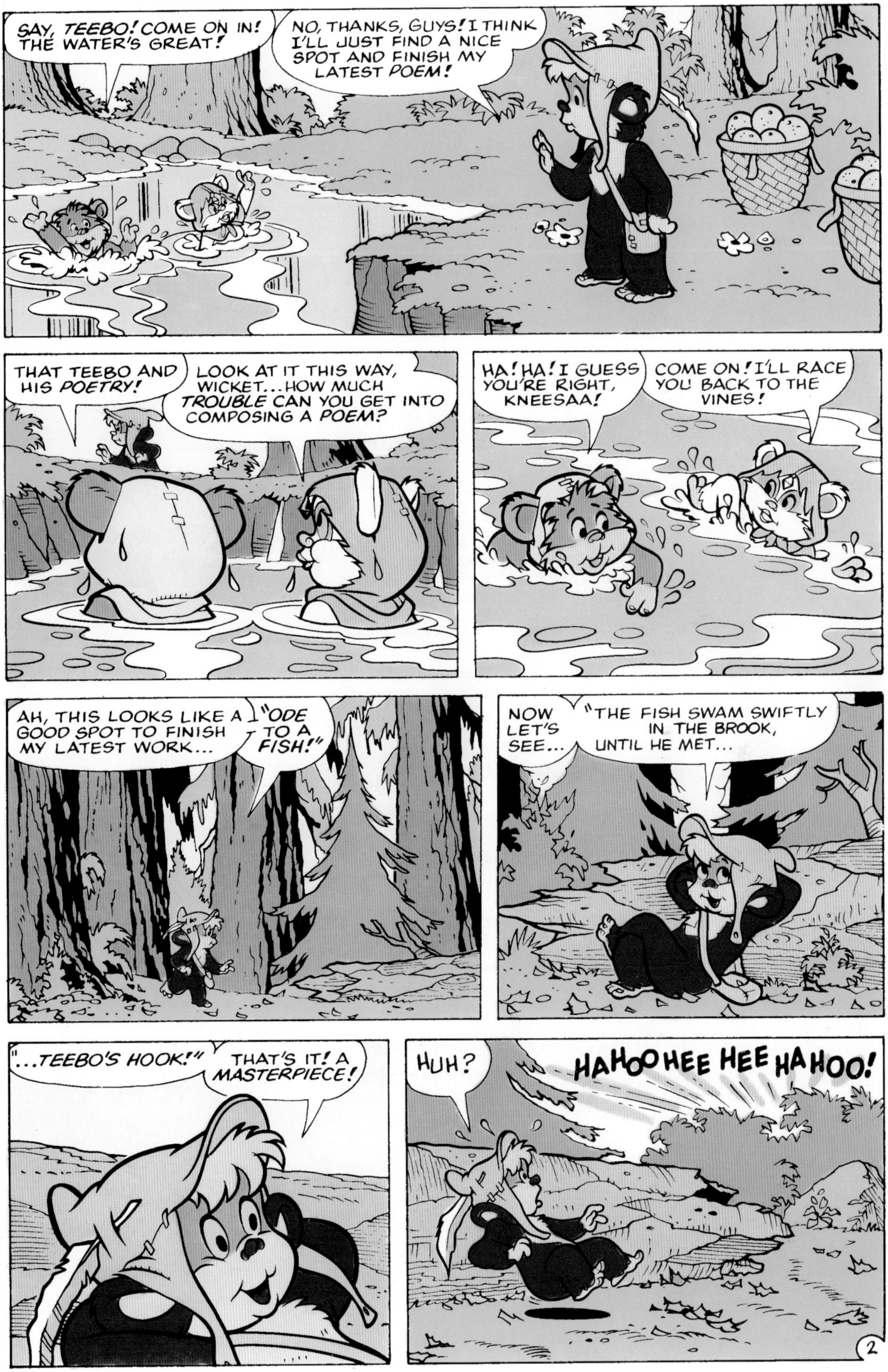
SAY, TEEBO! COME ON IN! THE WATER'S GREAT!
NO, THANKS, GUYS! I THINK I'LL JUST FIND A NICE SPOT AND FINISH MY LATEST POEM!
THAT TEEBO AND HIS POETRY!
LOOK AT IT THIS WAY, WICKET... HOW MUCH TROUBLE CAN YOU GET INTO COMPOSING A POEM?
HA! HA! I GUESS YOU'RE RIGHT, KNEESAA!
COME ON! I'LL RACE YOU BACK TO THE VINES!
AH, THIS LOOKS LIKE A GOOD SPOT TO FINISH MY LATEST WORK...
"ODE TO A FISH!"
NOW LET'S SEE...
"THE FISH SWAM SWIFTLY IN THE BROOK, UNTIL HE MET...
"...TEEBO'S HOOK!"
THAT'S IT! A MASTERPIECE!
HUH?
HAHOOHEE HEE HAHOO!
2

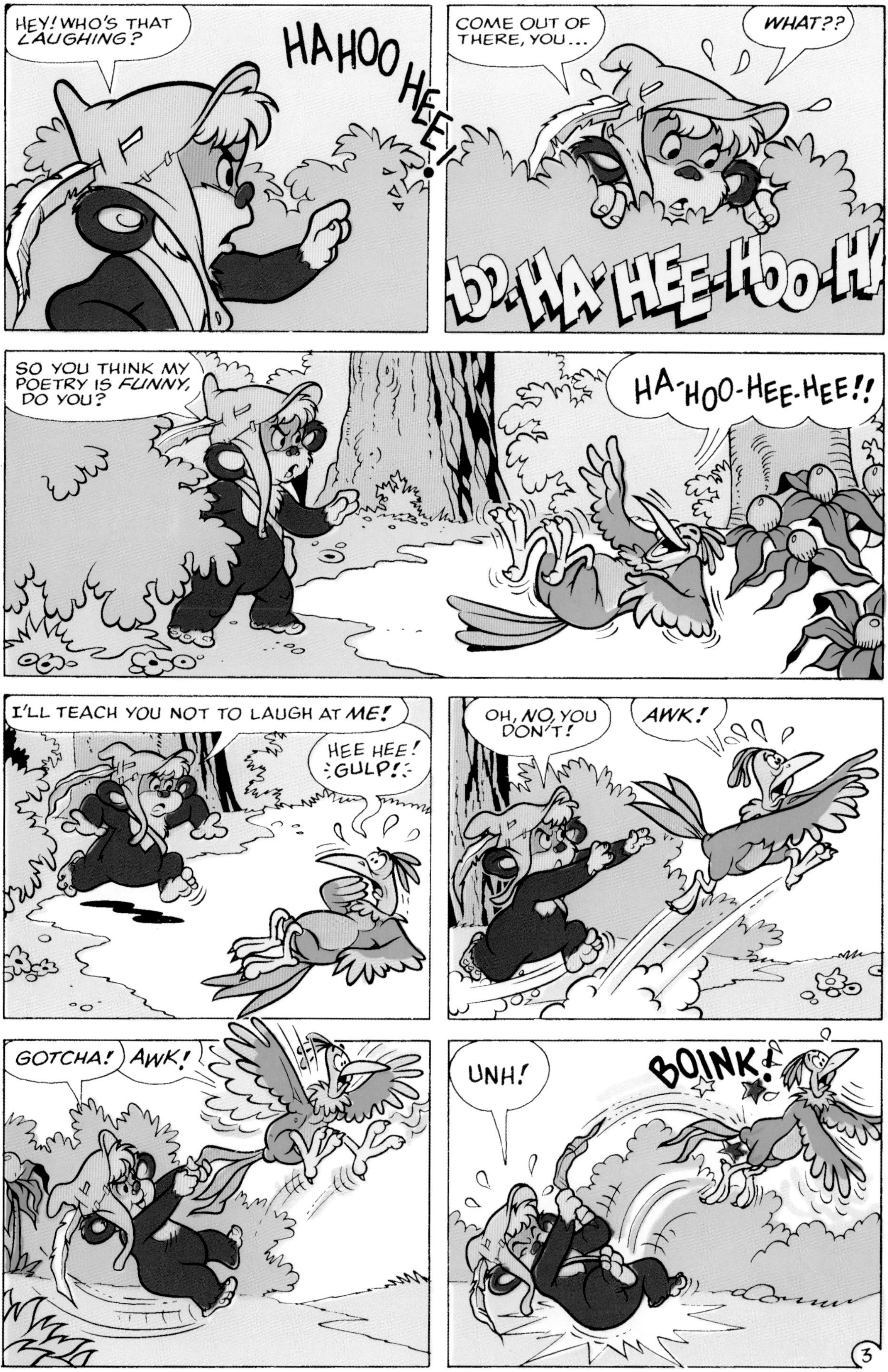
HEY! WHO'S THAT LAUGHING?
HAHOO HEE!
COME OUT OF THERE, YOU...
WHAT??
HOO-HA-HEE-HOO-HA
SO YOU THINK MY POETRY IS FUNNY, DO YOU?
HA-HOO-HEE-HEE!!
I'LL TEACH YOU NOT TO LAUGH AT ME!
HEE HEE! GULP!
OH, NO, YOU DON'T!
AWK!
GOTCHA!
AWK!
UNH!
BOINK!
3

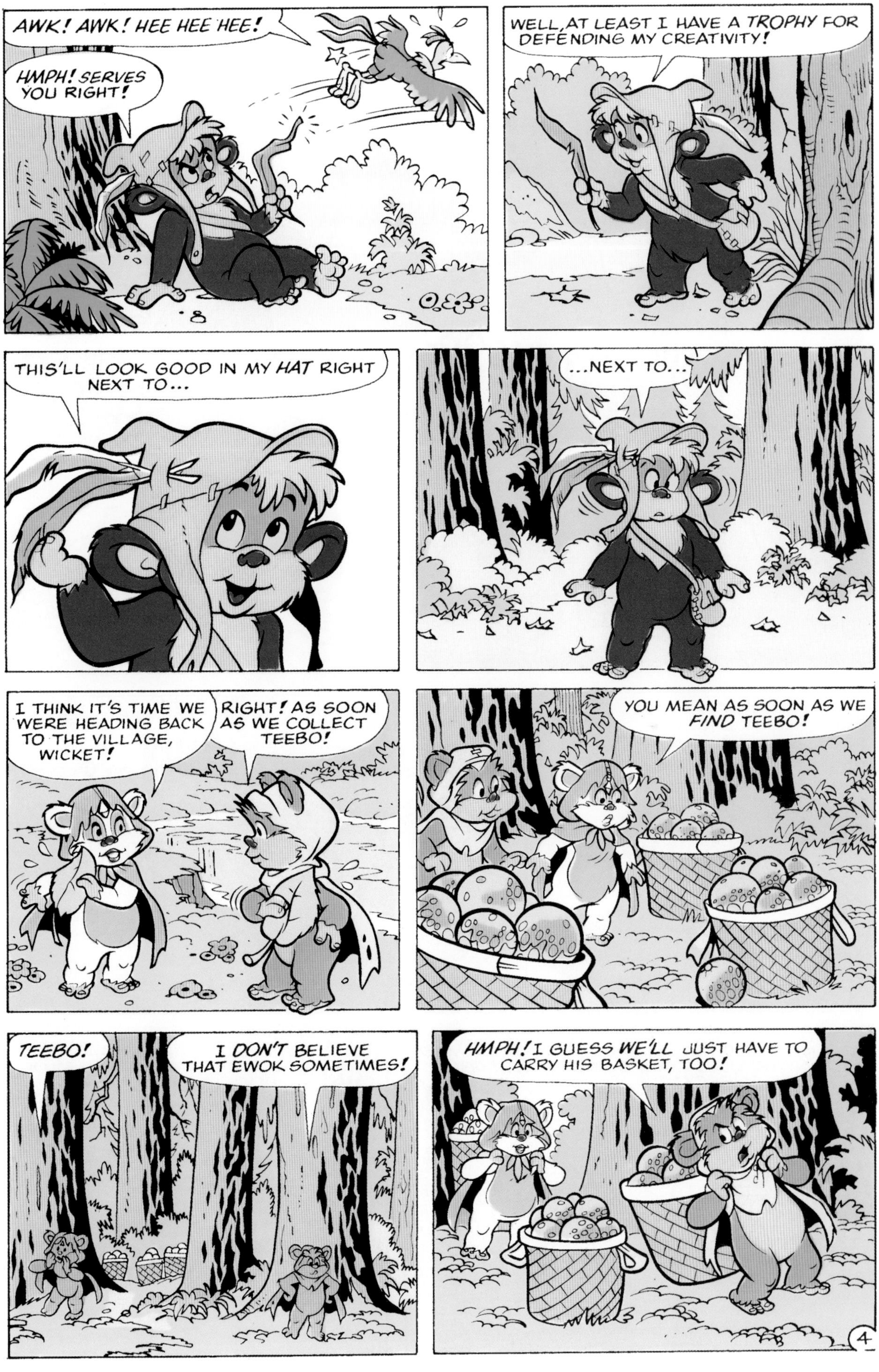
AWK! AWK! HEE HEE HEE!
HMPH! SERVES YOU RIGHT!
WELL, AT LEAST I HAVE A TROPHY FOR DEFENDING MY CREATIVITY!
THIS'LL LOOK GOOD IN MY HAT RIGHT NEXT TO...
...NEXT TO...
I THINK IT'S TIME WE WERE HEADING BACK TO THE VILLAGE, WICKET!
RIGHT! AS SOON AS WE COLLECT TEEBO!
YOU MEAN AS SOON AS WE FIND TEEBO!
TEEBO!
I DON'T BELIEVE THAT EWOK SOMETIMES!
HMPH! I GUESS WE'LL JUST HAVE TO CARRY HIS BASKET, TOO!
4

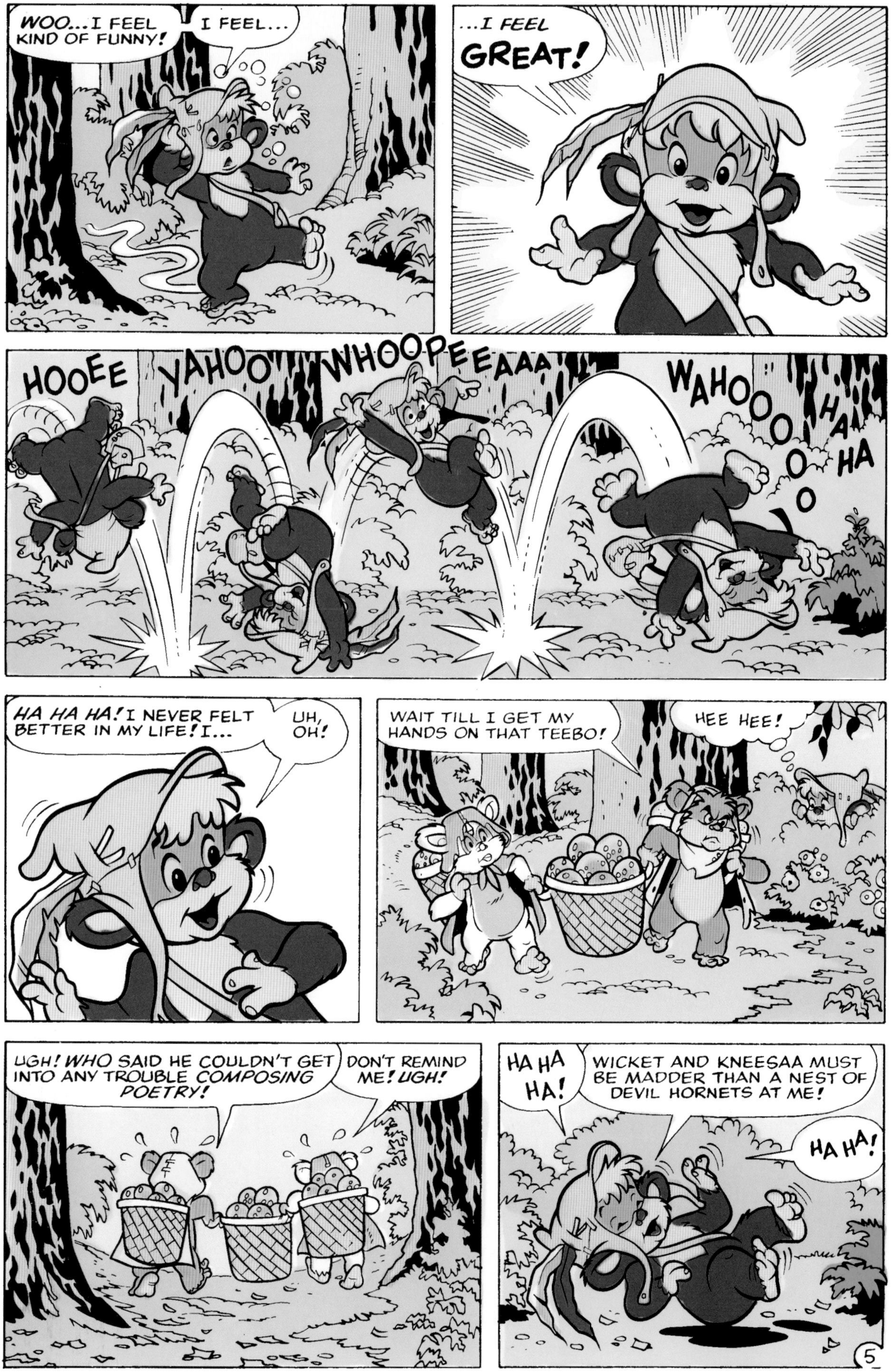
WOO...I FEEL KIND OF FUNNY!
I FEEL...
...I FEEL GREAT!
HOOEE
YAHOO
WHOOPEEAAA
WAHOOOOOO
HA HA HA
HA HA HA! I NEVER FELT BETTER IN MY LIFE! I...
UH, OH!
WAIT TILL I GET MY HANDS ON THAT TEEBO!
HEE HEE!
UGH! WHO SAID HE COULDN'T GET INTO ANY TROUBLE COMPOSING POETRY!
DON'T REMIND ME! UGH!
HA HA HA!
WICKET AND KNEESAA MUST BE MADDER THAN A NEST OF DEVIL HORNETS AT ME!
HA HA!
5

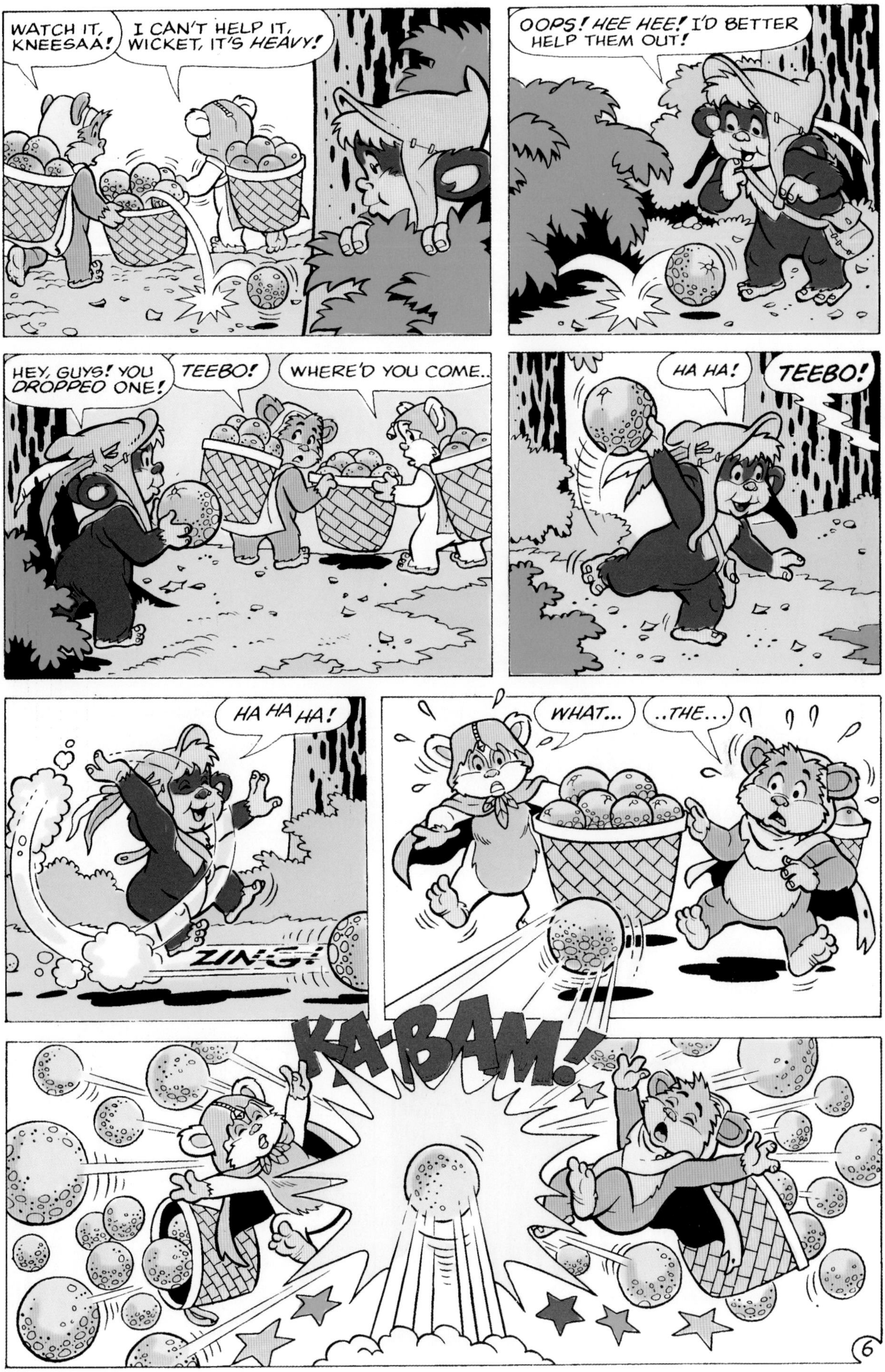
WATCH IT, KNEESAA!
I CAN'T HELP IT, WICKET, IT'S HEAVY!
OOPS! HEE HEE! I'D BETTER HELP THEM OUT!
HEY, GUYS! YOU DROPPED ONE!
TEEBO!
WHERE'D YOU COME..
HA HA!
TEEBO!
HA HA HA!
ZING!
WHAT...
..THE...
KA-BAM!
6

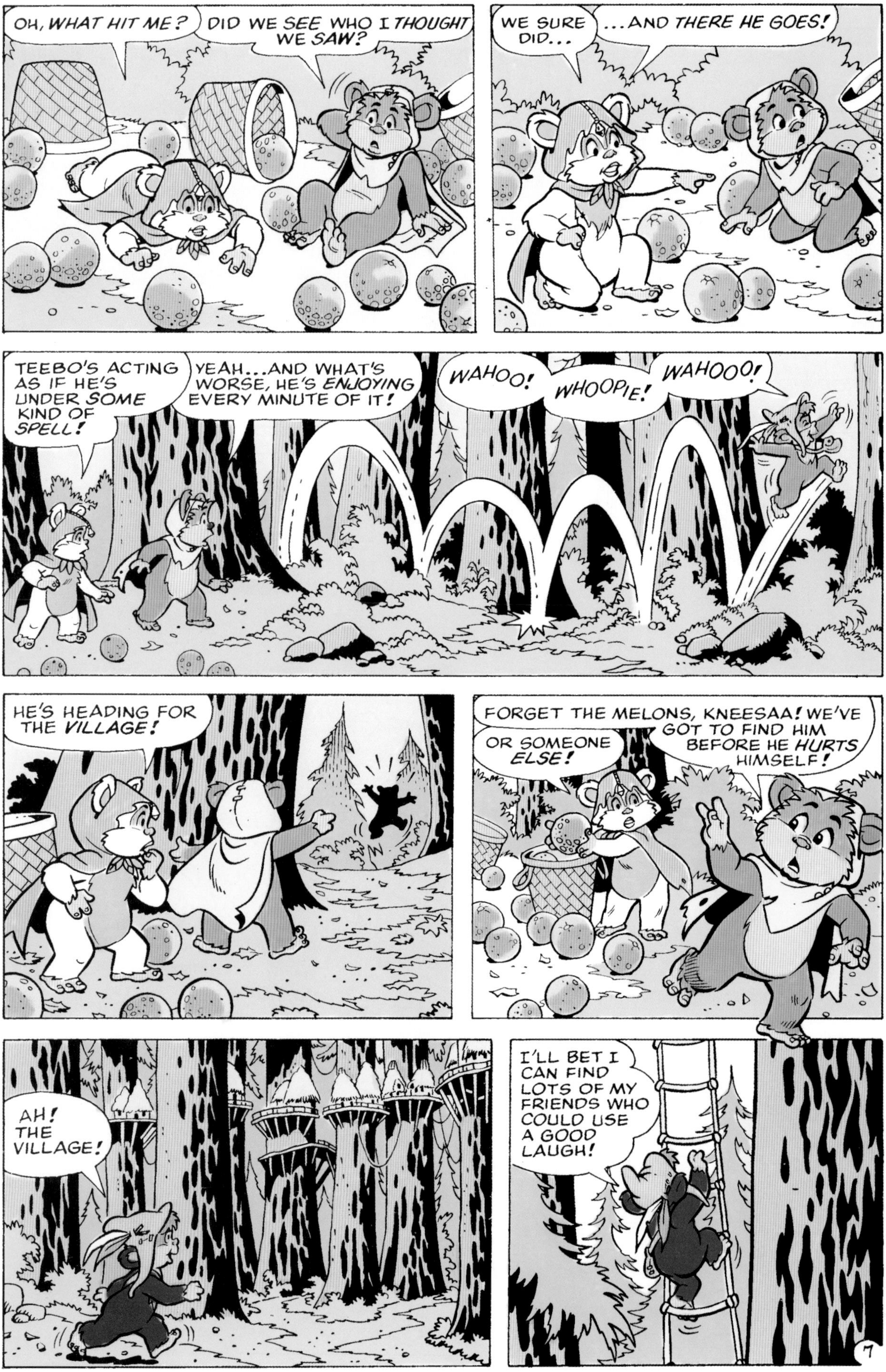
OH, WHAT HIT ME?
DID WE SEE WHO I THOUGHT WE SAW?
WE SURE DID...
...AND THERE HE GOES!
TEEBO'S ACTING AS IF HE'S UNDER SOME KIND OF SPELL!
YEAH...AND WHAT'S WORSE, HE'S ENJOYING EVERY MINUTE OF IT!
WAHOO!
WHOOPIE!
WAHOOO!
HE'S HEADING FOR THE VILLAGE!
FORGET THE MELONS, KNEESAA! WE'VE GOT TO FIND HIM BEFORE HE HURTS HIMSELF!
OR SOMEONE ELSE!
AH! THE VILLAGE!
I'LL BET I CAN FIND LOTS OF MY FRIENDS WHO COULD USE A GOOD LAUGH!
7

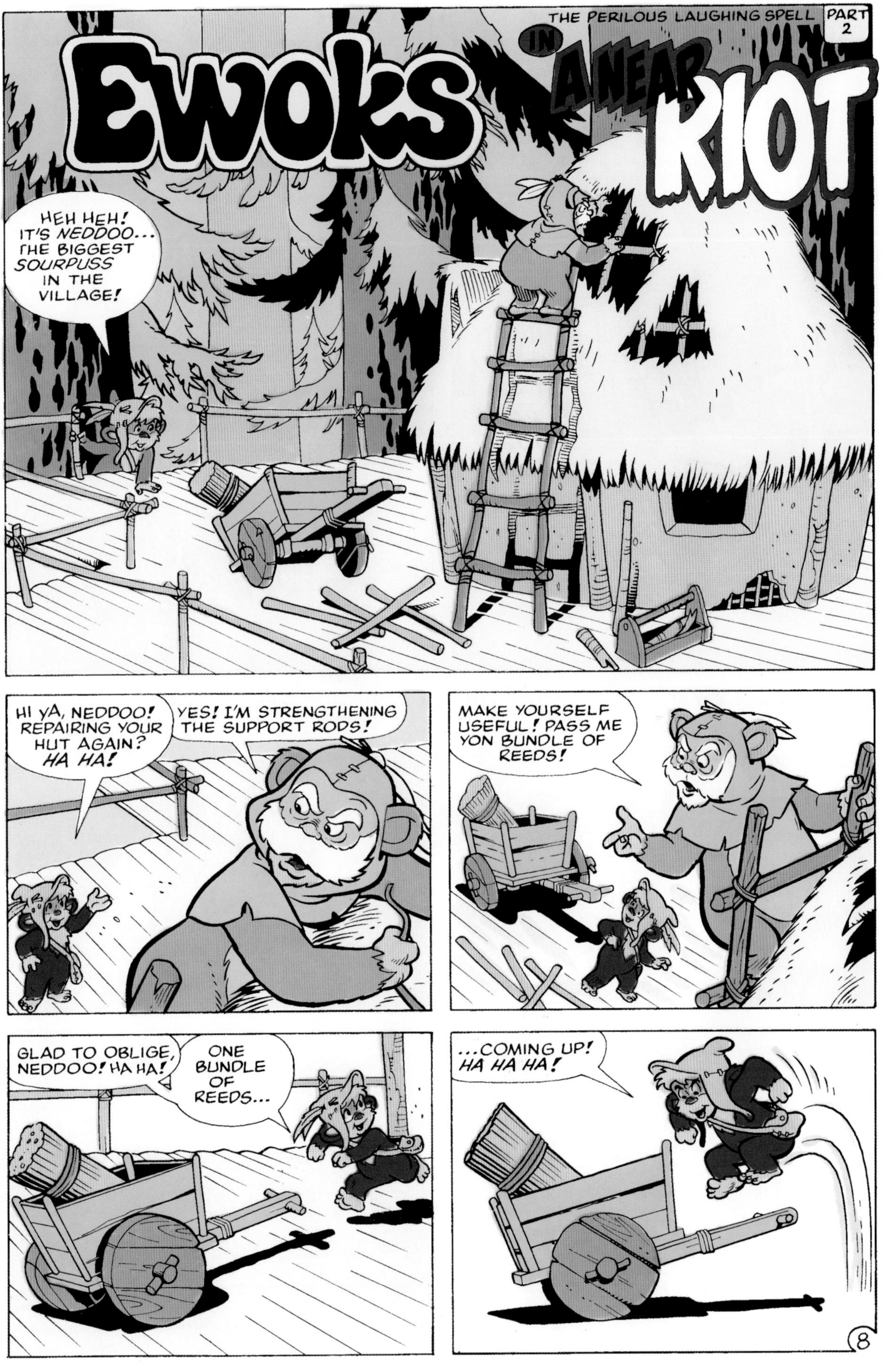
THE PERILOUS LAUGHING SPELL PART 2
EWOKS IN A NEAR RIOT
HEH HEH! IT'S NEDDOO... THE BIGGEST SOURPUSS IN THE VILLAGE!
HI yA, NEDDOO! REPAIRING YOUR HUT AGAIN? HA HA!
YES! I'M STRENGTHENING THE SUPPORT RODS!
MAKE YOURSELF USEFUL! PASS ME YON BUNDLE OF REEDS!
GLAD TO OBLIGE, NEDDOO! HA HA!
ONE BUNDLE OF REEDS...
...COMING UP! HA HA HA!
8

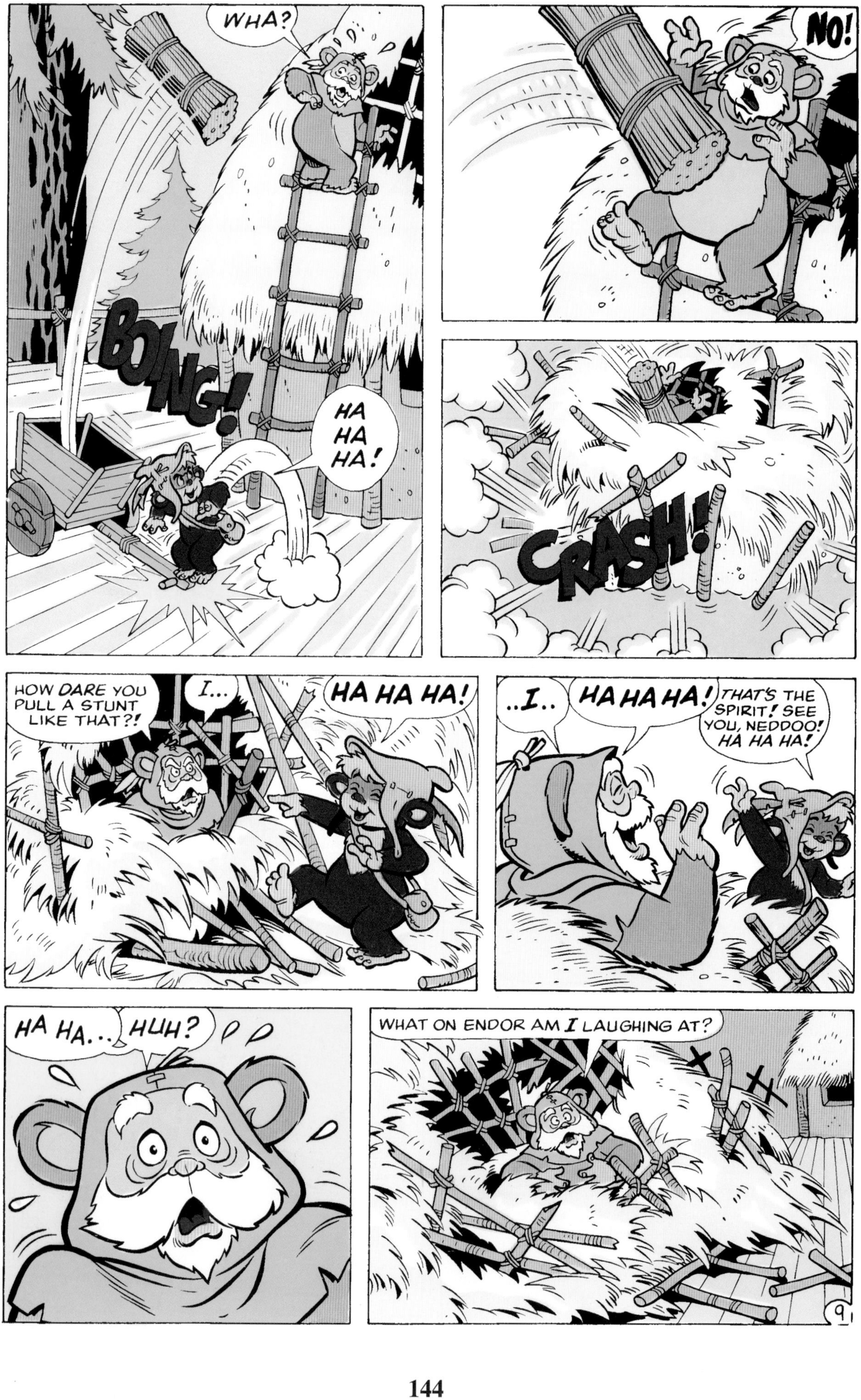
WHA?
NO!
BOING!
HA HA HA!
CRASH!
HOW DARE YOU PULL A STUNT LIKE THAT?!
I...
HA HA HA!
..I..
HA HA HA HA!
THAT'S THE SPIRIT! SEE YOU, NEDDOO! HA HA HA!
HA HA...
HUH?
WHAT ON ENDOR AM I LAUGHING AT?
9

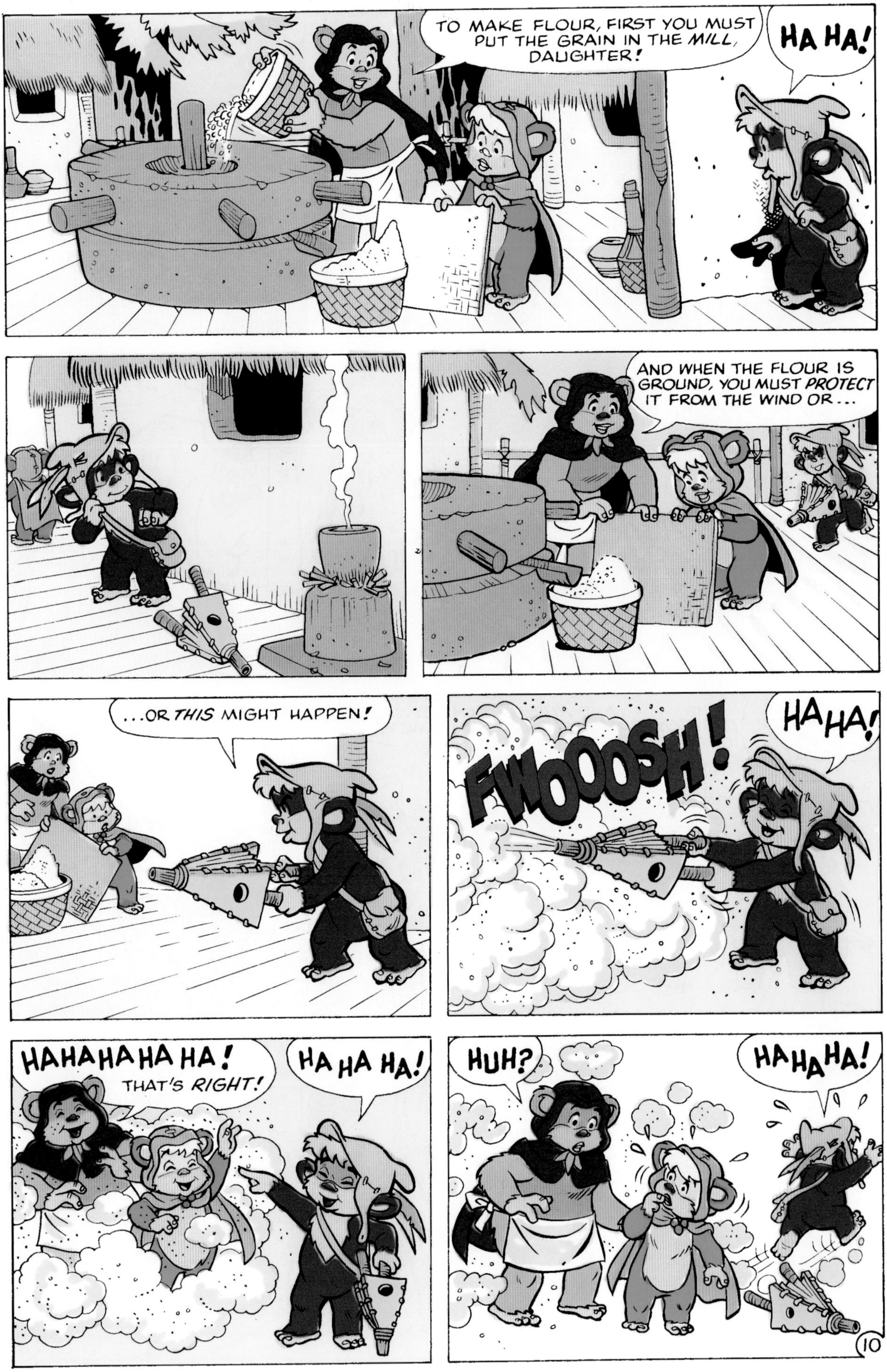
TO MAKE FLOUR, FIRST YOU MUST PUT THE GRAIN IN THE MILL, DAUGHTER!
HA HA!
AND WHEN THE FLOUR IS GROUND, YOU MUST PROTECT IT FROM THE WIND OR...
...OR THIS MIGHT HAPPEN!
FWOOOSH!
HAHA!
HAHAHAHAHA HA! THAT'S RIGHT!
HA HA HA!
HUH?
HAHAHA!
10

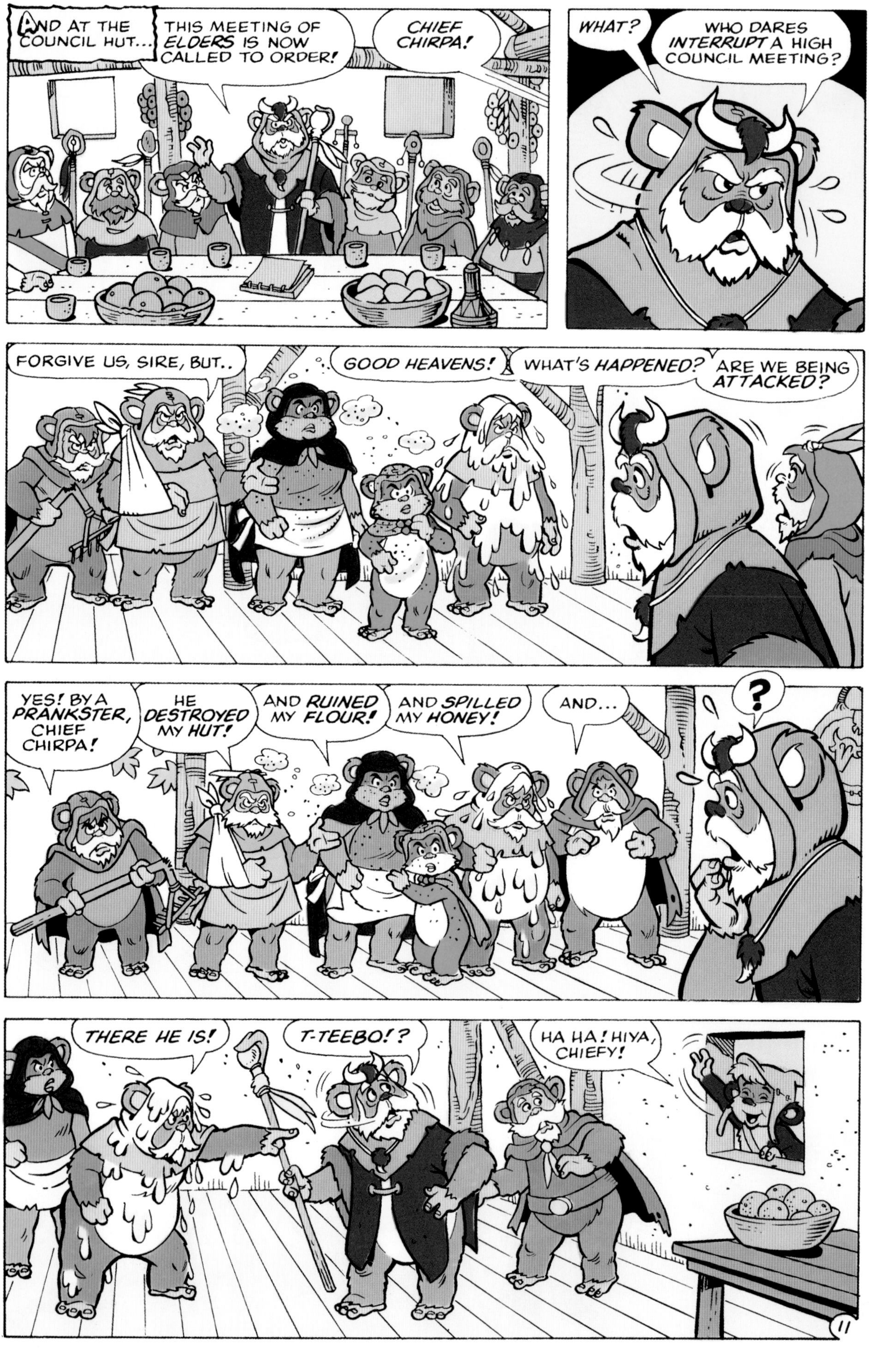
AND AT THE COUNCIL HUT...
THIS MEETING OF ELDERS IS NOW CALLED TO ORDER!
CHIEF CHIRPA!
WHAT?
WHO DARES INTERRUPT A HIGH COUNCIL MEETING?
FORGIVE US, SIRE, BUT..
GOOD HEAVENS!
WHAT'S HAPPENED?
ARE WE BEING ATTACKED?
YES! BY A PRANKSTER, CHIEF CHIRPA!
HE DESTROYED MY HUT!
AND RUINED MY FLOUR!
AND SPILLED MY HONEY!
AND...
?
THERE HE IS!
T-TEEBO!?
HA HA! HIYA, CHIEFY!
11

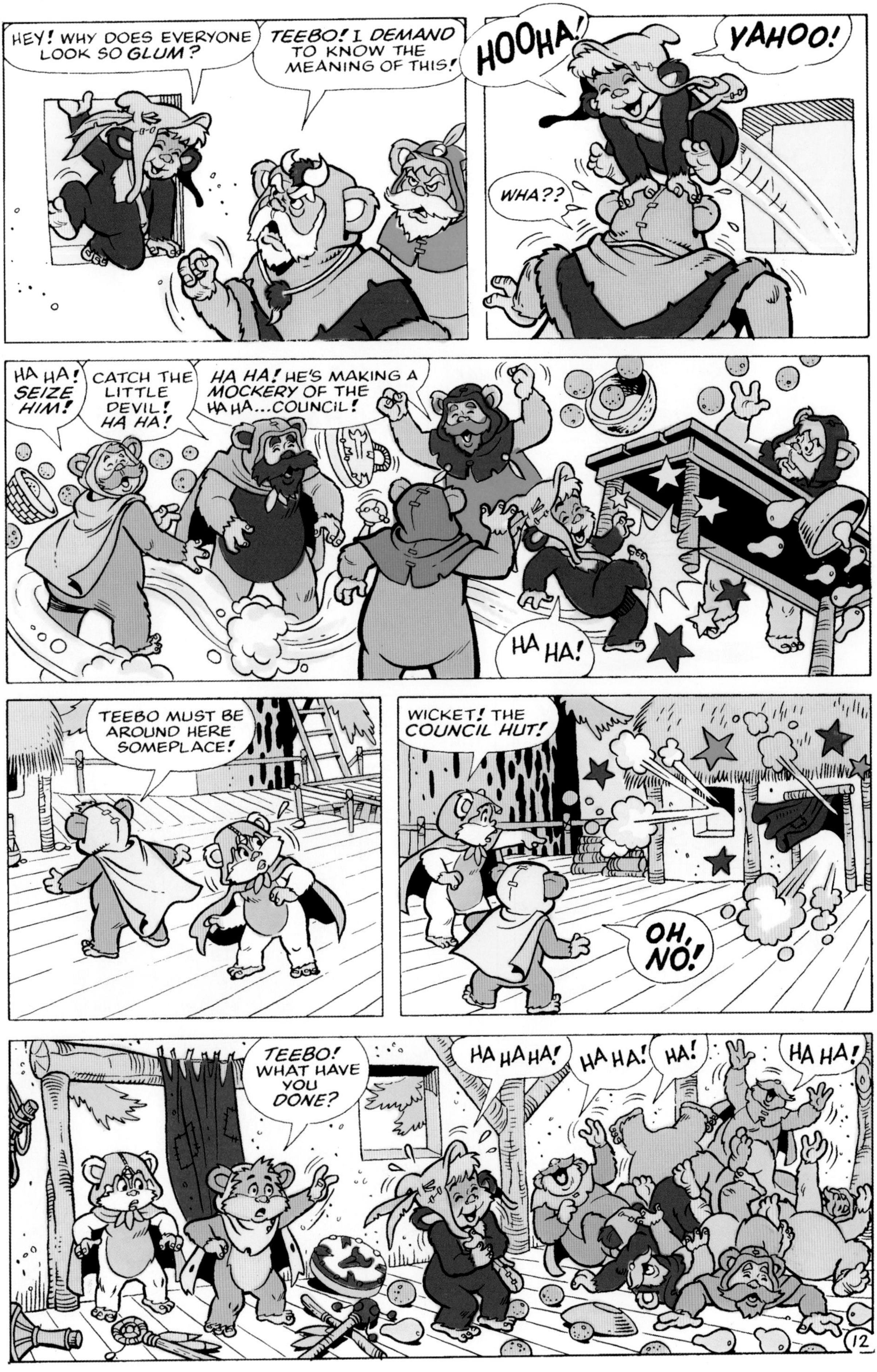
HEY! WHY DOES EVERYONE LOOK SO GLUM?
TEEBO! I DEMAND TO KNOW THE MEANING OF THIS!
HOOHA!
YAHOO!
WHA??
HA HA! SEIZE HIM!
CATCH THE LITTLE DEVIL! HA HA!
HA HA! HE'S MAKING A MOCKERY OF THE HA HA... COUNCIL!
HA HA!
TEEBO MUST BE AROUND HERE SOMEPLACE!
WICKET! THE COUNCIL HUT!
OH, NO!
TEEBO! WHAT HAVE YOU DONE?
HA HA HA!
HA HA!
HA!
HA HA!
12

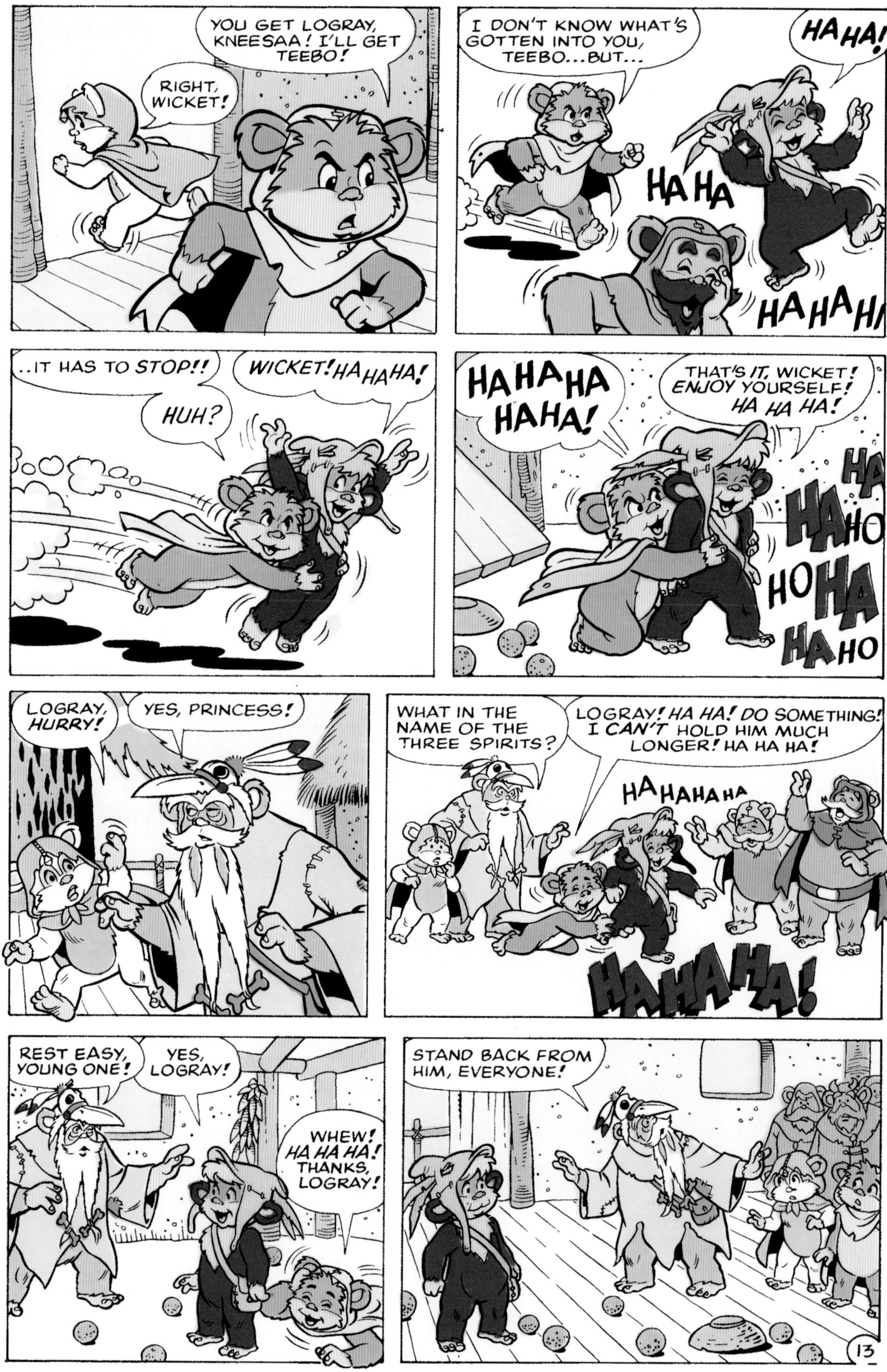
YOU GET LOGRAY, KNEESAA! I'LL GET TEEBO!
RIGHT, WICKET!
I DON'T KNOW WHAT'S GOTTEN INTO YOU, TEEBO...BUT...
HA HA!
HA HA
HA HA HA
..IT HAS TO STOP!!
WICKET! HA HA HA!
HUH?
HA HA HA HA HA!
THAT'S IT, WICKET! ENJOY YOURSELF! HA HA HA!
HA HA HO HO HA HA HO
LOGRAY, HURRY!
YES, PRINCESS!
WHAT IN THE NAME OF THE THREE SPIRITS?
LOGRAY! HA HA! DO SOMETHING! I CAN'T HOLD HIM MUCH LONGER! HA HA HA!
HA HA HA HA HA
HA HA HA HA!
REST EASY, YOUNG ONE!
YES, LOGRAY!
WHEW! HA HA HA! THANKS, LOGRAY!
STAND BACK FROM HIM, EVERYONE!
13

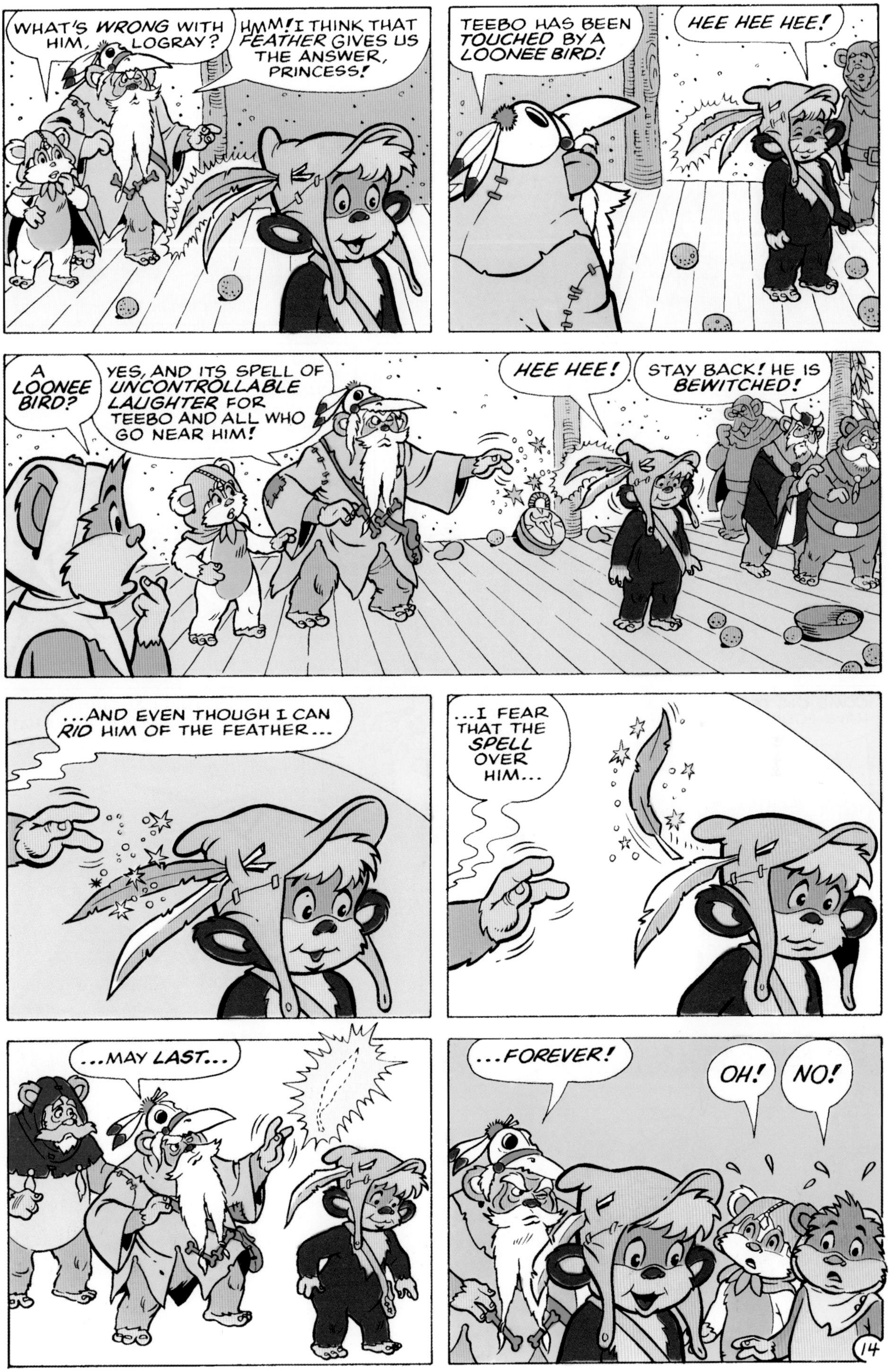

WHAT'S WRONG WITH HIM, LOGRAY?
HMM! I THINK THAT FEATHER GIVES US THE ANSWER, PRINCESS!
TEEBO HAS BEEN TOUCHED BY A LOONEE BIRD!
HEE HEE HEE!
A LOONEE BIRD?
YES, AND ITS SPELL OF UNCONTROLLABLE LAUGHTER FOR TEEBO AND ALL WHO GO NEAR HIM!
HEE HEE!
STAY BACK! HE IS BEWITCHED!
...AND EVEN THOUGH I CAN RID HIM OF THE FEATHER...
...I FEAR THAT THE SPELL OVER HIM...
...MAY LAST...
...FOREVER!
OH!
NO!
14

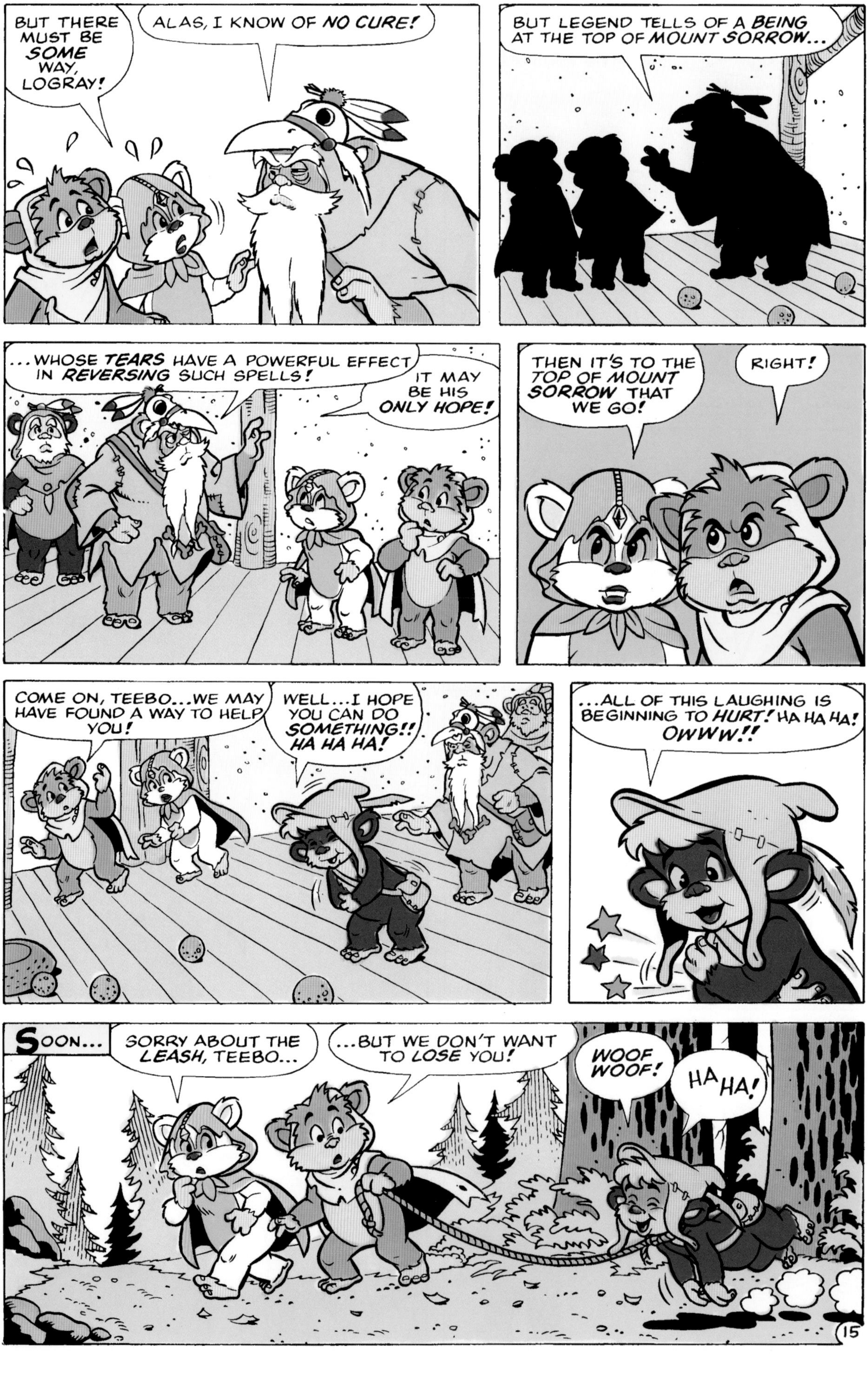
BUT THERE MUST BE SOME WAY, LOGRAY!
ALAS, I KNOW OF NO CURE!
BUT LEGEND TELLS OF A BEING AT THE TOP OF MOUNT SORROW...
...WHOSE TEARS HAVE A POWERFUL EFFECT IN REVERSING SUCH SPELLS!
IT MAY BE HIS ONLY HOPE!
THEN IT'S TO THE TOP OF MOUNT SORROW THAT WE GO!
RIGHT!
COME ON, TEEBO...WE MAY HAVE FOUND A WAY TO HELP YOU!
WELL...I HOPE YOU CAN DO SOMETHING!! HA HA HA!
...ALL OF THIS LAUGHING IS BEGINNING TO HURT! HA HA HA! OWWW!!
SOON...
SORRY ABOUT THE LEASH, TEEBO...
...BUT WE DON'T WANT TO LOSE YOU!
WOOF WOOF!
HA HA!
15

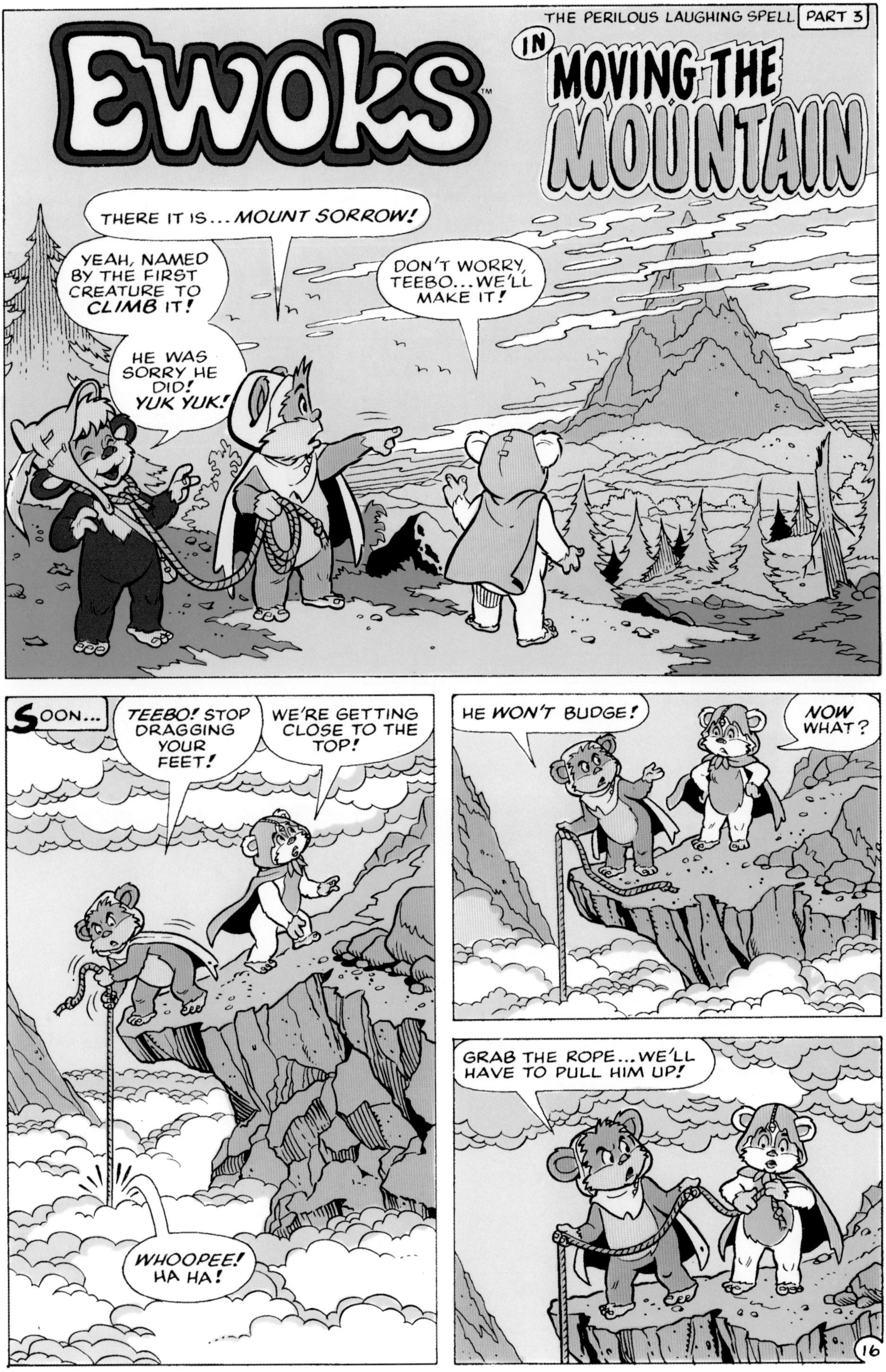
THE PERILOUS LAUGHING SPELL PART 3
EWOKS™ IN MOVING THE MOUNTAIN
THERE IT IS... MOUNT SORROW!
YEAH, NAMED BY THE FIRST CREATURE TO CLIMB IT!
HE WAS SORRY HE DID! YUK YUK!
DON'T WORRY, TEEBO... WE'LL MAKE IT!
SOON...
TEEBO! STOP DRAGGING YOUR FEET!
WE'RE GETTING CLOSE TO THE TOP!
WHOOPEE! HA HA!
HE WON'T BUDGE!
NOW WHAT?
GRAB THE ROPE... WE'LL HAVE TO PULL HIM UP!
16

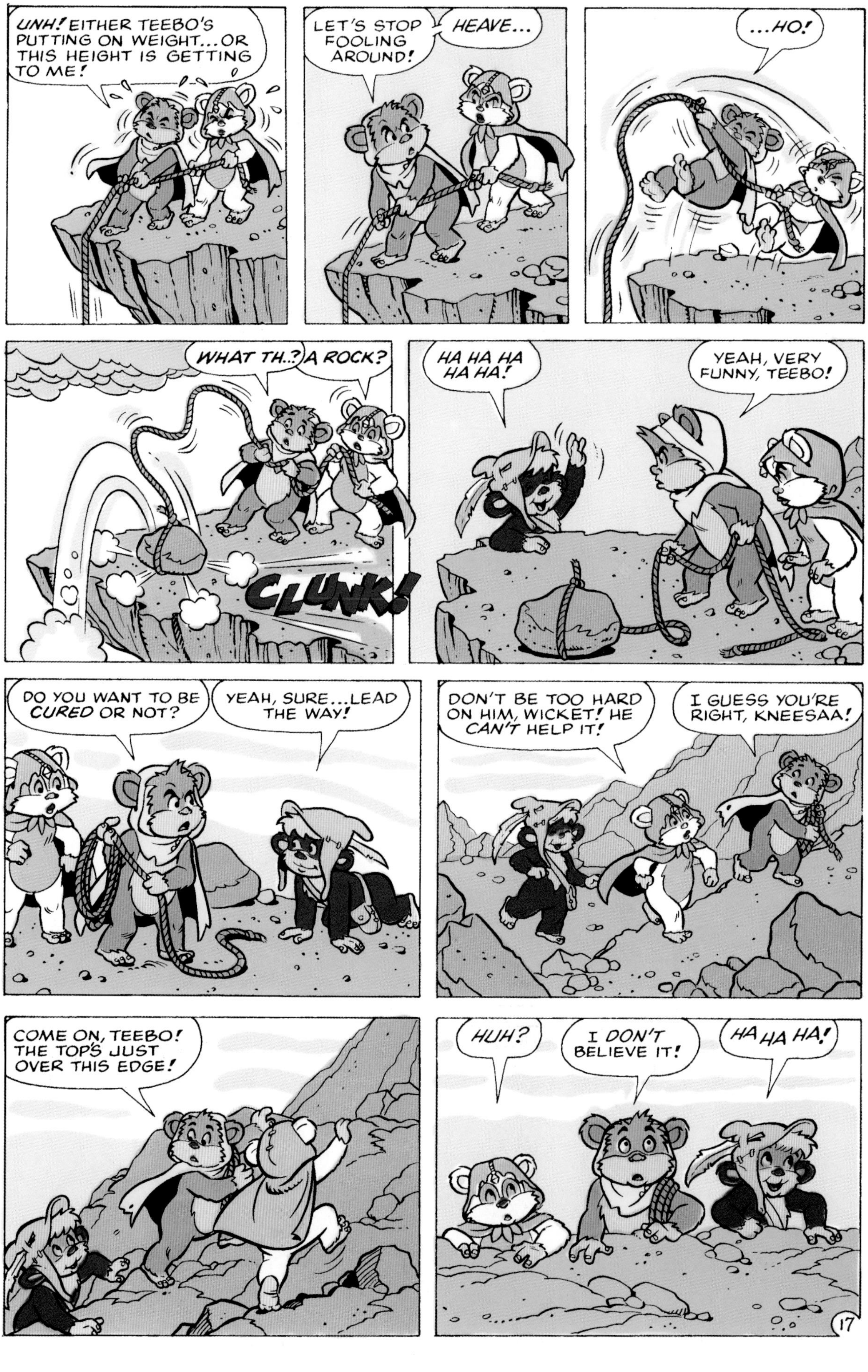
UNH! EITHER TEEBO'S PUTTING ON WEIGHT...OR THIS HEIGHT IS GETTING TO ME!
LET'S STOP FOOLING AROUND!
HEAVE...
...HO!
WHAT TH..?
A ROCK?
CLUNK!
HA HA HA HA HA!
YEAH, VERY FUNNY, TEEBO!
DO YOU WANT TO BE CURED OR NOT?
YEAH, SURE...LEAD THE WAY!
DON'T BE TOO HARD ON HIM, WICKET! HE CAN'T HELP IT!
I GUESS YOU'RE RIGHT, KNEESAA!
COME ON, TEEBO! THE TOP'S JUST OVER THIS EDGE!
HUH?
I DON'T BELIEVE IT!
HA HA HA!
17

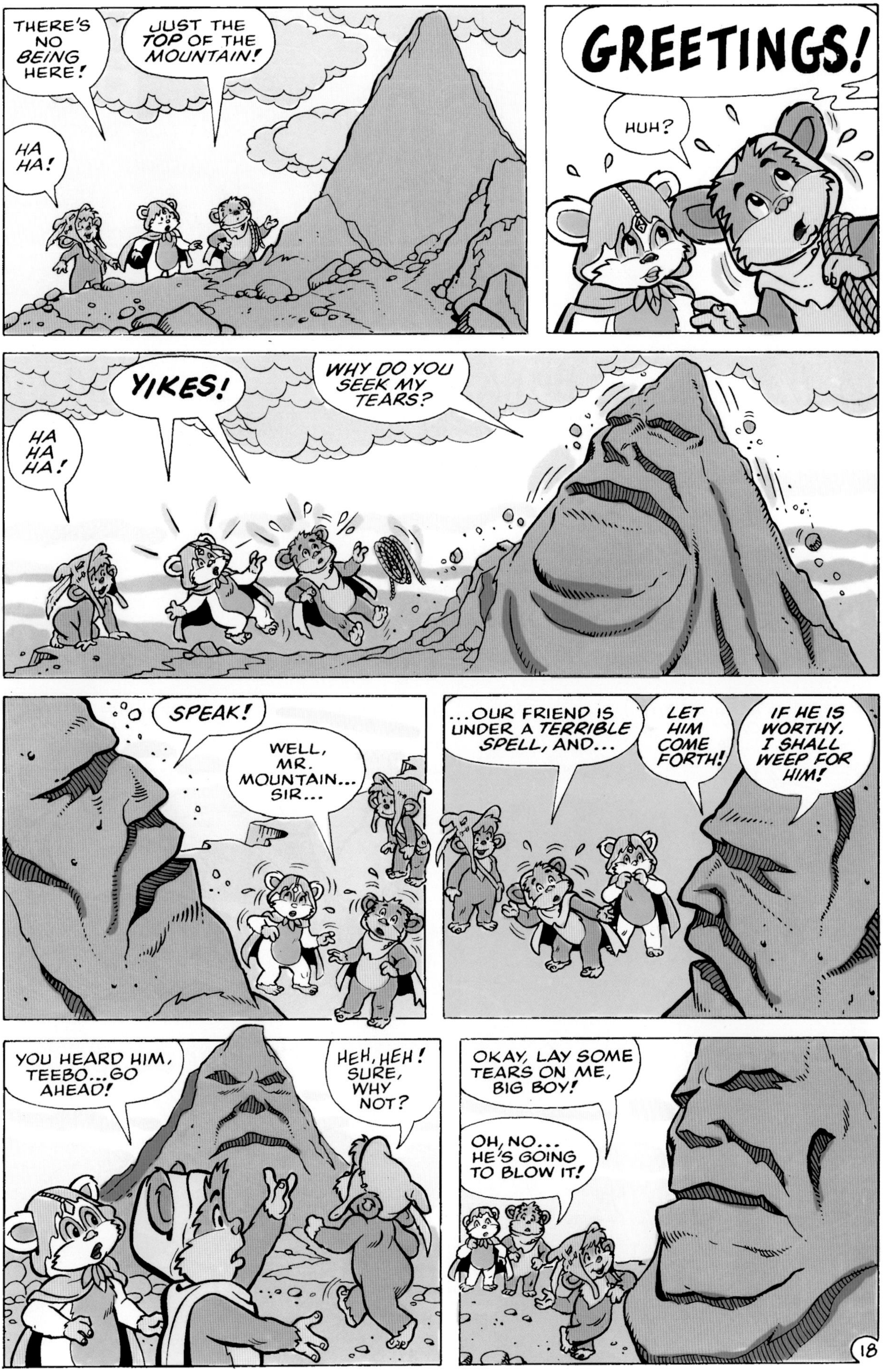

THERE'S NO BEING HERE!
JUST THE TOP OF THE MOUNTAIN!
HA HA!
GREETINGS!
HUH?
HA HA HA!
YIKES!
WHY DO YOU SEEK MY TEARS?
SPEAK!
WELL, MR. MOUNTAIN... SIR...
...OUR FRIEND IS UNDER A TERRIBLE SPELL, AND...
LET HIM COME FORTH!
IF HE IS WORTHY, I SHALL WEEP FOR HIM!
YOU HEARD HIM, TEEBO...GO AHEAD!
HEH, HEH! SURE, WHY NOT?
OKAY, LAY SOME TEARS ON ME, BIG BOY!
OH, NO... HE'S GOING TO BLOW IT!
18

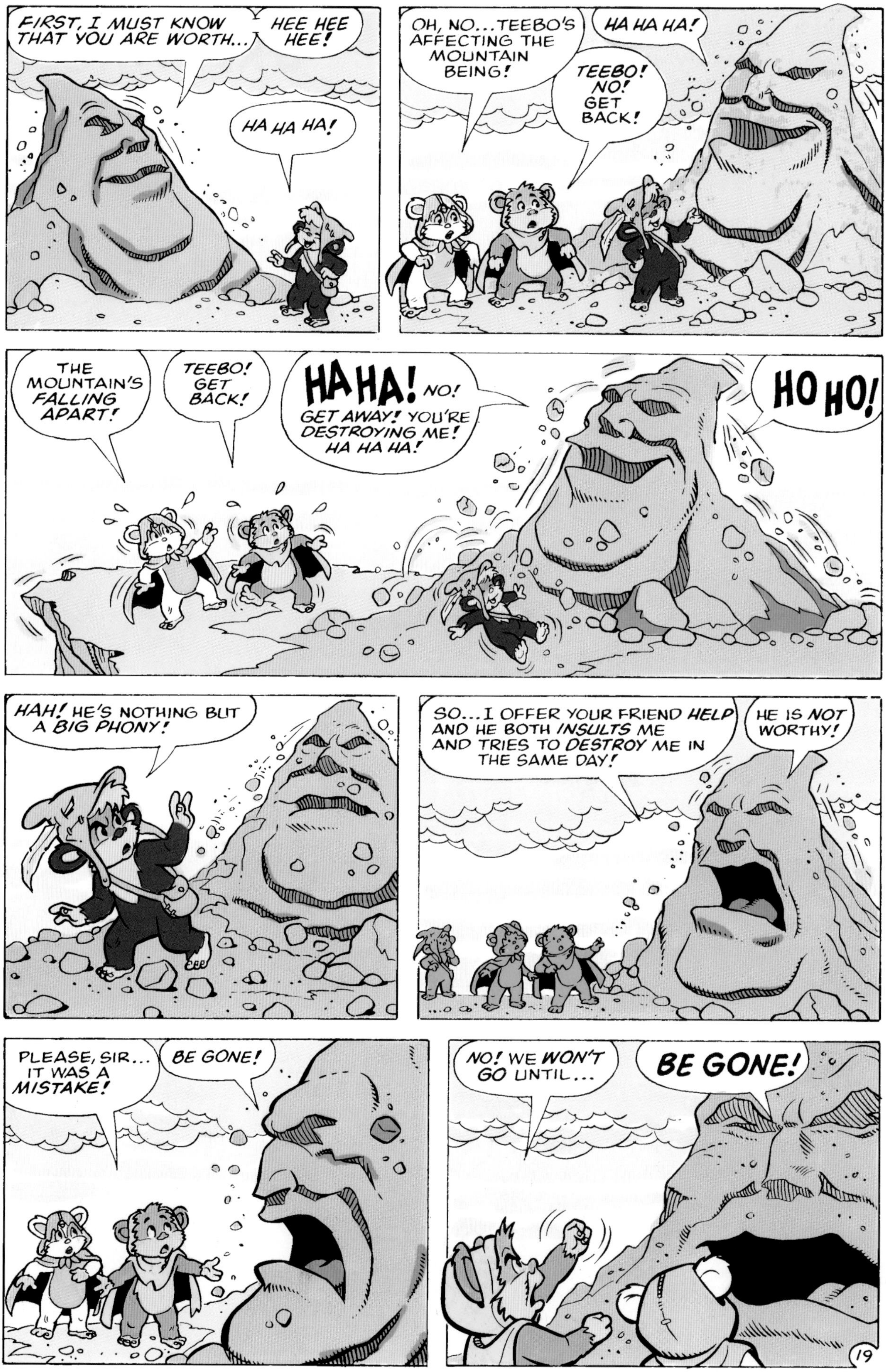
FIRST, I MUST KNOW THAT YOU ARE WORTH...
HEE HEE HEE!
HA HA HA!
OH, NO...TEEBO'S AFFECTING THE MOUNTAIN BEING!
HA HA HA!
TEEBO! NO! GET BACK!
THE MOUNTAIN'S FALLING APART!
TEEBO! GET BACK!
HAHA! NO! GET AWAY! YOU'RE DESTROYING ME! HA HA HA!
HO HO!
HAH! HE'S NOTHING BUT A BIG PHONY!
SO...I OFFER YOUR FRIEND HELP AND HE BOTH INSULTS ME AND TRIES TO DESTROY ME IN THE SAME DAY!
HE IS NOT WORTHY!
PLEASE, SIR... IT WAS A MISTAKE!
BE GONE!
NO! WE WON'T GO UNTIL...
BE GONE!
19

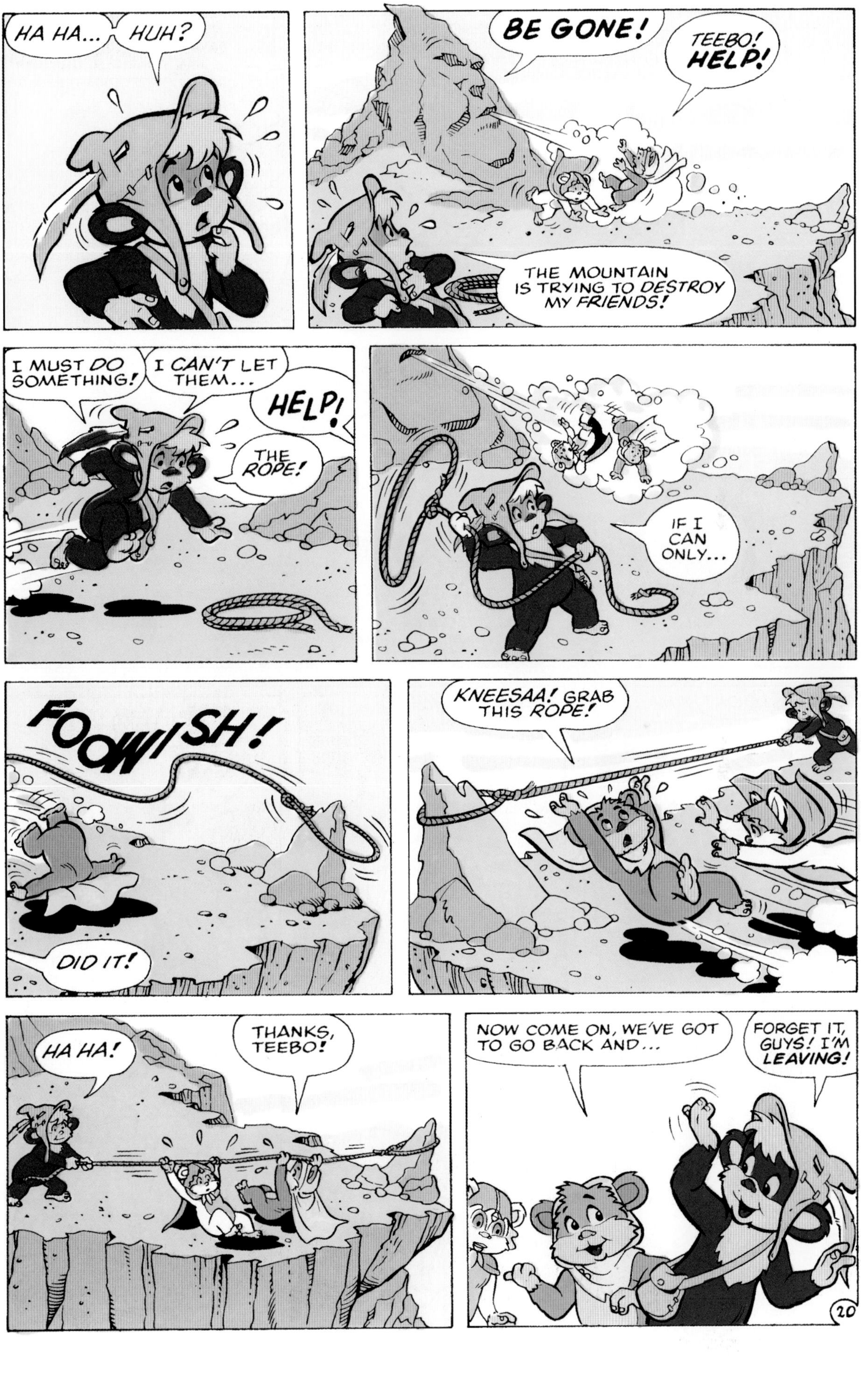
HA HA...
HUH?
BE GONE!
TEEBO! HELP!
THE MOUNTAIN IS TRYING TO DESTROY MY FRIENDS!
I MUST DO SOMETHING!
I CAN'T LET THEM...
HELP!
THE ROPE!
IF I CAN ONLY...
FOOWISH!
DID IT!
KNEESAA! GRAB THIS ROPE!
HA HA!
THANKS, TEEBO!
NOW COME ON, WE'VE GOT TO GO BACK AND...
FORGET IT, GUYS! I'M LEAVING!
20

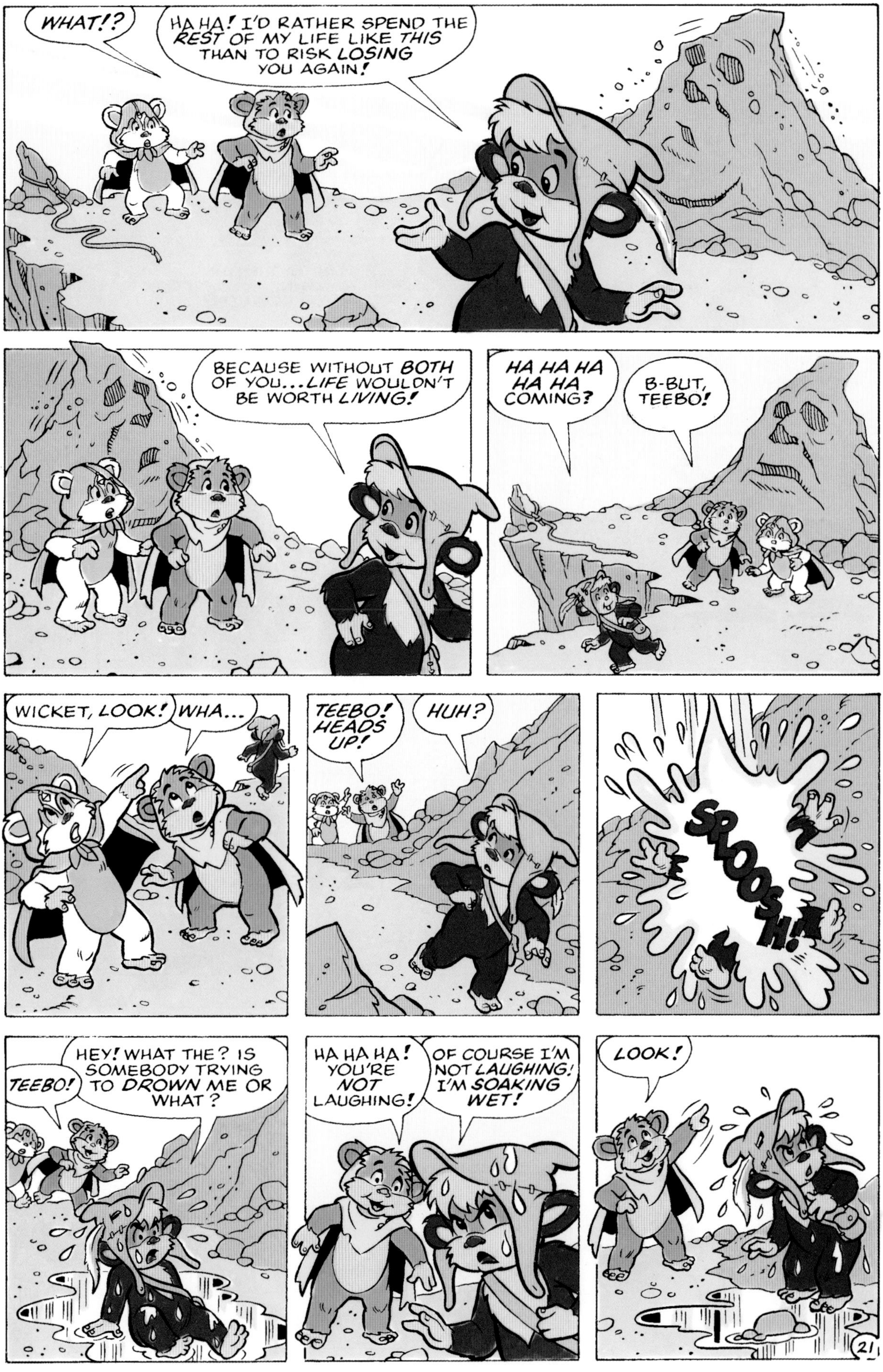
WHAT!?
HA HA! I'D RATHER SPEND THE REST OF MY LIFE LIKE THIS THAN TO RISK LOSING YOU AGAIN!
BECAUSE WITHOUT BOTH OF YOU...LIFE WOULDN'T BE WORTH LIVING!
HA HA HA HA HA COMING?
B-BUT, TEEBO!
WICKET, LOOK!
WHA...
TEEBO! HEADS UP!
HUH?
SPLOOSH!!
TEEBO!
HEY! WHAT THE? IS SOMEBODY TRYING TO DROWN ME OR WHAT?
HA HA HA! YOU'RE NOT LAUGHING!
OF COURSE I'M NOT LAUGHING! I'M SOAKING WET!
LOOK!
21

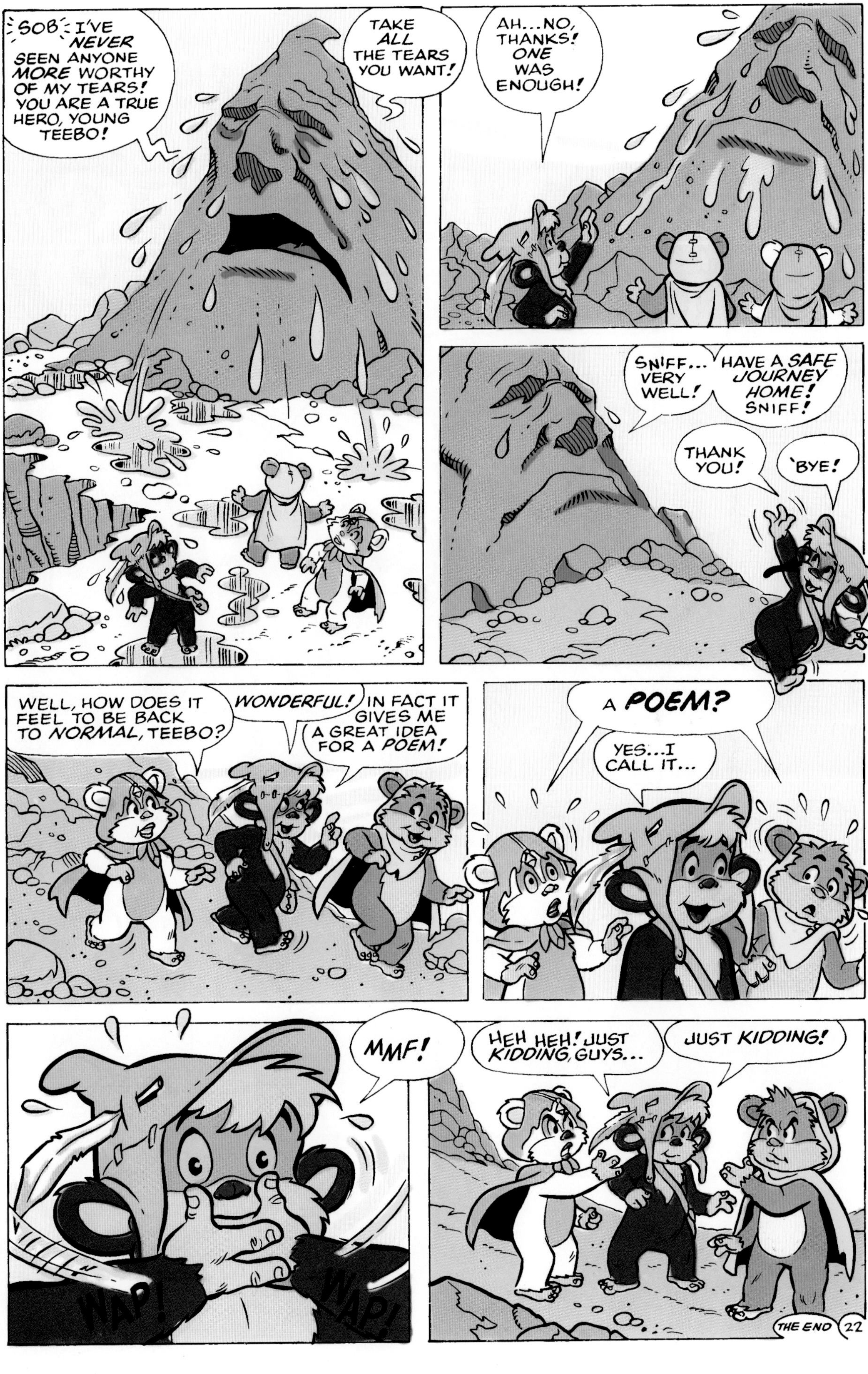
SOB I'VE NEVER SEEN ANYONE MORE WORTHY OF MY TEARS! YOU ARE A TRUE HERO, YOUNG TEEBO!
TAKE ALL THE TEARS YOU WANT!
AH...NO, THANKS! ONE WAS ENOUGH!
SNIFF... VERY WELL!
HAVE A SAFE JOURNEY HOME! SNIFF!
THANK YOU!
`BYE!
WELL, HOW DOES IT FEEL TO BE BACK TO NORMAL, TEEBO?
WONDERFUL!
IN FACT IT GIVES ME A GREAT IDEA FOR A POEM!
A POEM?
YES...I CALL IT...
MMF!
WAP!
WAP!
HEH HEH! JUST KIDDING, GUYS...
JUST KIDDING!
THE END
22

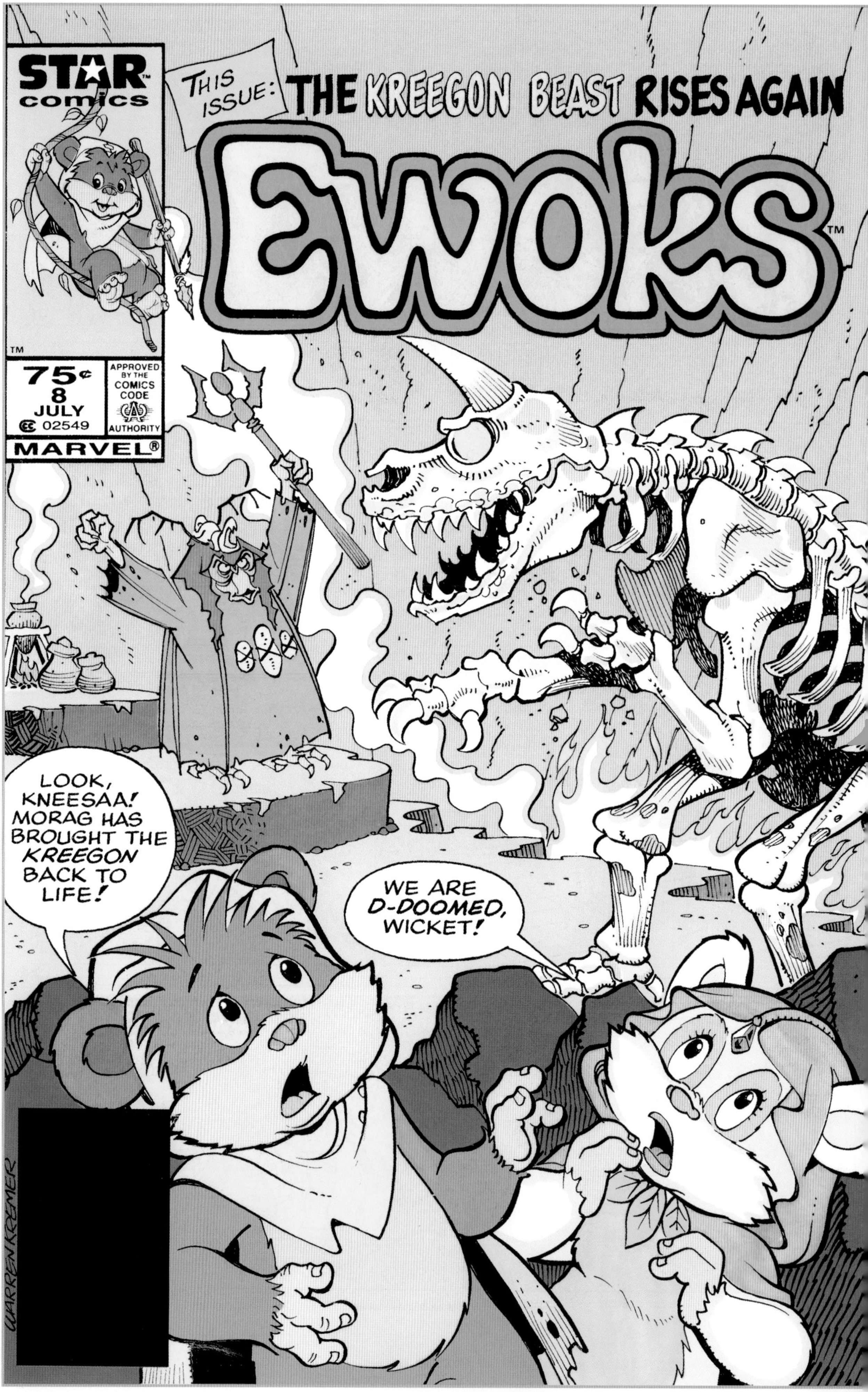
STAR comics
THIS ISSUE: THE KREEGON BEAST RISES AGAIN
EWOKS™
75¢
8
JULY
02549
APPROVED BY THE COMICS CODE AUTHORITY
MARVEL®
LOOK, KNEESAA! MORAG HAS BROUGHT THE KREEGON BACK TO LIFE!
WE ARE D-DOOMED, WICKET!
WARREN KREMER

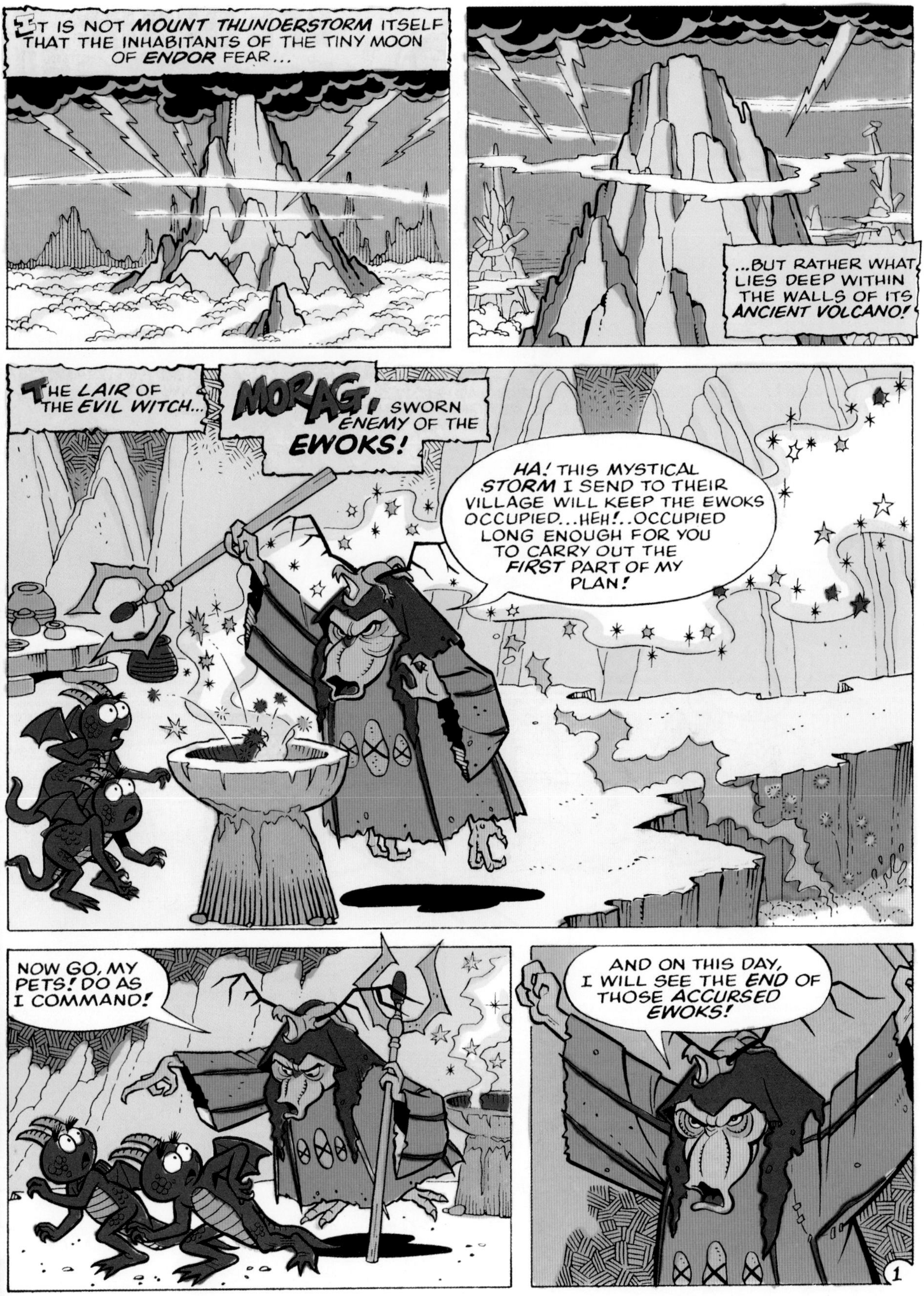
IT IS NOT MOUNT THUNDERSTORM ITSELF THAT THE INHABITANTS OF THE TINY MOON OF ENDOR FEAR...
...BUT RATHER WHAT LIES DEEP WITHIN THE WALLS OF ITS ANCIENT VOLCANO!
THE LAIR OF THE EVIL WITCH...
MORAG! SWORN ENEMY OF THE EWOKS!
HA! THIS MYSTICAL STORM I SEND TO THEIR VILLAGE WILL KEEP THE EWOKS OCCUPIED...HEH!..OCCUPIED LONG ENOUGH FOR YOU TO CARRY OUT THE FIRST PART OF MY PLAN!
NOW GO, MY PETS! DO AS I COMMAND!
AND ON THIS DAY, I WILL SEE THE END OF THOSE ACCURSED EWOKS!
1

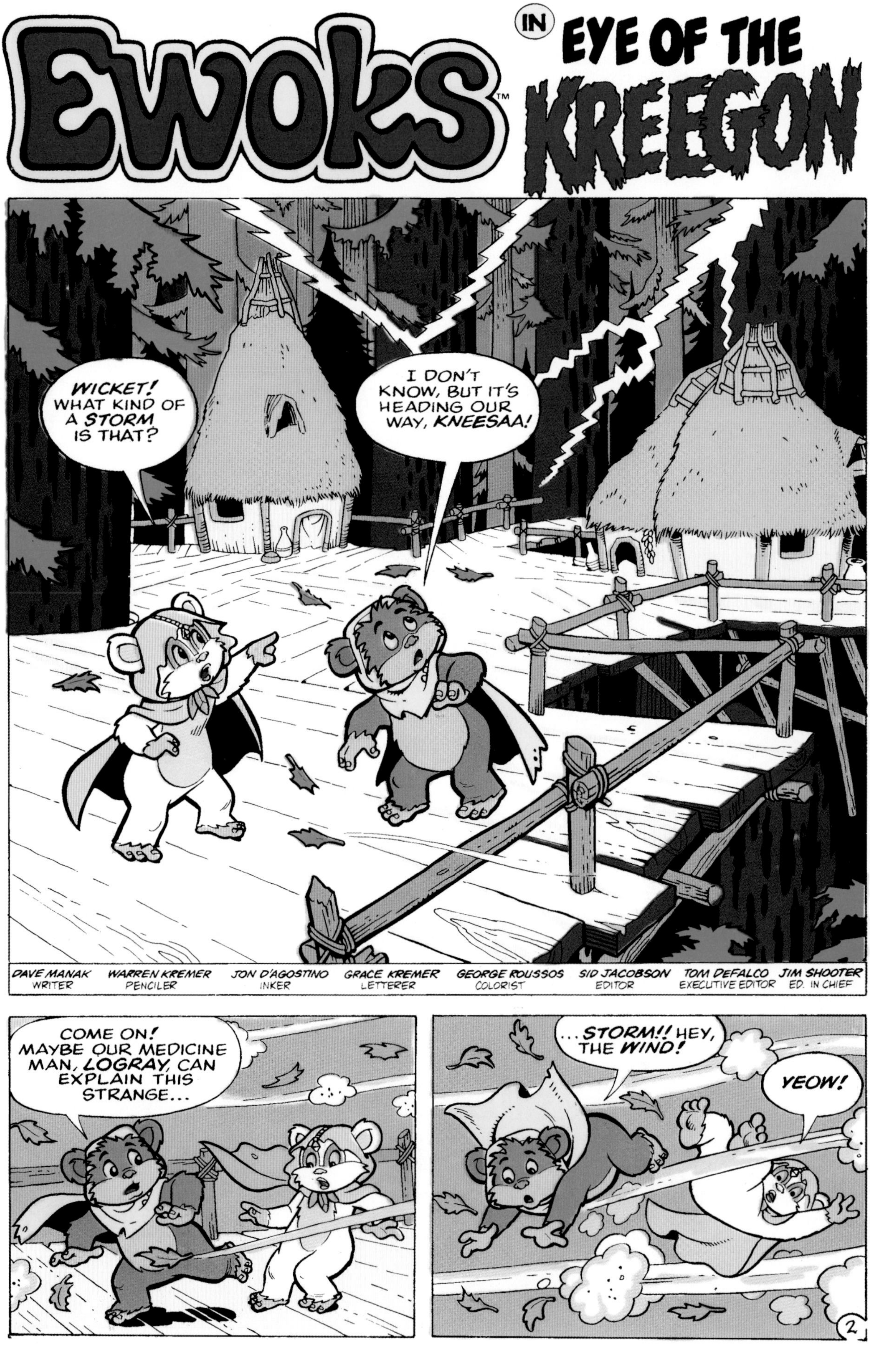
EWOKS™ IN EYE OF THE KREEGON
WICKET! WHAT KIND OF A STORM IS THAT?
I DON'T KNOW, BUT IT'S HEADING OUR WAY, KNEESAA!
DAVE MANAK WRITER
WARREN KREMER PENCILER
JON D'AGOSTINO INKER
GRACE KREMER LETTERER
GEORGE ROUSSOS COLORIST
SID JACOBSON EDITOR
TOM DEFALCO EXECUTIVE EDITOR
JIM SHOOTER ED. IN CHIEF
COME ON! MAYBE OUR MEDICINE MAN, LOGRAY, CAN EXPLAIN THIS STRANGE...
...STORM!! HEY, THE WIND!
YEOW!
2

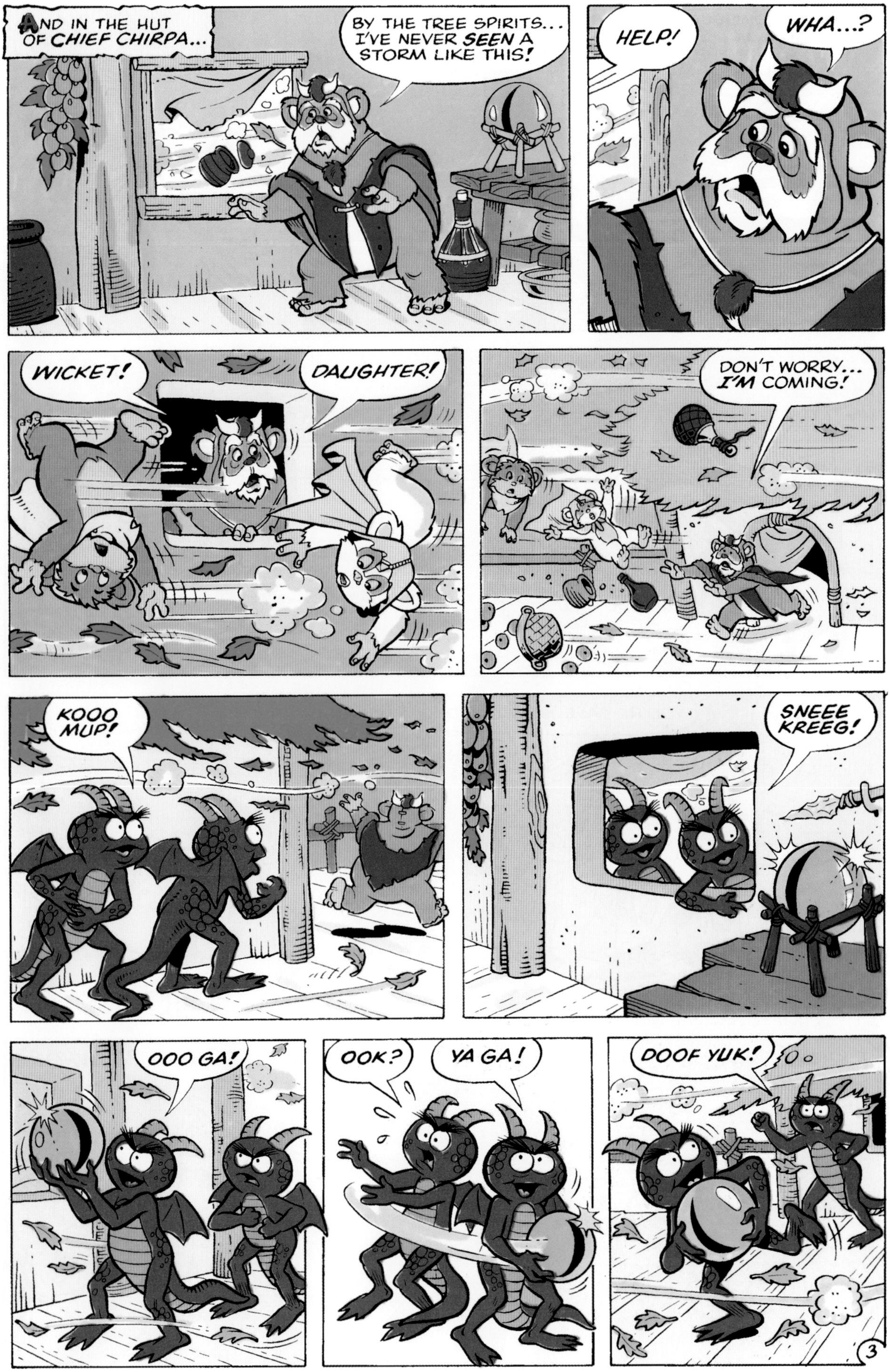
AND IN THE HUT OF CHIEF CHIRPA...
BY THE TREE SPIRITS... I'VE NEVER SEEN A STORM LIKE THIS!
HELP!
WHA...?
WICKET!
DAUGHTER!
DON'T WORRY... I'M COMING!
KOOO MUP!
SNEEE KREEG!
OOO GA!
OOK?
YA GA!
DOOF YUK!
3

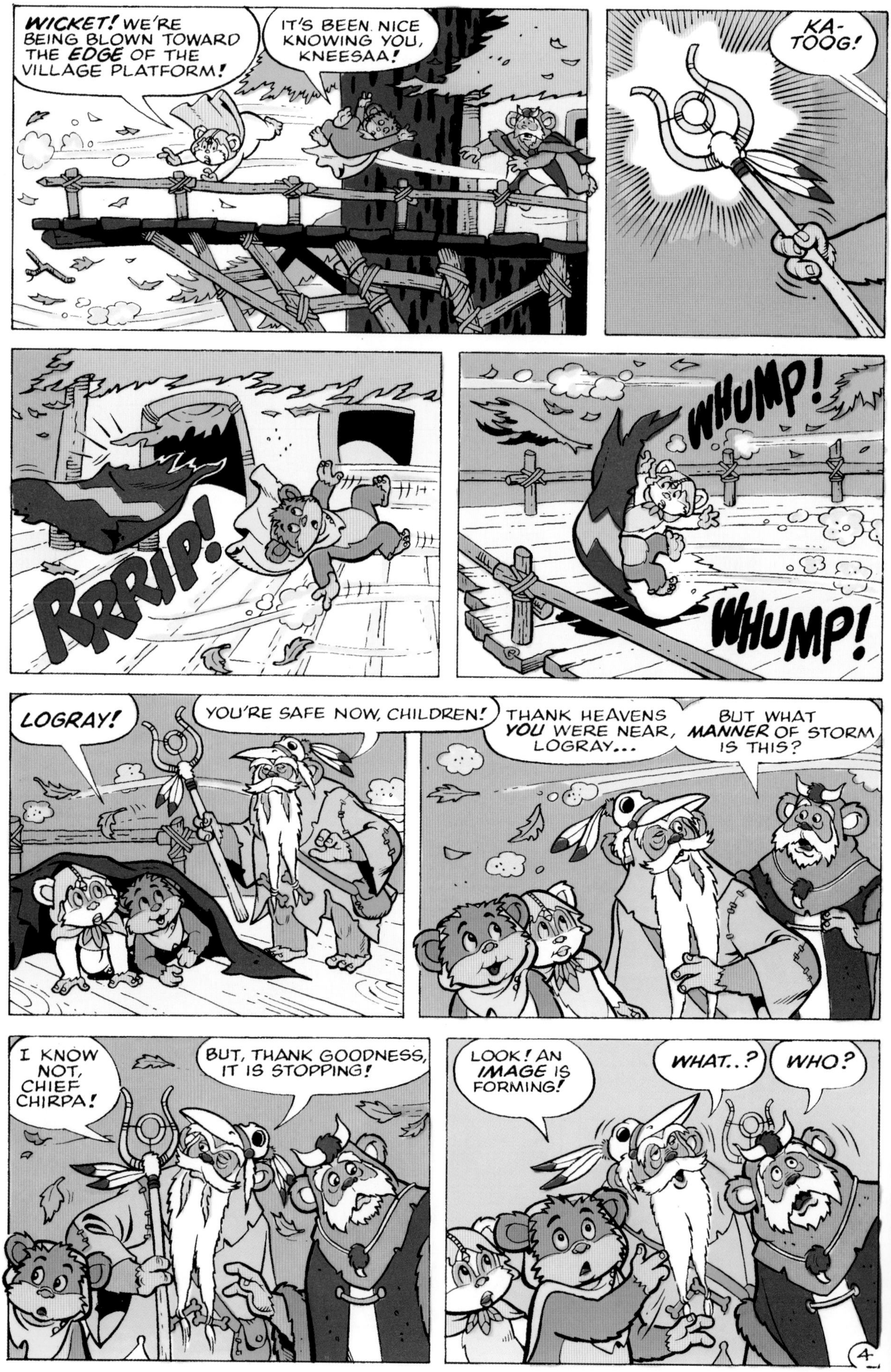
WICKET! WE'RE BEING BLOWN TOWARD THE EDGE OF THE VILLAGE PLATFORM!
IT'S BEEN NICE KNOWING YOU, KNEESAA!
KA-TOOG!
RRRIP!
WHUMP!
WHUMP!
LOGRAY!
YOU'RE SAFE NOW, CHILDREN!
THANK HEAVENS YOU WERE NEAR, LOGRAY...
BUT WHAT MANNER OF STORM IS THIS?
I KNOW NOT, CHIEF CHIRPA!
BUT, THANK GOODNESS, IT IS STOPPING!
LOOK! AN IMAGE IS FORMING!
WHAT..?
WHO?
4

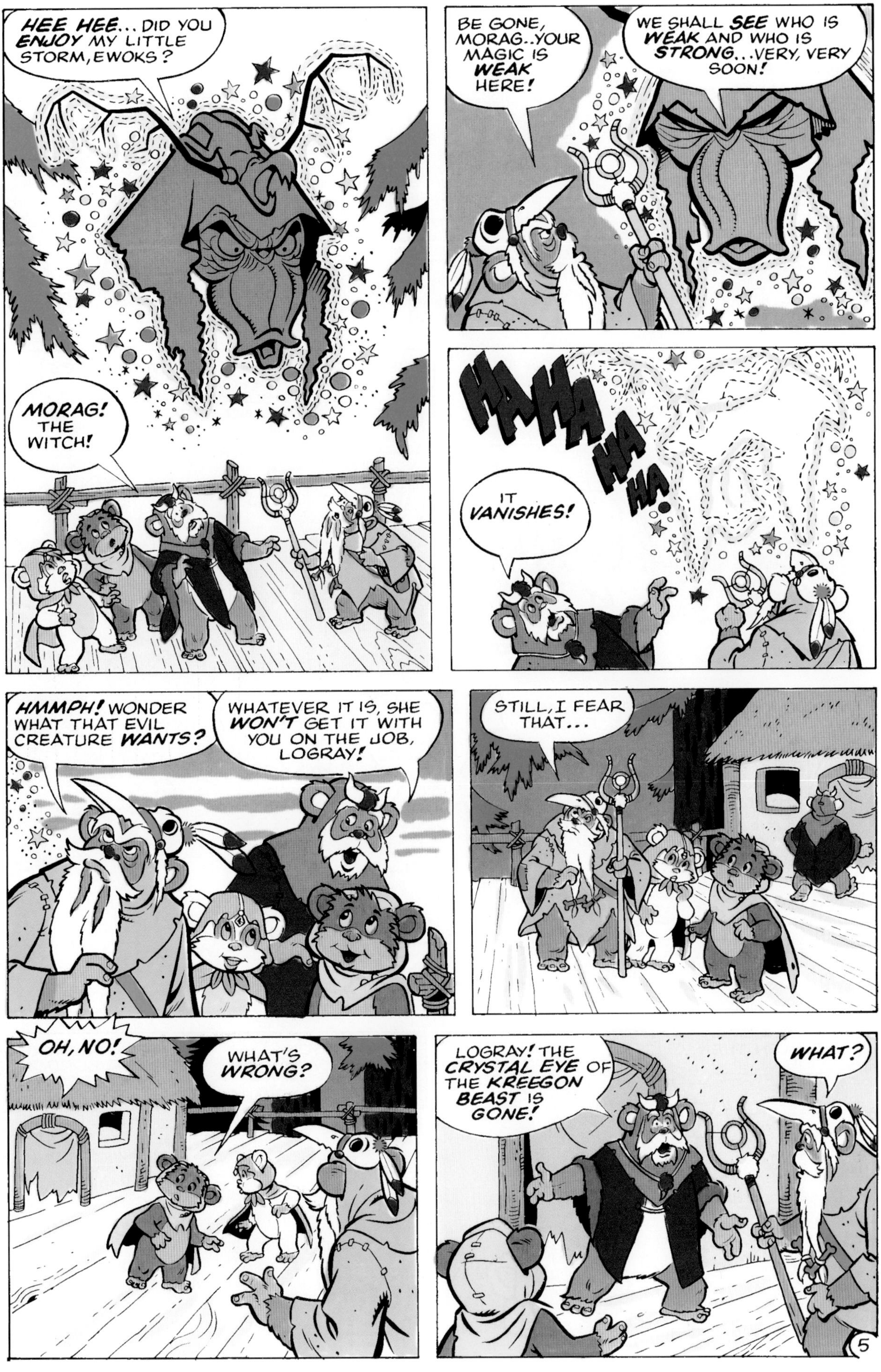
HEE HEE... DID YOU ENJOY MY LITTLE STORM, EWOKS?
MORAG! THE WITCH!
BE GONE, MORAG..YOUR MAGIC IS WEAK HERE!
WE SHALL SEE WHO IS WEAK AND WHO IS STRONG... VERY, VERY SOON!
HA HA HA HA HA HA
IT VANISHES!
HMMPH! WONDER WHAT THAT EVIL CREATURE WANTS?
WHATEVER IT IS, SHE WON'T GET IT WITH YOU ON THE JOB, LOGRAY!
STILL, I FEAR THAT...
OH, NO!
WHAT'S WRONG?
LOGRAY! THE CRYSTAL EYE OF THE KREEGON BEAST IS GONE!
WHAT?
5

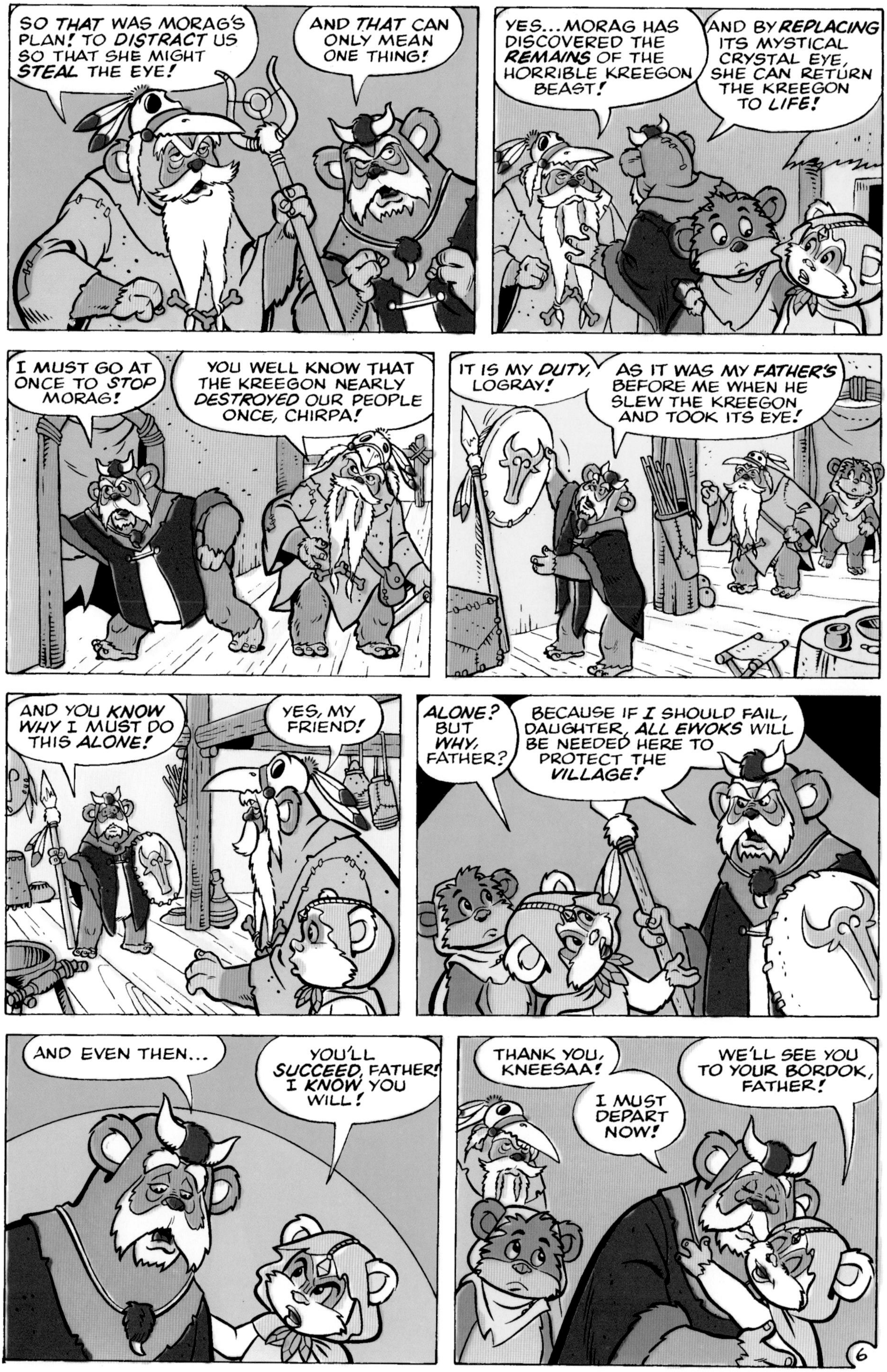
SO THAT WAS MORAG'S PLAN! TO DISTRACT US SO THAT SHE MIGHT STEAL THE EYE!
AND THAT CAN ONLY MEAN ONE THING!
YES... MORAG HAS DISCOVERED THE REMAINS OF THE HORRIBLE KREEGON BEAST!
AND BY REPLACING ITS MYSTICAL CRYSTAL EYE, SHE CAN RETURN THE KREEGON TO LIFE!
I MUST GO AT ONCE TO STOP MORAG!
YOU WELL KNOW THAT THE KREEGON NEARLY DESTROYED OUR PEOPLE ONCE, CHIRPA!
IT IS MY DUTY, LOGRAY!
AS IT WAS MY FATHER'S BEFORE ME WHEN HE SLEW THE KREEGON AND TOOK ITS EYE!
AND YOU KNOW WHY I MUST DO THIS ALONE!
YES, MY FRIEND!
ALONE? BUT WHY, FATHER?
BECAUSE IF I SHOULD FAIL, DAUGHTER, ALL EWOKS WILL BE NEEDED HERE TO PROTECT THE VILLAGE!
AND EVEN THEN...
YOU'LL SUCCEED, FATHER! I KNOW YOU WILL!
THANK YOU, KNEESAA!
I MUST DEPART NOW!
WE'LL SEE YOU TO YOUR BORDOK, FATHER!
6

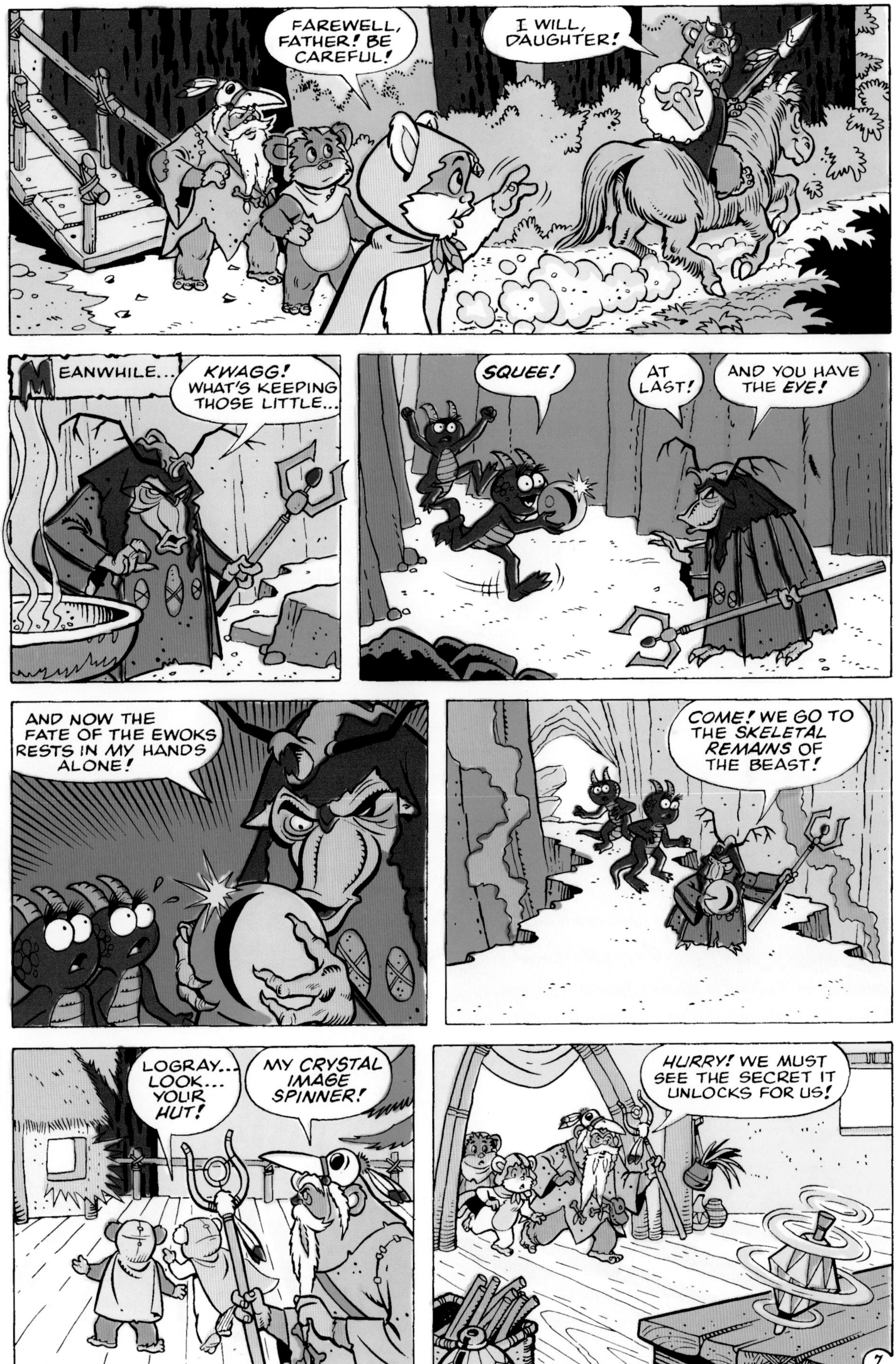
FAREWELL, FATHER! BE CAREFUL!
I WILL, DAUGHTER!
MEANWHILE...
KWAGG! WHAT'S KEEPING THOSE LITTLE...
SQUEE!
AT LAST!
AND YOU HAVE THE EYE!
AND NOW THE FATE OF THE EWOKS RESTS IN MY HANDS ALONE!
COME! WE GO TO THE SKELETAL REMAINS OF THE BEAST!
LOGRAY... LOOK... YOUR HUT!
MY CRYSTAL IMAGE SPINNER!
HURRY! WE MUST SEE THE SECRET IT UNLOCKS FOR US!
7

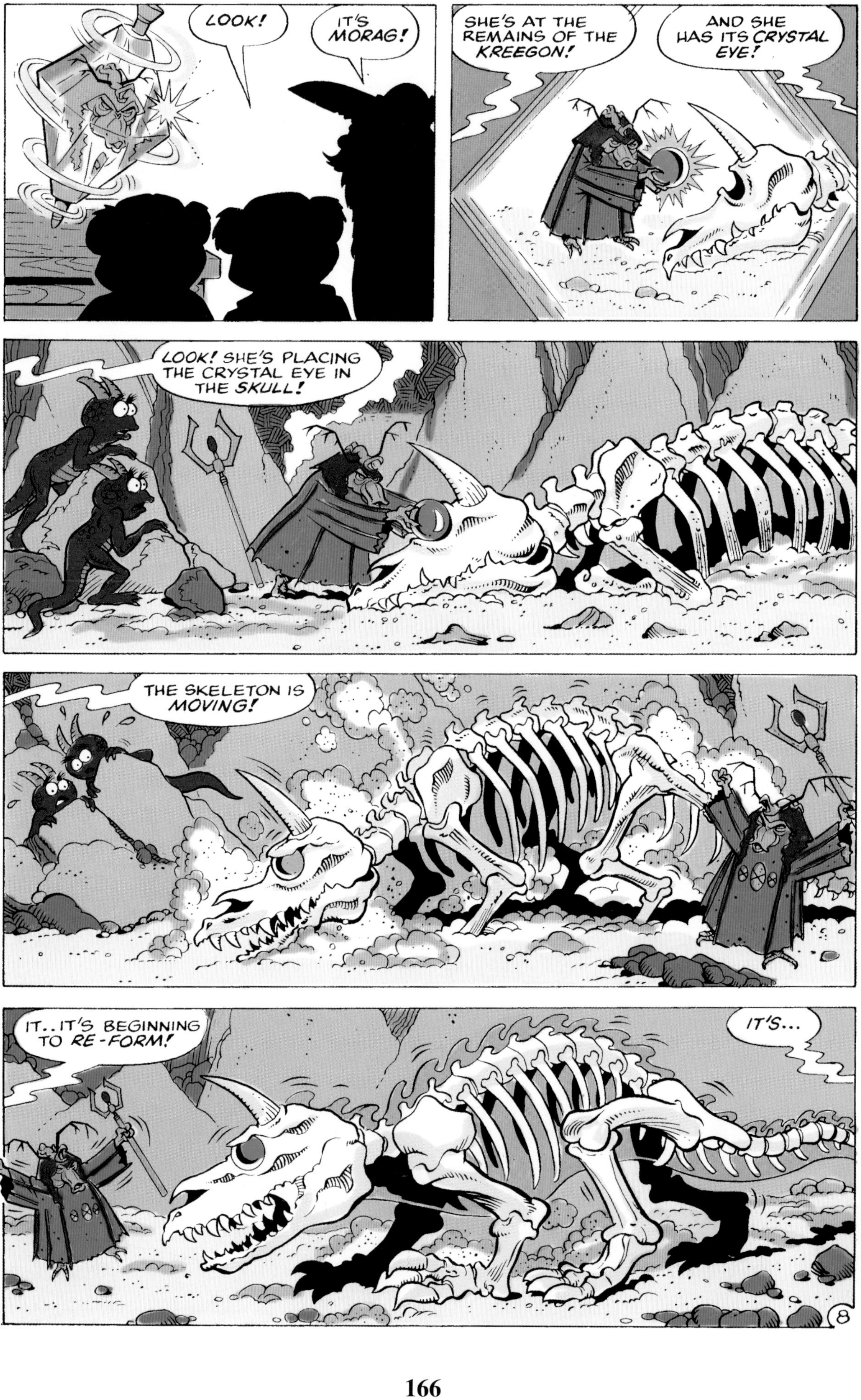
LOOK!
IT'S MORAG!
SHE'S AT THE REMAINS OF THE KREEGON!
AND SHE HAS ITS CRYSTAL EYE!
LOOK! SHE'S PLACING THE CRYSTAL EYE IN THE SKULL!
THE SKELETON IS MOVING!
IT..IT'S BEGINNING TO RE-FORM!
IT'S...
8

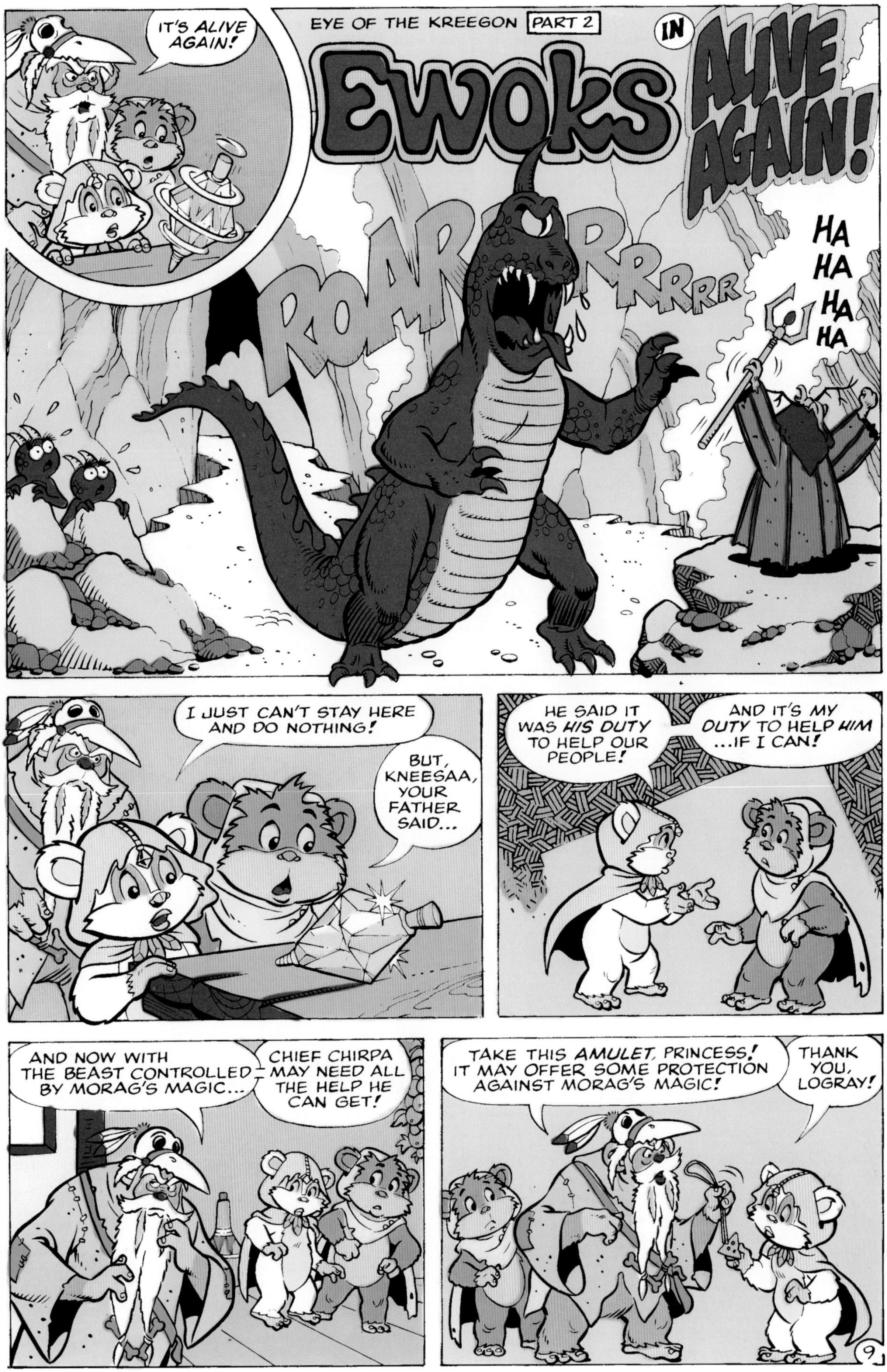
IT'S ALIVE AGAIN!
EYE OF THE KREEGON PART 2
Ewoks
IN
ALIVE AGAIN!
ROARRRRRRR
HA HA HA HA HA
I JUST CAN'T STAY HERE AND DO NOTHING!
BUT, KNEESAA, YOUR FATHER SAID...
HE SAID IT WAS HIS DUTY TO HELP OUR PEOPLE!
AND IT'S MY DUTY TO HELP HIM ...IF I CAN!
AND NOW WITH THE BEAST CONTROLLED BY MORAG'S MAGIC...
CHIEF CHIRPA MAY NEED ALL THE HELP HE CAN GET!
TAKE THIS AMULET, PRINCESS! IT MAY OFFER SOME PROTECTION AGAINST MORAG'S MAGIC!
THANK YOU, LOGRAY!
9

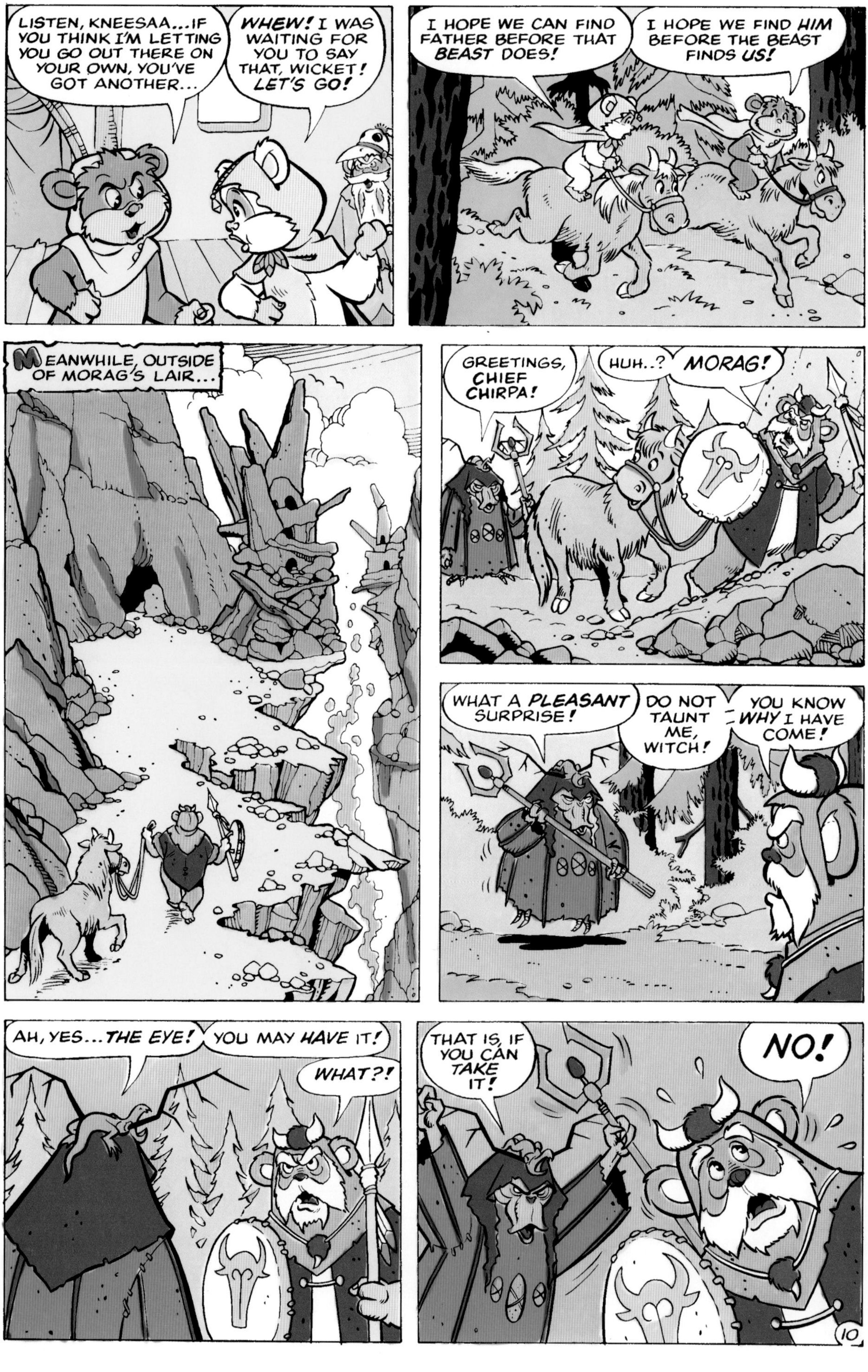

LISTEN, KNEESAA...IF YOU THINK I'M LETTING YOU GO OUT THERE ON YOUR OWN, YOU'VE GOT ANOTHER...
WHEW! I WAS WAITING FOR YOU TO SAY THAT, WICKET! LET'S GO!
I HOPE WE CAN FIND FATHER BEFORE THAT BEAST DOES!
I HOPE WE FIND HIM BEFORE THE BEAST FINDS US!
MEANWHILE, OUTSIDE OF MORAG'S LAIR...
GREETINGS, CHIEF CHIRPA!
HUH..?
MORAG!
WHAT A PLEASANT SURPRISE!
DO NOT TAUNT ME, WITCH!
YOU KNOW WHY I HAVE COME!
AH, YES...THE EYE!
YOU MAY HAVE IT!
WHAT?!
THAT IS, IF YOU CAN TAKE IT!
NO!
10

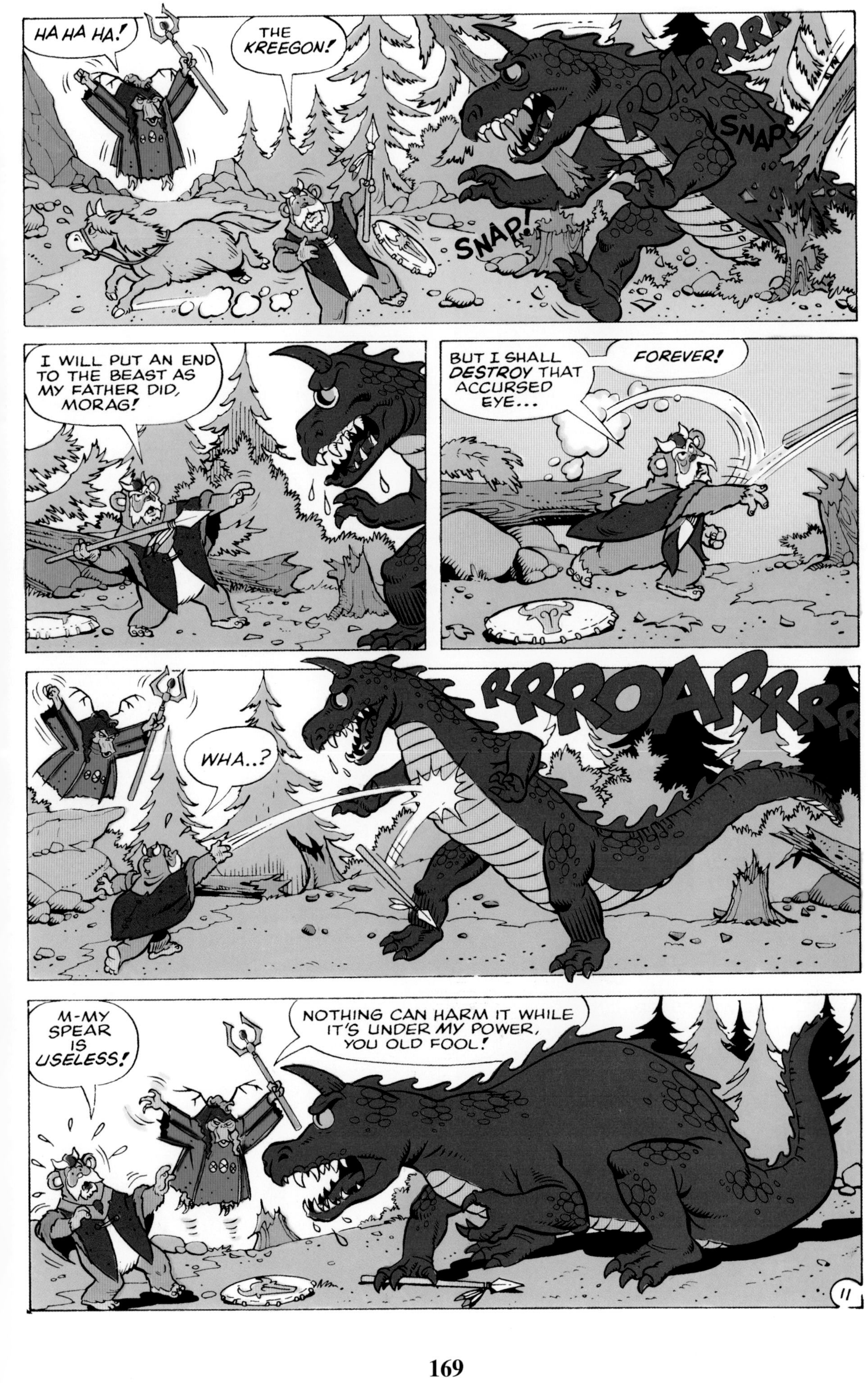
HA HA HA!
THE KREEGON!
ROARRRR
SNAP!
SNAP!
I WILL PUT AN END TO THE BEAST AS MY FATHER DID, MORAG!
BUT I SHALL DESTROY THAT ACCURSED EYE...
FOREVER!
WHA..?
RRROARRRR
M-MY SPEAR IS USELESS!
NOTHING CAN HARM IT WHILE IT'S UNDER MY POWER, YOU OLD FOOL!
11

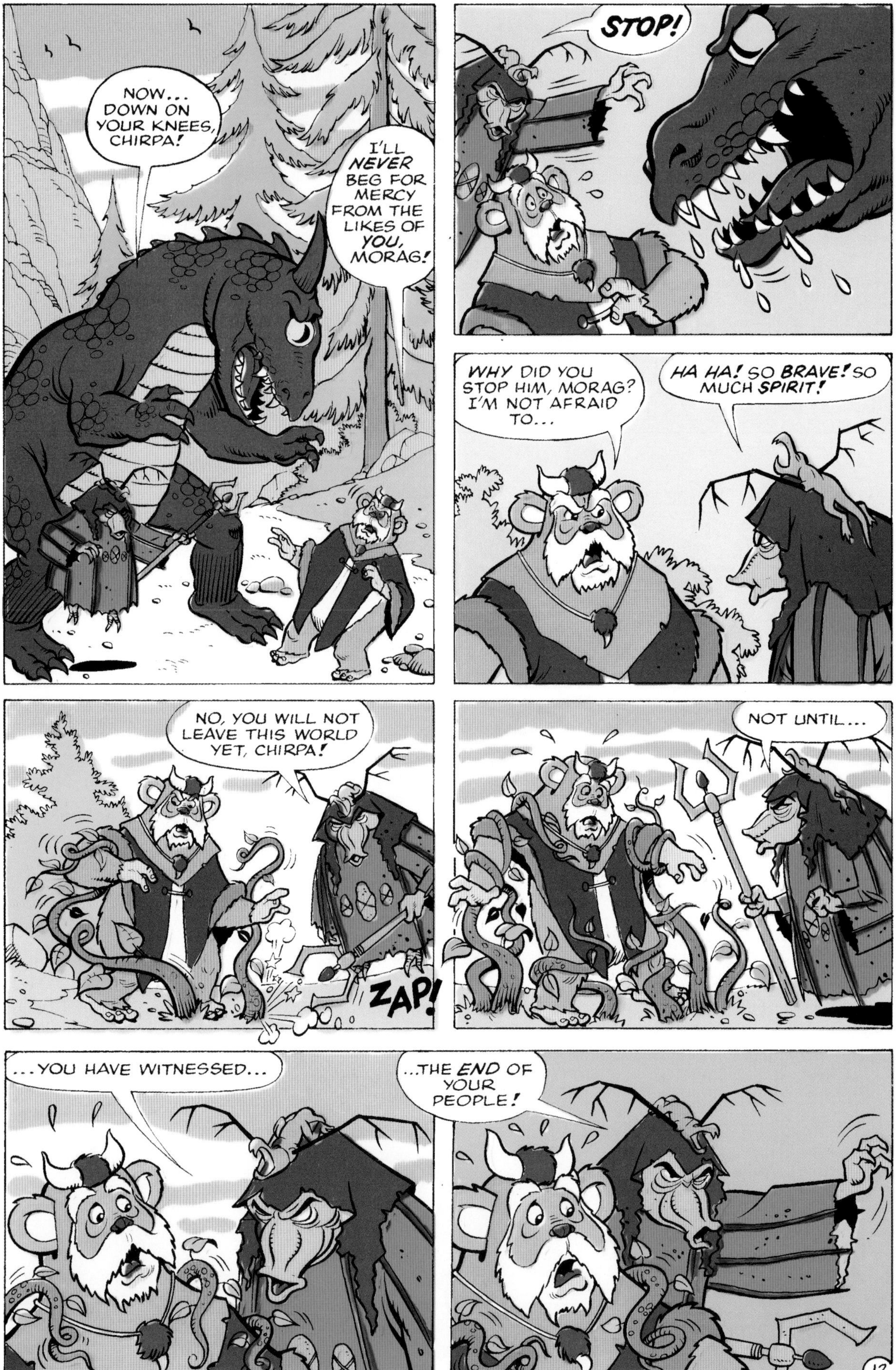
NOW... DOWN ON YOUR KNEES, CHIRPA!
I'LL NEVER BEG FOR MERCY FROM THE LIKES OF YOU, MORAG!
STOP!
WHY DID YOU STOP HIM, MORAG? I'M NOT AFRAID TO...
HA HA! SO BRAVE! SO MUCH SPIRIT!
NO, YOU WILL NOT LEAVE THIS WORLD YET, CHIRPA!
ZAP!
NOT UNTIL...
...YOU HAVE WITNESSED...
...THE END OF YOUR PEOPLE!
12

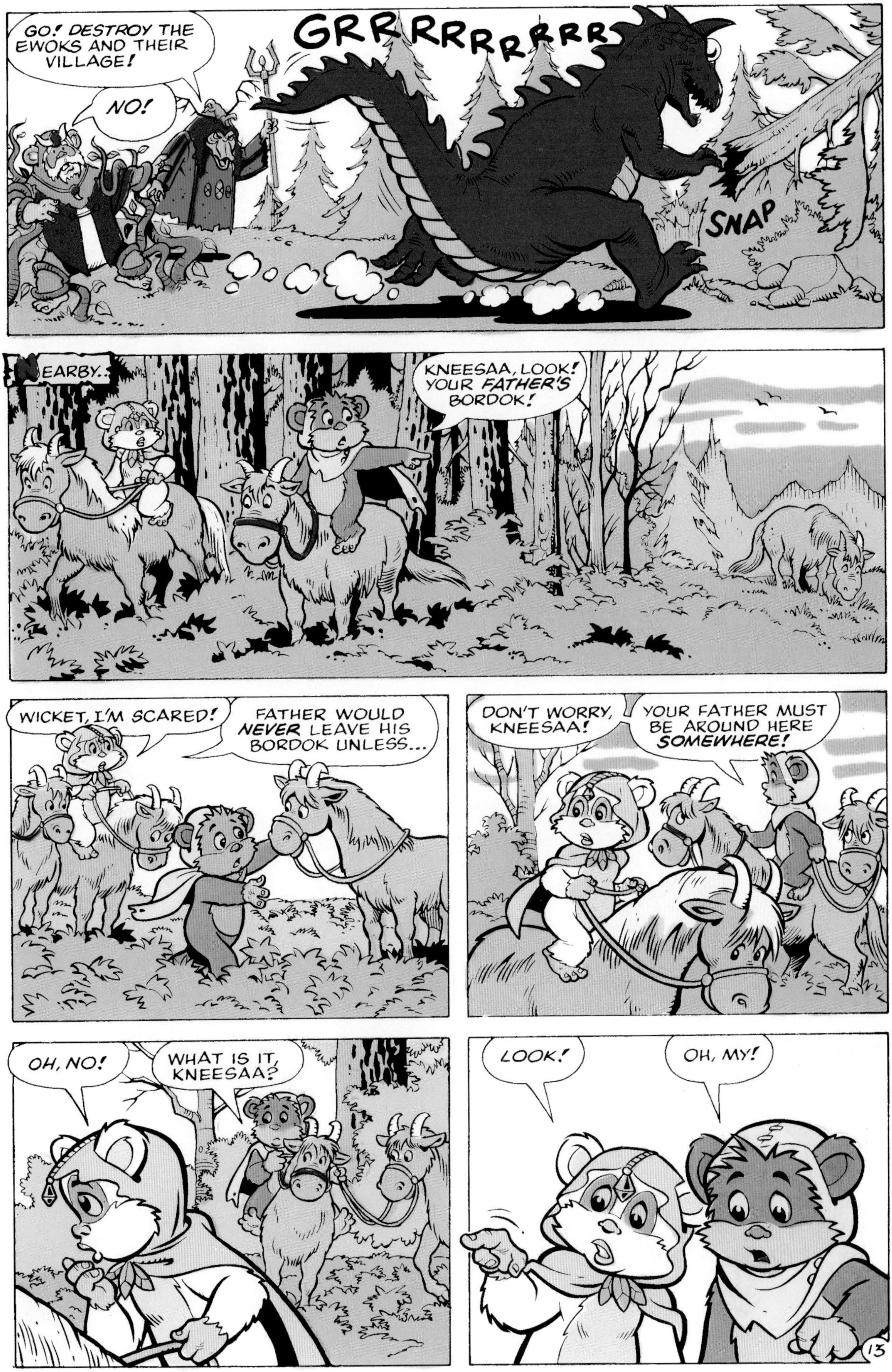
GO! DESTROY THE EWOKS AND THEIR VILLAGE!
NO!
GRRRRRRRRRR
SNAP
NEARBY...
KNEESAA, LOOK! YOUR FATHER'S BORDOK!
WICKET, I'M SCARED!
FATHER WOULD NEVER LEAVE HIS BORDOK UNLESS...
DON'T WORRY, KNEESAA!
YOUR FATHER MUST BE AROUND HERE SOMEWHERE!
OH, NO!
WHAT IS IT, KNEESAA?
LOOK!
OH, MY!
13

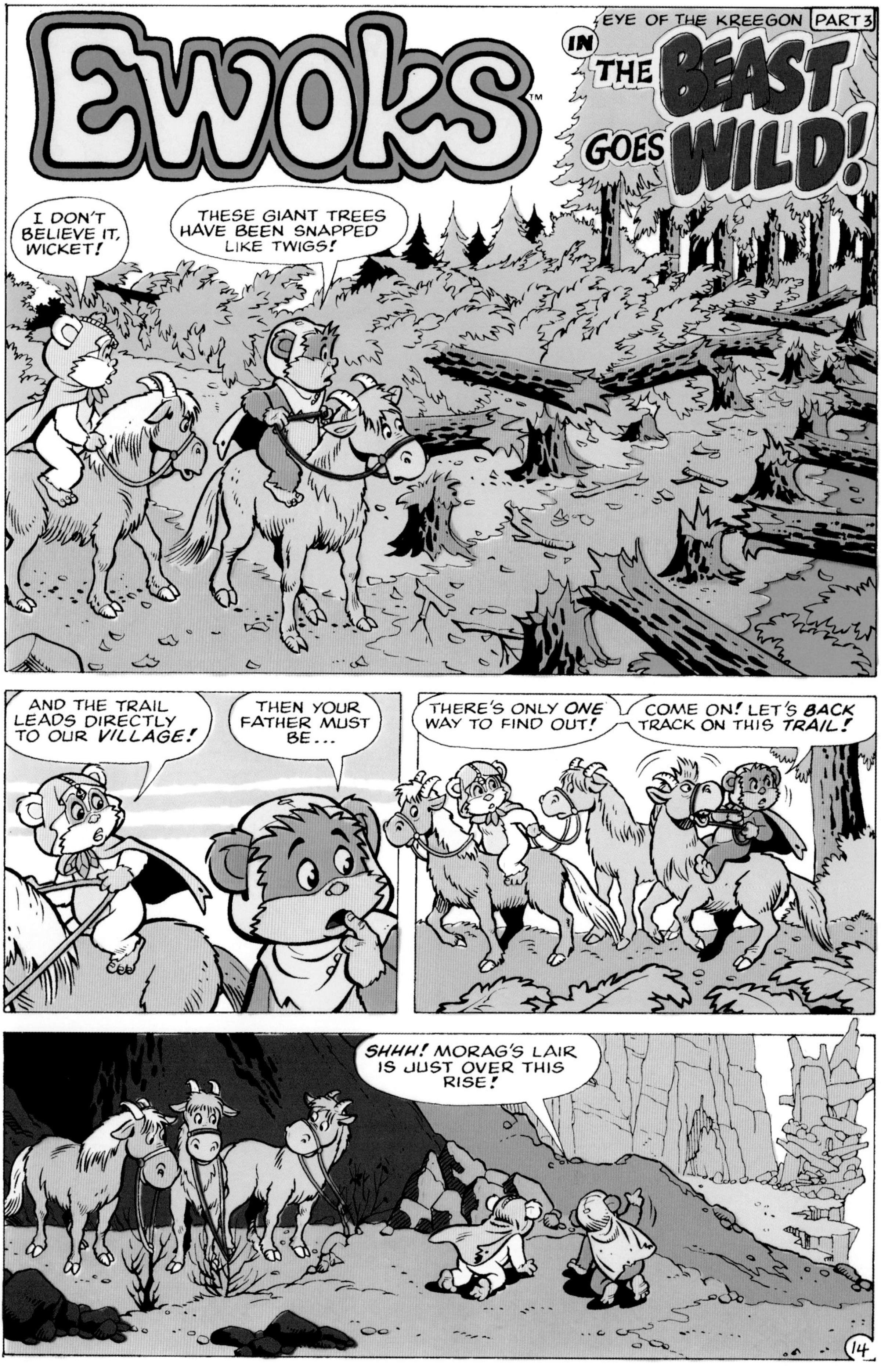
Ewoks™
in
EYE OF THE KREEGON PART 3
THE BEAST GOES WILD!
I DON'T BELIEVE IT, WICKET!
THESE GIANT TREES HAVE BEEN SNAPPED LIKE TWIGS!
AND THE TRAIL LEADS DIRECTLY TO OUR VILLAGE!
THEN YOUR FATHER MUST BE...
THERE'S ONLY ONE WAY TO FIND OUT!
COME ON! LET'S BACK TRACK ON THIS TRAIL!
SHHH! MORAG'S LAIR IS JUST OVER THIS RISE!
14

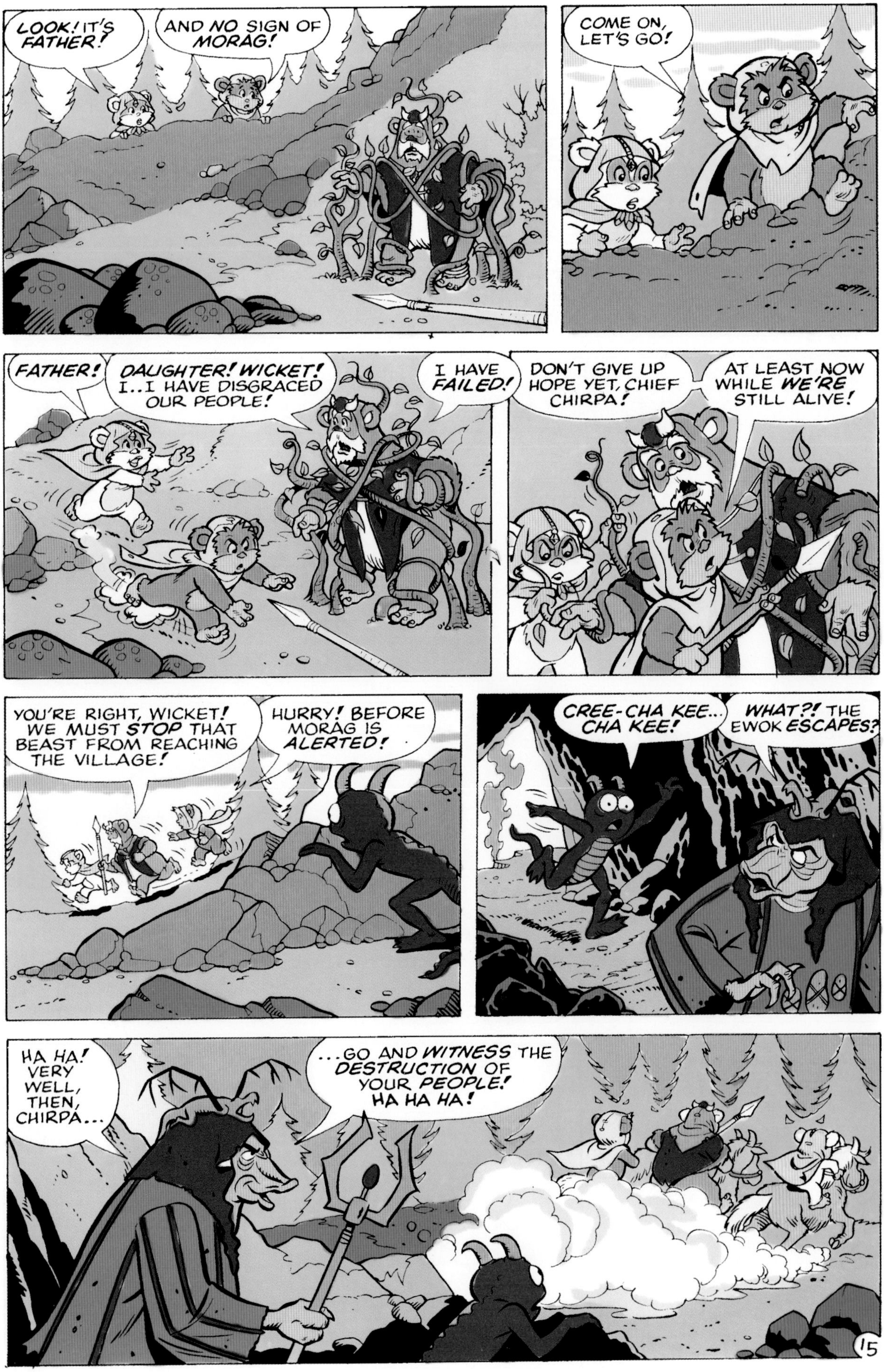
LOOK! IT'S FATHER!
AND NO SIGN OF MORAG!
COME ON, LET'S GO!
FATHER!
DAUGHTER! WICKET! I..I HAVE DISGRACED OUR PEOPLE!
I HAVE FAILED!
DON'T GIVE UP HOPE YET, CHIEF CHIRPA!
AT LEAST NOW WHILE WE'RE STILL ALIVE!
YOU'RE RIGHT, WICKET! WE MUST STOP THAT BEAST FROM REACHING THE VILLAGE!
HURRY! BEFORE MORAG IS ALERTED!
CREE-CHA KEE... CHA KEE!
WHAT?! THE EWOK ESCAPES?
HA HA! VERY WELL, THEN, CHIRPA...
...GO AND WITNESS THE DESTRUCTION OF YOUR PEOPLE! HA HA HA!
15

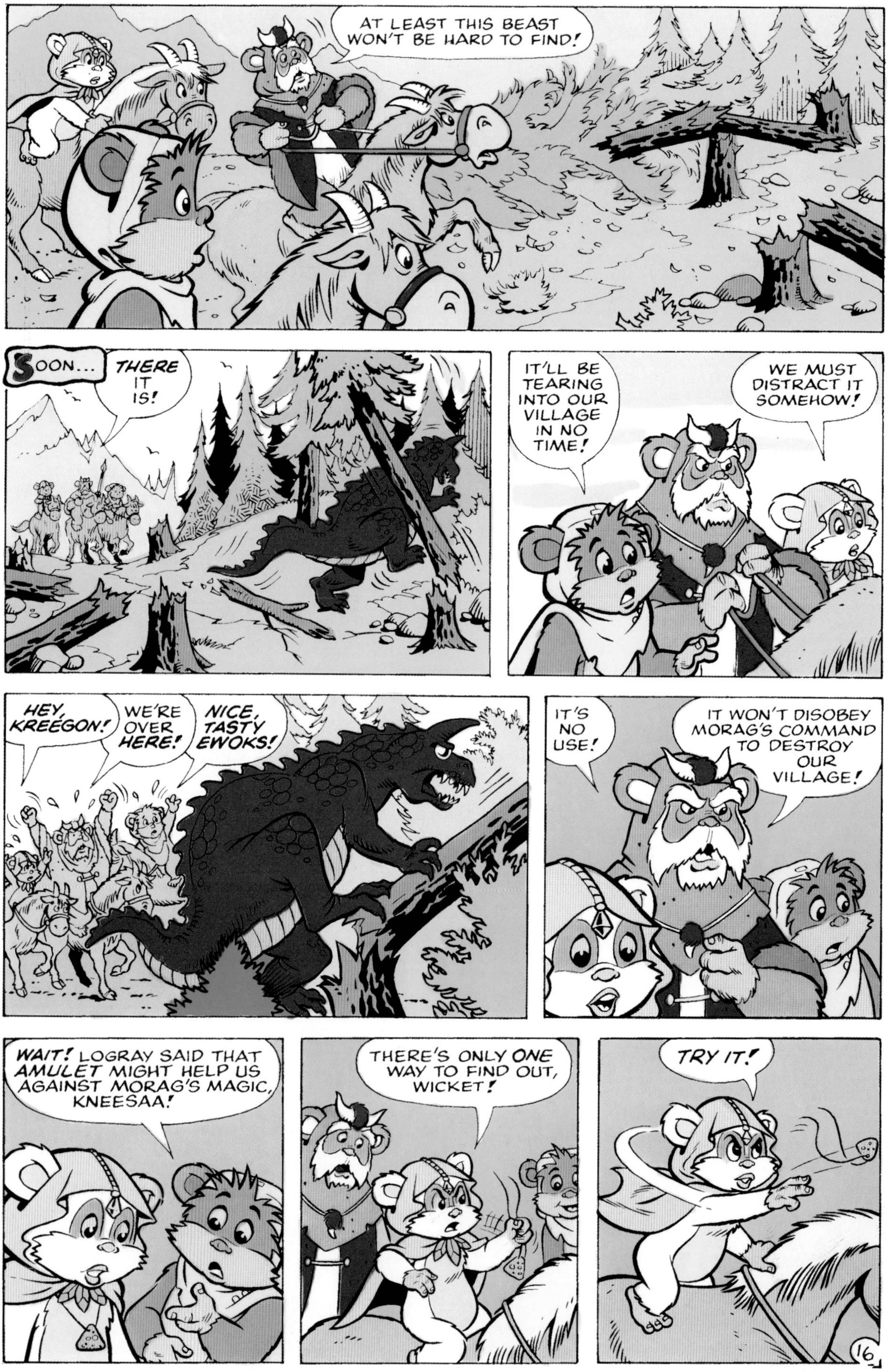
AT LEAST THIS BEAST WON'T BE HARD TO FIND!
SOON...
THERE IT IS!
IT'LL BE TEARING INTO OUR VILLAGE IN NO TIME!
WE MUST DISTRACT IT SOMEHOW!
HEY, KREEGON!
WE'RE OVER HERE!
NICE, TASTY EWOKS!
IT'S NO USE!
IT WON'T DISOBEY MORAG'S COMMAND TO DESTROY OUR VILLAGE!
WAIT! LOGRAY SAID THAT AMULET MIGHT HELP US AGAINST MORAG'S MAGIC, KNEESAA!
THERE'S ONLY ONE WAY TO FIND OUT, WICKET!
TRY IT!
16

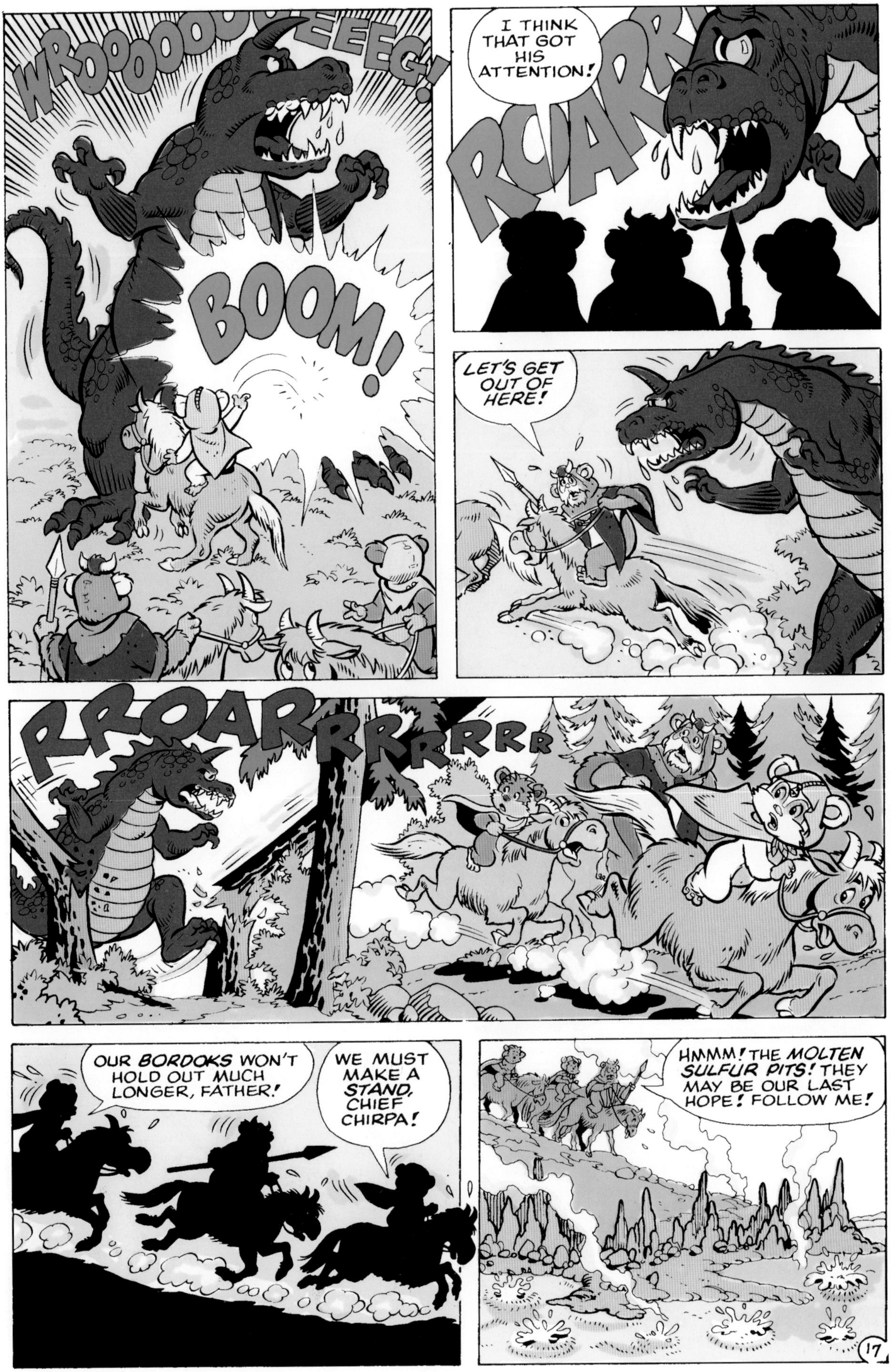

WROOOOOOOEEEEG!
BOOM!
I THINK THAT GOT HIS ATTENTION!
RCIARR
LET'S GET OUT OF HERE!
RROARRRRRRR
OUR BORDOKS WON'T HOLD OUT MUCH LONGER, FATHER!
WE MUST MAKE A STAND, CHIEF CHIRPA!
HMMM! THE MOLTEN SULFUR PITS! THEY MAY BE OUR LAST HOPE! FOLLOW ME!
17

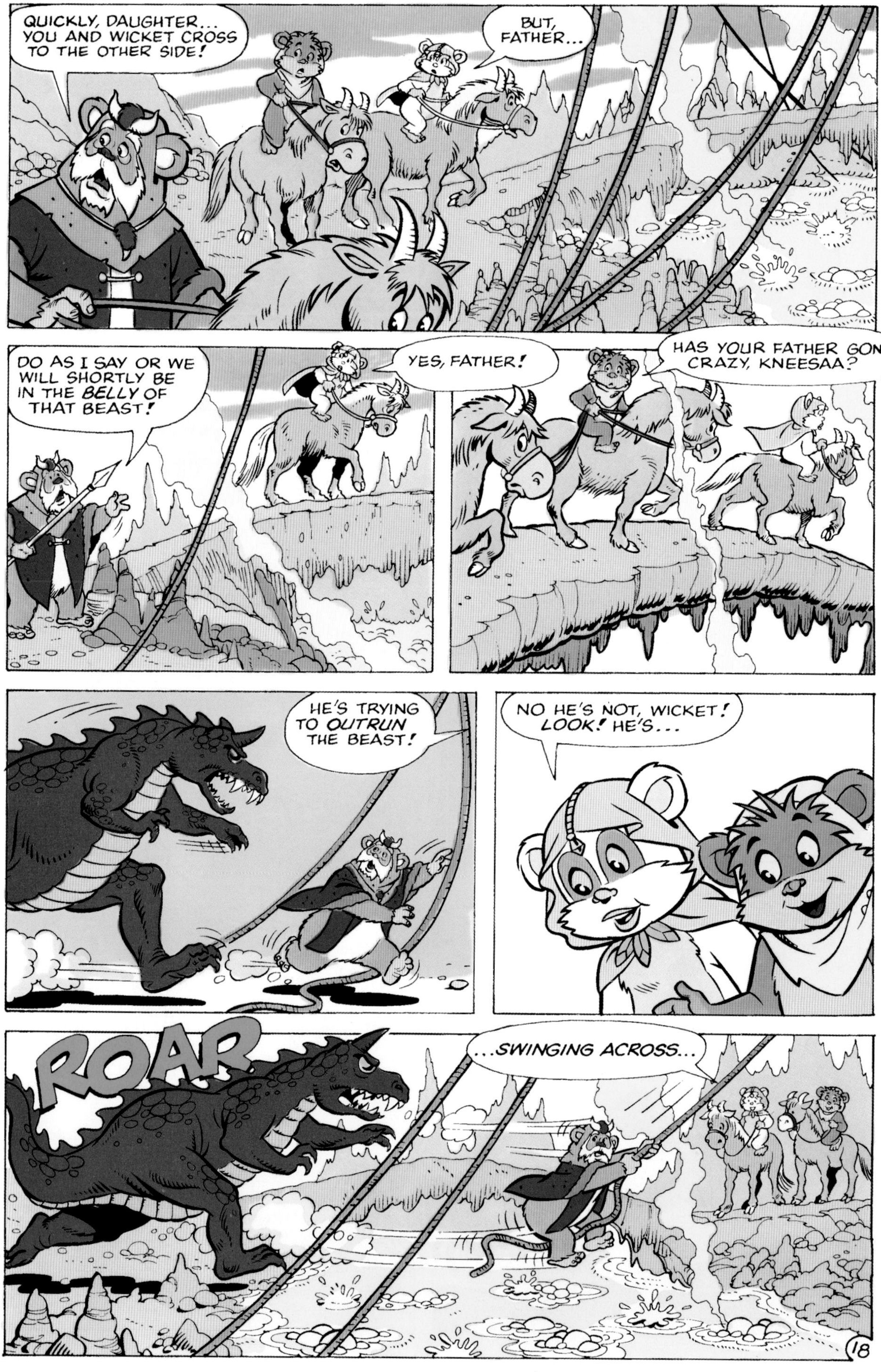
QUICKLY, DAUGHTER... YOU AND WICKET CROSS TO THE OTHER SIDE!
BUT, FATHER...
DO AS I SAY OR WE WILL SHORTLY BE IN THE BELLY OF THAT BEAST!
YES, FATHER!
HAS YOUR FATHER GONE CRAZY, KNEESAA?
HE'S TRYING TO OUTRUN THE BEAST!
NO HE'S NOT, WICKET! LOOK! HE'S...
ROAR
...SWINGING ACROSS...
18

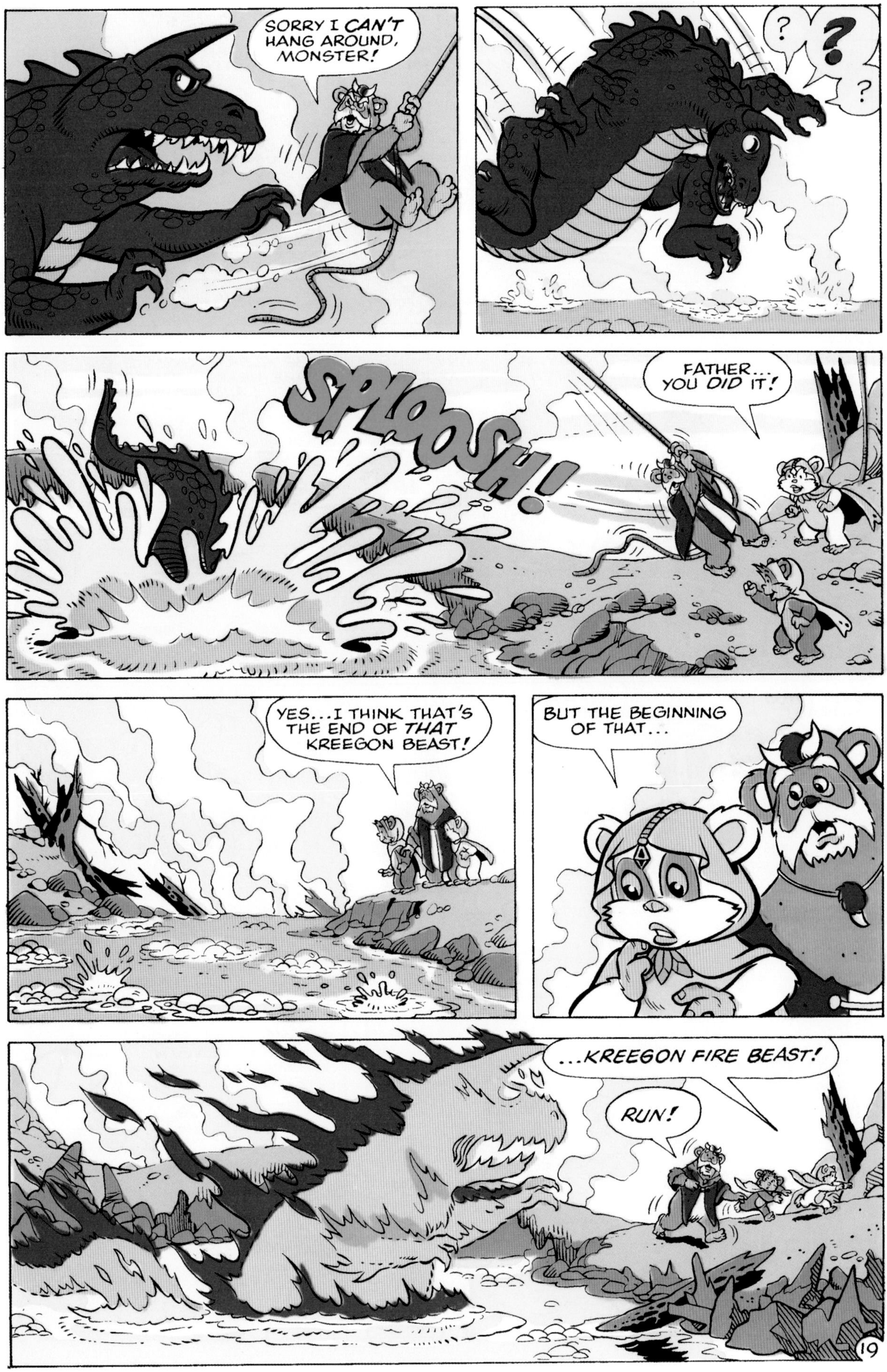
SORRY I CAN'T HANG AROUND, MONSTER!
? ? ?
SPLOOSH!
FATHER... YOU DID IT!
YES...I THINK THAT'S THE END OF THAT KREEGON BEAST!
BUT THE BEGINNING OF THAT...
...KREEGON FIRE BEAST!
RUN!
19

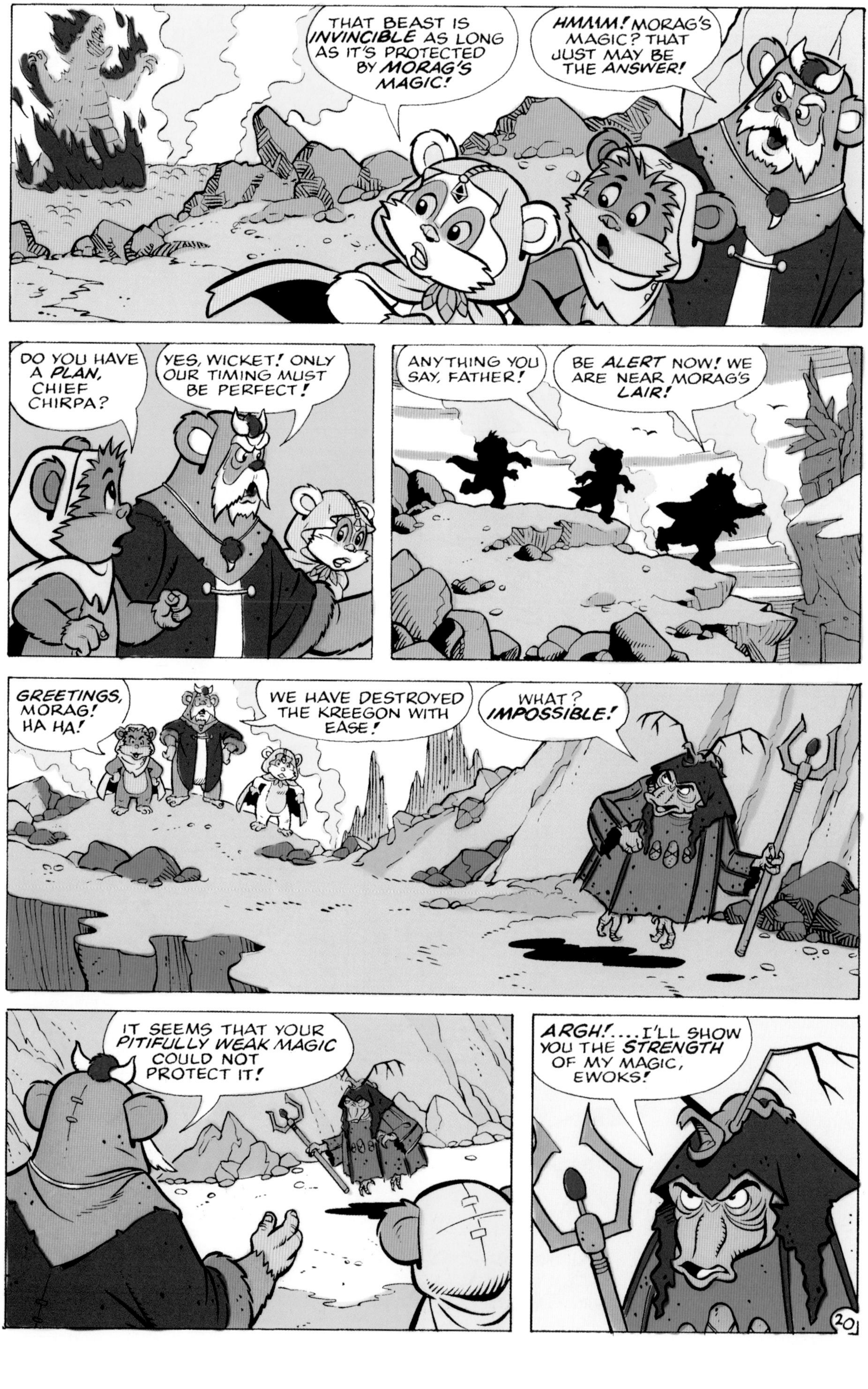
THAT BEAST IS INVINCIBLE AS LONG AS IT'S PROTECTED BY MORAG'S MAGIC!
HMMM! MORAG'S MAGIC? THAT JUST MAY BE THE ANSWER!
DO YOU HAVE A PLAN, CHIEF CHIRPA?
YES, WICKET! ONLY OUR TIMING MUST BE PERFECT!
ANYTHING YOU SAY, FATHER!
BE ALERT NOW! WE ARE NEAR MORAG'S LAIR!
GREETINGS, MORAG! HA HA!
WE HAVE DESTROYED THE KREEGON WITH EASE!
WHAT? IMPOSSIBLE!
IT SEEMS THAT YOUR PITIFULLY WEAK MAGIC COULD NOT PROTECT IT!
ARGH!....I'LL SHOW YOU THE STRENGTH OF MY MAGIC, EWOKS!
20

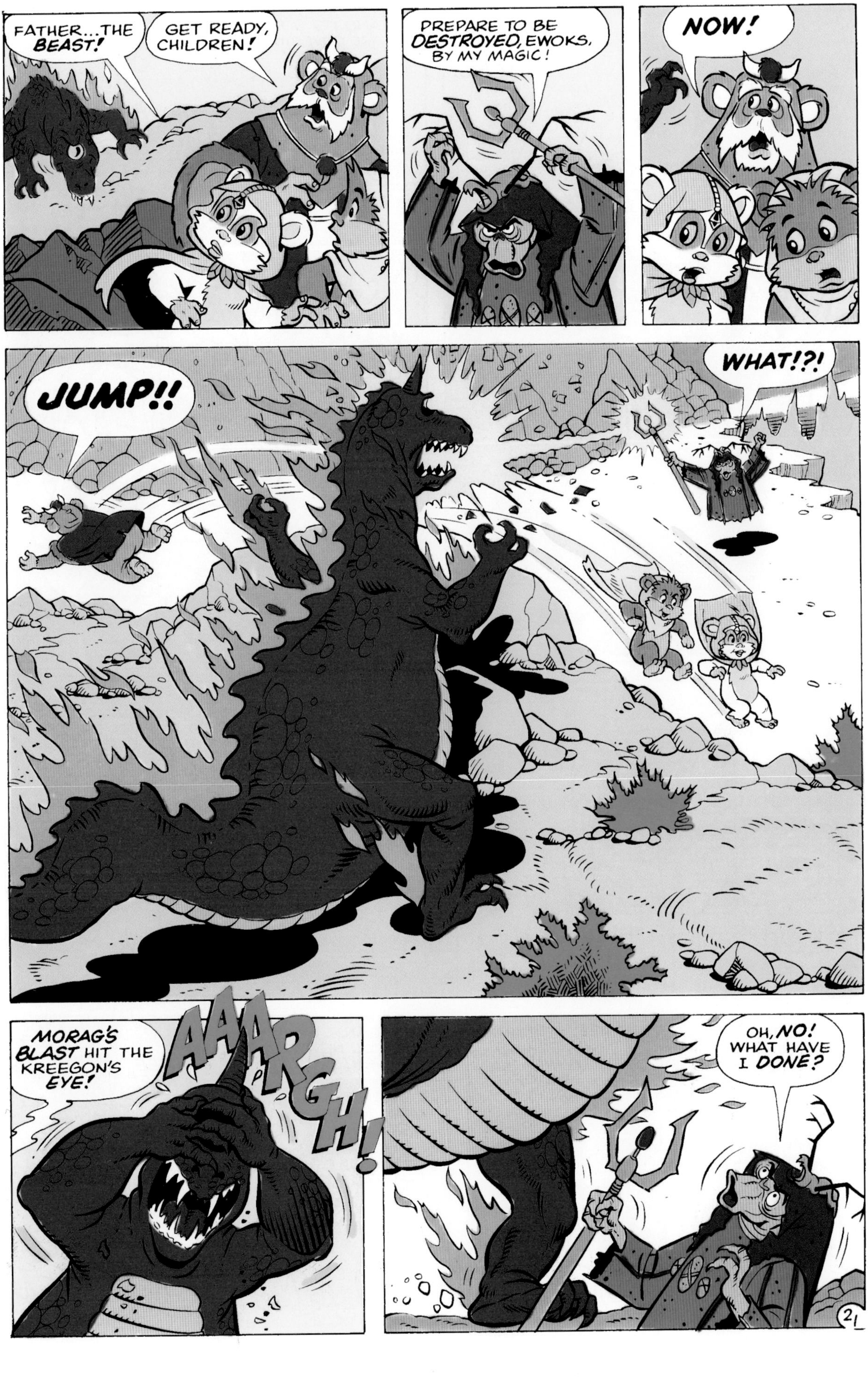
FATHER...THE BEAST!
GET READY, CHILDREN!
PREPARE TO BE DESTROYED, EWOKS, BY MY MAGIC!
NOW!
JUMP!!
WHAT!?!
MORAG'S BLAST HIT THE KREEGON'S EYE!
AAARGH!
OH, NO! WHAT HAVE I DONE?
21

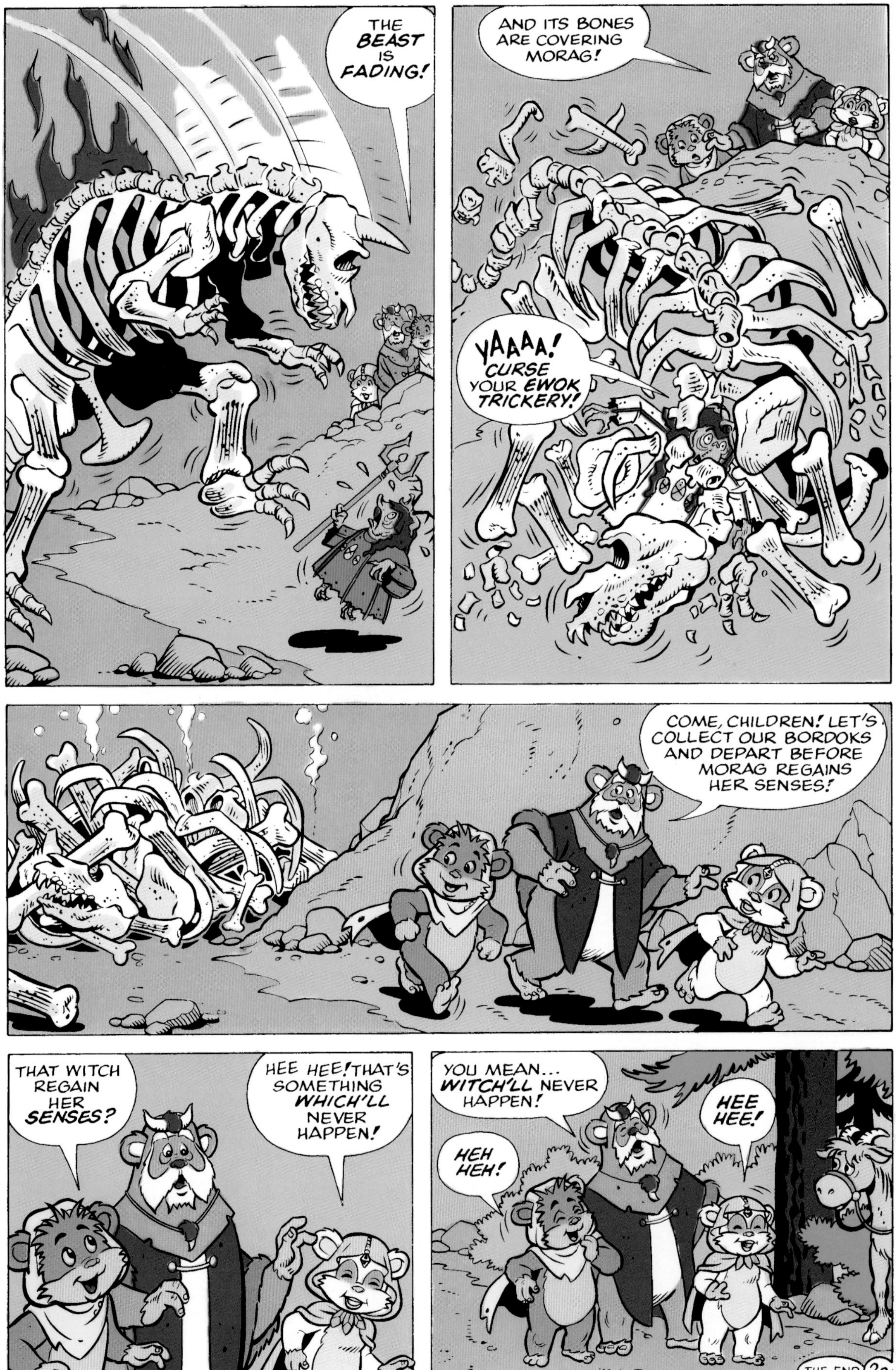
THE BEAST IS FADING!
AND ITS BONES ARE COVERING MORAG!
YAAAA! CURSE YOUR EWOK TRICKERY!
COME, CHILDREN! LET'S COLLECT OUR BORDOKS AND DEPART BEFORE MORAG REGAINS HER SENSES!
THAT WITCH REGAIN HER SENSES?
HEE HEE! THAT'S SOMETHING WHICH'LL NEVER HAPPEN!
YOU MEAN... WITCH'LL NEVER HAPPEN!
HEE HEE!
HEH HEH!
THE END 22

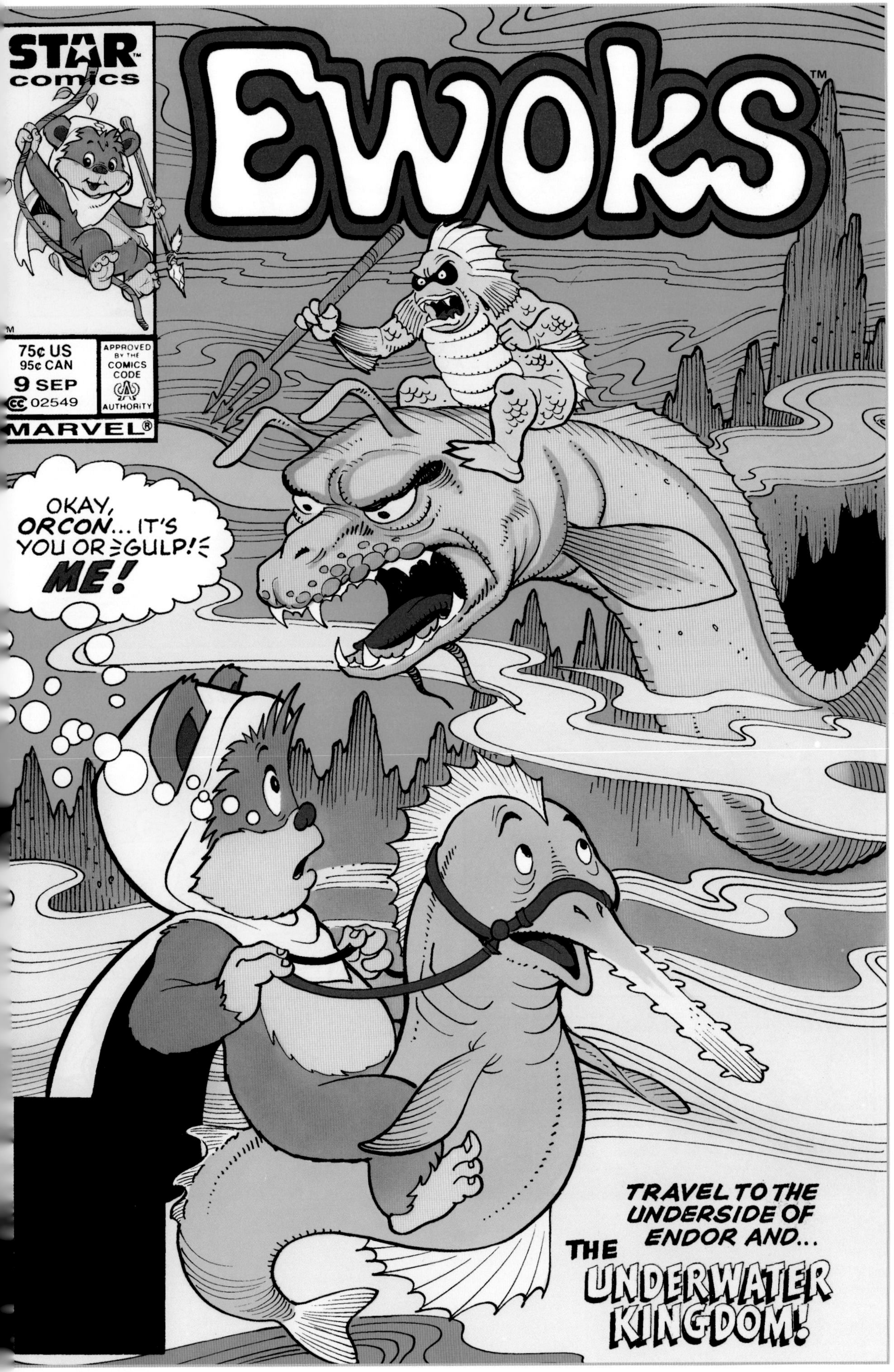
STAR comics
EWOKS™
75¢ US
95¢ CAN
9 SEP
02549
APPROVED BY THE COMICS CODE AUTHORITY
MARVEL®
OKAY, ORCON... IT'S YOU OR =GULP!= ME!
TRAVEL TO THE UNDERSIDE OF ENDOR AND...
THE UNDERWATER KINGDOM!

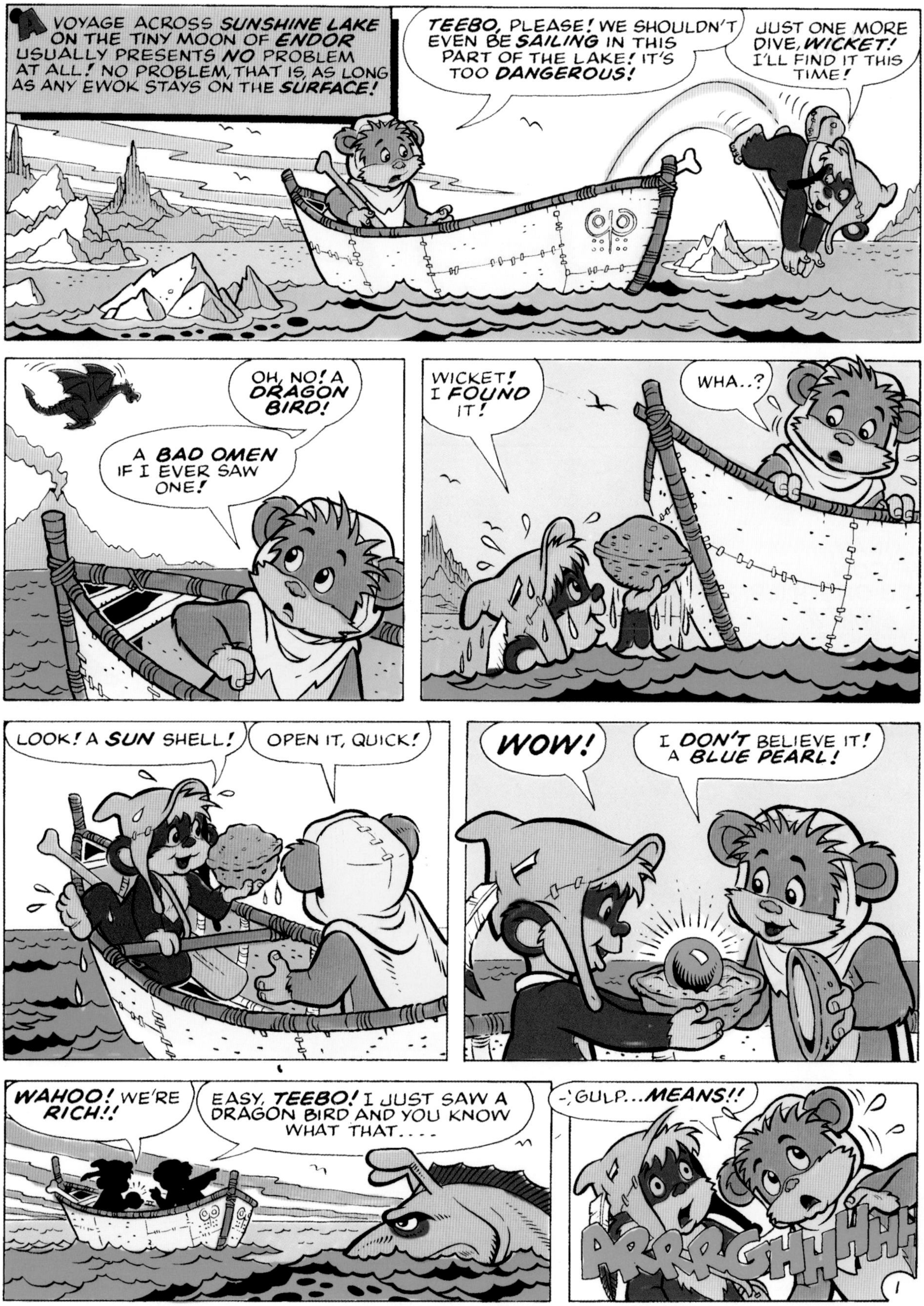
A VOYAGE ACROSS SUNSHINE LAKE ON THE TINY MOON OF ENDOR USUALLY PRESENTS NO PROBLEM AT ALL! NO PROBLEM, THAT IS, AS LONG AS ANY EWOK STAYS ON THE SURFACE!
TEEBO, PLEASE! WE SHOULDN'T EVEN BE SAILING IN THIS PART OF THE LAKE! IT'S TOO DANGEROUS!
JUST ONE MORE DIVE, WICKET! I'LL FIND IT THIS TIME!
OH, NO! A DRAGON BIRD!
A BAD OMEN IF I EVER SAW ONE!
WICKET! I FOUND IT!
WHA..?
LOOK! A SUN SHELL!
OPEN IT, QUICK!
WOW!
I DON'T BELIEVE IT! A BLUE PEARL!
WAHOO! WE'RE RICH!!
EASY, TEEBO! I JUST SAW A DRAGON BIRD AND YOU KNOW WHAT THAT....
-GULP...MEANS!!
ARRRGHHHHH

EWOKS™ IN THE Underwater KINGDOM!

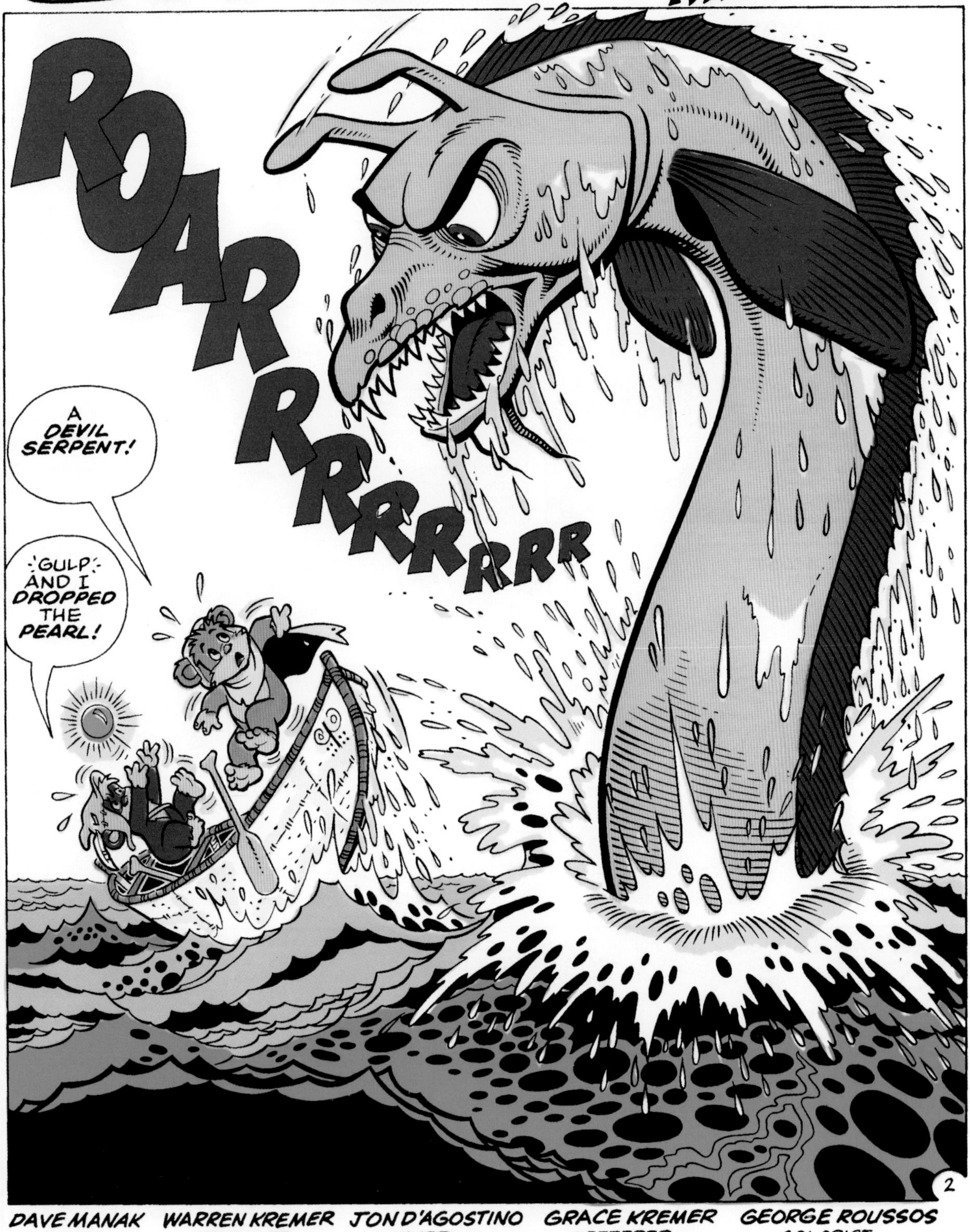
ROARRRRRRRR
A DEVIL SERPENT!
-GULP- AND I DROPPED THE PEARL!
2

DAVE MANAK, WRITER
WARREN KREMER, PENCILER
JON D'AGOSTINO, INKER
GRACE KREMER, LETTERER
GEORGE ROUSSOS, COLORIST
SID JACOBSON, EDITOR
TOM DEFALCO, EXECUTIVE EDITOR
JIM SHOOTER, EDITOR IN CHIEF

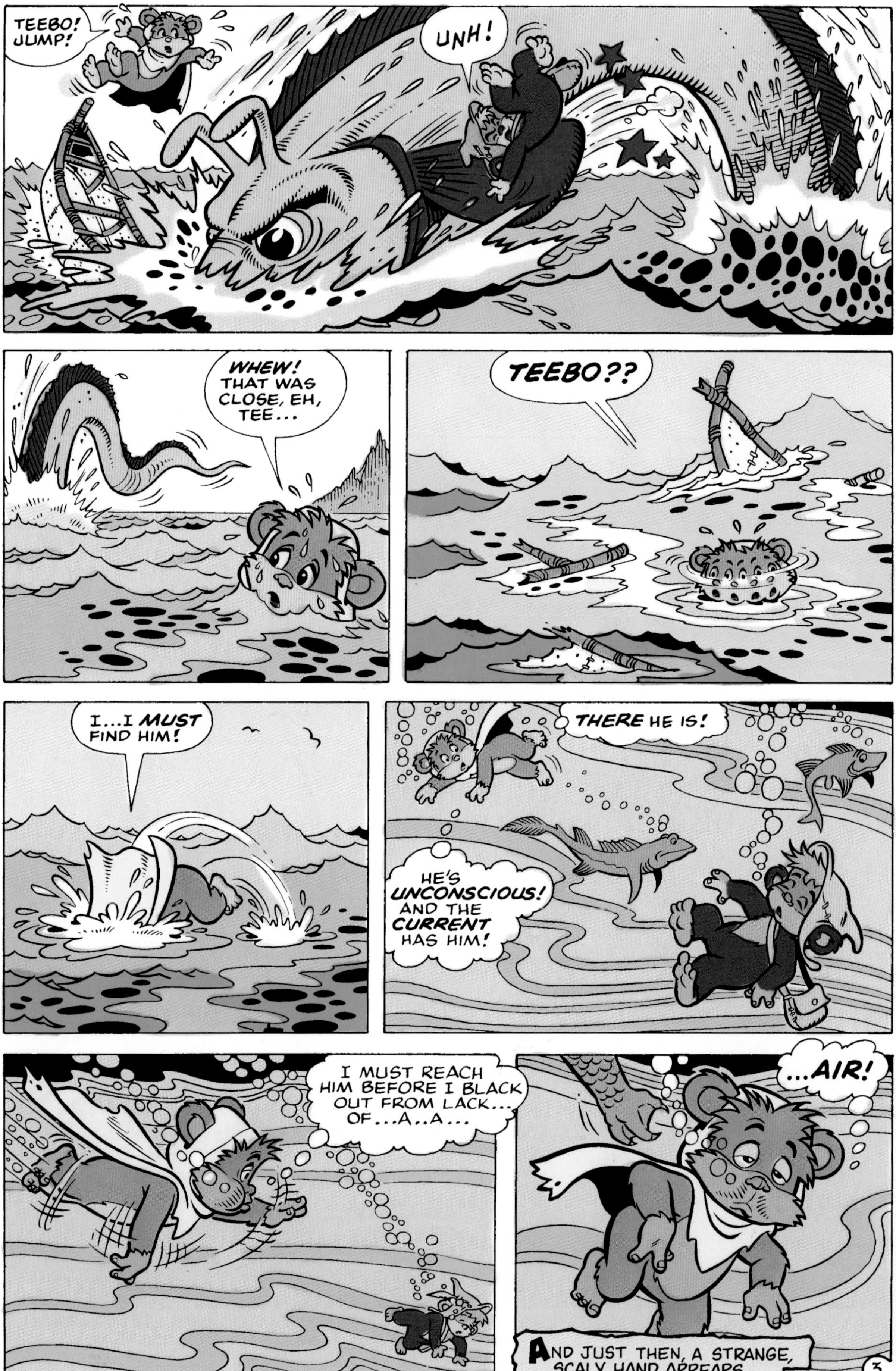
TEEBO! JUMP!
UNH!
WHEW! THAT WAS CLOSE, EH, TEE...
TEEBO??
I...I MUST FIND HIM!
THERE HE IS!
HE'S UNCONSCIOUS! AND THE CURRENT HAS HIM!
I MUST REACH HIM BEFORE I BLACK OUT FROM LACK... OF...A..A...
...AIR!
AND JUST THEN, A STRANGE, SCALY HAND APPEARS...
3

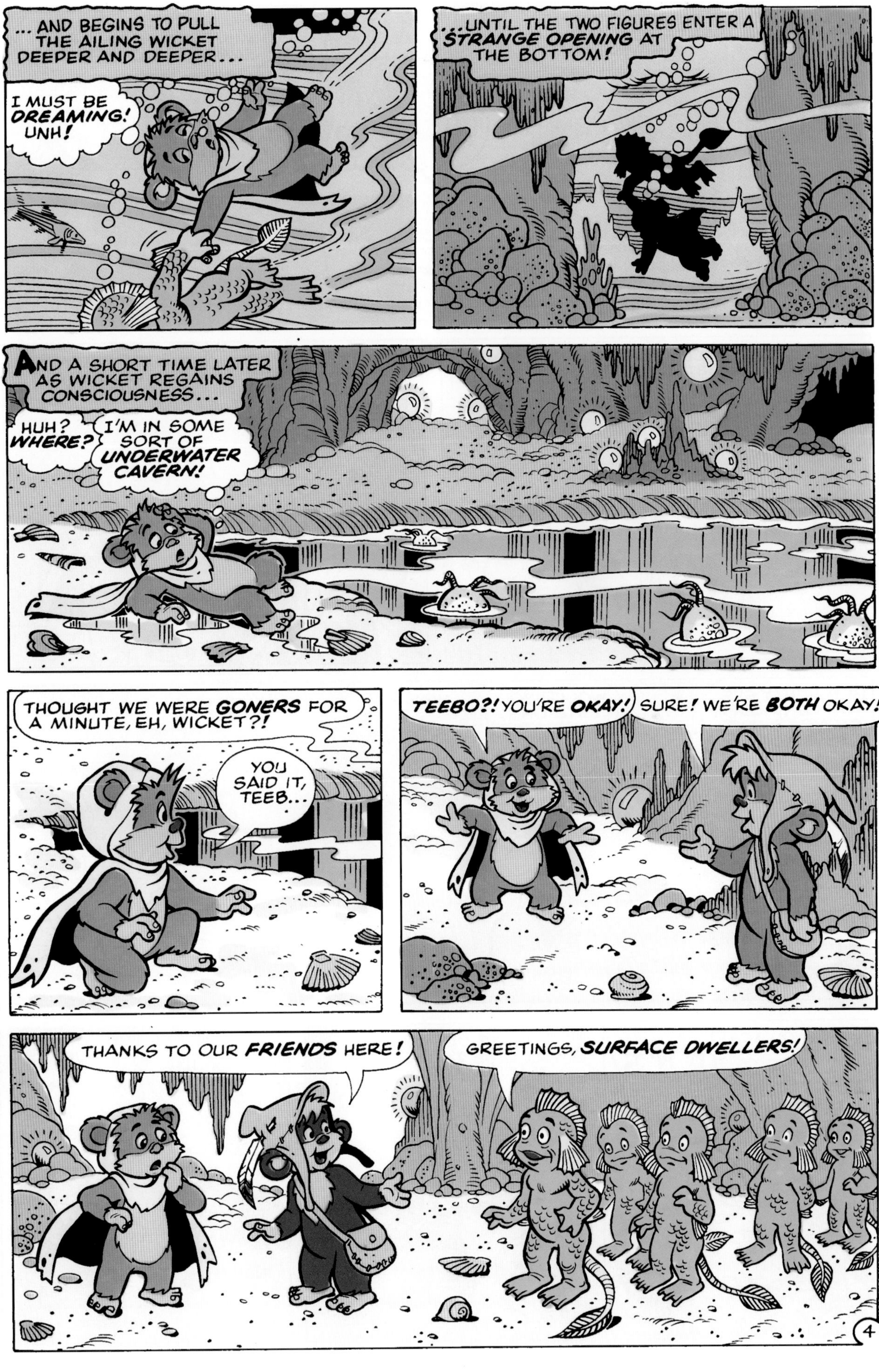
...AND BEGINS TO PULL THE AILING WICKET DEEPER AND DEEPER...
I MUST BE DREAMING! UNH!
...UNTIL THE TWO FIGURES ENTER A STRANGE OPENING AT THE BOTTOM!
AND A SHORT TIME LATER AS WICKET REGAINS CONSCIOUSNESS...
HUH? WHERE?
I'M IN SOME SORT OF UNDERWATER CAVERN!
THOUGHT WE WERE GONERS FOR A MINUTE, EH, WICKET?!
YOU SAID IT, TEEB...
TEEBO?! YOU'RE OKAY!
SURE! WE'RE BOTH OKAY!
THANKS TO OUR FRIENDS HERE!
GREETINGS, SURFACE DWELLERS!
4

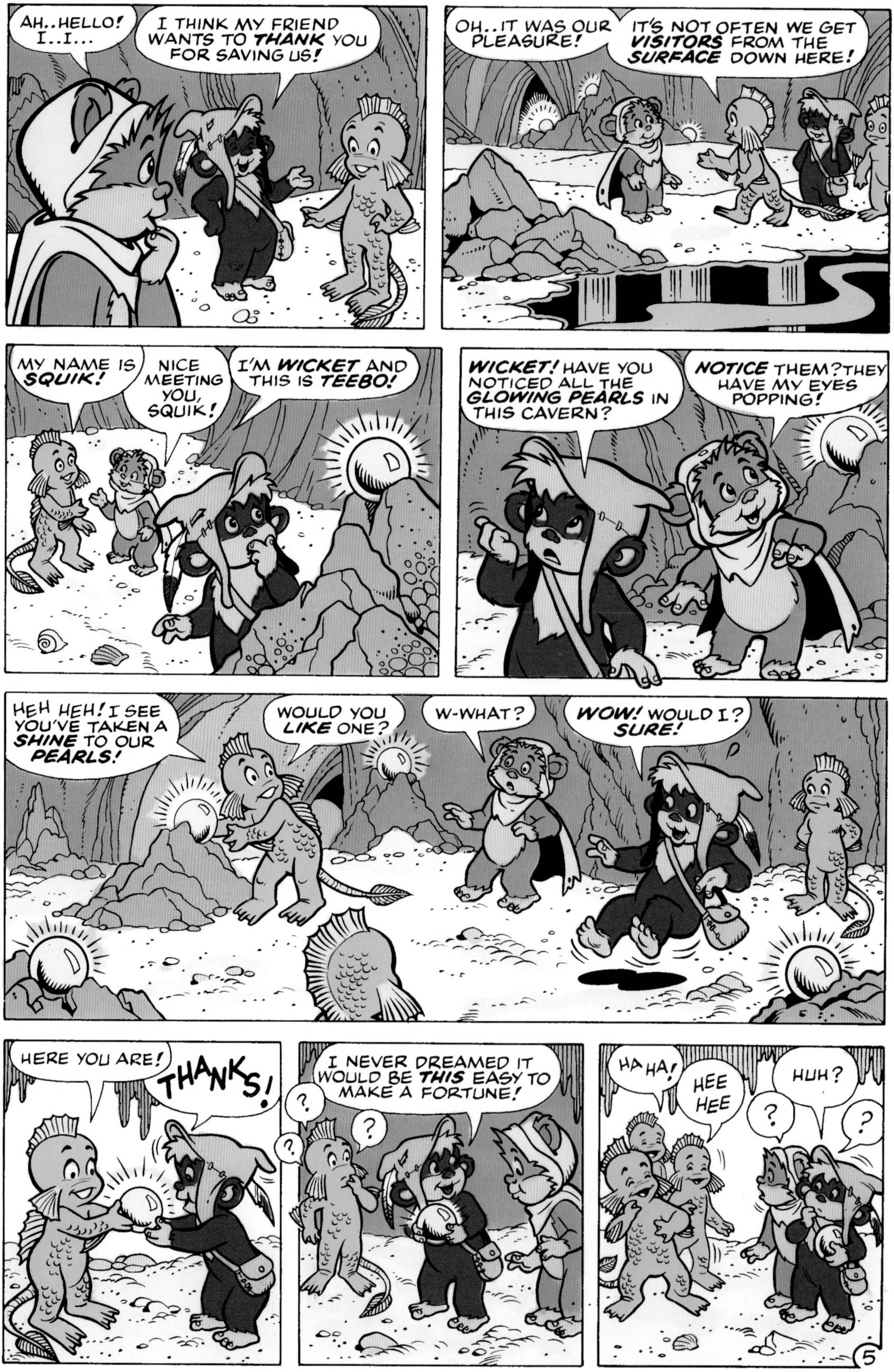
AH..HELLO! I..I...
I THINK MY FRIEND WANTS TO THANK YOU FOR SAVING US!
OH..IT WAS OUR PLEASURE!
IT'S NOT OFTEN WE GET VISITORS FROM THE SURFACE DOWN HERE!
MY NAME IS SQUIK!
NICE MEETING YOU, SQUIK!
I'M WICKET AND THIS IS TEEBO!
WICKET! HAVE YOU NOTICED ALL THE GLOWING PEARLS IN THIS CAVERN?
NOTICE THEM? THEY HAVE MY EYES POPPING!
HEH HEH! I SEE YOU'VE TAKEN A SHINE TO OUR PEARLS!
WOULD YOU LIKE ONE?
W-WHAT?
WOW! WOULD I? SURE!
HERE YOU ARE!
THANKS!
?
?
?
I NEVER DREAMED IT WOULD BE THIS EASY TO MAKE A FORTUNE!
HA HA!
HEE HEE
?
HUH?
?
5

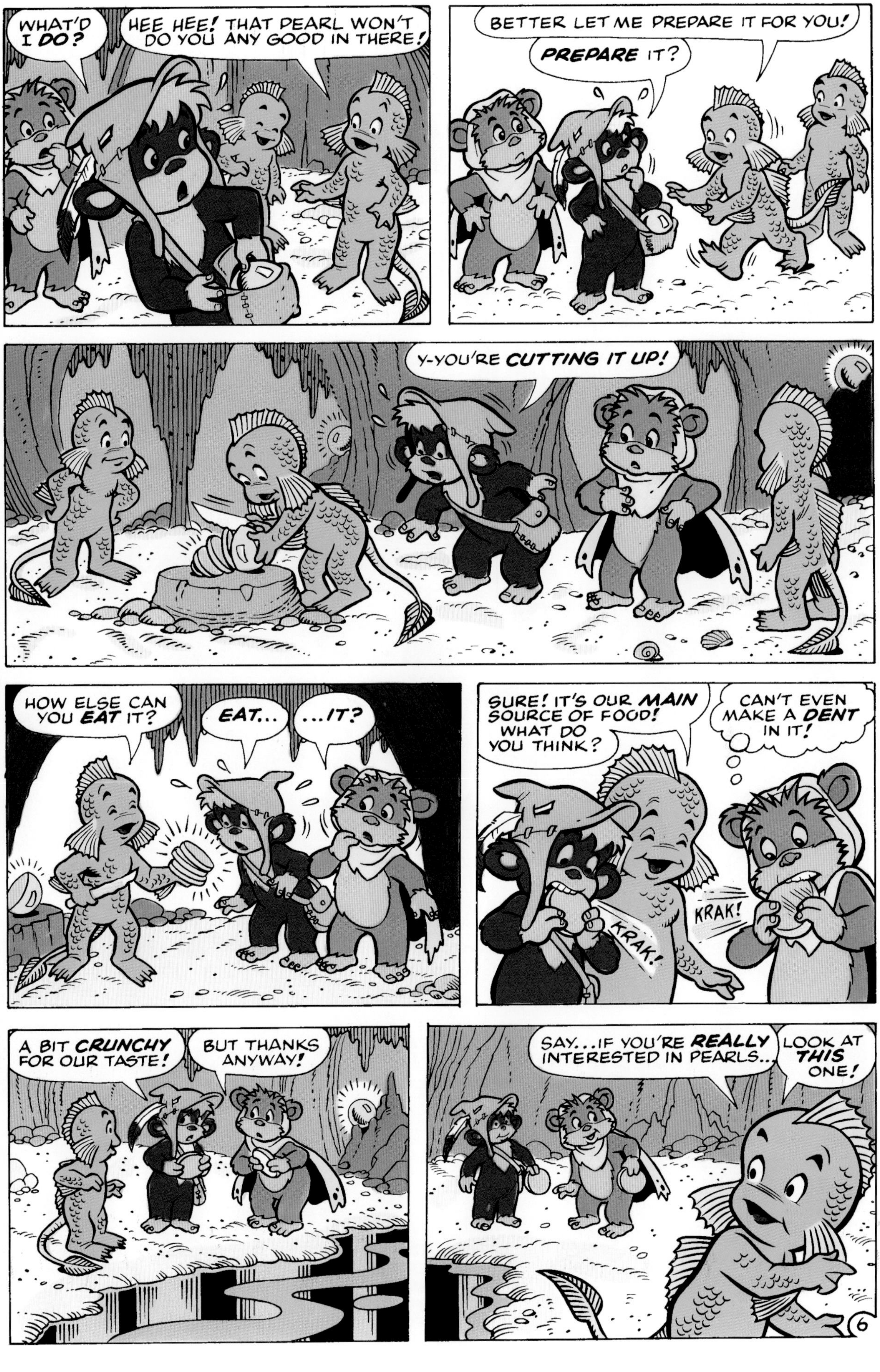
WHAT'D I DO?
HEE HEE! THAT PEARL WON'T DO YOU ANY GOOD IN THERE!
BETTER LET ME PREPARE IT FOR YOU!
PREPARE IT?
Y-YOU'RE CUTTING IT UP!
HOW ELSE CAN YOU EAT IT?
EAT...
...IT?
SURE! IT'S OUR MAIN SOURCE OF FOOD! WHAT DO YOU THINK?
CAN'T EVEN MAKE A DENT IN IT!
KRAK!
KRAK!
A BIT CRUNCHY FOR OUR TASTE!
BUT THANKS ANYWAY!
SAY...IF YOU'RE REALLY INTERESTED IN PEARLS...
LOOK AT THIS ONE!
6

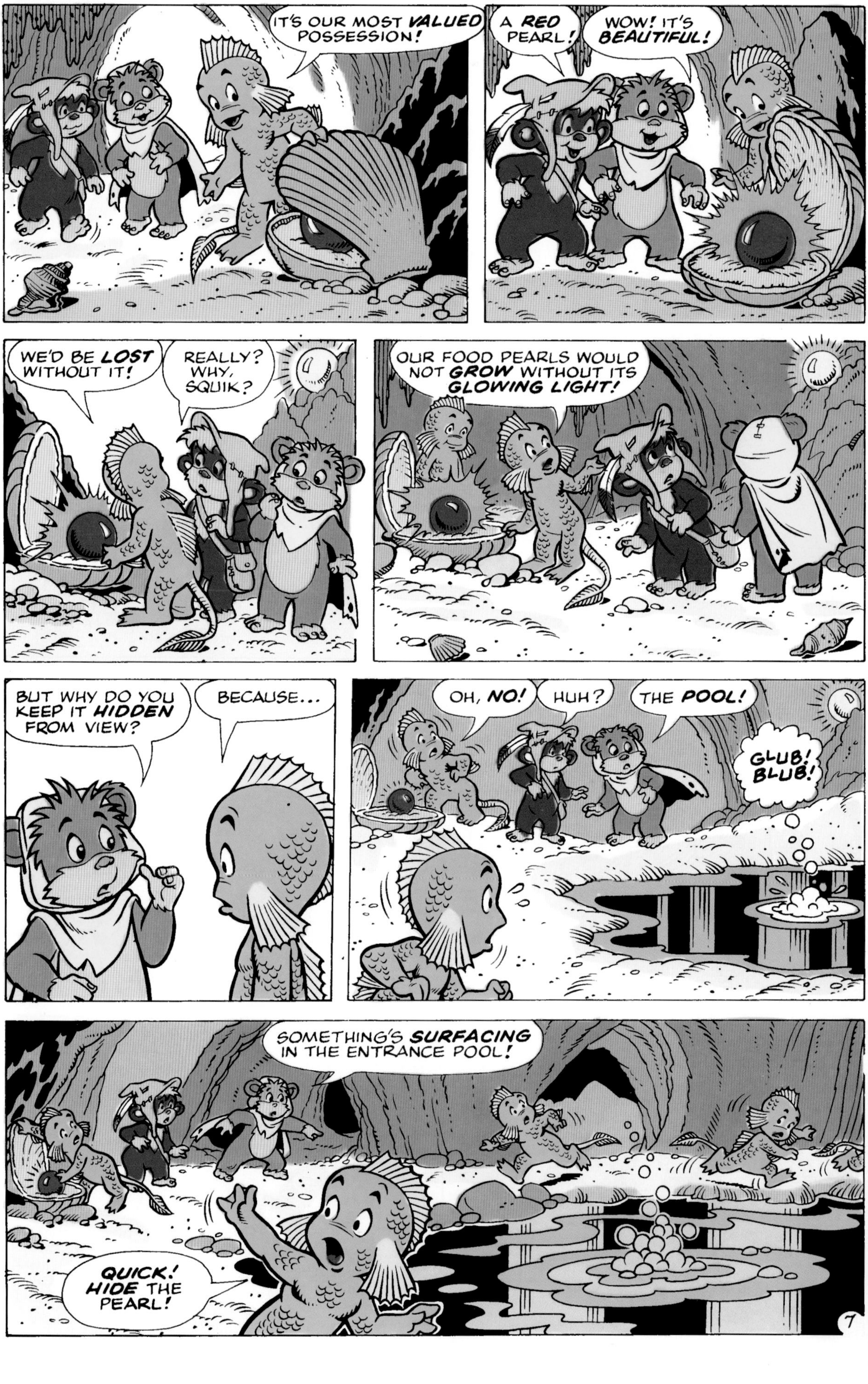
IT'S OUR MOST VALUED POSSESSION!
A RED PEARL!
WOW! IT'S BEAUTIFUL!
WE'D BE LOST WITHOUT IT!
REALLY? WHY, SQUIK?
OUR FOOD PEARLS WOULD NOT GROW WITHOUT ITS GLOWING LIGHT!
BUT WHY DO YOU KEEP IT HIDDEN FROM VIEW?
BECAUSE...
OH, NO!
HUH?
THE POOL!
GLUB! BLUB!
SOMETHING'S SURFACING IN THE ENTRANCE POOL!
QUICK! HIDE THE PEARL!
7

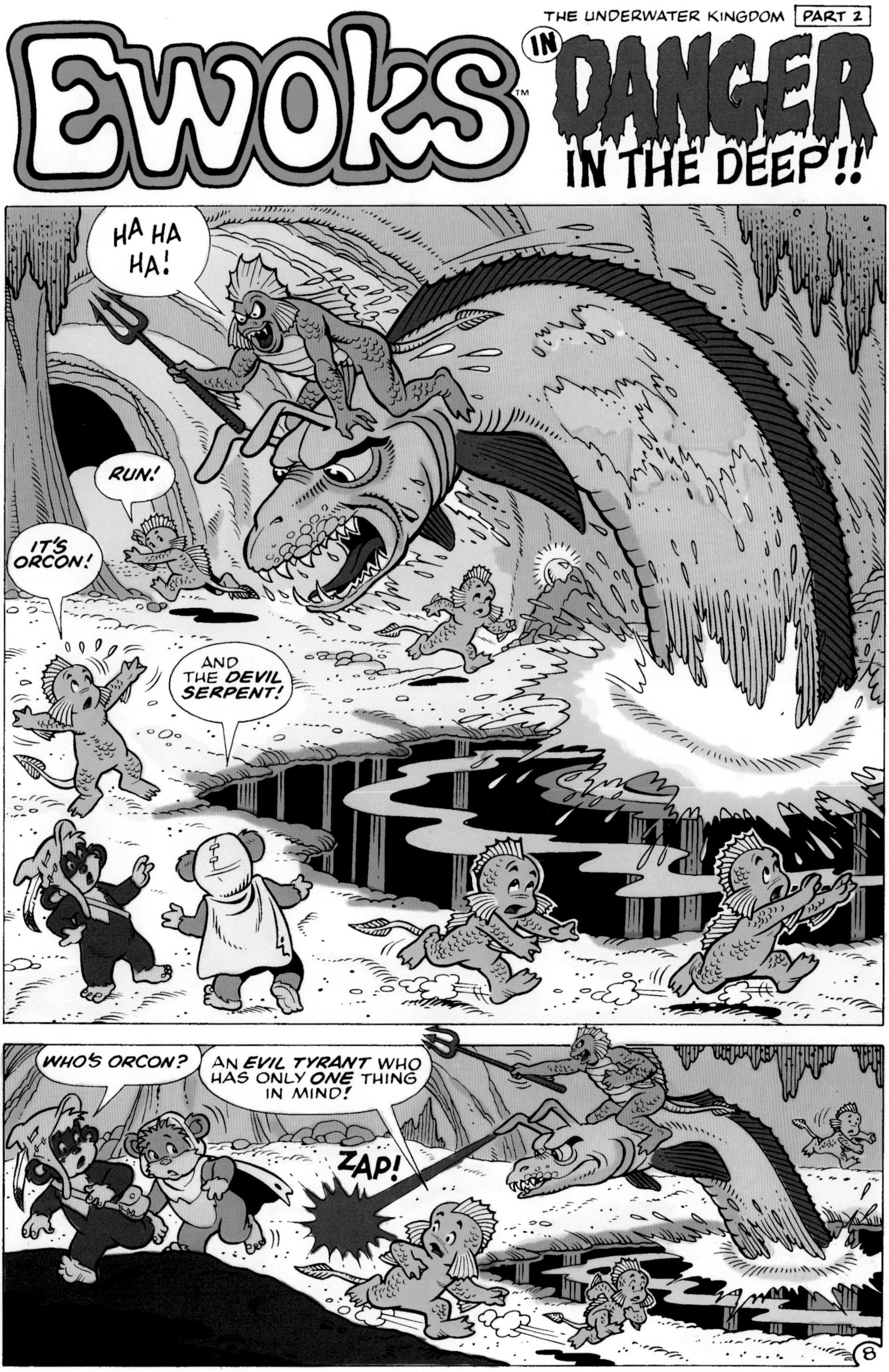
THE UNDERWATER KINGDOM PART 2
EWOKS IN DANGER IN THE DEEP!!
HA HA HA!
RUN!
IT'S ORCON!
AND THE DEVIL SERPENT!
WHO'S ORCON?
AN EVIL TYRANT WHO HAS ONLY ONE THING IN MIND!
ZAP!
8

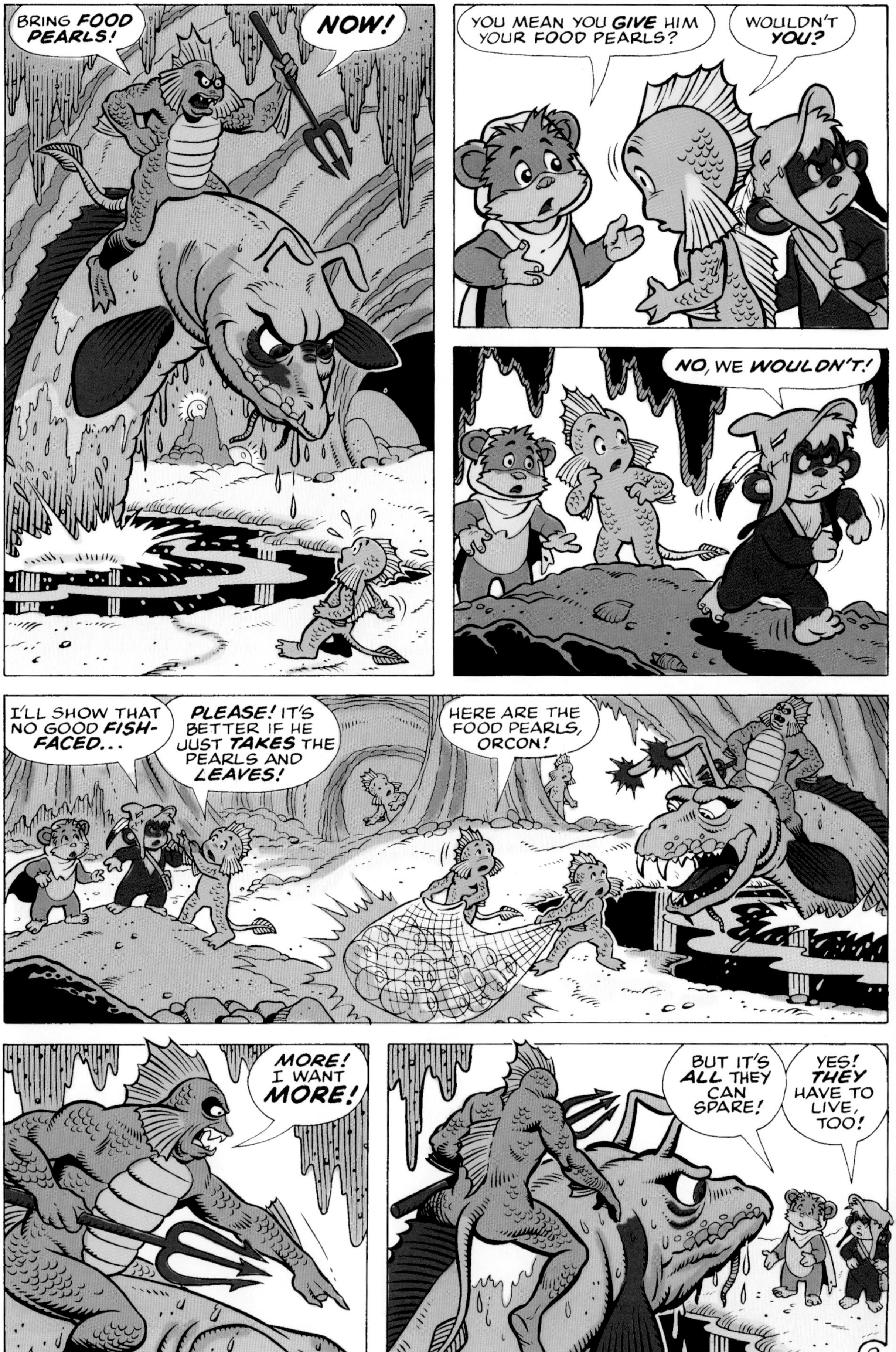
BRING FOOD PEARLS!
NOW!
YOU MEAN YOU GIVE HIM YOUR FOOD PEARLS?
WOULDN'T YOU?
NO, WE WOULDN'T!
I'LL SHOW THAT NO GOOD FISH-FACED...
PLEASE! IT'S BETTER IF HE JUST TAKES THE PEARLS AND LEAVES!
HERE ARE THE FOOD PEARLS, ORCON!
MORE! I WANT MORE!
BUT IT'S ALL THEY CAN SPARE!
YES! THEY HAVE TO LIVE, TOO!
9

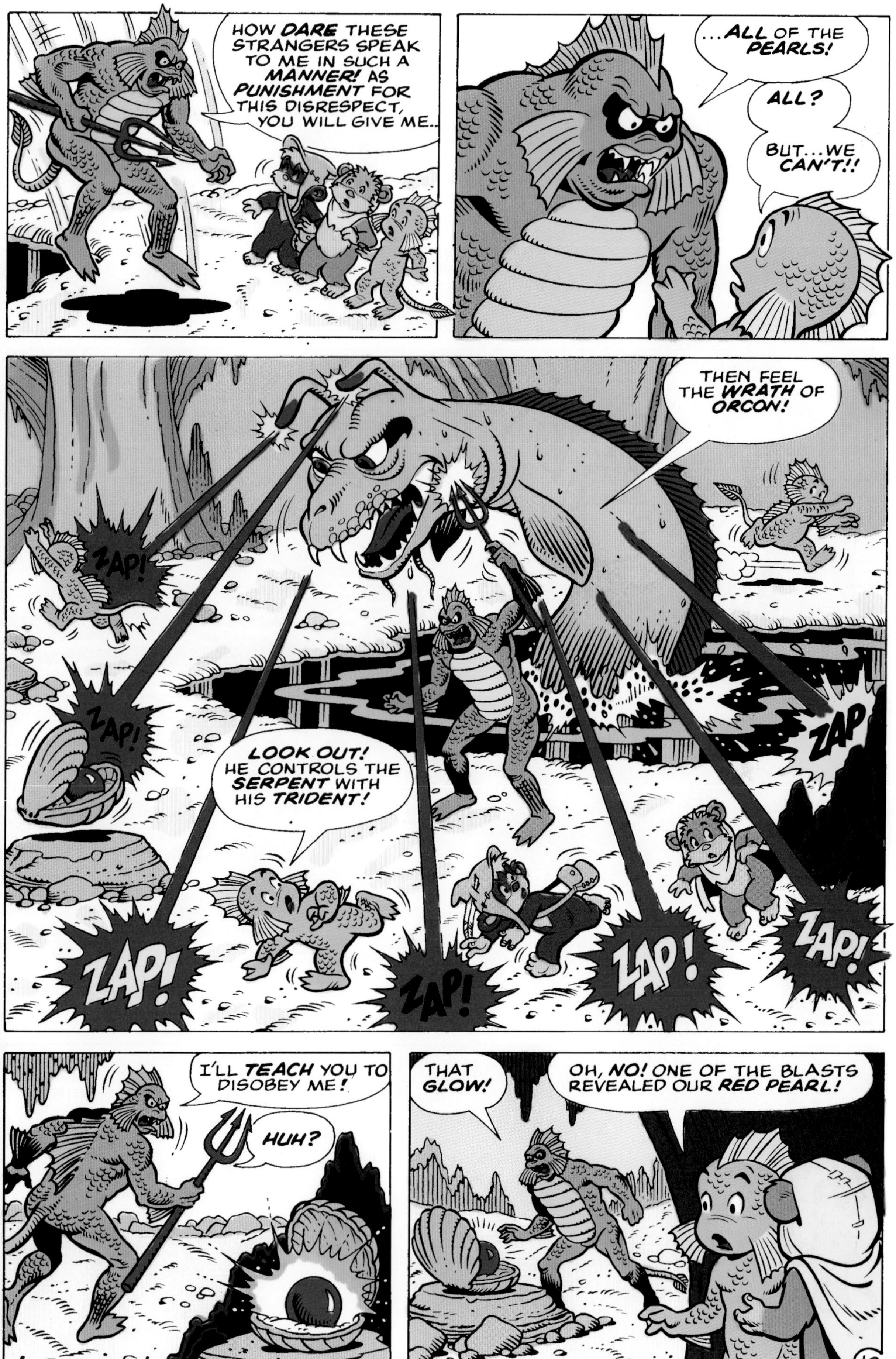
HOW DARE THESE STRANGERS SPEAK TO ME IN SUCH A MANNER! AS PUNISHMENT FOR THIS DISRESPECT, YOU WILL GIVE ME...
...ALL OF THE PEARLS!
ALL?
BUT...WE CAN'T!!
THEN FEEL THE WRATH OF ORCON!
ZAP!
ZAP!
LOOK OUT! HE CONTROLS THE SERPENT WITH HIS TRIDENT!
ZAP
ZAP!
ZAP!
ZAP!
ZAP!
I'LL TEACH YOU TO DISOBEY ME!
HUH?
THAT GLOW!
OH, NO! ONE OF THE BLASTS REVEALED OUR RED PEARL!
10

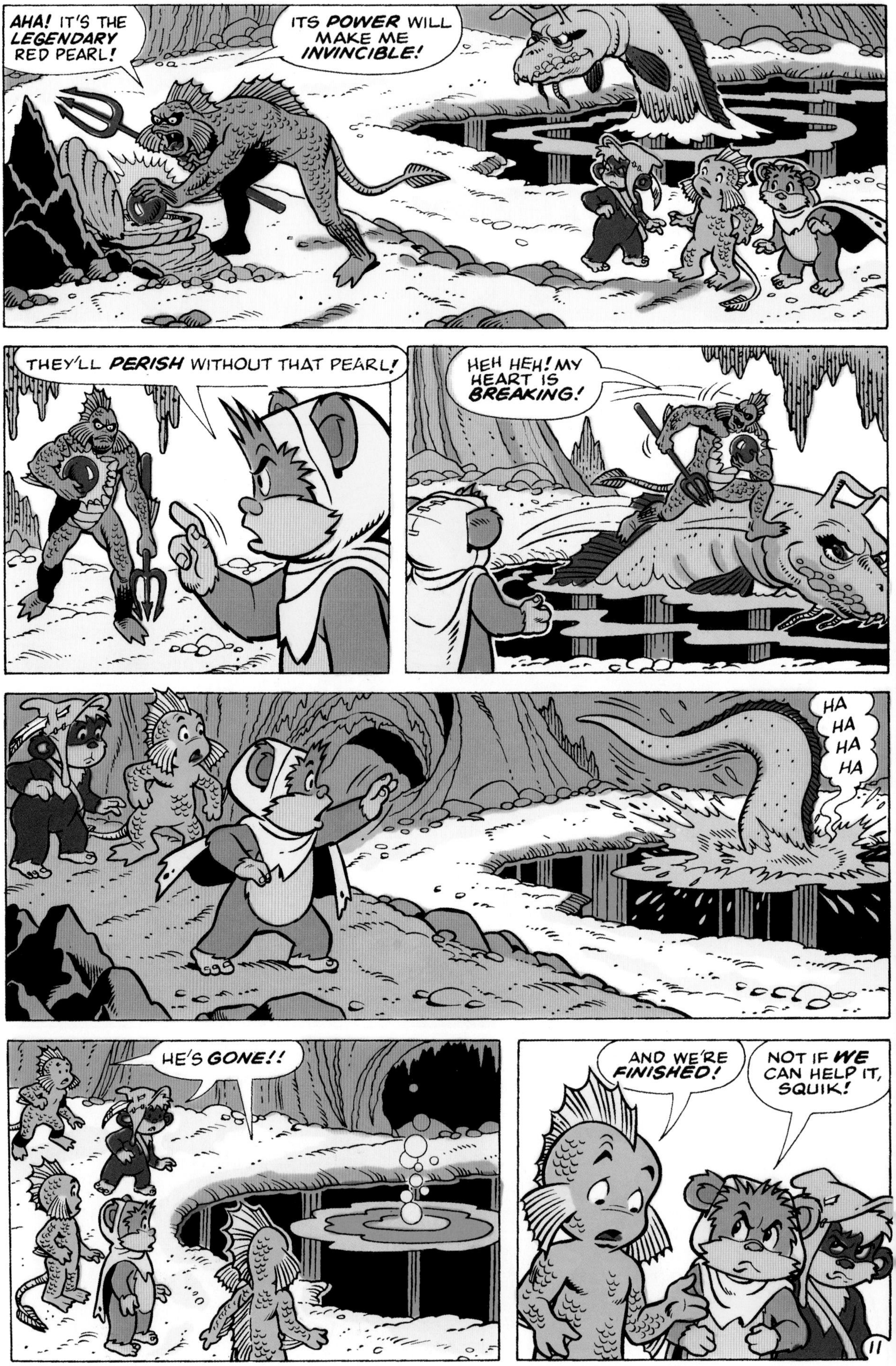

AHA! IT'S THE LEGENDARY RED PEARL!
ITS POWER WILL MAKE ME INVINCIBLE!
THEY'LL PERISH WITHOUT THAT PEARL!
HEH HEH! MY HEART IS BREAKING!
HA HA HA HA
HE'S GONE!!
AND WE'RE FINISHED!
NOT IF WE CAN HELP IT, SQUIK!
11

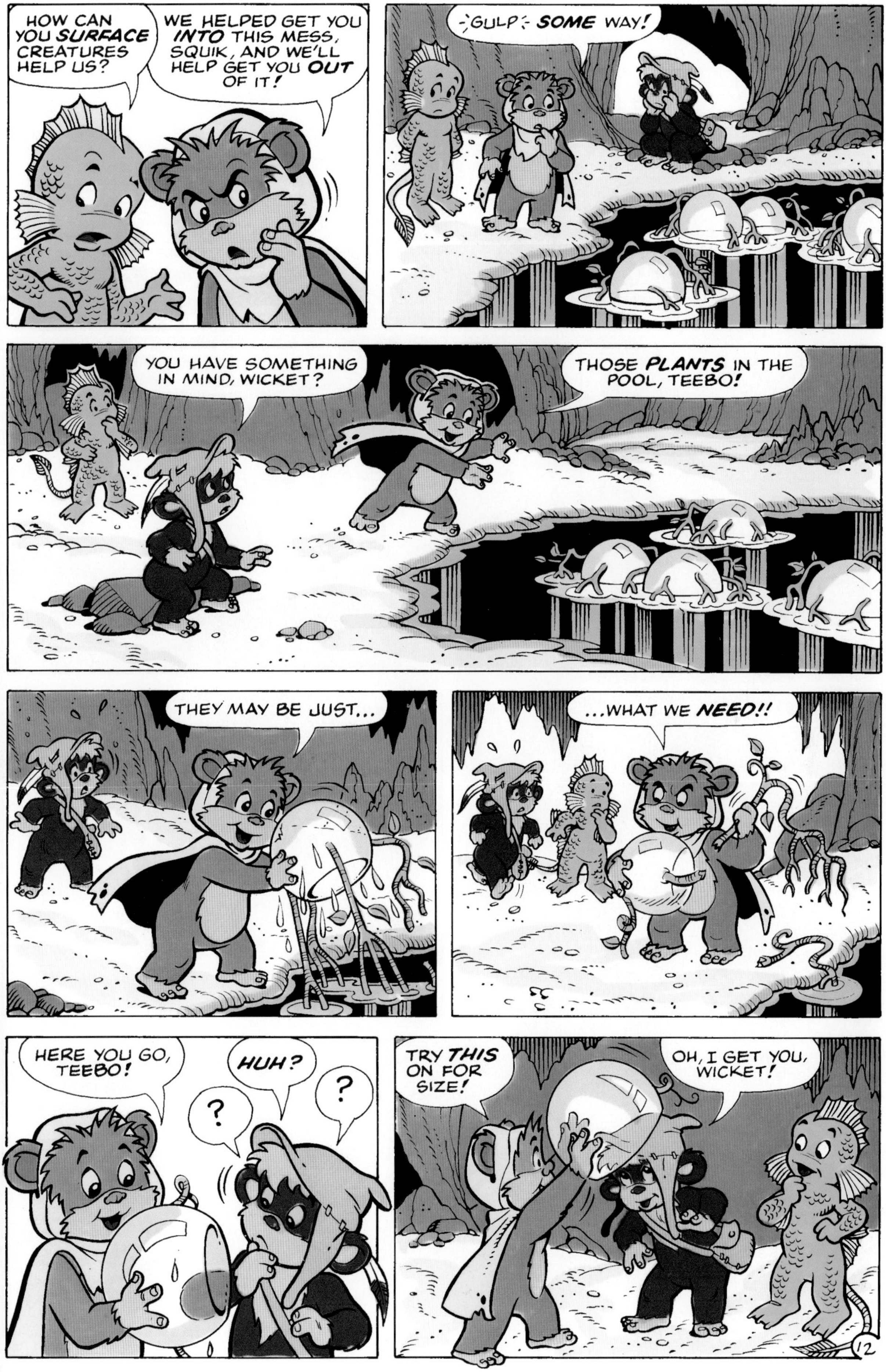
HOW CAN YOU *SURFACE* CREATURES HELP US?
WE HELPED GET YOU *INTO* THIS MESS, SQUIK, AND WE'LL HELP GET YOU *OUT* OF IT!
-GULP- *SOME* WAY!
YOU HAVE SOMETHING IN MIND, WICKET?
THOSE *PLANTS* IN THE POOL, TEEBO!
THEY MAY BE JUST...
...WHAT WE *NEED!!*
HERE YOU GO, TEEBO!
HUH?
?
?
TRY *THIS* ON FOR SIZE!
OH, I GET YOU, WICKET!
12

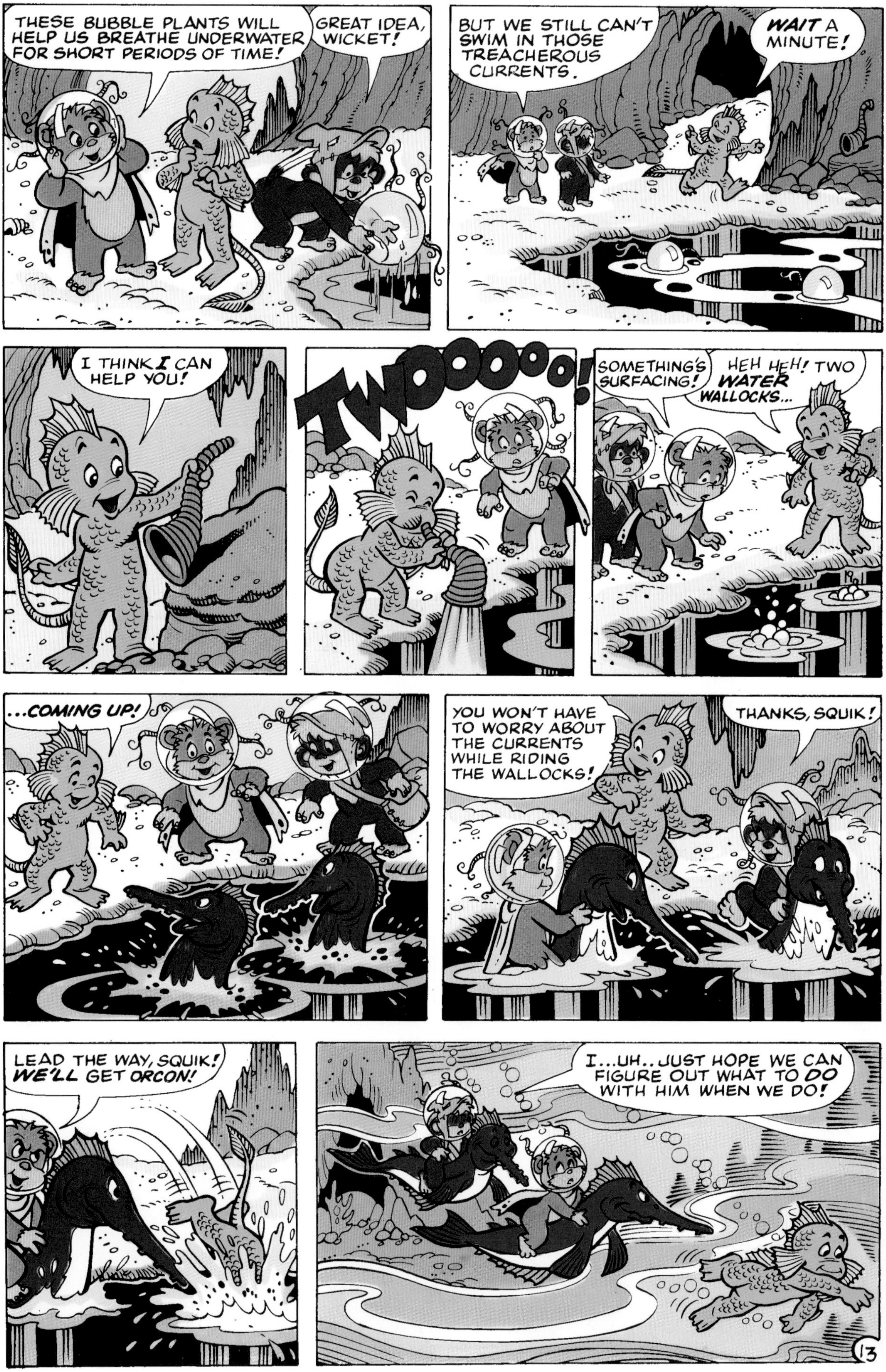
THESE BUBBLE PLANTS WILL HELP US BREATHE UNDERWATER FOR SHORT PERIODS OF TIME!
GREAT IDEA, WICKET!
BUT WE STILL CAN'T SWIM IN THOSE TREACHEROUS CURRENTS.
WAIT A MINUTE!
I THINK I CAN HELP YOU!
TWOOOOOO!
SOMETHING'S SURFACING!
HEH HEH! TWO WATER WALLOCKS...
...COMING UP!
YOU WON'T HAVE TO WORRY ABOUT THE CURRENTS WHILE RIDING THE WALLOCKS!
THANKS, SQUIK!
LEAD THE WAY, SQUIK! WE'LL GET ORCON!
I...UH..JUST HOPE WE CAN FIGURE OUT WHAT TO DO WITH HIM WHEN WE DO!
13

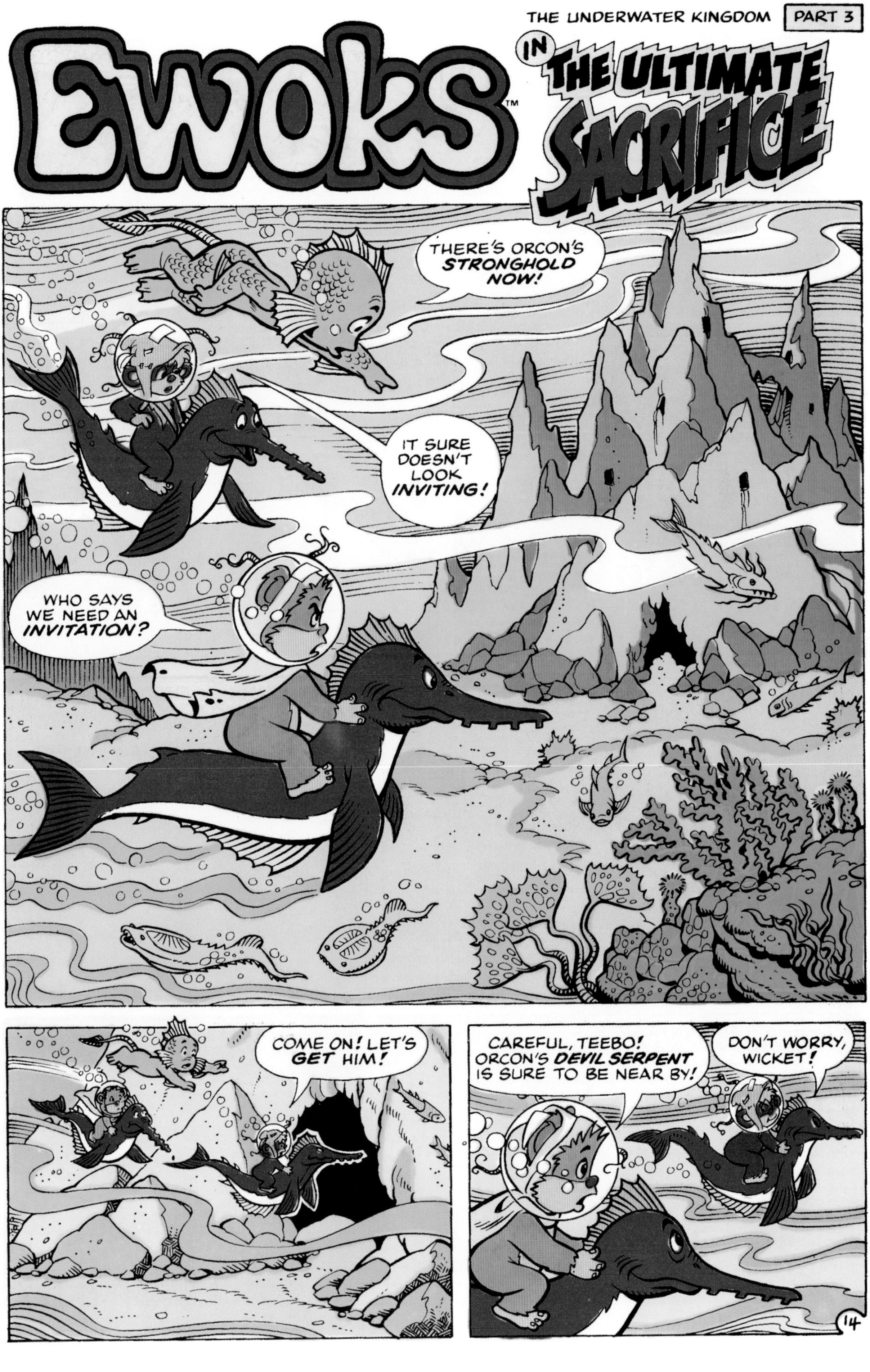
THE UNDERWATER KINGDOM
PART 3
Ewoks™
IN
THE ULTIMATE SACRIFICE
THERE'S ORCON'S STRONGHOLD NOW!
IT SURE DOESN'T LOOK INVITING!
WHO SAYS WE NEED AN INVITATION?
COME ON! LET'S GET HIM!
CAREFUL, TEEBO! ORCON'S DEVIL SERPENT IS SURE TO BE NEAR BY!
DON'T WORRY, WICKET!
14

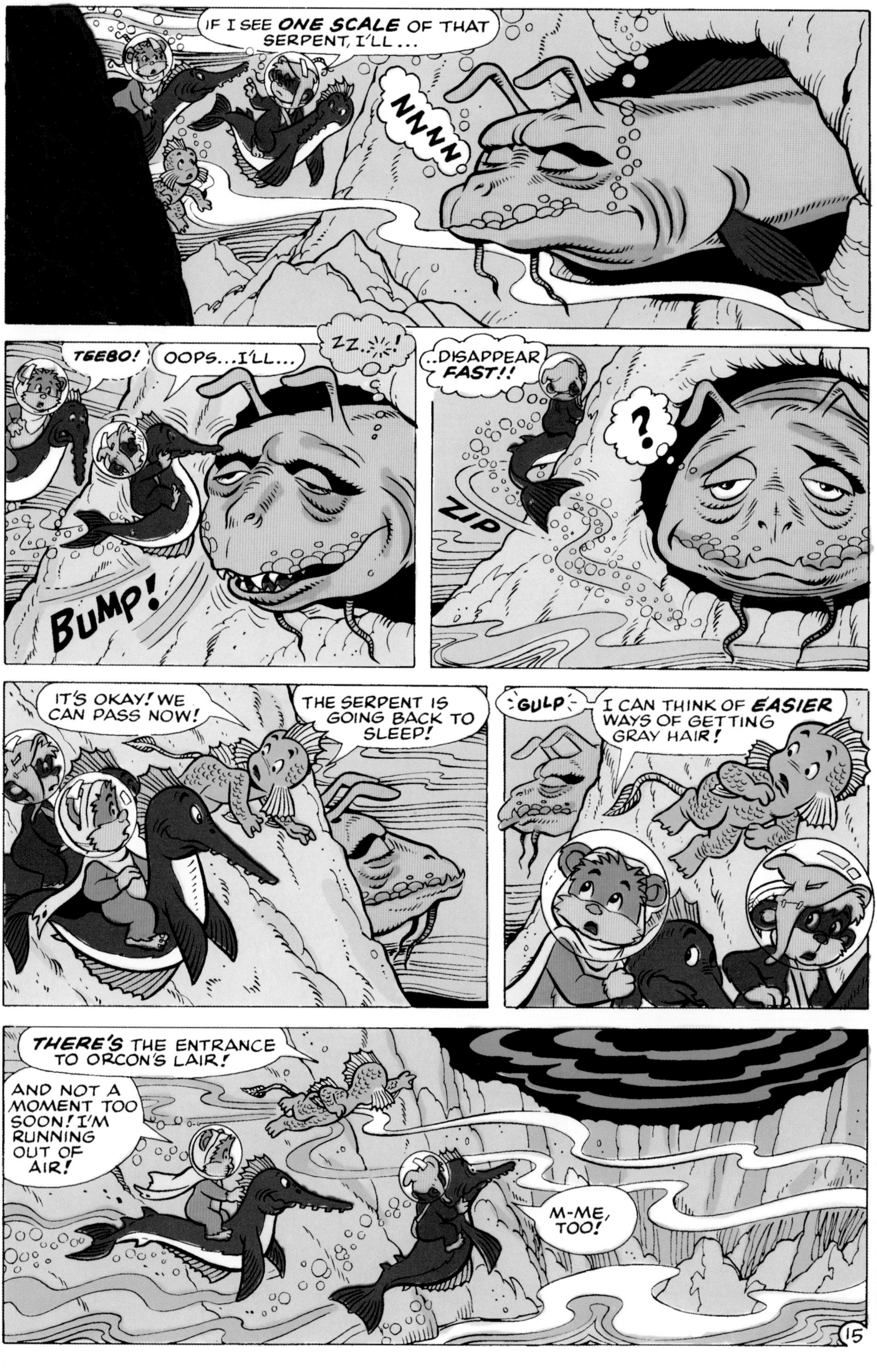
IF I SEE ONE SCALE OF THAT SERPENT, I'LL...
NNNN
TEEBO!
OOPS...I'LL...
ZZ...!
..DISAPPEAR FAST!!
?
ZIP
BUMP!
IT'S OKAY! WE CAN PASS NOW!
THE SERPENT IS GOING BACK TO SLEEP!
GULP
I CAN THINK OF EASIER WAYS OF GETTING GRAY HAIR!
THERE'S THE ENTRANCE TO ORCON'S LAIR!
AND NOT A MOMENT TOO SOON! I'M RUNNING OUT OF AIR!
M-ME, TOO!
15

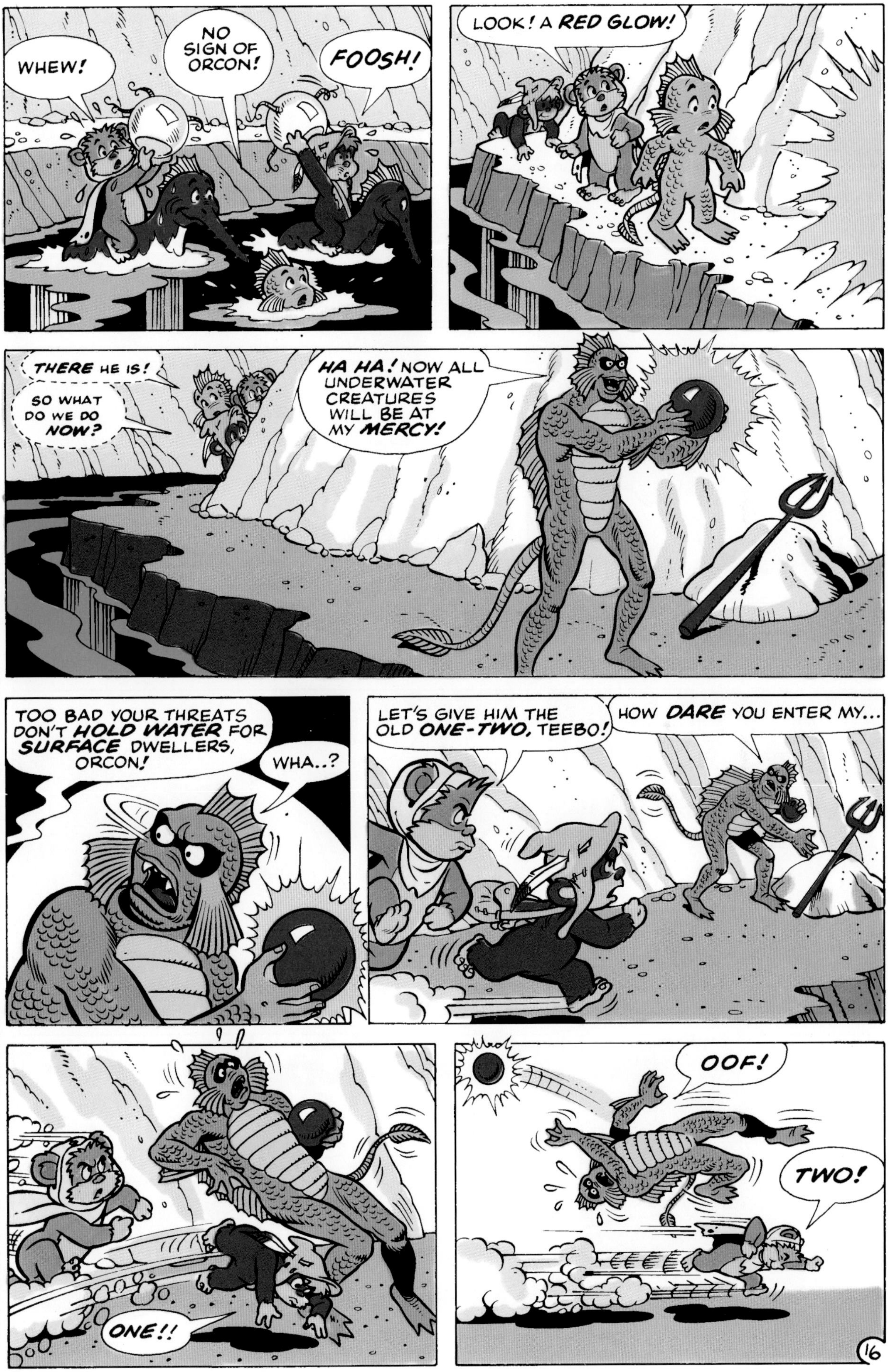
WHEW!
NO SIGN OF ORCON!
FOOSH!
LOOK! A RED GLOW!
THERE HE IS!
SO WHAT DO WE DO NOW?
HA HA! NOW ALL UNDERWATER CREATURES WILL BE AT MY MERCY!
TOO BAD YOUR THREATS DON'T HOLD WATER FOR SURFACE DWELLERS, ORCON!
WHA..?
LET'S GIVE HIM THE OLD ONE-TWO, TEEBO!
HOW DARE YOU ENTER MY...
ONE!!
OOF!
TWO!
16

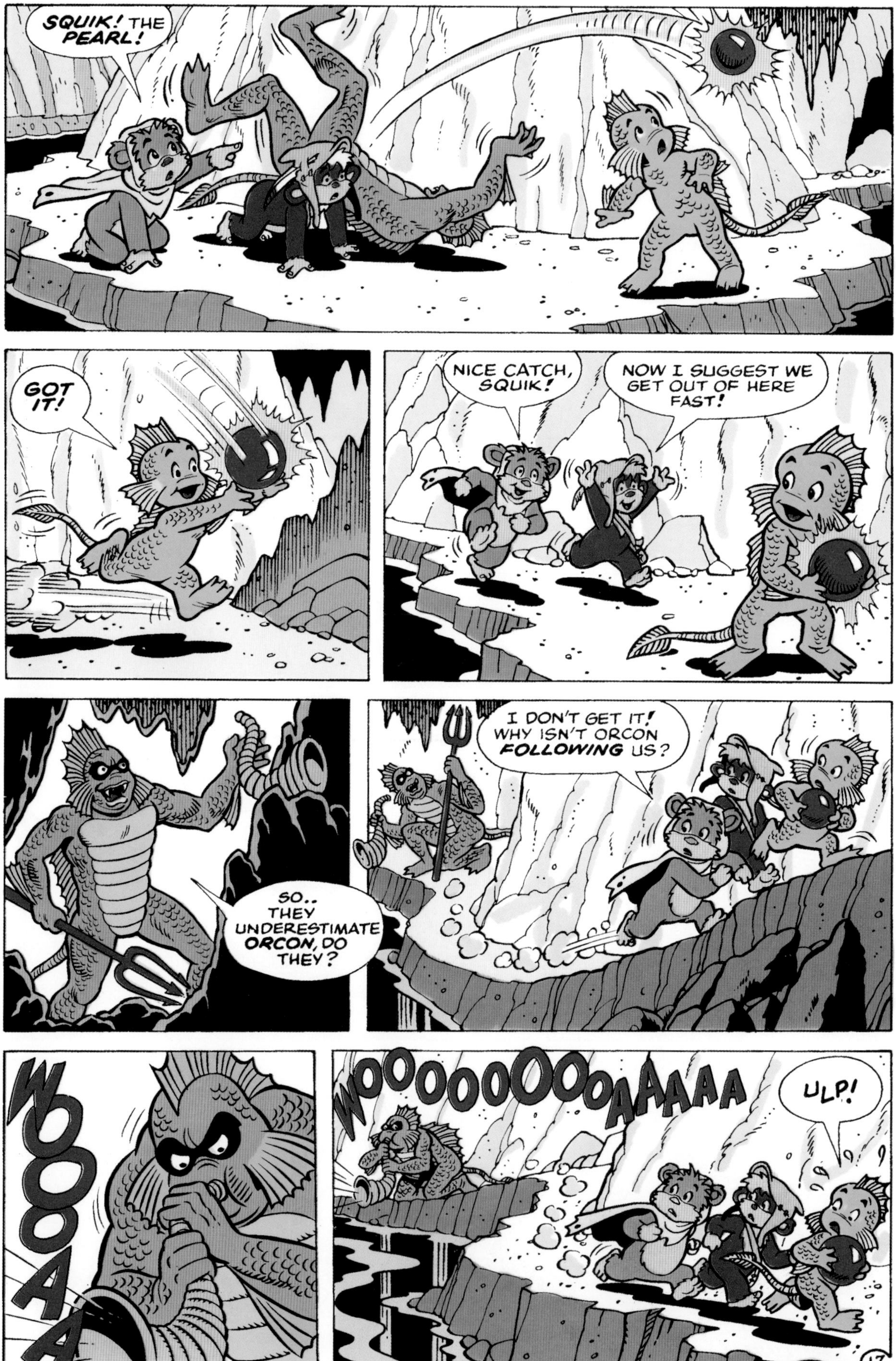
SQUIK! THE PEARL!
GOT IT!
NICE CATCH, SQUIK!
NOW I SUGGEST WE GET OUT OF HERE FAST!
SO.. THEY UNDERESTIMATE ORCON, DO THEY?
I DON'T GET IT! WHY ISN'T ORCON FOLLOWING US?
WOOOAAA
WOOOOOOOOOAAAAAA
ULP!
17

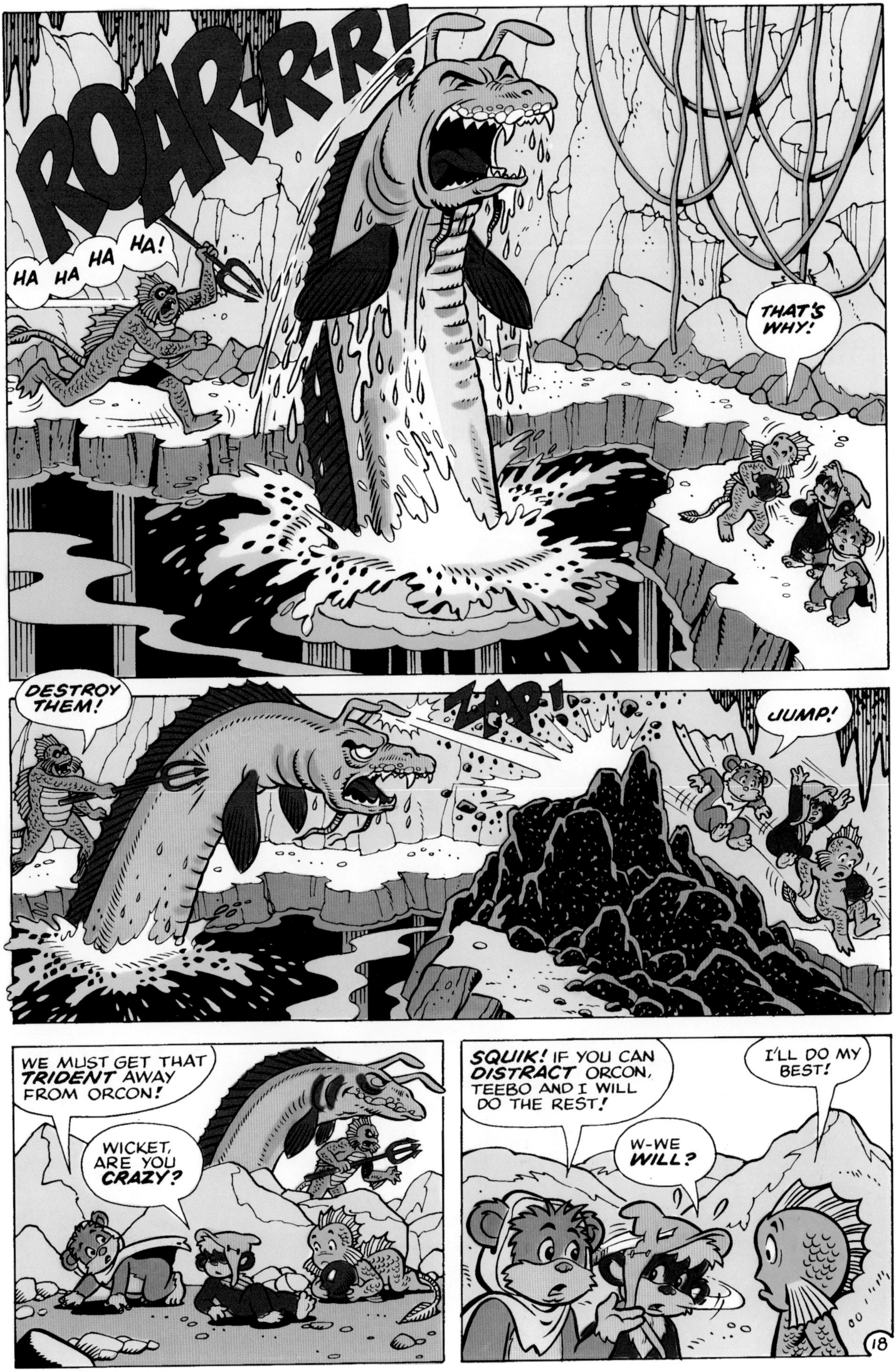
ROAR-R-R!
HA HA HA HA!
THAT'S WHY!
DESTROY THEM!
ZAP!
JUMP!
WE MUST GET THAT TRIDENT AWAY FROM ORCON!
WICKET, ARE YOU CRAZY?
SQUIK! IF YOU CAN DISTRACT ORCON, TEEBO AND I WILL DO THE REST!
W-WE WILL?
I'LL DO MY BEST!
18

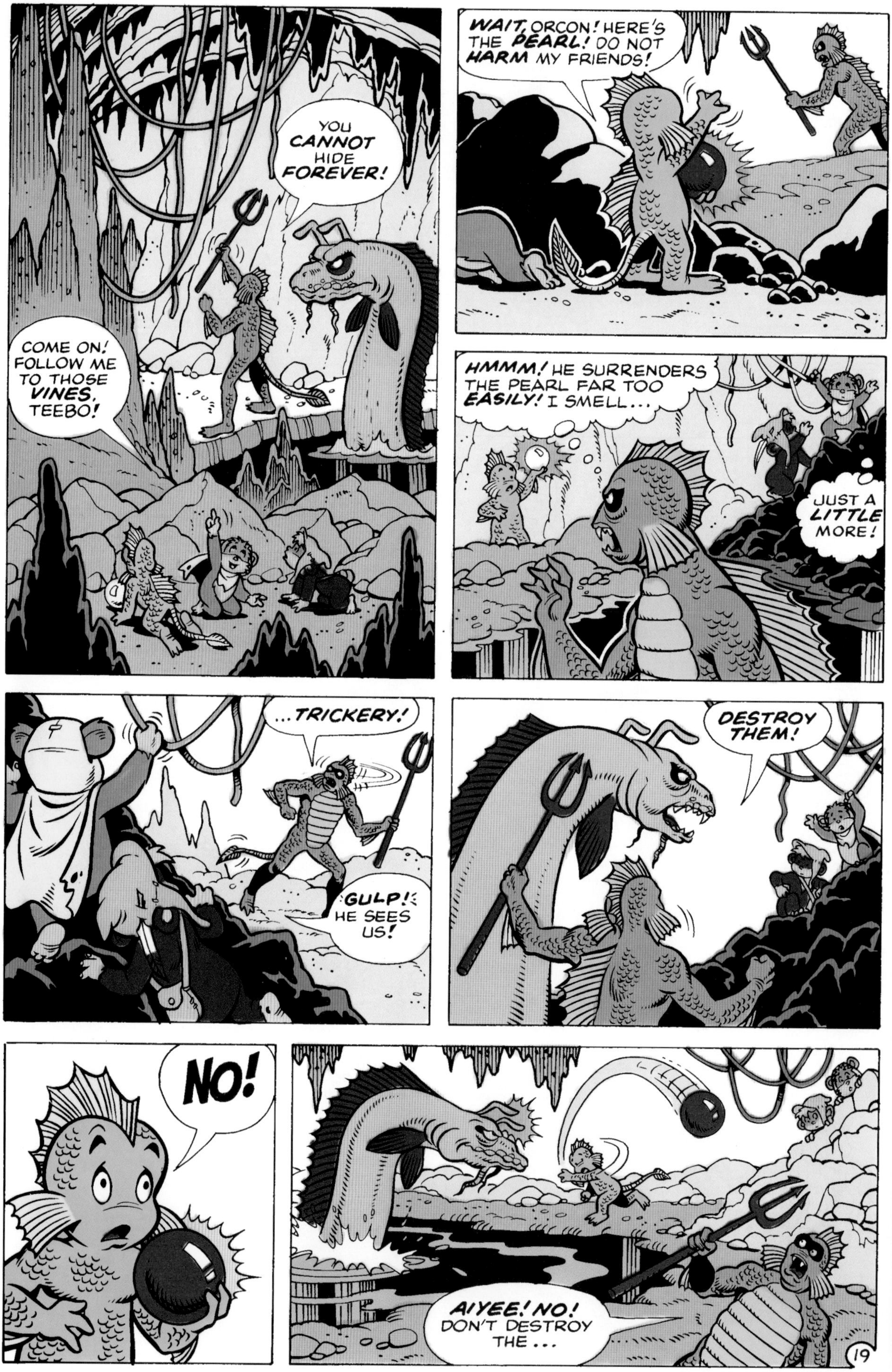
YOU CANNOT HIDE FOREVER!
COME ON! FOLLOW ME TO THOSE VINES, TEEBO!
WAIT, ORCON! HERE'S THE PEARL! DO NOT HARM MY FRIENDS!
HMMM! HE SURRENDERS THE PEARL FAR TOO EASILY! I SMELL...
JUST A LITTLE MORE!
...TRICKERY!
GULP! HE SEES US!
DESTROY THEM!
NO!
AIYEE! NO! DON'T DESTROY THE...
19

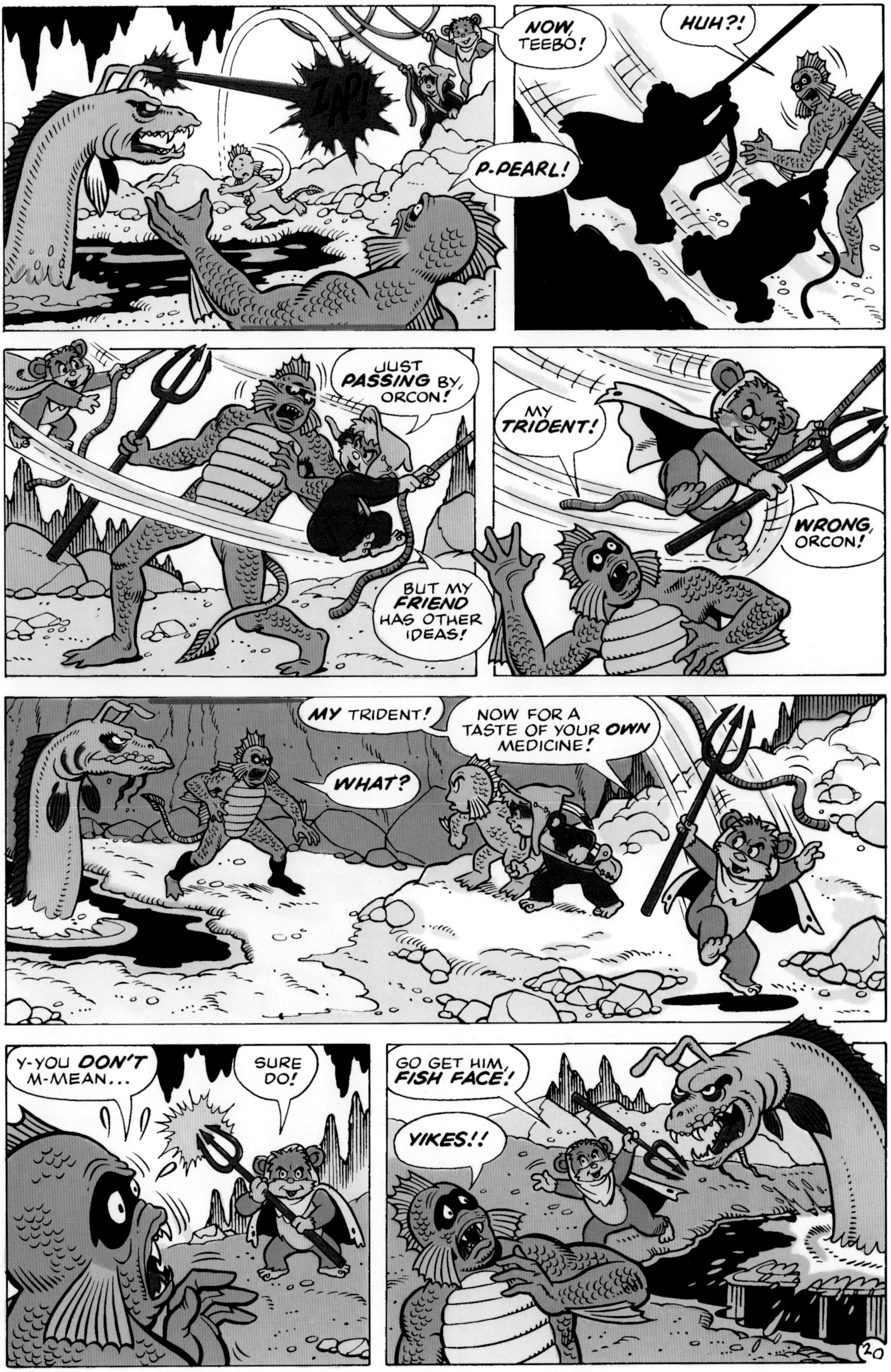
ZAP!
NOW, TEEBO!
P-PEARL!
HUH?!
JUST PASSING BY, ORCON!
BUT MY FRIEND HAS OTHER IDEAS!
MY TRIDENT!
WRONG, ORCON!
MY TRIDENT!
NOW FOR A TASTE OF YOUR OWN MEDICINE!
WHAT?
Y-YOU DON'T M-MEAN...
SURE DO!
GO GET HIM, FISH FACE!
YIKES!!
20

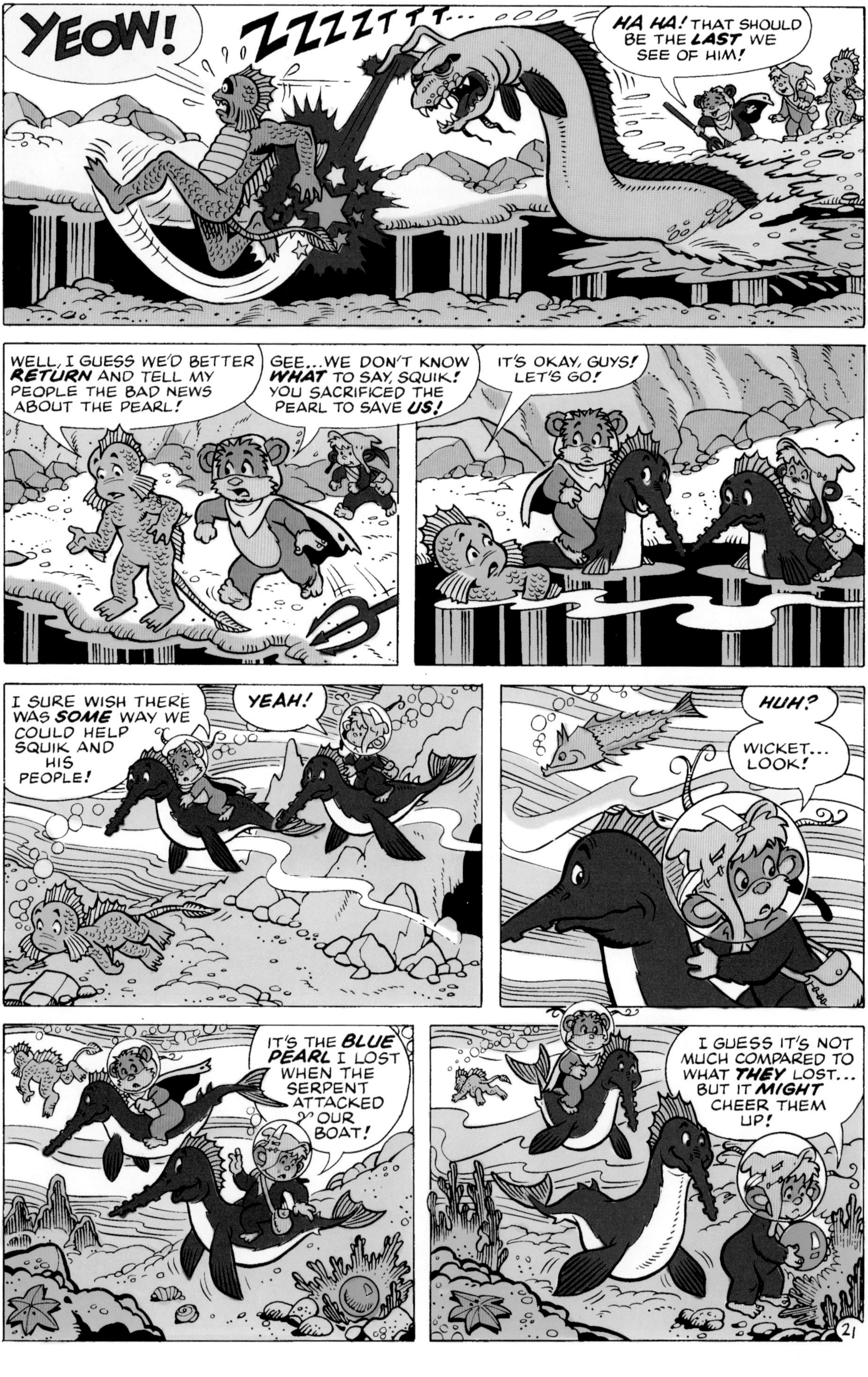
YEOW!
ZZZZZTTTT...
HA HA! THAT SHOULD BE THE LAST WE SEE OF HIM!
WELL, I GUESS WE'D BETTER RETURN AND TELL MY PEOPLE THE BAD NEWS ABOUT THE PEARL!
GEE...WE DON'T KNOW WHAT TO SAY, SQUIK! YOU SACRIFICED THE PEARL TO SAVE US!
IT'S OKAY, GUYS! LET'S GO!
I SURE WISH THERE WAS SOME WAY WE COULD HELP SQUIK AND HIS PEOPLE!
YEAH!
HUH?
WICKET... LOOK!
IT'S THE BLUE PEARL I LOST WHEN THE SERPENT ATTACKED OUR BOAT!
I GUESS IT'S NOT MUCH COMPARED TO WHAT THEY LOST... BUT IT MIGHT CHEER THEM UP!
21

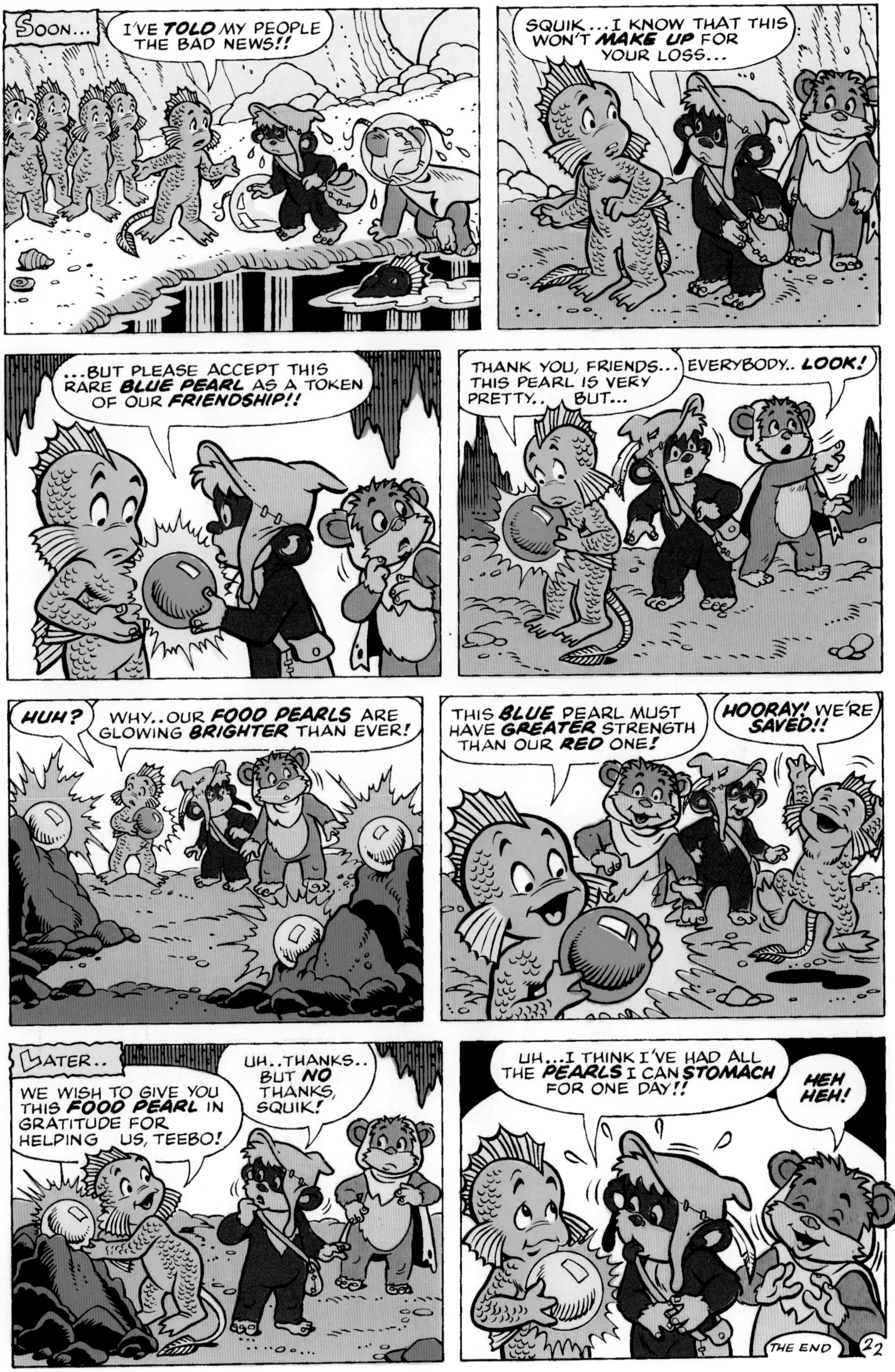
SOON...
I'VE TOLD MY PEOPLE THE BAD NEWS!!
SQUIK... I KNOW THAT THIS WON'T MAKE UP FOR YOUR LOSS...
...BUT PLEASE ACCEPT THIS RARE BLUE PEARL AS A TOKEN OF OUR FRIENDSHIP!!
THANK YOU, FRIENDS... THIS PEARL IS VERY PRETTY.. BUT...
EVERYBODY.. LOOK!
HUH?
WHY..OUR FOOD PEARLS ARE GLOWING BRIGHTER THAN EVER!
THIS BLUE PEARL MUST HAVE GREATER STRENGTH THAN OUR RED ONE!
HOORAY! WE'RE SAVED!!
LATER..
WE WISH TO GIVE YOU THIS FOOD PEARL IN GRATITUDE FOR HELPING US, TEEBO!
UH..THANKS.. BUT NO THANKS, SQUIK!
UH...I THINK I'VE HAD ALL THE PEARLS I CAN STOMACH FOR ONE DAY!!
HEH HEH!
THE END
22

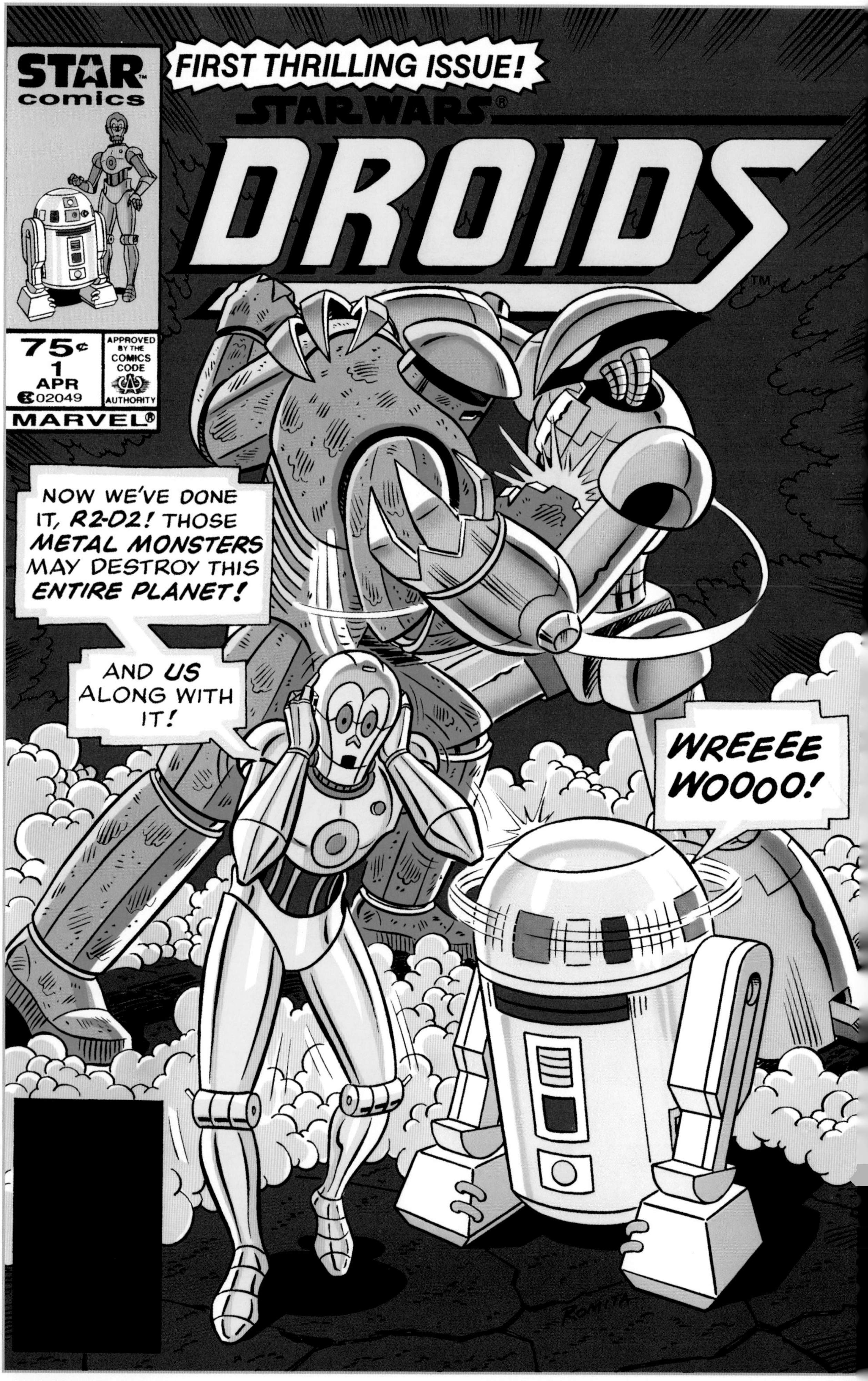
STAR comics
FIRST THRILLING ISSUE!
STAR WARS®
DROIDS™
75¢
1
APR
02049
APPROVED BY THE COMICS CODE AUTHORITY
MARVEL®
NOW WE'VE DONE IT, R2-D2! THOSE METAL MONSTERS MAY DESTROY THIS ENTIRE PLANET!
AND US ALONG WITH IT!
WREEEE WOOOO!
ROMITA

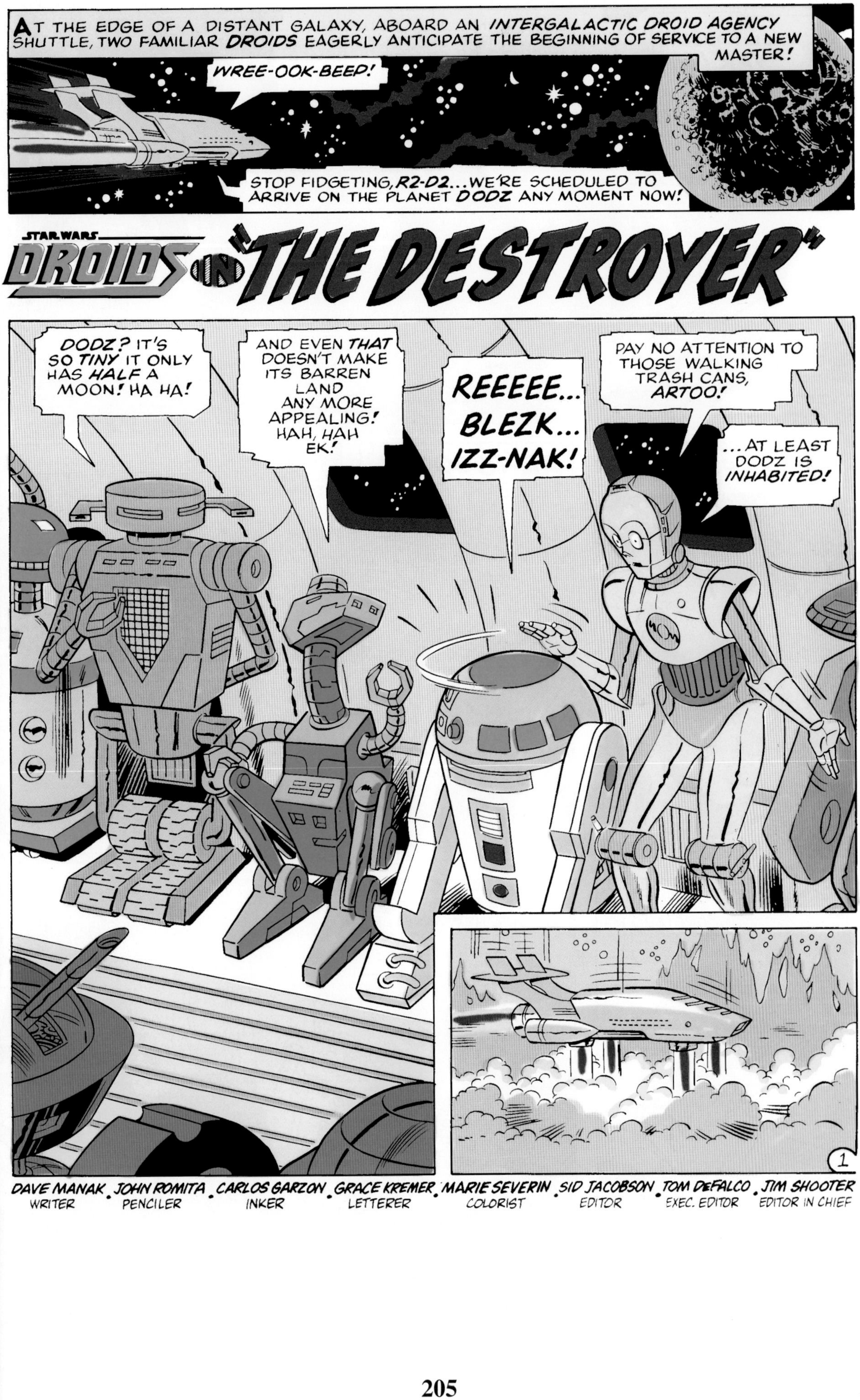

AT THE EDGE OF A DISTANT GALAXY, ABOARD AN INTERGALACTIC DROID AGENCY SHUTTLE, TWO FAMILIAR DROIDS EAGERLY ANTICIPATE THE BEGINNING OF SERVICE TO A NEW MASTER!
WREE-OOK-BEEP!
STOP FIDGETING, R2-D2... WE'RE SCHEDULED TO ARRIVE ON THE PLANET DODZ ANY MOMENT NOW!
STAR WARS DROIDS IN "THE DESTROYER"
DODZ? IT'S SO TINY IT ONLY HAS HALF A MOON! HA HA!
AND EVEN THAT DOESN'T MAKE ITS BARREN LAND ANY MORE APPEALING! HAH, HAH EK!
REEEEE... BLEZK... IZZ-NAK!
PAY NO ATTENTION TO THOSE WALKING TRASH CANS, ARTOO!
...AT LEAST DODZ IS INHABITED!
1
DAVE MANAK WRITER · JOHN ROMITA PENCILER · CARLOS GARZON INKER · GRACE KREMER LETTERER · MARIE SEVERIN COLORIST · SID JACOBSON EDITOR · TOM DeFALCO EXEC. EDITOR · JIM SHOOTER EDITOR IN CHIEF

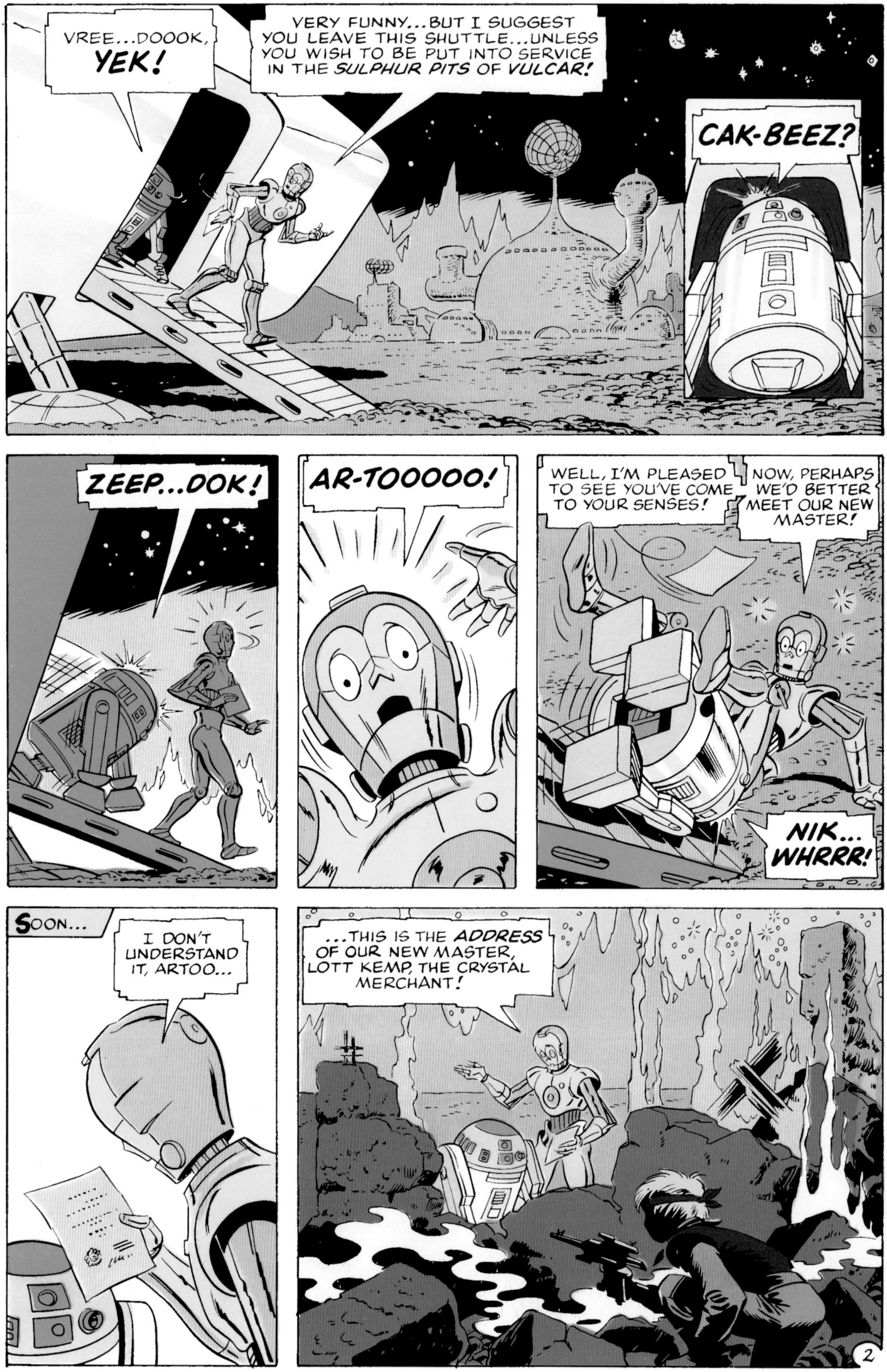
VREE...DOOOK, YEK!
VERY FUNNY...BUT I SUGGEST YOU LEAVE THIS SHUTTLE...UNLESS YOU WISH TO BE PUT INTO SERVICE IN THE SULPHUR PITS OF VULCAR!
CAK-BEEZ?
ZEEP...DOK!
AR-TOOOOO!
WELL, I'M PLEASED TO SEE YOU'VE COME TO YOUR SENSES!
NOW, PERHAPS WE'D BETTER MEET OUR NEW MASTER!
NIK... WHRRR!
SOON...
I DON'T UNDERSTAND IT, ARTOO...
...THIS IS THE ADDRESS OF OUR NEW MASTER, LOTT KEMP, THE CRYSTAL MERCHANT!
2

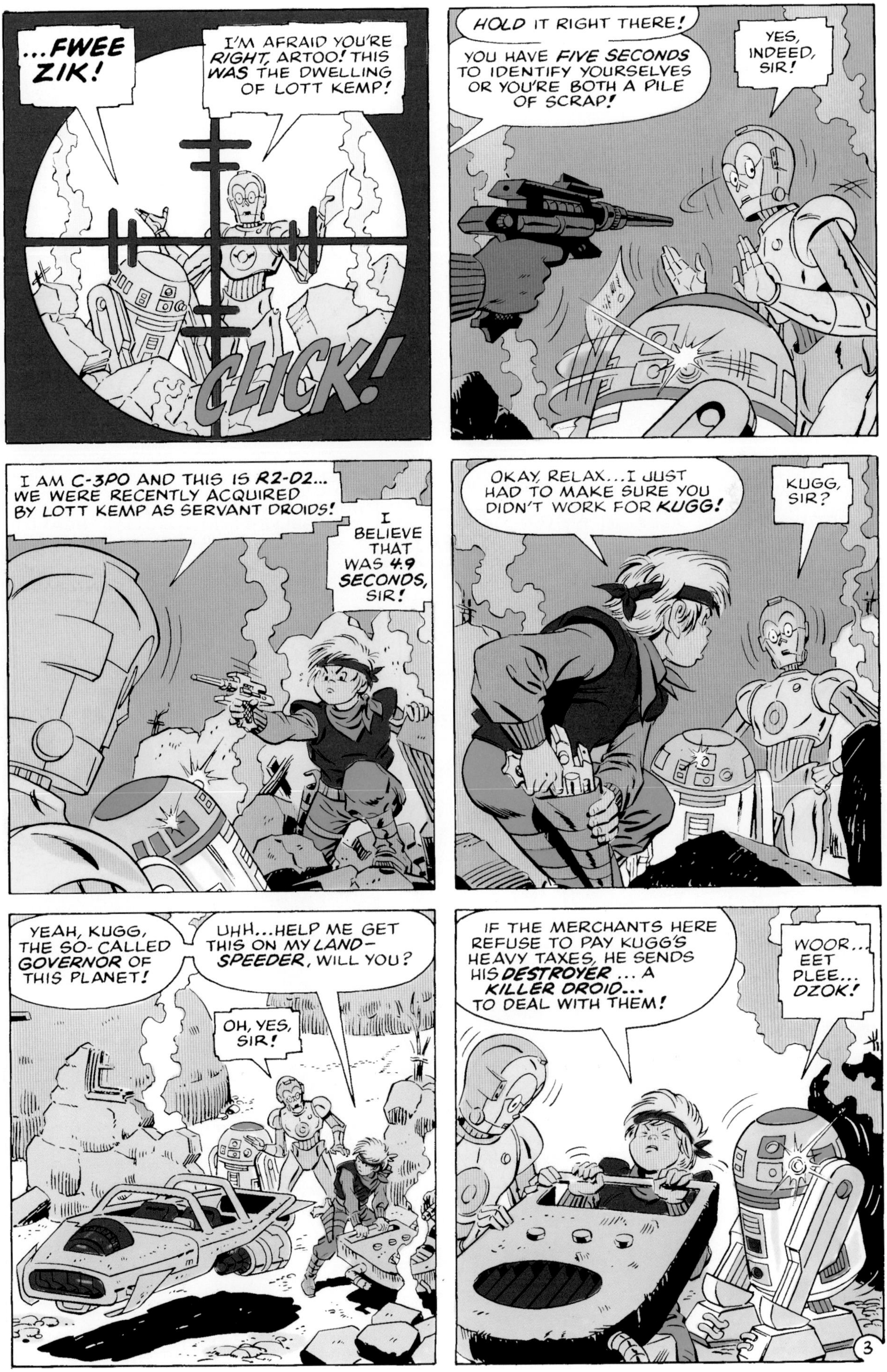
...FWEE ZIK!
I'M AFRAID YOU'RE RIGHT, ARTOO! THIS WAS THE DWELLING OF LOTT KEMP!
CLICK!
HOLD IT RIGHT THERE!
YOU HAVE FIVE SECONDS TO IDENTIFY YOURSELVES OR YOU'RE BOTH A PILE OF SCRAP!
YES, INDEED, SIR!
I AM C-3PO AND THIS IS R2-D2... WE WERE RECENTLY ACQUIRED BY LOTT KEMP AS SERVANT DROIDS!
I BELIEVE THAT WAS 4.9 SECONDS, SIR!
OKAY, RELAX...I JUST HAD TO MAKE SURE YOU DIDN'T WORK FOR KUGG!
KUGG, SIR?
YEAH, KUGG, THE SO-CALLED GOVERNOR OF THIS PLANET!
UHH...HELP ME GET THIS ON MY LAND-SPEEDER, WILL YOU?
OH, YES, SIR!
IF THE MERCHANTS HERE REFUSE TO PAY KUGG'S HEAVY TAXES, HE SENDS HIS DESTROYER ... A KILLER DROID... TO DEAL WITH THEM!
WOOR... EET PLEE... DZOK!
3

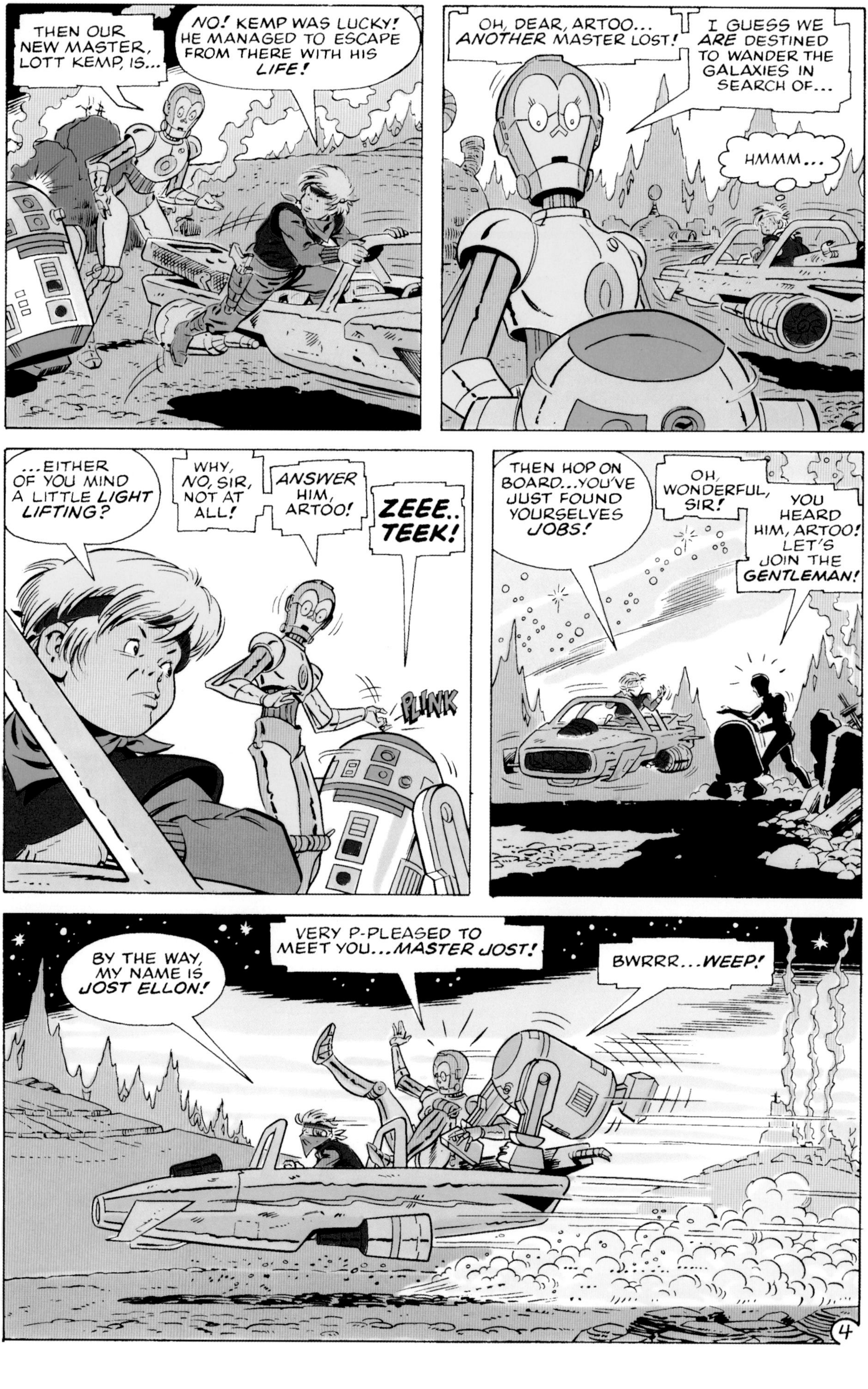
THEN OUR NEW MASTER, LOTT KEMP, IS...
NO! KEMP WAS LUCKY! HE MANAGED TO ESCAPE FROM THERE WITH HIS LIFE!
OH, DEAR, ARTOO... ANOTHER MASTER LOST!
I GUESS WE ARE DESTINED TO WANDER THE GALAXIES IN SEARCH OF...
HMMM...
...EITHER OF YOU MIND A LITTLE LIGHT LIFTING?
WHY, NO, SIR, NOT AT ALL!
ANSWER HIM, ARTOO!
ZEEE.. TEEK!
PLINK
THEN HOP ON BOARD...YOU'VE JUST FOUND YOURSELVES JOBS!
OH, WONDERFUL, SIR!
YOU HEARD HIM, ARTOO! LET'S JOIN THE GENTLEMAN!
BY THE WAY, MY NAME IS JOST ELLON!
VERY P-PLEASED TO MEET YOU... MASTER JOST!
BWRRR... WEEP!
4

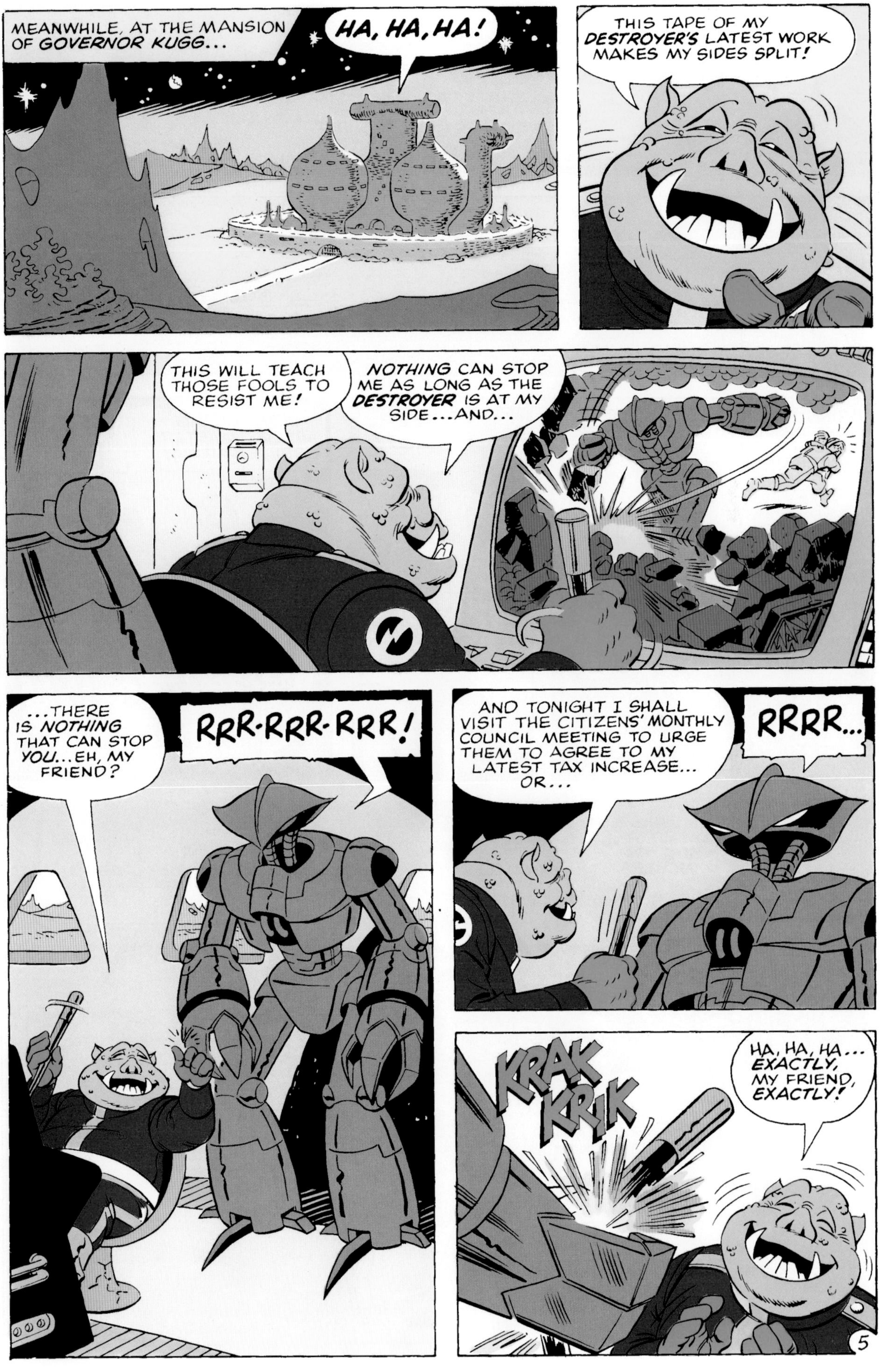
MEANWHILE, AT THE MANSION OF GOVERNOR KUGG...
HA, HA, HA!
THIS TAPE OF MY DESTROYER'S LATEST WORK MAKES MY SIDES SPLIT!
THIS WILL TEACH THOSE FOOLS TO RESIST ME!
NOTHING CAN STOP ME AS LONG AS THE DESTROYER IS AT MY SIDE...AND...
...THERE IS NOTHING THAT CAN STOP YOU...EH, MY FRIEND?
RRR-RRR-RRR!
AND TONIGHT I SHALL VISIT THE CITIZENS' MONTHLY COUNCIL MEETING TO URGE THEM TO AGREE TO MY LATEST TAX INCREASE... OR...
RRRR...
KRAK KRIK
HA, HA, HA... EXACTLY, MY FRIEND, EXACTLY!
5

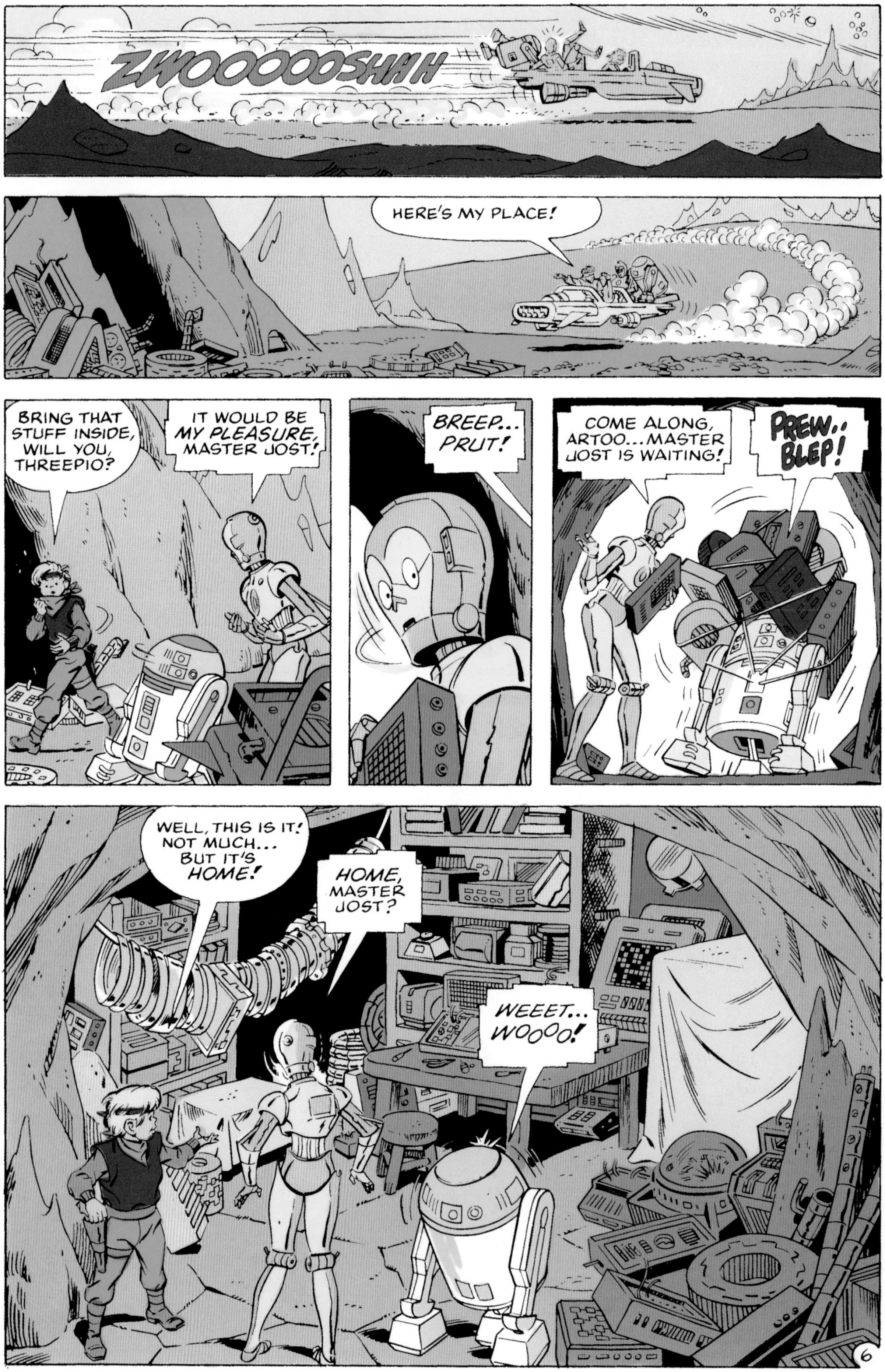
ZWOOOOOSHHH
HERE'S MY PLACE!
BRING THAT STUFF INSIDE, WILL YOU, THREEPIO?
IT WOULD BE MY PLEASURE, MASTER JOST!
BREEP... PRUT!
COME ALONG, ARTOO... MASTER JOST IS WAITING!
PREW.. BLEP!
WELL, THIS IS IT! NOT MUCH... BUT IT'S HOME!
HOME, MASTER JOST?
WEEET... WOOOO!
6

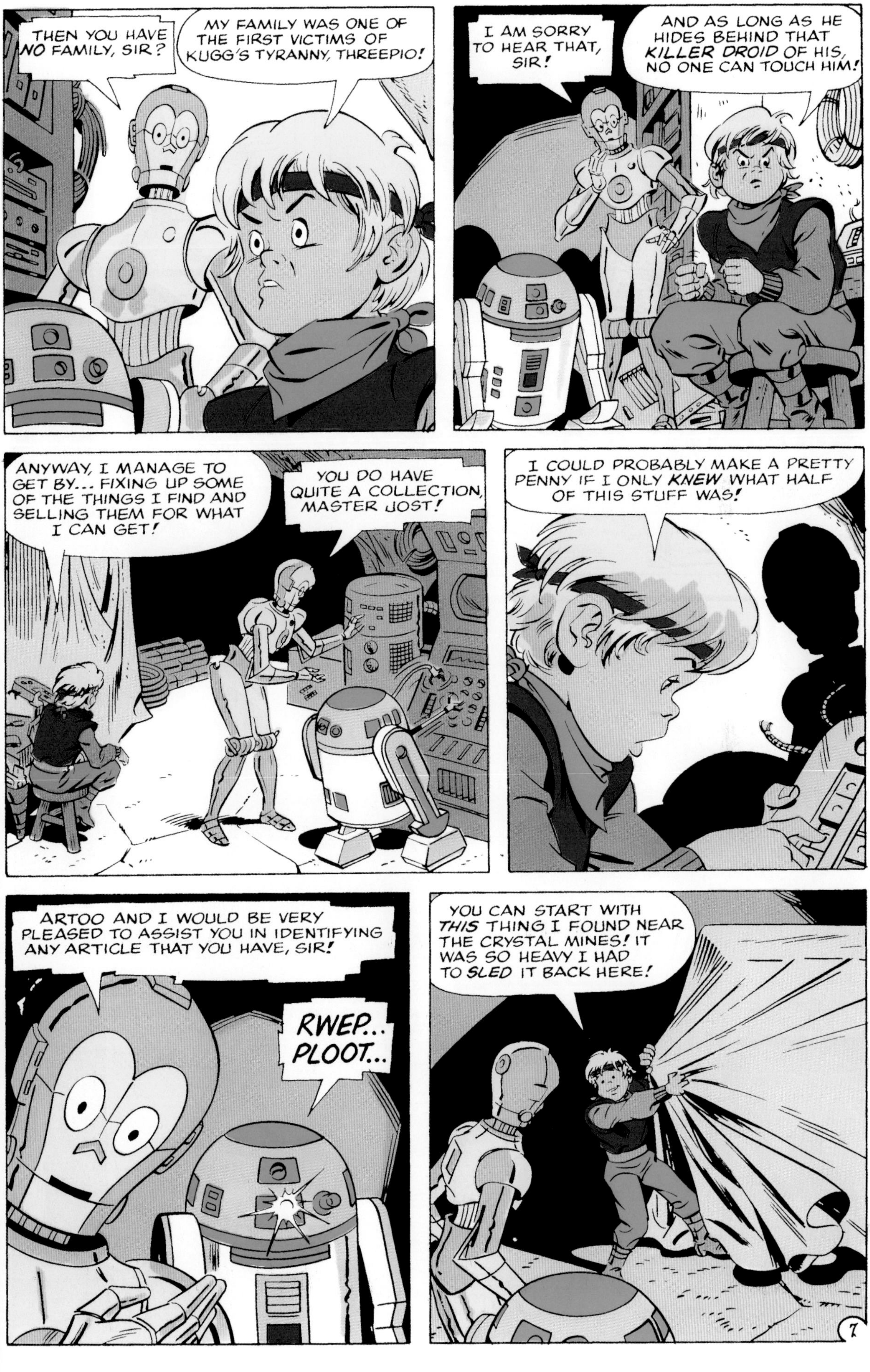
THEN YOU HAVE NO FAMILY, SIR?
MY FAMILY WAS ONE OF THE FIRST VICTIMS OF KUGG'S TYRANNY, THREEPIO!
I AM SORRY TO HEAR THAT, SIR!
AND AS LONG AS HE HIDES BEHIND THAT KILLER DROID OF HIS, NO ONE CAN TOUCH HIM!
ANYWAY, I MANAGE TO GET BY... FIXING UP SOME OF THE THINGS I FIND AND SELLING THEM FOR WHAT I CAN GET!
YOU DO HAVE QUITE A COLLECTION, MASTER JOST!
I COULD PROBABLY MAKE A PRETTY PENNY IF I ONLY KNEW WHAT HALF OF THIS STUFF WAS!
ARTOO AND I WOULD BE VERY PLEASED TO ASSIST YOU IN IDENTIFYING ANY ARTICLE THAT YOU HAVE, SIR!
RWEP... PLOOT...
YOU CAN START WITH THIS THING I FOUND NEAR THE CRYSTAL MINES! IT WAS SO HEAVY I HAD TO SLED IT BACK HERE!
7

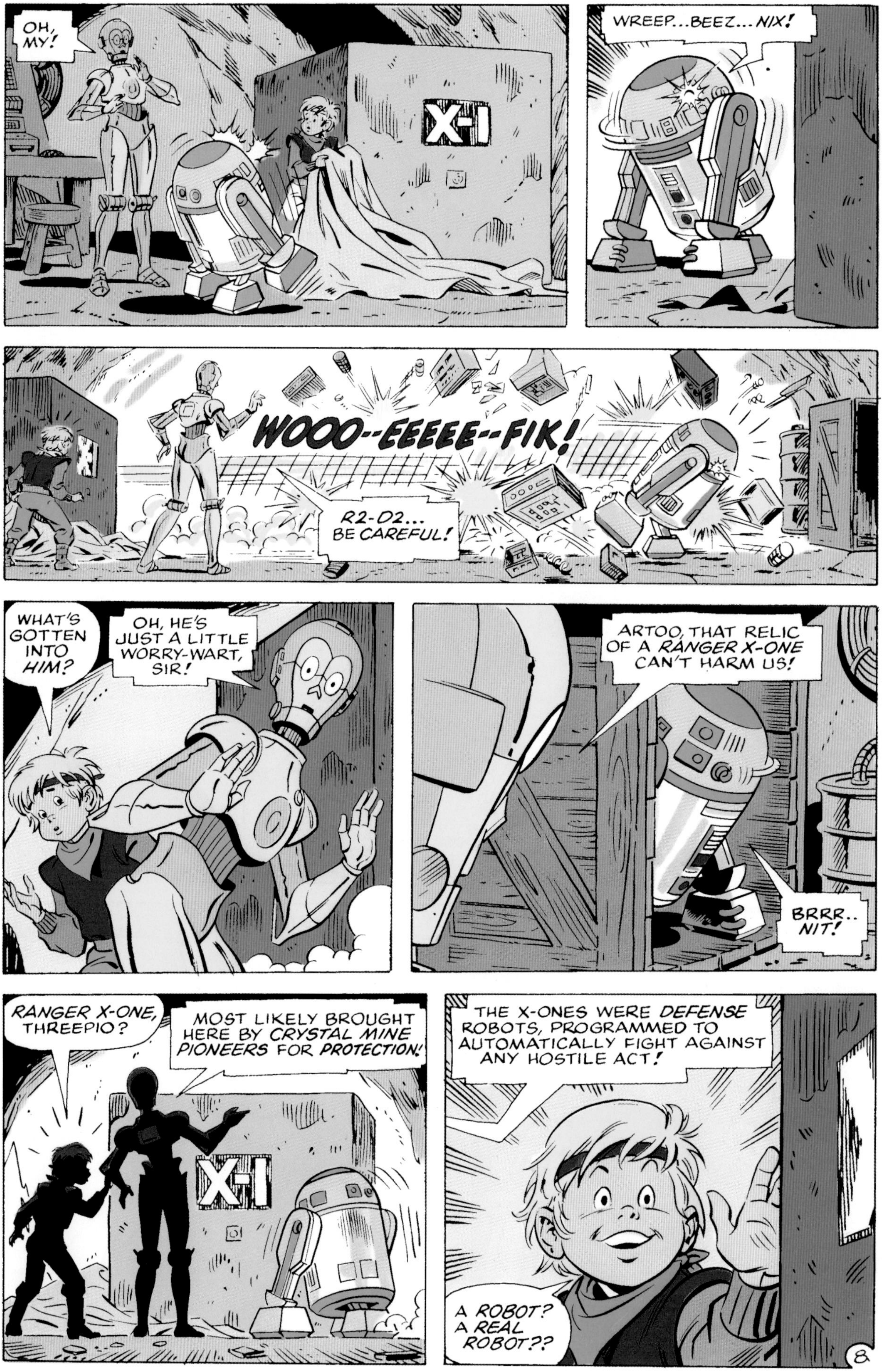
OH, MY!
WREEP...BEEZ...NIX!
WOOO--EEEEE--FIK!
R2-D2... BE CAREFUL!
WHAT'S GOTTEN INTO HIM?
OH, HE'S JUST A LITTLE WORRY-WART, SIR!
ARTOO, THAT RELIC OF A RANGER X-ONE CAN'T HARM US!
BRRR.. NIT!
RANGER X-ONE, THREEPIO?
MOST LIKELY BROUGHT HERE BY CRYSTAL MINE PIONEERS FOR PROTECTION!
THE X-ONES WERE DEFENSE ROBOTS, PROGRAMMED TO AUTOMATICALLY FIGHT AGAINST ANY HOSTILE ACT!
A ROBOT? A REAL ROBOT??
8

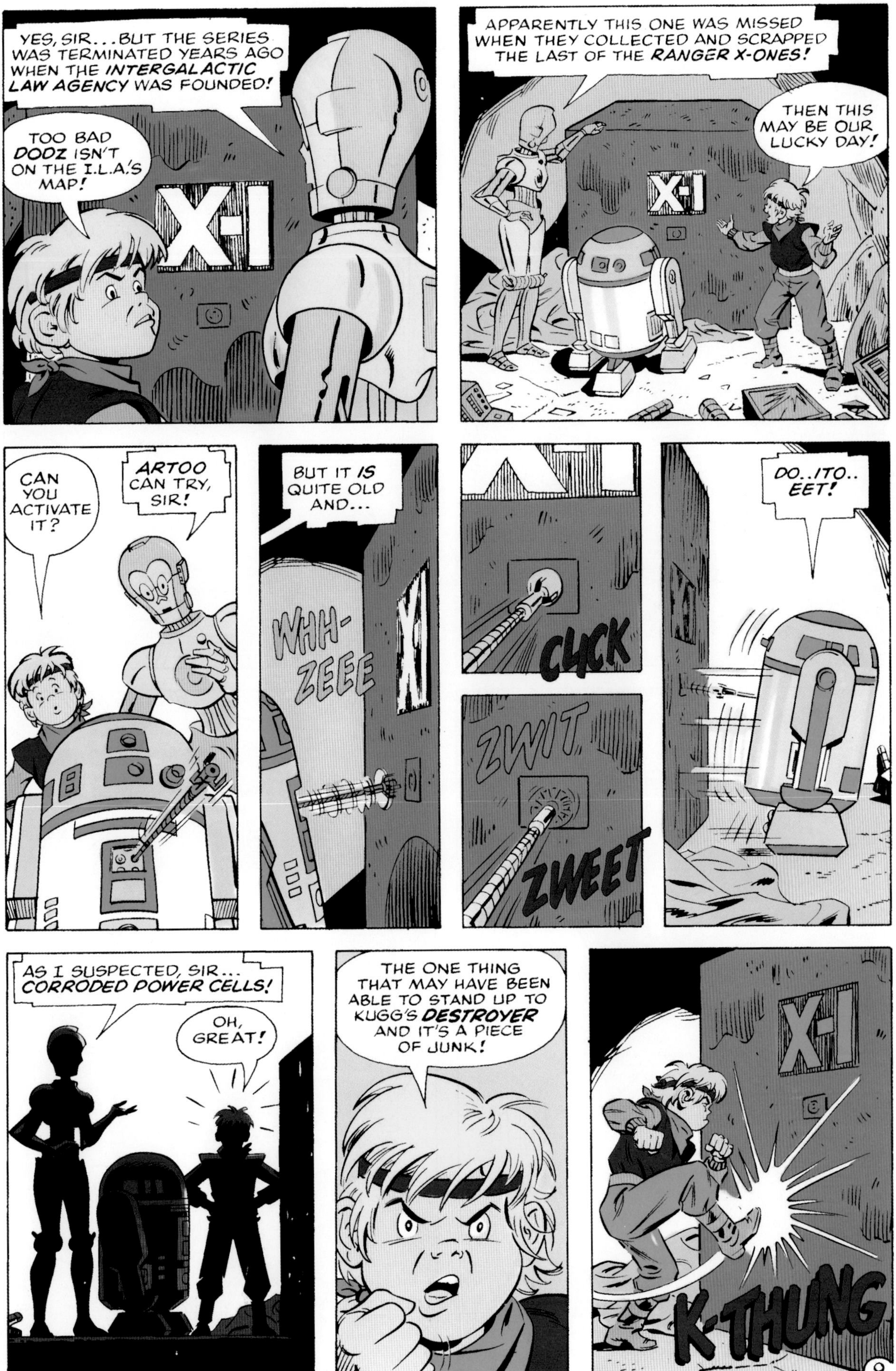
YES, SIR... BUT THE SERIES WAS TERMINATED YEARS AGO WHEN THE INTERGALACTIC LAW AGENCY WAS FOUNDED!
TOO BAD DOOZ ISN'T ON THE I.L.A.'S MAP!
X-I
APPARENTLY THIS ONE WAS MISSED WHEN THEY COLLECTED AND SCRAPPED THE LAST OF THE RANGER X-ONES!
THEN THIS MAY BE OUR LUCKY DAY!
X-I
CAN YOU ACTIVATE IT?
ARTOO CAN TRY, SIR!
BUT IT IS QUITE OLD AND...
WHH-ZEEE
CLICK
ZWIT
ZWEET
DO..ITO.. EET!
AS I SUSPECTED, SIR... CORRODED POWER CELLS!
OH, GREAT!
THE ONE THING THAT MAY HAVE BEEN ABLE TO STAND UP TO KUGG'S DESTROYER AND IT'S A PIECE OF JUNK!
X-I
K-THUNG
9

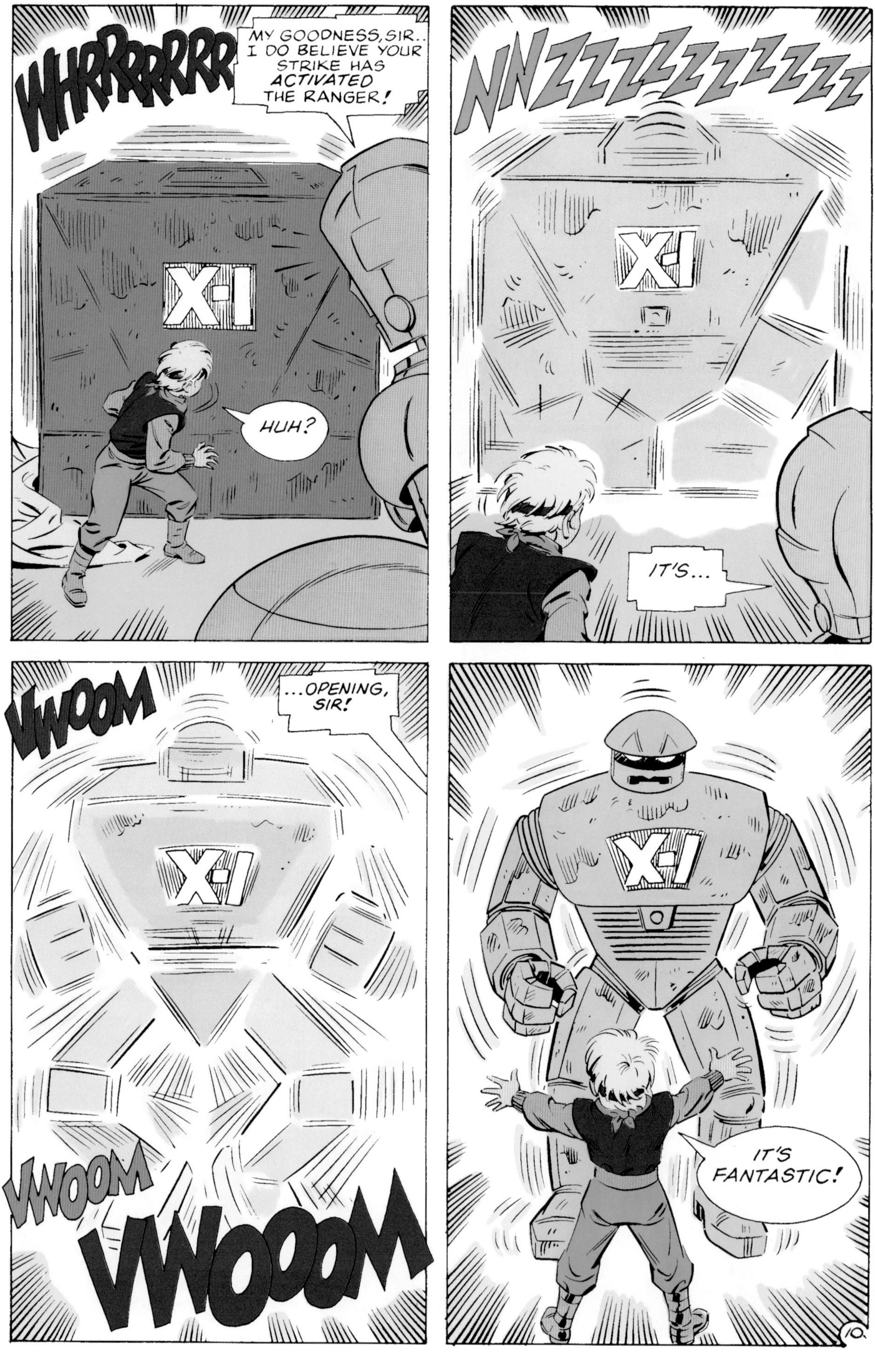
WHRRRRRRR
MY GOODNESS, SIR.. I DO BELIEVE YOUR STRIKE HAS ACTIVATED THE RANGER!
HUH?
NNZZZZZZZZZZZ
IT'S...
VWOOM
...OPENING, SIR!
VWOOM
VWOOOM
IT'S FANTASTIC!
10

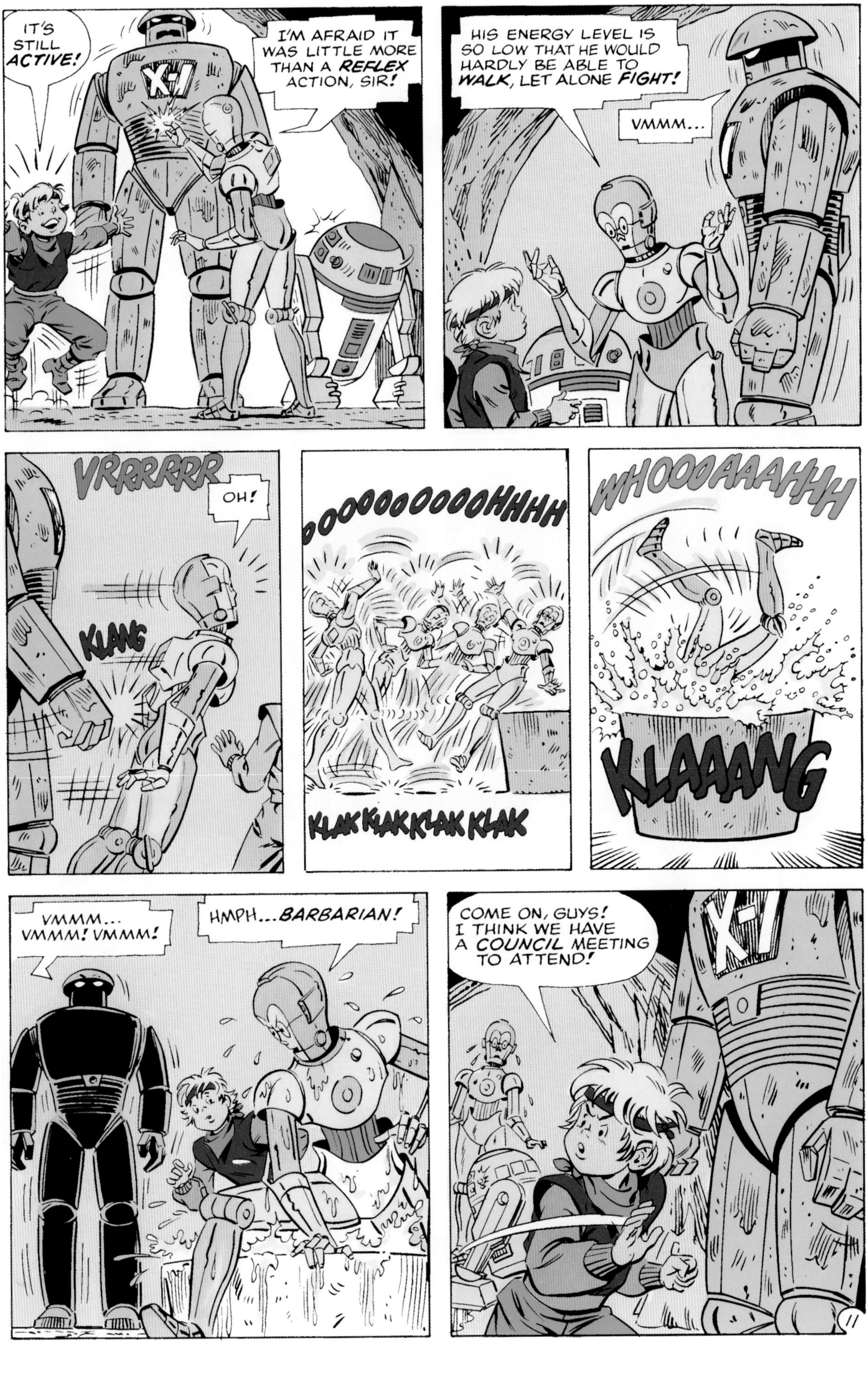
IT'S STILL ACTIVE!
I'M AFRAID IT WAS LITTLE MORE THAN A REFLEX ACTION, SIR!
HIS ENERGY LEVEL IS SO LOW THAT HE WOULD HARDLY BE ABLE TO WALK, LET ALONE FIGHT!
VMMM...
VRRRRRR
OH!
KLANG
OOOOOOOOOOOHHHH
KLAK KLAK KLAK KLAK
WHOOOAAAAHHH
KLAAAANG
VMMM... VMMM! VMMM!
HMPH... BARBARIAN!
COME ON, GUYS! I THINK WE HAVE A COUNCIL MEETING TO ATTEND!
11

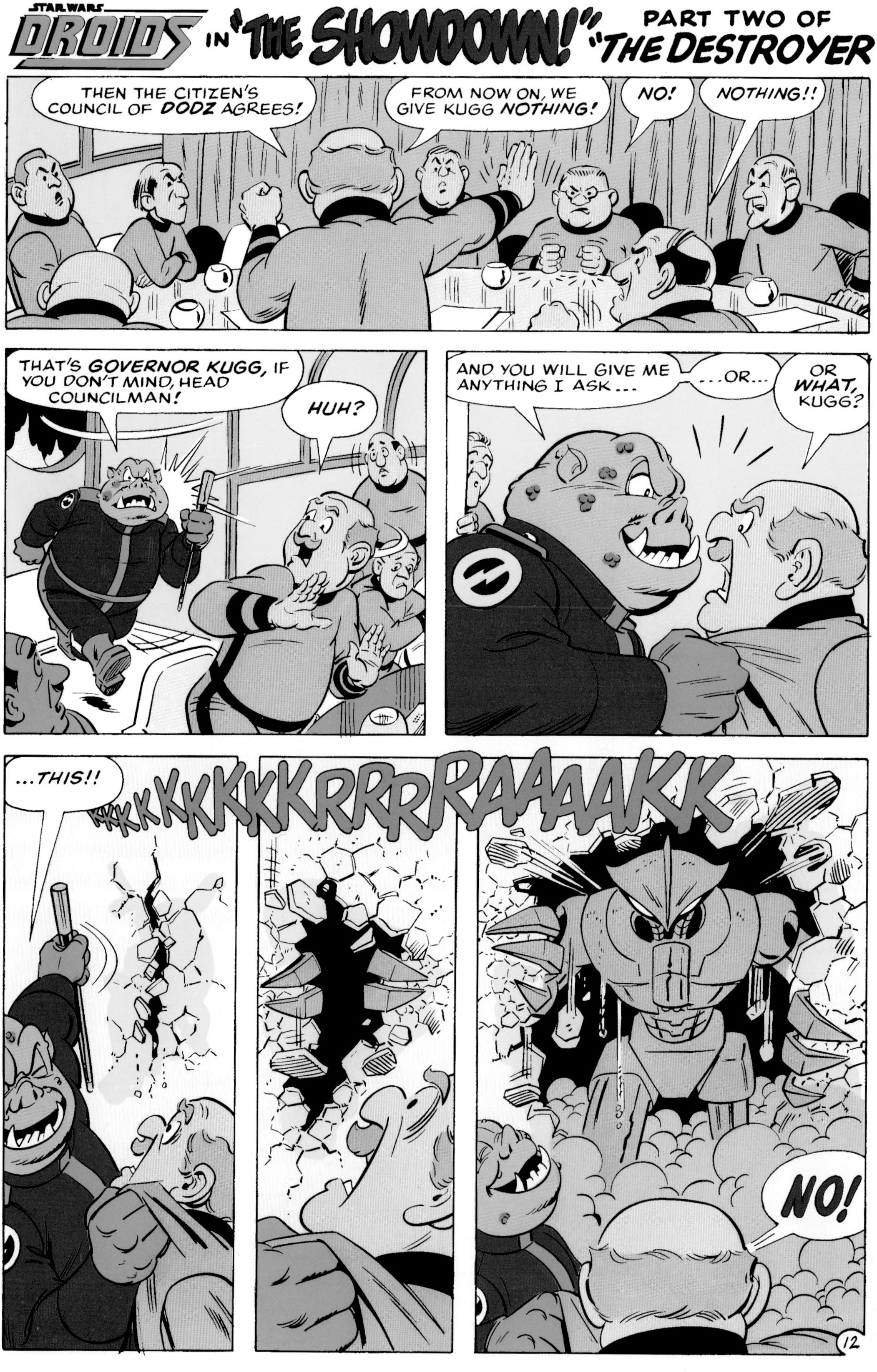
STAR WARS
DROIDS in "THE SHOWDOWN!" PART TWO OF "THE DESTROYER"
THEN THE CITIZEN'S COUNCIL OF DODZ AGREES!
FROM NOW ON, WE GIVE KUGG NOTHING!
NO!
NOTHING!!
THAT'S GOVERNOR KUGG, IF YOU DON'T MIND, HEAD COUNCILMAN!
HUH?
AND YOU WILL GIVE ME ANYTHING I ASK...
...OR...
OR WHAT, KUGG?
...THIS!!
KKKKKKKKRRRRAAAAAKK
NO!
12

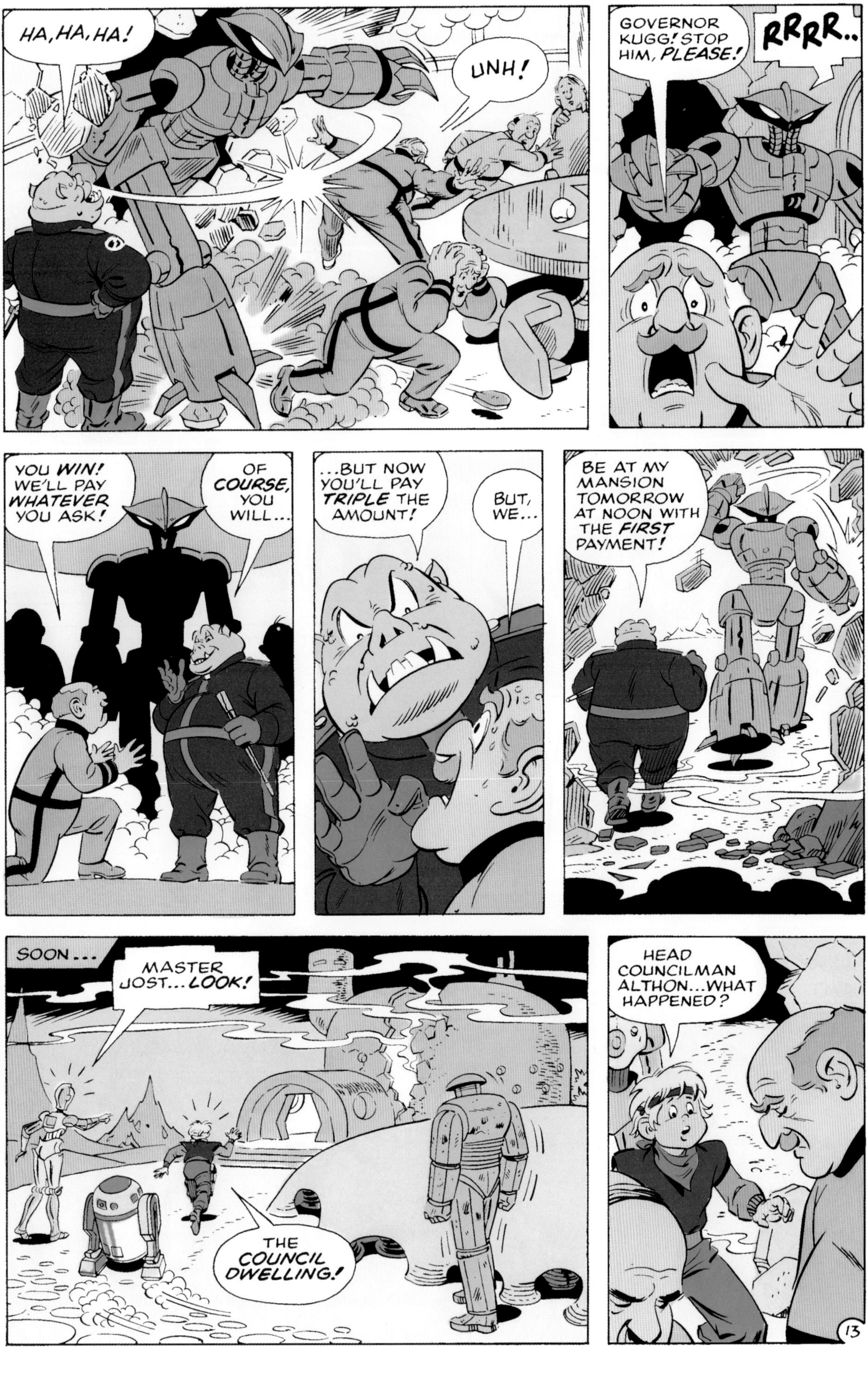
HA, HA, HA!
UNH!
GOVERNOR KUGG! STOP HIM, PLEASE!
RRRR..
YOU WIN! WE'LL PAY WHATEVER YOU ASK!
OF COURSE, YOU WILL...
...BUT NOW YOU'LL PAY TRIPLE THE AMOUNT!
BUT, WE...
BE AT MY MANSION TOMORROW AT NOON WITH THE FIRST PAYMENT!
SOON...
MASTER JOST... LOOK!
THE COUNCIL DWELLING!
HEAD COUNCILMAN ALTHON... WHAT HAPPENED?
13

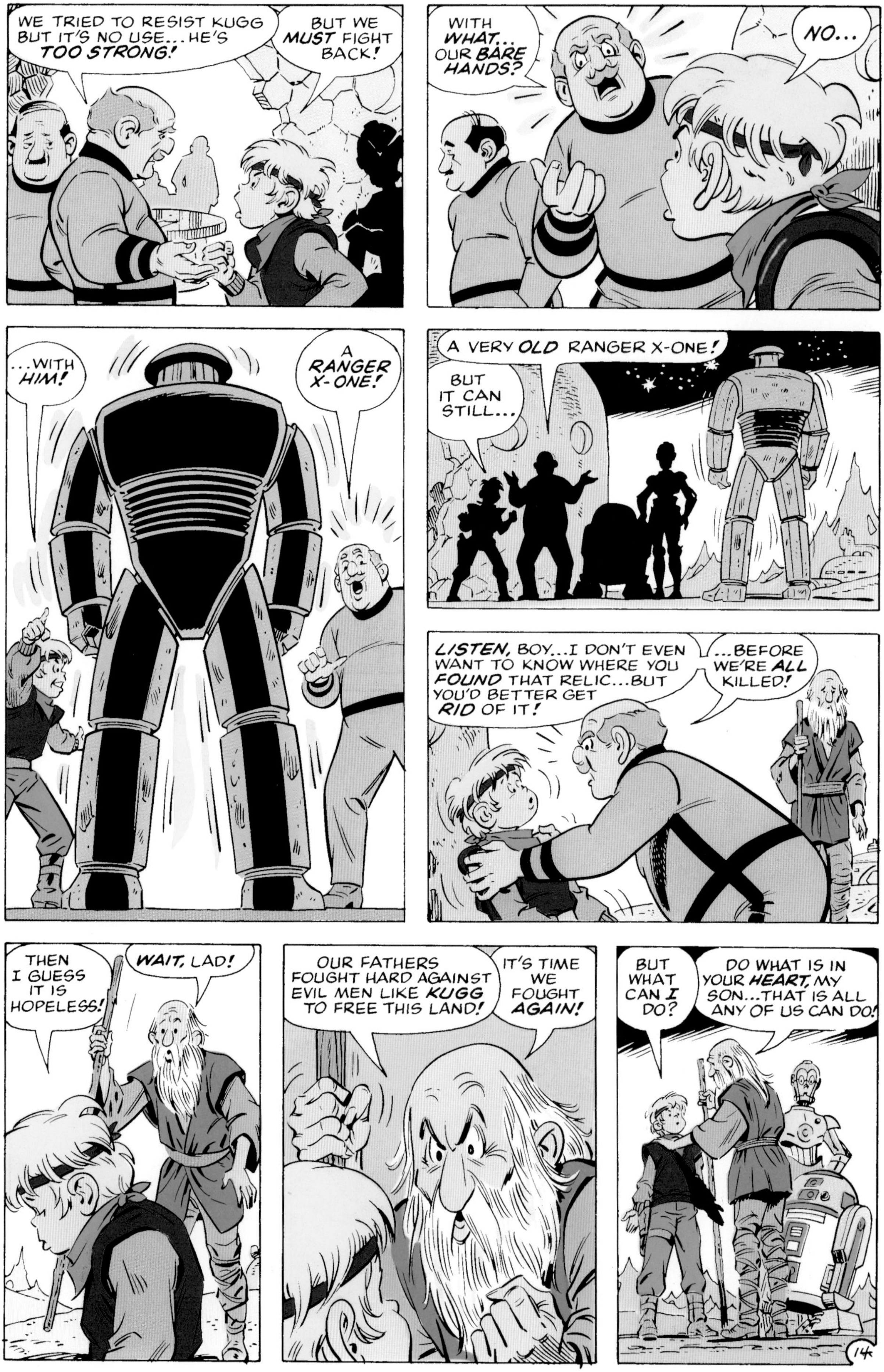
WE TRIED TO RESIST KUGG BUT IT'S NO USE... HE'S TOO STRONG!
BUT WE MUST FIGHT BACK!
WITH WHAT... OUR BARE HANDS?
NO...
...WITH HIM!
A RANGER X-ONE!
A VERY OLD RANGER X-ONE!
BUT IT CAN STILL...
LISTEN, BOY...I DON'T EVEN WANT TO KNOW WHERE YOU FOUND THAT RELIC...BUT YOU'D BETTER GET RID OF IT!
...BEFORE WE'RE ALL KILLED!
THEN I GUESS IT IS HOPELESS!
WAIT, LAD!
OUR FATHERS FOUGHT HARD AGAINST EVIL MEN LIKE KUGG TO FREE THIS LAND!
IT'S TIME WE FOUGHT AGAIN!
BUT WHAT CAN I DO?
DO WHAT IS IN YOUR HEART, MY SON...THAT IS ALL ANY OF US CAN DO!
14

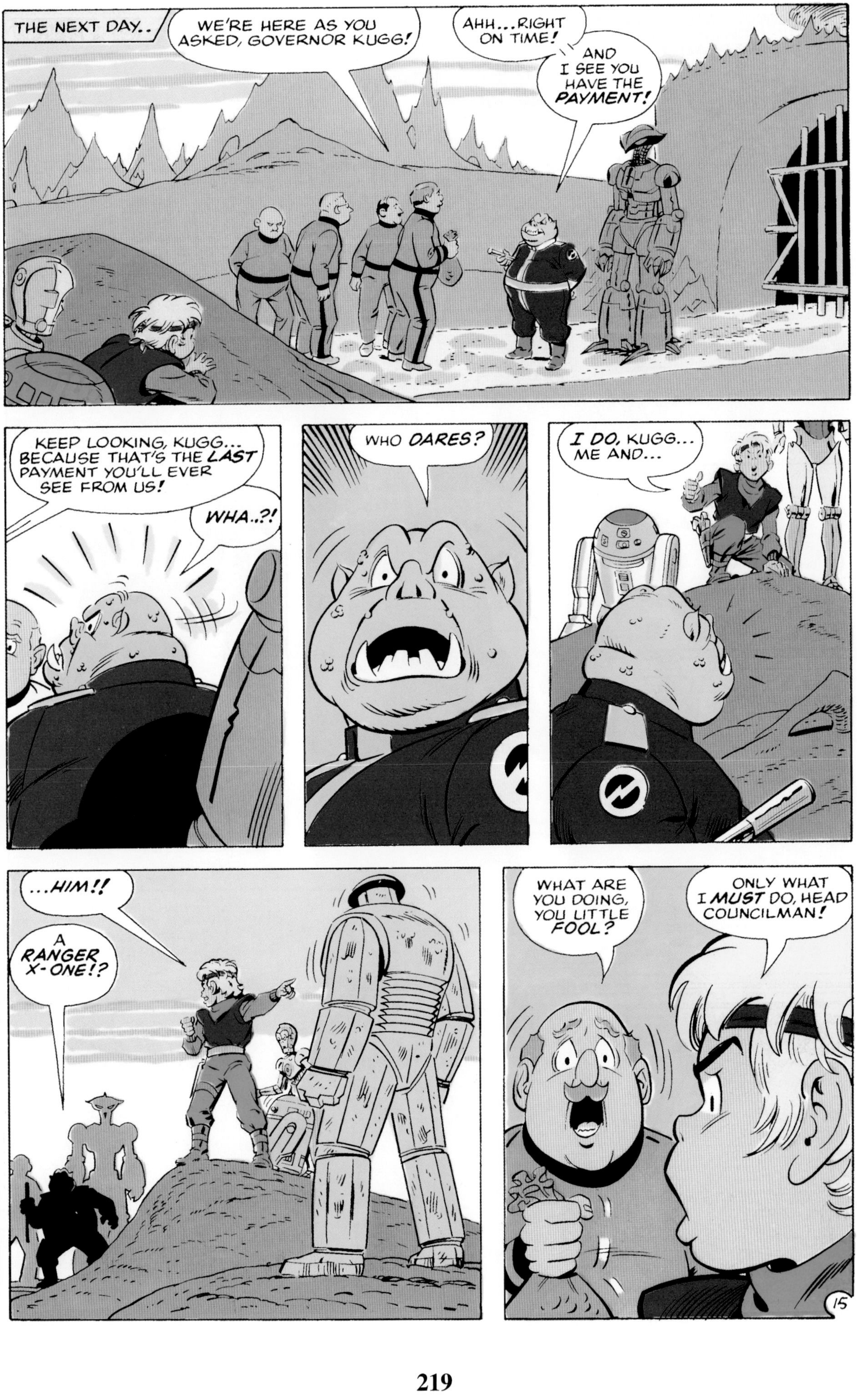
THE NEXT DAY..
WE'RE HERE AS YOU ASKED, GOVERNOR KUGG!
AHH...RIGHT ON TIME!
AND I SEE YOU HAVE THE PAYMENT!
KEEP LOOKING, KUGG... BECAUSE THAT'S THE LAST PAYMENT YOU'LL EVER SEE FROM US!
WHA..?!
WHO DARES?
I DO, KUGG... ME AND...
...HIM!!
A RANGER X-ONE!?
WHAT ARE YOU DOING, YOU LITTLE FOOL?
ONLY WHAT I MUST DO, HEAD COUNCILMAN!
15

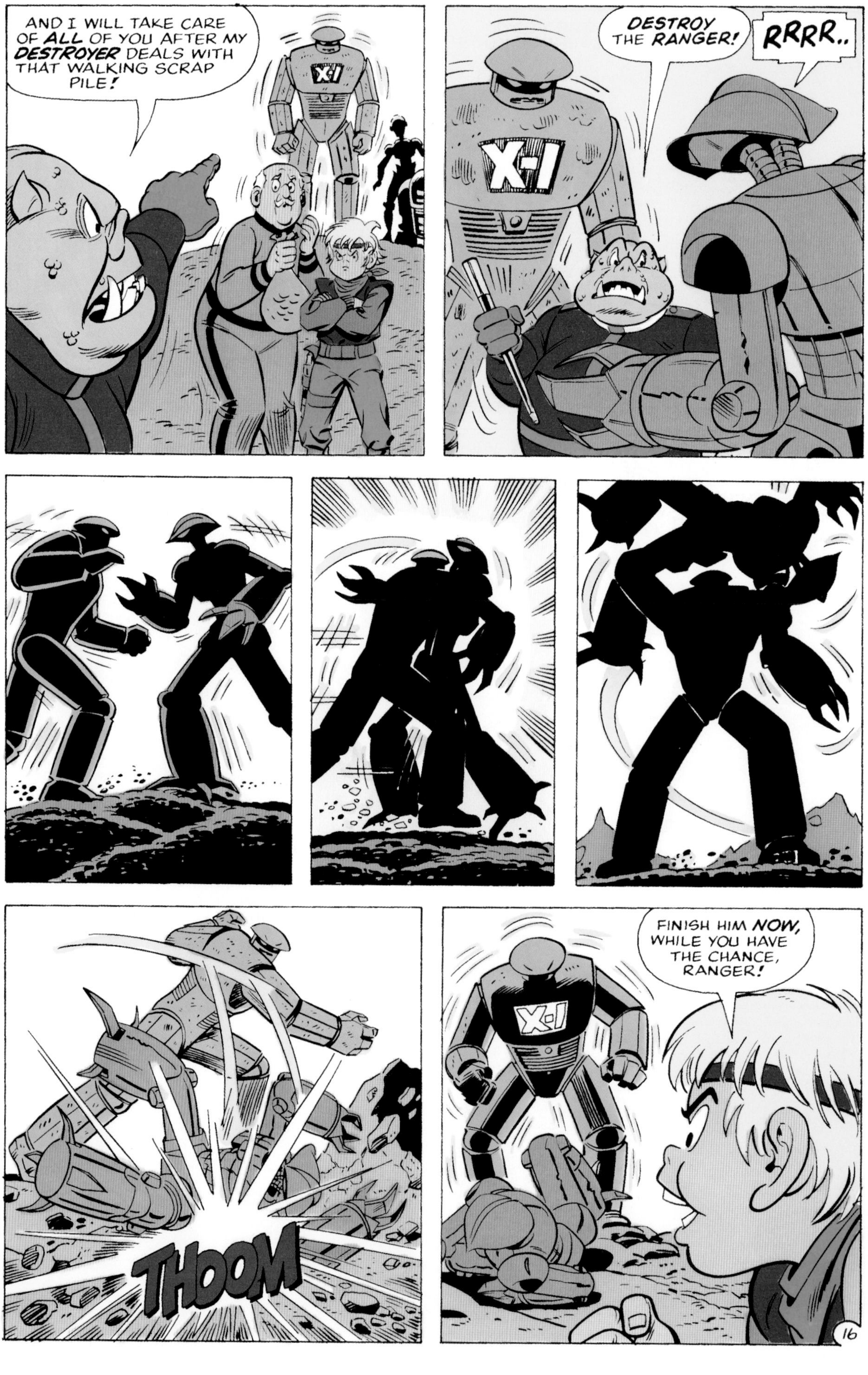
AND I WILL TAKE CARE OF ALL OF YOU AFTER MY DESTROYER DEALS WITH THAT WALKING SCRAP PILE!
X-1
DESTROY THE RANGER!
RRRR..
X-1
THOOM
FINISH HIM NOW, WHILE YOU HAVE THE CHANCE, RANGER!
X-1
16

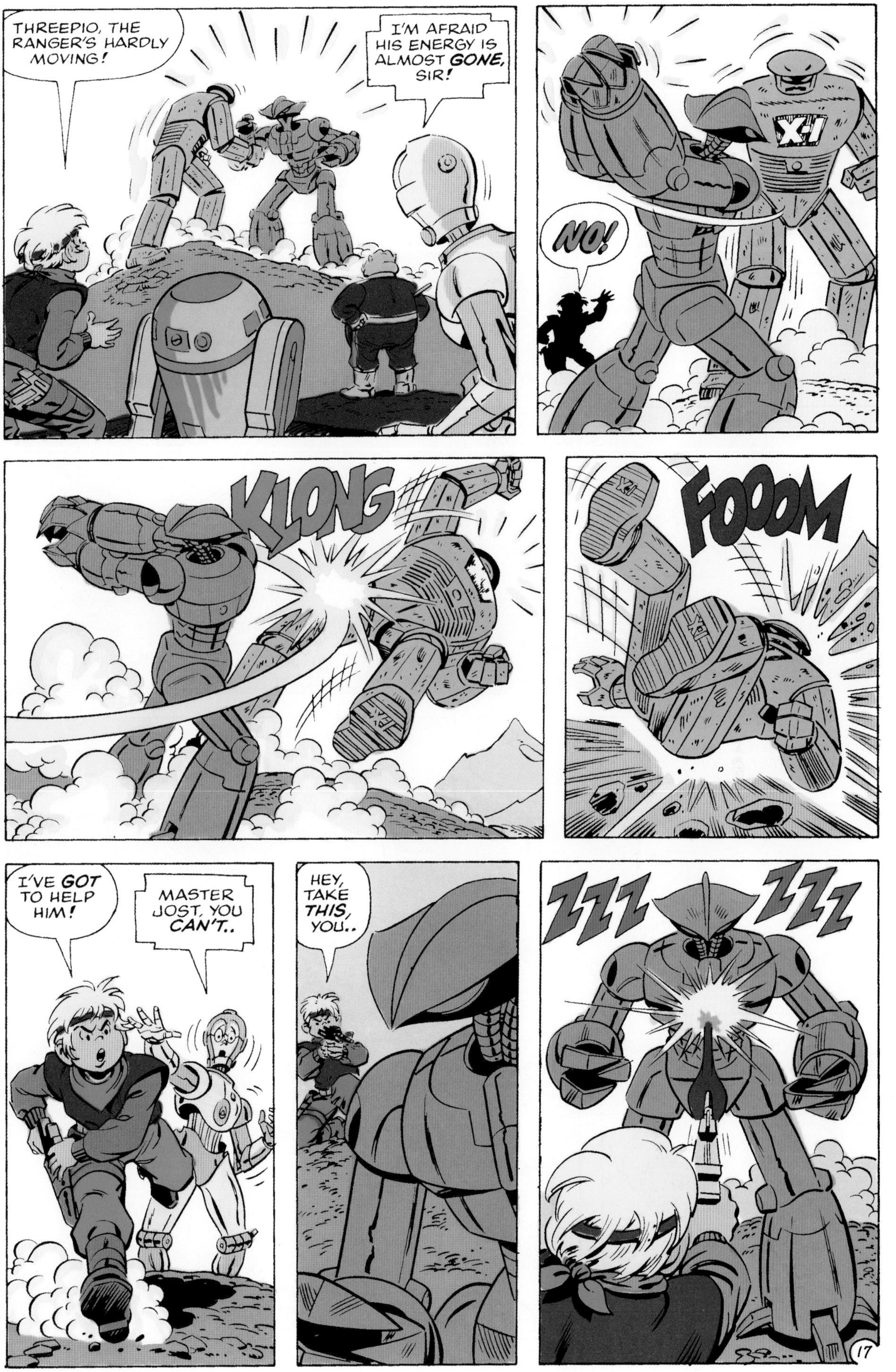
THREEPIO, THE RANGER'S HARDLY MOVING!
I'M AFRAID HIS ENERGY IS ALMOST GONE, SIR!
NO!
KLONG
FOOOM
I'VE GOT TO HELP HIM!
MASTER JOST, YOU CAN'T..
HEY, TAKE THIS, YOU..
ZZZ
ZZZ
17

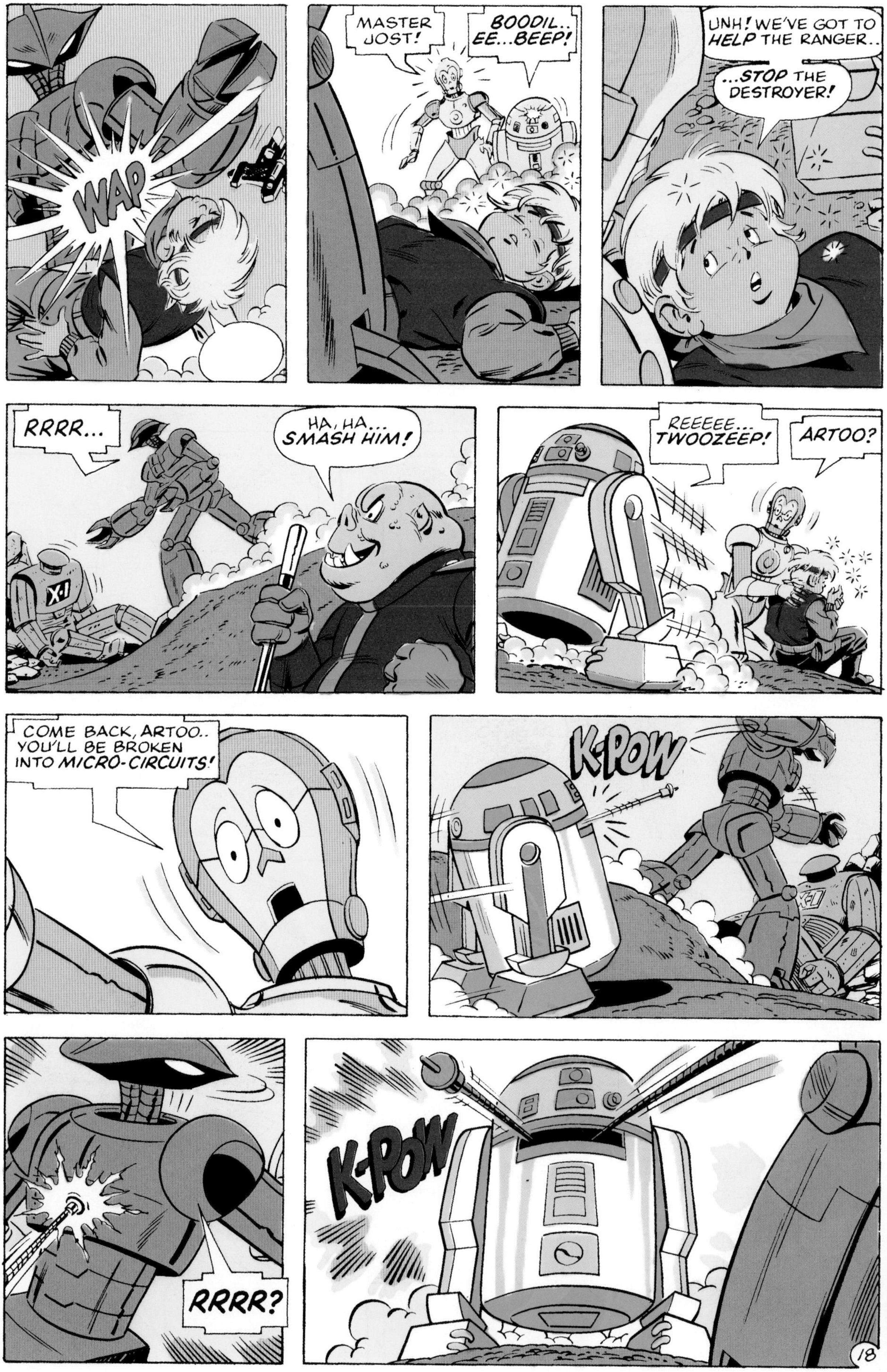
WAP
MASTER JOST!
BOODIL.. EE...BEEP!
UNH! WE'VE GOT TO HELP THE RANGER..
...STOP THE DESTROYER!
RRRR...
HA, HA... SMASH HIM!
X-1
REEEEE... TWOOZEEP!
ARTOO?
COME BACK, ARTOO.. YOU'LL BE BROKEN INTO MICRO-CIRCUITS!
K-POW
K-POW
RRRR?
18

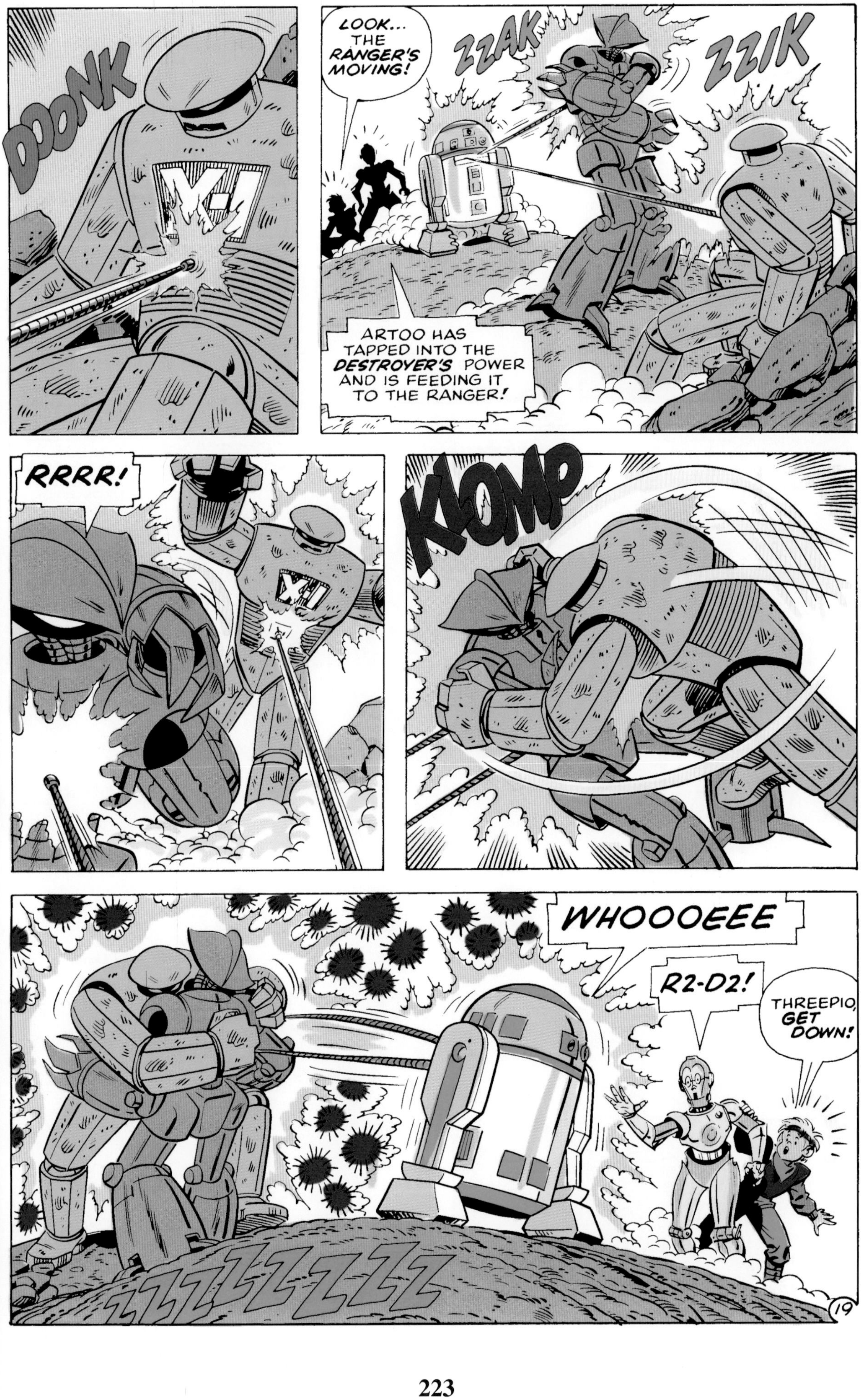
DOONK
LOOK... THE RANGER'S MOVING!
ZZAK
ZZIK
ARTOO HAS TAPPED INTO THE DESTROYER'S POWER AND IS FEEDING IT TO THE RANGER!
RRRR!
KLOMP
WHOOOEEE
R2-D2!
THREEPIO, GET DOWN!
ZZZZZZZZZ
19

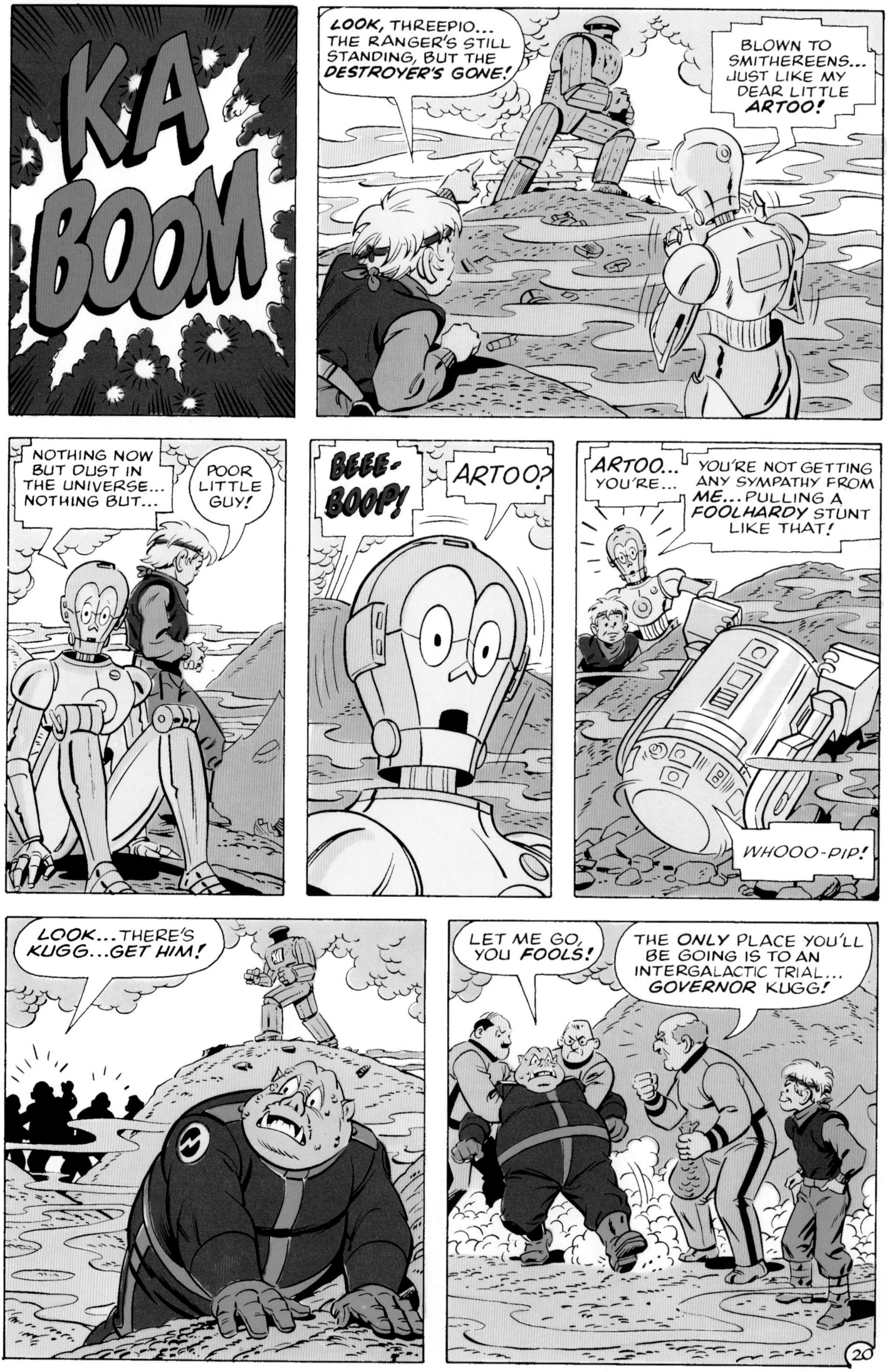
KA BOOM
LOOK, THREEPIO... THE RANGER'S STILL STANDING, BUT THE DESTROYER'S GONE!
BLOWN TO SMITHEREENS... JUST LIKE MY DEAR LITTLE ARTOO!
NOTHING NOW BUT DUST IN THE UNIVERSE... NOTHING BUT...
POOR LITTLE GUY!
BEEE-BOOP!
ARTOO?
ARTOO... YOU'RE...
YOU'RE NOT GETTING ANY SYMPATHY FROM ME... PULLING A FOOLHARDY STUNT LIKE THAT!
WHOOO-PIP!
LOOK... THERE'S KUGG... GET HIM!
LET ME GO, YOU FOOLS!
THE ONLY PLACE YOU'LL BE GOING IS TO AN INTERGALACTIC TRIAL... GOVERNOR KUGG!
20

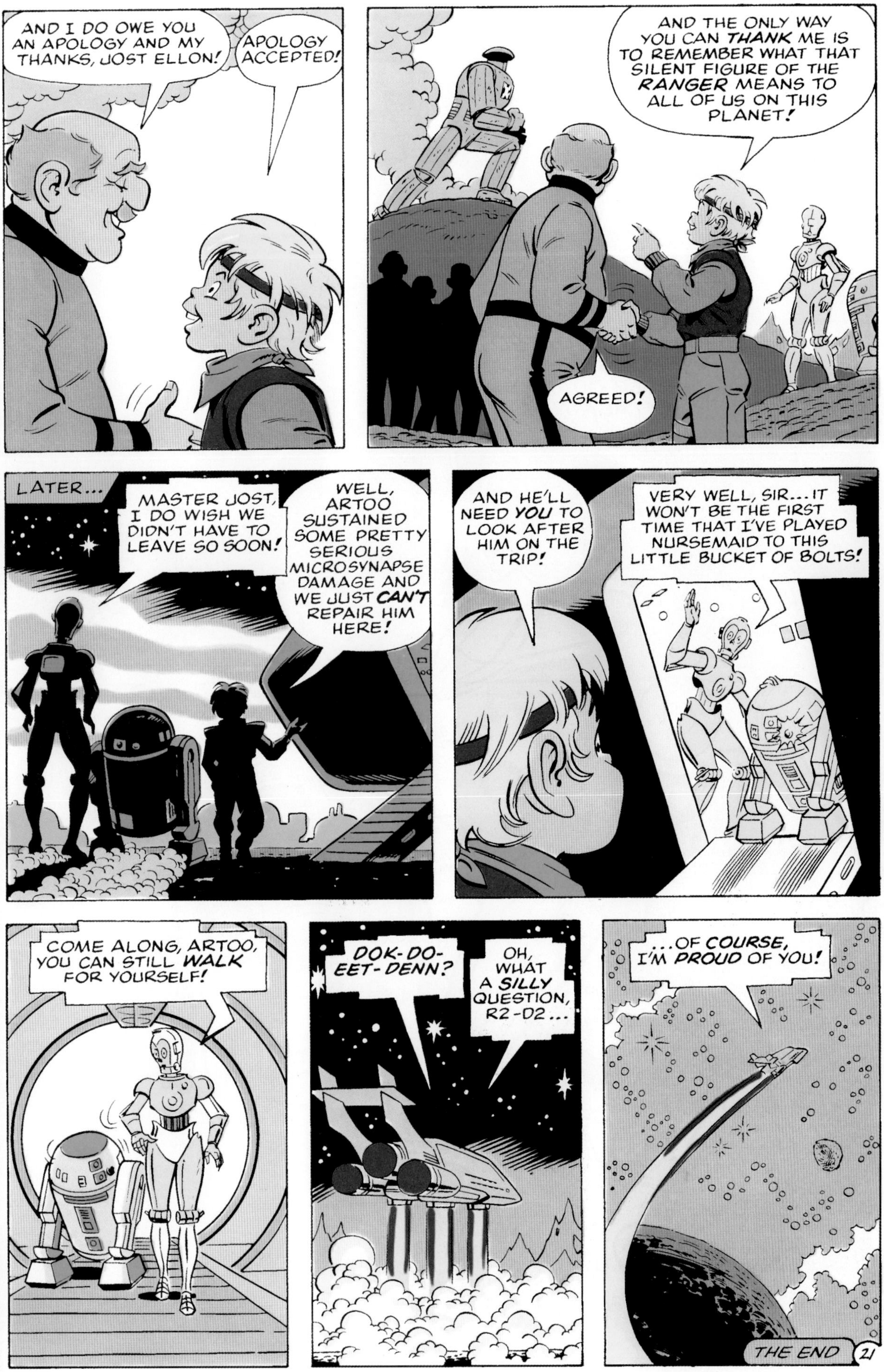
AND I DO OWE YOU AN APOLOGY AND MY THANKS, JOST ELLON!
APOLOGY ACCEPTED!
AND THE ONLY WAY YOU CAN THANK ME IS TO REMEMBER WHAT THAT SILENT FIGURE OF THE RANGER MEANS TO ALL OF US ON THIS PLANET!
AGREED!
LATER...
MASTER JOST, I DO WISH WE DIDN'T HAVE TO LEAVE SO SOON!
WELL, ARTOO SUSTAINED SOME PRETTY SERIOUS MICROSYNAPSE DAMAGE AND WE JUST CAN'T REPAIR HIM HERE!
AND HE'LL NEED YOU TO LOOK AFTER HIM ON THE TRIP!
VERY WELL, SIR... IT WON'T BE THE FIRST TIME THAT I'VE PLAYED NURSEMAID TO THIS LITTLE BUCKET OF BOLTS!
COME ALONG, ARTOO, YOU CAN STILL WALK FOR YOURSELF!
DOK-DO-EET-DENN?
OH, WHAT A SILLY QUESTION, R2-D2...
...OF COURSE, I'M PROUD OF YOU!
THE END
21

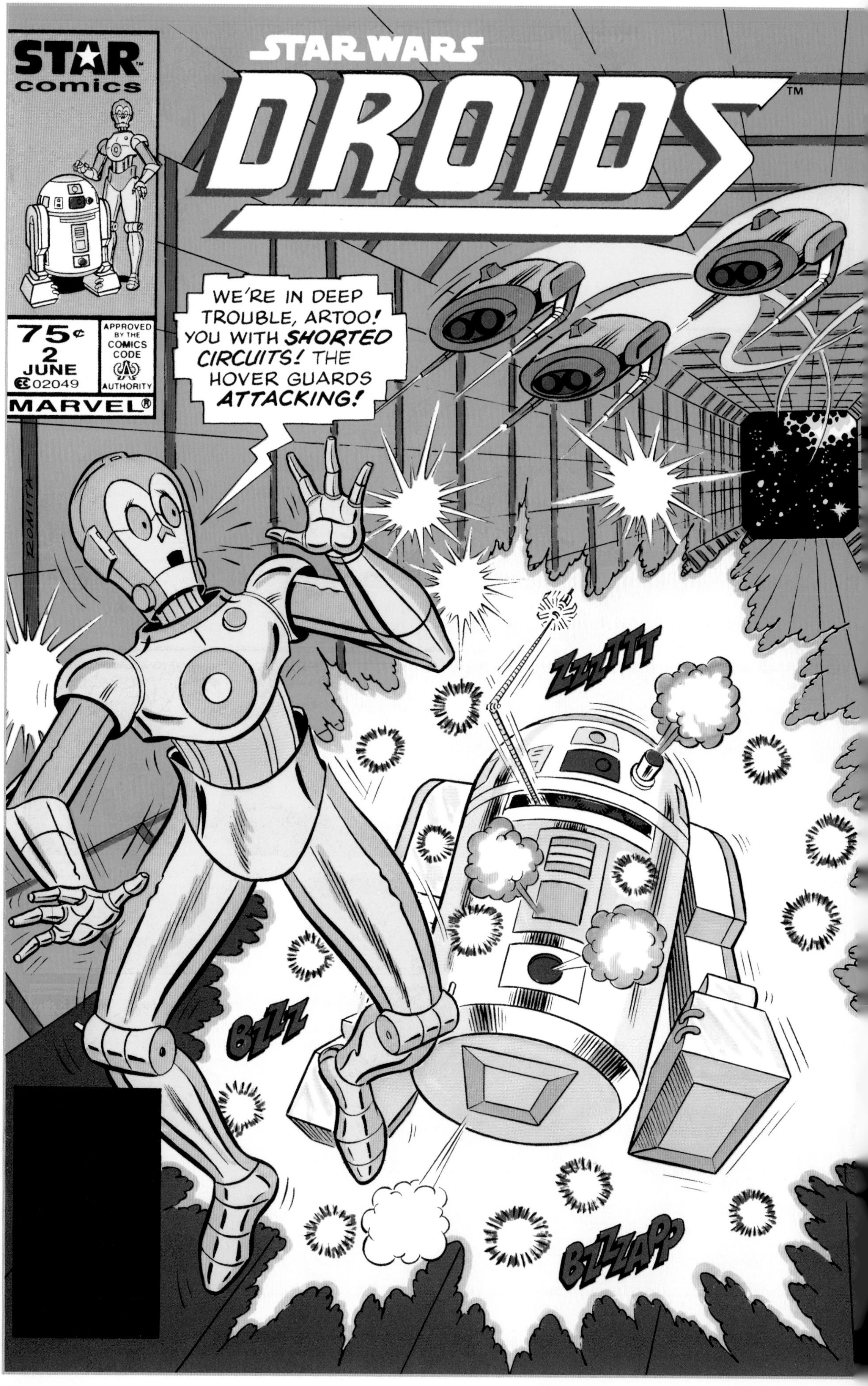
STAR comics
STAR WARS
DROIDS
75¢
2
JUNE
02049
APPROVED BY THE COMICS CODE AUTHORITY
MARVEL
WE'RE IN DEEP TROUBLE, ARTOO! YOU WITH SHORTED CIRCUITS! THE HOVER GUARDS ATTACKING!
ROMITA
ZZZTTT
BZZZ
BZZZAPP

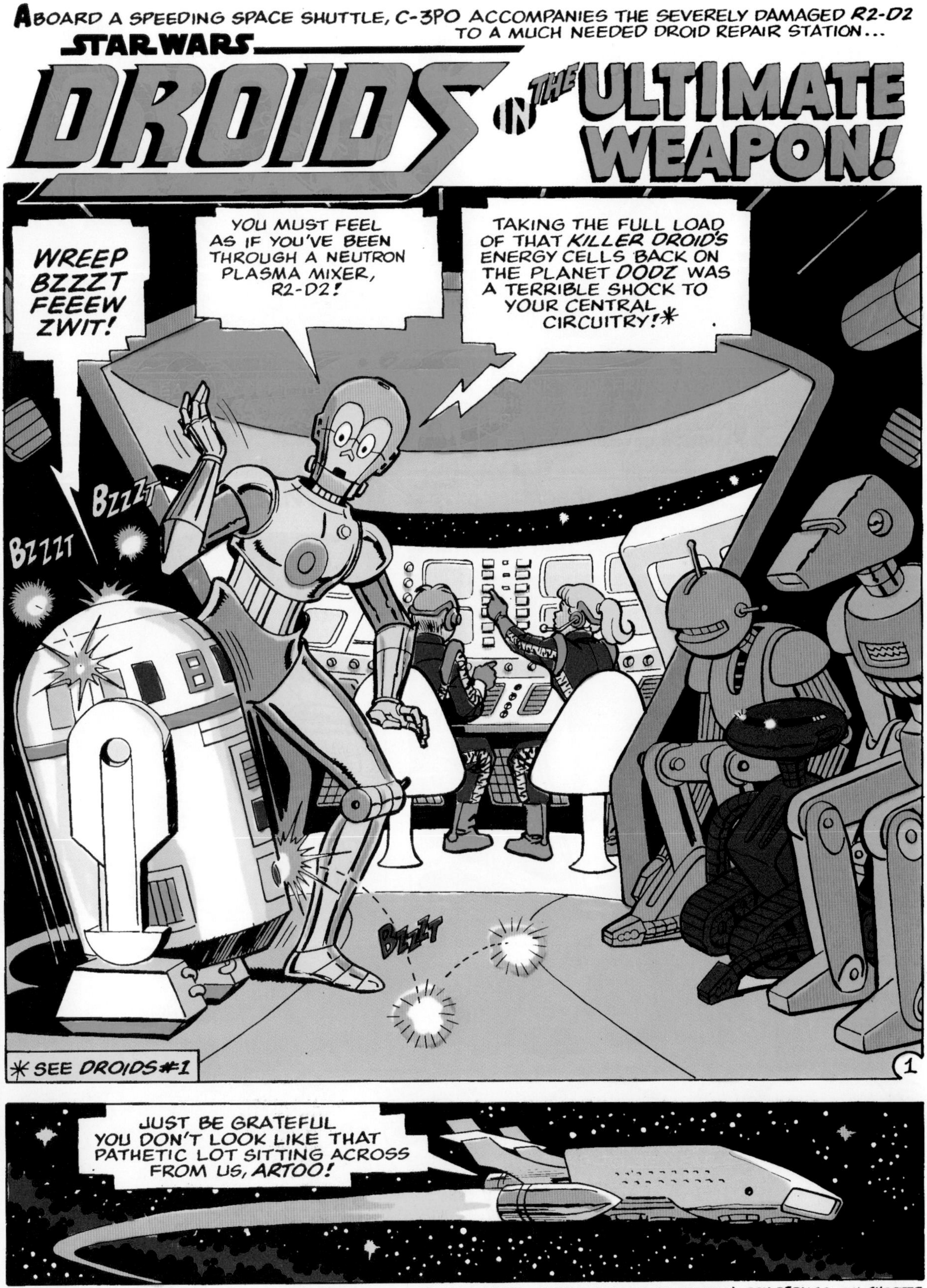
ABOARD A SPEEDING SPACE SHUTTLE, C-3PO ACCOMPANIES THE SEVERELY DAMAGED R2-D2 TO A MUCH NEEDED DROID REPAIR STATION...
STAR WARS
DROIDS
IN THE ULTIMATE WEAPON!
WREEP BZZZT FEEEW ZWIT!
YOU MUST FEEL AS IF YOU'VE BEEN THROUGH A NEUTRON PLASMA MIXER, R2-D2!
TAKING THE FULL LOAD OF THAT KILLER DROID'S ENERGY CELLS BACK ON THE PLANET DODZ WAS A TERRIBLE SHOCK TO YOUR CENTRAL CIRCUITRY!*
BZZZT
BZZZT
BZZZT
* SEE DROIDS #1
1
JUST BE GRATEFUL YOU DON'T LOOK LIKE THAT PATHETIC LOT SITTING ACROSS FROM US, ARTOO!
DAVE MANAK WRITER . JOHN ROMITA PENCILER . AL WILLIAMSON & J. D'AGOSTINO INKERS . GRACE KREMER LETTERER . GEORGE ROUSSOS COLORIST . SID JACOBSON EDITOR . TOM DEFALCO EXEC. EDITOR . JIM SHOOTER ED-IN-CHIEF

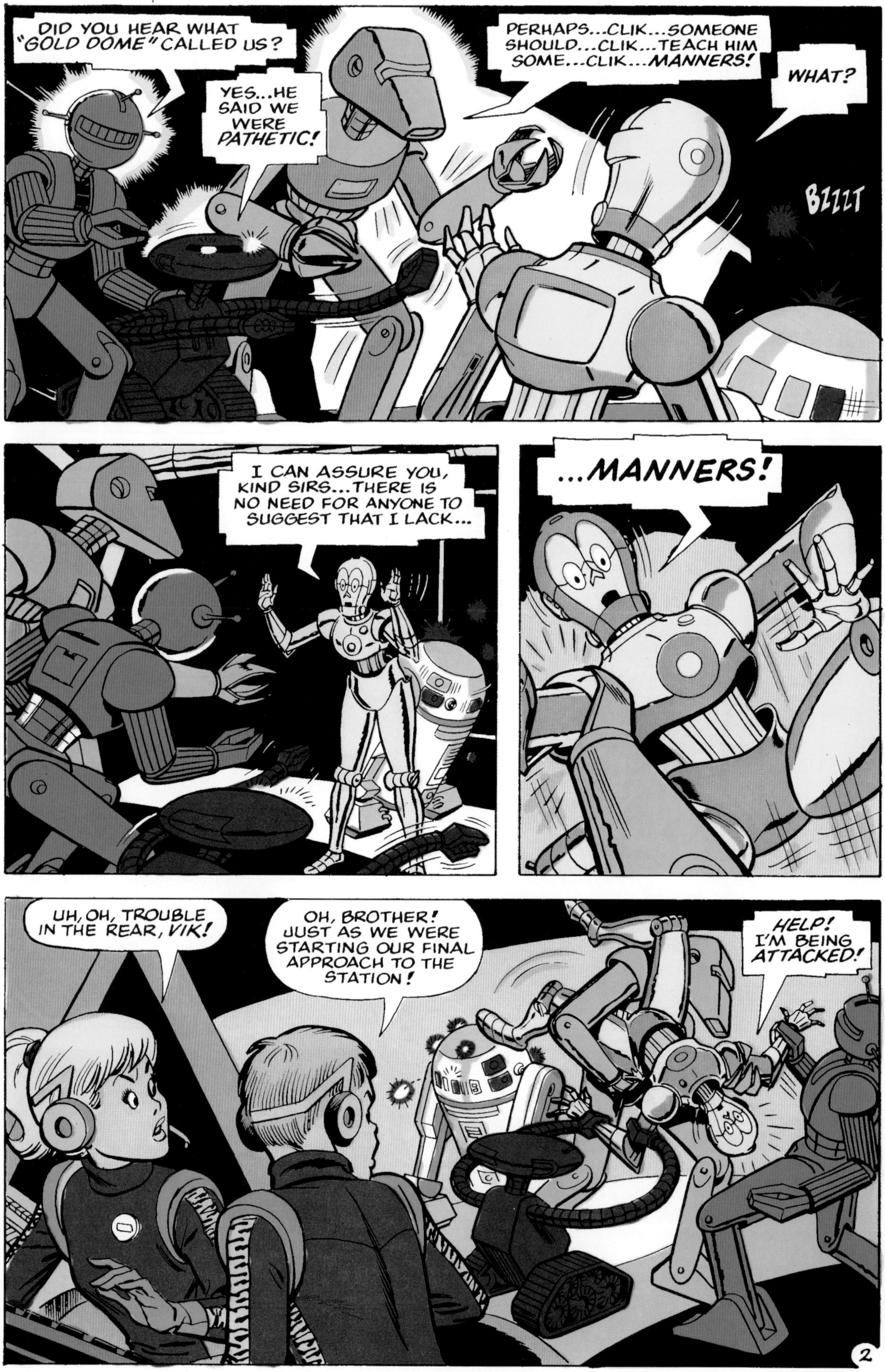
DID YOU HEAR WHAT "GOLD DOME" CALLED US?
YES...HE SAID WE WERE PATHETIC!
PERHAPS...CLIK...SOMEONE SHOULD...CLIK...TEACH HIM SOME...CLIK...MANNERS!
WHAT?
BZZZT
I CAN ASSURE YOU, KIND SIRS...THERE IS NO NEED FOR ANYONE TO SUGGEST THAT I LACK...
...MANNERS!
UH, OH, TROUBLE IN THE REAR, VIK!
OH, BROTHER! JUST AS WE WERE STARTING OUR FINAL APPROACH TO THE STATION!
HELP! I'M BEING ATTACKED!
2

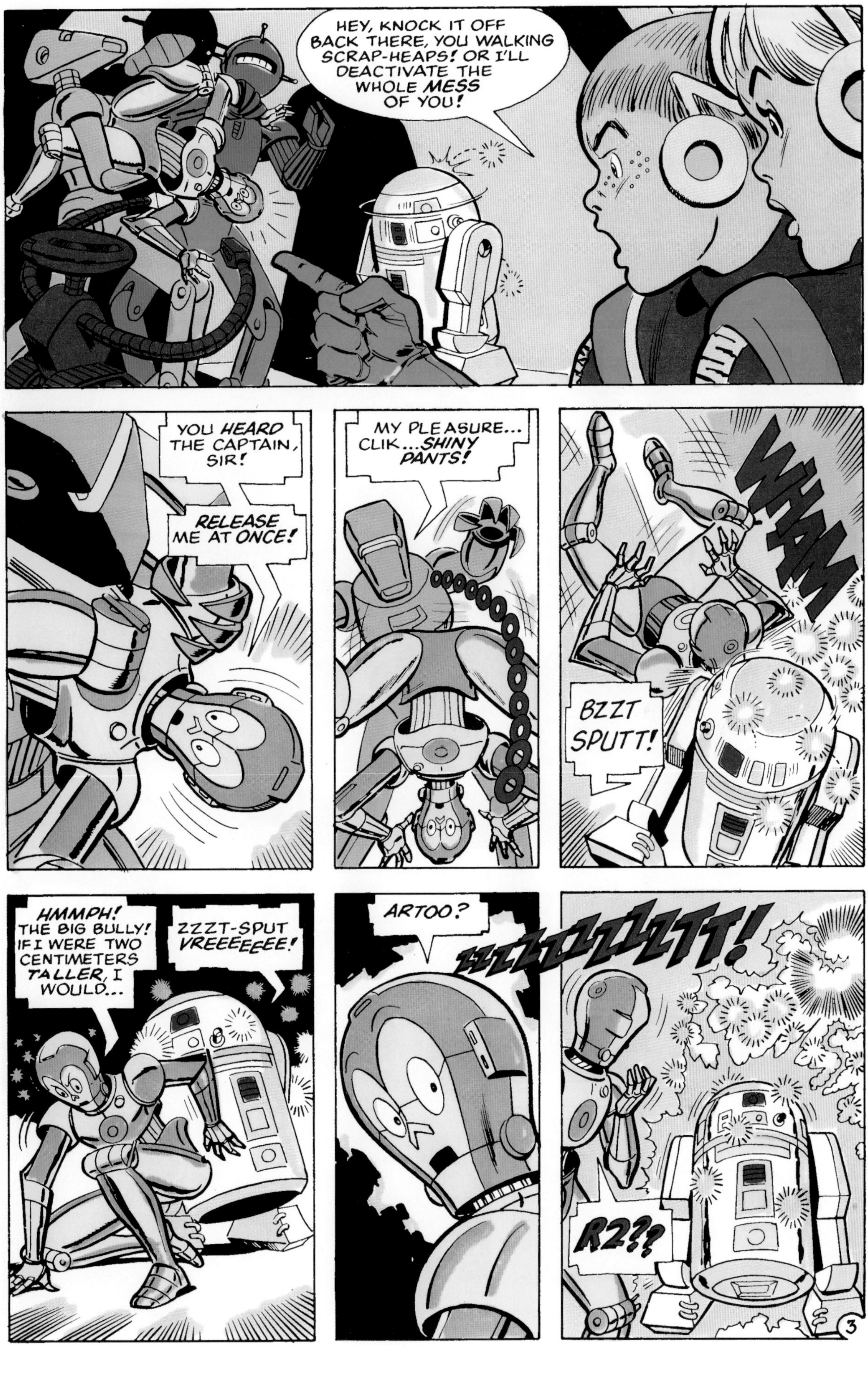
HEY, KNOCK IT OFF BACK THERE, YOU WALKING SCRAP-HEAPS! OR I'LL DEACTIVATE THE WHOLE MESS OF YOU!
YOU HEARD THE CAPTAIN, SIR!
RELEASE ME AT ONCE!
MY PLEASURE... CLIK...SHINY PANTS!
WHAM
BZZT SPUTT!
HMMPH! THE BIG BULLY! IF I WERE TWO CENTIMETERS TALLER, I WOULD...
ZZZT-SPUT VREEEEEEEE!
ARTOO?
ZZZZZZZZZTT!
R2??
3

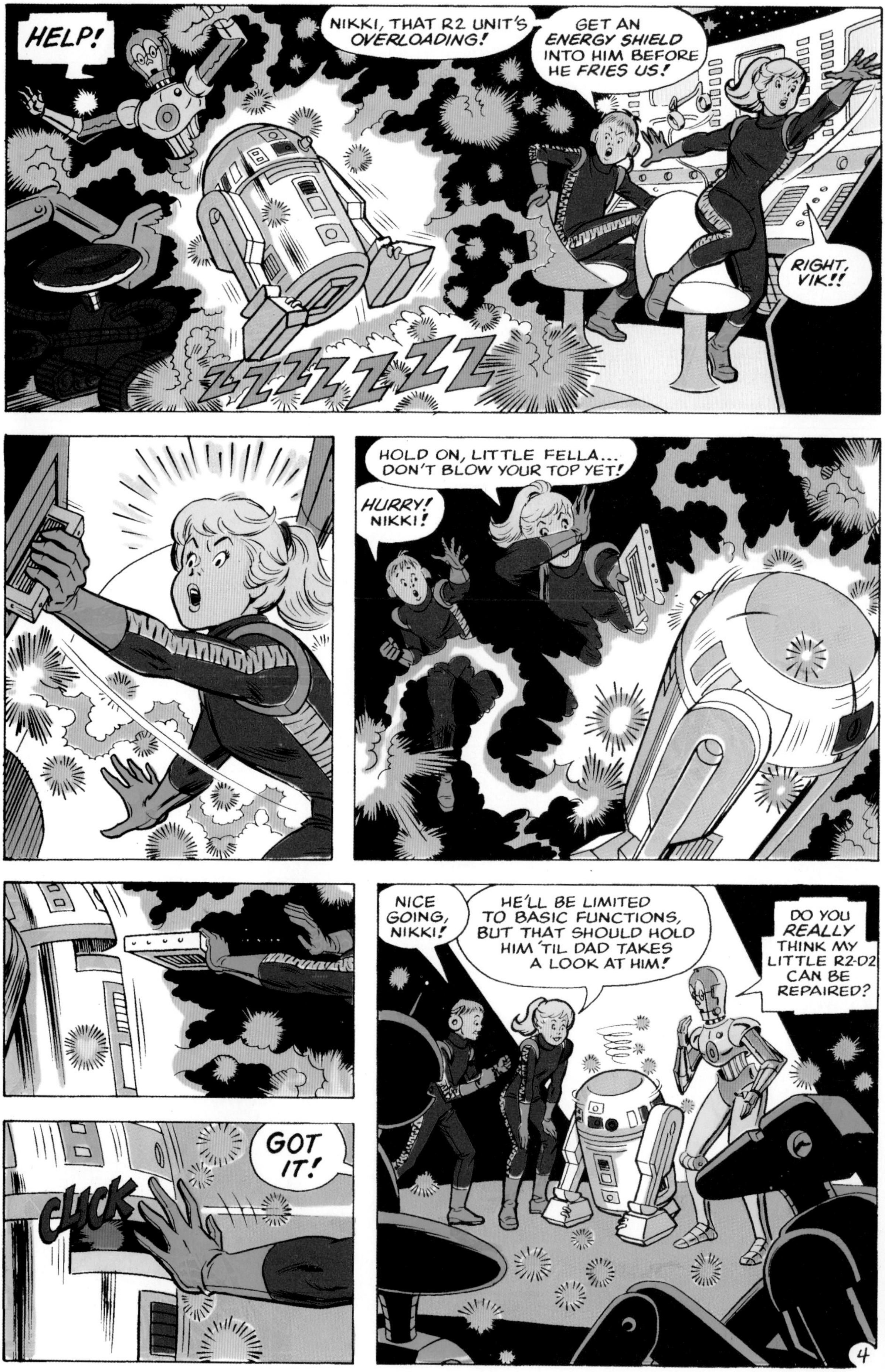
HELP!
NIKKI, THAT R2 UNIT'S OVERLOADING!
GET AN ENERGY SHIELD INTO HIM BEFORE HE FRIES US!
RIGHT, VIK!!
ZZZZZZZZ
HOLD ON, LITTLE FELLA... DON'T BLOW YOUR TOP YET!
HURRY! NIKKI!
GOT IT!
CLICK
NICE GOING, NIKKI!
HE'LL BE LIMITED TO BASIC FUNCTIONS, BUT THAT SHOULD HOLD HIM 'TIL DAD TAKES A LOOK AT HIM!
DO YOU REALLY THINK MY LITTLE R2-D2 CAN BE REPAIRED?
4

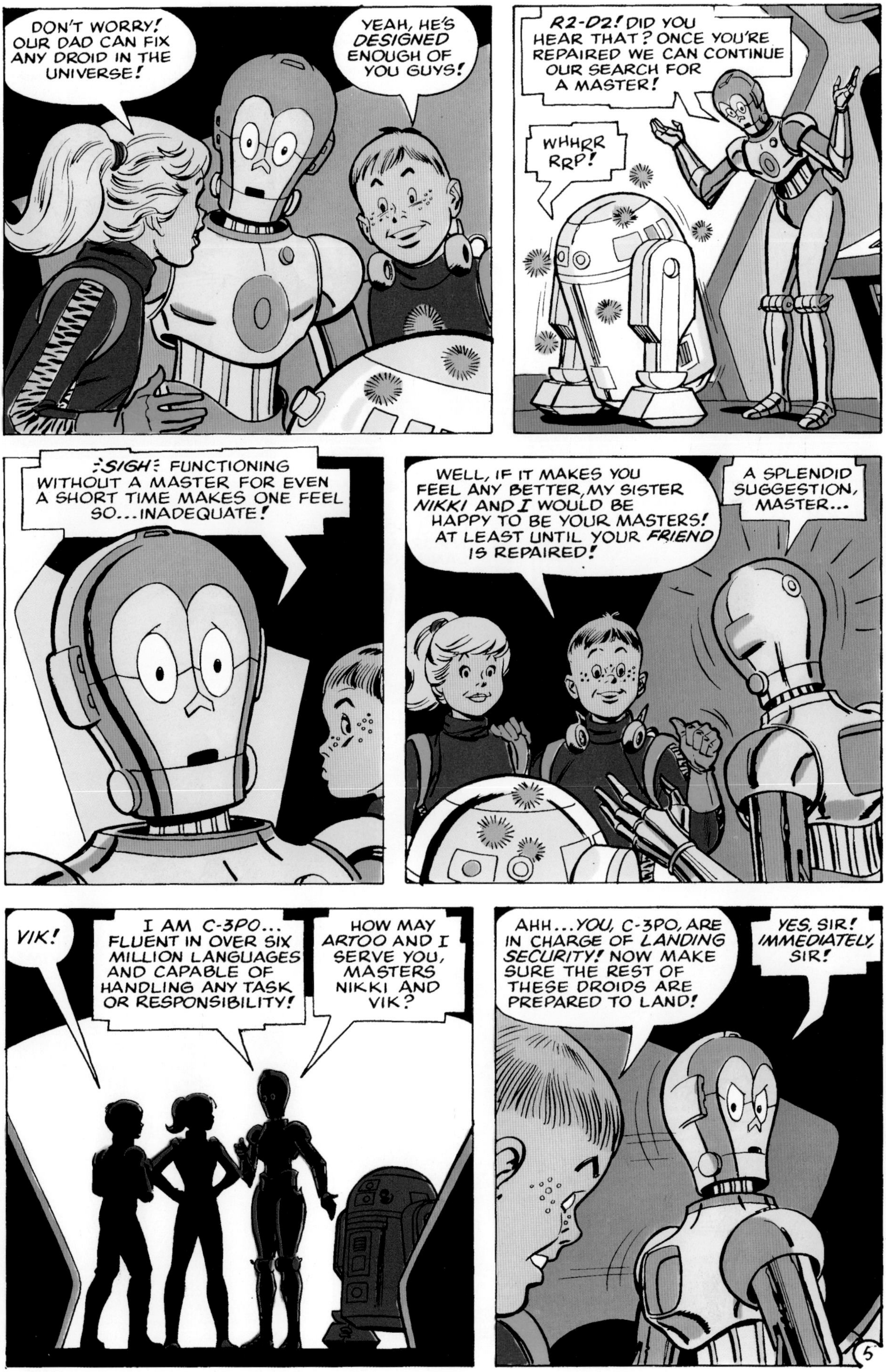
DON'T WORRY! OUR DAD CAN FIX ANY DROID IN THE UNIVERSE!
YEAH, HE'S DESIGNED ENOUGH OF YOU GUYS!
R2-D2! DID YOU HEAR THAT? ONCE YOU'RE REPAIRED WE CAN CONTINUE OUR SEARCH FOR A MASTER!
WHHRR RRP!
:SIGH: FUNCTIONING WITHOUT A MASTER FOR EVEN A SHORT TIME MAKES ONE FEEL SO...INADEQUATE!
WELL, IF IT MAKES YOU FEEL ANY BETTER, MY SISTER NIKKI AND I WOULD BE HAPPY TO BE YOUR MASTERS! AT LEAST UNTIL YOUR FRIEND IS REPAIRED!
A SPLENDID SUGGESTION, MASTER...
VIK!
I AM C-3PO... FLUENT IN OVER SIX MILLION LANGUAGES AND CAPABLE OF HANDLING ANY TASK OR RESPONSIBILITY!
HOW MAY ARTOO AND I SERVE YOU, MASTERS NIKKI AND VIK?
AHH...YOU, C-3PO, ARE IN CHARGE OF LANDING SECURITY! NOW MAKE SURE THE REST OF THESE DROIDS ARE PREPARED TO LAND!
YES, SIR! IMMEDIATELY, SIR!
5

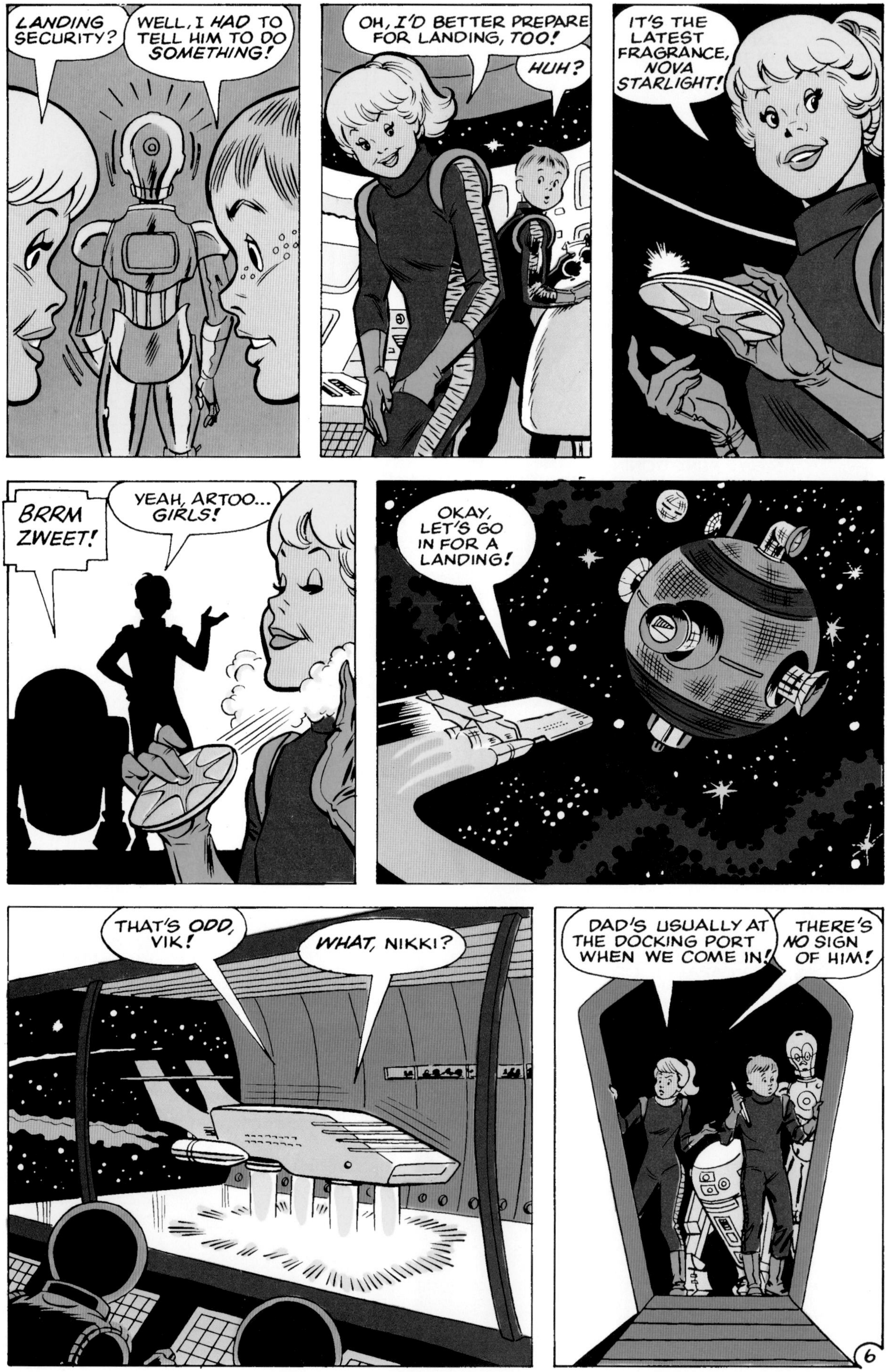
LANDING SECURITY?
WELL, I HAD TO TELL HIM TO DO SOMETHING!
OH, I'D BETTER PREPARE FOR LANDING, TOO!
HUH?
IT'S THE LATEST FRAGRANCE, NOVA STARLIGHT!
BRRM ZWEET!
YEAH, ARTOO... GIRLS!
OKAY, LET'S GO IN FOR A LANDING!
THAT'S ODD, VIK!
WHAT, NIKKI?
DAD'S USUALLY AT THE DOCKING PORT WHEN WE COME IN!
THERE'S NO SIGN OF HIM!
6

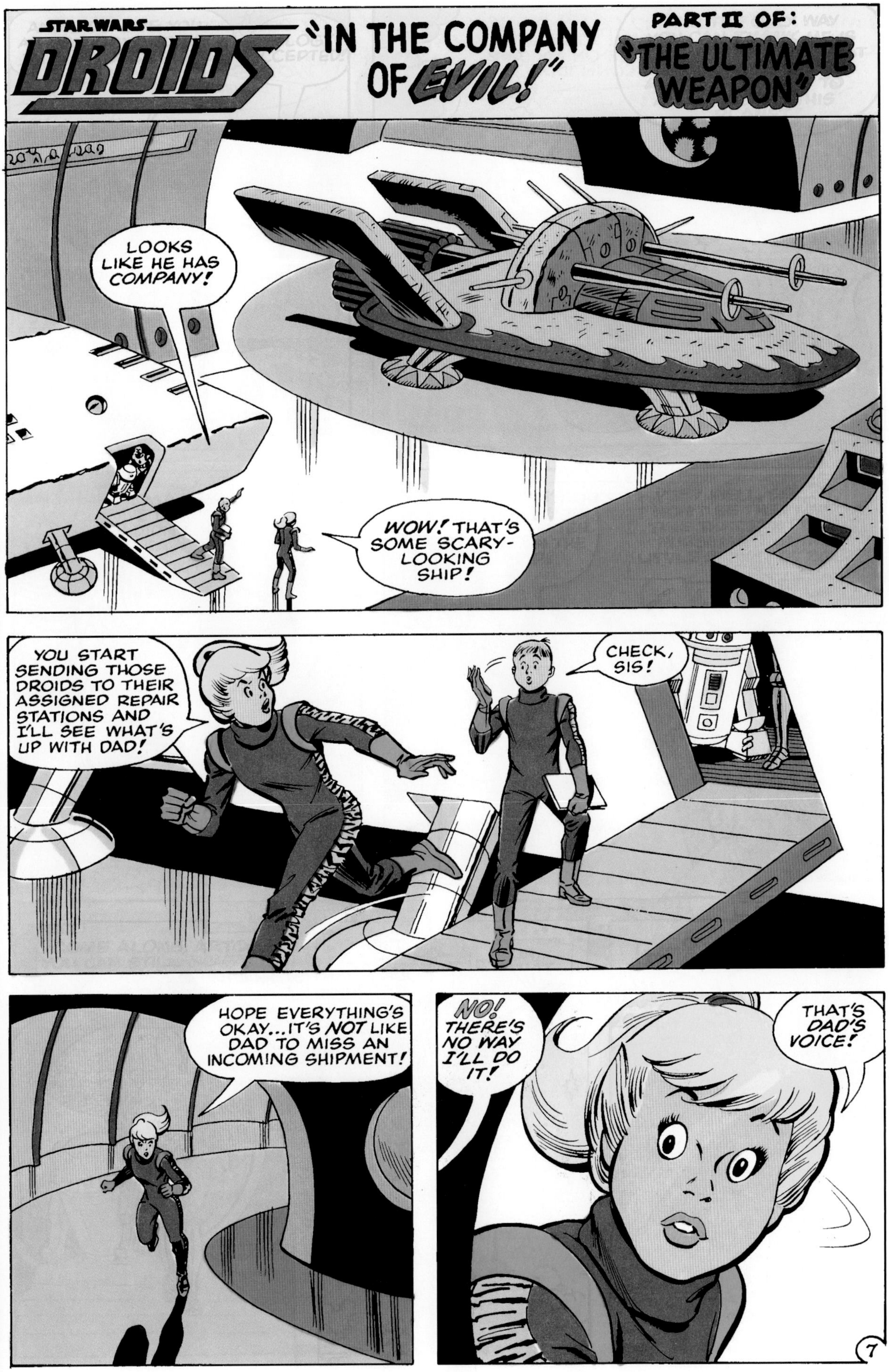
STAR WARS
DROIDS
"IN THE COMPANY OF EVIL!"
PART II OF: "THE ULTIMATE WEAPON"
LOOKS LIKE HE HAS COMPANY!
WOW! THAT'S SOME SCARY-LOOKING SHIP!
YOU START SENDING THOSE DROIDS TO THEIR ASSIGNED REPAIR STATIONS AND I'LL SEE WHAT'S UP WITH DAD!
CHECK, SIS!
HOPE EVERYTHING'S OKAY...IT'S NOT LIKE DAD TO MISS AN INCOMING SHIPMENT!
NO! THERE'S NO WAY I'LL DO IT!
THAT'S DAD'S VOICE!
7

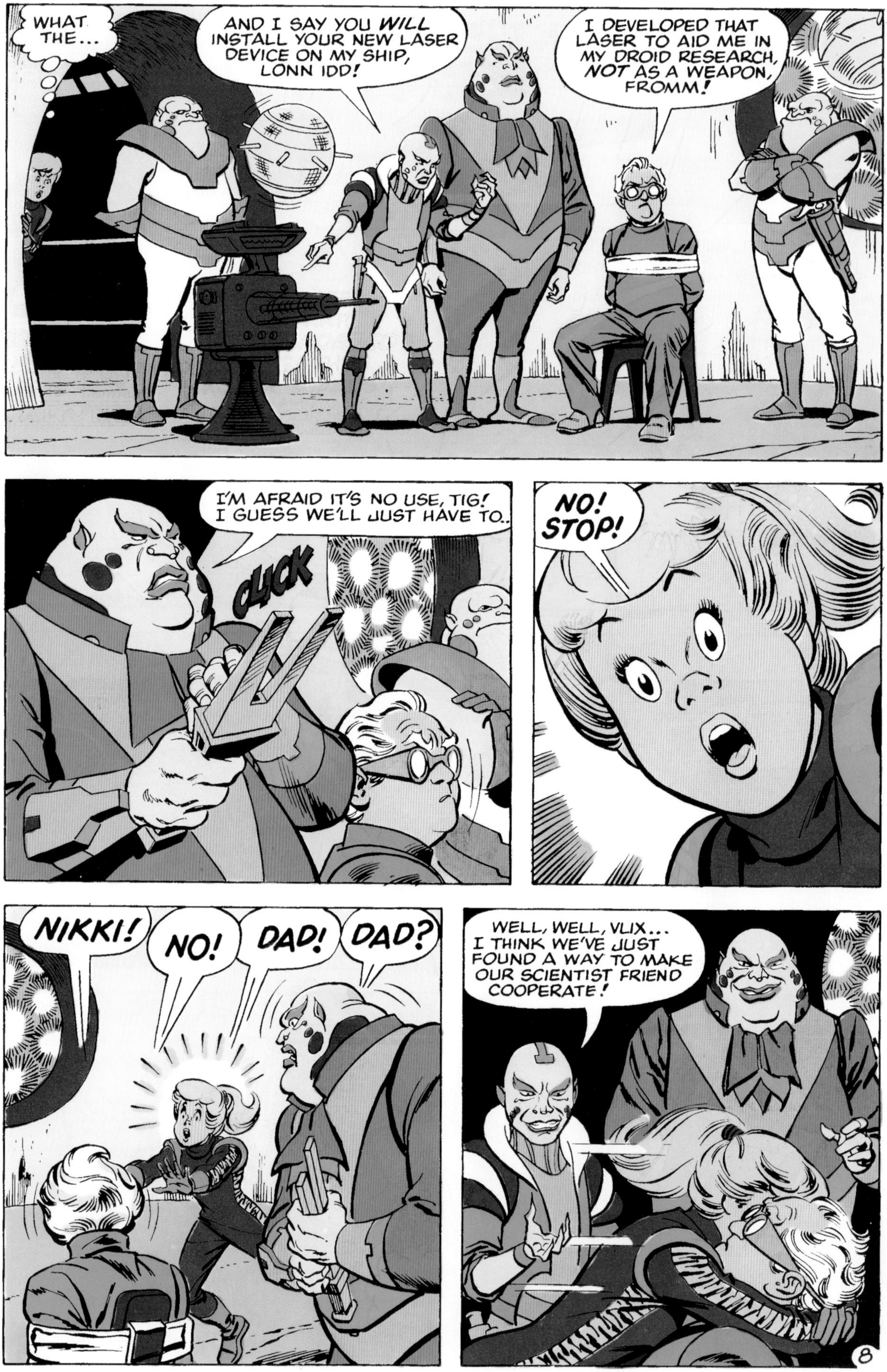
WHAT THE...
AND I SAY YOU WILL INSTALL YOUR NEW LASER DEVICE ON MY SHIP, LONN IDD!
I DEVELOPED THAT LASER TO AID ME IN MY DROID RESEARCH, NOT AS A WEAPON, FROMM!
I'M AFRAID IT'S NO USE, TIG! I GUESS WE'LL JUST HAVE TO..
CLICK
NO! STOP!
NIKKI!
NO!
DAD!
DAD?
WELL, WELL, VLIX... I THINK WE'VE JUST FOUND A WAY TO MAKE OUR SCIENTIST FRIEND COOPERATE!
8

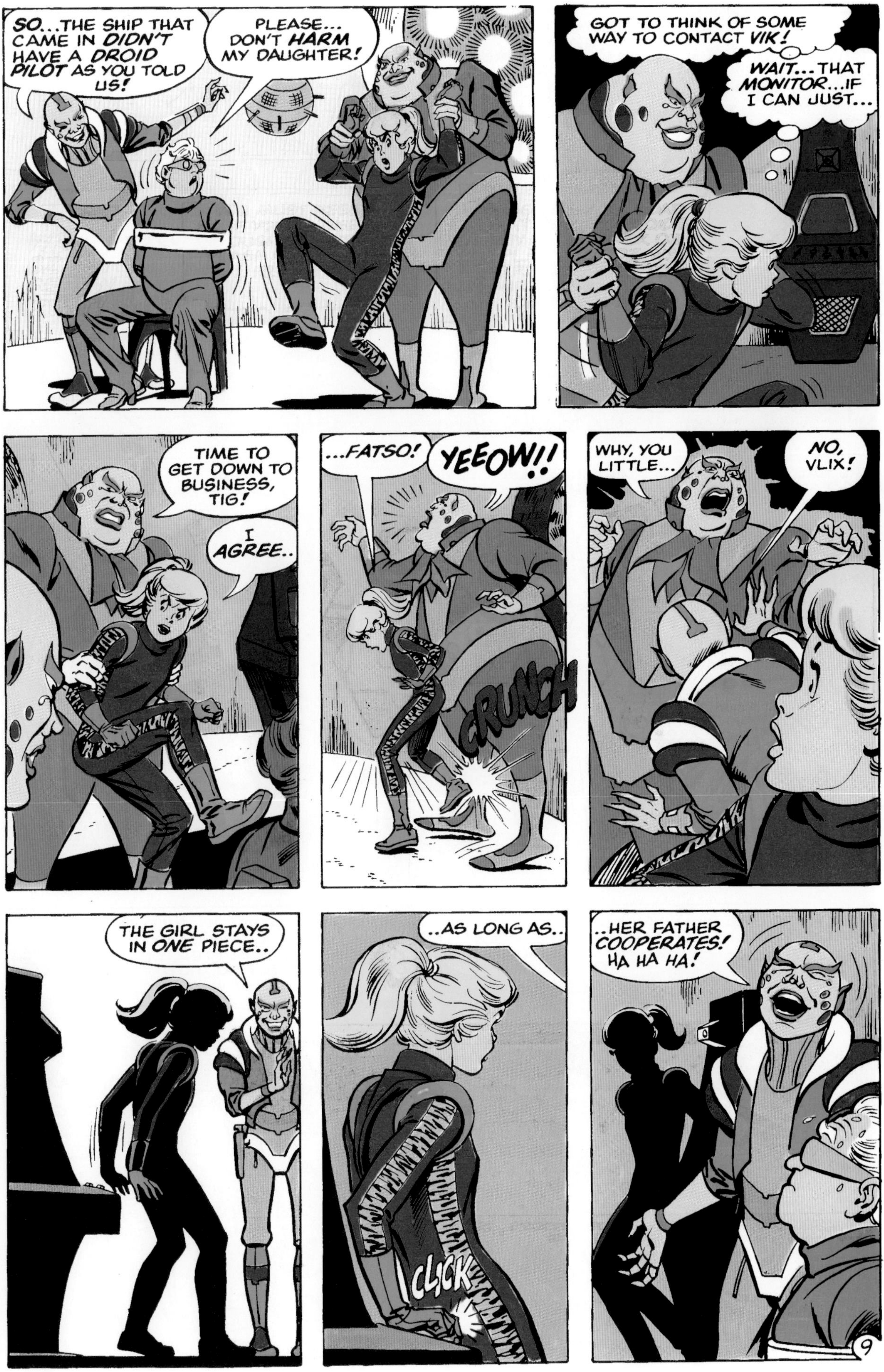
SO...THE SHIP THAT CAME IN DIDN'T HAVE A DROID PILOT AS YOU TOLD US!
PLEASE... DON'T HARM MY DAUGHTER!
GOT TO THINK OF SOME WAY TO CONTACT VIK!
WAIT...THAT MONITOR...IF I CAN JUST...
TIME TO GET DOWN TO BUSINESS, TIG!
I AGREE..
...FATSO!
YEEOW!!
CRUNCH
WHY, YOU LITTLE...
NO, VLIX!
THE GIRL STAYS IN ONE PIECE..
..AS LONG AS..
CLICK
..HER FATHER COOPERATES! HA HA HA!
9

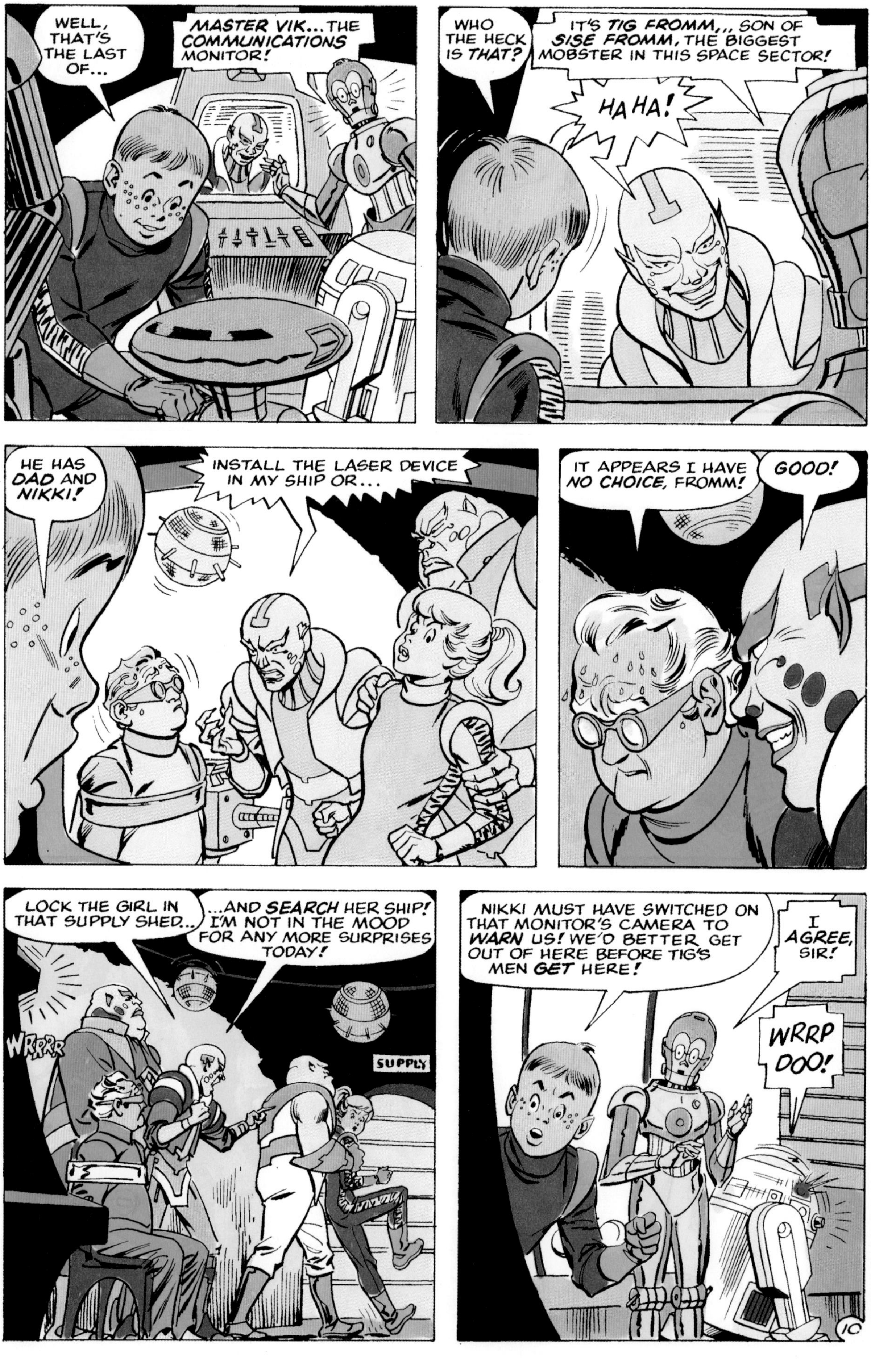
WELL, THAT'S THE LAST OF...
MASTER VIK... THE COMMUNICATIONS MONITOR!
WHO THE HECK IS THAT?
IT'S TIG FROMM,, SON OF SISE FROMM, THE BIGGEST MOBSTER IN THIS SPACE SECTOR!
HA HA!
HE HAS DAD AND NIKKI!
INSTALL THE LASER DEVICE IN MY SHIP OR...
IT APPEARS I HAVE NO CHOICE, FROMM!
GOOD!
LOCK THE GIRL IN THAT SUPPLY SHED...
...AND SEARCH HER SHIP! I'M NOT IN THE MOOD FOR ANY MORE SURPRISES TODAY!
WRRRR
SUPPLY
NIKKI MUST HAVE SWITCHED ON THAT MONITOR'S CAMERA TO WARN US! WE'D BETTER GET OUT OF HERE BEFORE TIG'S MEN GET HERE!
I AGREE, SIR!
WRRP DOO!
10

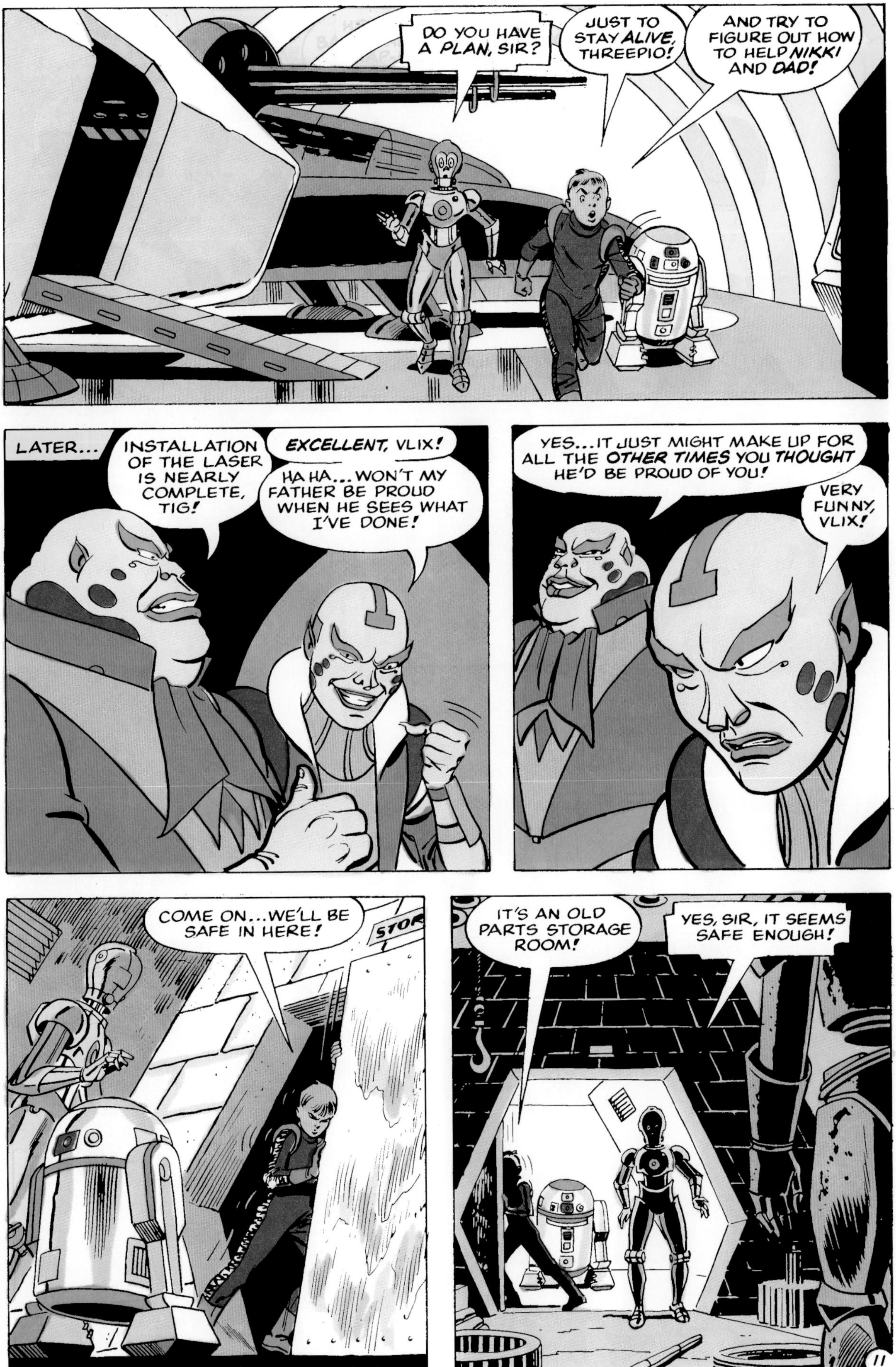
DO YOU HAVE A PLAN, SIR?
JUST TO STAY ALIVE, THREEPIO!
AND TRY TO FIGURE OUT HOW TO HELP NIKKI AND DAD!
LATER...
INSTALLATION OF THE LASER IS NEARLY COMPLETE, TIG!
EXCELLENT, VLIX!
HA HA... WON'T MY FATHER BE PROUD WHEN HE SEES WHAT I'VE DONE!
YES... IT JUST MIGHT MAKE UP FOR ALL THE OTHER TIMES YOU THOUGHT HE'D BE PROUD OF YOU!
VERY FUNNY, VLIX!
COME ON... WE'LL BE SAFE IN HERE!
IT'S AN OLD PARTS STORAGE ROOM!
YES, SIR, IT SEEMS SAFE ENOUGH!
11

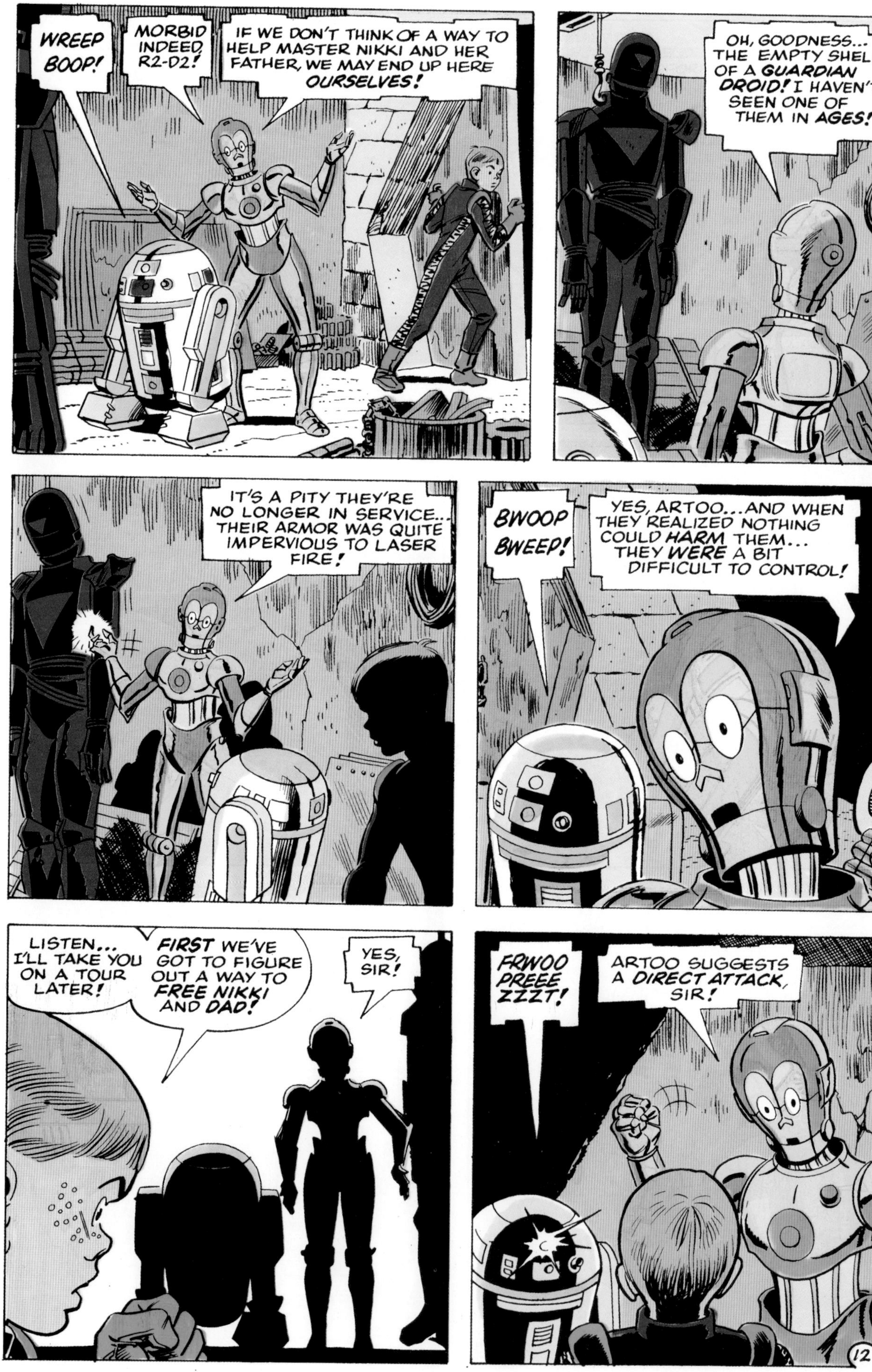
WREEP BOOP!
MORBID INDEED, R2-D2!
IF WE DON'T THINK OF A WAY TO HELP MASTER NIKKI AND HER FATHER, WE MAY END UP HERE OURSELVES!
OH, GOODNESS... THE EMPTY SHELL OF A GUARDIAN DROID! I HAVEN'T SEEN ONE OF THEM IN AGES!
IT'S A PITY THEY'RE NO LONGER IN SERVICE... THEIR ARMOR WAS QUITE IMPERVIOUS TO LASER FIRE!
BWOOP BWEEP!
YES, ARTOO... AND WHEN THEY REALIZED NOTHING COULD HARM THEM... THEY WERE A BIT DIFFICULT TO CONTROL!
LISTEN... I'LL TAKE YOU ON A TOUR LATER!
FIRST WE'VE GOT TO FIGURE OUT A WAY TO FREE NIKKI AND DAD!
YES, SIR!
FRWOO PREEE ZZZT!
ARTOO SUGGESTS A DIRECT ATTACK, SIR!
12

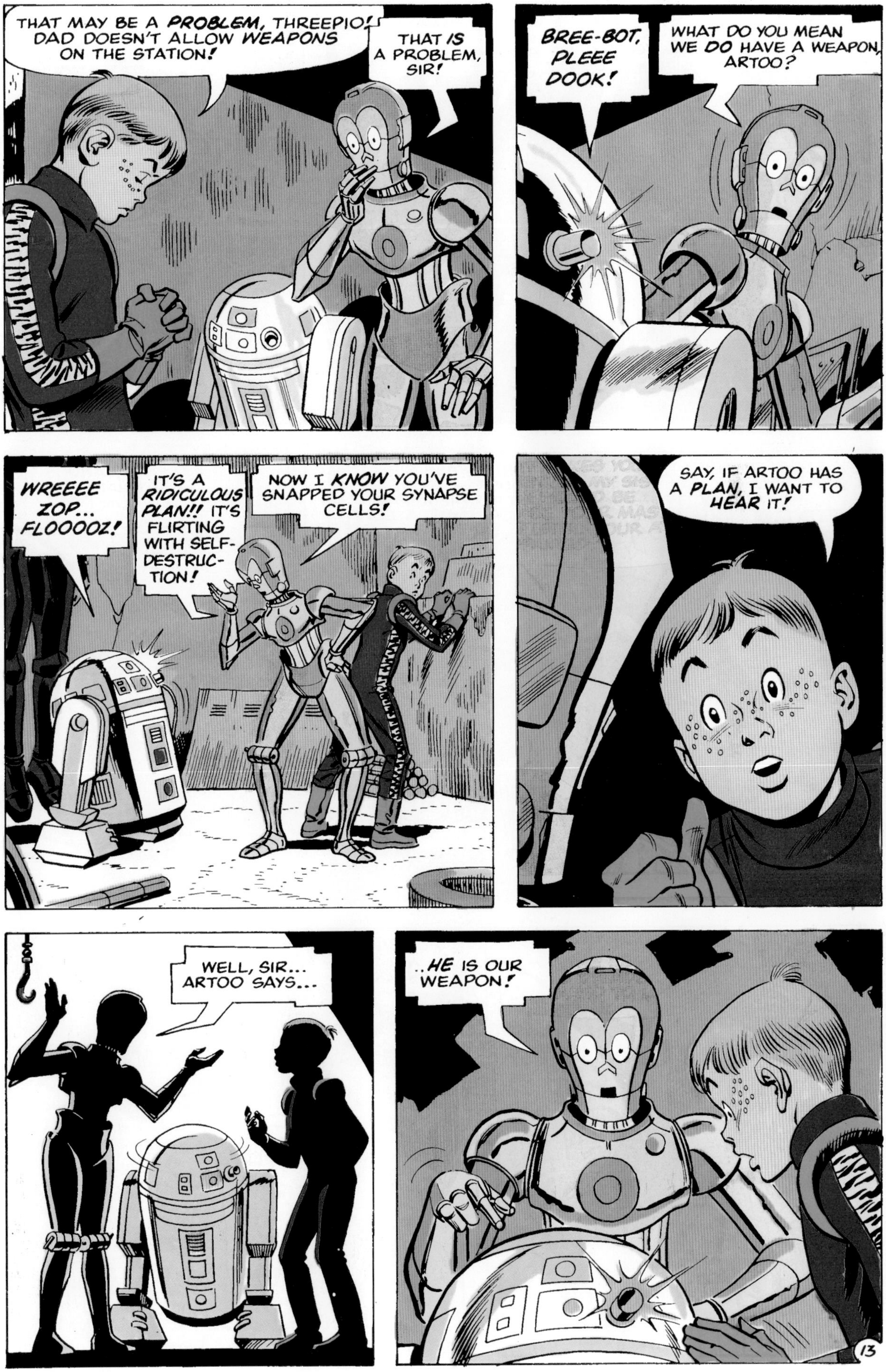
THAT MAY BE A PROBLEM, THREEPIO! DAD DOESN'T ALLOW WEAPONS ON THE STATION!
THAT IS A PROBLEM, SIR!
BREE-BOT, PLEEE DOOK!
WHAT DO YOU MEAN WE DO HAVE A WEAPON, ARTOO?
WREEEE ZOP... FLOOOOZ!
IT'S A RIDICULOUS PLAN!! IT'S FLIRTING WITH SELF-DESTRUCTION!
NOW I KNOW YOU'VE SNAPPED YOUR SYNAPSE CELLS!
SAY, IF ARTOO HAS A PLAN, I WANT TO HEAR IT!
WELL, SIR... ARTOO SAYS...
..HE IS OUR WEAPON!
13

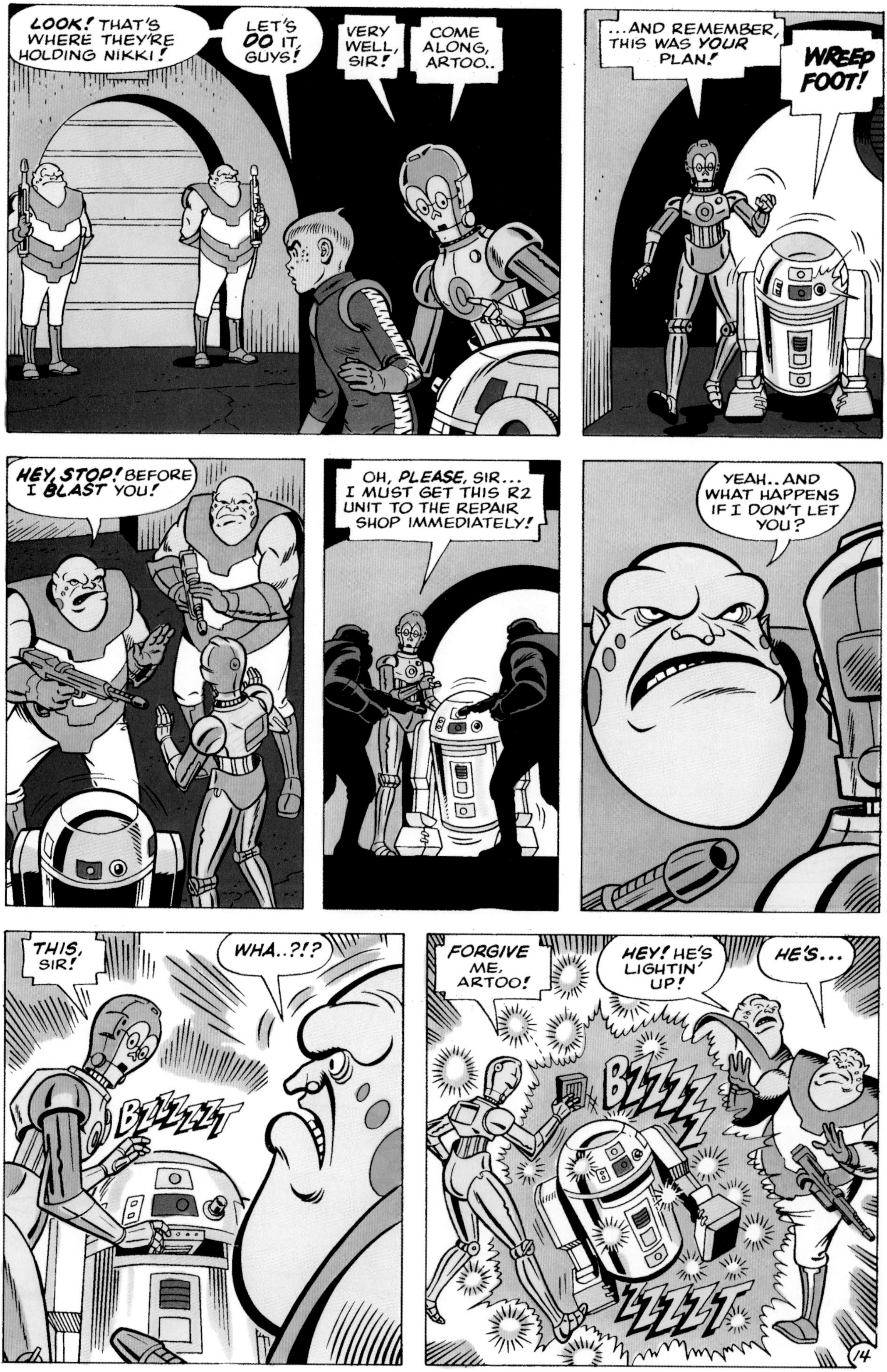
LOOK! THAT'S WHERE THEY'RE HOLDING NIKKI!
LET'S DO IT, GUYS!
VERY WELL, SIR!
COME ALONG, ARTOO..
...AND REMEMBER, THIS WAS YOUR PLAN!
WREEP FOOT!
HEY, STOP! BEFORE I BLAST YOU!
OH, PLEASE, SIR... I MUST GET THIS R2 UNIT TO THE REPAIR SHOP IMMEDIATELY!
YEAH..AND WHAT HAPPENS IF I DON'T LET YOU?
THIS, SIR!
WHA..?!?
BZZZZZT
FORGIVE ME, ARTOO!
HEY! HE'S LIGHTIN' UP!
HE'S...
BZZZZ
ZZZZT
14

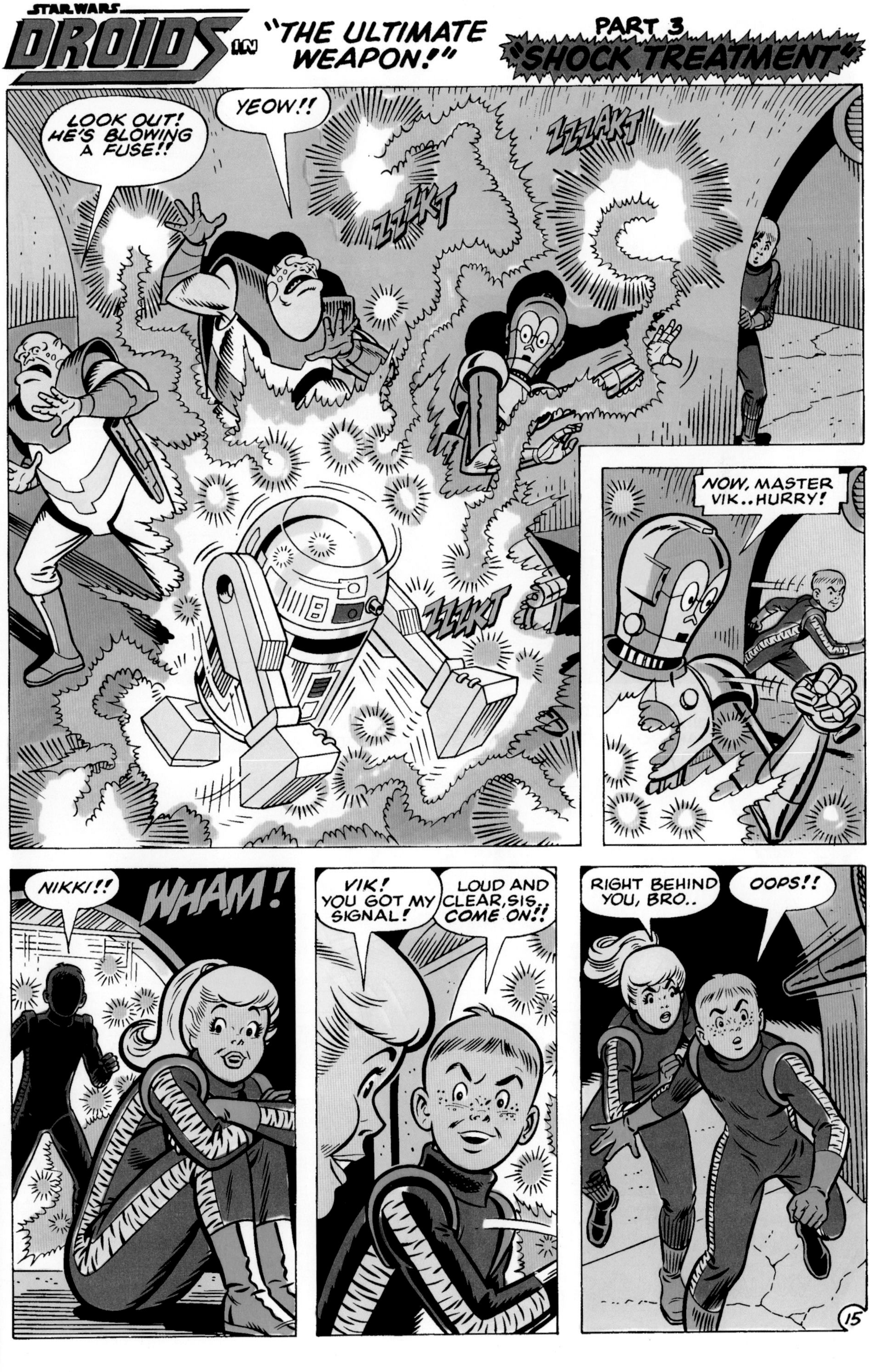
STAR WARS
DROIDS in "THE ULTIMATE WEAPON!"
PART 3 "SHOCK TREATMENT"
LOOK OUT! HE'S BLOWING A FUSE!!
YEOW!!
ZZZAKT
ZZZAKT
ZZZAKT
NOW, MASTER VIK.. HURRY!
NIKKI!!
WHAM!
VIK! YOU GOT MY SIGNAL!
LOUD AND CLEAR, SIS.. COME ON!!
RIGHT BEHIND YOU, BRO..
OOPS!!
15

A HOVER GUARD!
WHRRRR
HELP!! WE'RE TRAPPED!
WHRRRRRR
ARTOO!
WHRRRRRRZZZZZZZZZZZZ
BOOM
OH..POOR ARTOO!
WREEE!
WE'D BETTER TAKE THOSE TWO TO TIG!
CLUNK
OH, I DO FEEL DREADFUL FOR YOU, ARTOO!
BUT I MUST DO SOMETHING TO HELP MASTERS NIKKI AND VIK!
MASTERS ARE SO HARD TO COME BY THESE DAYS!
THEY DESERVE MY TAKING GULP THIS CHANCE!
CLIK
CLIK
16

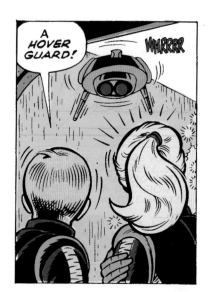

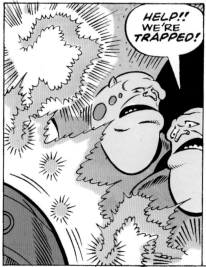

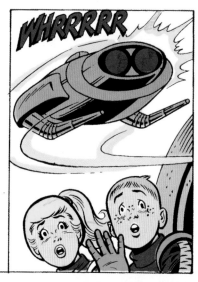

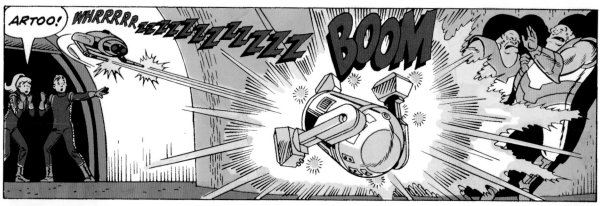

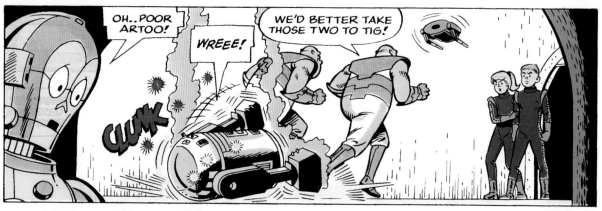

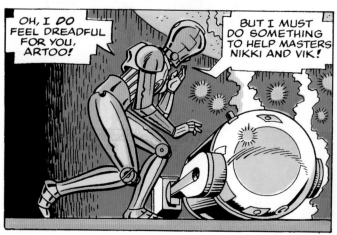

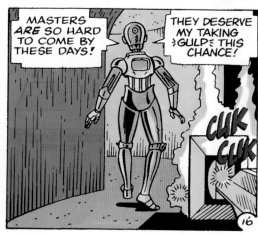

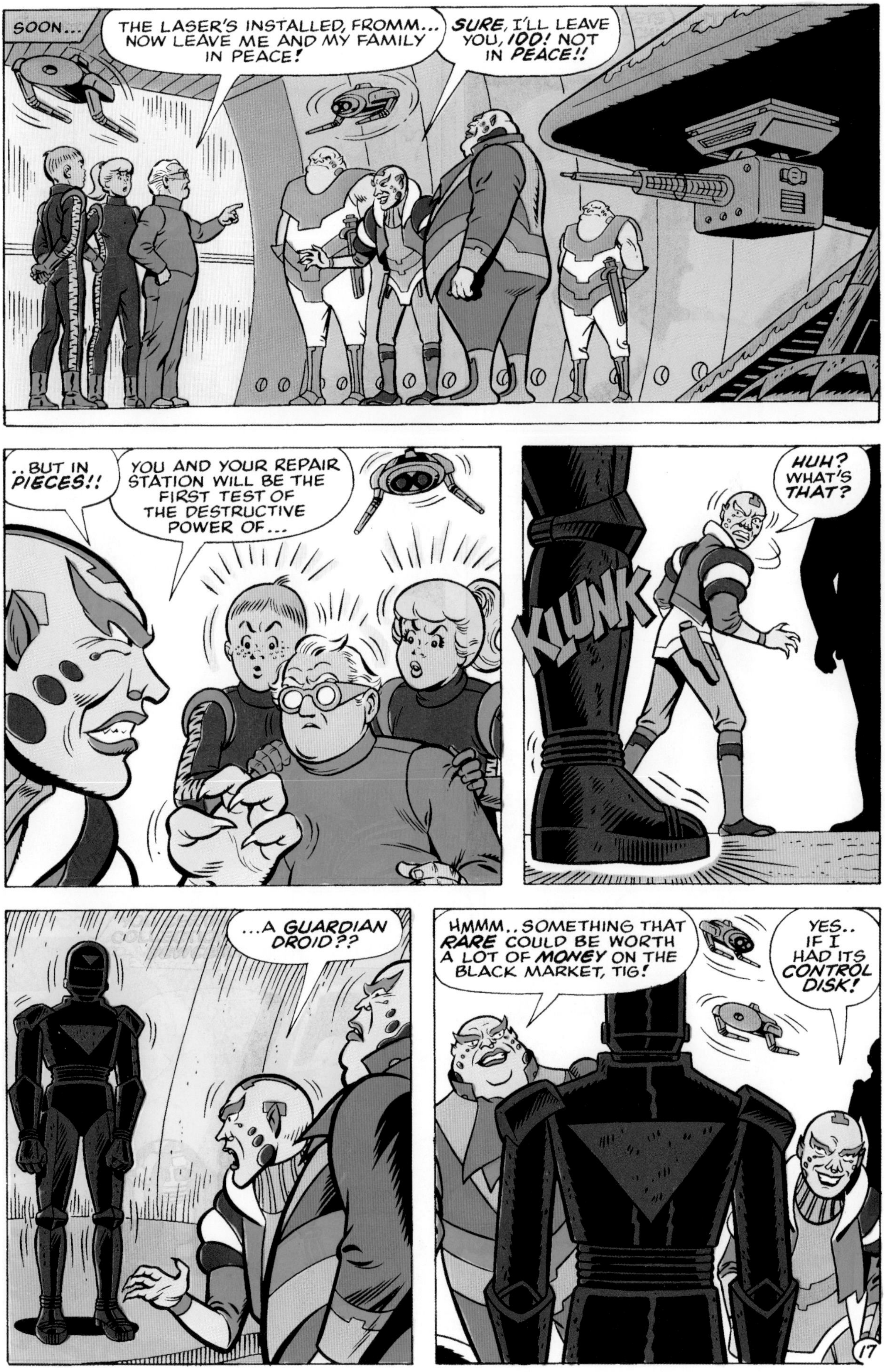
SOON...
THE LASER'S INSTALLED, FROMM... NOW LEAVE ME AND MY FAMILY IN PEACE!
SURE, I'LL LEAVE YOU, IOD! NOT IN PEACE!!
..BUT IN PIECES!!
YOU AND YOUR REPAIR STATION WILL BE THE FIRST TEST OF THE DESTRUCTIVE POWER OF...
KLUNK
HUH? WHAT'S THAT?
...A GUARDIAN DROID??
HMMM..SOMETHING THAT RARE COULD BE WORTH A LOT OF MONEY ON THE BLACK MARKET, TIG!
YES.. IF I HAD ITS CONTROL DISK!
17

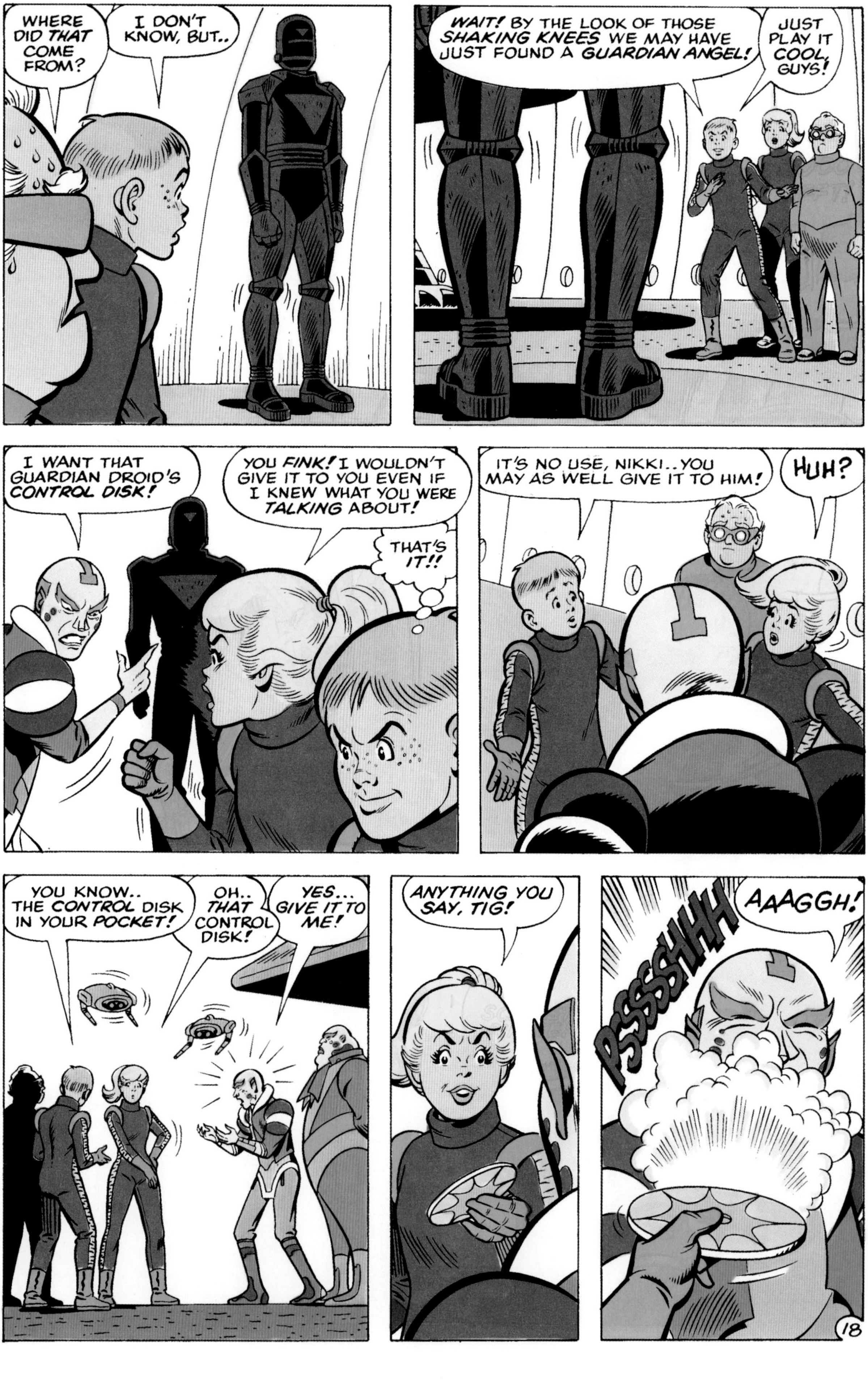
WHERE DID THAT COME FROM?
I DON'T KNOW, BUT..
WAIT! BY THE LOOK OF THOSE SHAKING KNEES WE MAY HAVE JUST FOUND A GUARDIAN ANGEL!
JUST PLAY IT COOL, GUYS!
I WANT THAT GUARDIAN DROID'S CONTROL DISK!
YOU FINK! I WOULDN'T GIVE IT TO YOU EVEN IF I KNEW WHAT YOU WERE TALKING ABOUT!
THAT'S IT!!
IT'S NO USE, NIKKI..YOU MAY AS WELL GIVE IT TO HIM!
HUH?
YOU KNOW.. THE CONTROL DISK IN YOUR POCKET!
OH.. THAT CONTROL DISK!
YES... GIVE IT TO ME!
ANYTHING YOU SAY, TIG!
PSSSSHHH
AAAGGH!
18

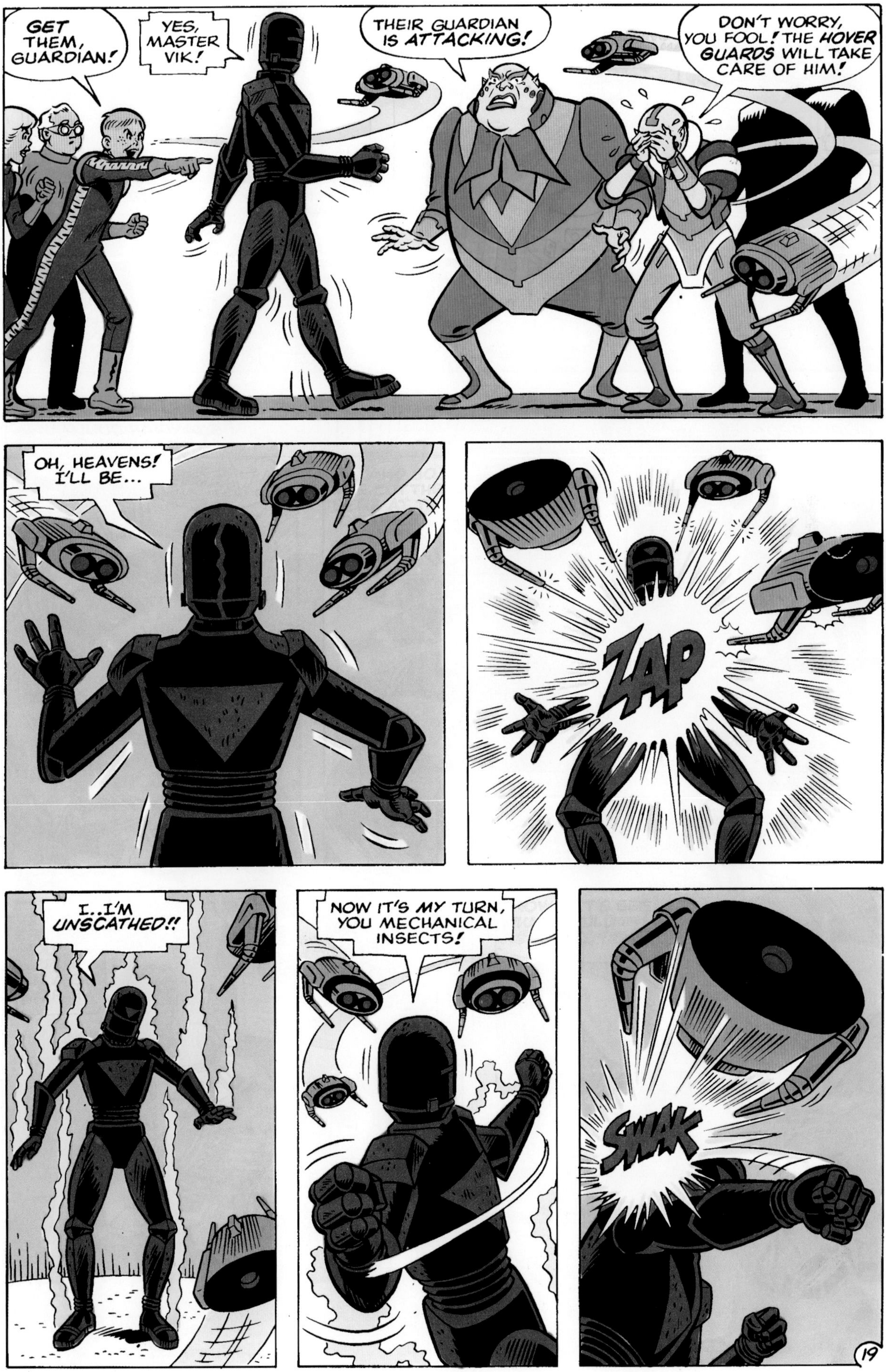

GET THEM, GUARDIAN!
YES, MASTER VIK!
THEIR GUARDIAN IS ATTACKING!
DON'T WORRY, YOU FOOL! THE HOVER GUARDS WILL TAKE CARE OF HIM!
OH, HEAVENS! I'LL BE...
ZAP
I..I'M UNSCATHED!!
NOW IT'S MY TURN, YOU MECHANICAL INSECTS!
SWAK
19

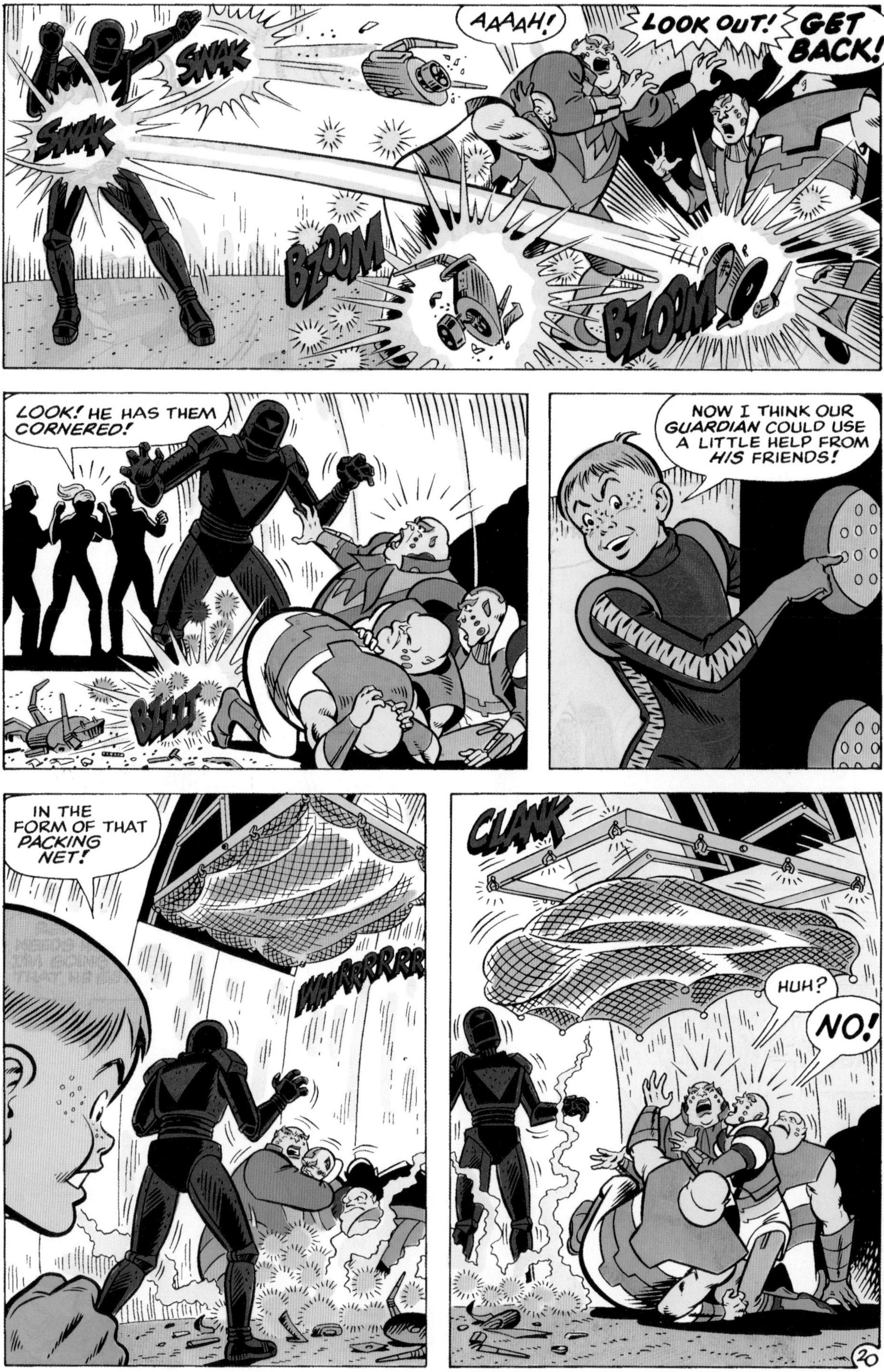
SWAK
SWAK
AAAAH!
LOOK OUT!
GET BACK!
BZOOM
BZOOM
LOOK! HE HAS THEM CORNERED!
BZZZT
NOW I THINK OUR GUARDIAN COULD USE A LITTLE HELP FROM HIS FRIENDS!
IN THE FORM OF THAT PACKING NET!
WHIRRRRR
CLANK
HUH?
NO!
20

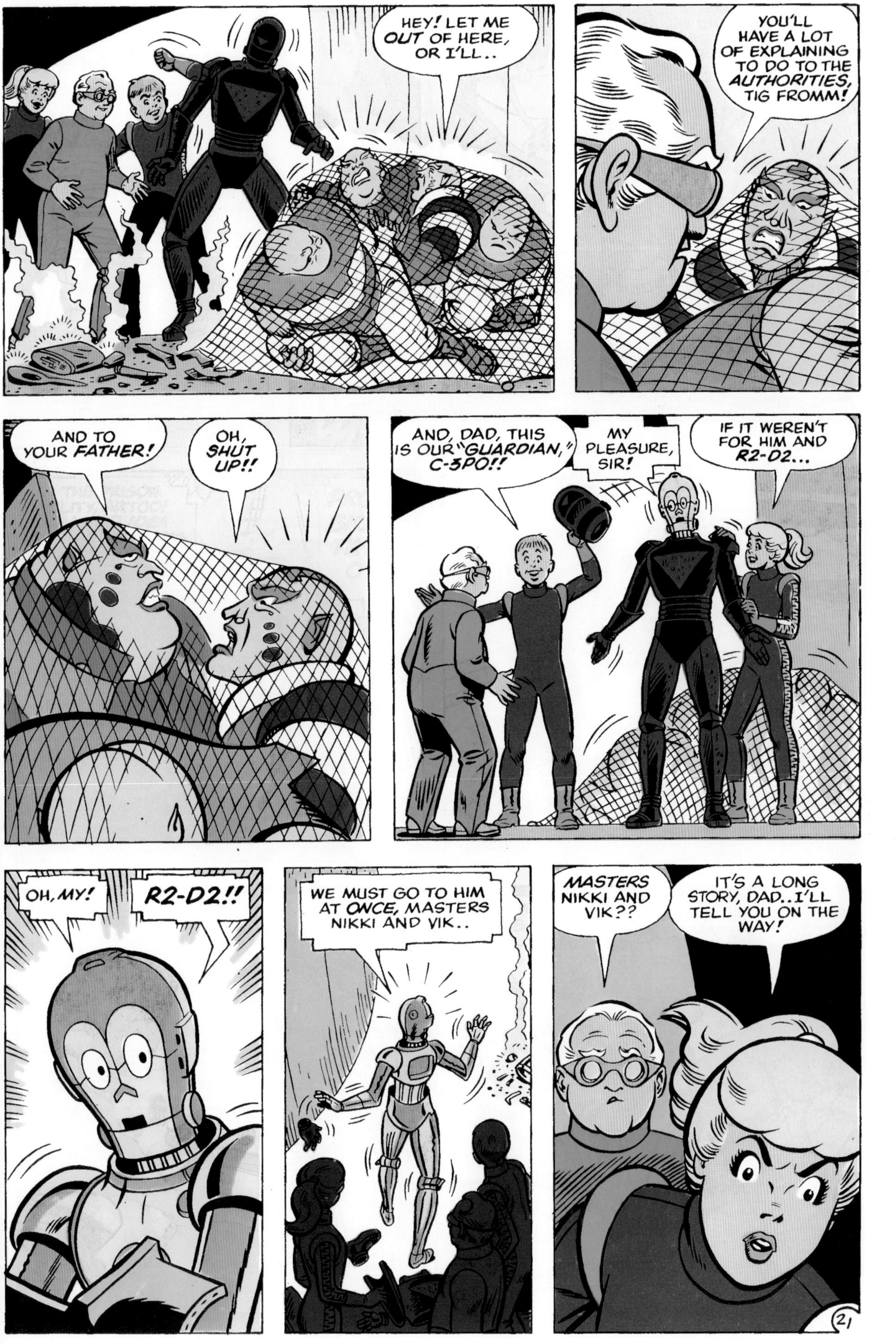
HEY! LET ME OUT OF HERE, OR I'LL..
YOU'LL HAVE A LOT OF EXPLAINING TO DO TO THE AUTHORITIES, TIG FROMM!
AND TO YOUR FATHER!
OH, SHUT UP!!
AND, DAD, THIS IS OUR "GUARDIAN," C-3PO!!
MY PLEASURE, SIR!
IF IT WEREN'T FOR HIM AND R2-D2...
OH, MY!
R2-D2!!
WE MUST GO TO HIM AT ONCE, MASTERS NIKKI AND VIK..
MASTERS NIKKI AND VIK??
IT'S A LONG STORY, DAD..I'LL TELL YOU ON THE WAY!
21

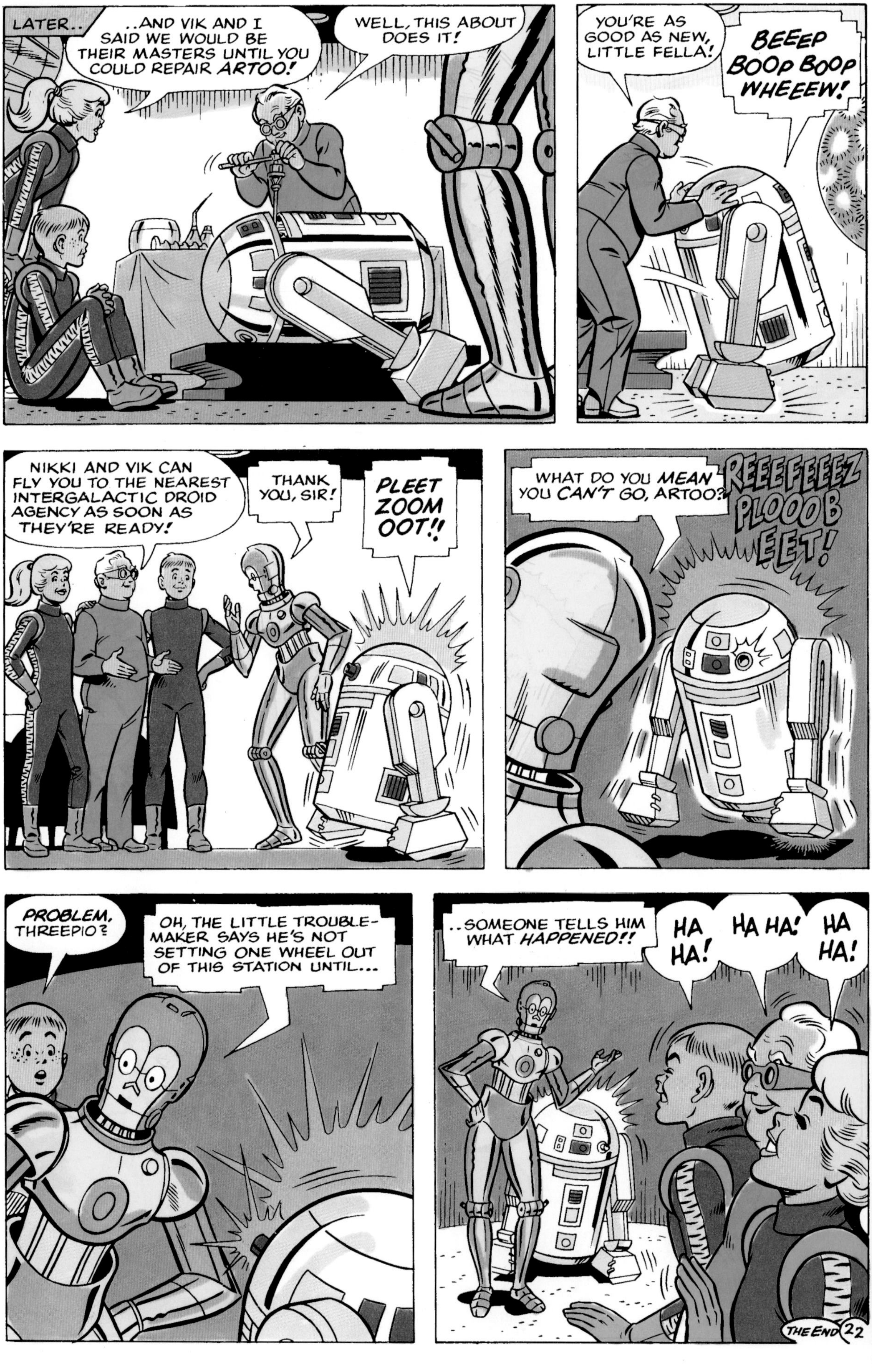
LATER..
..AND VIK AND I SAID WE WOULD BE THEIR MASTERS UNTIL YOU COULD REPAIR ARTOO!
WELL, THIS ABOUT DOES IT!
YOU'RE AS GOOD AS NEW, LITTLE FELLA!
BEEEP BOOp BOOp WHEEEW!
NIKKI AND VIK CAN FLY YOU TO THE NEAREST INTERGALACTIC DROID AGENCY AS SOON AS THEY'RE READY!
THANK YOU, SIR!
PLEET ZOOM OOT!!
WHAT DO YOU MEAN YOU CAN'T GO, ARTOO?
REEEFEEEZ PLOOOB EET!
PROBLEM, THREEPIO?
OH, THE LITTLE TROUBLE-MAKER SAYS HE'S NOT SETTING ONE WHEEL OUT OF THIS STATION UNTIL...
..SOMEONE TELLS HIM WHAT HAPPENED!!
HA HA!
HA HA!
HA HA!
THE END 22

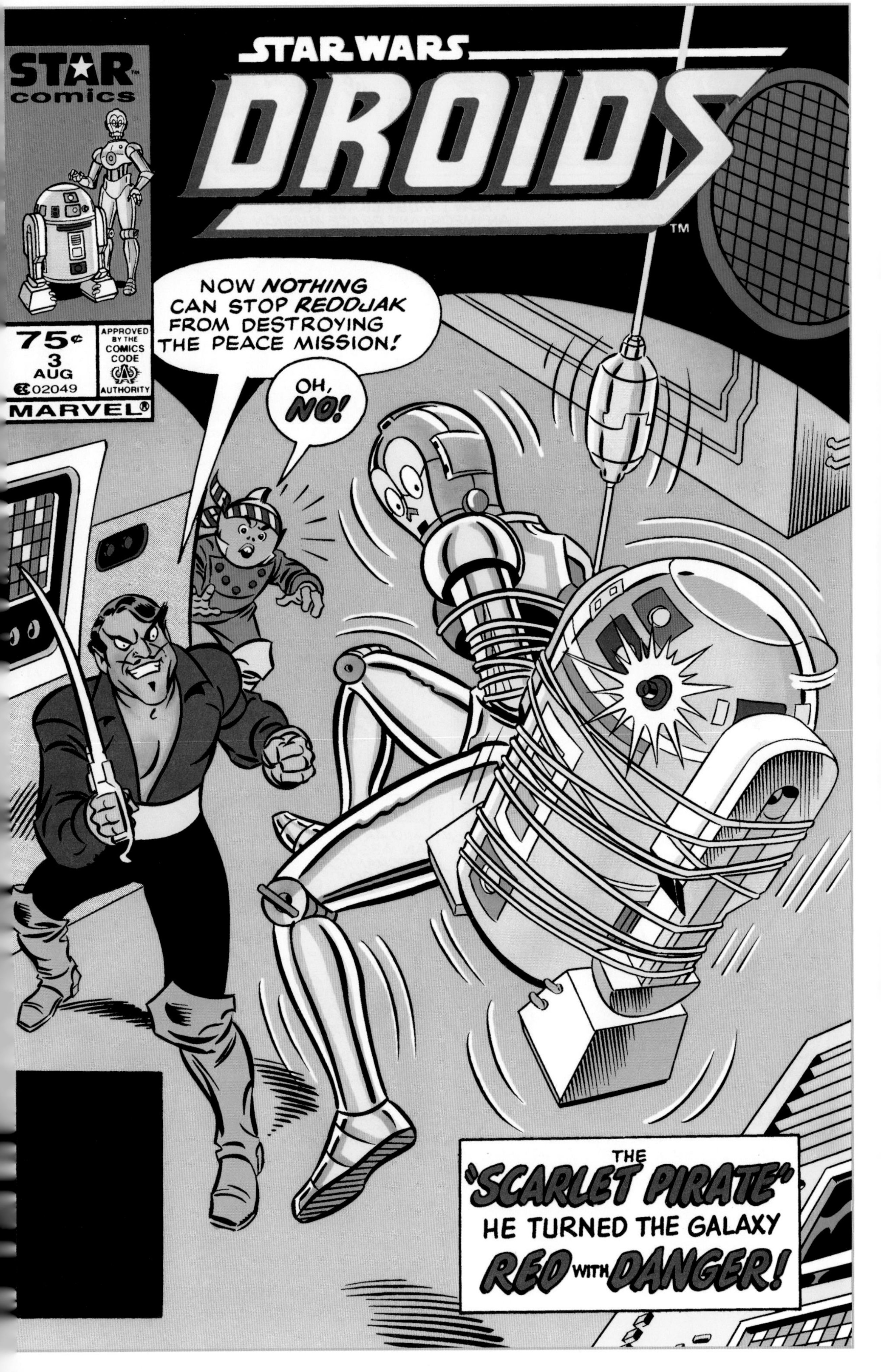
STAR WARS
DROIDS™
STAR™ comics
75¢
3
AUG
02049
APPROVED BY THE COMICS CODE AUTHORITY
MARVEL®
NOW NOTHING CAN STOP REDDJAK FROM DESTROYING THE PEACE MISSION!
OH, NO!
THE "SCARLET PIRATE" HE TURNED THE GALAXY RED WITH DANGER!

PURCHASED BY A WEALTHY GOVERNMENT OFFICIAL ON THE PLANET *MAJOOR*, THE *DROIDS R2-D2* AND *C-3PO* HAVE FINALLY FOUND A POSITION OF DIGNITY... AND *DUTIES* THAT MAY BRING THEIR *END!*

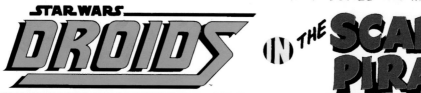

STAR WARS

DROIDS IN THE SCARLET PIRATE!

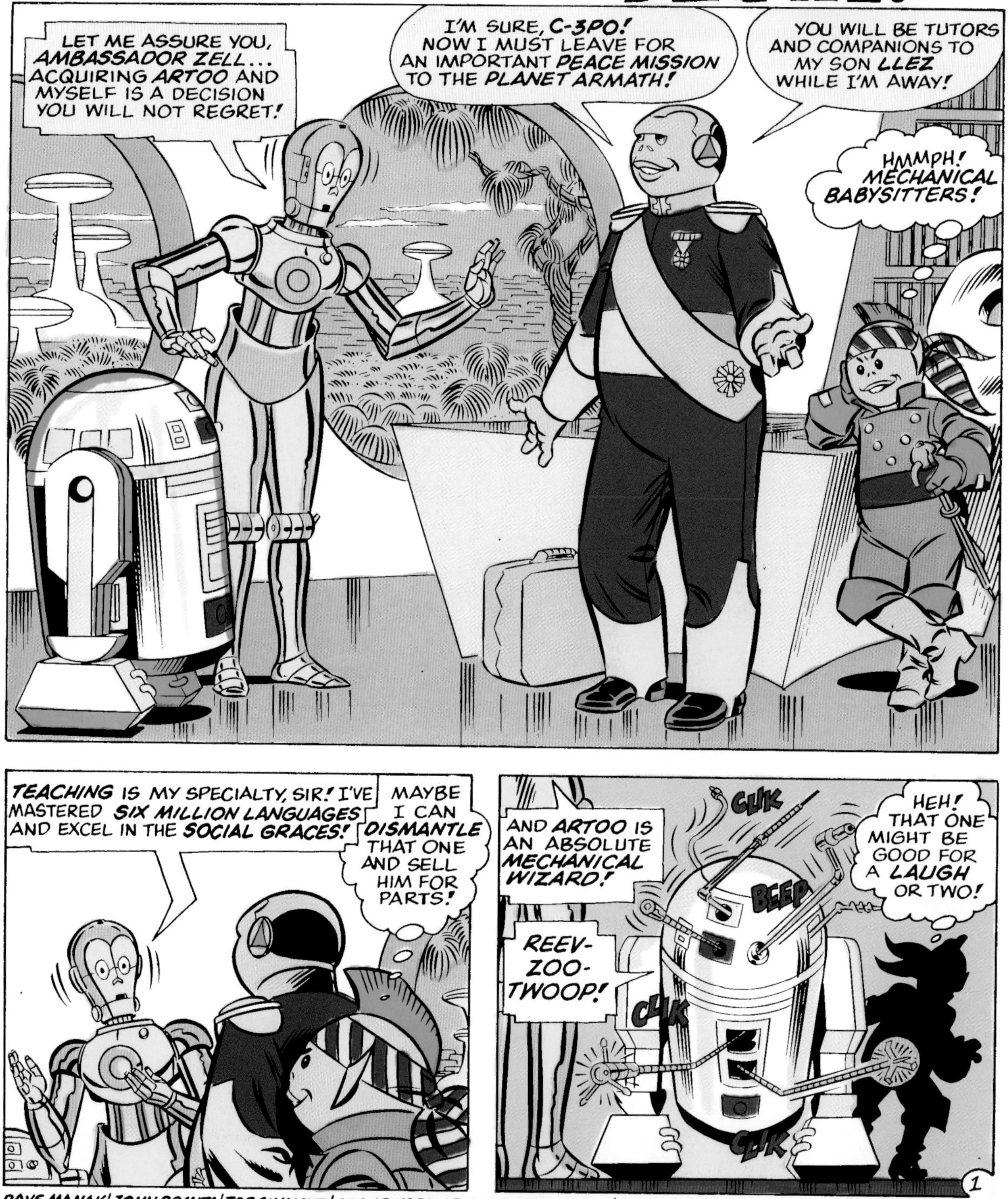

LET ME ASSURE YOU, AMBASSADOR ZELL... ACQUIRING ARTOO AND MYSELF IS A DECISION YOU WILL NOT REGRET!
I'M SURE, C-3PO! NOW I MUST LEAVE FOR AN IMPORTANT PEACE MISSION TO THE PLANET ARMATH!
YOU WILL BE TUTORS AND COMPANIONS TO MY SON LLEZ WHILE I'M AWAY!
HMMPH! MECHANICAL BABYSITTERS!
TEACHING IS MY SPECIALTY, SIR! I'VE MASTERED SIX MILLION LANGUAGES AND EXCEL IN THE SOCIAL GRACES!
MAYBE I CAN DISMANTLE THAT ONE AND SELL HIM FOR PARTS!
AND ARTOO IS AN ABSOLUTE MECHANICAL WIZARD!
CLIK
BEEP
REEV-ZOO-TWOOP!
CLIK
CLIK
HEH! THAT ONE MIGHT BE GOOD FOR A LAUGH OR TWO!
1

DAVE MANAK WRITER / JOHN ROMITA PENCILER / JOE SINNOTT INKER / GRACE KREMER LETTERER / GEORGE ROUSSOS COLORIST / SID JACOBSON EDITOR / TOM DeFALCO EXEC. EDITOR / JIM SHOOTER EDITOR IN CHIEF

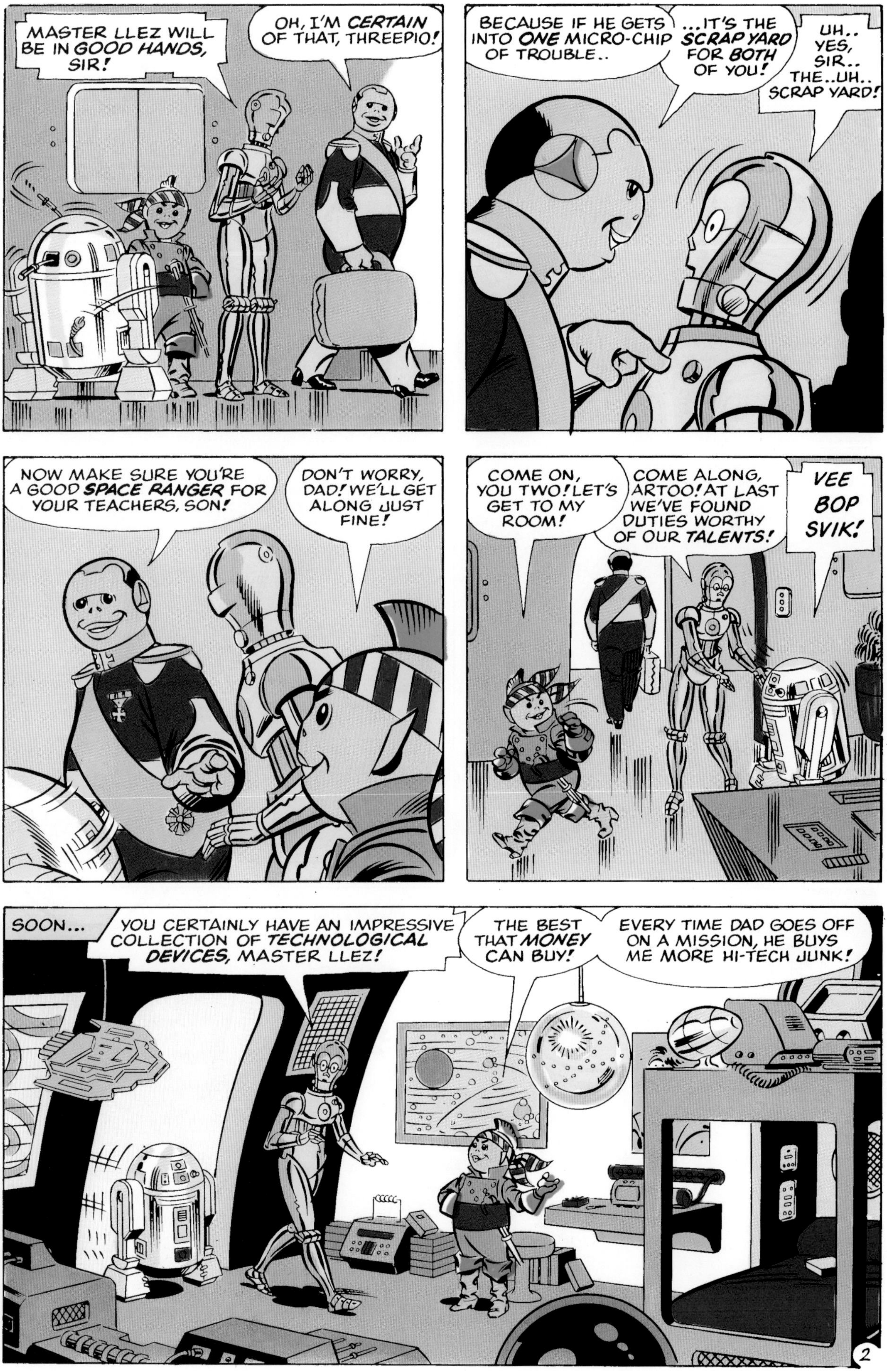
MASTER LLEZ WILL BE IN GOOD HANDS, SIR!
OH, I'M CERTAIN OF THAT, THREEPIO!
BECAUSE IF HE GETS INTO ONE MICRO-CHIP OF TROUBLE..
...IT'S THE SCRAP YARD FOR BOTH OF YOU!
UH.. YES, SIR.. THE..UH.. SCRAP YARD!
NOW MAKE SURE YOU'RE A GOOD SPACE RANGER FOR YOUR TEACHERS, SON!
DON'T WORRY, DAD! WE'LL GET ALONG JUST FINE!
COME ON, YOU TWO! LET'S GET TO MY ROOM!
COME ALONG, ARTOO! AT LAST WE'VE FOUND DUTIES WORTHY OF OUR TALENTS!
VEE BOP SVIK!
SOON...
YOU CERTAINLY HAVE AN IMPRESSIVE COLLECTION OF TECHNOLOGICAL DEVICES, MASTER LLEZ!
THE BEST THAT MONEY CAN BUY!
EVERY TIME DAD GOES OFF ON A MISSION, HE BUYS ME MORE HI-TECH JUNK!
2

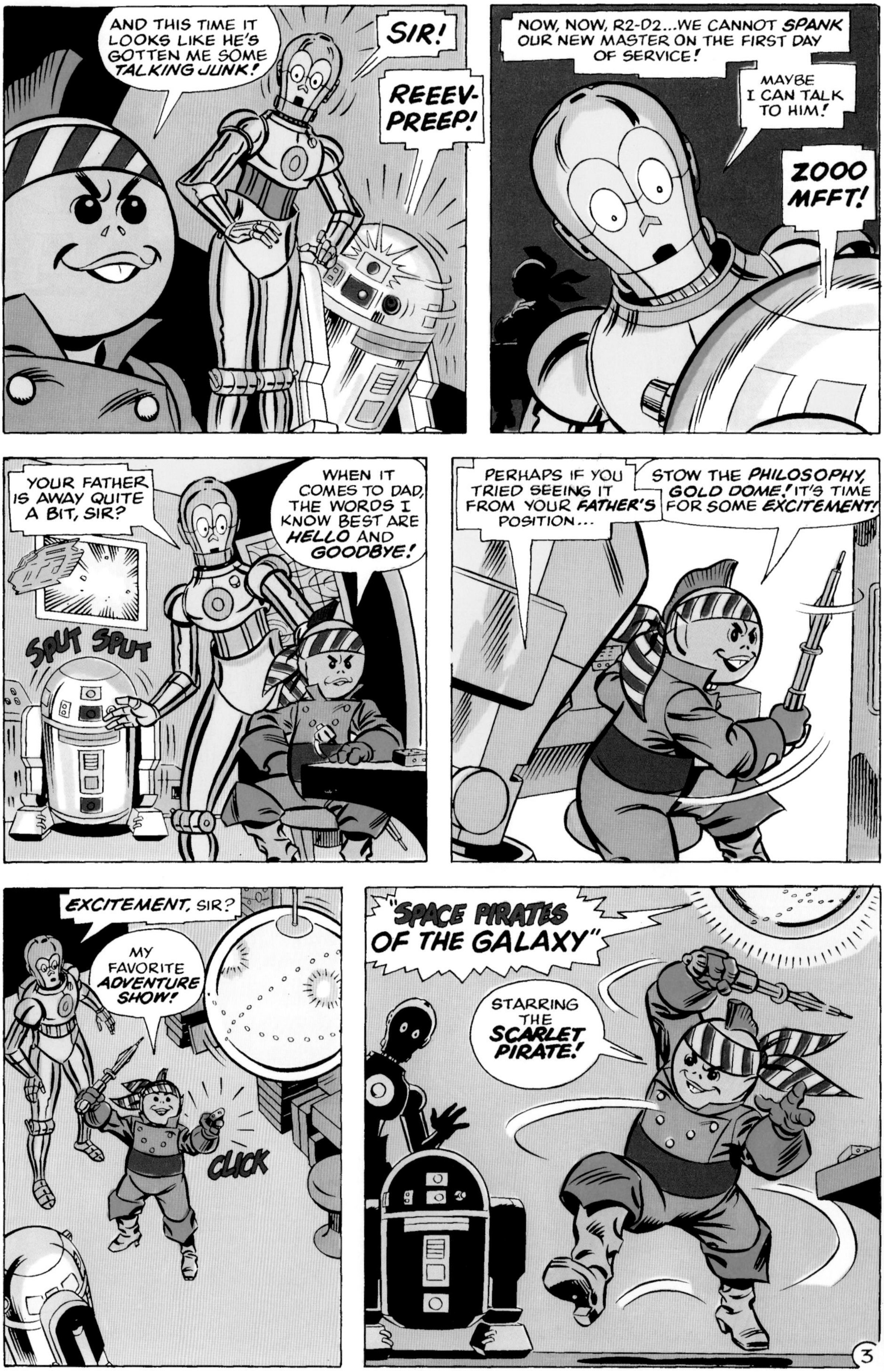
AND THIS TIME IT LOOKS LIKE HE'S GOTTEN ME SOME TALKING JUNK!
SIR!
REEEV-PREEP!
NOW, NOW, R2-D2...WE CANNOT SPANK OUR NEW MASTER ON THE FIRST DAY OF SERVICE!
MAYBE I CAN TALK TO HIM!
ZOOO MFFT!
YOUR FATHER IS AWAY QUITE A BIT, SIR?
WHEN IT COMES TO DAD, THE WORDS I KNOW BEST ARE HELLO AND GOODBYE!
SPUT SPUT
PERHAPS IF YOU TRIED SEEING IT FROM YOUR FATHER'S POSITION...
STOW THE PHILOSOPHY, GOLD DOME! IT'S TIME FOR SOME EXCITEMENT!
EXCITEMENT, SIR?
MY FAVORITE ADVENTURE SHOW!
CLICK
"SPACE PIRATES OF THE GALAXY"
STARRING THE SCARLET PIRATE!
3

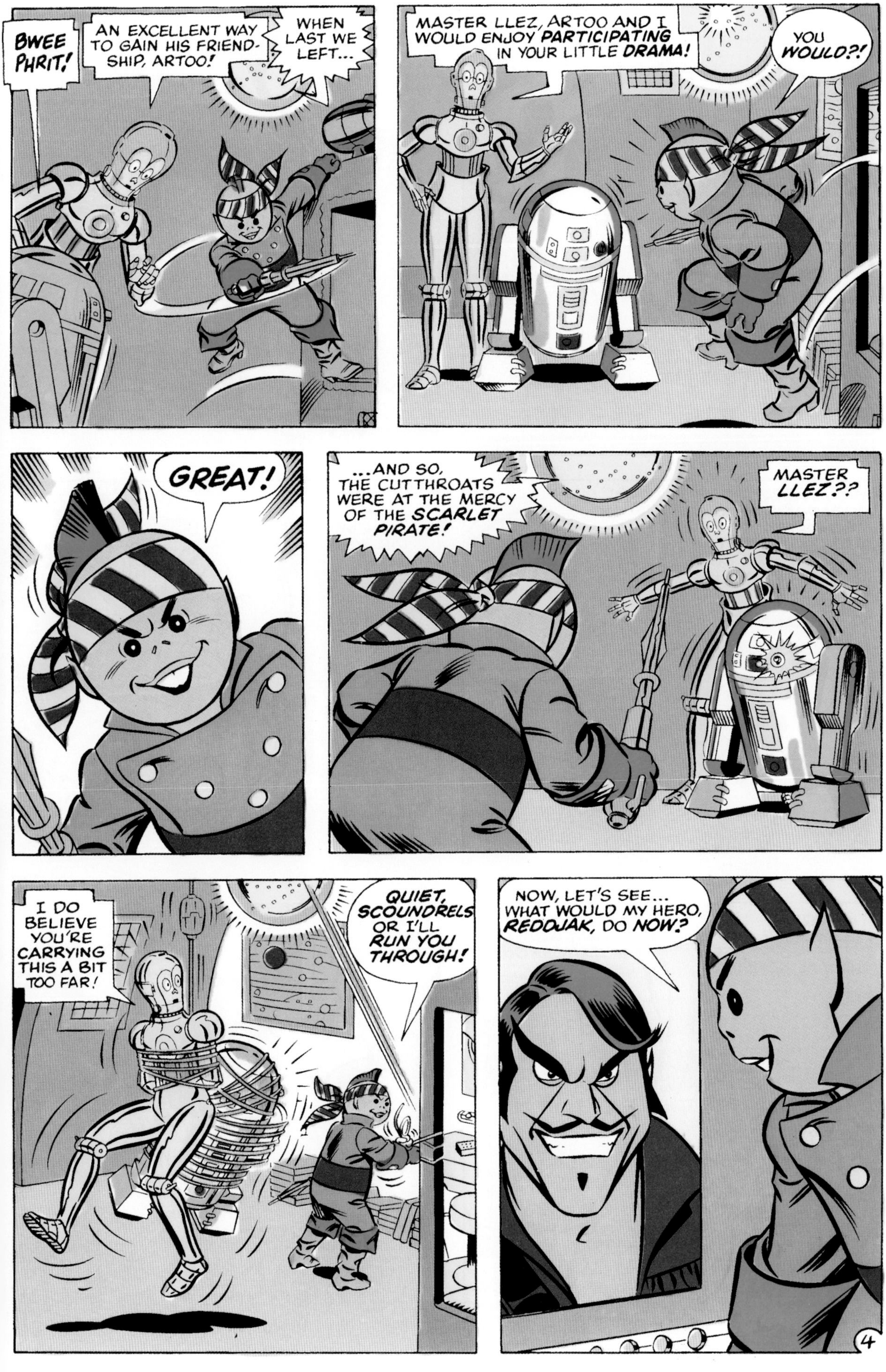
BWEE PHRIT!
AN EXCELLENT WAY TO GAIN HIS FRIENDSHIP, ARTOO!
WHEN LAST WE LEFT...
MASTER LLEZ, ARTOO AND I WOULD ENJOY PARTICIPATING IN YOUR LITTLE DRAMA!
YOU WOULD?!
GREAT!
...AND SO, THE CUTTHROATS WERE AT THE MERCY OF THE SCARLET PIRATE!
MASTER LLEZ??
I DO BELIEVE YOU'RE CARRYING THIS A BIT TOO FAR!
QUIET, SCOUNDRELS OR I'LL RUN YOU THROUGH!
NOW, LET'S SEE... WHAT WOULD MY HERO, REDDJAK, DO NOW?
4

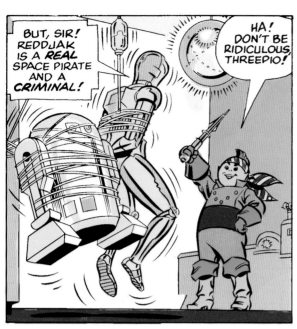

BUT, SIR! REDDJAK IS A *REAL* SPACE PIRATE AND A *CRIMINAL!*

HA! DON'T BE RIDICULOUS, THREEPIO!

HE'S A MAN OF *ADVENTURE!*

IF ONLY I HAD A CHANCE TO BE LIKE HIM, I'D...

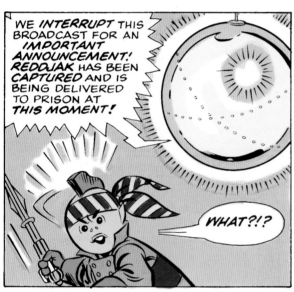

WE *INTERRUPT* THIS BROADCAST FOR AN *IMPORTANT ANNOUNCEMENT!* REDDJAK HAS BEEN *CAPTURED* AND IS BEING DELIVERED TO PRISON AT *THIS MOMENT!*

WHAT?!?

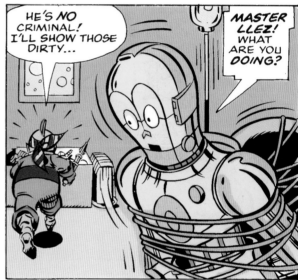

HE'S NO CRIMINAL! I'LL SHOW THOSE DIRTY...

MASTER LLEZ! WHAT ARE YOU *DOING?*

REDDJAK NEEDS HELP AND I'M GOING TO SEE THAT HE *GETS* IT!

BUT, SIR! THAT WOULD BE DANGEROUS!

NOT WITH THIS LITTLE BAG OF *HI-TECH* TRICKS!

SEE YOU!

SIR, PLEASE! DON'T GO!

PLEEP ZWUT!

ZWEP TOOOM!

ARTOO, RELEASE US FROM THESE BONDS AT ONCE!

CLICK

ZWEEEEEEEEEE

THAT'S IT, R2-D2! WE'RE FREE!

CLUNK

TO THE PRISON FACILITY, ARTOO! HE HAS NO IDEA WHAT HE'S GETTING HIMSELF INTO!

PROOP SKAZ TWEE-OT!

ALMOST THERE!

ONLY HOPE I'M IN TIME TO...

UH-OH! A DROID GUARD SHIP!

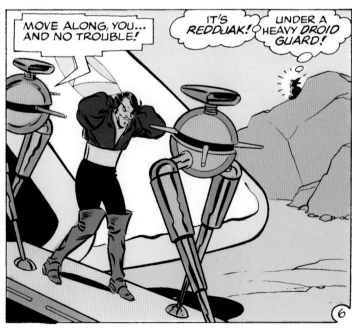

MOVE ALONG, YOU... AND NO TROUBLE!

IT'S REDDJAK!

UNDER A HEAVY DROID GUARD!

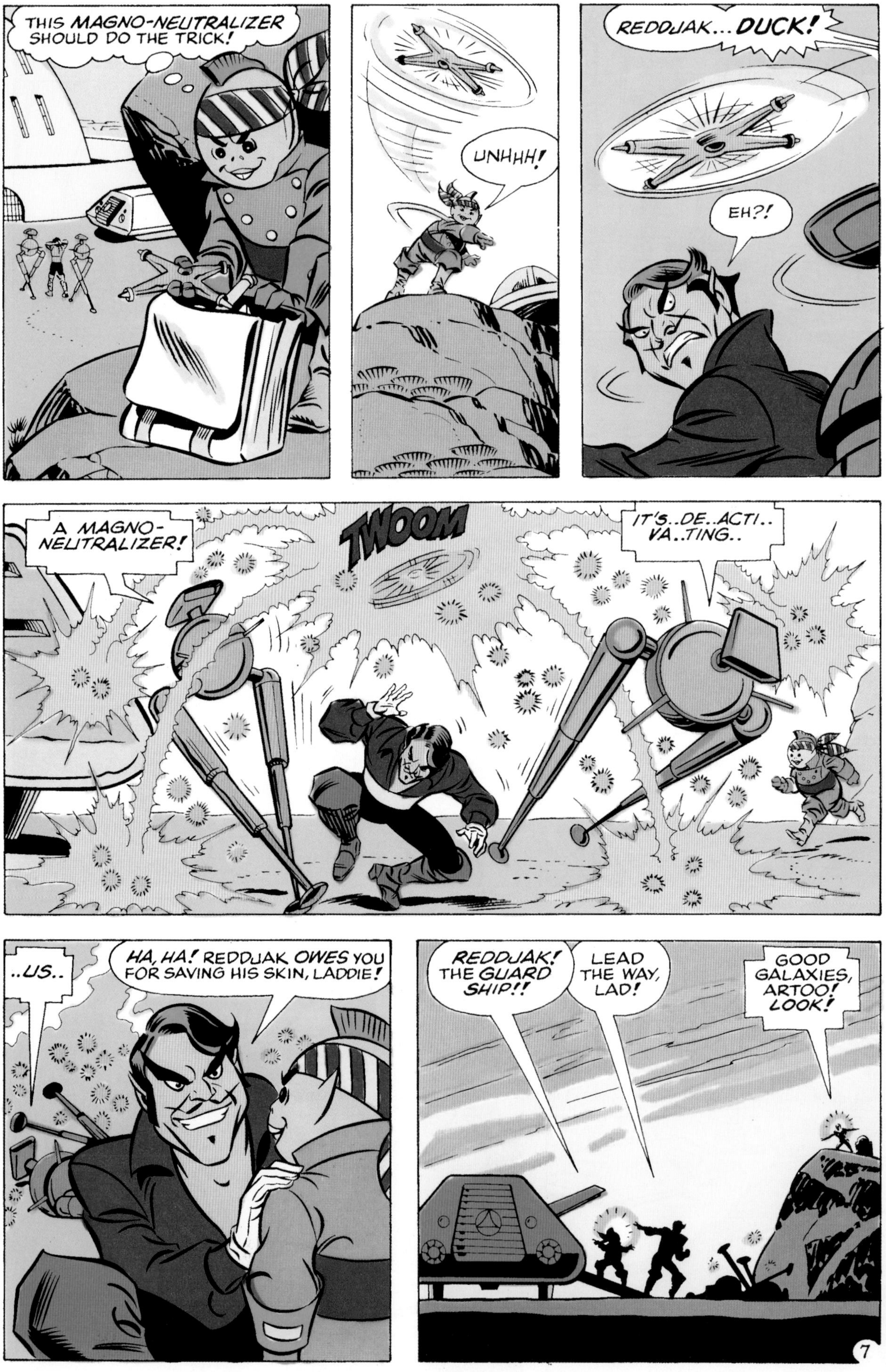
THIS MAGNO-NEUTRALIZER SHOULD DO THE TRICK!
UNHHH!
REDDJAK... DUCK!
EH?!
A MAGNO-NEUTRALIZER!
TWOOM
IT'S..DE..ACTI.. VA..TING..
..US..
HA, HA! REDDJAK OWES YOU FOR SAVING HIS SKIN, LADDIE!
REDDJAK! THE GUARD SHIP!!
LEAD THE WAY, LAD!
GOOD GALAXIES, ARTOO! LOOK!
7

MASTER LLEZ IS LEAVING WITH THAT TERRIBLE PIRATE!

HURRY! IF WE CAN'T STOP HIM, PERHAPS WE CAN AT LEAST KEEP A LENS ON HIM!

WHHHOOOOSHHH

INTO THE CARGO BAY, ARTOO...

...BEFORE...

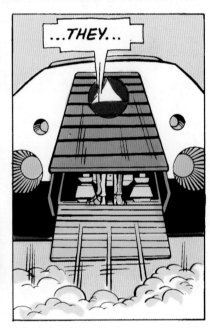

...THEY...

WWWEEEEEEEEEE

TAKE OFF!!

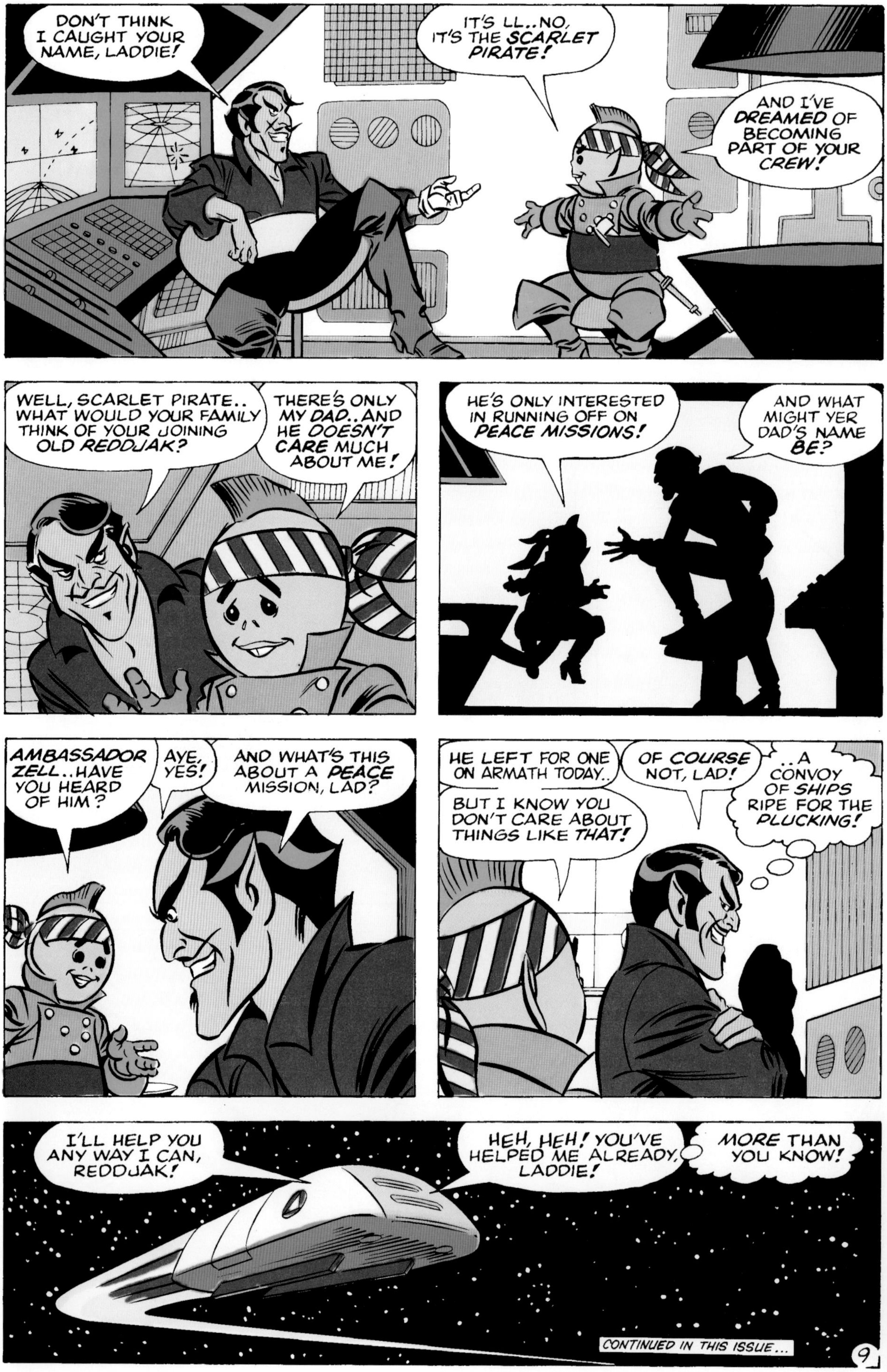
DON'T THINK I CAUGHT YOUR NAME, LADDIE!
IT'S LL..NO, IT'S THE SCARLET PIRATE!
AND I'VE DREAMED OF BECOMING PART OF YOUR CREW!
WELL, SCARLET PIRATE.. WHAT WOULD YOUR FAMILY THINK OF YOUR JOINING OLD REDDJAK?
THERE'S ONLY MY DAD..AND HE DOESN'T CARE MUCH ABOUT ME!
HE'S ONLY INTERESTED IN RUNNING OFF ON PEACE MISSIONS!
AND WHAT MIGHT YER DAD'S NAME BE?
AMBASSADOR ZELL..HAVE YOU HEARD OF HIM?
AYE, YES!
AND WHAT'S THIS ABOUT A PEACE MISSION, LAD?
HE LEFT FOR ONE ON ARMATH TODAY..
BUT I KNOW YOU DON'T CARE ABOUT THINGS LIKE THAT!
OF COURSE NOT, LAD!
..A CONVOY OF SHIPS RIPE FOR THE PLUCKING!
I'LL HELP YOU ANY WAY I CAN, REDDJAK!
HEH, HEH! YOU'VE HELPED ME ALREADY, LADDIE!
MORE THAN YOU KNOW!
CONTINUED IN THIS ISSUE...
9

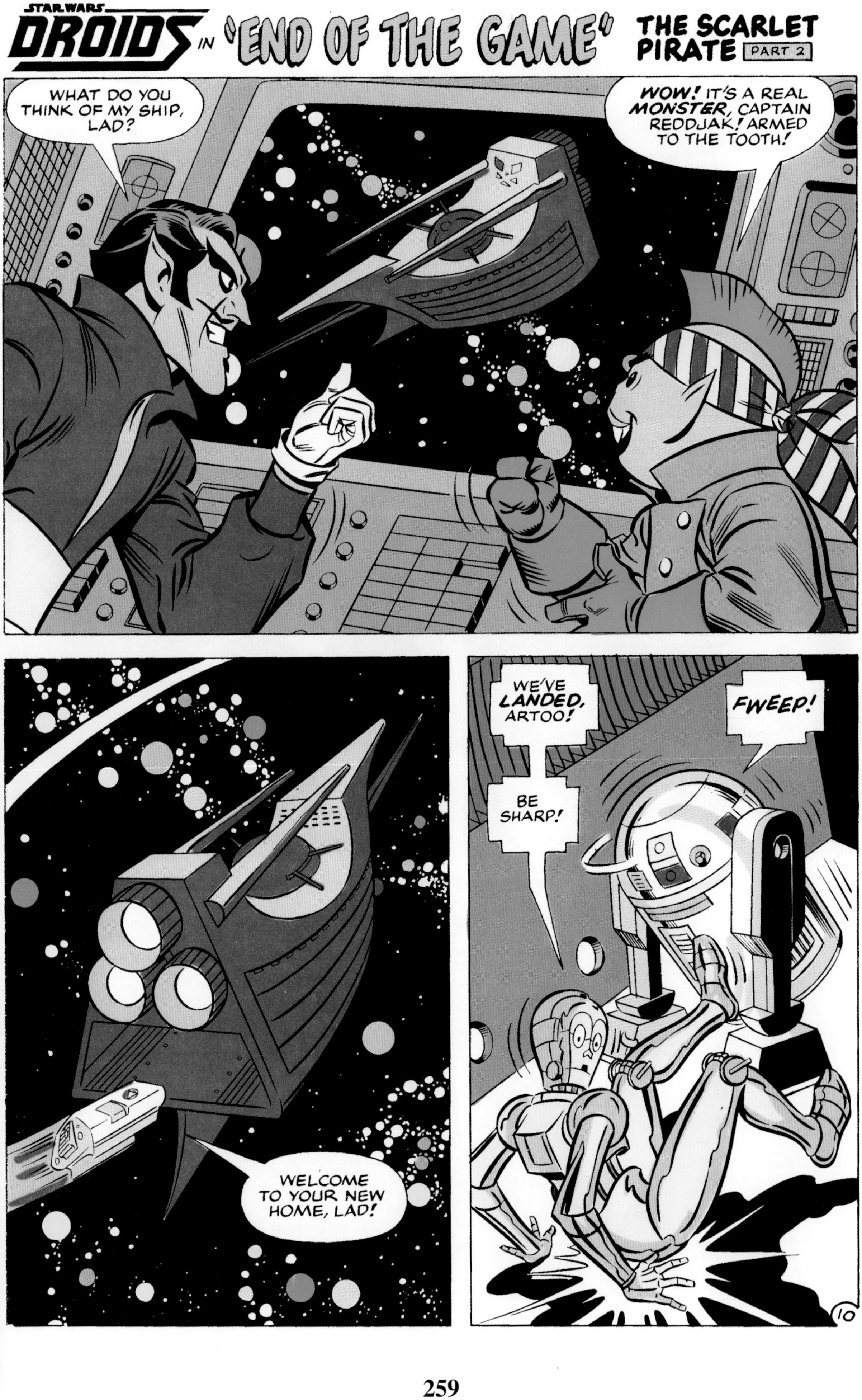
STAR WARS DROIDS IN "END OF THE GAME"
THE SCARLET PIRATE PART 2
WHAT DO YOU THINK OF MY SHIP, LAD?
WOW! IT'S A REAL MONSTER, CAPTAIN REDDJAK! ARMED TO THE TOOTH!
WELCOME TO YOUR NEW HOME, LAD!
WE'VE LANDED, ARTOO!
FWEEP!
BE SHARP!
10

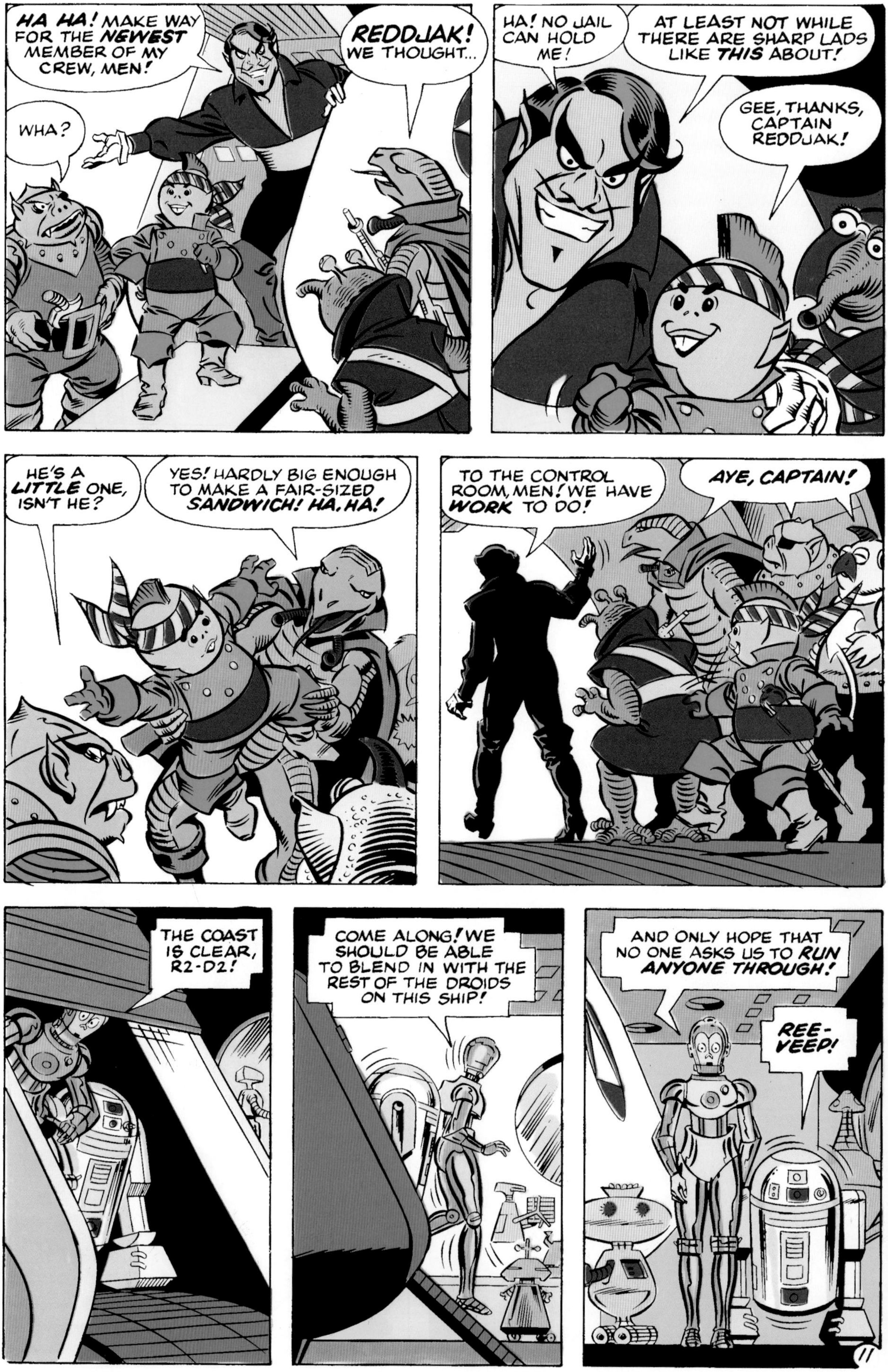
HA HA! MAKE WAY FOR THE NEWEST MEMBER OF MY CREW, MEN!
WHA?
REDDJAK! WE THOUGHT...
HA! NO JAIL CAN HOLD ME!
AT LEAST NOT WHILE THERE ARE SHARP LADS LIKE THIS ABOUT!
GEE, THANKS, CAPTAIN REDDJAK!
HE'S A LITTLE ONE, ISN'T HE?
YES! HARDLY BIG ENOUGH TO MAKE A FAIR-SIZED SANDWICH! HA, HA!
TO THE CONTROL ROOM, MEN! WE HAVE WORK TO DO!
AYE, CAPTAIN!
THE COAST IS CLEAR, R2-D2!
COME ALONG! WE SHOULD BE ABLE TO BLEND IN WITH THE REST OF THE DROIDS ON THIS SHIP!
AND ONLY HOPE THAT NO ONE ASKS US TO RUN ANYONE THROUGH!
REE-VEEP!
11

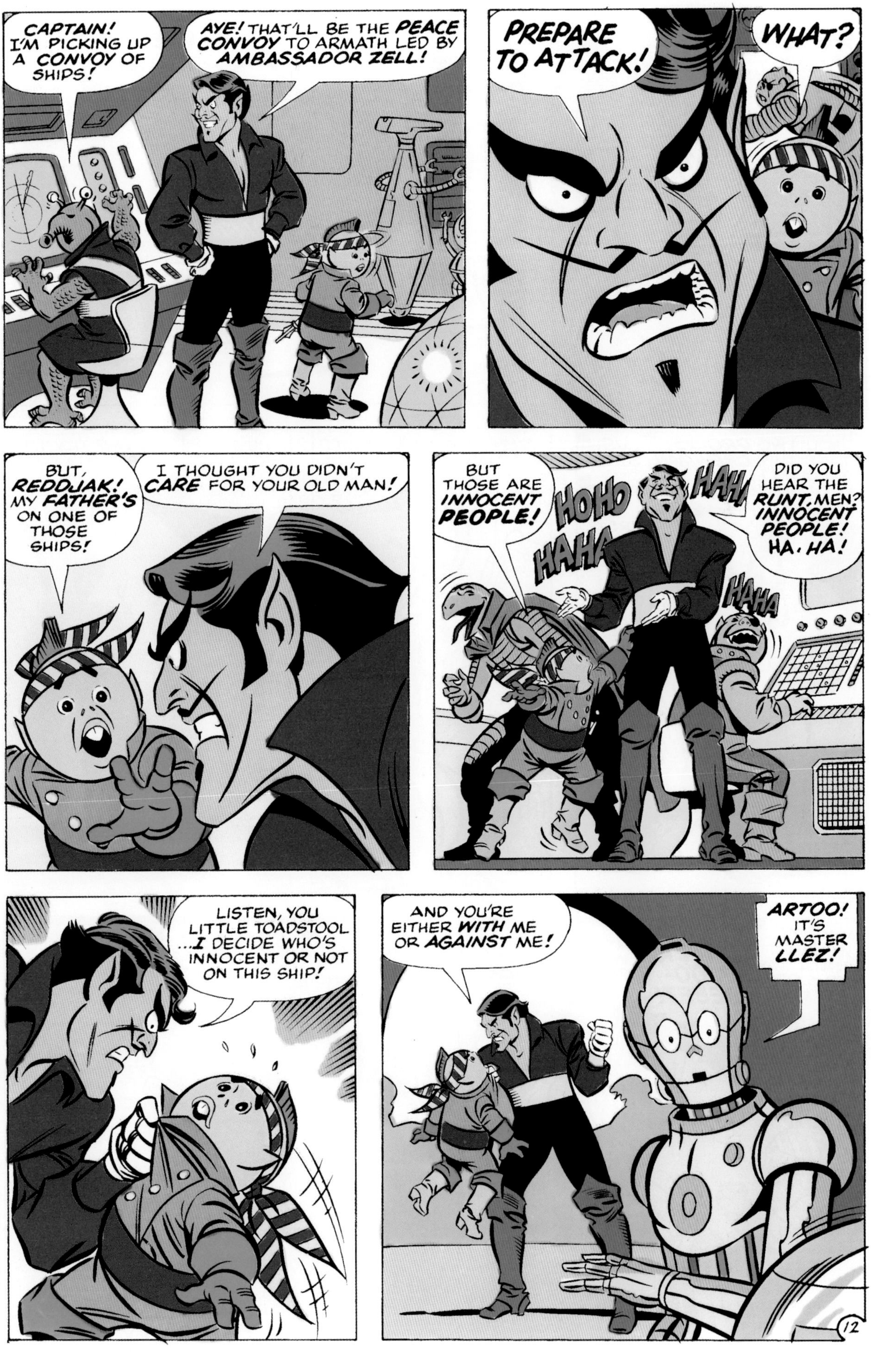
CAPTAIN! I'M PICKING UP A CONVOY OF SHIPS!
AYE! THAT'LL BE THE PEACE CONVOY TO ARMATH LED BY AMBASSADOR ZELL!
PREPARE TO ATTACK!
WHAT?
BUT, REDDJAK! MY FATHER'S ON ONE OF THOSE SHIPS!
I THOUGHT YOU DIDN'T CARE FOR YOUR OLD MAN!
BUT THOSE ARE INNOCENT PEOPLE!
HOHO
HAHA
HAHA
DID YOU HEAR THE RUNT, MEN? INNOCENT PEOPLE! HA, HA!
HAHA
LISTEN, YOU LITTLE TOADSTOOL ...I DECIDE WHO'S INNOCENT OR NOT ON THIS SHIP!
AND YOU'RE EITHER WITH ME OR AGAINST ME!
ARTOO! IT'S MASTER LLEZ!
12

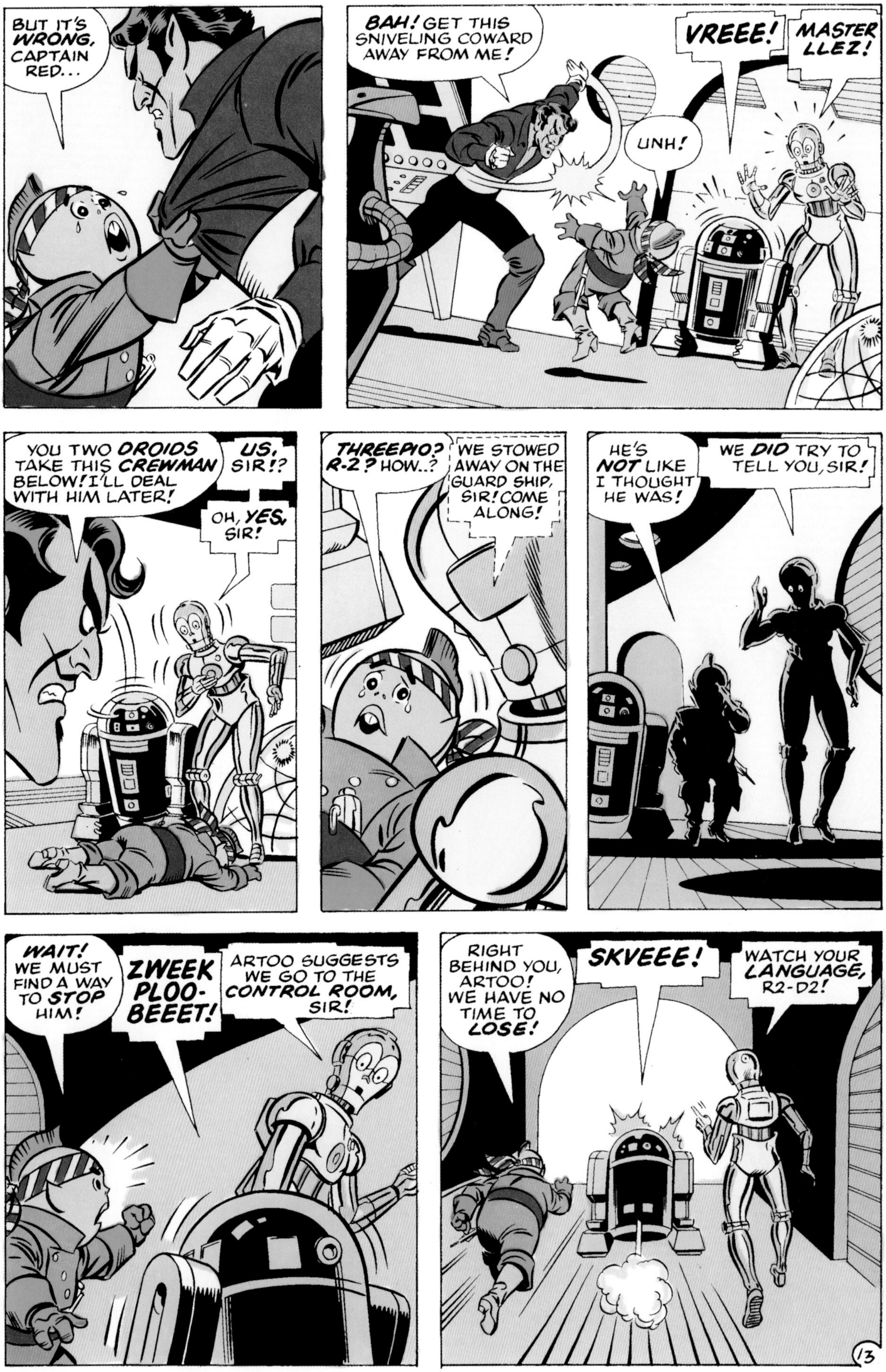
BUT IT'S WRONG, CAPTAIN RED...
BAH! GET THIS SNIVELING COWARD AWAY FROM ME!
VREEE!
MASTER LLEZ!
UNH!
YOU TWO DROIDS TAKE THIS CREWMAN BELOW! I'LL DEAL WITH HIM LATER!
US, SIR!?
OH, YES, SIR!
THREEPIO? R-2? HOW..?
WE STOWED AWAY ON THE GUARD SHIP, SIR! COME ALONG!
HE'S NOT LIKE I THOUGHT HE WAS!
WE DID TRY TO TELL YOU, SIR!
WAIT! WE MUST FIND A WAY TO STOP HIM!
ZWEEK PLOO-BEEET!
ARTOO SUGGESTS WE GO TO THE CONTROL ROOM, SIR!
RIGHT BEHIND YOU, ARTOO! WE HAVE NO TIME TO LOSE!
SKVEEE!
WATCH YOUR LANGUAGE, R2-D2!
13

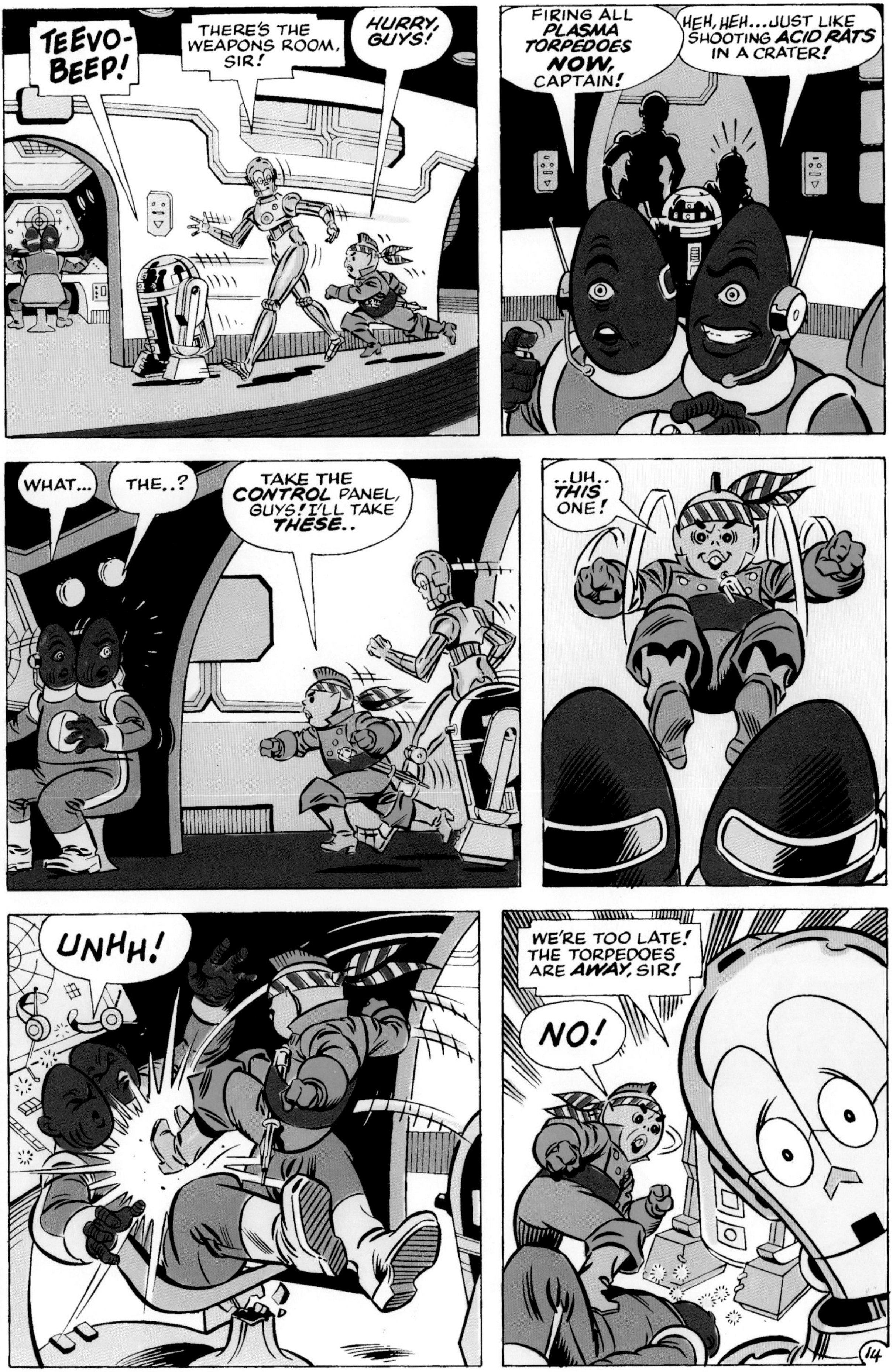
TEEVO-BEEP!
THERE'S THE WEAPONS ROOM, SIR!
HURRY, GUYS!
FIRING ALL PLASMA TORPEDOES NOW, CAPTAIN!
HEH, HEH...JUST LIKE SHOOTING ACID RATS IN A CRATER!
WHAT...
THE..?
TAKE THE CONTROL PANEL, GUYS! I'LL TAKE THESE..
..UH.. THIS ONE!
UNHH!
WE'RE TOO LATE! THE TORPEDOES ARE AWAY, SIR!
NO!
14

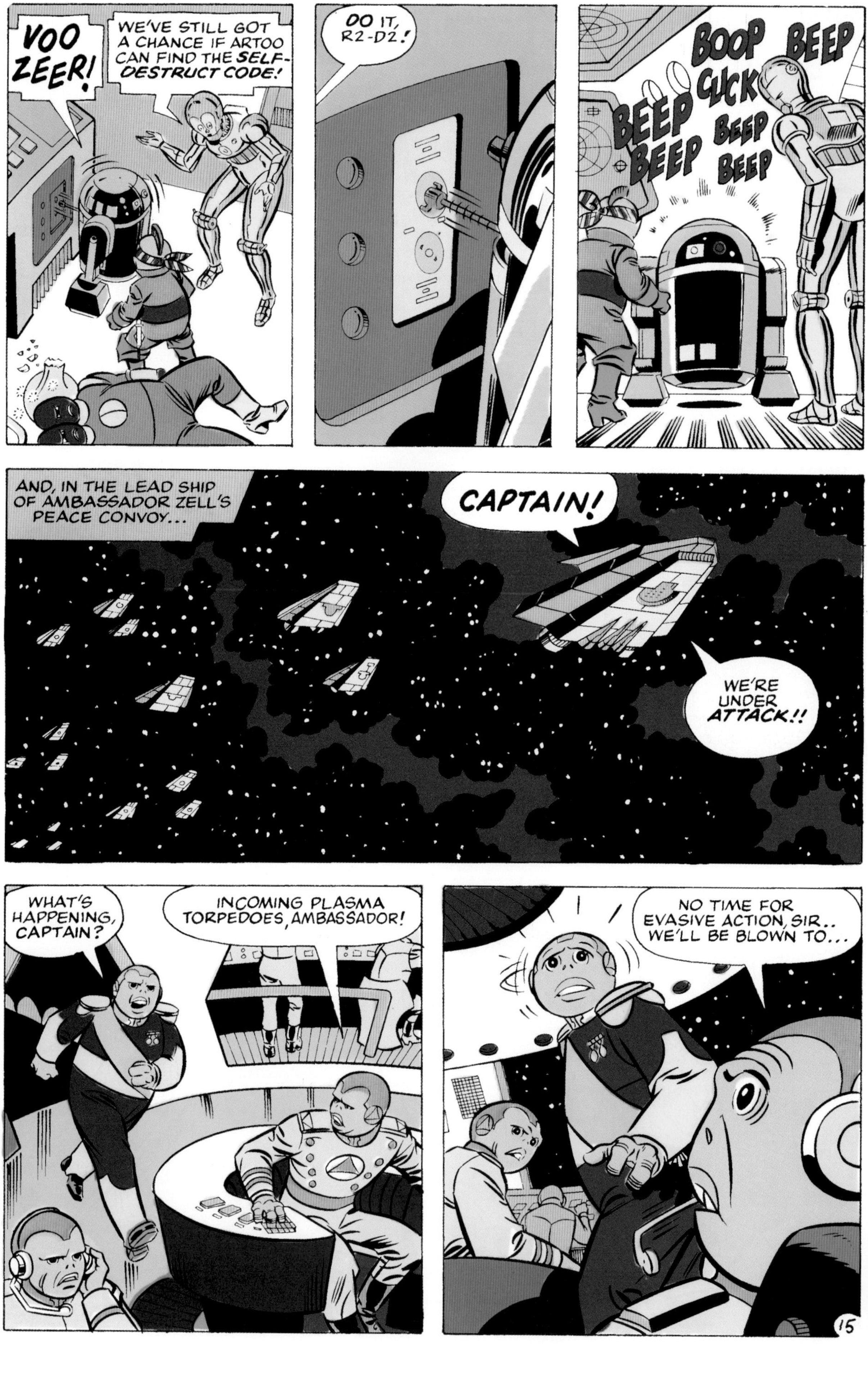
VOO ZEER!
WE'VE STILL GOT A CHANCE IF ARTOO CAN FIND THE SELF-DESTRUCT CODE!
DO IT, R2-D2!
BOOP BEEP
CLICK
BEEP BEEP
BEEP BEEP
BEEP
AND, IN THE LEAD SHIP OF AMBASSADOR ZELL'S PEACE CONVOY...
CAPTAIN!
WE'RE UNDER ATTACK!!
WHAT'S HAPPENING, CAPTAIN?
INCOMING PLASMA TORPEDOES, AMBASSADOR!
NO TIME FOR EVASIVE ACTION, SIR.. WE'LL BE BLOWN TO...
15

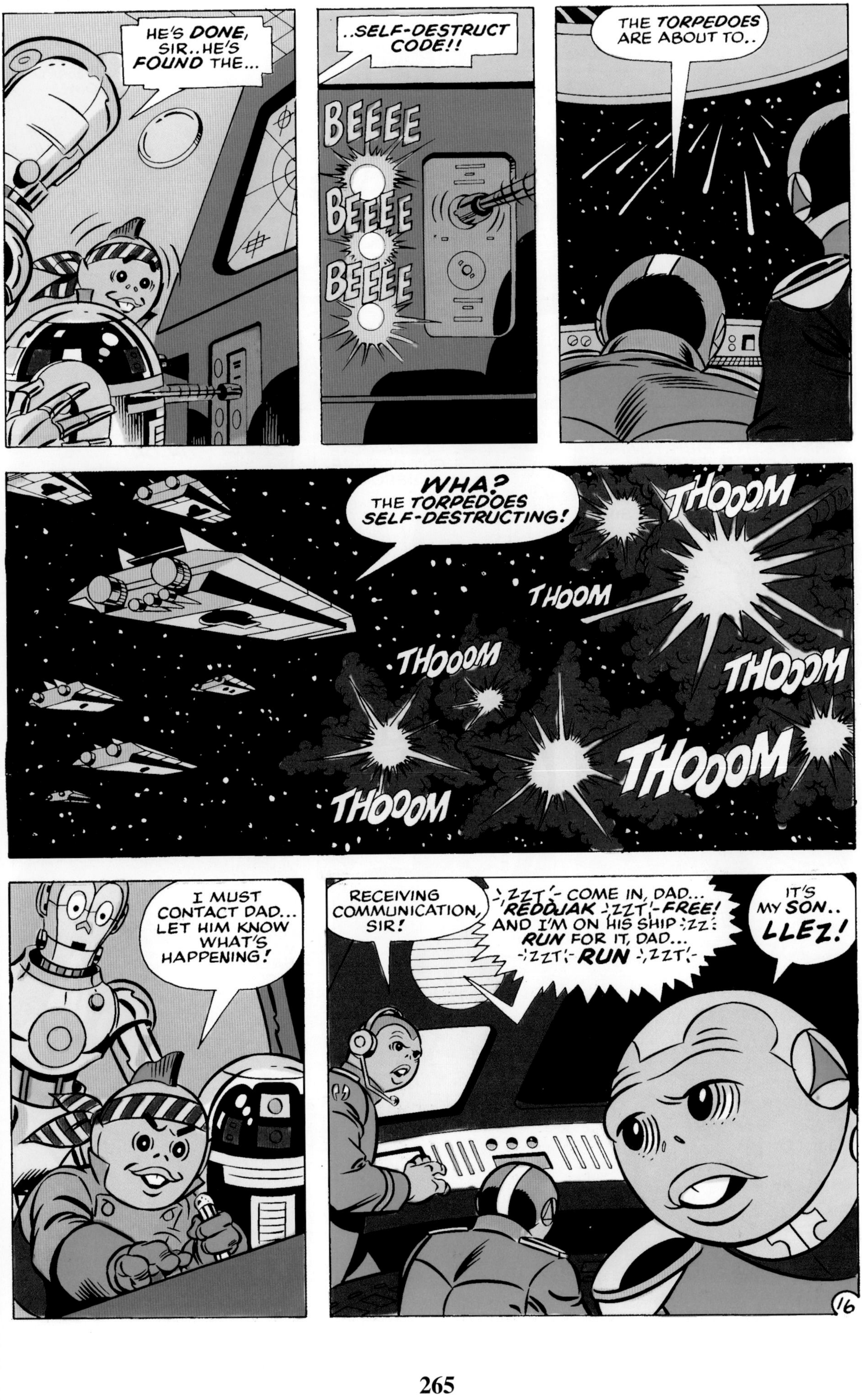
HE'S DONE, SIR..HE'S FOUND THE...
..SELF-DESTRUCT CODE!!
BEEEE
BEEEE
BEEEE
THE TORPEDOES ARE ABOUT TO..
WHA? THE TORPEDOES SELF-DESTRUCTING!
THOOOM
THOOM
THOOOM
THOOOM
THOOOM
THOOOM
I MUST CONTACT DAD... LET HIM KNOW WHAT'S HAPPENING!
RECEIVING COMMUNICATION, SIR!
-ZZT- COME IN, DAD... REDDJAK -ZZT- FREE! AND I'M ON HIS SHIP -ZZ- RUN FOR IT, DAD... -ZZT- RUN -ZZT-
IT'S MY SON.. LLEZ!
16

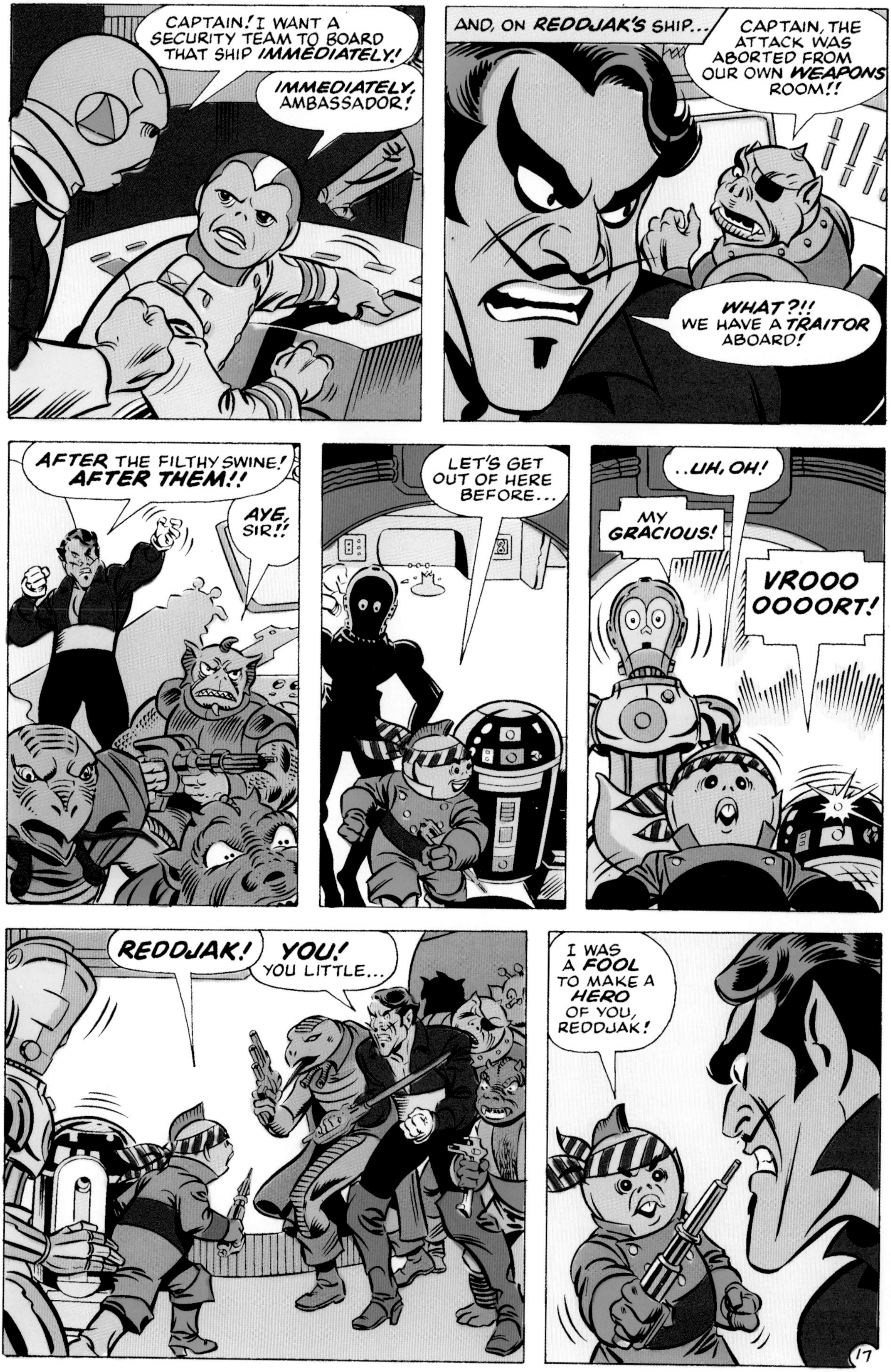
CAPTAIN! I WANT A SECURITY TEAM TO BOARD THAT SHIP IMMEDIATELY!
IMMEDIATELY, AMBASSADOR!
AND, ON REDDJAK'S SHIP...
CAPTAIN, THE ATTACK WAS ABORTED FROM OUR OWN WEAPONS ROOM!!
WHAT?!! WE HAVE A TRAITOR ABOARD!
AFTER THE FILTHY SWINE! AFTER THEM!!
AYE, SIR!!
LET'S GET OUT OF HERE BEFORE...
..UH, OH!
MY GRACIOUS!
VROOO OOOORT!
REDDJAK!
YOU! YOU LITTLE...
I WAS A FOOL TO MAKE A HERO OF YOU, REDDJAK!
17

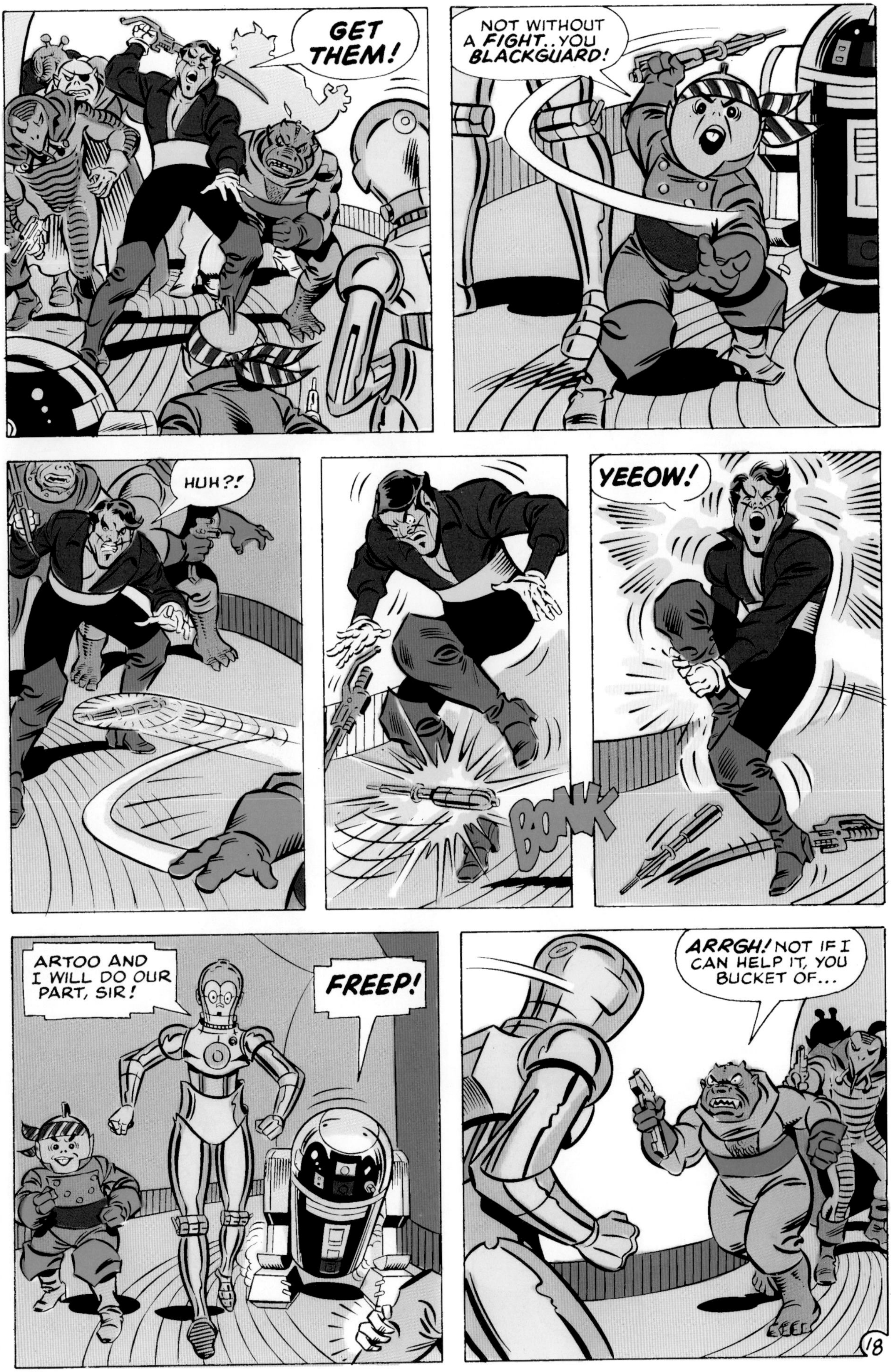
GET THEM!
NOT WITHOUT A FIGHT..YOU BLACKGUARD!
HUH?!
YEEOW!
BONK
ARTOO AND I WILL DO OUR PART, SIR!
FREEP!
ARRGH! NOT IF I CAN HELP IT, YOU BUCKET OF...
18

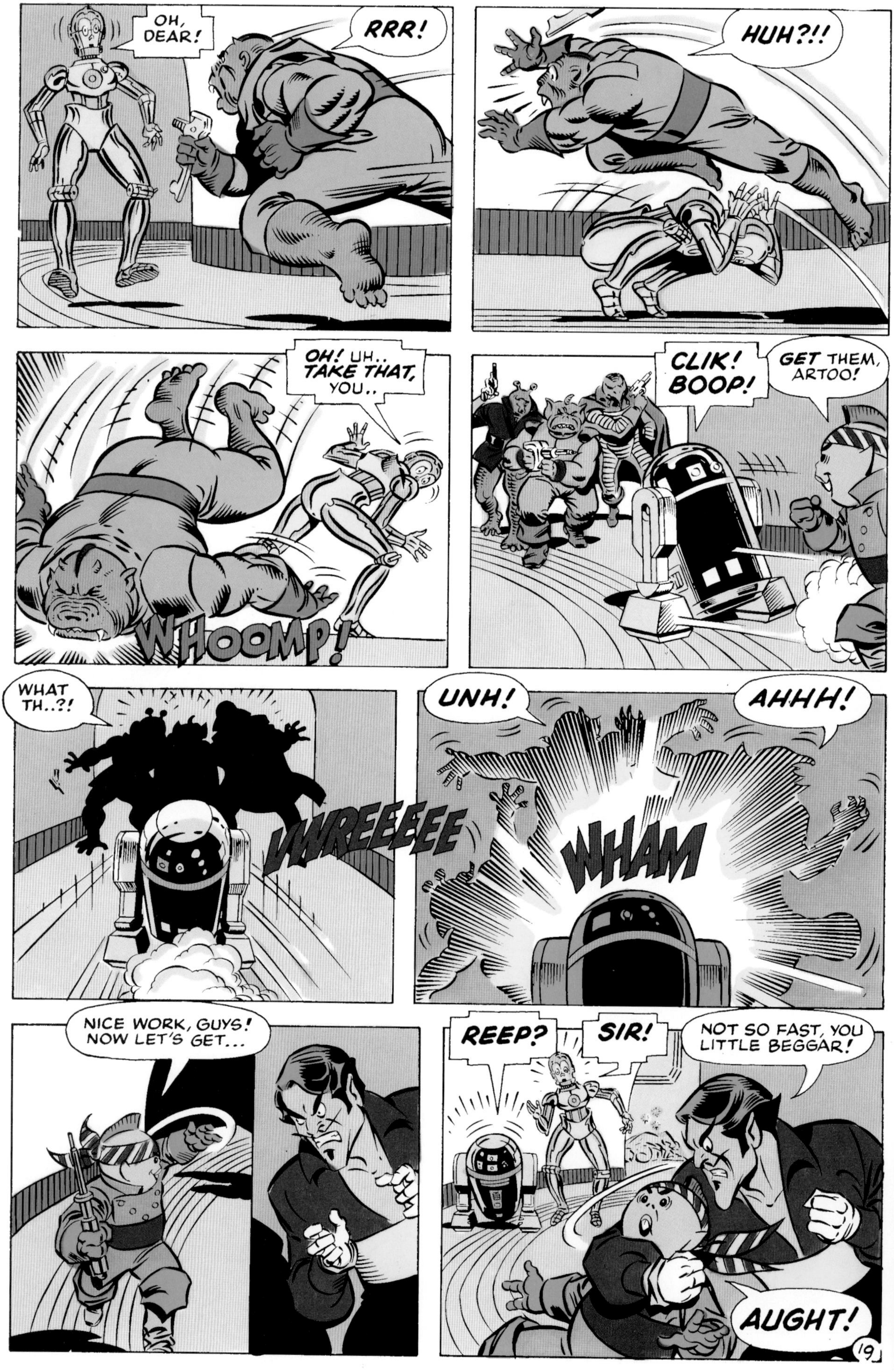
OH, DEAR!
RRR!
HUH?!!
OH! UH.. TAKE THAT, YOU..
WHOOMP!
CLIK! BOOP!
GET THEM, ARTOO!
WHAT TH..?!
VWREEEEEE
UNH!
AHHH!
WHAM
NICE WORK, GUYS! NOW LET'S GET...
REEP?
SIR!
NOT SO FAST, YOU LITTLE BEGGAR!
AUGHT!
19

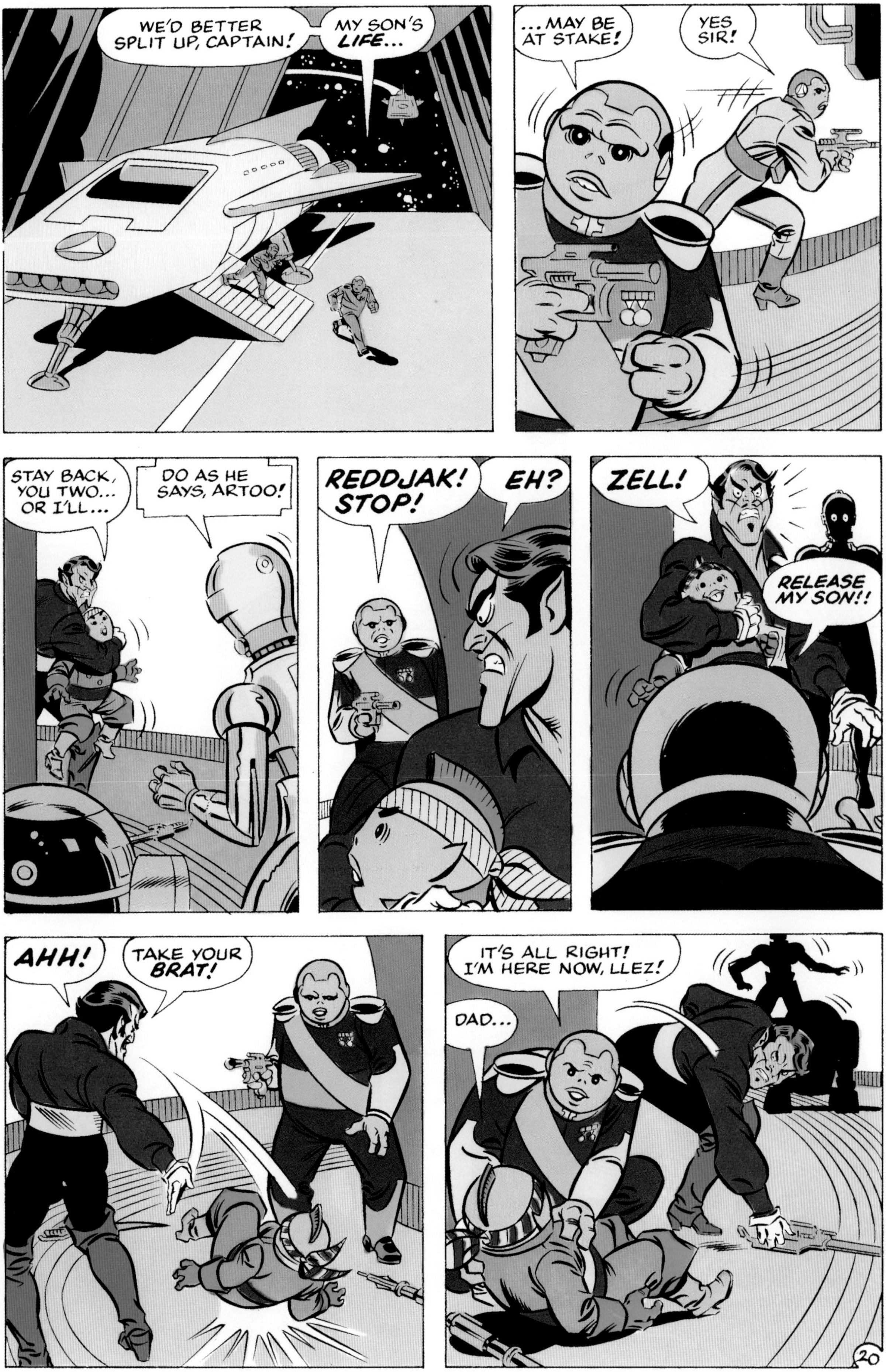
WE'D BETTER SPLIT UP, CAPTAIN!
MY SON'S LIFE...
...MAY BE AT STAKE!
YES SIR!
STAY BACK, YOU TWO... OR I'LL...
DO AS HE SAYS, ARTOO!
REDDJAK! STOP!
EH?
ZELL!
RELEASE MY SON!!
AHH!
TAKE YOUR BRAT!
IT'S ALL RIGHT! I'M HERE NOW, LLEZ!
DAD...
20

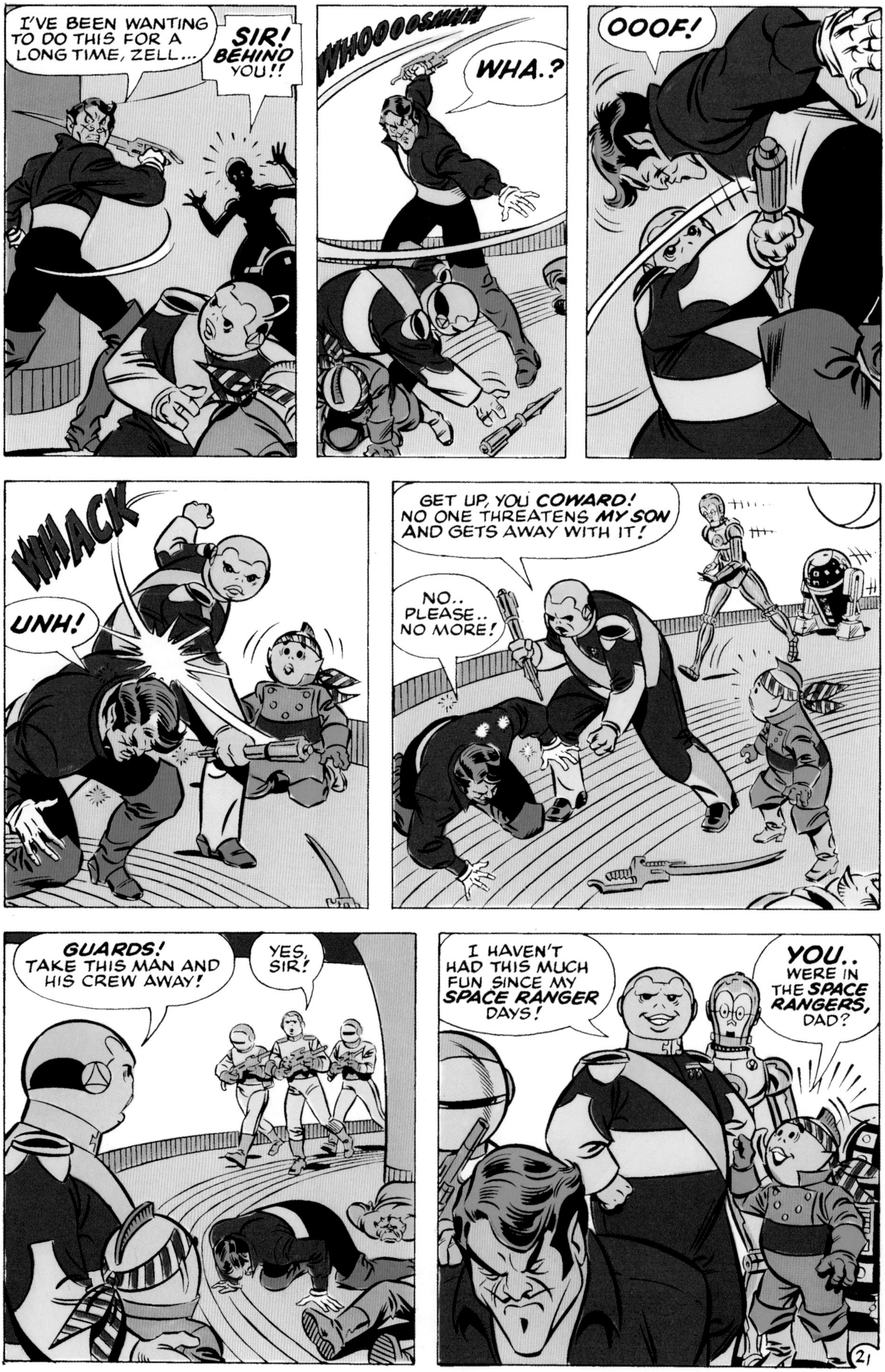
I'VE BEEN WANTING TO DO THIS FOR A LONG TIME, ZELL...
SIR! BEHIND YOU!!
WHOOOOOSHHHH
WHA.?
OOOF!
WHACK
UNH!
GET UP, YOU COWARD! NO ONE THREATENS MY SON AND GETS AWAY WITH IT!
NO.. PLEASE.. NO MORE!
GUARDS! TAKE THIS MAN AND HIS CREW AWAY!
YES, SIR!
I HAVEN'T HAD THIS MUCH FUN SINCE MY SPACE RANGER DAYS!
YOU.. WERE IN THE SPACE RANGERS, DAD?
21

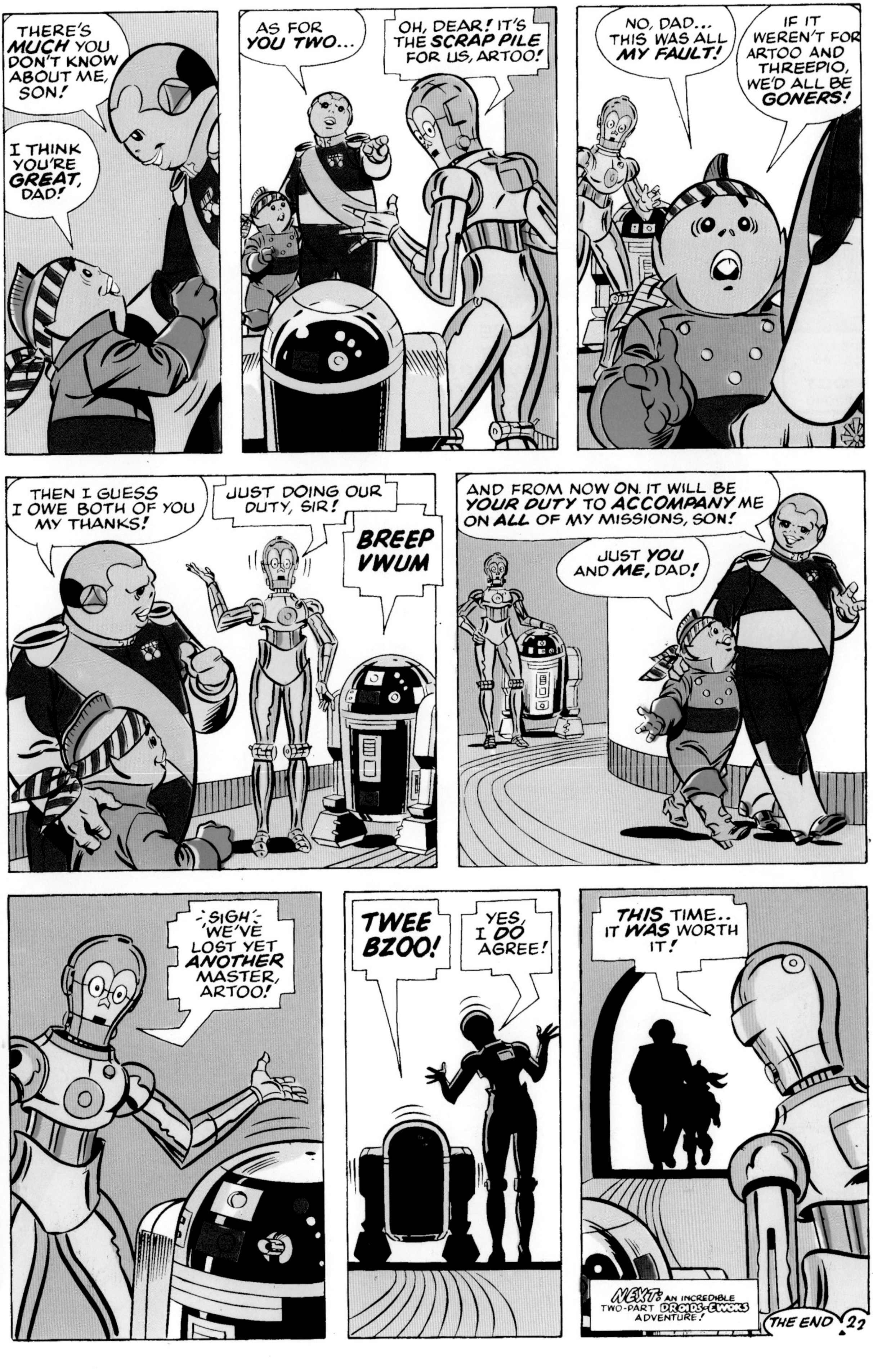
THERE'S MUCH YOU DON'T KNOW ABOUT ME, SON!
I THINK YOU'RE GREAT, DAD!
AS FOR YOU TWO...
OH, DEAR! IT'S THE SCRAP PILE FOR US, ARTOO!
NO, DAD... THIS WAS ALL MY FAULT!
IF IT WEREN'T FOR ARTOO AND THREEPIO, WE'D ALL BE GONERS!
THEN I GUESS I OWE BOTH OF YOU MY THANKS!
JUST DOING OUR DUTY, SIR!
BREEP VWUM
AND FROM NOW ON IT WILL BE YOUR DUTY TO ACCOMPANY ME ON ALL OF MY MISSIONS, SON!
JUST YOU AND ME, DAD!
SIGH WE'VE LOST YET ANOTHER MASTER, ARTOO!
TWEE BZOO!
YES, I DO AGREE!
THIS TIME.. IT WAS WORTH IT!
NEXT: AN INCREDIBLE TWO-PART DROIDS-EWOKS ADVENTURE!
THE END 22

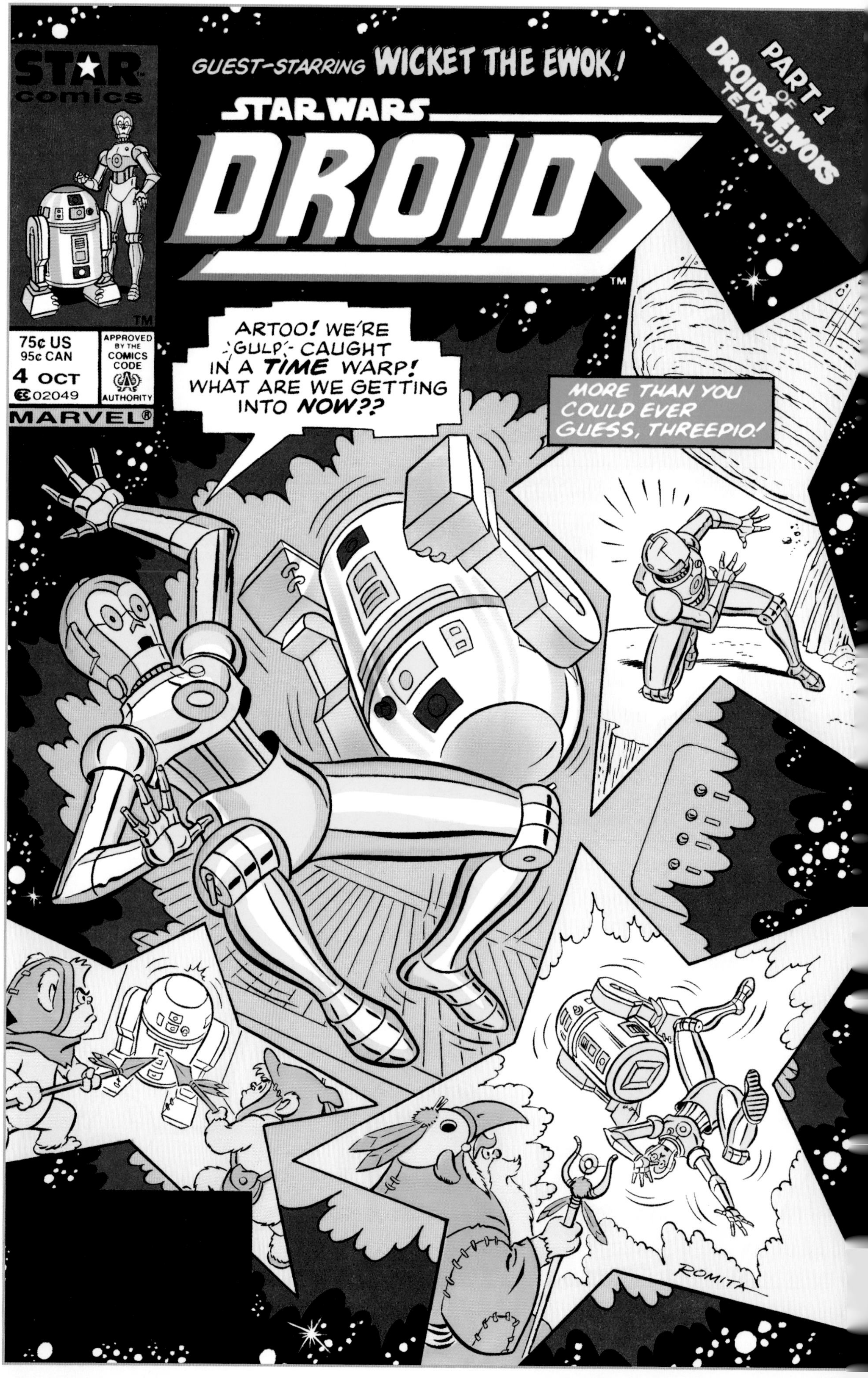
STAR comics
GUEST-STARRING WICKET THE EWOK!
STAR WARS
DROIDS
PART 1 OF DROIDS-EWOKS TEAM-UP
75¢ US
95¢ CAN
4 OCT
APPROVED BY THE COMICS CODE AUTHORITY
MARVEL
ARTOO! WE'RE -GULP- CAUGHT IN A TIME WARP! WHAT ARE WE GETTING INTO NOW??
MORE THAN YOU COULD EVER GUESS, THREEPIO!
ROMITA

STAR WARS DROIDS AND EWOKS IN LOST IN TIME!

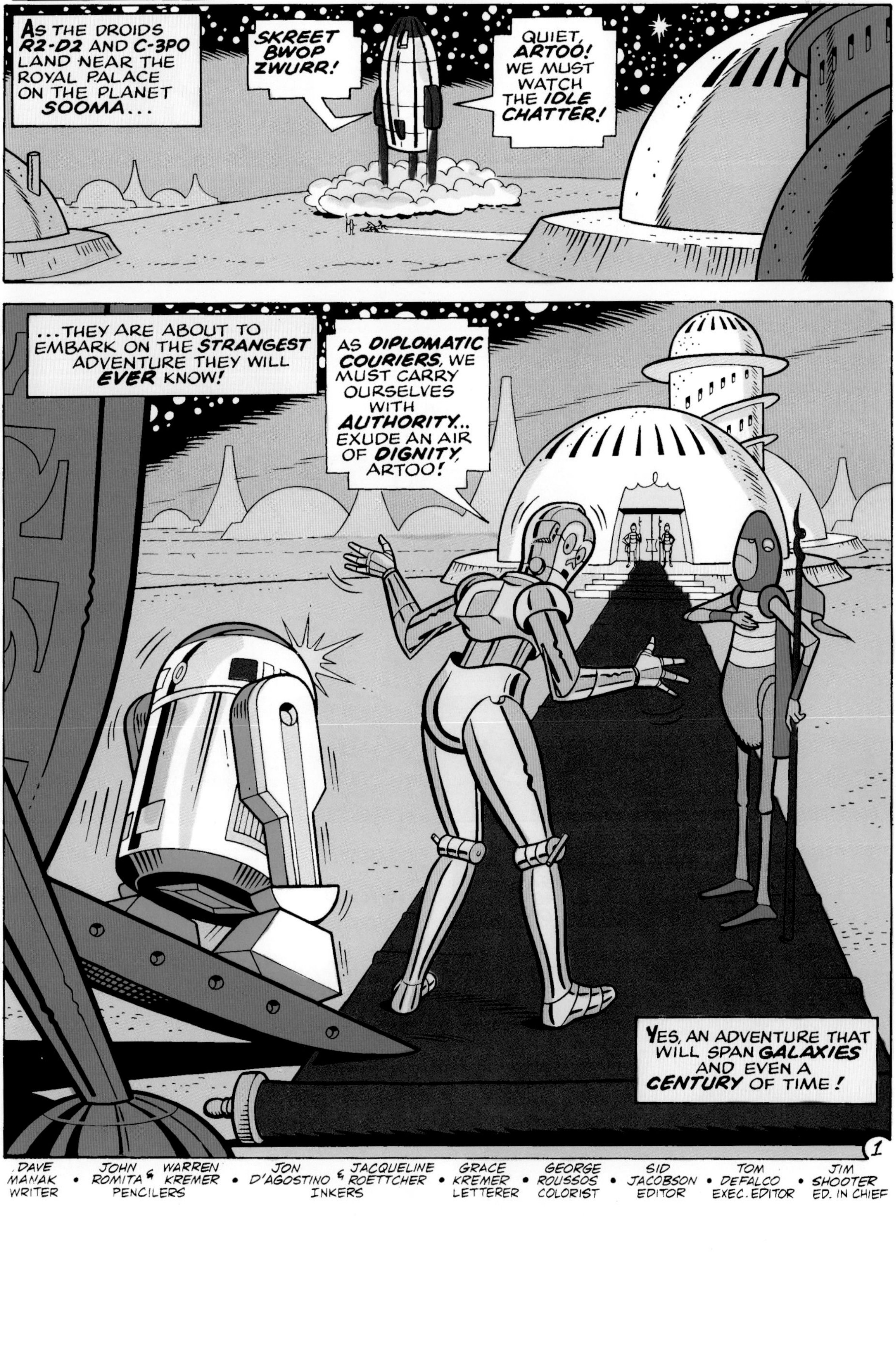

AS THE DROIDS R2-D2 AND C-3PO LAND NEAR THE ROYAL PALACE ON THE PLANET SOOMA...
SKREET BWOP ZWURR!
QUIET, ARTOO! WE MUST WATCH THE IDLE CHATTER!
...THEY ARE ABOUT TO EMBARK ON THE STRANGEST ADVENTURE THEY WILL EVER KNOW!
AS DIPLOMATIC COURIERS, WE MUST CARRY OURSELVES WITH AUTHORITY... EXUDE AN AIR OF DIGNITY, ARTOO!
YES, AN ADVENTURE THAT WILL SPAN GALAXIES AND EVEN A CENTURY OF TIME!
1

DAVE MANAK WRITER • JOHN ROMITA & WARREN KREMER PENCILERS • JON D'AGOSTINO & JACQUELINE ROETTCHER INKERS • GRACE KREMER LETTERER • GEORGE ROUSSOS COLORIST • SID JACOBSON EDITOR • TOM DEFALCO EXEC. EDITOR • JIM SHOOTER ED. IN CHIEF

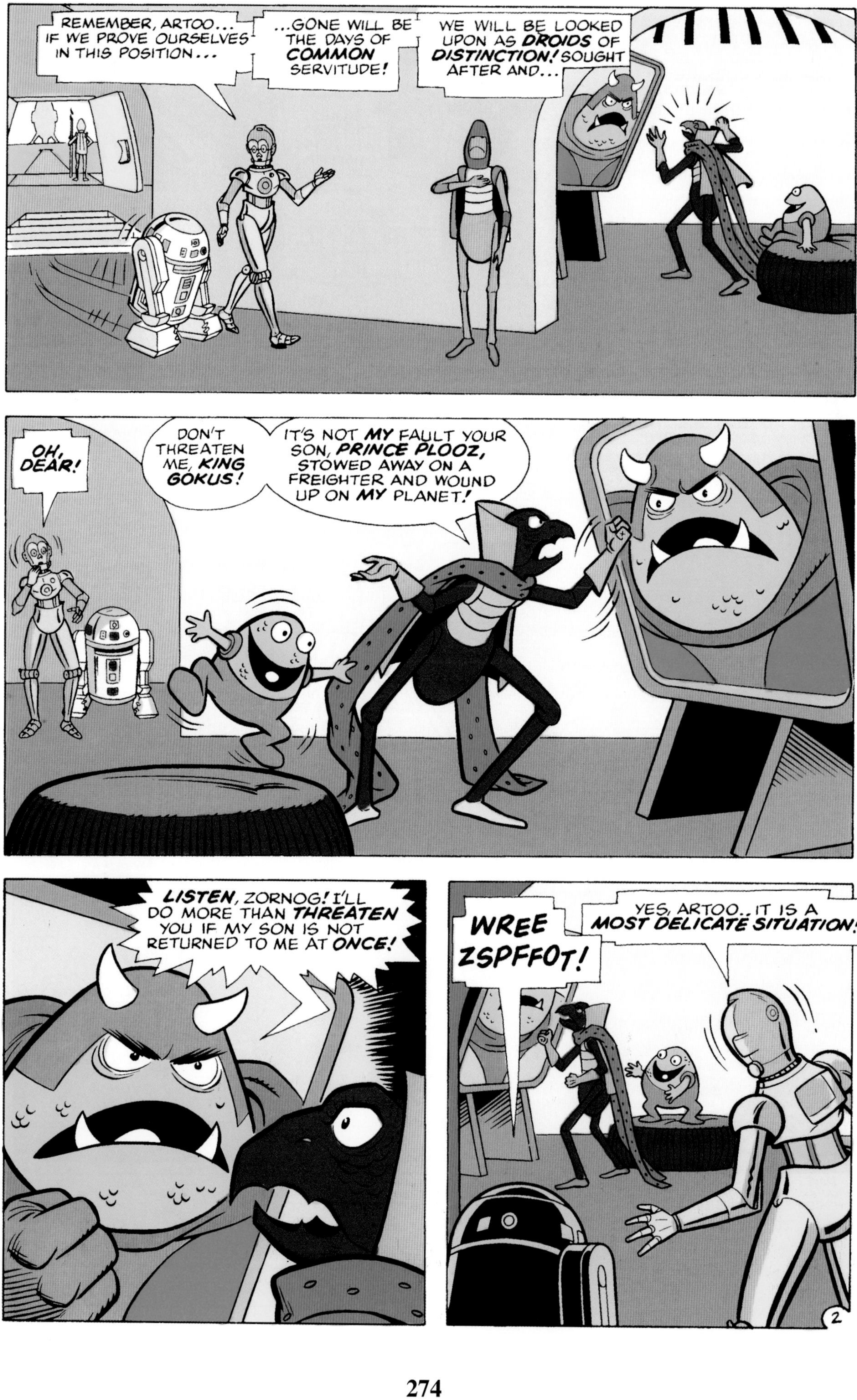
REMEMBER, ARTOO... IF WE PROVE OURSELVES IN THIS POSITION...
...GONE WILL BE THE DAYS OF COMMON SERVITUDE!
WE WILL BE LOOKED UPON AS DROIDS OF DISTINCTION! SOUGHT AFTER AND...
OH, DEAR!
DON'T THREATEN ME, KING GOKUS!
IT'S NOT MY FAULT YOUR SON, PRINCE PLOOZ, STOWED AWAY ON A FREIGHTER AND WOUND UP ON MY PLANET!
LISTEN, ZORNOG! I'LL DO MORE THAN THREATEN YOU IF MY SON IS NOT RETURNED TO ME AT ONCE!
WREE ZSPFFOT!
YES, ARTOO.. IT IS A MOST DELICATE SITUATION!
2

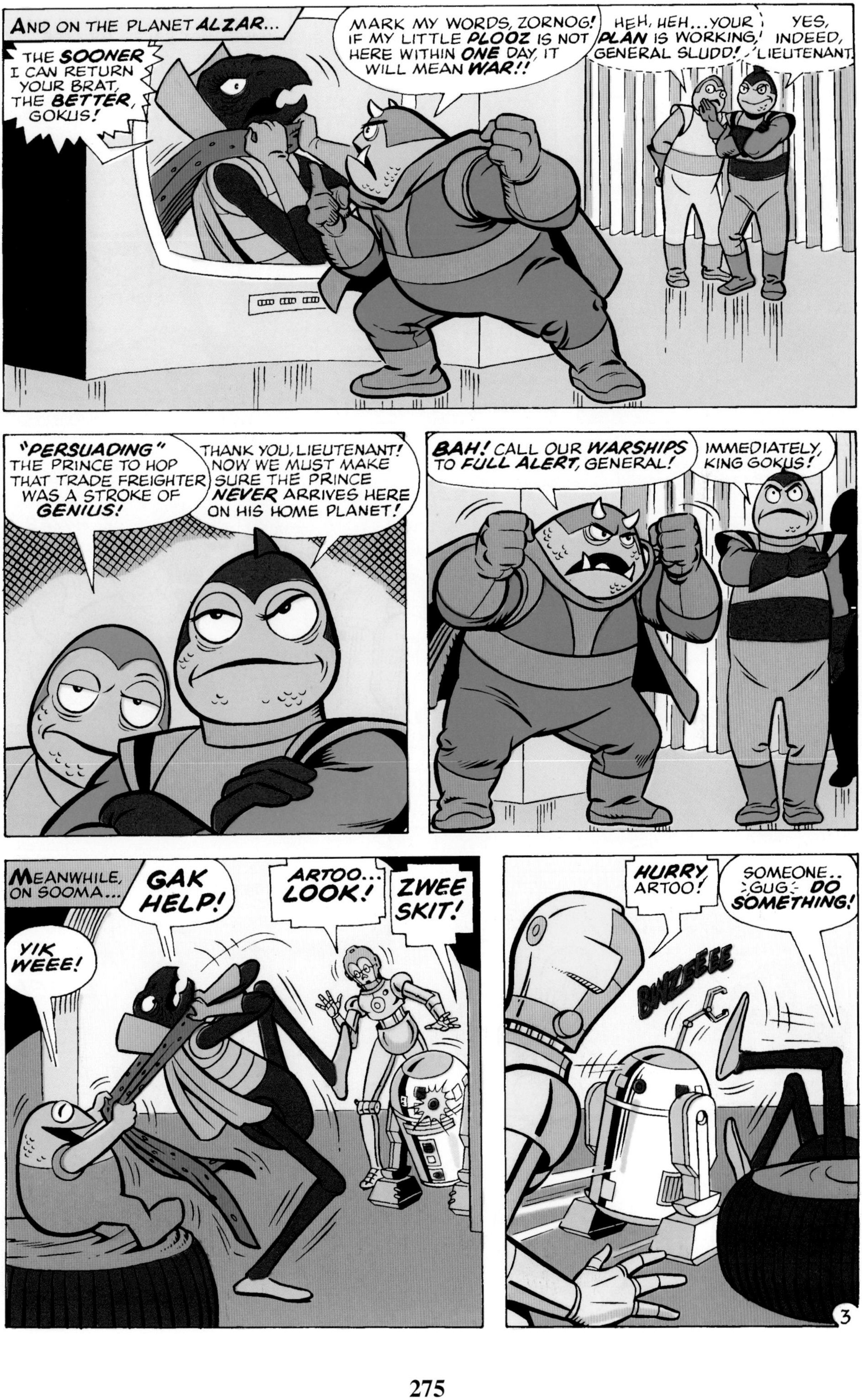
AND ON THE PLANET ALZAR...
THE SOONER I CAN RETURN YOUR BRAT, THE BETTER, GOKUS!
MARK MY WORDS, ZORNOG! IF MY LITTLE PLOOZ IS NOT HERE WITHIN ONE DAY, IT WILL MEAN WAR!!
HEH, HEH... YOUR PLAN IS WORKING, GENERAL SLUDD!
YES, INDEED, LIEUTENANT.
"PERSUADING" THE PRINCE TO HOP THAT TRADE FREIGHTER WAS A STROKE OF GENIUS!
THANK YOU, LIEUTENANT! NOW WE MUST MAKE SURE THE PRINCE NEVER ARRIVES HERE ON HIS HOME PLANET!
BAH! CALL OUR WARSHIPS TO FULL ALERT, GENERAL!
IMMEDIATELY, KING GOKUS!
MEANWHILE, ON SOOMA...
GAK HELP!
YIK WEEE!
ARTOO... LOOK!
ZWEE SKIT!
HURRY ARTOO!
SOMEONE.. GUG.. DO SOMETHING!
BWZEEEE
3

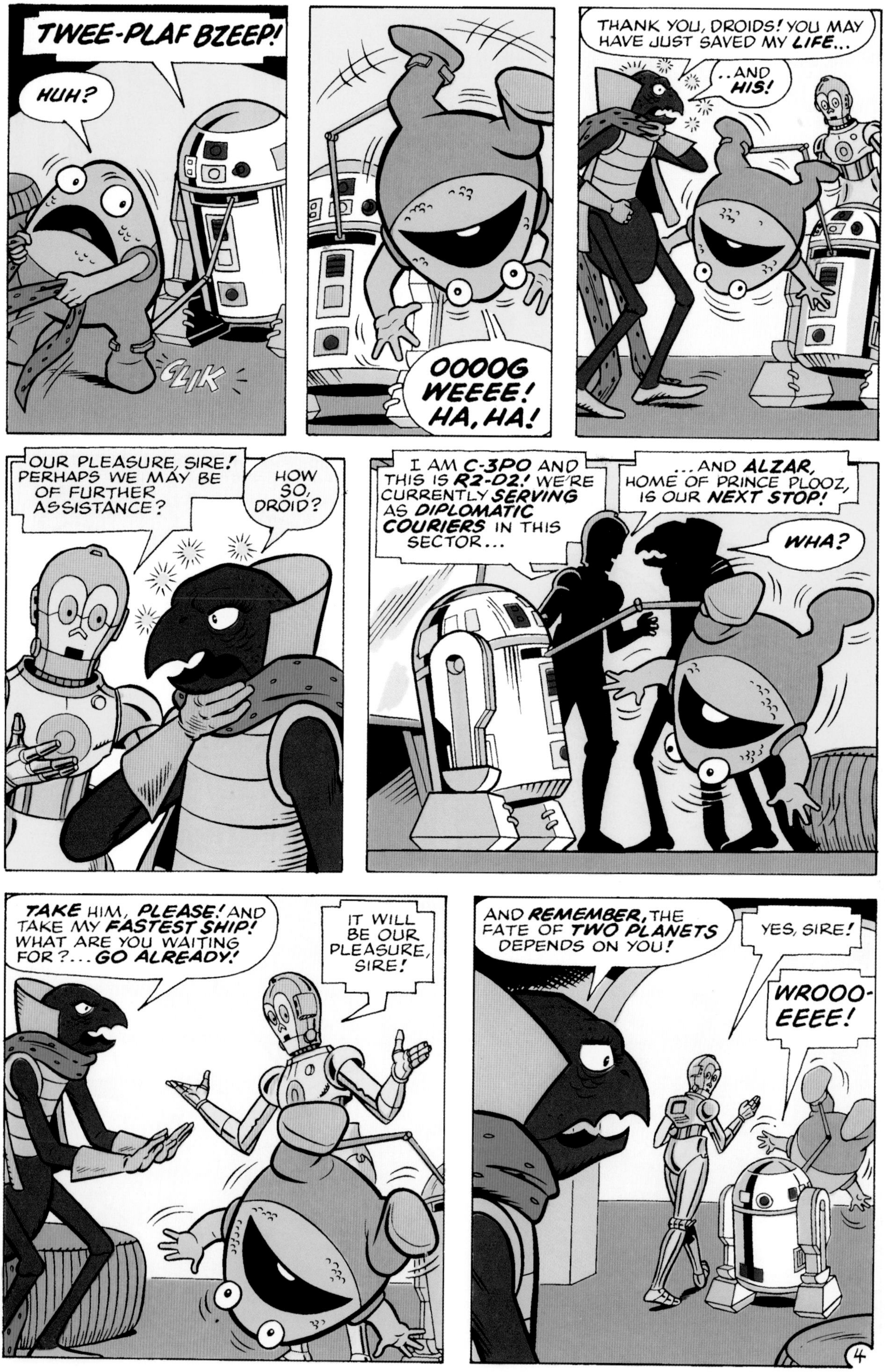
TWEE-PLAF BZEEP!
HUH?
CLIK
OOOOG WEEEE! HA, HA!
THANK YOU, DROIDS! YOU MAY HAVE JUST SAVED MY LIFE...
..AND HIS!
OUR PLEASURE, SIRE! PERHAPS WE MAY BE OF FURTHER ASSISTANCE?
HOW SO, DROID?
I AM C-3PO AND THIS IS R2-D2! WE'RE CURRENTLY SERVING AS DIPLOMATIC COURIERS IN THIS SECTOR...
...AND ALZAR, HOME OF PRINCE PLOOZ, IS OUR NEXT STOP!
WHA?
TAKE HIM, PLEASE! AND TAKE MY FASTEST SHIP! WHAT ARE YOU WAITING FOR?... GO ALREADY!
IT WILL BE OUR PLEASURE, SIRE!
AND REMEMBER, THE FATE OF TWO PLANETS DEPENDS ON YOU!
YES, SIRE!
WROOO-EEEE!
4

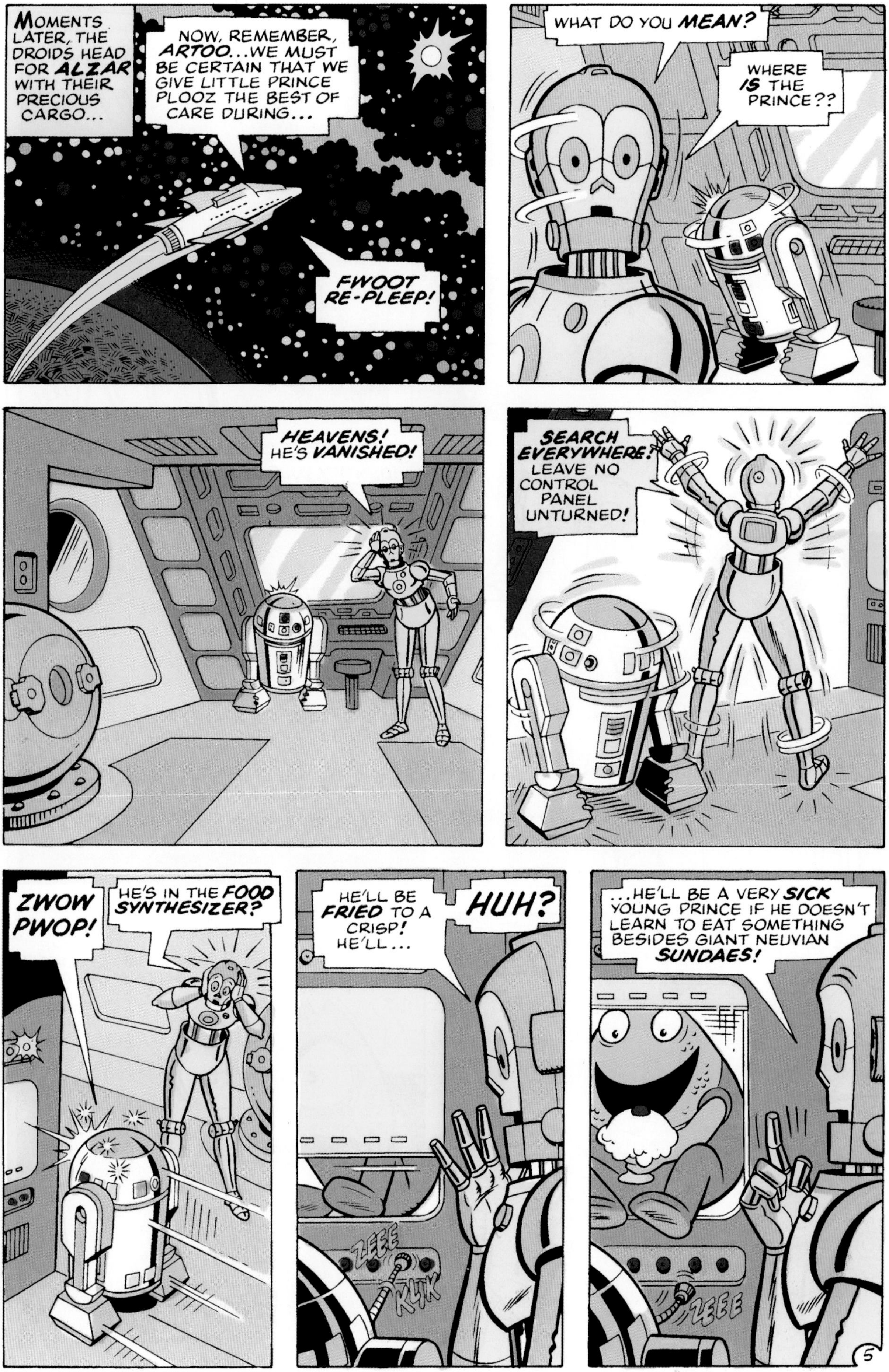
MOMENTS LATER, THE DROIDS HEAD FOR ALZAR WITH THEIR PRECIOUS CARGO...
NOW, REMEMBER, ARTOO...WE MUST BE CERTAIN THAT WE GIVE LITTLE PRINCE PLOOZ THE BEST OF CARE DURING...
FWOOT RE-PLEEP!
WHAT DO YOU MEAN?
WHERE IS THE PRINCE??
HEAVENS! HE'S VANISHED!
SEARCH EVERYWHERE! LEAVE NO CONTROL PANEL UNTURNED!
ZWOW PWOP!
HE'S IN THE FOOD SYNTHESIZER?
HE'LL BE FRIED TO A CRISP! HE'LL...
HUH?
ZEEE
KLIK
...HE'LL BE A VERY SICK YOUNG PRINCE IF HE DOESN'T LEARN TO EAT SOMETHING BESIDES GIANT NEUVIAN SUNDAES!
ZEEE
5

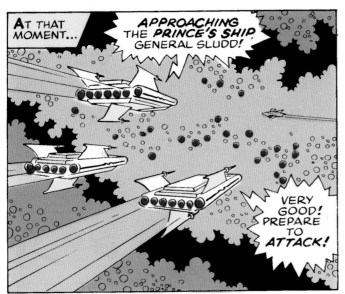

AT THAT MOMENT... APPROACHING THE **PRINCE'S SHIP**, GENERAL SLUDD!

VERY GOOD! PREPARE TO **ATTACK!**

FREE-OP BLWEEP!

BEEP BEEP BEEP

WHAT'S THAT, ARTOO? **SHIPS** APPROACHING OUR PORT SIDE...

...IN **ATTACK FORMATION??!**

ATT.. TAK?

IDENTIFY YOURSELVES AT **ONCE!** WE ARE UNARMED...

..AND CARRY THE **ROYAL PRINCE** OF **ALZAR!**

BZZZT! NOT FOR **LONG**, IF I HAVE MY WAY!

PRINCE PLOOZ, IT'S YOUR FATHER'S **FIRST GENERAL!**

SLUDD?

HA, HA! THE SOONER LITTLE LORD PLOOZ IS OUT OF THE WAY AND **WAR** IS DECLARED..

..THE SOONER I WILL HAVE THE **POWER** TO CONQUER **BOTH** WORLDS!

6

278

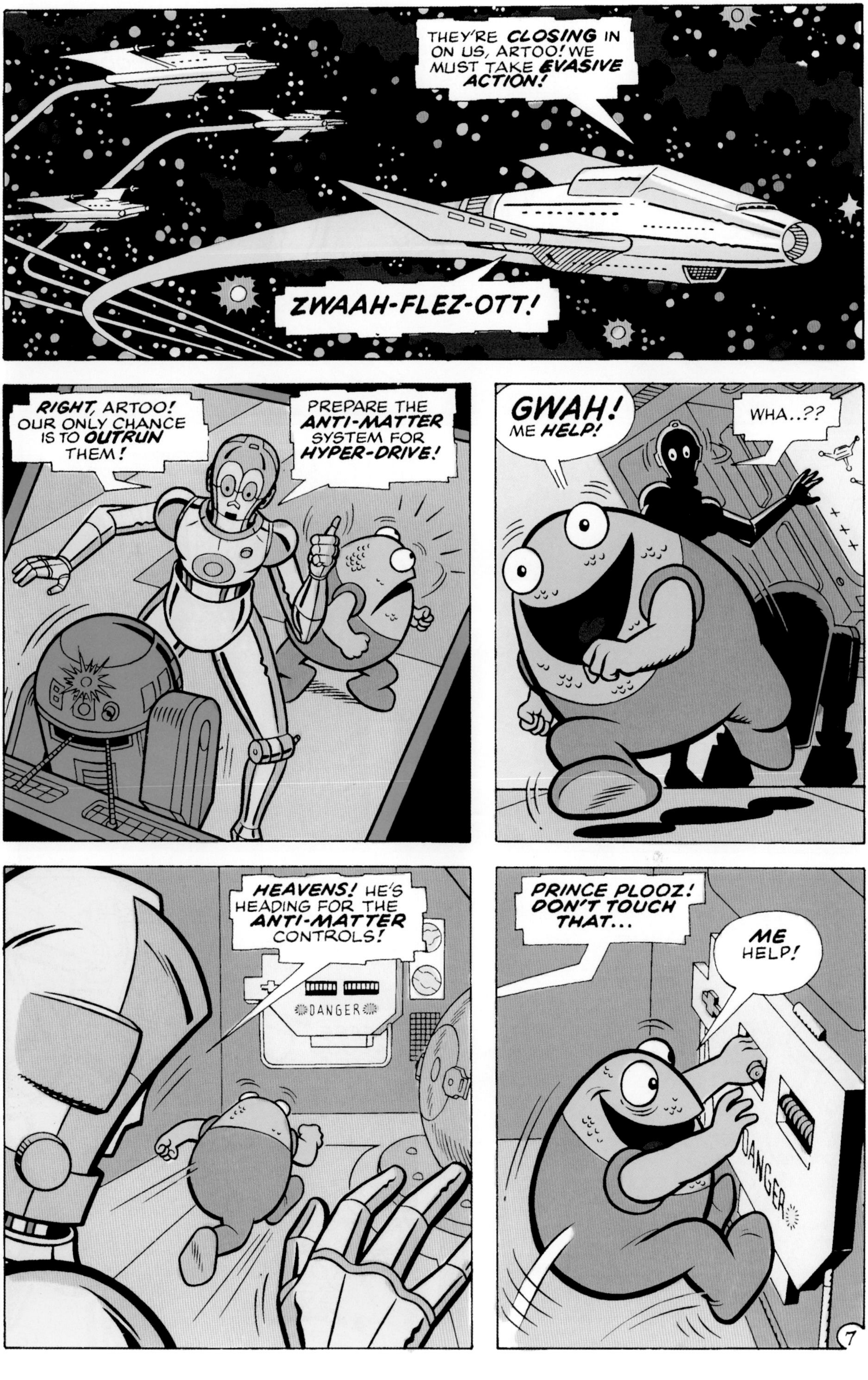
THEY'RE CLOSING IN ON US, ARTOO! WE MUST TAKE EVASIVE ACTION!
ZWAAH-FLEZ-OTT!
RIGHT, ARTOO! OUR ONLY CHANCE IS TO OUTRUN THEM!
PREPARE THE ANTI-MATTER SYSTEM FOR HYPER-DRIVE!
GWAH! ME HELP!
WHA..??
HEAVENS! HE'S HEADING FOR THE ANTI-MATTER CONTROLS!
DANGER
PRINCE PLOOZ! DON'T TOUCH THAT...
ME HELP!
DANGER
7

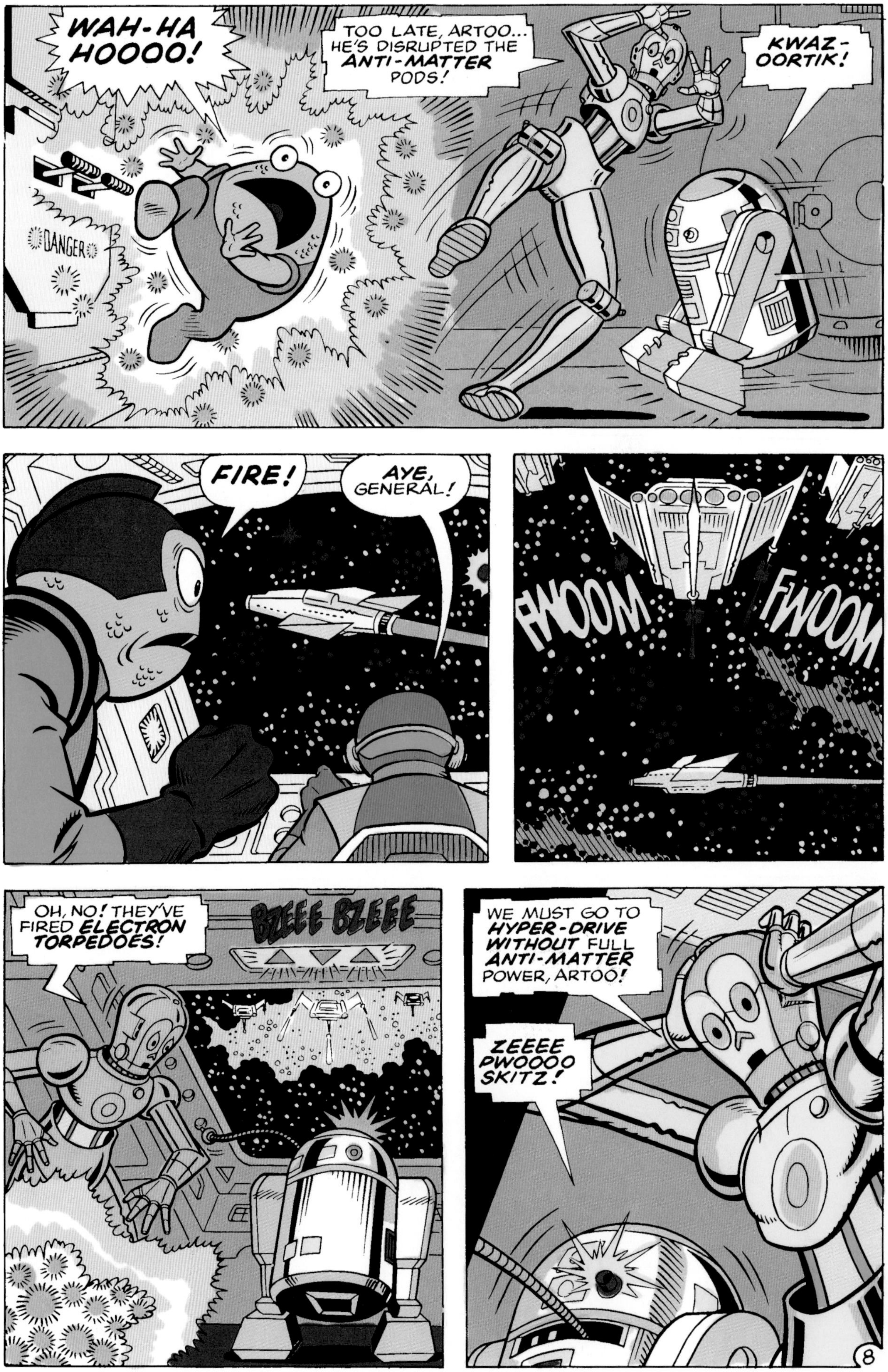
WAH-HA HOOOO!
TOO LATE, ARTOO... HE'S DISRUPTED THE ANTI-MATTER PODS!
KWAZ-OORTIK!
DANGER
FIRE!
AYE, GENERAL!
FWOOM
FWOOM
OH, NO! THEY'VE FIRED ELECTRON TORPEDOES!
BZEEE BZEEE
WE MUST GO TO HYPER-DRIVE WITHOUT FULL ANTI-MATTER POWER, ARTOO!
ZEEEE PWOOOO SKITZ!
8

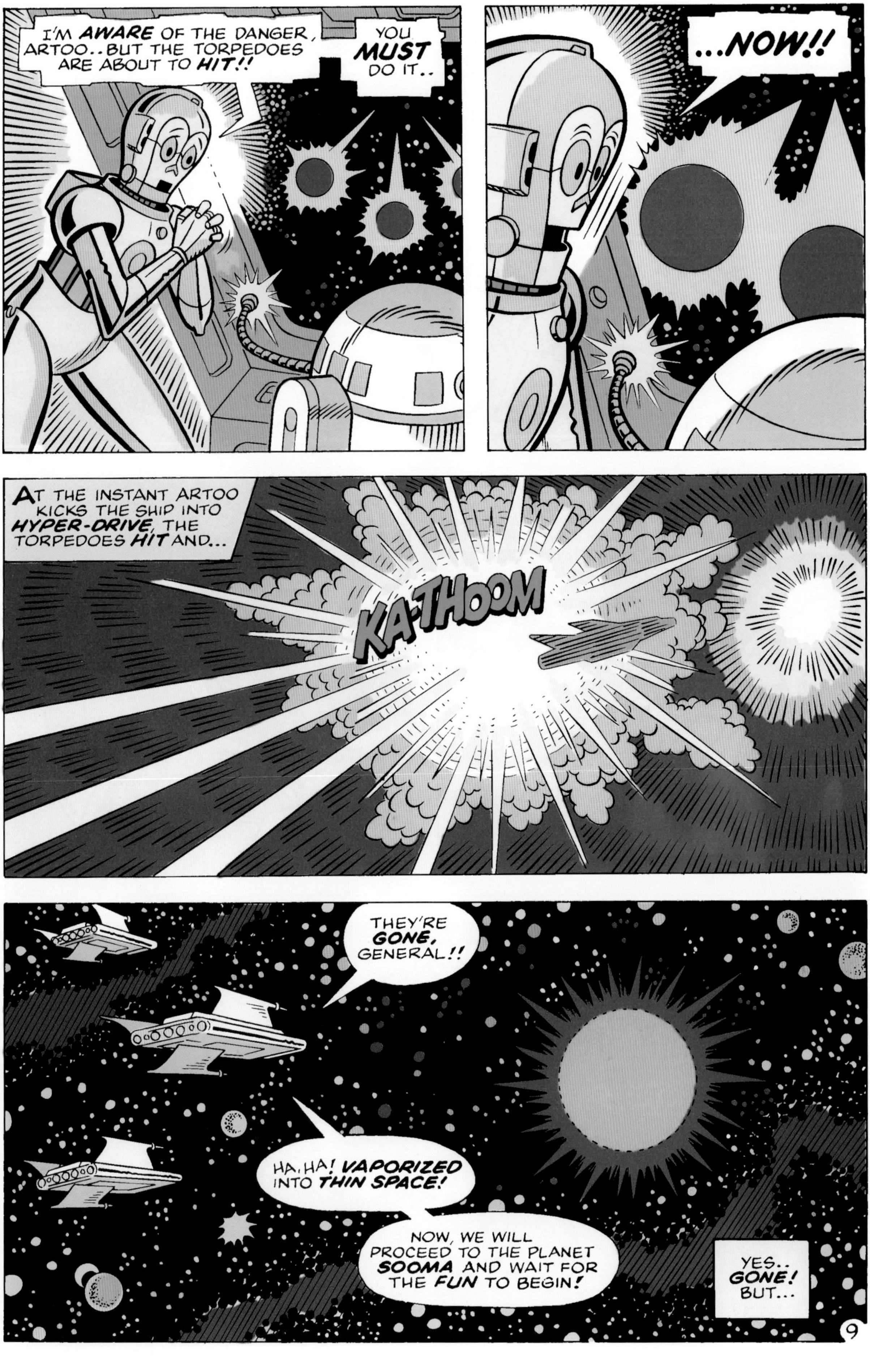
I'M AWARE OF THE DANGER, ARTOO.. BUT THE TORPEDOES ARE ABOUT TO HIT!!
YOU MUST DO IT..
...NOW!!
AT THE INSTANT ARTOO KICKS THE SHIP INTO HYPER-DRIVE, THE TORPEDOES HIT AND...
KA-THOOM
THEY'RE GONE, GENERAL!!
HA, HA! VAPORIZED INTO THIN SPACE!
NOW, WE WILL PROCEED TO THE PLANET SOOMA AND WAIT FOR THE FUN TO BEGIN!
YES.. GONE! BUT...
9

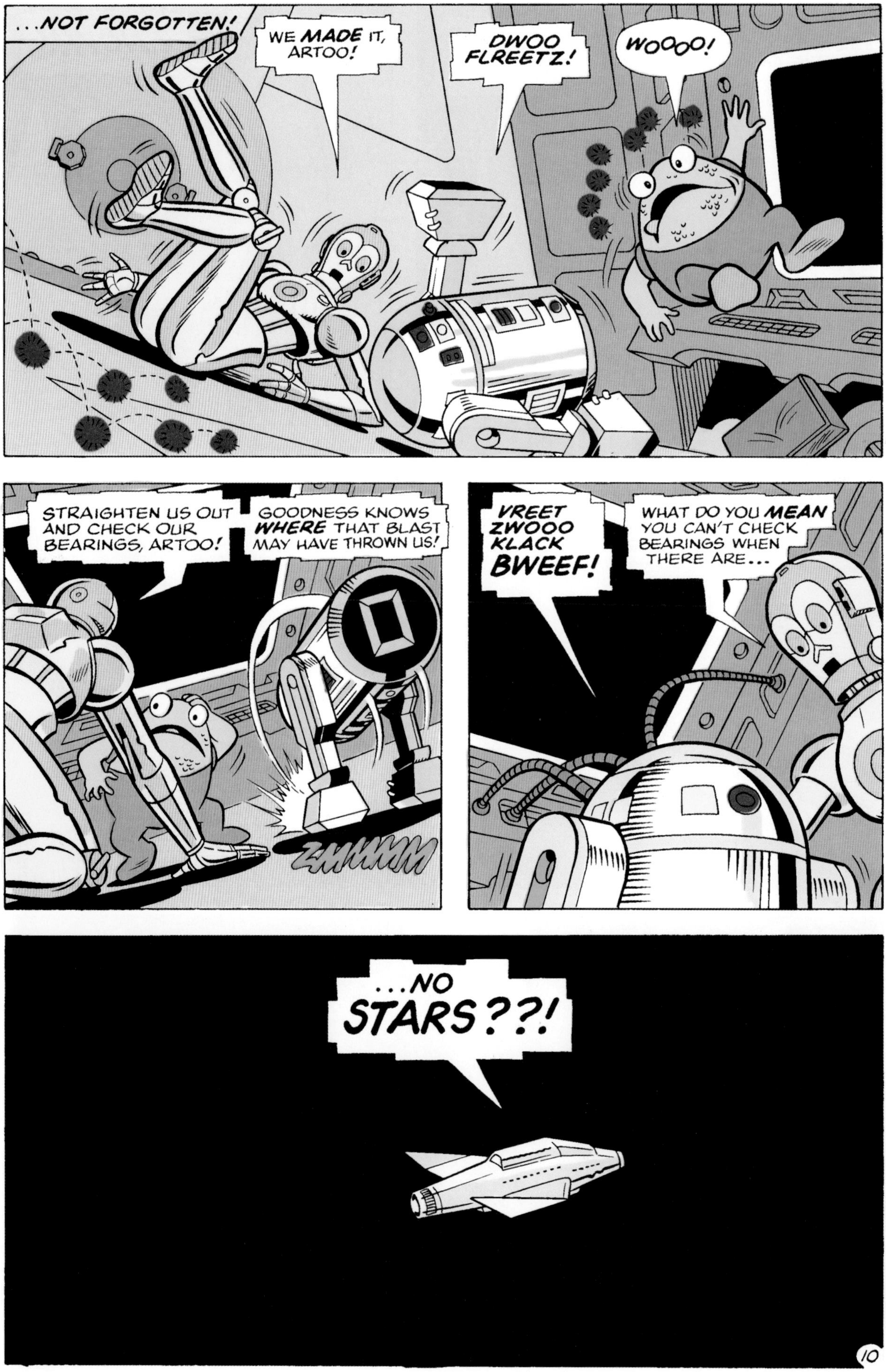
...NOT FORGOTTEN!
WE MADE IT, ARTOO!
DWOO FLREETZ!
WOOOOO!
STRAIGHTEN US OUT AND CHECK OUR BEARINGS, ARTOO!
GOODNESS KNOWS WHERE THAT BLAST MAY HAVE THROWN US!
ZMMMM
VREET ZWOOO KLACK BWEEF!
WHAT DO YOU MEAN YOU CAN'T CHECK BEARINGS WHEN THERE ARE...
...NO STARS??!
10

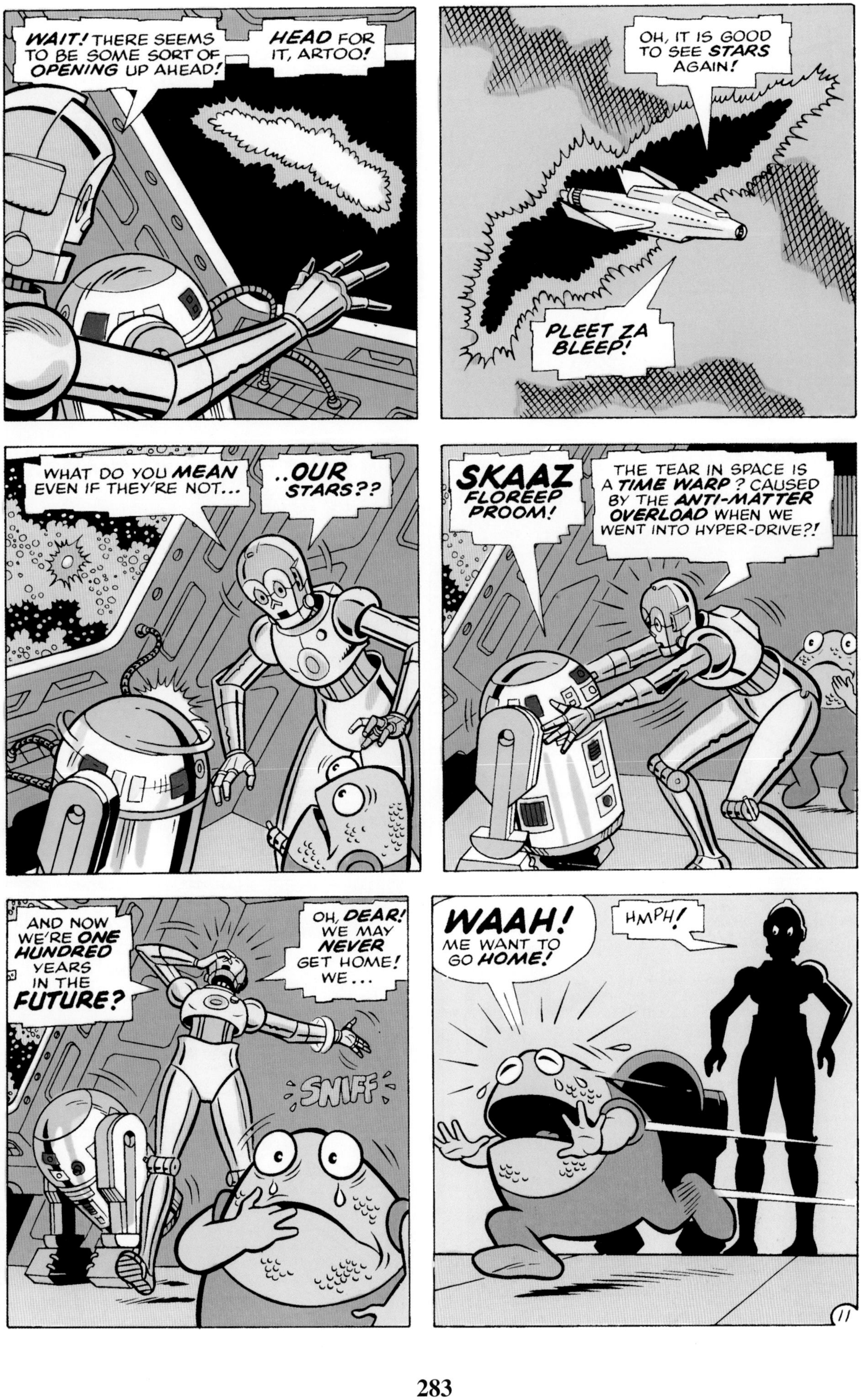
WAIT! THERE SEEMS TO BE SOME SORT OF OPENING UP AHEAD!
HEAD FOR IT, ARTOO!
OH, IT IS GOOD TO SEE STARS AGAIN!
PLEET ZA BLEEP!
WHAT DO YOU MEAN EVEN IF THEY'RE NOT...
..OUR STARS??
SKAAZ FLOREEP PROOM!
THE TEAR IN SPACE IS A TIME WARP? CAUSED BY THE ANTI-MATTER OVERLOAD WHEN WE WENT INTO HYPER-DRIVE?!
AND NOW WE'RE ONE HUNDRED YEARS IN THE FUTURE?
OH, DEAR! WE MAY NEVER GET HOME! WE...
SNIFF
WAAH! ME WANT TO GO HOME!
HMPH!
11

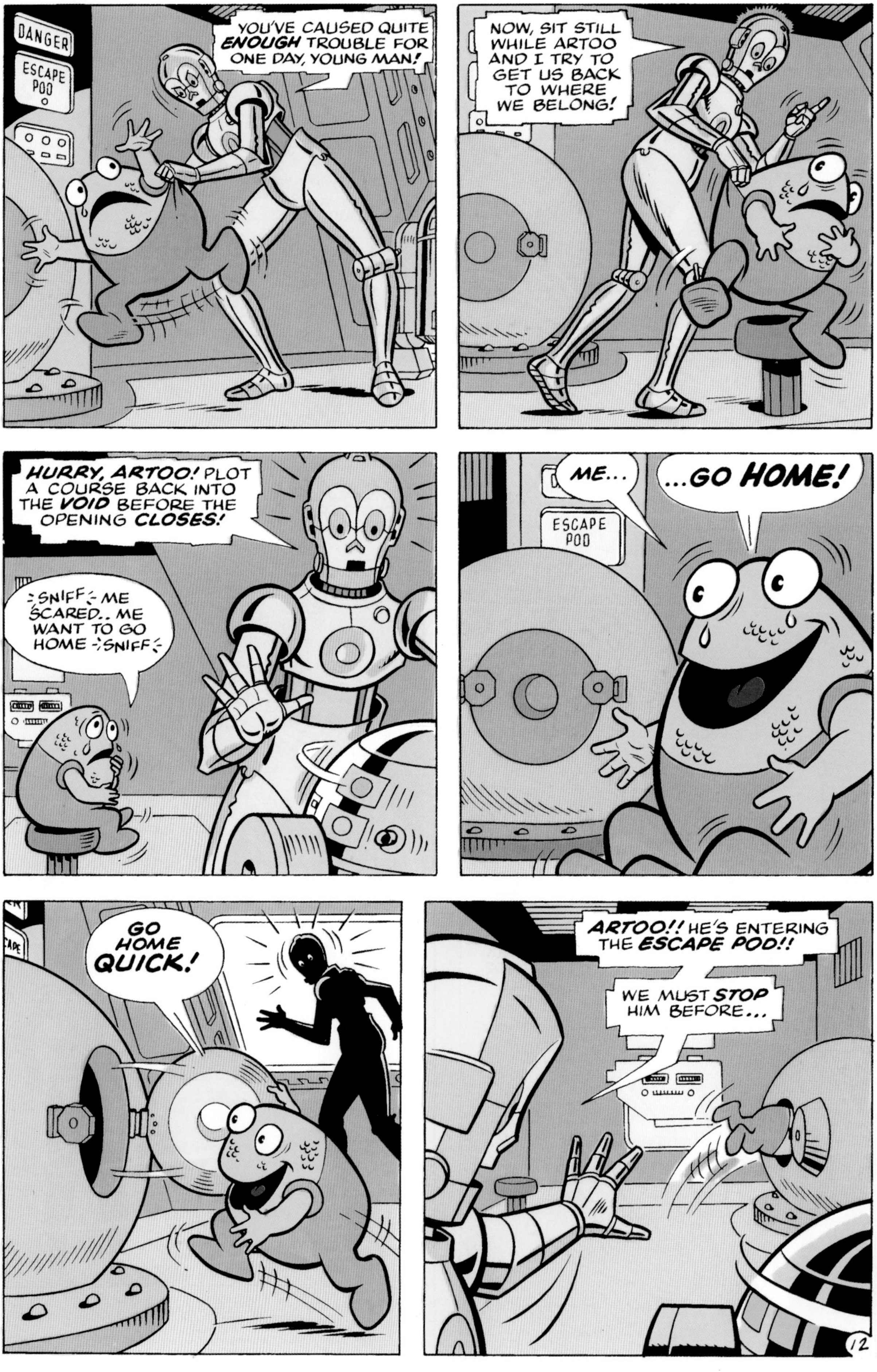
DANGER
ESCAPE POD
YOU'VE CAUSED QUITE ENOUGH TROUBLE FOR ONE DAY, YOUNG MAN!
NOW, SIT STILL WHILE ARTOO AND I TRY TO GET US BACK TO WHERE WE BELONG!
HURRY, ARTOO! PLOT A COURSE BACK INTO THE VOID BEFORE THE OPENING CLOSES!
-SNIFF- ME SCARED.. ME WANT TO GO HOME -SNIFF-
ME...
...GO HOME!
ESCAPE POD
GO HOME QUICK!
ARTOO!! HE'S ENTERING THE ESCAPE POD!!
WE MUST STOP HIM BEFORE...
12

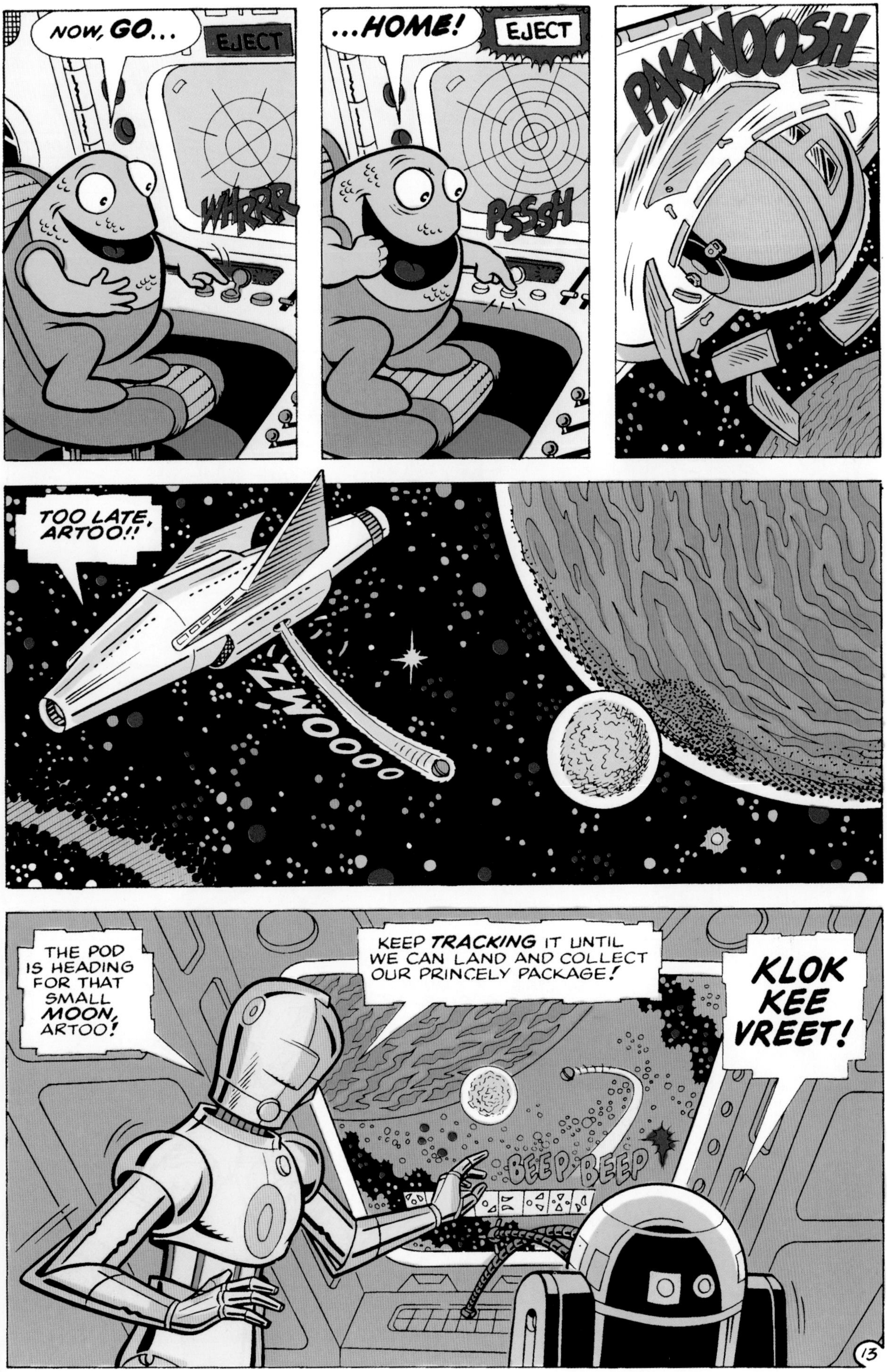
NOW, GO...
EJECT
WHRRR
...HOME!
EJECT
PSSSH
PAKWOOSH
TOO LATE, ARTOO!!
ZWOOOOO
THE POD IS HEADING FOR THAT SMALL MOON, ARTOO!
KEEP TRACKING IT UNTIL WE CAN LAND AND COLLECT OUR PRINCELY PACKAGE!
KLOK KEE VREET!
BEEP BEEP
13

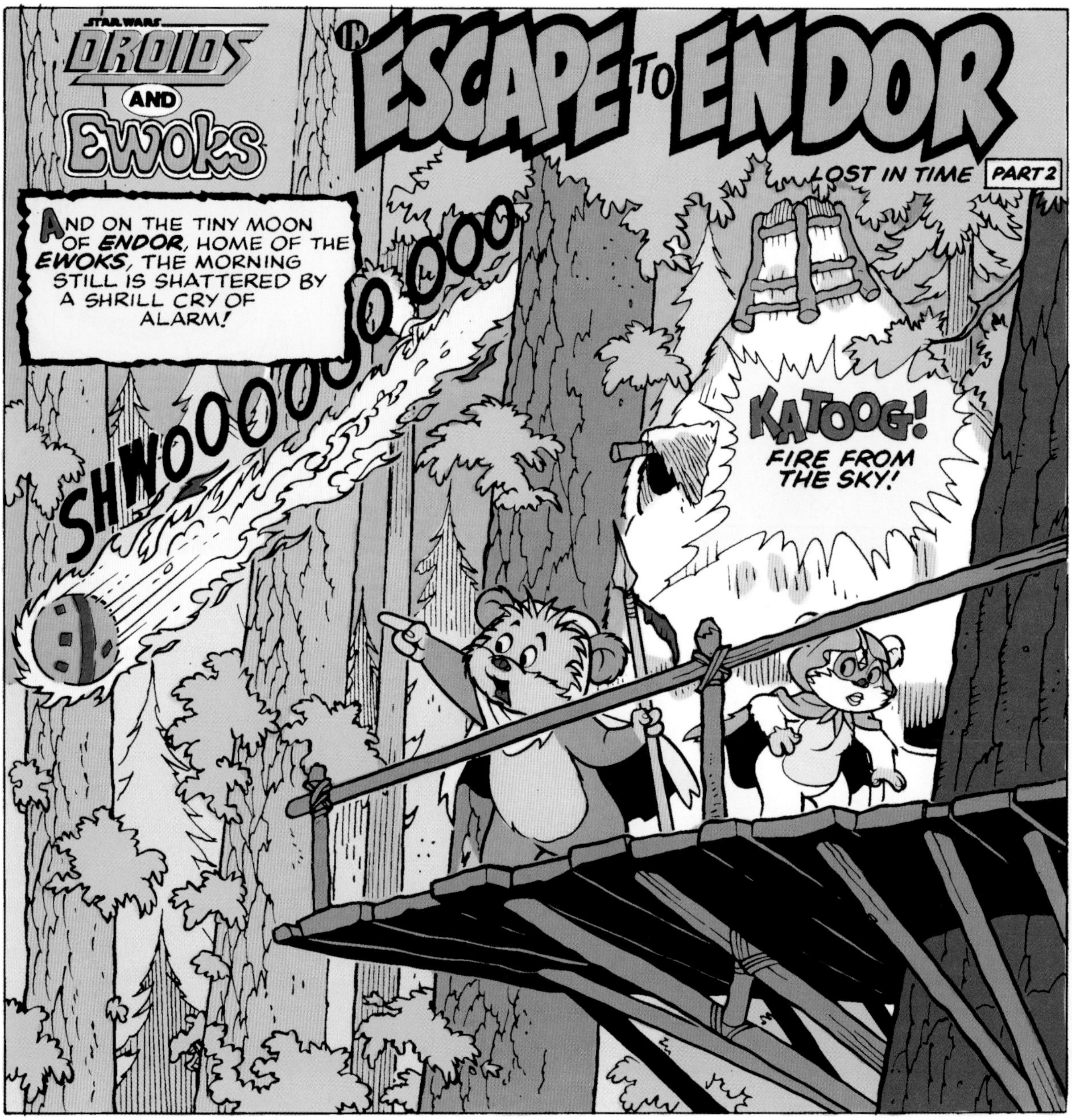
STAR WARS
DROIDS
AND
Ewoks
IN
ESCAPE TO ENDOR
LOST IN TIME
PART 2
AND ON THE TINY MOON OF ENDOR, HOME OF THE EWOKS, THE MORNING STILL IS SHATTERED BY A SHRILL CRY OF ALARM!
SHWOOOOOOOO OOOO
KATOOG! FIRE FROM THE SKY!

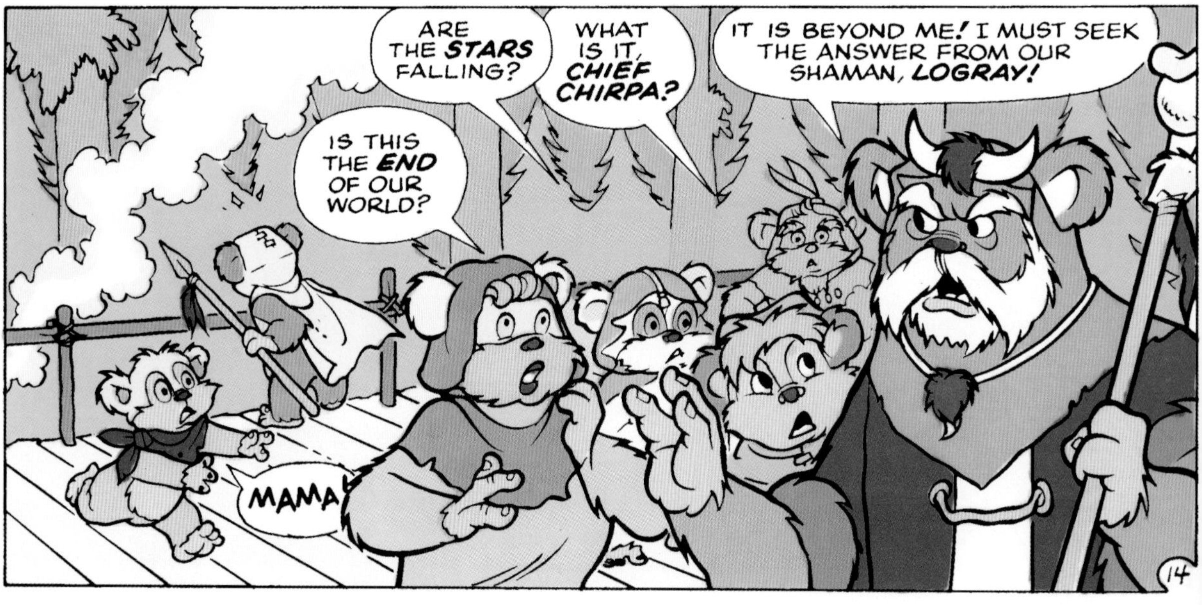
ARE THE STARS FALLING?
WHAT IS IT, CHIEF CHIRPA?
IT IS BEYOND ME! I MUST SEEK THE ANSWER FROM OUR SHAMAN, LOGRAY!
IS THIS THE END OF OUR WORLD?
MAMA!
14

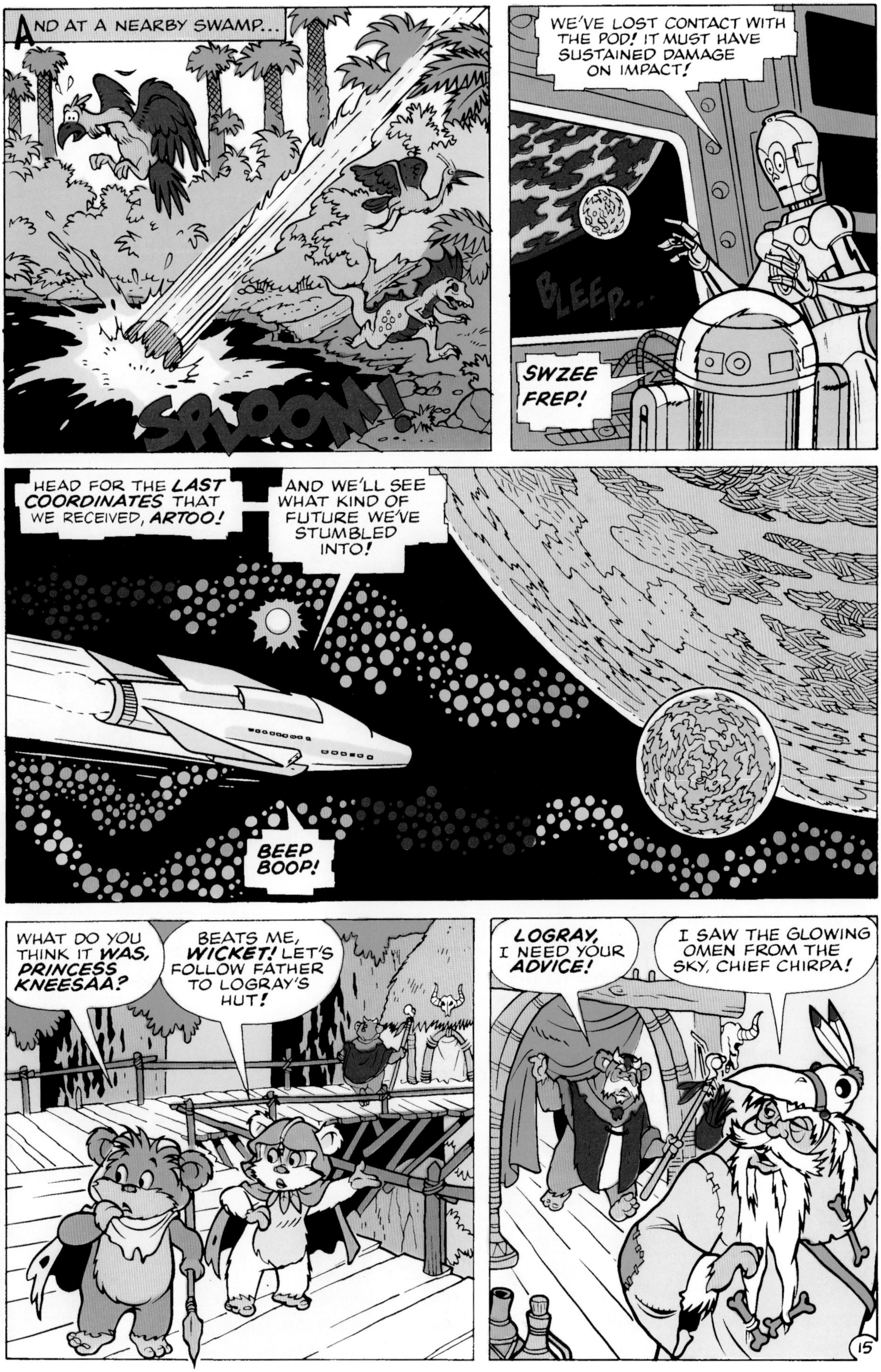
AND AT A NEARBY SWAMP...
SPLOOM!
WE'VE LOST CONTACT WITH THE POD! IT MUST HAVE SUSTAINED DAMAGE ON IMPACT!
BLEEP...
SWZEE FREP!
HEAD FOR THE LAST COORDINATES THAT WE RECEIVED, ARTOO!
AND WE'LL SEE WHAT KIND OF FUTURE WE'VE STUMBLED INTO!
BEEP BOOP!
WHAT DO YOU THINK IT WAS, PRINCESS KNEESAA?
BEATS ME, WICKET! LET'S FOLLOW FATHER TO LOGRAY'S HUT!
LOGRAY, I NEED YOUR ADVICE!
I SAW THE GLOWING OMEN FROM THE SKY, CHIEF CHIRPA!
15

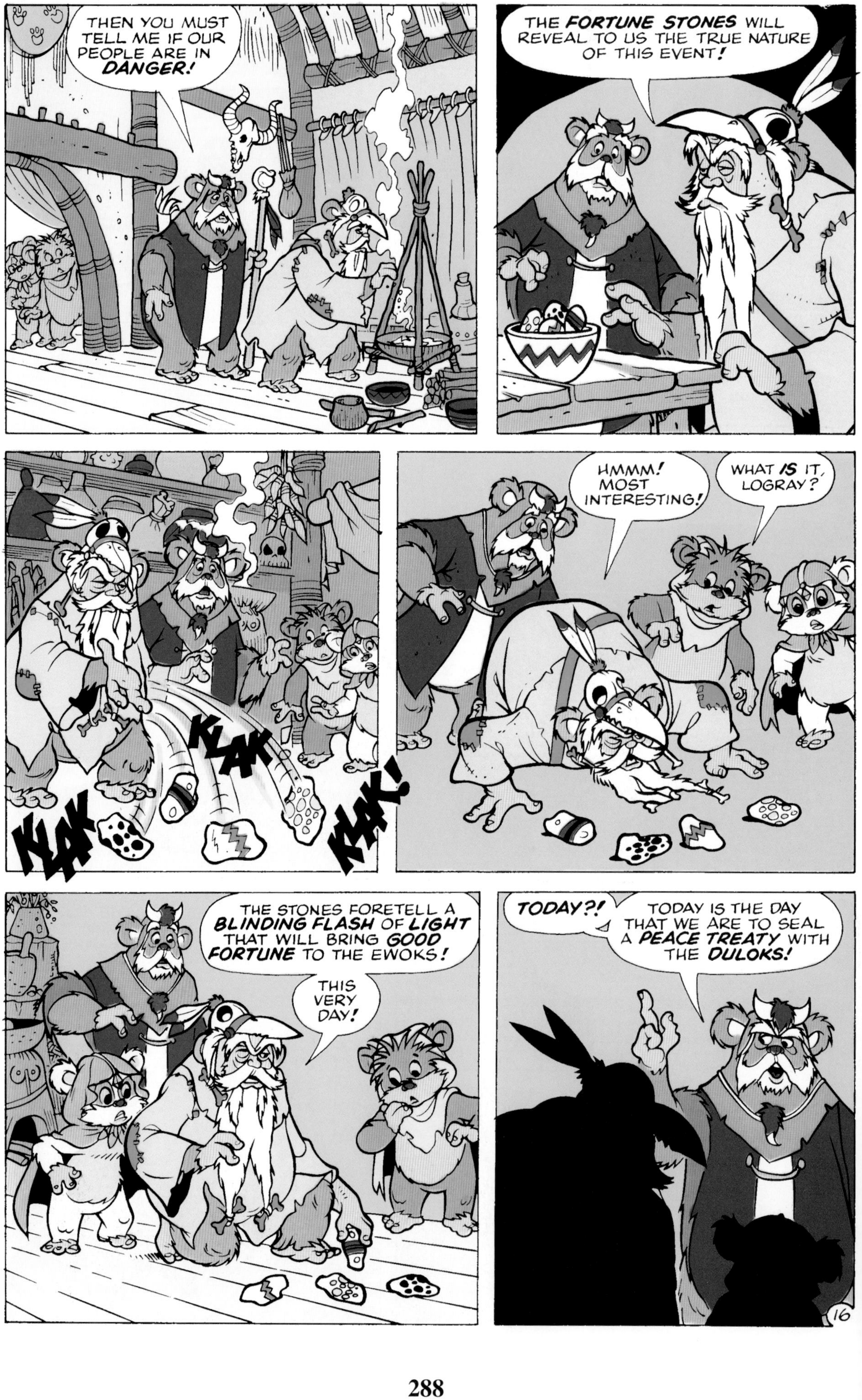
THEN YOU MUST TELL ME IF OUR PEOPLE ARE IN DANGER!
THE FORTUNE STONES WILL REVEAL TO US THE TRUE NATURE OF THIS EVENT!
KLAK
KLAK
KLAK!
HMMM! MOST INTERESTING!
WHAT IS IT, LOGRAY?
THE STONES FORETELL A BLINDING FLASH OF LIGHT THAT WILL BRING GOOD FORTUNE TO THE EWOKS!
THIS VERY DAY!
TODAY?!
TODAY IS THE DAY THAT WE ARE TO SEAL A PEACE TREATY WITH THE DULOKS!
16

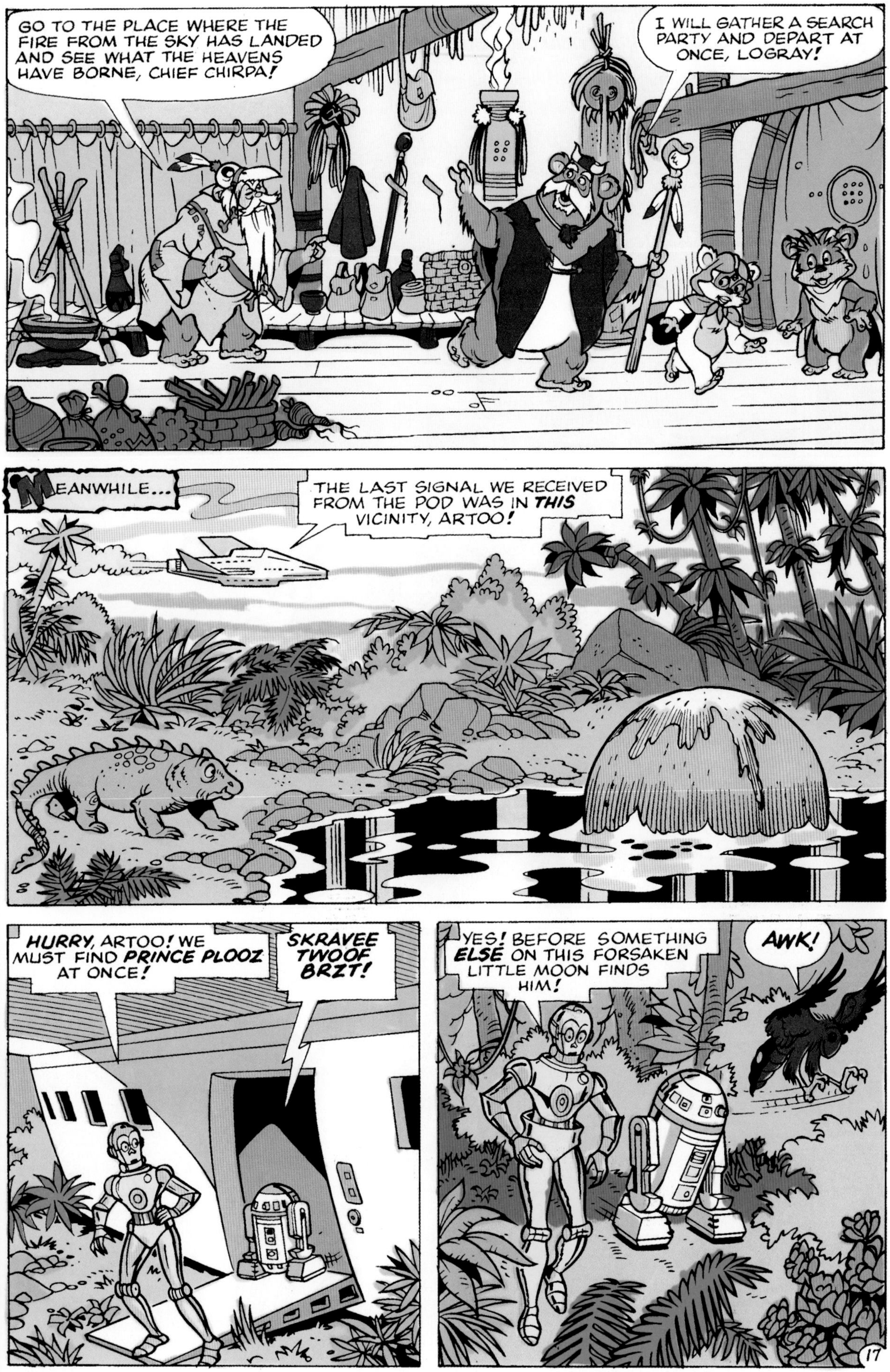
GO TO THE PLACE WHERE THE FIRE FROM THE SKY HAS LANDED AND SEE WHAT THE HEAVENS HAVE BORNE, CHIEF CHIRPA!
I WILL GATHER A SEARCH PARTY AND DEPART AT ONCE, LOGRAY!
MEANWHILE...
THE LAST SIGNAL WE RECEIVED FROM THE POD WAS IN THIS VICINITY, ARTOO!
HURRY, ARTOO! WE MUST FIND PRINCE PLOOZ AT ONCE!
SKRAVEE TWOOF BRZT!
YES! BEFORE SOMETHING ELSE ON THIS FORSAKEN LITTLE MOON FINDS HIM!
AWK!
17

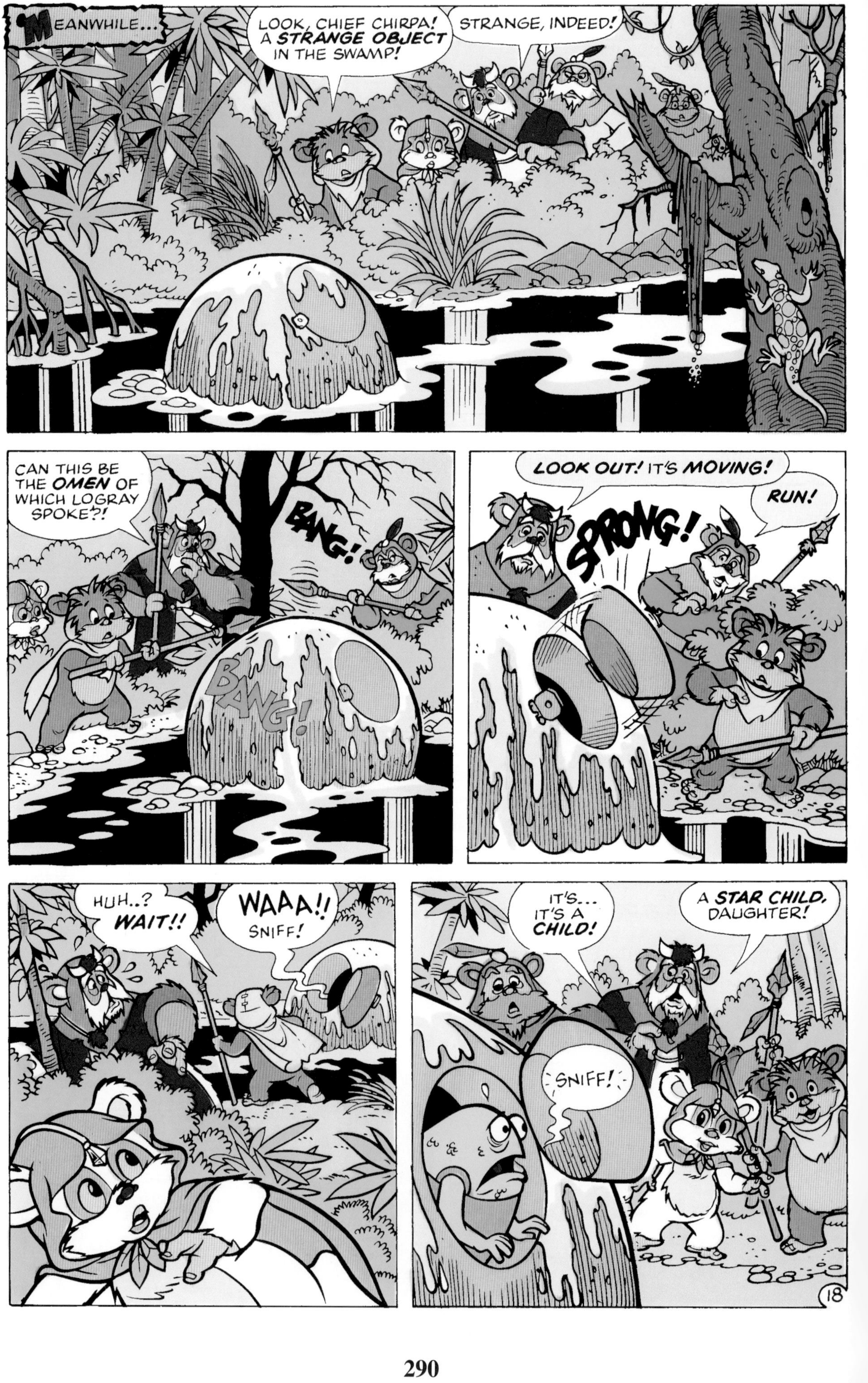
MEANWHILE...
LOOK, CHIEF CHIRPA! A STRANGE OBJECT IN THE SWAMP!
STRANGE, INDEED!
CAN THIS BE THE OMEN OF WHICH LOGRAY SPOKE?!
BANG!
BANG!
LOOK OUT! IT'S MOVING!
RUN!
SPRONG!
HUH..? WAIT!!
WAAA!! SNIFF!
IT'S... IT'S A CHILD!
A STAR CHILD, DAUGHTER!
SNIFF!
18

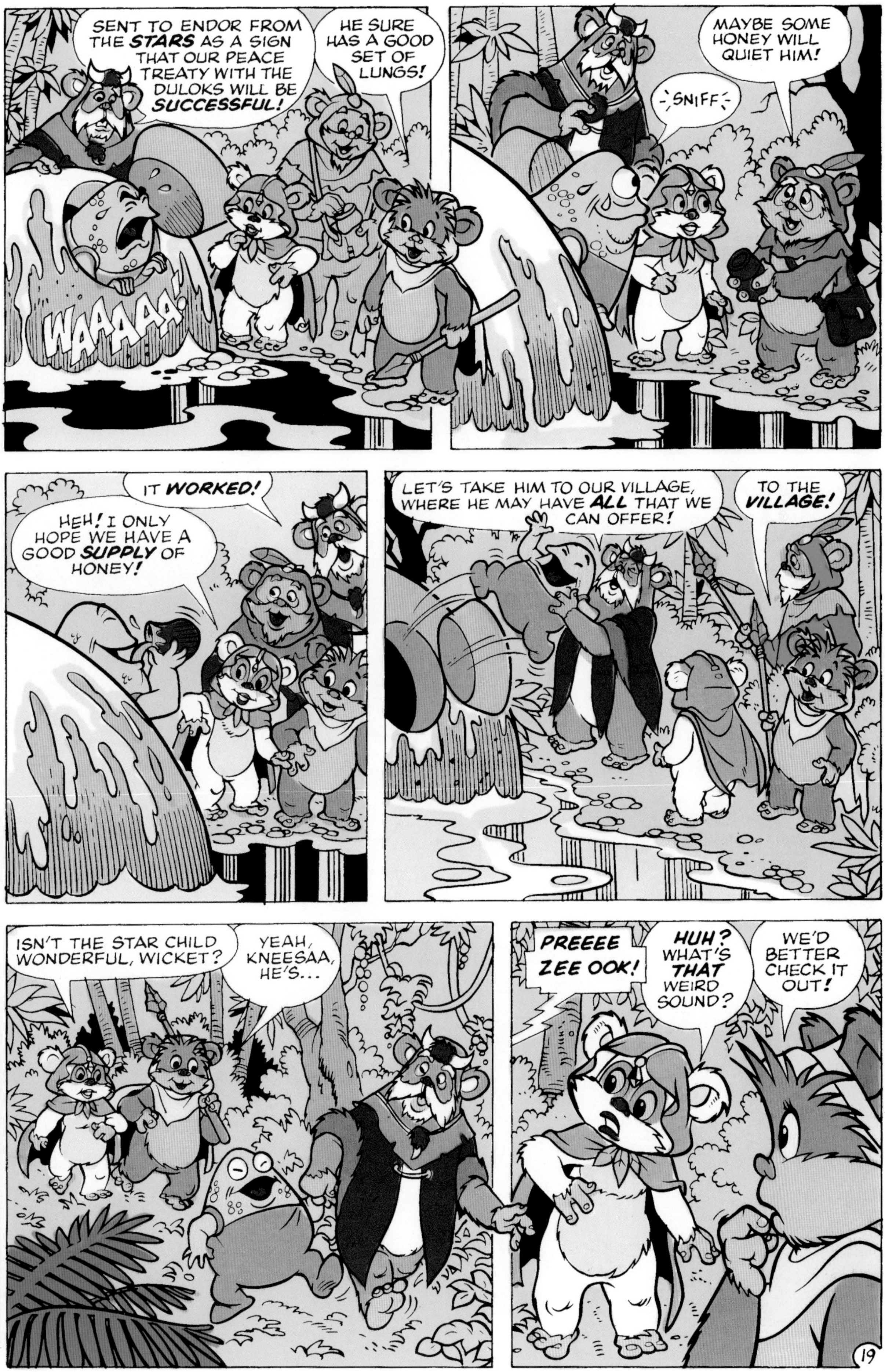
SENT TO ENDOR FROM THE STARS AS A SIGN THAT OUR PEACE TREATY WITH THE DULOKS WILL BE SUCCESSFUL!
HE SURE HAS A GOOD SET OF LUNGS!
WAAAAA!
SNIFF
MAYBE SOME HONEY WILL QUIET HIM!
IT WORKED!
HEH! I ONLY HOPE WE HAVE A GOOD SUPPLY OF HONEY!
LET'S TAKE HIM TO OUR VILLAGE, WHERE HE MAY HAVE ALL THAT WE CAN OFFER!
TO THE VILLAGE!
ISN'T THE STAR CHILD WONDERFUL, WICKET?
YEAH, KNEESAA, HE'S...
PREEEE ZEE OOK!
HUH? WHAT'S THAT WEIRD SOUND?
WE'D BETTER CHECK IT OUT!
19

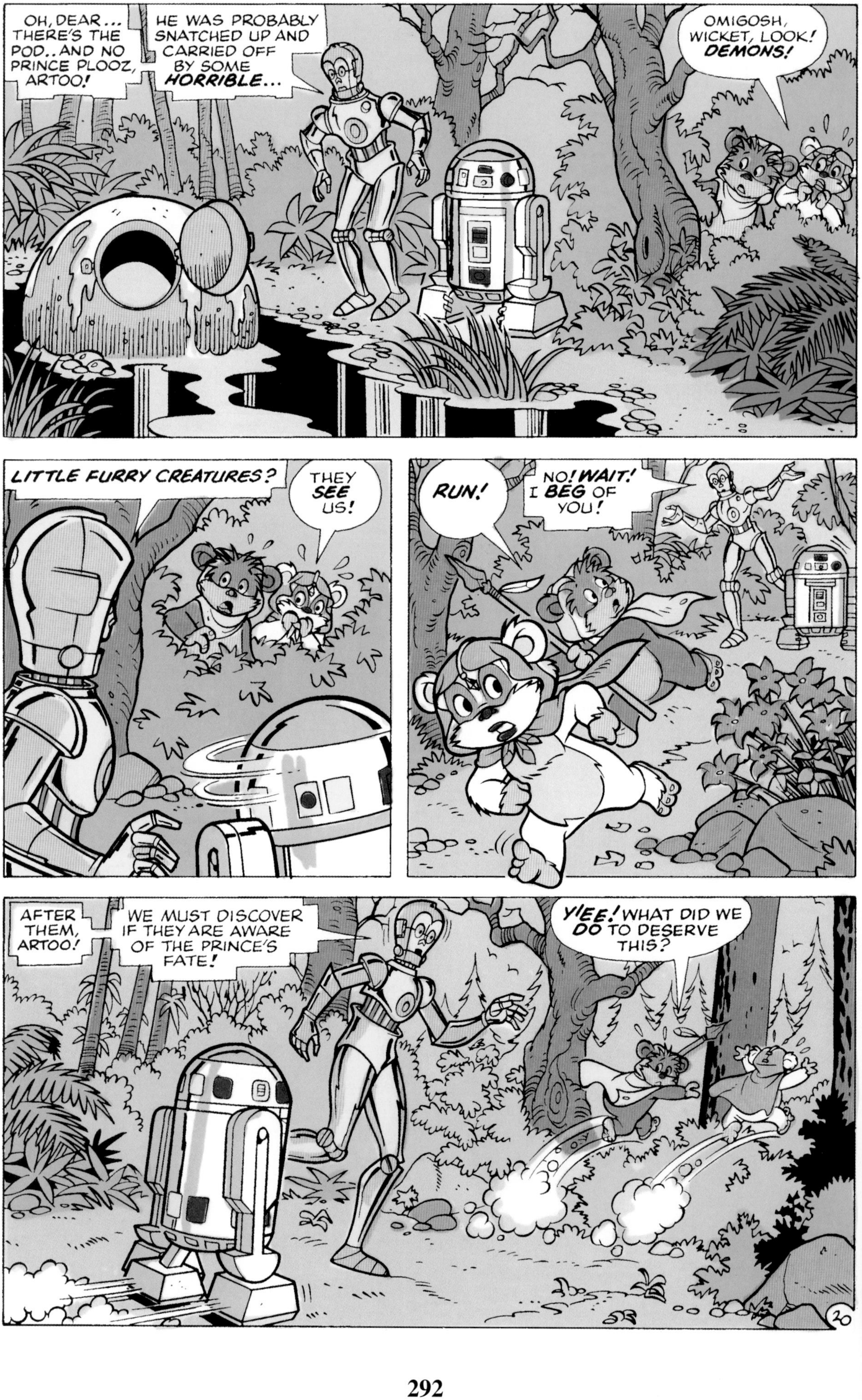
OH, DEAR... THERE'S THE POD.. AND NO PRINCE PLOOZ, ARTOO!
HE WAS PROBABLY SNATCHED UP AND CARRIED OFF BY SOME HORRIBLE...
OMIGOSH, WICKET, LOOK! DEMONS!
LITTLE FURRY CREATURES?
THEY SEE US!
RUN!
NO! WAIT! I BEG OF YOU!
AFTER THEM, ARTOO!
WE MUST DISCOVER IF THEY ARE AWARE OF THE PRINCE'S FATE!
YIEE! WHAT DID WE DO TO DESERVE THIS?
20

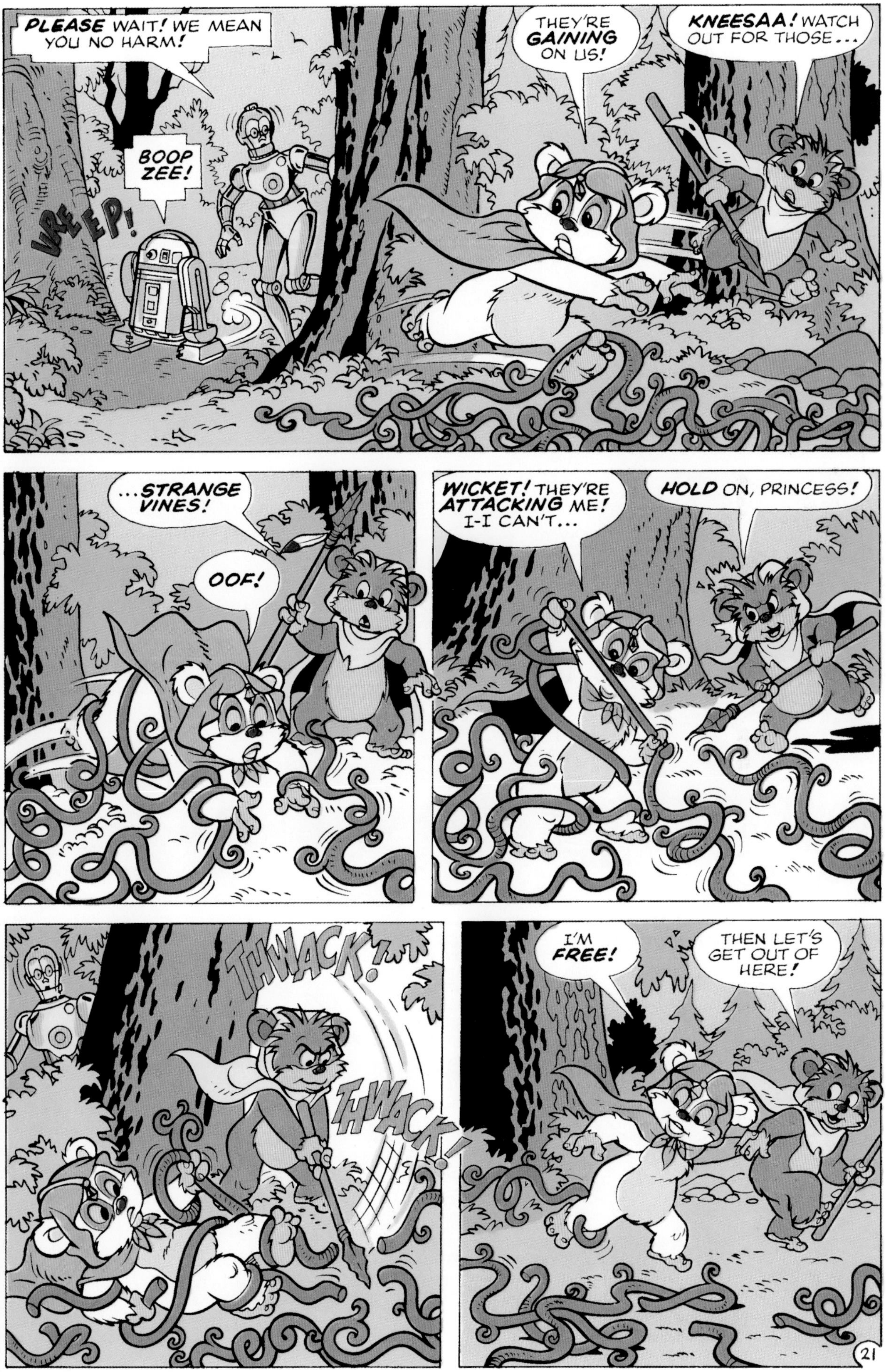
PLEASE WAIT! WE MEAN YOU NO HARM!
BOOP ZEE!
VREEP!
THEY'RE GAINING ON US!
KNEESAA! WATCH OUT FOR THOSE...
...STRANGE VINES!
OOF!
WICKET! THEY'RE ATTACKING ME! I-I CAN'T...
HOLD ON, PRINCESS!
THWACK!
THWACK!
I'M FREE!
THEN LET'S GET OUT OF HERE!
21

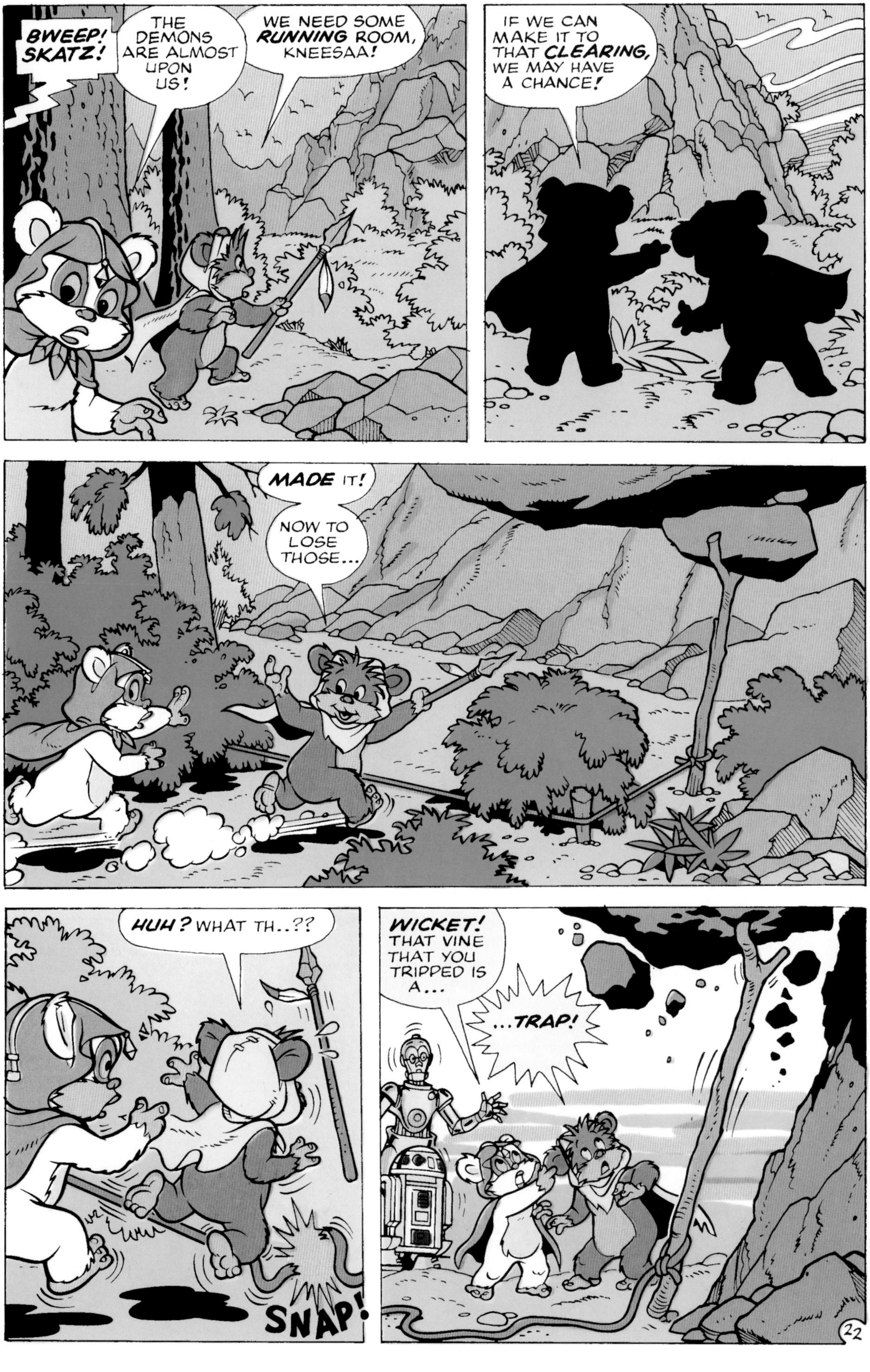
BWEEP! SKATZ!
THE DEMONS ARE ALMOST UPON US!
WE NEED SOME RUNNING ROOM, KNEESAA!
IF WE CAN MAKE IT TO THAT CLEARING, WE MAY HAVE A CHANCE!
MADE IT!
NOW TO LOSE THOSE...
HUH? WHAT TH..??
SNAP!
WICKET! THAT VINE THAT YOU TRIPPED IS A...
...TRAP!
22

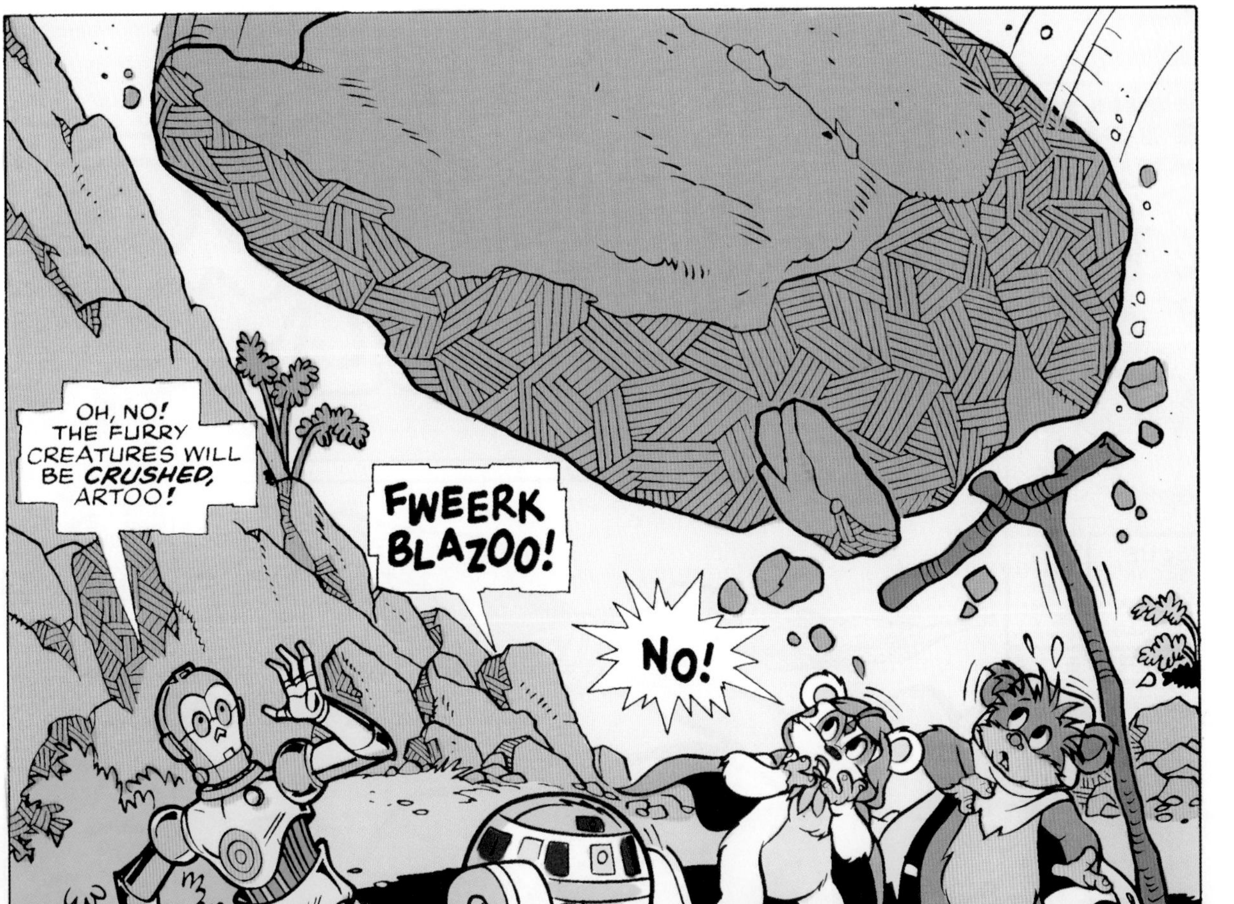
OH, NO! THE FURRY CREATURES WILL BE CRUSHED, ARTOO!
FWEERK BLAZOO!
NO!
GOOD HEAVENS, YES! AND SO WILL WE!
TO BE CONTINUED...
23

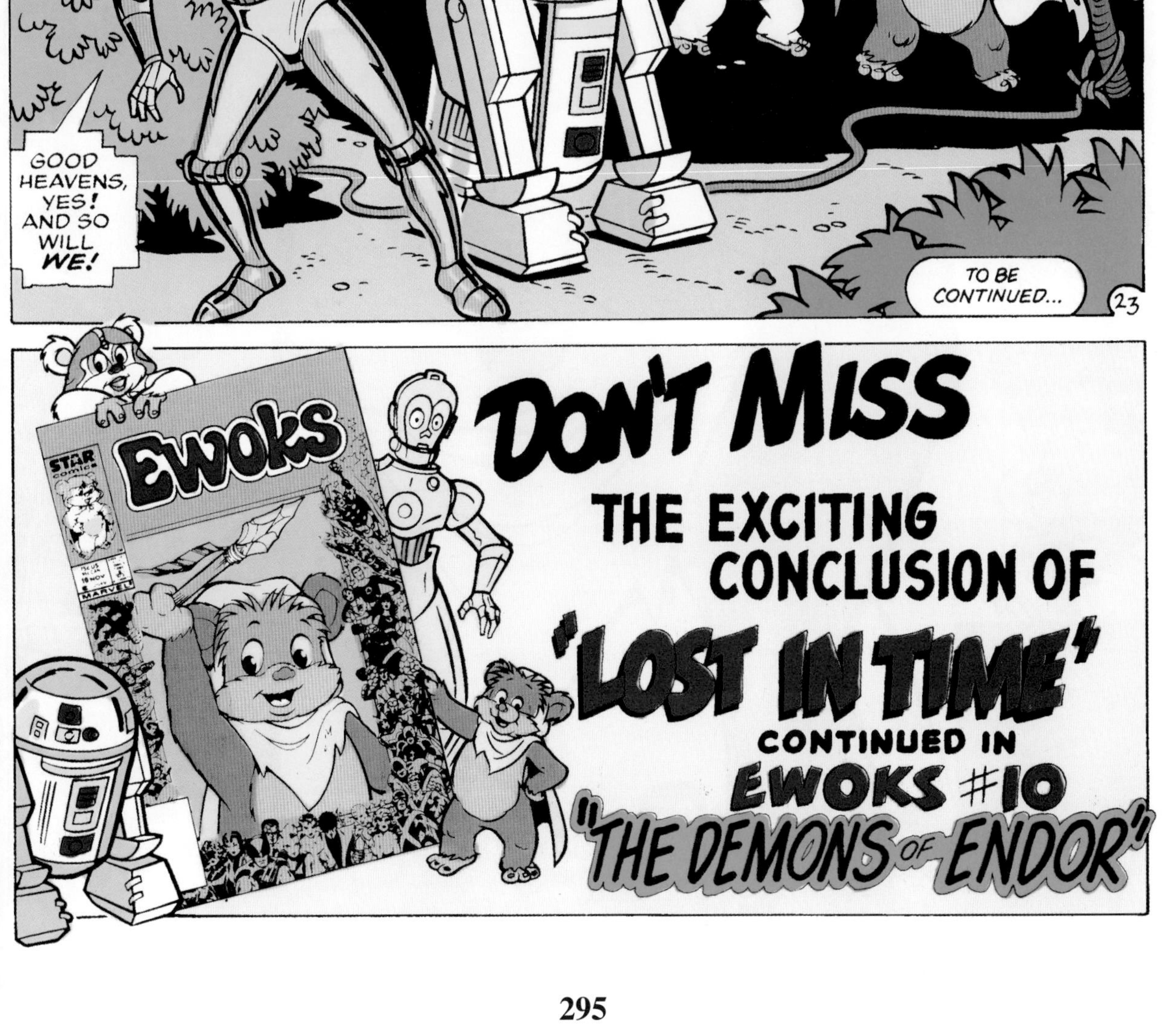
EWOKS
STAR comics
MARVEL
DON'T MISS
THE EXCITING CONCLUSION OF
"LOST IN TIME"
CONTINUED IN EWOKS #10
"THE DEMONS OF ENDOR"

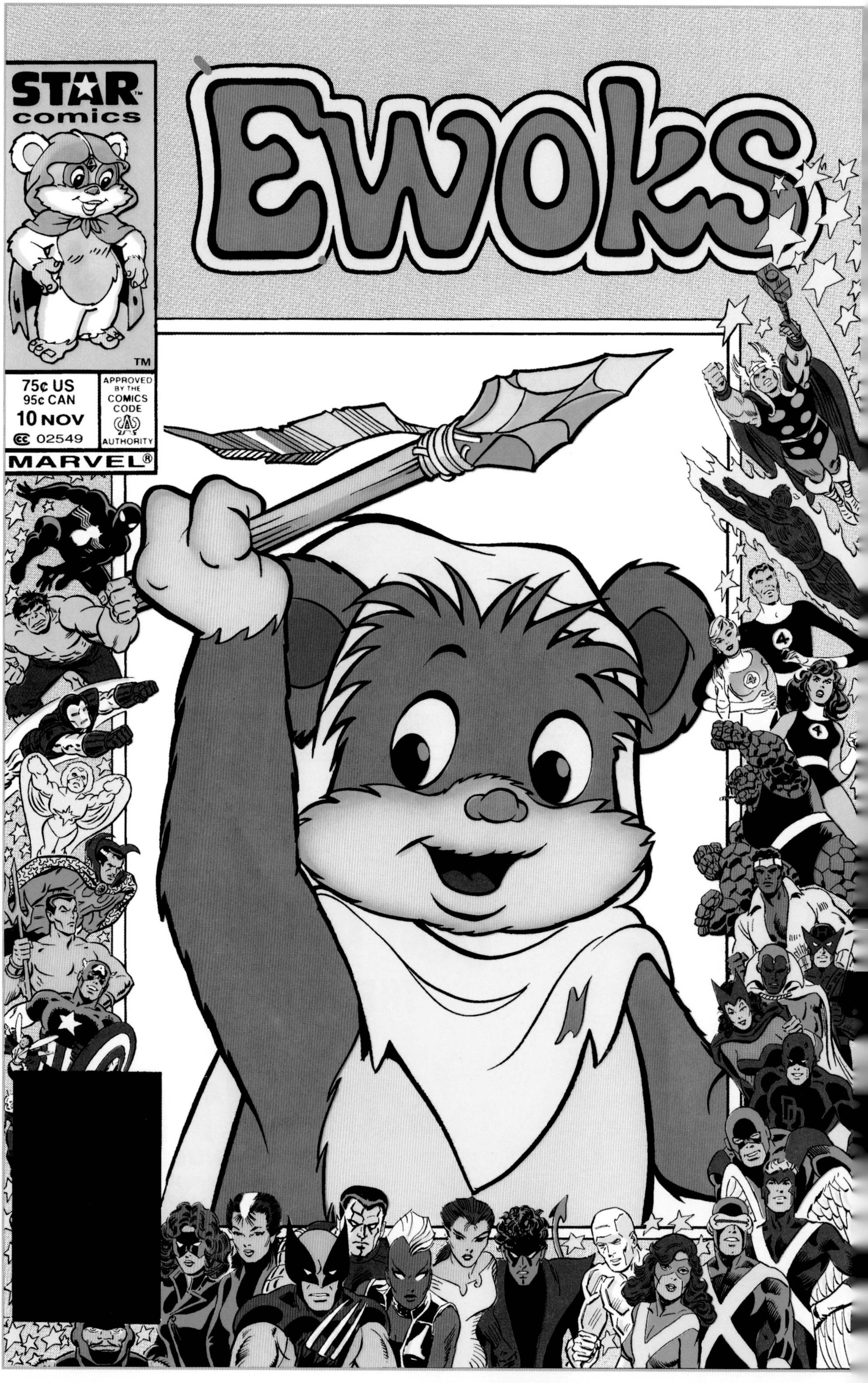
STAR comics
TM
Ewoks
75¢ US
95¢ CAN
10 NOV
02549
APPROVED BY THE COMICS CODE AUTHORITY
MARVEL®

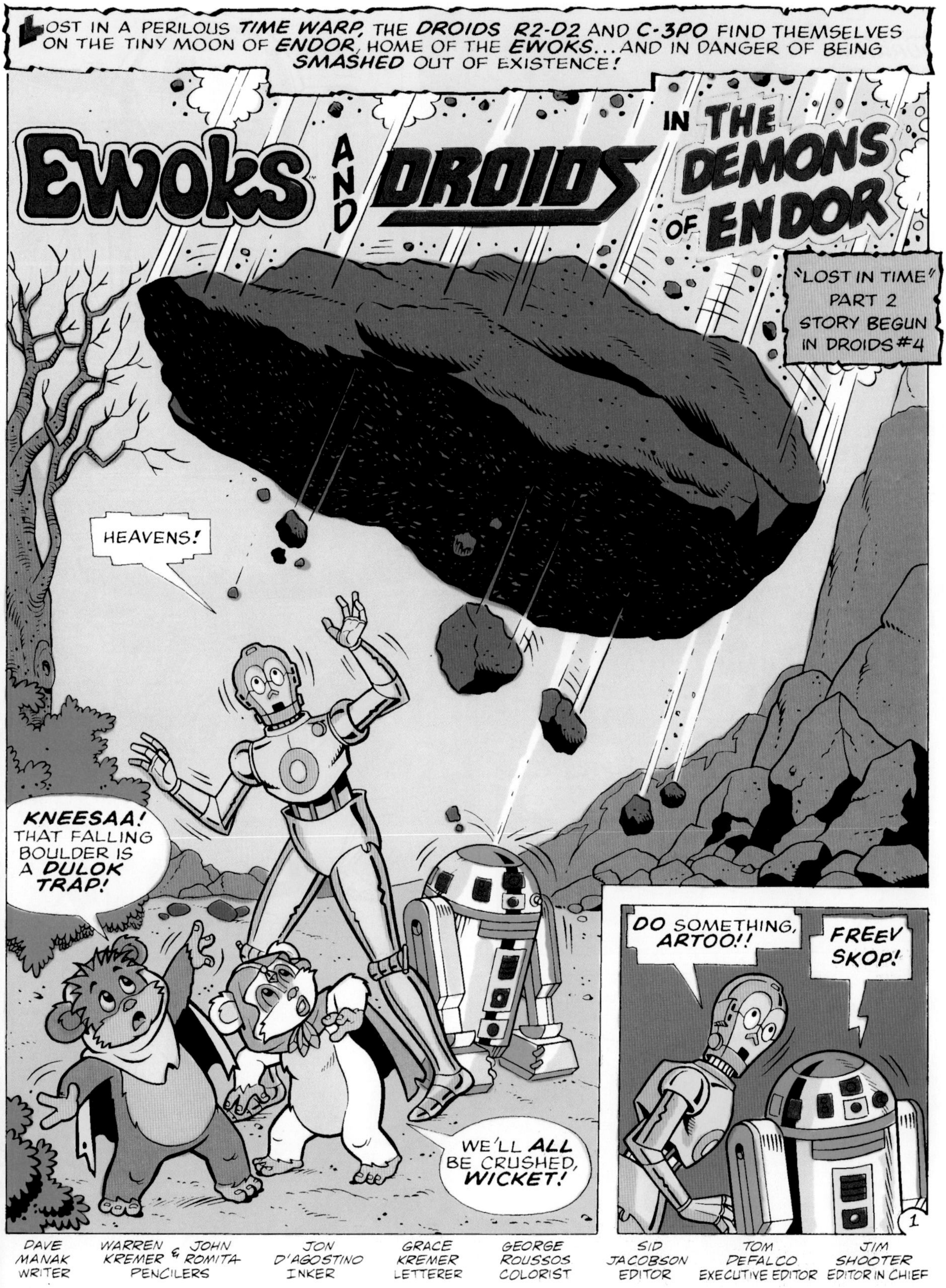
LOST IN A PERILOUS TIME WARP, THE DROIDS R2-D2 AND C-3PO FIND THEMSELVES ON THE TINY MOON OF ENDOR, HOME OF THE EWOKS... AND IN DANGER OF BEING SMASHED OUT OF EXISTENCE!
EWOKS AND DROIDS IN THE DEMONS OF ENDOR
"LOST IN TIME" PART 2 STORY BEGUN IN DROIDS #4
HEAVENS!
KNEESAA! THAT FALLING BOULDER IS A DULOK TRAP!
WE'LL ALL BE CRUSHED, WICKET!
DO SOMETHING, ARTOO!!
FREEV SKOP!
1
DAVE MANAK WRITER
WARREN KREMER & JOHN ROMITA PENCILERS
JON D'AGOSTINO INKER
GRACE KREMER LETTERER
GEORGE ROUSSOS COLORIST
SID JACOBSON EDITOR
TOM DEFALCO EXECUTIVE EDITOR
JIM SHOOTER EDITOR IN CHIEF

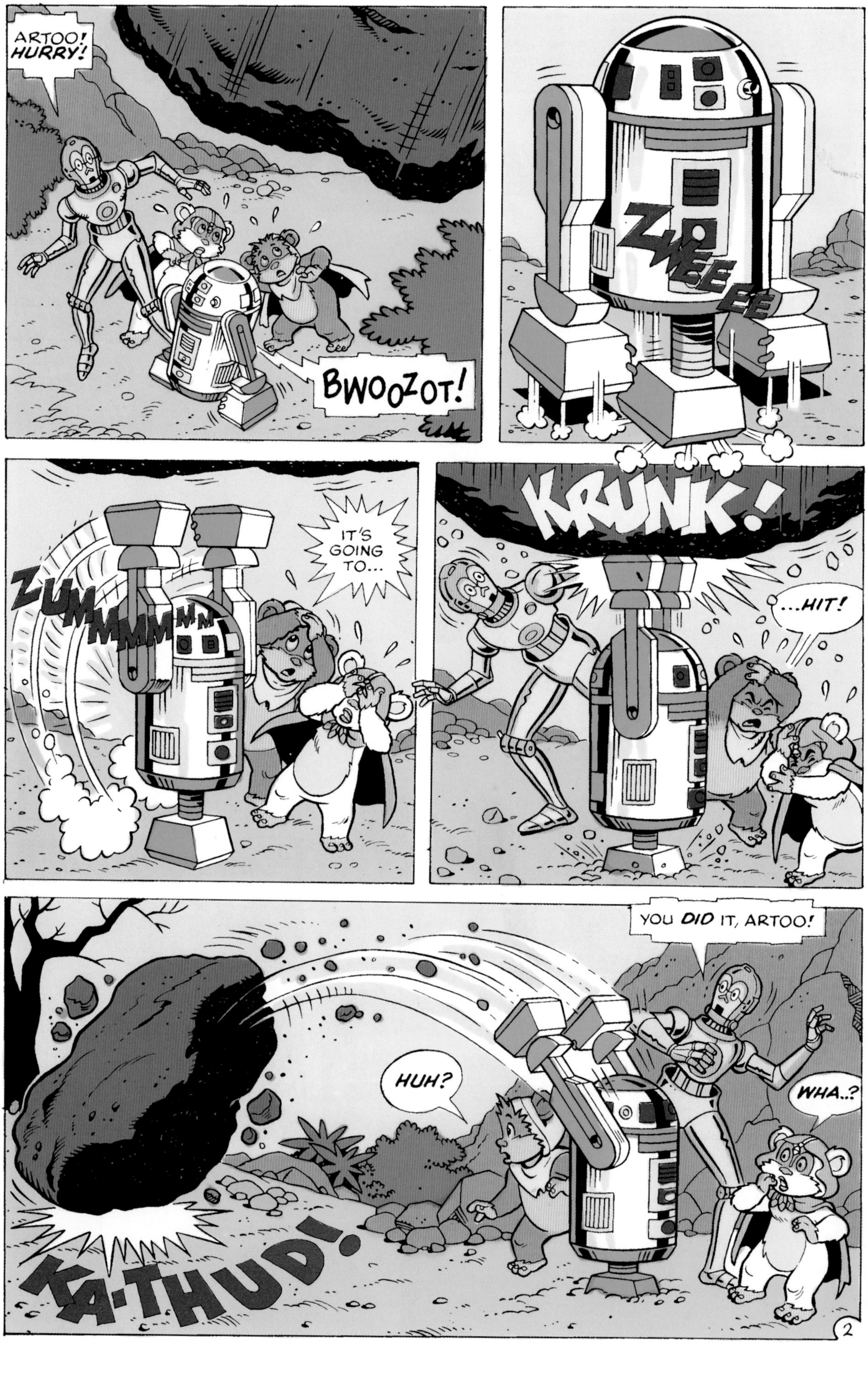
ARTOO! HURRY!
BWOOZOT!
ZWEEEEE
ZUMMMMMMM
IT'S GOING TO...
KRUNK!
...HIT!
YOU DID IT, ARTOO!
HUH?
WHA..?
KA-THUD!
2

WICKET! THE DEMONS SAVED US!

DEMONS? MY WORD! WE'RE ANYTHING BUT THAT!

I'M C-3PO AND THIS IS R2-D2...SIMPLE SPACE TRAVELERS IN SEARCH OF A LOST COMPANION!

I ASSURE YOU THERE IS NO NEED TO BE AFRAID!

YOU SPEAK OUR LANGUAGE!

OF COURSE! THOUGH IT IS AN OBSCURE DIALECT OF THE INNER ZUMA REGION, I HAPPEN TO BE FLUENT IN SIX MILLION FORMS OF LANGUAGES, AND...

FZZZOT NEE SPLOFZ!

OH, YES! FORGIVE ME! BACK TO THE POINT!

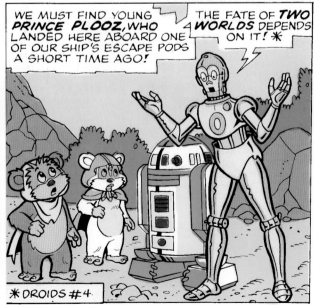

WE MUST FIND YOUNG PRINCE PLOOZ, WHO LANDED HERE ABOARD ONE OF OUR SHIP'S ESCAPE PODS A SHORT TIME AGO!

THE FATE OF TWO WORLDS DEPENDS ON IT! *

* DROIDS #4

WICKET! THEY MUST BE SPEAKING OF THE STAR CHILD!

SPAX ZOOT?

STAR CHILD?

3

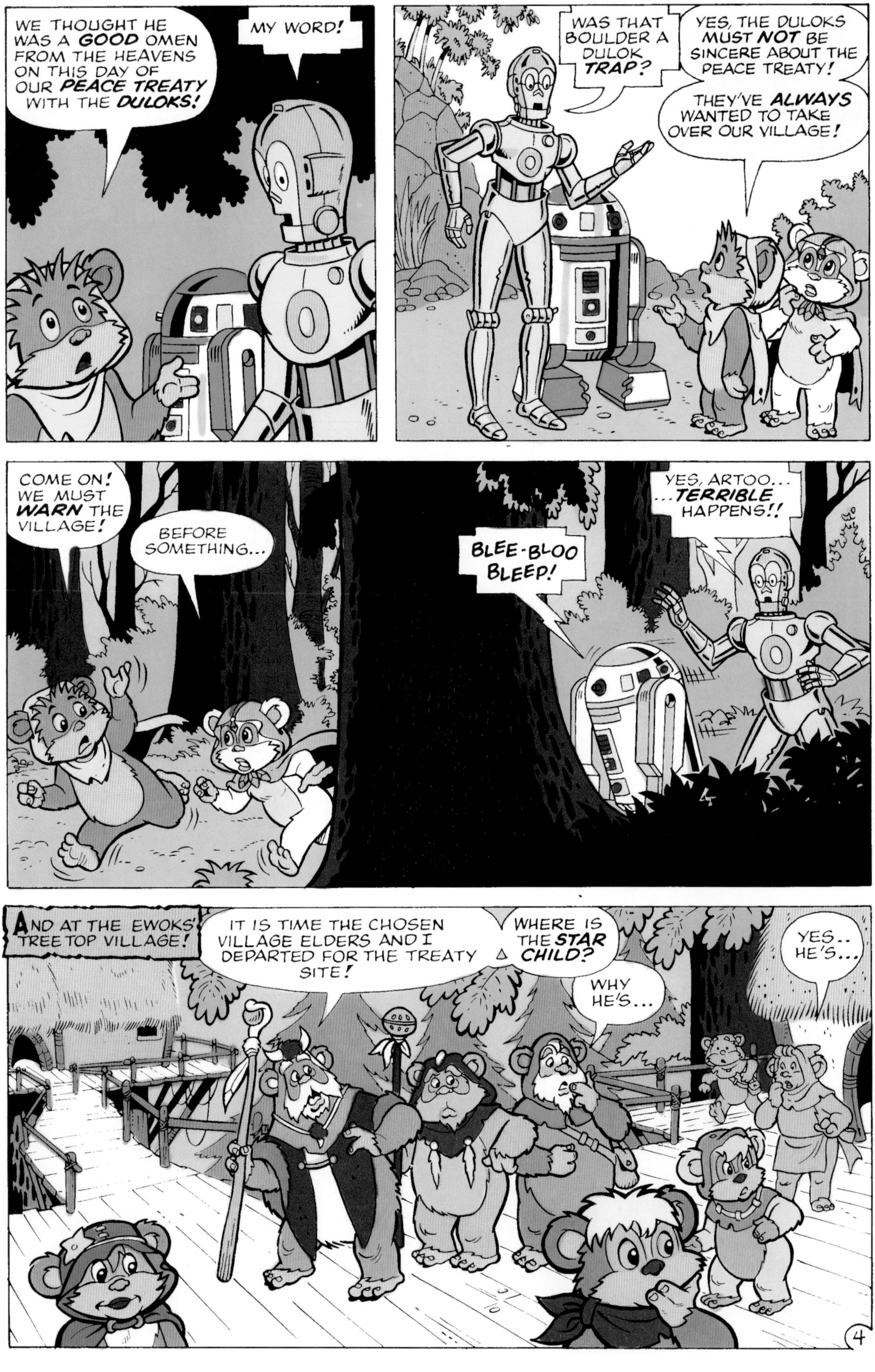
WE THOUGHT HE WAS A GOOD OMEN FROM THE HEAVENS ON THIS DAY OF OUR PEACE TREATY WITH THE DULOKS!
MY WORD!
WAS THAT BOULDER A DULOK TRAP?
YES, THE DULOKS MUST NOT BE SINCERE ABOUT THE PEACE TREATY!
THEY'VE ALWAYS WANTED TO TAKE OVER OUR VILLAGE!
COME ON! WE MUST WARN THE VILLAGE!
BEFORE SOMETHING...
BLEE-BLOO BLEEP!
YES, ARTOO... ...TERRIBLE HAPPENS!!
AND AT THE EWOKS' TREE TOP VILLAGE!
IT IS TIME THE CHOSEN VILLAGE ELDERS AND I DEPARTED FOR THE TREATY SITE!
WHERE IS THE STAR CHILD?
WHY HE'S...
YES.. HE'S...
4

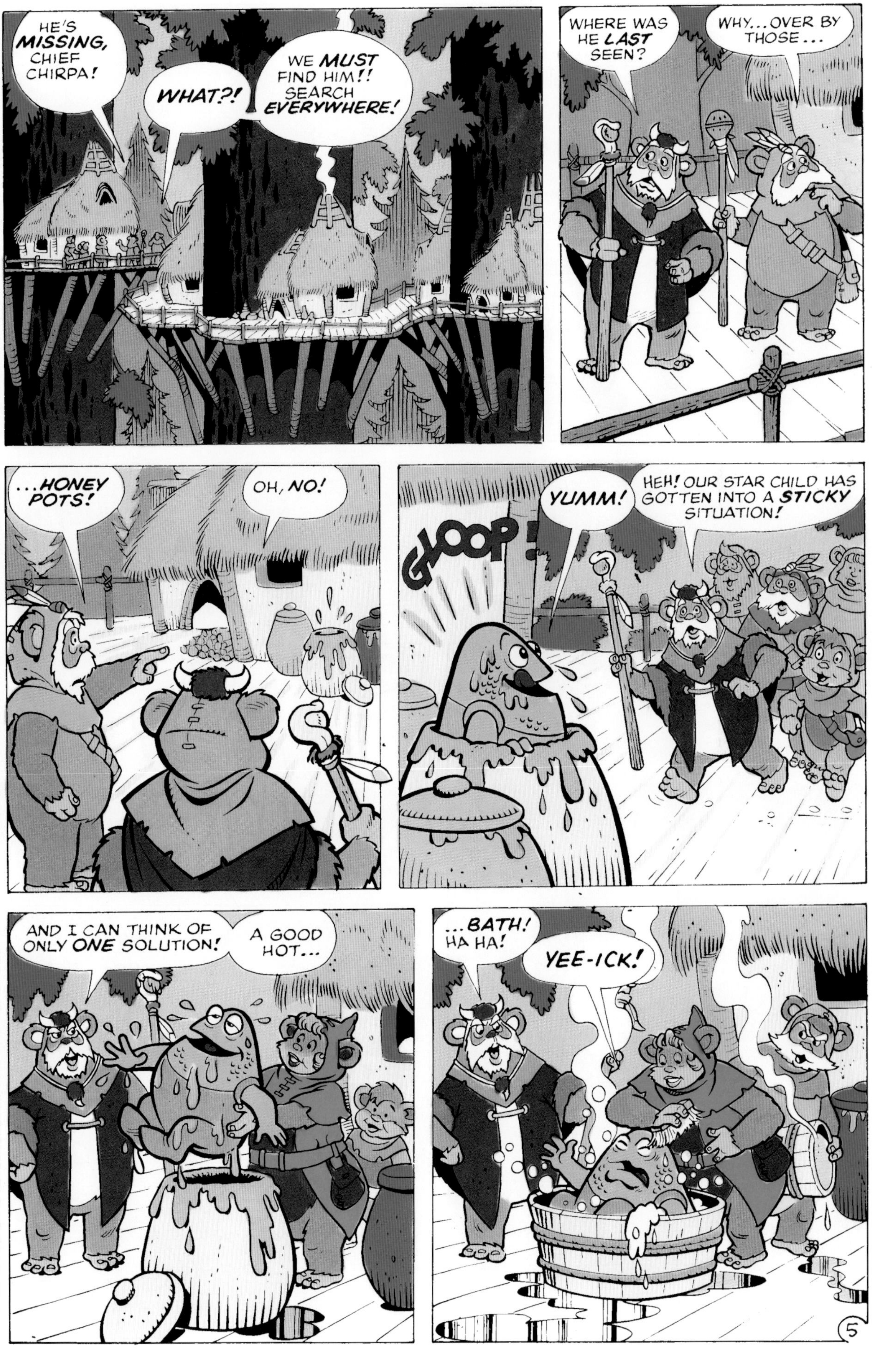
HE'S MISSING, CHIEF CHIRPA!
WHAT?!
WE MUST FIND HIM!! SEARCH EVERYWHERE!
WHERE WAS HE LAST SEEN?
WHY... OVER BY THOSE...
...HONEY POTS!
OH, NO!
GLOOP!
YUMM!
HEH! OUR STAR CHILD HAS GOTTEN INTO A STICKY SITUATION!
AND I CAN THINK OF ONLY ONE SOLUTION!
A GOOD HOT...
...BATH! HA HA!
YEE-ICK!
5

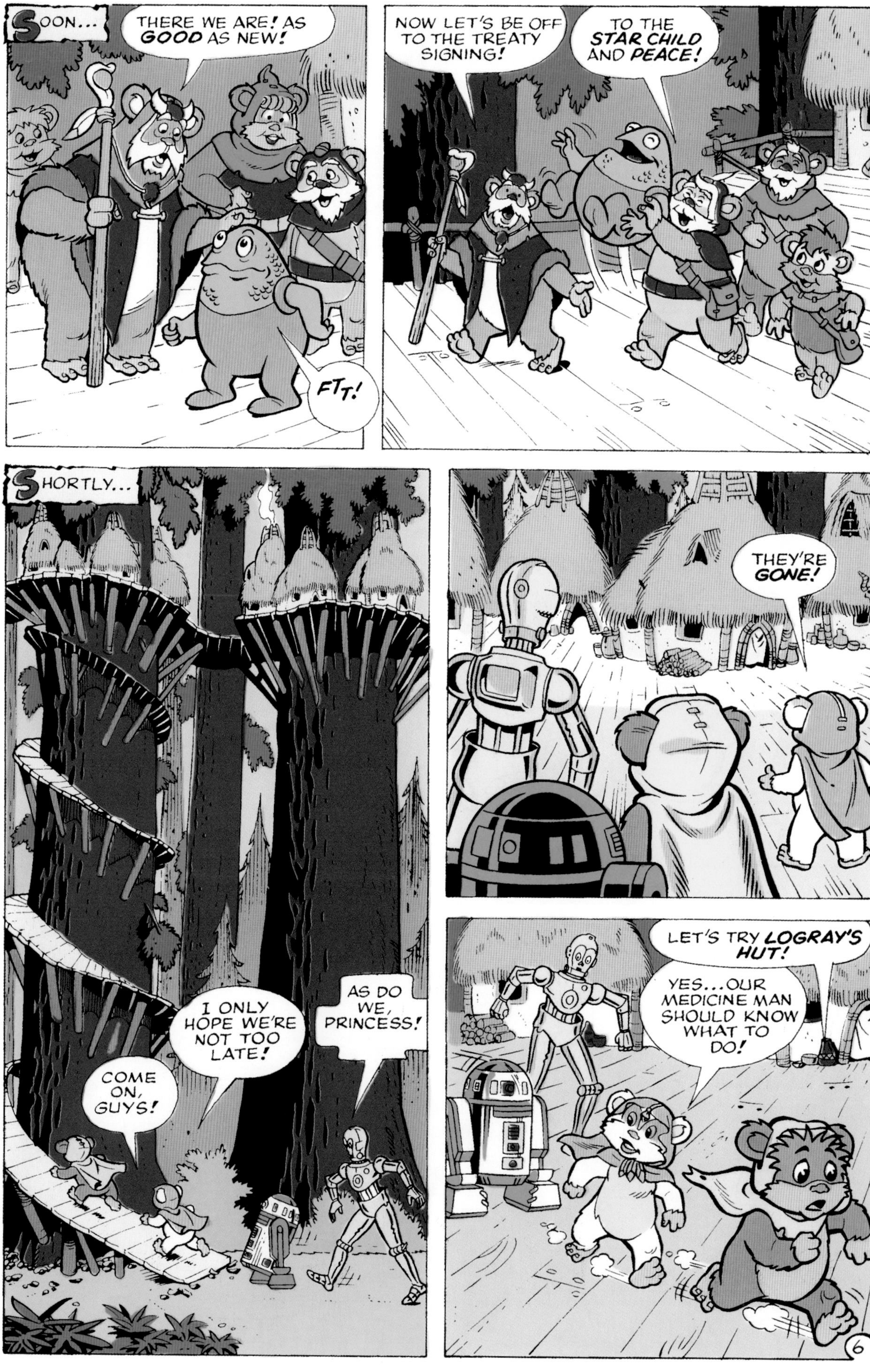
SOON...
THERE WE ARE! AS GOOD AS NEW!
FTT!
NOW LET'S BE OFF TO THE TREATY SIGNING!
TO THE STAR CHILD AND PEACE!
SHORTLY...
COME ON, GUYS!
I ONLY HOPE WE'RE NOT TOO LATE!
AS DO WE, PRINCESS!
THEY'RE GONE!
LET'S TRY LOGRAY'S HUT!
YES...OUR MEDICINE MAN SHOULD KNOW WHAT TO DO!
6

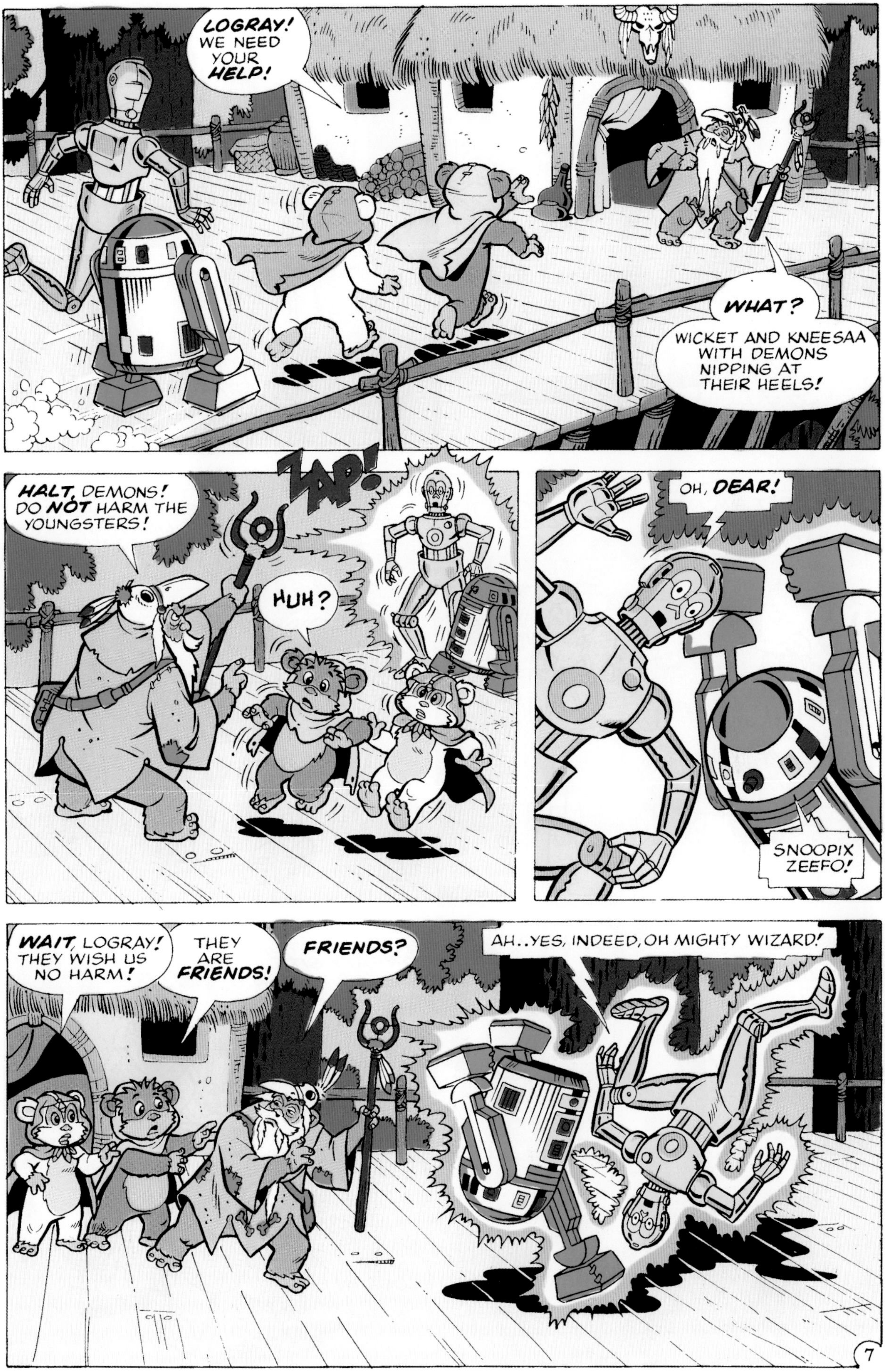
LOGRAY! WE NEED YOUR HELP!
WHAT?
WICKET AND KNEESAA WITH DEMONS NIPPING AT THEIR HEELS!
HALT, DEMONS! DO NOT HARM THE YOUNGSTERS!
ZAP!
HUH?
OH, DEAR!
SNOOPIX ZEEFO!
WAIT, LOGRAY! THEY WISH US NO HARM!
THEY ARE FRIENDS!
FRIENDS?
AH..YES, INDEED, OH MIGHTY WIZARD!
7

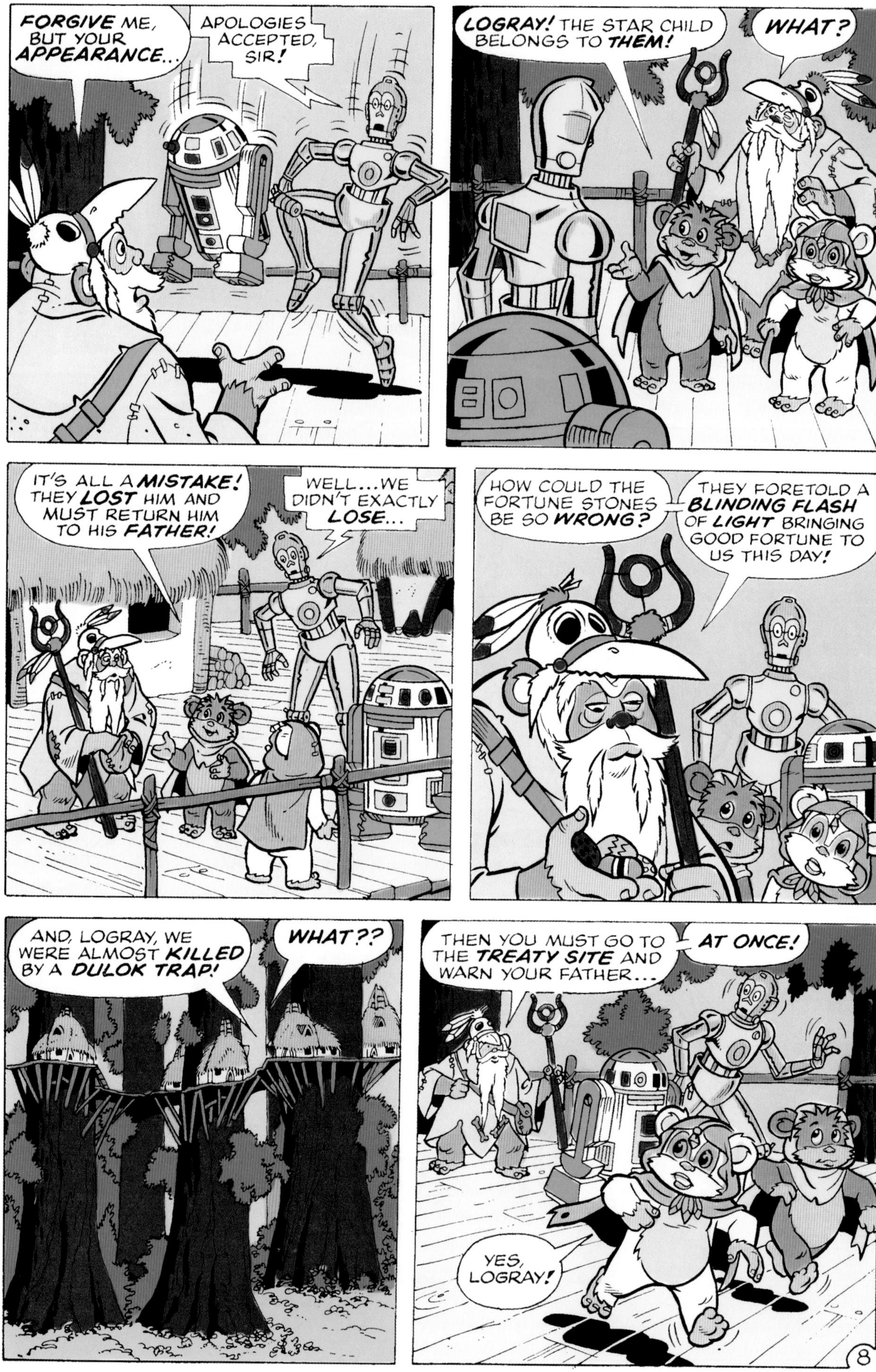
FORGIVE ME, BUT YOUR APPEARANCE...
APOLOGIES ACCEPTED, SIR!
LOGRAY! THE STAR CHILD BELONGS TO THEM!
WHAT?
IT'S ALL A MISTAKE! THEY LOST HIM AND MUST RETURN HIM TO HIS FATHER!
WELL...WE DIDN'T EXACTLY LOSE...
HOW COULD THE FORTUNE STONES BE SO WRONG?
THEY FORETOLD A BLINDING FLASH OF LIGHT BRINGING GOOD FORTUNE TO US THIS DAY!
AND, LOGRAY, WE WERE ALMOST KILLED BY A DULOK TRAP!
WHAT??
THEN YOU MUST GO TO THE TREATY SITE AND WARN YOUR FATHER...
AT ONCE!
YES, LOGRAY!
8

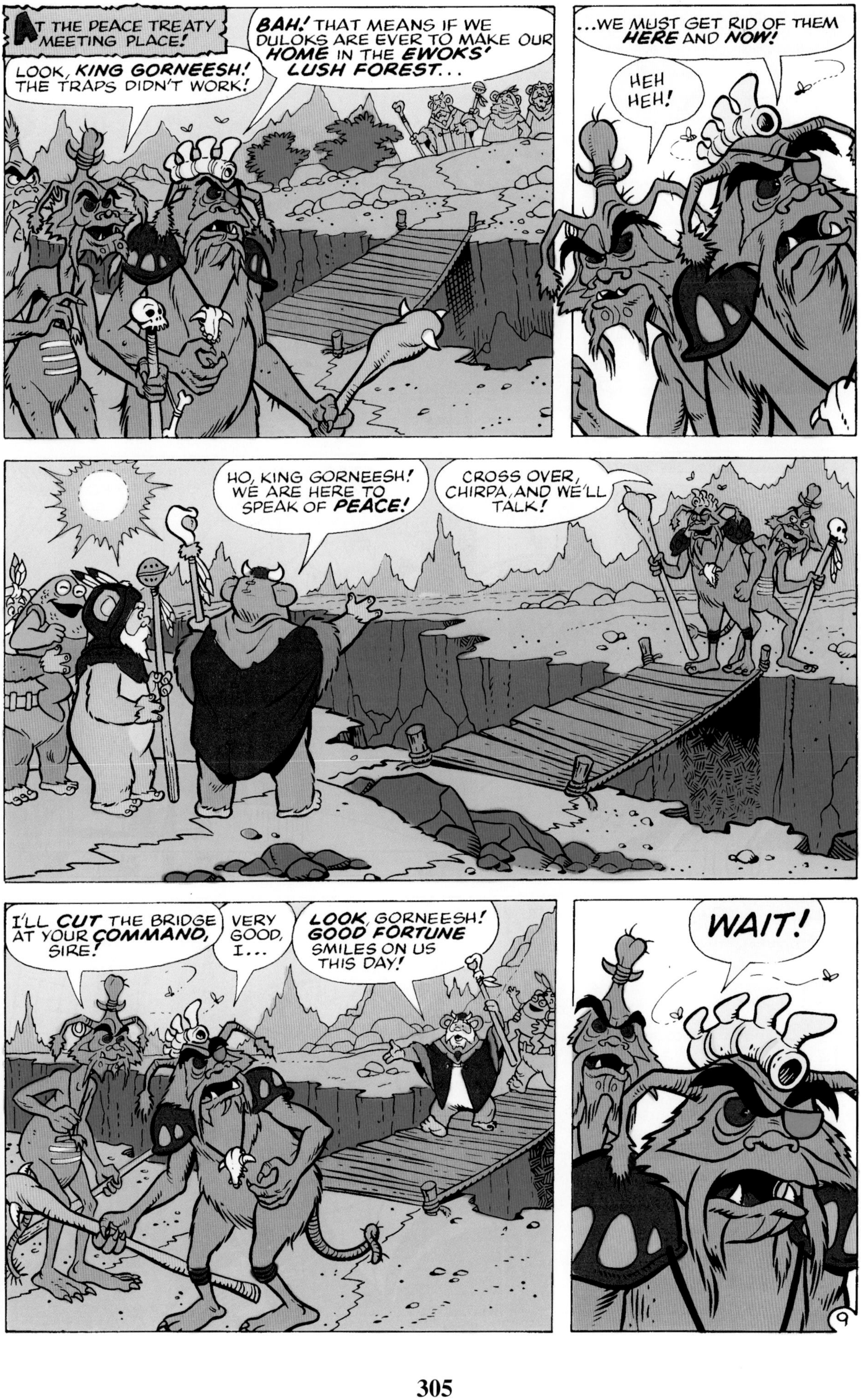
AT THE PEACE TREATY MEETING PLACE!
LOOK, KING GORNEESH! THE TRAPS DIDN'T WORK!
BAH! THAT MEANS IF WE DULOKS ARE EVER TO MAKE OUR HOME IN THE EWOKS' LUSH FOREST...
...WE MUST GET RID OF THEM HERE AND NOW!
HEH HEH!
HO, KING GORNEESH! WE ARE HERE TO SPEAK OF PEACE!
CROSS OVER, CHIRPA, AND WE'LL TALK!
I'LL CUT THE BRIDGE AT YOUR COMMAND, SIRE!
VERY GOOD, I...
LOOK, GORNEESH! GOOD FORTUNE SMILES ON US THIS DAY!
WAIT!
9

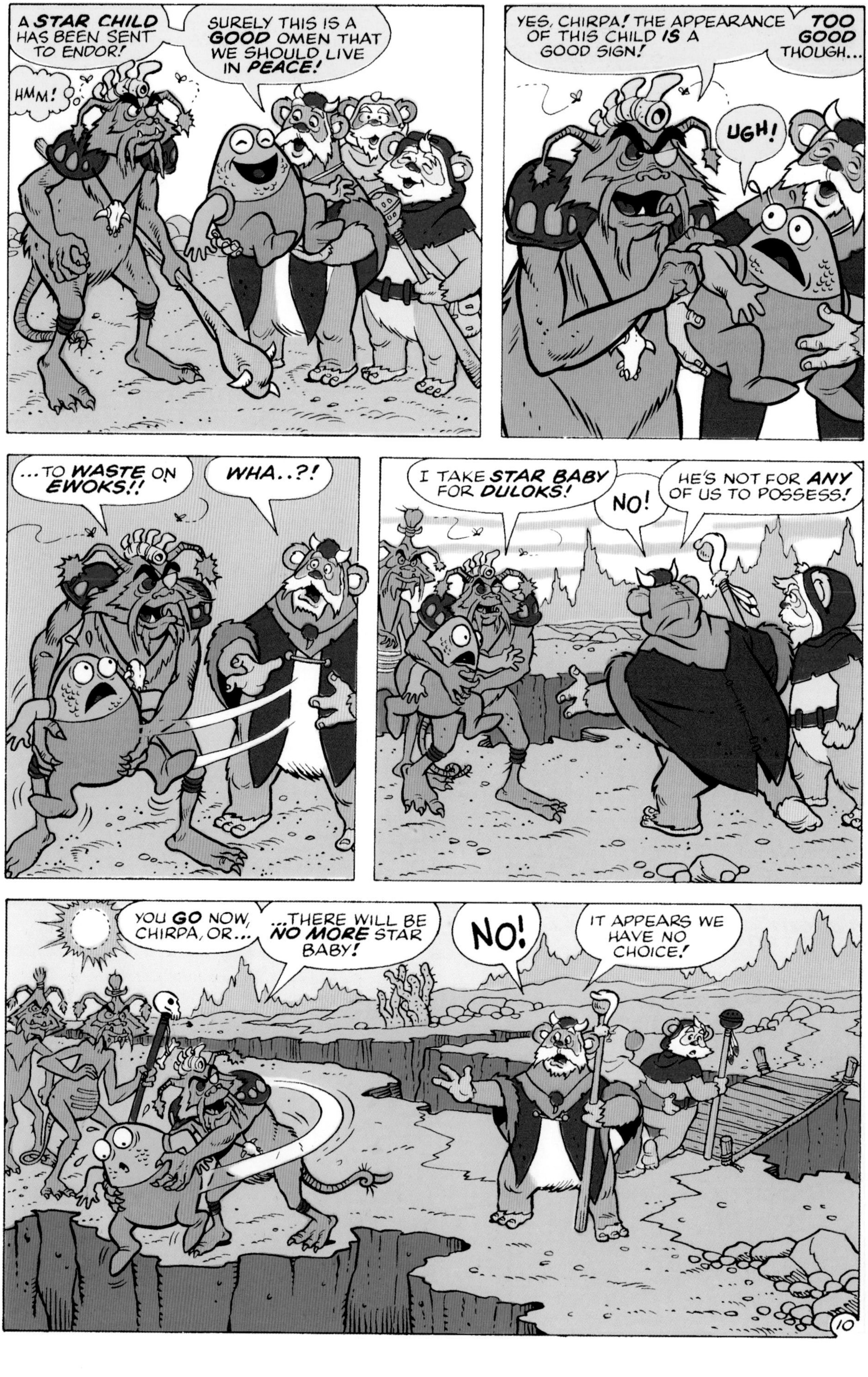
A STAR CHILD HAS BEEN SENT TO ENDOR!
HMM!
SURELY THIS IS A GOOD OMEN THAT WE SHOULD LIVE IN PEACE!
YES, CHIRPA! THE APPEARANCE OF THIS CHILD IS A GOOD SIGN!
TOO GOOD THOUGH...
UGH!
...TO WASTE ON EWOKS!!
WHA..?!
I TAKE STAR BABY FOR DULOKS!
NO!
HE'S NOT FOR ANY OF US TO POSSESS!
YOU GO NOW, CHIRPA, OR...
...THERE WILL BE NO MORE STAR BABY!
NO!
IT APPEARS WE HAVE NO CHOICE!
10

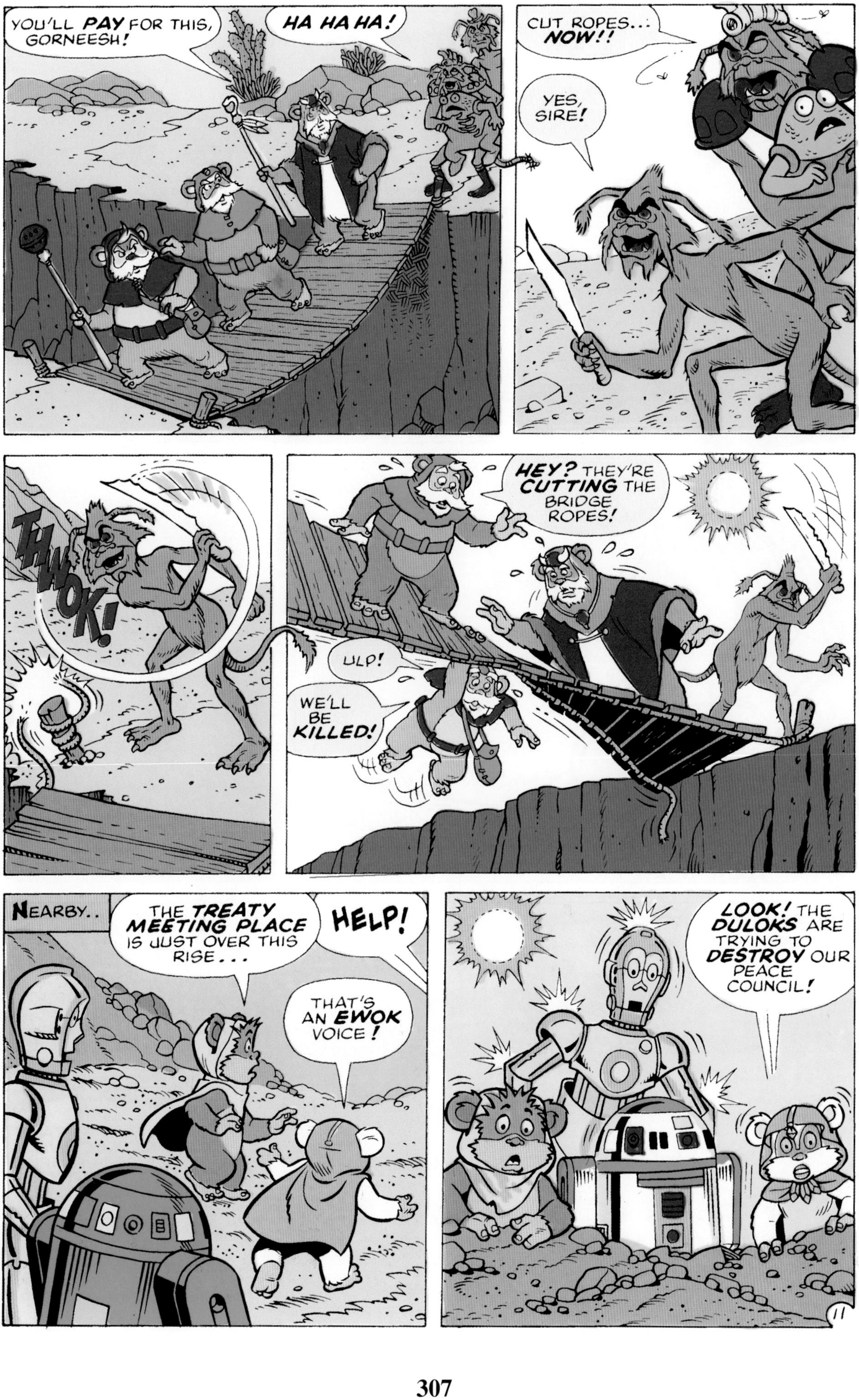
YOU'LL PAY FOR THIS, GORNEESH!
HA HA HA!
CUT ROPES... NOW!!
YES, SIRE!
THWOK!
HEY? THEY'RE CUTTING THE BRIDGE ROPES!
ULP!
WE'LL BE KILLED!
NEARBY..
THE TREATY MEETING PLACE IS JUST OVER THIS RISE...
HELP!
THAT'S AN EWOK VOICE!
LOOK! THE DULOKS ARE TRYING TO DESTROY OUR PEACE COUNCIL!
11

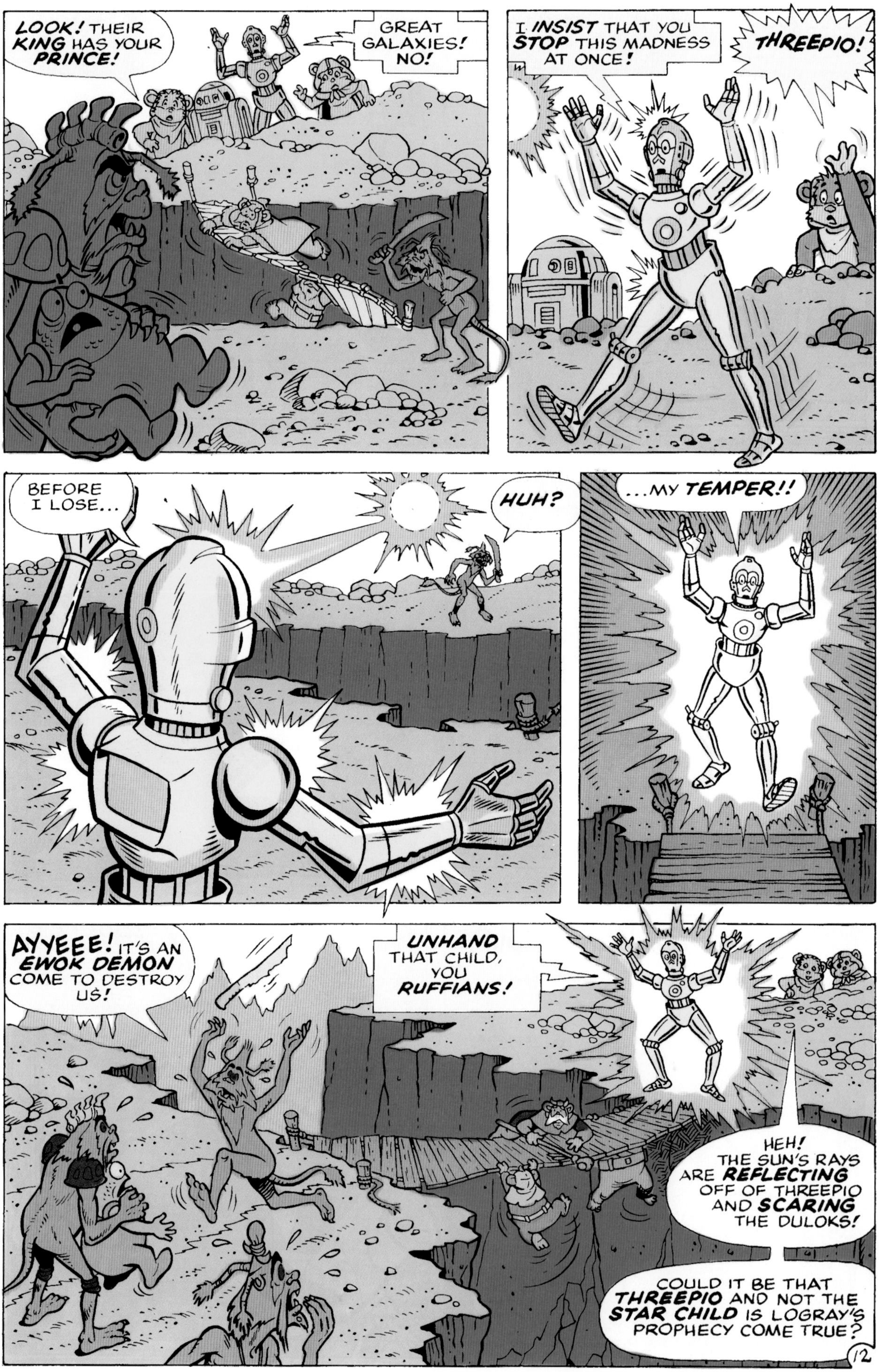
LOOK! THEIR KING HAS YOUR PRINCE!
GREAT GALAXIES! NO!
I INSIST THAT YOU STOP THIS MADNESS AT ONCE!
THREEPIO!
BEFORE I LOSE...
HUH?
...MY TEMPER!!
AYYEEE! IT'S AN EWOK DEMON COME TO DESTROY US!
UNHAND THAT CHILD, YOU RUFFIANS!
HEH! THE SUN'S RAYS ARE REFLECTING OFF OF THREEPIO AND SCARING THE DULOKS!
COULD IT BE THAT THREEPIO AND NOT THE STAR CHILD IS LOGRAY'S PROPHECY COME TRUE?
12

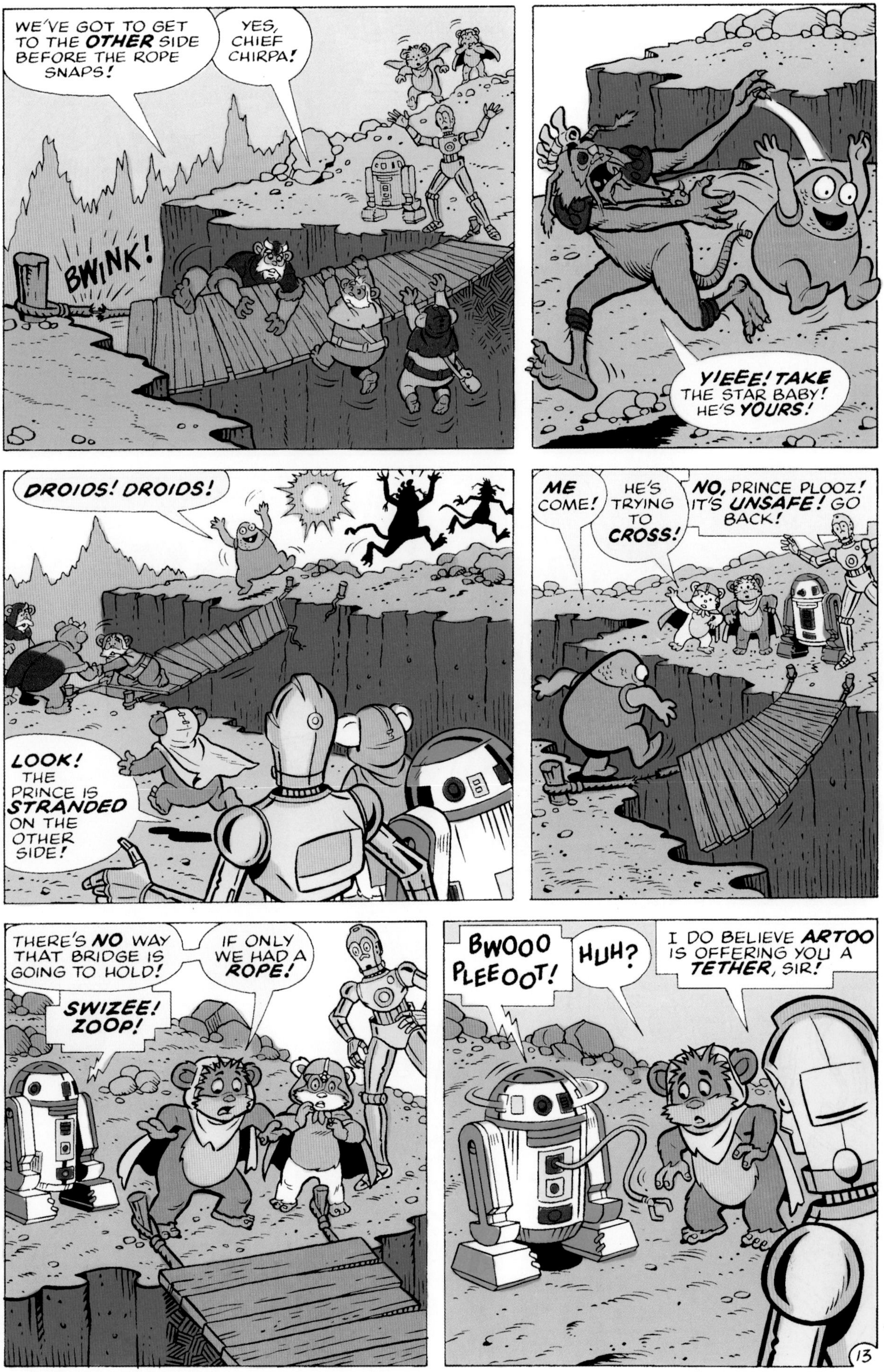
WE'VE GOT TO GET TO THE OTHER SIDE BEFORE THE ROPE SNAPS!
YES, CHIEF CHIRPA!
BWINK!
YIEEE! TAKE THE STAR BABY! HE'S YOURS!
DROIDS! DROIDS!
LOOK! THE PRINCE IS STRANDED ON THE OTHER SIDE!
ME COME!
HE'S TRYING TO CROSS!
NO, PRINCE PLOOZ! IT'S UNSAFE! GO BACK!
THERE'S NO WAY THAT BRIDGE IS GOING TO HOLD!
IF ONLY WE HAD A ROPE!
SWIZEE! ZOOP!
BWOOO PLEEOOT!
HUH?
I DO BELIEVE ARTOO IS OFFERING YOU A TETHER, SIR!
13

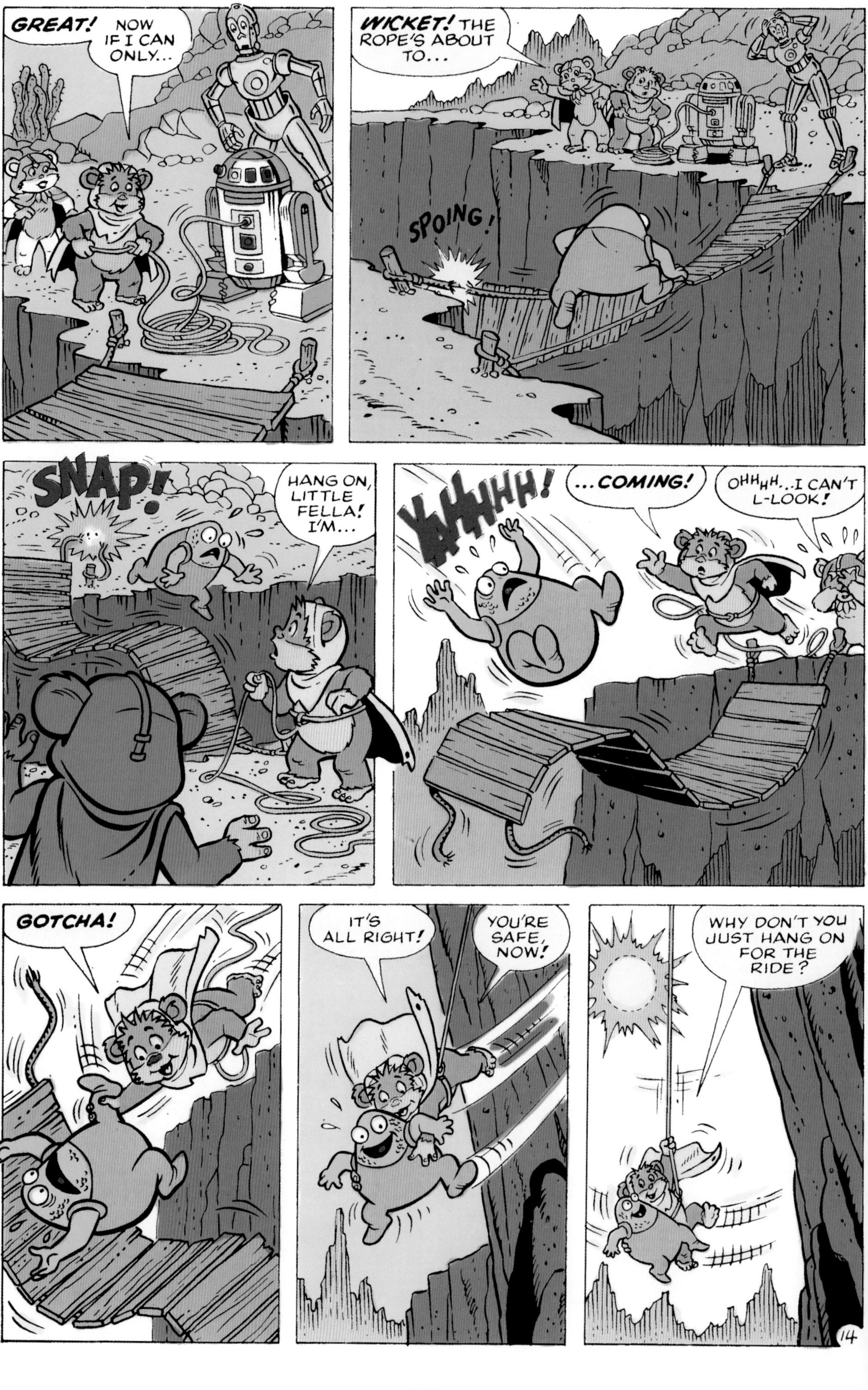
GREAT! NOW IF I CAN ONLY...
WICKET! THE ROPE'S ABOUT TO...
SPOING!
SNAP!
HANG ON, LITTLE FELLA! I'M...
YAAHHH!
...COMING!
OHHHH...I CAN'T L-LOOK!
GOTCHA!
IT'S ALL RIGHT!
YOU'RE SAFE, NOW!
WHY DON'T YOU JUST HANG ON FOR THE RIDE?
14

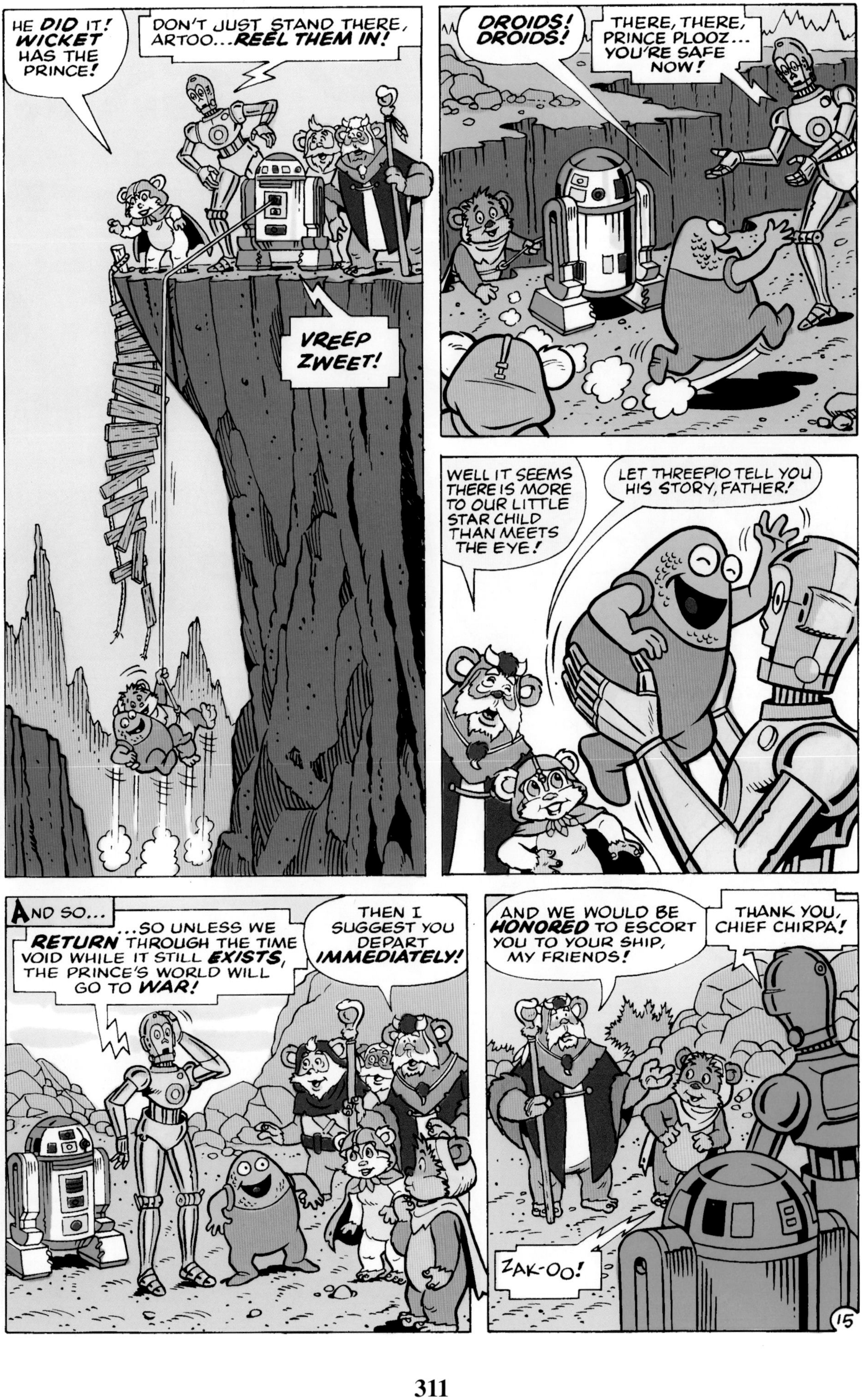
HE DID IT! WICKET HAS THE PRINCE!
DON'T JUST STAND THERE, ARTOO...REEL THEM IN!
VREEP ZWEET!
DROIDS! DROIDS!
THERE, THERE, PRINCE PLOOZ... YOU'RE SAFE NOW!
WELL IT SEEMS THERE IS MORE TO OUR LITTLE STAR CHILD THAN MEETS THE EYE!
LET THREEPIO TELL YOU HIS STORY, FATHER!
AND SO...
...SO UNLESS WE RETURN THROUGH THE TIME VOID WHILE IT STILL EXISTS, THE PRINCE'S WORLD WILL GO TO WAR!
THEN I SUGGEST YOU DEPART IMMEDIATELY!
AND WE WOULD BE HONORED TO ESCORT YOU TO YOUR SHIP, MY FRIENDS!
THANK YOU, CHIEF CHIRPA!
ZAK-OO!
15

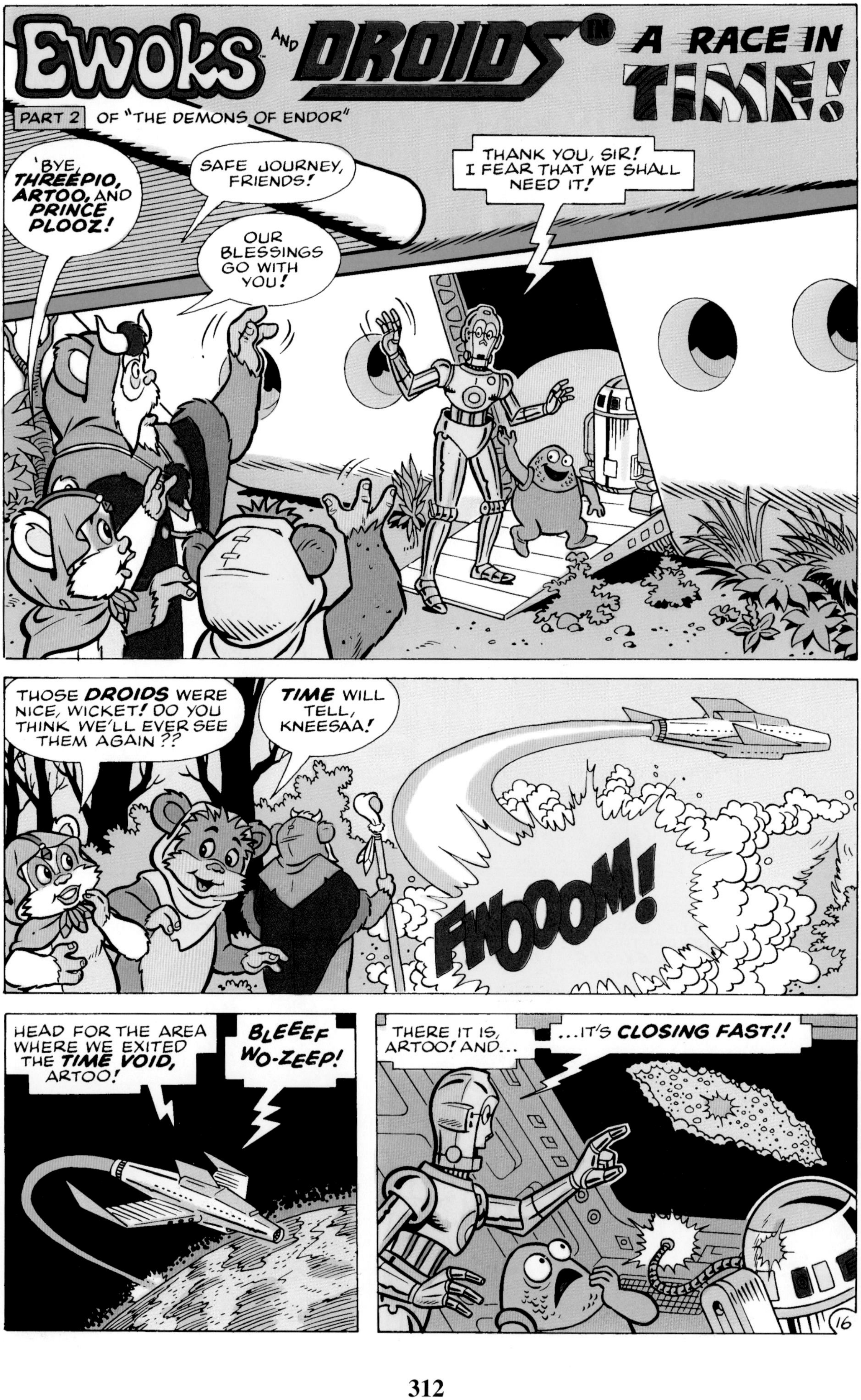
Ewoks AND DROIDS IN A RACE IN TIME!
PART 2 OF "THE DEMONS OF ENDOR"
'BYE, THREEPIO, ARTOO, AND PRINCE PLOOZ!
SAFE JOURNEY, FRIENDS!
OUR BLESSINGS GO WITH YOU!
THANK YOU, SIR! I FEAR THAT WE SHALL NEED IT!
THOSE DROIDS WERE NICE, WICKET! DO YOU THINK WE'LL EVER SEE THEM AGAIN??
TIME WILL TELL, KNEESAA!
FWOOOM!
HEAD FOR THE AREA WHERE WE EXITED THE TIME VOID, ARTOO!
BLEEEF WO-ZEEP!
THERE IT IS, ARTOO! AND...
...IT'S CLOSING FAST!!
16

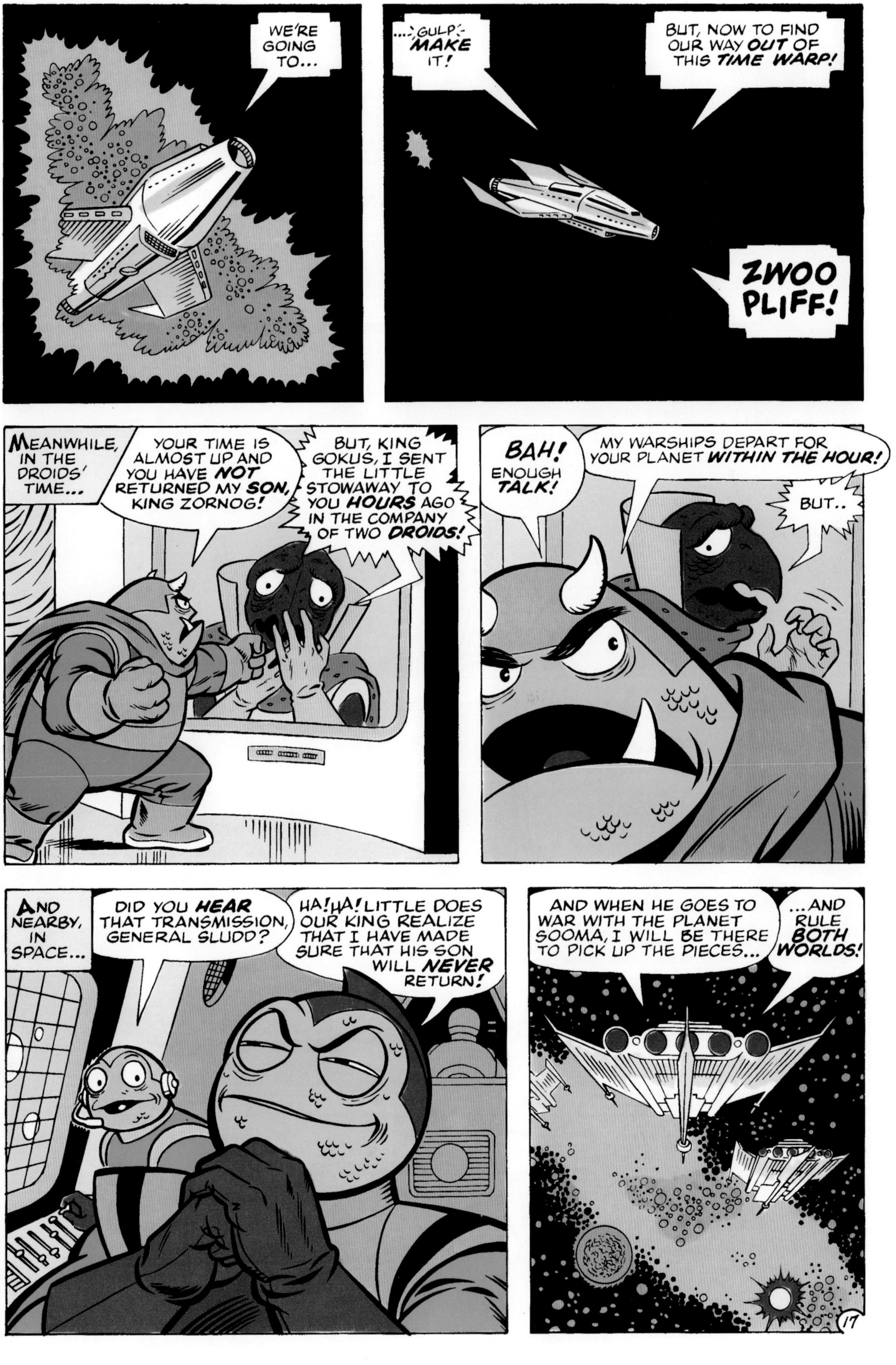
WE'RE GOING TO...
...GULP- MAKE IT!
BUT, NOW TO FIND OUR WAY OUT OF THIS TIME WARP!
ZWOO PLIFF!
MEANWHILE, IN THE DROIDS' TIME...
YOUR TIME IS ALMOST UP AND YOU HAVE NOT RETURNED MY SON, KING ZORNOG!
BUT, KING GOKUS, I SENT THE LITTLE STOWAWAY TO YOU HOURS AGO IN THE COMPANY OF TWO DROIDS!
BAH! ENOUGH TALK!
MY WARSHIPS DEPART FOR YOUR PLANET WITHIN THE HOUR!
BUT..
AND NEARBY, IN SPACE...
DID YOU HEAR THAT TRANSMISSION, GENERAL SLUDD?
HA! HA! LITTLE DOES OUR KING REALIZE THAT I HAVE MADE SURE THAT HIS SON WILL NEVER RETURN!
AND WHEN HE GOES TO WAR WITH THE PLANET SOOMA, I WILL BE THERE TO PICK UP THE PIECES...
...AND RULE BOTH WORLDS!
17

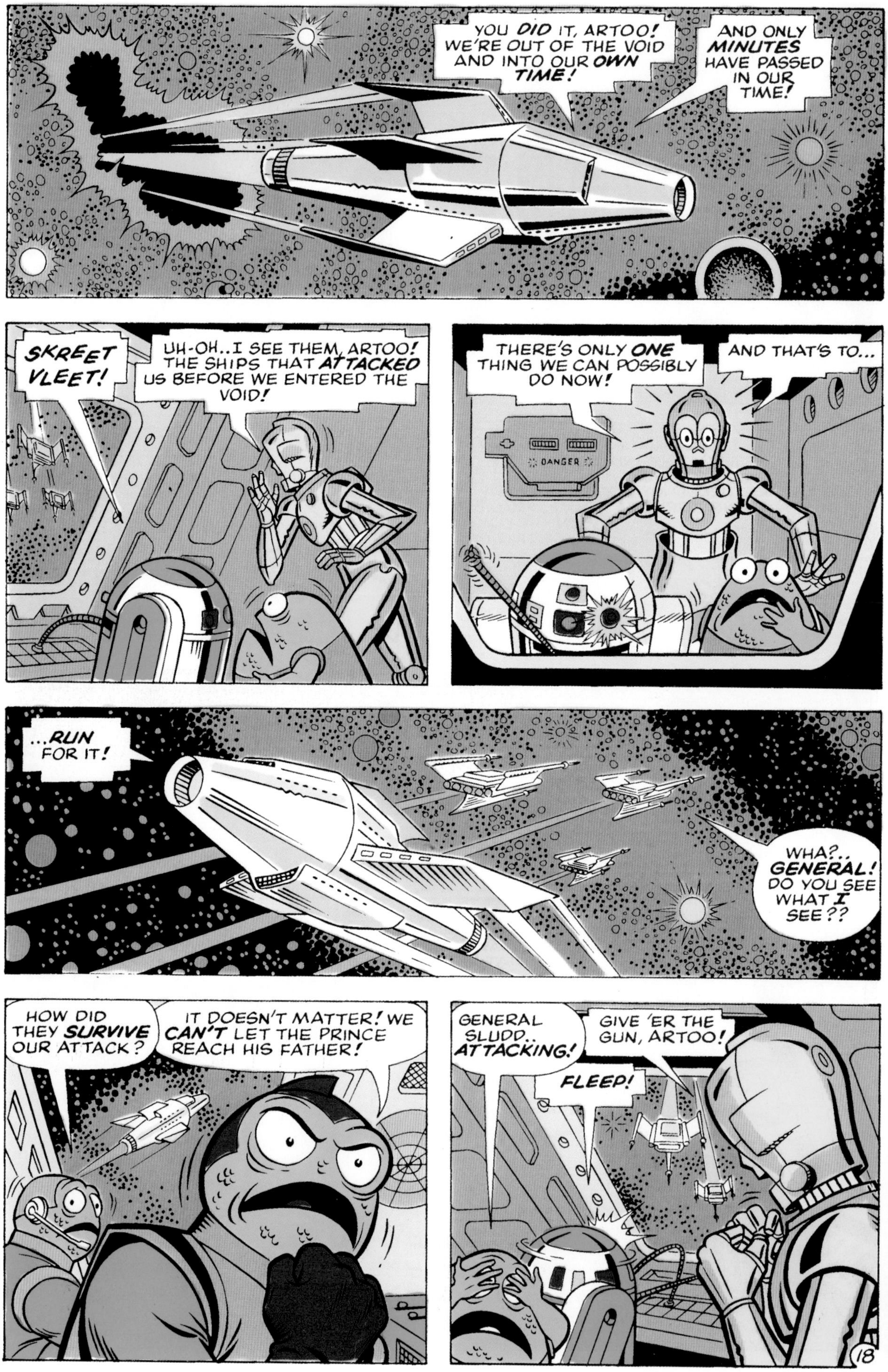

YOU **DID** IT, ARTOO! WE'RE OUT OF THE VOID AND INTO OUR **OWN TIME!**
AND ONLY **MINUTES** HAVE PASSED IN OUR TIME!
SKREEET VLEET!
UH-OH.. I SEE THEM, ARTOO! THE SHIPS THAT **ATTACKED** US BEFORE WE ENTERED THE VOID!
THERE'S ONLY **ONE** THING WE CAN POSSIBLY DO NOW!
DANGER
AND THAT'S TO...
...**RUN** FOR IT!
WHA?.. **GENERAL!** DO YOU SEE WHAT **I** SEE??
HOW DID THEY **SURVIVE** OUR ATTACK?
IT DOESN'T MATTER! WE **CAN'T** LET THE PRINCE REACH HIS FATHER!
GENERAL SLUDD.. **ATTACKING!**
GIVE 'ER THE GUN, ARTOO!
FLEEP!
18

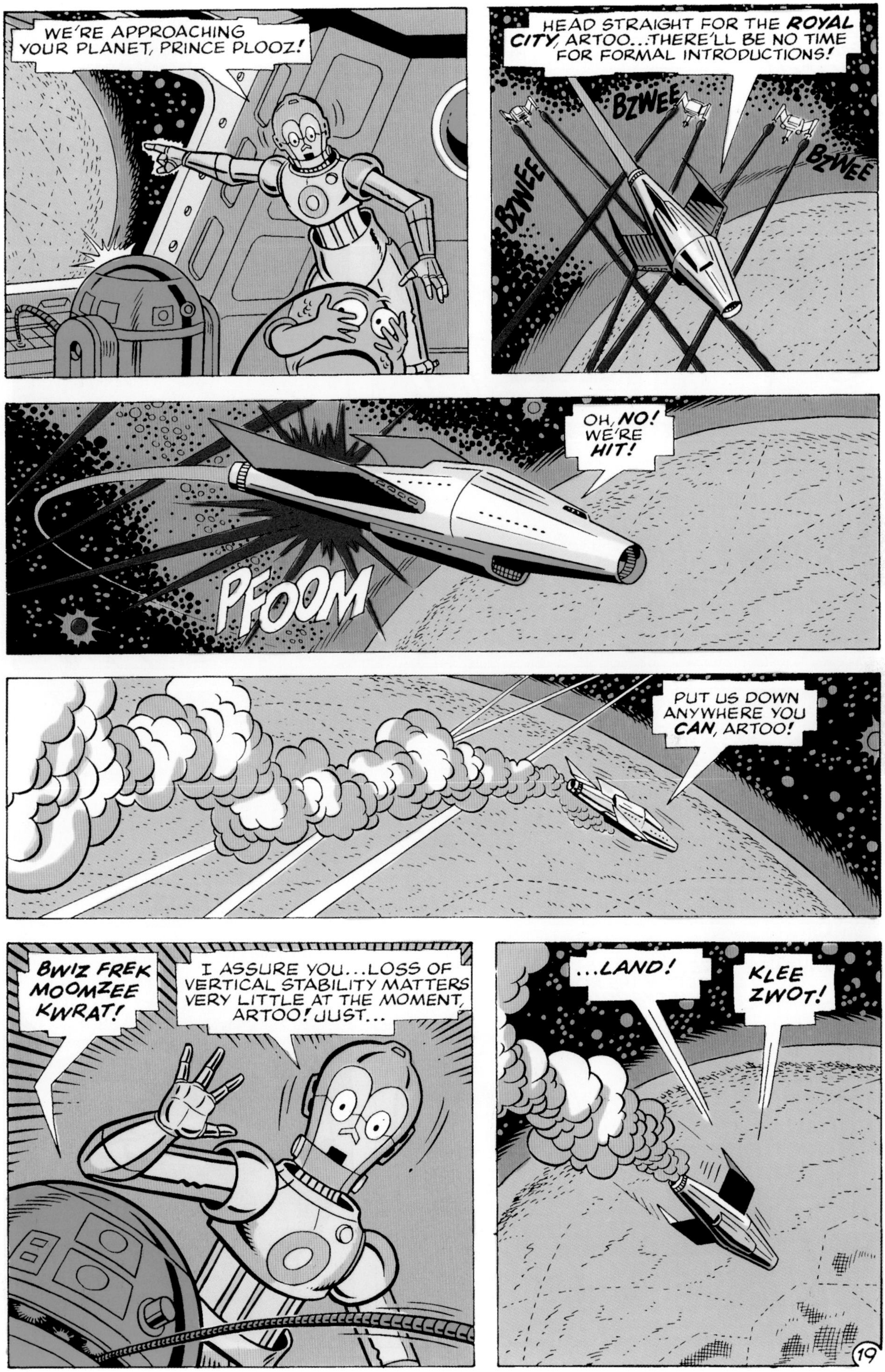

WE'RE APPROACHING YOUR PLANET, PRINCE PLOOZ!
HEAD STRAIGHT FOR THE ROYAL CITY, ARTOO...THERE'LL BE NO TIME FOR FORMAL INTRODUCTIONS!
BZWEE
BZWEE
BZWEE
OH, NO! WE'RE HIT!
PFOOM
PUT US DOWN ANYWHERE YOU CAN, ARTOO!
BWIZ FREK MOOMZEE KWRAT!
I ASSURE YOU...LOSS OF VERTICAL STABILITY MATTERS VERY LITTLE AT THE MOMENT, ARTOO! JUST...
...LAND!
KLEE ZWOT!
19

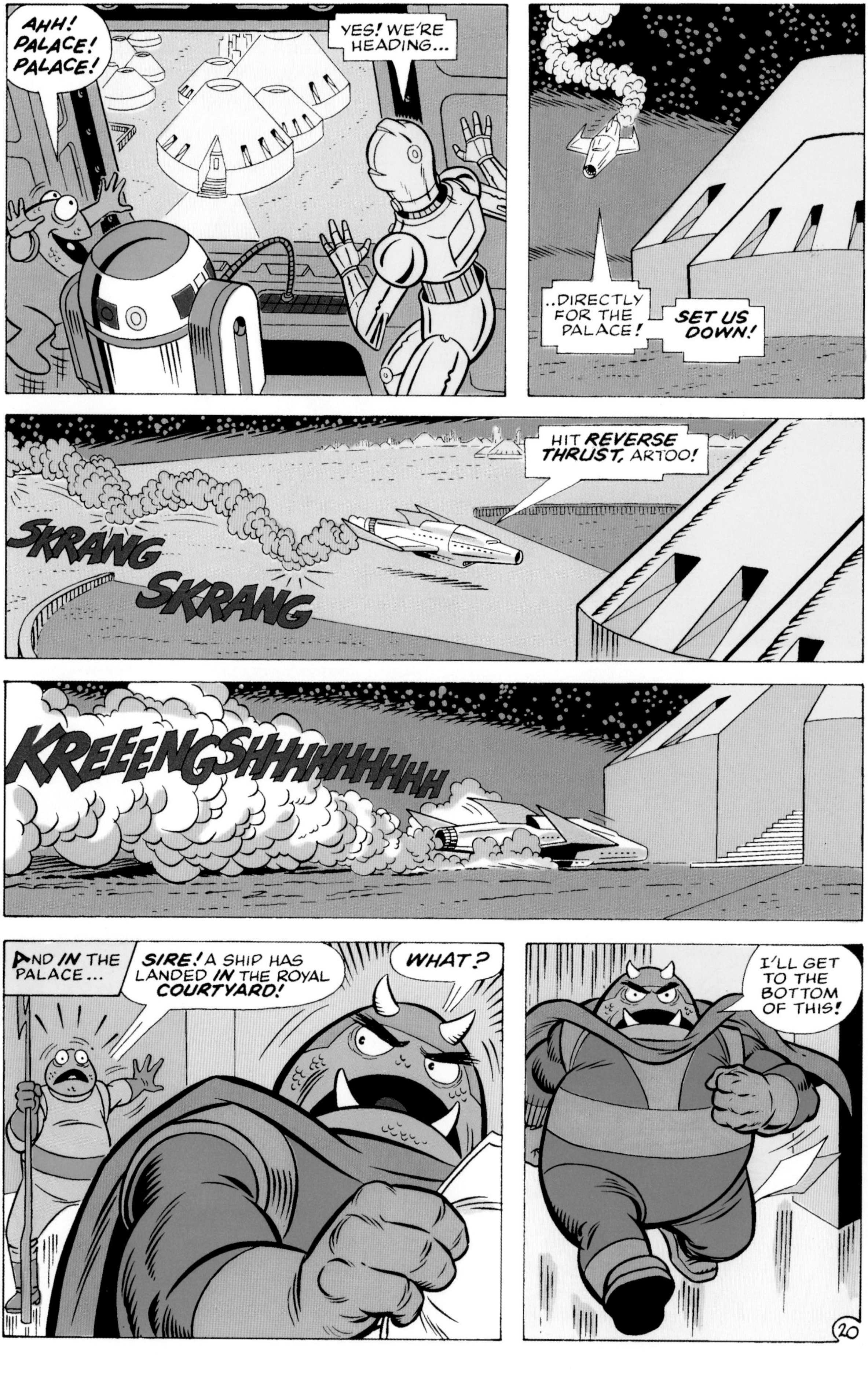
AHH! PALACE! PALACE!
YES! WE'RE HEADING...
..DIRECTLY FOR THE PALACE!
SET US DOWN!
HIT REVERSE THRUST, ARTOO!
SKRANG
SKRANG
KREEENGSHHHHHHHHH
AND IN THE PALACE...
SIRE! A SHIP HAS LANDED IN THE ROYAL COURTYARD!
WHAT?
I'LL GET TO THE BOTTOM OF THIS!
20

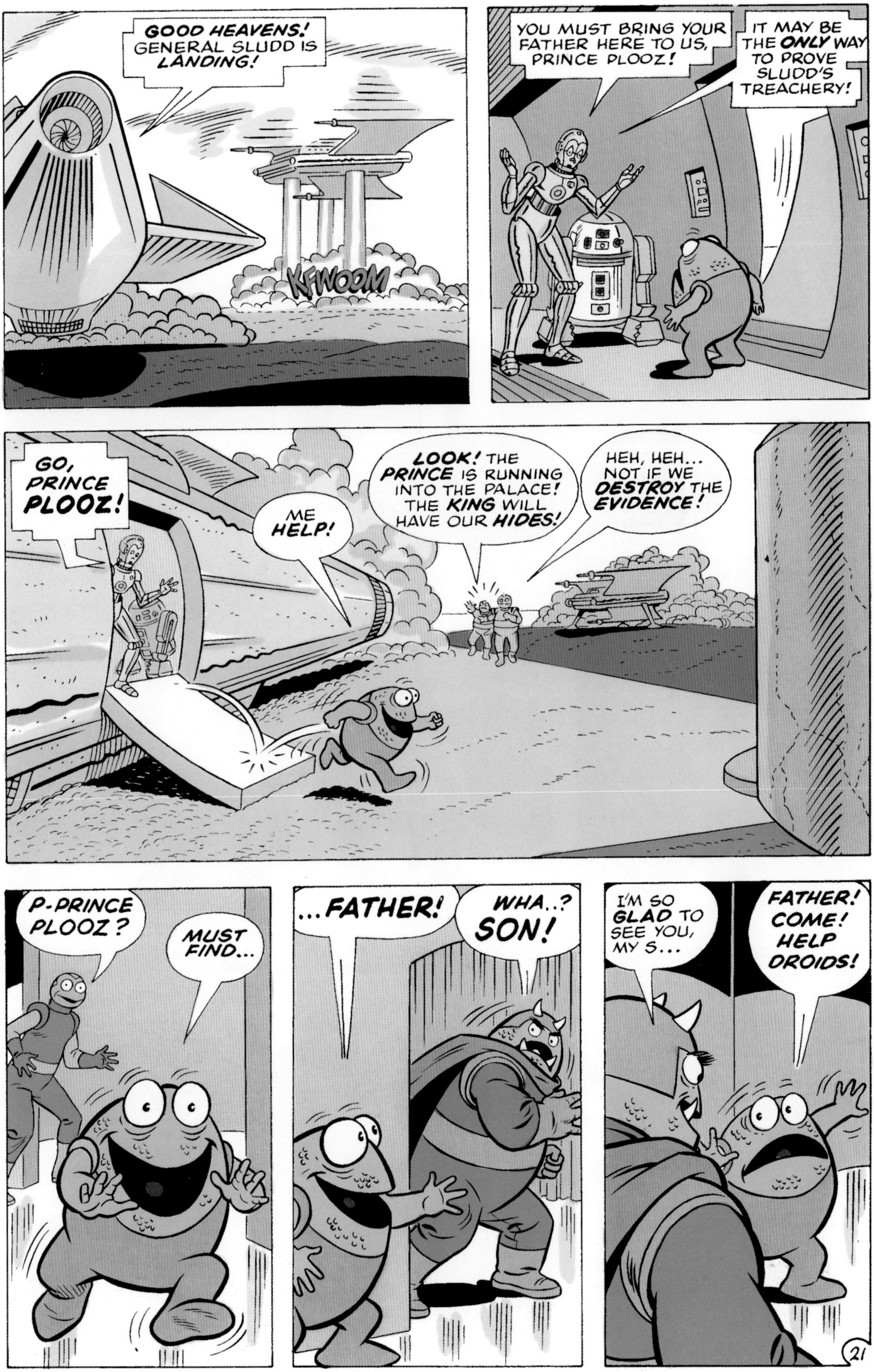
GOOD HEAVENS! GENERAL SLUDD IS LANDING!
KFWOOM
YOU MUST BRING YOUR FATHER HERE TO US, PRINCE PLOOZ!
IT MAY BE THE ONLY WAY TO PROVE SLUDD'S TREACHERY!
GO, PRINCE PLOOZ!
ME HELP!
LOOK! THE PRINCE IS RUNNING INTO THE PALACE! THE KING WILL HAVE OUR HIDES!
HEH, HEH... NOT IF WE DESTROY THE EVIDENCE!
P-PRINCE PLOOZ?
MUST FIND...
...FATHER!
WHA..? SON!
I'M SO GLAD TO SEE YOU, MY S...
FATHER! COME! HELP DROIDS!
21

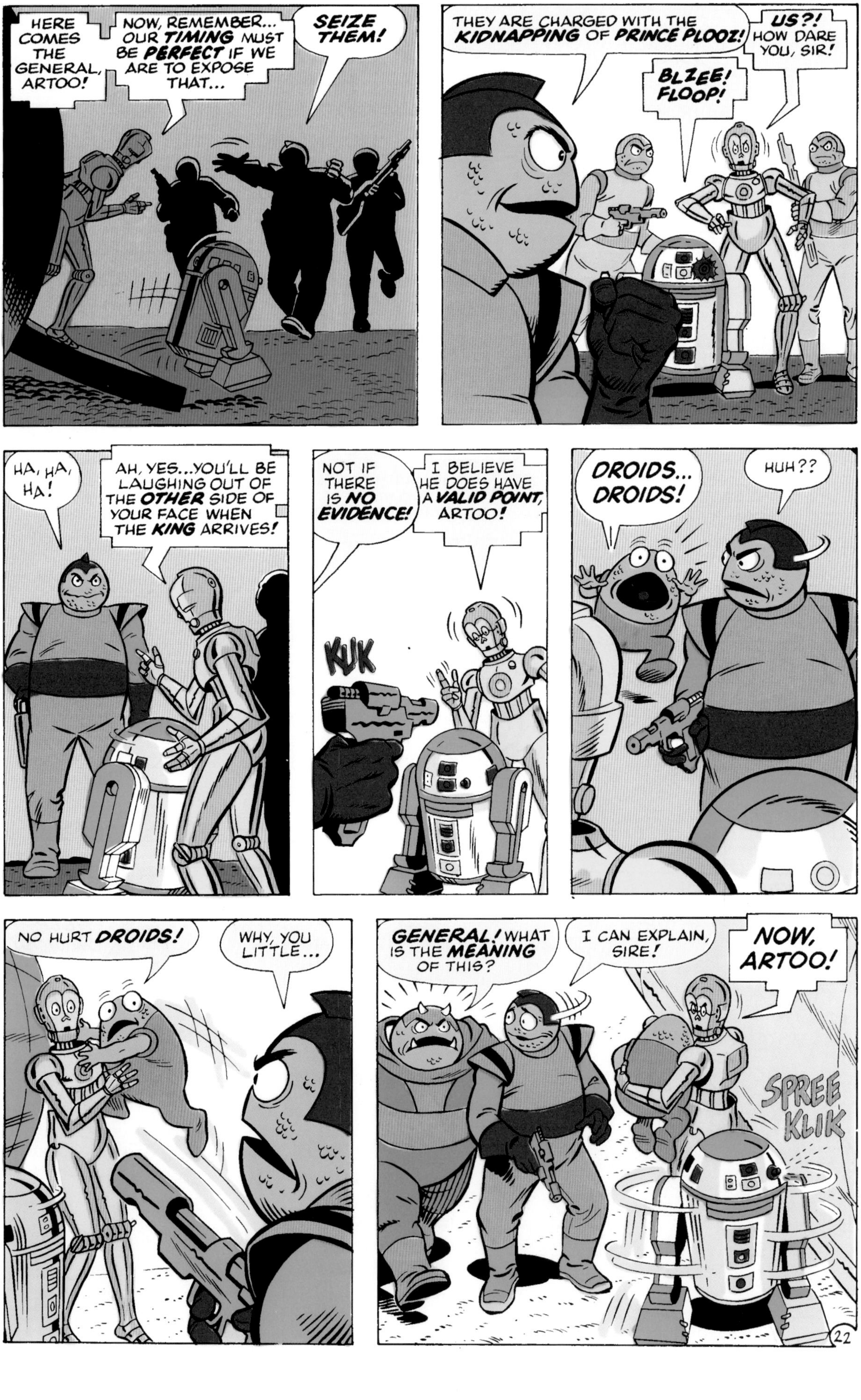
HERE COMES THE GENERAL, ARTOO!
NOW, REMEMBER... OUR TIMING MUST BE PERFECT IF WE ARE TO EXPOSE THAT...
SEIZE THEM!
THEY ARE CHARGED WITH THE KIDNAPPING OF PRINCE PLOOZ!
US?! HOW DARE YOU, SIR!
BLZEE! FLOOP!
HA, HA, HA!
AH, YES...YOU'LL BE LAUGHING OUT OF THE OTHER SIDE OF YOUR FACE WHEN THE KING ARRIVES!
NOT IF THERE IS NO EVIDENCE!
I BELIEVE HE DOES HAVE A VALID POINT, ARTOO!
KUK
DROIDS... DROIDS!
HUH??
NO HURT DROIDS!
WHY, YOU LITTLE...
GENERAL! WHAT IS THE MEANING OF THIS?
I CAN EXPLAIN, SIRE!
NOW, ARTOO!
SPREE KLIK
22

EXPLAIN YOUR WAY OUT OF THIS **RECORD TAPE** FROM OUR SHIP, GENERAL!

THE SOONER LITTLE **LORD PLOOZ** IS OUT OF THE WAY AND **WAR** IS DECLARED... THE SOONER **I** WILL HAVE THE POWER TO CONQUER **BOTH** WORLDS!

WHAT??

LOOKS LIKE YOU'LL BE DOING YOUR EXPLAINING FROM **PRISON**!

TAKE **GENERAL SLUDD** AND HIS MEN AWAY!

YES, SIRE!

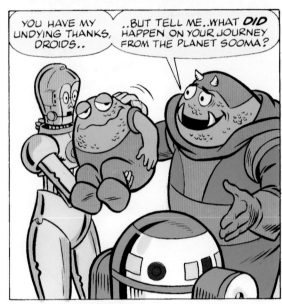

YOU HAVE MY UNDYING THANKS, DROIDS..

..BUT TELL ME..WHAT **DID** HAPPEN ON YOUR JOURNEY FROM THE PLANET SOOMA?

WELL, SIRE..THE ONLY WAY TO START IS BY SAYING IT'S BEEN..

...A **LONG, LONG DAY!**

ZZZZZ

THE END 23

319

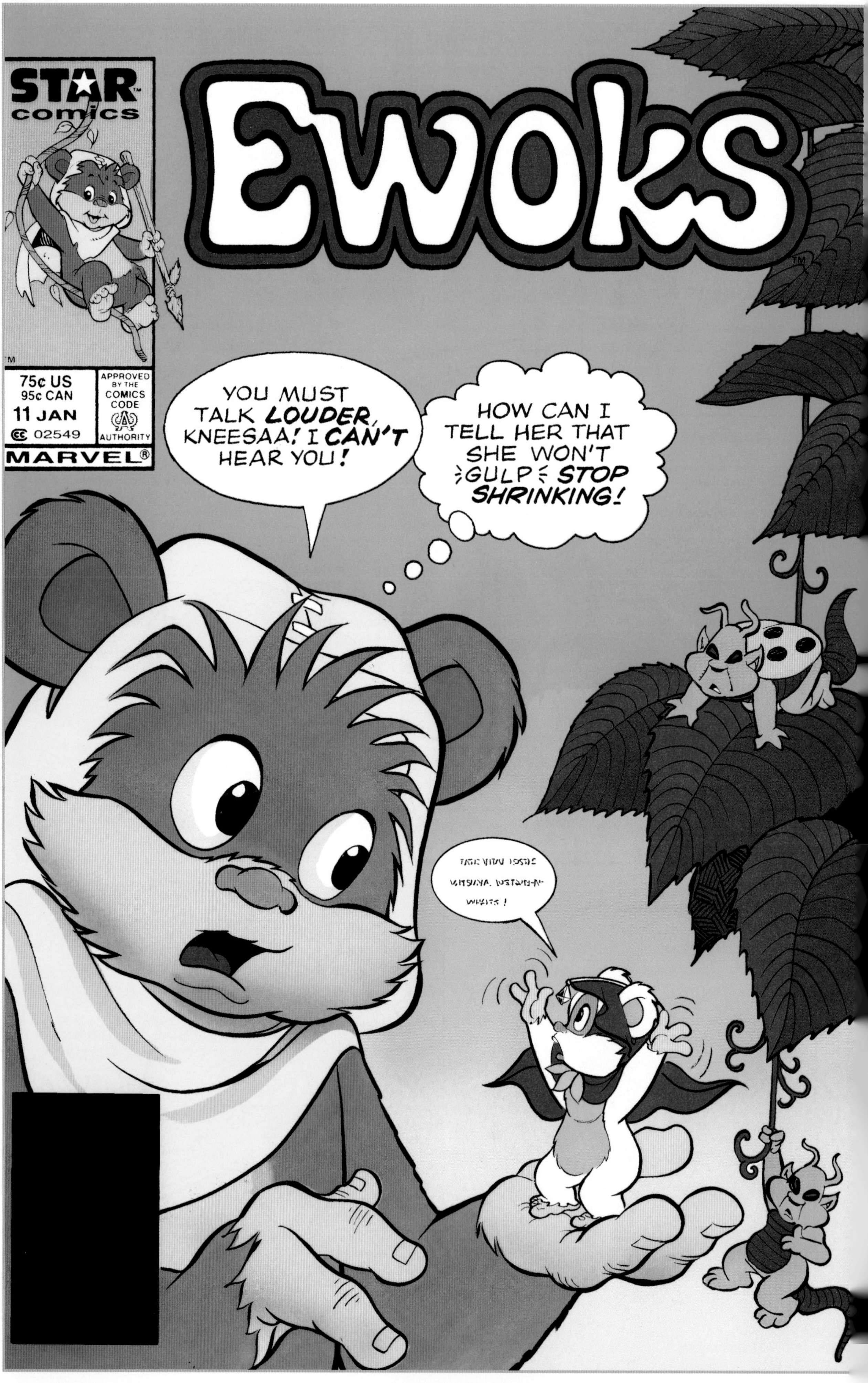
STAR comics
EWOKS
75¢ US
95¢ CAN
11 JAN
02549
APPROVED BY THE COMICS CODE AUTHORITY
MARVEL
YOU MUST TALK LOUDER, KNEESAA! I CAN'T HEAR YOU!
HOW CAN I TELL HER THAT SHE WON'T GULP STOP SHRINKING!

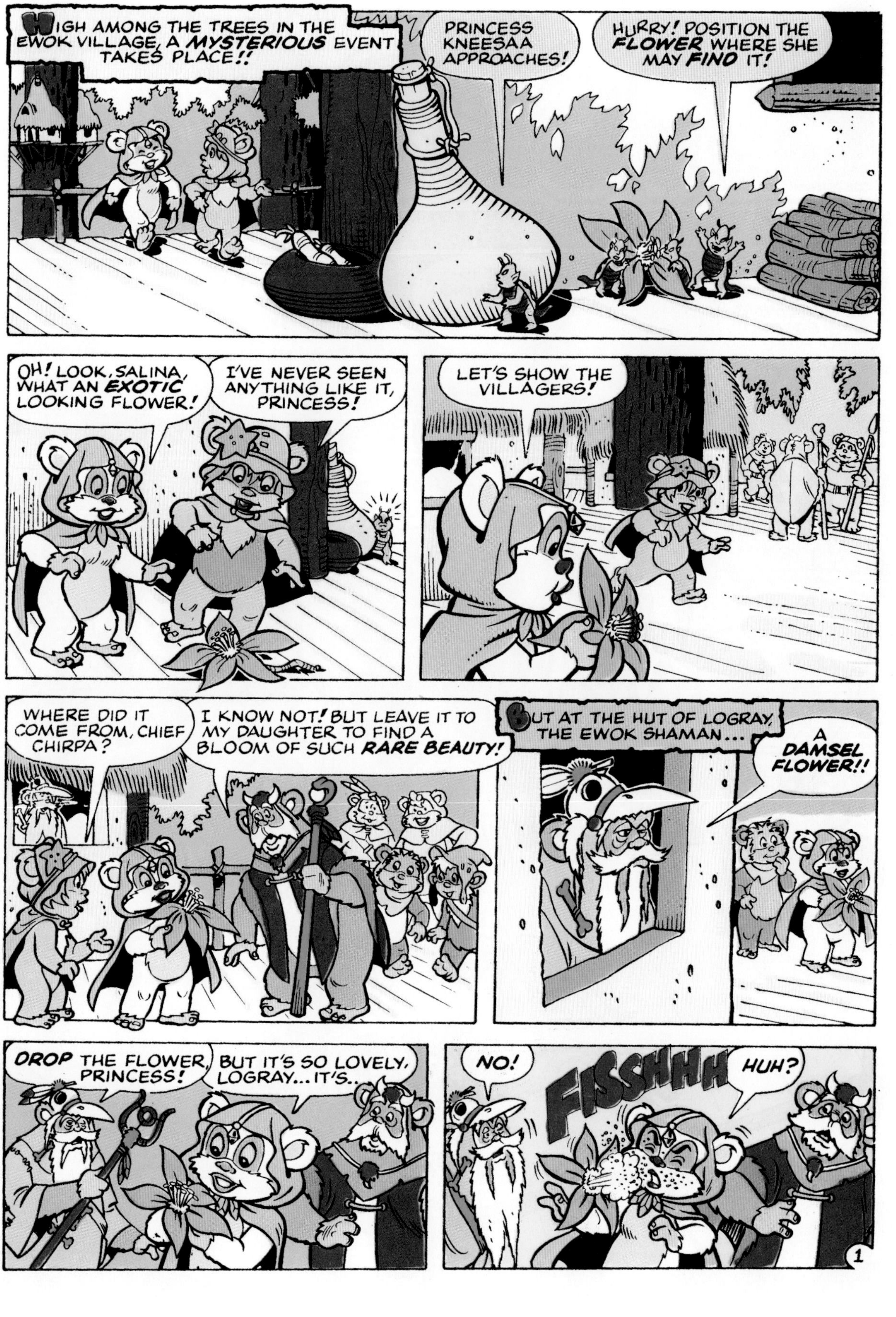
HIGH AMONG THE TREES IN THE EWOK VILLAGE, A MYSTERIOUS EVENT TAKES PLACE!!
PRINCESS KNEESAA APPROACHES!
HURRY! POSITION THE FLOWER WHERE SHE MAY FIND IT!
OH! LOOK, SALINA, WHAT AN EXOTIC LOOKING FLOWER!
I'VE NEVER SEEN ANYTHING LIKE IT, PRINCESS!
LET'S SHOW THE VILLAGERS!
WHERE DID IT COME FROM, CHIEF CHIRPA?
I KNOW NOT! BUT LEAVE IT TO MY DAUGHTER TO FIND A BLOOM OF SUCH RARE BEAUTY!
BUT AT THE HUT OF LOGRAY, THE EWOK SHAMAN...
A DAMSEL FLOWER!!
DROP THE FLOWER, PRINCESS!
BUT IT'S SO LOVELY, LOGRAY... IT'S...
NO!
FISSHHH
HUH?
1

Ewoks™ in The Incredible Shrinking Princess

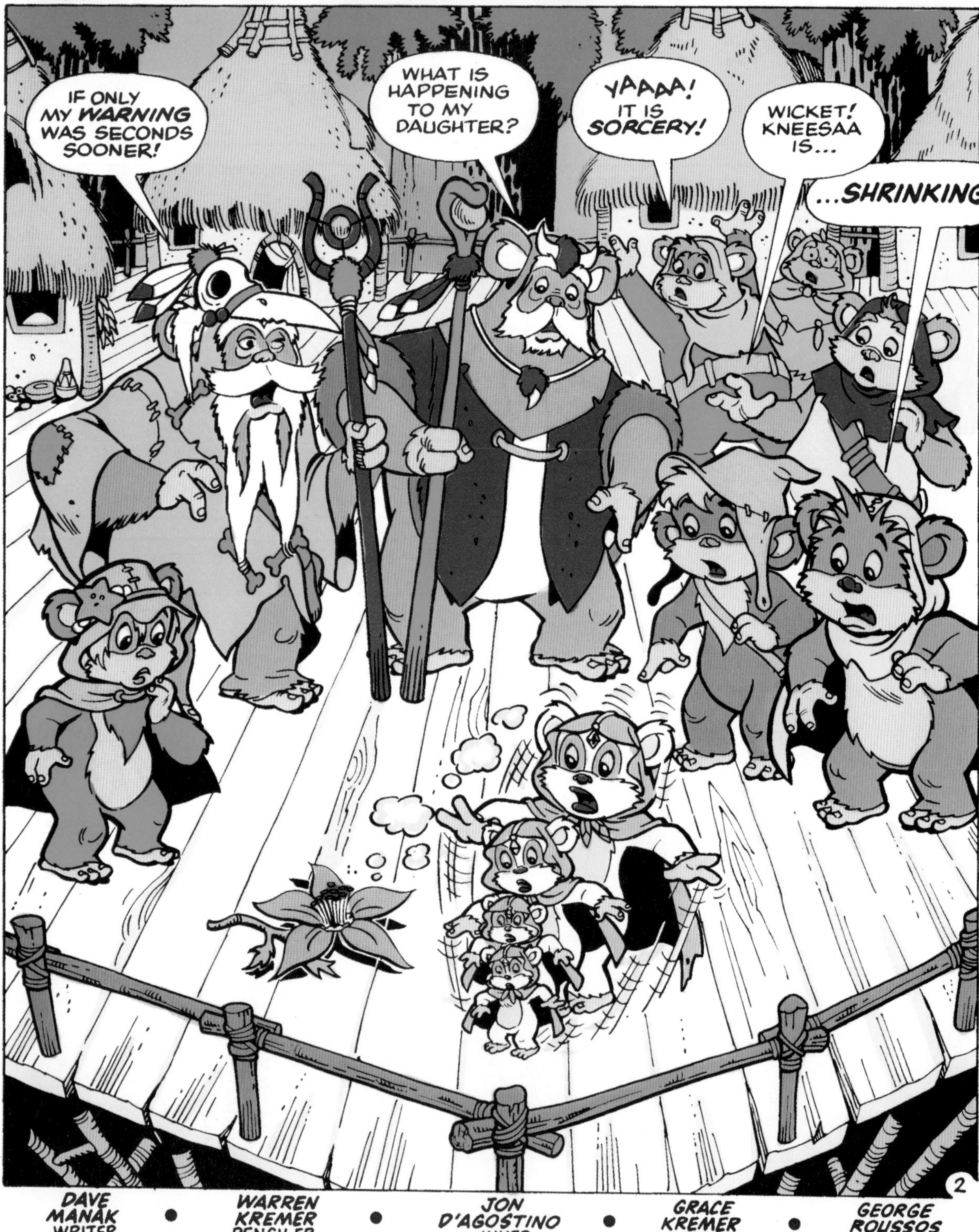
IF ONLY MY WARNING WAS SECONDS SOONER!
WHAT IS HAPPENING TO MY DAUGHTER?
YAAAA! IT IS SORCERY!
WICKET! KNEESAA IS...
...SHRINKING!
2

DAVE MANAK WRITER • WARREN KREMER PENCILER • JON D'AGOSTINO INKER • GRACE KREMER LETTERER • GEORGE ROUSSOS COLORIST

SID JACOBSON EDITOR • TOM DE FALCO EXECUTIVE EDITOR • JIM SHOOTER EDITOR IN CHIEF

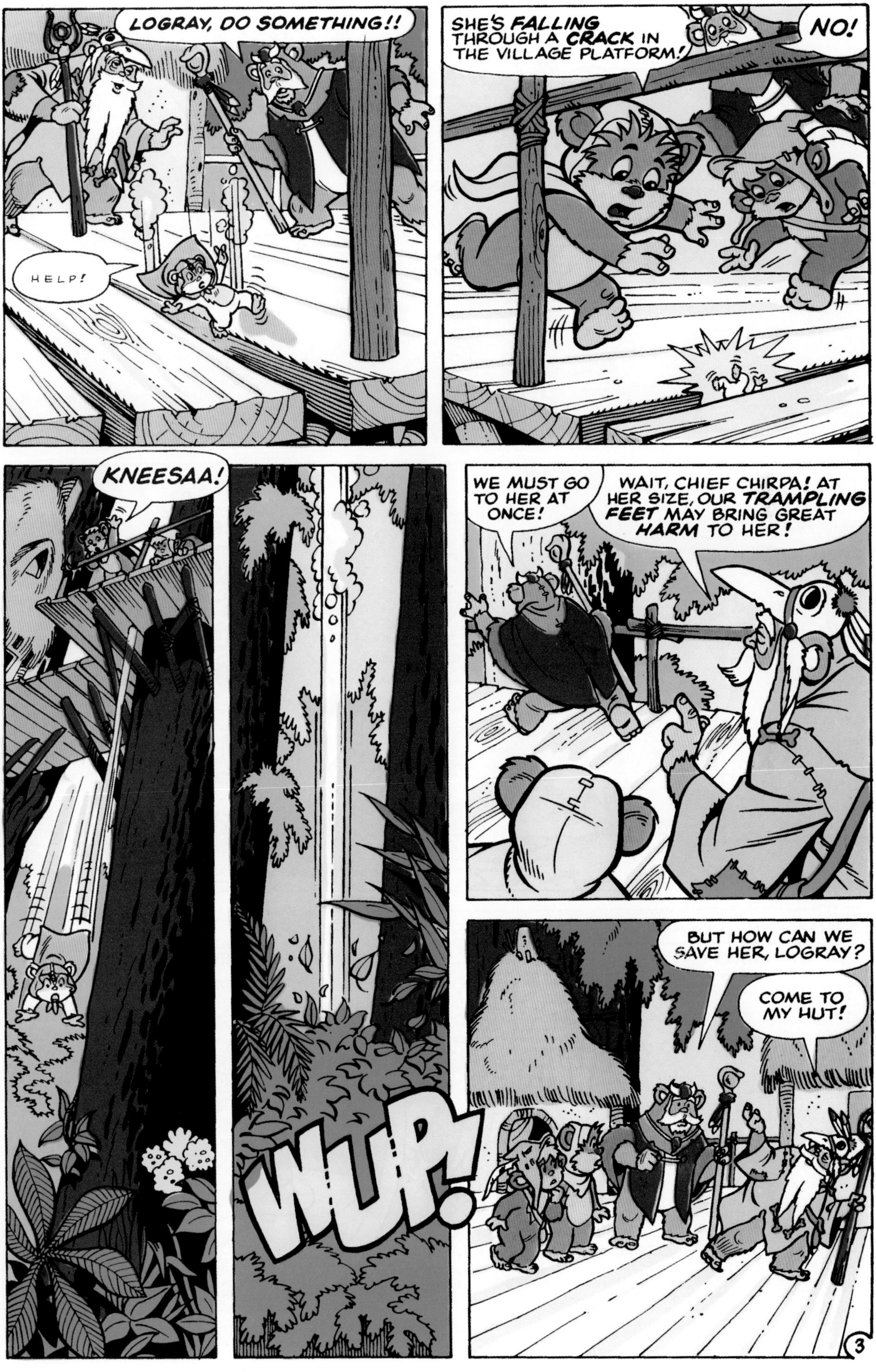
LOGRAY, DO SOMETHING!!
HELP!
SHE'S FALLING THROUGH A CRACK IN THE VILLAGE PLATFORM!
NO!
KNEESAA!
WUP!
WE MUST GO TO HER AT ONCE!
WAIT, CHIEF CHIRPA! AT HER SIZE, OUR TRAMPLING FEET MAY BRING GREAT HARM TO HER!
BUT HOW CAN WE SAVE HER, LOGRAY?
COME TO MY HUT!
3

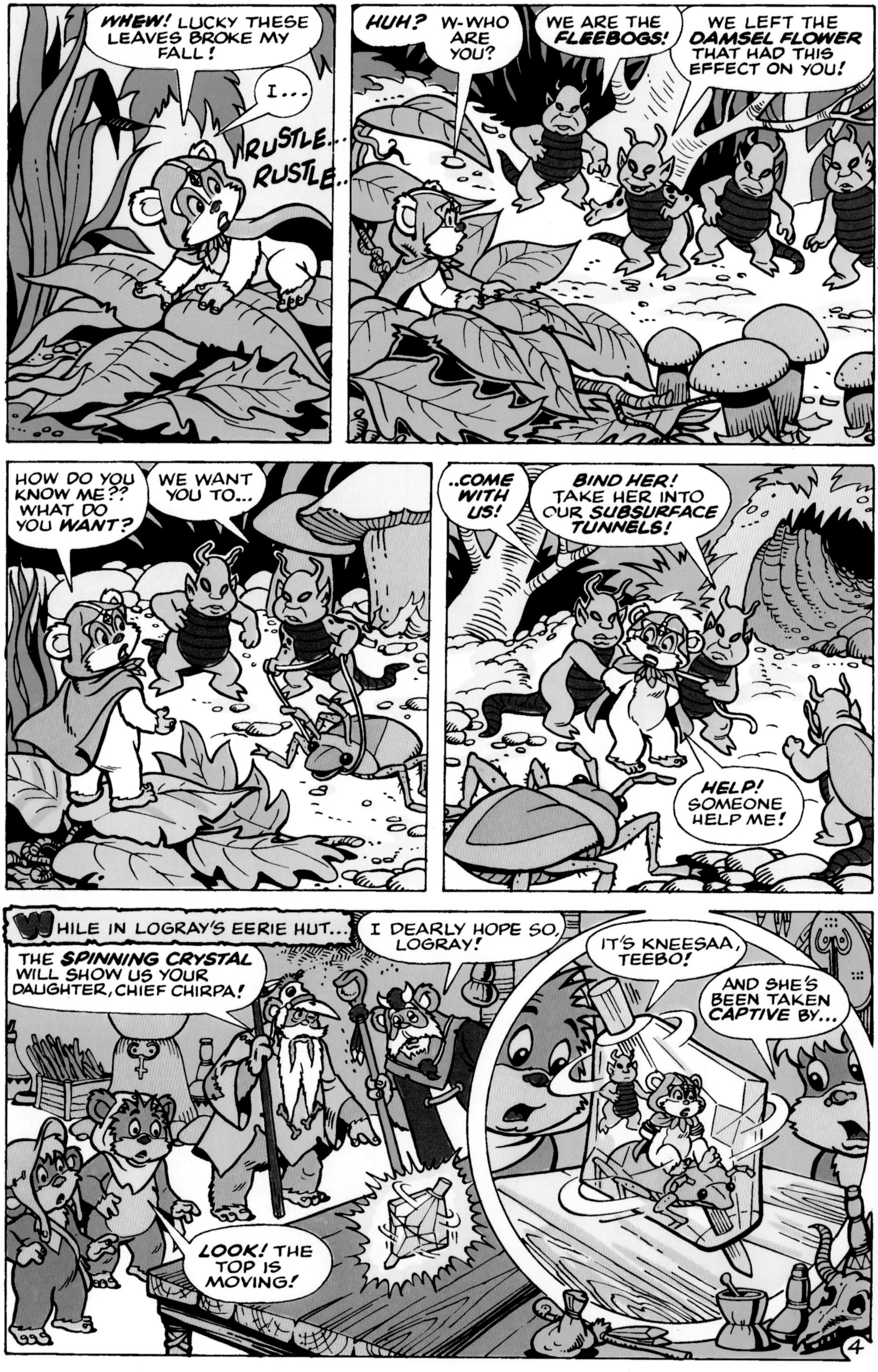
WHEW! LUCKY THESE LEAVES BROKE MY FALL!
I...
RUSTLE... RUSTLE...
HUH? W-WHO ARE YOU?
WE ARE THE FLEEBOGS!
WE LEFT THE DAMSEL FLOWER THAT HAD THIS EFFECT ON YOU!
HOW DO YOU KNOW ME?? WHAT DO YOU WANT?
WE WANT YOU TO...
..COME WITH US!
BIND HER! TAKE HER INTO OUR SUBSURFACE TUNNELS!
HELP! SOMEONE HELP ME!
WHILE IN LOGRAY'S EERIE HUT...
THE SPINNING CRYSTAL WILL SHOW US YOUR DAUGHTER, CHIEF CHIRPA!
I DEARLY HOPE SO, LOGRAY!
IT'S KNEESAA, TEEBO!
AND SHE'S BEEN TAKEN CAPTIVE BY...
LOOK! THE TOP IS MOVING!
4

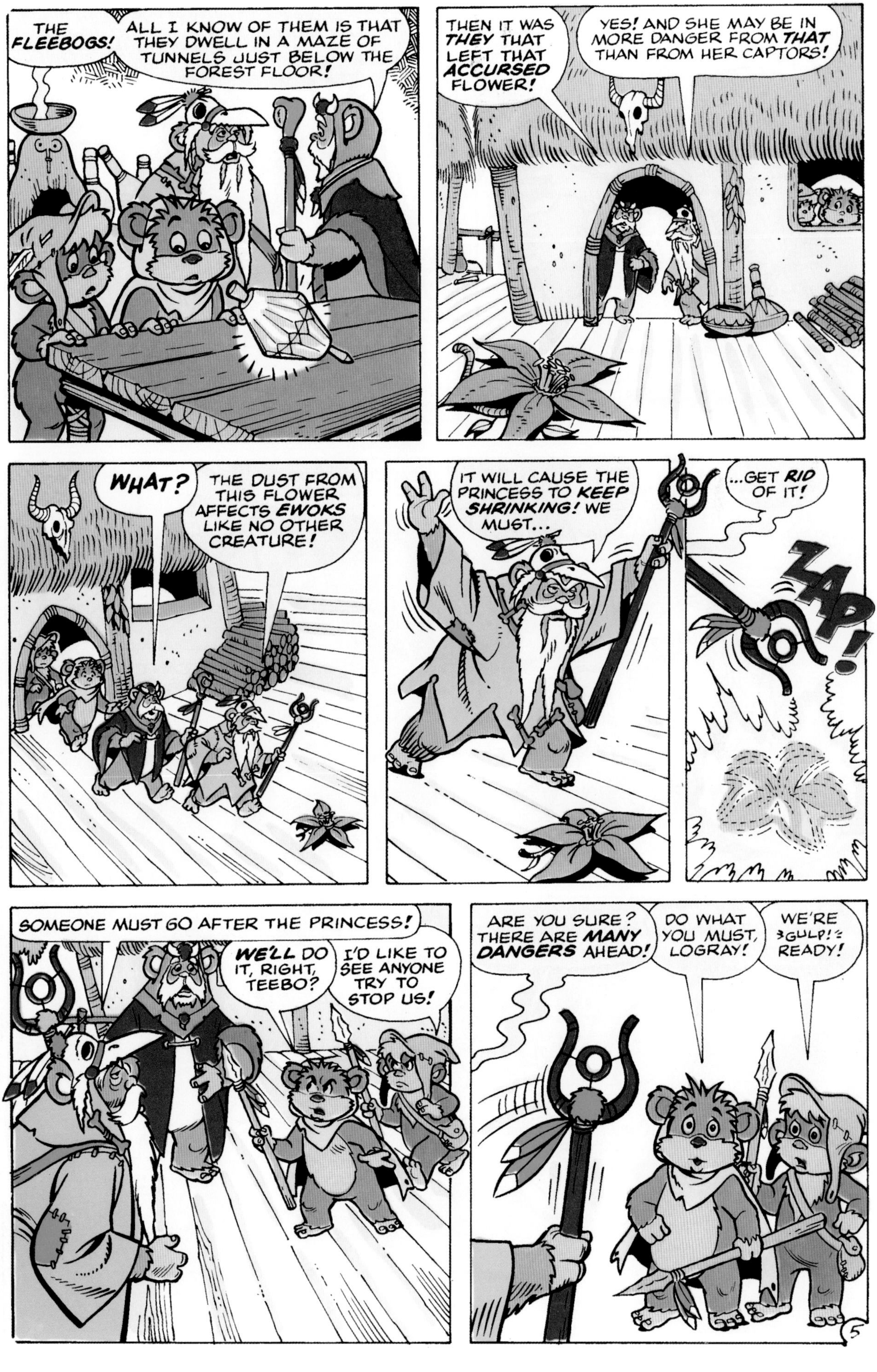
THE FLEEBOGS!
ALL I KNOW OF THEM IS THAT THEY DWELL IN A MAZE OF TUNNELS JUST BELOW THE FOREST FLOOR!
THEN IT WAS THEY THAT LEFT THAT ACCURSED FLOWER!
YES! AND SHE MAY BE IN MORE DANGER FROM THAT THAN FROM HER CAPTORS!
WHAT?
THE DUST FROM THIS FLOWER AFFECTS EWOKS LIKE NO OTHER CREATURE!
IT WILL CAUSE THE PRINCESS TO KEEP SHRINKING! WE MUST...
...GET RID OF IT!
ZAP!
SOMEONE MUST GO AFTER THE PRINCESS!
WE'LL DO IT, RIGHT, TEEBO?
I'D LIKE TO SEE ANYONE TRY TO STOP US!
ARE YOU SURE? THERE ARE MANY DANGERS AHEAD!
DO WHAT YOU MUST, LOGRAY!
WE'RE GULP! READY!
5

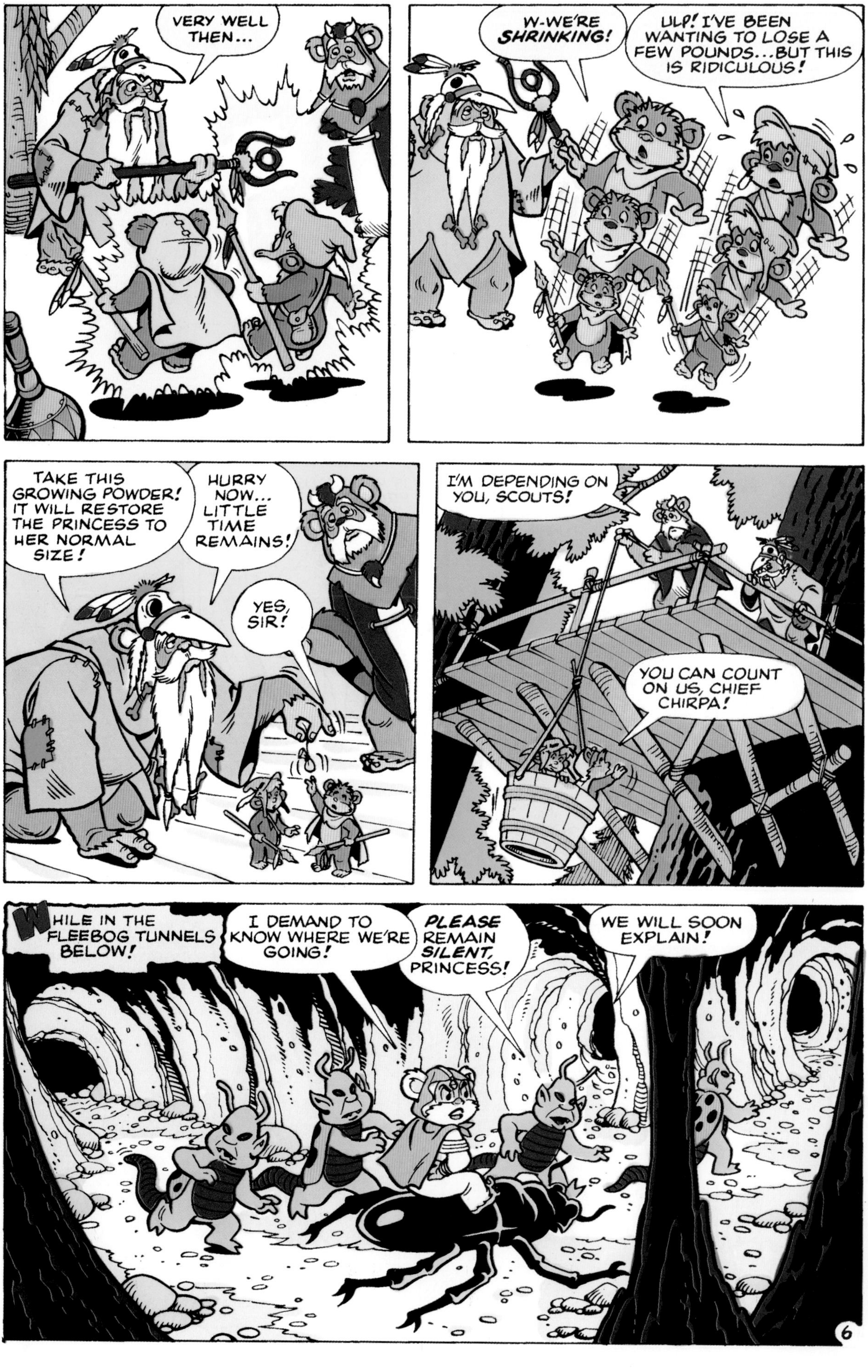
VERY WELL THEN...
W-WE'RE SHRINKING!
ULP! I'VE BEEN WANTING TO LOSE A FEW POUNDS...BUT THIS IS RIDICULOUS!
TAKE THIS GROWING POWDER! IT WILL RESTORE THE PRINCESS TO HER NORMAL SIZE!
HURRY NOW... LITTLE TIME REMAINS!
YES, SIR!
I'M DEPENDING ON YOU, SCOUTS!
YOU CAN COUNT ON US, CHIEF CHIRPA!
WHILE IN THE FLEEBOG TUNNELS BELOW!
I DEMAND TO KNOW WHERE WE'RE GOING!
PLEASE REMAIN SILENT, PRINCESS!
WE WILL SOON EXPLAIN!
6

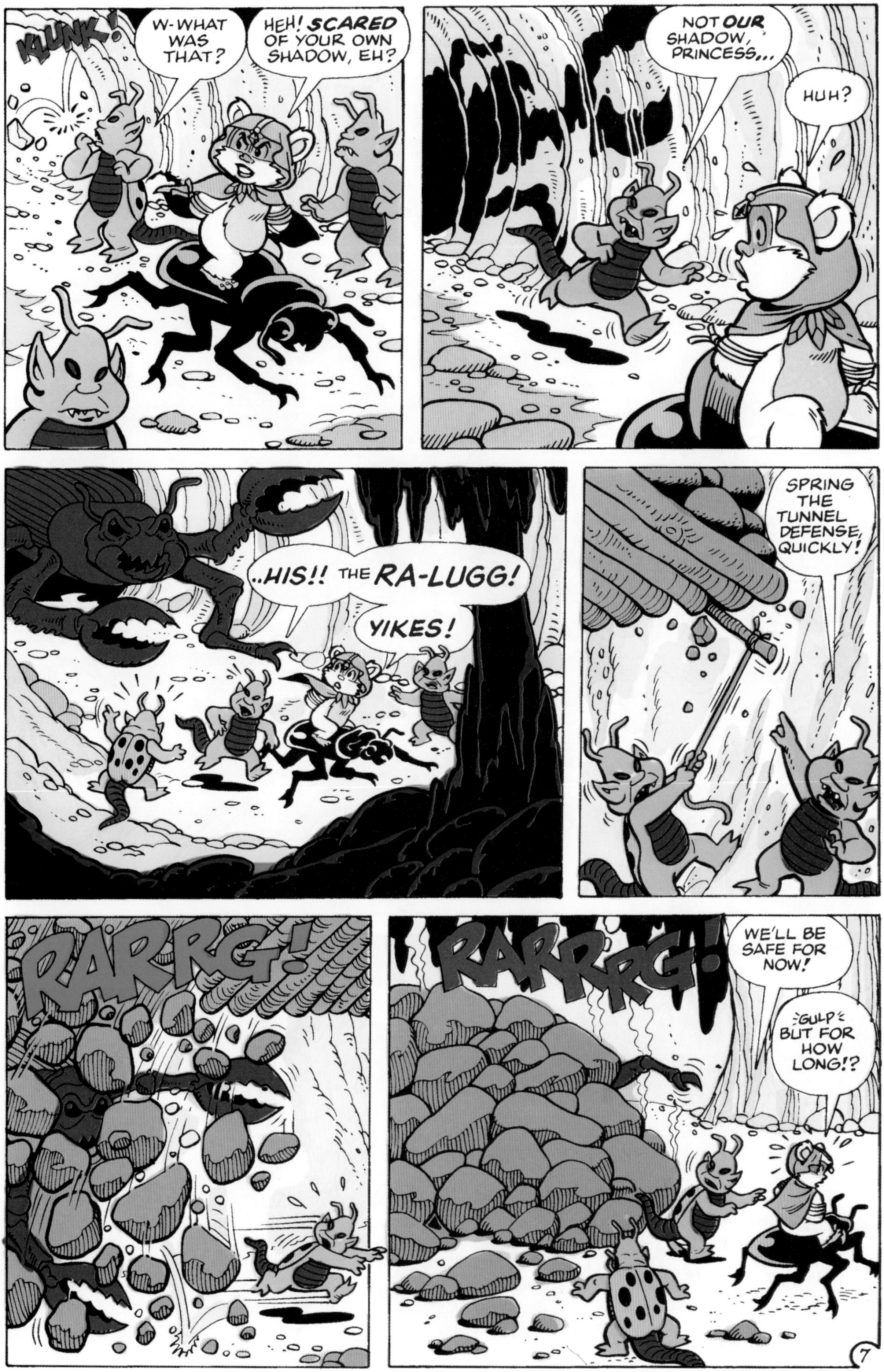
KLUNK!
W-WHAT WAS THAT?
HEH! SCARED OF YOUR OWN SHADOW, EH?
NOT OUR SHADOW, PRINCESS...
HUH?
..HIS!! THE RA-LUGG!
YIKES!
SPRING THE TUNNEL DEFENSE, QUICKLY!
RARRG!
RARRRG!
WE'LL BE SAFE FOR NOW!
GULP BUT FOR HOW LONG!?
7

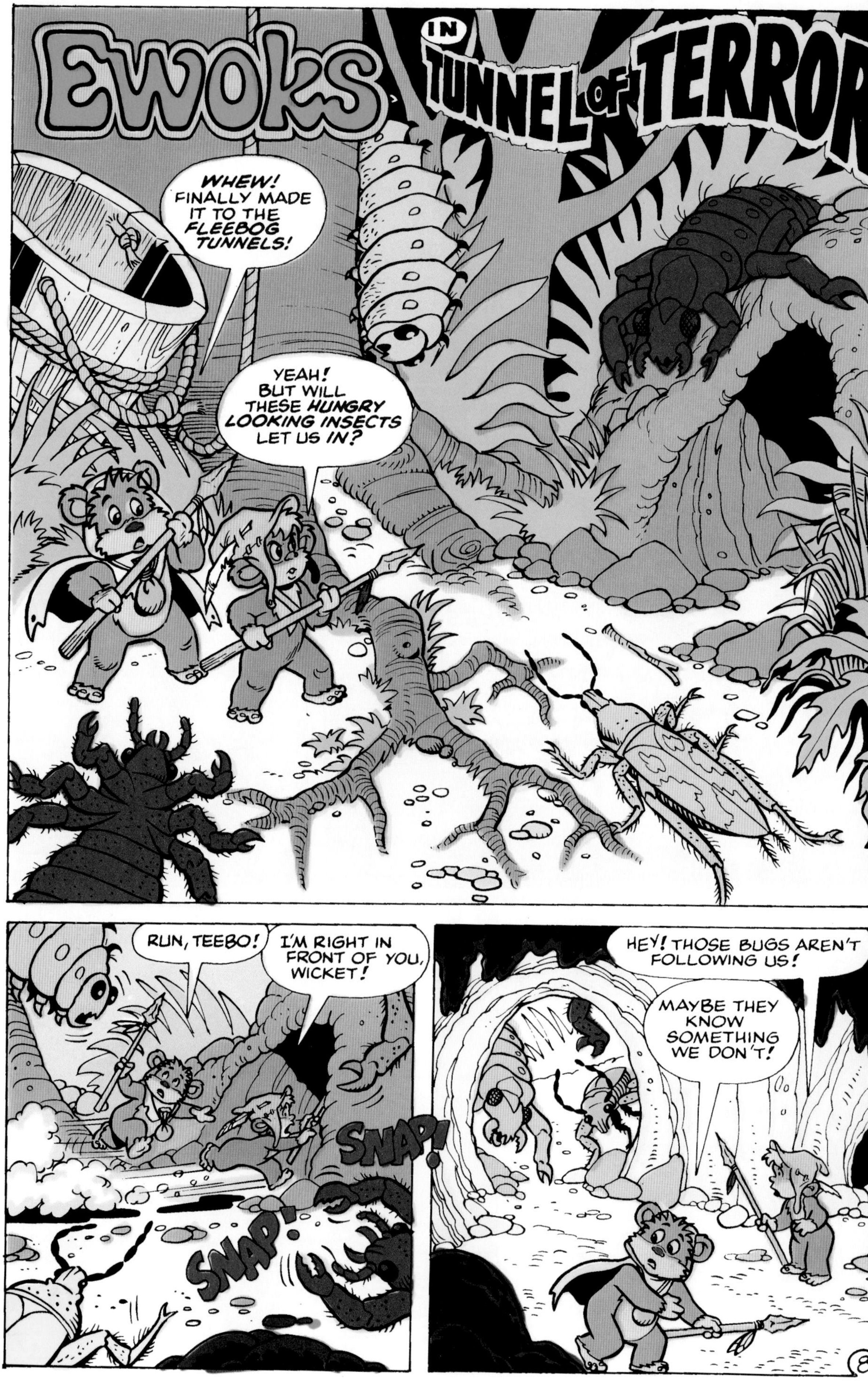
Ewoks
IN
TUNNEL OF TERROR
WHEW! FINALLY MADE IT TO THE FLEEBOG TUNNELS!
YEAH! BUT WILL THESE HUNGRY LOOKING INSECTS LET US IN?
RUN, TEEBO!
I'M RIGHT IN FRONT OF YOU, WICKET!
SNAP!
SNAP!
HEY! THOSE BUGS AREN'T FOLLOWING US!
MAYBE THEY KNOW SOMETHING WE DON'T!
8

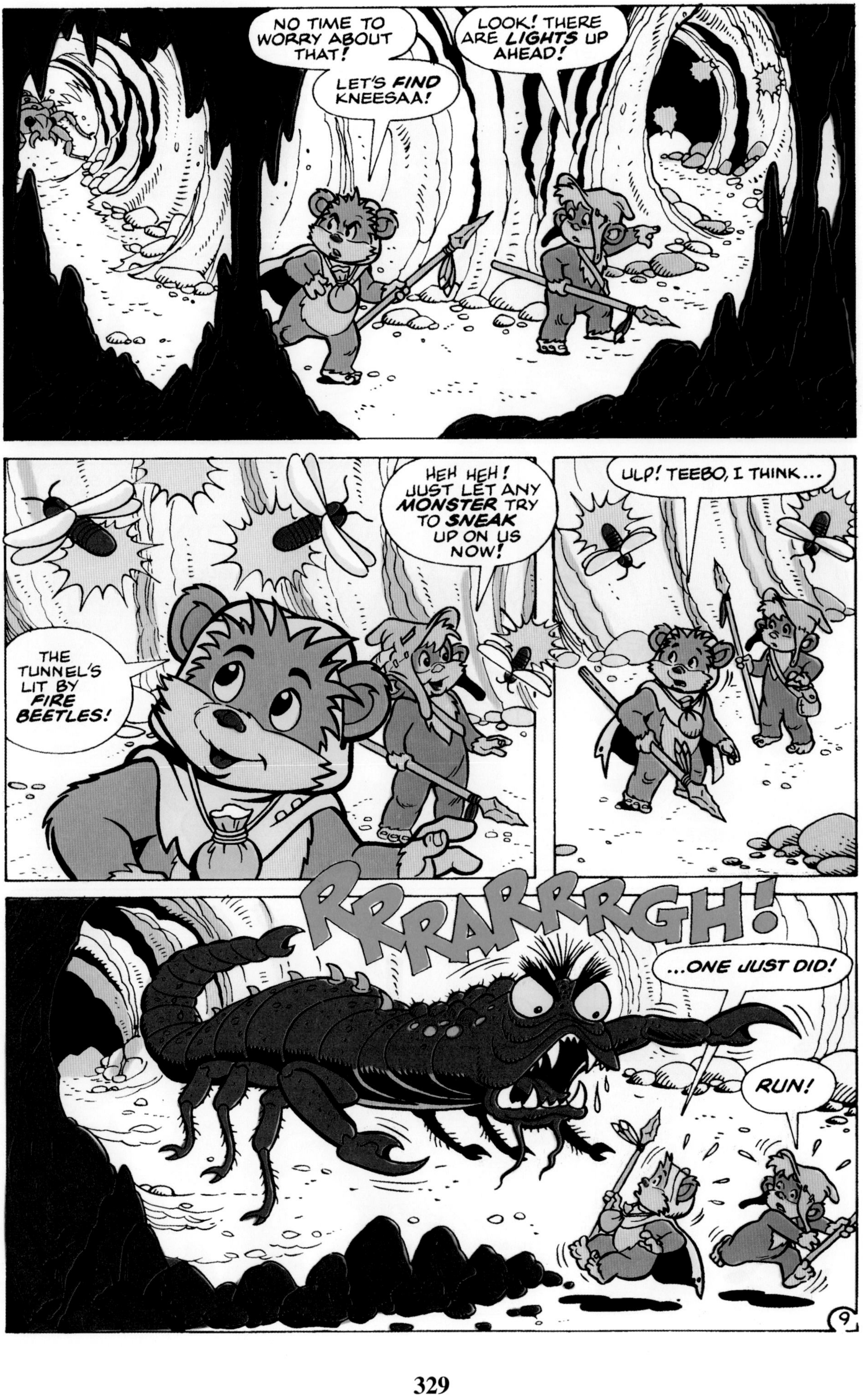
NO TIME TO WORRY ABOUT THAT!
LET'S FIND KNEESAA!
LOOK! THERE ARE LIGHTS UP AHEAD!
THE TUNNEL'S LIT BY FIRE BEETLES!
HEH HEH! JUST LET ANY MONSTER TRY TO SNEAK UP ON US NOW!
ULP! TEEBO, I THINK...
RRRARRRRGH!
...ONE JUST DID!
RUN!
9

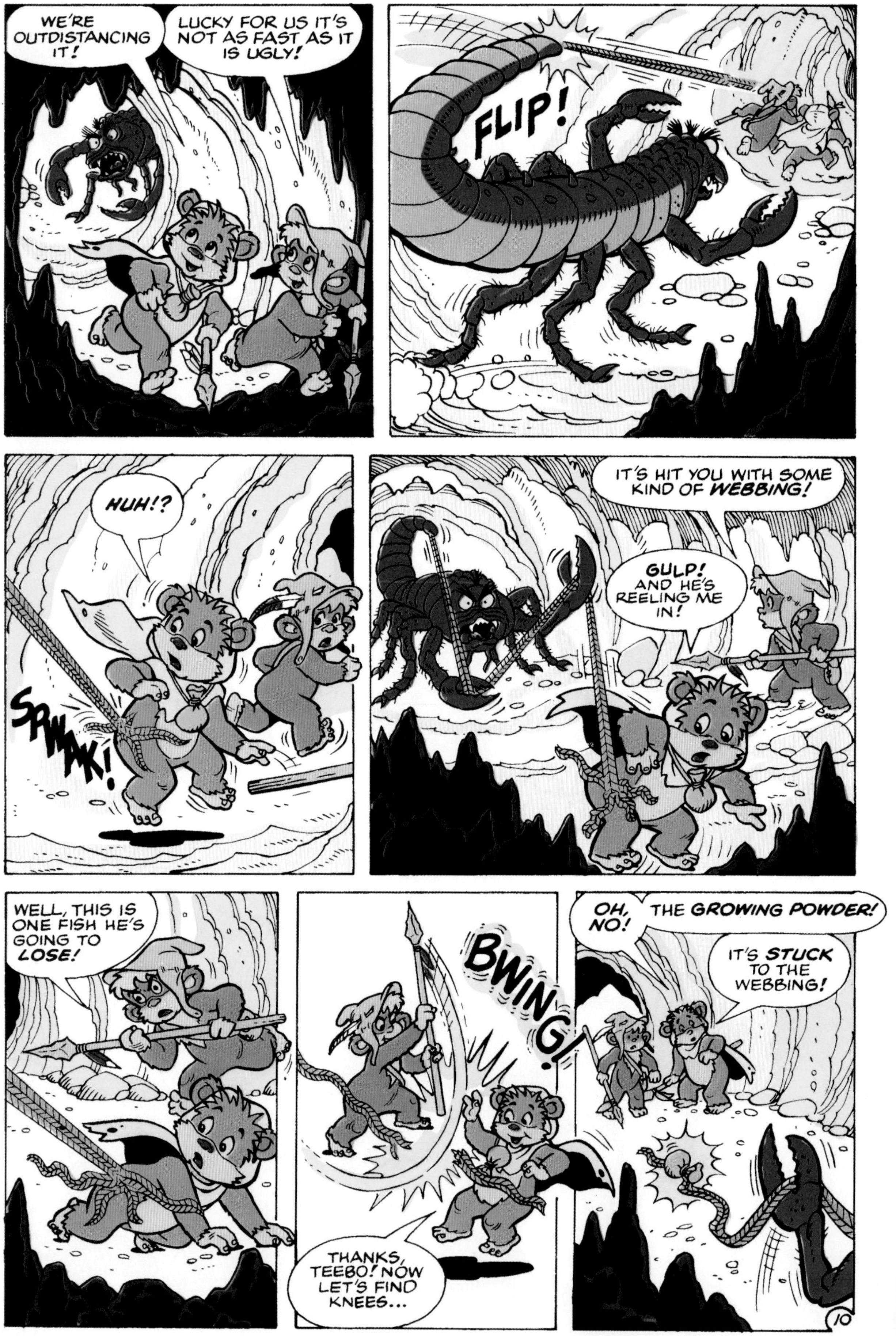
WE'RE OUTDISTANCING IT!
LUCKY FOR US IT'S NOT AS FAST AS IT IS UGLY!
FLIP!
HUH!?
SPWAAK!
IT'S HIT YOU WITH SOME KIND OF WEBBING!
GULP! AND HE'S REELING ME IN!
WELL, THIS IS ONE FISH HE'S GOING TO LOSE!
BWING!
THANKS, TEEBO! NOW LET'S FIND KNEES...
OH, NO!
THE GROWING POWDER!
IT'S STUCK TO THE WEBBING!
10

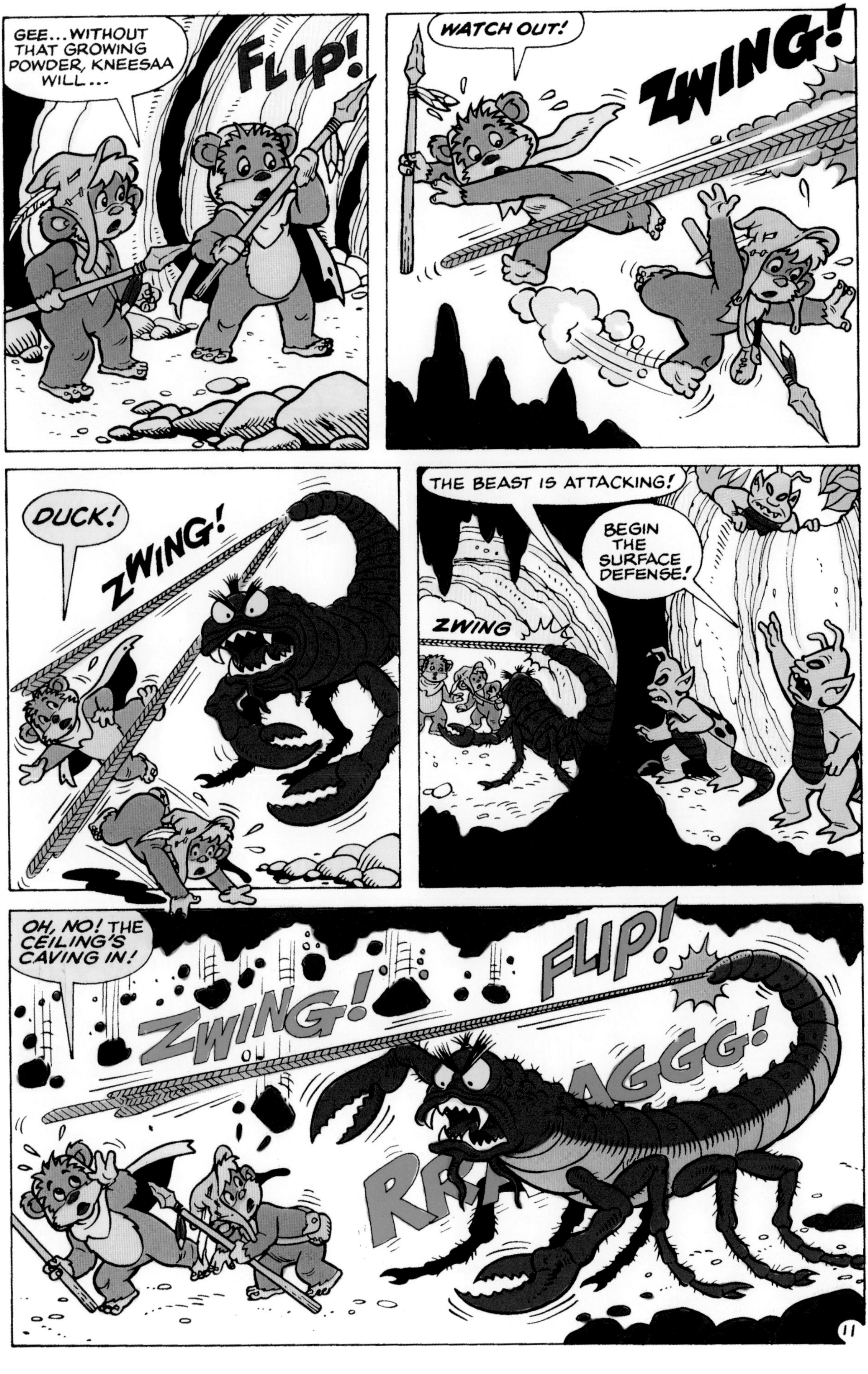
GEE... WITHOUT THAT GROWING POWDER, KNEESAA WILL...
FLIP!
WATCH OUT!
ZWING!
DUCK!
ZWING!
THE BEAST IS ATTACKING!
BEGIN THE SURFACE DEFENSE!
ZWING
OH, NO! THE CEILING'S CAVING IN!
FLIP!
ZWING!
AGGGG!
11

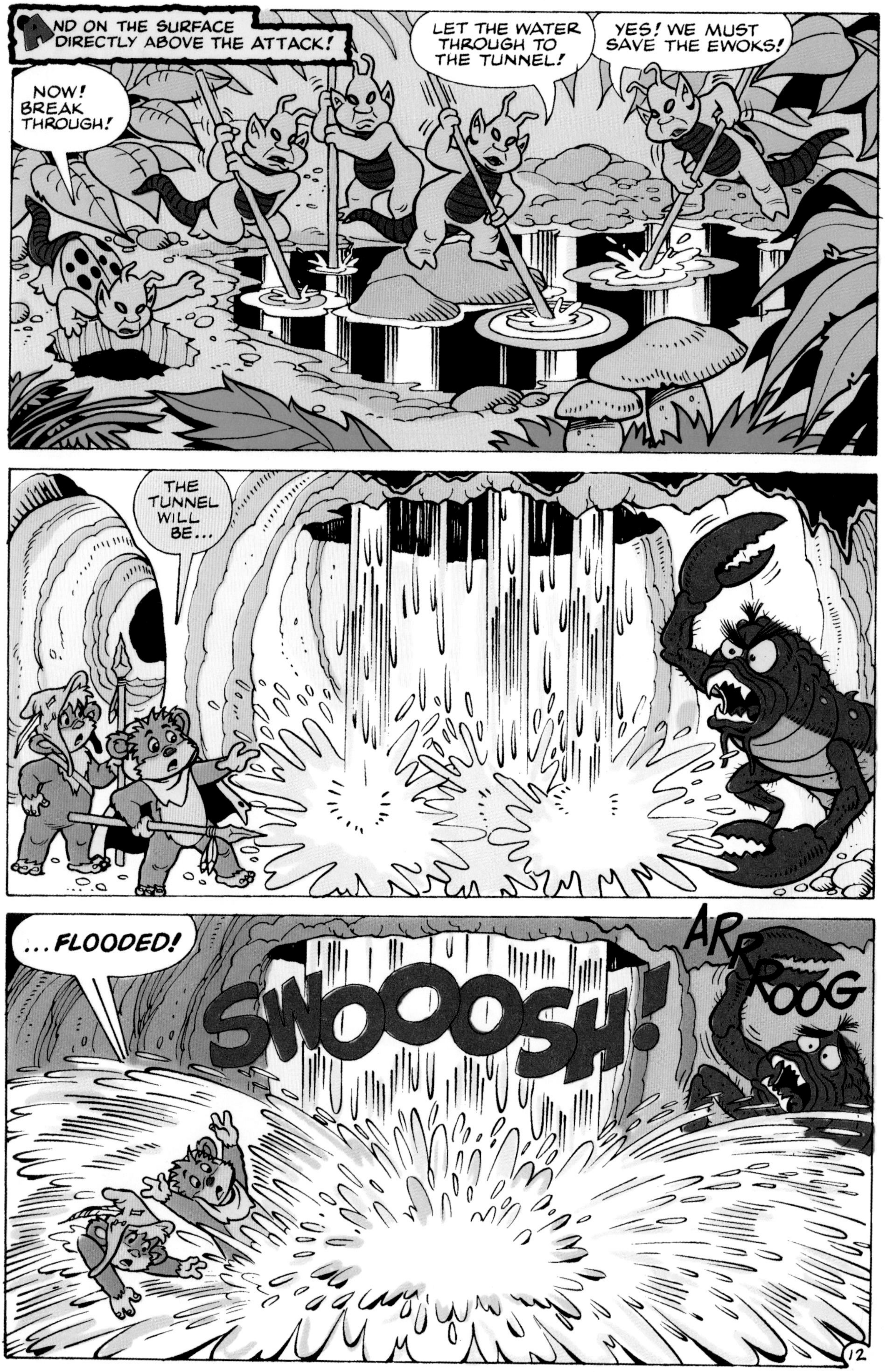
AND ON THE SURFACE DIRECTLY ABOVE THE ATTACK!
NOW! BREAK THROUGH!
LET THE WATER THROUGH TO THE TUNNEL!
YES! WE MUST SAVE THE EWOKS!
THE TUNNEL WILL BE...
...FLOODED!
SWOOOSH!
ARRROOG
12

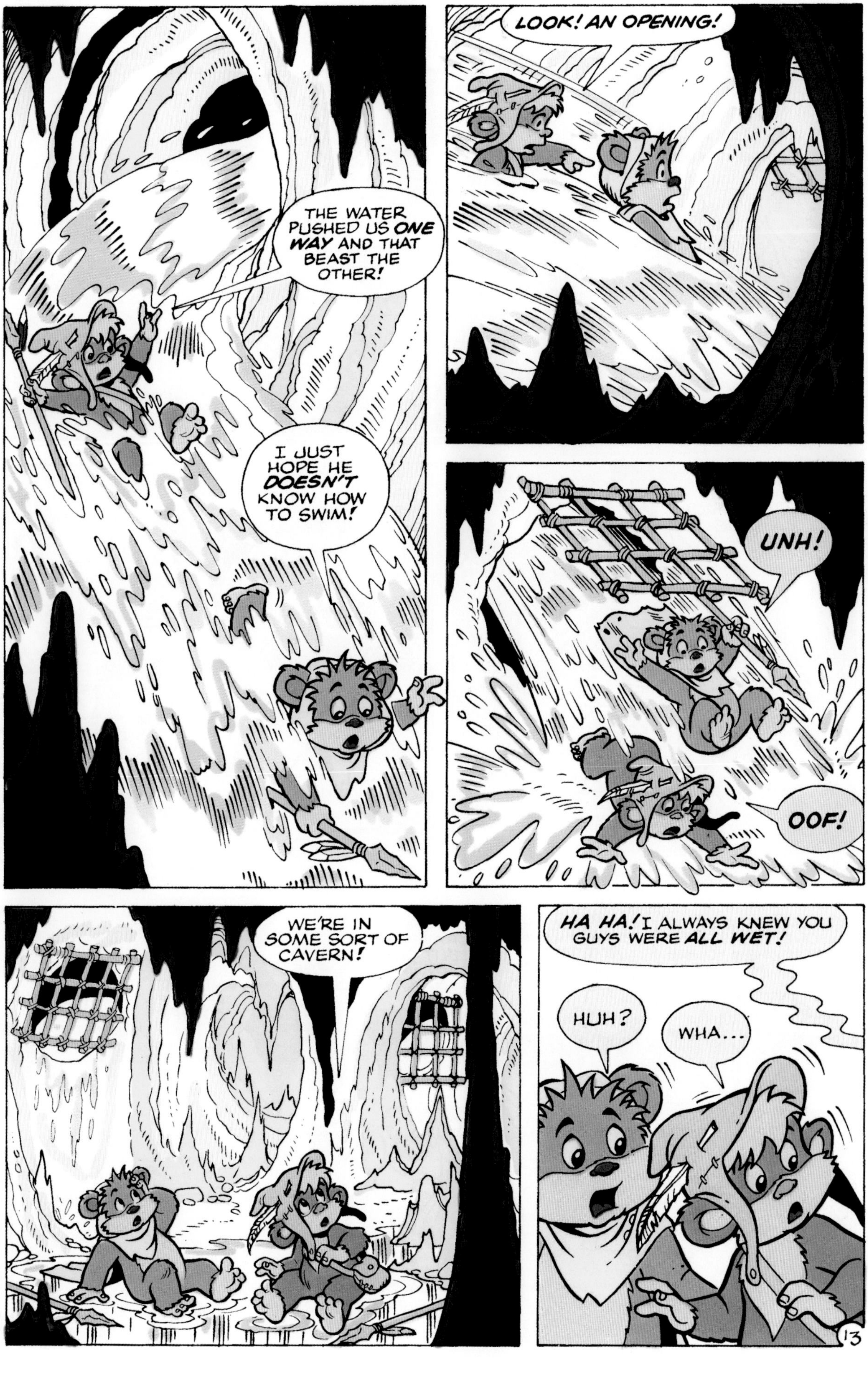
THE WATER PUSHED US ONE WAY AND THAT BEAST THE OTHER!
I JUST HOPE HE DOESN'T KNOW HOW TO SWIM!
LOOK! AN OPENING!
UNH!
OOF!
WE'RE IN SOME SORT OF CAVERN!
HA HA! I ALWAYS KNEW YOU GUYS WERE ALL WET!
HUH?
WHA...
13

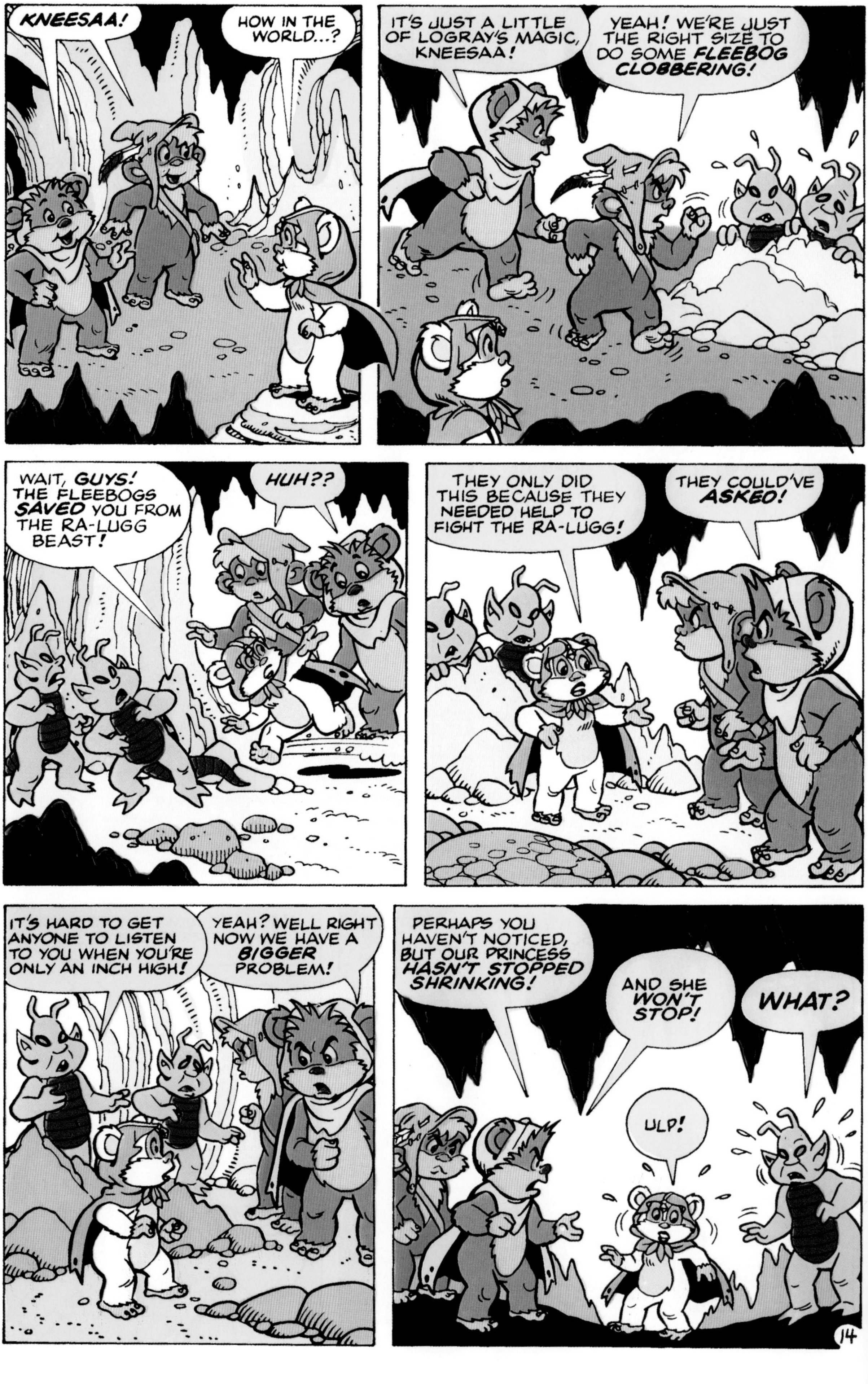
KNEESAA!
HOW IN THE WORLD...?
IT'S JUST A LITTLE OF LOGRAY'S MAGIC, KNEESAA!
YEAH! WE'RE JUST THE RIGHT SIZE TO DO SOME FLEEBOG CLOBBERING!
WAIT, GUYS! THE FLEEBOGS SAVED YOU FROM THE RA-LUGG BEAST!
HUH??
THEY ONLY DID THIS BECAUSE THEY NEEDED HELP TO FIGHT THE RA-LUGG!
THEY COULD'VE ASKED!
IT'S HARD TO GET ANYONE TO LISTEN TO YOU WHEN YOU'RE ONLY AN INCH HIGH!
YEAH? WELL RIGHT NOW WE HAVE A BIGGER PROBLEM!
PERHAPS YOU HAVEN'T NOTICED, BUT OUR PRINCESS HASN'T STOPPED SHRINKING!
AND SHE WON'T STOP!
WHAT?
ULP!
14

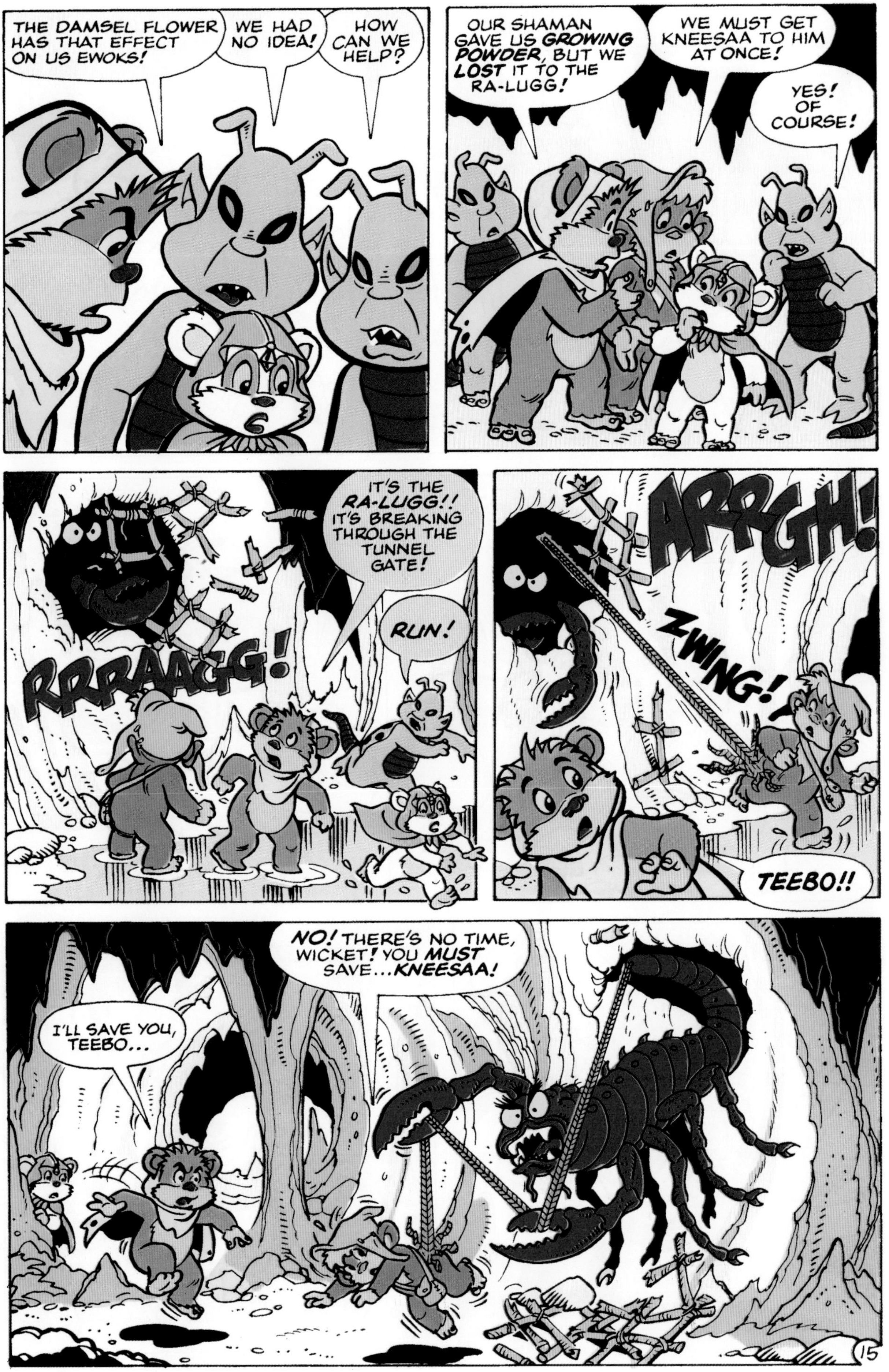
THE DAMSEL FLOWER HAS THAT EFFECT ON US EWOKS!
WE HAD NO IDEA!
HOW CAN WE HELP?
OUR SHAMAN GAVE US GROWING POWDER, BUT WE LOST IT TO THE RA-LUGG!
WE MUST GET KNEESAA TO HIM AT ONCE!
YES! OF COURSE!
IT'S THE RA-LUGG!! IT'S BREAKING THROUGH THE TUNNEL GATE!
RRRAAGG!
RUN!
ARRGH!
ZWING!
TEEBO!!
NO! THERE'S NO TIME, WICKET! YOU MUST SAVE... KNEESAA!
I'LL SAVE YOU, TEEBO...
15

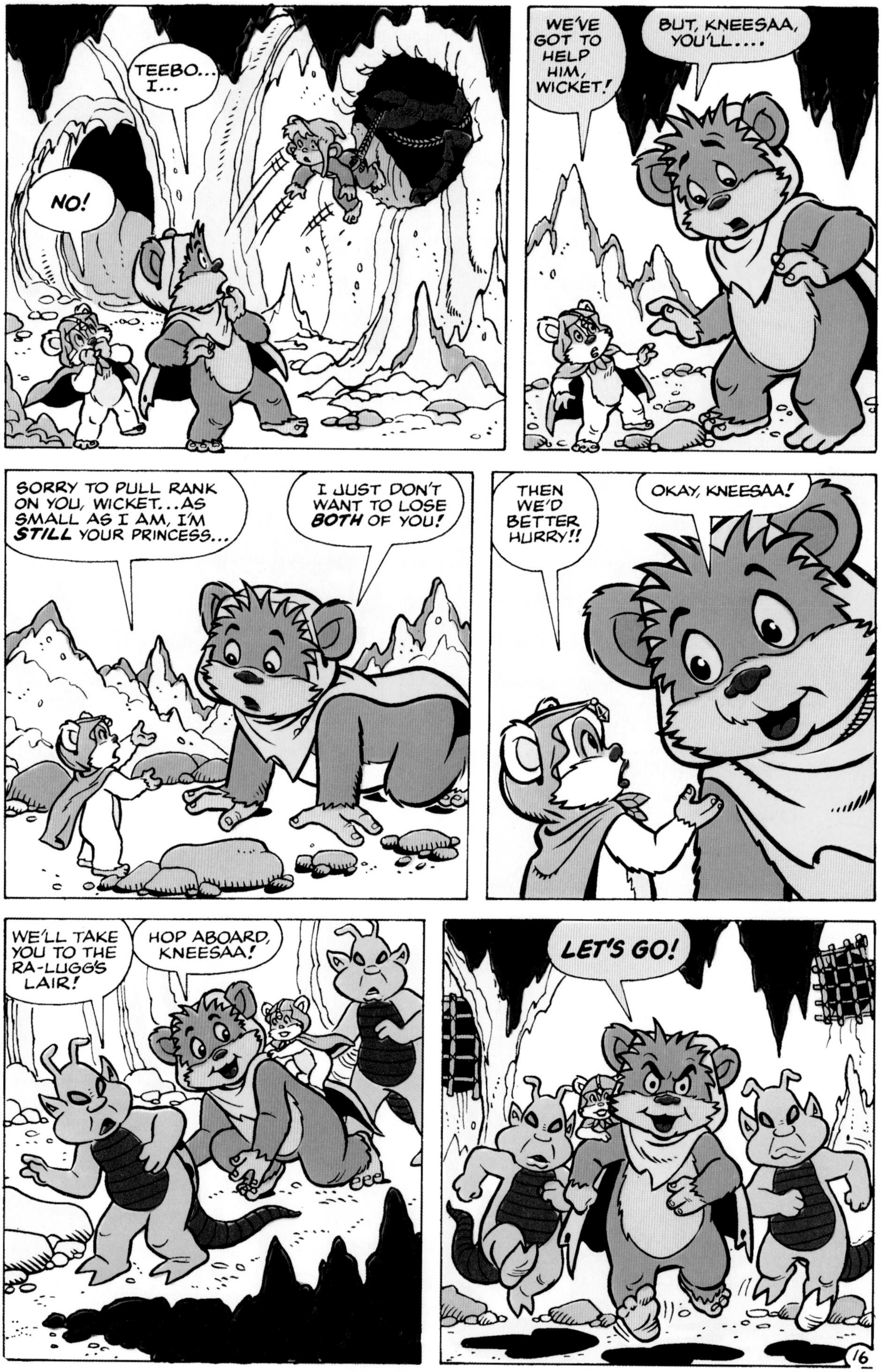

TEEBO... I...
NO!
WE'VE GOT TO HELP HIM, WICKET!
BUT, KNEESAA, YOU'LL....
SORRY TO PULL RANK ON YOU, WICKET...AS SMALL AS I AM, I'M STILL YOUR PRINCESS...
I JUST DON'T WANT TO LOSE BOTH OF YOU!
THEN WE'D BETTER HURRY!!
OKAY, KNEESAA!
WE'LL TAKE YOU TO THE RA-LUGG'S LAIR!
HOP ABOARD, KNEESAA!
LET'S GO!
16

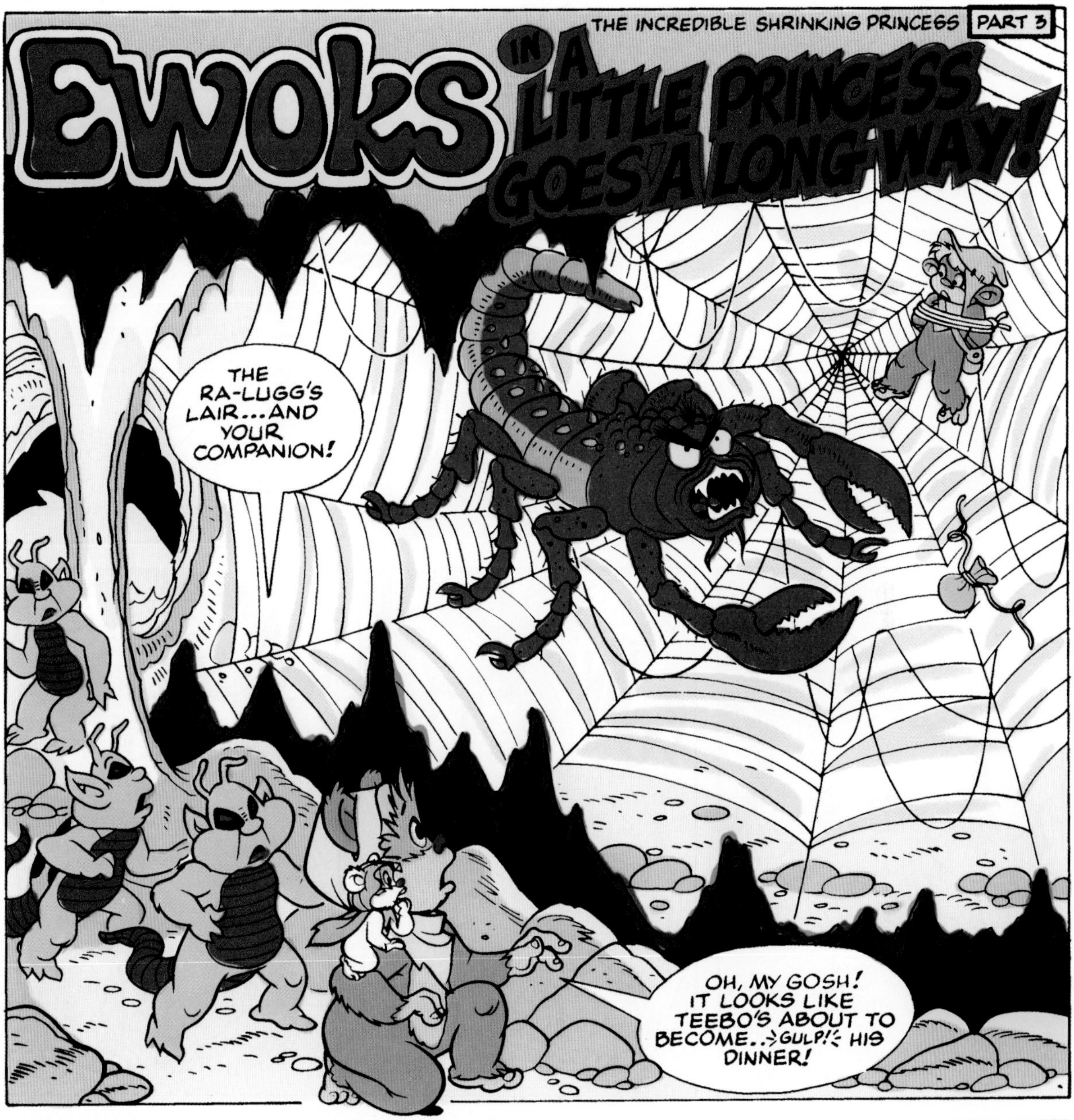
THE INCREDIBLE SHRINKING PRINCESS
PART 3
EWOKS IN A LITTLE PRINCESS GOES A LONG WAY!
THE RA-LUGG'S LAIR...AND YOUR COMPANION!
OH, MY GOSH! IT LOOKS LIKE TEEBO'S ABOUT TO BECOME...GULP! HIS DINNER!

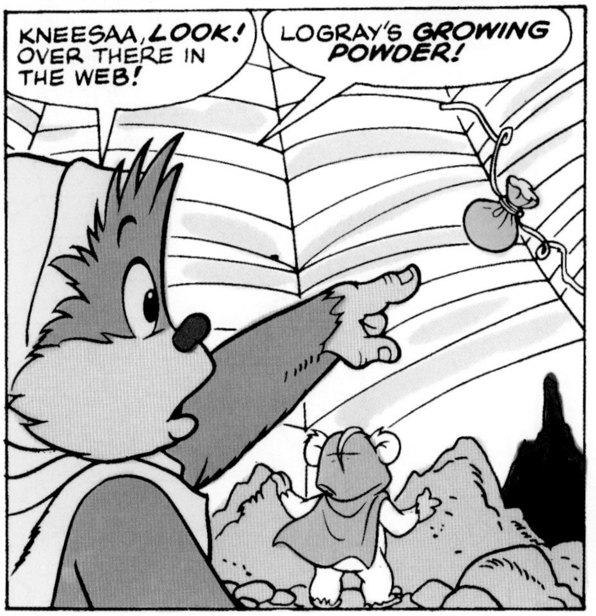
KNEESAA, LOOK! OVER THERE IN THE WEB!
LOGRAY'S GROWING POWDER!

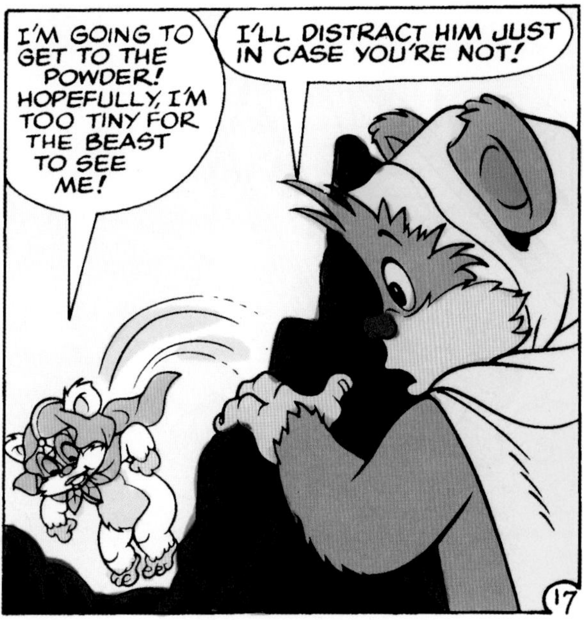
I'M GOING TO GET TO THE POWDER! HOPEFULLY, I'M TOO TINY FOR THE BEAST TO SEE ME!
I'LL DISTRACT HIM JUST IN CASE YOU'RE NOT!
17

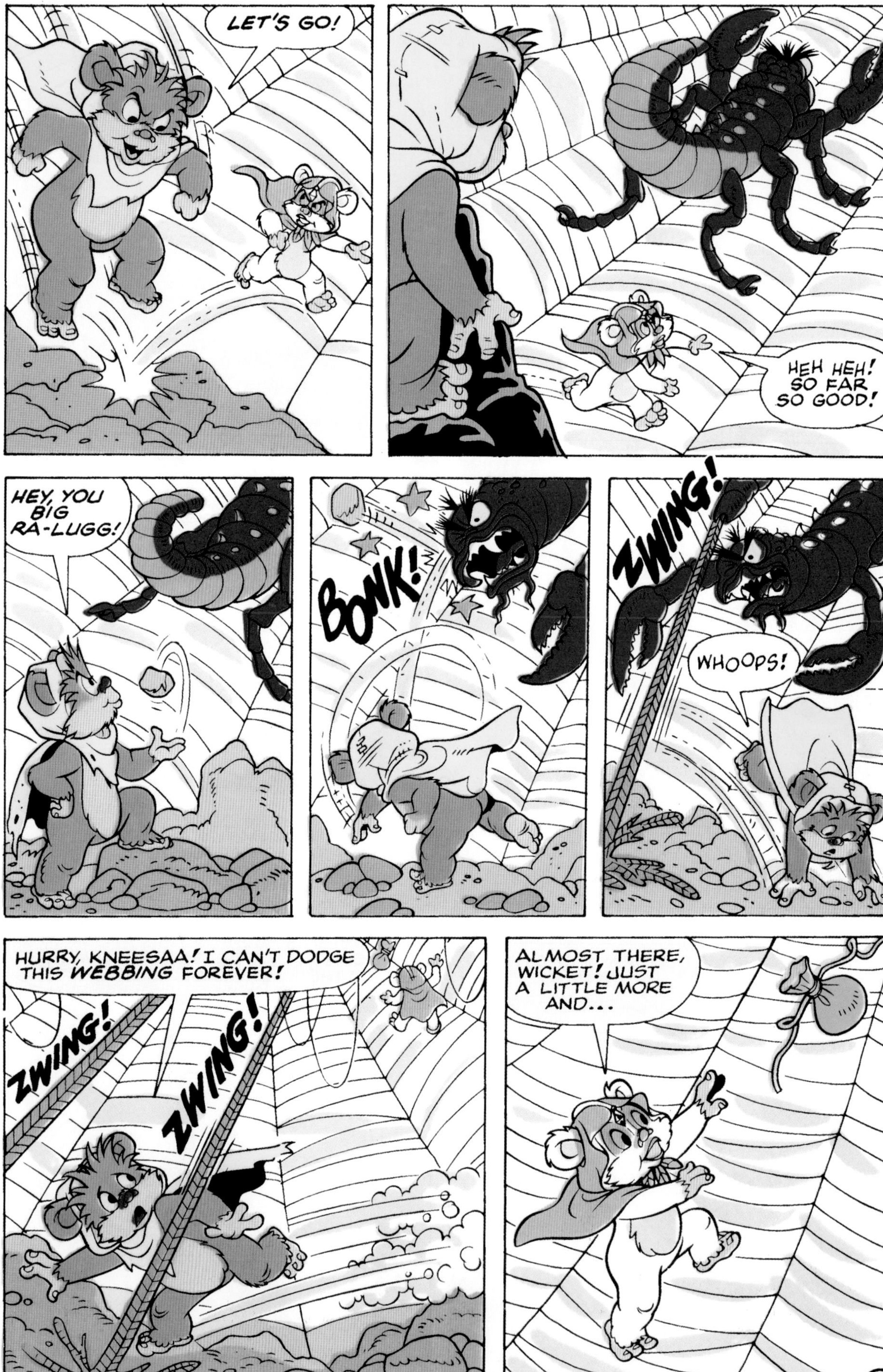
LET'S GO!
HEH HEH! SO FAR SO GOOD!
HEY, YOU BIG RA-LUGG!
BONK!
ZWING!
WHOOPS!
HURRY, KNEESAA! I CAN'T DODGE THIS WEBBING FOREVER!
ZWING!
ZWING!
ALMOST THERE, WICKET! JUST A LITTLE MORE AND...
18

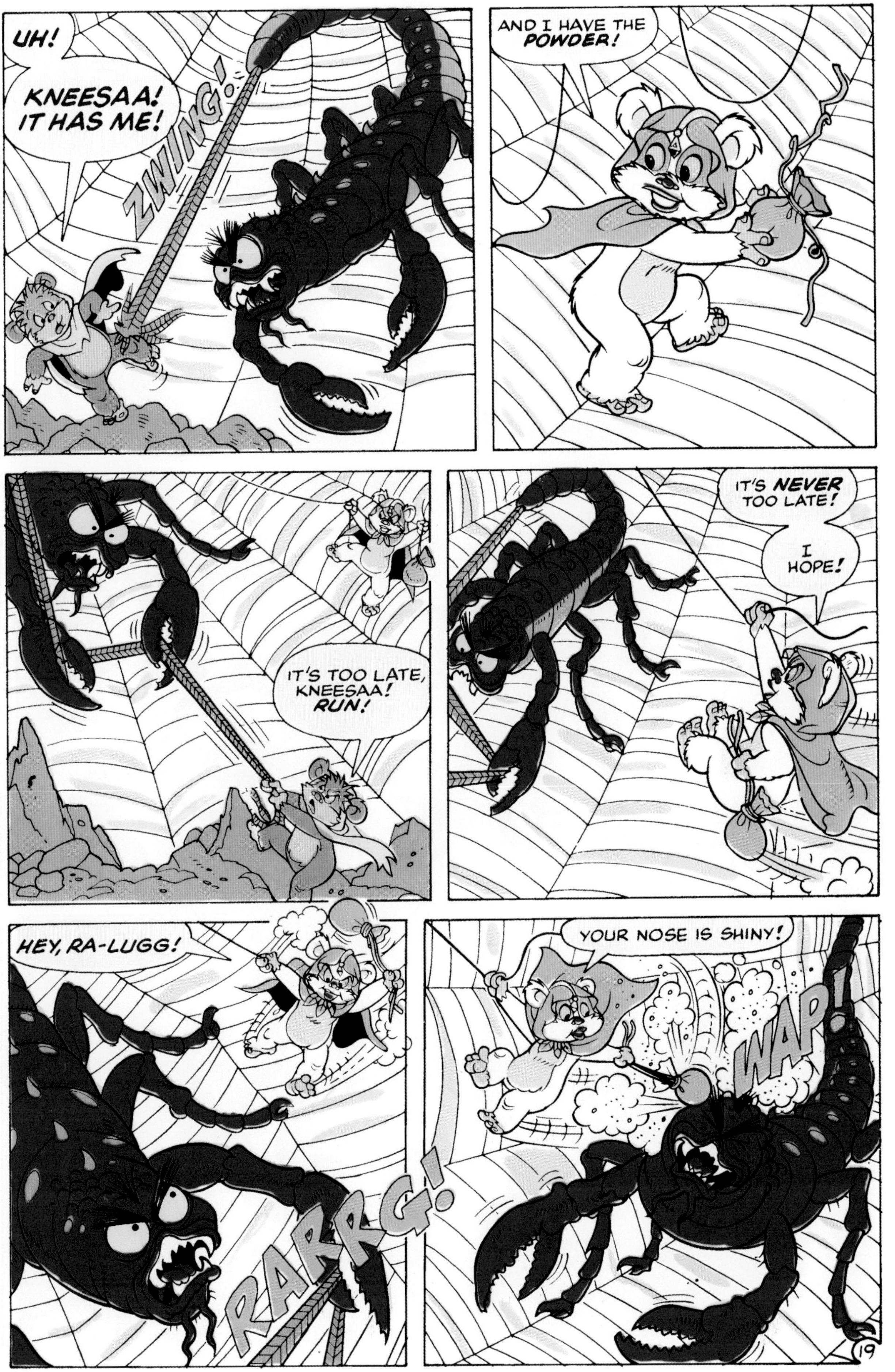
UH!
KNEESAA! IT HAS ME!
ZWING!
AND I HAVE THE POWDER!
IT'S TOO LATE, KNEESAA! RUN!
IT'S NEVER TOO LATE!
I HOPE!
HEY, RA-LUGG!
RARRG!
YOUR NOSE IS SHINY!
WAP!
19

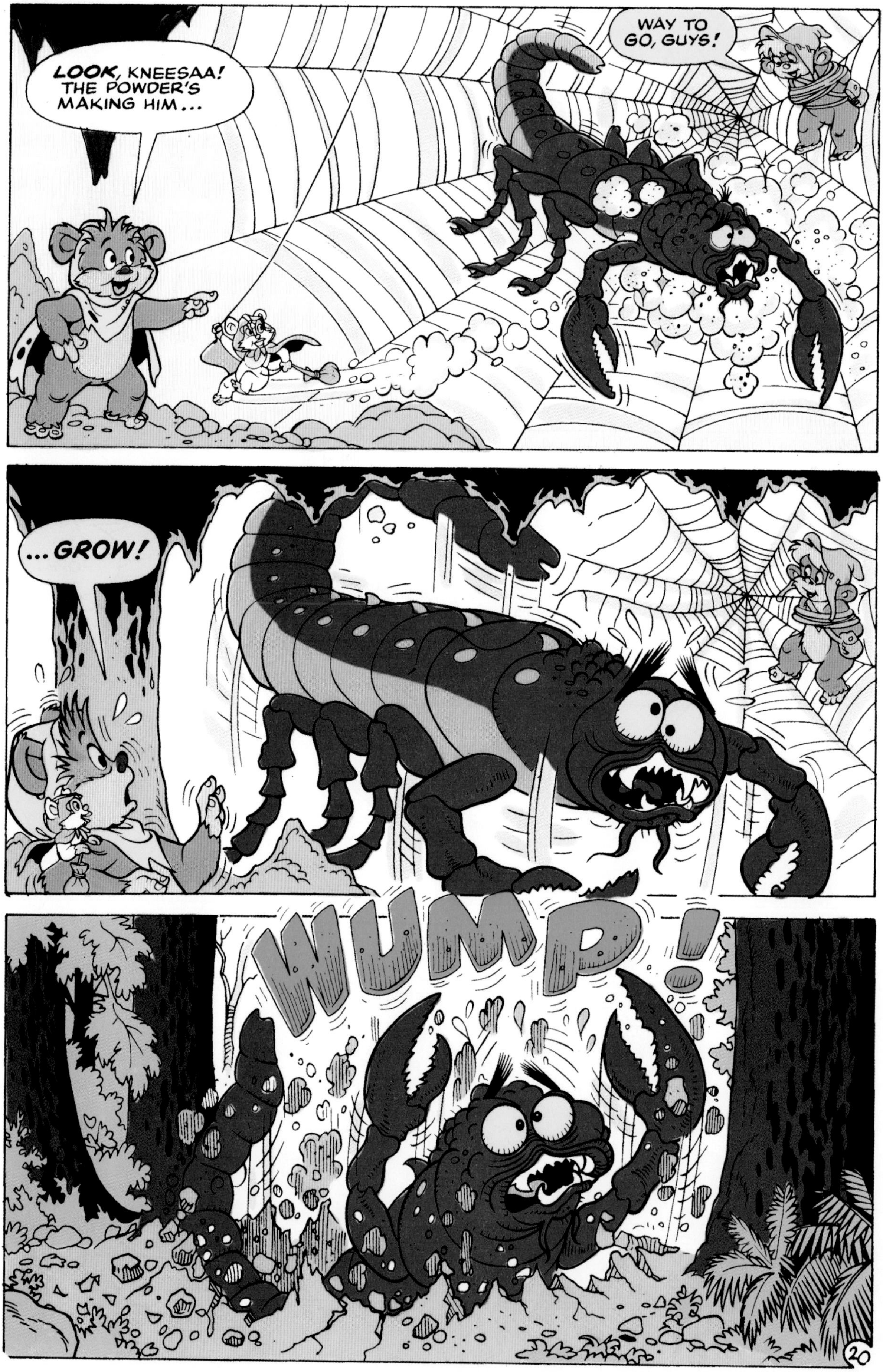
LOOK, KNEESAA! THE POWDER'S MAKING HIM...
WAY TO GO, GUYS!
...GROW!
WUMP!
20

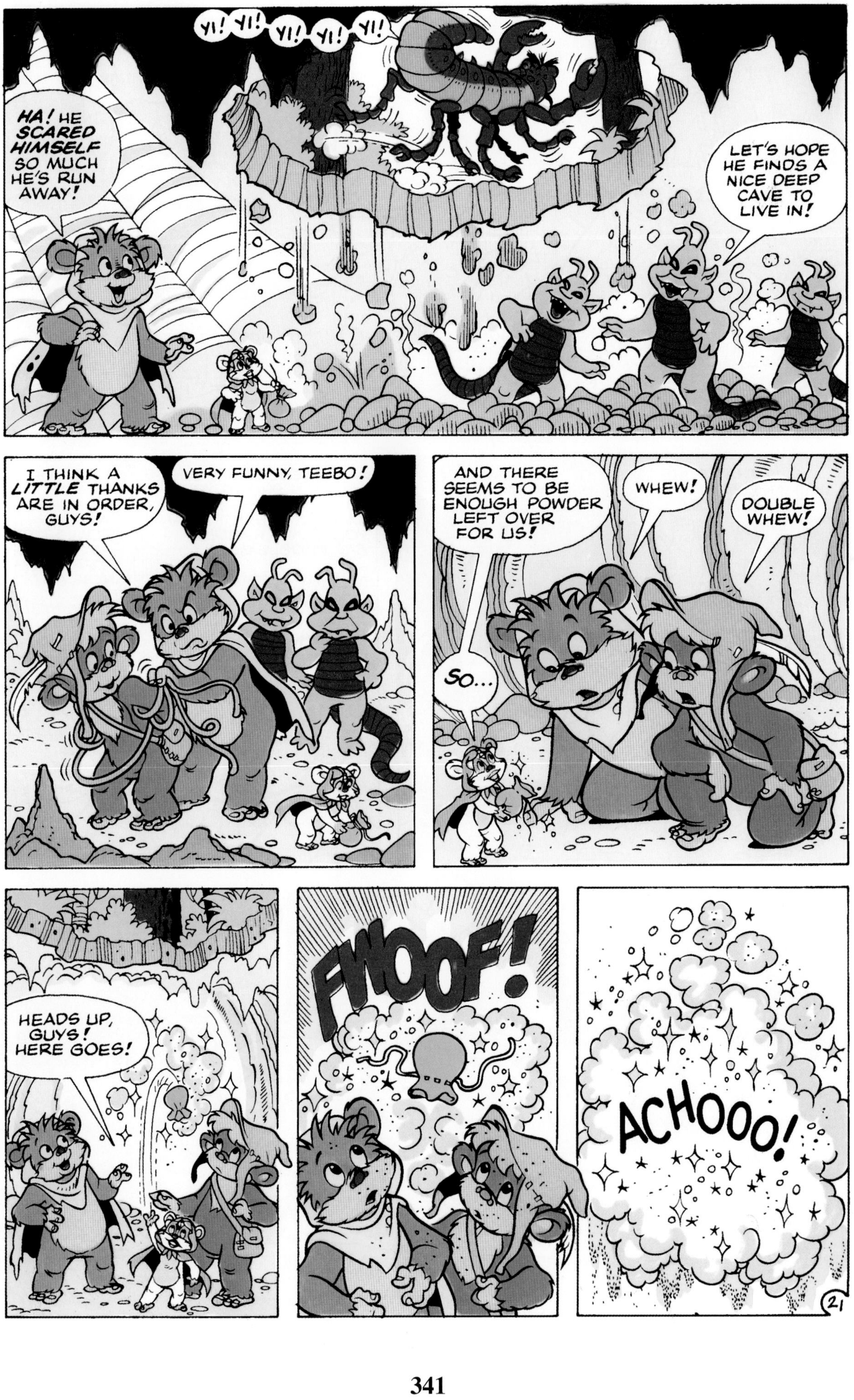
YI! YI! YI! YI! YI!
HA! HE SCARED HIMSELF SO MUCH HE'S RUN AWAY!
LET'S HOPE HE FINDS A NICE DEEP CAVE TO LIVE IN!
I THINK A LITTLE THANKS ARE IN ORDER, GUYS!
VERY FUNNY, TEEBO!
AND THERE SEEMS TO BE ENOUGH POWDER LEFT OVER FOR US!
WHEW!
DOUBLE WHEW!
SO...
HEADS UP, GUYS! HERE GOES!
FWOOF!
ACHOOO!
21

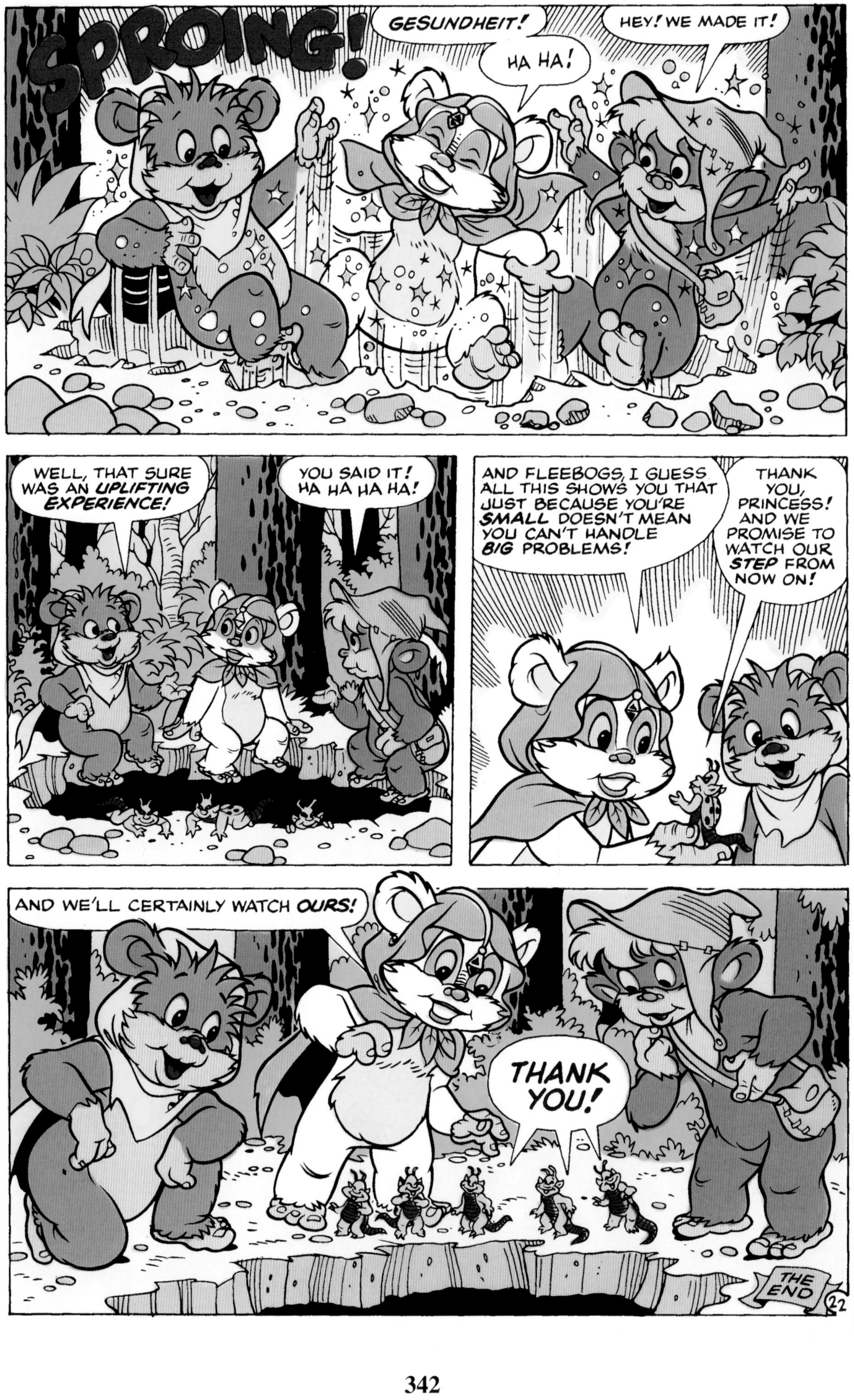
SPROING!
GESUNDHEIT!
HA HA!
HEY! WE MADE IT!
WELL, THAT SURE WAS AN UPLIFTING EXPERIENCE!
YOU SAID IT! HA HA HA HA!
AND FLEEBOGS, I GUESS ALL THIS SHOWS YOU THAT JUST BECAUSE YOU'RE SMALL DOESN'T MEAN YOU CAN'T HANDLE BIG PROBLEMS!
THANK YOU, PRINCESS! AND WE PROMISE TO WATCH OUR STEP FROM NOW ON!
AND WE'LL CERTAINLY WATCH OURS!
THANK YOU!
THE END
22

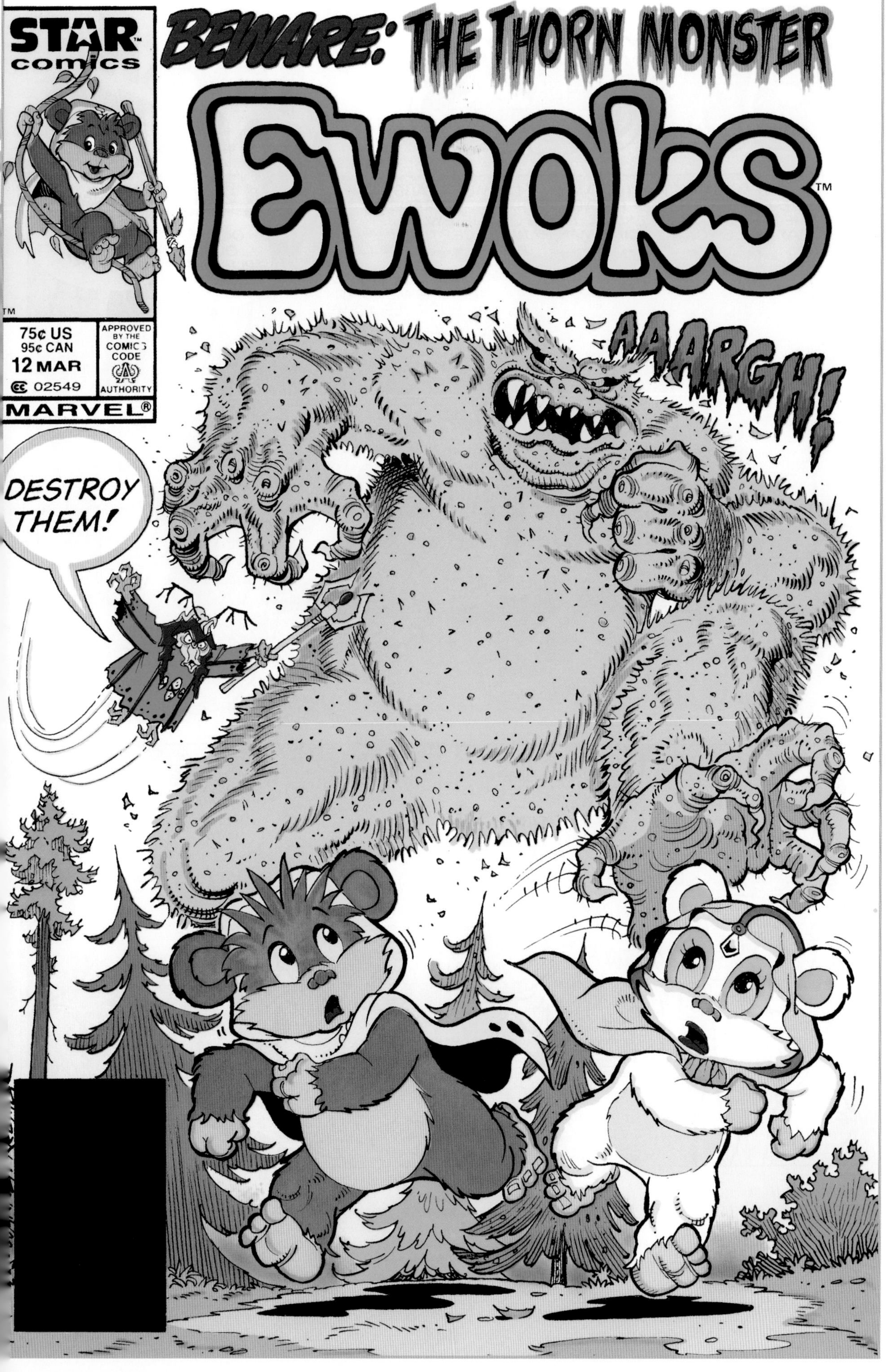
STAR comics
BEWARE: THE THORN MONSTER
EWOKS™
75¢ US
95¢ CAN
12 MAR
02549
APPROVED BY THE COMICS CODE AUTHORITY
MARVEL®
AAARGH!
DESTROY THEM!

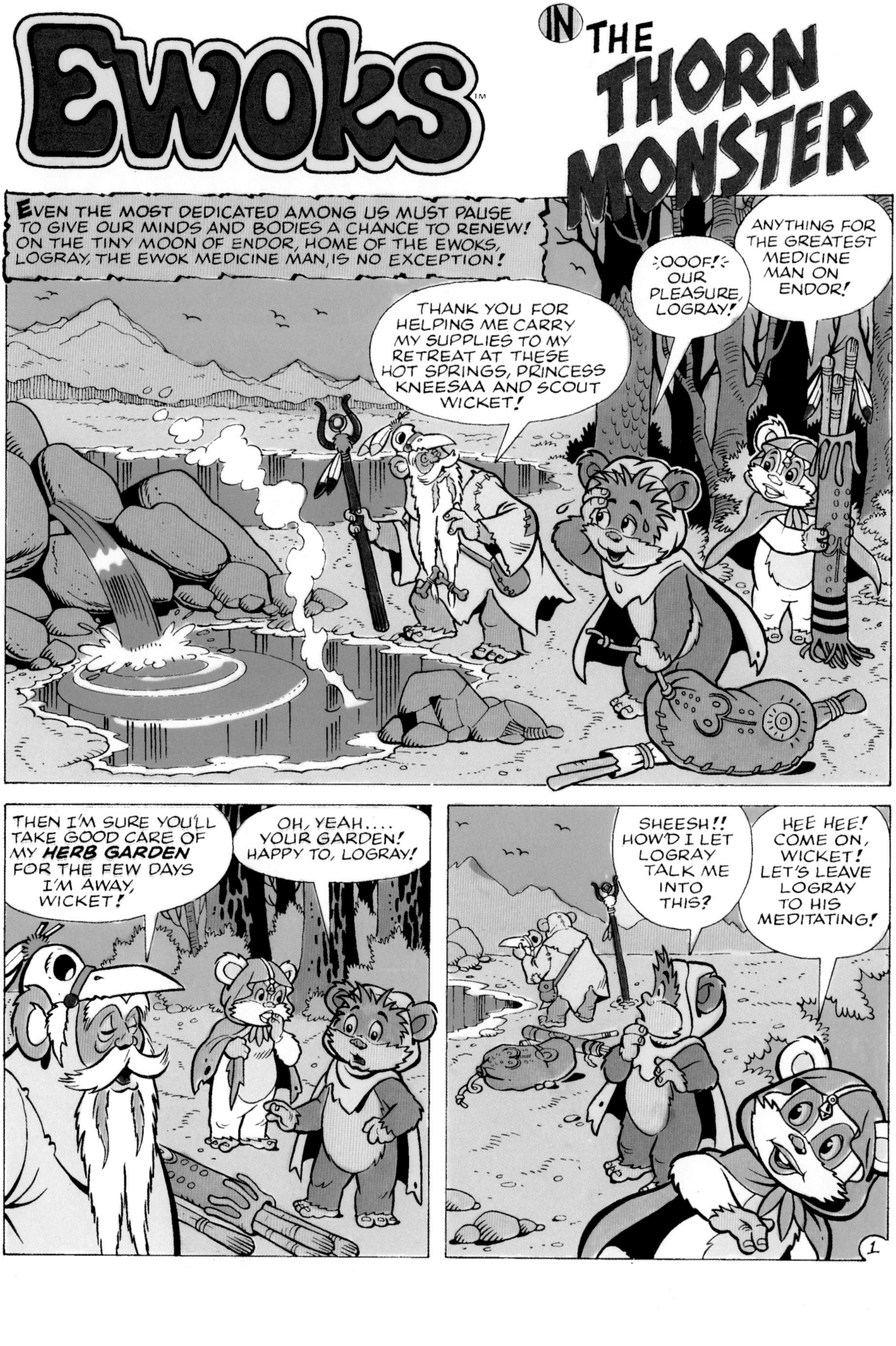
EWOKS
IN THE THORN MONSTER
EVEN THE MOST DEDICATED AMONG US MUST PAUSE TO GIVE OUR MINDS AND BODIES A CHANCE TO RENEW! ON THE TINY MOON OF ENDOR, HOME OF THE EWOKS, LOGRAY, THE EWOK MEDICINE MAN, IS NO EXCEPTION!
THANK YOU FOR HELPING ME CARRY MY SUPPLIES TO MY RETREAT AT THESE HOT SPRINGS, PRINCESS KNEESAA AND SCOUT WICKET!
OOOF! OUR PLEASURE, LOGRAY!
ANYTHING FOR THE GREATEST MEDICINE MAN ON ENDOR!
THEN I'M SURE YOU'LL TAKE GOOD CARE OF MY HERB GARDEN FOR THE FEW DAYS I'M AWAY, WICKET!
OH, YEAH.... YOUR GARDEN! HAPPY TO, LOGRAY!
SHEESH!! HOW'D I LET LOGRAY TALK ME INTO THIS?
HEE HEE! COME ON, WICKET! LET'S LEAVE LOGRAY TO HIS MEDITATING!
1

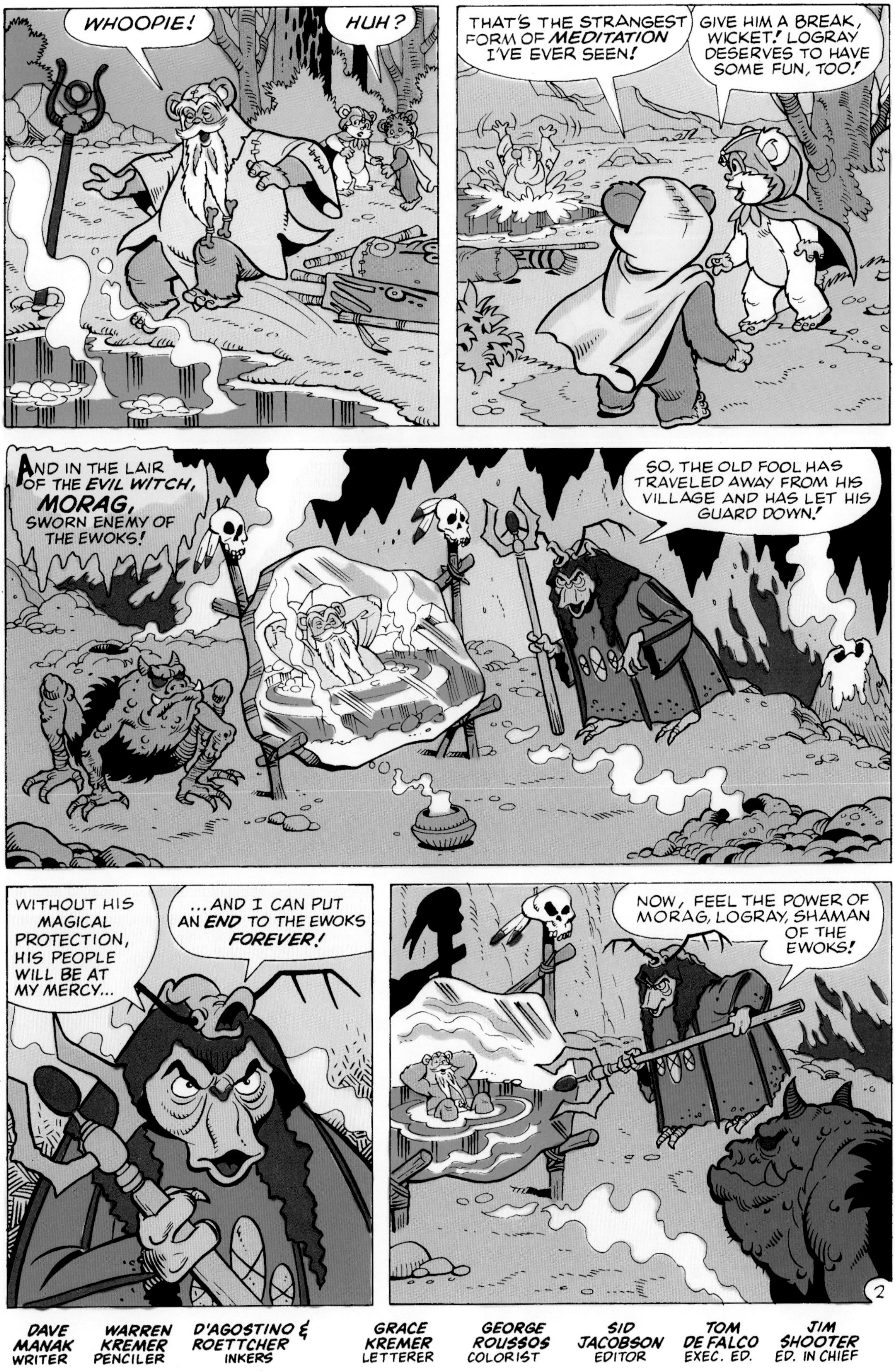

WHOOPIE!
HUH?
THAT'S THE STRANGEST FORM OF MEDITATION I'VE EVER SEEN!
GIVE HIM A BREAK, WICKET! LOGRAY DESERVES TO HAVE SOME FUN, TOO!
AND IN THE LAIR OF THE EVIL WITCH, MORAG, SWORN ENEMY OF THE EWOKS!
SO, THE OLD FOOL HAS TRAVELED AWAY FROM HIS VILLAGE AND HAS LET HIS GUARD DOWN!
WITHOUT HIS MAGICAL PROTECTION, HIS PEOPLE WILL BE AT MY MERCY...
...AND I CAN PUT AN END TO THE EWOKS FOREVER!
NOW, FEEL THE POWER OF MORAG, LOGRAY, SHAMAN OF THE EWOKS!
2

DAVE MANAK WRITER · WARREN KREMER PENCILER · D'AGOSTINO & ROETTCHER INKERS · GRACE KREMER LETTERER · GEORGE ROUSSOS COLORIST · SID JACOBSON EDITOR · TOM DE FALCO EXEC. ED. · JIM SHOOTER ED. IN CHIEF

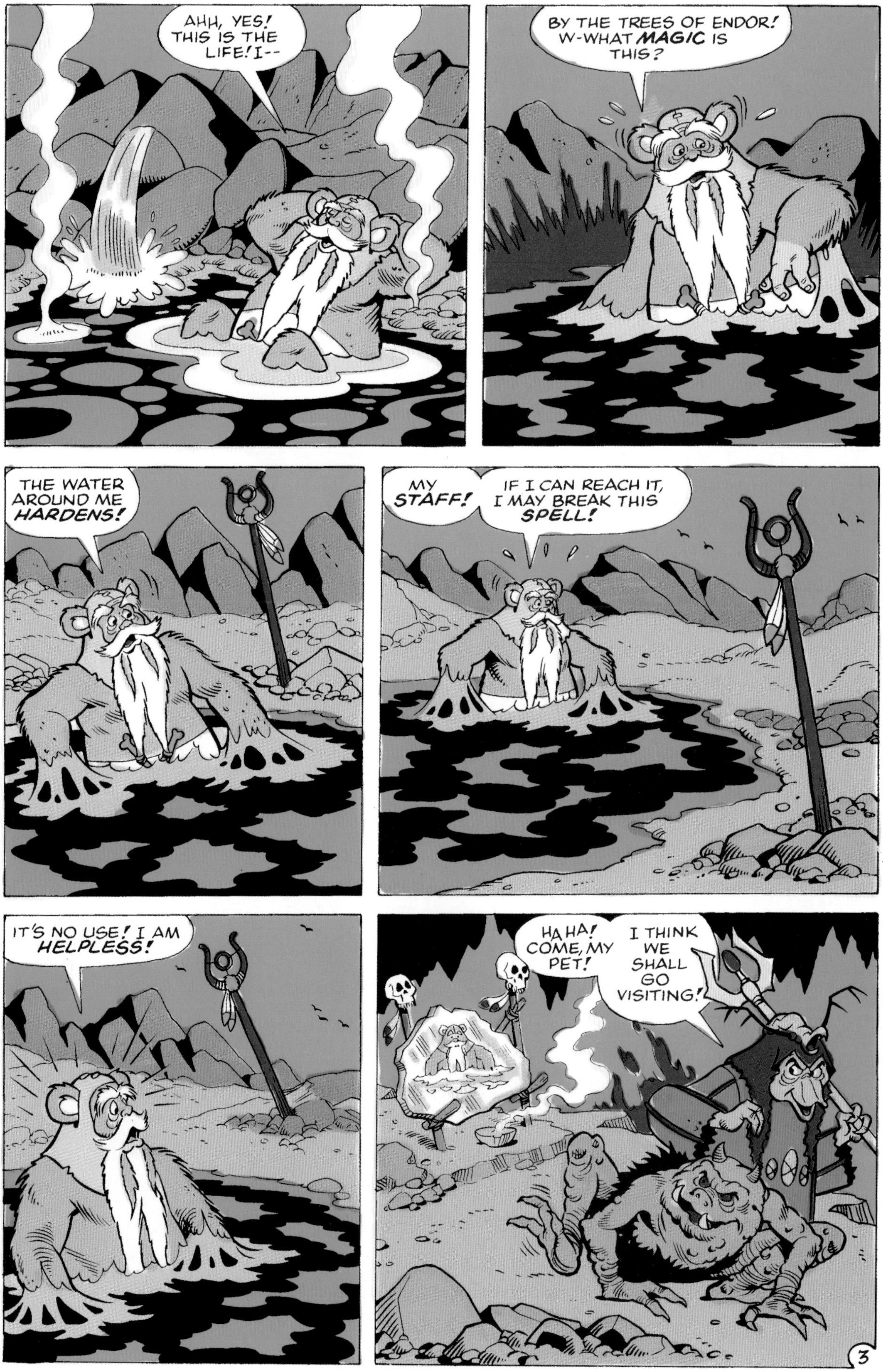
AHH, YES! THIS IS THE LIFE! I--
BY THE TREES OF ENDOR! W-WHAT MAGIC IS THIS?
THE WATER AROUND ME HARDENS!
MY STAFF!
IF I CAN REACH IT, I MAY BREAK THIS SPELL!
IT'S NO USE! I AM HELPLESS!
HA HA! COME, MY PET!
I THINK WE SHALL GO VISITING!
3

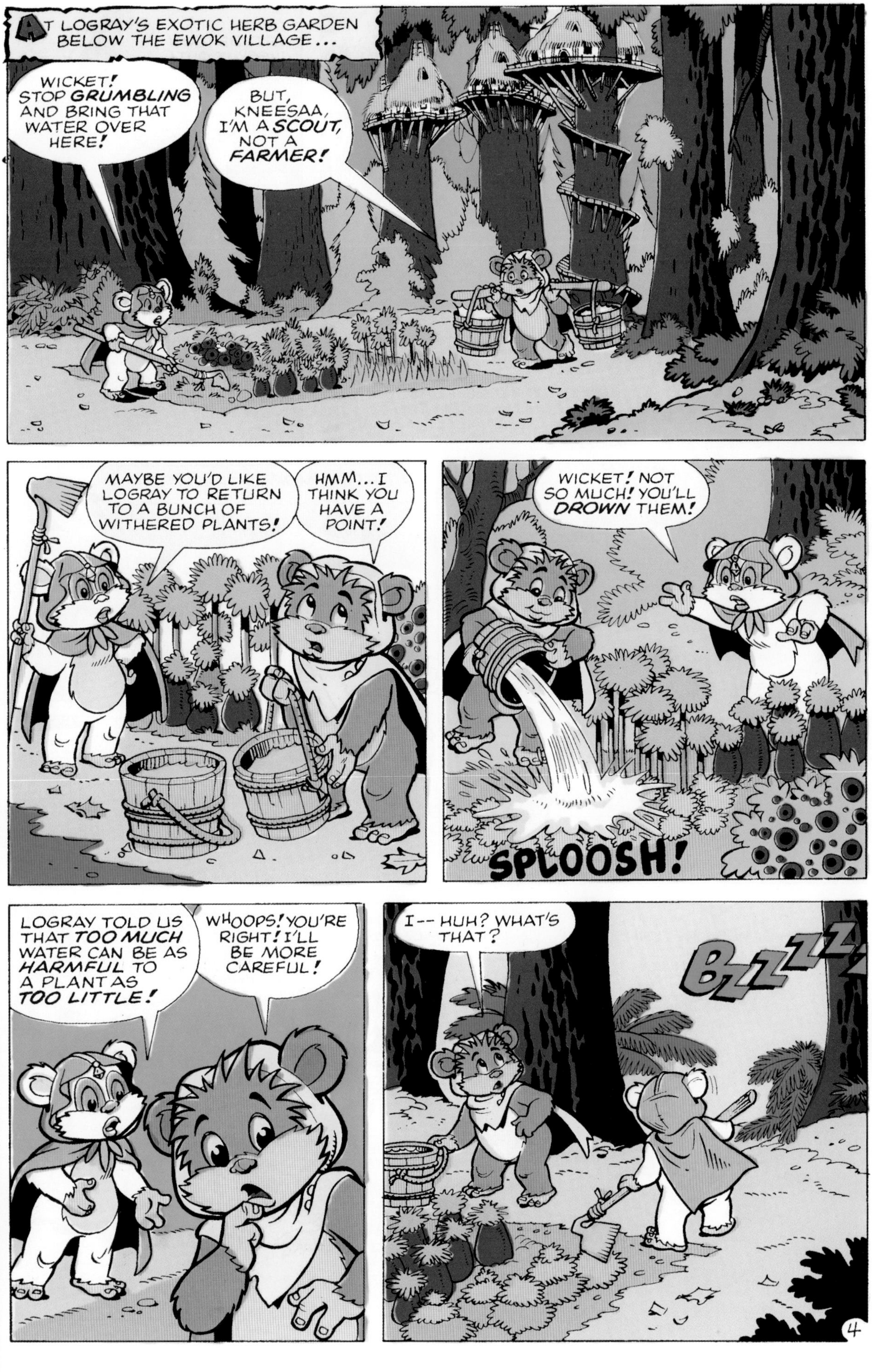
AT LOGRAY'S EXOTIC HERB GARDEN BELOW THE EWOK VILLAGE...
WICKET! STOP GRUMBLING AND BRING THAT WATER OVER HERE!
BUT, KNEESAA, I'M A SCOUT, NOT A FARMER!
MAYBE YOU'D LIKE LOGRAY TO RETURN TO A BUNCH OF WITHERED PLANTS!
HMM... I THINK YOU HAVE A POINT!
WICKET! NOT SO MUCH! YOU'LL DROWN THEM!
SPLOOSH!
LOGRAY TOLD US THAT TOO MUCH WATER CAN BE AS HARMFUL TO A PLANT AS TOO LITTLE!
WHOOPS! YOU'RE RIGHT! I'LL BE MORE CAREFUL!
I-- HUH? WHAT'S THAT?
BZZZZZ
4

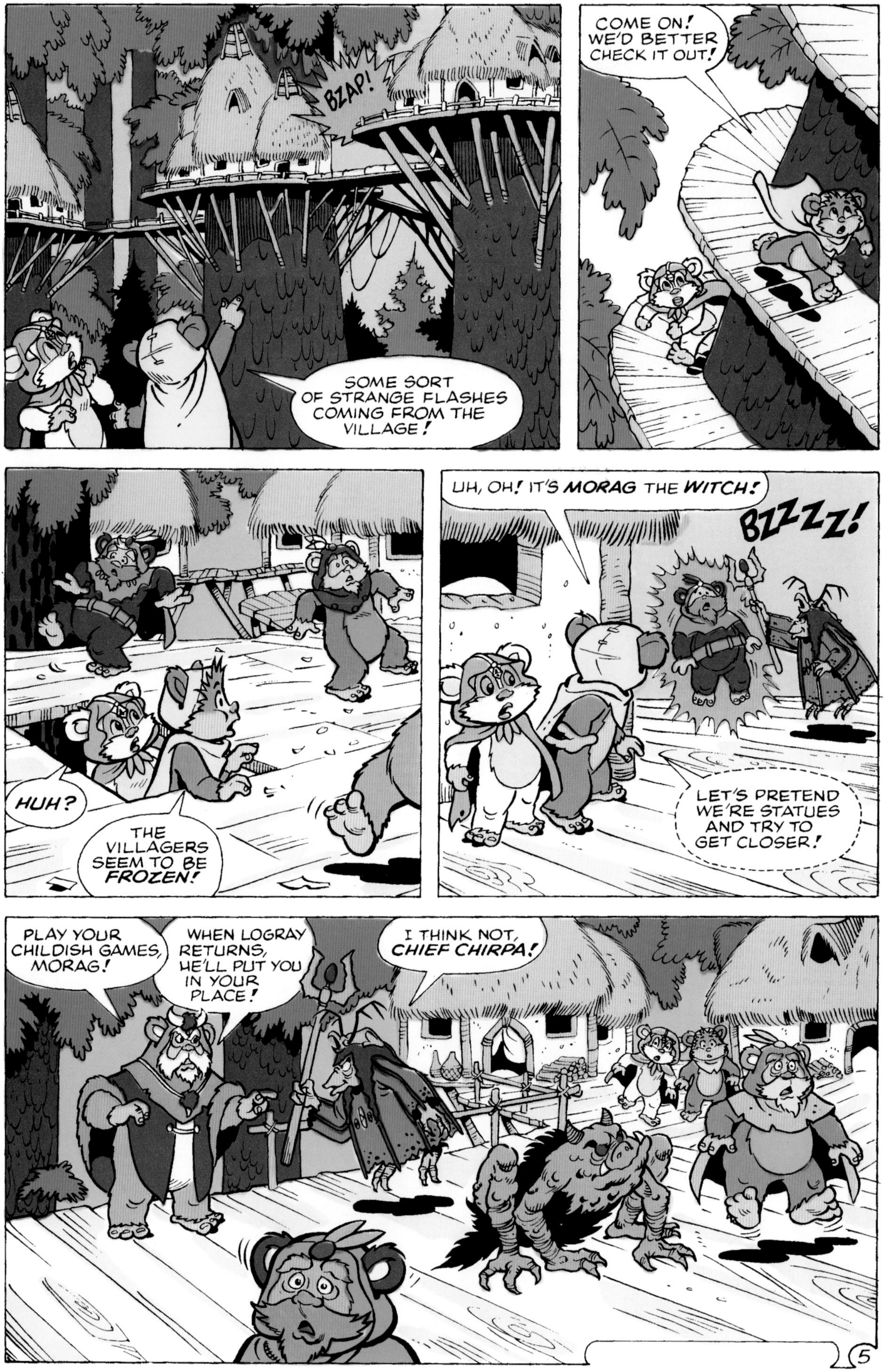
BZAP!
SOME SORT OF STRANGE FLASHES COMING FROM THE VILLAGE!
COME ON! WE'D BETTER CHECK IT OUT!
HUH?
THE VILLAGERS SEEM TO BE FROZEN!
UH, OH! IT'S MORAG THE WITCH!
BZZZZ!
LET'S PRETEND WE'RE STATUES AND TRY TO GET CLOSER!
PLAY YOUR CHILDISH GAMES, MORAG!
WHEN LOGRAY RETURNS, HE'LL PUT YOU IN YOUR PLACE!
I THINK NOT, CHIEF CHIRPA!
5

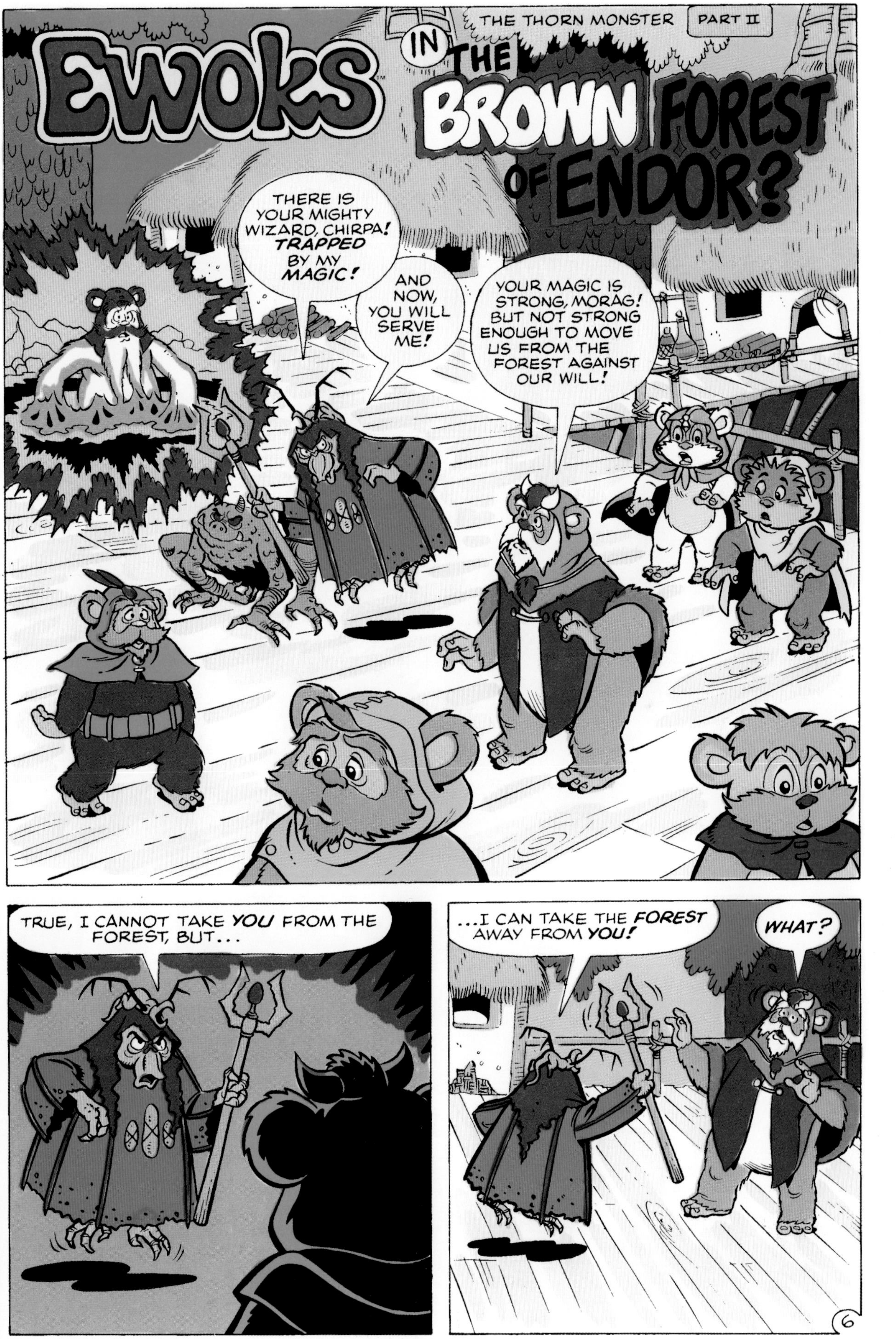
THE THORN MONSTER
PART II
EWOKS™
IN
THE BROWN FOREST OF ENDOR?
THERE IS YOUR MIGHTY WIZARD, CHIRPA! TRAPPED BY MY MAGIC!
AND NOW, YOU WILL SERVE ME!
YOUR MAGIC IS STRONG, MORAG! BUT NOT STRONG ENOUGH TO MOVE US FROM THE FOREST AGAINST OUR WILL!
TRUE, I CANNOT TAKE YOU FROM THE FOREST, BUT...
...I CAN TAKE THE FOREST AWAY FROM YOU!
WHAT?
6

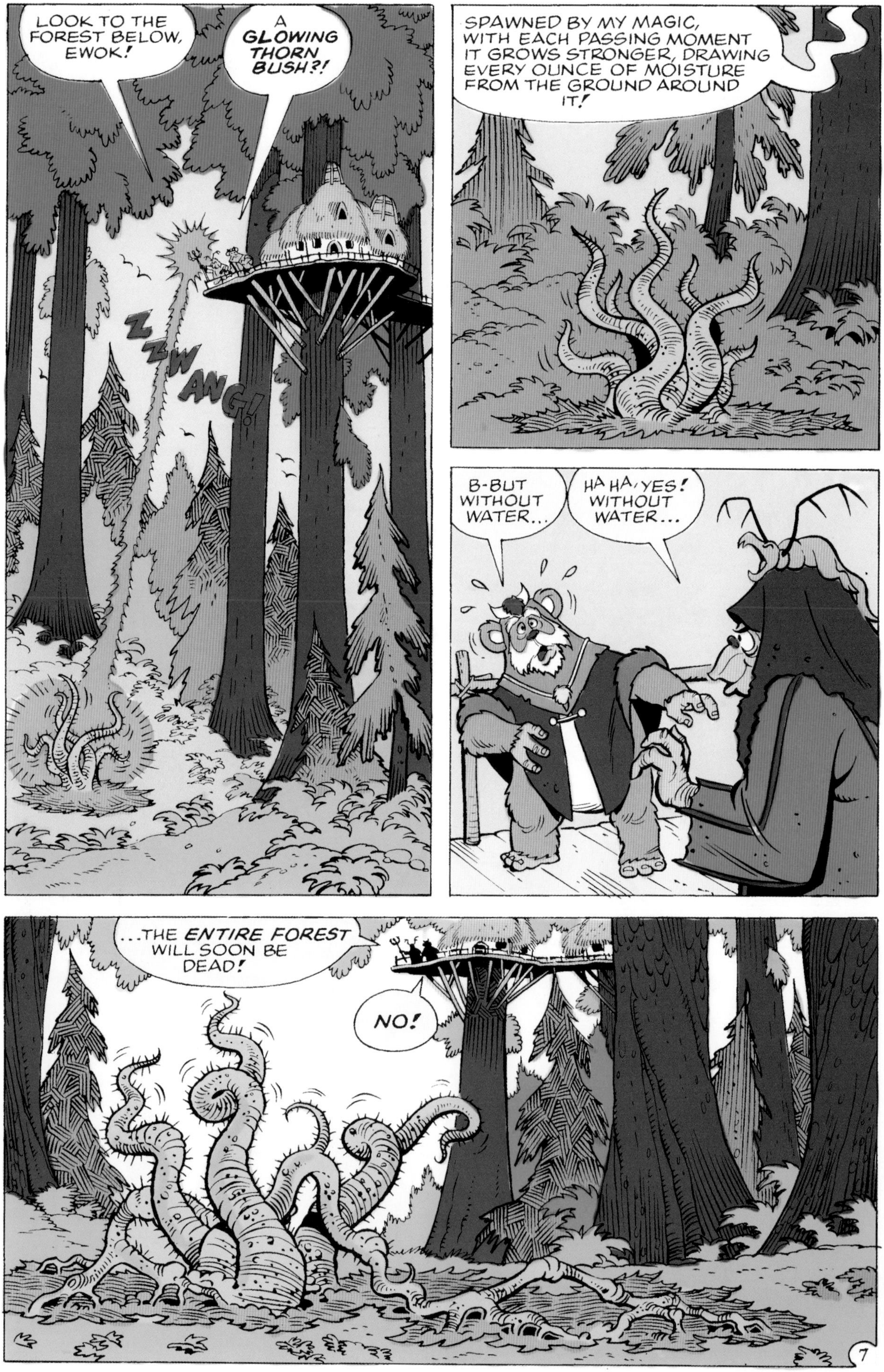
LOOK TO THE FOREST BELOW, EWOK!
A GLOWING THORN BUSH?!
ZZWANG!
SPAWNED BY MY MAGIC, WITH EACH PASSING MOMENT IT GROWS STRONGER, DRAWING EVERY OUNCE OF MOISTURE FROM THE GROUND AROUND IT!
B-BUT WITHOUT WATER...
HA HA, YES! WITHOUT WATER...
...THE ENTIRE FOREST WILL SOON BE DEAD!
NO!
7

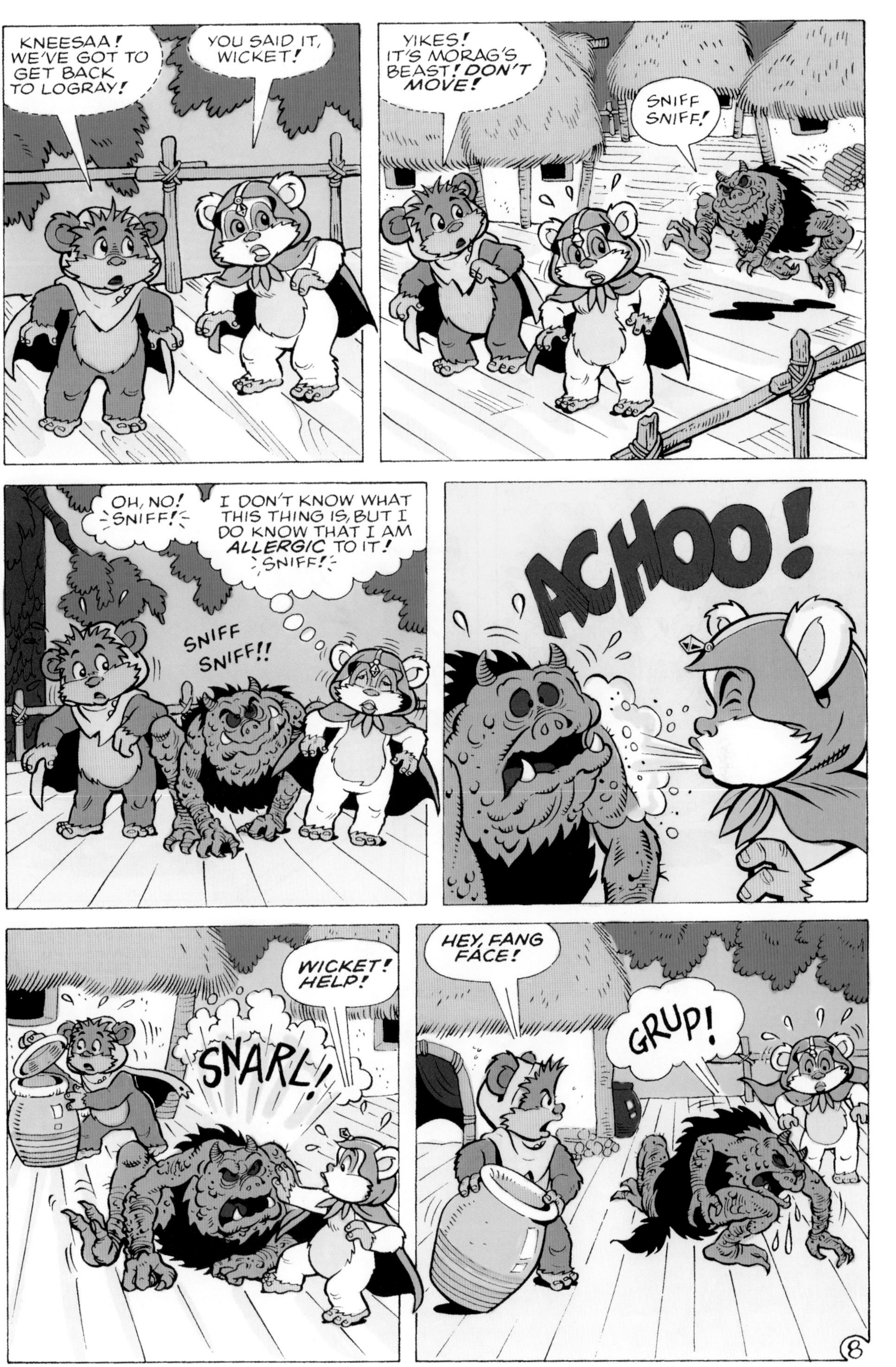
KNEESAA! WE'VE GOT TO GET BACK TO LOGRAY!
YOU SAID IT, WICKET!
YIKES! IT'S MORAG'S BEAST! DON'T MOVE!
SNIFF SNIFF!
OH, NO! SNIFF!
I DON'T KNOW WHAT THIS THING IS, BUT I DO KNOW THAT I AM ALLERGIC TO IT! SNIFF!
SNIFF SNIFF!!
ACHOO!
SNARL!
WICKET! HELP!
HEY, FANG FACE!
GRUP!
8

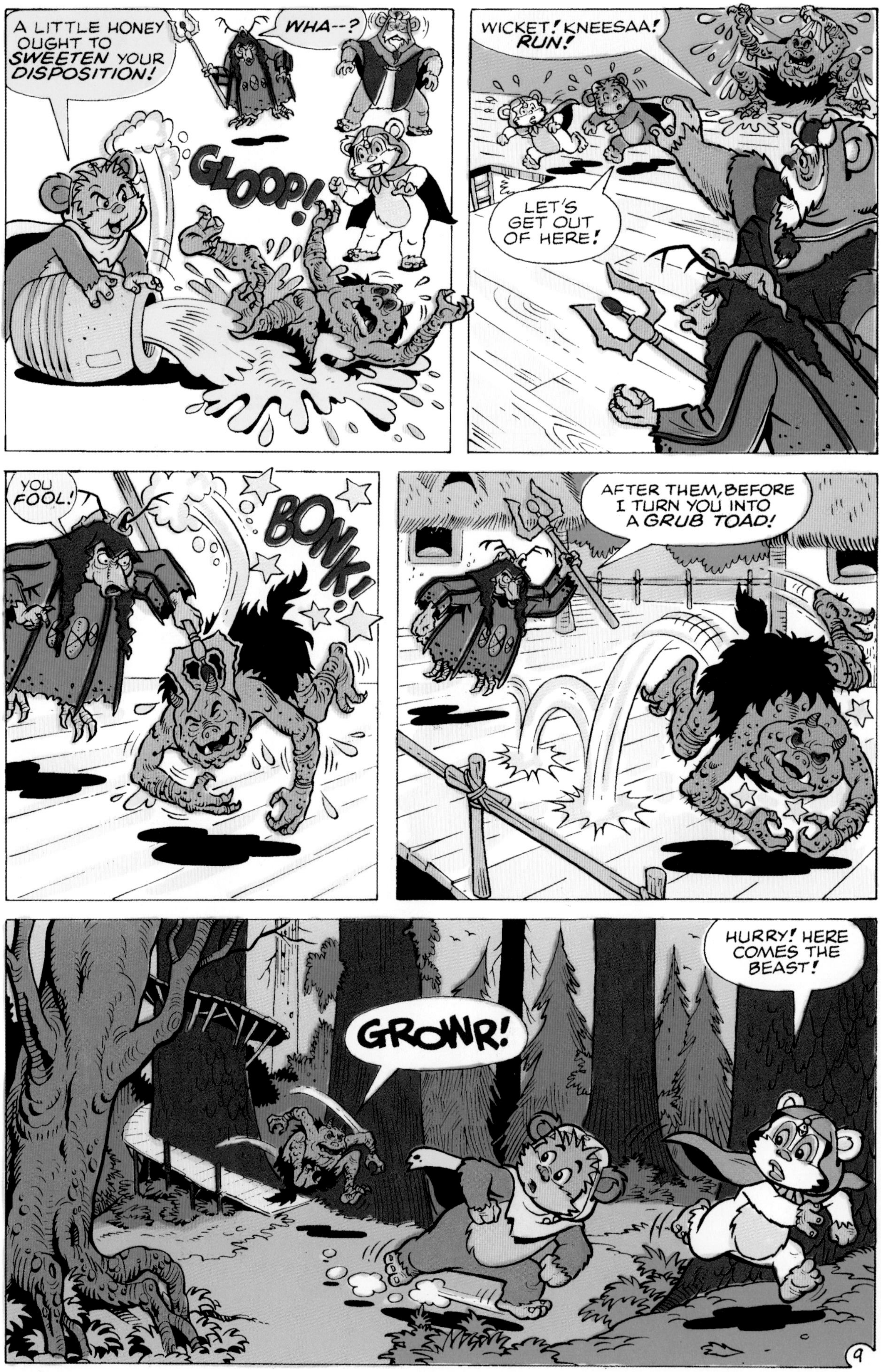

A LITTLE HONEY OUGHT TO SWEETEN YOUR DISPOSITION!
WHA--?
GLOOP!
WICKET! KNEESAA! RUN!
LET'S GET OUT OF HERE!
YOU FOOL!
BONK!
AFTER THEM, BEFORE I TURN YOU INTO A GRUB TOAD!
HURRY! HERE COMES THE BEAST!
GROWR!
9

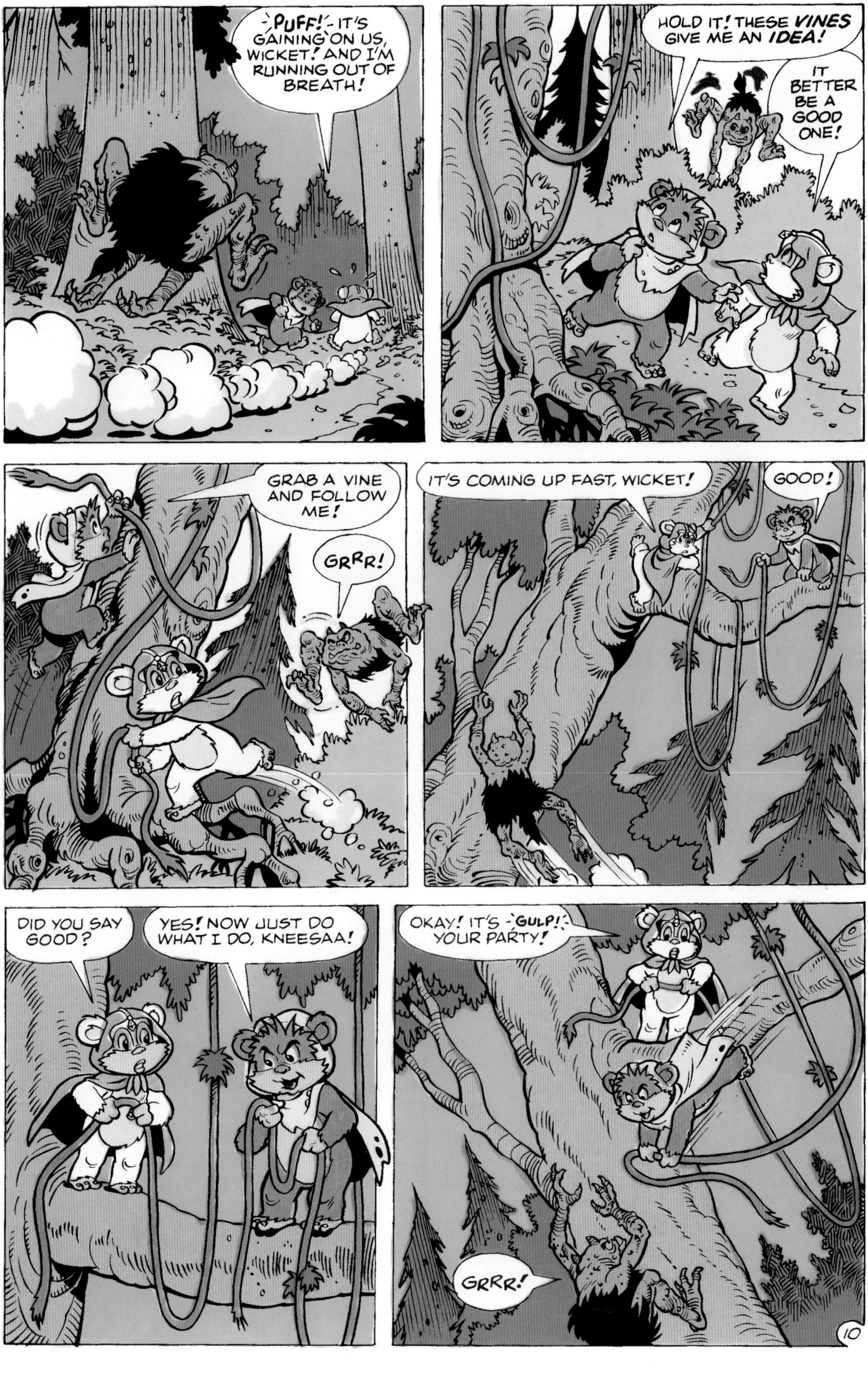
-PUFF!- IT'S GAINING ON US, WICKET! AND I'M RUNNING OUT OF BREATH!
HOLD IT! THESE VINES GIVE ME AN IDEA!
IT BETTER BE A GOOD ONE!
GRAB A VINE AND FOLLOW ME!
GRRR!
IT'S COMING UP FAST, WICKET!
GOOD!
DID YOU SAY GOOD?
YES! NOW JUST DO WHAT I DO, KNEESAA!
OKAY! IT'S -GULP!- YOUR PARTY!
GRRR!
10

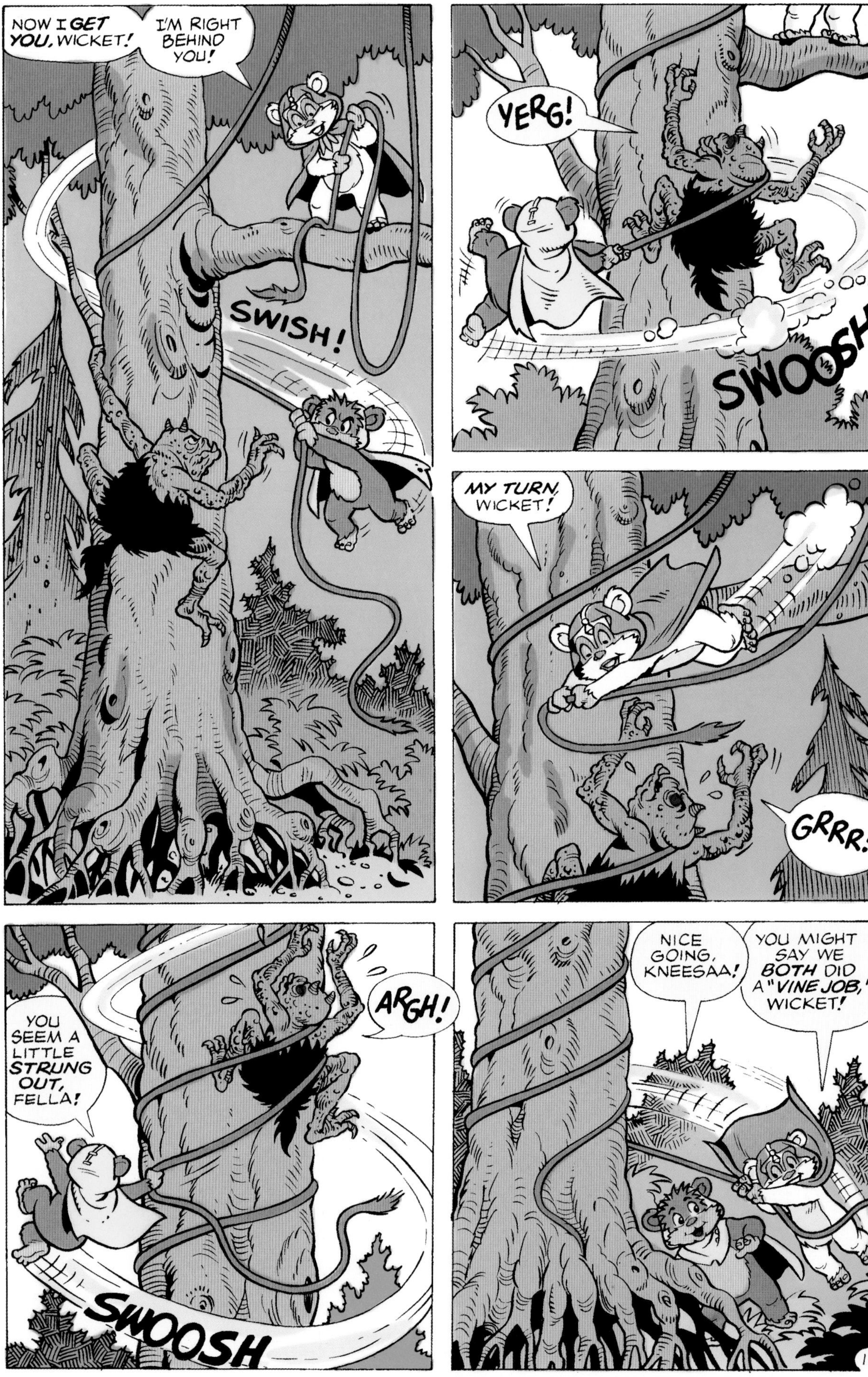

NOW I **GET YOU,** WICKET!
I'M RIGHT BEHIND YOU!
SWISH!
YERG!
SWOOSH!
MY TURN, WICKET!
GRRR!
YOU SEEM A LITTLE **STRUNG OUT,** FELLA!
ARGH!
SWOOSH
NICE GOING, KNEESAA!
YOU MIGHT SAY WE **BOTH** DID A "**VINE JOB,**" WICKET!
11

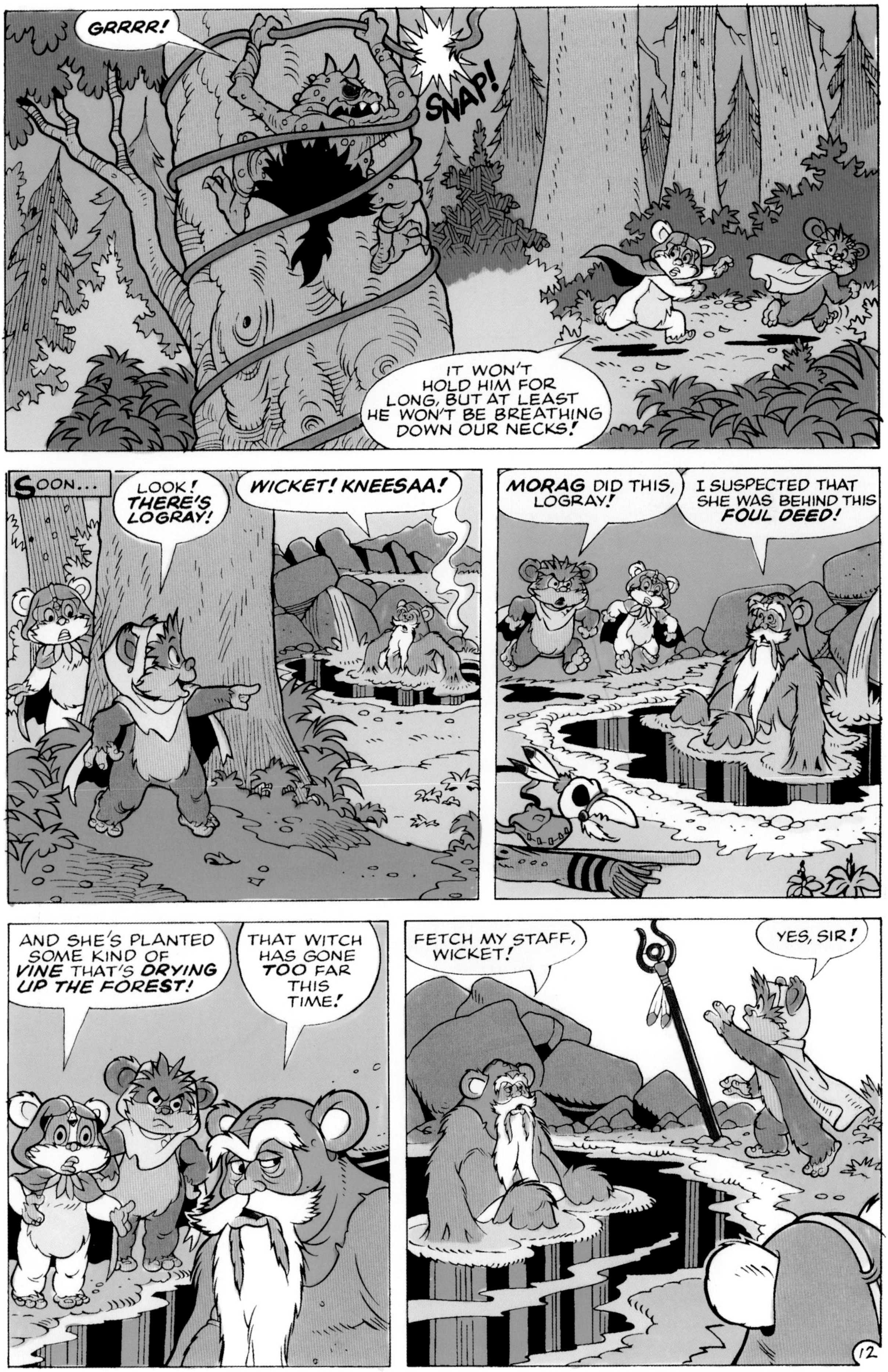
GRRRR!
SNAP!
IT WON'T HOLD HIM FOR LONG, BUT AT LEAST HE WON'T BE BREATHING DOWN OUR NECKS!
SOON...
LOOK! THERE'S LOGRAY!
WICKET! KNEESAA!
MORAG DID THIS, LOGRAY!
I SUSPECTED THAT SHE WAS BEHIND THIS FOUL DEED!
AND SHE'S PLANTED SOME KIND OF VINE THAT'S DRYING UP THE FOREST!
THAT WITCH HAS GONE TOO FAR THIS TIME!
FETCH MY STAFF, WICKET!
YES, SIR!
12

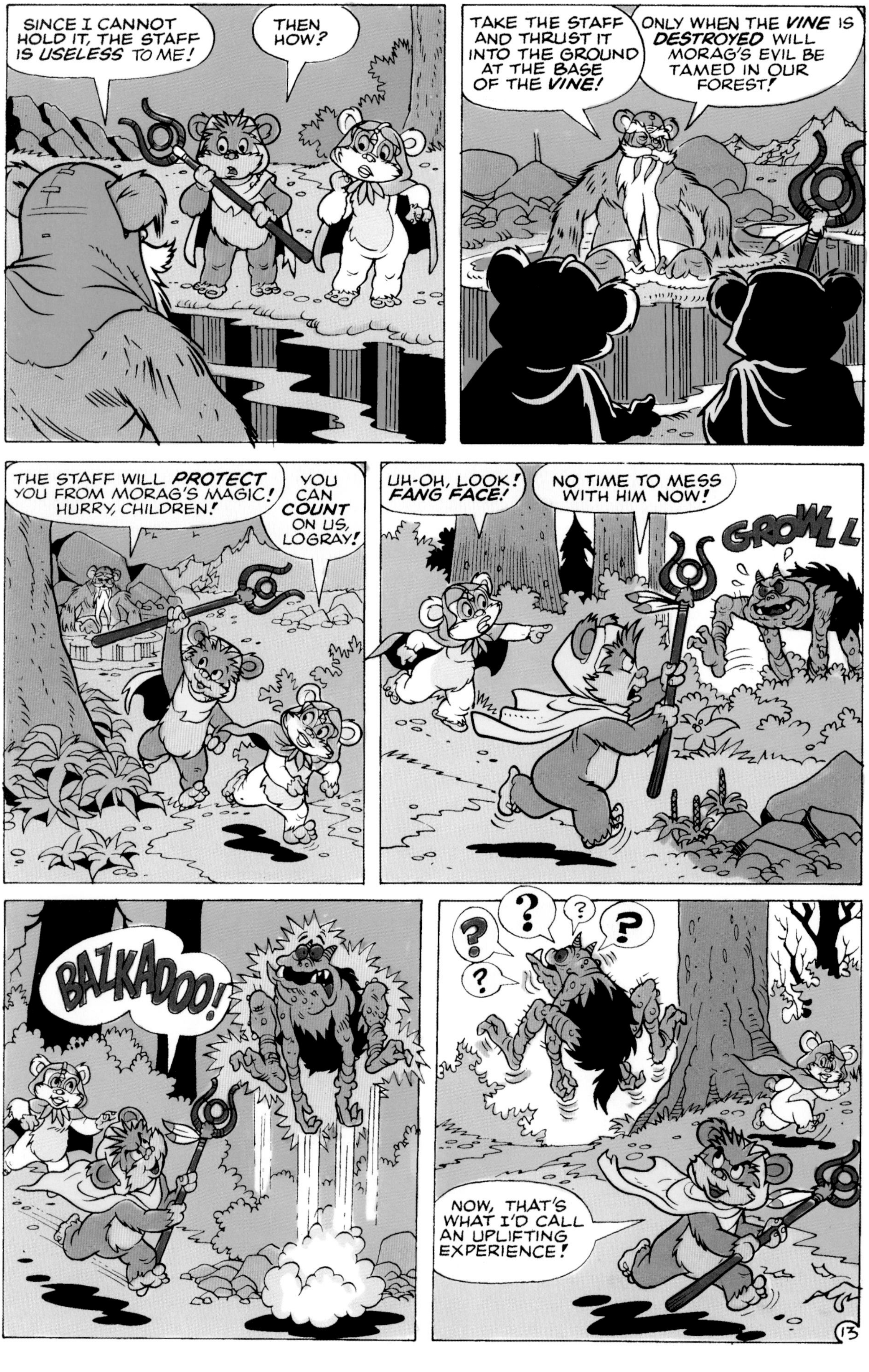
SINCE I CANNOT HOLD IT, THE STAFF IS USELESS TO ME!
THEN HOW?
TAKE THE STAFF AND THRUST IT INTO THE GROUND AT THE BASE OF THE VINE!
ONLY WHEN THE VINE IS DESTROYED WILL MORAG'S EVIL BE TAMED IN OUR FOREST!
THE STAFF WILL PROTECT YOU FROM MORAG'S MAGIC! HURRY, CHILDREN!
YOU CAN COUNT ON US, LOGRAY!
UH-OH, LOOK! FANG FACE!
NO TIME TO MESS WITH HIM NOW!
GROWLL
BAZKADOO!
?
?
?
?
?
NOW, THAT'S WHAT I'D CALL AN UPLIFTING EXPERIENCE!
13

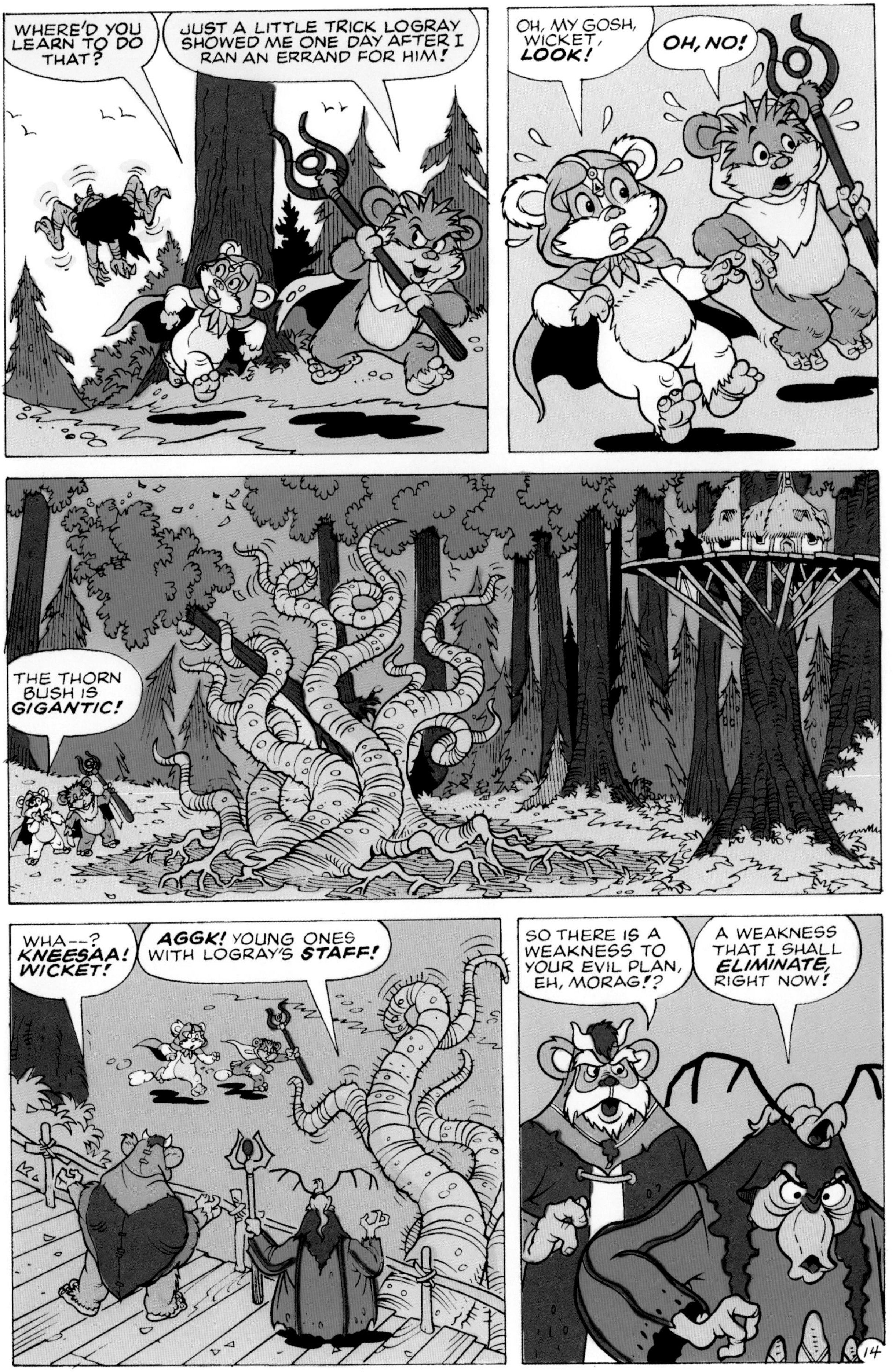
WHERE'D YOU LEARN TO DO THAT?
JUST A LITTLE TRICK LOGRAY SHOWED ME ONE DAY AFTER I RAN AN ERRAND FOR HIM!
OH, MY GOSH, WICKET, LOOK!
OH, NO!
THE THORN BUSH IS GIGANTIC!
WHA--? KNEESAA! WICKET!
AGGK! YOUNG ONES WITH LOGRAY'S STAFF!
SO THERE IS A WEAKNESS TO YOUR EVIL PLAN, EH, MORAG!?
A WEAKNESS THAT I SHALL ELIMINATE, RIGHT NOW!
14

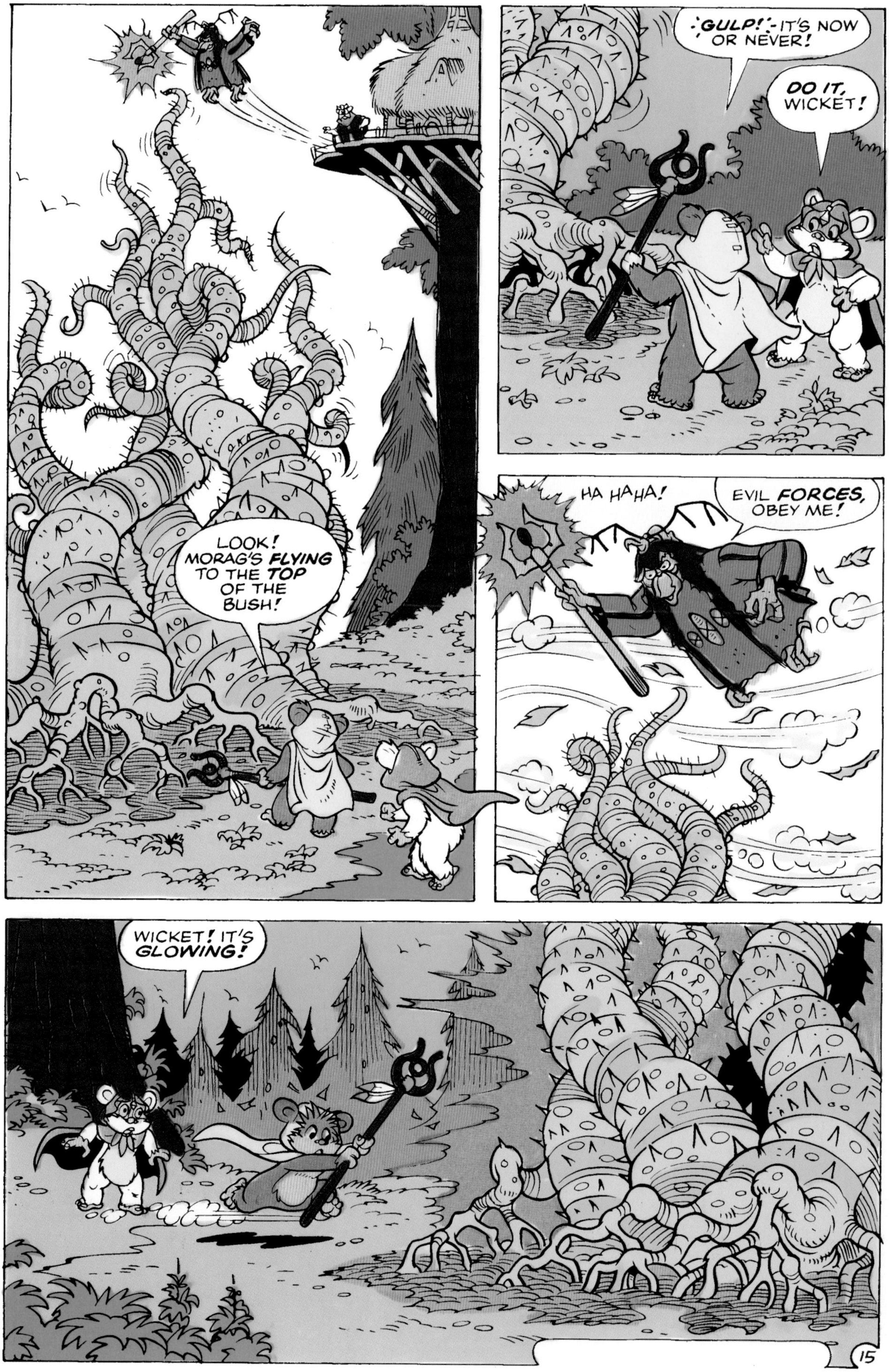
LOOK! MORAG'S FLYING TO THE TOP OF THE BUSH!
:GULP!: - IT'S NOW OR NEVER!
DO IT, WICKET!
HA HAHA!
EVIL FORCES, OBEY ME!
WICKET! IT'S GLOWING!
15

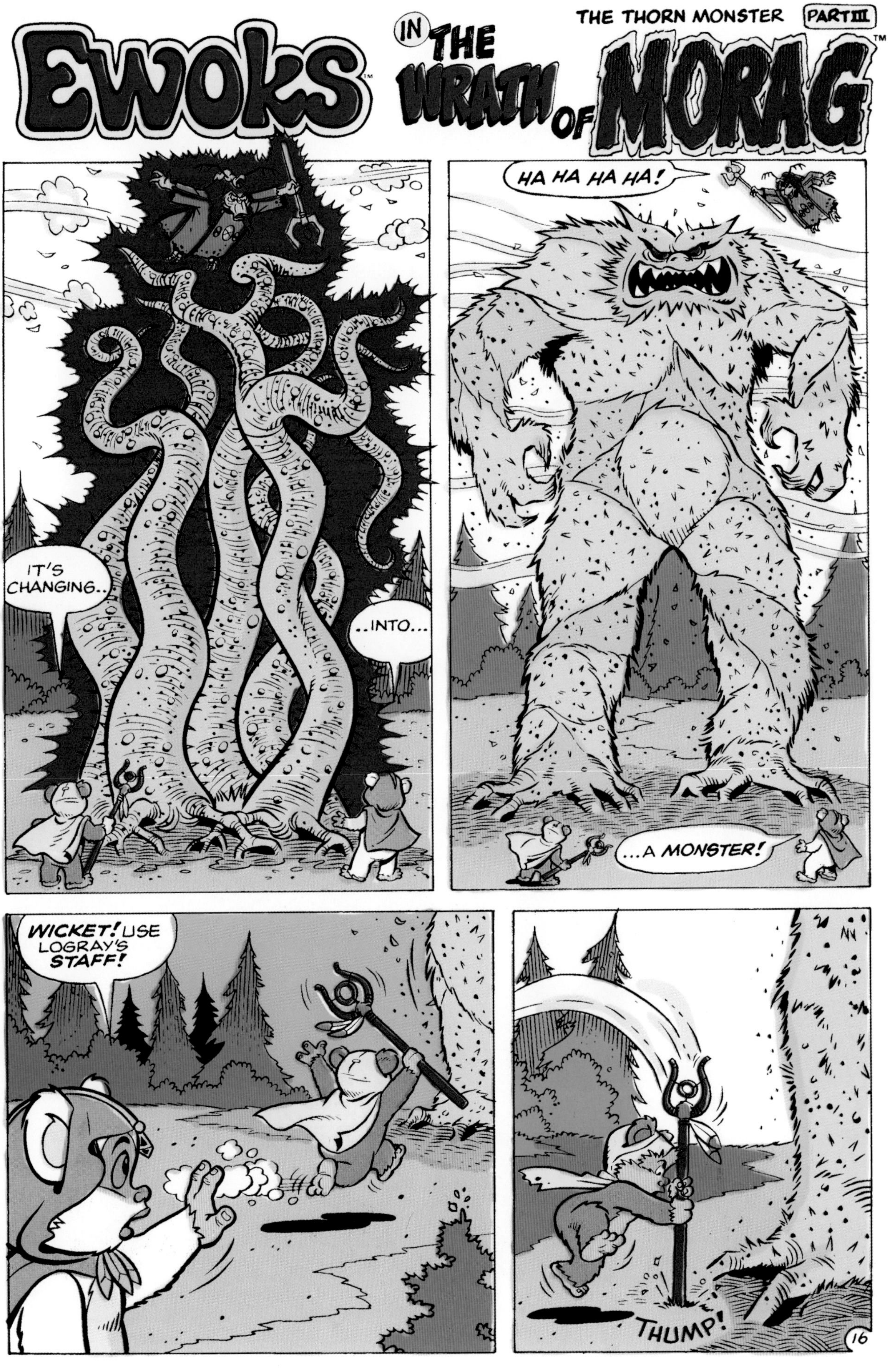

THE THORN MONSTER PART III
EWOKS™ IN THE WRATH OF MORAG™
IT'S CHANGING..
..INTO...
HA HA HA HA!
...A MONSTER!
WICKET! USE LOGRAY'S STAFF!
THUMP!
16

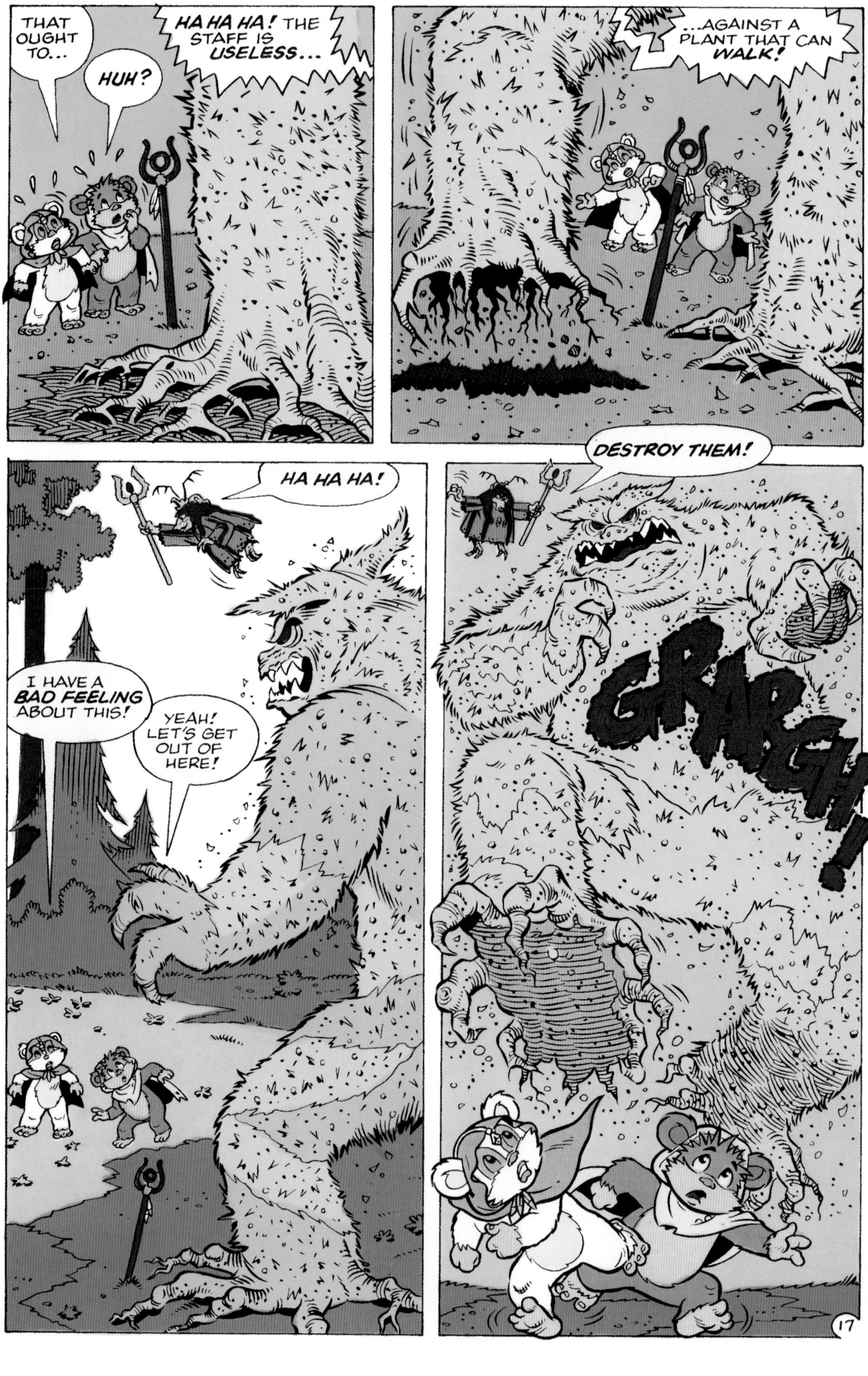
THAT OUGHT TO...
HUH?
HA HA HA! THE STAFF IS USELESS...
...AGAINST A PLANT THAT CAN WALK!
HA HA HA!
I HAVE A BAD FEELING ABOUT THIS!
YEAH! LET'S GET OUT OF HERE!
DESTROY THEM!
GRRARGH!!
17

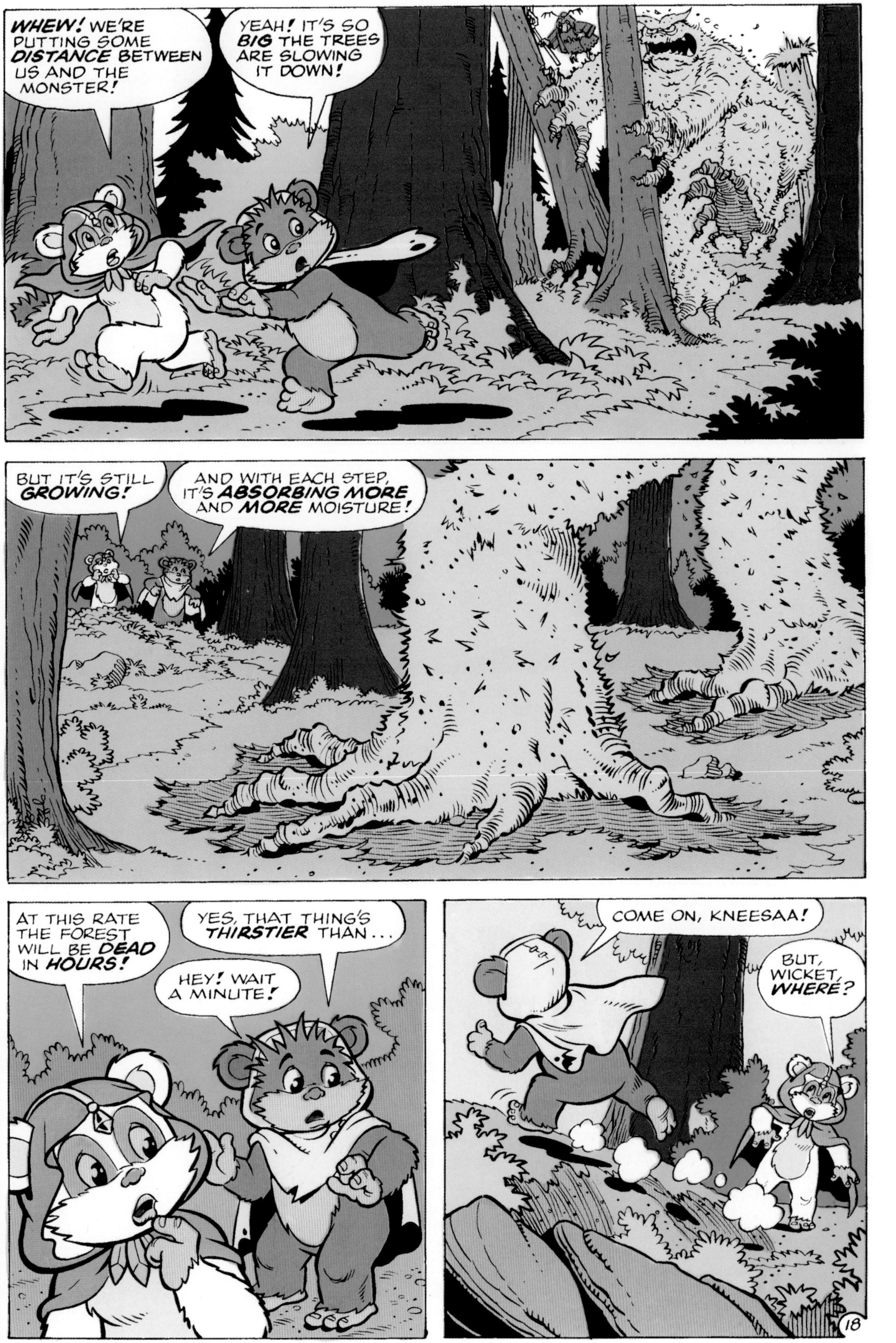
WHEW! WE'RE PUTTING SOME DISTANCE BETWEEN US AND THE MONSTER!
YEAH! IT'S SO BIG THE TREES ARE SLOWING IT DOWN!
BUT IT'S STILL GROWING!
AND WITH EACH STEP, IT'S ABSORBING MORE AND MORE MOISTURE!
AT THIS RATE THE FOREST WILL BE DEAD IN HOURS!
YES, THAT THING'S THIRSTIER THAN...
HEY! WAIT A MINUTE!
COME ON, KNEESAA!
BUT, WICKET, WHERE?
18

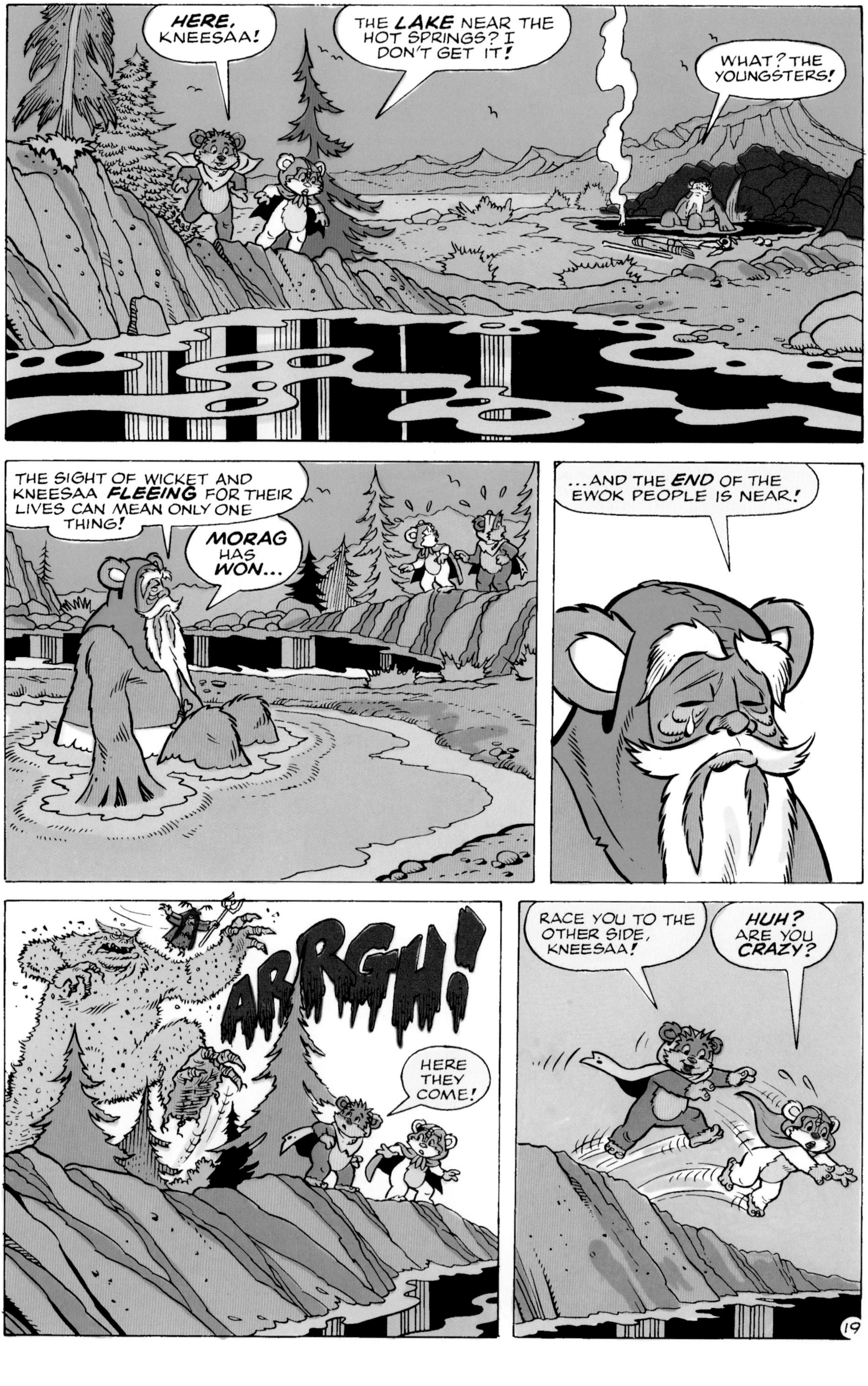
HERE, KNEESAA!
THE LAKE NEAR THE HOT SPRINGS? I DON'T GET IT!
WHAT? THE YOUNGSTERS!
THE SIGHT OF WICKET AND KNEESAA FLEEING FOR THEIR LIVES CAN MEAN ONLY ONE THING!
MORAG HAS WON...
...AND THE END OF THE EWOK PEOPLE IS NEAR!
ARRGH!
HERE THEY COME!
RACE YOU TO THE OTHER SIDE, KNEESAA!
HUH? ARE YOU CRAZY?
19

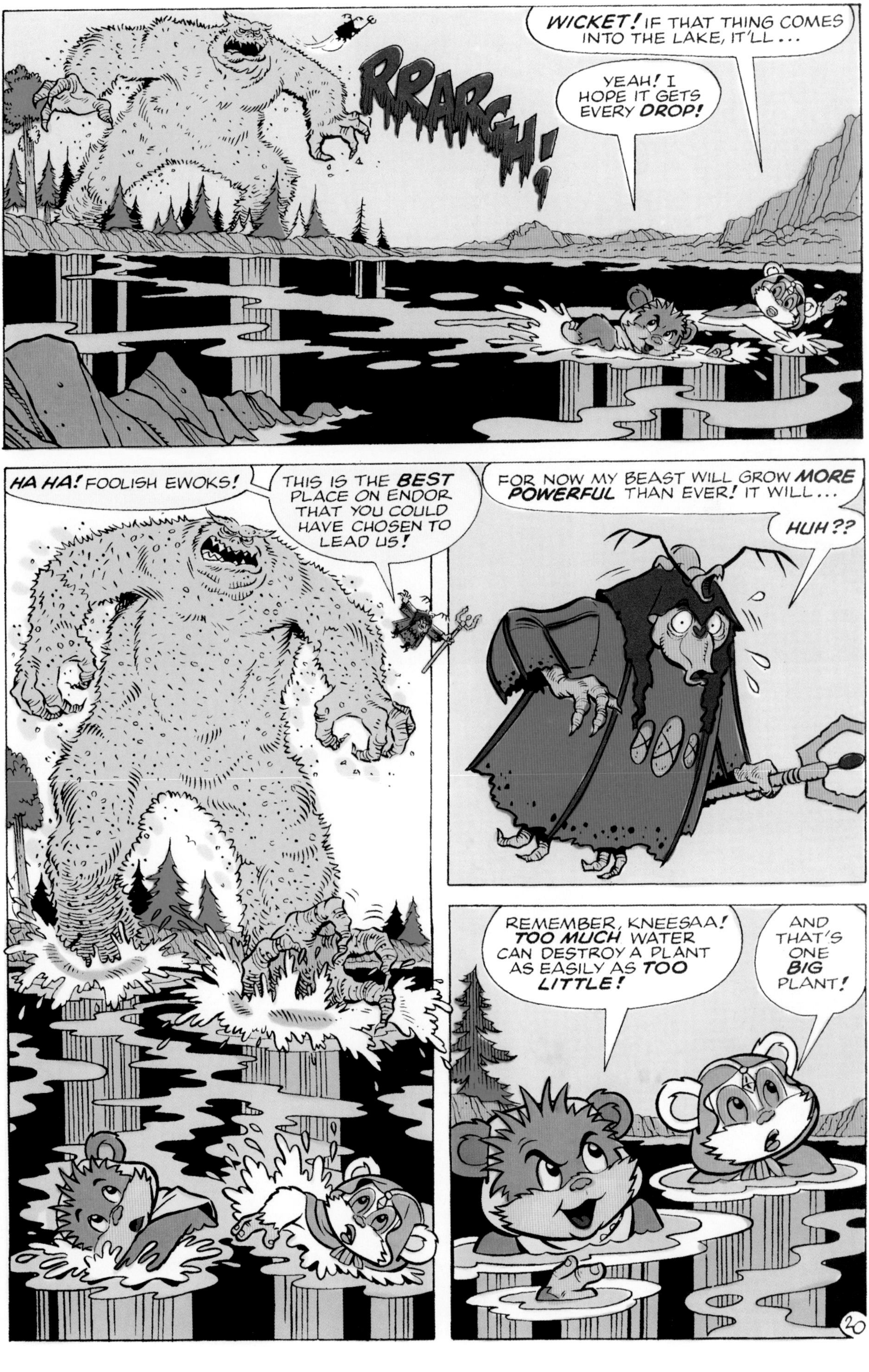

WICKET! IF THAT THING COMES INTO THE LAKE, IT'LL . . .
YEAH! I HOPE IT GETS EVERY DROP!
RRARGH!
HA HA! FOOLISH EWOKS!
THIS IS THE BEST PLACE ON ENDOR THAT YOU COULD HAVE CHOSEN TO LEAD US!
FOR NOW MY BEAST WILL GROW MORE POWERFUL THAN EVER! IT WILL . . .
HUH??
REMEMBER, KNEESAA! TOO MUCH WATER CAN DESTROY A PLANT AS EASILY AS TOO LITTLE!
AND THAT'S ONE BIG PLANT!
20

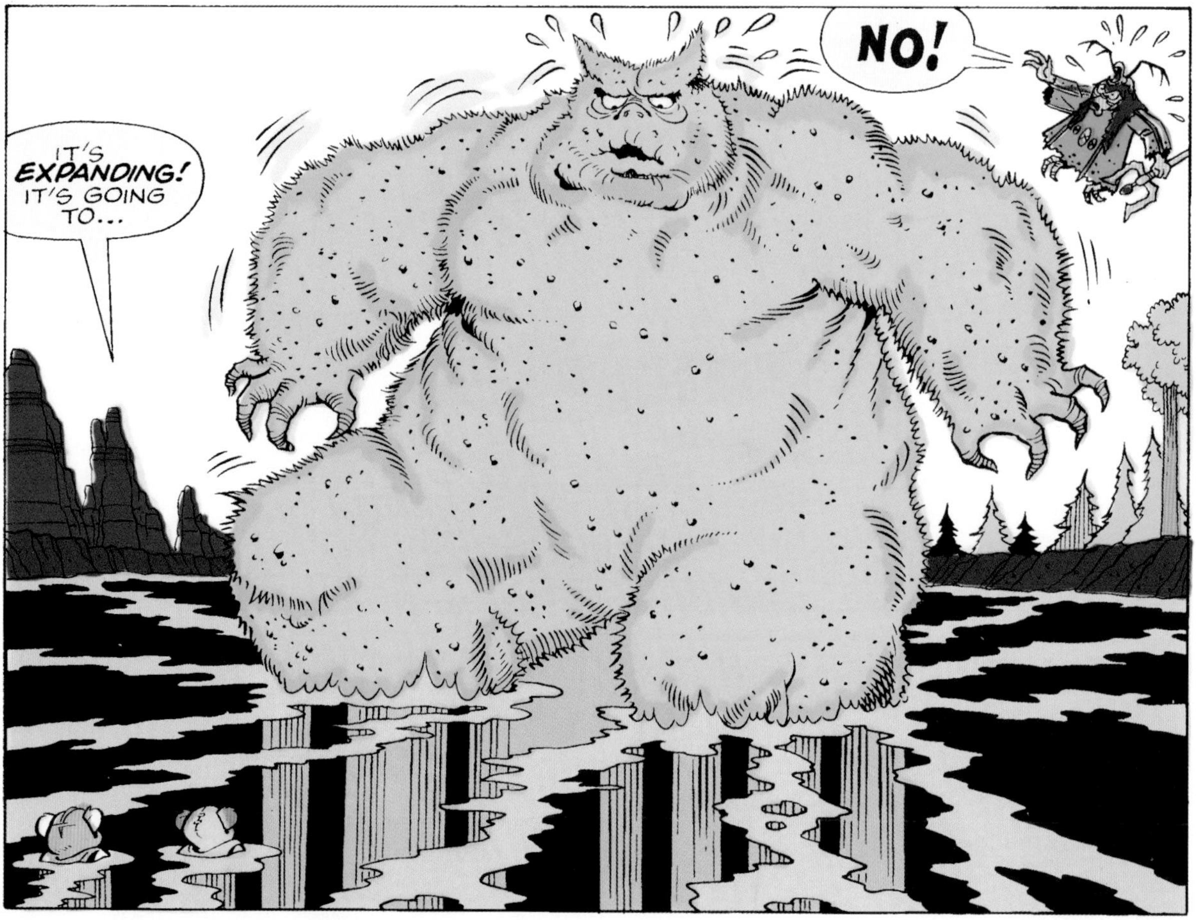
IT'S EXPANDING! IT'S GOING TO...
NO!

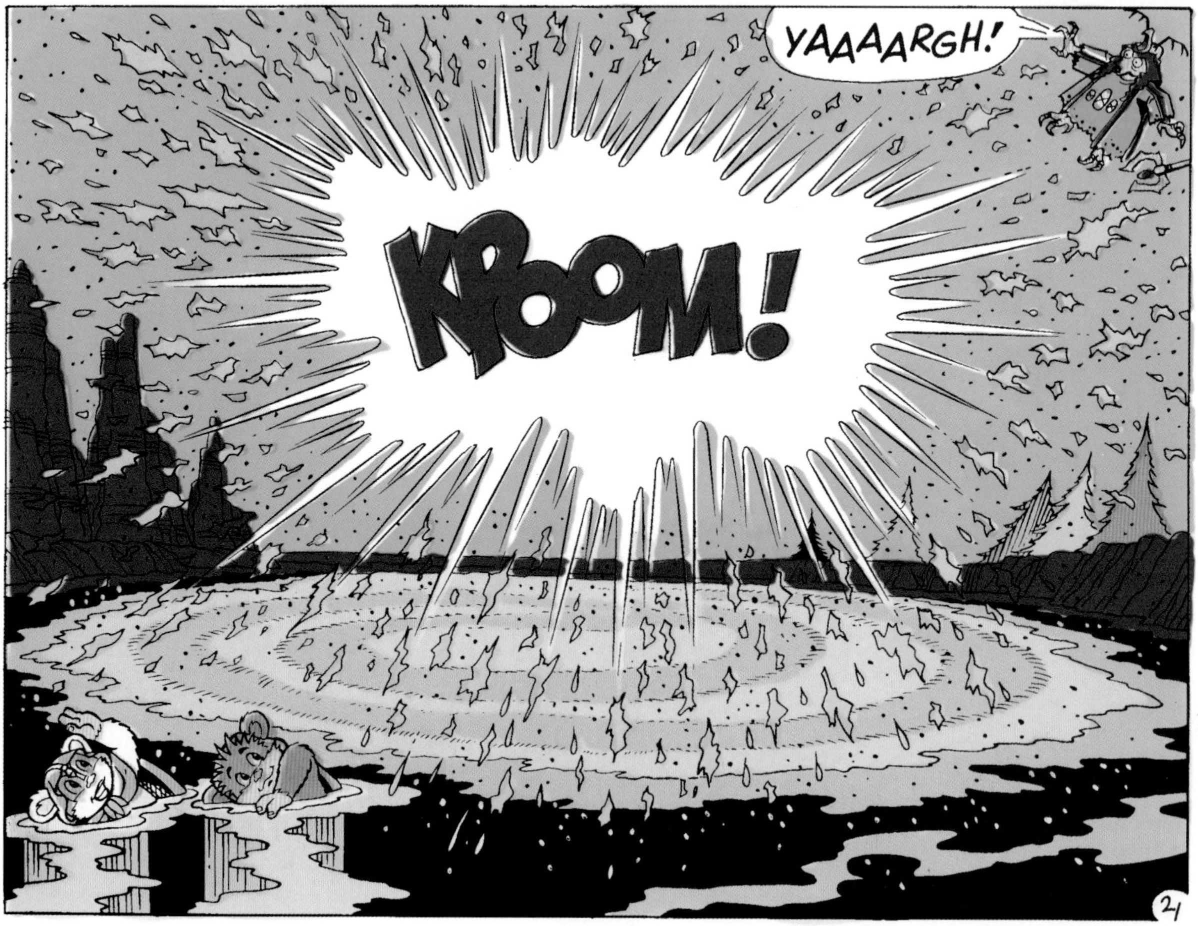
YAAAARGH!
KBOOM!
24

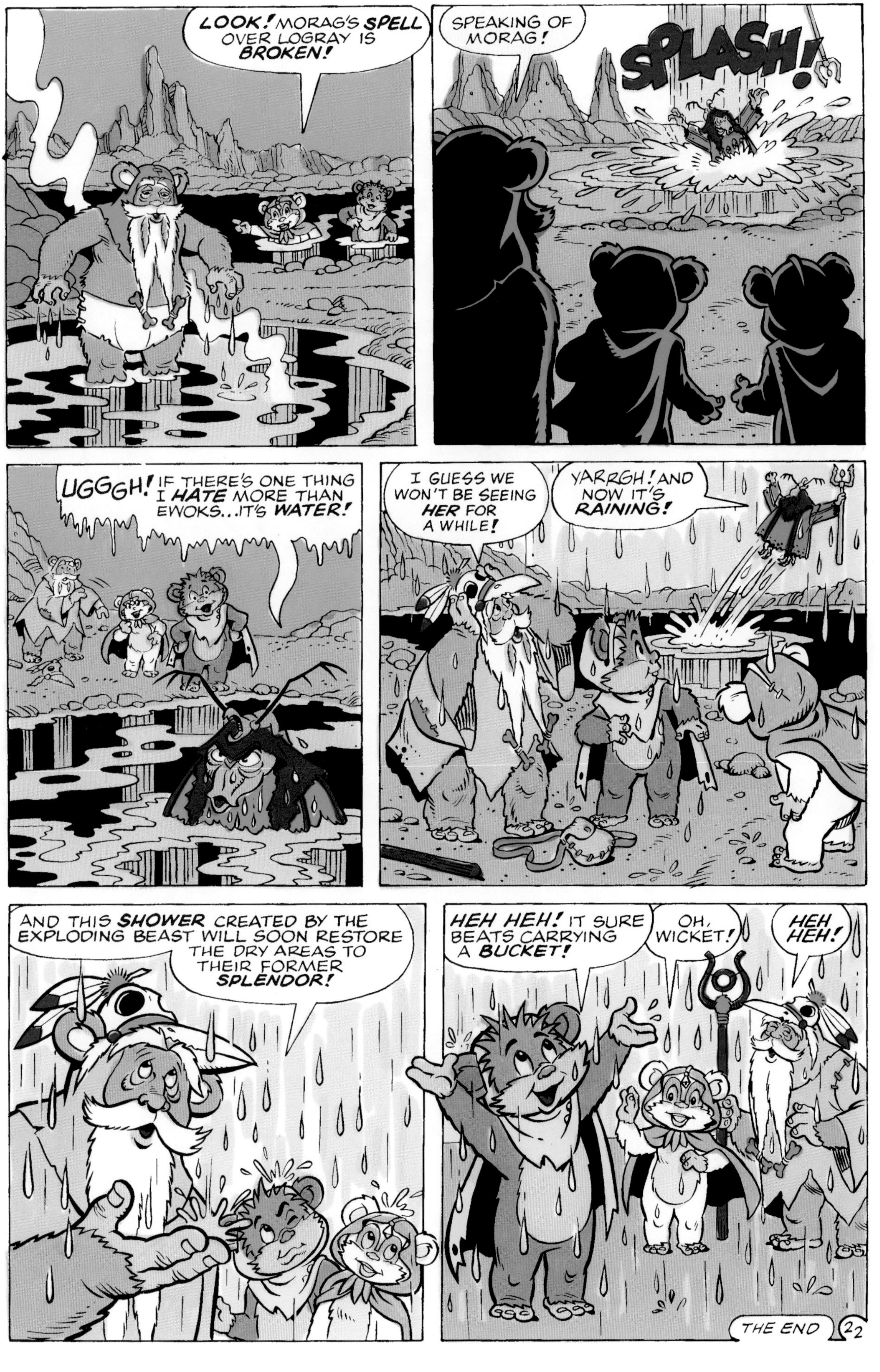
LOOK! MORAG'S SPELL OVER LOGRAY IS BROKEN!
SPEAKING OF MORAG!
SPLASH!
UGGGH! IF THERE'S ONE THING I HATE MORE THAN EWOKS...IT'S WATER!
I GUESS WE WON'T BE SEEING HER FOR A WHILE!
YARRGH! AND NOW IT'S RAINING!
AND THIS SHOWER CREATED BY THE EXPLODING BEAST WILL SOON RESTORE THE DRY AREAS TO THEIR FORMER SPLENDOR!
HEH HEH! IT SURE BEATS CARRYING A BUCKET!
OH, WICKET!
HEH HEH!
THE END
22

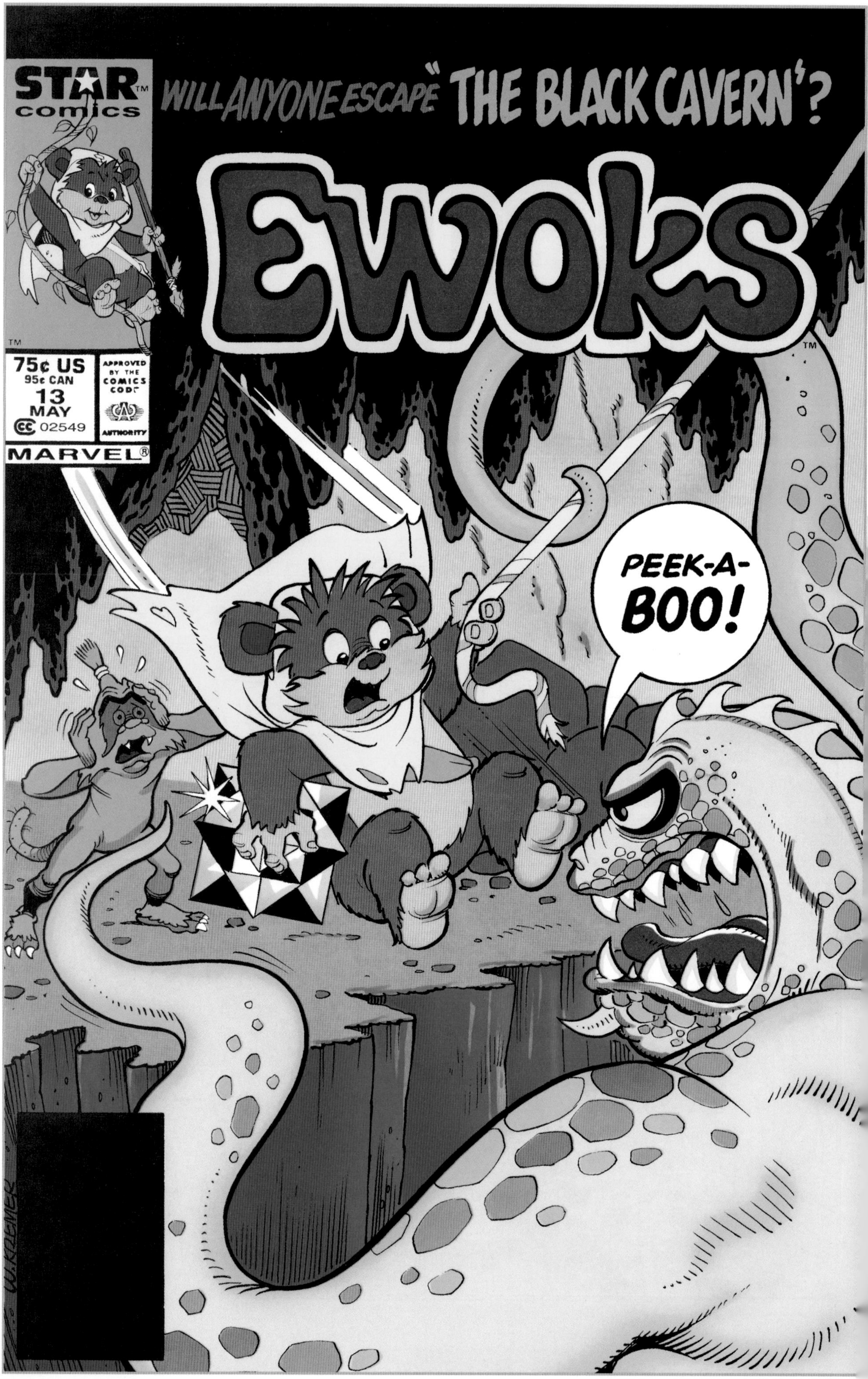
STAR comics
WILL ANYONE ESCAPE "THE BLACK CAVERN"?
Ewoks
75¢ US
95¢ CAN
13
MAY
CC 02549
APPROVED BY THE COMICS CODE AUTHORITY
MARVEL
PEEK-A-BOO!

Ewoks™ in THE BLACK CAVERN

ON THE TINY MOON OF ENDOR, HOME OF THE EWOKS, A MOST IMPORTANT CEREMONY IS ABOUT TO TAKE PLACE...A CEREMONY THAT WILL LEAD ONE EWOK AND HIS ENEMY INTO A WHIRLPOOL OF TERROR!!

WHO COMES TO TEST HIS *COURAGE* TODAY?

IT IS I, *HEAD ELDER KAZAK,* WICKET, THE SCOUT!

THEN, AS WE STAND BEFORE THE GLOWING LIGHT OF THE *SUN CRYSTAL,* SYMBOL OF EWOK BRAVERY... LET THE TEST *BEGIN!*

AND I, CHIEF CHIRPA, WILL EXPLAIN YOUR CHALLENGE, WICKET!

DAVE MANAK WRITER	WARREN KREMER PENCILER	JON D'AGOSTINO INKER	GRACE KREMER LETTERER
GEORGE ROUSSOS COLORIST	SID JACOBSON EDITOR	TOM DE FALCO EXECUTIVE EDITOR	JIM SHOOTER ED. IN CHIEF

1

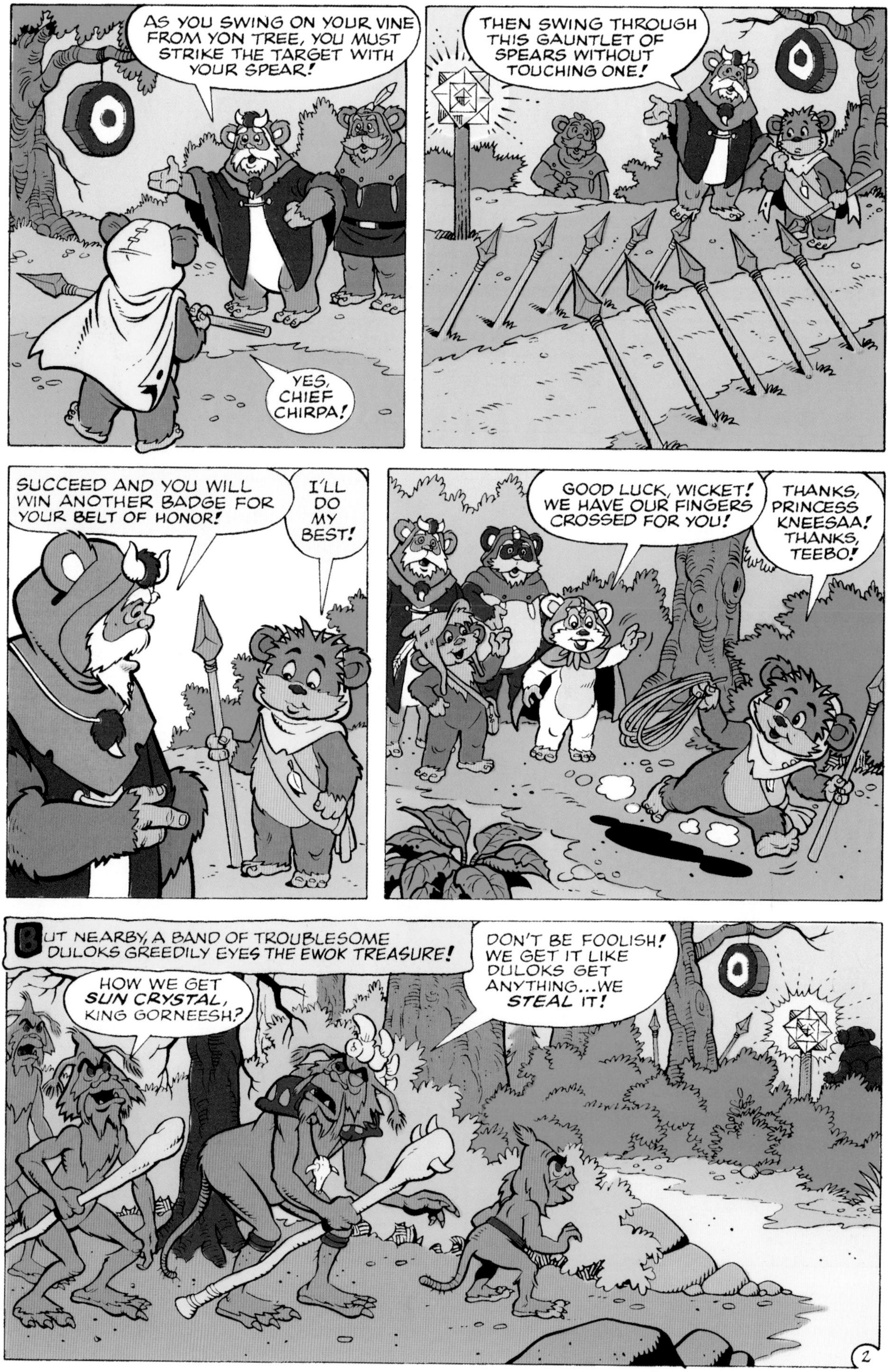

AS YOU SWING ON YOUR VINE FROM YON TREE, YOU MUST STRIKE THE TARGET WITH YOUR SPEAR!
YES, CHIEF CHIRPA!
THEN SWING THROUGH THIS GAUNTLET OF SPEARS WITHOUT TOUCHING ONE!
SUCCEED AND YOU WILL WIN ANOTHER BADGE FOR YOUR BELT OF HONOR!
I'LL DO MY BEST!
GOOD LUCK, WICKET! WE HAVE OUR FINGERS CROSSED FOR YOU!
THANKS, PRINCESS KNEESAA! THANKS, TEEBO!
BUT NEARBY, A BAND OF TROUBLESOME DULOKS GREEDILY EYES THE EWOK TREASURE!
HOW WE GET SUN CRYSTAL, KING GORNEESH?
DON'T BE FOOLISH! WE GET IT LIKE DULOKS GET ANYTHING...WE STEAL IT!
2

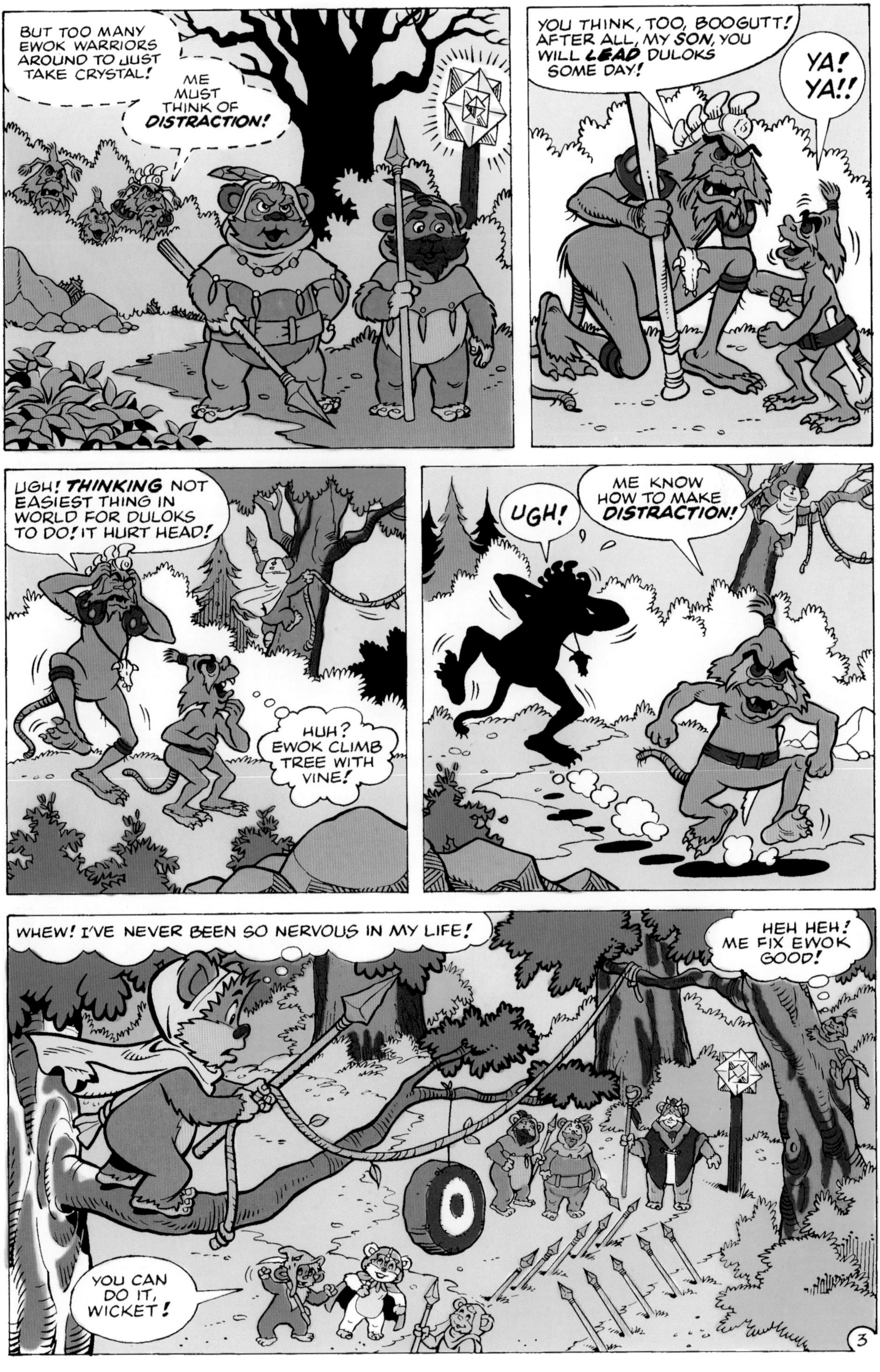
BUT TOO MANY EWOK WARRIORS AROUND TO JUST TAKE CRYSTAL!
ME MUST THINK OF DISTRACTION!
YOU THINK, TOO, BOOGUTT! AFTER ALL, MY SON, YOU WILL LEAD DULOKS SOME DAY!
YA! YA!!
UGH! THINKING NOT EASIEST THING IN WORLD FOR DULOKS TO DO! IT HURT HEAD!
HUH? EWOK CLIMB TREE WITH VINE!
UGH!
ME KNOW HOW TO MAKE DISTRACTION!
WHEW! I'VE NEVER BEEN SO NERVOUS IN MY LIFE!
HEH HEH! ME FIX EWOK GOOD!
YOU CAN DO IT, WICKET!
3

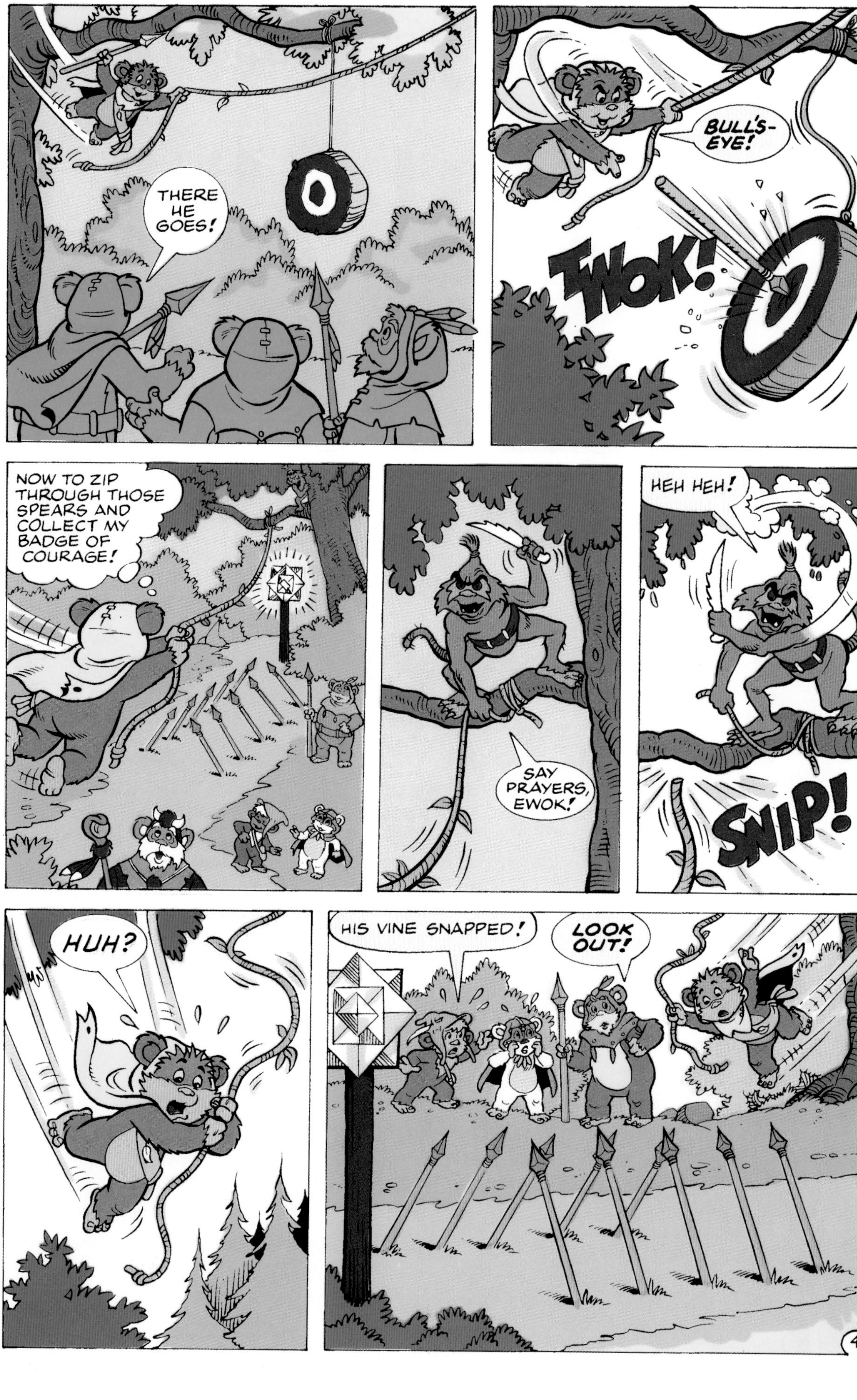
THERE HE GOES!
BULL'S-EYE!
TWOK!
NOW TO ZIP THROUGH THOSE SPEARS AND COLLECT MY BADGE OF COURAGE!
SAY PRAYERS, EWOK!
HEH HEH!
SNIP!
HUH?
HIS VINE SNAPPED!
LOOK OUT!
4

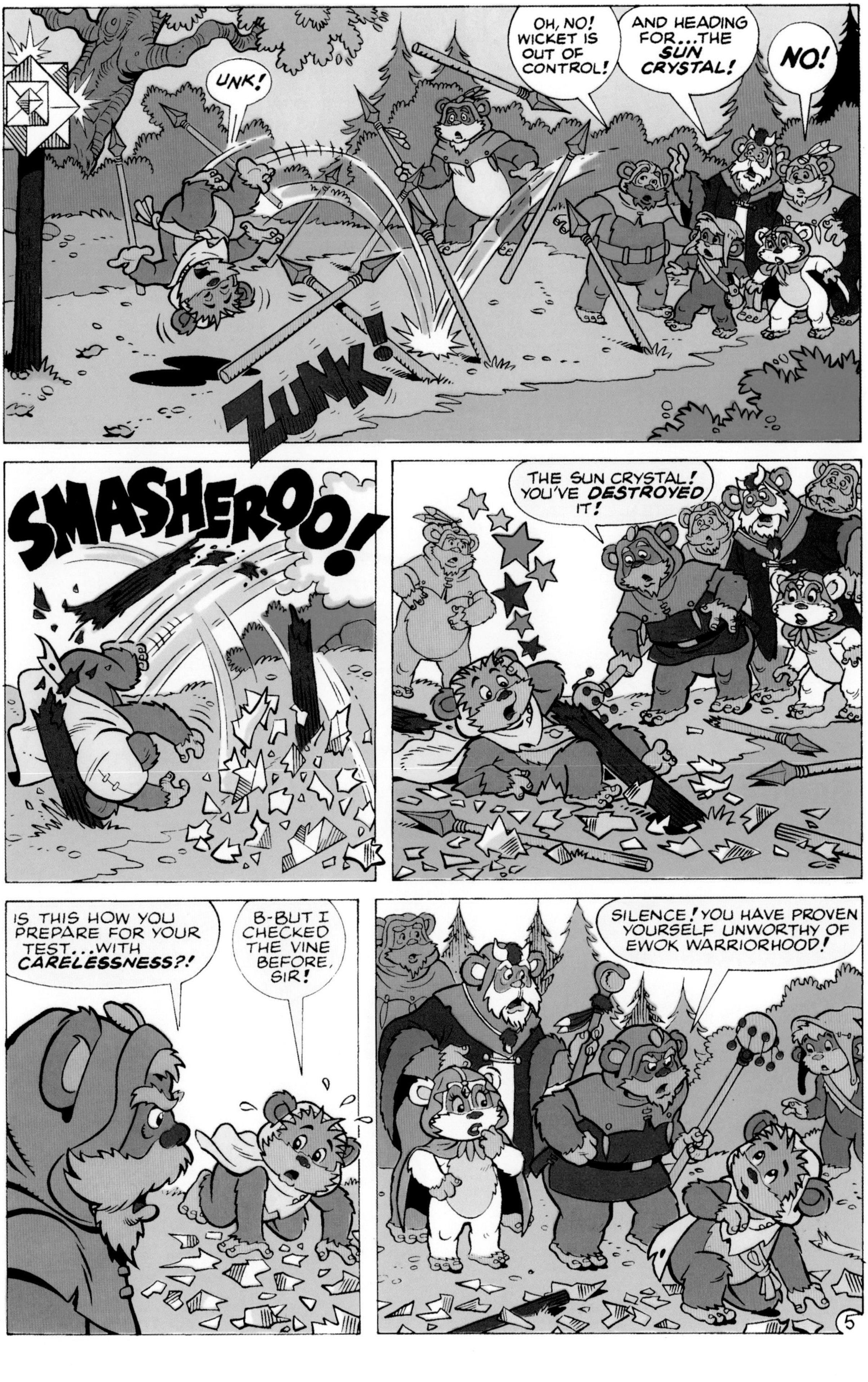
UNK!
OH, NO! WICKET IS OUT OF CONTROL!
AND HEADING FOR...THE SUN CRYSTAL!
NO!
ZUNK!
SMASHEROO!
THE SUN CRYSTAL! YOU'VE DESTROYED IT!
IS THIS HOW YOU PREPARE FOR YOUR TEST...WITH CARELESSNESS?!
B-BUT I CHECKED THE VINE BEFORE, SIR!
SILENCE! YOU HAVE PROVEN YOURSELF UNWORTHY OF EWOK WARRIORHOOD!
5

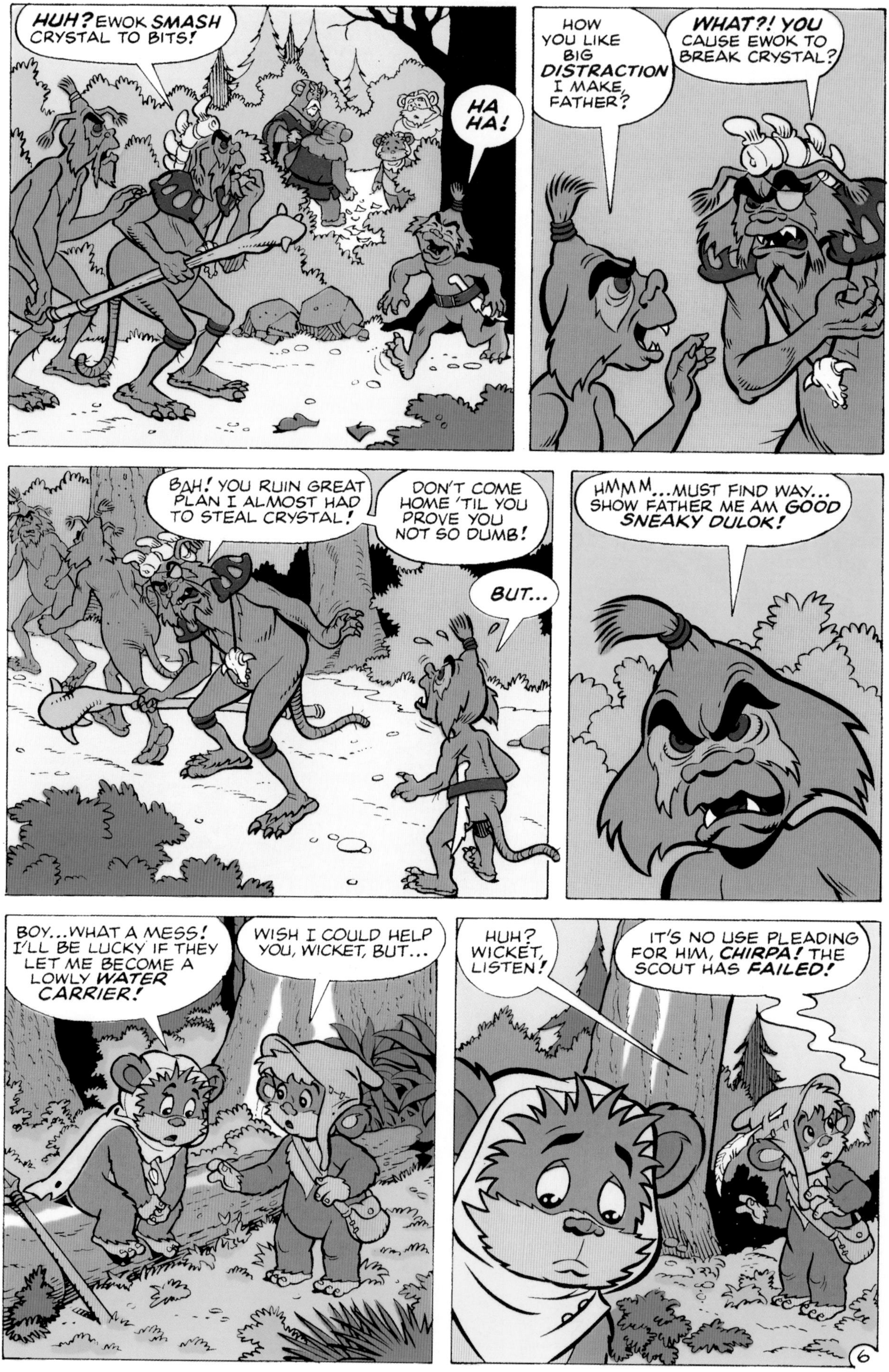
HUH? EWOK SMASH CRYSTAL TO BITS!
HA HA!
HOW YOU LIKE BIG DISTRACTION I MAKE, FATHER?
WHAT?! YOU CAUSE EWOK TO BREAK CRYSTAL?
BAH! YOU RUIN GREAT PLAN I ALMOST HAD TO STEAL CRYSTAL!
DON'T COME HOME 'TIL YOU PROVE YOU NOT SO DUMB!
BUT...
HMMM...MUST FIND WAY... SHOW FATHER ME AM GOOD SNEAKY DULOK!
BOY...WHAT A MESS! I'LL BE LUCKY IF THEY LET ME BECOME A LOWLY WATER CARRIER!
WISH I COULD HELP YOU, WICKET, BUT...
HUH? WICKET, LISTEN!
IT'S NO USE PLEADING FOR HIM, CHIRPA! THE SCOUT HAS FAILED!
6

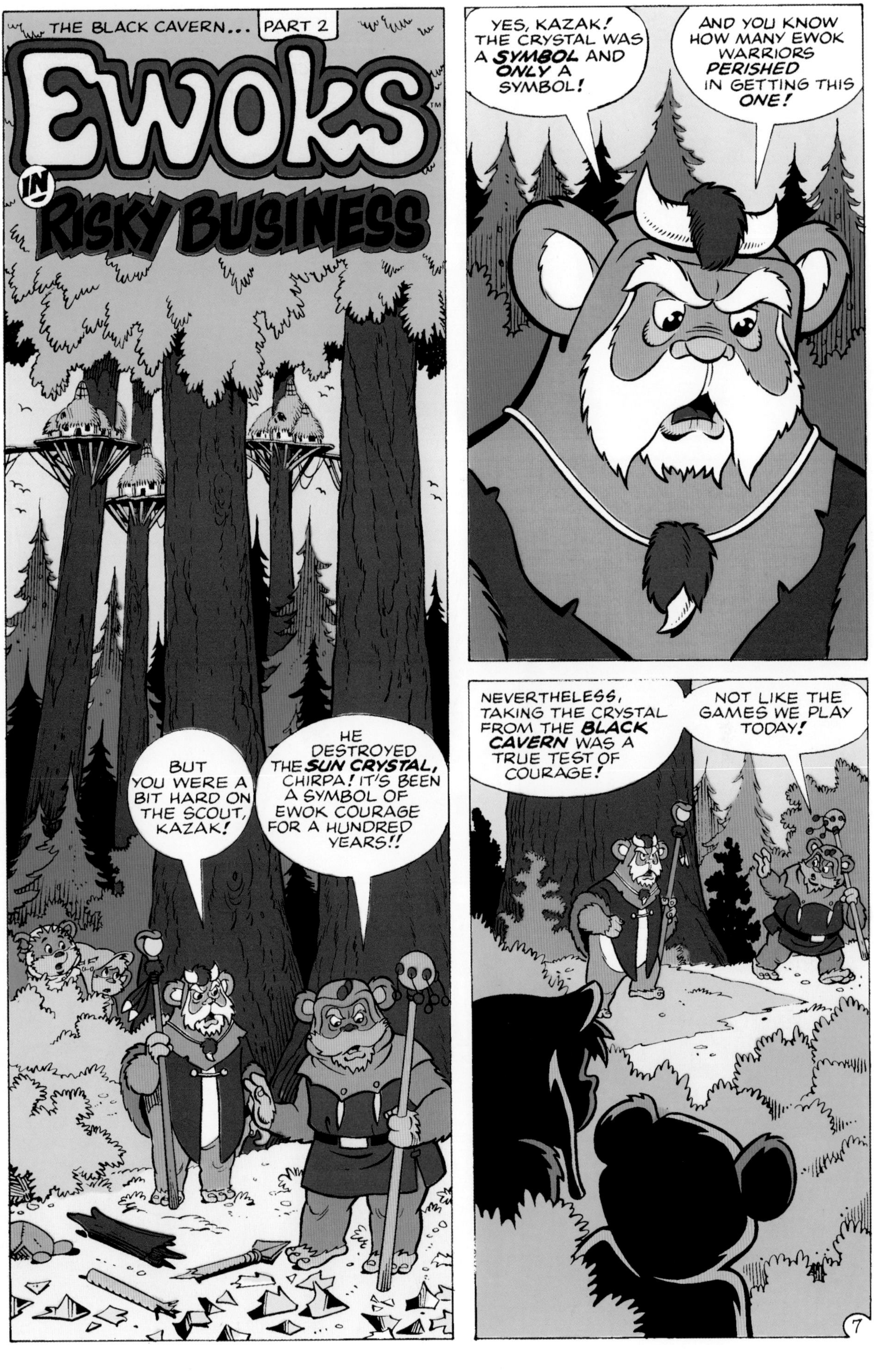
THE BLACK CAVERN... PART 2
Ewoks
IN RISKY BUSINESS
BUT YOU WERE A BIT HARD ON THE SCOUT, KAZAK!
HE DESTROYED THE SUN CRYSTAL, CHIRPA! IT'S BEEN A SYMBOL OF EWOK COURAGE FOR A HUNDRED YEARS!!
YES, KAZAK! THE CRYSTAL WAS A SYMBOL AND ONLY A SYMBOL!
AND YOU KNOW HOW MANY EWOK WARRIORS PERISHED IN GETTING THIS ONE!
NEVERTHELESS, TAKING THE CRYSTAL FROM THE BLACK CAVERN WAS A TRUE TEST OF COURAGE!
NOT LIKE THE GAMES WE PLAY TODAY!
7

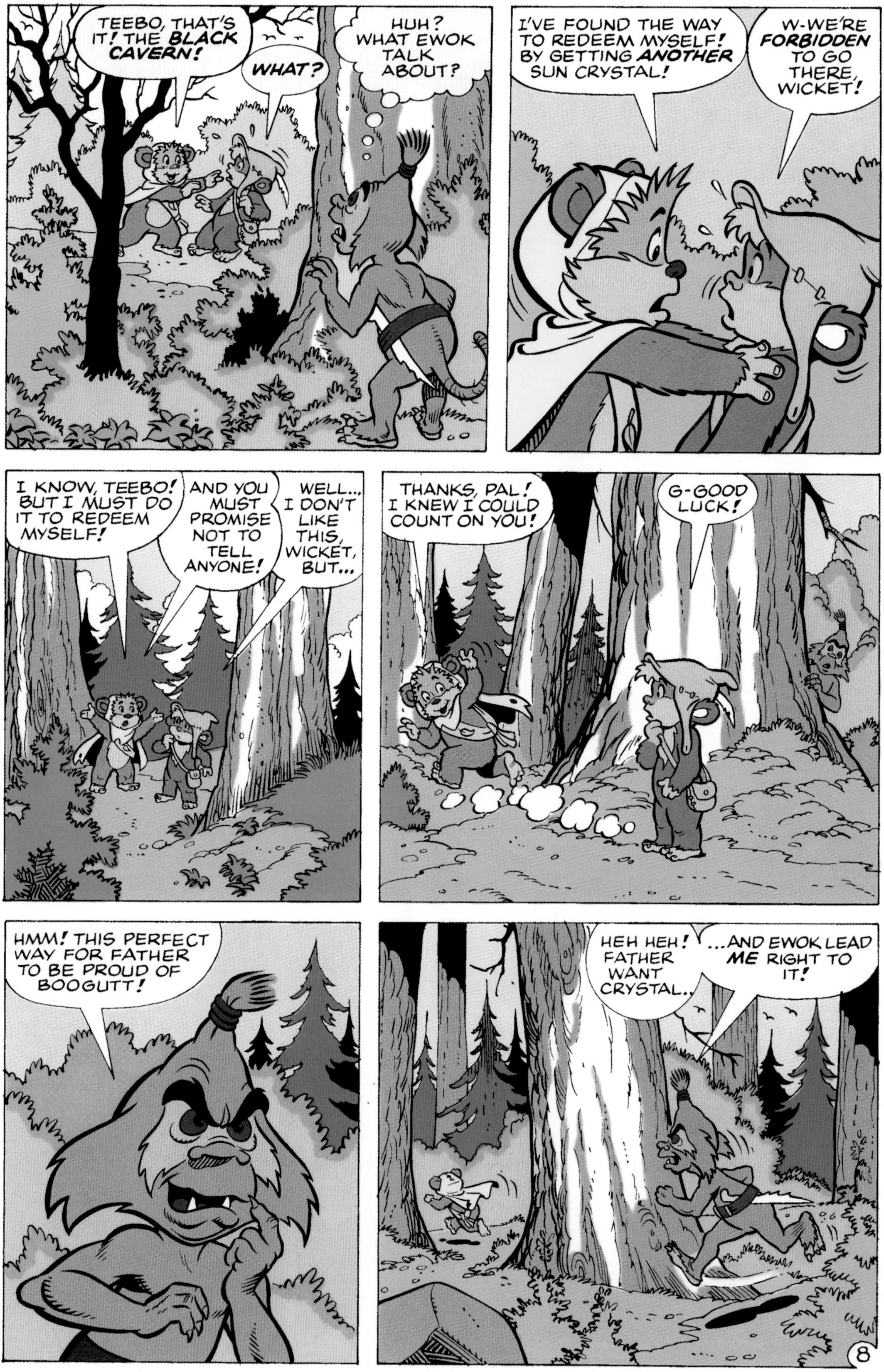
TEEBO, THAT'S IT! THE BLACK CAVERN!
WHAT?
HUH? WHAT EWOK TALK ABOUT?
I'VE FOUND THE WAY TO REDEEM MYSELF! BY GETTING ANOTHER SUN CRYSTAL!
W-WE'RE FORBIDDEN TO GO THERE, WICKET!
I KNOW, TEEBO! BUT I MUST DO IT TO REDEEM MYSELF!
AND YOU MUST PROMISE NOT TO TELL ANYONE!
WELL... I DON'T LIKE THIS, WICKET, BUT...
THANKS, PAL! I KNEW I COULD COUNT ON YOU!
G-GOOD LUCK!
HMM! THIS PERFECT WAY FOR FATHER TO BE PROUD OF BOOGUTT!
HEH HEH! FATHER WANT CRYSTAL...
...AND EWOK LEAD ME RIGHT TO IT!
8

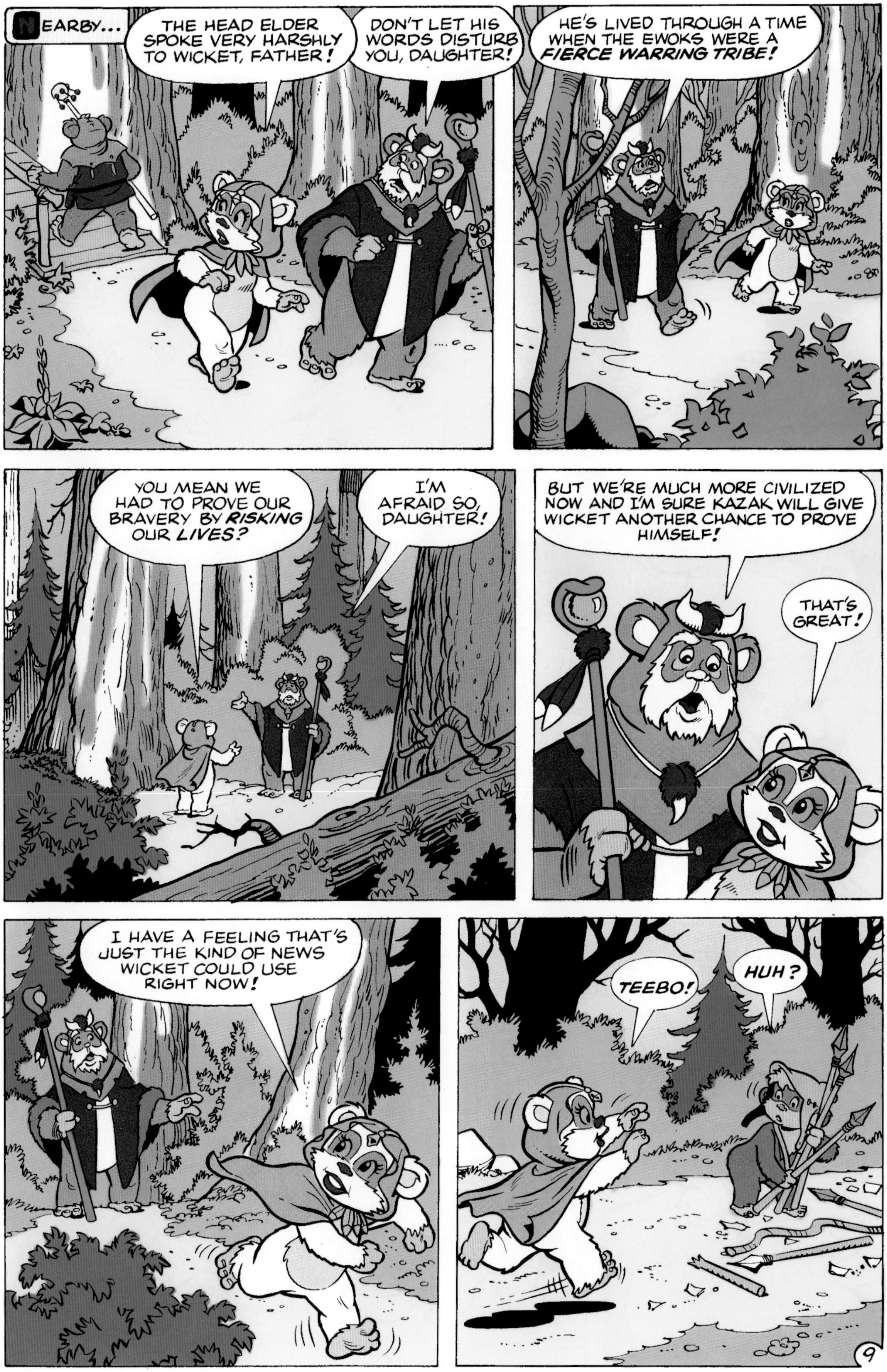
NEARBY...
THE HEAD ELDER SPOKE VERY HARSHLY TO WICKET, FATHER!
DON'T LET HIS WORDS DISTURB YOU, DAUGHTER!
HE'S LIVED THROUGH A TIME WHEN THE EWOKS WERE A FIERCE WARRING TRIBE!
YOU MEAN WE HAD TO PROVE OUR BRAVERY BY RISKING OUR LIVES?
I'M AFRAID SO, DAUGHTER!
BUT WE'RE MUCH MORE CIVILIZED NOW AND I'M SURE KAZAK WILL GIVE WICKET ANOTHER CHANCE TO PROVE HIMSELF!
THAT'S GREAT!
I HAVE A FEELING THAT'S JUST THE KIND OF NEWS WICKET COULD USE RIGHT NOW!
TEEBO!
HUH?
9

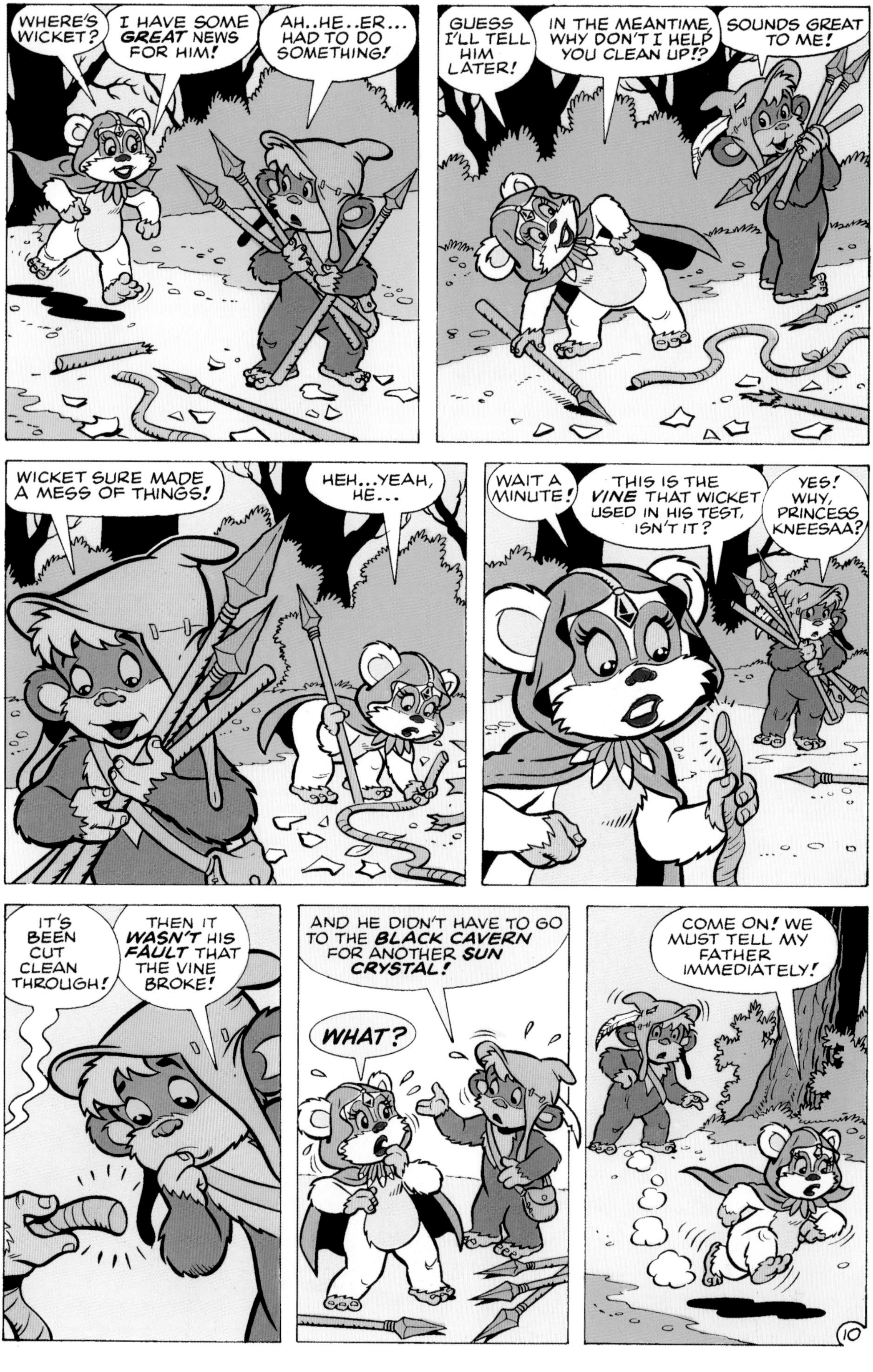

WHERE'S WICKET?
I HAVE SOME GREAT NEWS FOR HIM!
AH..HE..ER... HAD TO DO SOMETHING!
GUESS I'LL TELL HIM LATER!
IN THE MEANTIME, WHY DON'T I HELP YOU CLEAN UP!?
SOUNDS GREAT TO ME!
WICKET SURE MADE A MESS OF THINGS!
HEH...YEAH, HE...
WAIT A MINUTE!
THIS IS THE VINE THAT WICKET USED IN HIS TEST, ISN'T IT?
YES! WHY, PRINCESS KNEESAA?
IT'S BEEN CUT CLEAN THROUGH!
THEN IT WASN'T HIS FAULT THAT THE VINE BROKE!
AND HE DIDN'T HAVE TO GO TO THE BLACK CAVERN FOR ANOTHER SUN CRYSTAL!
WHAT?
COME ON! WE MUST TELL MY FATHER IMMEDIATELY!
10

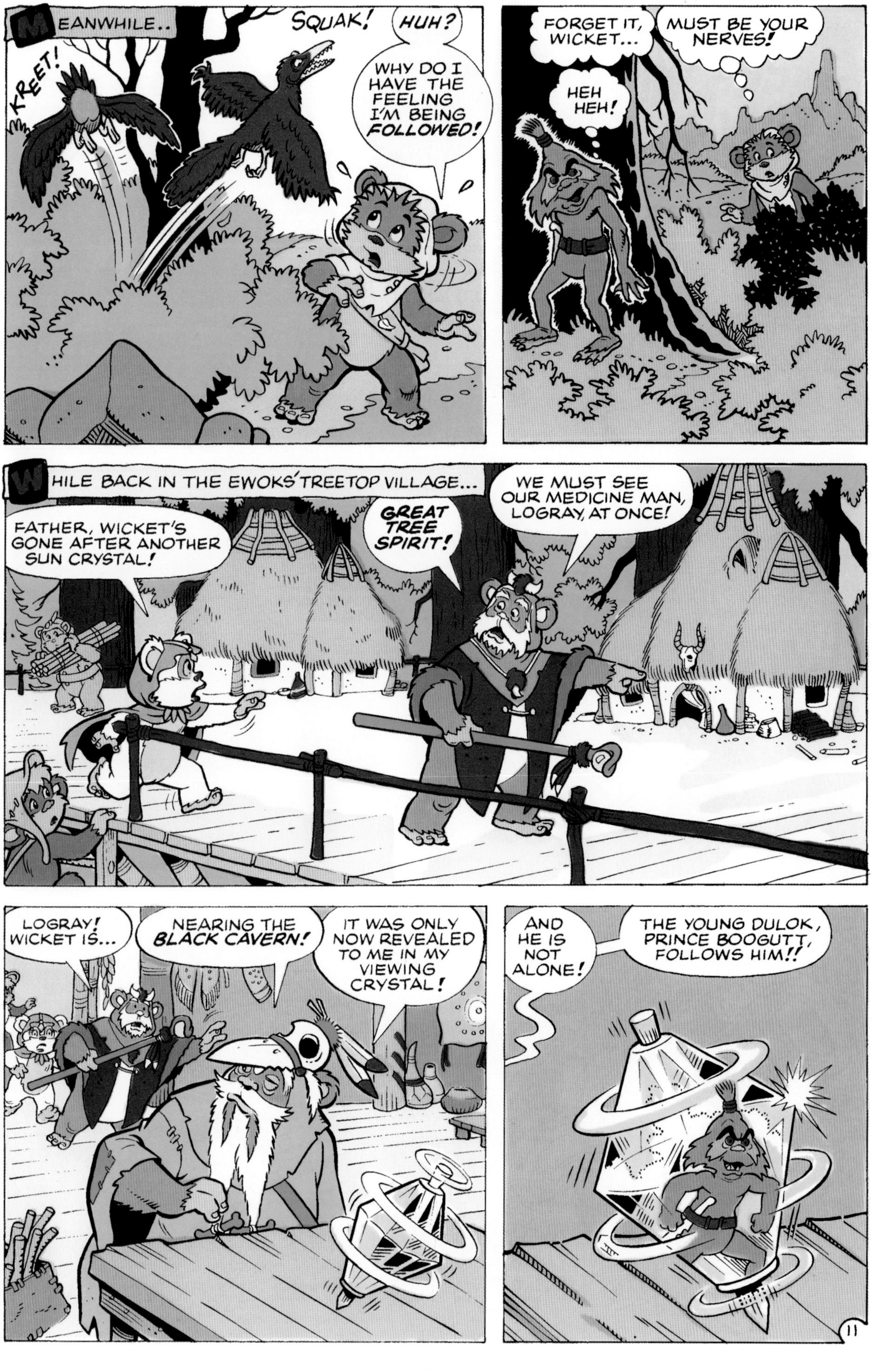
MEANWHILE..
KREET!
SQUAK!
HUH?
WHY DO I HAVE THE FEELING I'M BEING FOLLOWED!
FORGET IT, WICKET...
MUST BE YOUR NERVES!
HEH HEH!
WHILE BACK IN THE EWOKS' TREETOP VILLAGE...
FATHER, WICKET'S GONE AFTER ANOTHER SUN CRYSTAL!
GREAT TREE SPIRIT!
WE MUST SEE OUR MEDICINE MAN, LOGRAY, AT ONCE!
LOGRAY! WICKET IS...
NEARING THE BLACK CAVERN!
IT WAS ONLY NOW REVEALED TO ME IN MY VIEWING CRYSTAL!
AND HE IS NOT ALONE!
THE YOUNG DULOK, PRINCE BOOGUTT, FOLLOWS HIM!!
11

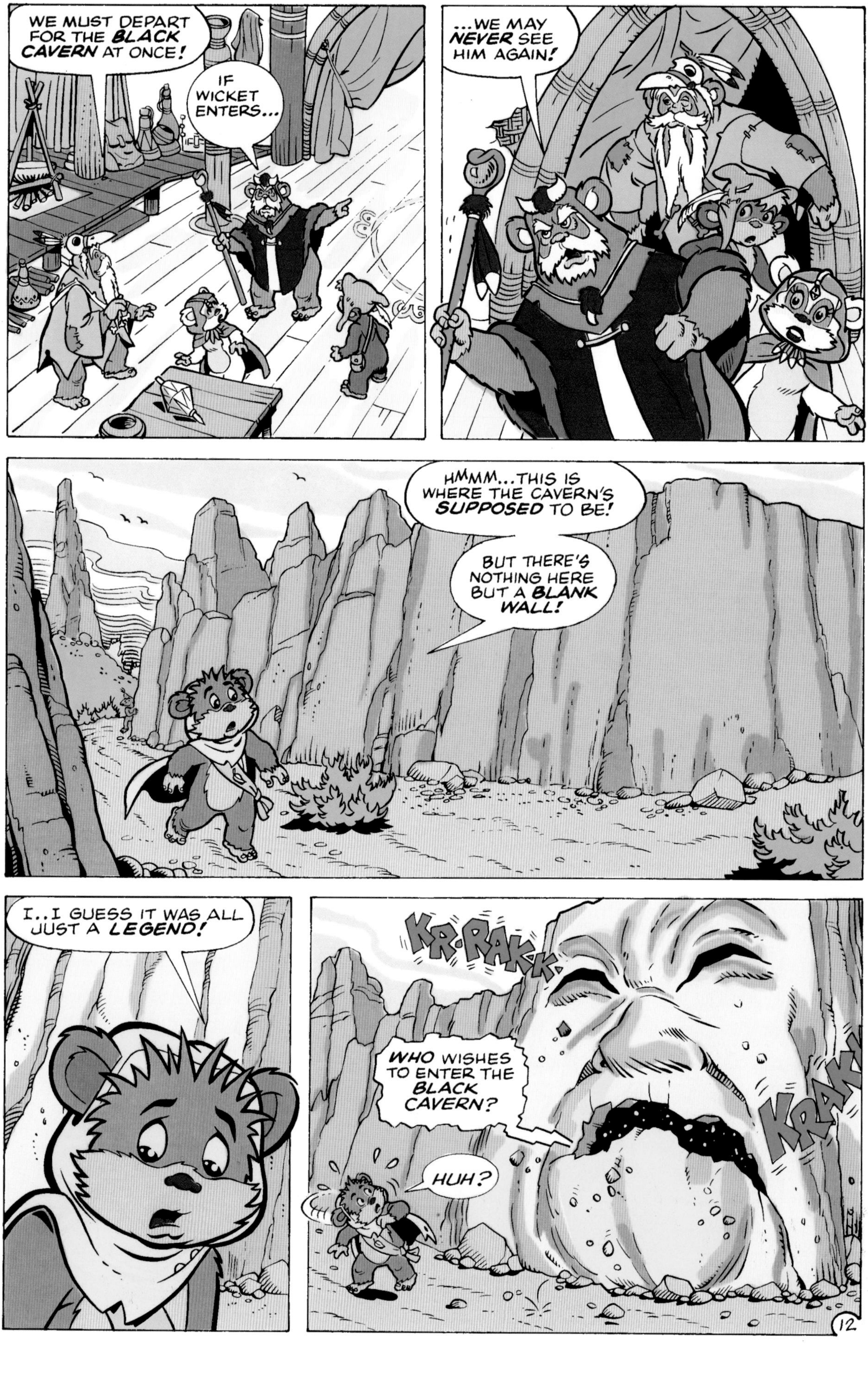
WE MUST DEPART FOR THE BLACK CAVERN AT ONCE!
IF WICKET ENTERS...
...WE MAY NEVER SEE HIM AGAIN!
HMMM...THIS IS WHERE THE CAVERN'S SUPPOSED TO BE!
BUT THERE'S NOTHING HERE BUT A BLANK WALL!
I..I GUESS IT WAS ALL JUST A LEGEND!
KR-RAKK
WHO WISHES TO ENTER THE BLACK CAVERN?
HUH?
12

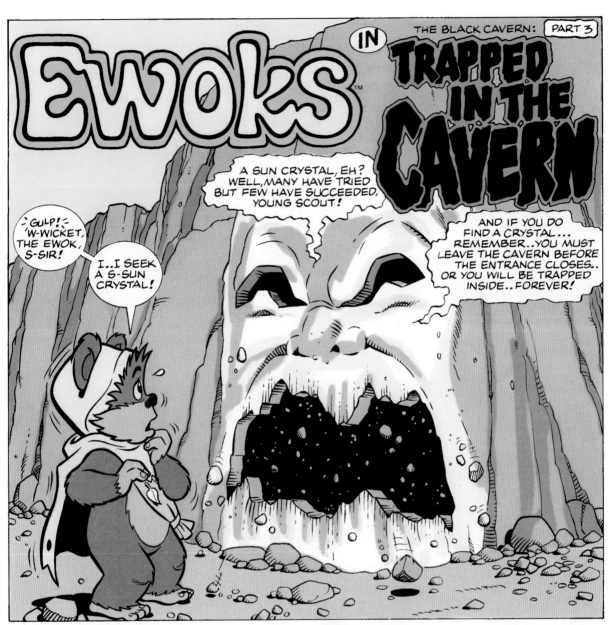

Ewoks IN

TRAPPED IN THE CAVERN

A SUN CRYSTAL, EH? WELL, MANY HAVE TRIED BUT FEW HAVE SUCCEEDED, YOUNG SCOUT!

-GULP!- 'W-WICKET, THE EWOK, S-SIR!

I..I SEEK A S-SUN CRYSTAL!

AND IF YOU DO FIND A CRYSTAL... REMEMBER..YOU MUST LEAVE THE CAVERN BEFORE THE ENTRANCE CLOSES.. OR YOU WILL BE TRAPPED INSIDE...FOREVER!

I..I MUST TRY!

THE CHOICE IS YOURS! ENTER!

AND NEARBY...

HUH? EWOK GO IN CAVE!

13

379

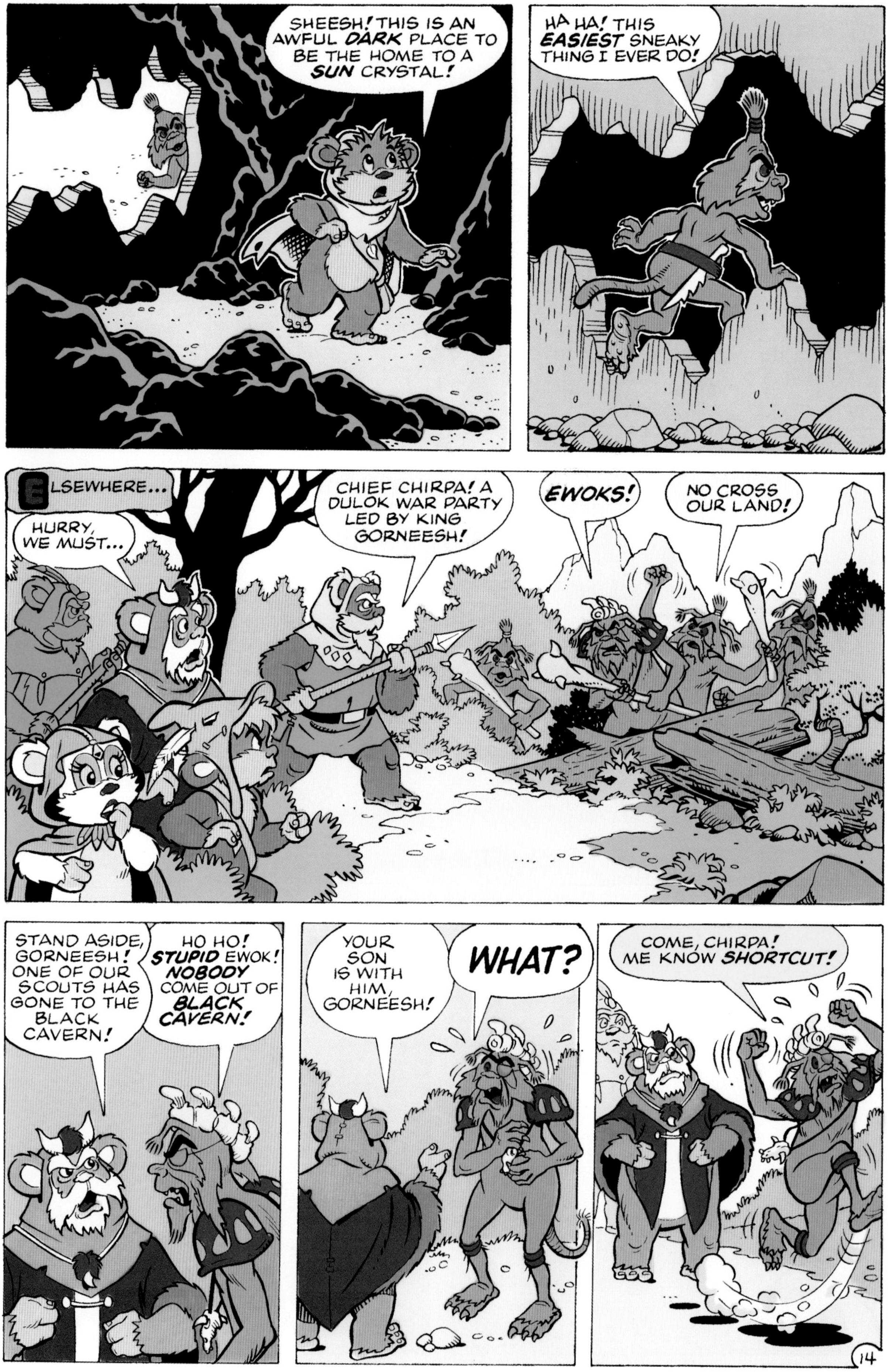
SHEESH! THIS IS AN AWFUL DARK PLACE TO BE THE HOME TO A SUN CRYSTAL!
HA HA! THIS EASIEST SNEAKY THING I EVER DO!
ELSEWHERE...
HURRY, WE MUST...
CHIEF CHIRPA! A DULOK WAR PARTY LED BY KING GORNEESH!
EWOKS!
NO CROSS OUR LAND!
STAND ASIDE, GORNEESH! ONE OF OUR SCOUTS HAS GONE TO THE BLACK CAVERN!
HO HO! STUPID EWOK! NOBODY COME OUT OF BLACK CAVERN!
YOUR SON IS WITH HIM, GORNEESH!
WHAT?
COME, CHIRPA! ME KNOW SHORTCUT!
14

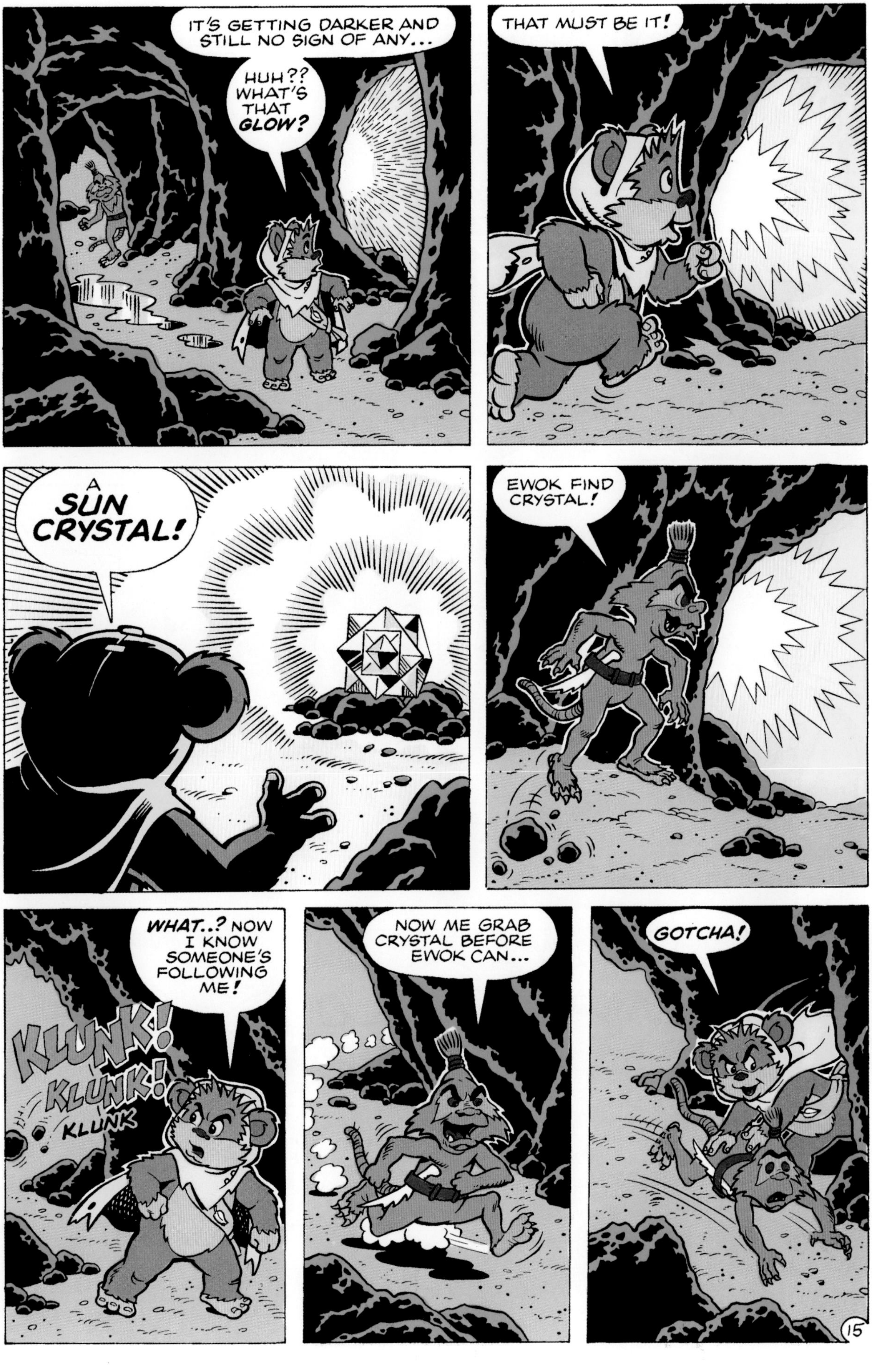
IT'S GETTING DARKER AND STILL NO SIGN OF ANY...
HUH?? WHAT'S THAT GLOW?
THAT MUST BE IT!
A SUN CRYSTAL!
EWOK FIND CRYSTAL!
WHAT..? NOW I KNOW SOMEONE'S FOLLOWING ME!
KLUNK! KLUNK! KLUNK
NOW ME GRAB CRYSTAL BEFORE EWOK CAN...
GOTCHA!
15

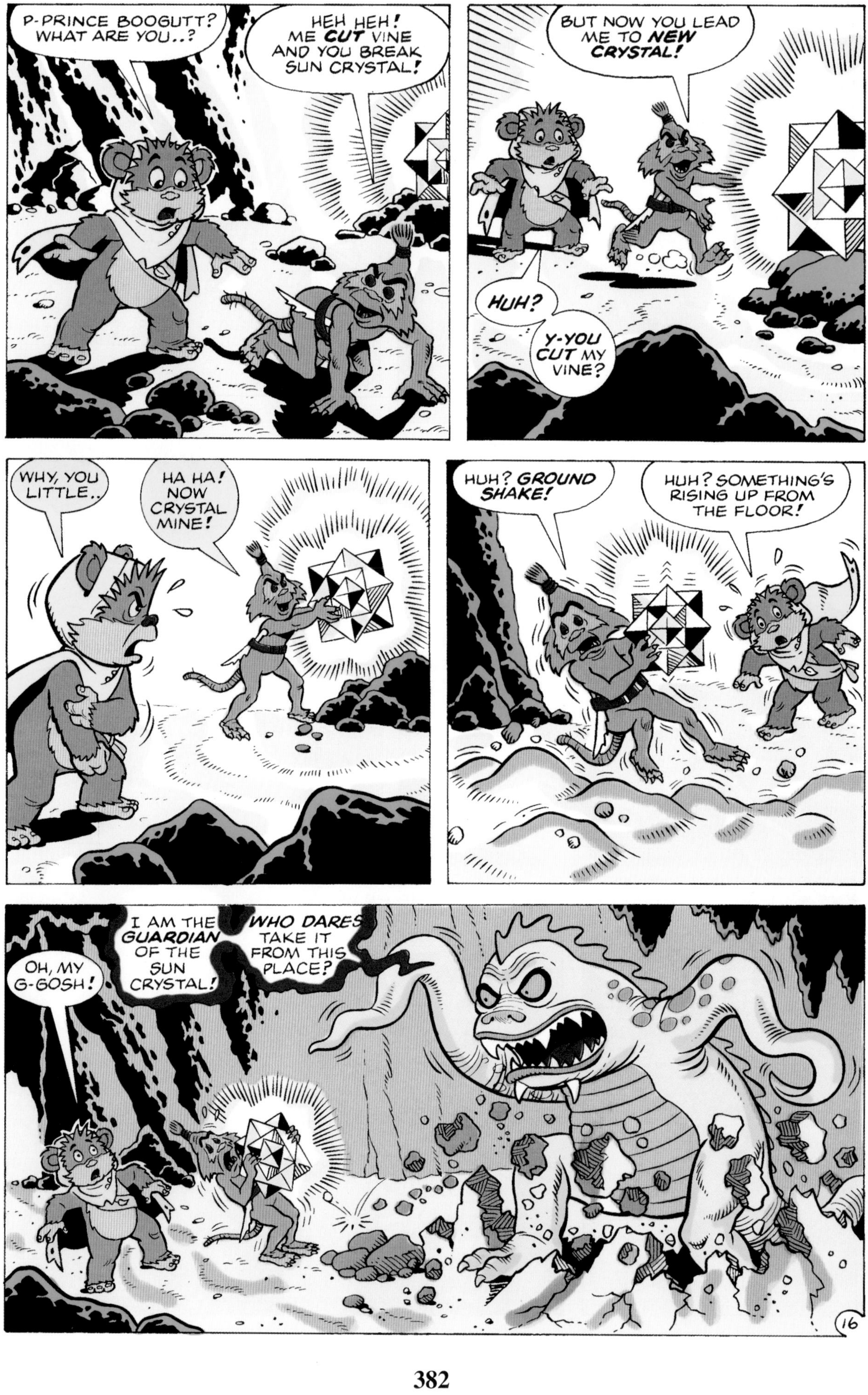
P-PRINCE BOOGUTT? WHAT ARE YOU..?
HEH HEH! ME CUT VINE AND YOU BREAK SUN CRYSTAL!
BUT NOW YOU LEAD ME TO NEW CRYSTAL!
HUH?
Y-YOU CUT MY VINE?
WHY, YOU LITTLE..
HA HA! NOW CRYSTAL MINE!
HUH? GROUND SHAKE!
HUH? SOMETHING'S RISING UP FROM THE FLOOR!
OH, MY G-GOSH!
I AM THE GUARDIAN OF THE SUN CRYSTAL!
WHO DARES TAKE IT FROM THIS PLACE?
16

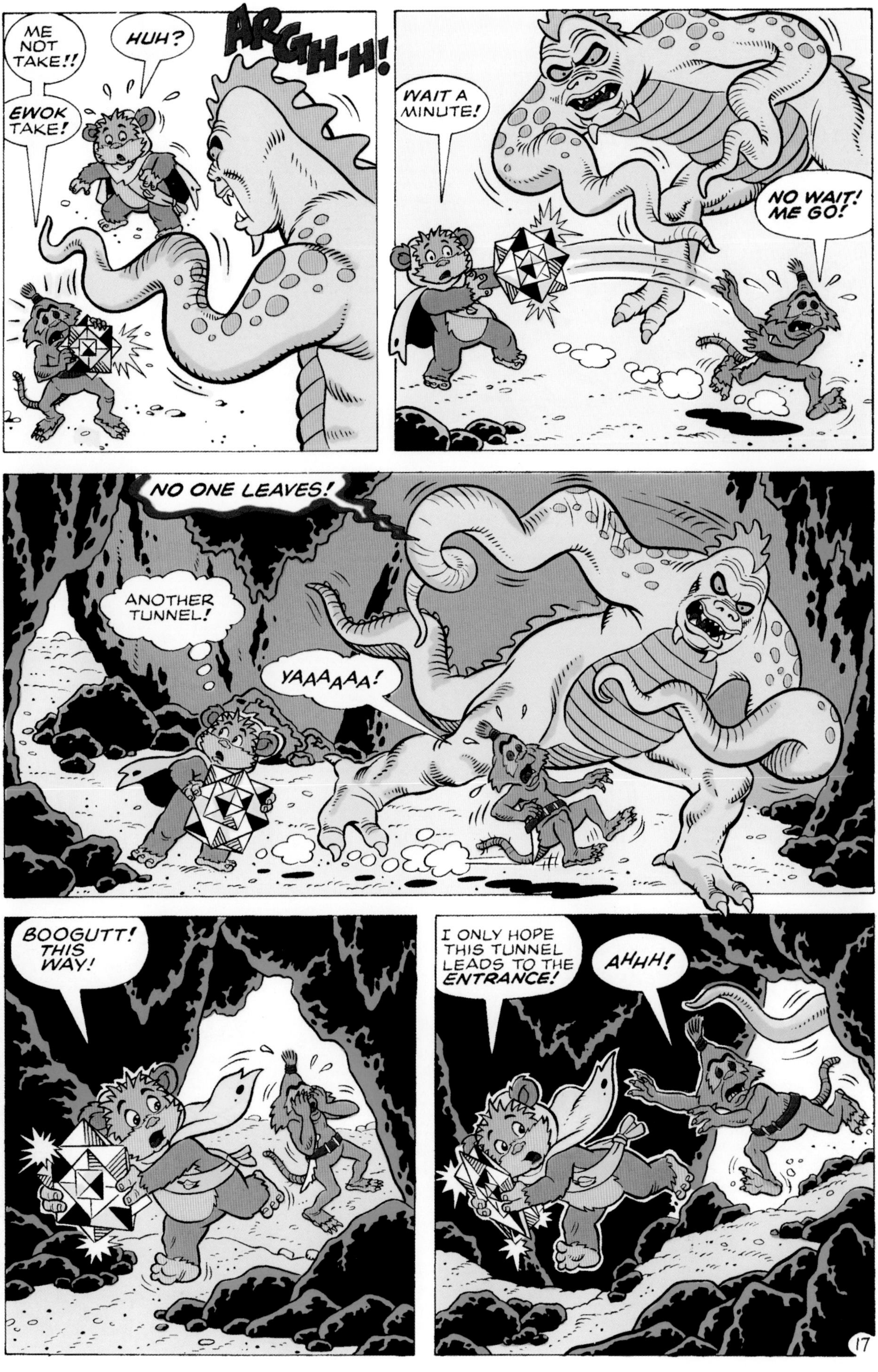

ME NOT TAKE!!
EWOK TAKE!
HUH?
ARGH-H!
WAIT A MINUTE!
NO WAIT! ME GO!
NO ONE LEAVES!
ANOTHER TUNNEL!
YAAAAAA!
BOOGUTT! THIS WAY!
I ONLY HOPE THIS TUNNEL LEADS TO THE ENTRANCE!
AHHH!
17

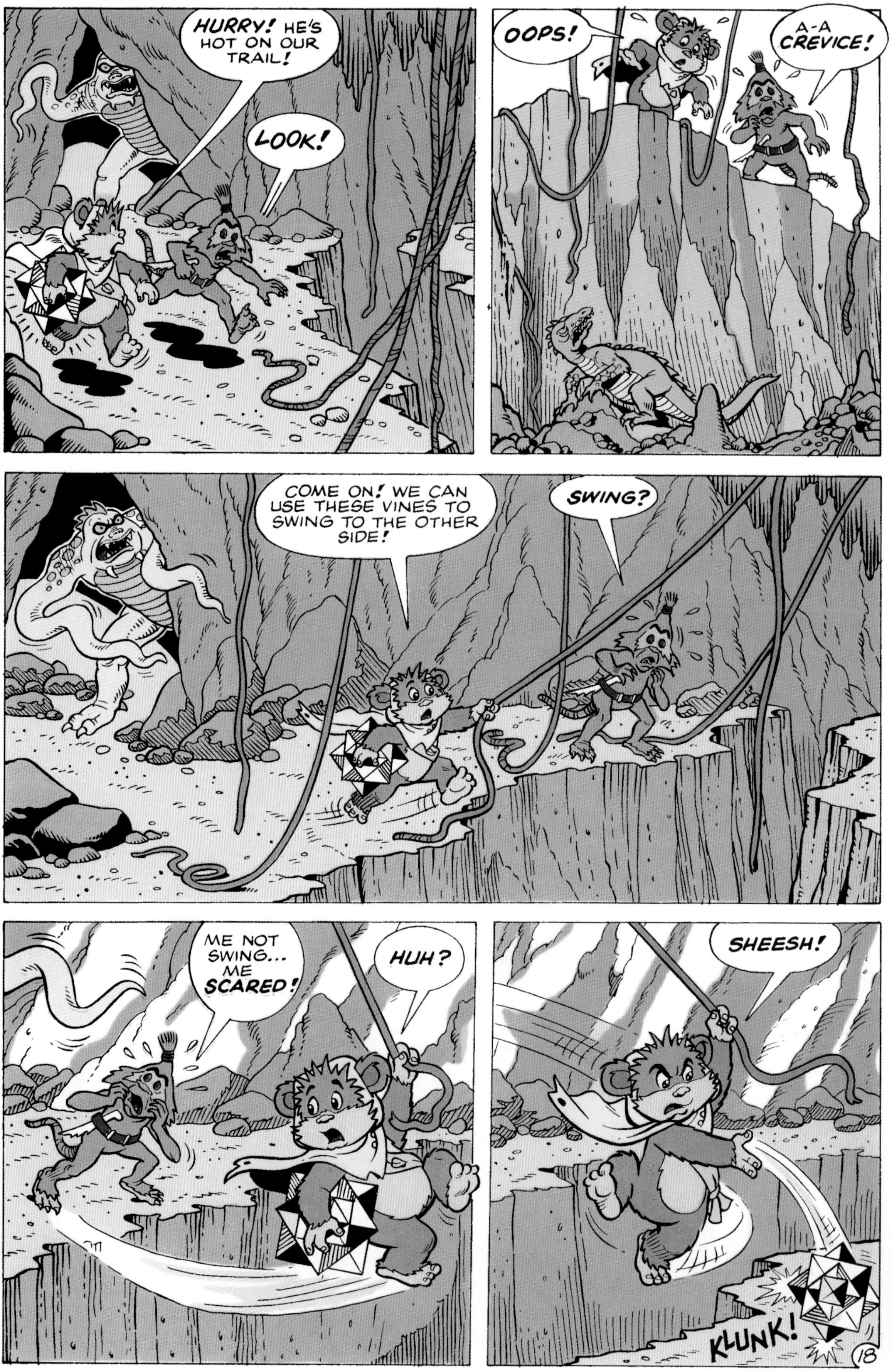
HURRY! HE'S HOT ON OUR TRAIL!
LOOK!
OOPS!
A-A CREVICE!
COME ON! WE CAN USE THESE VINES TO SWING TO THE OTHER SIDE!
SWING?
ME NOT SWING... ME SCARED!
HUH?
SHEESH!
KLUNK!
18

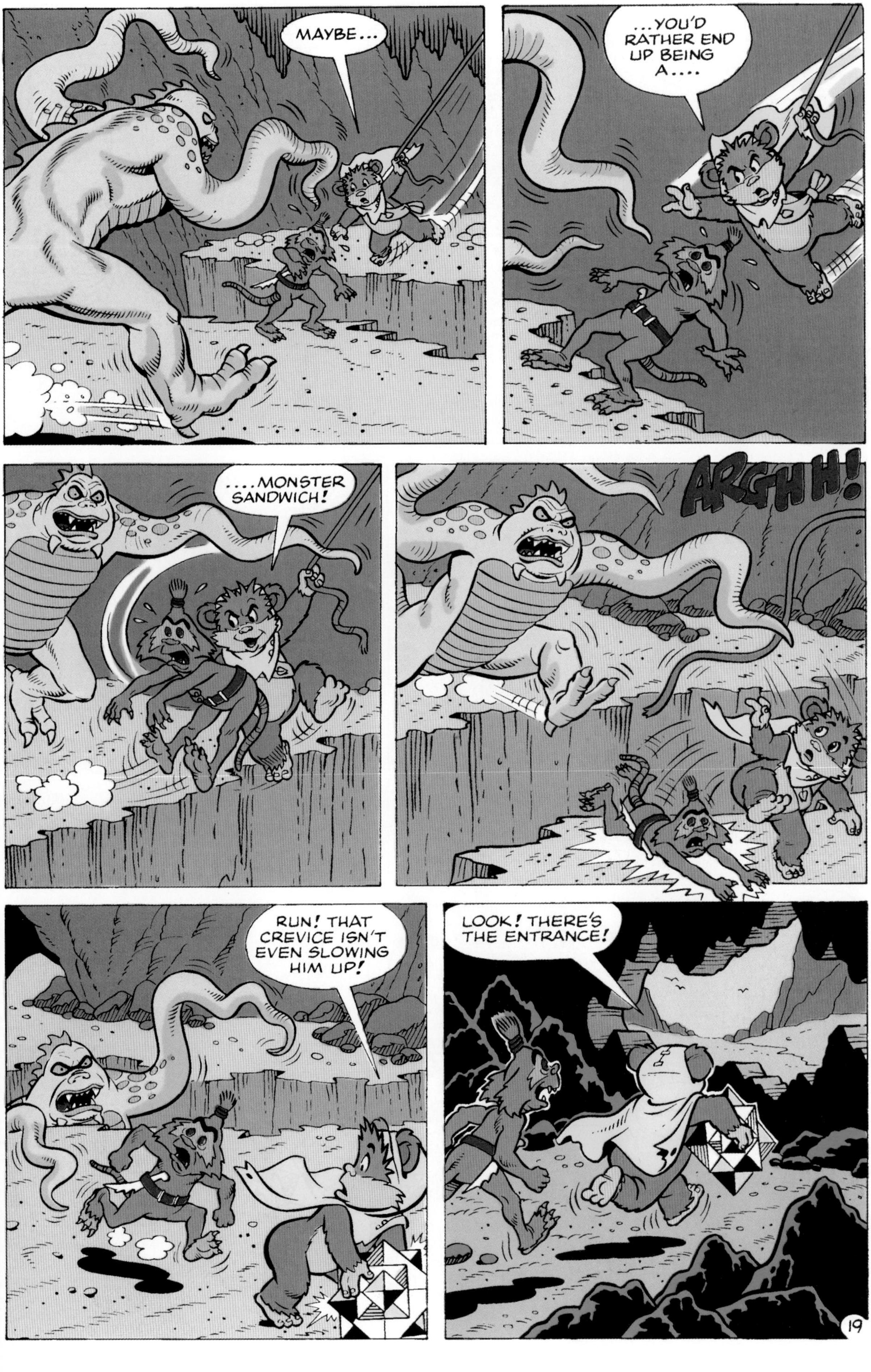
MAYBE...
...YOU'D RATHER END UP BEING A....
....MONSTER SANDWICH!
ARGHH!
RUN! THAT CREVICE ISN'T EVEN SLOWING HIM UP!
LOOK! THERE'S THE ENTRANCE!
19

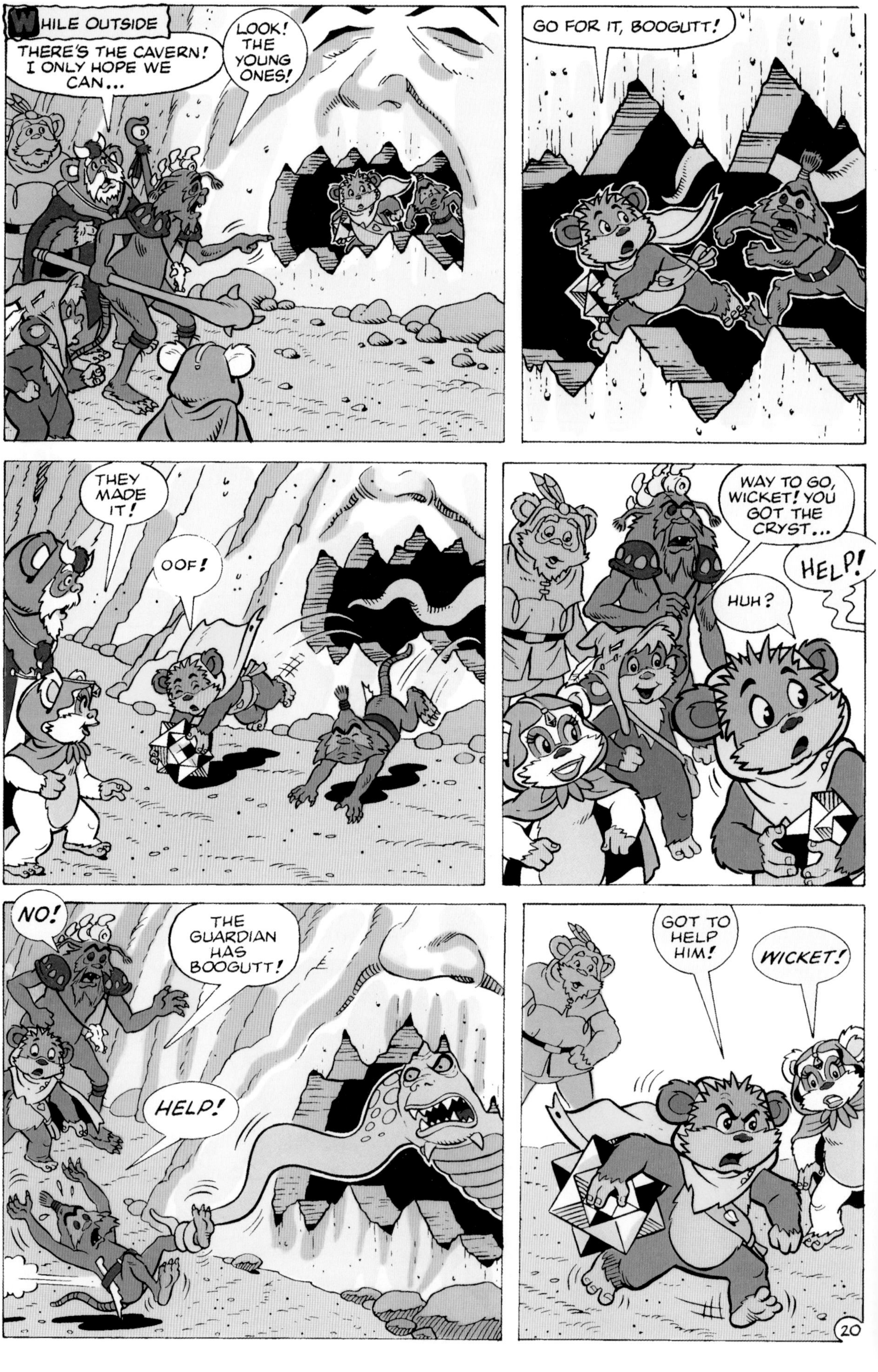
WHILE OUTSIDE
THERE'S THE CAVERN! I ONLY HOPE WE CAN...
LOOK! THE YOUNG ONES!
GO FOR IT, BOOGUTT!
THEY MADE IT!
OOF!
WAY TO GO, WICKET! YOU GOT THE CRYST...
HELP!
HUH?
NO!
THE GUARDIAN HAS BOOGUTT!
HELP!
GOT TO HELP HIM!
WICKET!
20

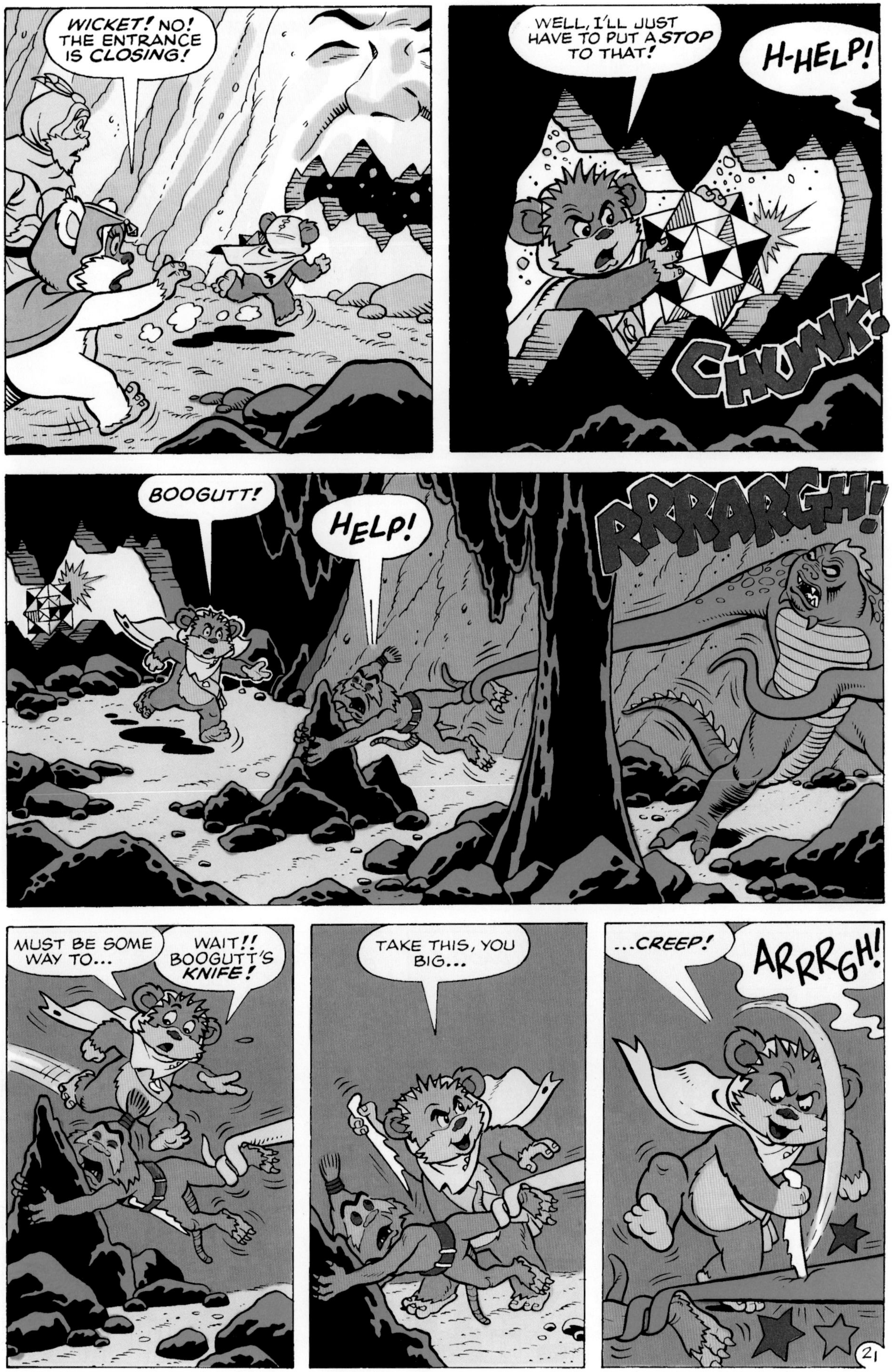
WICKET! NO! THE ENTRANCE IS CLOSING!
WELL, I'LL JUST HAVE TO PUT A STOP TO THAT!
H-HELP!
CHUNK!
BOOGUTT!
HELP!
RRRARGH!
MUST BE SOME WAY TO...
WAIT!! BOOGUTT'S KNIFE!
TAKE THIS, YOU BIG...
...CREEP!
ARRRGH!
21

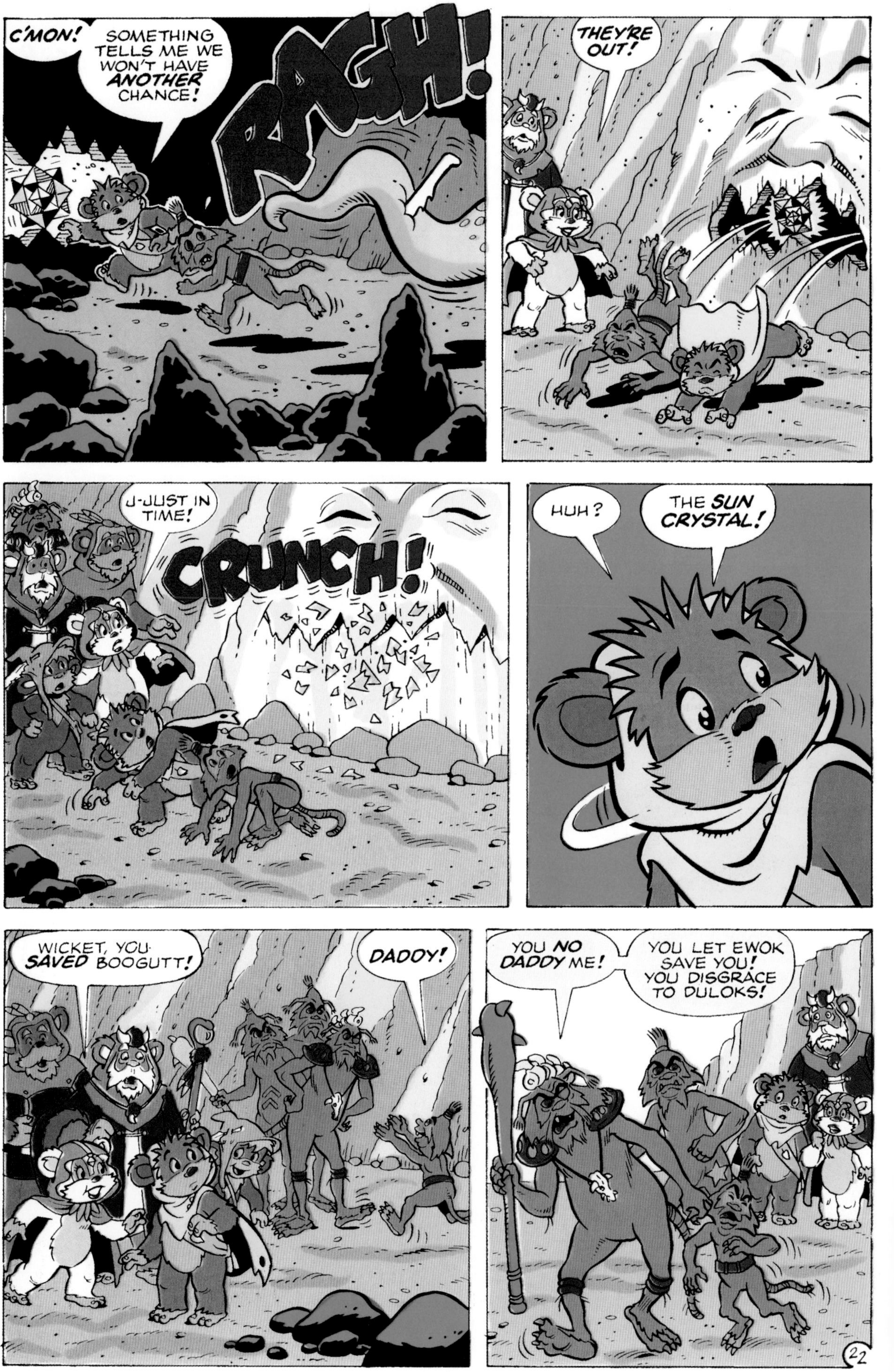
C'MON!
SOMETHING TELLS ME WE WON'T HAVE ANOTHER CHANCE!
RAGH!
THEY'RE OUT!
J-JUST IN TIME!
CRUNCH!
HUH?
THE SUN CRYSTAL!
WICKET, YOU SAVED BOOGUTT!
DADDY!
YOU NO DADDY ME!
YOU LET EWOK SAVE YOU! YOU DISGRACE TO DULOKS!
22

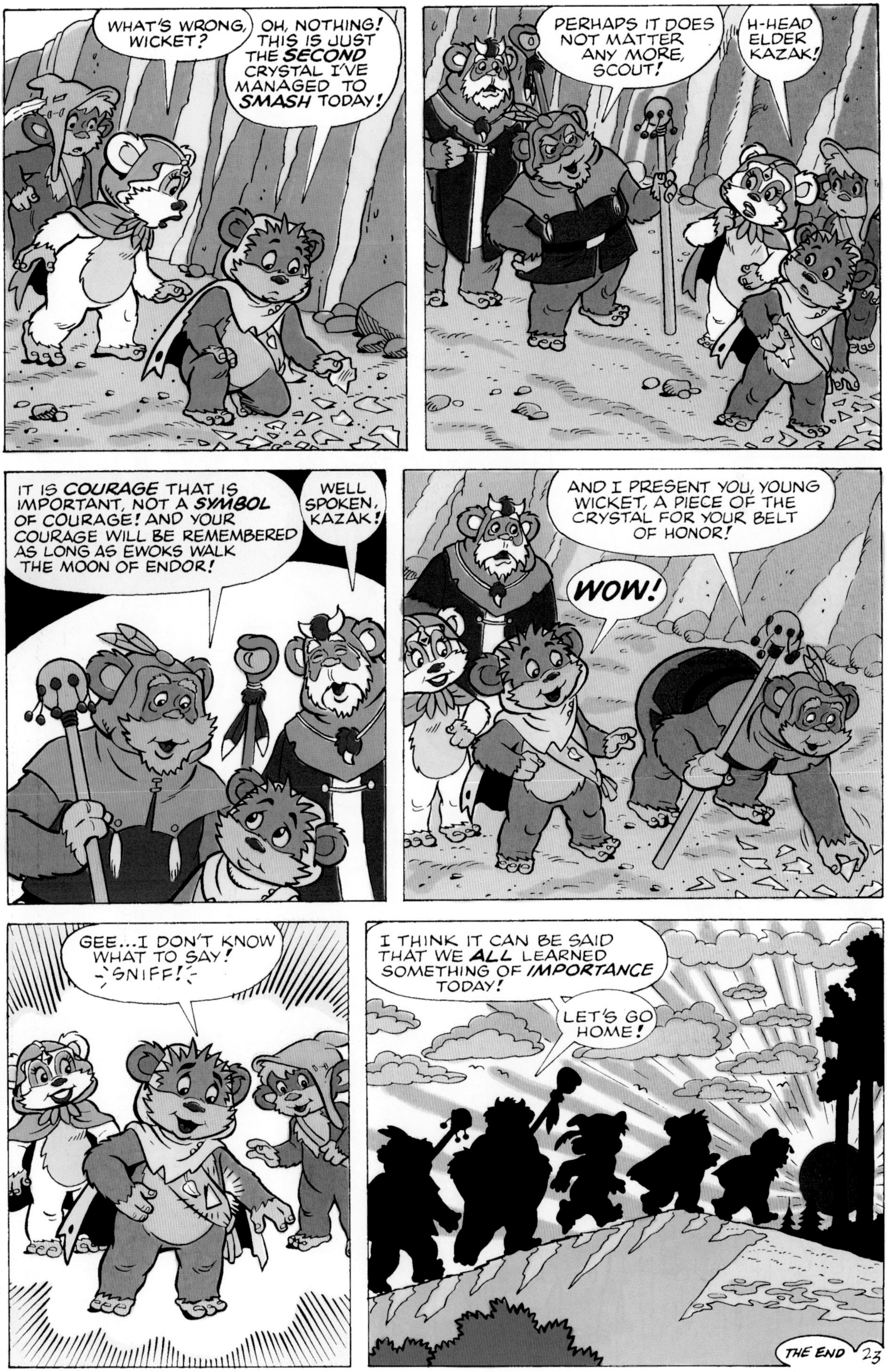
WHAT'S WRONG, WICKET?
OH, NOTHING! THIS IS JUST THE SECOND CRYSTAL I'VE MANAGED TO SMASH TODAY!
PERHAPS IT DOES NOT MATTER ANY MORE, SCOUT!
H-HEAD ELDER KAZAK!
IT IS COURAGE THAT IS IMPORTANT, NOT A SYMBOL OF COURAGE! AND YOUR COURAGE WILL BE REMEMBERED AS LONG AS EWOKS WALK THE MOON OF ENDOR!
WELL SPOKEN, KAZAK!
AND I PRESENT YOU, YOUNG WICKET, A PIECE OF THE CRYSTAL FOR YOUR BELT OF HONOR!
WOW!
GEE...I DON'T KNOW WHAT TO SAY! SNIFF!
I THINK IT CAN BE SAID THAT WE ALL LEARNED SOMETHING OF IMPORTANCE TODAY!
LET'S GO HOME!
THE END 23

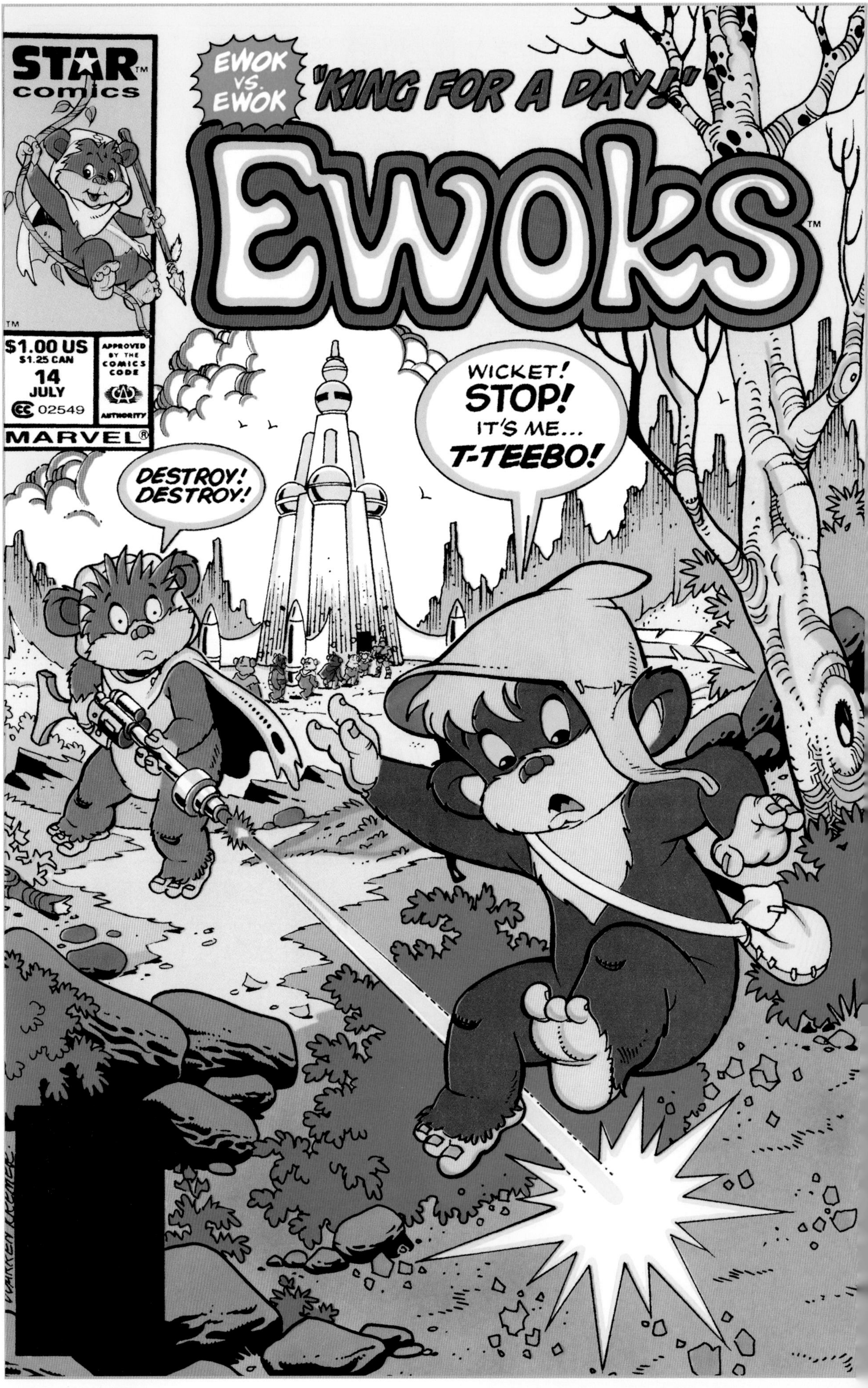
STAR comics™
EWOK vs. EWOK
"KING FOR A DAY!"
EWOKS™
$1.00 US
$1.25 CAN
14
JULY
02549
APPROVED BY THE COMICS CODE AUTHORITY
MARVEL®
DESTROY! DESTROY!
WICKET! STOP! IT'S ME... T-TEEBO!
WARREN KREMER

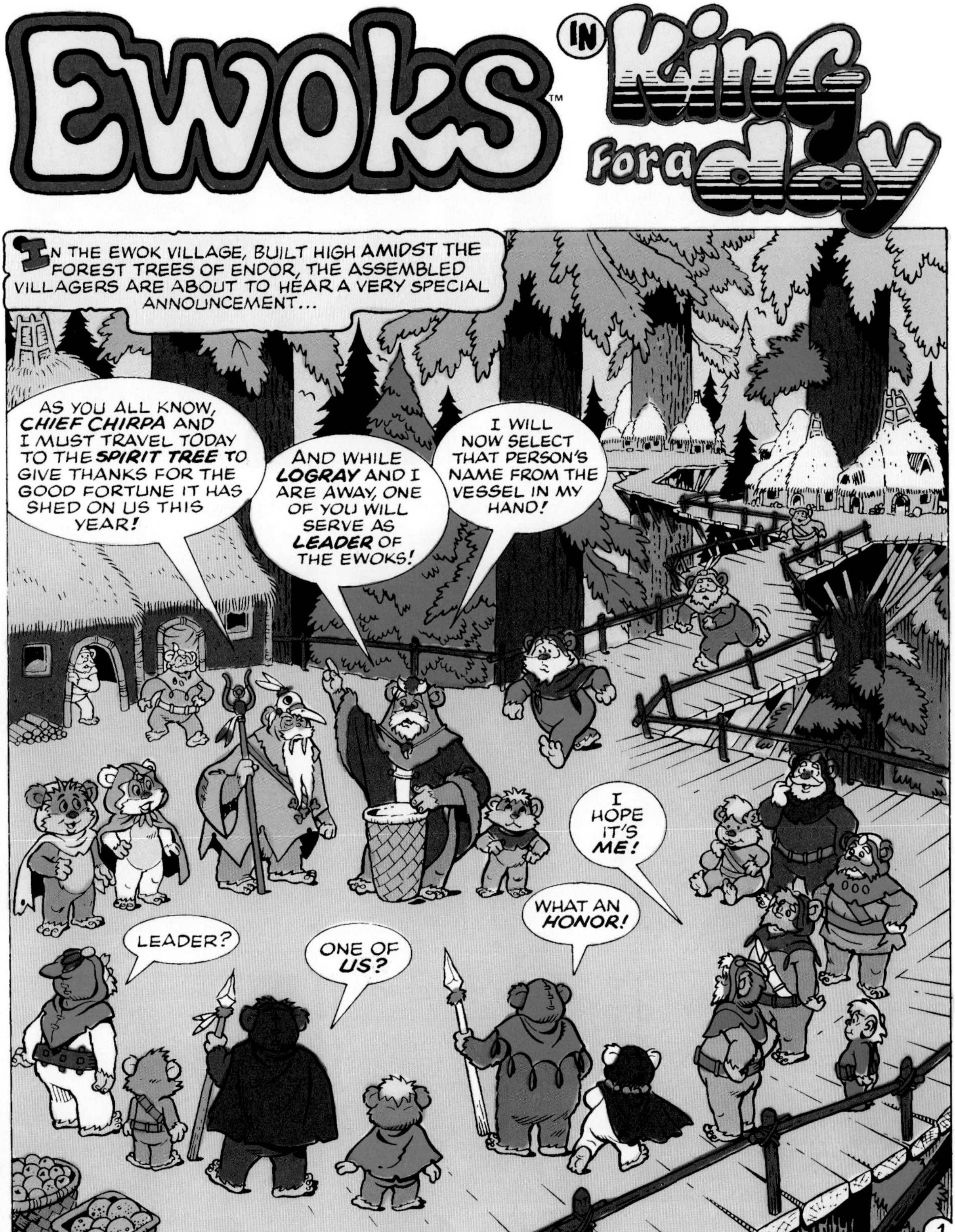
EWOKS™ IN KING FOR A DAY
IN THE EWOK VILLAGE, BUILT HIGH AMIDST THE FOREST TREES OF ENDOR, THE ASSEMBLED VILLAGERS ARE ABOUT TO HEAR A VERY SPECIAL ANNOUNCEMENT...
AS YOU ALL KNOW, CHIEF CHIRPA AND I MUST TRAVEL TODAY TO THE SPIRIT TREE TO GIVE THANKS FOR THE GOOD FORTUNE IT HAS SHED ON US THIS YEAR!
AND WHILE LOGRAY AND I ARE AWAY, ONE OF YOU WILL SERVE AS LEADER OF THE EWOKS!
I WILL NOW SELECT THAT PERSON'S NAME FROM THE VESSEL IN MY HAND!
I HOPE IT'S ME!
WHAT AN HONOR!
LEADER?
ONE OF US?
1

DAVE MANAK STORY · WARREN KREMER PENCILS · D'AGOSTINO & ROETTCHER INKS · GRACE KREMER LETTERS · GEORGE ROUSSOS COLORS · SID JACOBSON EDITOR · TOM DE FALCO EXEC. EDITOR · JIM SHOOTER ED. IN CHIEF

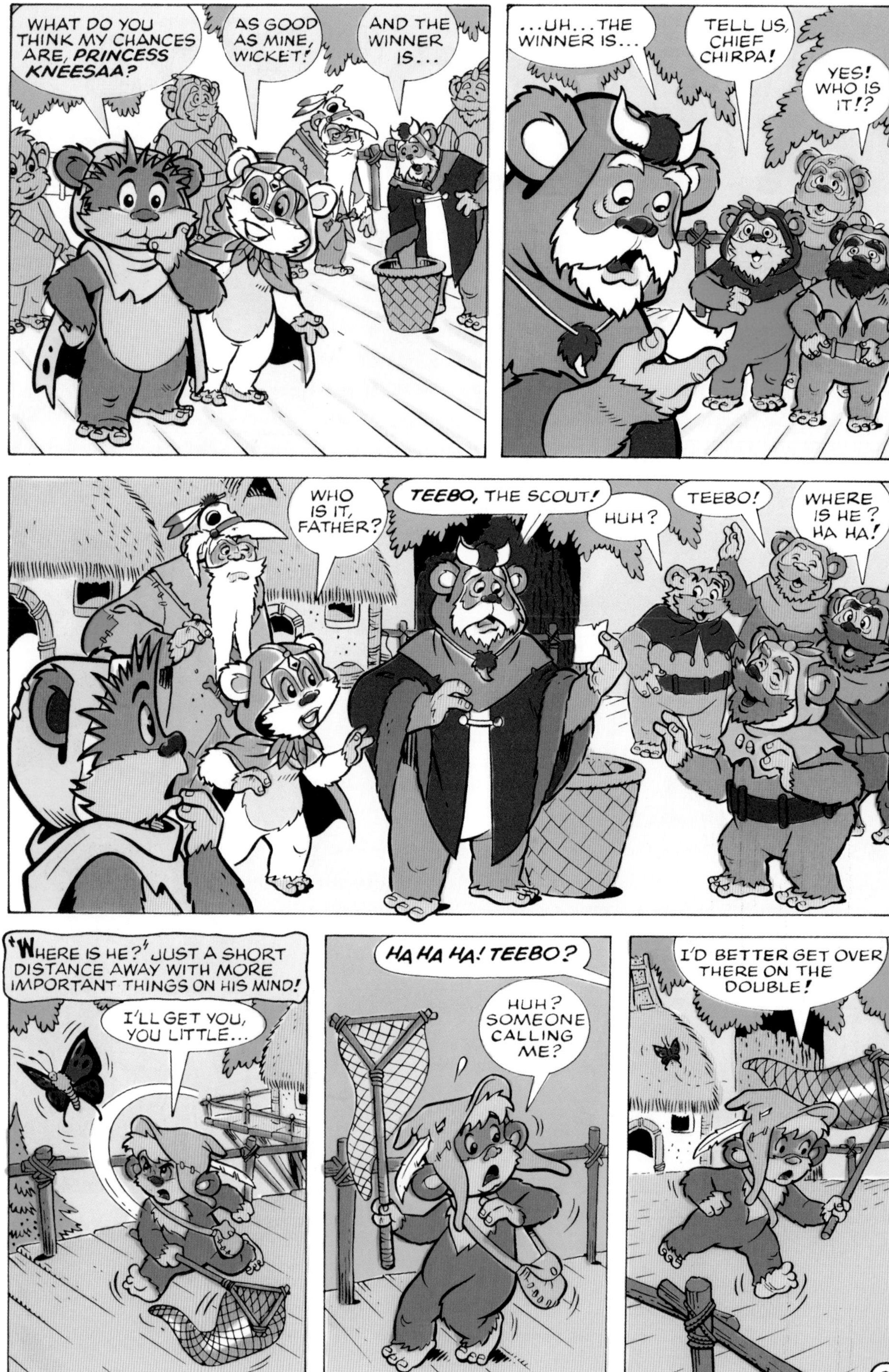
WHAT DO YOU THINK MY CHANCES ARE, PRINCESS KNEESAA?
AS GOOD AS MINE, WICKET!
AND THE WINNER IS...
...UH...THE WINNER IS...
TELL US, CHIEF CHIRPA!
YES! WHO IS IT!?
WHO IS IT, FATHER?
TEEBO, THE SCOUT!
HUH?
TEEBO!
WHERE IS HE? HA HA!
"WHERE IS HE?" JUST A SHORT DISTANCE AWAY WITH MORE IMPORTANT THINGS ON HIS MIND!
I'LL GET YOU, YOU LITTLE...
HA HA HA! TEEBO?
HUH? SOMEONE CALLING ME?
I'D BETTER GET OVER THERE ON THE DOUBLE!
2

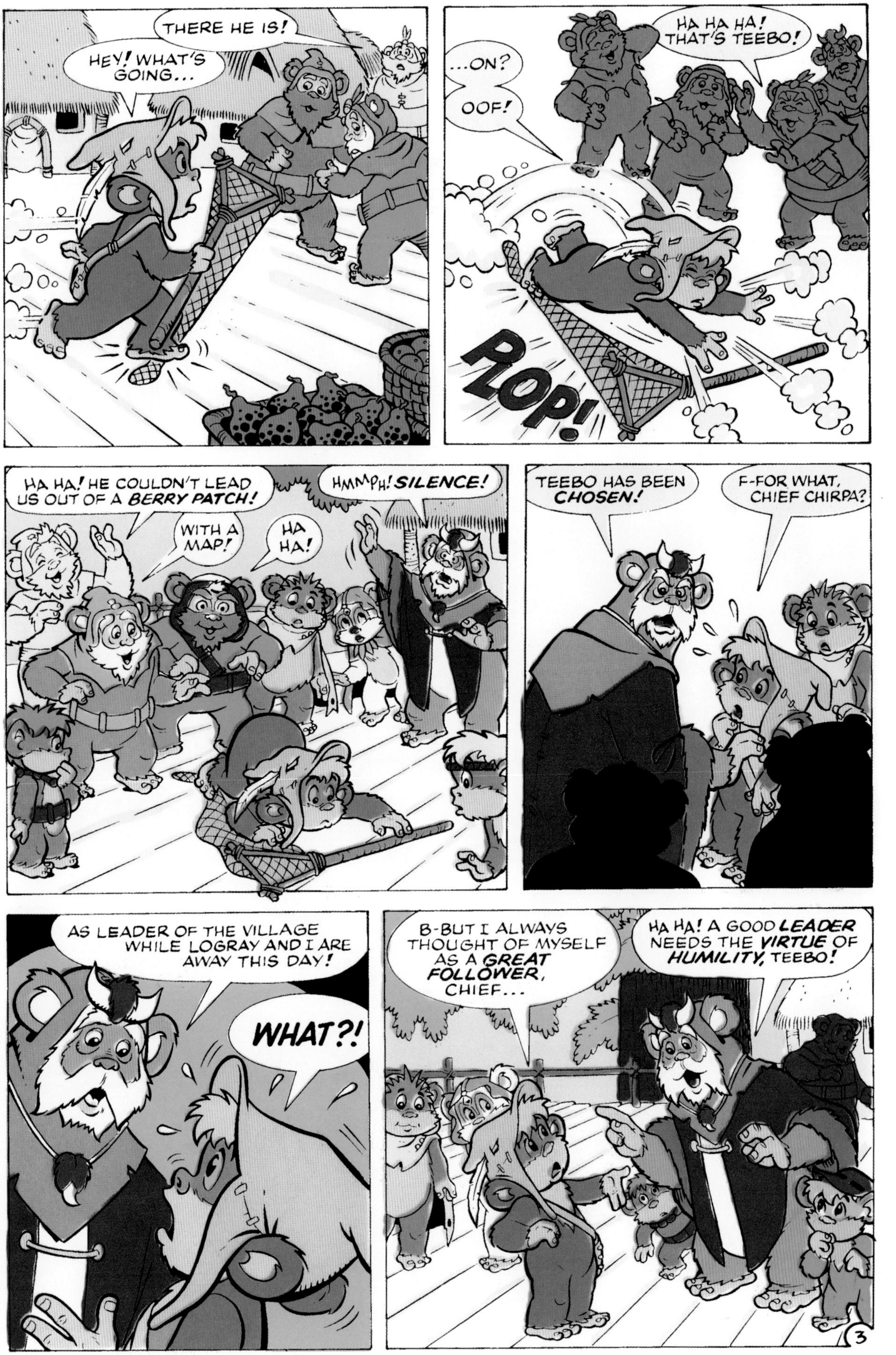
HEY! WHAT'S GOING...
THERE HE IS!
...ON?
OOF!
HA HA HA! THAT'S TEEBO!
PLOP!
HA HA! HE COULDN'T LEAD US OUT OF A BERRY PATCH!
WITH A MAP!
HA HA!
HMMPH! SILENCE!
TEEBO HAS BEEN CHOSEN!
F-FOR WHAT, CHIEF CHIRPA?
AS LEADER OF THE VILLAGE WHILE LOGRAY AND I ARE AWAY THIS DAY!
WHAT?!
B-BUT I ALWAYS THOUGHT OF MYSELF AS A GREAT FOLLOWER, CHIEF...
HA HA! A GOOD LEADER NEEDS THE VIRTUE OF HUMILITY, TEEBO!
3

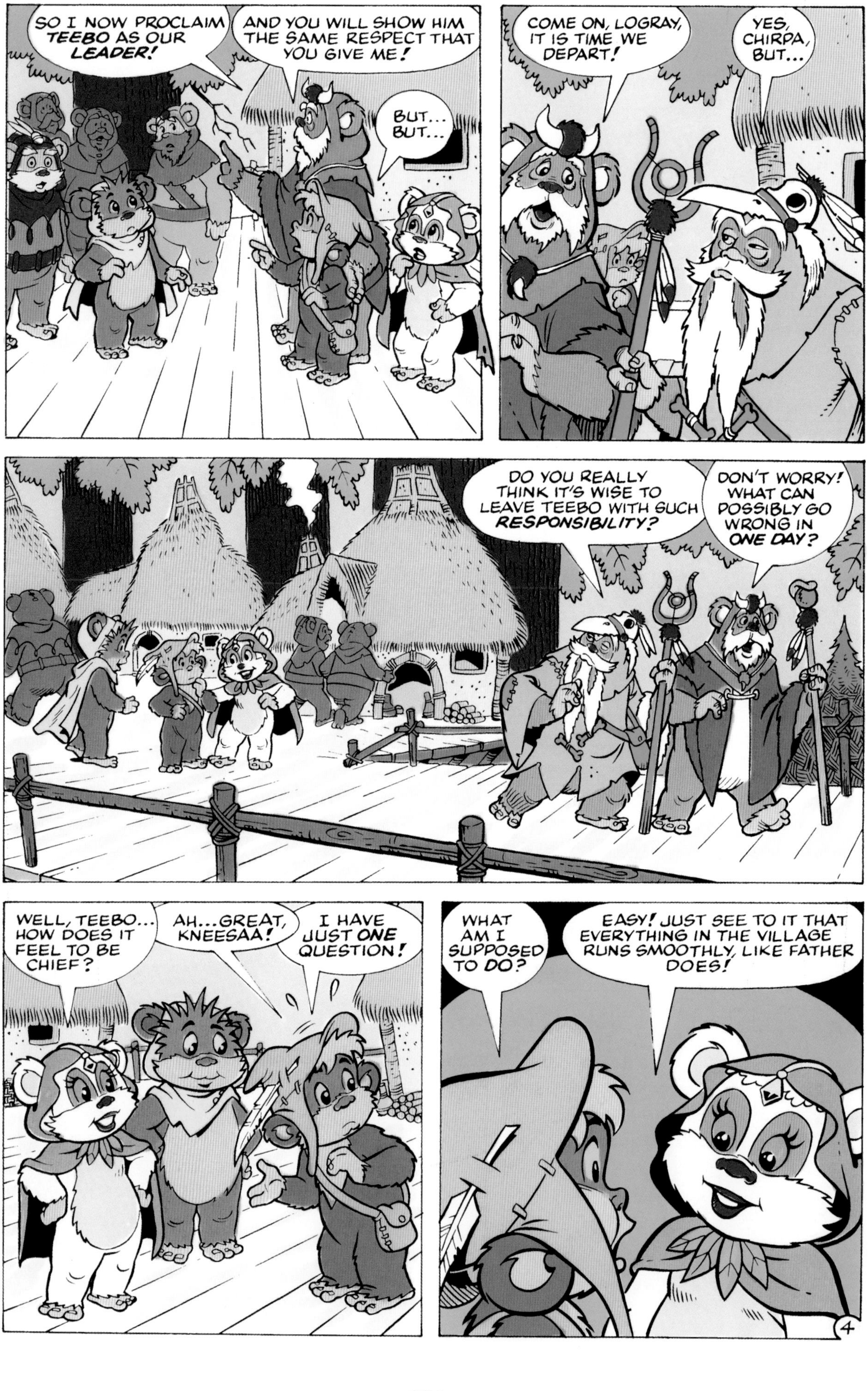
SO I NOW PROCLAIM TEEBO AS OUR LEADER!
AND YOU WILL SHOW HIM THE SAME RESPECT THAT YOU GIVE ME!
BUT... BUT...
COME ON, LOGRAY, IT IS TIME WE DEPART!
YES, CHIRPA, BUT...
DO YOU REALLY THINK IT'S WISE TO LEAVE TEEBO WITH SUCH RESPONSIBILITY?
DON'T WORRY! WHAT CAN POSSIBLY GO WRONG IN ONE DAY?
WELL, TEEBO... HOW DOES IT FEEL TO BE CHIEF?
AH...GREAT, KNEESAA!
I HAVE JUST ONE QUESTION!
WHAT AM I SUPPOSED TO DO?
EASY! JUST SEE TO IT THAT EVERYTHING IN THE VILLAGE RUNS SMOOTHLY, LIKE FATHER DOES!
4

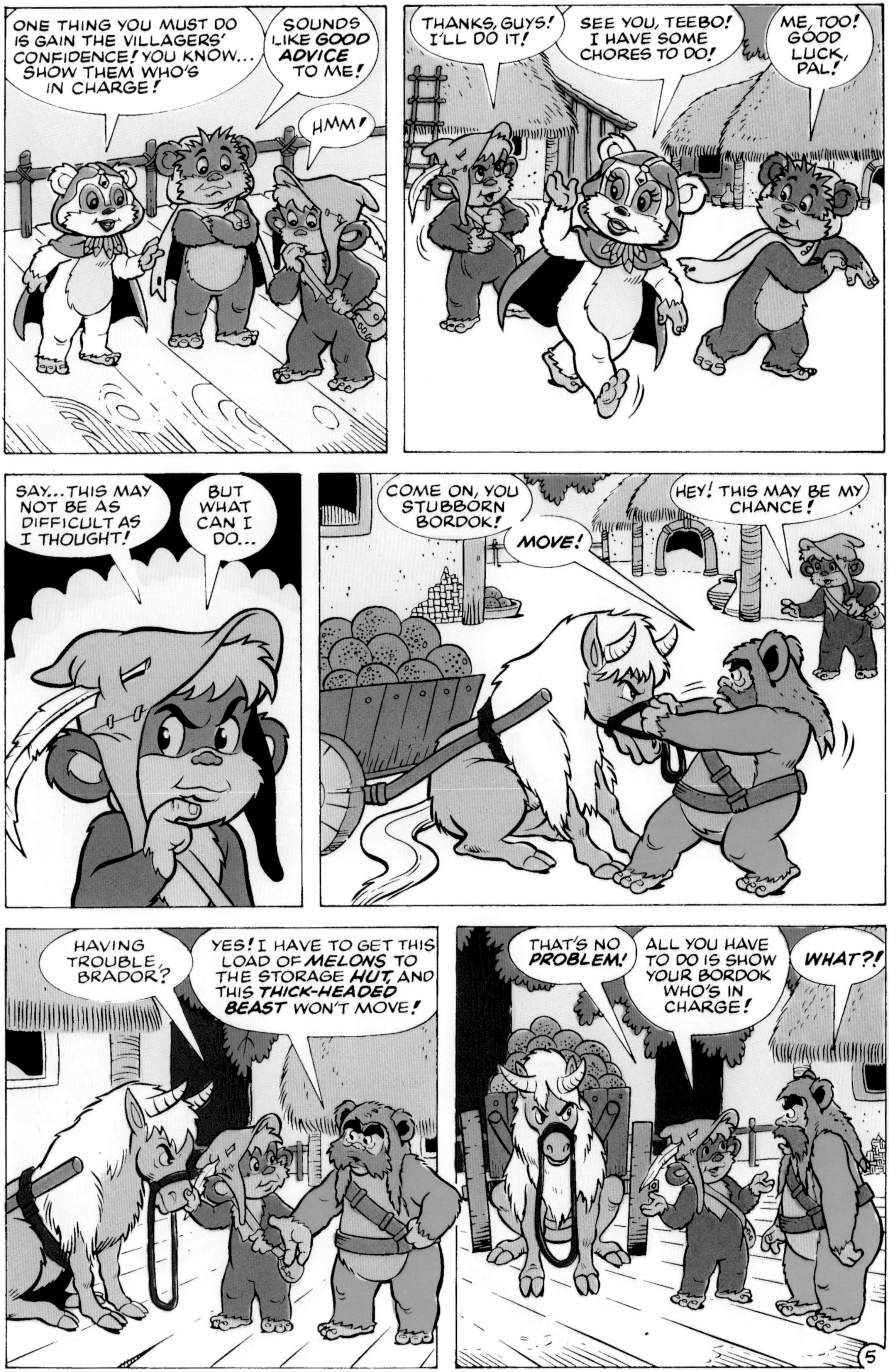
ONE THING YOU MUST DO IS GAIN THE VILLAGERS' CONFIDENCE! YOU KNOW... SHOW THEM WHO'S IN CHARGE!
SOUNDS LIKE GOOD ADVICE TO ME!
HMM!
THANKS, GUYS! I'LL DO IT!
SEE YOU, TEEBO! I HAVE SOME CHORES TO DO!
ME, TOO! GOOD LUCK, PAL!
SAY... THIS MAY NOT BE AS DIFFICULT AS I THOUGHT!
BUT WHAT CAN I DO...
COME ON, YOU STUBBORN BORDOK!
MOVE!
HEY! THIS MAY BE MY CHANCE!
HAVING TROUBLE, BRADOR?
YES! I HAVE TO GET THIS LOAD OF MELONS TO THE STORAGE HUT, AND THIS THICK-HEADED BEAST WON'T MOVE!
THAT'S NO PROBLEM!
ALL YOU HAVE TO DO IS SHOW YOUR BORDOK WHO'S IN CHARGE!
WHAT?!
5

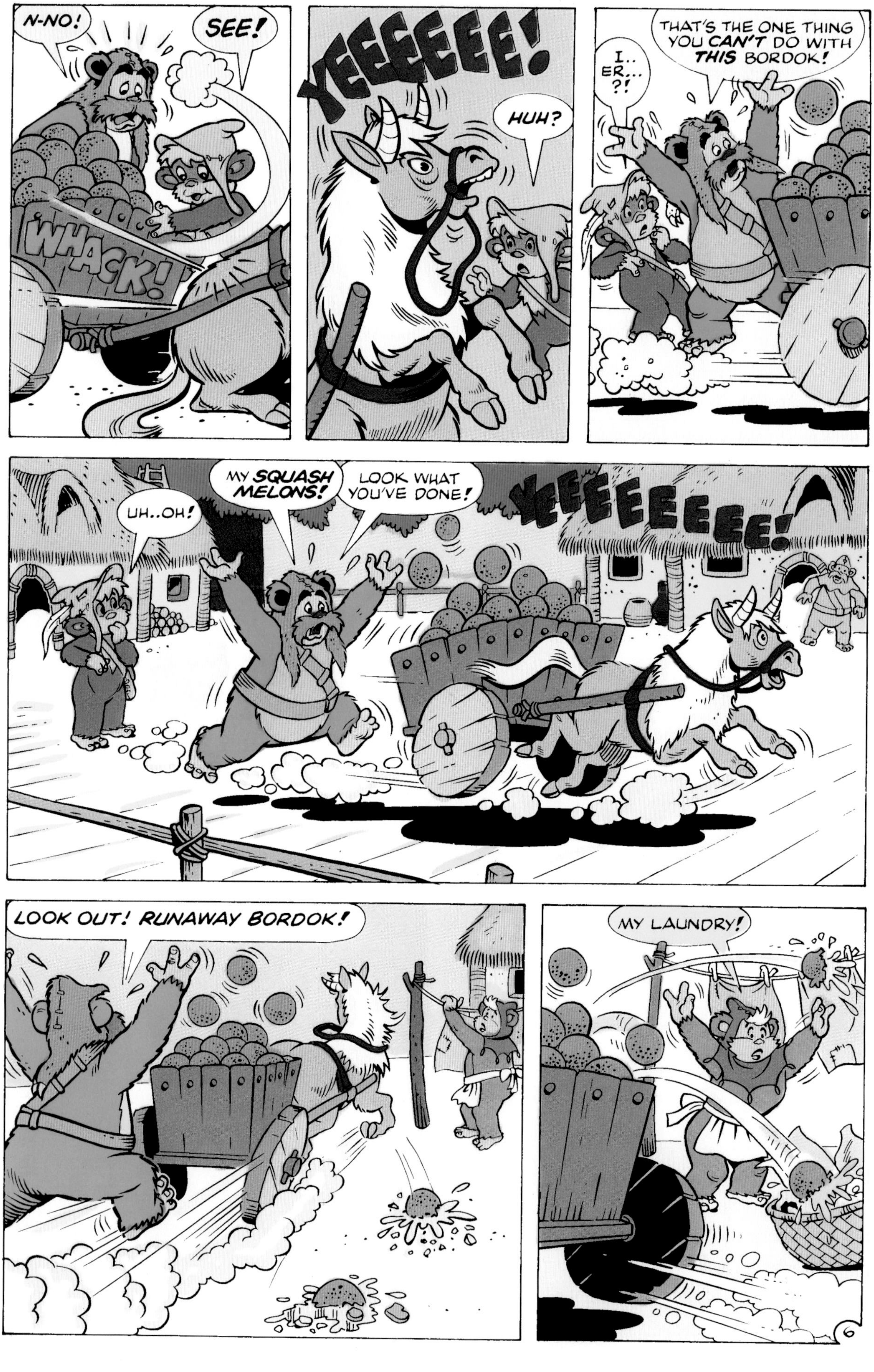
N-NO!
SEE!
WHACK!
YEEEEEEE!
HUH?
THAT'S THE ONE THING YOU CAN'T DO WITH THIS BORDOK!
I.. ER... ?!
UH..OH!
MY SQUASH MELONS!
LOOK WHAT YOU'VE DONE!
YEEEEEEEE!
LOOK OUT! RUNAWAY BORDOK!
MY LAUNDRY!
6

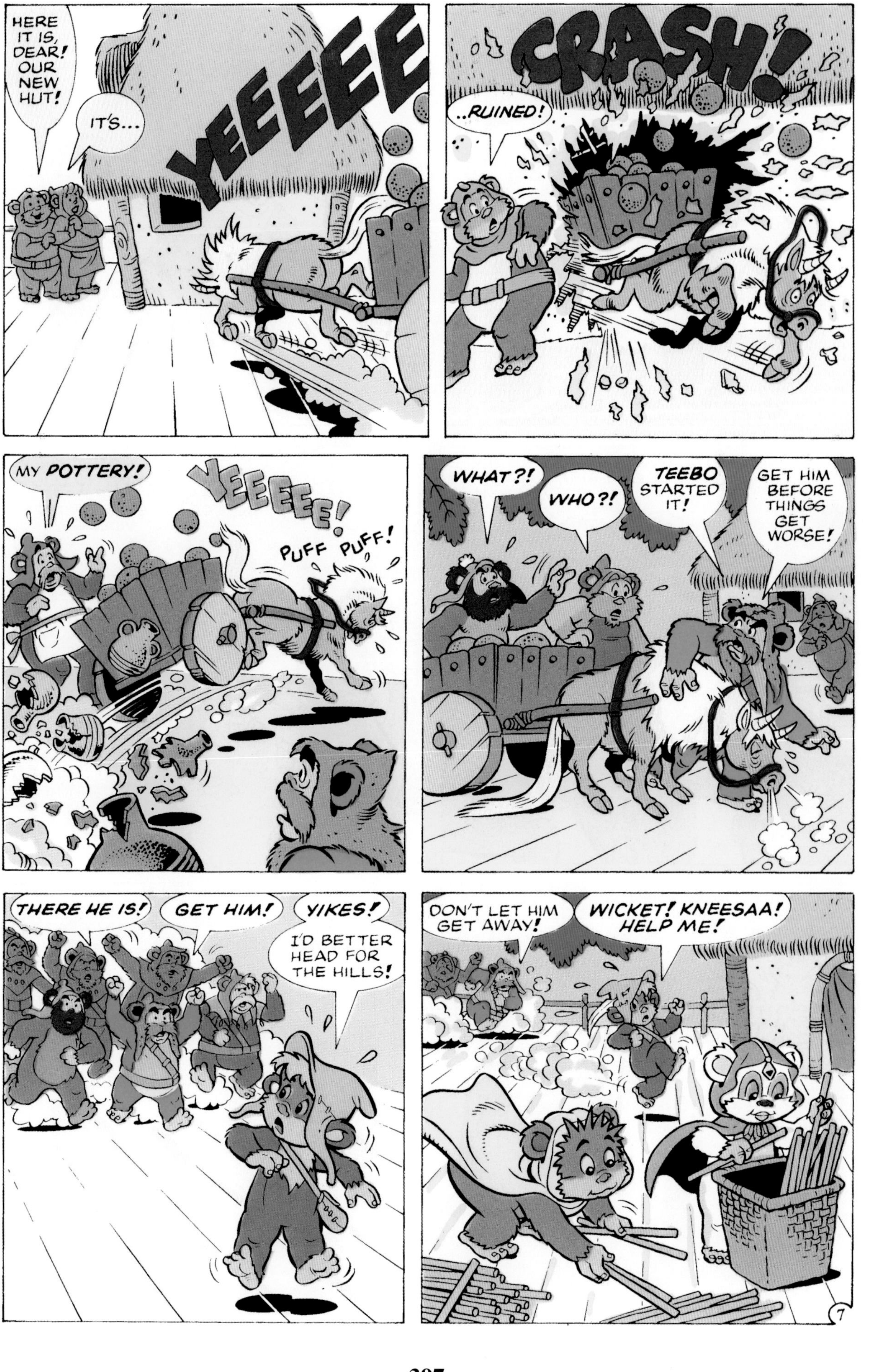
HERE IT IS, DEAR! OUR NEW HUT!
IT'S...
YEEEEE
CRASH!
..RUINED!
MY POTTERY!
YEEEEEE!
PUFF PUFF!
WHAT?!
WHO?!
TEEBO STARTED IT!
GET HIM BEFORE THINGS GET WORSE!
THERE HE IS!
GET HIM!
YIKES!
I'D BETTER HEAD FOR THE HILLS!
DON'T LET HIM GET AWAY!
WICKET! KNEESAA! HELP ME!
7

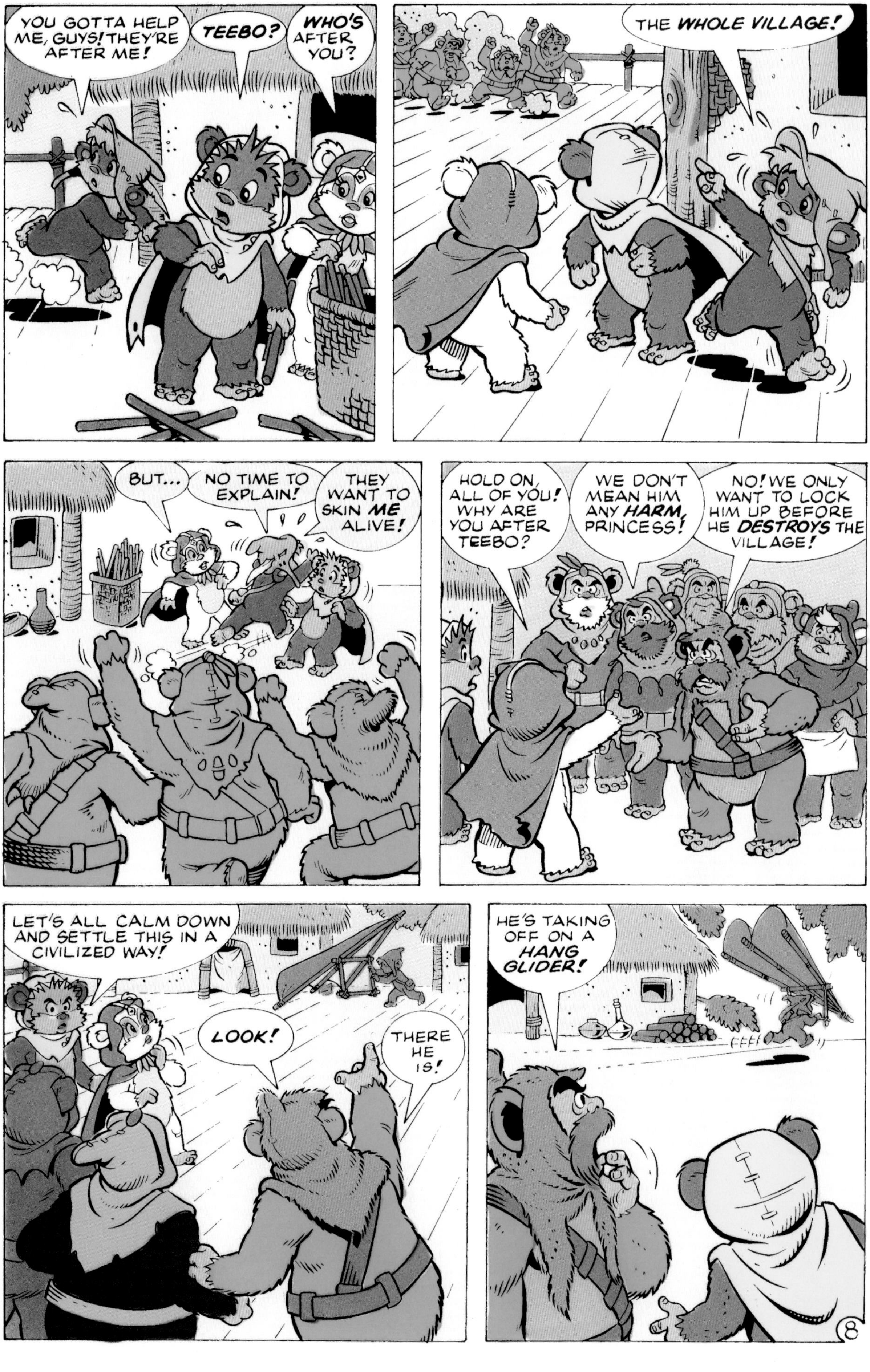

YOU GOTTA HELP ME, GUYS! THEY'RE AFTER ME!
TEEBO?
WHO'S AFTER YOU?
THE WHOLE VILLAGE!
BUT...
NO TIME TO EXPLAIN!
THEY WANT TO SKIN ME ALIVE!
HOLD ON, ALL OF YOU! WHY ARE YOU AFTER TEEBO?
WE DON'T MEAN HIM ANY HARM, PRINCESS!
NO! WE ONLY WANT TO LOCK HIM UP BEFORE HE DESTROYS THE VILLAGE!
LET'S ALL CALM DOWN AND SETTLE THIS IN A CIVILIZED WAY!
LOOK!
THERE HE IS!
HE'S TAKING OFF ON A HANG GLIDER!
8

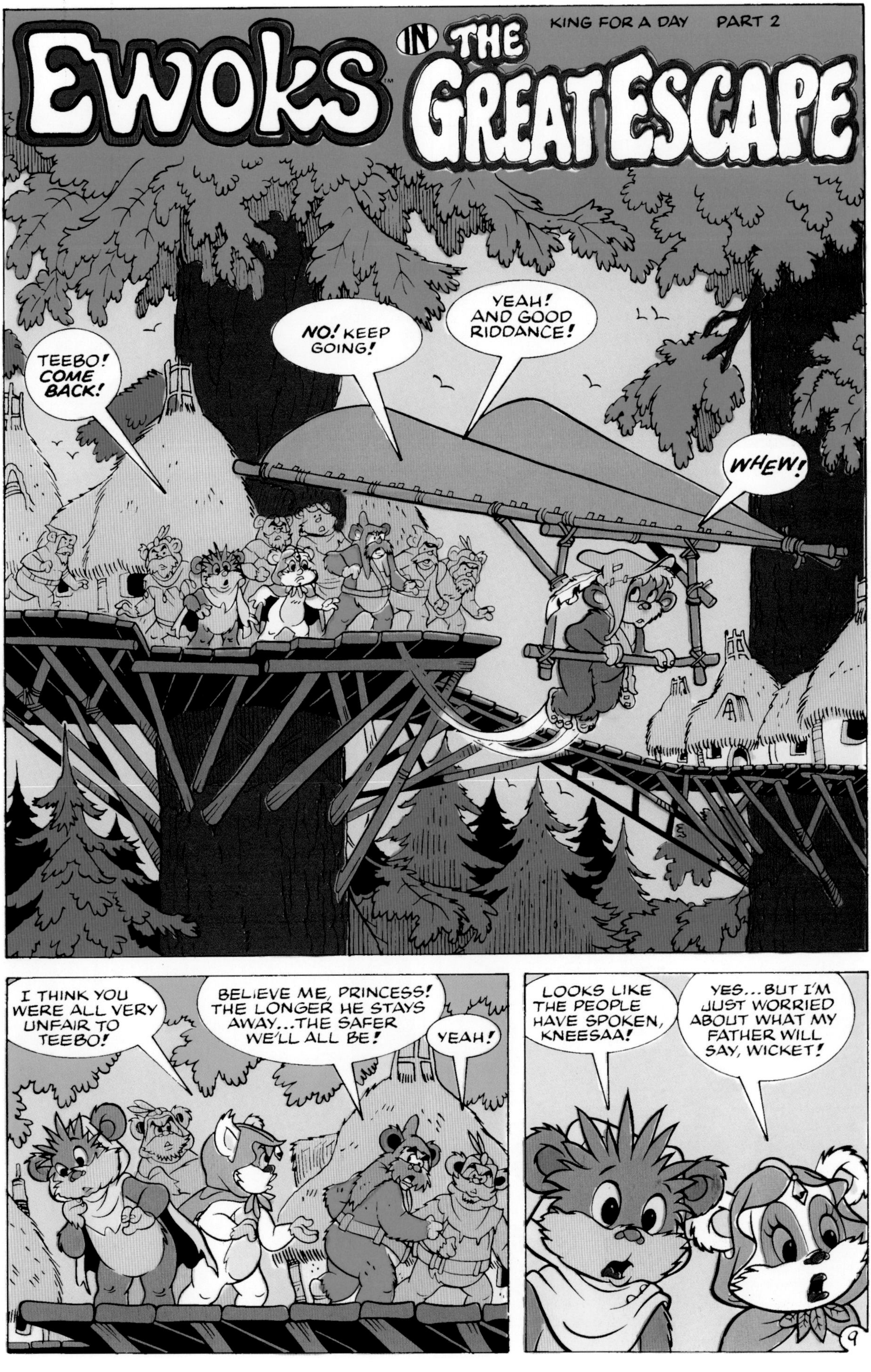

KING FOR A DAY PART 2
EWOKS™ IN THE GREAT ESCAPE
TEEBO! COME BACK!
NO! KEEP GOING!
YEAH! AND GOOD RIDDANCE!
WHEW!
I THINK YOU WERE ALL VERY UNFAIR TO TEEBO!
BELIEVE ME, PRINCESS! THE LONGER HE STAYS AWAY...THE SAFER WE'LL ALL BE!
YEAH!
LOOKS LIKE THE PEOPLE HAVE SPOKEN, KNEESAA!
YES...BUT I'M JUST WORRIED ABOUT WHAT MY FATHER WILL SAY, WICKET!
9

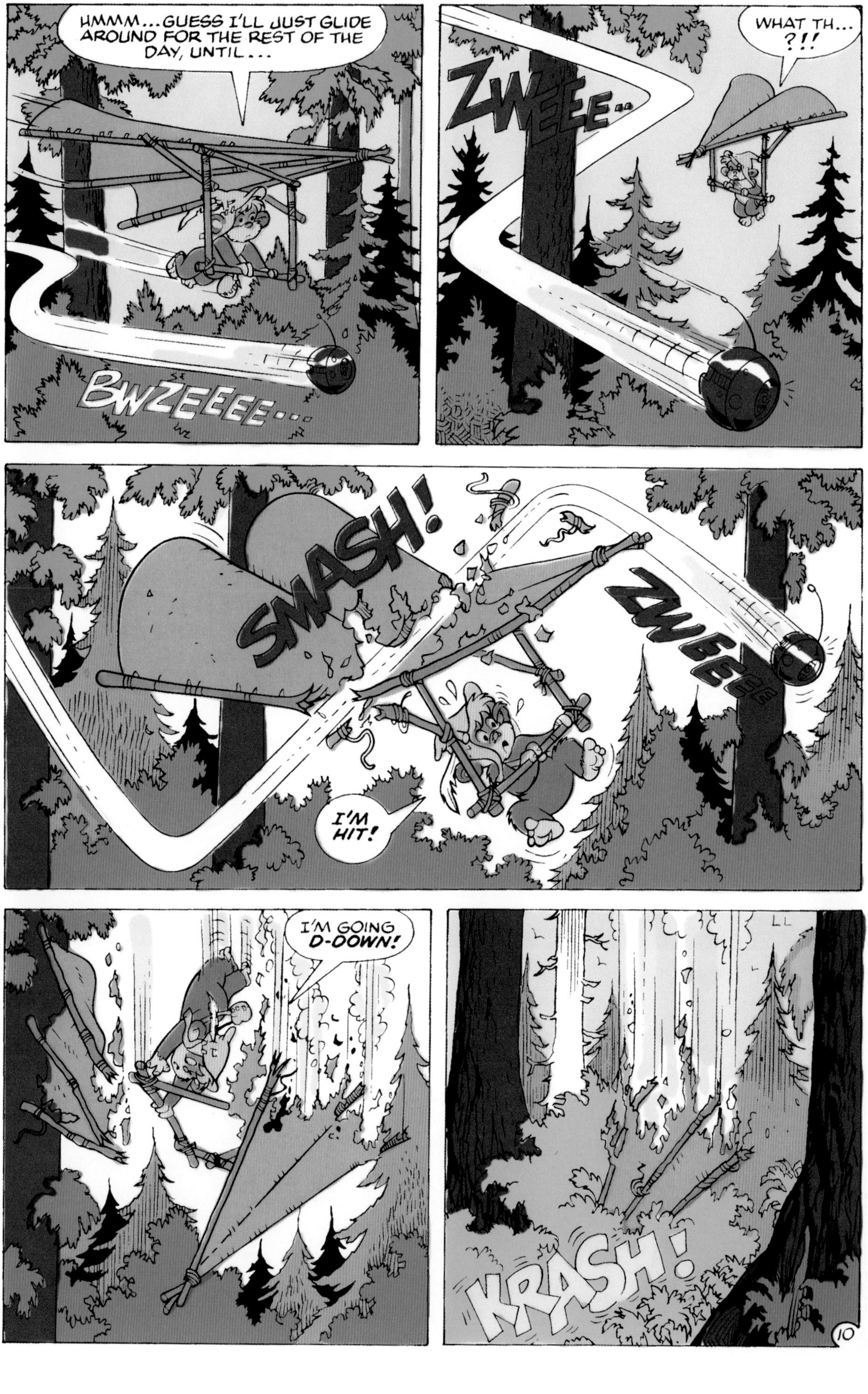
HMMM...GUESS I'LL JUST GLIDE AROUND FOR THE REST OF THE DAY, UNTIL...
BWZEEEEE...
ZWEEE...
WHAT TH... ?!!
SMASH!
ZWEEE
I'M HIT!
I'M GOING D-DOWN!
KRASH!
10

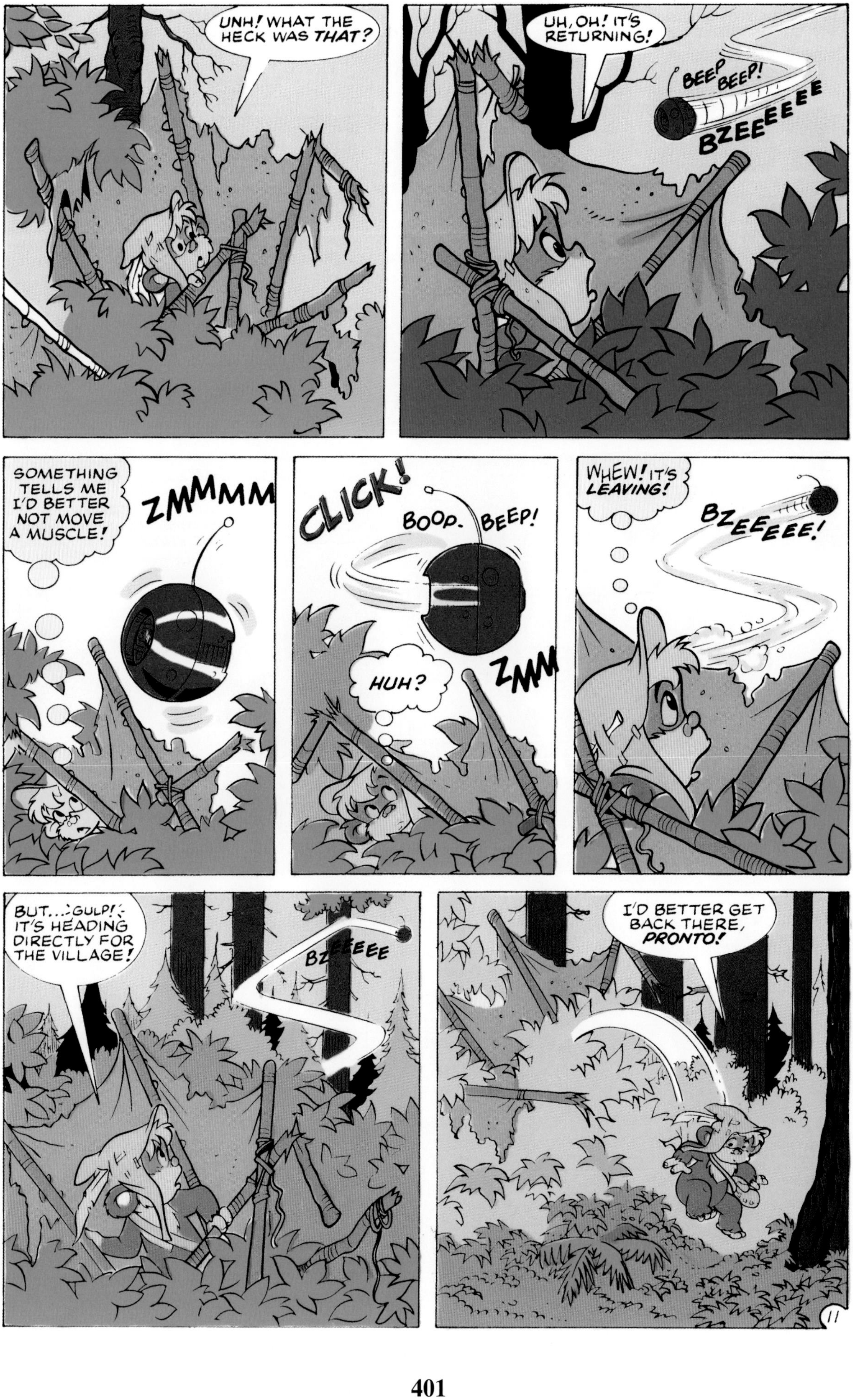
UNH! WHAT THE HECK WAS THAT?
UH, OH! IT'S RETURNING!
BEEP BEEP!
BZEEEEEEE
SOMETHING TELLS ME I'D BETTER NOT MOVE A MUSCLE!
ZMMMMM
CLICK!
BOOP. BEEP!
HUH?
ZMM
WHEW! IT'S LEAVING!
BZEEEEEE!
BUT...GULP!.. IT'S HEADING DIRECTLY FOR THE VILLAGE!
BZEEEEE
I'D BETTER GET BACK THERE, PRONTO!
11

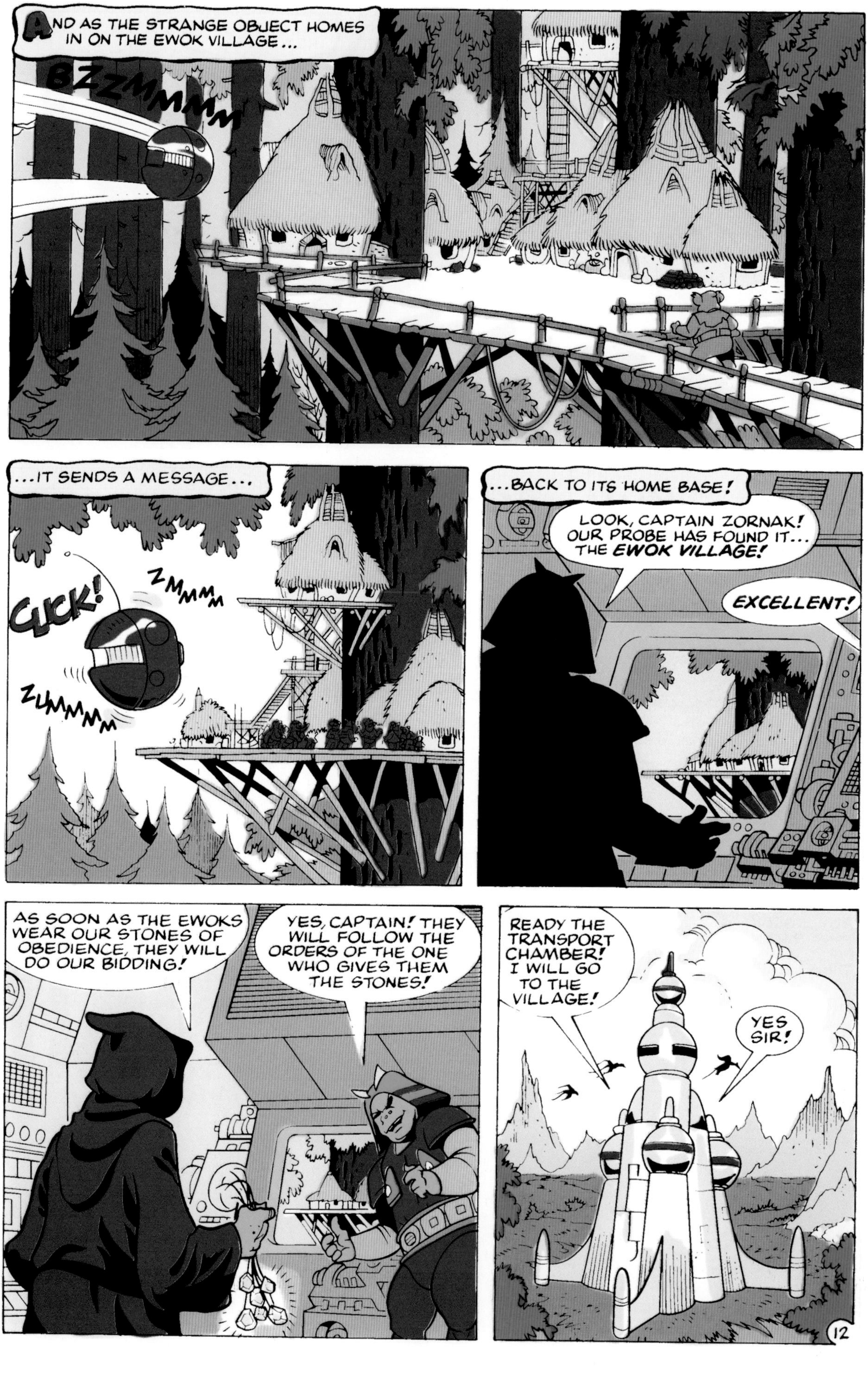
AND AS THE STRANGE OBJECT HOMES IN ON THE EWOK VILLAGE...
BZZMMMM
...IT SENDS A MESSAGE...
CLICK!
ZMMMM
ZUMMMM
...BACK TO ITS HOME BASE!
LOOK, CAPTAIN ZORNAK! OUR PROBE HAS FOUND IT... THE EWOK VILLAGE!
EXCELLENT!
AS SOON AS THE EWOKS WEAR OUR STONES OF OBEDIENCE, THEY WILL DO OUR BIDDING!
YES, CAPTAIN! THEY WILL FOLLOW THE ORDERS OF THE ONE WHO GIVES THEM THE STONES!
READY THE TRANSPORT CHAMBER! I WILL GO TO THE VILLAGE!
YES SIR!
12

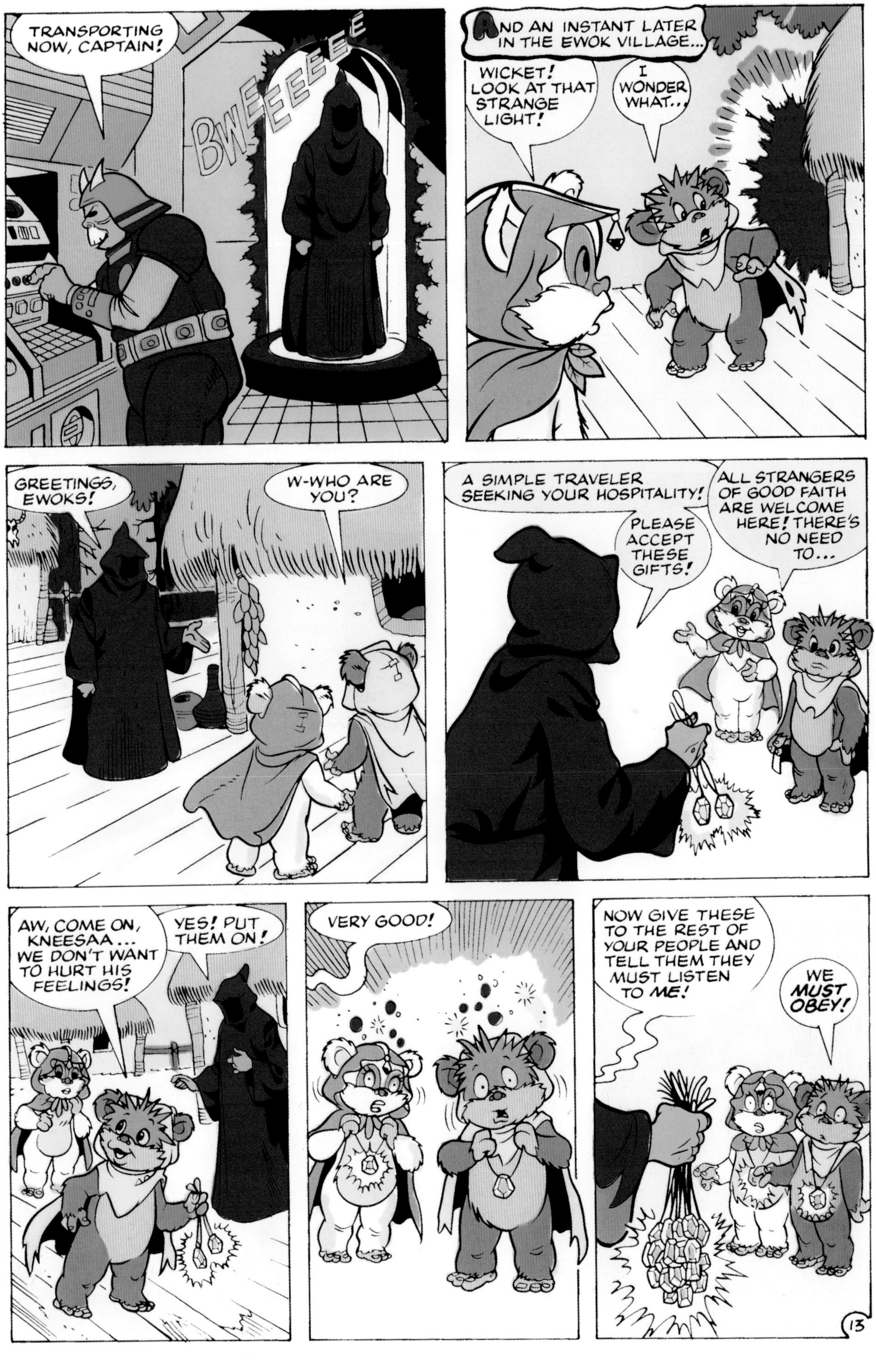
TRANSPORTING NOW, CAPTAIN!
BWEEEEEEE
AND AN INSTANT LATER IN THE EWOK VILLAGE...
WICKET! LOOK AT THAT STRANGE LIGHT!
I WONDER WHAT...
GREETINGS, EWOKS!
W-WHO ARE YOU?
A SIMPLE TRAVELER SEEKING YOUR HOSPITALITY!
PLEASE ACCEPT THESE GIFTS!
ALL STRANGERS OF GOOD FAITH ARE WELCOME HERE! THERE'S NO NEED TO...
AW, COME ON, KNEESAA... WE DON'T WANT TO HURT HIS FEELINGS!
YES! PUT THEM ON!
VERY GOOD!
NOW GIVE THESE TO THE REST OF YOUR PEOPLE AND TELL THEM THEY MUST LISTEN TO ME!
WE MUST OBEY!
13

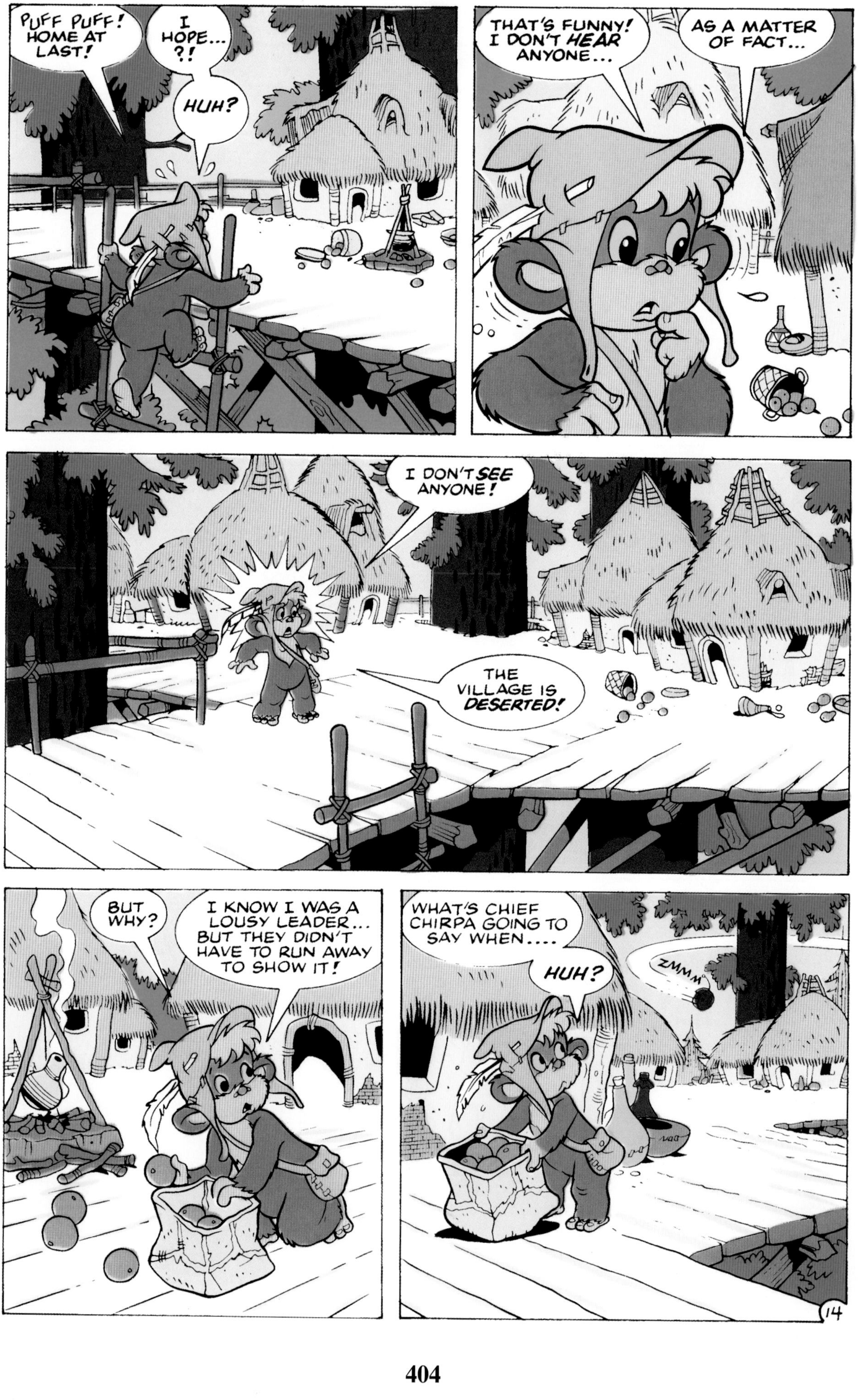
PUFF PUFF! HOME AT LAST!
I HOPE... ?!
HUH?
THAT'S FUNNY! I DON'T HEAR ANYONE...
AS A MATTER OF FACT...
I DON'T SEE ANYONE!
THE VILLAGE IS DESERTED!
BUT WHY?
I KNOW I WAS A LOUSY LEADER... BUT THEY DIDN'T HAVE TO RUN AWAY TO SHOW IT!
WHAT'S CHIEF CHIRPA GOING TO SAY WHEN....
HUH?
ZMMM
14

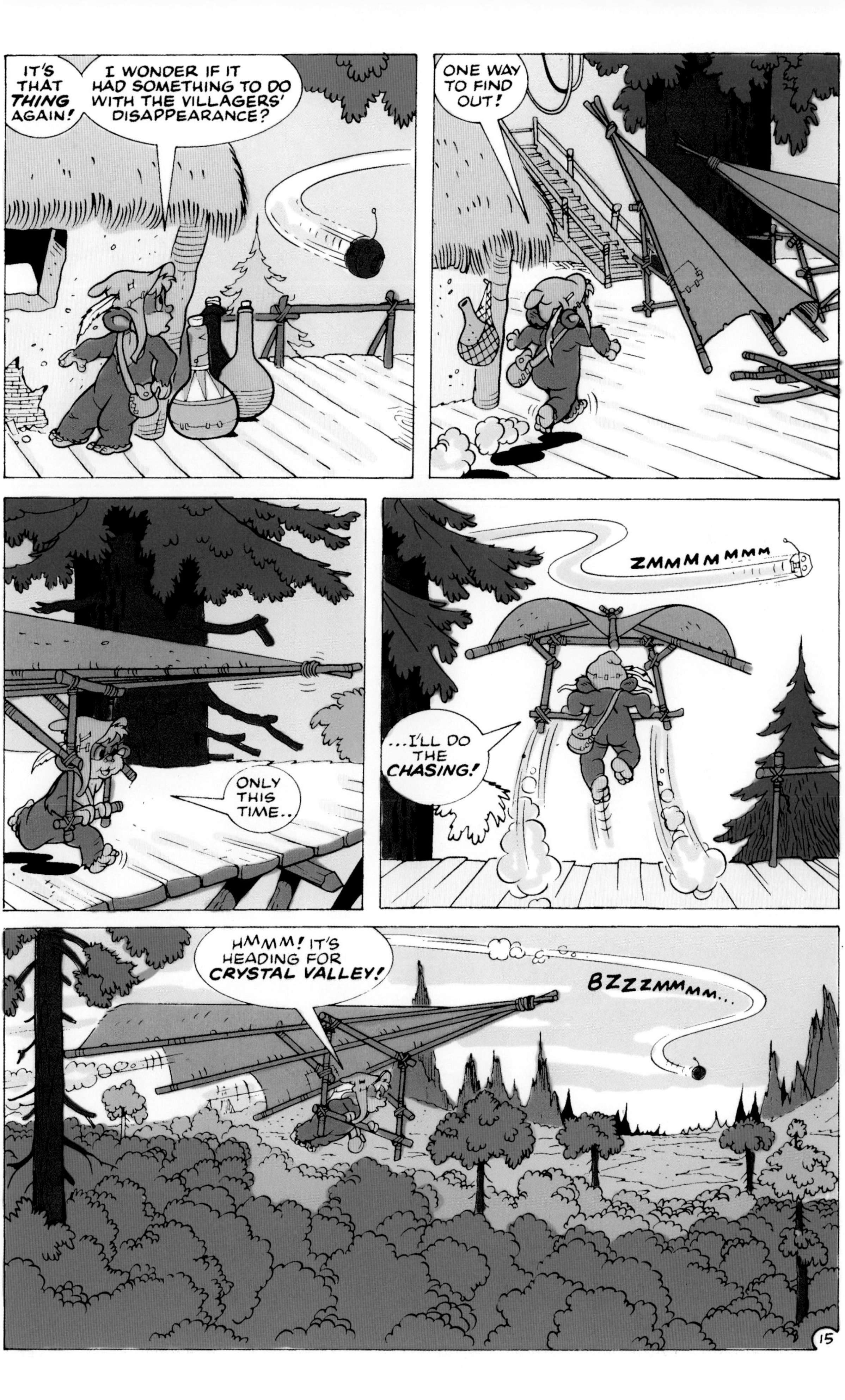
IT'S THAT THING AGAIN!
I WONDER IF IT HAD SOMETHING TO DO WITH THE VILLAGERS' DISAPPEARANCE?
ONE WAY TO FIND OUT!
ONLY THIS TIME..
ZMMMMMMM
...I'LL DO THE CHASING!
HMMM! IT'S HEADING FOR CRYSTAL VALLEY!
BZZZMMMM...
15

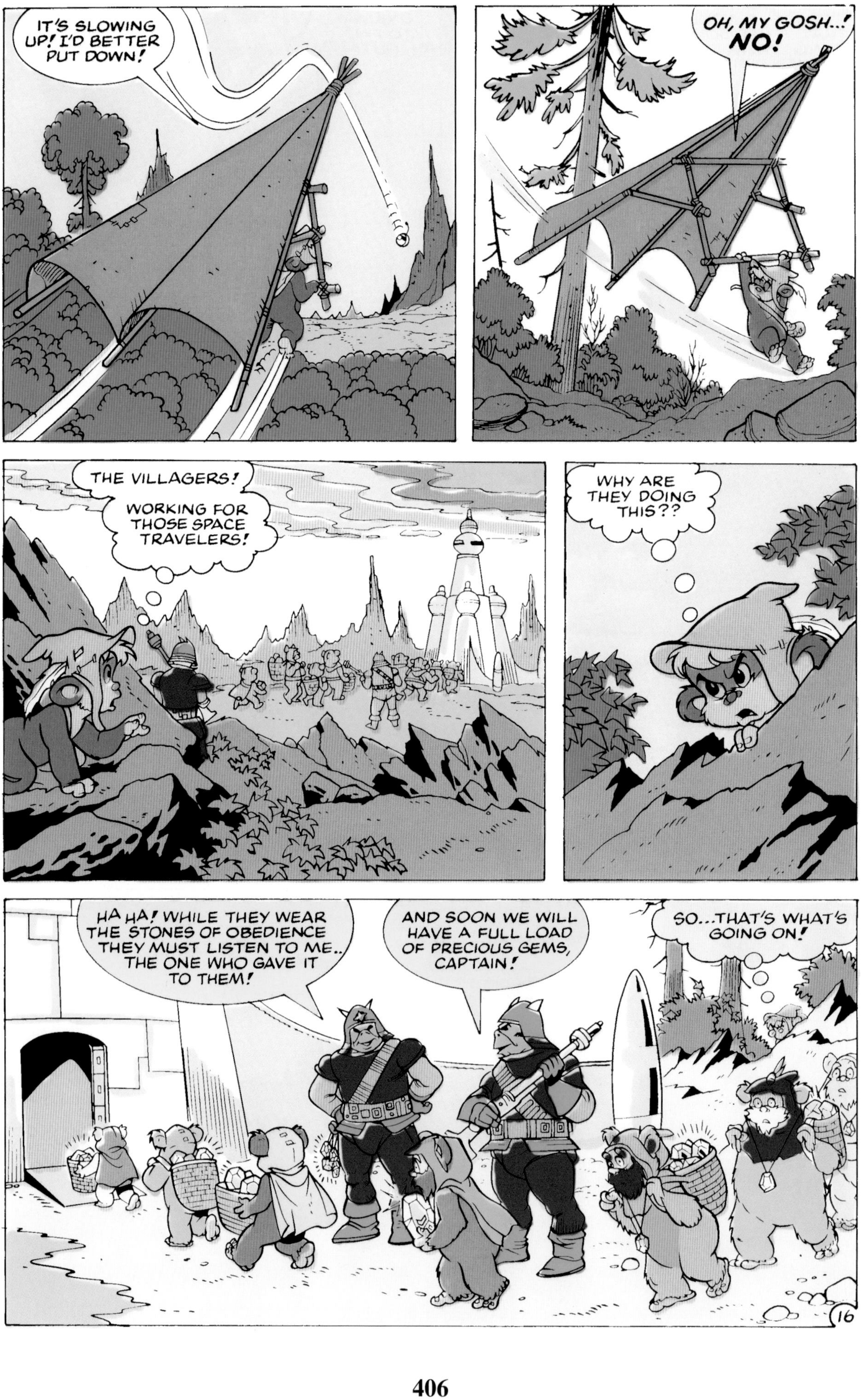
IT'S SLOWING UP! I'D BETTER PUT DOWN!
OH, MY GOSH..! NO!
THE VILLAGERS!
WORKING FOR THOSE SPACE TRAVELERS!
WHY ARE THEY DOING THIS??
HA HA! WHILE THEY WEAR THE STONES OF OBEDIENCE THEY MUST LISTEN TO ME.. THE ONE WHO GAVE IT TO THEM!
AND SOON WE WILL HAVE A FULL LOAD OF PRECIOUS GEMS, CAPTAIN!
SO...THAT'S WHAT'S GOING ON!
16

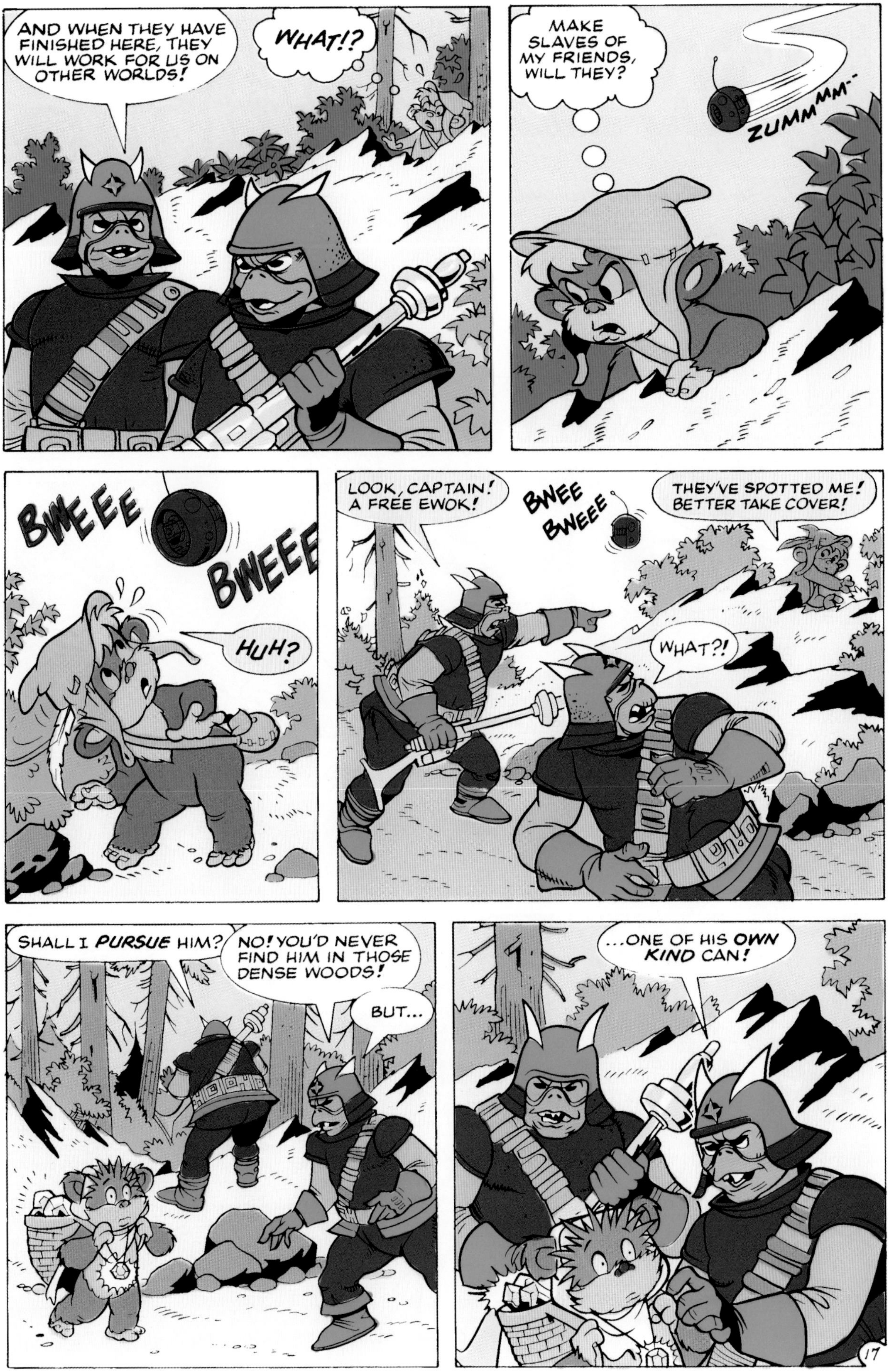
AND WHEN THEY HAVE FINISHED HERE, THEY WILL WORK FOR US ON OTHER WORLDS!
WHAT!?
MAKE SLAVES OF MY FRIENDS, WILL THEY?
ZUMMMM--
BWEEEE
BWEEEE
HUH?
LOOK, CAPTAIN! A FREE EWOK!
BWEE BWEEE
THEY'VE SPOTTED ME! BETTER TAKE COVER!
WHAT?!
SHALL I PURSUE HIM?
NO! YOU'D NEVER FIND HIM IN THOSE DENSE WOODS!
BUT...
...ONE OF HIS OWN KIND CAN!
17

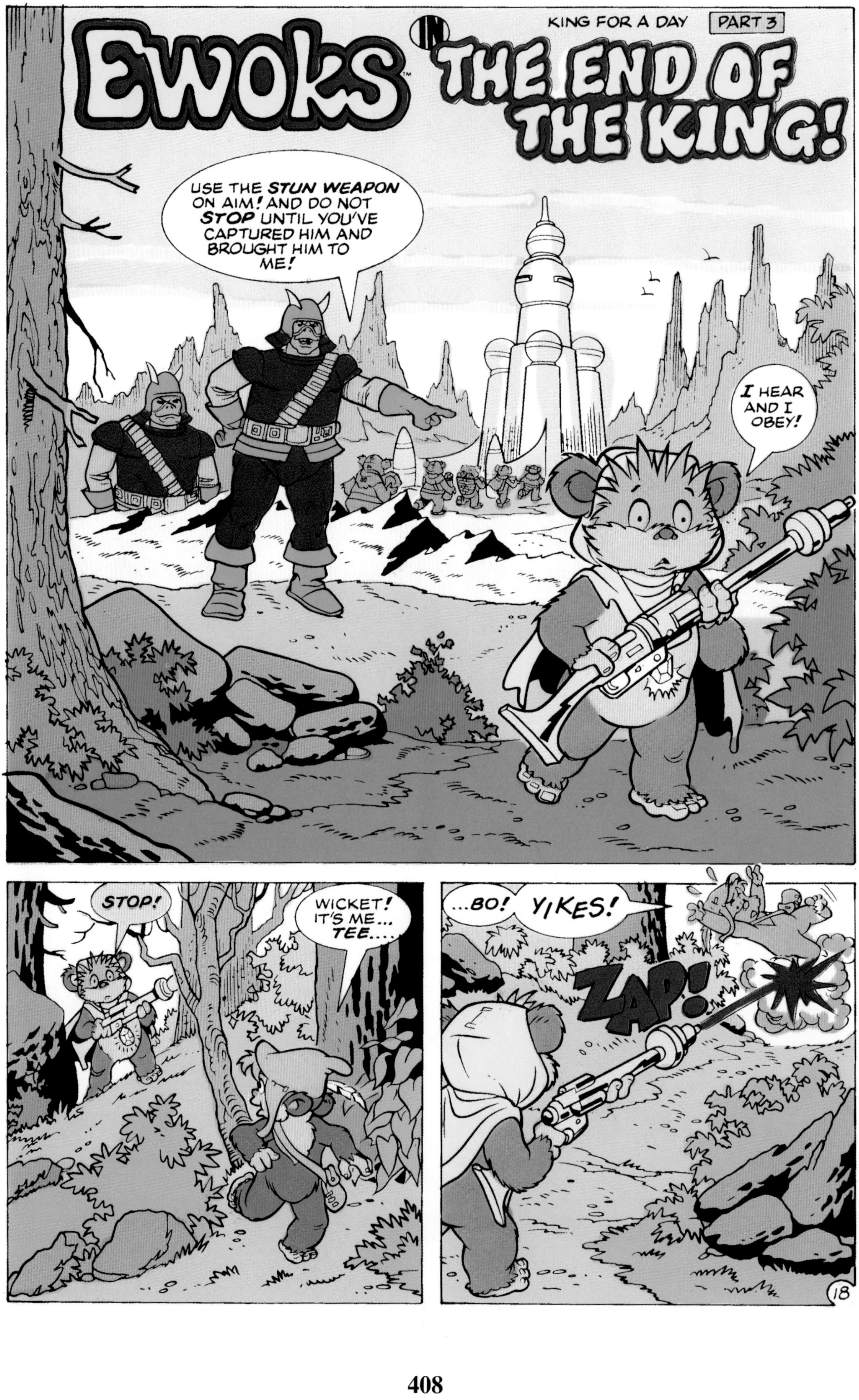
KING FOR A DAY
PART 3
Ewoks
IN
THE END OF THE KING!
USE THE STUN WEAPON ON AIM! AND DO NOT STOP UNTIL YOU'VE CAPTURED HIM AND BROUGHT HIM TO ME!
I HEAR AND I OBEY!
STOP!
WICKET! IT'S ME... TEE....
...BO!
YIKES!
ZAP!
18

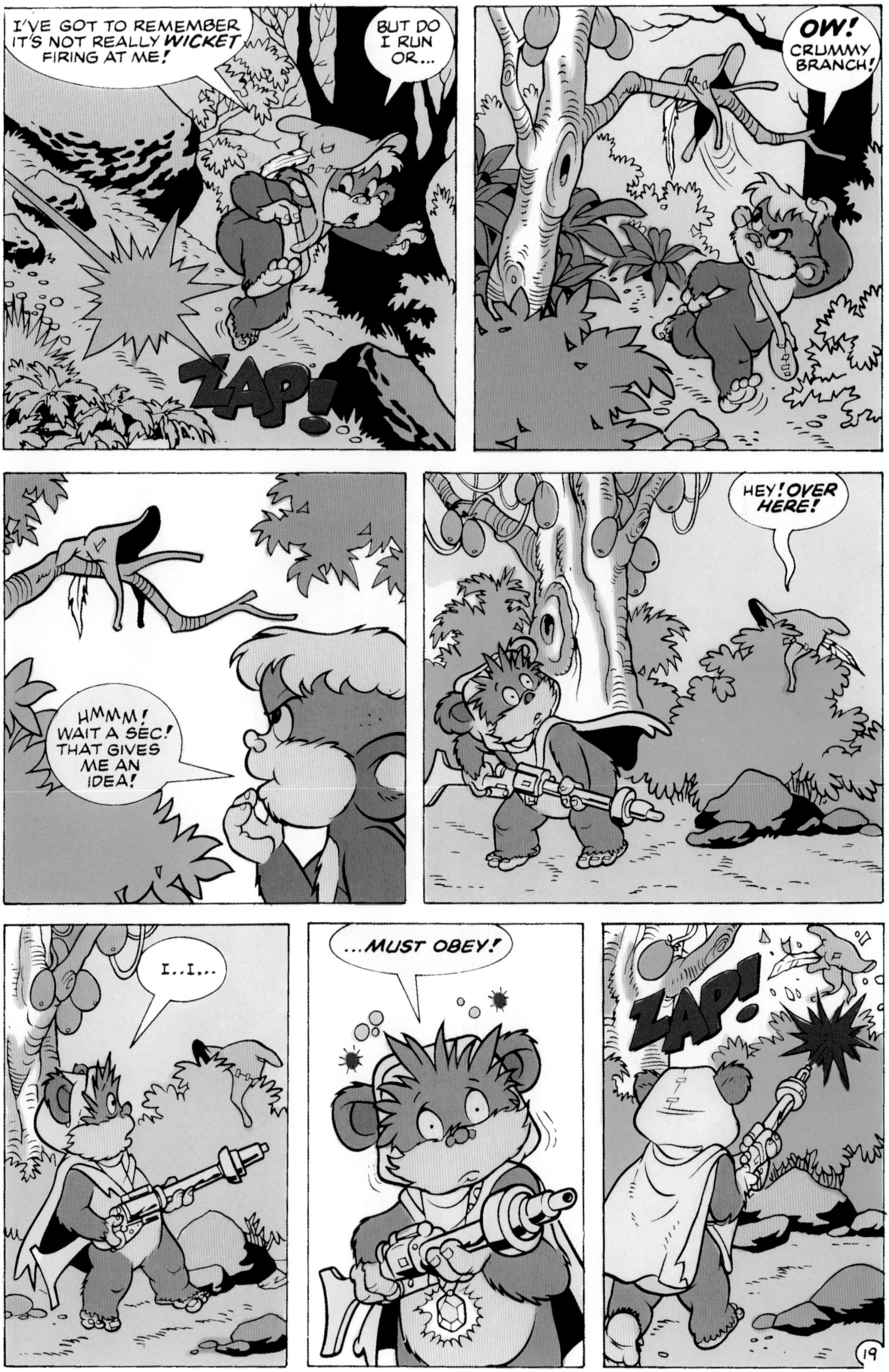
I'VE GOT TO REMEMBER IT'S NOT REALLY WICKET FIRING AT ME!
BUT DO I RUN OR...
ZAP!
OW! CRUMMY BRANCH!
HMMM! WAIT A SEC! THAT GIVES ME AN IDEA!
HEY! OVER HERE!
I..I...
...MUST OBEY!
ZAP!
19

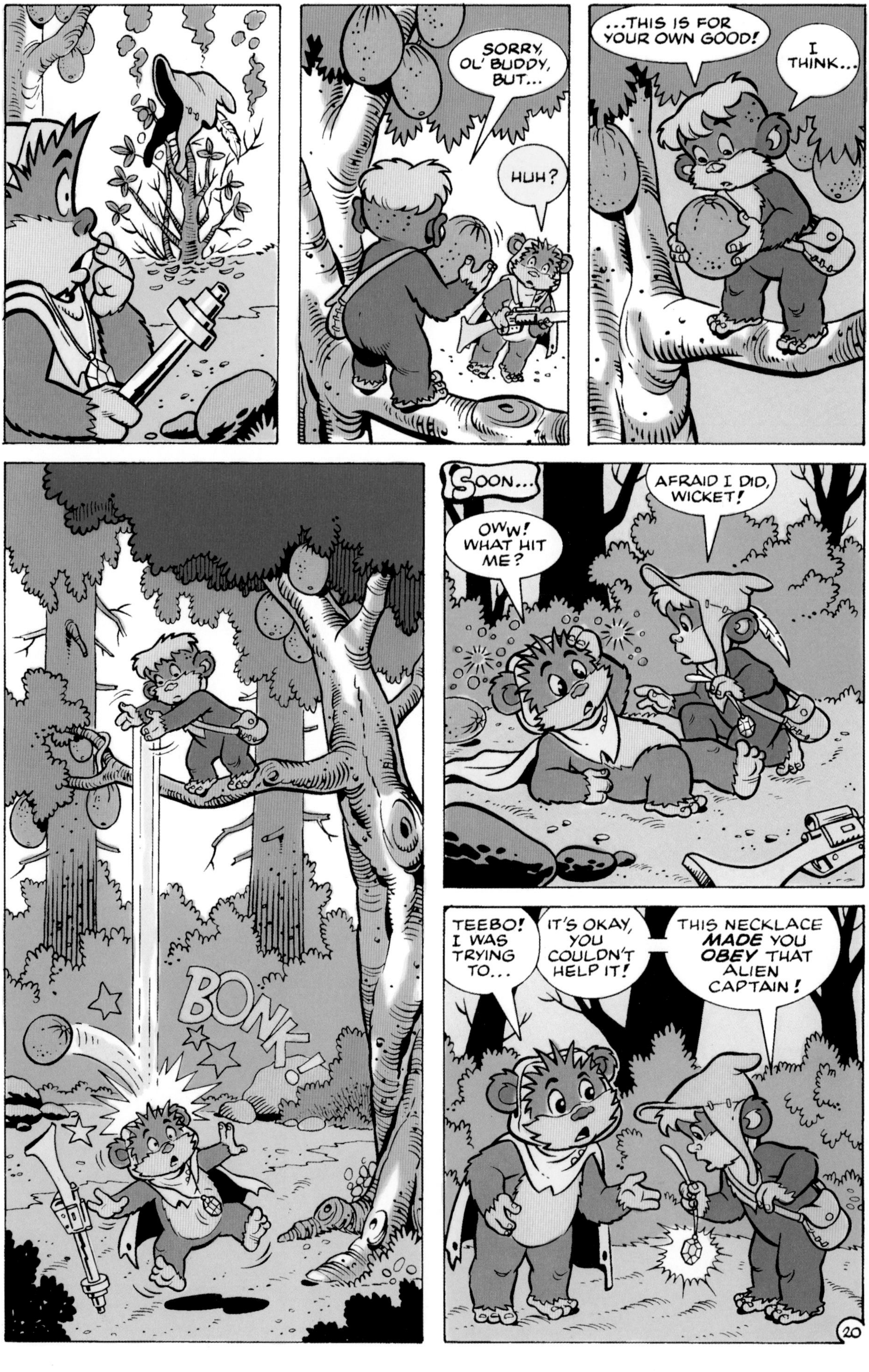
SORRY, OL' BUDDY, BUT...
HUH?
...THIS IS FOR YOUR OWN GOOD!
I THINK...
BONK!
SOON...
OWW! WHAT HIT ME?
AFRAID I DID, WICKET!
TEEBO! I WAS TRYING TO...
IT'S OKAY, YOU COULDN'T HELP IT!
THIS NECKLACE MADE YOU OBEY THAT ALIEN CAPTAIN!
20

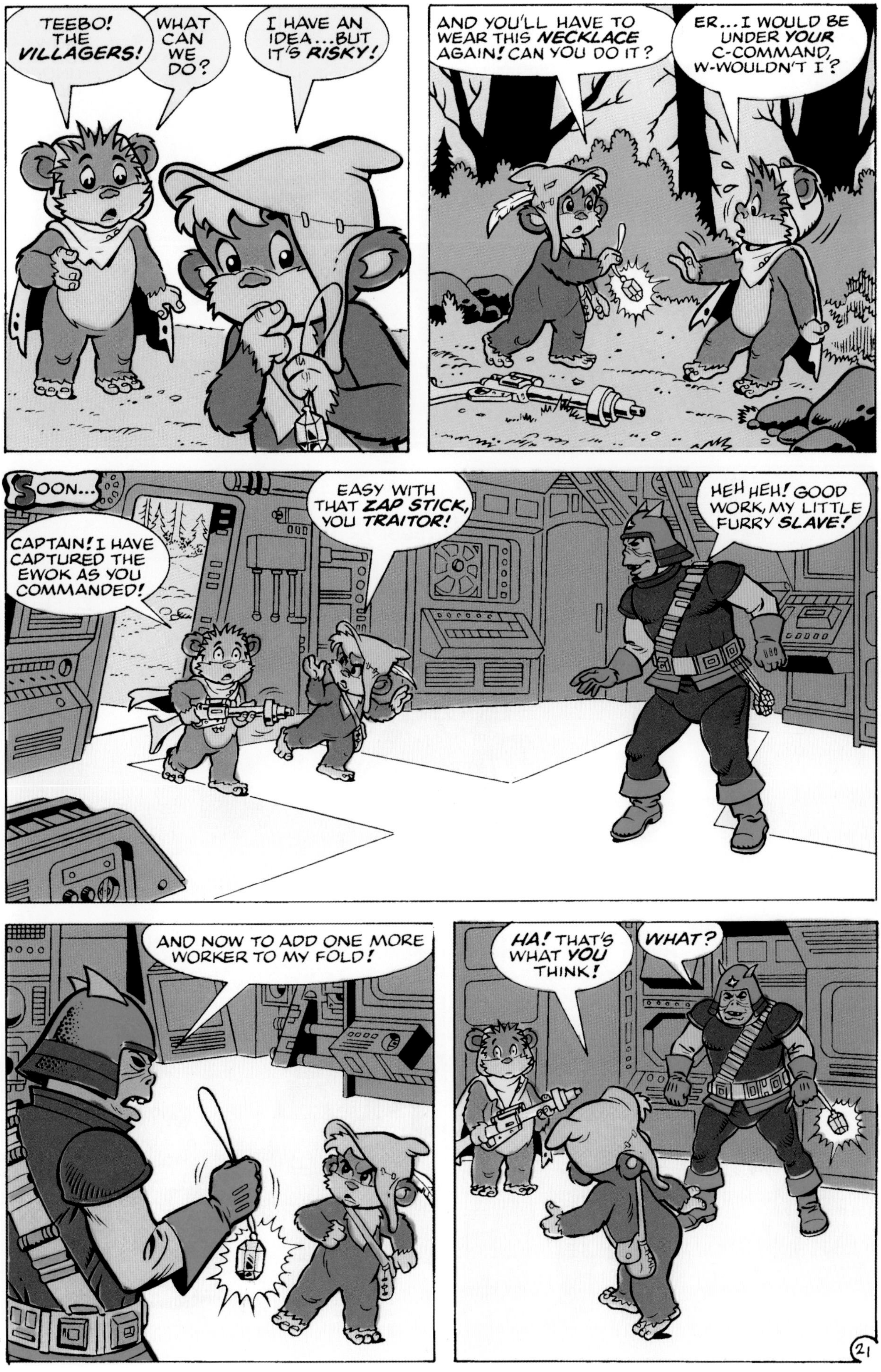
TEEBO! THE VILLAGERS!
WHAT CAN WE DO?
I HAVE AN IDEA...BUT IT'S RISKY!
AND YOU'LL HAVE TO WEAR THIS NECKLACE AGAIN! CAN YOU DO IT?
ER...I WOULD BE UNDER YOUR C-COMMAND, W-WOULDN'T I?
SOON...
CAPTAIN! I HAVE CAPTURED THE EWOK AS YOU COMMANDED!
EASY WITH THAT ZAP STICK, YOU TRAITOR!
HEH HEH! GOOD WORK, MY LITTLE FURRY SLAVE!
AND NOW TO ADD ONE MORE WORKER TO MY FOLD!
HA! THAT'S WHAT YOU THINK!
WHAT?
21

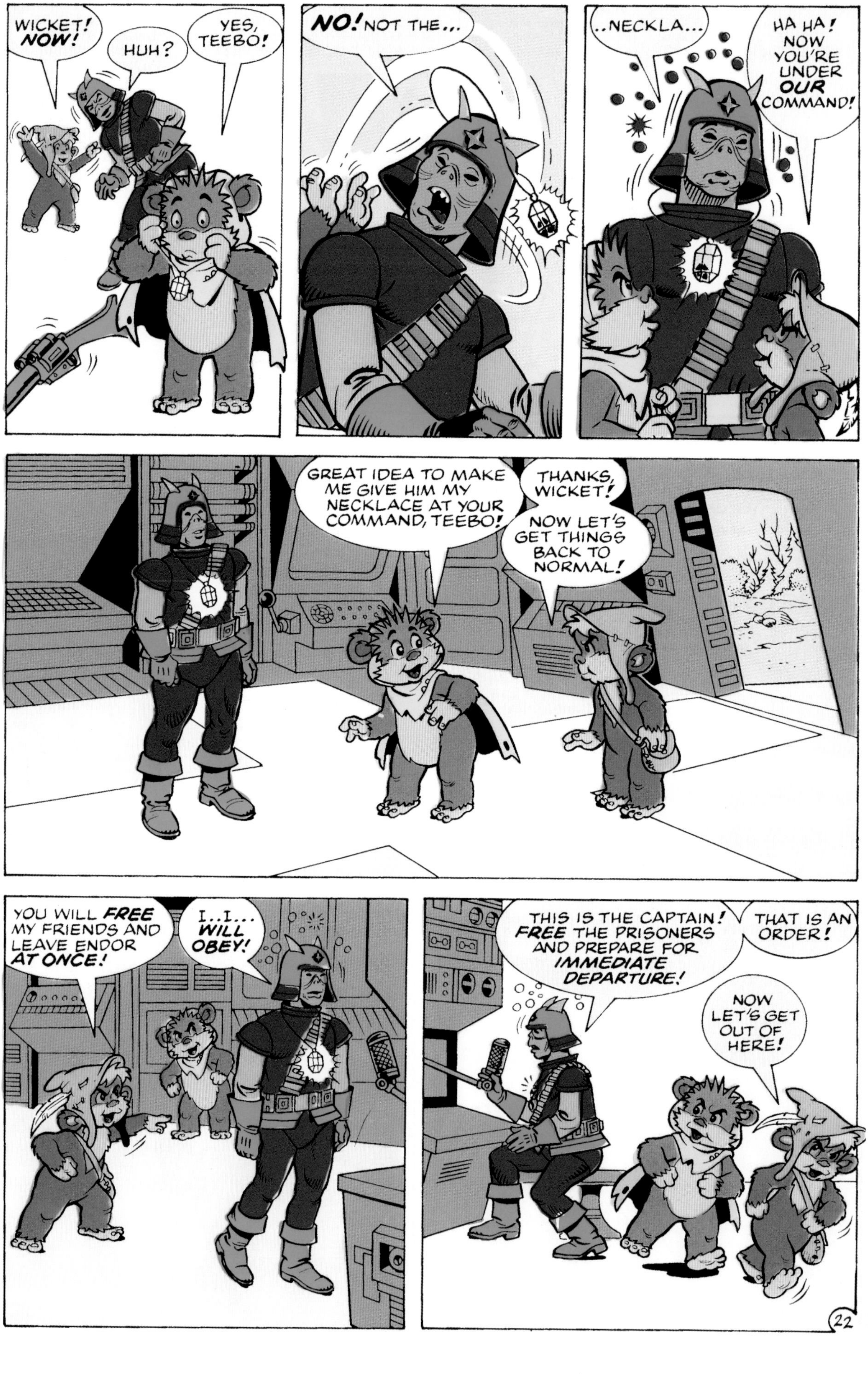
WICKET! NOW!
HUH?
YES, TEEBO!
NO! NOT THE...
..NECKLA...
HA HA! NOW YOU'RE UNDER OUR COMMAND!
GREAT IDEA TO MAKE ME GIVE HIM MY NECKLACE AT YOUR COMMAND, TEEBO!
THANKS, WICKET!
NOW LET'S GET THINGS BACK TO NORMAL!
YOU WILL FREE MY FRIENDS AND LEAVE ENDOR AT ONCE!
I..I... WILL OBEY!
THIS IS THE CAPTAIN! FREE THE PRISONERS AND PREPARE FOR IMMEDIATE DEPARTURE!
THAT IS AN ORDER!
NOW LET'S GET OUT OF HERE!
22

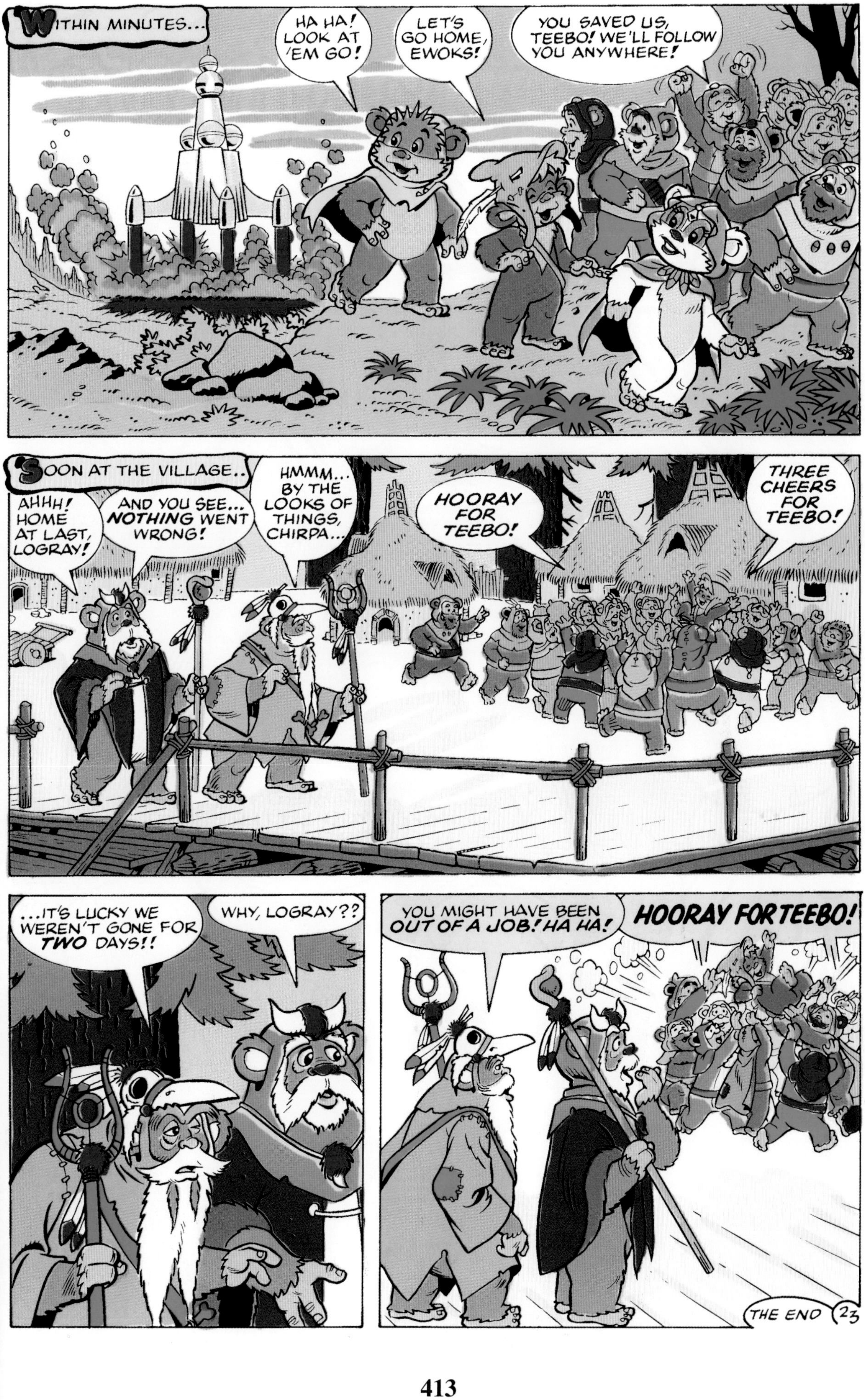
WITHIN MINUTES...
HA HA! LOOK AT 'EM GO!
LET'S GO HOME, EWOKS!
YOU SAVED US, TEEBO! WE'LL FOLLOW YOU ANYWHERE!
SOON AT THE VILLAGE..
AHHH! HOME AT LAST, LOGRAY!
AND YOU SEE... NOTHING WENT WRONG!
HMMM... BY THE LOOKS OF THINGS, CHIRPA...
HOORAY FOR TEEBO!
THREE CHEERS FOR TEEBO!
...IT'S LUCKY WE WEREN'T GONE FOR TWO DAYS!!
WHY, LOGRAY??
YOU MIGHT HAVE BEEN OUT OF A JOB! HA HA!
HOORAY FOR TEEBO!
THE END
23

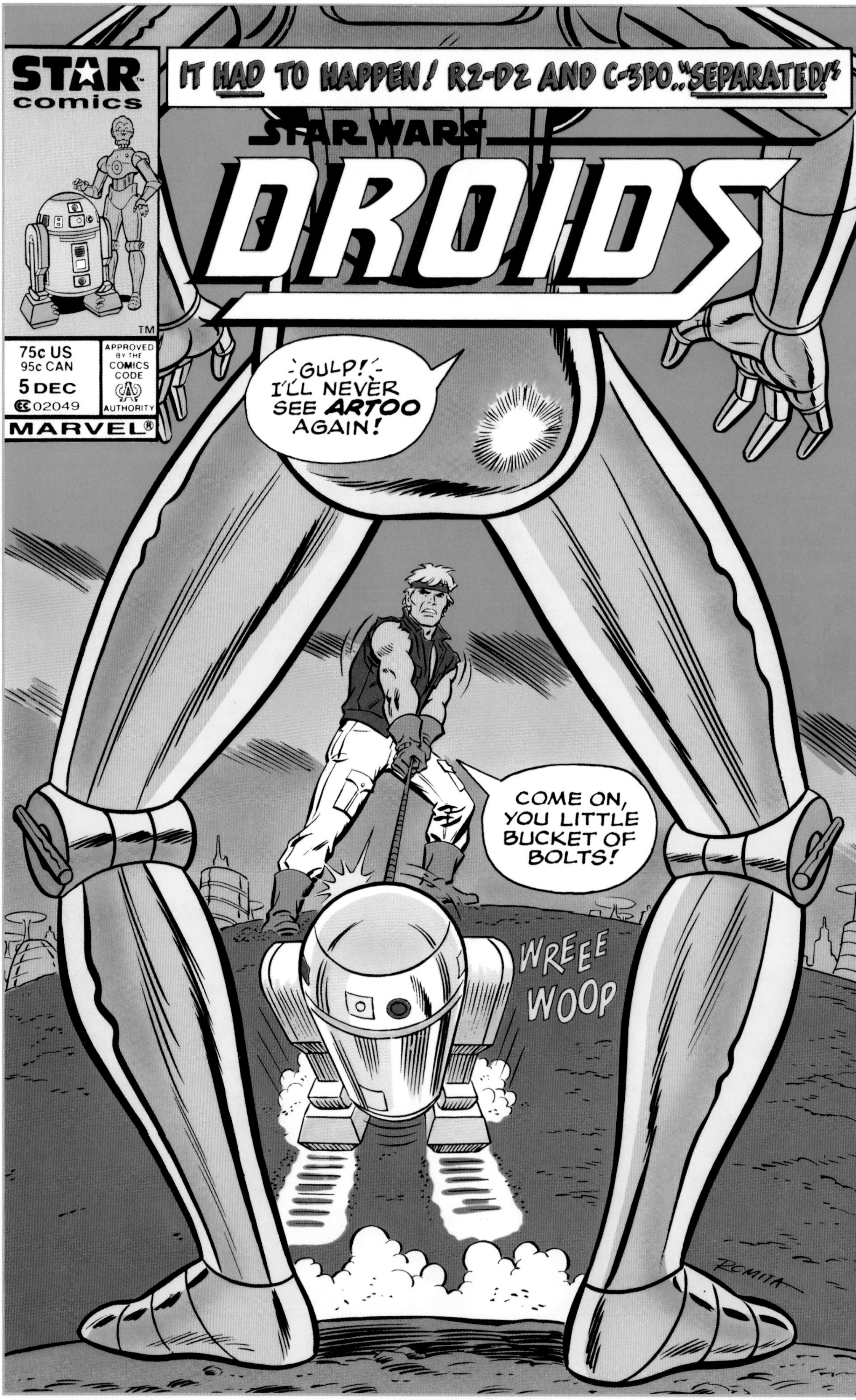

STAR comics
IT HAD TO HAPPEN! R2-D2 AND C-3PO..."SEPARATED!"
STAR WARS
DROIDS
75¢ US
95¢ CAN
5 DEC
02049
APPROVED BY THE COMICS CODE AUTHORITY
MARVEL®
-GULP!- I'LL NEVER SEE ARTOO AGAIN!
COME ON, YOU LITTLE BUCKET OF BOLTS!
WREEE
WOOP
ROMITA

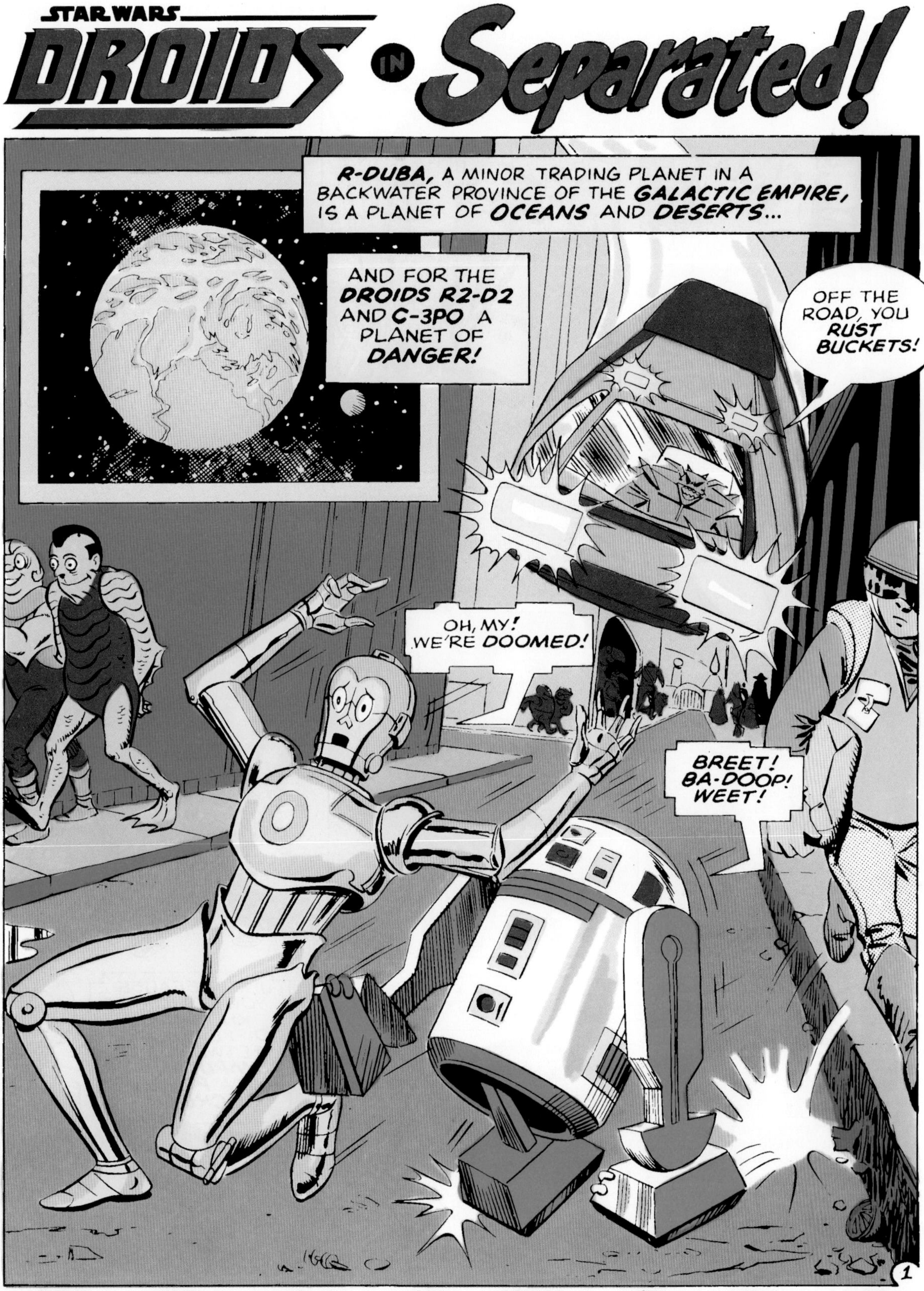
STAR WARS
DROIDS IN Separated!
R-DUBA, A MINOR TRADING PLANET IN A BACKWATER PROVINCE OF THE GALACTIC EMPIRE, IS A PLANET OF OCEANS AND DESERTS...
AND FOR THE DROIDS R2-D2 AND C-3PO A PLANET OF DANGER!
OFF THE ROAD, YOU RUST BUCKETS!
OH, MY! WE'RE DOOMED!
BREET! BA-DOOP! WEET!
1

GEORGE CARRAGONE WRITER · MARY WILSHIRE PENCILER · AL WILLIAMSON INKER · GRACE KREMER LETTERER · GEORGE ROUSSOS COLORIST · SID JACOBSON EDITOR · TOM DE FALCO EXECUTIVE EDITOR · JIM SHOOTER ED. IN CHIEF

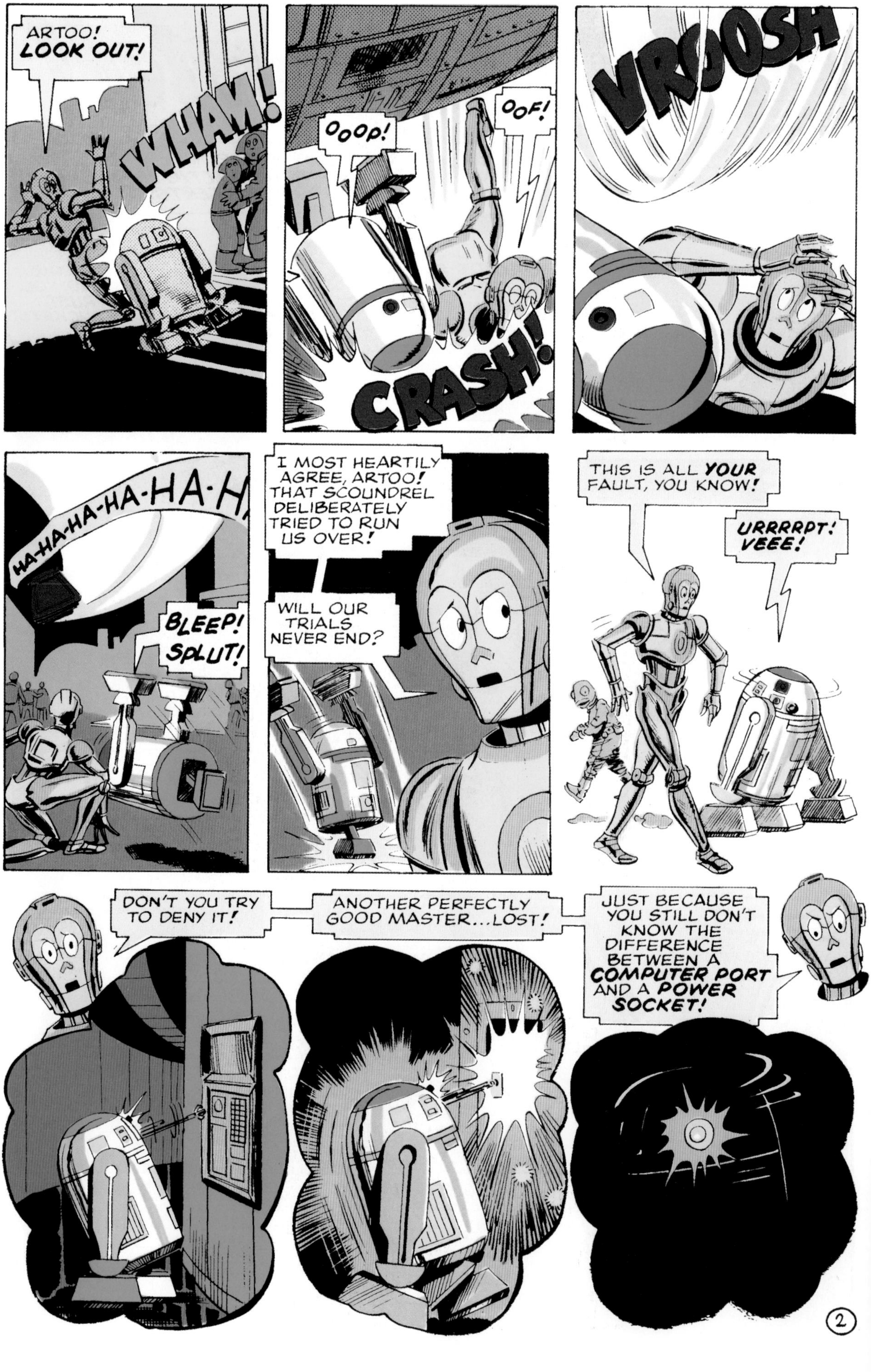
ARTOO! LOOK OUT!
WHAM!
OOOP!
OOF!
CRASH!
VROOSH
HA-HA-HA-HA-HA-H
BLEEP! SPLUT!
I MOST HEARTILY AGREE, ARTOO! THAT SCOUNDREL DELIBERATELY TRIED TO RUN US OVER!
WILL OUR TRIALS NEVER END?
THIS IS ALL YOUR FAULT, YOU KNOW!
URRRRPT! VEEE!
DON'T YOU TRY TO DENY IT!
ANOTHER PERFECTLY GOOD MASTER...LOST!
JUST BECAUSE YOU STILL DON'T KNOW THE DIFFERENCE BETWEEN A COMPUTER PORT AND A POWER SOCKET!
2

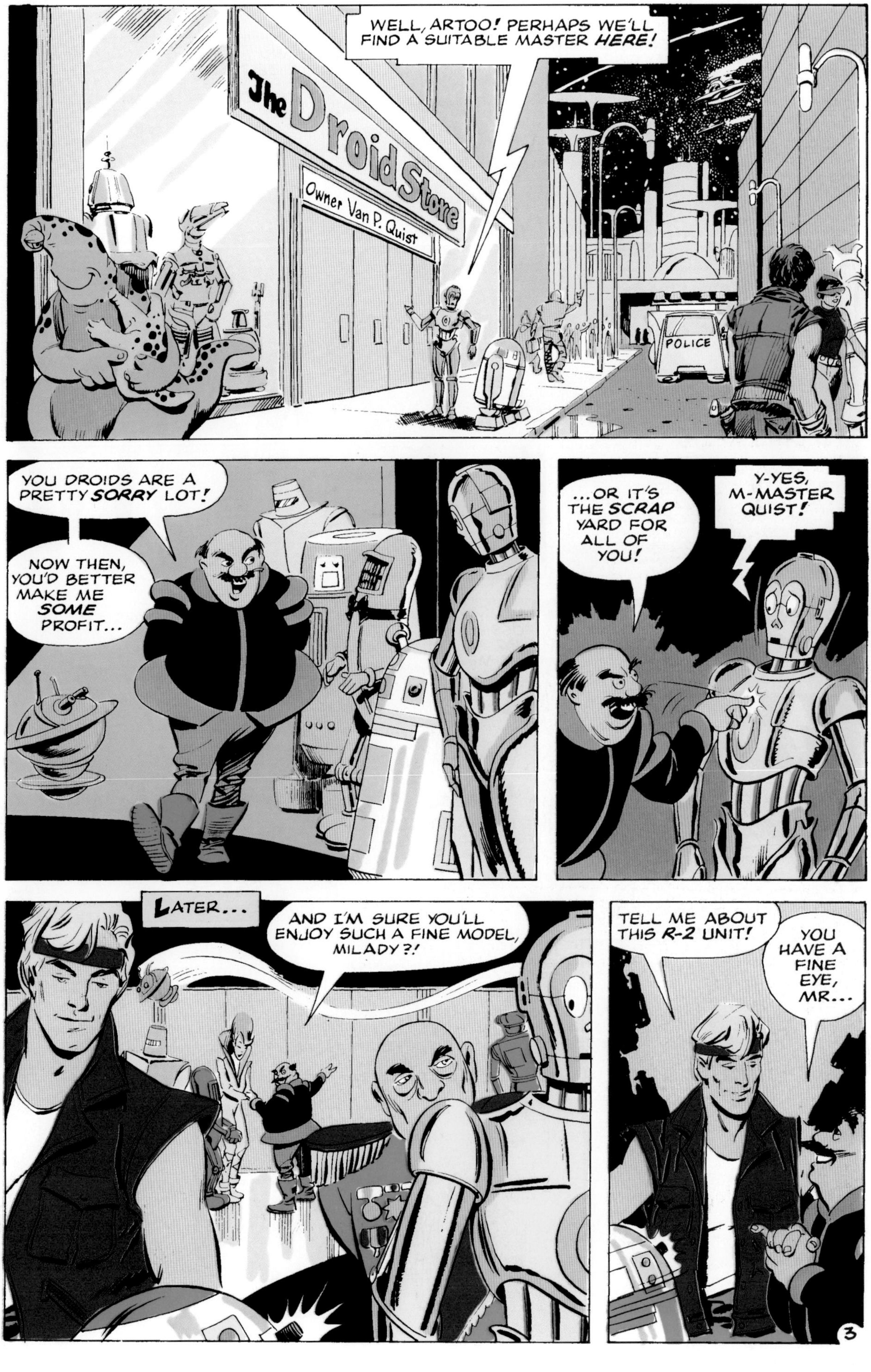
WELL, ARTOO! PERHAPS WE'LL FIND A SUITABLE MASTER HERE!
The Droid Store
Owner Van P. Quist
POLICE
YOU DROIDS ARE A PRETTY SORRY LOT!
NOW THEN, YOU'D BETTER MAKE ME SOME PROFIT...
...OR IT'S THE SCRAP YARD FOR ALL OF YOU!
Y-YES, M-MASTER QUIST!
LATER...
AND I'M SURE YOU'LL ENJOY SUCH A FINE MODEL, MILADY?!
TELL ME ABOUT THIS R-2 UNIT!
YOU HAVE A FINE EYE, MR...
3

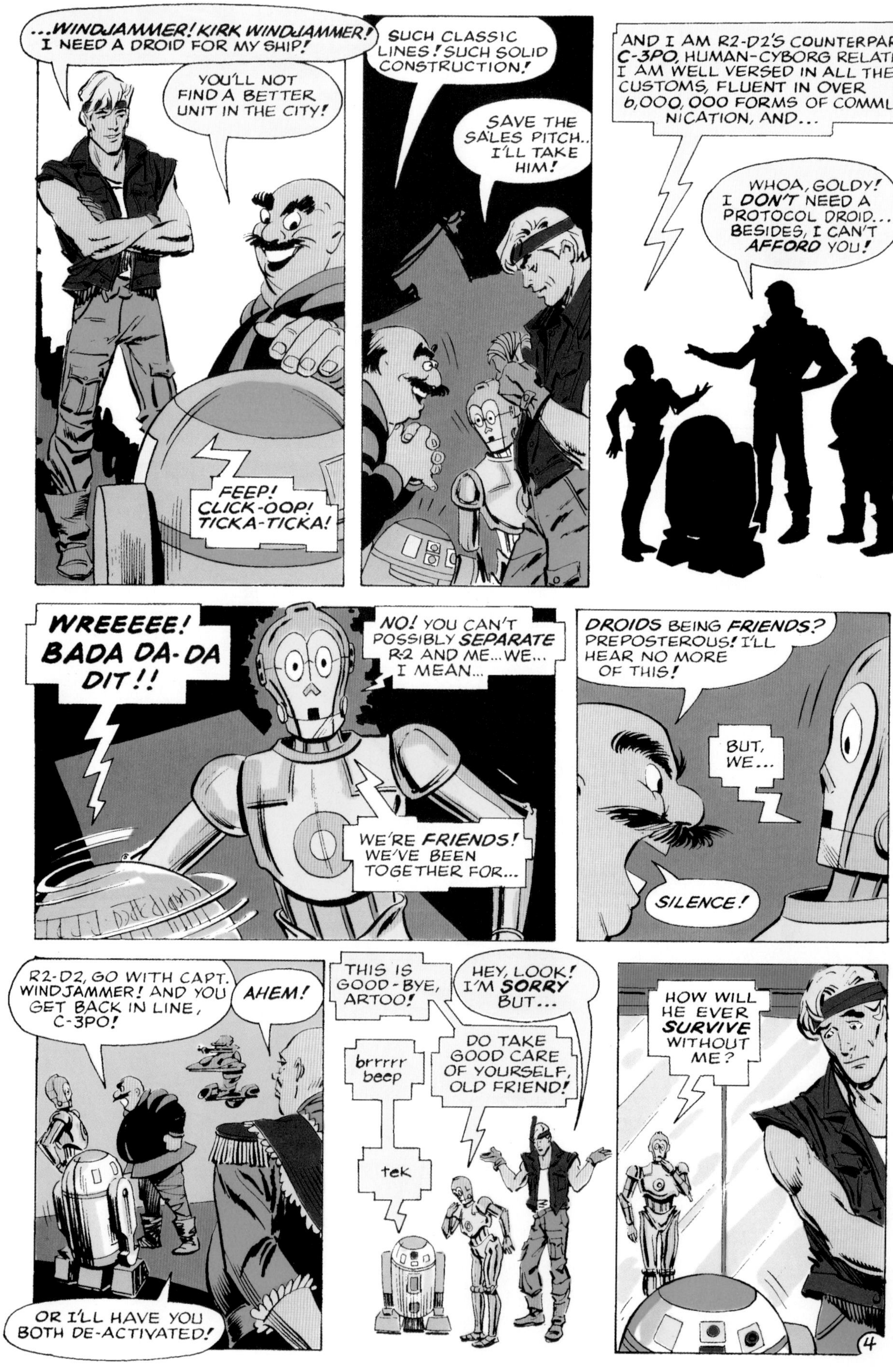
...WINDJAMMER! KIRK WINDJAMMER! I NEED A DROID FOR MY SHIP!
YOU'LL NOT FIND A BETTER UNIT IN THE CITY!
FEEP! CLICK-OOP! TICKA-TICKA!
SUCH CLASSIC LINES! SUCH SOLID CONSTRUCTION!
SAVE THE SALES PITCH.. I'LL TAKE HIM!
AND I AM R2-D2'S COUNTERPART! C-3PO, HUMAN-CYBORG RELATIONS! I AM WELL VERSED IN ALL THE CUSTOMS, FLUENT IN OVER 6,000,000 FORMS OF COMMUNICATION, AND...
WHOA, GOLDY! I DON'T NEED A PROTOCOL DROID... BESIDES, I CAN'T AFFORD YOU!
WREEEEE! BADA DA-DA DIT!!
NO! YOU CAN'T POSSIBLY SEPARATE R-2 AND ME... WE... I MEAN...
WE'RE FRIENDS! WE'VE BEEN TOGETHER FOR...
DROIDS BEING FRIENDS? PREPOSTEROUS! I'LL HEAR NO MORE OF THIS!
BUT, WE...
SILENCE!
R2-D2, GO WITH CAPT. WINDJAMMER! AND YOU GET BACK IN LINE, C-3PO!
AHEM!
OR I'LL HAVE YOU BOTH DE-ACTIVATED!
THIS IS GOOD-BYE, ARTOO!
HEY, LOOK! I'M SORRY BUT...
DO TAKE GOOD CARE OF YOURSELF, OLD FRIEND!
brrrrr beep
tek
HOW WILL HE EVER SURVIVE WITHOUT ME?
4

WELL, THREEPIO, YOU'RE IN LUCK! *BARON STARLOCK*, ADVISOR TO OUR RULER, *PRINCE JAGODA*, WAS IMPRESSED BY YOUR CREDENTIALS, AND HAS PURCHASED YOU!

YOU WILL BOARD HIS HOVERCRAFT...

...OUT FRONT!

HELLO AGAIN, *RUST BUCKET!*

GET IN THE *BACK!* HA-HA-HA-HA-HA!

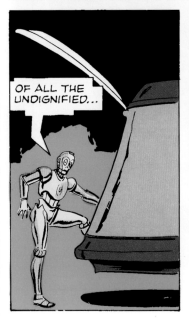

OF ALL THE UNDIGNIFIED...

BUMP

OWW!

HEE-HEE HEE-HEE!

⑤

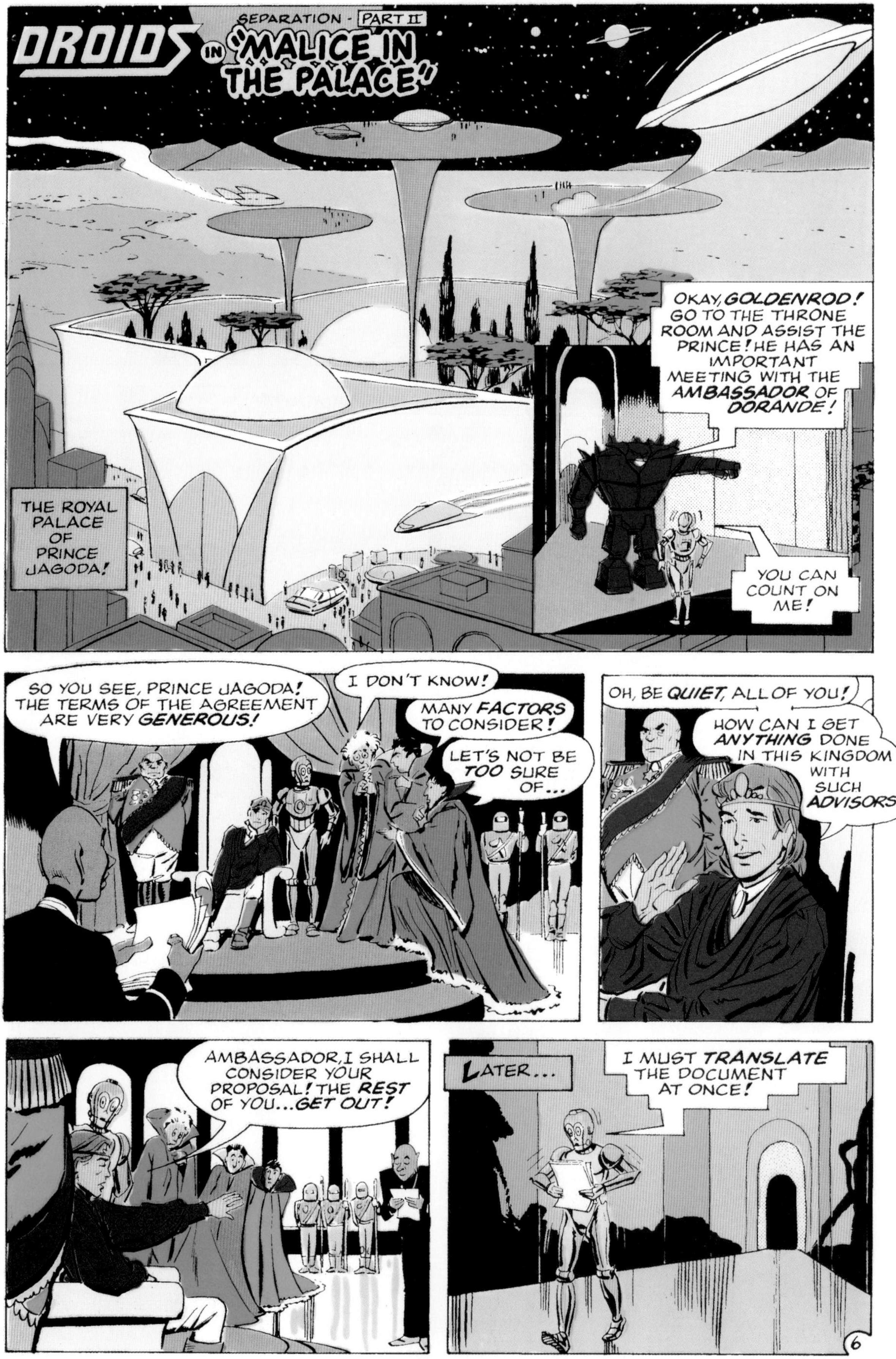
SEPARATION - PART II
DROIDS in "MALICE IN THE PALACE"
THE ROYAL PALACE OF PRINCE JAGODA!
OKAY, GOLDENROD! GO TO THE THRONE ROOM AND ASSIST THE PRINCE! HE HAS AN IMPORTANT MEETING WITH THE AMBASSADOR OF DORANDE!
YOU CAN COUNT ON ME!
SO YOU SEE, PRINCE JAGODA! THE TERMS OF THE AGREEMENT ARE VERY GENEROUS!
I DON'T KNOW!
MANY FACTORS TO CONSIDER!
LET'S NOT BE TOO SURE OF...
OH, BE QUIET, ALL OF YOU!
HOW CAN I GET ANYTHING DONE IN THIS KINGDOM WITH SUCH ADVISORS?
AMBASSADOR, I SHALL CONSIDER YOUR PROPOSAL! THE REST OF YOU...GET OUT!
LATER...
I MUST TRANSLATE THE DOCUMENT AT ONCE!
6

WHAT'S THAT I'M HEARING?

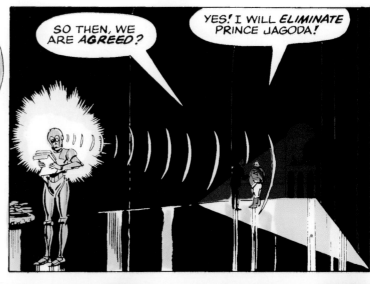

SO THEN, WE ARE *AGREED?*

YES! I WILL *ELIMINATE* PRINCE JAGODA!

OH, MY *GOODNESS!*

MY ADVANCED HEARING SOMETIMES TELLS ME *TOO* MUCH!

WITH THAT FOOL OUT OF THE WAY, I CAN SEIZE POWER!

THEN A *STRIKE FORCE* FROM MY PLANET WILL MOVE IN!

WITH THE ELEMENT OF SURPRISE, THE PLANET WILL BE *OURS...* IN THE NAME OF *DORANDE*, OF COURSE!

NATURALLY!

AND I SHALL RECEIVE THE *MONEY* WE AGREED ON?

WHEN DO WE STRIKE?

MY DROID, *BX-OO,* IS READY TO ATTACK ON MY COMMAND!

I MUST GO TO THE PRINCE AT *ONCE* TO *PROTECT* HIM!

OH, WHERE IS *ARTOO* WHEN I NEED HIM!?

7

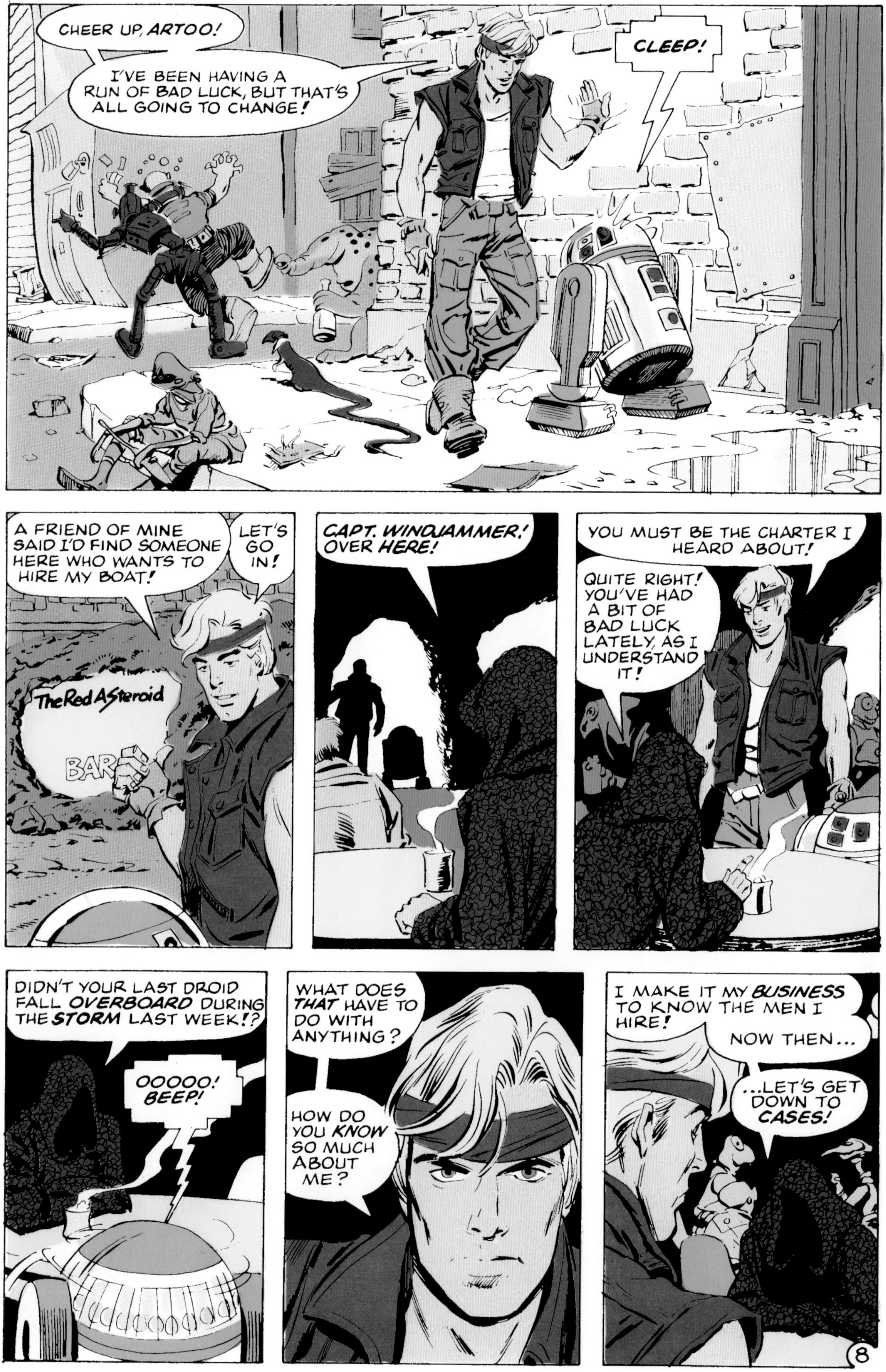
CHEER UP, ARTOO!
I'VE BEEN HAVING A RUN OF BAD LUCK, BUT THAT'S ALL GOING TO CHANGE!
CLEEP!
A FRIEND OF MINE SAID I'D FIND SOMEONE HERE WHO WANTS TO HIRE MY BOAT!
LET'S GO IN!
The Red Asteroid
BAR
CAPT. WINDJAMMER! OVER HERE!
YOU MUST BE THE CHARTER I HEARD ABOUT!
QUITE RIGHT! YOU'VE HAD A BIT OF BAD LUCK LATELY, AS I UNDERSTAND IT!
DIDN'T YOUR LAST DROID FALL OVERBOARD DURING THE STORM LAST WEEK!?
OOOOO! BEEP!
WHAT DOES THAT HAVE TO DO WITH ANYTHING?
HOW DO YOU KNOW SO MUCH ABOUT ME?
I MAKE IT MY BUSINESS TO KNOW THE MEN I HIRE!
NOW THEN...
...LET'S GET DOWN TO CASES!
8

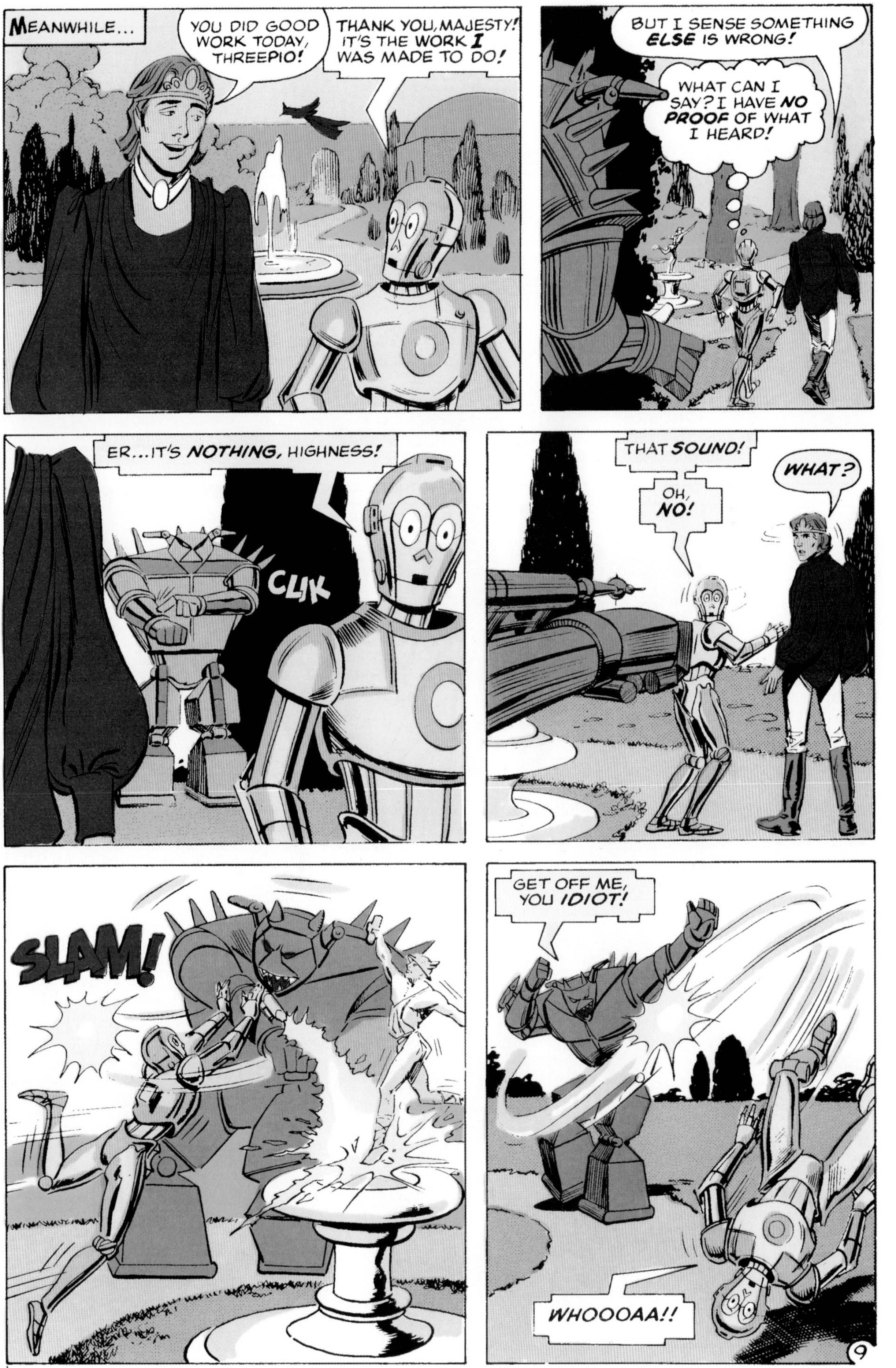
MEANWHILE...
YOU DID GOOD WORK TODAY, THREEPIO!
THANK YOU, MAJESTY! IT'S THE WORK I WAS MADE TO DO!
BUT I SENSE SOMETHING ELSE IS WRONG!
WHAT CAN I SAY? I HAVE NO PROOF OF WHAT I HEARD!
ER...IT'S NOTHING, HIGHNESS!
CLIK
THAT SOUND!
OH, NO!
WHAT?
SLAM!
GET OFF ME, YOU IDIOT!
WHOOOAA!!
9

WHAT IS THE *MEANING* OF THIS!?

I'M JUST FOLLOWING ORDERS, "YOUR *MAJESTY*"!

AND NOW, "YOUR *HIGHNESS*"..!

BZZZT!

I *D-DID* IT! I *G-GOT* HIM!

THREEPIO! YOU *SAVED* MY LIFE!

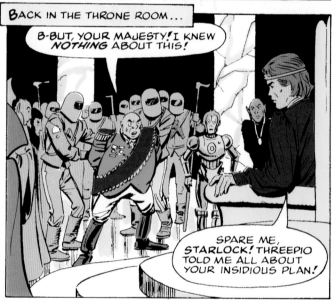

BACK IN THE THRONE ROOM...

B-BUT, YOUR MAJESTY! I KNEW *NOTHING* ABOUT THIS!

SPARE ME, STARLOCK! THREEPIO TOLD ME ALL ABOUT YOUR *INSIDIOUS* PLAN!

SURELY YOU WOULDN'T TAKE THE WORD OF A *MERE DROID* OVER MINE!

TOO TRUE!

HE HAS A POINT!

THAT *MERE DROID* SAVED MY *LIFE!*

STARLOCK, YOU ARE HEREBY *BANISHED* FROM R-DUBA *FOREVER!*

10

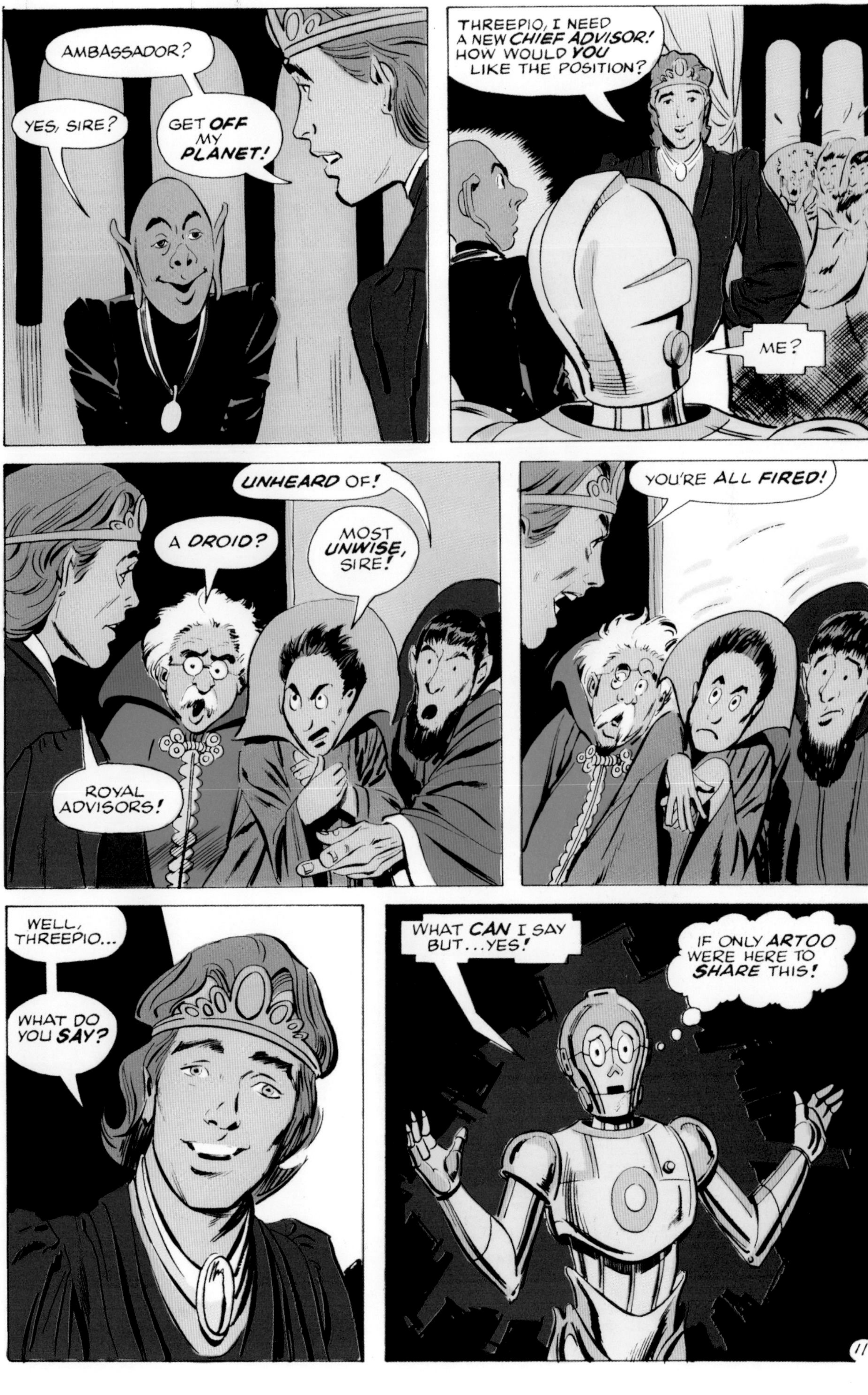
AMBASSADOR?
YES, SIRE?
GET OFF MY PLANET!
THREEPIO, I NEED A NEW CHIEF ADVISOR! HOW WOULD YOU LIKE THE POSITION?
ME?
ROYAL ADVISORS!
A DROID?
UNHEARD OF!
MOST UNWISE, SIRE!
YOU'RE ALL FIRED!
WELL, THREEPIO...
WHAT DO YOU SAY?
WHAT CAN I SAY BUT...YES!
IF ONLY ARTOO WERE HERE TO SHARE THIS!
11

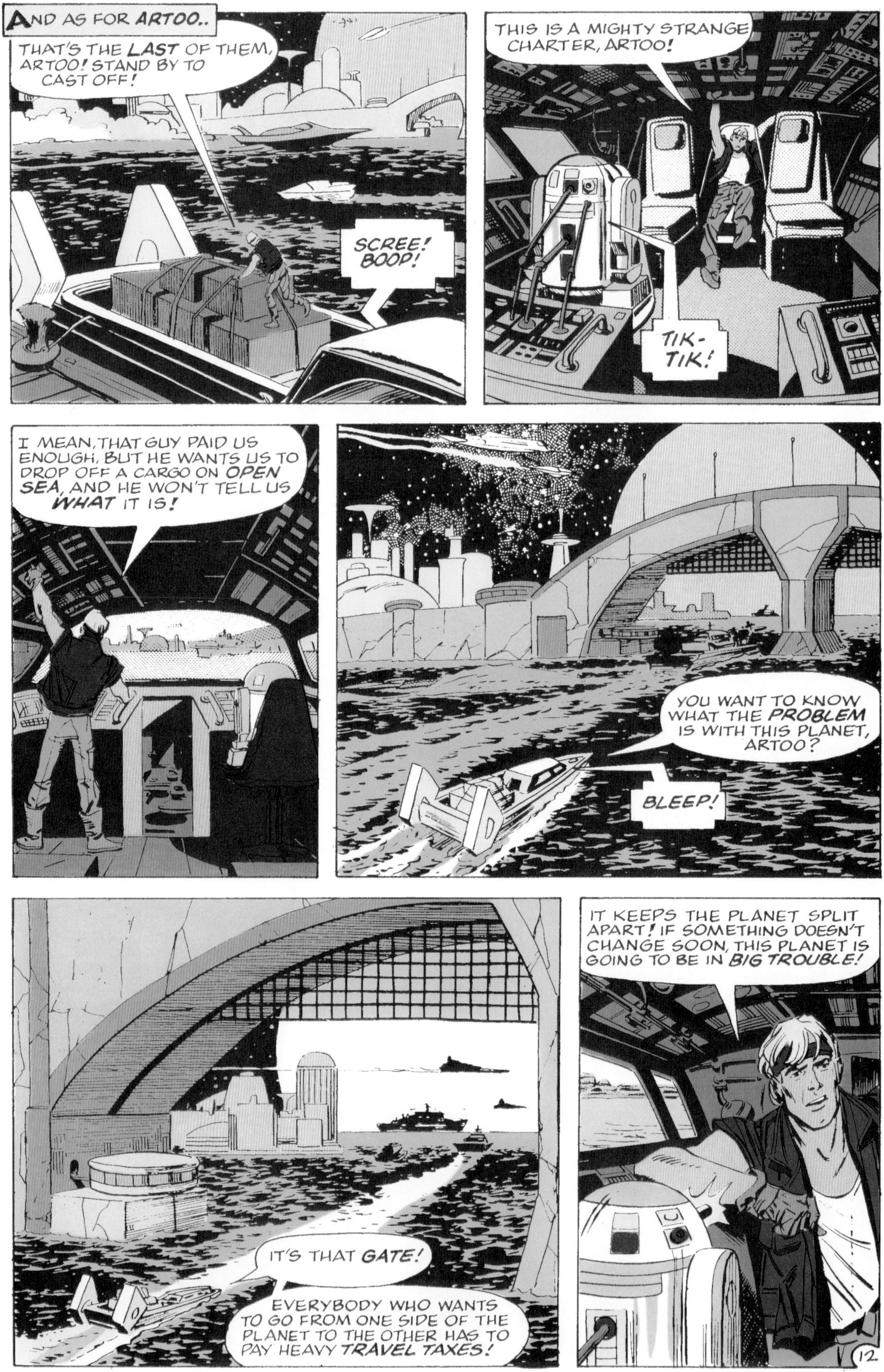
AND AS FOR ARTOO..
THAT'S THE LAST OF THEM, ARTOO! STAND BY TO CAST OFF!
SCREE! BOOP!
THIS IS A MIGHTY STRANGE CHARTER, ARTOO!
TIK-TIK!
I MEAN, THAT GUY PAID US ENOUGH, BUT HE WANTS US TO DROP OFF A CARGO ON OPEN SEA, AND HE WON'T TELL US WHAT IT IS!
YOU WANT TO KNOW WHAT THE PROBLEM IS WITH THIS PLANET, ARTOO?
BLEEP!
IT'S THAT GATE!
EVERYBODY WHO WANTS TO GO FROM ONE SIDE OF THE PLANET TO THE OTHER HAS TO PAY HEAVY TRAVEL TAXES!
IT KEEPS THE PLANET SPLIT APART! IF SOMETHING DOESN'T CHANGE SOON, THIS PLANET IS GOING TO BE IN BIG TROUBLE!
12

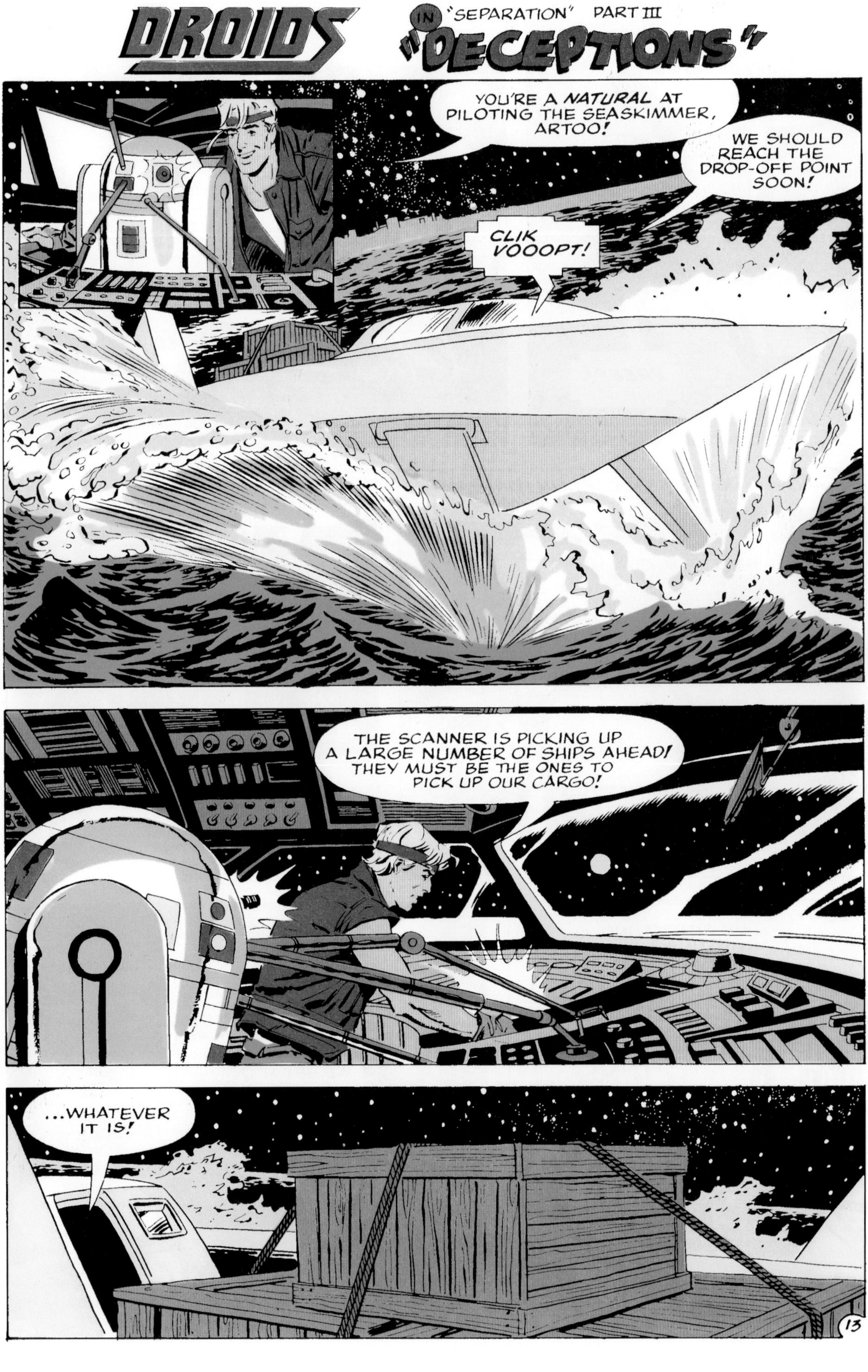
DROIDS
IN "SEPARATION" PART III
"DECEPTIONS"
YOU'RE A *NATURAL* AT PILOTING THE SEASKIMMER, ARTOO!
WE SHOULD REACH THE DROP-OFF POINT SOON!
CLIK VOOOPT!
THE SCANNER IS PICKING UP A LARGE NUMBER OF SHIPS AHEAD! THEY MUST BE THE ONES TO PICK UP OUR CARGO!
...WHATEVER IT IS!
13

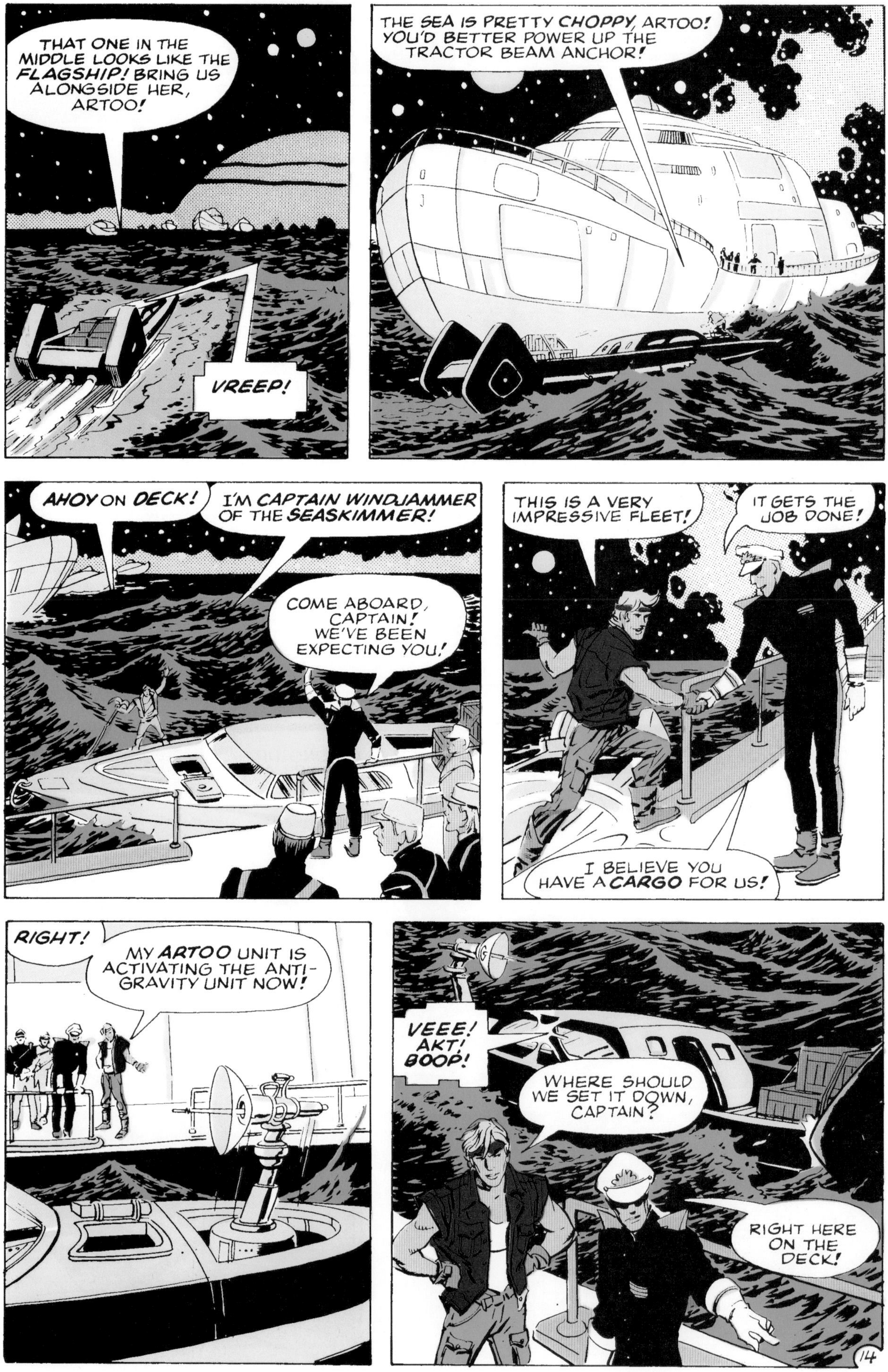
THAT ONE IN THE MIDDLE LOOKS LIKE THE FLAGSHIP! BRING US ALONGSIDE HER, ARTOO!
VREEP!
THE SEA IS PRETTY CHOPPY, ARTOO! YOU'D BETTER POWER UP THE TRACTOR BEAM ANCHOR!
AHOY ON DECK!
I'M CAPTAIN WINDJAMMER OF THE SEASKIMMER!
COME ABOARD, CAPTAIN! WE'VE BEEN EXPECTING YOU!
THIS IS A VERY IMPRESSIVE FLEET!
IT GETS THE JOB DONE!
I BELIEVE YOU HAVE A CARGO FOR US!
RIGHT!
MY ARTOO UNIT IS ACTIVATING THE ANTI-GRAVITY UNIT NOW!
VEEE! AKT! BOOP!
WHERE SHOULD WE SET IT DOWN, CAPTAIN?
RIGHT HERE ON THE DECK!
14

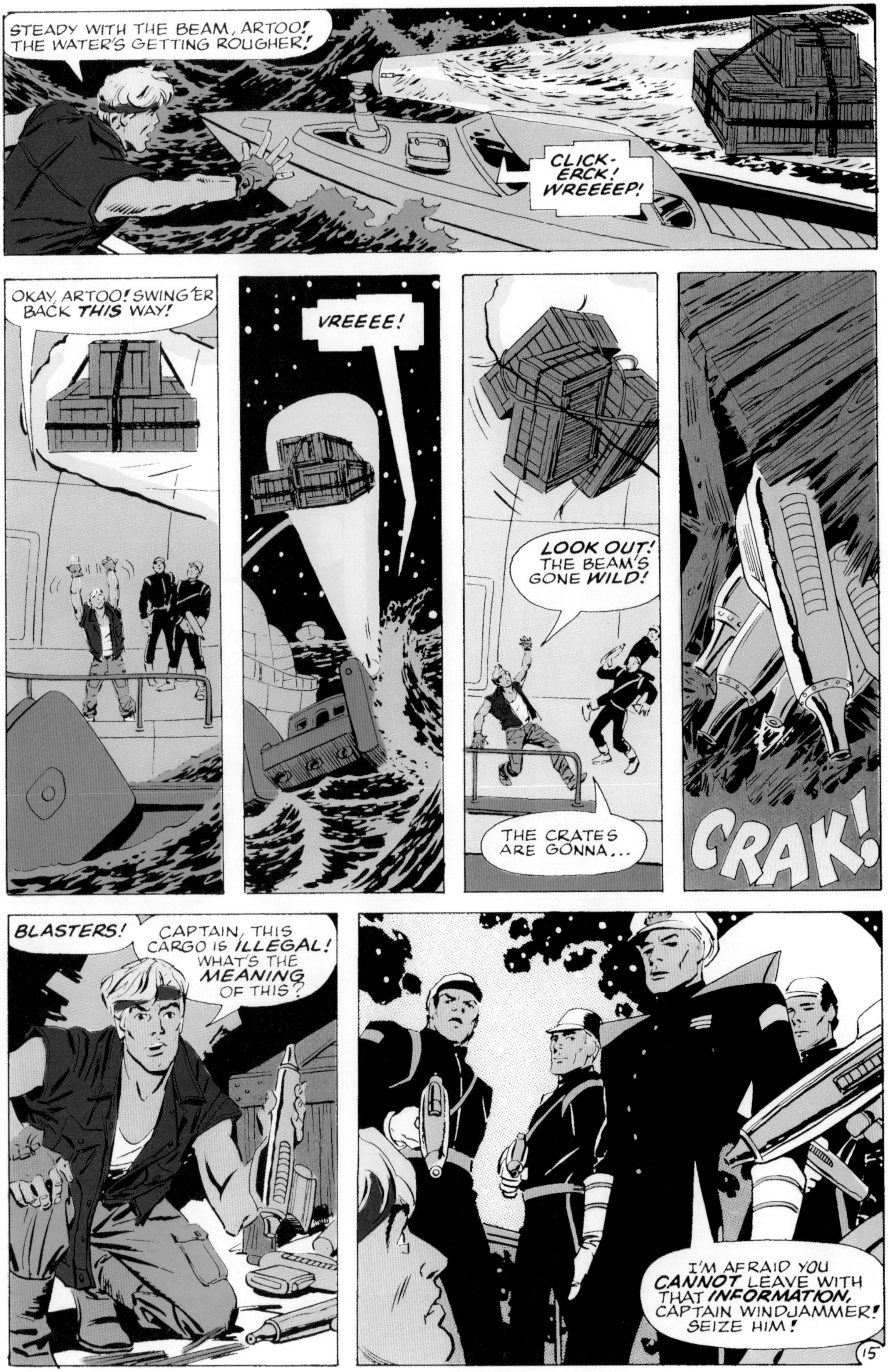
STEADY WITH THE BEAM, ARTOO! THE WATER'S GETTING ROUGHER!
CLICK-ERCK! WREEEEP!
OKAY, ARTOO! SWING 'ER BACK THIS WAY!
VREEEE!
LOOK OUT! THE BEAM'S GONE WILD!
THE CRATES ARE GONNA...
CRAK!
BLASTERS!
CAPTAIN, THIS CARGO IS ILLEGAL! WHAT'S THE MEANING OF THIS?
I'M AFRAID YOU CANNOT LEAVE WITH THAT INFORMATION, CAPTAIN WINDJAMMER! SEIZE HIM!
15

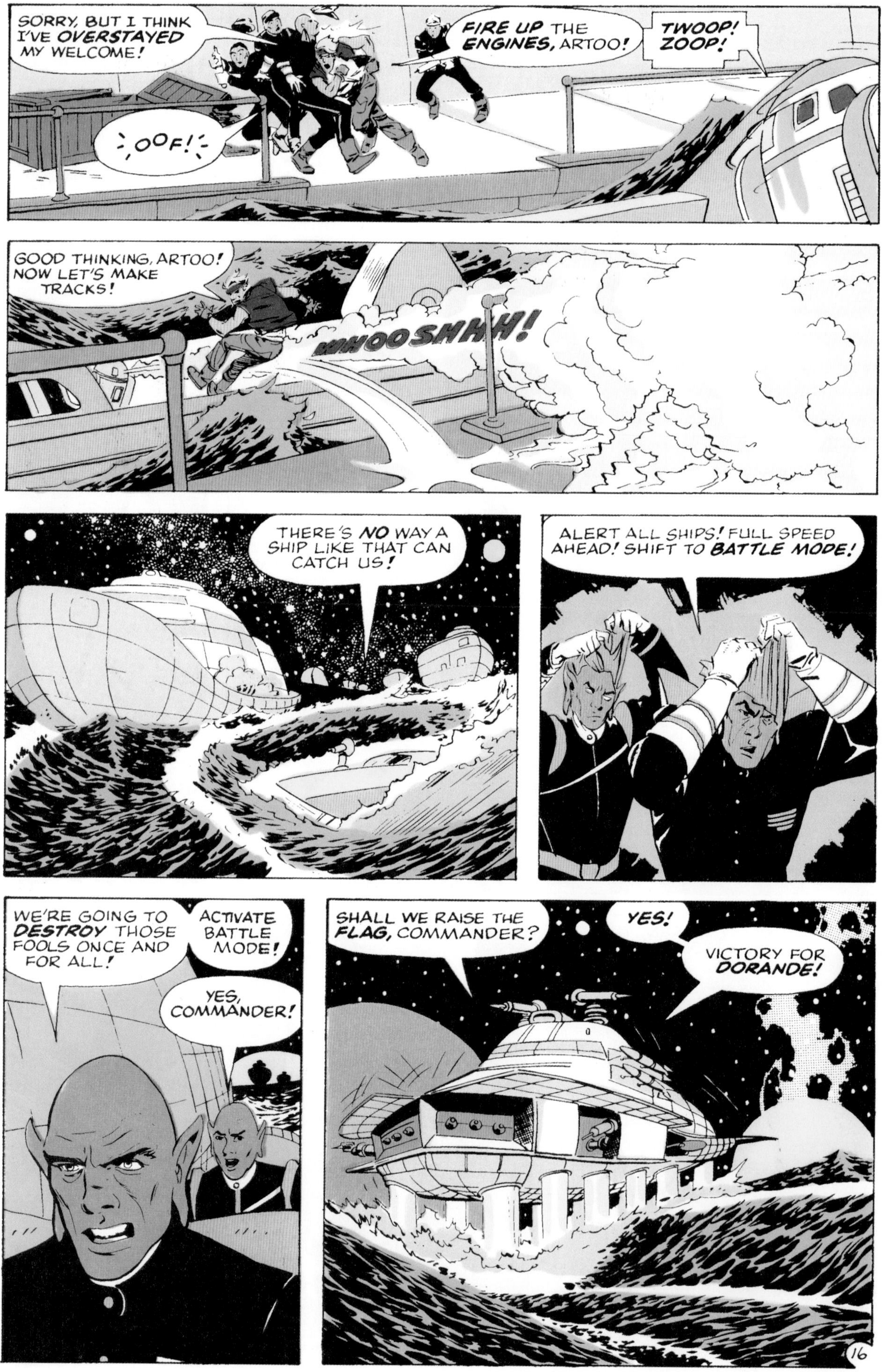
SORRY, BUT I THINK I'VE OVERSTAYED MY WELCOME!
OOF!
FIRE UP THE ENGINES, ARTOO!
TWOOP! ZOOP!
GOOD THINKING, ARTOO! NOW LET'S MAKE TRACKS!
WHOOSHHH!
THERE'S NO WAY A SHIP LIKE THAT CAN CATCH US!
ALERT ALL SHIPS! FULL SPEED AHEAD! SHIFT TO BATTLE MODE!
WE'RE GOING TO DESTROY THOSE FOOLS ONCE AND FOR ALL!
ACTIVATE BATTLE MODE!
YES, COMMANDER!
SHALL WE RAISE THE FLAG, COMMANDER?
YES!
VICTORY FOR DORANDE!
16

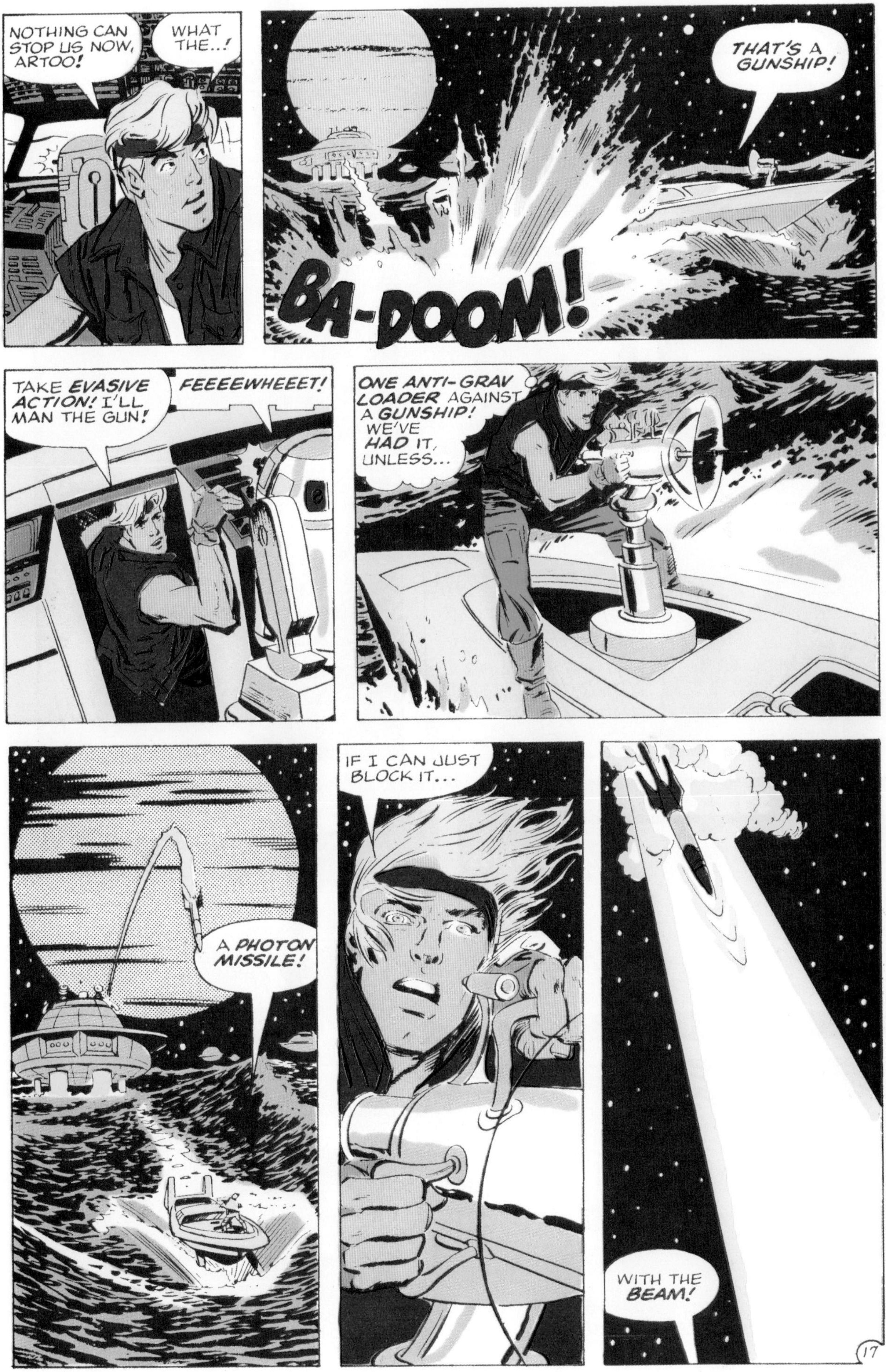
NOTHING CAN STOP US NOW, ARTOO!
WHAT THE...!
THAT'S A GUNSHIP!
BA-DOOM!
TAKE EVASIVE ACTION! I'LL MAN THE GUN!
FEEEEWHEEET!
ONE ANTI-GRAV LOADER AGAINST A GUNSHIP! WE'VE HAD IT, UNLESS...
A PHOTON MISSILE!
IF I CAN JUST BLOCK IT...
WITH THE BEAM!
17

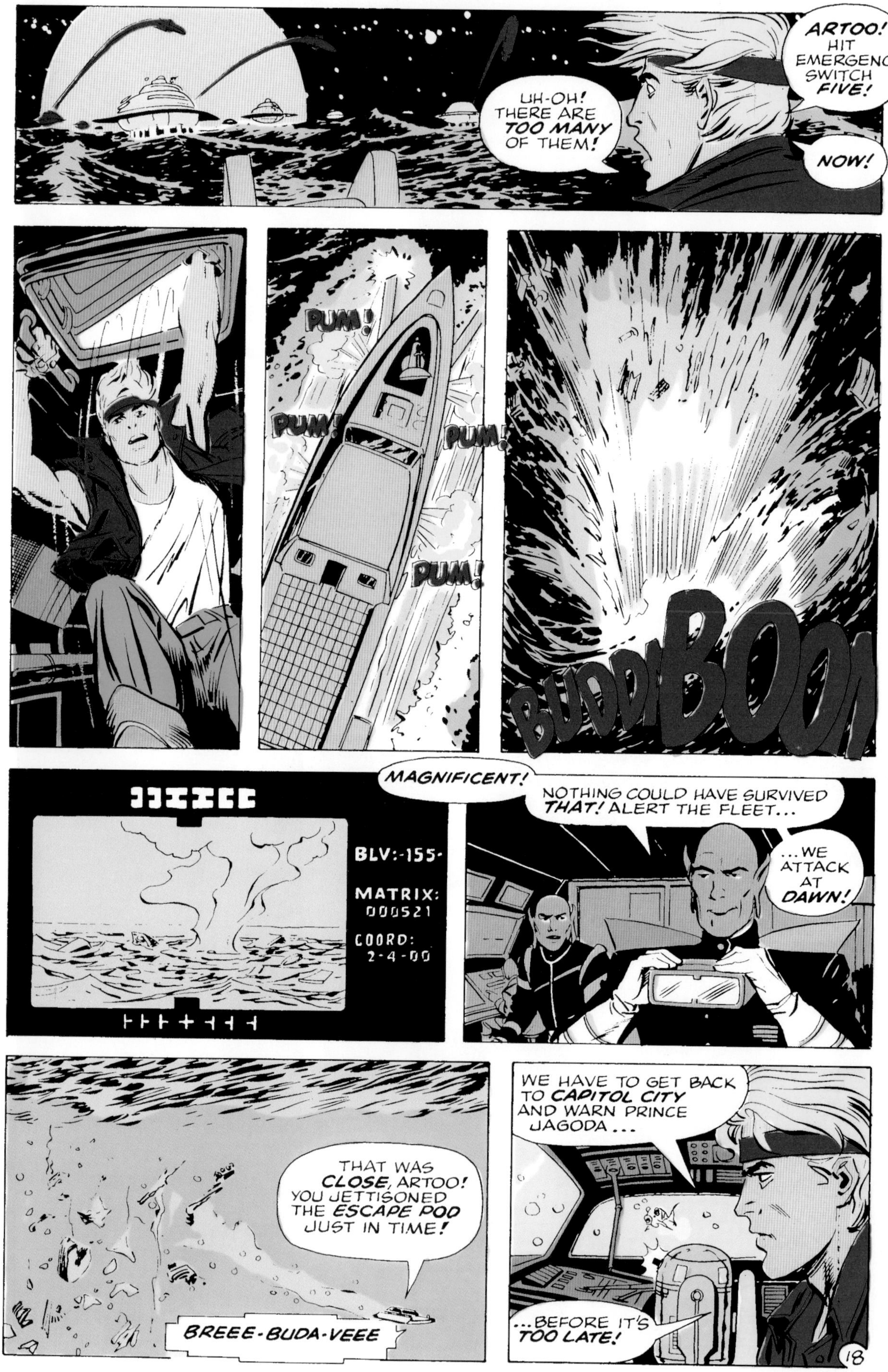
UH-OH! THERE ARE TOO MANY OF THEM!
ARTOO! HIT EMERGENCY SWITCH FIVE!
NOW!
PUM!
PUM!
PUM!
PUM!
BUDDIBOOM
BLV:-155-
MATRIX: 000521
COORD: 2-4-00
MAGNIFICENT!
NOTHING COULD HAVE SURVIVED THAT! ALERT THE FLEET...
...WE ATTACK AT DAWN!
THAT WAS CLOSE, ARTOO! YOU JETTISONED THE ESCAPE POD JUST IN TIME!
BREEE-BUDA-VEEE
WE HAVE TO GET BACK TO CAPITOL CITY AND WARN PRINCE JAGODA...
...BEFORE IT'S TOO LATE!
18

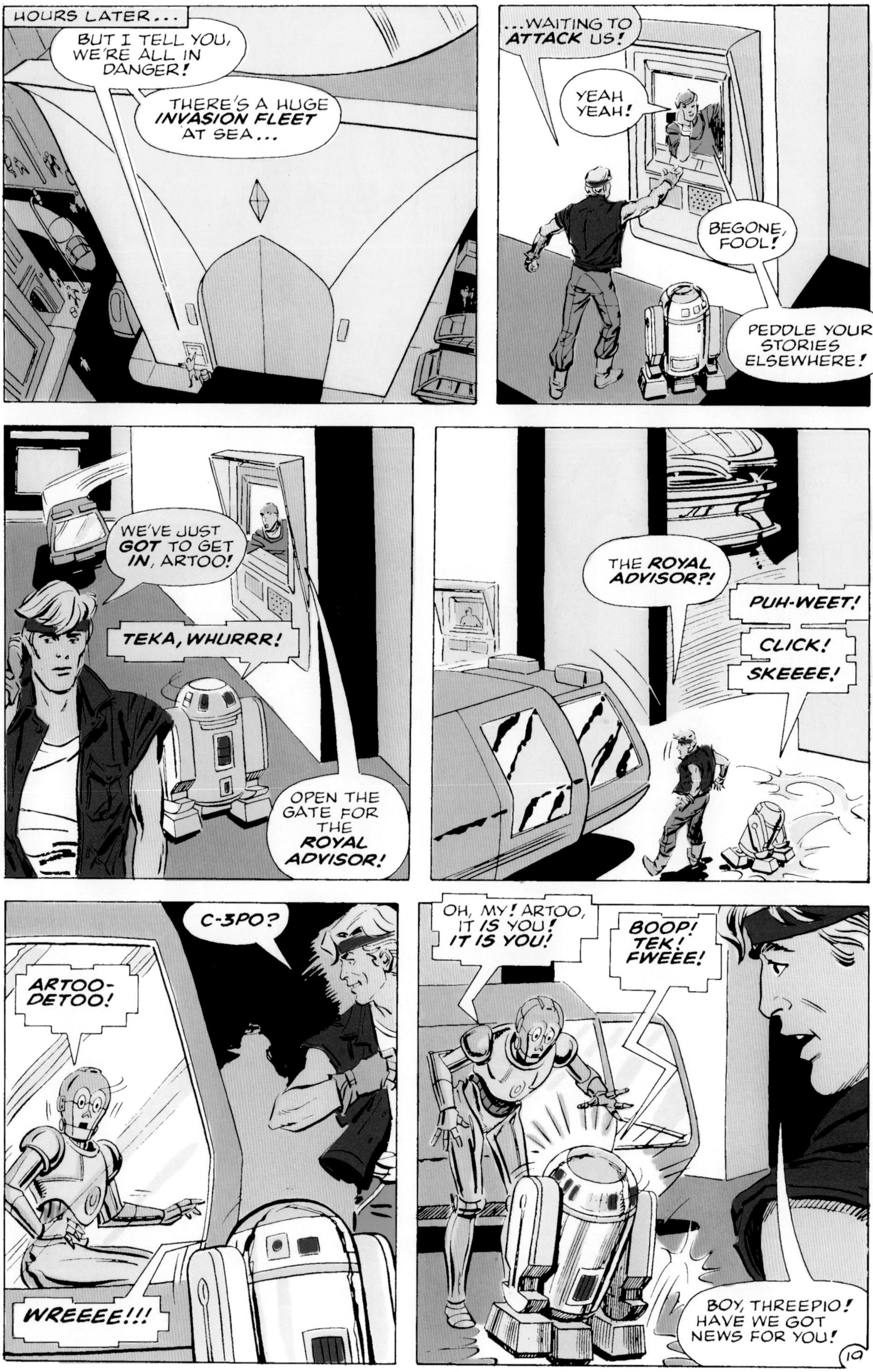
HOURS LATER...
BUT I TELL YOU, WE'RE ALL IN DANGER!
THERE'S A HUGE INVASION FLEET AT SEA...
...WAITING TO ATTACK US!
YEAH YEAH!
BEGONE, FOOL!
PEDDLE YOUR STORIES ELSEWHERE!
WE'VE JUST GOT TO GET IN, ARTOO!
TEKA, WHURRR!
OPEN THE GATE FOR THE ROYAL ADVISOR!
THE ROYAL ADVISOR?!
PUH-WEET!
CLICK!
SKEEEE!
C-3PO?
ARTOO-DETOO!
WREEEE!!!
OH, MY! ARTOO, IT IS YOU! IT IS YOU!
BOOP! TEK! FWEEE!
BOY, THREEPIO! HAVE WE GOT NEWS FOR YOU!
10

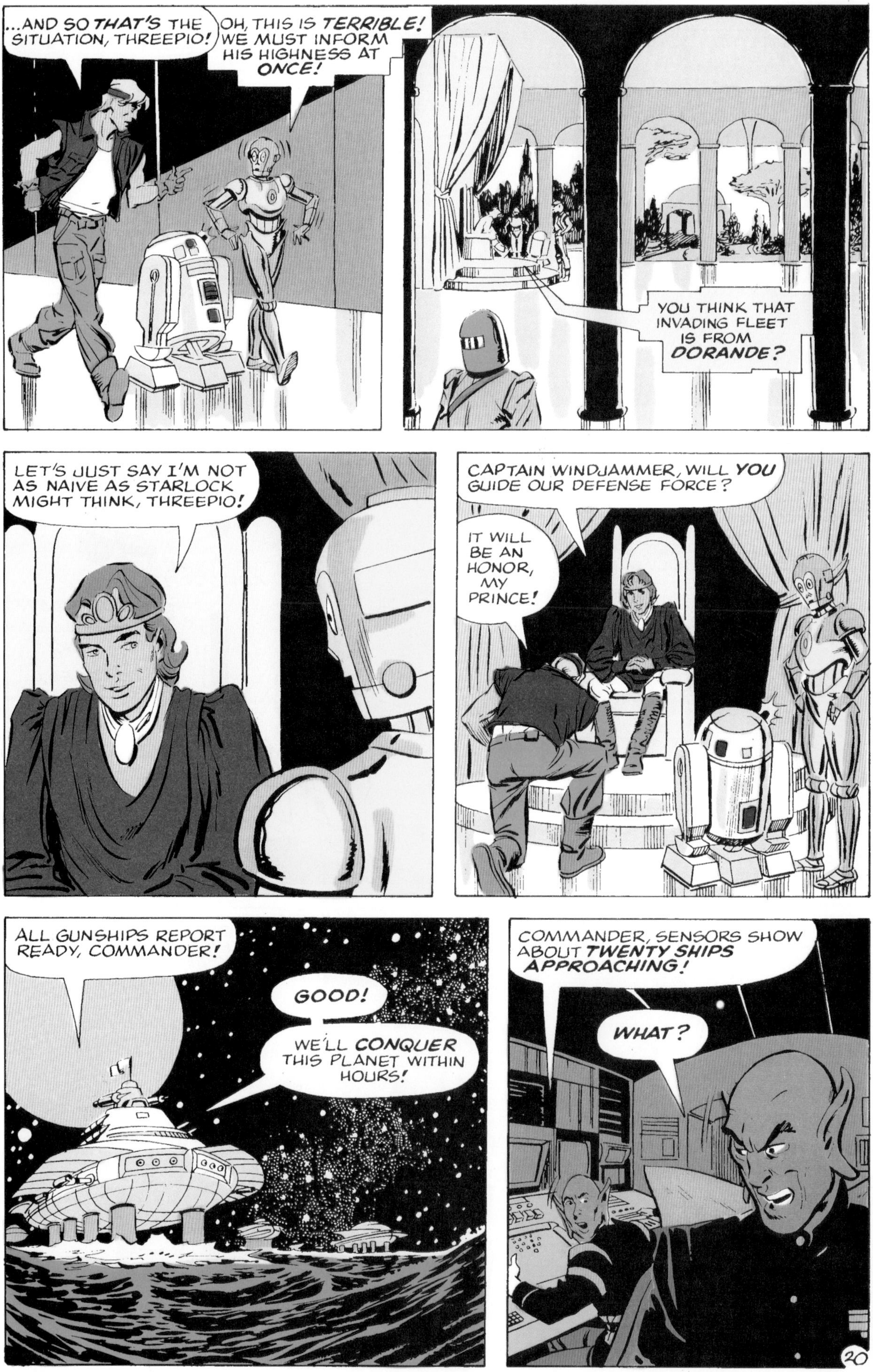
...AND SO THAT'S THE SITUATION, THREEPIO!
OH, THIS IS TERRIBLE! WE MUST INFORM HIS HIGHNESS AT ONCE!
YOU THINK THAT INVADING FLEET IS FROM DORANDE?
LET'S JUST SAY I'M NOT AS NAIVE AS STARLOCK MIGHT THINK, THREEPIO!
CAPTAIN WINDJAMMER, WILL YOU GUIDE OUR DEFENSE FORCE?
IT WILL BE AN HONOR, MY PRINCE!
ALL GUNSHIPS REPORT READY, COMMANDER!
GOOD!
WE'LL CONQUER THIS PLANET WITHIN HOURS!
COMMANDER, SENSORS SHOW ABOUT TWENTY SHIPS APPROACHING!
WHAT?
20

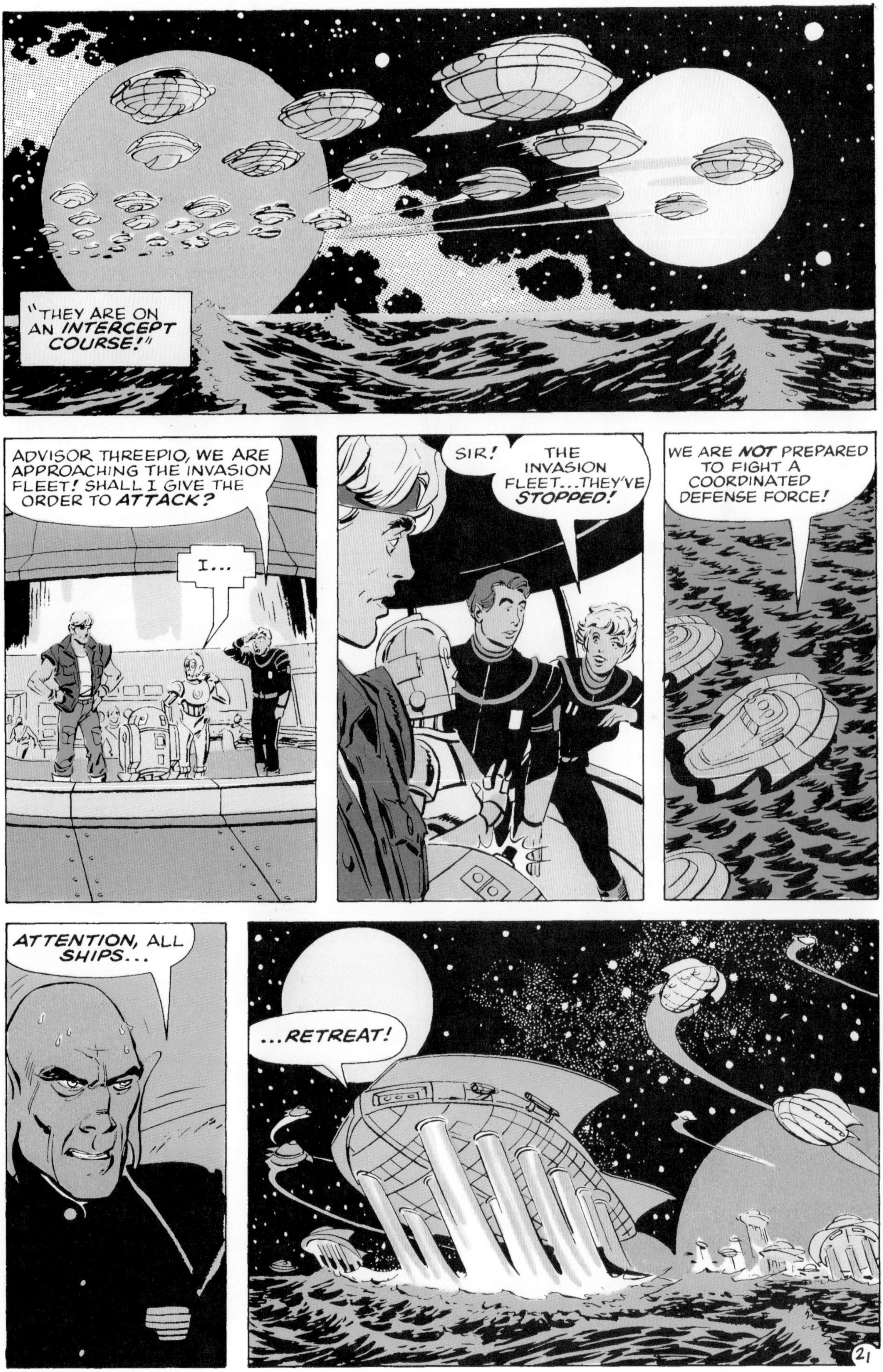
"THEY ARE ON AN *INTERCEPT COURSE!*"
ADVISOR THREEPIO, WE ARE APPROACHING THE INVASION FLEET! SHALL I GIVE THE ORDER TO *ATTACK?*
I...
SIR!
THE INVASION FLEET...THEY'VE *STOPPED!*
WE ARE *NOT* PREPARED TO FIGHT A COORDINATED DEFENSE FORCE!
ATTENTION, ALL SHIPS...
...*RETREAT!*
21

AND THAT'S WHEN THEY *RAN!*

CAPTAIN, ARTOO, THREEPIO...

...YOUR ACTIONS HAVE *SAVED* R-DUBA! YOU HAVE OUR UNDYING THANKS!

WHAT WILL YOU DO NOW, CAPTAIN, SINCE YOUR SHIP HAS BEEN *DESTROYED?*

I'LL SURVIVE, SIRE! I'VE STARTED WITH NOTHING BEFORE, AND I'LL DO IT AGAIN!

SURELY I CAN DO *SOMETHING* FOR YOU!

WELL, THERE *IS* SOMETHING YOU CAN DO...FOR *EVERYONE!*

NAME IT!

"LIFT THE *TRAVEL TAXES*, SIRE! WHAT THIS PLANET NEEDS IS TO BE *CLOSER TOGETHER*, NOT SPLIT APART! THE SEA CAN DO A LOT FOR THE DESERT AS THE DESERT CAN DO A LOT FOR THE OCEAN!"

YOU MAY BE RIGHT, WINDJAMMER!

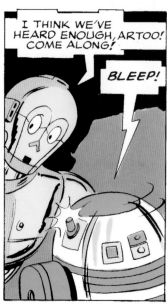

I THINK WE'VE HEARD ENOUGH, ARTOO! COME ALONG!

BLEEP!

NEXT MORNING...

YOU CALLED FOR ME, SIRE!

YES, COME IN, KIRK!

22

436

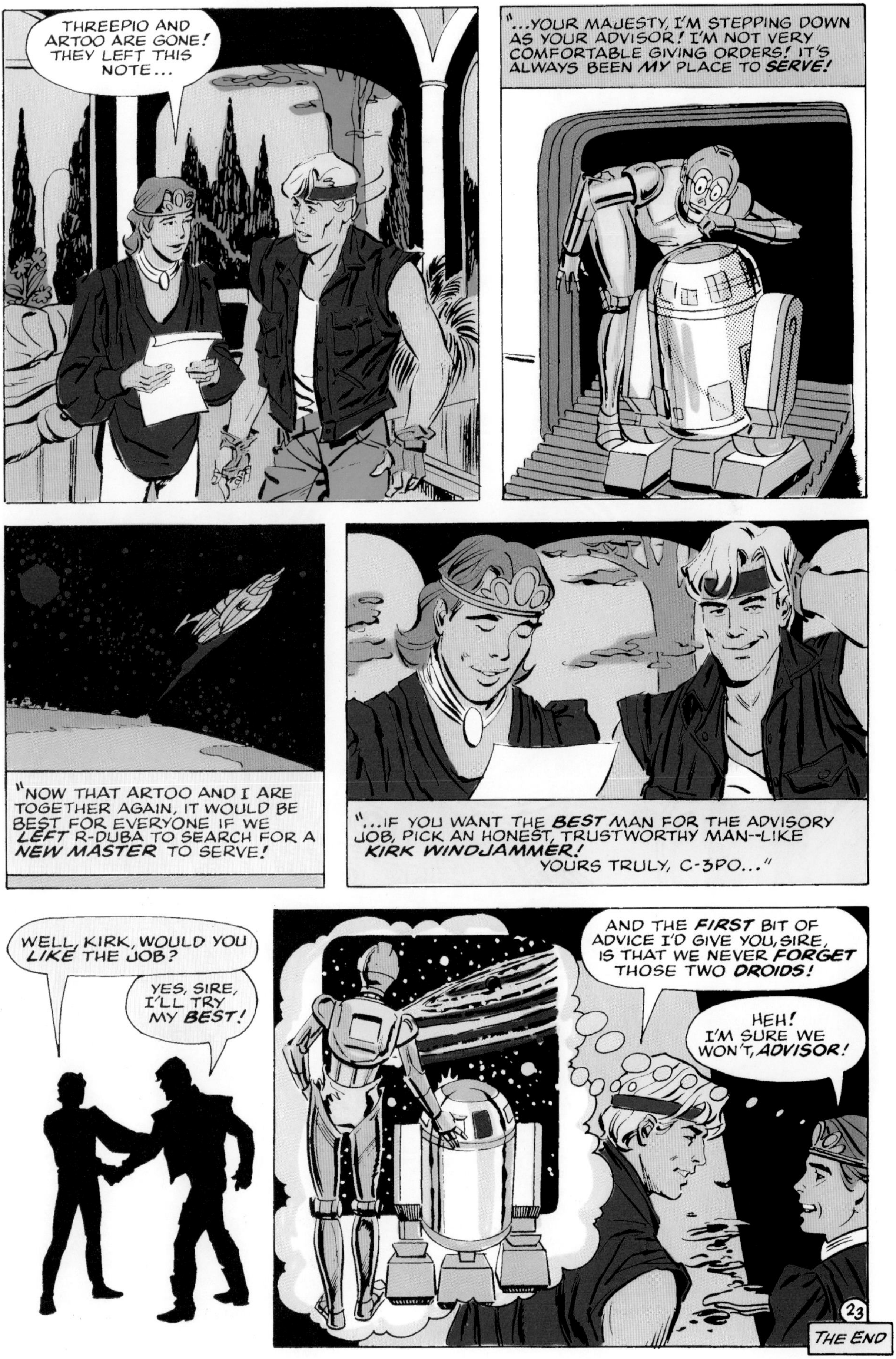
THREEPIO AND ARTOO ARE GONE! THEY LEFT THIS NOTE...
"...YOUR MAJESTY, I'M STEPPING DOWN AS YOUR ADVISOR! I'M NOT VERY COMFORTABLE GIVING ORDERS! IT'S ALWAYS BEEN MY PLACE TO SERVE!
"NOW THAT ARTOO AND I ARE TOGETHER AGAIN, IT WOULD BE BEST FOR EVERYONE IF WE LEFT R-DUBA TO SEARCH FOR A NEW MASTER TO SERVE!
"...IF YOU WANT THE BEST MAN FOR THE ADVISORY JOB, PICK AN HONEST, TRUSTWORTHY MAN--LIKE KIRK WINDJAMMER! YOURS TRULY, C-3PO..."
WELL, KIRK, WOULD YOU LIKE THE JOB?
YES, SIRE, I'LL TRY MY BEST!
AND THE FIRST BIT OF ADVICE I'D GIVE YOU, SIRE, IS THAT WE NEVER FORGET THOSE TWO DROIDS!
HEH! I'M SURE WE WON'T, ADVISOR!
23
THE END

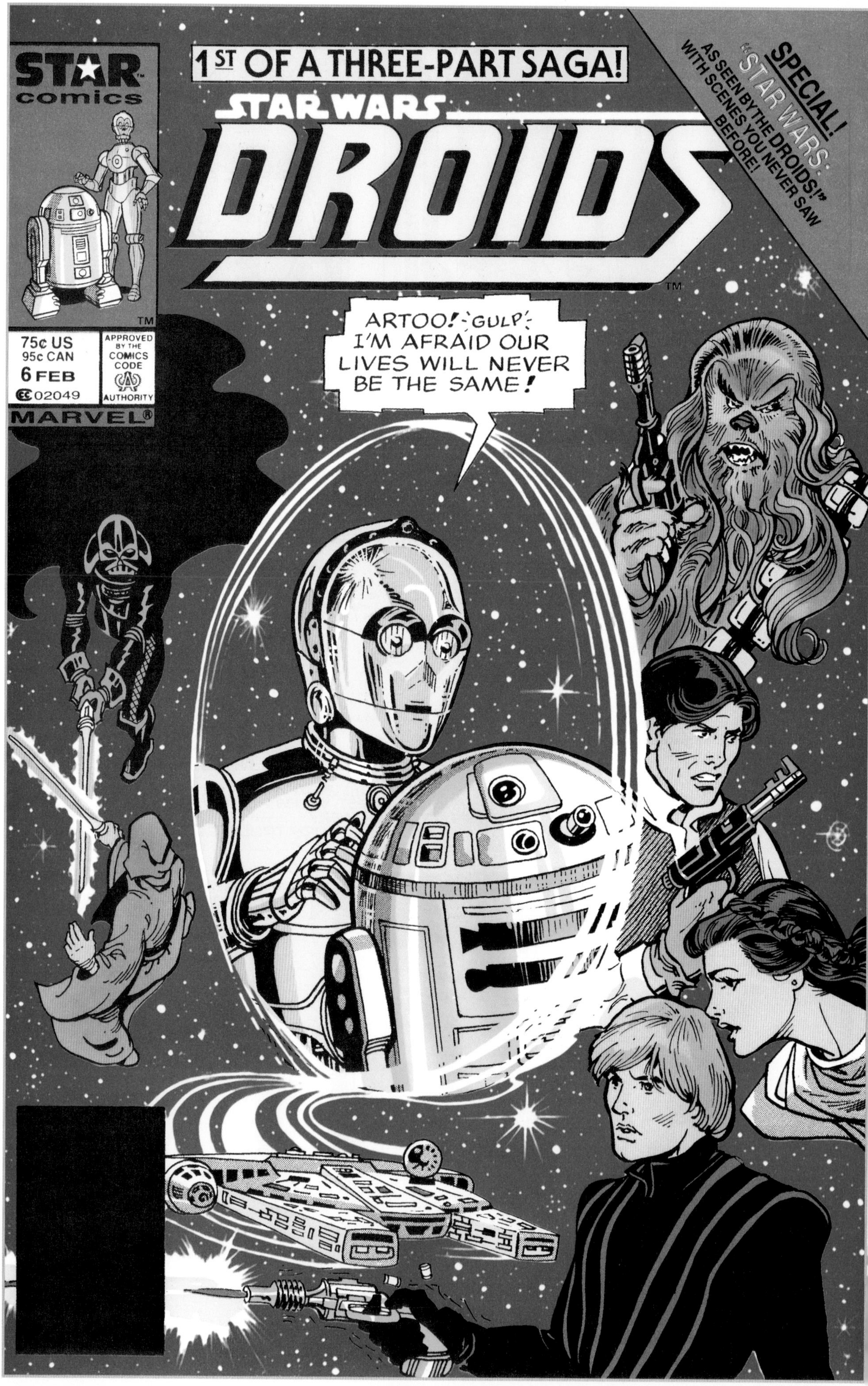
STAR comics
1ST OF A THREE-PART SAGA!
STAR WARS
DROIDS
SPECIAL! "STAR WARS: AS SEEN BY THE DROIDS!" WITH SCENES YOU NEVER SAW BEFORE!
75¢ US 95¢ CAN 6 FEB 02049
APPROVED BY THE COMICS CODE AUTHORITY
MARVEL
ARTOO! -GULP- I'M AFRAID OUR LIVES WILL NEVER BE THE SAME!

STAR WARS DROIDS IN

STAR WARS: ACCORDING TO THE DROIDS

A LONG, LONG TIME AGO, IN A GALAXY FAR AWAY... TWO DROIDS, *R2-D2* AND *C-3PO*, ARE IN SERVICE ABOARD A ROYAL TRANSPORT -- A TRANSPORT UNDER ATTACK BY AN IMPERIAL BATTLE CRUISER.

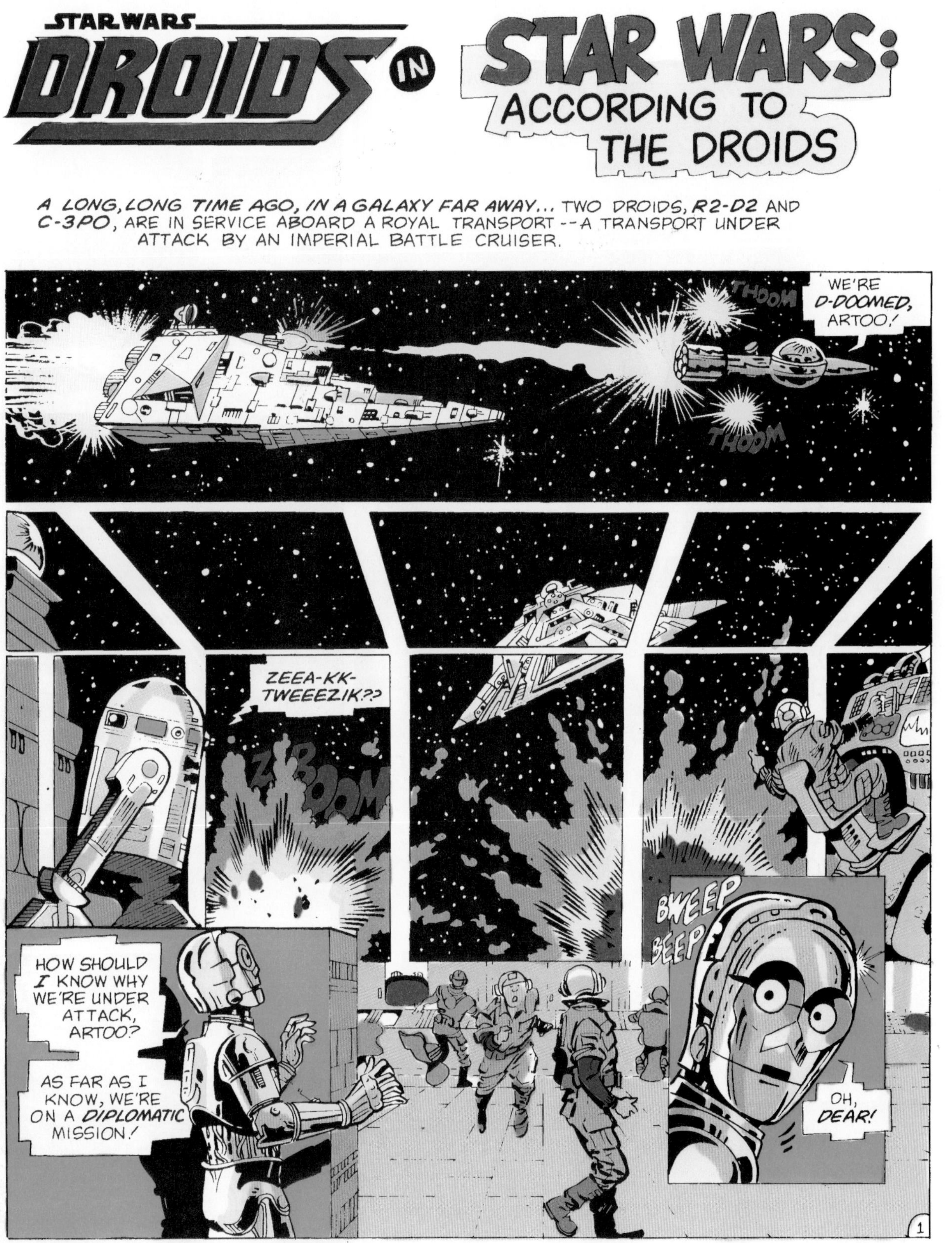
THOOM
WE'RE D-DOOMED, ARTOO!
THOOM
ZEEA-KK-TWEEEZIK??
ZIBOOM
HOW SHOULD I KNOW WHY WE'RE UNDER ATTACK, ARTOO?
AS FAR AS I KNOW, WE'RE ON A DIPLOMATIC MISSION!
BWEEP BEEP
OH, DEAR!
1

DAVE MANAK	ERNIE COLÓN	MARIE SEVERIN	ED KING	SID JACOBSON	TOM DEFALCO	JIM SHOOTER
WRITER	PENCILER	INKER/COLORIST	LETTERER	EDITOR	EXECUTIVE EDITOR	ED. IN CHIEF

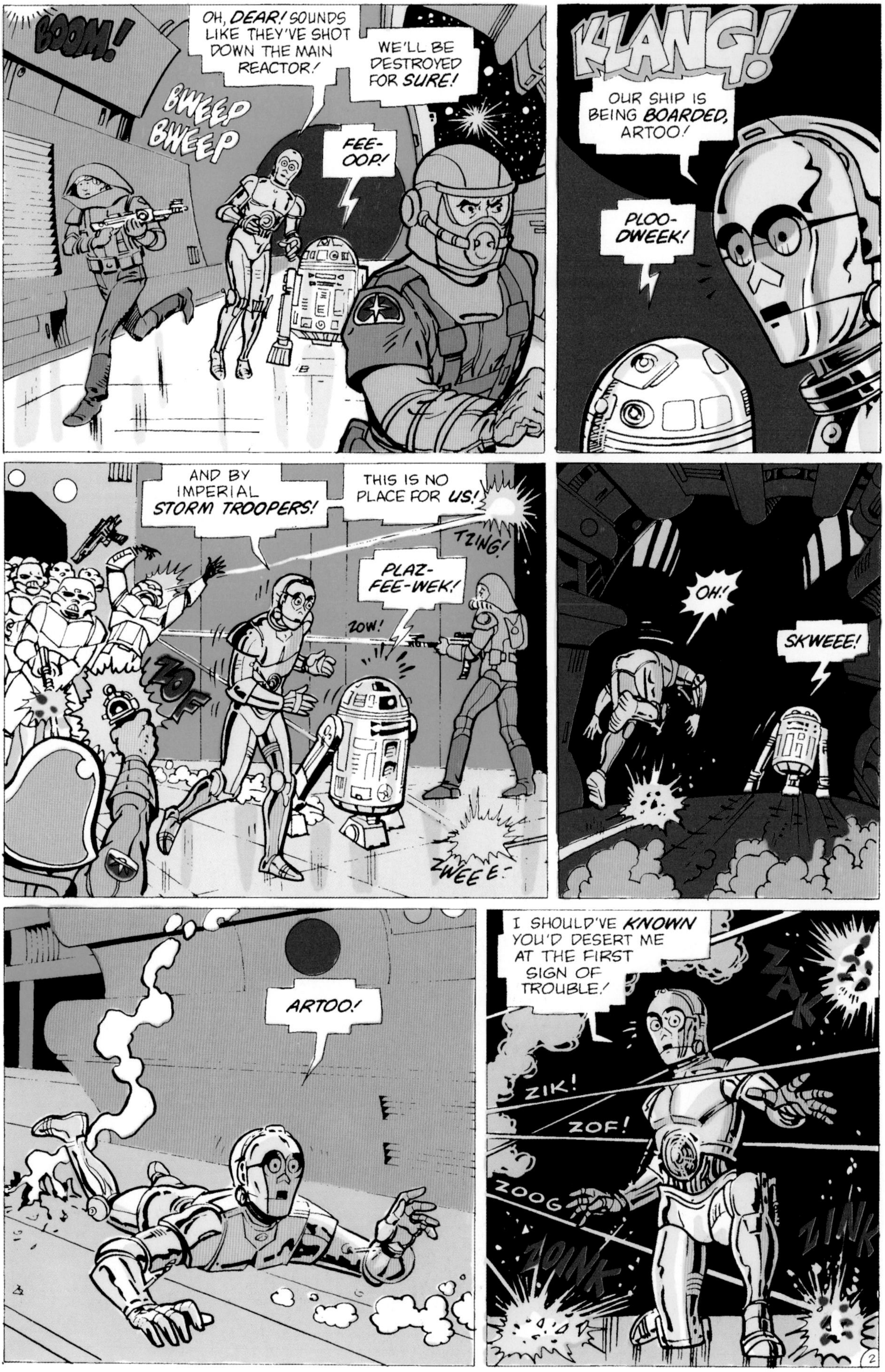
BOOM!
OH, DEAR! SOUNDS LIKE THEY'VE SHOT DOWN THE MAIN REACTOR!
WE'LL BE DESTROYED FOR SURE!
BWEEP BWEEP
FEE-OOP!
KLANG!
OUR SHIP IS BEING BOARDED, ARTOO!
PLOO-DWEEK!
AND BY IMPERIAL STORM TROOPERS!
THIS IS NO PLACE FOR US!
TZING!
PLAZ-FEE-WEK!
ZOW!
ZOF
ZWEEE
OH!
SKWEEE!
ARTOO!
I SHOULD'VE KNOWN YOU'D DESERT ME AT THE FIRST SIGN OF TROUBLE!
ZAK
ZIK!
ZOF!
ZOOG
ZOINK
ZINK
2

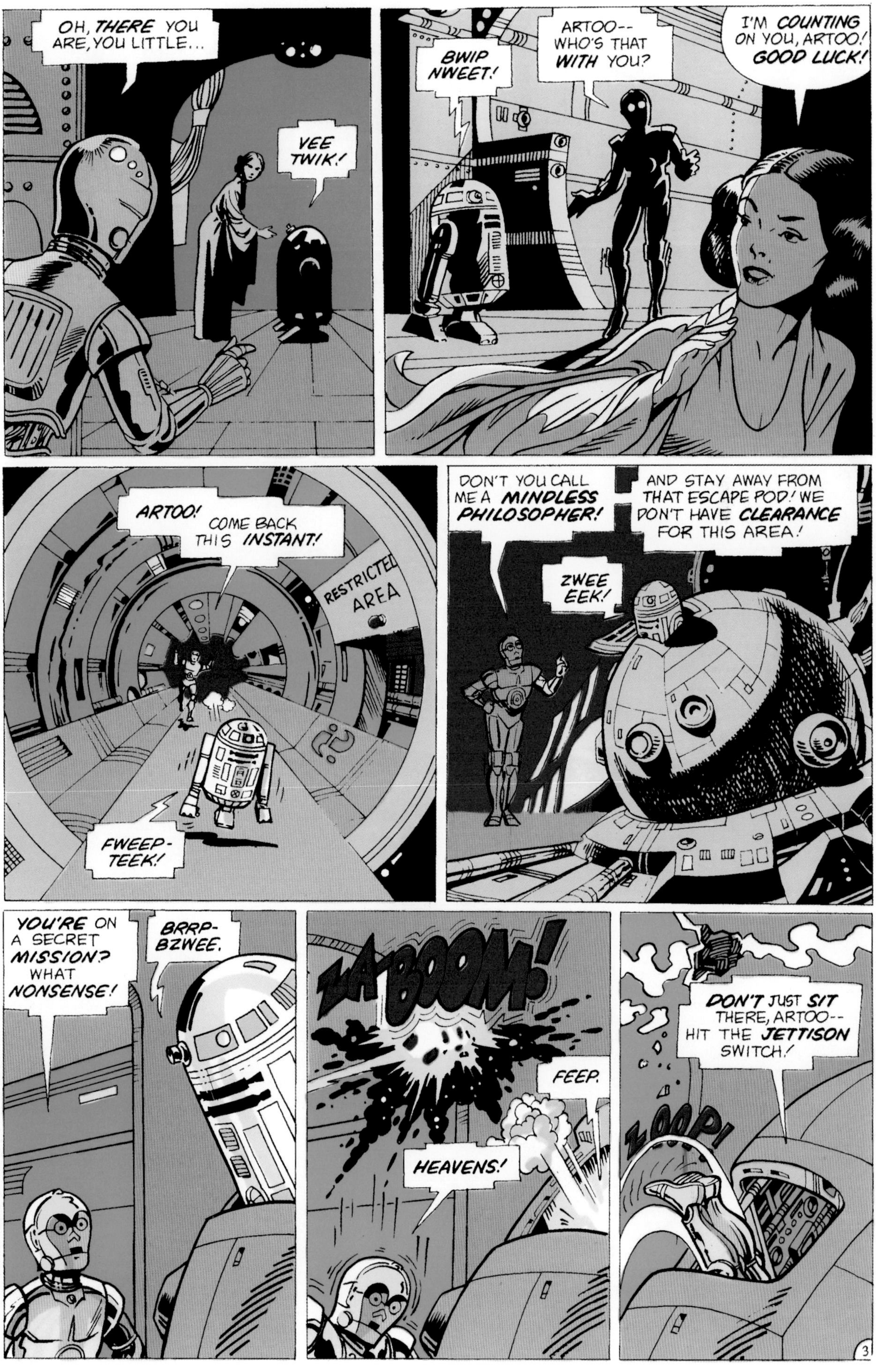

OH, THERE YOU ARE, YOU LITTLE...
VEE TWIK!
BWIP NWEET!
ARTOO-- WHO'S THAT WITH YOU?
I'M COUNTING ON YOU, ARTOO! GOOD LUCK!
ARTOO! COME BACK THIS INSTANT!
RESTRICTED AREA
FWEEP-TEEK!
DON'T YOU CALL ME A MINDLESS PHILOSOPHER!
AND STAY AWAY FROM THAT ESCAPE POD! WE DON'T HAVE CLEARANCE FOR THIS AREA!
ZWEE EEK!
YOU'RE ON A SECRET MISSION? WHAT NONSENSE!
BRRP-BZWEE.
KA-BOOM!
FEEP.
HEAVENS!
DON'T JUST SIT THERE, ARTOO-- HIT THE JETTISON SWITCH!
ZOOP!
3

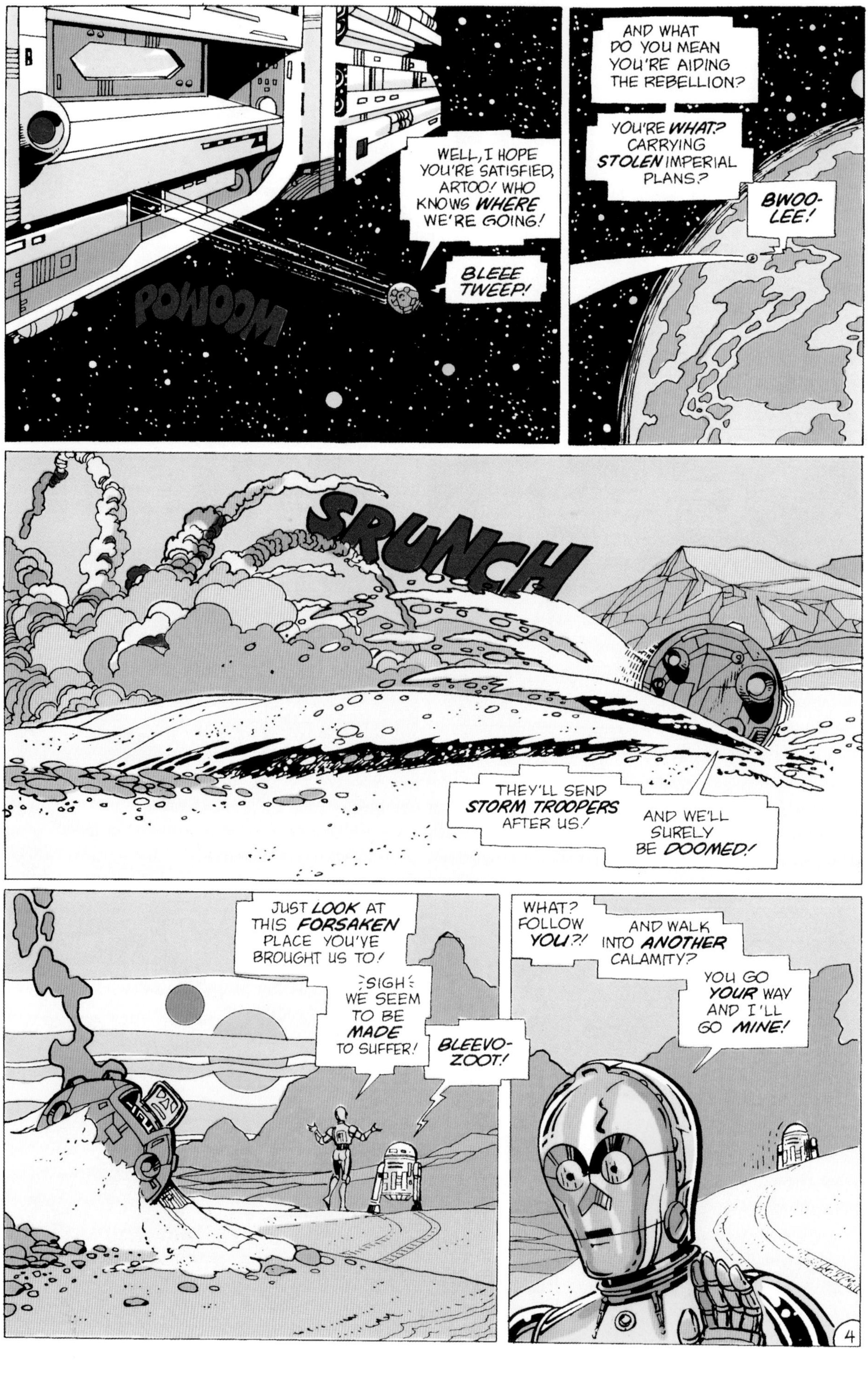
POWOOM
WELL, I HOPE YOU'RE SATISFIED, ARTOO! WHO KNOWS WHERE WE'RE GOING!
BLEEE TWEEP!
AND WHAT DO YOU MEAN YOU'RE AIDING THE REBELLION?
YOU'RE WHAT? CARRYING STOLEN IMPERIAL PLANS?
BWOO-LEE!
SRUNCH
THEY'LL SEND STORM TROOPERS AFTER US!
AND WE'LL SURELY BE DOOMED!
JUST LOOK AT THIS FORSAKEN PLACE YOU'VE BROUGHT US TO!
SIGH WE SEEM TO BE MADE TO SUFFER!
BLEEVO-ZOOT!
WHAT? FOLLOW YOU?!
AND WALK INTO ANOTHER CALAMITY?
YOU GO YOUR WAY AND I'LL GO MINE!
4

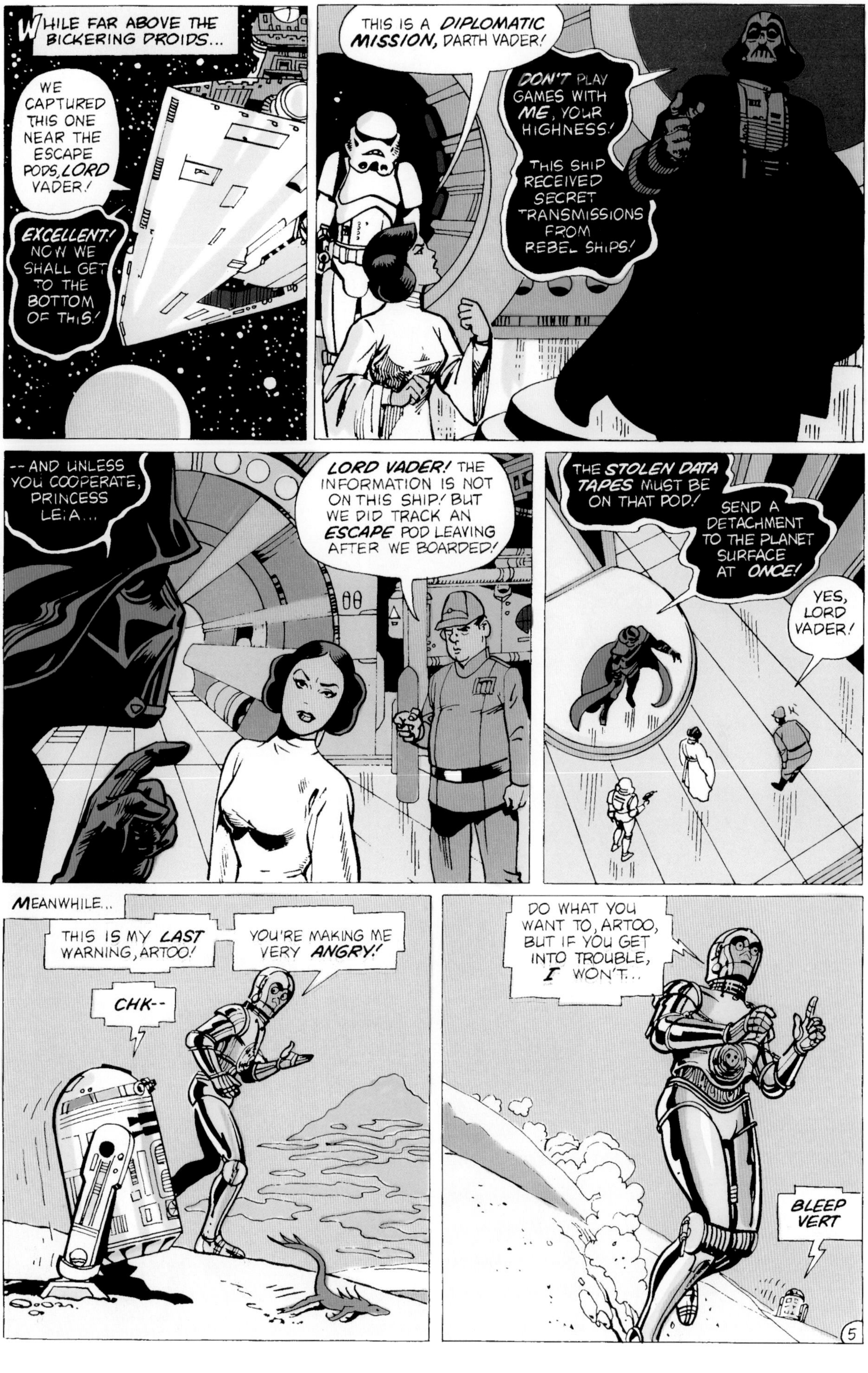
WHILE FAR ABOVE THE BICKERING DROIDS...
WE CAPTURED THIS ONE NEAR THE ESCAPE PODS, LORD VADER!
EXCELLENT! NOW WE SHALL GET TO THE BOTTOM OF THIS!
THIS IS A DIPLOMATIC MISSION, DARTH VADER!
DON'T PLAY GAMES WITH ME, YOUR HIGHNESS!
THIS SHIP RECEIVED SECRET TRANSMISSIONS FROM REBEL SHIPS!
-- AND UNLESS YOU COOPERATE, PRINCESS LEIA...
LORD VADER! THE INFORMATION IS NOT ON THIS SHIP! BUT WE DID TRACK AN ESCAPE POD LEAVING AFTER WE BOARDED!
THE STOLEN DATA TAPES MUST BE ON THAT POD!
SEND A DETACHMENT TO THE PLANET SURFACE AT ONCE!
YES, LORD VADER!
MEANWHILE...
THIS IS MY LAST WARNING, ARTOO!
YOU'RE MAKING ME VERY ANGRY!
CHK--
DO WHAT YOU WANT TO, ARTOO, BUT IF YOU GET INTO TROUBLE, I WON'T...
BLEEP VERT
5

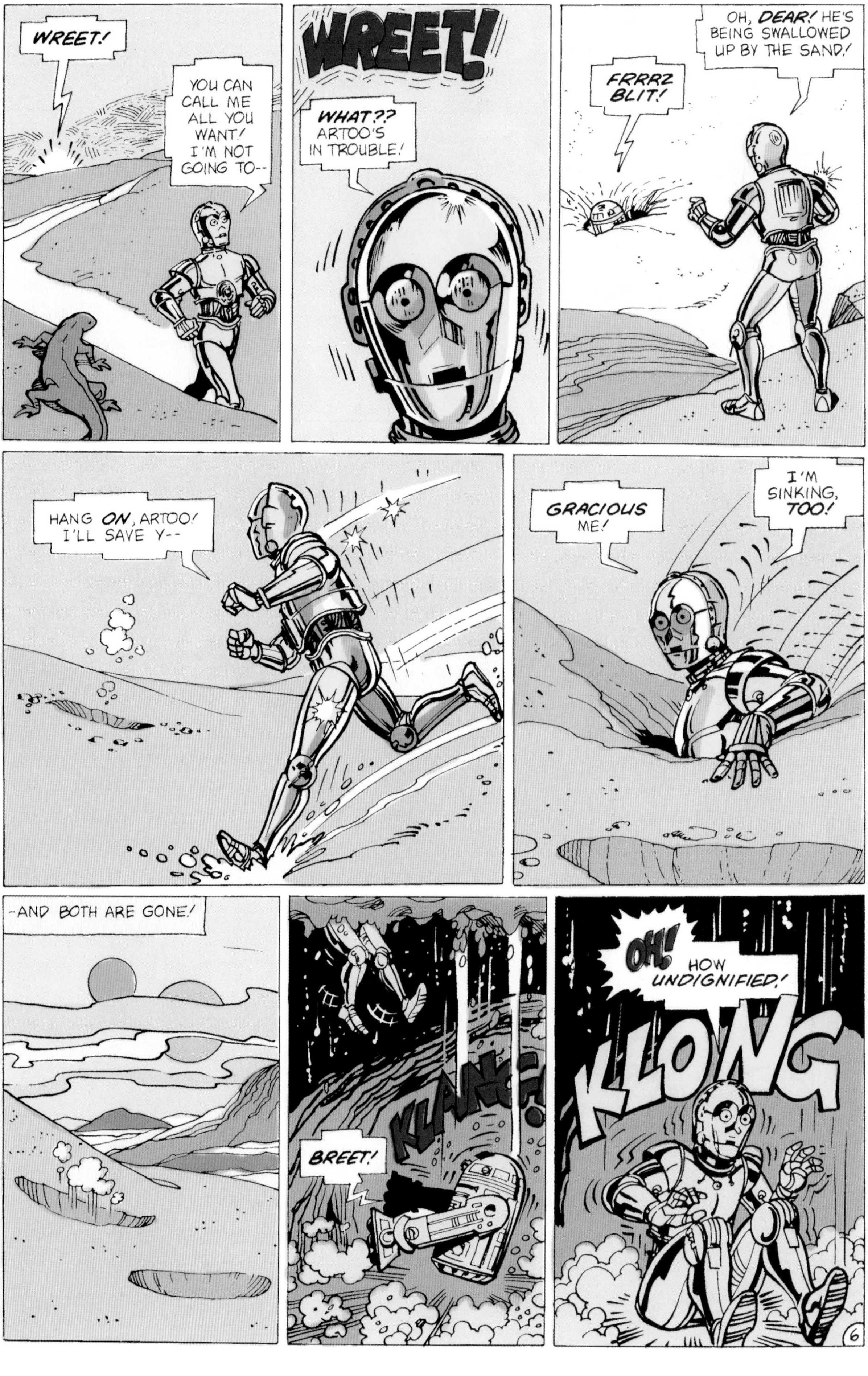
WREET!
YOU CAN CALL ME ALL YOU WANT! I'M NOT GOING TO--
WREET!
WHAT?? ARTOO'S IN TROUBLE!
OH, DEAR! HE'S BEING SWALLOWED UP BY THE SAND!
FRRRZ BLIT!
HANG ON, ARTOO! I'LL SAVE Y--
GRACIOUS ME!
I'M SINKING, TOO!
-AND BOTH ARE GONE!
KLANG!
BREET!
OH! HOW UNDIGNIFIED!
KLONG
6

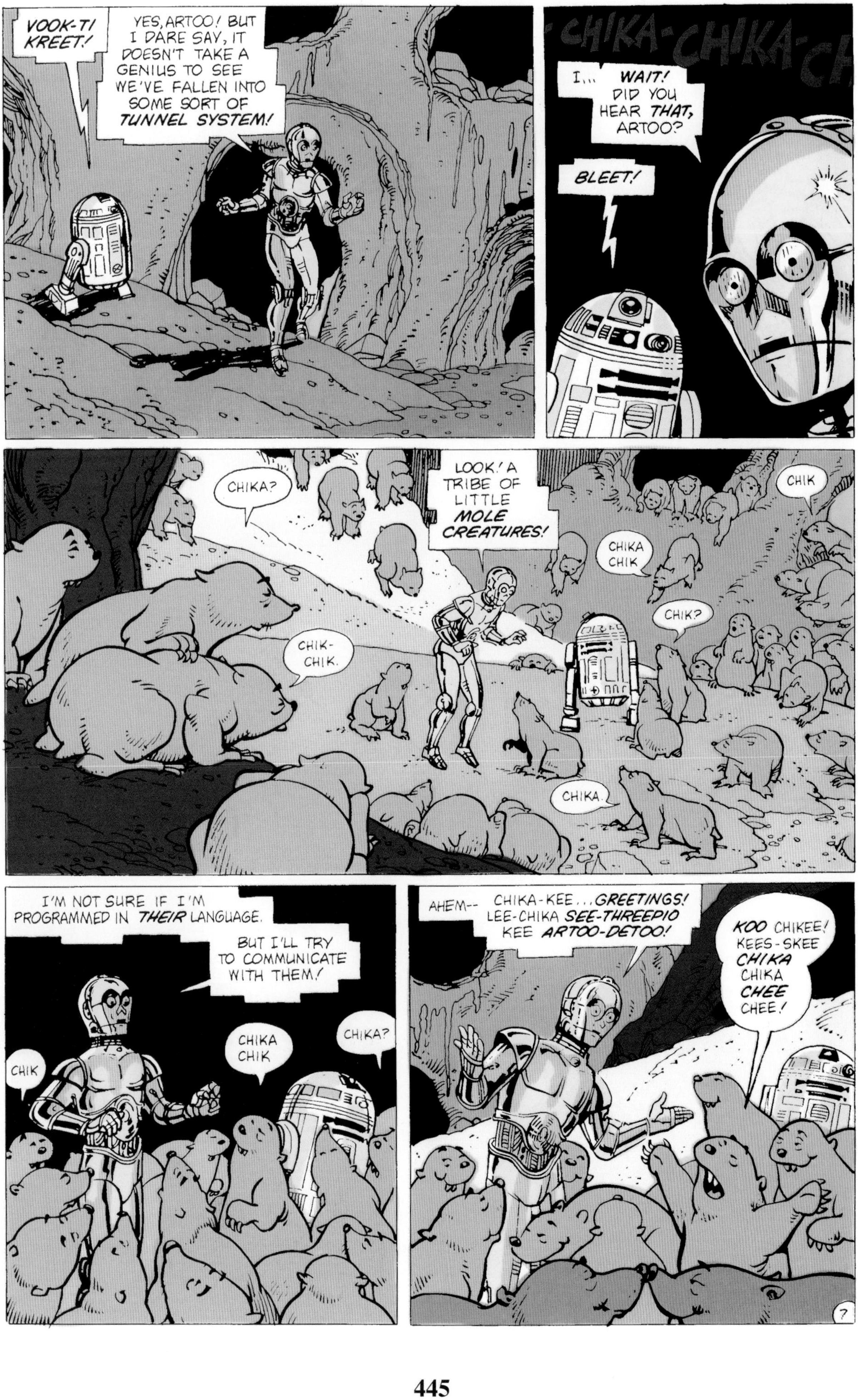
VOOK-TI KREET!
YES, ARTOO! BUT I DARE SAY, IT DOESN'T TAKE A GENIUS TO SEE WE'VE FALLEN INTO SOME SORT OF TUNNEL SYSTEM!
CHIKA-CHIKA-CH
I... WAIT! DID YOU HEAR THAT, ARTOO?
BLEET!
CHIKA?
LOOK! A TRIBE OF LITTLE MOLE CREATURES!
CHIK
CHIKA CHIK
CHIK?
CHIK-CHIK.
CHIKA.
I'M NOT SURE IF I'M PROGRAMMED IN THEIR LANGUAGE.
BUT I'LL TRY TO COMMUNICATE WITH THEM!
CHIK
CHIKA CHIK
CHIKA?
AHEM-- CHIKA-KEE...GREETINGS! LEE-CHIKA SEE-THREEPIO KEE ARTOO-DETOO!
KOO CHIKEE! KEES-SKEE CHIKA CHIKA CHEE CHEE!
7

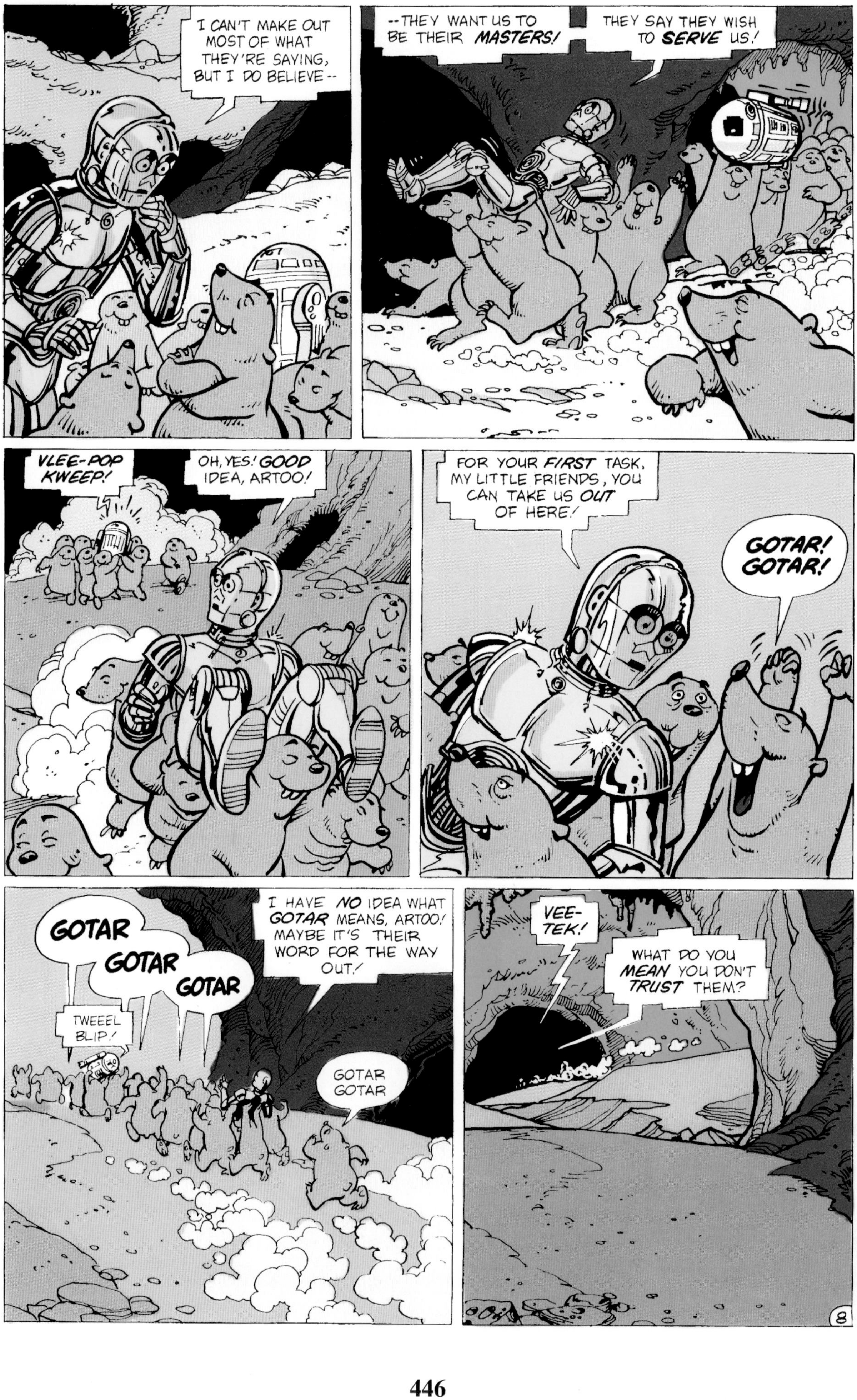

I CAN'T MAKE OUT MOST OF WHAT THEY'RE SAYING, BUT I DO BELIEVE --
--THEY WANT US TO BE THEIR MASTERS!
THEY SAY THEY WISH TO SERVE US!
VLEE-POP KWEEP!
OH, YES! GOOD IDEA, ARTOO!
FOR YOUR FIRST TASK, MY LITTLE FRIENDS, YOU CAN TAKE US OUT OF HERE!
GOTAR! GOTAR!
GOTAR
GOTAR
GOTAR
TWEEEL BLIP!
I HAVE NO IDEA WHAT GOTAR MEANS, ARTOO! MAYBE IT'S THEIR WORD FOR THE WAY OUT!
GOTAR GOTAR
VEE-TEK!
WHAT DO YOU MEAN YOU DON'T TRUST THEM?
8

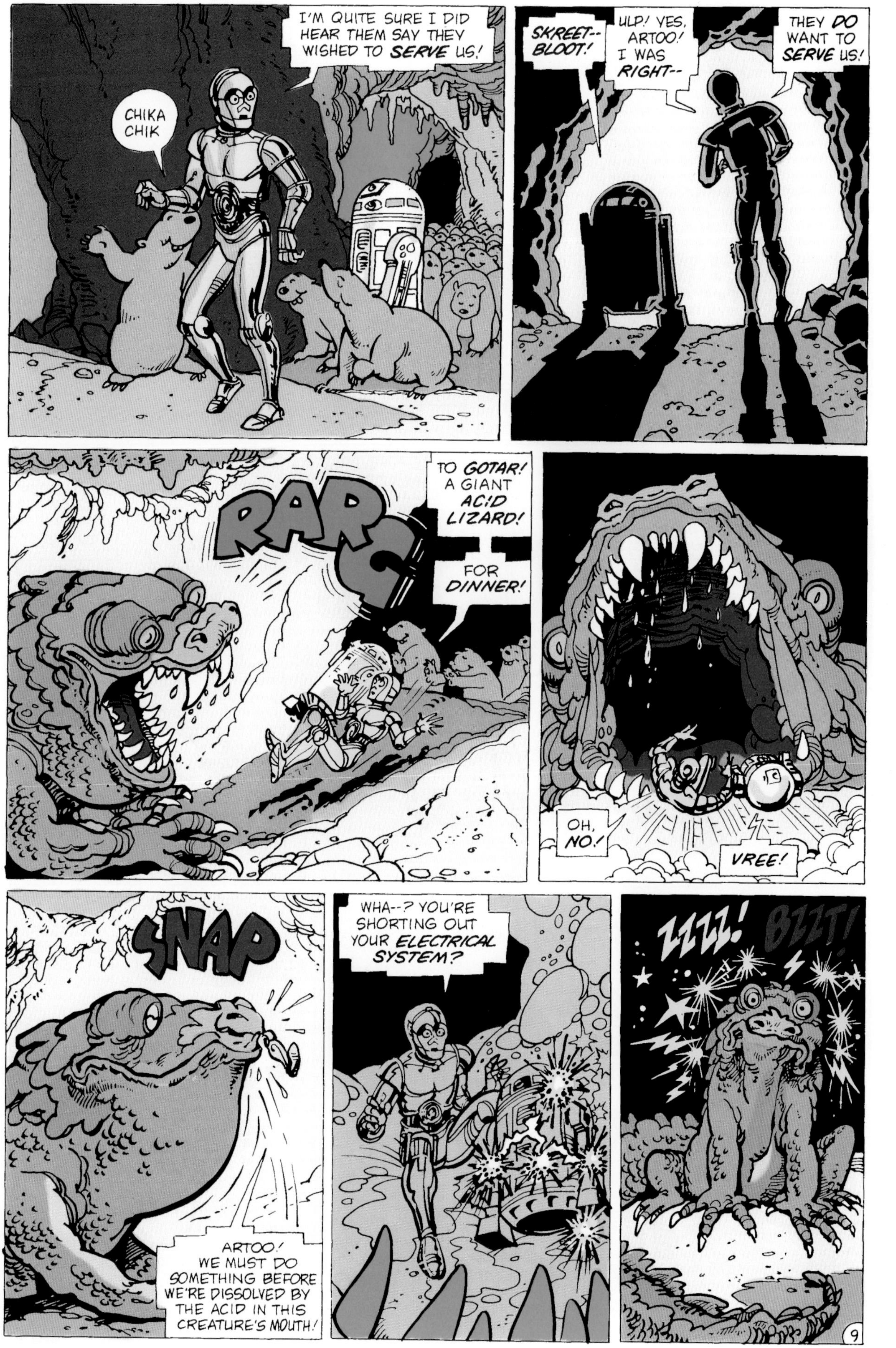

I'M QUITE SURE I DID HEAR THEM SAY THEY WISHED TO **SERVE** US!
CHIKA CHIK
SKREET-- BLOOT!
ULP! YES, ARTOO! I WAS **RIGHT--**
THEY **DO** WANT TO **SERVE** US!
RARG
TO **GOTAR!** A GIANT **ACID LIZARD!**
FOR **DINNER!**
OH, **NO!**
VREE!
SNAP
ARTOO! WE MUST DO SOMETHING BEFORE WE'RE DISSOLVED BY THE ACID IN THIS CREATURE'S MOUTH!
WHA--? YOU'RE SHORTING OUT YOUR **ELECTRICAL SYSTEM?**
ZZZZ! BZZT!
9

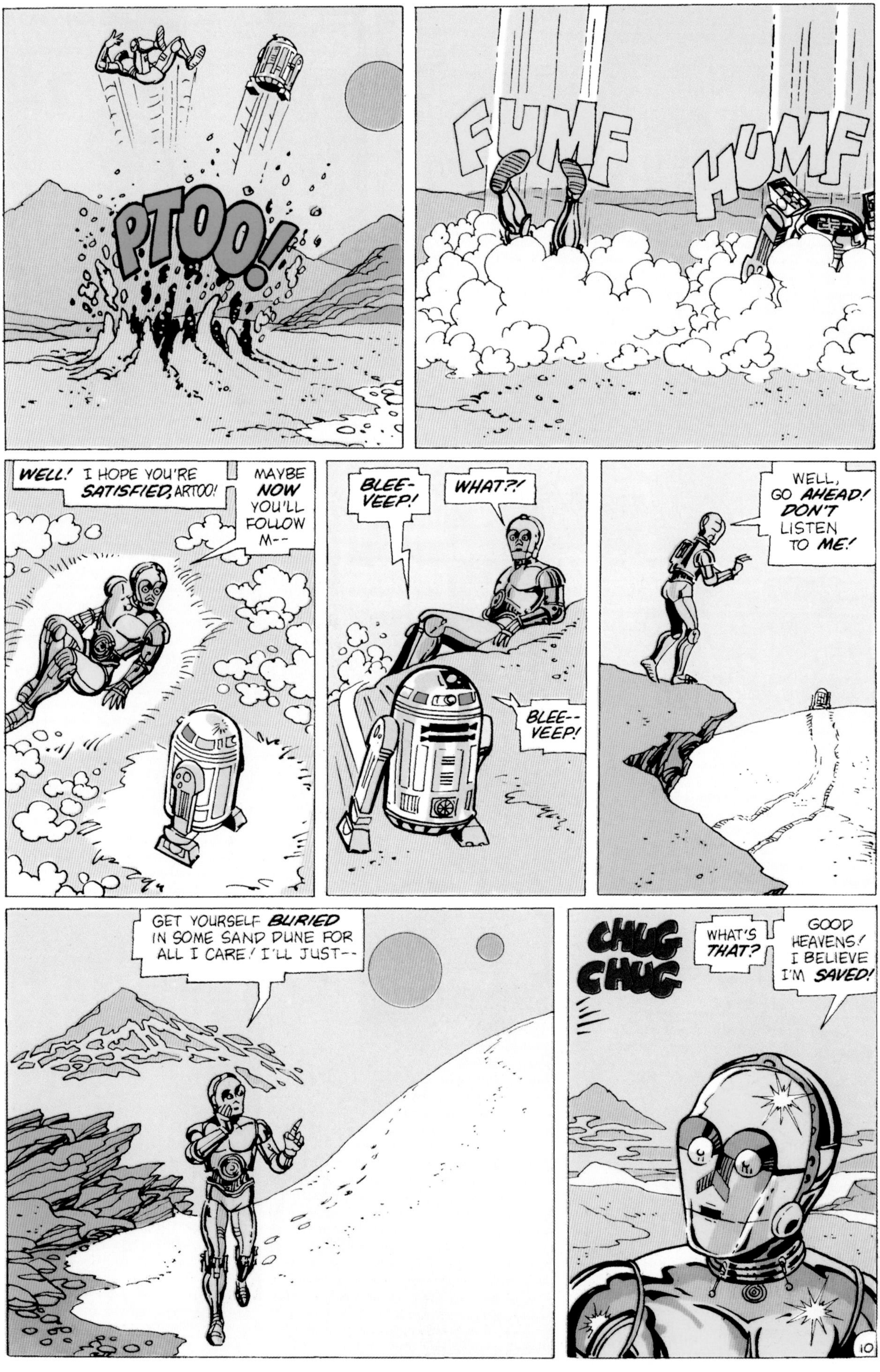
PTOO!
FUMF
HUMF
WELL! I HOPE YOU'RE SATISFIED, ARTOO!
MAYBE NOW YOU'LL FOLLOW M--
BLEE-VEEP!
WHAT?!
BLEE--VEEP!
WELL, GO AHEAD! DON'T LISTEN TO ME!
GET YOURSELF BURIED IN SOME SAND DUNE FOR ALL I CARE! I'LL JUST--
CHUG CHUG
WHAT'S THAT?
GOOD HEAVENS! I BELIEVE I'M SAVED!
10

AS A LUMBERING LAND TRANSPORT SLOWLY APPROACHES THREEPIO...

RUMBLE RUMB

I'M *SAVED!* I'M *SAVED!*

GWEE, ZOOOK!

I--

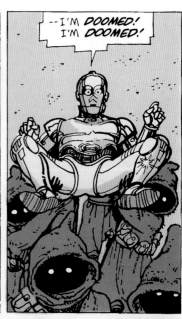

--I'M *DOOMED!* I'M *DOOMED!*

OH, *DEAR!* CAPTURED BY *JAWAS!* THE MOST DISGUSTING LITTLE DESERT RATS IN THE GALAXY!

AT LEAST ARTOO HAS ESCAPED THIS *HUMILIATION!*

BEEP VEEP

VREEE!

WHA--? THAT *VOICE!*

THWOONG

ARTOO-DETOO!

PLOOT-- DEEK!

KLONG

DON'T BE SILLY, ARTOO! OF COURSE I'M *GLAD* TO SEE YOU!

BUT I AM *DISAPPOINTED* THAT YOU WERE CAPTURED SO *EASILY!*

PLEET-- TIK!

KLAK KLAK

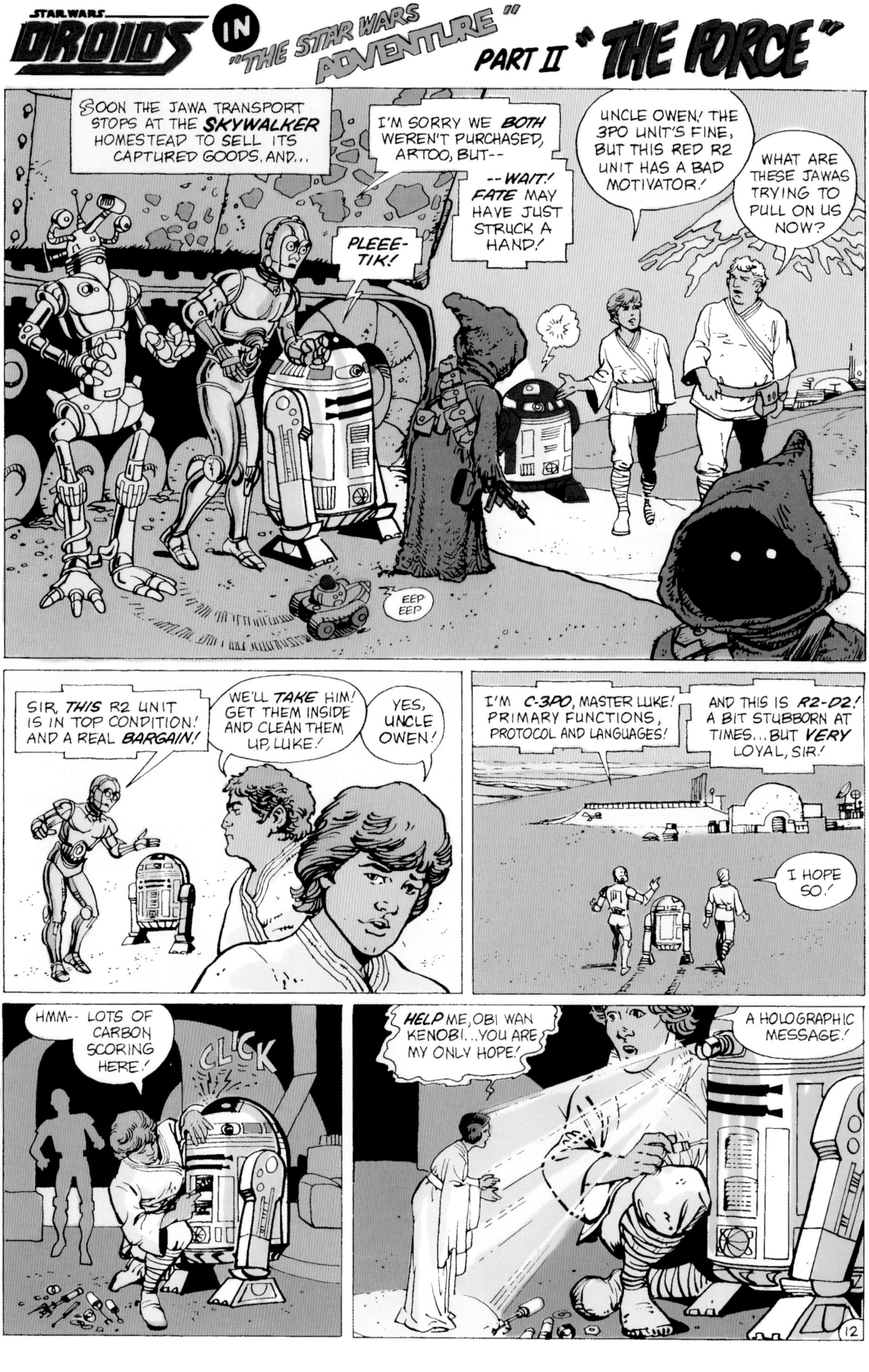
STAR WARS DROIDS IN "THE STAR WARS ADVENTURE" PART II "THE FORCE"
SOON THE JAWA TRANSPORT STOPS AT THE SKYWALKER HOMESTEAD TO SELL ITS CAPTURED GOODS, AND...
I'M SORRY WE BOTH WEREN'T PURCHASED, ARTOO, BUT--
--WAIT! FATE MAY HAVE JUST STRUCK A HAND!
PLEEE-TIK!
UNCLE OWEN! THE 3PO UNIT'S FINE, BUT THIS RED R2 UNIT HAS A BAD MOTIVATOR!
WHAT ARE THESE JAWAS TRYING TO PULL ON US NOW?
EEP EEP
SIR, THIS R2 UNIT IS IN TOP CONDITION! AND A REAL BARGAIN!
WE'LL TAKE HIM! GET THEM INSIDE AND CLEAN THEM UP, LUKE!
YES, UNCLE OWEN!
I'M C-3PO, MASTER LUKE! PRIMARY FUNCTIONS, PROTOCOL AND LANGUAGES!
AND THIS IS R2-D2! A BIT STUBBORN AT TIMES... BUT VERY LOYAL, SIR!
I HOPE SO!
HMM-- LOTS OF CARBON SCORING HERE!
CLICK
HELP ME, OBI WAN KENOBI... YOU ARE MY ONLY HOPE!
A HOLOGRAPHIC MESSAGE!
12

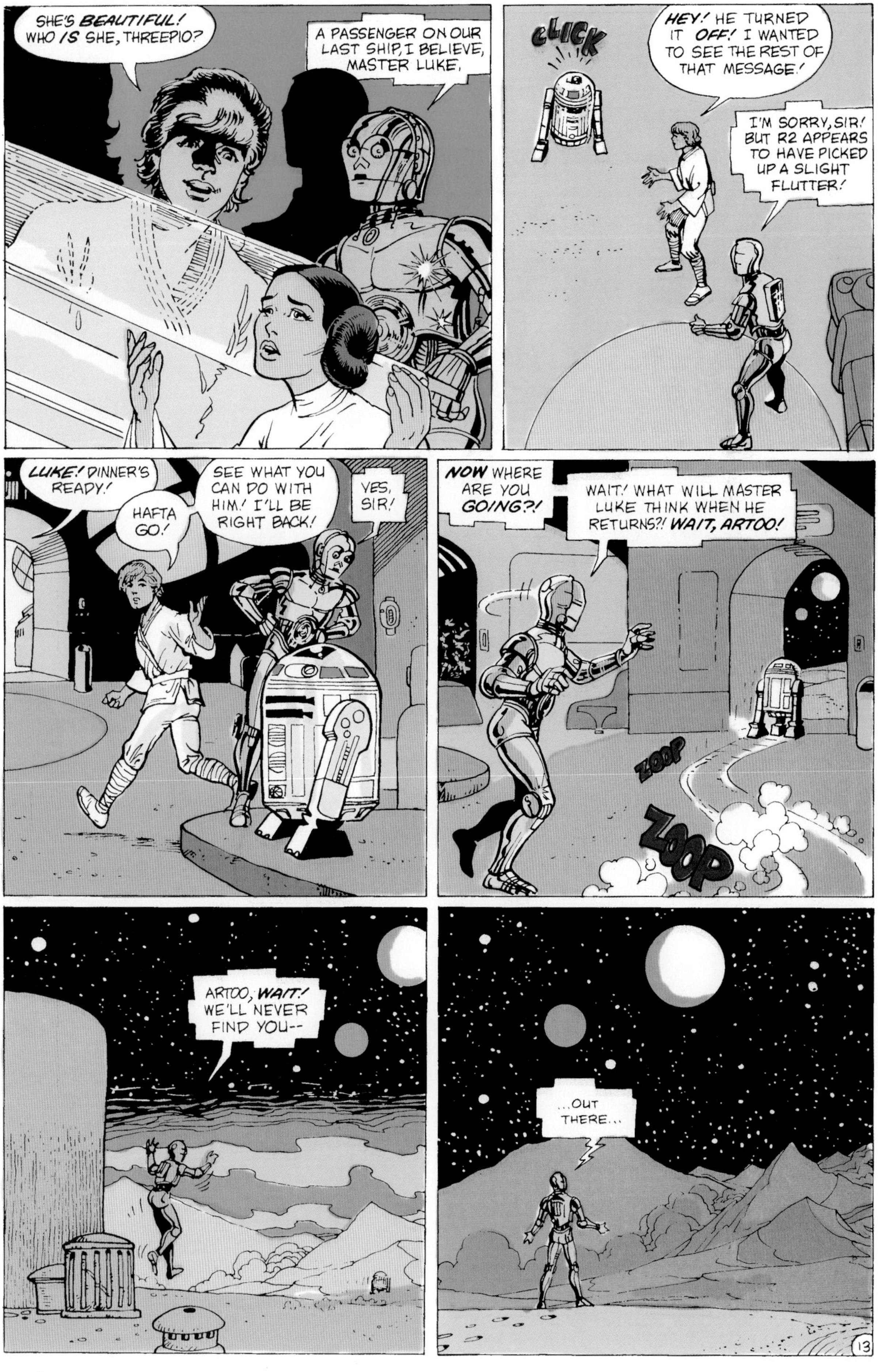
SHE'S BEAUTIFUL! WHO IS SHE, THREEPIO?
A PASSENGER ON OUR LAST SHIP, I BELIEVE, MASTER LUKE.
CLICK
HEY! HE TURNED IT OFF! I WANTED TO SEE THE REST OF THAT MESSAGE!
I'M SORRY, SIR! BUT R2 APPEARS TO HAVE PICKED UP A SLIGHT FLUTTER!
LUKE! DINNER'S READY!
HAFTA GO!
SEE WHAT YOU CAN DO WITH HIM! I'LL BE RIGHT BACK!
YES, SIR!
NOW WHERE ARE YOU GOING?!
WAIT! WHAT WILL MASTER LUKE THINK WHEN HE RETURNS?! WAIT, ARTOO!
ZOOP
ZOOP
ARTOO, WAIT! WE'LL NEVER FIND YOU--
...OUT THERE...
13

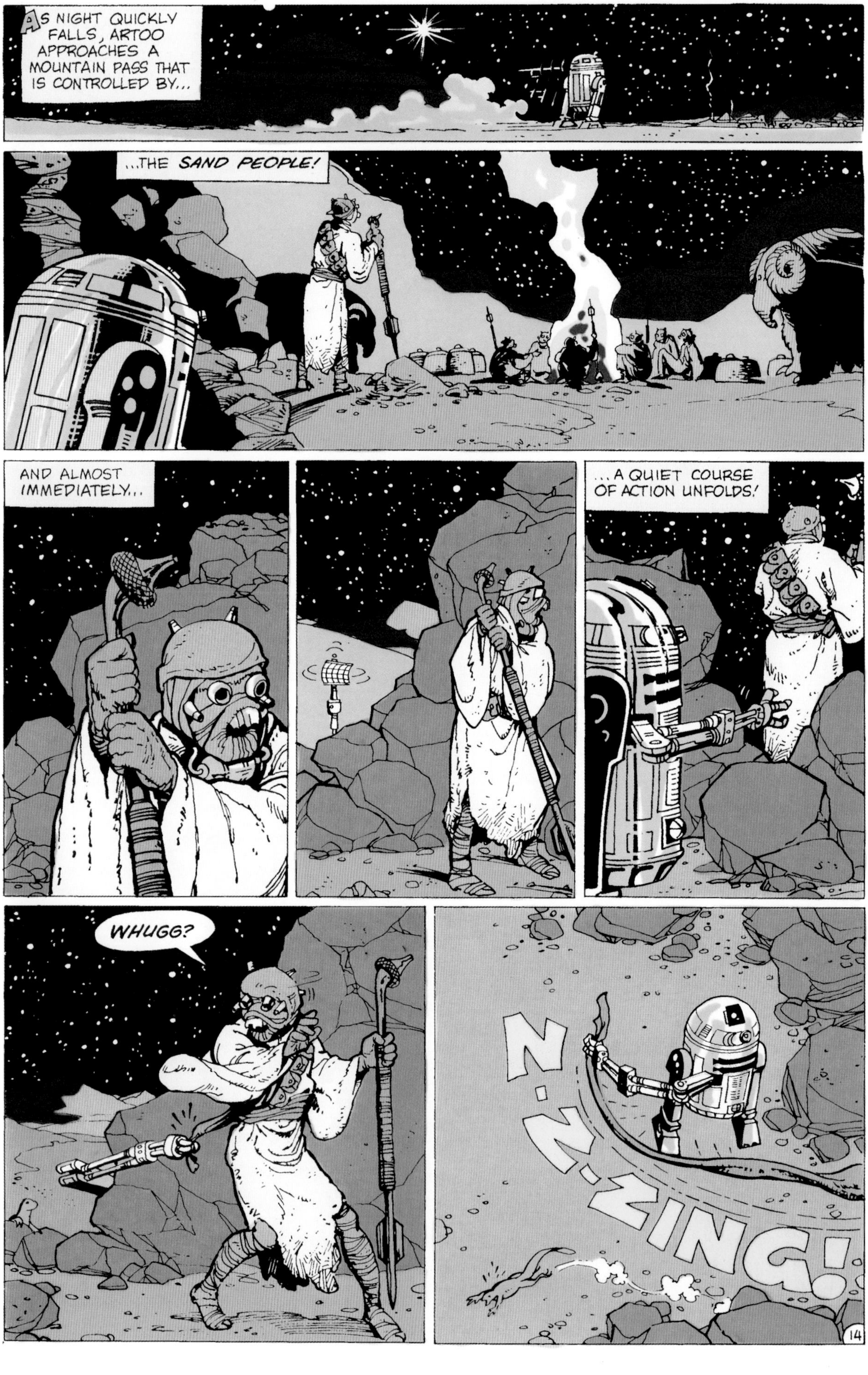

AS NIGHT QUICKLY FALLS, ARTOO APPROACHES A MOUNTAIN PASS THAT IS CONTROLLED BY...
...THE SAND PEOPLE!
AND ALMOST IMMEDIATELY...
...A QUIET COURSE OF ACTION UNFOLDS!
WHUGG?
N-N-N-ZING!
14

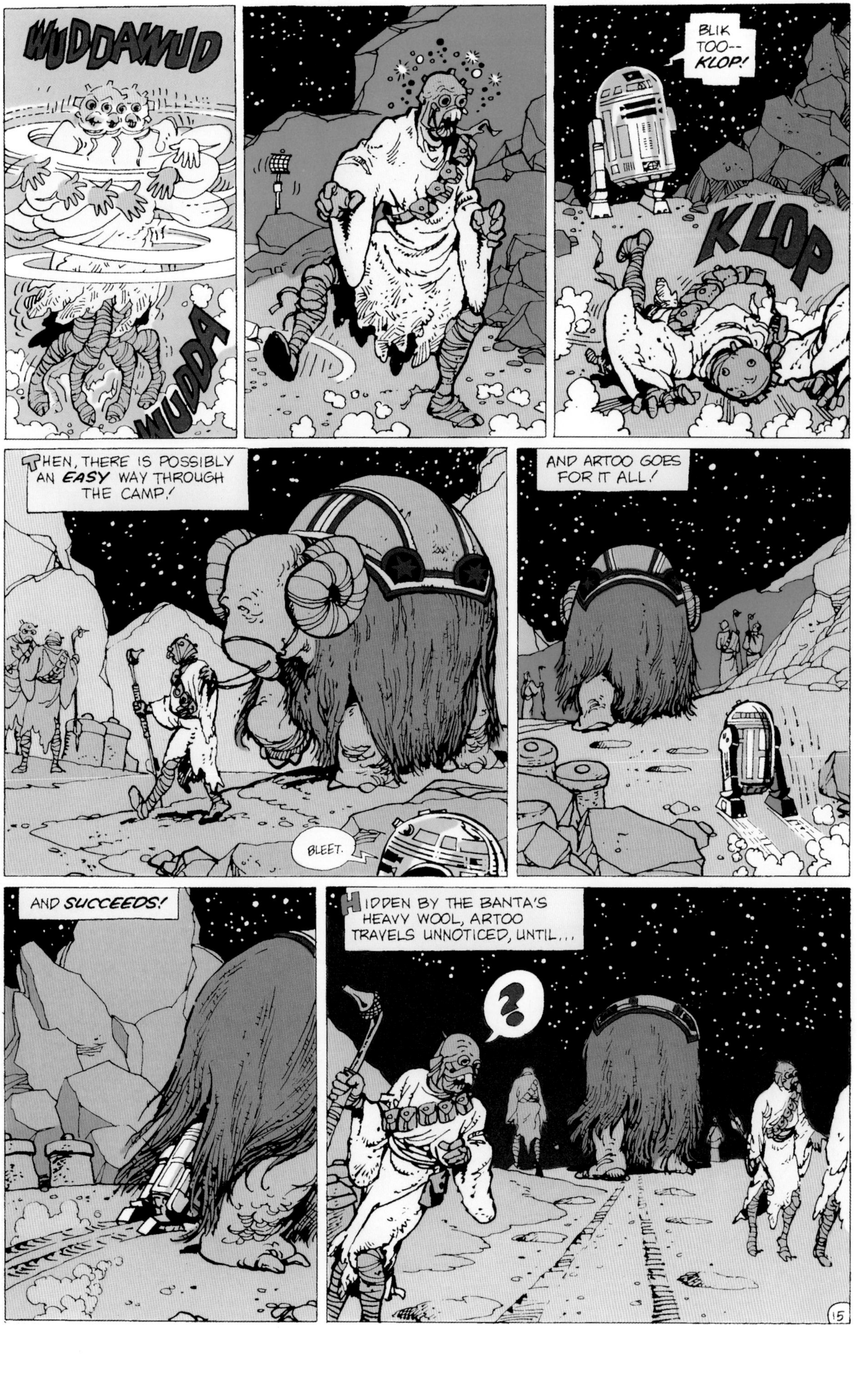
WUDDAWUD
WUDDA
BLIK TOO-- KLOP!
KLOP
THEN, THERE IS POSSIBLY AN EASY WAY THROUGH THE CAMP!
BLEET.
AND ARTOO GOES FOR IT ALL!
AND SUCCEEDS!
HIDDEN BY THE BANTA'S HEAVY WOOL, ARTOO TRAVELS UNNOTICED, UNTIL...
?
15

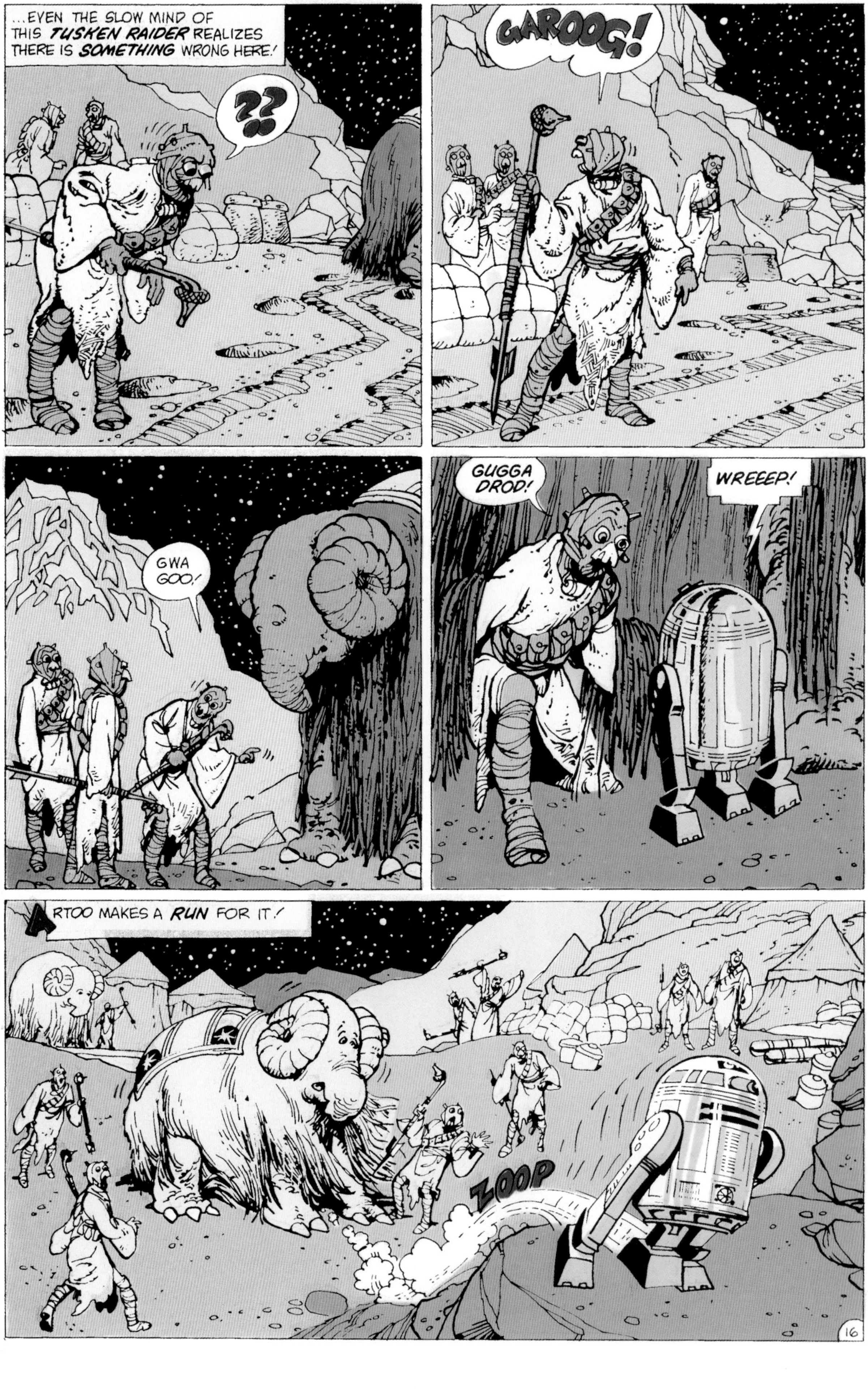
...EVEN THE SLOW MIND OF THIS TUSKEN RAIDER REALIZES THERE IS SOMETHING WRONG HERE!
??
GAROOG!
GWA GOO!
GUGGA DROD!
WREEEP!
ARTOO MAKES A RUN FOR IT!
ZOOP
16

AND THEN *STOPS!*

ARRUGKA
AGGH HAJ HAROOM

SKEEK!

REACHING INTO HIS MEMORY BANK, THE LITTLE DROID PROJECTS AN IMAGE:

RAZA BAZA RA--!!

KLIK

AN *AWESOME IMAGE* TO THE SAND PEOPLE!

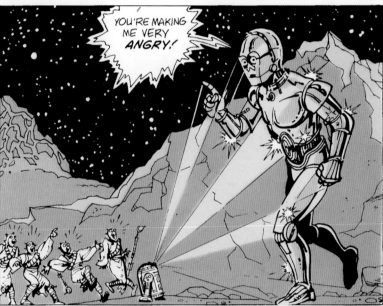

YOU'RE MAKING ME VERY *ANGRY!*

SENDING THE TERRIFIED SAND PEOPLE *SCAMPERING* INTO THE NIGHT!

KLIK!

AND ALLOWING THE SMALL DROID TO *CONTINUE* ON HIS *DESPERATE MISSION!*

17

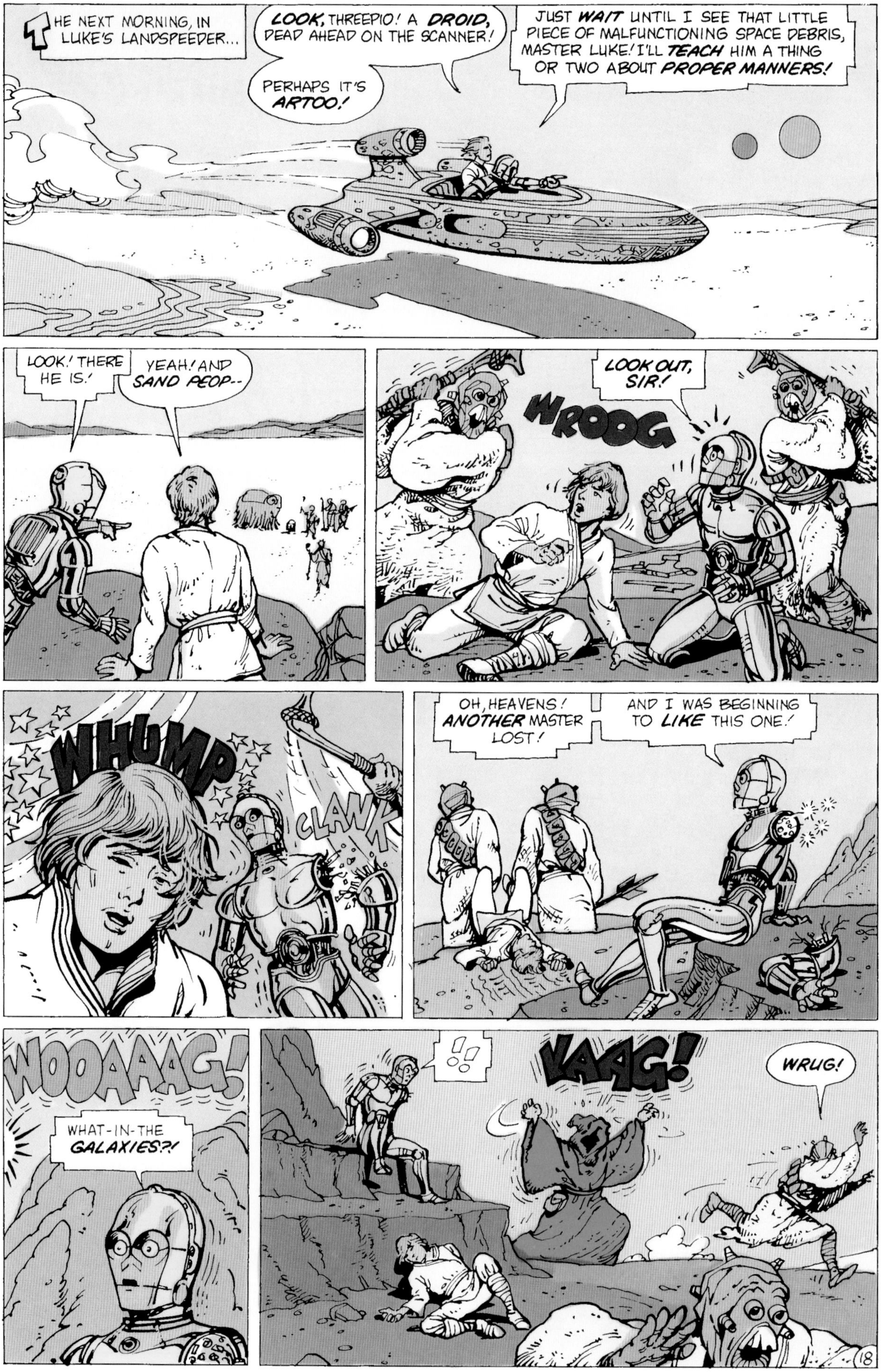

THE NEXT MORNING, IN LUKE'S LANDSPEEDER...
LOOK, THREEPIO! A DROID, DEAD AHEAD ON THE SCANNER!
PERHAPS IT'S ARTOO!
JUST WAIT UNTIL I SEE THAT LITTLE PIECE OF MALFUNCTIONING SPACE DEBRIS, MASTER LUKE! I'LL TEACH HIM A THING OR TWO ABOUT PROPER MANNERS!
LOOK! THERE HE IS!
YEAH! AND SAND PEOP--
WROOG
LOOK OUT, SIR!
WHUMP
CLANK
OH, HEAVENS! ANOTHER MASTER LOST!
AND I WAS BEGINNING TO LIKE THIS ONE!
WOOAAAG!
WHAT-IN-THE GALAXIES?!
!!
VAAG!
WRUG!
18

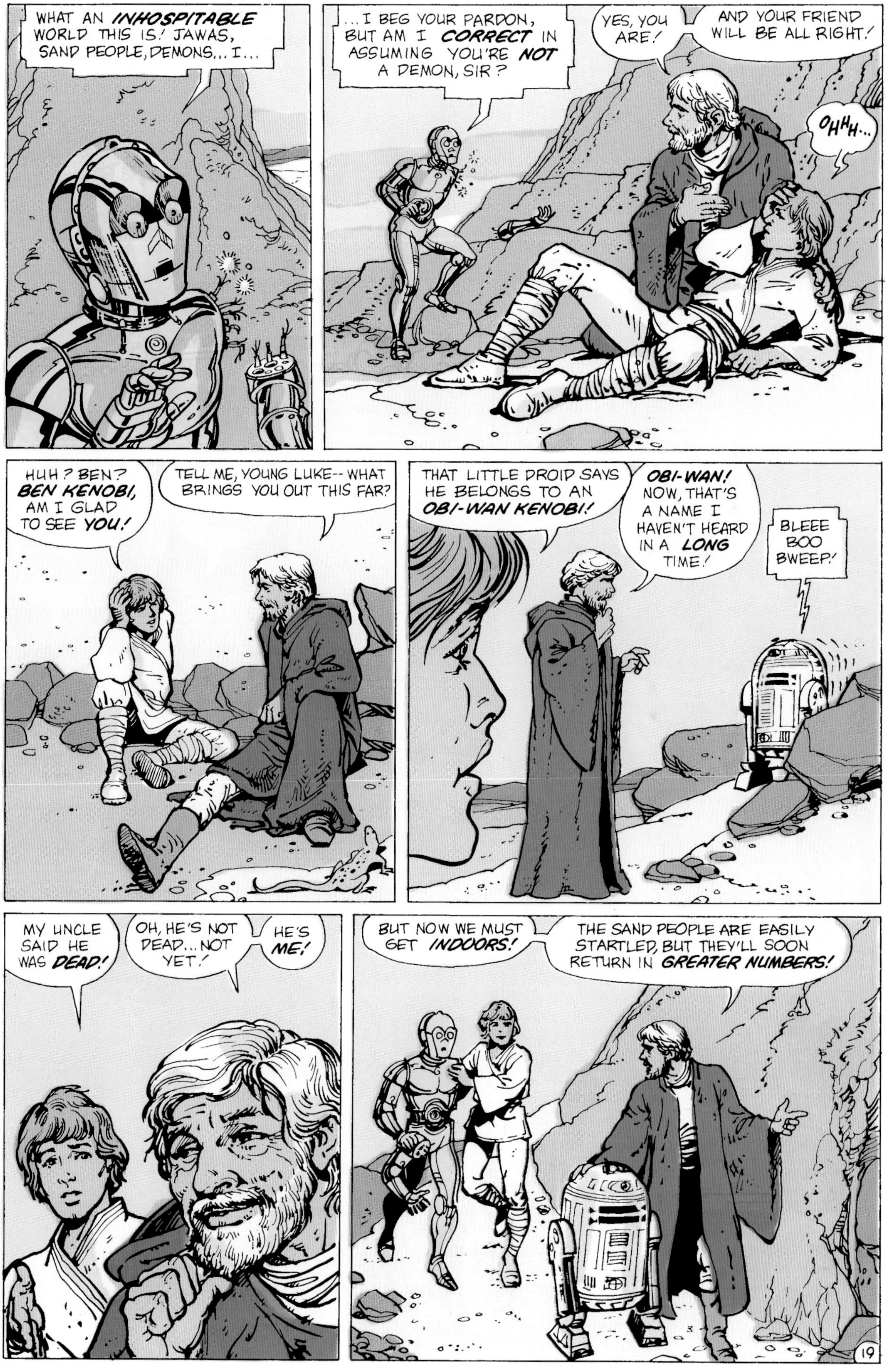

WHAT AN INHOSPITABLE WORLD THIS IS! JAWAS, SAND PEOPLE, DEMONS... I...
...I BEG YOUR PARDON, BUT AM I CORRECT IN ASSUMING YOU'RE NOT A DEMON, SIR?
YES, YOU ARE!
AND YOUR FRIEND WILL BE ALL RIGHT!
OHHH...
HUH? BEN? BEN KENOBI, AM I GLAD TO SEE YOU!
TELL ME, YOUNG LUKE-- WHAT BRINGS YOU OUT THIS FAR?
THAT LITTLE DROID SAYS HE BELONGS TO AN OBI-WAN KENOBI!
OBI-WAN! NOW, THAT'S A NAME I HAVEN'T HEARD IN A LONG TIME!
BLEEE BOO BWEEP!
MY UNCLE SAID HE WAS DEAD!
OH, HE'S NOT DEAD... NOT YET!
HE'S ME!
BUT NOW WE MUST GET INDOORS!
THE SAND PEOPLE ARE EASILY STARTLED, BUT THEY'LL SOON RETURN IN GREATER NUMBERS!
19

I FEEL POSITIVELY *DREADFUL* ABOUT THIS WHOLE TURN OF EVENTS, MASTER LUKE!

RELAX, THREEPIO! YOU'LL FEEL BETTER ONCE I GET YOU BACK IN *ONE PIECE!*

SOON--

MASTER LUKE WAS RIGHT! I *DO* FEEL BETTER!

YOU FOUGHT IN THE *CLONE WARS,* BEN?

INDEED! I WAS A *JEDI KNIGHT,* THE SAME AS YOUR *FATHER!* AND HE WAS A GOOD FRIEND!

YOUR FATHER WANTED YOU TO HAVE THIS WHEN YOU WERE OLD ENOUGH!

WHAT *IS* IT?

HIS *LIGHT SABER!* AN ELEGANT WEAPON OF A MORE CIVILIZED AGE!

CLICK

WZZZZ

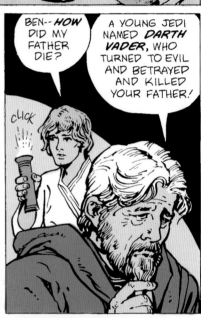

BEN-- *HOW* DID MY FATHER *DIE?*

A YOUNG JEDI NAMED *DARTH VADER,* WHO TURNED TO EVIL AND BETRAYED AND KILLED YOUR FATHER!

CLICK

VADER WAS SEDUCED BY THE DARK SIDE OF THE *"FORCE"!*

AND USED THIS GREAT *ENERGY FIELD,* CREATED BY ALL LIVING THINGS, FOR NAUGHT BUT *EVIL!*

BREEE BWOOO!

NOW LET'S SEE WHAT OUR LITTLE FRIEND WANTS TO *TELL* US!

WROOO VLEEPO BEEP!

CLICK!

20

458

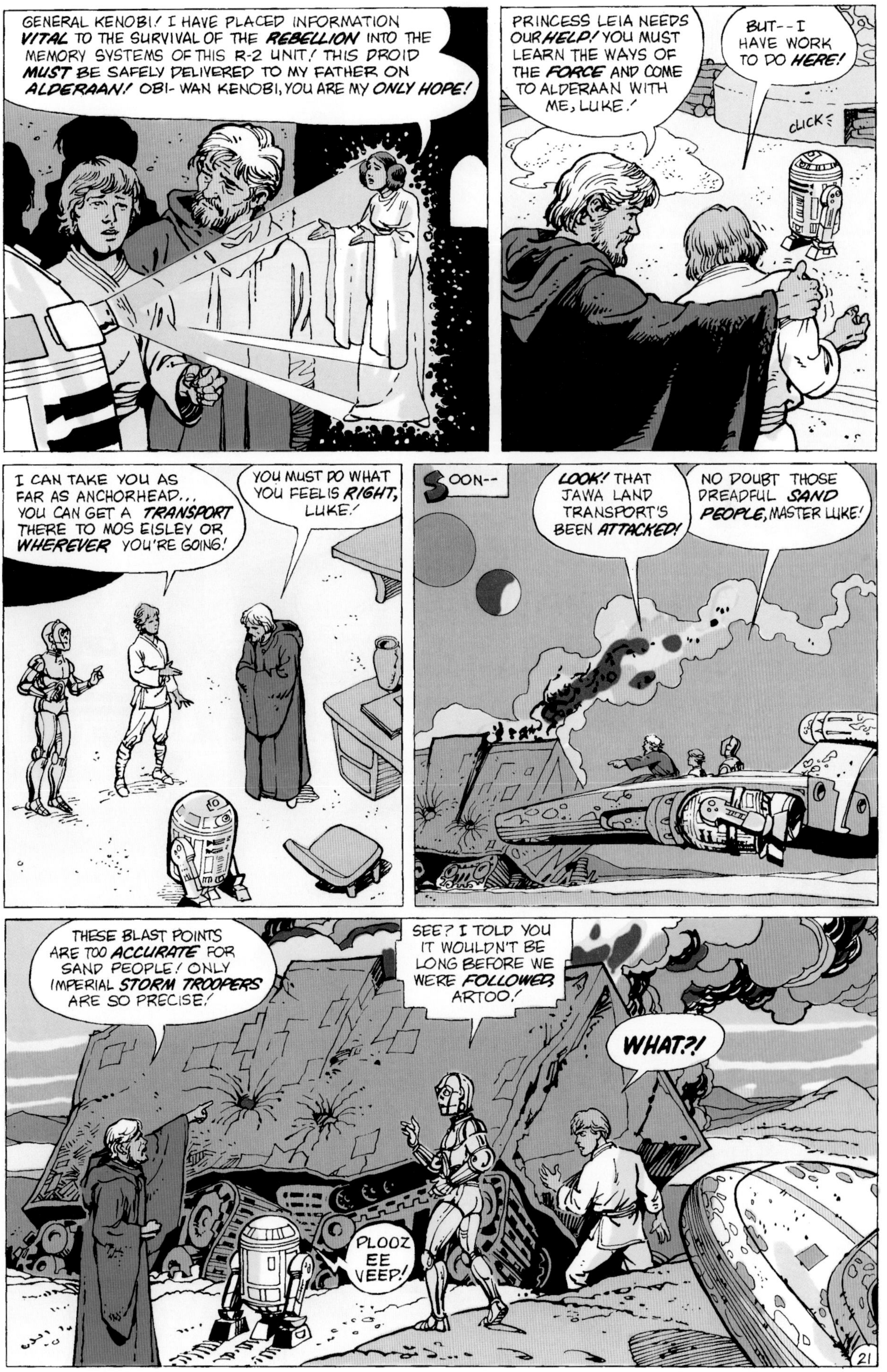
GENERAL KENOBI! I HAVE PLACED INFORMATION VITAL TO THE SURVIVAL OF THE REBELLION INTO THE MEMORY SYSTEMS OF THIS R-2 UNIT! THIS DROID MUST BE SAFELY DELIVERED TO MY FATHER ON ALDERAAN! OBI-WAN KENOBI, YOU ARE MY ONLY HOPE!
PRINCESS LEIA NEEDS OUR HELP! YOU MUST LEARN THE WAYS OF THE FORCE AND COME TO ALDERAAN WITH ME, LUKE!
BUT--I HAVE WORK TO DO HERE!
CLICK
I CAN TAKE YOU AS FAR AS ANCHORHEAD... YOU CAN GET A TRANSPORT THERE TO MOS EISLEY OR WHEREVER YOU'RE GOING!
YOU MUST DO WHAT YOU FEEL IS RIGHT, LUKE!
SOON--
LOOK! THAT JAWA LAND TRANSPORT'S BEEN ATTACKED!
NO DOUBT THOSE DREADFUL SAND PEOPLE, MASTER LUKE!
THESE BLAST POINTS ARE TOO ACCURATE FOR SAND PEOPLE! ONLY IMPERIAL STORM TROOPERS ARE SO PRECISE!
SEE? I TOLD YOU IT WOULDN'T BE LONG BEFORE WE WERE FOLLOWED, ARTOO!
WHAT?!
PLOOZ EE VEEP!
21

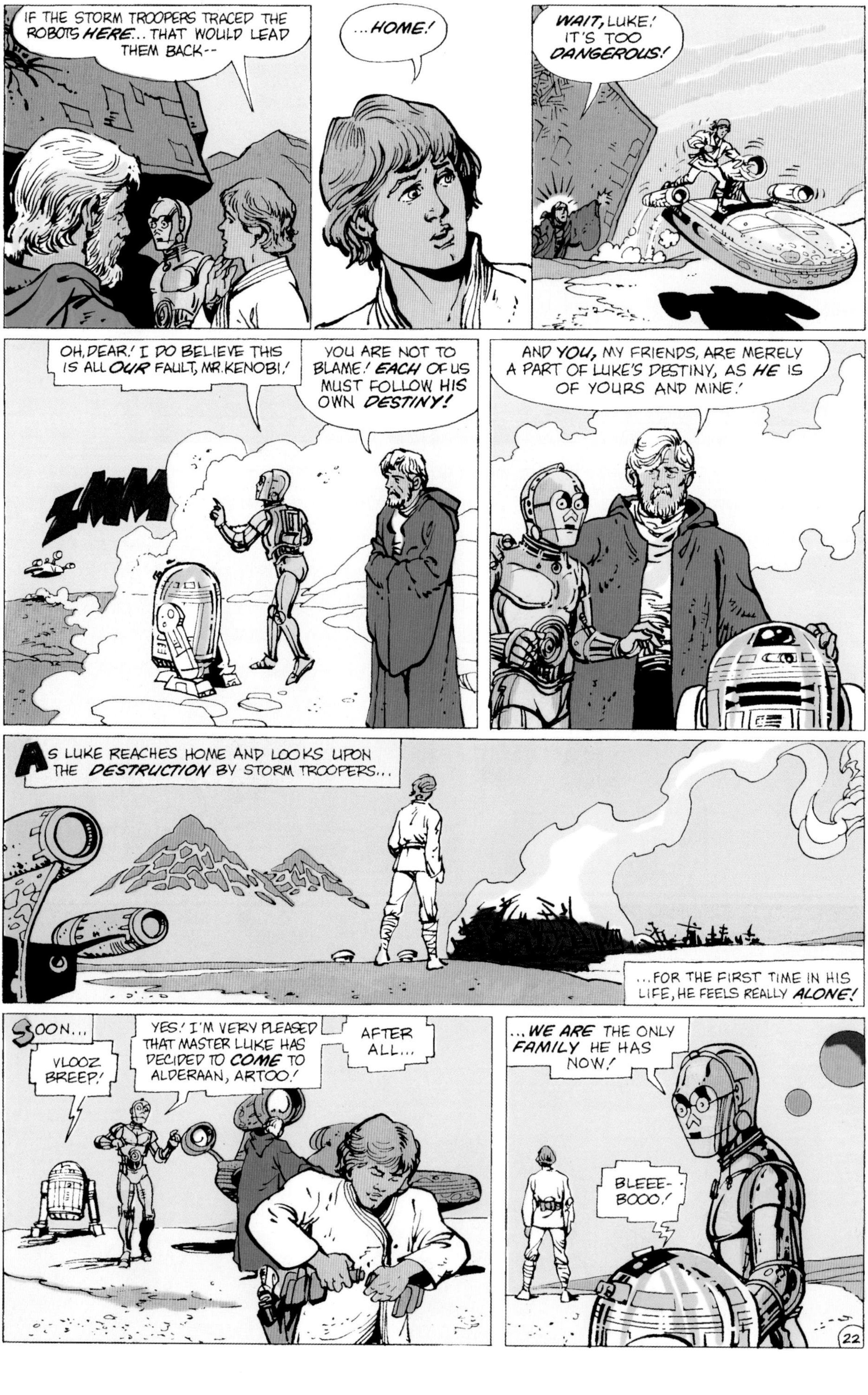
IF THE STORM TROOPERS TRACED THE ROBOTS HERE... THAT WOULD LEAD THEM BACK--
...HOME!
WAIT, LUKE! IT'S TOO DANGEROUS!
OH, DEAR! I DO BELIEVE THIS IS ALL OUR FAULT, MR. KENOBI!
YOU ARE NOT TO BLAME! EACH OF US MUST FOLLOW HIS OWN DESTINY!
ZMM
AND YOU, MY FRIENDS, ARE MERELY A PART OF LUKE'S DESTINY, AS HE IS OF YOURS AND MINE!
AS LUKE REACHES HOME AND LOOKS UPON THE DESTRUCTION BY STORM TROOPERS...
...FOR THE FIRST TIME IN HIS LIFE, HE FEELS REALLY ALONE!
SOON...
VLOOZ BREEP!
YES! I'M VERY PLEASED THAT MASTER LUKE HAS DECIDED TO COME TO ALDERAAN, ARTOO!
AFTER ALL...
...WE ARE THE ONLY FAMILY HE HAS NOW!
BLEEE-BOOO!
22

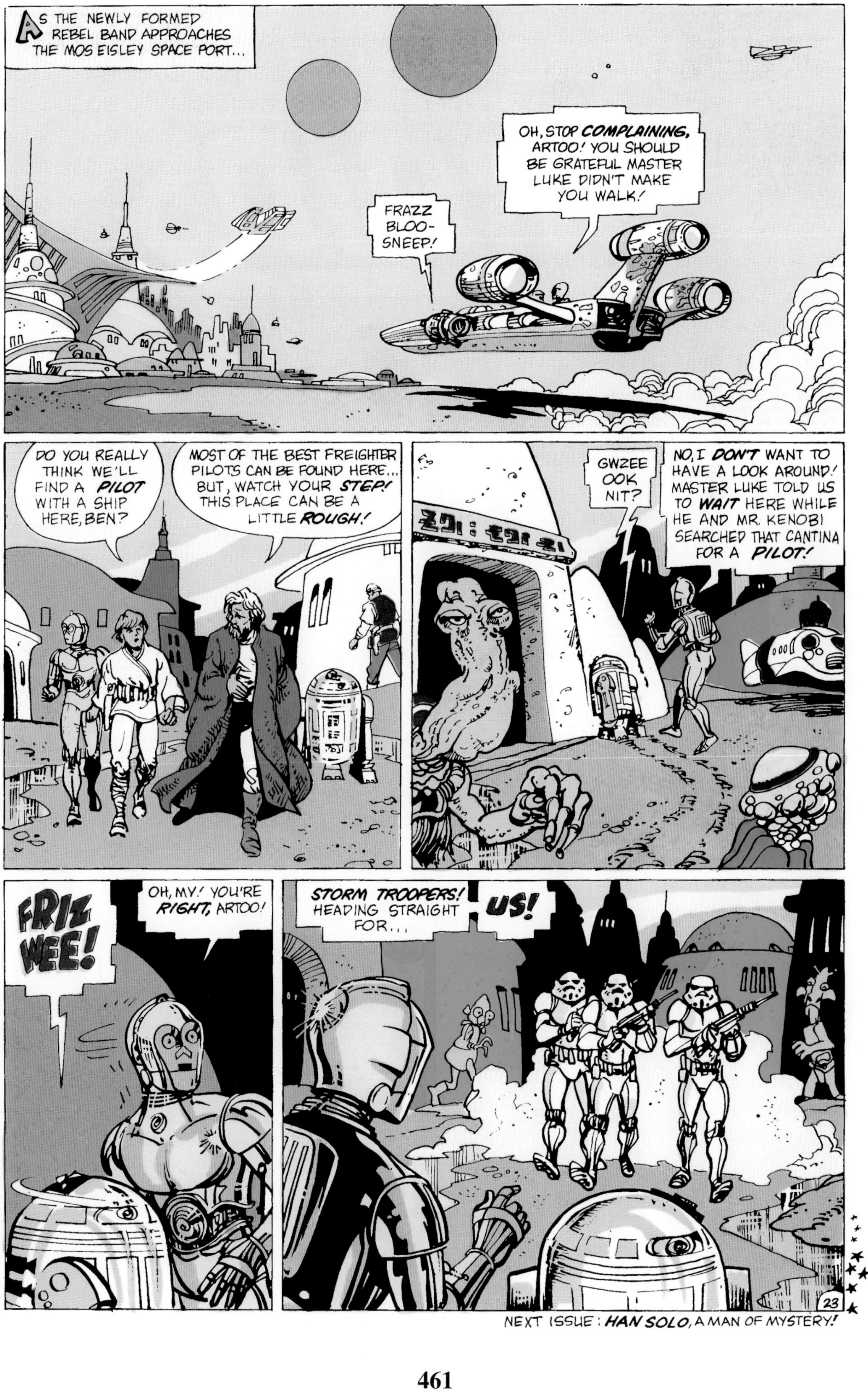
AS THE NEWLY FORMED REBEL BAND APPROACHES THE MOS EISLEY SPACE PORT...
OH, STOP COMPLAINING, ARTOO! YOU SHOULD BE GRATEFUL MASTER LUKE DIDN'T MAKE YOU WALK!
FRAZZ BLOO-SNEEP!
DO YOU REALLY THINK WE'LL FIND A PILOT WITH A SHIP HERE, BEN?
MOST OF THE BEST FREIGHTER PILOTS CAN BE FOUND HERE... BUT, WATCH YOUR STEP! THIS PLACE CAN BE A LITTLE ROUGH!
GWZEE OOK NIT?
NO, I DON'T WANT TO HAVE A LOOK AROUND! MASTER LUKE TOLD US TO WAIT HERE WHILE HE AND MR. KENOBI SEARCHED THAT CANTINA FOR A PILOT!
FRIZ WEE!
OH, MY! YOU'RE RIGHT, ARTOO!
STORM TROOPERS! HEADING STRAIGHT FOR...
US!
23

NEXT ISSUE: ***HAN SOLO***, A MAN OF MYSTERY!

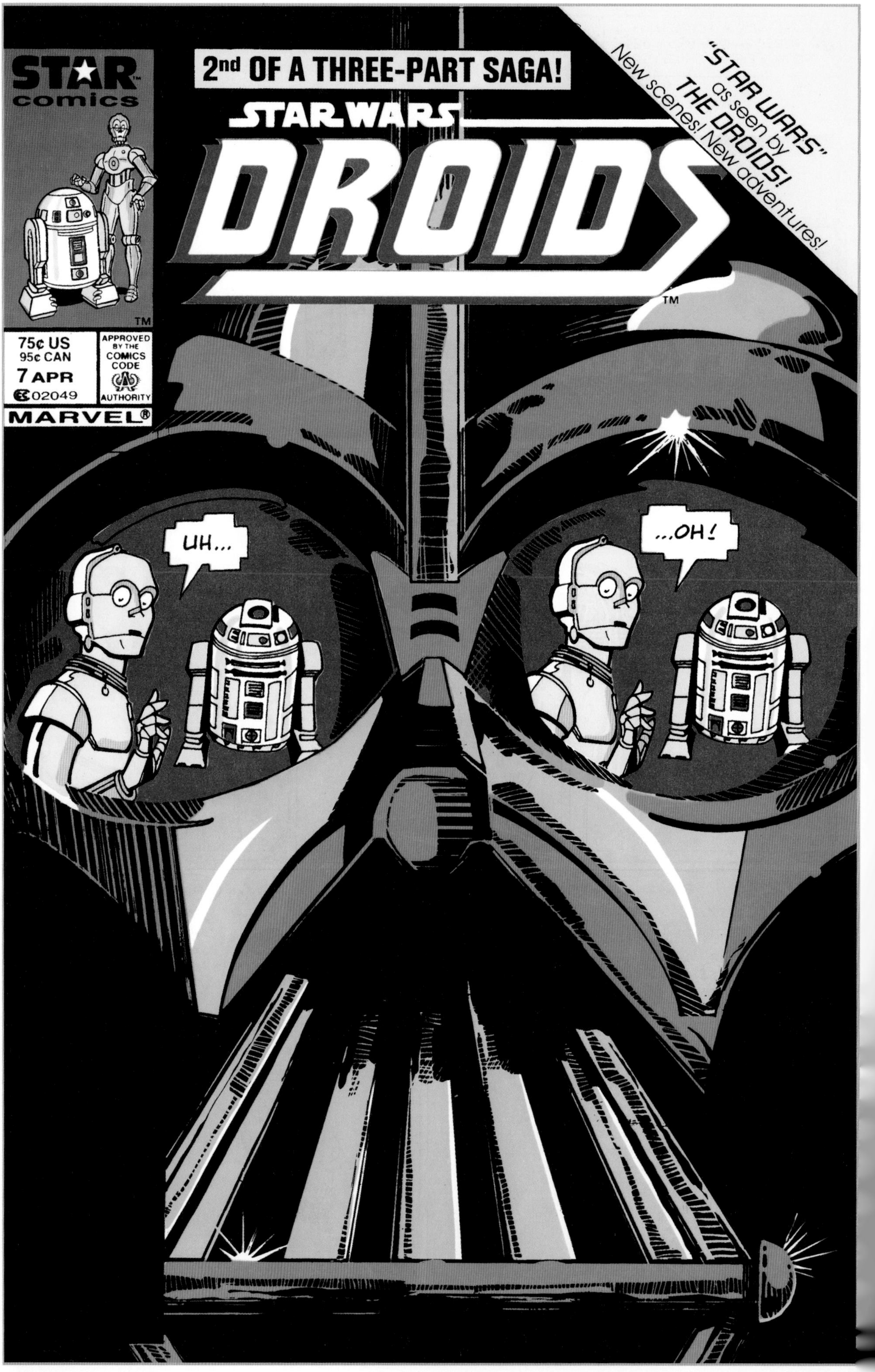
STAR comics
2nd OF A THREE-PART SAGA!
STAR WARS
DROIDS
"STAR WARS" as seen by THE DROIDS! New scenes! New adventures!
75¢ US
95¢ CAN
7 APR
02049
APPROVED BY THE COMICS CODE AUTHORITY
MARVEL
UH...
...OH!

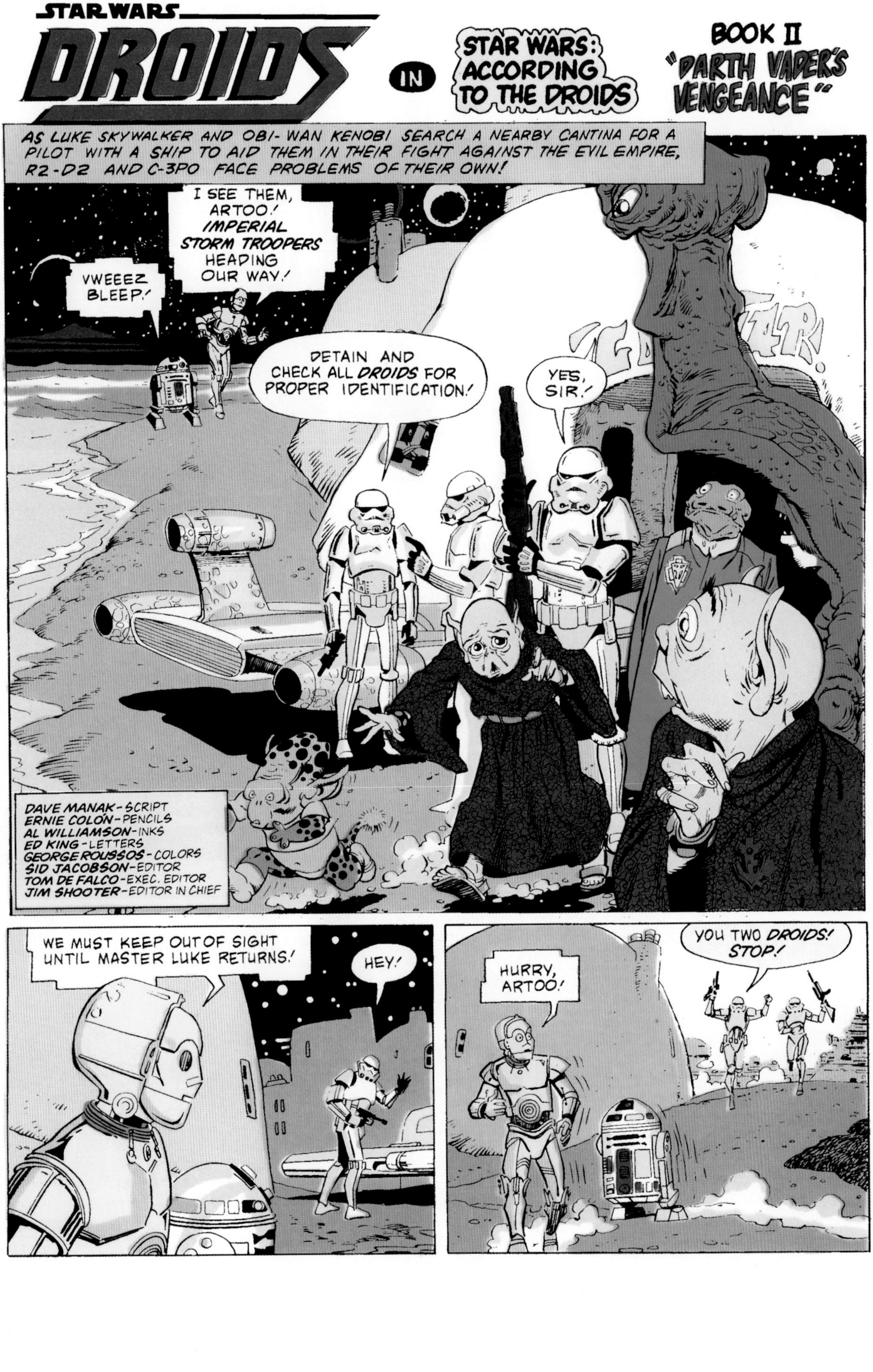
STAR WARS
DROIDS
IN
STAR WARS: ACCORDING TO THE DROIDS
BOOK II "DARTH VADER'S VENGEANCE"
AS LUKE SKYWALKER AND OBI-WAN KENOBI SEARCH A NEARBY CANTINA FOR A PILOT WITH A SHIP TO AID THEM IN THEIR FIGHT AGAINST THE EVIL EMPIRE, R2-D2 AND C-3PO FACE PROBLEMS OF THEIR OWN!
VWEEEZ BLEEP!
I SEE THEM, ARTOO! IMPERIAL STORM TROOPERS HEADING OUR WAY!
DETAIN AND CHECK ALL DROIDS FOR PROPER IDENTIFICATION!
YES, SIR!
DAVE MANAK-SCRIPT
ERNIE COLON-PENCILS
AL WILLIAMSON-INKS
ED KING-LETTERS
GEORGE ROUSSOS-COLORS
SID JACOBSON-EDITOR
TOM DE FALCO-EXEC. EDITOR
JIM SHOOTER-EDITOR IN CHIEF
WE MUST KEEP OUT OF SIGHT UNTIL MASTER LUKE RETURNS!
HEY!
HURRY, ARTOO!
YOU TWO DROIDS! STOP!

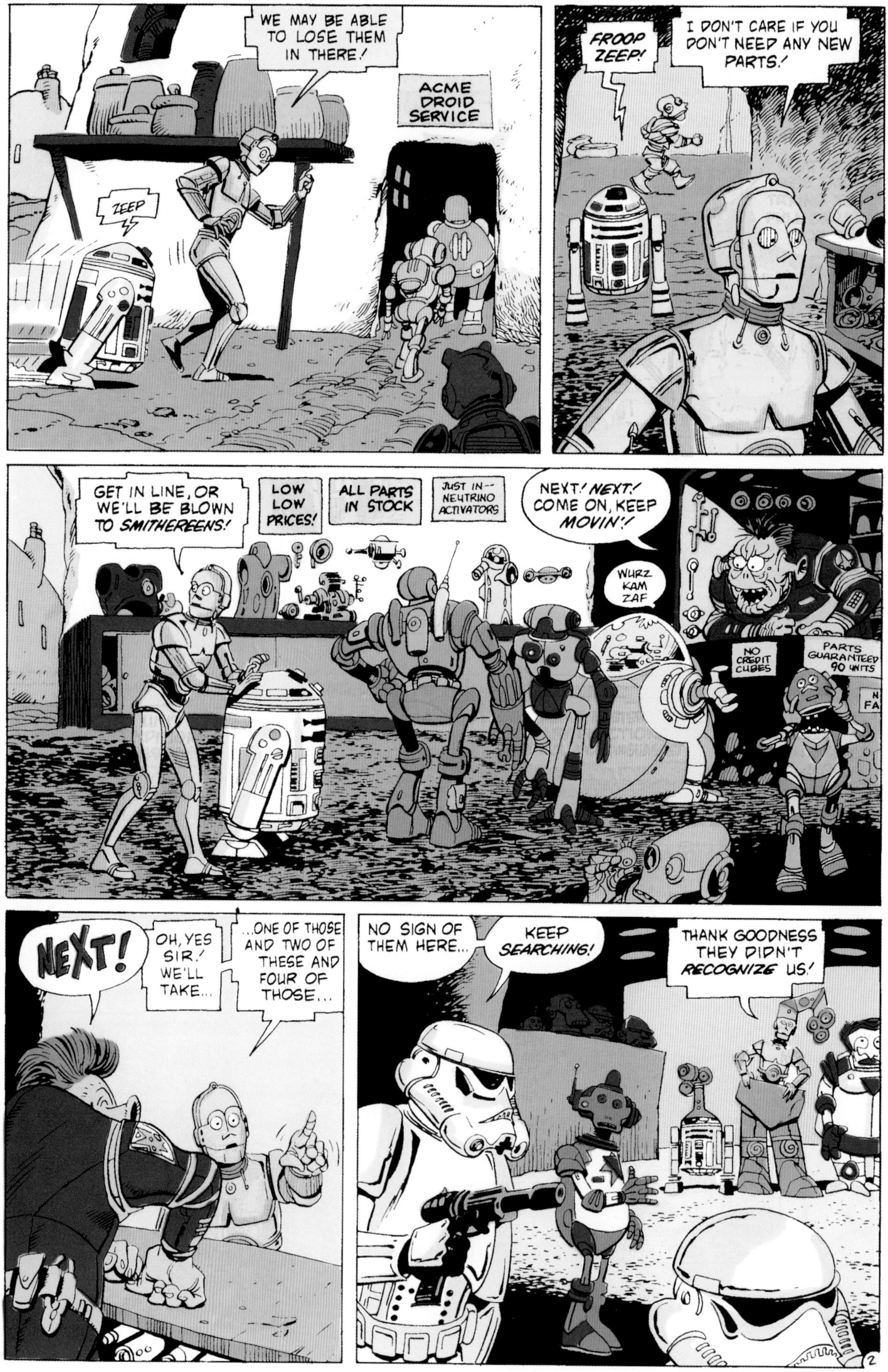
WE MAY BE ABLE TO LOSE THEM IN THERE!
ACME DROID SERVICE
ZEEP
FROOP ZEEP!
I DON'T CARE IF YOU DON'T NEED ANY NEW PARTS!
GET IN LINE, OR WE'LL BE BLOWN TO SMITHEREENS!
LOW LOW PRICES!
ALL PARTS IN STOCK
JUST IN-- NEUTRINO ACTIVATORS
NEXT! NEXT! COME ON, KEEP MOVIN'!
WURZ KAM ZAF
NO CREDIT CUBES
PARTS GUARANTEED 90 UNITS
NEXT!
OH, YES SIR! WE'LL TAKE...
...ONE OF THOSE AND TWO OF THESE AND FOUR OF THOSE...
NO SIGN OF THEM HERE...
KEEP SEARCHING!
THANK GOODNESS THEY DIDN'T RECOGNIZE US!
2

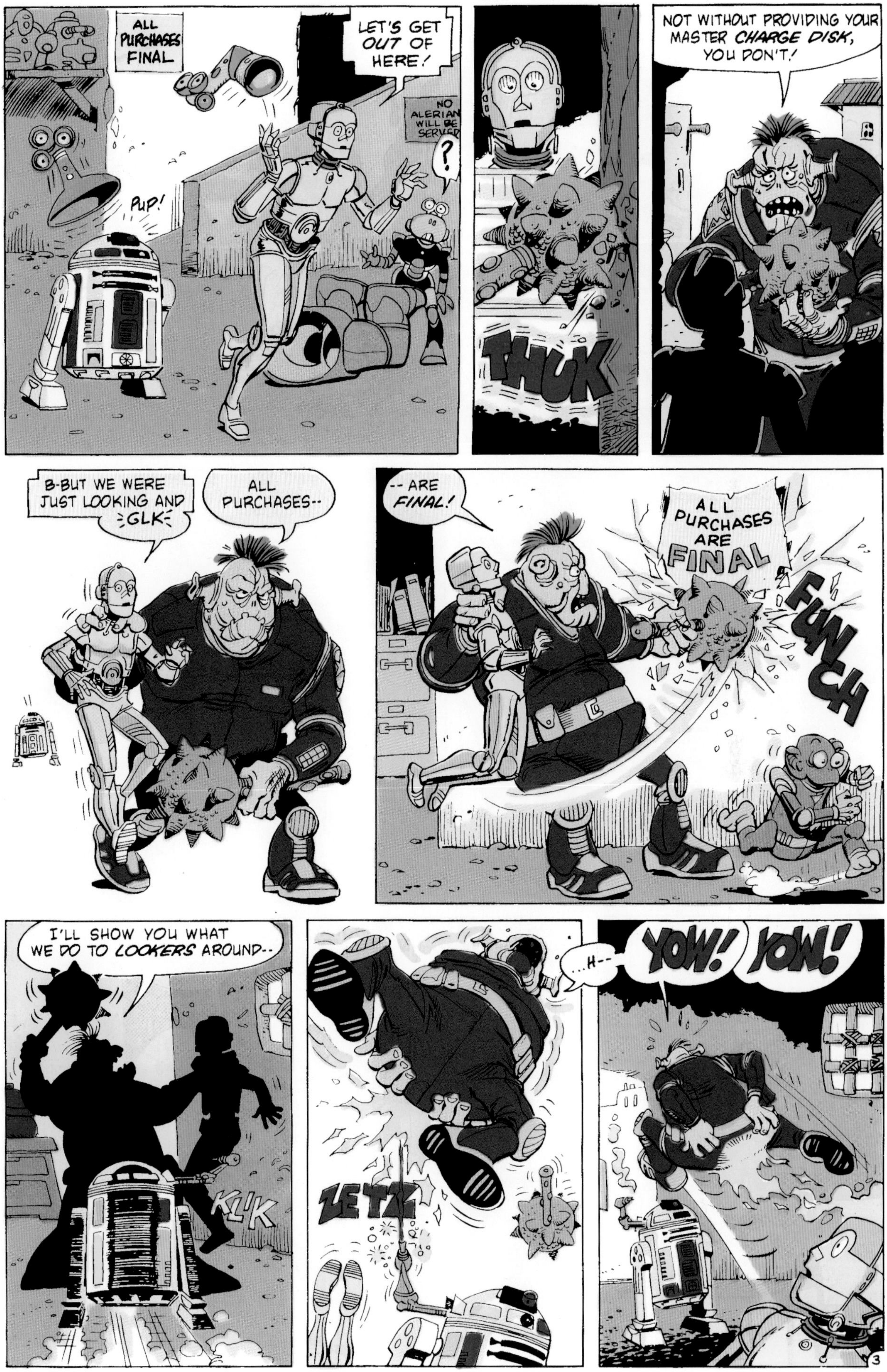

ALL PURCHASES FINAL
LET'S GET OUT OF HERE!
NO ALERIAN WILL BE SERVED
?
PUP!
THUK
NOT WITHOUT PROVIDING YOUR MASTER CHARGE DISK, YOU DON'T!
B-BUT WE WERE JUST LOOKING AND GLK
ALL PURCHASES--
--ARE FINAL!
ALL PURCHASES ARE FINAL
FUNCH
I'LL SHOW YOU WHAT WE DO TO LOOKERS AROUND--
KLIK
...H--
ZETZ
YOW! YOW!
3

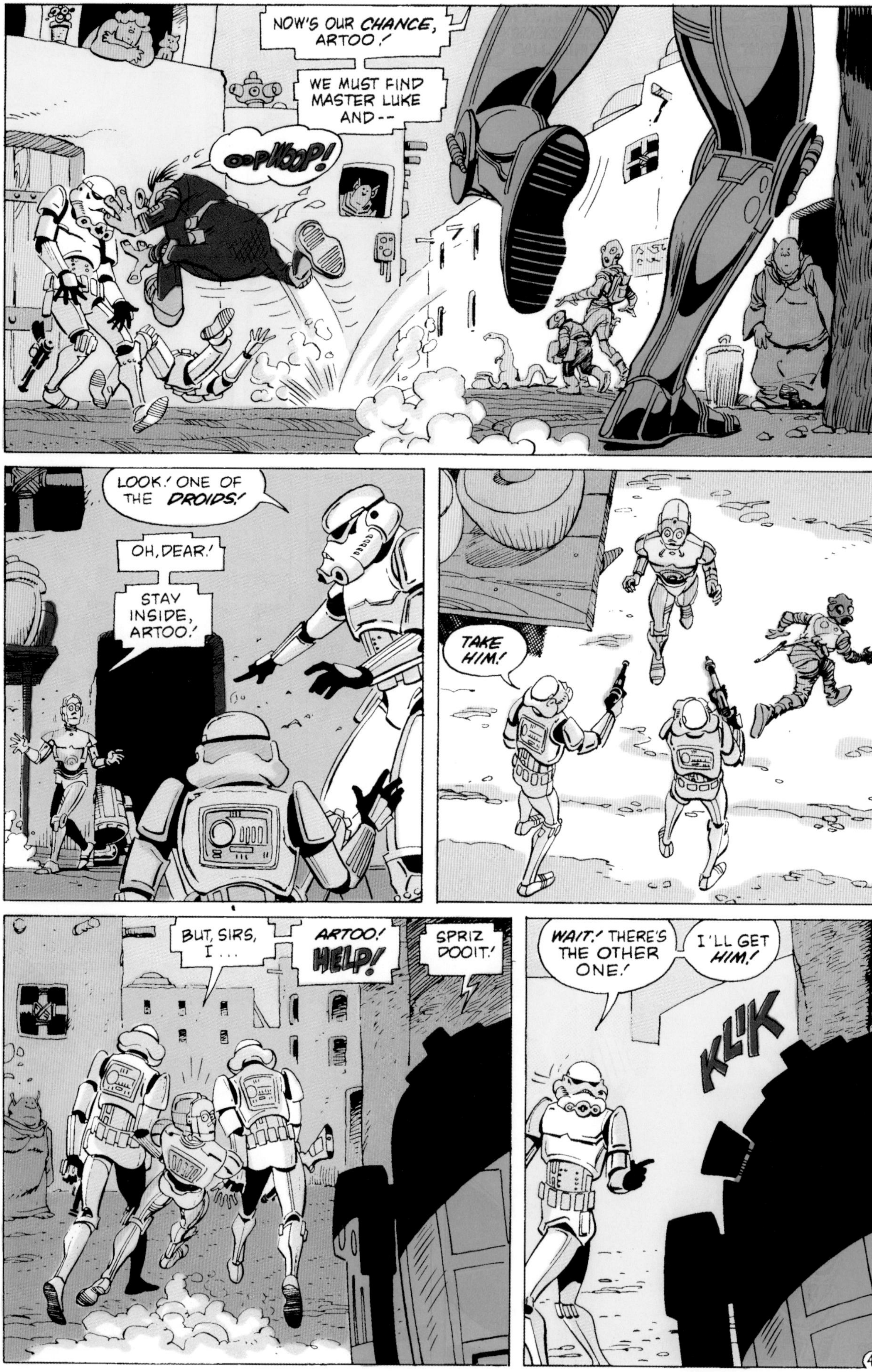
NOW'S OUR CHANCE, ARTOO!
WE MUST FIND MASTER LUKE AND--
OOPWOOP!
LOOK! ONE OF THE DROIDS!
OH, DEAR!
STAY INSIDE, ARTOO!
TAKE HIM!
BUT, SIRS, I ...
ARTOO! HELP!
SPRIZ DOOIT!
WAIT! THERE'S THE OTHER ONE!
I'LL GET HIM!
KLIK
4

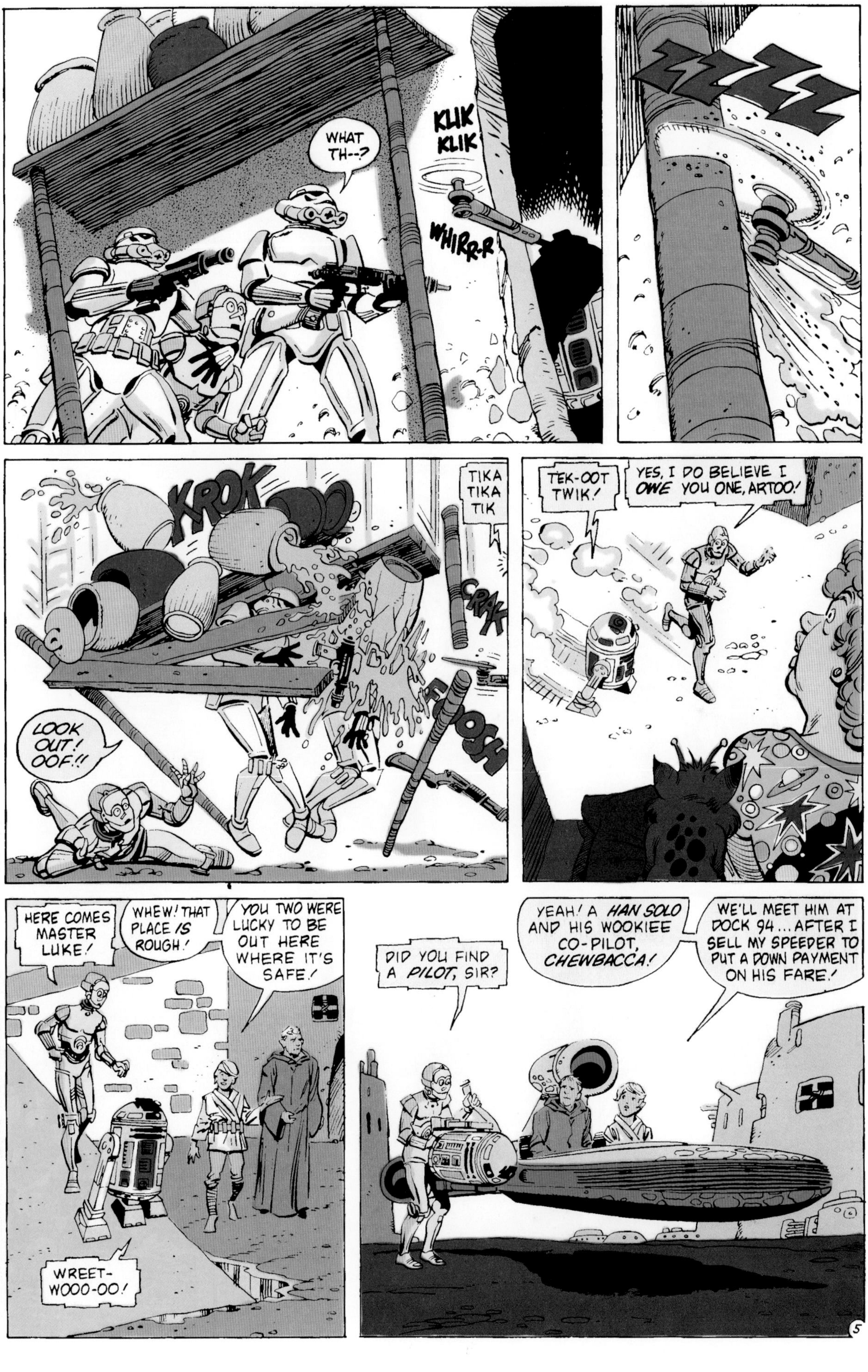
WHAT TH--?
KLIK KLIK
WHIRR-R
ZZZZ
KROK
TIKA TIKA TIK
CRAK
FOOSH
LOOK OUT! OOF!!
TEK-OOT TWIK!
YES, I DO BELIEVE I OWE YOU ONE, ARTOO!
HERE COMES MASTER LUKE!
WHEW! THAT PLACE IS ROUGH!
YOU TWO WERE LUCKY TO BE OUT HERE WHERE IT'S SAFE!
WREET-WOOO-OO!
DID YOU FIND A PILOT, SIR?
YEAH! A HAN SOLO AND HIS WOOKIEE CO-PILOT, CHEWBACCA!
WE'LL MEET HIM AT DOCK 94... AFTER I SELL MY SPEEDER TO PUT A DOWN PAYMENT ON HIS FARE!
5

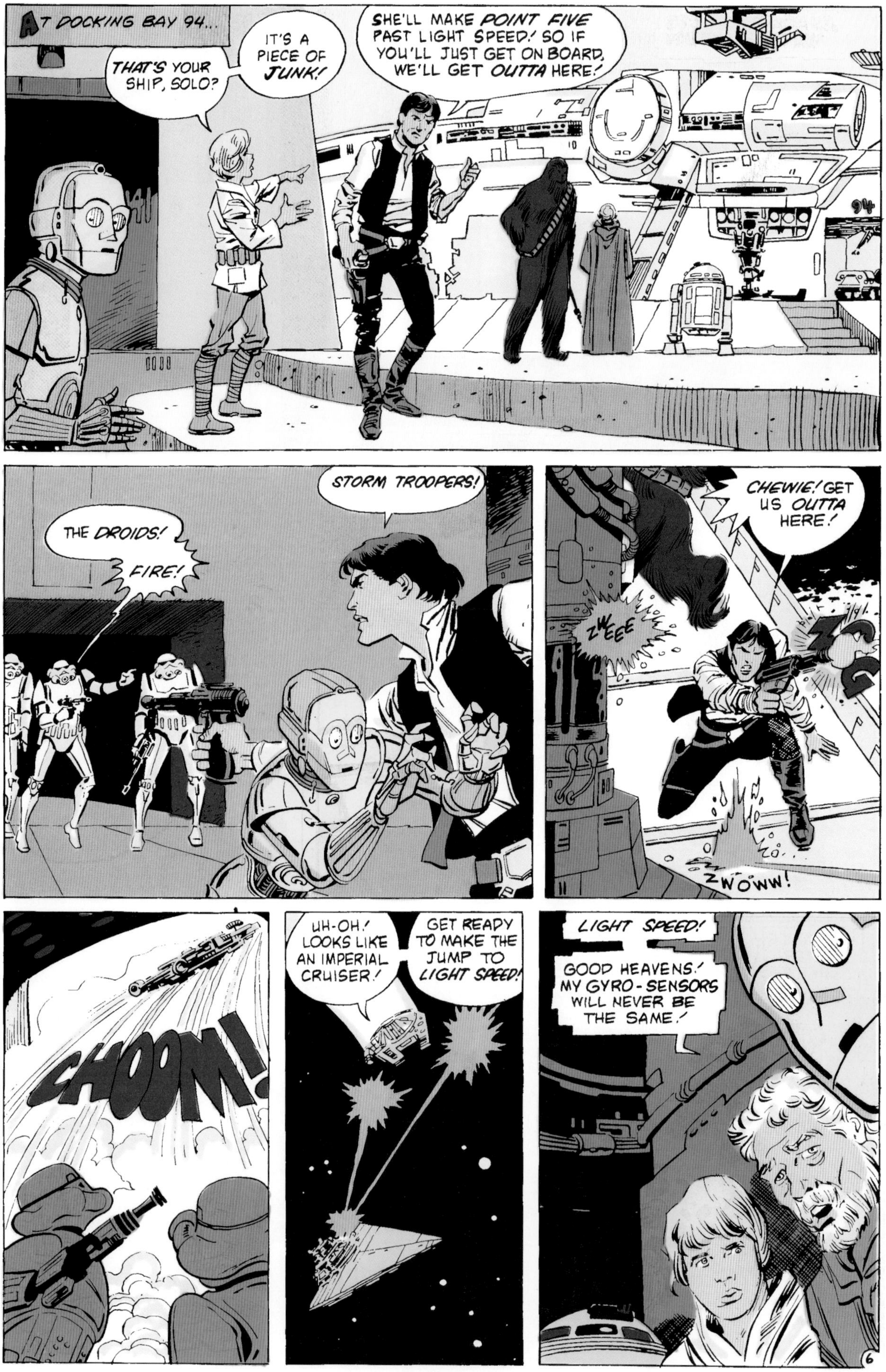
AT DOCKING BAY 94...
THAT'S YOUR SHIP, SOLO?
IT'S A PIECE OF JUNK!
SHE'LL MAKE POINT FIVE PAST LIGHT SPEED! SO IF YOU'LL JUST GET ON BOARD, WE'LL GET OUTTA HERE!
STORM TROOPERS!
THE DROIDS!
FIRE!
CHEWIE! GET US OUTTA HERE!
ZWEEE
ZWOWW!
CHOOM!
UH-OH! LOOKS LIKE AN IMPERIAL CRUISER!
GET READY TO MAKE THE JUMP TO LIGHT SPEED!
LIGHT SPEED!
GOOD HEAVENS! MY GYRO-SENSORS WILL NEVER BE THE SAME!
6

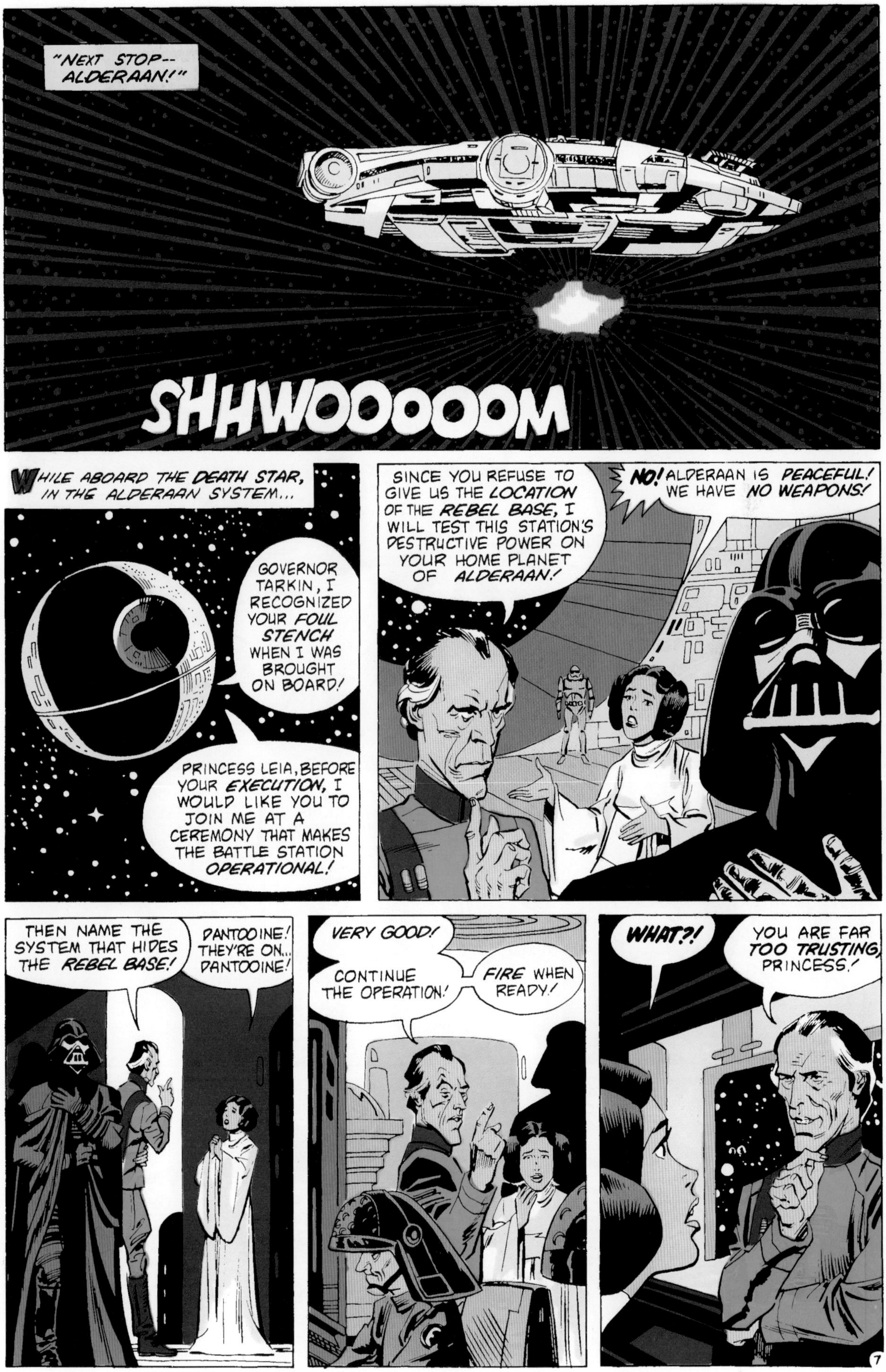
"NEXT STOP-- ALDERAAN!"
SHHWOOOOOM
WHILE ABOARD THE DEATH STAR, IN THE ALDERAAN SYSTEM...
GOVERNOR TARKIN, I RECOGNIZED YOUR FOUL STENCH WHEN I WAS BROUGHT ON BOARD!
PRINCESS LEIA, BEFORE YOUR EXECUTION, I WOULD LIKE YOU TO JOIN ME AT A CEREMONY THAT MAKES THE BATTLE STATION OPERATIONAL!
SINCE YOU REFUSE TO GIVE US THE LOCATION OF THE REBEL BASE, I WILL TEST THIS STATION'S DESTRUCTIVE POWER ON YOUR HOME PLANET OF ALDERAAN!
NO! ALDERAAN IS PEACEFUL! WE HAVE NO WEAPONS!
THEN NAME THE SYSTEM THAT HIDES THE REBEL BASE!
DANTOOINE! THEY'RE ON... DANTOOINE!
VERY GOOD!
CONTINUE THE OPERATION!
FIRE WHEN READY!
WHAT?!
YOU ARE FAR TOO TRUSTING, PRINCESS!
7

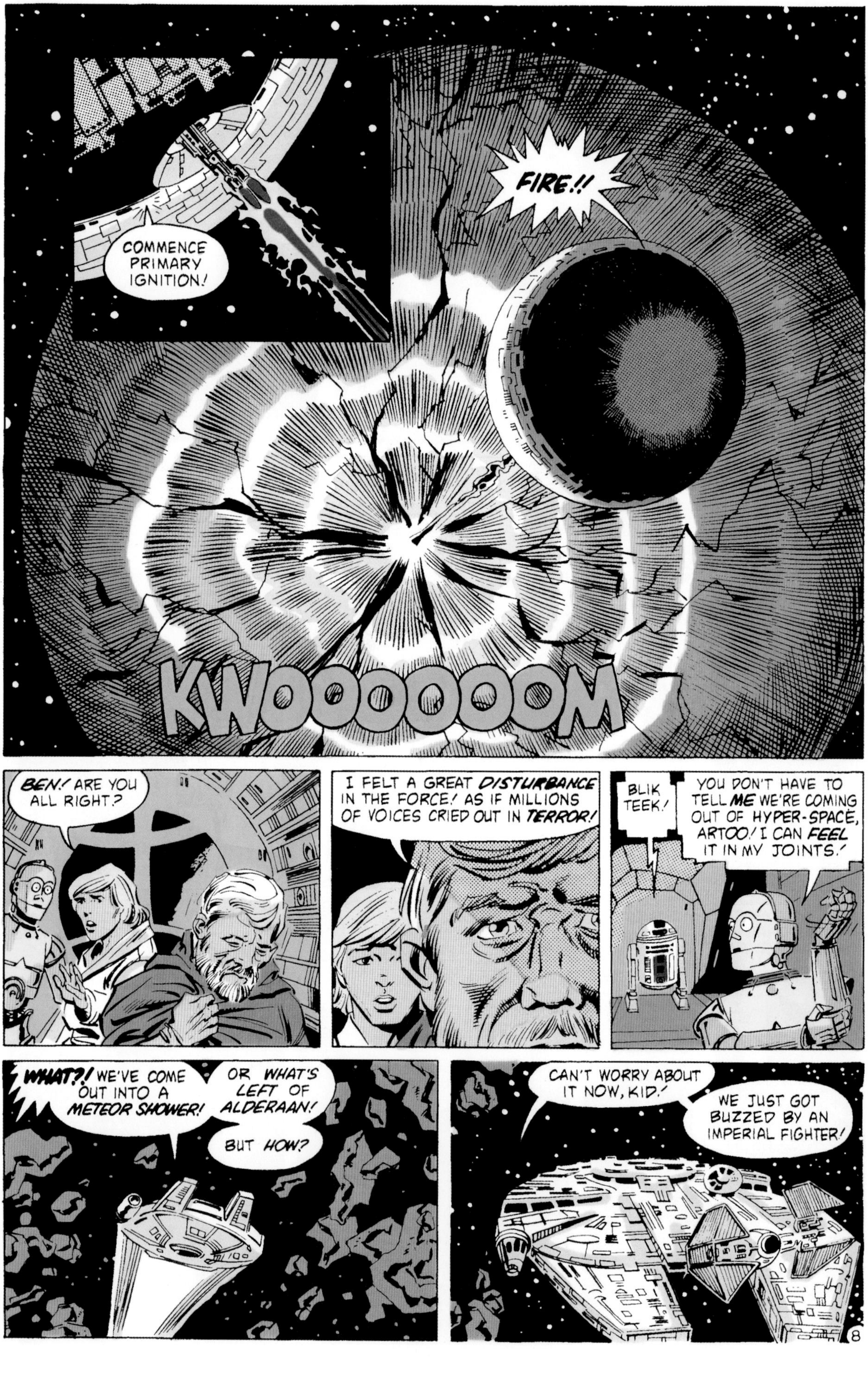
COMMENCE PRIMARY IGNITION!
FIRE!!
KWOOOOOOOM
BEN! ARE YOU ALL RIGHT?
I FELT A GREAT DISTURBANCE IN THE FORCE! AS IF MILLIONS OF VOICES CRIED OUT IN TERROR!
BLIK TEEK!
YOU DON'T HAVE TO TELL ME WE'RE COMING OUT OF HYPER-SPACE, ARTOO! I CAN FEEL IT IN MY JOINTS!
WHAT?! WE'VE COME OUT INTO A METEOR SHOWER!
OR WHAT'S LEFT OF ALDERAAN!
BUT HOW?
CAN'T WORRY ABOUT IT NOW, KID!
WE JUST GOT BUZZED BY AN IMPERIAL FIGHTER!
8

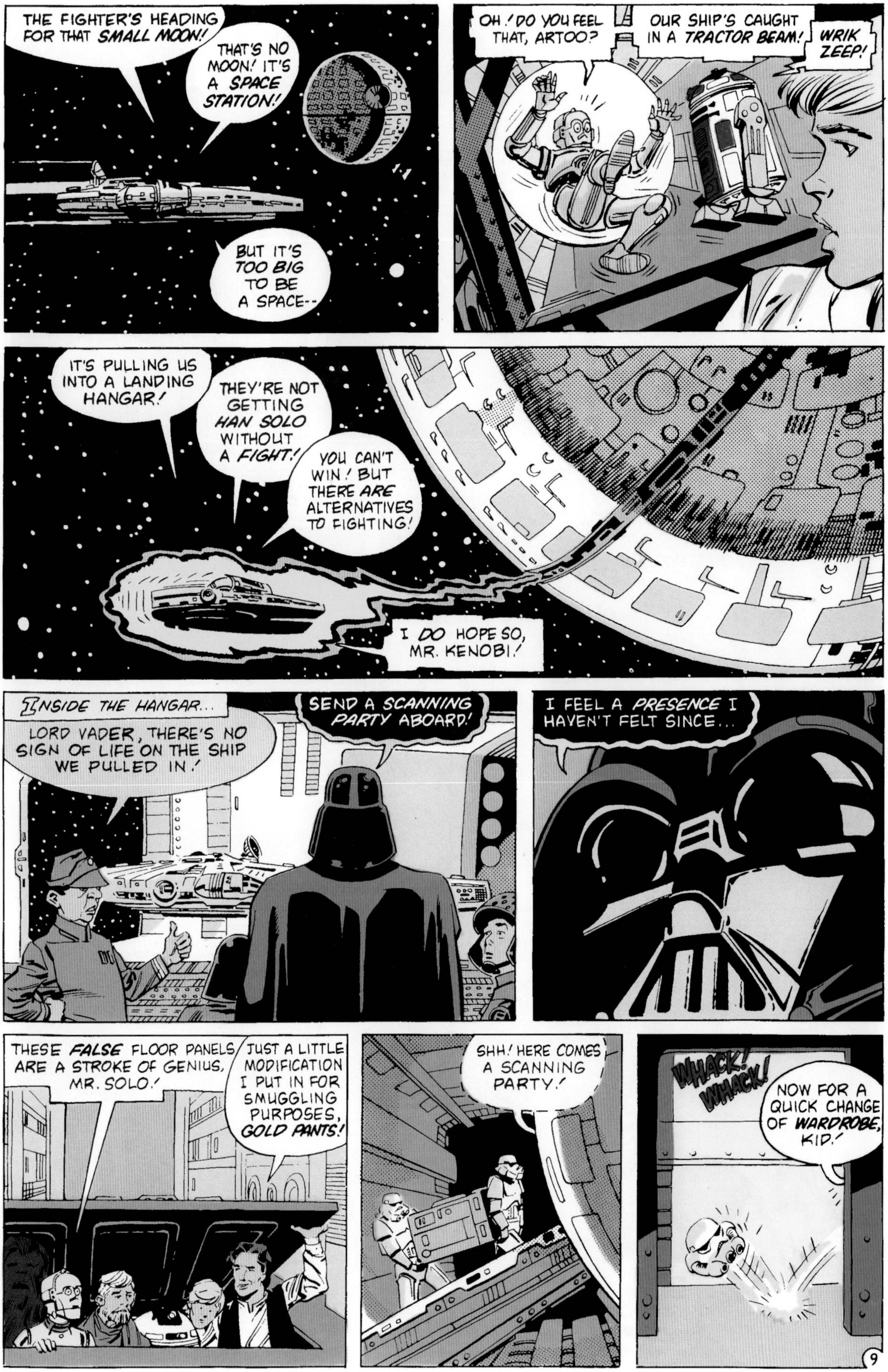
THE FIGHTER'S HEADING FOR THAT SMALL MOON!
THAT'S NO MOON! IT'S A SPACE STATION!
BUT IT'S TOO BIG TO BE A SPACE--
OH! DO YOU FEEL THAT, ARTOO?
OUR SHIP'S CAUGHT IN A TRACTOR BEAM!
WRIK ZEEP!
IT'S PULLING US INTO A LANDING HANGAR!
THEY'RE NOT GETTING HAN SOLO WITHOUT A FIGHT!
YOU CAN'T WIN! BUT THERE ARE ALTERNATIVES TO FIGHTING!
I DO HOPE SO, MR. KENOBI!
INSIDE THE HANGAR...
LORD VADER, THERE'S NO SIGN OF LIFE ON THE SHIP WE PULLED IN!
SEND A SCANNING PARTY ABOARD!
I FEEL A PRESENCE I HAVEN'T FELT SINCE...
THESE FALSE FLOOR PANELS ARE A STROKE OF GENIUS, MR. SOLO!
JUST A LITTLE MODIFICATION I PUT IN FOR SMUGGLING PURPOSES, GOLD PANTS!
SHH! HERE COMES A SCANNING PARTY!
WHACK! WHACK!
NOW FOR A QUICK CHANGE OF WARDROBE, KID!
9

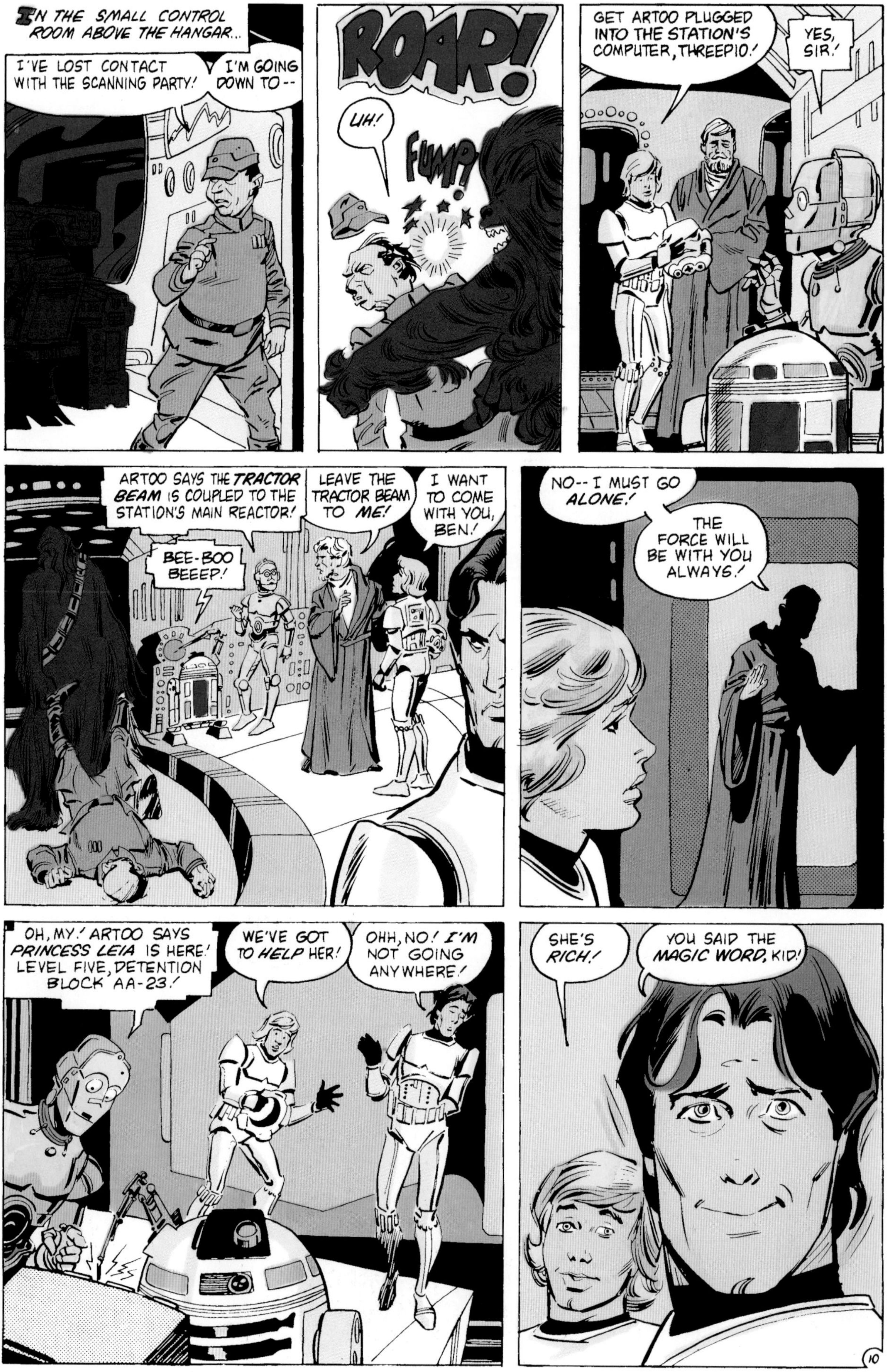
IN THE SMALL CONTROL ROOM ABOVE THE HANGAR...
I'VE LOST CONTACT WITH THE SCANNING PARTY!
I'M GOING DOWN TO --
ROAR!
UH!
FUMP!
GET ARTOO PLUGGED INTO THE STATION'S COMPUTER, THREEPIO!
YES, SIR!
ARTOO SAYS THE TRACTOR BEAM IS COUPLED TO THE STATION'S MAIN REACTOR!
BEE-BOO BEEEP!
LEAVE THE TRACTOR BEAM TO ME!
I WANT TO COME WITH YOU, BEN!
NO-- I MUST GO ALONE!
THE FORCE WILL BE WITH YOU ALWAYS!
OH, MY! ARTOO SAYS PRINCESS LEIA IS HERE! LEVEL FIVE, DETENTION BLOCK AA-23!
WE'VE GOT TO HELP HER!
OHH, NO! I'M NOT GOING ANYWHERE!
SHE'S RICH!
YOU SAID THE MAGIC WORD, KID!
10

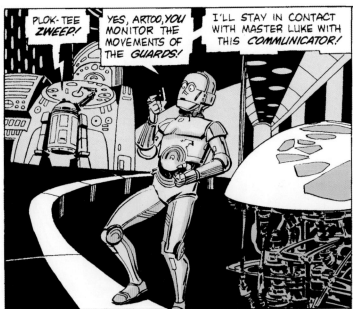

PLOK-TEE ZWEEP!

YES, ARTOO, YOU MONITOR THE MOVEMENTS OF THE GUARDS!

I'LL STAY IN CONTACT WITH MASTER LUKE WITH THIS COMMUNICATOR!

SOON...

ARTOO! THEY'VE BROKEN INTO THE DETENTION BLOCK AND HAVE FOUND THE PRINCESS'S CELL!

BLEE-BOOP BEEEP!

PRINCESS LEIA! I'M LUKE SKYWALKER! I'M HERE TO RESCUE YOU!

YOU DID SEEM A LITTLE SHORT TO BE A STORM TROOPER!

I'M HERE WITH BEN KENOBI!

BEN KENOBI?!

LET'S GO!

HE IS HERE!

OBI-WAN KENOBI? WHAT MAKES YOU THINK SO?

A TREMOR IN THE FORCE! THE LAST TIME I FELT IT WAS IN THE PRESENCE OF MY OLD MASTER!

SURELY HE MUST BE DEAD BY NOW!

OBI-WAN IS HERE! THE FORCE IS WITH HIM!

I MUST FACE HIM ALONE!

11

473

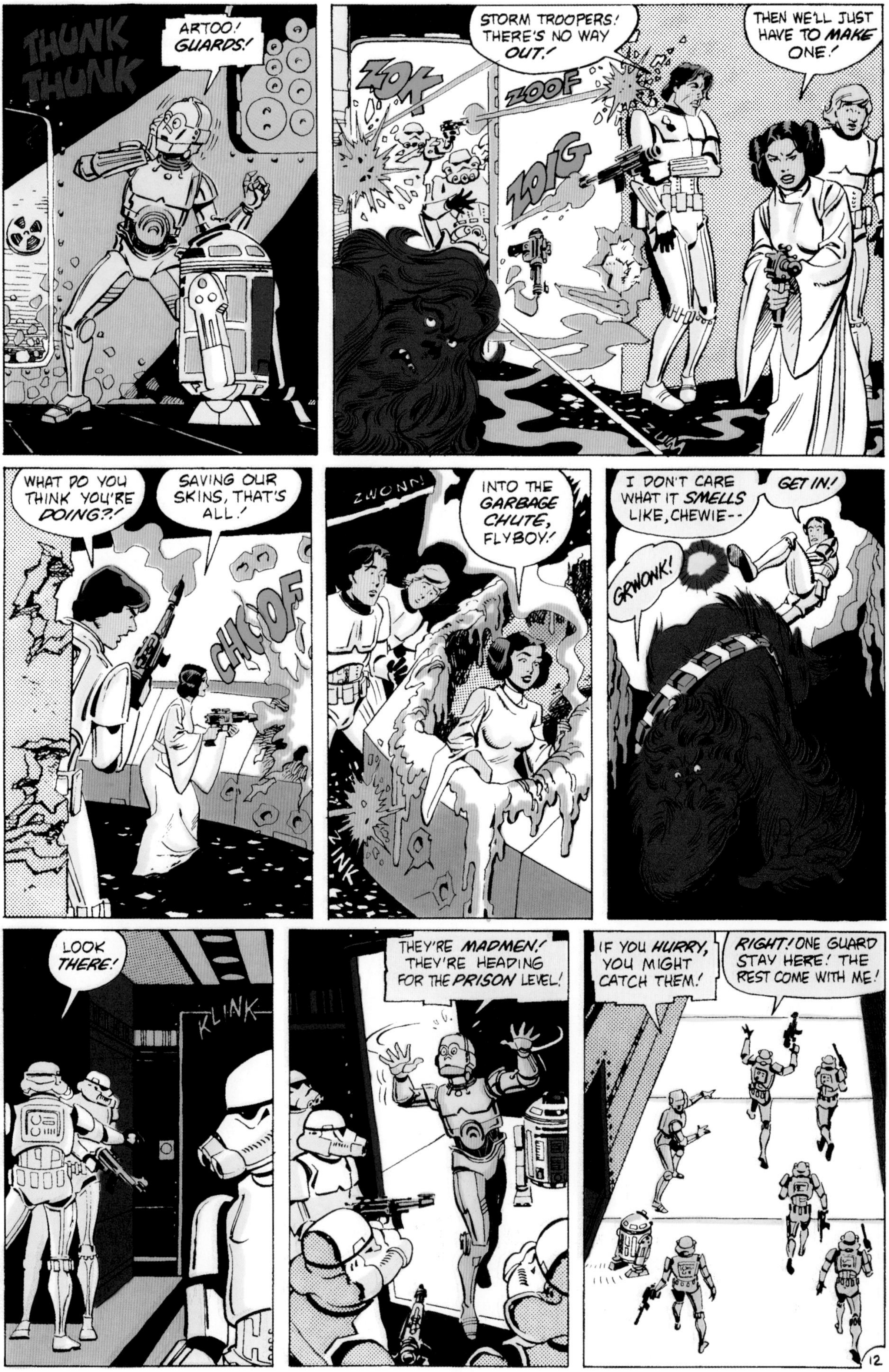
THUNK THUNK
ARTOO! GUARDS!
ZOK
ZOOF
STORM TROOPERS! THERE'S NO WAY OUT!
ZOIG
THEN WE'LL JUST HAVE TO MAKE ONE!
ZUM
WHAT DO YOU THINK YOU'RE DOING?!
SAVING OUR SKINS, THAT'S ALL!
CHOOF
ZWONN!
INTO THE GARBAGE CHUTE, FLYBOY!
ZINK
I DON'T CARE WHAT IT SMELLS LIKE, CHEWIE--
GET IN!
GRWONK!
LOOK THERE!
KLINK
THEY'RE MADMEN! THEY'RE HEADING FOR THE PRISON LEVEL!
IF YOU HURRY, YOU MIGHT CATCH THEM!
RIGHT! ONE GUARD STAY HERE! THE REST COME WITH ME!
12

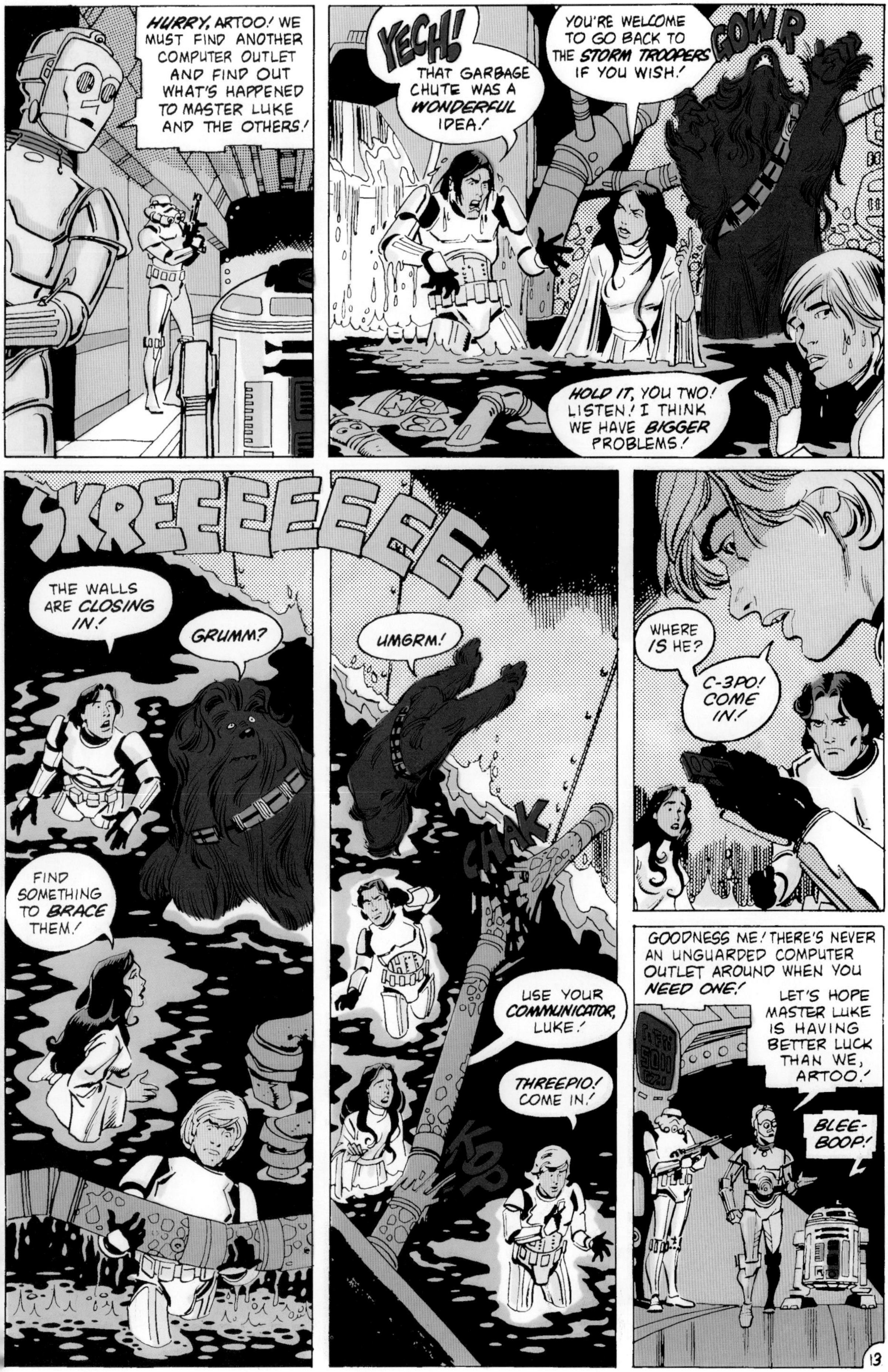
HURRY, ARTOO! WE MUST FIND ANOTHER COMPUTER OUTLET AND FIND OUT WHAT'S HAPPENED TO MASTER LUKE AND THE OTHERS!
YECH!
THAT GARBAGE CHUTE WAS A WONDERFUL IDEA!
YOU'RE WELCOME TO GO BACK TO THE STORM TROOPERS IF YOU WISH!
GOWR
HOLD IT, YOU TWO! LISTEN! I THINK WE HAVE BIGGER PROBLEMS!
SKREEEEEEEE!
THE WALLS ARE CLOSING IN!
GRUMM?
FIND SOMETHING TO BRACE THEM!
UMGRM!
CHAK
USE YOUR COMMUNICATOR, LUKE!
THREEPIO! COME IN!
KLOP
WHERE IS HE?
C-3PO! COME IN!
GOODNESS ME! THERE'S NEVER AN UNGUARDED COMPUTER OUTLET AROUND WHEN YOU NEED ONE!
LET'S HOPE MASTER LUKE IS HAVING BETTER LUCK THAN WE, ARTOO!
BLEE-BOOP!
13

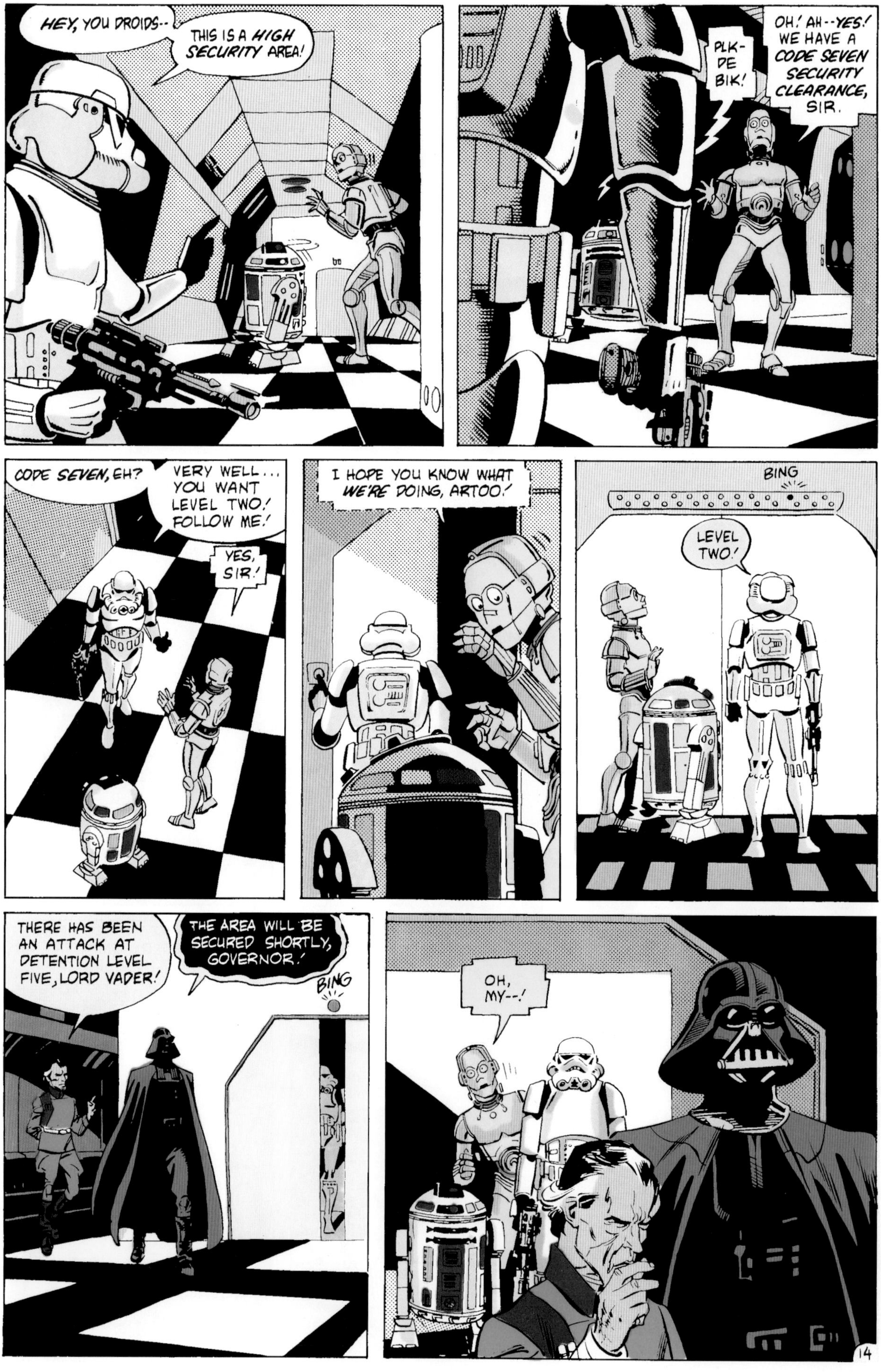

HEY, YOU DROIDS--
THIS IS A HIGH SECURITY AREA!
PLK-DE BIK!
OH! AH--YES! WE HAVE A CODE SEVEN SECURITY CLEARANCE, SIR.
CODE SEVEN, EH?
VERY WELL... YOU WANT LEVEL TWO! FOLLOW ME!
YES, SIR!
I HOPE YOU KNOW WHAT WE'RE DOING, ARTOO!
BING
LEVEL TWO!
THERE HAS BEEN AN ATTACK AT DETENTION LEVEL FIVE, LORD VADER!
THE AREA WILL BE SECURED SHORTLY, GOVERNOR!
BING
OH, MY--!
14

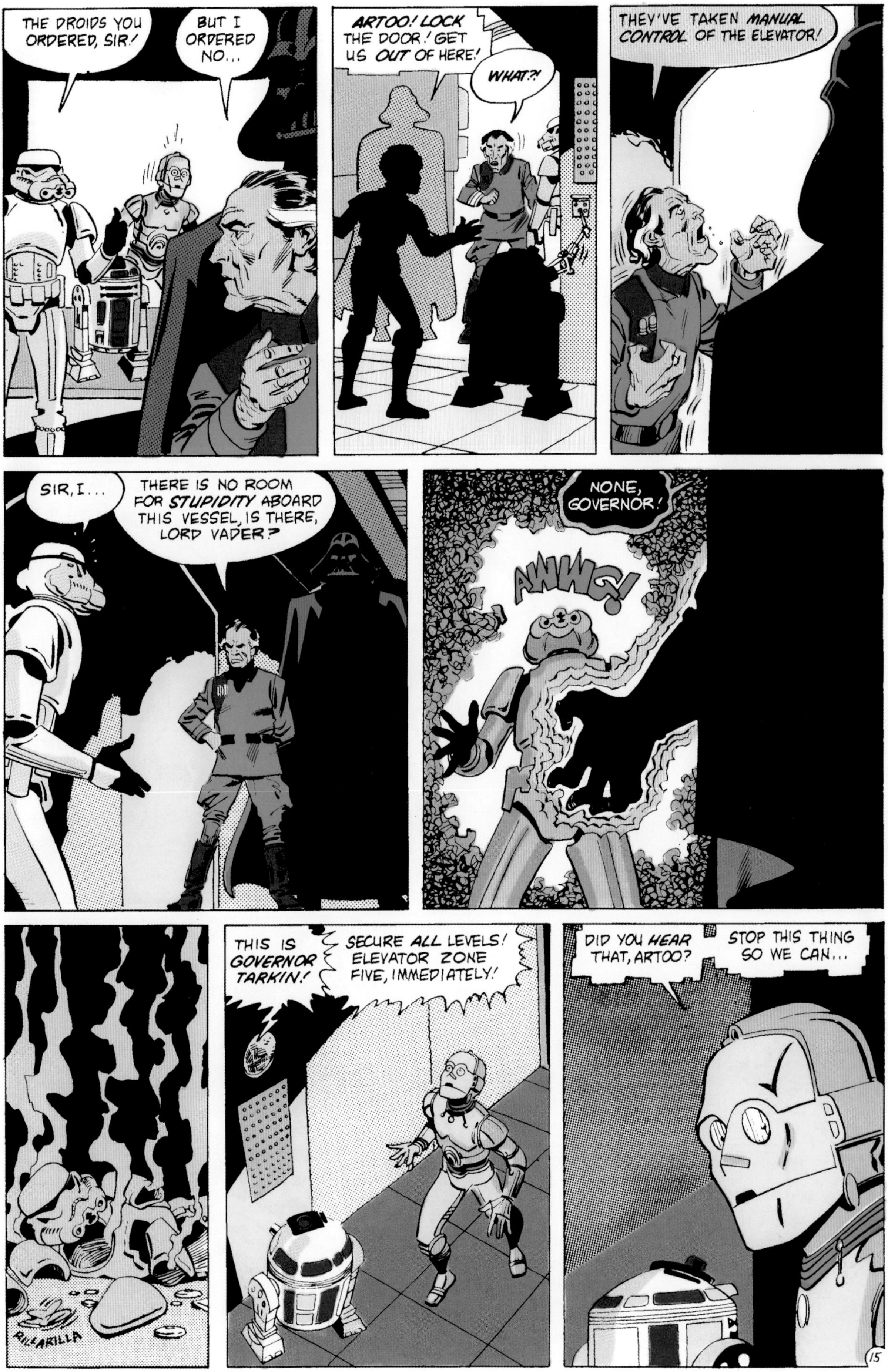

THE DROIDS YOU ORDERED, SIR!
BUT I ORDERED NO...
ARTOO! LOCK THE DOOR! GET US OUT OF HERE!
WHAT?!
THEY'VE TAKEN MANUAL CONTROL OF THE ELEVATOR!
SIR, I...
THERE IS NO ROOM FOR STUPIDITY ABOARD THIS VESSEL, IS THERE, LORD VADER?
NONE, GOVERNOR!
AWWG!
RIL-ARILLA
THIS IS GOVERNOR TARKIN!
SECURE ALL LEVELS! ELEVATOR ZONE FIVE, IMMEDIATELY!
DID YOU HEAR THAT, ARTOO?
STOP THIS THING SO WE CAN...
15

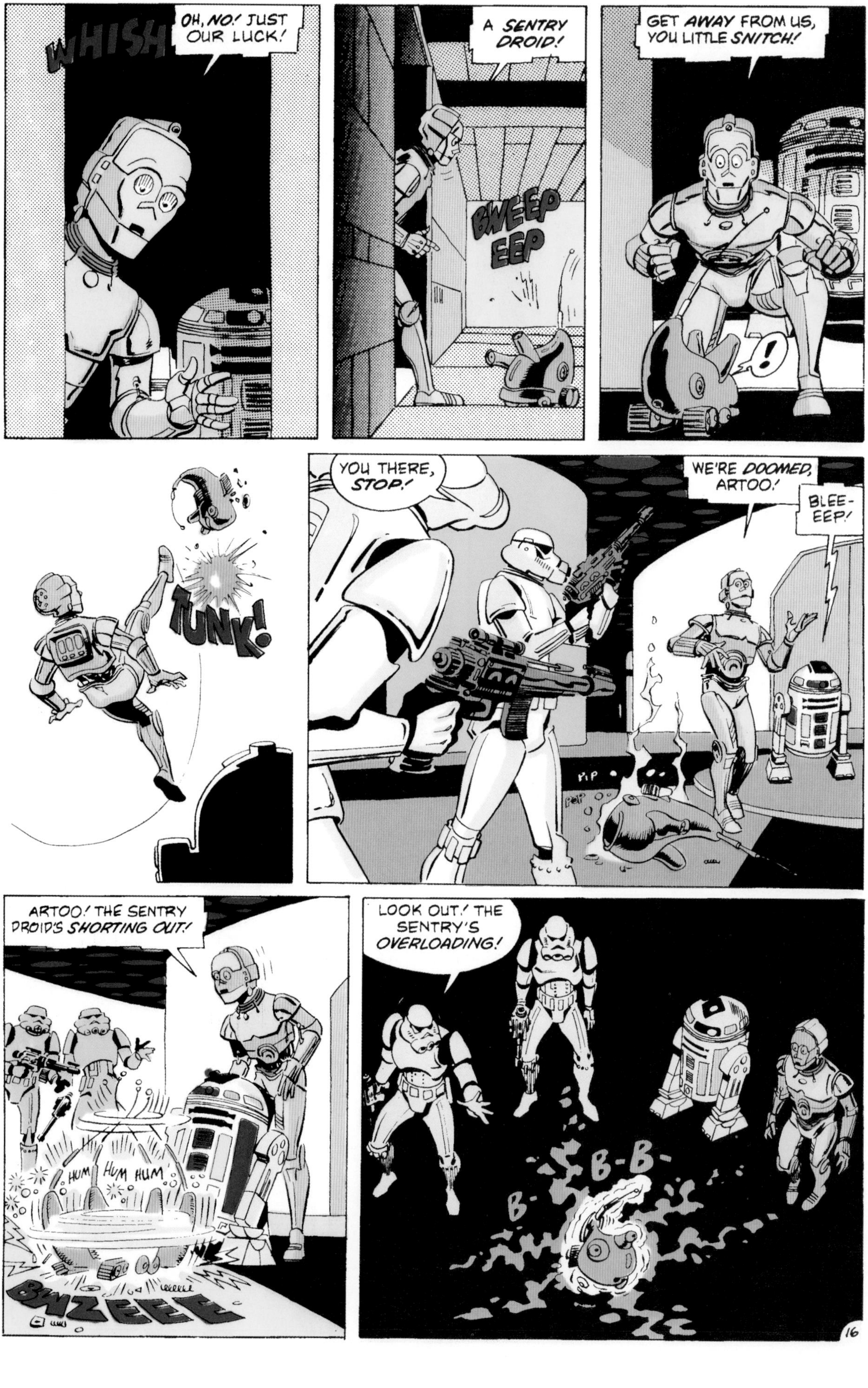
WHISH
OH, NO! JUST OUR LUCK!
A SENTRY DROID!
BWEEP EEP
GET AWAY FROM US, YOU LITTLE SNITCH!
!
TUNK!
YOU THERE, STOP!
WE'RE DOOMED, ARTOO!
BLEE-EEP!
ARTOO! THE SENTRY DROID'S SHORTING OUT!
HUM HUM HUM
BWZEEE
LOOK OUT! THE SENTRY'S OVERLOADING!
B- B-B-
16

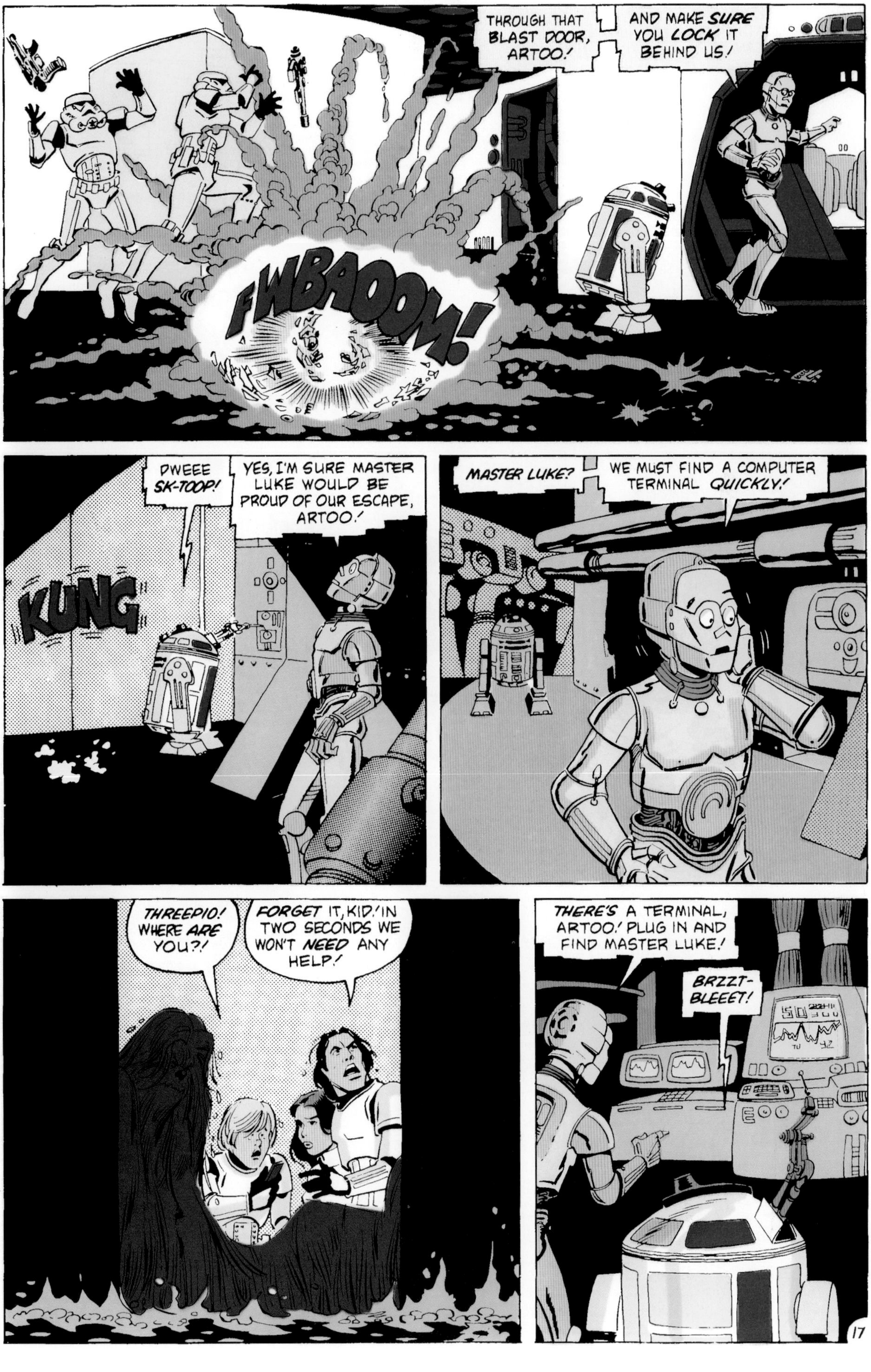
THROUGH THAT BLAST DOOR, ARTOO!
AND MAKE SURE YOU LOCK IT BEHIND US!
FWBAOOM!
DWEEE SK-TOOP!
KUNG
YES, I'M SURE MASTER LUKE WOULD BE PROUD OF OUR ESCAPE, ARTOO!
MASTER LUKE?
WE MUST FIND A COMPUTER TERMINAL QUICKLY!
THREEPIO! WHERE ARE YOU?!
FORGET IT, KID! IN TWO SECONDS WE WON'T NEED ANY HELP!
THERE'S A TERMINAL, ARTOO! PLUG IN AND FIND MASTER LUKE!
BRZZT-BLEEET!
17

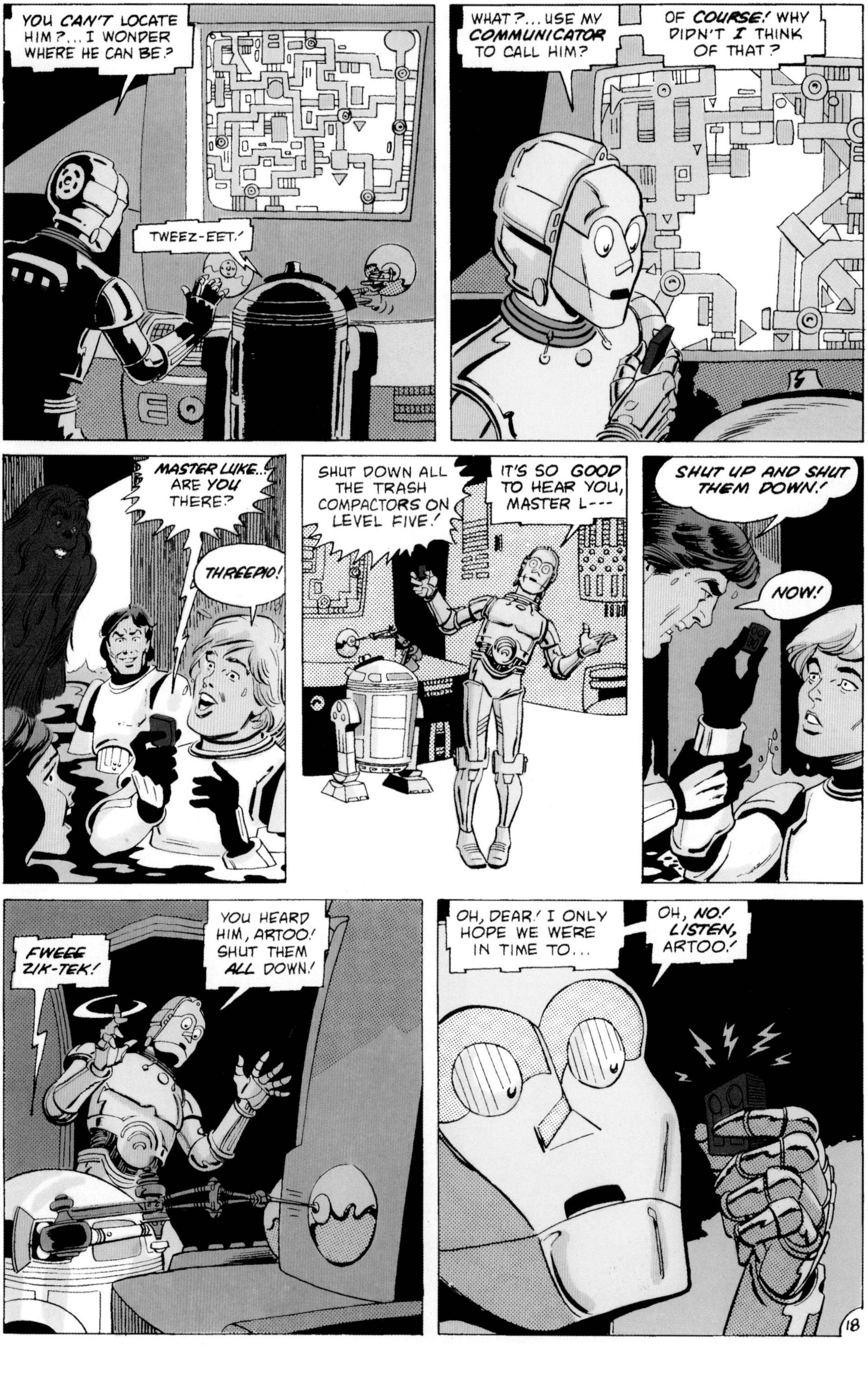
YOU CAN'T LOCATE HIM?... I WONDER WHERE HE CAN BE?
TWEEZ-EET!
WHAT?... USE MY COMMUNICATOR TO CALL HIM?
OF COURSE! WHY DIDN'T I THINK OF THAT?
MASTER LUKE... ARE YOU THERE?
THREEPIO!
IT'S SO GOOD TO HEAR YOU, MASTER L---
SHUT DOWN ALL THE TRASH COMPACTORS ON LEVEL FIVE!
SHUT UP AND SHUT THEM DOWN!
NOW!
FWEEE ZIK-TEK!
YOU HEARD HIM, ARTOO! SHUT THEM ALL DOWN!
OH, DEAR! I ONLY HOPE WE WERE IN TIME TO...
OH, NO! LISTEN, ARTOO!
18

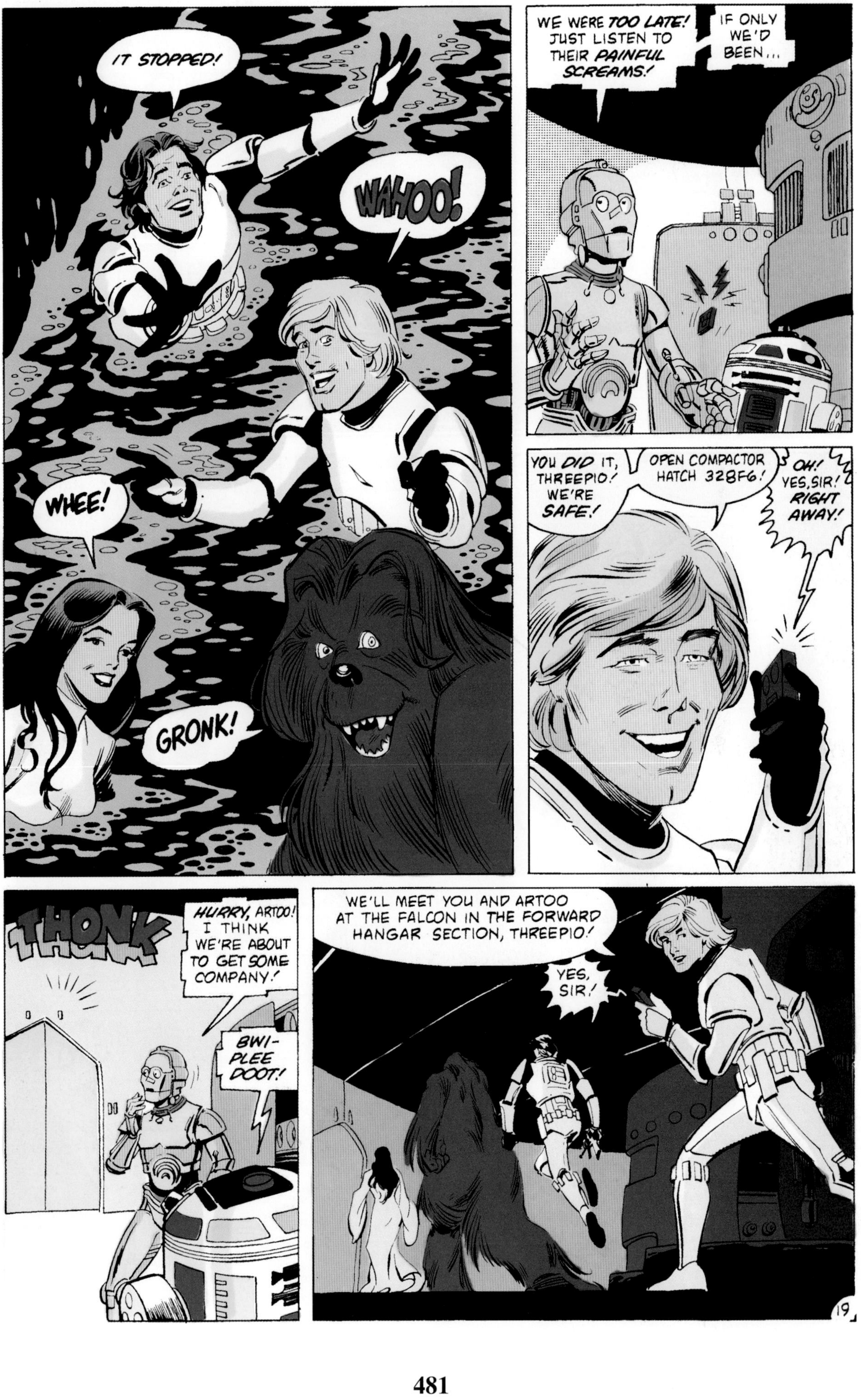
IT STOPPED!
WAHOO!
WHEE!
GRONK!
WE WERE TOO LATE! JUST LISTEN TO THEIR PAINFUL SCREAMS!
IF ONLY WE'D BEEN...
YOU DID IT, THREEPIO! WE'RE SAFE!
OPEN COMPACTOR HATCH 328F6!
OH! YES, SIR! RIGHT AWAY!
THONK
HURRY, ARTOO! I THINK WE'RE ABOUT TO GET SOME COMPANY!
BWI-PLEE DOOT!
WE'LL MEET YOU AND ARTOO AT THE FALCON IN THE FORWARD HANGAR SECTION, THREEPIO!
YES, SIR!
19

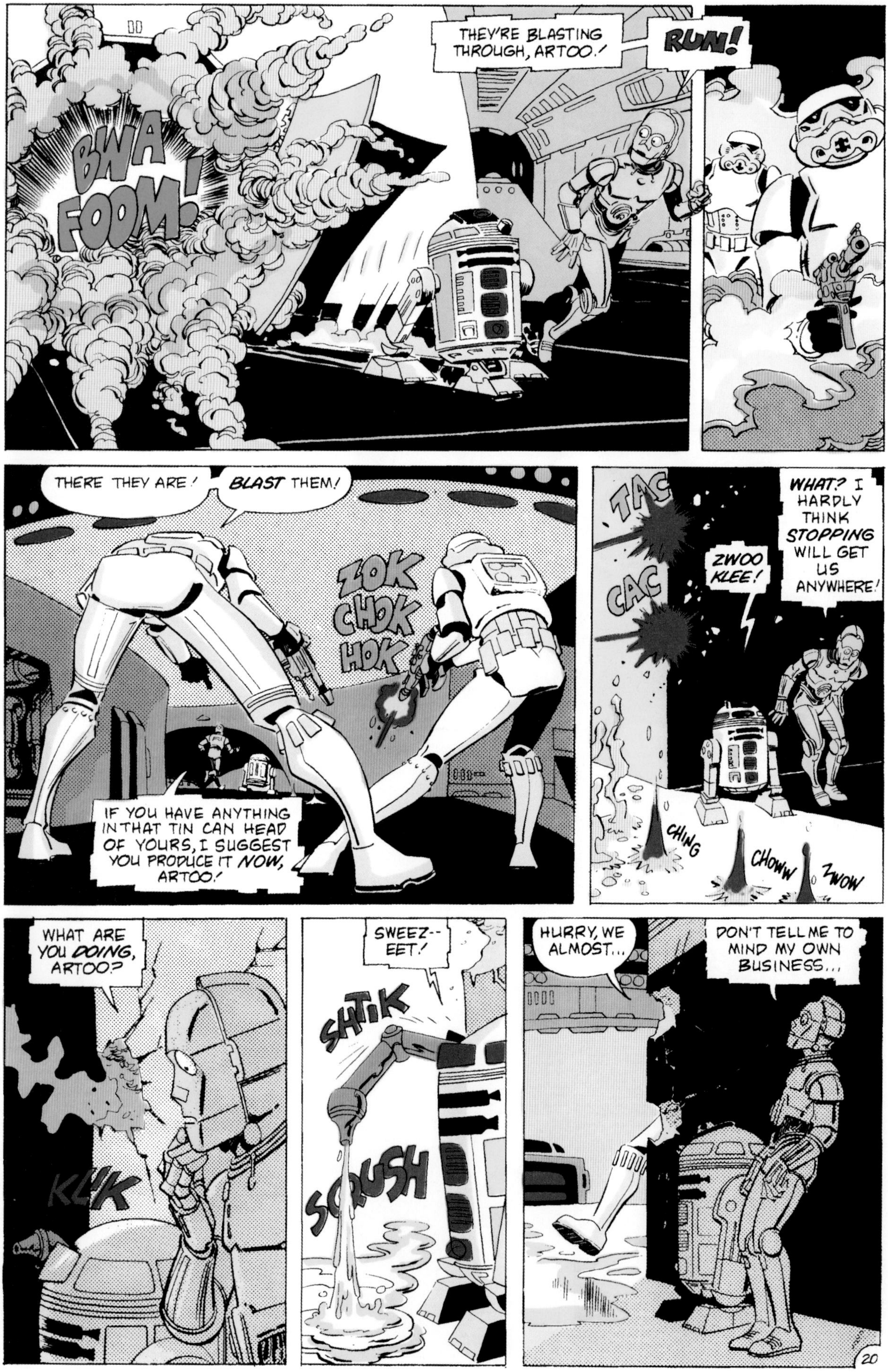
BWA FOOM!
THEY'RE BLASTING THROUGH, ARTOO!
RUN!
THERE THEY ARE!
BLAST THEM!
ZOK CHOK HOK
IF YOU HAVE ANYTHING IN THAT TIN CAN HEAD OF YOURS, I SUGGEST YOU PRODUCE IT NOW, ARTOO!
TAC
CAC
ZWOO KLEE!
WHAT? I HARDLY THINK STOPPING WILL GET US ANYWHERE!
CHING
CHOWW
ZWOW
WHAT ARE YOU DOING, ARTOO?
KLIK
SWEEZ--EET!
SHTIK
SQUSH
HURRY, WE ALMOST...
DON'T TELL ME TO MIND MY OWN BUSINESS...
20

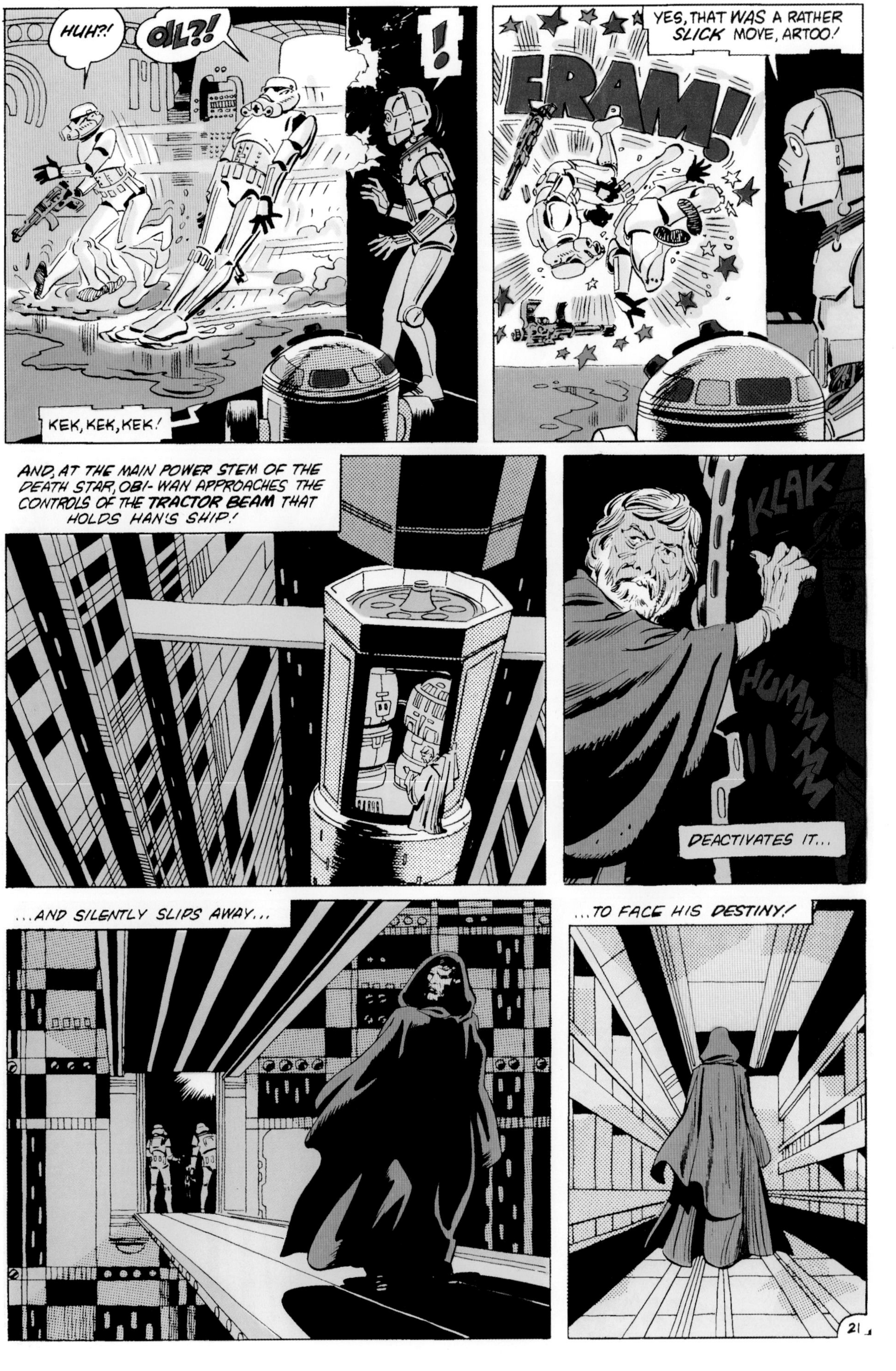
HUH?!
OIL?!
!
KEK, KEK, KEK!
YES, THAT WAS A RATHER SLICK MOVE, ARTOO!
FRAM!
AND, AT THE MAIN POWER STEM OF THE DEATH STAR, OBI-WAN APPROACHES THE CONTROLS OF THE TRACTOR BEAM THAT HOLDS HAN'S SHIP!
KLAK
HUMMMM
DEACTIVATES IT...
...AND SILENTLY SLIPS AWAY...
...TO FACE HIS DESTINY!
21

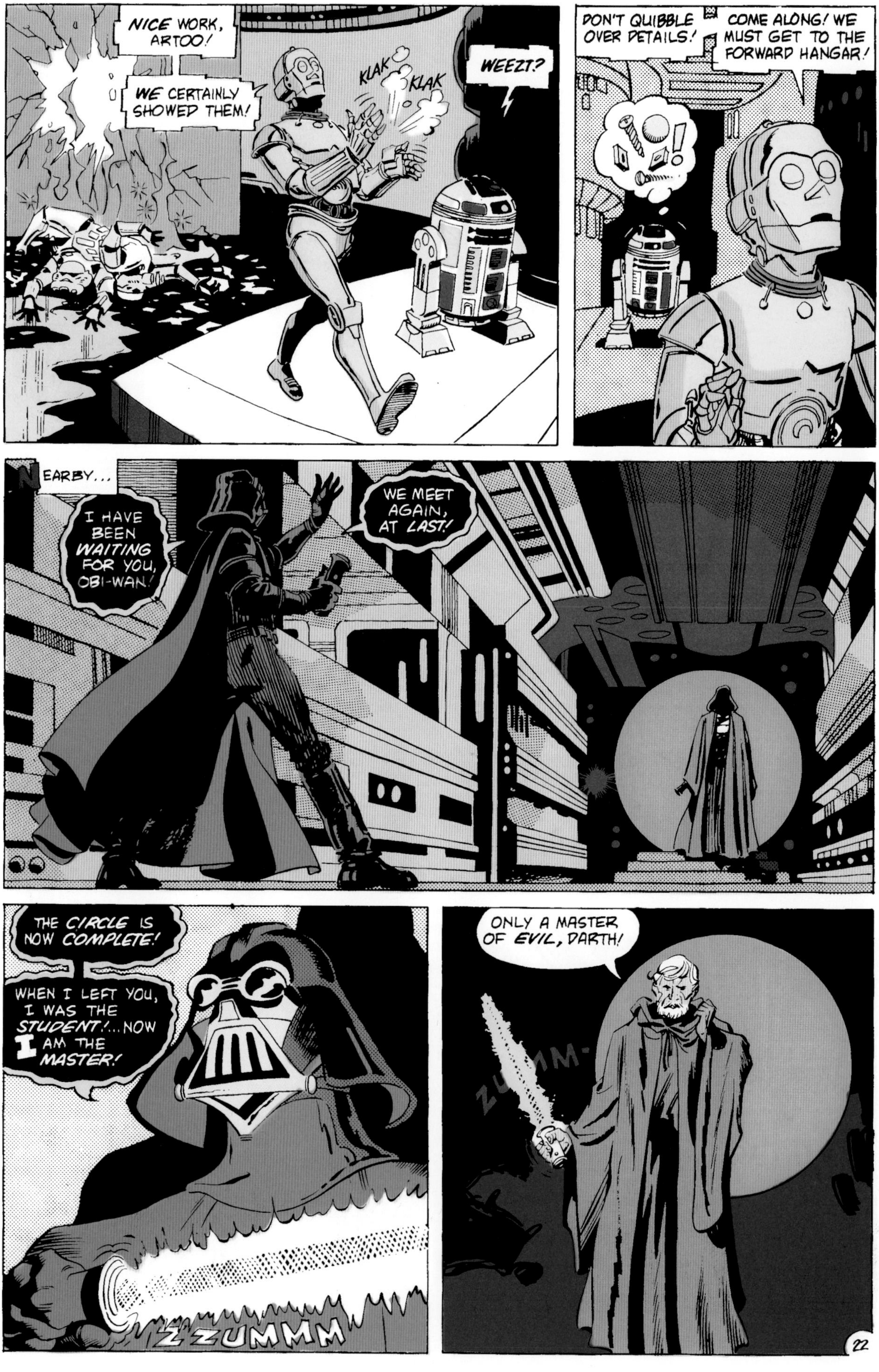
NICE WORK, ARTOO!
WE CERTAINLY SHOWED THEM!
KLAK KLAK
WEEZT?
DON'T QUIBBLE OVER DETAILS!
COME ALONG! WE MUST GET TO THE FORWARD HANGAR!
NEARBY...
I HAVE BEEN WAITING FOR YOU, OBI-WAN!
WE MEET AGAIN, AT LAST!
THE CIRCLE IS NOW COMPLETE!
WHEN I LEFT YOU, I WAS THE STUDENT!...NOW I AM THE MASTER!
ZZUMMM
ONLY A MASTER OF EVIL, DARTH!
ZUMMM-
22

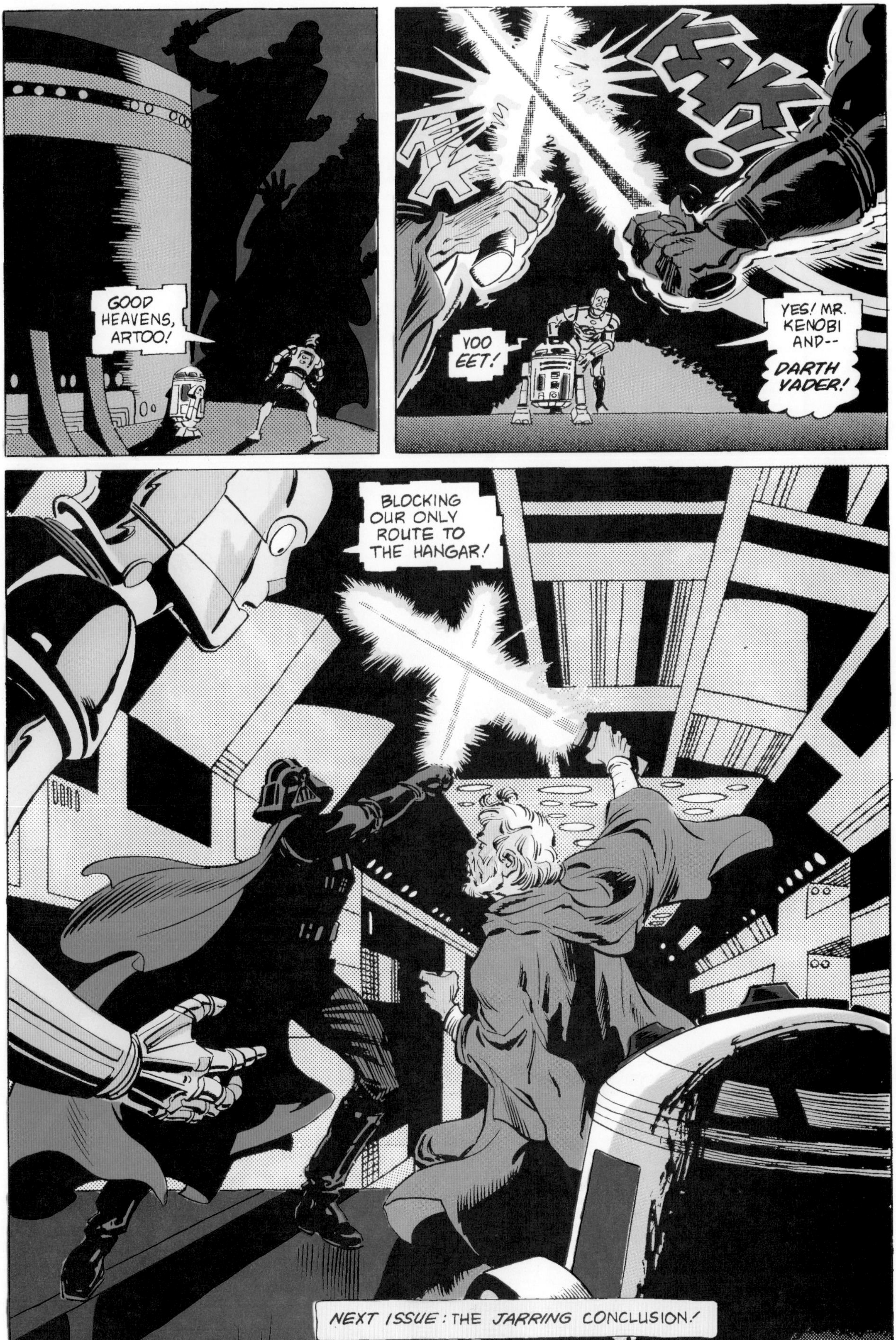
GOOD HEAVENS, ARTOO!
KAK!
KAK!
YOO EET!
YES! MR. KENOBI AND--
DARTH VADER!
BLOCKING OUR ONLY ROUTE TO THE HANGAR!
NEXT ISSUE: THE JARRING CONCLUSION!
23

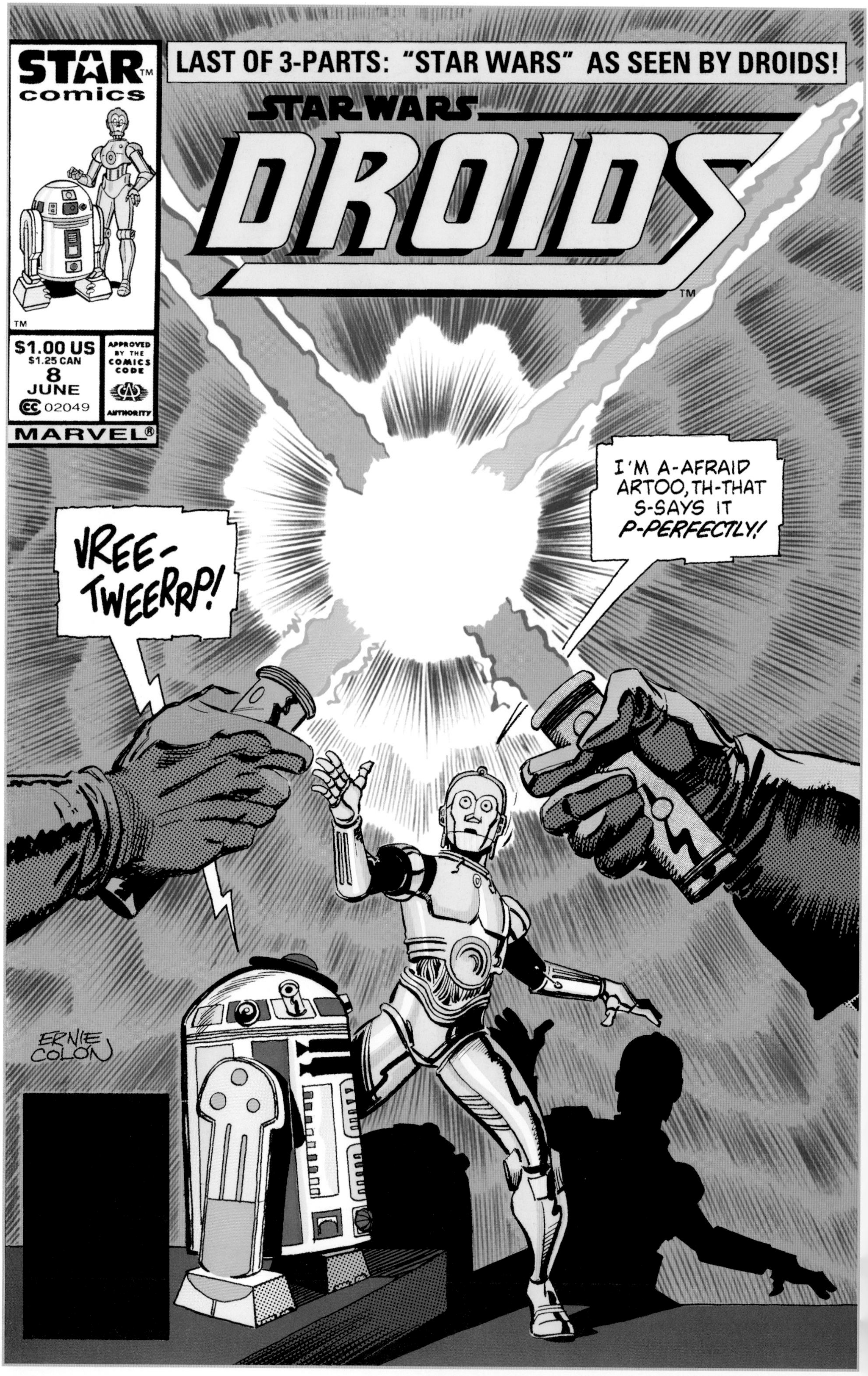
STAR™ comics
LAST OF 3-PARTS: "STAR WARS" AS SEEN BY DROIDS!
STAR WARS
DROIDS™
$1.00 US
$1.25 CAN
8
JUNE
02049
APPROVED BY THE COMICS CODE AUTHORITY
MARVEL®
VREE-TWEERRP!
I'M A-AFRAID ARTOO, TH-THAT S-SAYS IT P-PERFECTLY!
ERNIE COLON

STAR WARS DROIDS

IN "THE STAR WARS ADVENTURE"

BOOK THREE
THE LAST JEDI!

ABOARD THE *DEATH STAR*, A DESPERATE RACE TAKES PLACE...*LUKE SKYWALKER* HAS ORDERED THE DROIDS *R2-D2* AND *C-3PO* TO MEET HIM, *PRINCESS LEIA*, AND *HAN SOLO* AT THE *MILLENNIUM FALCON* AT ONCE, OR THE REBELLION AGAINST THE EVIL EMPIRE MAY BE LOST!

SKWEE-ZOO-EET!

YES! *DARTH VADER* AND *OBI-WAN* ARE BLOCKING THE ONLY ROUTE TO OUR SHIP, ARTOO!

AND MASTER LUKE CAN'T TAKE OFF *WITHOUT* YOU!

WUSSMM

| DAVID MANAK WRITER | ERNIE COLÓN PENCILER | AL WILLIAMSON INKER | GEORGE ROUSSOS COLORIST | ED KING LETTERER | SID JACOBSON EDITOR | TOM DE FALCO EXECUTIVE EDITOR | JIM SHOOTER EDITOR-IN-CHIEF |

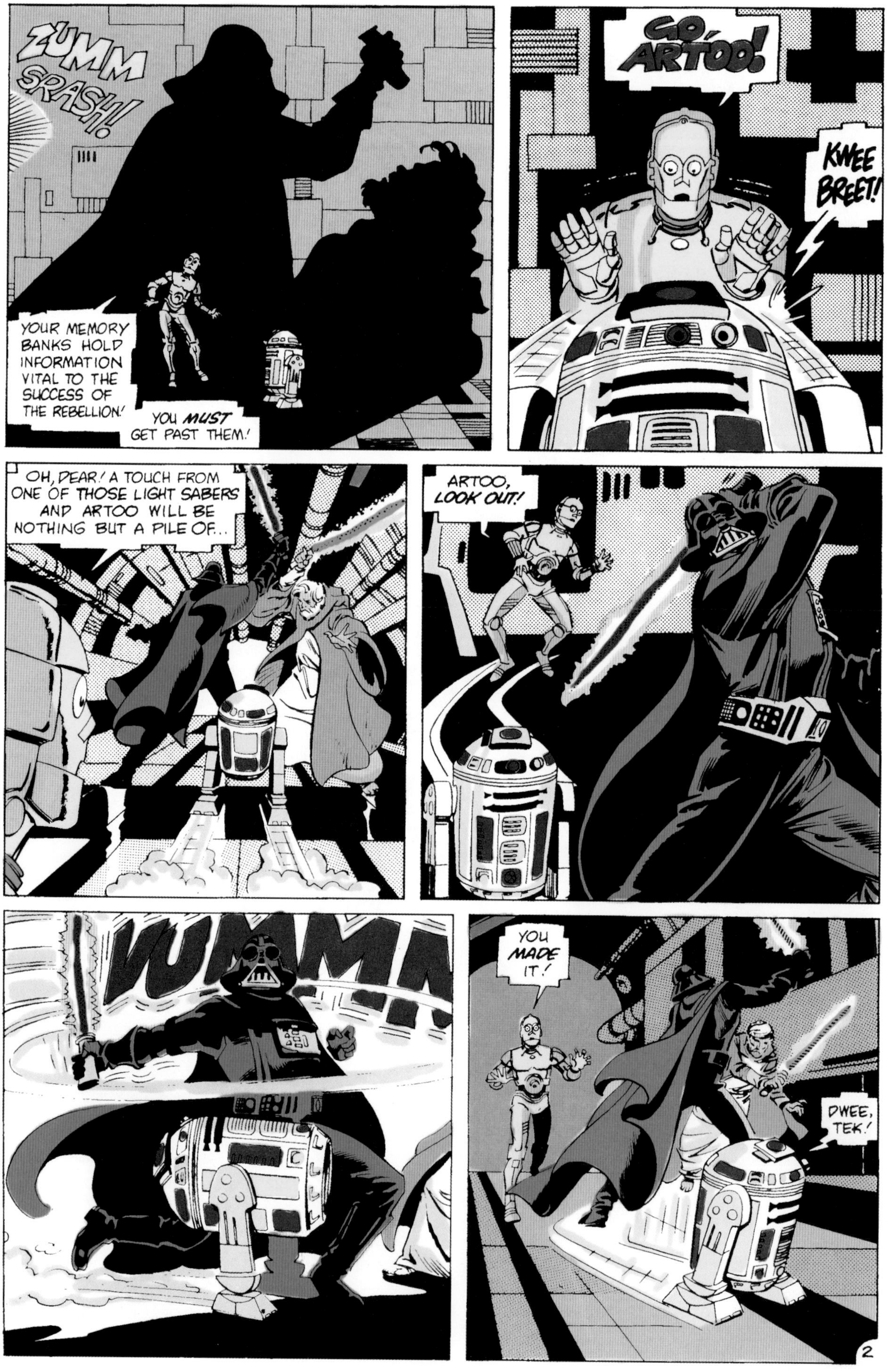
ZUMM
SRASH!
YOUR MEMORY BANKS HOLD INFORMATION VITAL TO THE SUCCESS OF THE REBELLION!
YOU MUST GET PAST THEM!
GO, ARTOO!
KWEE BREET!
OH, DEAR! A TOUCH FROM ONE OF THOSE LIGHT SABERS AND ARTOO WILL BE NOTHING BUT A PILE OF...
ARTOO, LOOK OUT!
VUMM
YOU MADE IT!
DWEE, TEK!
2

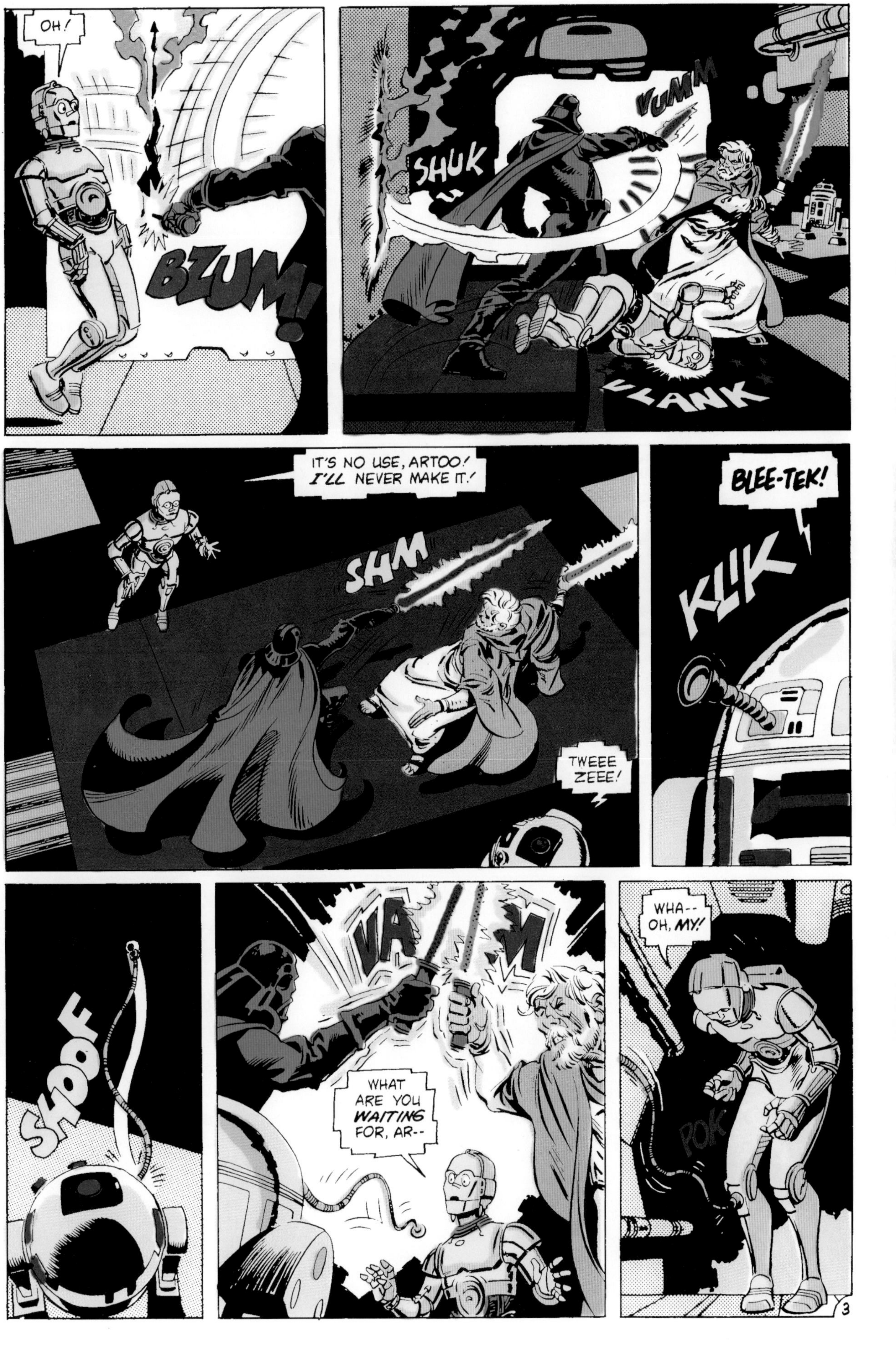
OH!
BZUM!
SHUK
VUMM
CLANK
IT'S NO USE, ARTOO! I'LL NEVER MAKE IT.!
SHM
TWEEE ZEEE!
BLEE-TEK!
KLIK
SHOOF
VA M
WHAT ARE YOU WAITING FOR, AR--
WHA-- OH, MY!
POK
3

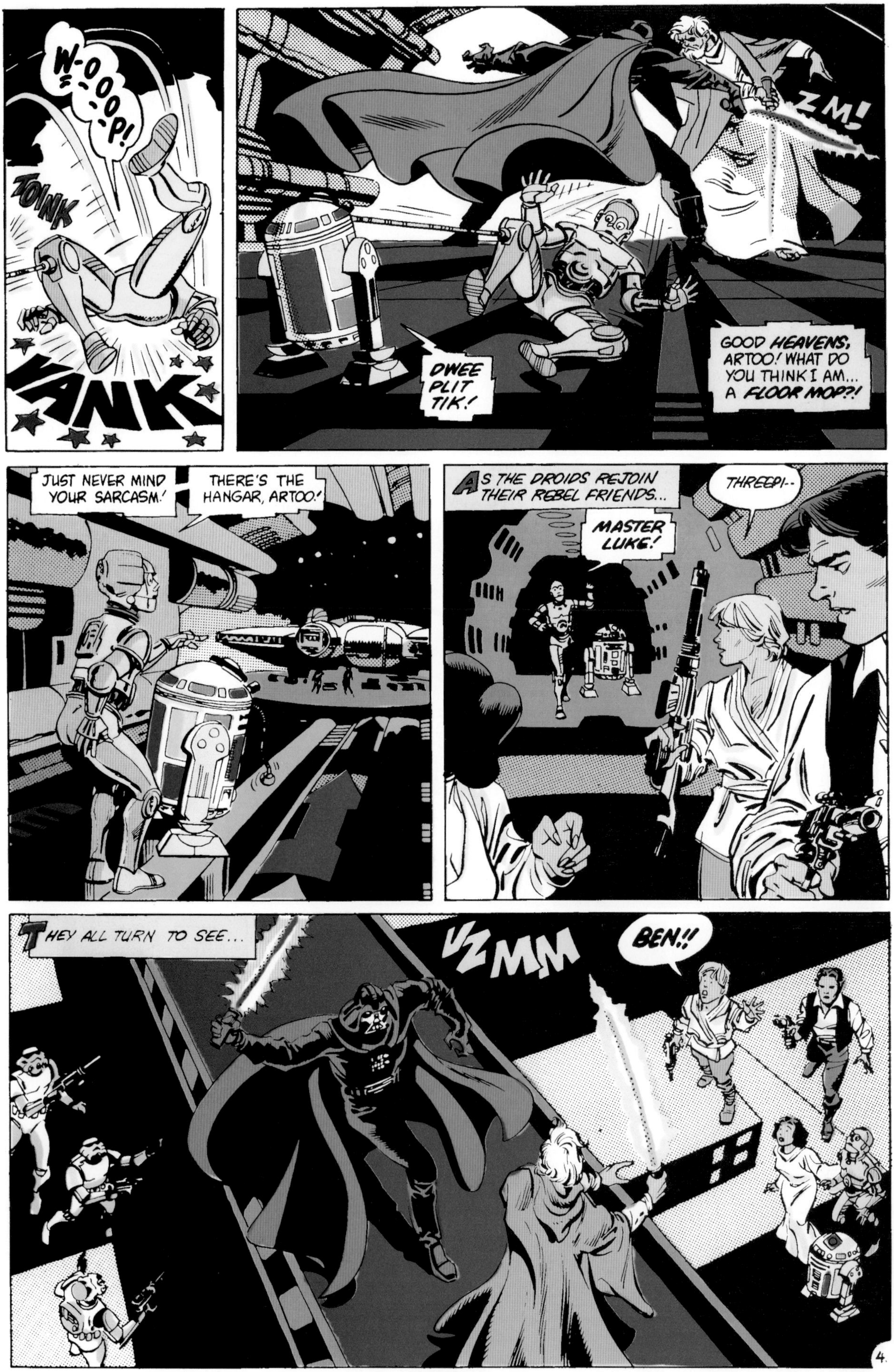
W-O-O-O-P!
TOINK
YANK
ZM!
DWEE PLIT TIK!
GOOD HEAVENS, ARTOO! WHAT DO YOU THINK I AM... A FLOOR MOP?!
JUST NEVER MIND YOUR SARCASM!
THERE'S THE HANGAR, ARTOO!
AS THE DROIDS REJOIN THEIR REBEL FRIENDS...
THREEPI--
MASTER LUKE!
THEY ALL TURN TO SEE...
VZMM
BEN!!
4.

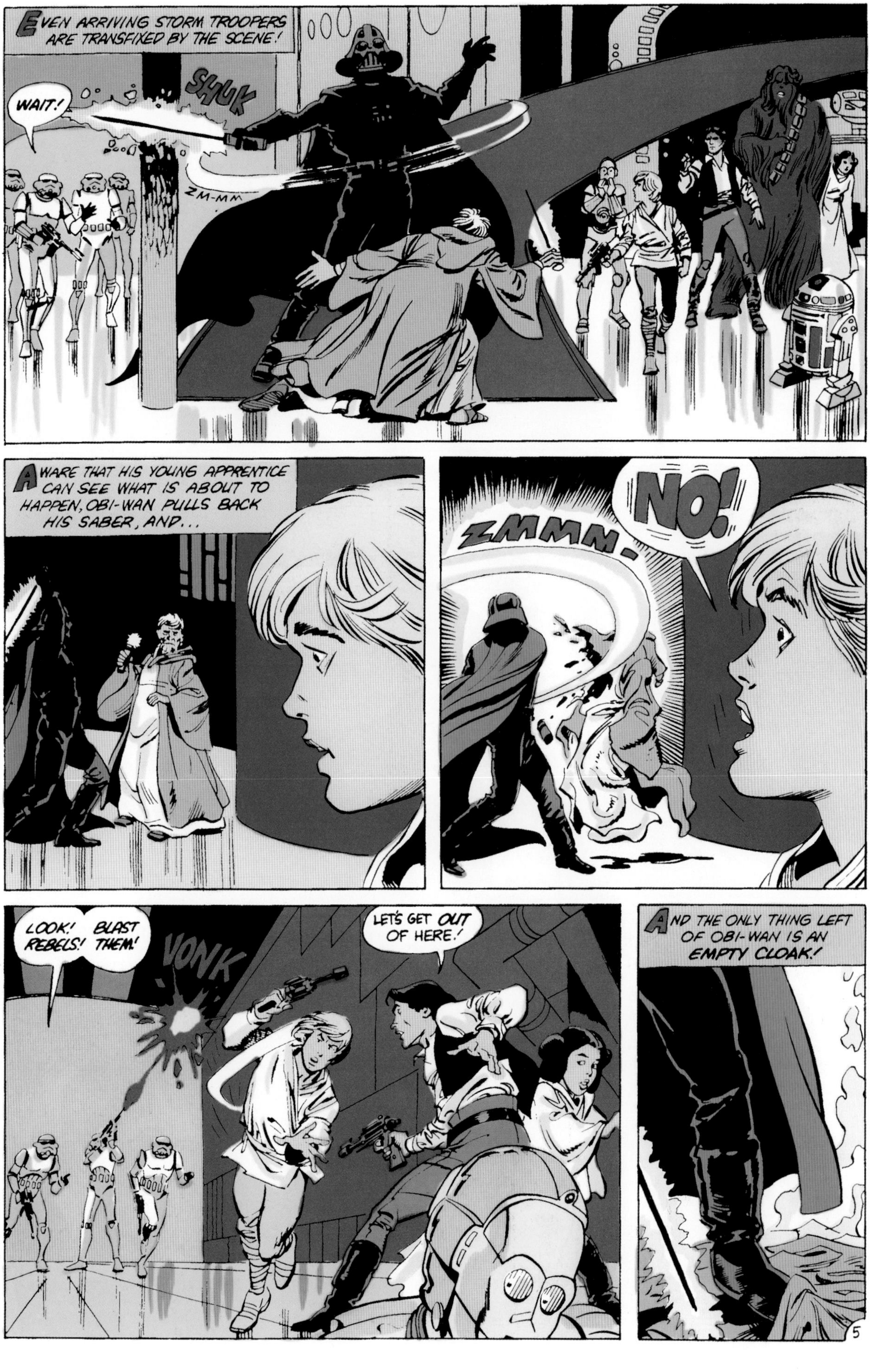
EVEN ARRIVING STORM TROOPERS ARE TRANSFIXED BY THE SCENE!
WAIT!
SHUK
ZM-MM
AWARE THAT HIS YOUNG APPRENTICE CAN SEE WHAT IS ABOUT TO HAPPEN, OBI-WAN PULLS BACK HIS SABER, AND...
ZMMM-
NO!
LOOK! REBELS!
BLAST THEM!
VONK
LET'S GET OUT OF HERE!
AND THE ONLY THING LEFT OF OBI-WAN IS AN EMPTY CLOAK!
5

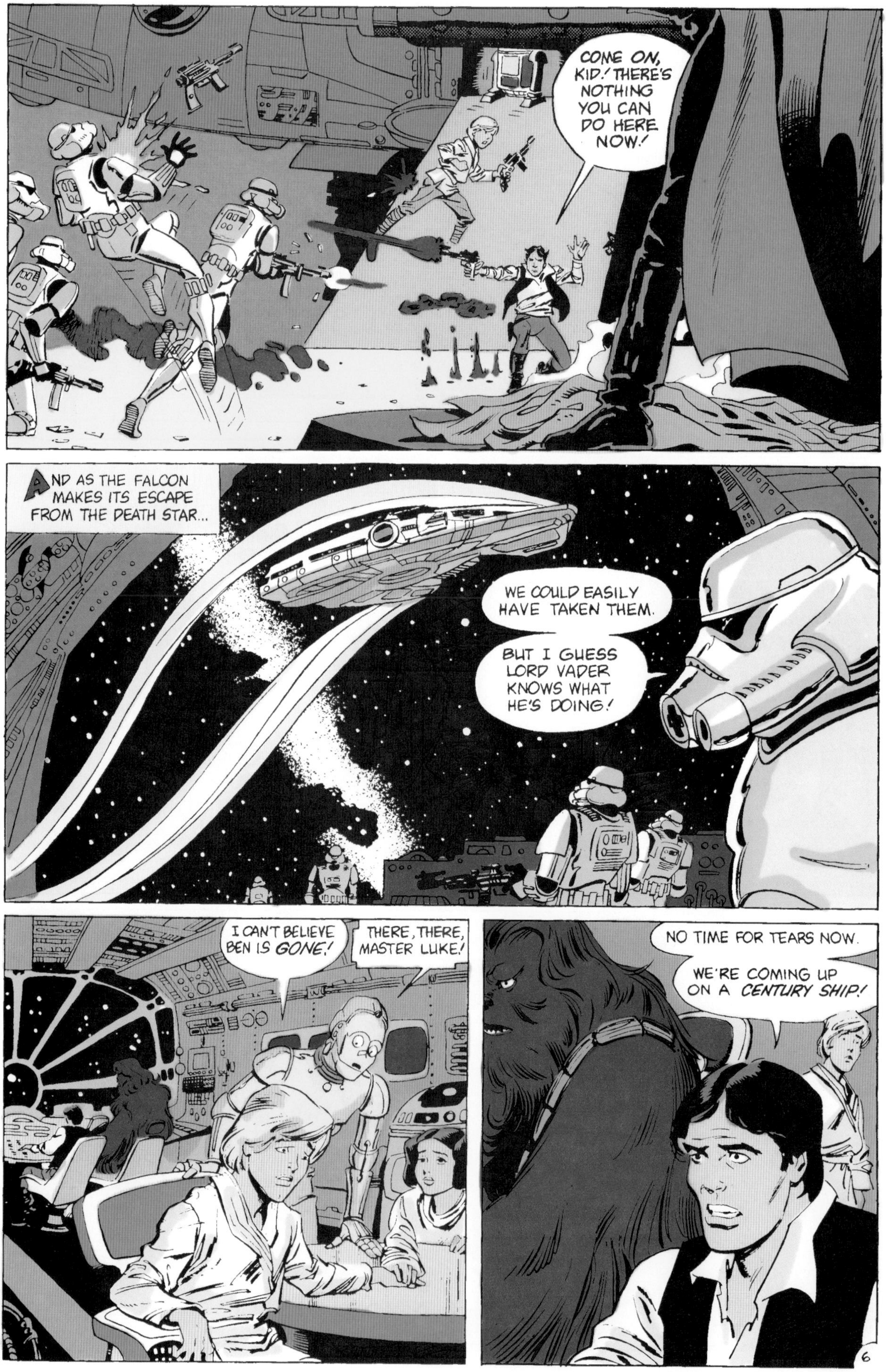
COME ON, KID! THERE'S NOTHING YOU CAN DO HERE NOW!
AND AS THE FALCON MAKES ITS ESCAPE FROM THE DEATH STAR...
WE COULD EASILY HAVE TAKEN THEM.
BUT I GUESS LORD VADER KNOWS WHAT HE'S DOING!
I CAN'T BELIEVE BEN IS GONE!
THERE, THERE, MASTER LUKE!
NO TIME FOR TEARS NOW.
WE'RE COMING UP ON A CENTURY SHIP!
6

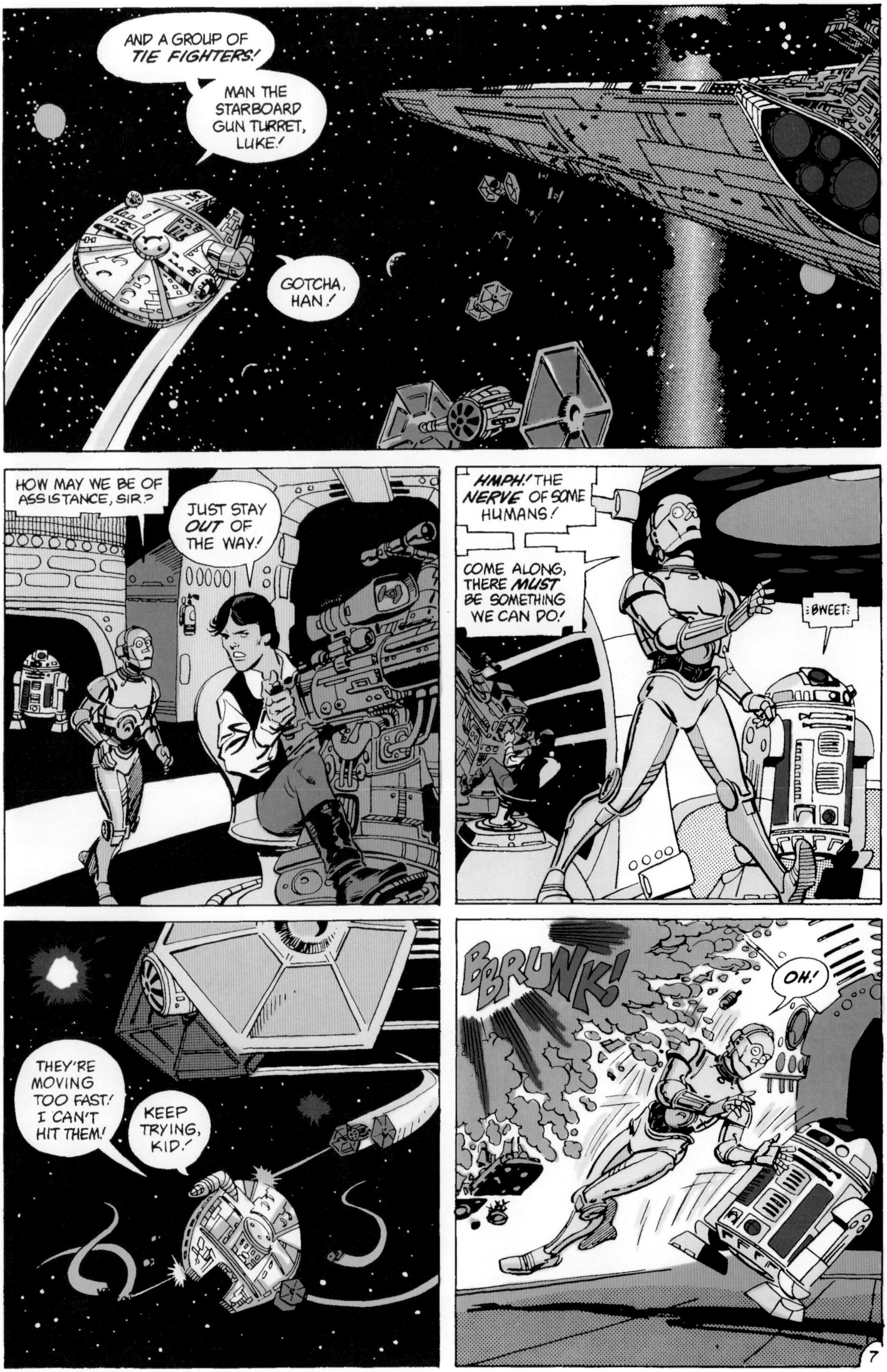
AND A GROUP OF TIE FIGHTERS!
MAN THE STARBOARD GUN TURRET, LUKE!
GOTCHA, HAN!
HOW MAY WE BE OF ASSISTANCE, SIR?
JUST STAY OUT OF THE WAY!
HMPH! THE NERVE OF SOME HUMANS!
COME ALONG, THERE MUST BE SOMETHING WE CAN DO!
BWEET
THEY'RE MOVING TOO FAST! I CAN'T HIT THEM!
KEEP TRYING, KID!
BBRUNK!
OH!
7

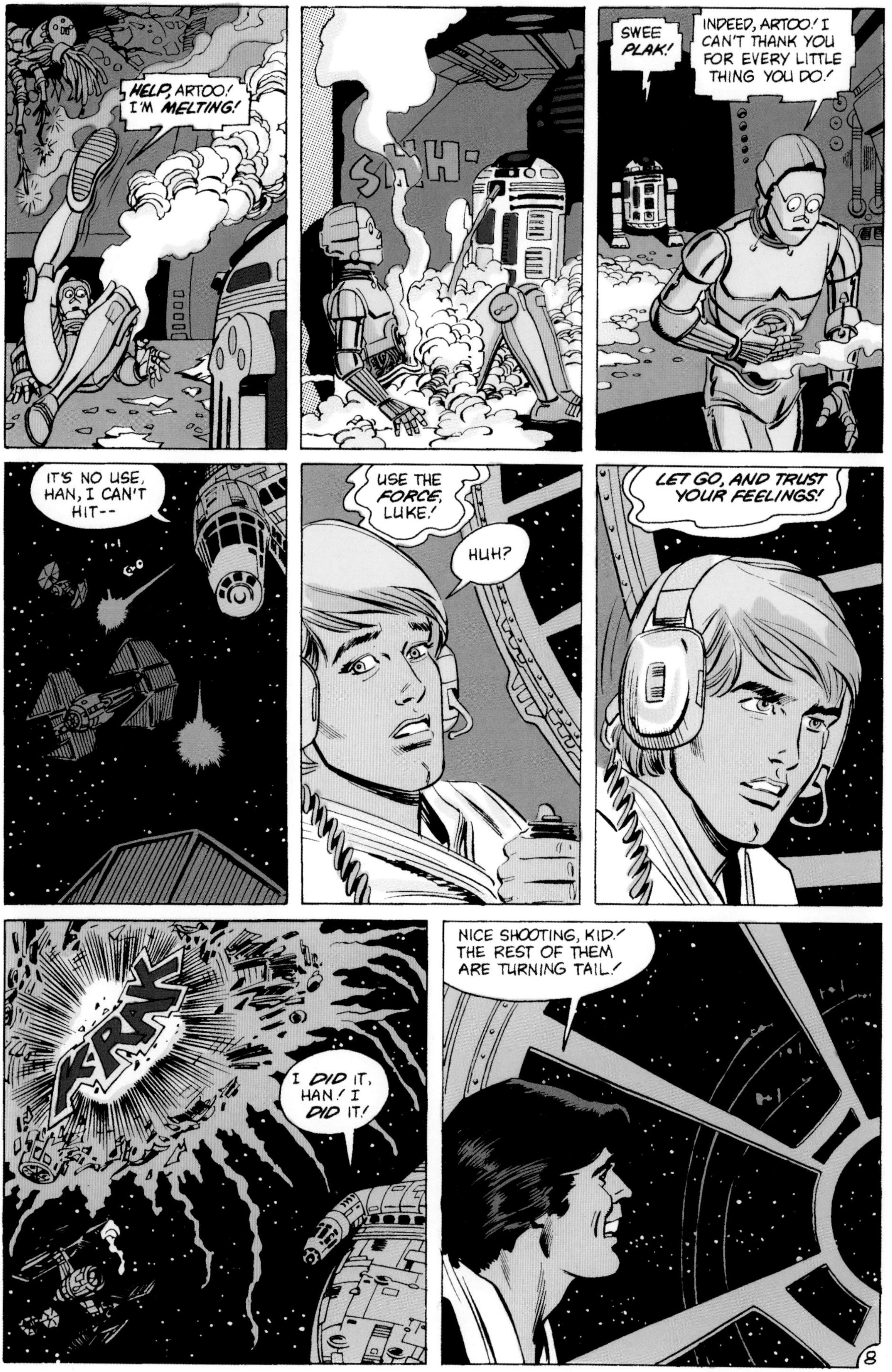
HELP, ARTOO! I'M MELTING!
SHH-
SWEE PLAK!
INDEED, ARTOO! I CAN'T THANK YOU FOR EVERY LITTLE THING YOU DO!
IT'S NO USE, HAN, I CAN'T HIT--
USE THE FORCE, LUKE!
HUH?
LET GO, AND TRUST YOUR FEELINGS!
KRAK
I DID IT, HAN! I DID IT!
NICE SHOOTING, KID! THE REST OF THEM ARE TURNING TAIL!
8

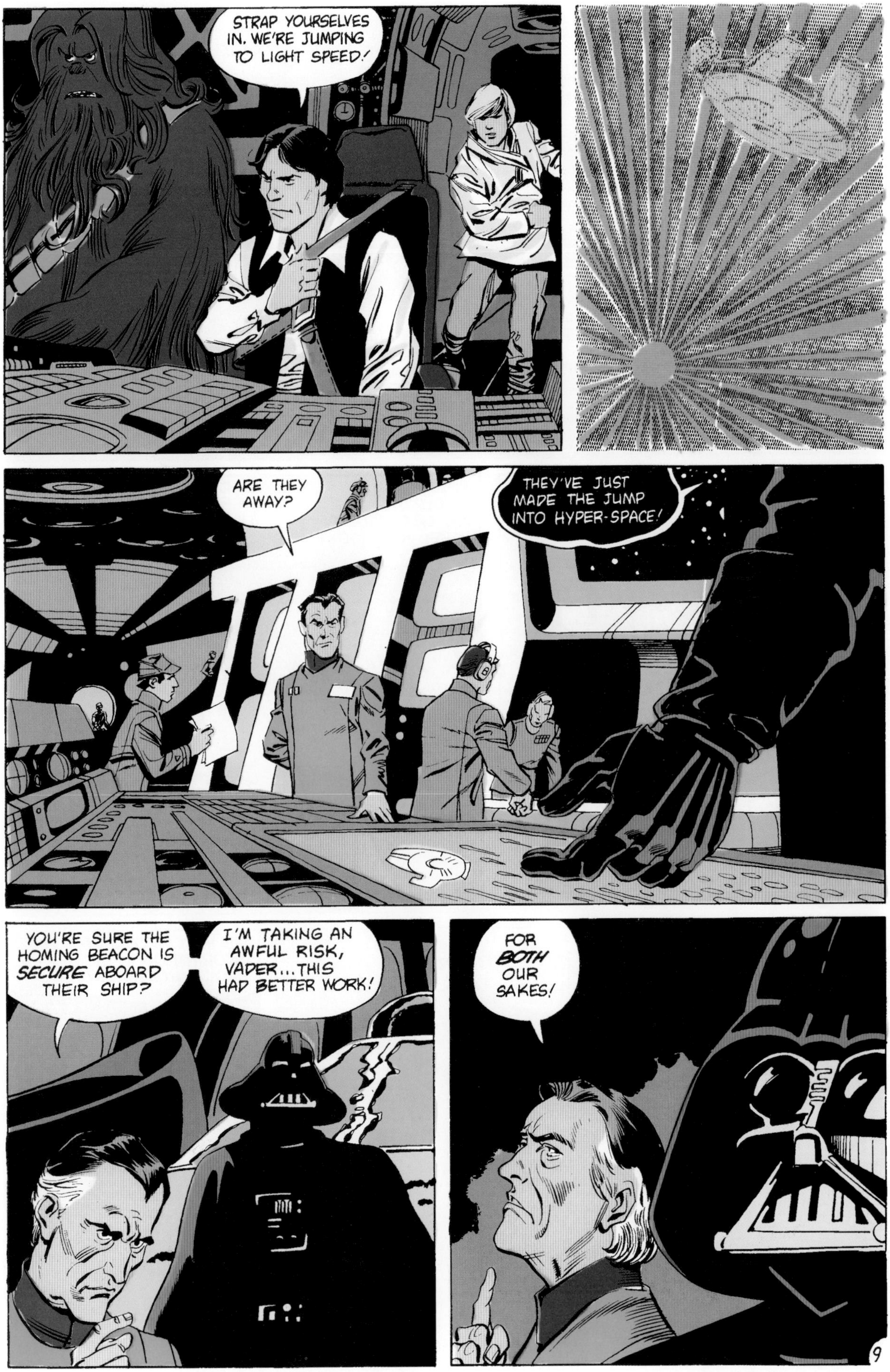
STRAP YOURSELVES IN. WE'RE JUMPING TO LIGHT SPEED!
ARE THEY AWAY?
THEY'VE JUST MADE THE JUMP INTO HYPER-SPACE!
YOU'RE SURE THE HOMING BEACON IS SECURE ABOARD THEIR SHIP?
I'M TAKING AN AWFUL RISK, VADER... THIS HAD BETTER WORK!
FOR BOTH OUR SAKES!
9

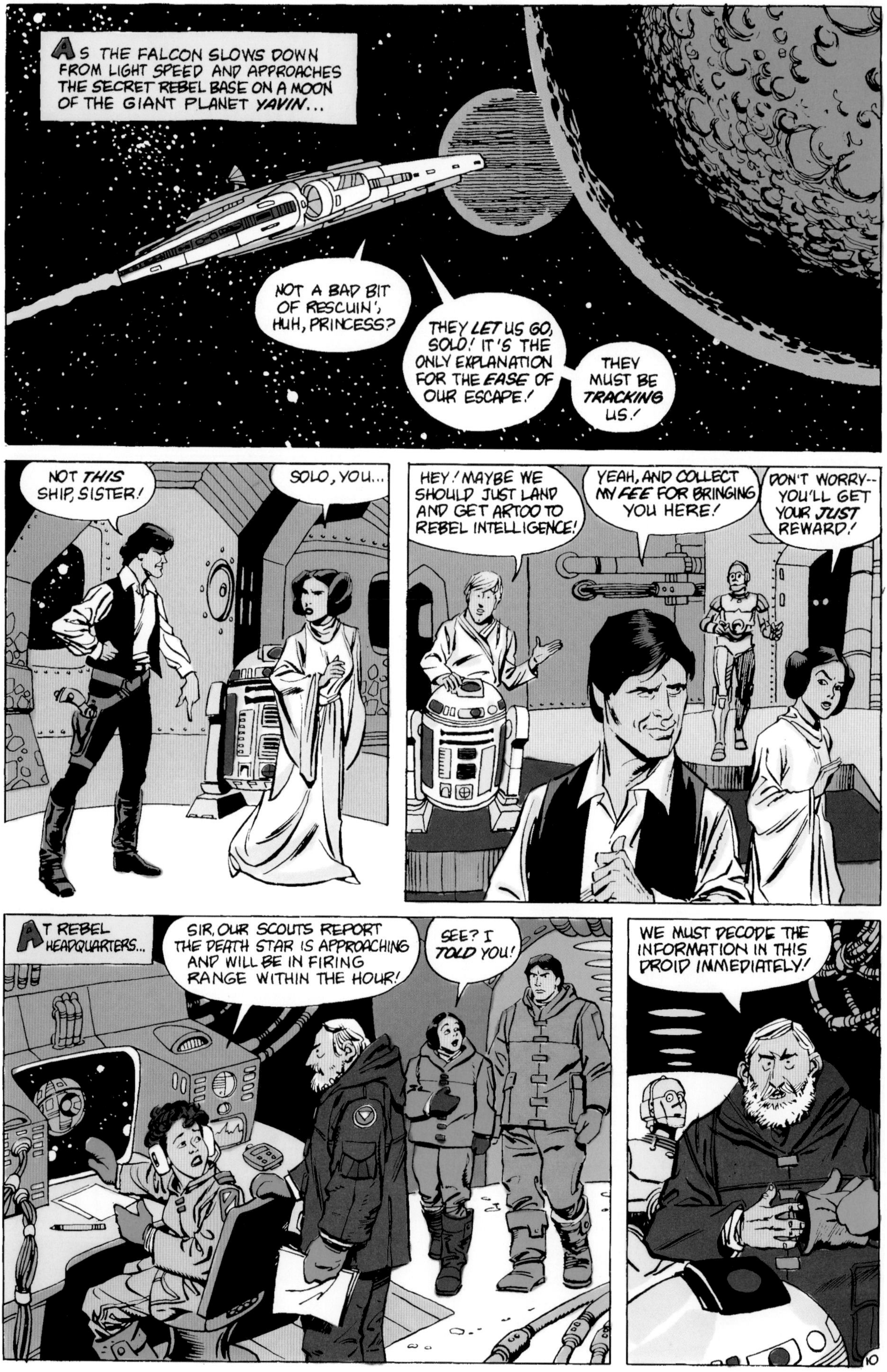

AS THE FALCON SLOWS DOWN FROM LIGHT SPEED AND APPROACHES THE SECRET REBEL BASE ON A MOON OF THE GIANT PLANET YAVIN...
NOT A BAD BIT OF RESCUIN', HUH, PRINCESS?
THEY LET US GO, SOLO! IT'S THE ONLY EXPLANATION FOR THE EASE OF OUR ESCAPE!
THEY MUST BE TRACKING US!
NOT THIS SHIP, SISTER!
SOLO, YOU...
HEY! MAYBE WE SHOULD JUST LAND AND GET ARTOO TO REBEL INTELLIGENCE!
YEAH, AND COLLECT MY FEE FOR BRINGING YOU HERE!
DON'T WORRY-- YOU'LL GET YOUR JUST REWARD!
AT REBEL HEADQUARTERS...
SIR, OUR SCOUTS REPORT THE DEATH STAR IS APPROACHING AND WILL BE IN FIRING RANGE WITHIN THE HOUR!
SEE? I TOLD YOU!
WE MUST DECODE THE INFORMATION IN THIS DROID IMMEDIATELY!
10

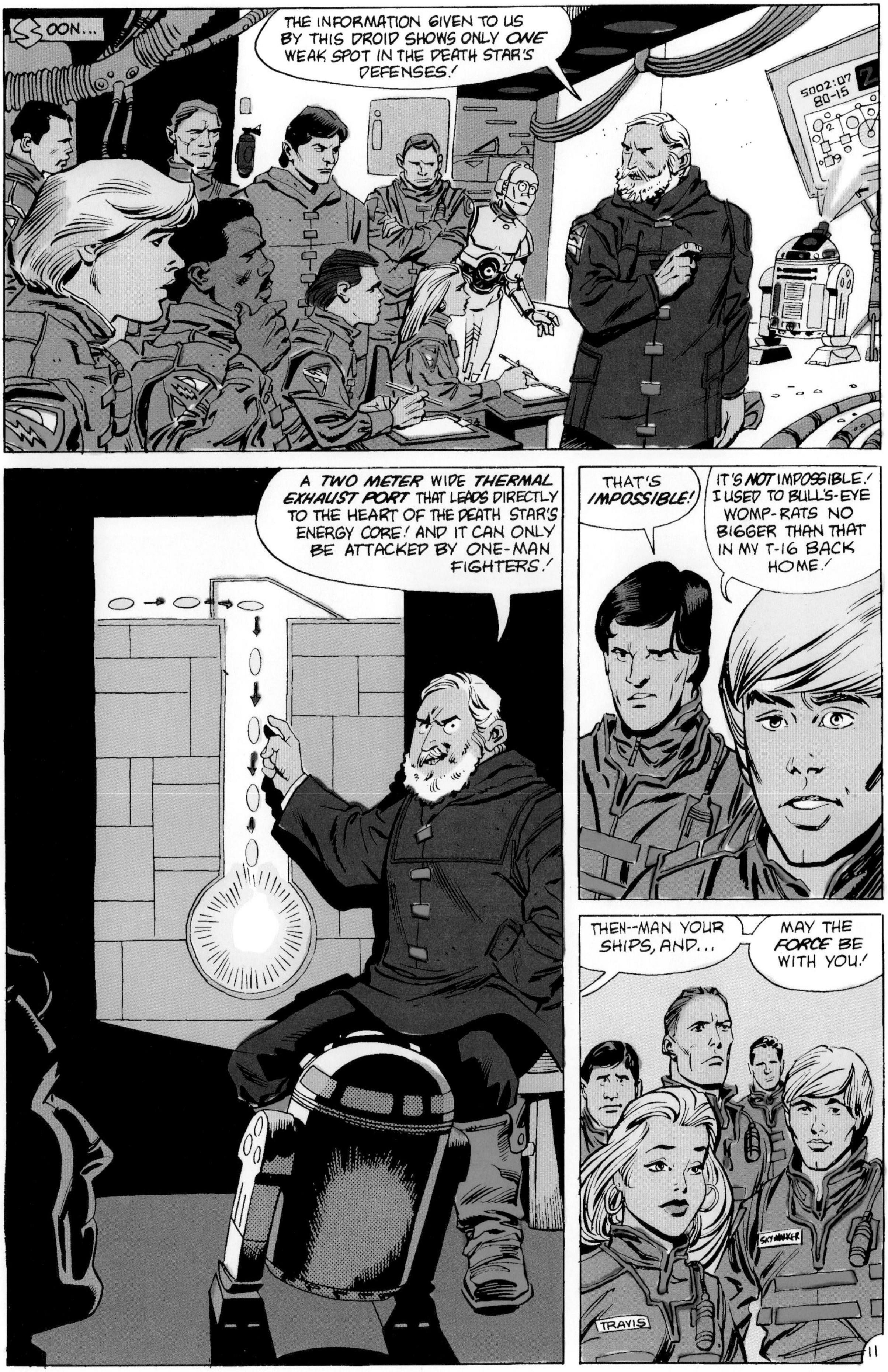
SOON...
THE INFORMATION GIVEN TO US BY THIS DROID SHOWS ONLY ONE WEAK SPOT IN THE DEATH STAR'S DEFENSES!
5002:07 80-15
A TWO METER WIDE THERMAL EXHAUST PORT THAT LEADS DIRECTLY TO THE HEART OF THE DEATH STAR'S ENERGY CORE! AND IT CAN ONLY BE ATTACKED BY ONE-MAN FIGHTERS!
THAT'S IMPOSSIBLE!
IT'S NOT IMPOSSIBLE! I USED TO BULL'S-EYE WOMP-RATS NO BIGGER THAN THAT IN MY T-16 BACK HOME!
THEN--MAN YOUR SHIPS, AND...
MAY THE FORCE BE WITH YOU!
SKYWALKER
TRAVIS
11

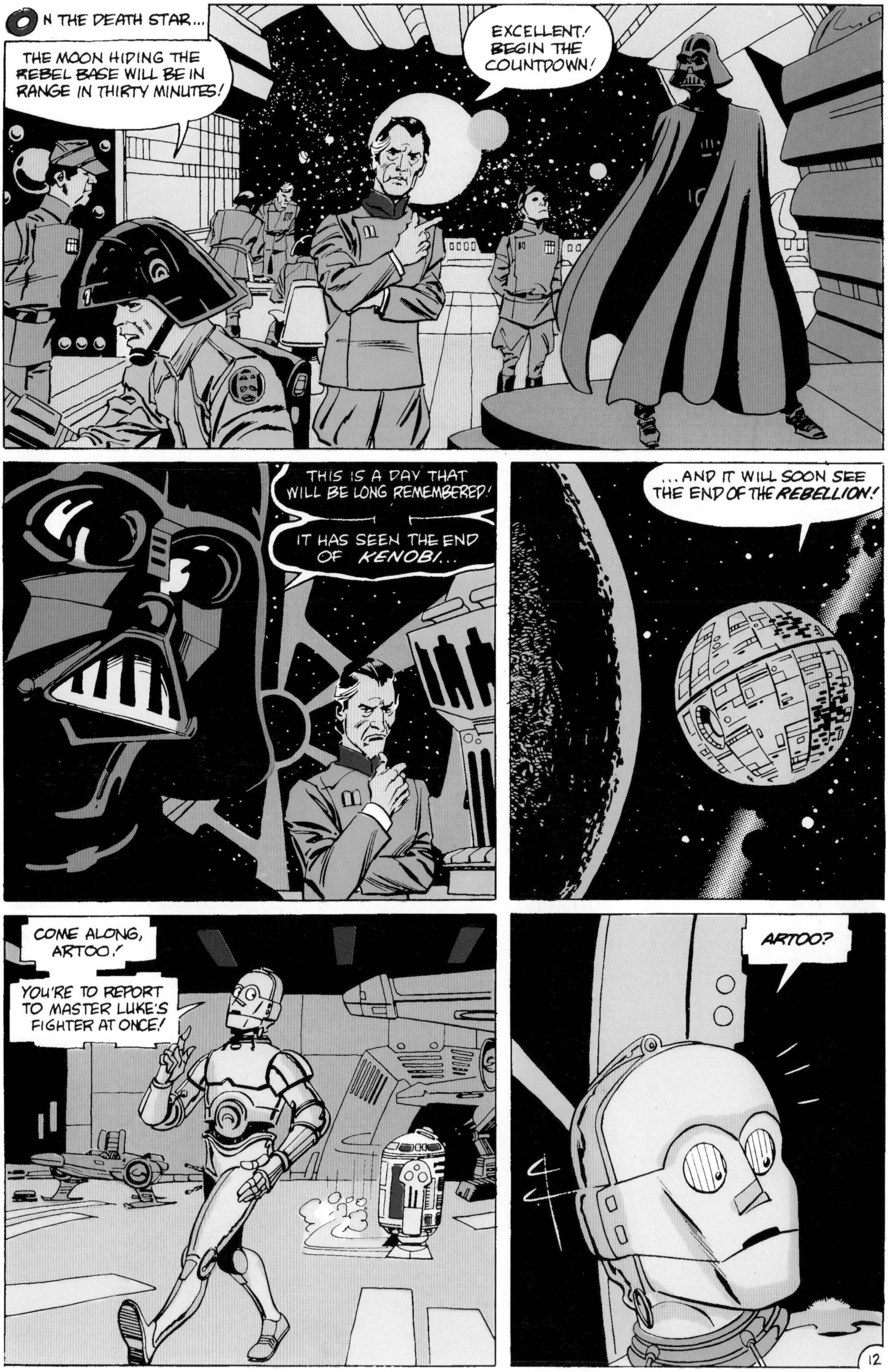
ON THE DEATH STAR...
THE MOON HIDING THE REBEL BASE WILL BE IN RANGE IN THIRTY MINUTES!
EXCELLENT! BEGIN THE COUNTDOWN!
THIS IS A DAY THAT WILL BE LONG REMEMBERED!
IT HAS SEEN THE END OF KENOBI...
...AND IT WILL SOON SEE THE END OF THE REBELLION!
COME ALONG, ARTOO!
YOU'RE TO REPORT TO MASTER LUKE'S FIGHTER AT ONCE!
ARTOO?
12

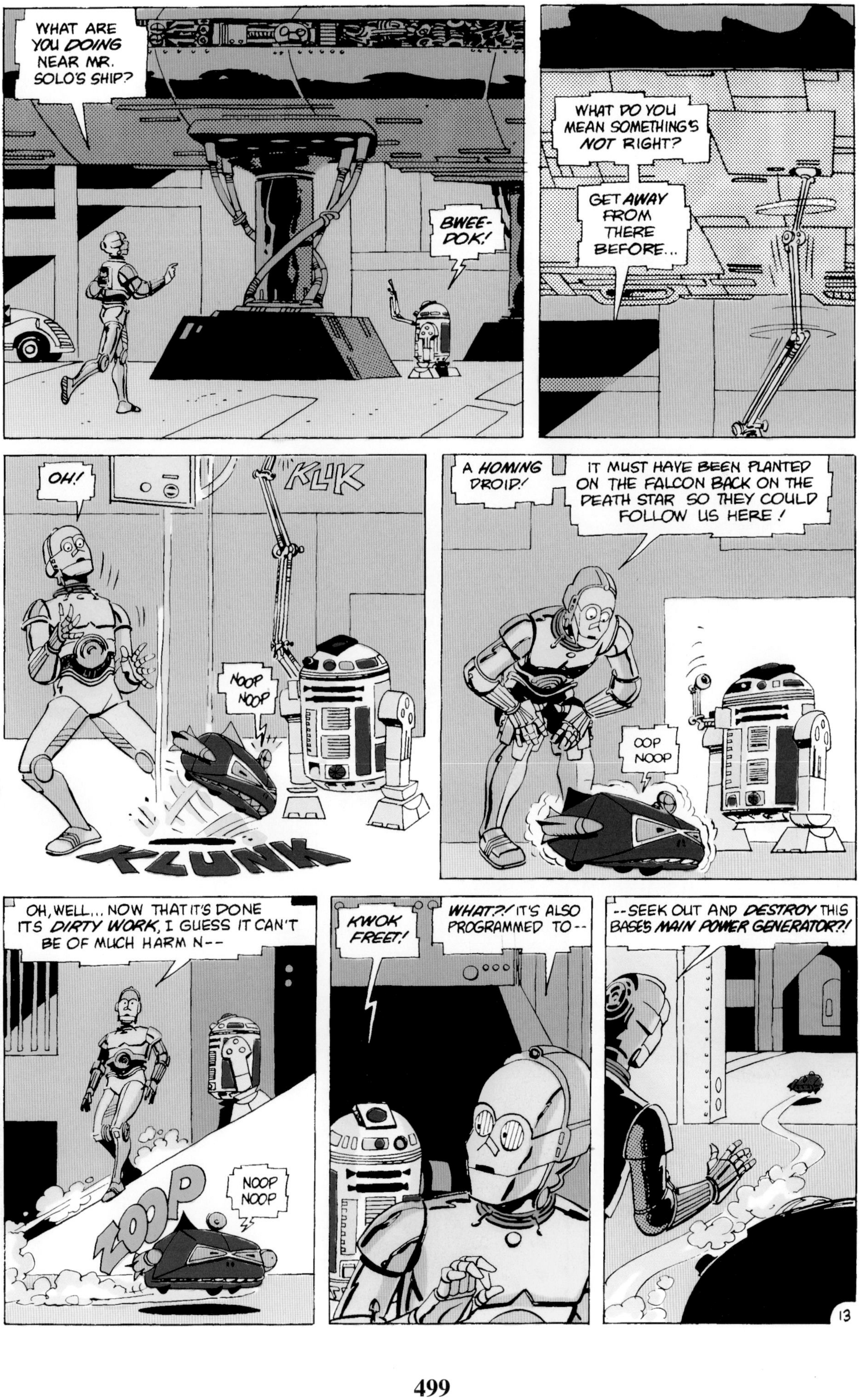
WHAT ARE YOU *DOING* NEAR MR. SOLO'S SHIP?
BWEE-DOK!
WHAT DO YOU MEAN SOMETHING'S *NOT* RIGHT?
GET *AWAY* FROM THERE BEFORE...
OH!
KLIK
NOOP NOOP
KLUNK
A *HOMING* DROID!
IT MUST HAVE BEEN PLANTED ON THE FALCON BACK ON THE DEATH STAR SO THEY COULD FOLLOW US HERE!
OOP NOOP
OH, WELL... NOW THAT IT'S DONE ITS *DIRTY WORK*, I GUESS IT CAN'T BE OF MUCH HARM N--
ZOOP
NOOP NOOP
KWOK FREET!
WHAT?! IT'S ALSO PROGRAMMED TO--
--SEEK OUT AND *DESTROY* THIS BASE'S *MAIN POWER GENERATOR?!*
13

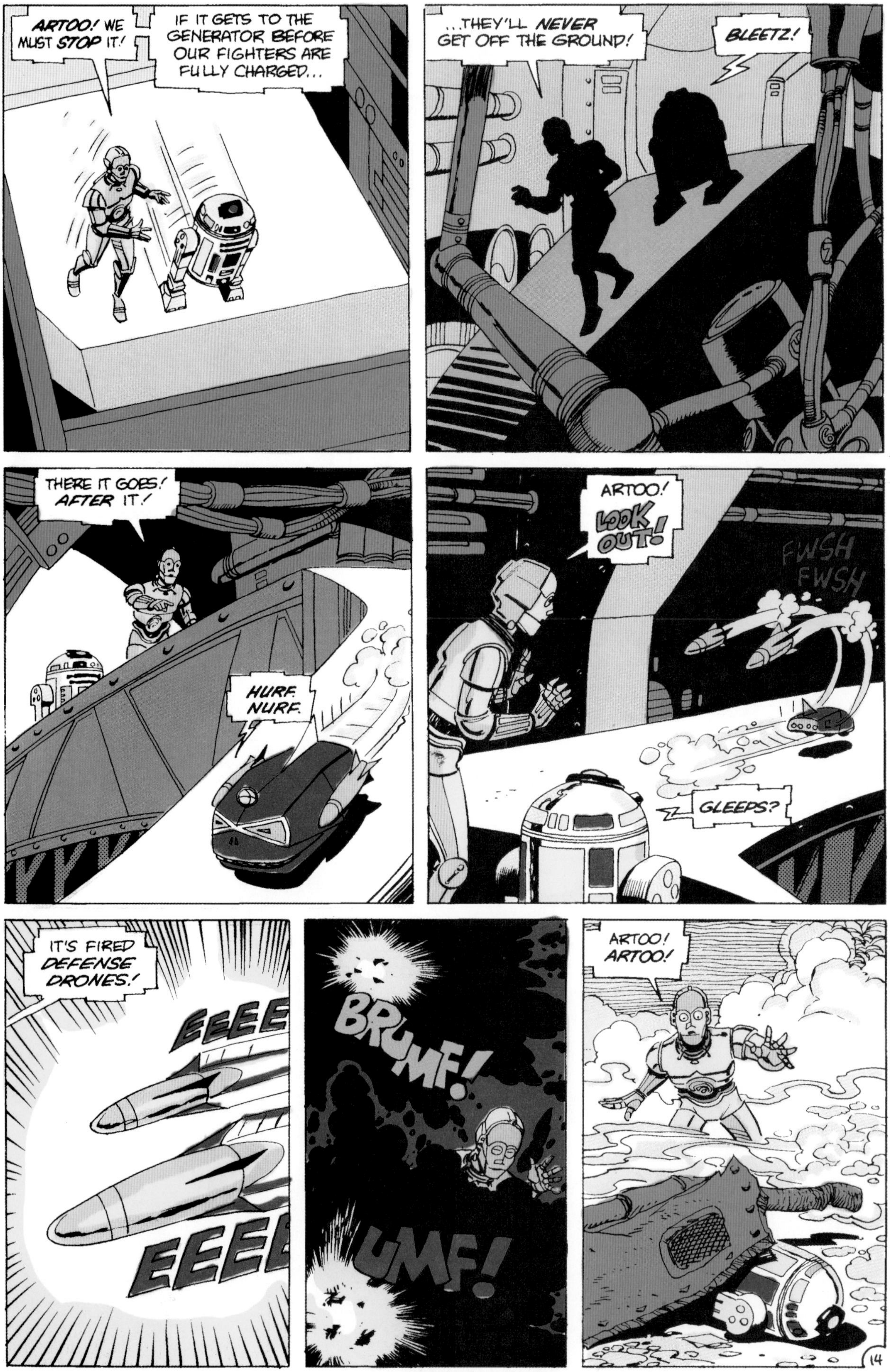
ARTOO! WE MUST STOP IT!
IF IT GETS TO THE GENERATOR BEFORE OUR FIGHTERS ARE FULLY CHARGED...
...THEY'LL NEVER GET OFF THE GROUND!
BLEETZ!
THERE IT GOES! AFTER IT!
HURF. NURF.
ARTOO! LOOK OUT!
FWSH FWSH
GLEEPS?
IT'S FIRED DEFENSE DRONES!
EEEE
EEEE
BRUMF!
UMF!
ARTOO! ARTOO!
14

I'LL TEACH YOU TO HARM MY LITTLE ARTOO, YOU--

BASE POWER →

OOP NOOP

ZOOP

OH! IT'S USED *ACID* TO EAT THROUGH THE GENERATOR SECURITY DOOR!

NOW IT'S ATTEMPTING TO DISRUPT THE BASE'S POWER SUPPLY!

SSSS-

GET *AWAY* FROM THERE, YOU LITTLE SABOTEUR!

FAP!

ARP!

OH, MY!

HURF NURF

FST!

ACID!

I'M *DOOMED!* DOOMED!

HURF URF

FST

FST

TSF

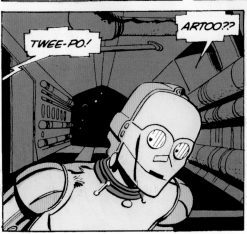

TWEE-PO!

ARTOO??

PREET GLIP!

OF *COURSE* I KNOW I'M STANDING NEXT TO THESE BLAST DOORS!

URF DURF

15

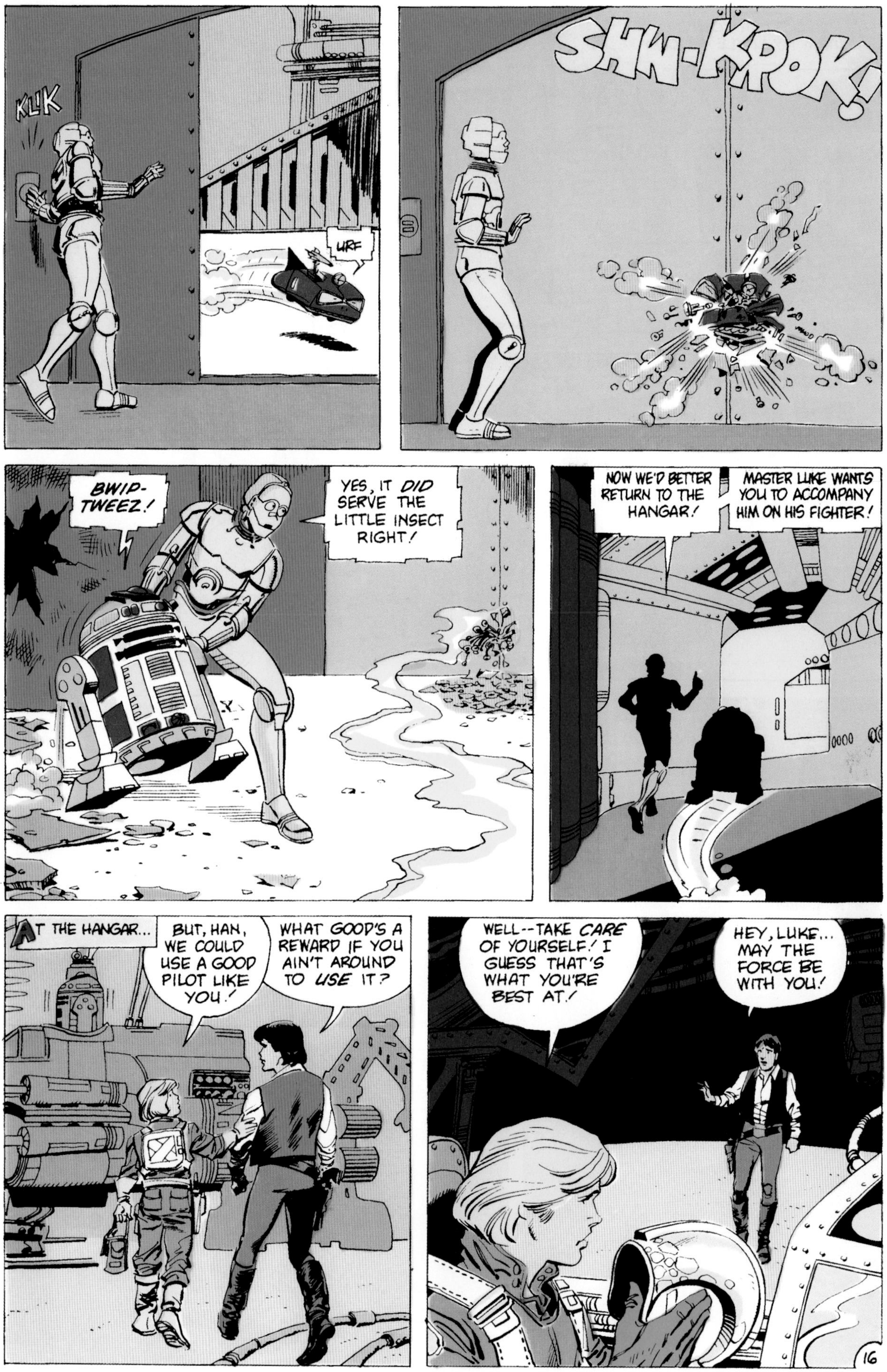
KLIK
URF
SHW-KROOK!
BWIP-TWEEZ!
YES, IT DID SERVE THE LITTLE INSECT RIGHT!
NOW WE'D BETTER RETURN TO THE HANGAR!
MASTER LUKE WANTS YOU TO ACCOMPANY HIM ON HIS FIGHTER!
AT THE HANGAR...
BUT, HAN, WE COULD USE A GOOD PILOT LIKE YOU!
WHAT GOOD'S A REWARD IF YOU AIN'T AROUND TO USE IT?
WELL--TAKE CARE OF YOURSELF! I GUESS THAT'S WHAT YOU'RE BEST AT!
HEY, LUKE... MAY THE FORCE BE WITH YOU!
16

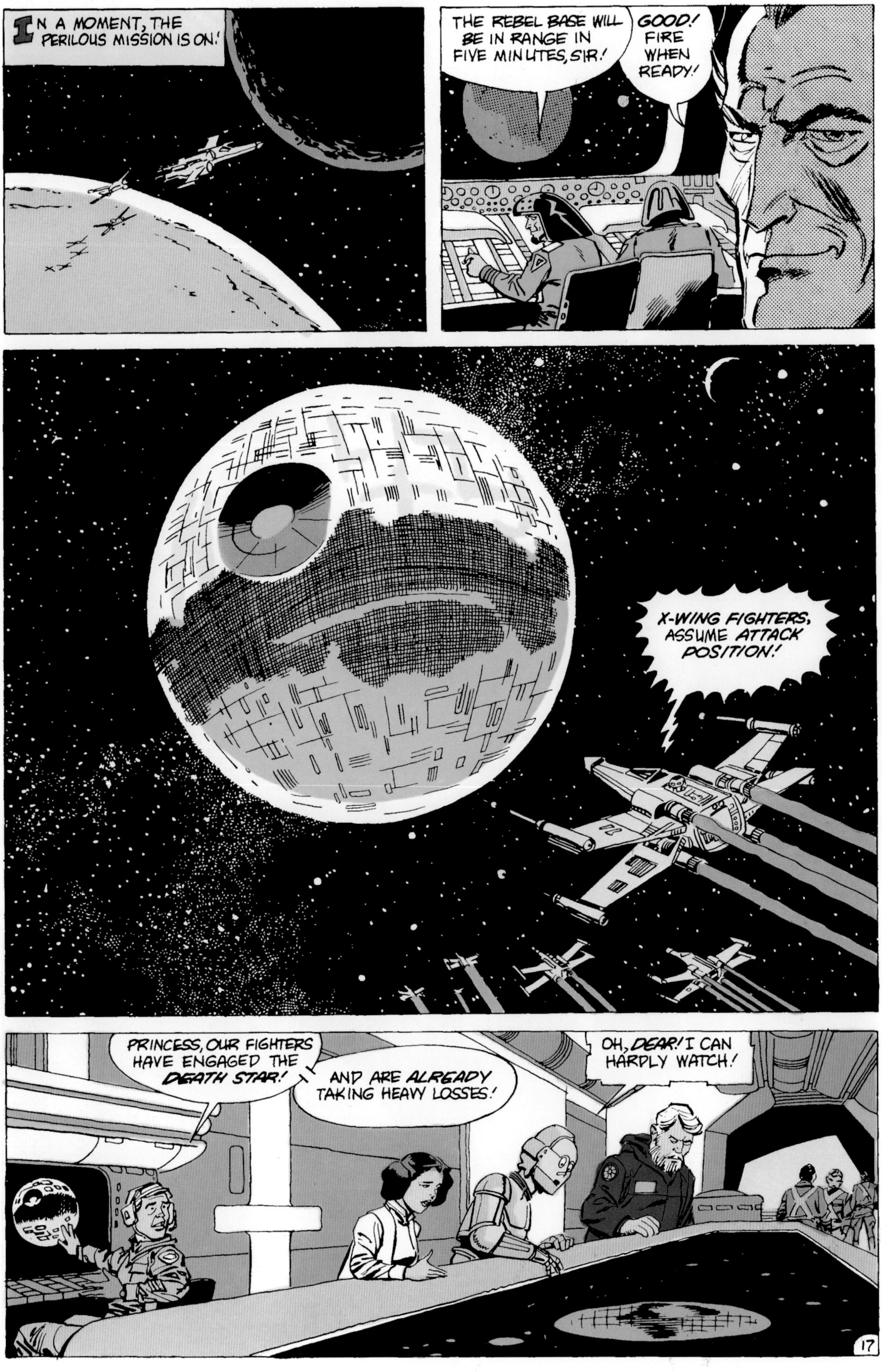
IN A MOMENT, THE PERILOUS MISSION IS ON!
THE REBEL BASE WILL BE IN RANGE IN FIVE MINUTES, SIR!
GOOD! FIRE WHEN READY!
X-WING FIGHTERS, ASSUME ATTACK POSITION!
PRINCESS, OUR FIGHTERS HAVE ENGAGED THE DEATH STAR!
AND ARE ALREADY TAKING HEAVY LOSSES!
OH, DEAR! I CAN HARDLY WATCH!
17

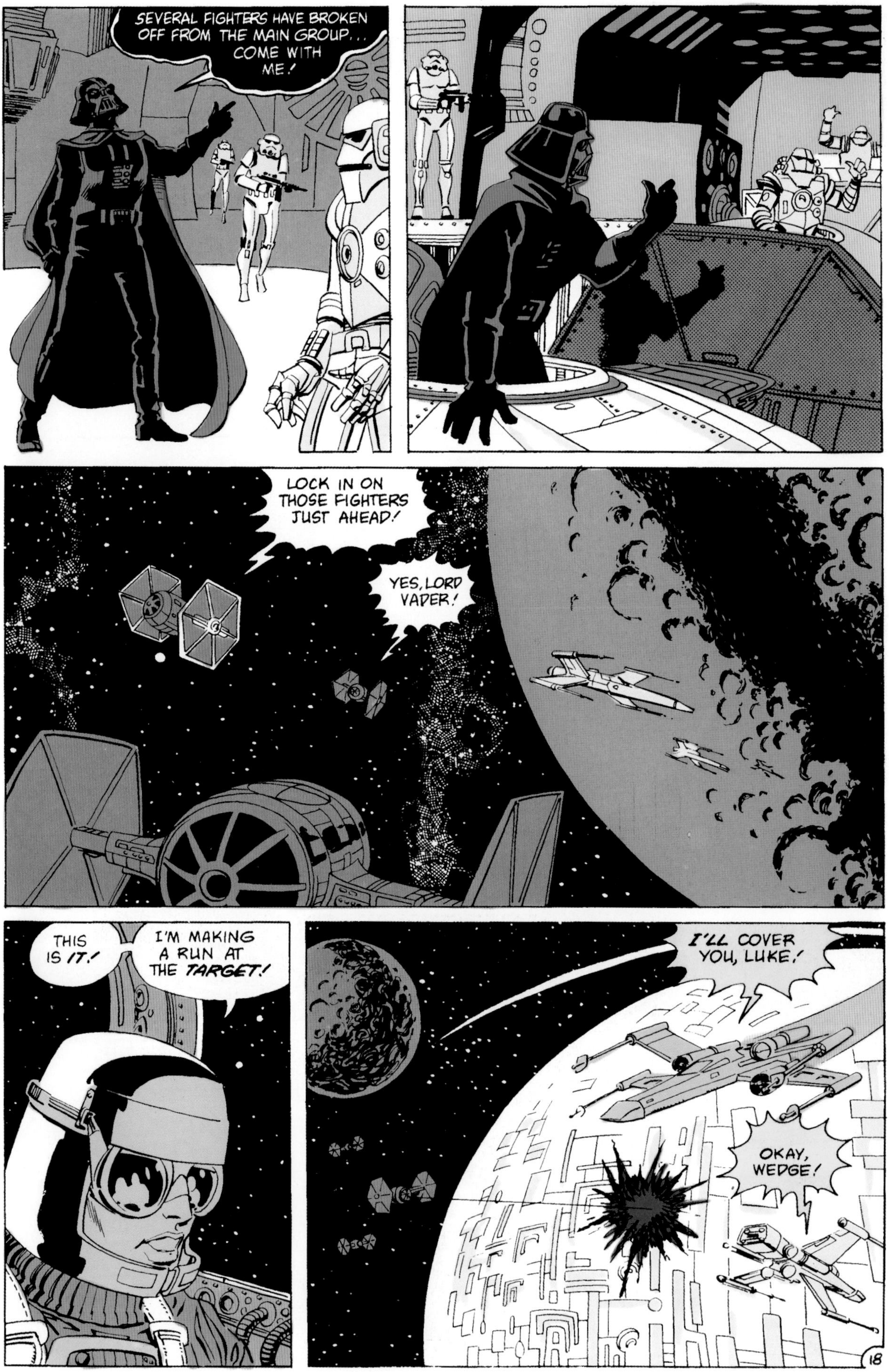
SEVERAL FIGHTERS HAVE BROKEN OFF FROM THE MAIN GROUP... COME WITH ME!
LOCK IN ON THOSE FIGHTERS JUST AHEAD!
YES, LORD VADER!
THIS IS IT!
I'M MAKING A RUN AT THE TARGET!
I'LL COVER YOU, LUKE!
OKAY, WEDGE!
18

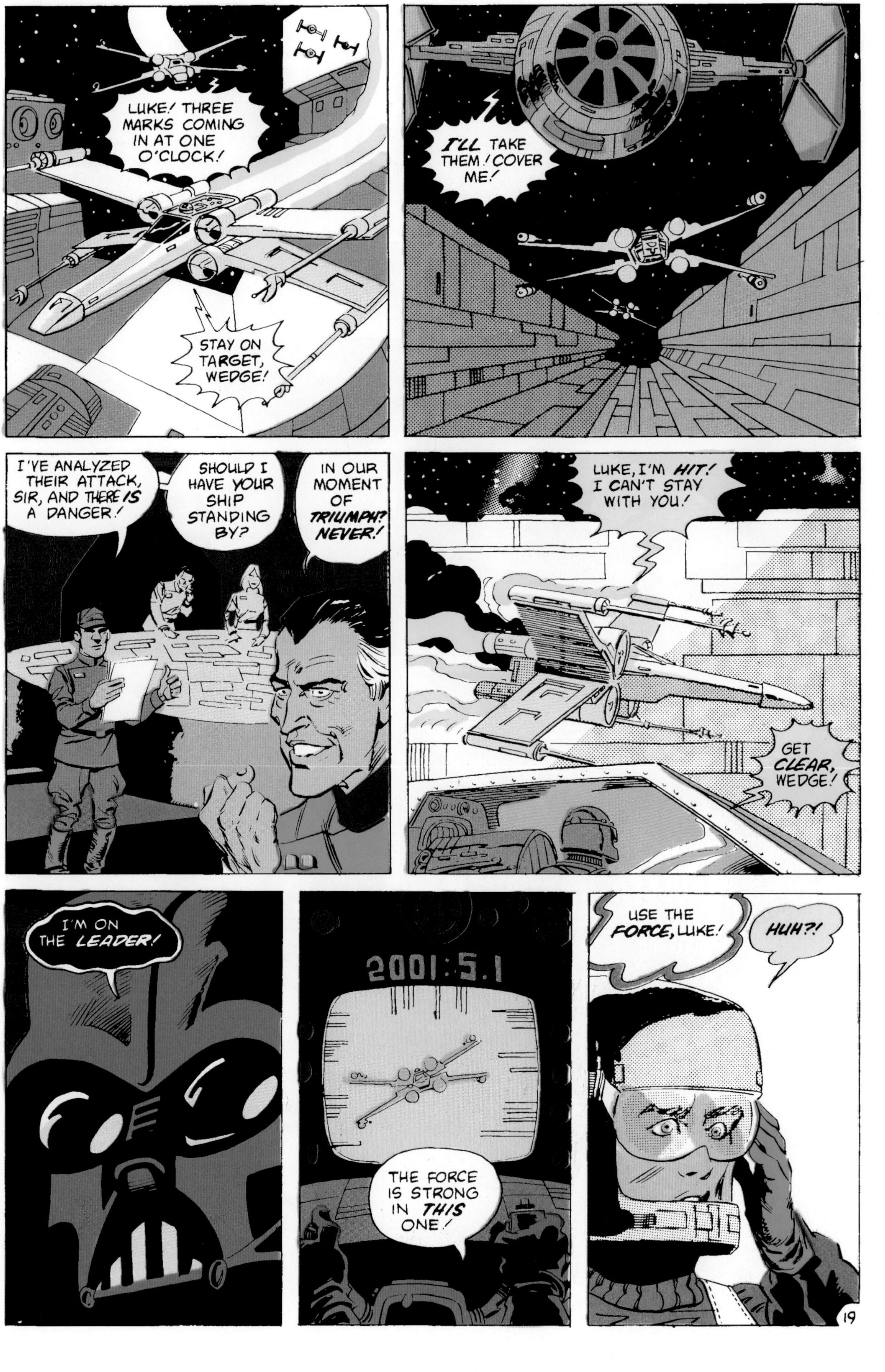
LUKE! THREE MARKS COMING IN AT ONE O'CLOCK!
STAY ON TARGET, WEDGE!
I'LL TAKE THEM! COVER ME!
I'VE ANALYZED THEIR ATTACK, SIR, AND THERE IS A DANGER!
SHOULD I HAVE YOUR SHIP STANDING BY?
IN OUR MOMENT OF TRIUMPH? NEVER!
LUKE, I'M HIT! I CAN'T STAY WITH YOU!
GET CLEAR, WEDGE!
I'M ON THE LEADER!
2001:5.1
THE FORCE IS STRONG IN THIS ONE!
USE THE FORCE, LUKE!
HUH?!
19

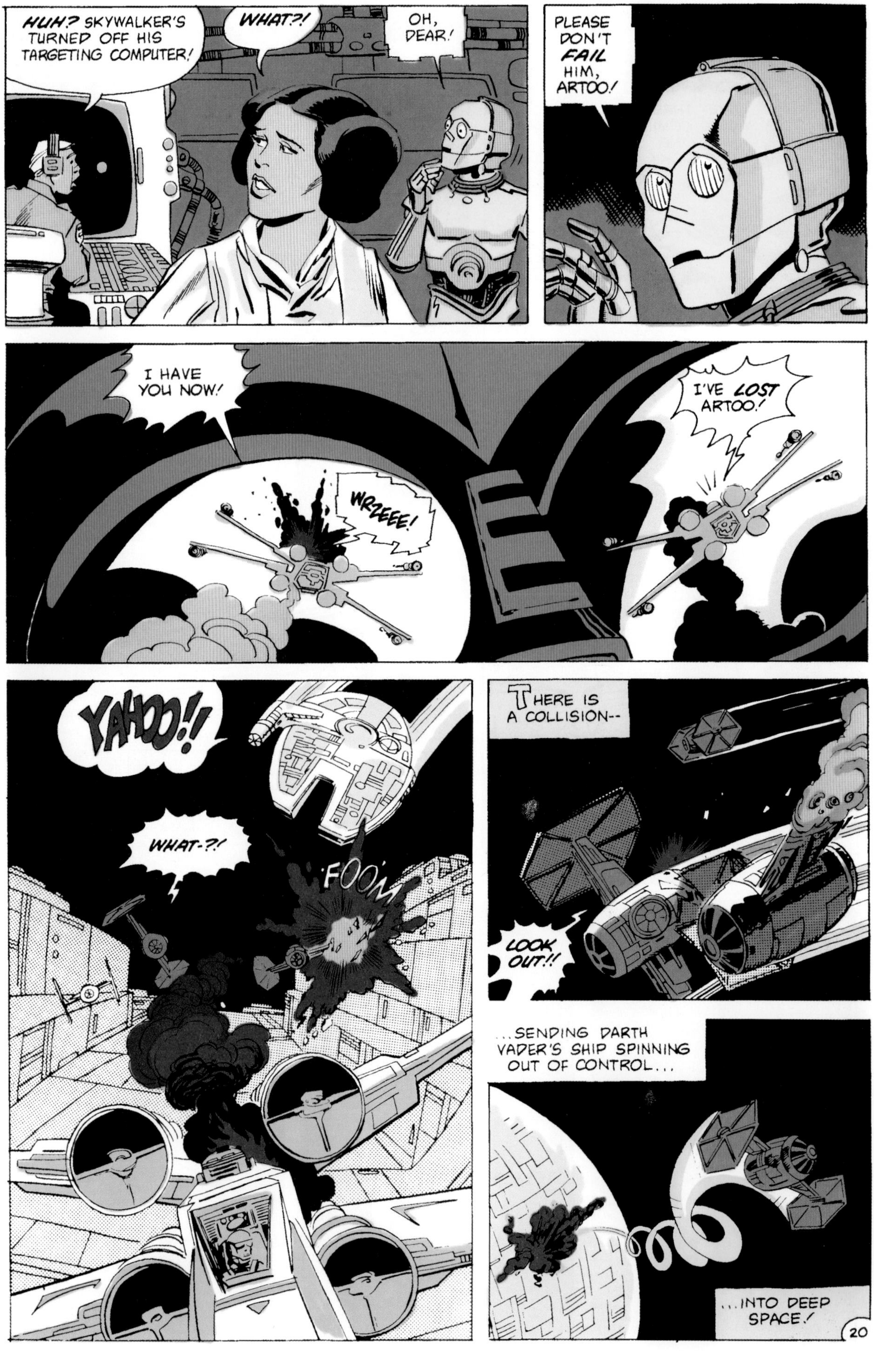

HUH? SKYWALKER'S TURNED OFF HIS TARGETING COMPUTER!
WHAT?!
OH, DEAR!
PLEASE DON'T FAIL HIM, ARTOO!
I HAVE YOU NOW!
WRZEEE!
I'VE LOST ARTOO!
YAHOO!!
WHAT-?!
FOOM
THERE IS A COLLISION--
LOOK OUT!!
...SENDING DARTH VADER'S SHIP SPINNING OUT OF CONTROL...
...INTO DEEP SPACE!
20

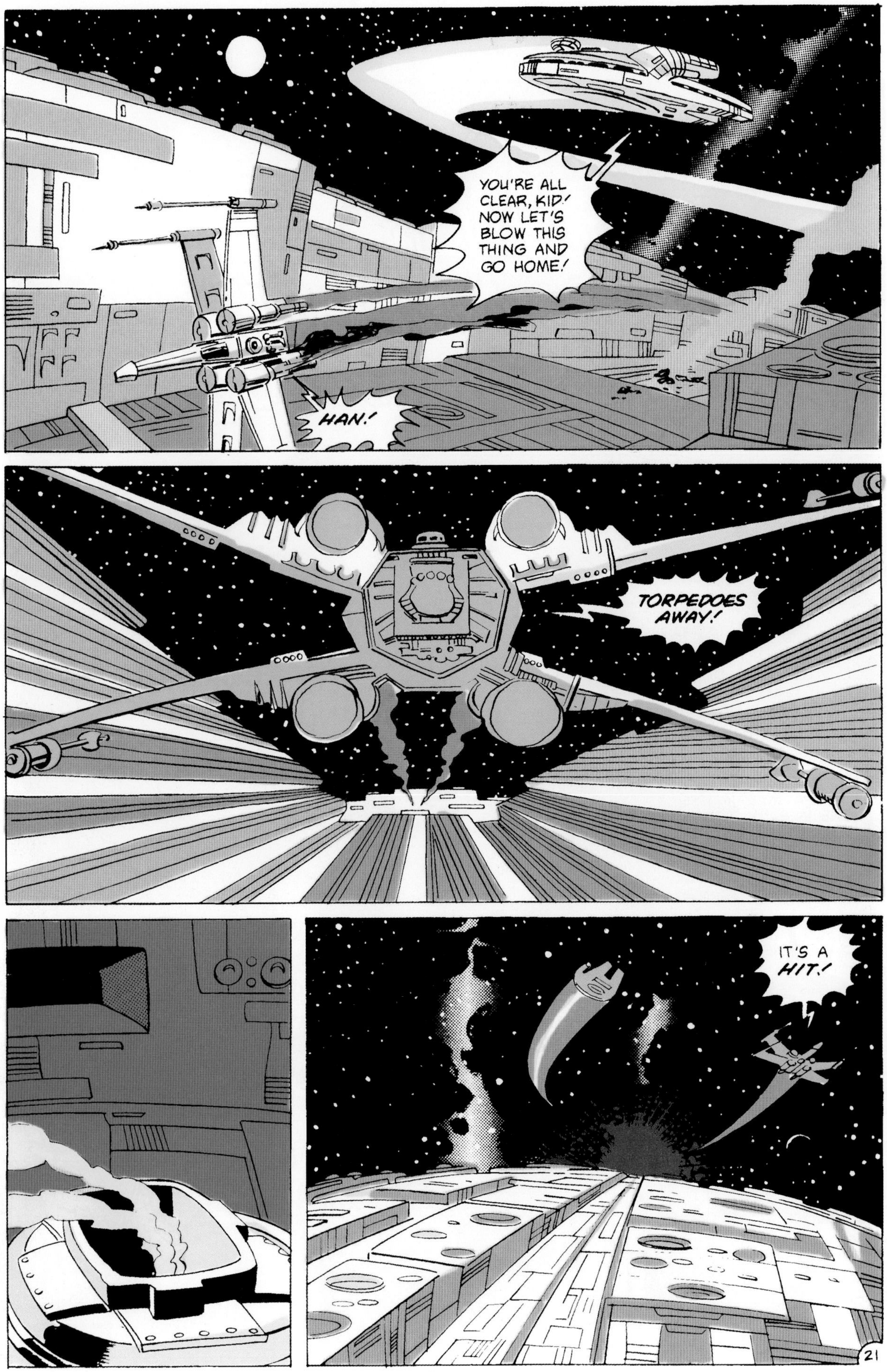
YOU'RE ALL CLEAR, KID! NOW LET'S BLOW THIS THING AND GO HOME!
HAN!
TORPEDOES AWAY!
IT'S A HIT!
21

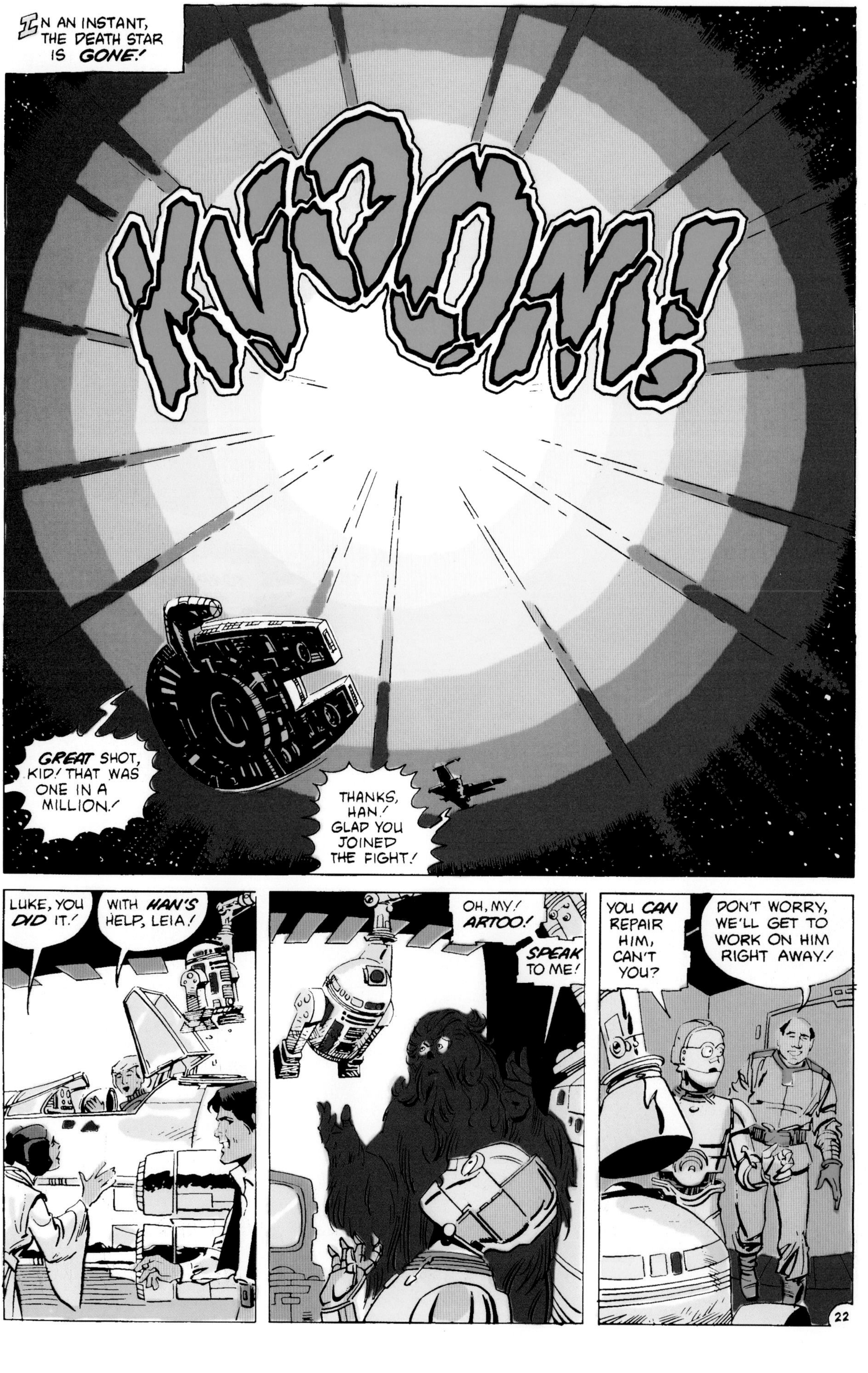
IN AN INSTANT, THE DEATH STAR IS GONE!
KVOOM!
GREAT SHOT, KID! THAT WAS ONE IN A MILLION!
THANKS, HAN! GLAD YOU JOINED THE FIGHT!
LUKE, YOU DID IT!
WITH HAN'S HELP, LEIA!
OH, MY! ARTOO!
SPEAK TO ME!
YOU CAN REPAIR HIM, CAN'T YOU?
DON'T WORRY, WE'LL GET TO WORK ON HIM RIGHT AWAY!
22

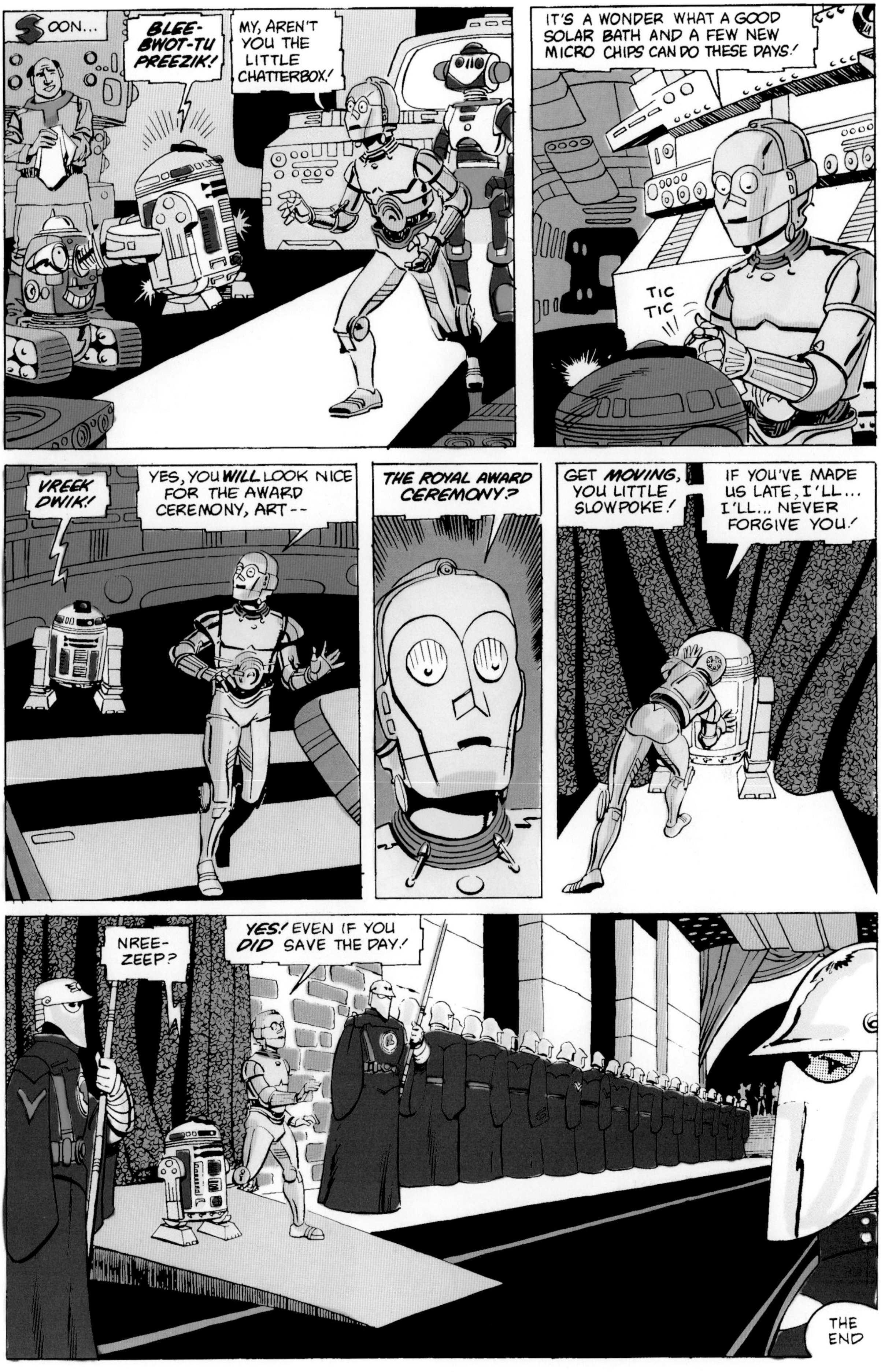
SOON...
BLEE-BWOT-TU PREEZIK!
MY, AREN'T YOU THE LITTLE CHATTERBOX!
IT'S A WONDER WHAT A GOOD SOLAR BATH AND A FEW NEW MICRO CHIPS CAN DO THESE DAYS!
TIC TIC
VREEK DWIK!
YES, YOU WILL LOOK NICE FOR THE AWARD CEREMONY, ART--
THE ROYAL AWARD CEREMONY?
GET MOVING, YOU LITTLE SLOWPOKE!
IF YOU'VE MADE US LATE, I'LL... I'LL... NEVER FORGIVE YOU!
NREE-ZEEP?
YES! EVEN IF YOU DID SAVE THE DAY!
THE END

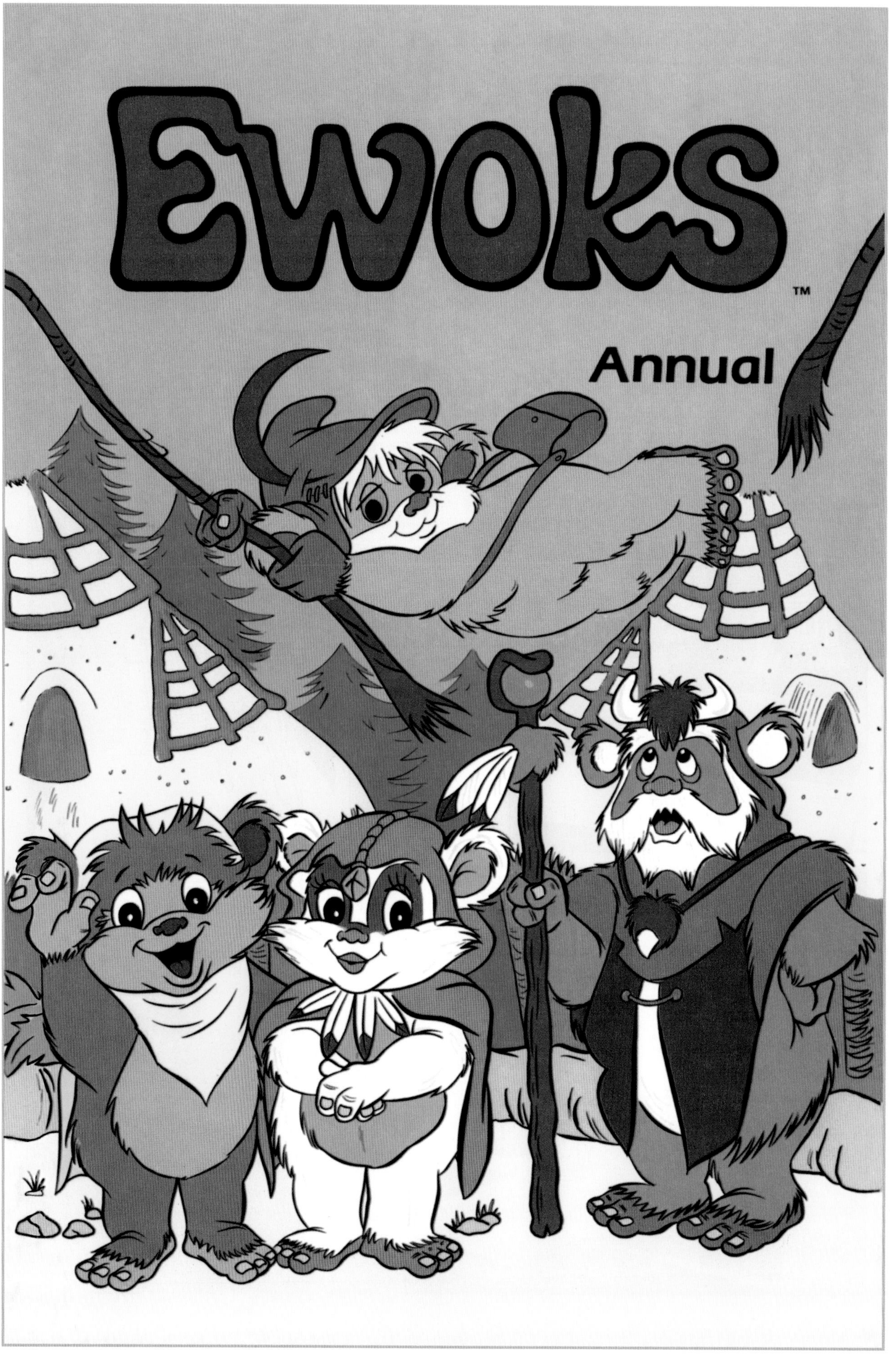
Ewoks™
Annual

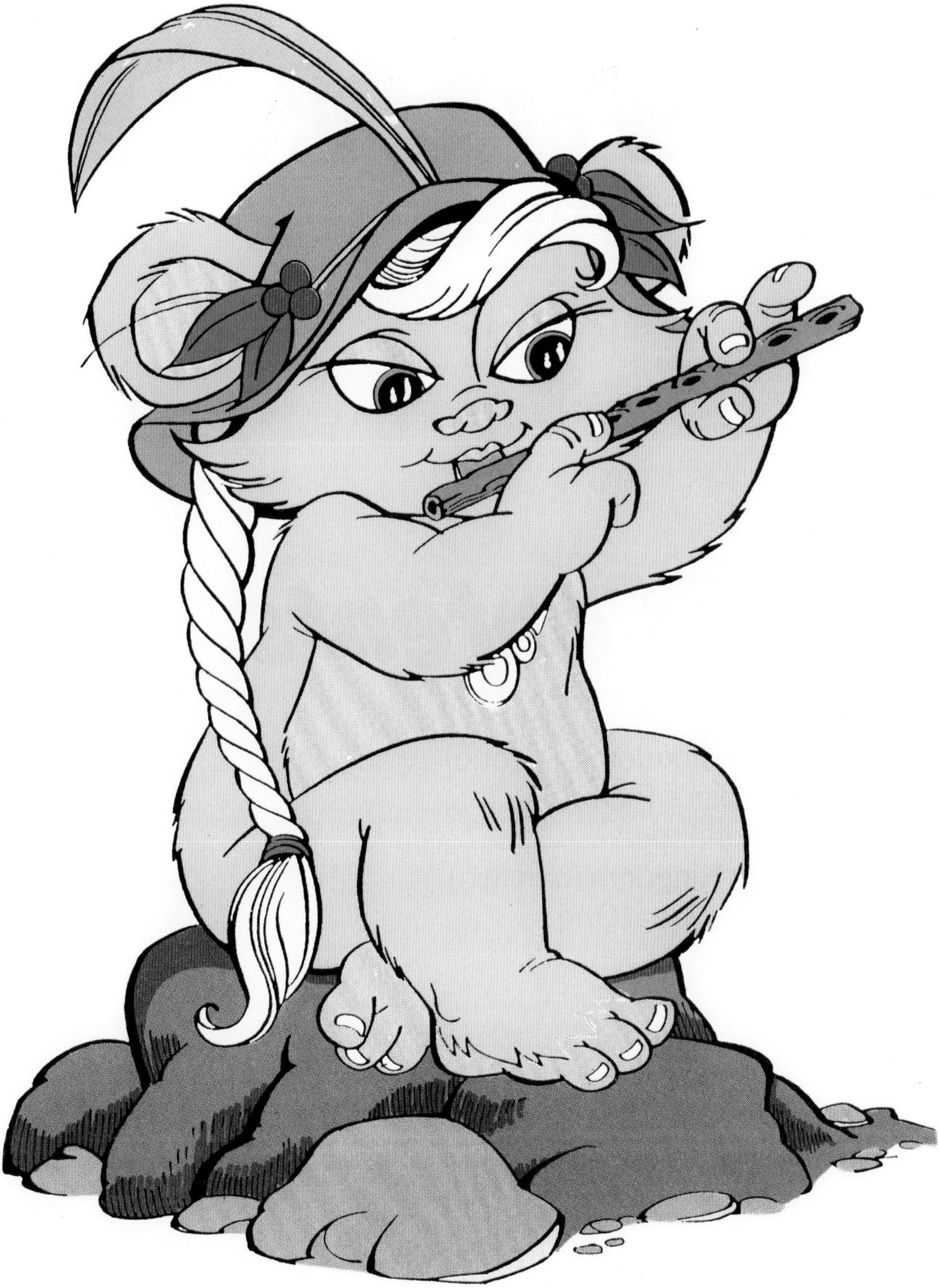

Ewoks™
ANNUAL

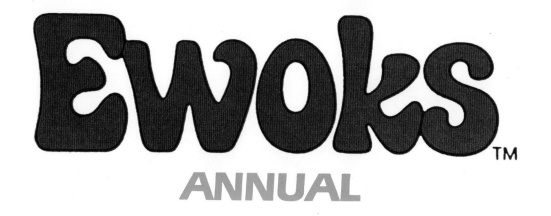

Contents

Chief Chirpa Kidnapped!

The whole of the woodland clearing rang with the sound of laughter. All the Ewoks had dressed up as ghosts and were having a wonderful time at their annual Hallowe'en party – one of the best events of their year.

"Arroo!"

"Whazzat?" gasped Wicket, almost jumping out of his costume as a spooky spectre reared up in front of him.

"It's only me," giggled Teebo. "This party is great fun, isn't it?"

"Y-yes?" said Wicket, but he was obviously not too sure.

Just then Princess Kneesaa danced across the clearing, giggling merrily. "Look at that," she laughed, pointing to a huge, red creature standing at the edge of the clearing. "Someone's dressed up as a Hanadak."

"I wonder who it is," said Teebo. "Danger!" cried Wicket. "That's no fancy-dress costume. That's a real Hanadak. Look at the fangs."

Suddenly the atmosphere changed as fear spread through the village. Wicket rallied the Ewoks behind him, cried "Charge!" and the brave Ewoks ran into the attack.

With one swipe of its enormous tail, the Hanadak sent the courageous Ewoks flying. "Come on," said Wicket picking himself up. "I've got an idea."

Teebo and Kneesaa followed him across the village to where the Hanadak now stood.

"Gather as many blue dlock leaves as you can carry," he said, pointing to a tall plant heavy with large leaves.

The three Ewoks soon stripped the plant bare and then Wicket led the others right up to the Hanadak.

"Now throw them over the

beast," he ordered, and in an instant the Hanadak was covered with the foliage. The air was filled with a heady aroma for the dlock plant leaves were the most fragrant and soothing of all the plants in the forest.

Before you could say "Dangar!" a wide grin spread across the Hanadak's ugly face and it lopped off into the forest. Wicket, Teebo and Kneesaa were also grinning widely as they went back to the other Ewoks who cheered them loudly.

"On with the party," giggled Kneesaa and soon the Ewoks were enjoying themselves hugely again.

While all this had been going on, Chief Chirpa had been in the harvest store getting the food ready for the party. He was so involved in what he was doing that he had not heard the sounds of the battle that had raged. Neither had he heard a Dulok sneak into the

harvest store.

The Dulok and his two companions outside had known about the Hallowe'en party and had decided that, with all the Ewoks busy enjoying themselves, it would be a good time to raid the harvest store.

It was very gloomy in the store and the Dulok didn't see Chief Chirpa who was busy at his task. Thinking that the coast was clear he beckoned his two accomplices inside.

The three tip-toed deep inside the gloomy store. It was so gloomy that they didn't see the ladder on top of which Chief Chirpa was reaching for some crunch-tree nuts. The first Dulok tripped over the ladder. The second Dulok tripped over the first Dulok. And the third Dulok tripped over the other two and sent the ladder wobbling wildly as he stumbled.

Chief Chirpa tried desperately to

keep his balance and grasped hold of the corner of a heavy sack on the top shelf. But it was no good! Woosh! he flew through the air taking the sack with him. There was a loud 'plop' as he landed in a wooden box. The sack fell on top of him, covering him completely.

The dazed Duloks picked themselves up. By now their eyes were accustomed to the gloom and they could see the sack of food sitting in the box. But, of course, they couldn't see Chief Chirpa underneath it.

"Look!" said one of the Duloks gleefully. 'A box of food. Let's sneak it back to our camp for our supper."

By this time the Ewoks' party was in full swing again, and no one noticed as the three Duloks, staggering under the weight of the box, skirted the clearing and headed back to their camp.

"I wish Father would bring on the food," said Princess Kneesaa. "I'm starving."

"Let's go and find him," said Teebo.

Wicket, Teebo and the princess made their way to the harvest store and peered inside.

"Can't see a thing," said Kneesaa. "Bring me a lantern."

A few minutes later, Kneesaa was holding a lantern aloft and was peering round the harvest store.

"He's not here!" she said. "And look!" She pointed to the ladder and then down to the floor. "There's something odd. These are Duloks' footprints."

"They can't have kidnapped him, can they?" gasped Wicket in astonishment.

"What else could have happened to him?" asked Teebo.

"Let's follow the tracks," said Kneesaa.

Even as the three Ewoks were speaking, the Dulok trio had reached their camp. They placed the box in front of their chief.

"Open the sack!" he commanded.

The three Dulok raiders pulled the sack from the box and there, staring up at them was a furious Chief Chirpa.

"Take him!" roared the chief.

"Take him yourself," quivered a cowardly Dulok.

"Dolt!" said the chief, jumping on top of Chief Chirpa, pinning him inside the box. "Bring me some rope."

Chief Chirpa had almost pushed the Dulok chief from his chest by the time a huge length of rope was brought forward. But although he heaved and heaved, he was outnumbered and was soon tied up.

"Drag him to the tree and tie him to it."

A few minutes later Chief Chirpa was securely tied to a huge baccy tree. "Just wait!" roared Chirpa.

"When I'm free, I'll have you for breakfast, lunch and dinner."

The Duloks danced around their prisoner, laughing and jeering at him.

"We'll get a ransom. We'll get a ransom," they taunted him.

Chirpa roared and bellowed so loudly that even though he was tied to the tree, the Duloks fell back in fear.

"All this noise is giving me a headache!" said the Dulok chief. "Let's leave him and have something to eat."

The Duloks retreated to their tables and were soon tucking into a hearty meal. Still Chirpa roared and shouted.

"He'll give me indigestion," complained the Dulok chief. "Can't someone shut him up."

"Shut him up yourself!" said a Dulok.

"I'll shut you up," roared the chief, and soon all the Duloks were scrapping amongst themselves.

The sound of the fighting filled the forest. "Listen!" said Teebo, who, with his two friends, was still following the tracks.

"Duloks! We must be near their camp."

They followed the sounds and soon they were on the edge of the Duloks' camp. "There's Father," whispered Kneesaa. "Over there."

The Duloks were still fighting each other and didn't notice Wicket as he made his way stealthily to Chief Chirpa and cut him free.

"Aagghh!" With a mighty roar, Chief Chirpa charged into the fray, knocking his enemies hither and thither until they were all scattered around the clearing, so dazed they were seeing stars.

"Back to our village," he said to the others, and led them through the forest to their homes.

The Ewoks were so delighted to see their chief again that, although it was very late, a great feast was prepared.

Meanwhile, back at the Duloks' camp, their chief and his men were a very sorry sight. They were bruised and bandaged.

"Thank goodness he's gone," said the chief. "I couldn't have taken much more of all that bellowing. What an old windbag. You men should count yourselves lucky at having me as your leader and not that bad-tempered old Chirpa."

"Yes," agreed a nearby Dulok. "You're much more of a pushover than he."

"Careful," said the chief. "Or else I might make a truce with the Ewoks and ask Chirpa to be our leader, too."

"You wouldn't!" gasped the Duloks in one voice. "That would be . . ."

"Unthinkable?" suggested the chief.

"Yes!" they chorused.

"In that case, we'll have no more in . . . subordiwhat's-it-called," he continued.

". . . ination," said the only Dulok with more than a hundredth of a brain.

"Bless you!" said the chief. "You'd better go and see the shaman and get something for that cold."

Match the Princess's Pictures!

The Forest of Endor where the Ewoks live is full of beautiful flowers and Princess Kneesa loves to go out and gather them. Chief Chirpa had a series of pictures painted showing his daughter holding a bunch of blooms. Only two of them are identical. Can you spot which two they are?

1
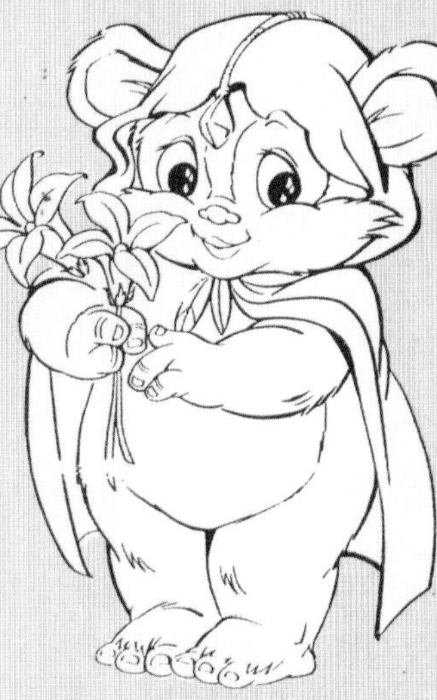

2
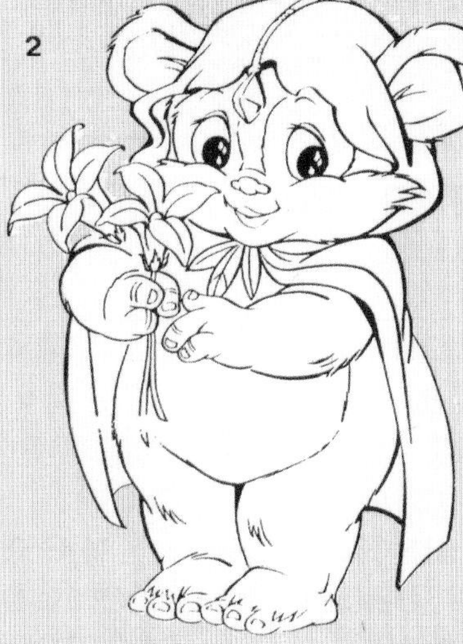

3
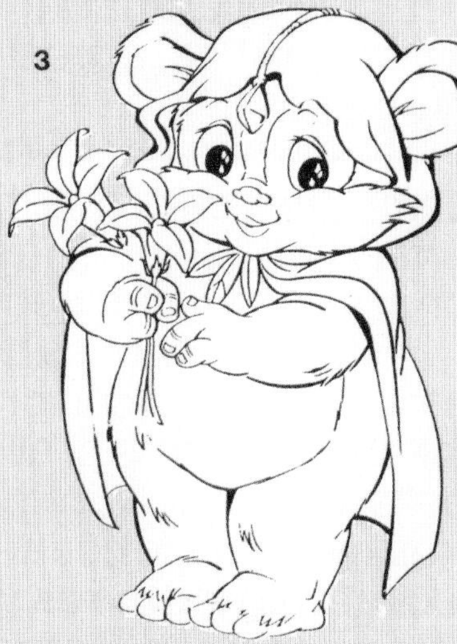

4
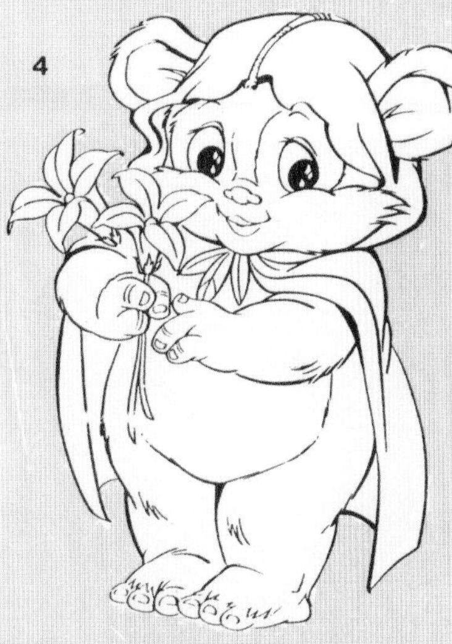

5
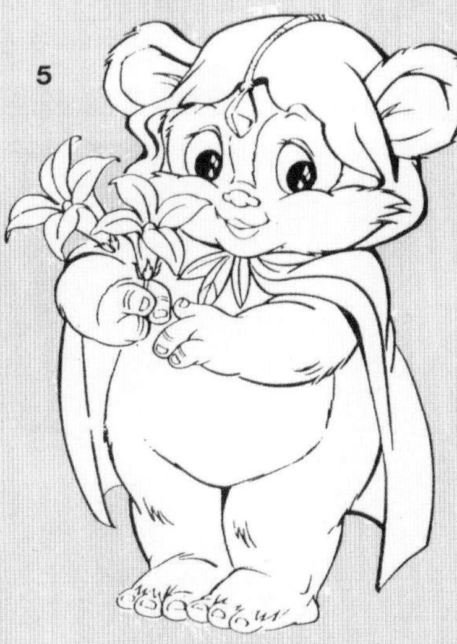

6
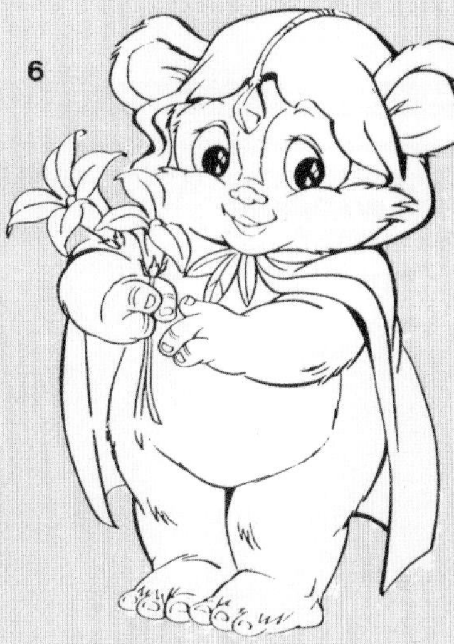

7
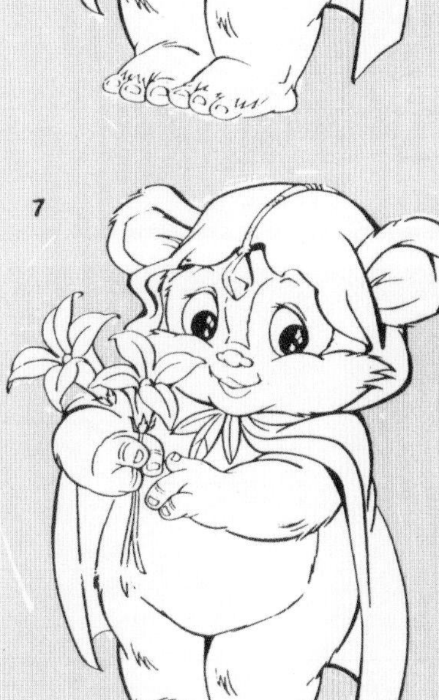

8
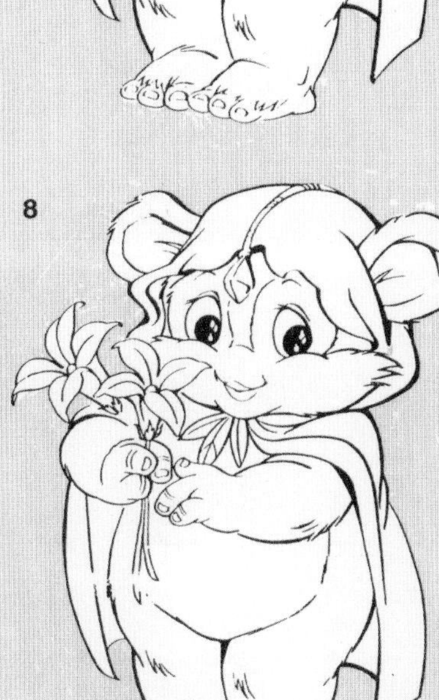

9
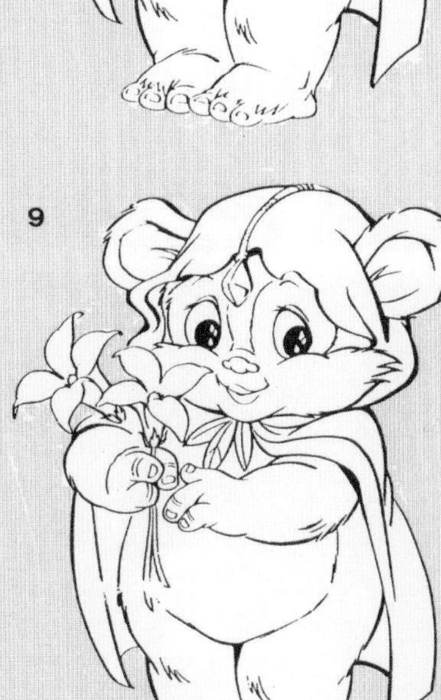

Answer: 2,7

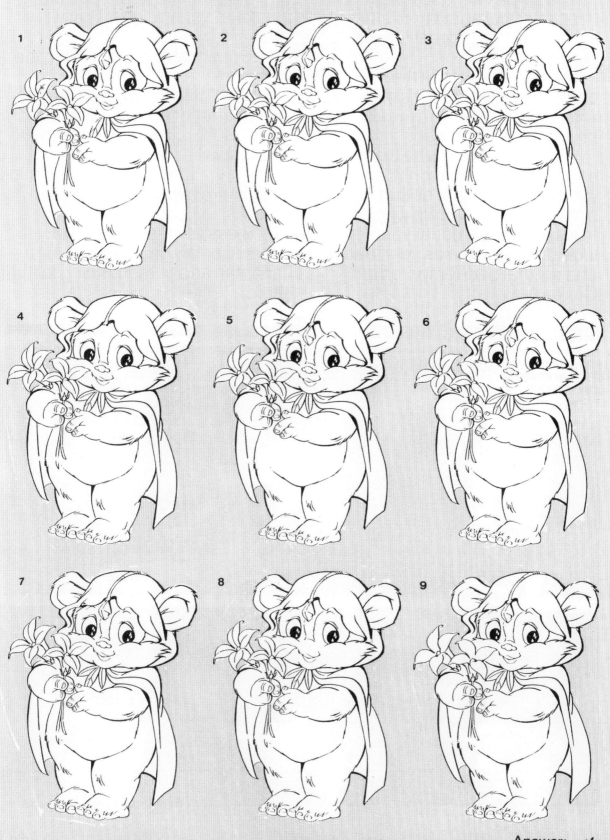

Return of the Great One!

Wicket lay beside his friend on the soft grass of the forest. He yawned and said, "There's nothing like the peace and quiet of the forest in the Sun Season, eh, Teebo?"

Teebo stood up. "Except it's too hot. Come on! I'll race you to the dam. We can cool off there."

The two Ewoks sped through the forest towards the dam which was high above the village.

"Cudvarrk!" gasped Wicket, stopping to get his breath back. "Slow down!"

"Dangar!" cried Teebo, stopping suddenly, for the hard ground of the forest had suddenly become completely water-logged. There was squelchy mud where there should have been sun-baked soil.

Before Wicket could say anything there was a loud crashing sound and the air was filled with the sound of running water.

"It's the dam!" cried Wicket.

"The Duloks must have breached it. They're trying to flood us out."

"We must get back to the village as quickly as possible," gasped Teebo. "We must warn Chief Chirpa." As he spoke he ran towards a Snarlf horse that was grazing nearby. "Come on, Wicket. We'll ride this beauty back."

The two Ewoks jumped on to the horse's back and galloped towards the village.

As soon as he heard what had happened, Chief Chirpa summoned Chukha-Trok, the woodsman.

"We need to build a breakwater immediately," he told the burly Ewok. "The dam's been sabotaged."

"Leave it to me," said Chukha-Trok. A few moments later there came the sound of two mighty blows of the woodsman's axe followed by a loud crashing as

Chukha-Trok felled a gigantic tree.

Not a moment too soon, it landed just in front of the gushing waters that were threatening to deluge the village.

"Veek!" gasped Teebo in relief, as the waters ran round the tree and cascaded over a cliff to create a spectacular waterfall. "Now we have time to repair the dam."

The Ewoks had lived in the forest for hundreds of years and thought that they knew everything that there was to know about it . . . but what they didn't know was that deep beneath the forest floor there was a vast, dark cavern. For thousands of years nothing had penetrated the eerie silence, but on the day the dam broke a drop of water seeped deep down through the earth and landed with a loud "plop" which echoed through the cavern. Then another . . . then another.

Suddenly another sound shuddered through the cavern. There was a loud very loud

'Urrrrgggghhhhh!'; so loud was it that the cavern walls began to shake: so loud was it that far above in the forest the Ewoks trembled with fear.

"What's that?" gasped Teebo as the ground shook so violently that he had to hold on to a tree to stay on his feet.

"Kffllnnnch!" It was as if the forest had been hit by an earthquake as trees tumbled and debris was scattered all around. A huge hole appeared in the ground and the Ewoks stared in disbelief as a monstrous head appeared from it. Steam poured from the creature's awesome nostrils. Its mouth opened wide and the Ewoks were terrified by the dreadful fangs that lashed out. Each fang was as big as a fully-grown Ewok!

Chief Chirpa gasped. "I-i-i-i-t's a k-k-k-k-radak," he stammered. "One of the g-g-g-reat ones. They've been extinct for thousands of years."

Teebo hugged Wicket for comfort as the huge monster

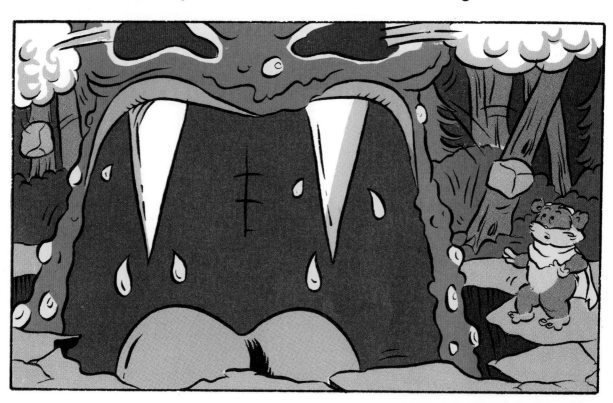

heaved itself from the ground. With each swing of its terrible neck, a forest tree crashed to the ground.

"If it breaks our support tree, we are doomed!" cried Chief Chirpa. "Logray!" he shouted. "Do something."

Logray, the Ewoks' wise old sage, came running out of his hut. As he ran towards the chief, a branch fell from a tree and knocked him senseless. Princess Kneesaa rushed to the old Ewok's side and knelt over him. When she realized that he wasn't seriously hurt she darted into his hut. Teebo and Wicket ran after her and found her mixing a potion from the herbs and waters that Logray stored there.

"What are you doing?" asked Wicket.

"I have often watched Logray mix his potions," replied the princess. "I think I know how to deal with the monster."

Teebo looked out of the hut. The monster had now pulled itself right out of the hole in the ground and was so tall that Teebo had to crane his neck skywards to see its head.

Great jets of fire spouted from its nostrils. All around, brave Ewoks were hitting and kicking it, but the monster didn't even notice them.

"Hurry, Kneesaa!" Teebo shouted.

"Finished!" cried Princess Kneesaa, running out of the hut, clasping a large bowl of steaming green liquid. "This should calm the monster down."

In her haste, the princess didn't notice a bundle of twigs. "Oh no!" she wept as the bowl slipped from her hands, sending its contents splashing over all the Ewoks on the ground below.

One by one, the Ewoks dropped to the ground and lay motionless where they fell.

"Kneesaa, you chook," said Wicket. "You've mixed a sleeping potion. Everyone's unconscious apart from you, me and Teebo . . ."

"And the monster!" exclaimed Teebo.

A loud roar from the ferocious beast shook the leaves from the trees, covering the three friends with foliage.

"Let's get out of here," gasped Teebo.

"Don't be such a drongo," barked Wicket. "If we don't do something, our village will be destroyed."

Meanwhile Kneesaa had rushed back to Logray's hut and was busy mixing another potion. "Keep the monster busy," she shouted.

"Keep it busy?" groaned Teebo. "What does she want us to do? Play Monopoly with it?"

Just then, Princess Kneesaa came running from the hut carrying another bowl. This time the liquid inside it was yellow. "I think this should be strong enough to send the kradak to sleep . . ." and as she spoke she slipped on a damp leaf and slithered along the branch. The bowl fell from her grip and its contents poured right down the monster's back.

It let out an angry roar as the scalding liquid burned into its flesh.

"Look!" cried the princess, pointing at the kradak.

The three Ewoks watched in astonishment as the creature started to shrink. It got smaller . . . and smaller . . . and smaller, until it was no bigger than an Ewok's hand.

"Kneesaa, you're wonderful," cheered Wicket. "You mixed a shrinking potion, not a sleeping one. We're saved."

By the time the other Ewoks had come to their senses, Wicket and the princess had built a tiny cage for the little monster which was looking very sorry for itself.

"You know, Teebo," said Wicket. "If we diverted some of the water from the breakwater to the hole before we repaired the dam, we could make a super swimming pool."

"What a great idea," agreed Teebo. "But let's do it tomorrow. I've had enough for one day."

Spot the Names!

The names of five Ewoks are hidden in the square below. They read either across the page or from top to bottom. The chief of the Duloks is so silly that he can't even spot the word 'Duloks' in the square. But Duloks aren't noted for their intelligence. Can you help him?

P	P	R	I	N	A	A	M	C	E	F	U	T	R	G
R	O	A	E	E	A	D	U	L	O	K	S	N	S	W
H	N	W	I	T	W	U	T	U	R	G	P	S	K	V
P	R	I	N	C	E	S	S	K	N	E	E	S	A	A
A	C	C	H	I	E	F	C	H	I	R	P	A	F	S
E	S	K	Q	J	H	D	A	V	L	O	G	R	A	Y
W	P	E	R	B	K	L	C	L	X	W	I	C	T	T
M	S	T	E	E	B	O	E	B	C	E	C	K	E	B
J	Q	H	D	G	O	N	F	K	C	H	Y	Z	E	O

The Ice Princess!

The Season of Snow had come around again on Endor. Usually the forest rang with the laughter of the Ewoks as they played in the snow, but not this year. The Ewoks were in mourning.

When the first snows had come, Princess Kneesaa, Wicket and Teebo had been making a slide when the princess had tumbled over and had been bitten by an ice-beetle.

Wicket was broken-hearted and stood sobbing as he and Teebo looked at the beautiful princess, encased in a tomb of ice crystals. Chief Chirpa knelt by his daughter's side, his hands covering his swollen eyes.

"Is there nothing we can do?" asked Teebo.

"I don't know," said Wicket. "Master Logray is going through all his parchments. Maybe he will come up with something."

Just then the old sage approached the three mourners.

"Have you found an answer?" wept Chief Chirpa.

"There is a way," said Logray. "But it is fraught with danger. The ice-beetle's poison can only be combated by the juice of the fire plant . . ."

"But that is only found on the Mountain of Doom," wailed Chief Chirpa.

The Mountain of Doom was the home of the Frost Giants. None of the Ewoks who had set out to journey there had ever been seen again.

"Even if there was a way, I can't spare my men," said the chief. "The Duloks are hungry. They were too lazy to harvest their crops this year and already they have begun to attack our store-houses. I need all my men to fend them off."

"You must spare Teebo and

me," said Wicket bravely. "*We* shall go to the mountain."

"Shall we?" squeaked Teebo. "How?"

"By glider!" said Wicket bravely. "And we shall succeed."

A few days later, after an uneventful flight, Wicket and Teebo landed their glider at the base of the Mountain of Doom. It was much too high for them to contemplate flying to the top, so with ice-clamps attached to their feet to give them some grip on the smooth mountain face, they set off to scale the peak.

"Wicket," said Teebo as they struggled up the steep slope. "What's big, red, flies and eats Ewoks for dinner?"

"This is no time for jokes," snapped Wicket.

"Who's joking?" gulped Teebo, pointing to a deadly, red dragon-bird that was swooping towards them.

With a blood-curdling squawk the dragon-bird zoomed towards the two Ewoks. Teebo clutched the mountain-face for safety but the dragon-bird's wings clipped his back and knocked him off his balance.

"Yeeeooow!" his cry filled the air as he plunged down towards the jagged rocks far below.

A few feet further down the mountain, Wicket watched in horror as his friend fell towards him. Clinging precariously to a tufty plant with one hand, he somehow managed to grab hold of Teebo's leg as he flashed by. The force almost pulled Wicket off the mountain, but he held on with grim determination as Teebo scrambled for safety.

"This makes a change," giggled Wicket nervously. "It's usually you who pulls my leg!"

Teebo was much too shocked to think of something funny to say, and the two continued climbing in silence until they reached a ledge.

With a great whoosh of wings, the dragon-bird swooped in again. Just in time, Wicket spotted a cranny in the rock-face and he and Teebo pressed themselves into it. Imagine their surprise when they found that the cranny was, in fact, the entrance to a cave.

"Come on," said Wicket. "I'd rather face whatever's in there, than stand up to the dragon-bird."

A few minutes later, Teebo's voice echoed through a maze of tunnels. "At least if we'd stayed out there, we'd have been killed quickly. Now we're lost and will probably starve to death slowly and miserably!"

"We may as well press on," said Wicket.

It seemed to Teebo that they had been in the tunnels for hours before they turned a dark corner and stopped in amazement. For there in front of them, was an enormous cave lit by hundreds of shining crystals. At one end there was a table laden with delicious-looking food.

"At least we won't starve to death," said Teebo, scurrying towards the table.

"Come back, Teebo!" ordered Wicket. "We don't have any time to eat. We must find the fire plant and we won't find it here. That's for sure!"

"How do you know?" asked Teebo.

"Because I think this must be the throne-room of the Frost Giants' king, and Frost Giants are obviously unlikely to have the fire plant."

"Why?"

"It would melt them, silly."

"No need to be quite so hot-tempered," snapped Teebo. "All right. Let's go."

But it was too late, for as Teebo spoke a procession of Frost Giants entered the cavern, heralding the arrival of the king.

The Ewoks gulped at what they saw, for the Frost Giants were indeed gigantic, at least eight times the size of an Ewok.

"Run," cried Wicket. But before they could move Wicket and Teebo were surrounded by a circle of Frost Giants.

"Trespassers!" roared the king.

"Your Majesty," gulped Wicket, bowing low. "We did not intend to trespass. We were trying to . . ."

But before Wicket could finish, the Frost Giant king scooped him up in his icy hand.

"You are doomed," he said. "We have a special way of dealing with uninvited guests. We breathe on them."

"Oh well," said Teebo. "As long as you haven't had too much garlic, it can't be all that bad."

But Wicket had heard the legend of the Frost Giants' breath. Anyone who was touched by it was instantly turned into a block of ice.

Just as it seemed the Ewoks were doomed, two guards rushed into the throne-room. "Sire," gasped one. "The devil-bird has returned. We are being attacked."

Wicket realized that the guard was talking about the dragon-bird, and he could see that the Frost Giants were terrified: with good reason, for one puff of the dragon-bird's breath and the giants would melt.

"Sire," said Wicket. "Teebo and I will deal with it. I have a plan."

Wicket quickly put his plan into action. He ordered the giants to build a huge wall of ice on the very edge of the mountain summit. Then he asked one of them to lead him back to the entrance to the maze, which was just below the summit. He could see the fearsome bird flying nearby.

Wicket made a very rude noise at the dragon-bird which swooped down towards him. Just as it looked as if the bird would have the courageous Ewok in its grasp, Wicket shouted "Now!" and darted backwards into the tunnel. Above, on the summit, the Frost Giants pushed with all their might against the towering wall, and before you could say, "Ewok!" it cascaded down the mountain in an enormous avalanche and smashed into the ledge.

The dragon-bird squawked as it was buried beneath tons of ice, and then was heard no more.

Teebo looked down and started to sob, for he thought that his friend had died along with the dragon-bird.

"Gone!" he sobbed. "Wicket's gone!"

"Well, I think that was very successful," said a voice behind the weeping Ewok. He spun round and there, standing quite calmly, was Wicket, looking for all the world as though nothing had happened.

"How . . ." started Teebo.

"I'll explain later," said Wicket.

"Ewoks," said the Frost Giant king.."You have saved us. How can we reward you?"

"If it please Your Majesty," said Wicket. "All we want is to be shown where the fire plant grows . . ."

"We will show you, but we dare not go near it," said the king. . .

When Wicket and Teebo returned to the village with the fire plant, Logray immediately consulted his parchments and began to mix a steaming potion. When it was bubbling furiously he poured it over Kneesaa's icy form.

All the Ewoks watched impatiently and then there was a huge sigh of relief as the ice began to melt. Soon she was free of her frozen prison and a great cheer rang out through the forest.

Chief Chirpa was so grateful that he could hardly speak. But eventually he got his tongue back and thanked his two faithful Ewoks time and time again.

"It was nothing," said Wicket modestly.

"Any time," said Teebo bravely.

"Let's go and play in the snow," said Princess Kneesaa smilingly.

A few minutes later the Ewoks were having the time of their lives as they zoomed down the snowy slopes on their sledges – apart from Wicket and Teebo. They'd had enough of snow and ice for one season!

Colour Chief Chirpa!

Here's a picture of Chief Chirpa for you to colour. So get your crayons out and get to work!

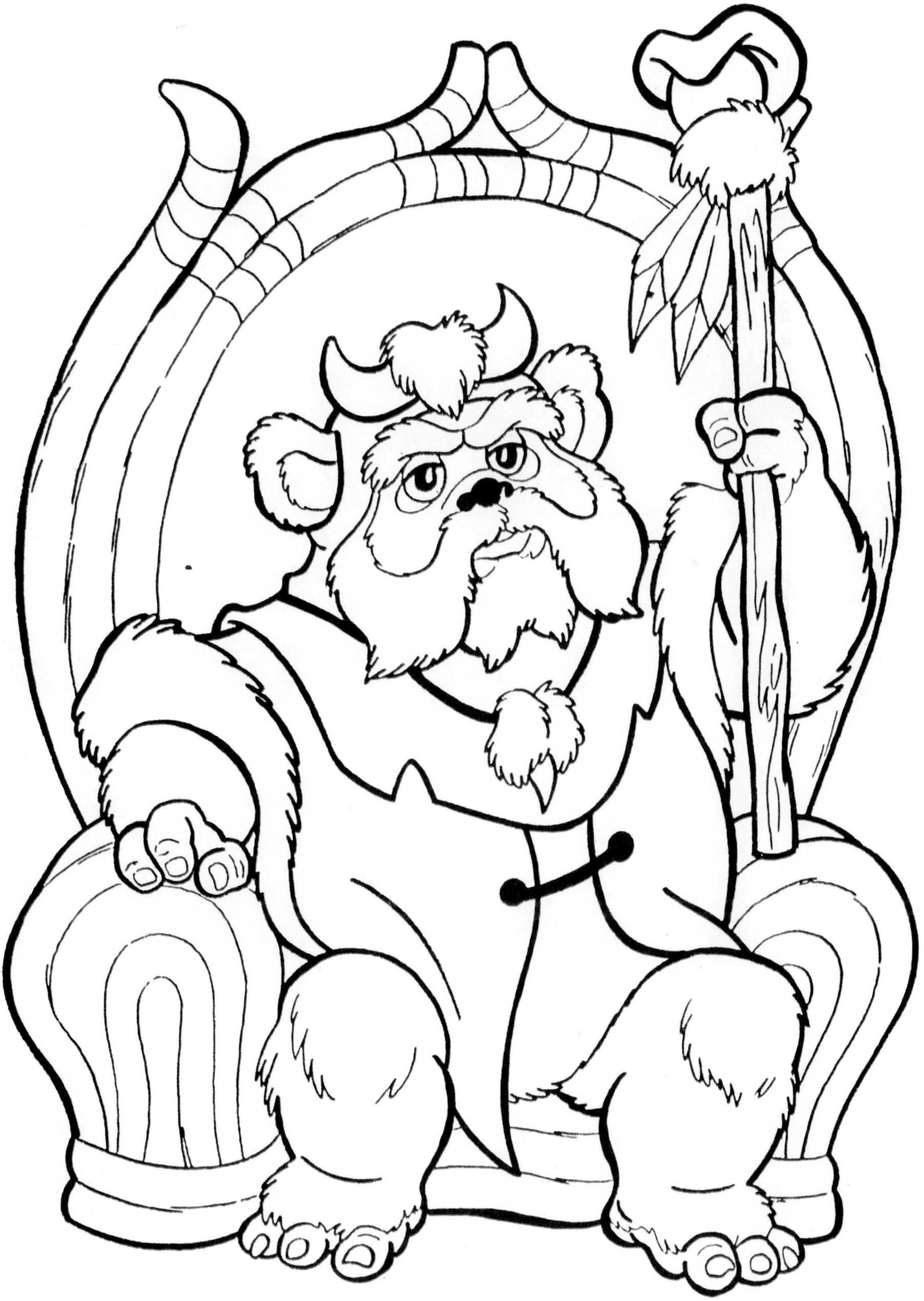

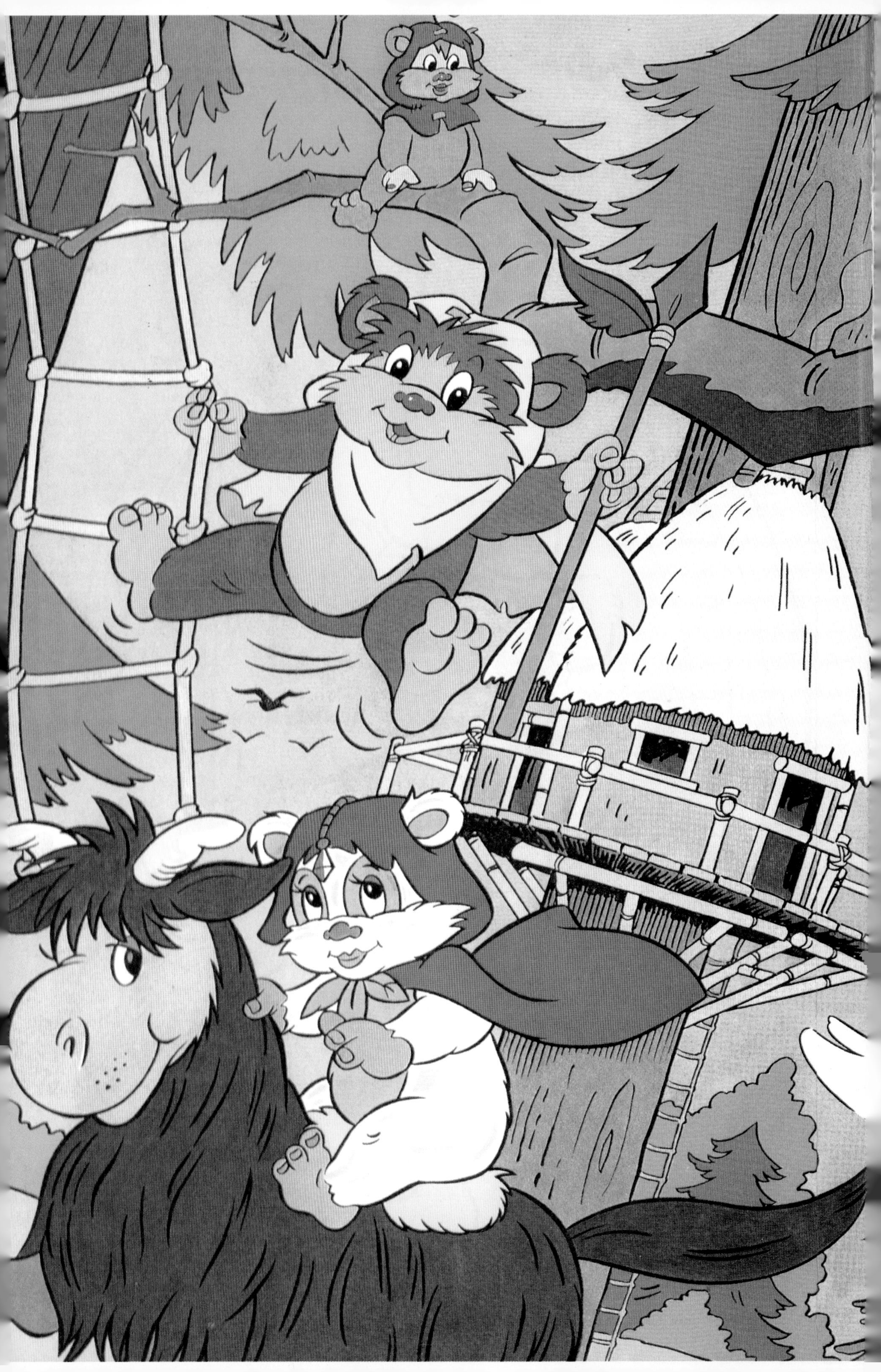

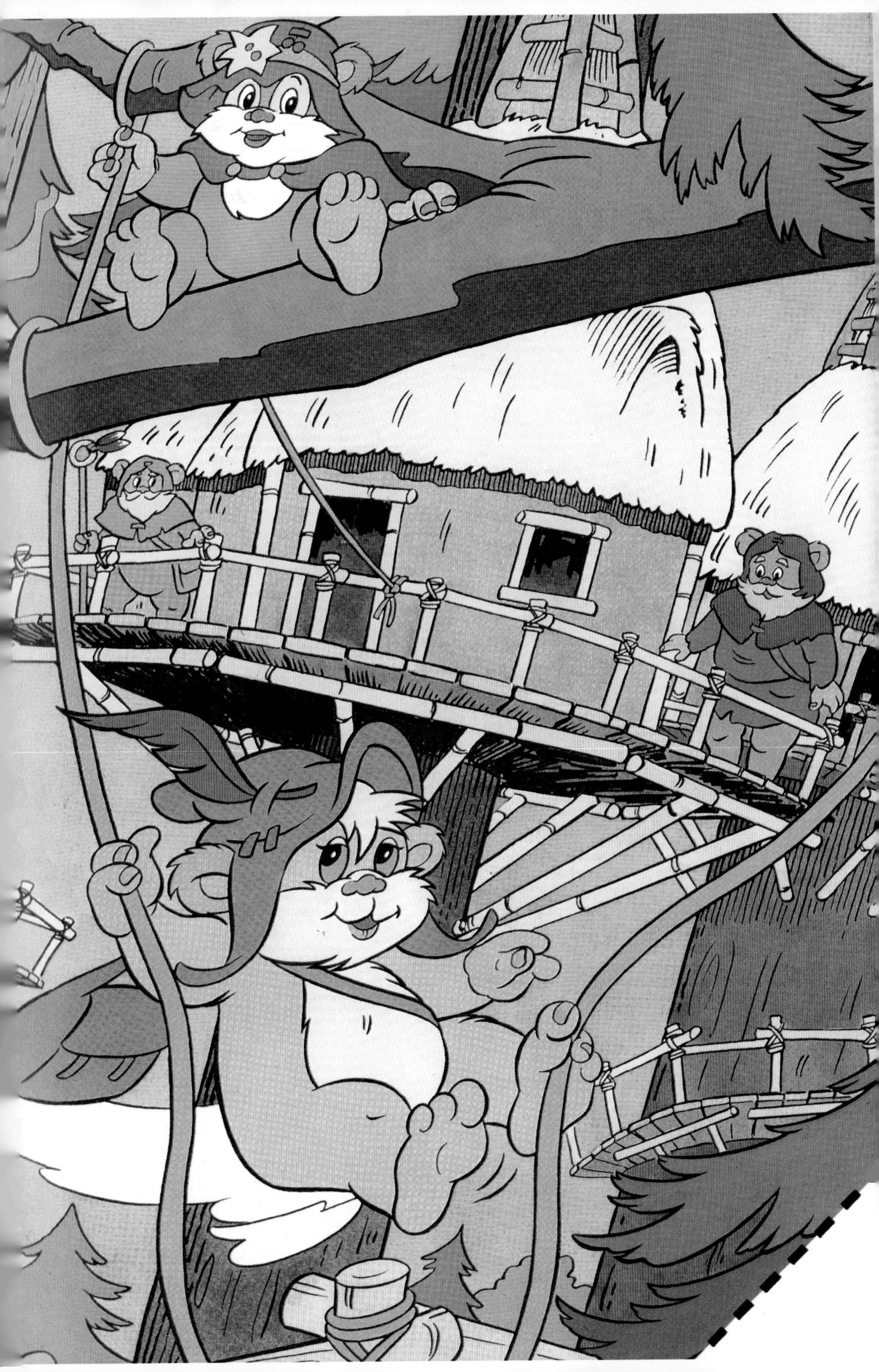

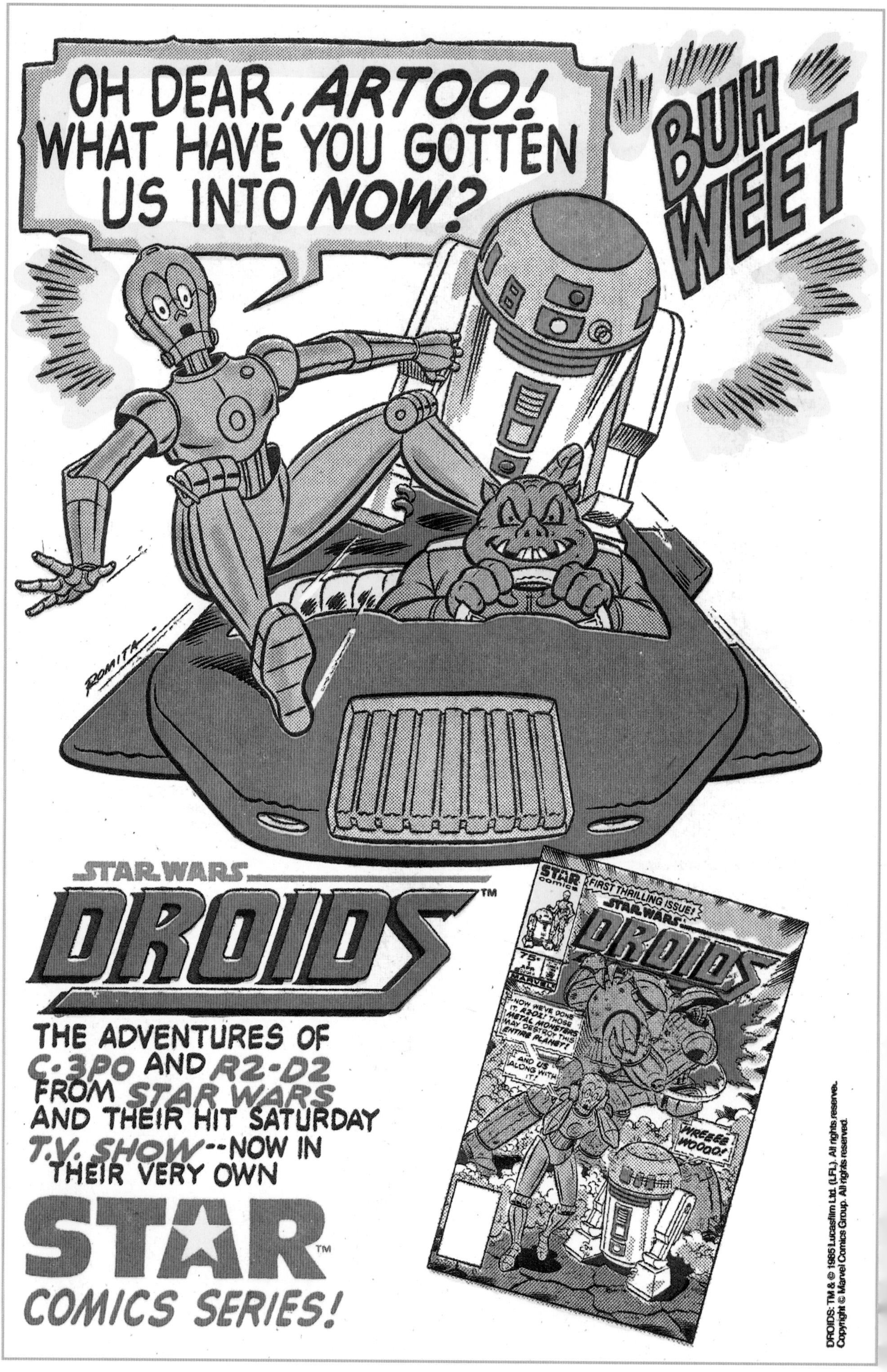
OH DEAR, ARTOO! WHAT HAVE YOU GOTTEN US INTO NOW?
BUH WEET
ROMITA
STAR WARS
DROIDS™
THE ADVENTURES OF C-3PO AND R2-D2 FROM STAR WARS AND THEIR HIT SATURDAY T.V. SHOW--NOW IN THEIR VERY OWN
STAR™
COMICS SERIES!
STAR COMICS
FIRST THRILLING ISSUE!
STAR WARS
DROIDS
75¢
NOW WE'VE DONE IT, R2D2! THOSE METAL MONSTERS MAY DESTROY THE ENTIRE PLANET!
AND US ALONG WITH IT!
WREEEE WOOOO!
DROIDS: TM & © 1985 Lucasfilm Ltd. (LFL). All rights reserve.
Copyright © Marvel Comics Group. All rights reserved.

Droids house ad by John Romita Sr.

STAR SPOTLIGHT ON . . .

by **Sandy Hausler**

LET'S GET OUT OF HERE!

The whole world seems to be **Ewoks** crazy! You can't go anywhere without seeing the images of those cute, little, furry creatures emblazoned on lunchboxes, T-shirts and other miscellaneous objects. Now Star Comics proudly presents **the Ewoks** in a brand new comic book all their own.

The roots of **the Ewoks**, of course, come from **George Lucas's** classic *Star Wars* movies. **Lucas** wanted to make a series of films that would couple the feeling of wonder that he found in the old **Flash Gordon** and **Buck Rogers** serials years ago with state-of-the-art special effects. He succeeded beyond his wildest dreams. There is probably not a person in America who has not heard of *Star Wars*, *The Empire Strikes Back*, and *Return of the Jedi*.

In the course of making these films, **Lucas** created a number of strange and bizarre creatures. Who can recall without affection **Chewbacca the Wookiee**? Can anyone forget the detestable **Jabba the Hut**? And what of the incredible Jedi-master **Yoda**? Without a doubt, however, the most loveable creatures to come out of this classic film trilogy are **the Ewoks**.

The Ewoks are the small, furry inhabitants of the planet Endor. Their help was instrumental in the victory of the Rebellion over the forces of the Empire. While they appear harmless, **the Ewoks** were able to assist **Han Solo**, **Chewie**, **Princess Leia**, and the droids in putting the Empire's shielding device for the new Deathstar out of commission, allowing the Rebels to destroy it.

It was soon clear to everyone that **the Ewoks** had won not only the hearts of **Luke Skywalker** and company, but of movie viewers as well. **Lucas**, realizing that the public was demanding to see more of **the Ewoks**, set to work to develop an **Ewoks** movie for television, a series of books from Random House about **the Ewoks**, and other special projects designed to satisfy an **Ewoks**-starved public. Now **Ewoks** fans will be able to read Star Comics' **THE EWOKS**, written by **Dave Manak**, penciled by **Warren Kremer** and inked by **Marie Severin**.

Dave Manak is a well-known freelance cartoonist. Since 1971 he has lived in New York writing and drawing his own material. Between 1971 and 1980 he did a lot of humor material for such magazines as **PLOP**, **SICK**, **MAD**, and Marvel's **CRAZY Magazine**. He then took a staff job at DC working as the special projects editor. He developed various projects involving licensed materials and worked on some of the regular books as well. **Dave** heard of Star Comics from **Ernie Colon**, an editor at DC and longtime friend of **Sid Jacobson**, editor of Star Comics. **Dave** was ready to try something new and went to see **Sid**. As a result, **Dave** is now doing extensive work for Star Comics including a tremendous job on **THE EWOKS**.

Dave was not especially knowledgeable about **the Ewoks** when he started out. "I knew about as much as anybody," he told **MARVEL AGE MAGAZINE**. "I read the Random House books and Lucasfilm sent the preproduction material for the movie and a glossary."

Nevertheless, **Manak** quickly became an **Ewoks** fan. He has developed a rich cultural mythology for the little creatures. He plans to slowly unfold a world of wonder and surprises on which **the Ewoks** live. Among the characters who appear in the book are **Princess Kneesaa** and her friends, **Teebo** and **Wicket**, **Chief Chirpa**, and **Logray the Medicine Man**. Among the more bizarre characters in the book are **Gantu the Ogre** and the zany **Zandor Rockers**. Magic crystals, rainbow bridges and glowing healing fluid also play parts in the series. You can count on encountering the unexpected in the pages of **THE EWOKS**.

Dave is very excited about the whole Star Comics line. He has great admiration for editor **Sid Jacobson**. "He doesn't let me get away with anything," **Dave** confided. "Even if there's a panel or two I'm not completely satisfied with, **Sid** will pick up on it and help me tighten it up and make it better." This obviously results in better comics and Star Comics are the best comics that **Sid** and his team can produce. That devotion to quality is certainly apparent in the pages of **THE EWOKS**. Don't miss it!

STAR SPOTLIGHT

STAR WARS DROIDS™

There's some good news and some bad news for fans of Marvel's exciting Star Comics line.

The good news is the debut of the newest comic book sensation from Star—DROIDS.

DROIDS, of course, features the cybernetic shenanigans of those lovable droids of Star Wars fame, **C-3PO** and **R2-D2**. So popular have the Star Wars characters become since that blockbuster motion picture exploded onto the silver screen that there has been an overwhelming demand for more and more exposure of the thrilling adventures of the Star Wars crew. Marvel has for years been producing the official comic book version of *Star Wars*. Star Comics' EWOKS, featuring the furry woodland creatures from the third Star Wars movie, *Return of the Jedi*, has in a short time become one of its most popular titles. DROIDS will undoubtedly be a worthy companion to both of those exciting books.

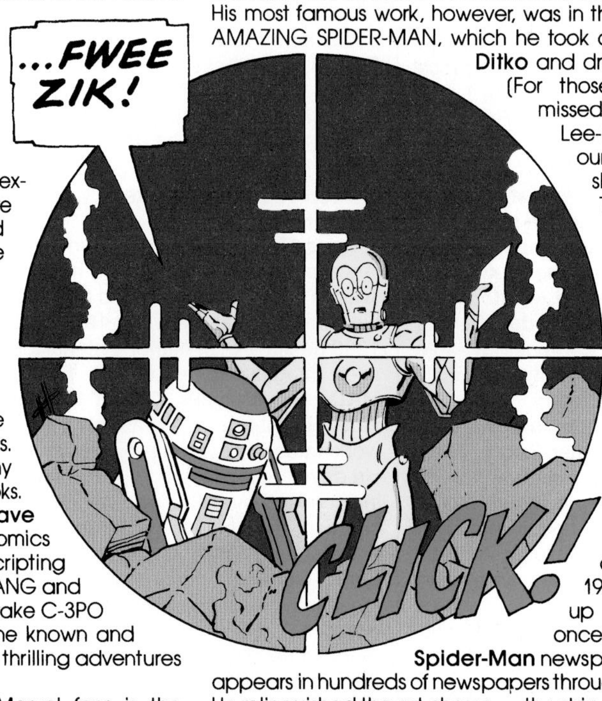
...FWEE ZIK!
CLICK!

The writer for DROIDS will be **Dave Manak**, who's no stranger to Star Comics fans. He's one of Star's busiest writers, scripting such books as EWOKS, GETALONG GANG and PLANET TERRY. His exciting stories will take C-3PO and R2-D2 on adventures through the known and unknown universe finding strange and thrilling adventures wherever they go.

Of special interest to long-time Marvel fans is the DROIDS' artist—none other than Jazzy **John Romita, Sr.** who is not to be confused with **John Romita, Jr.**, his talented son, whose pulse-pounding pencils can be seen each month in the pages of THE X-MEN.

John is one of the mainstays of Marvel. He has been drawing comics since 1949 when a friend asked him to ghost pencil a comic book assignment. He drew comics in just about every conceivable genre—mystery, crime, science fiction, war, romance, western and jungle adventure. He even did a one-year stint on CAPTAIN AMERICA in the 1950's.

When the Marvel Age of Comics exploded in the 1950's, John found himself in the thick of things. He started off inking an issue of THE AVENGERS, then went on to draw such favorites as DAREDEVIL, HULK and CAPTAIN AMERICA. His most famous work, however, was in the pages of THE AMAZING SPIDER-MAN, which he took over from **Steve Ditko** and drew for six years. (For those of you who missed the sensational Lee-Romita years on our favorite web-slinger, fret not. Those stories are currently being reprinted in the pages of MARVEL TALES!

For the past few years, John has served as Marvel's Art Director, overseeing at different times all of Marvel's covers and Special Projects. In 1977 he teamed up with **Stan Lee** once again on the **Spider-Man** newspaper strip which appears in hundreds of newspapers throughout the world. He relinquished the art chores on the strip in 1980.

Currently John directs the apprentice program (known around the Bullpen as Romita's Raiders) in addition to doing cover sketches and character designs.

John is very excited about drawing DROIDS. Despite

the extensive and varied experience he has had in the comics field, John has never done anything resembling a Star Comic. When he expressed a desire to try something along those lines, editors **Tom DeFalco** and **Sid Jacobson** were quick to convince him to give it a whirl. John agreed.

"I didn't expect to be doing robots and spaceships," John told MARVEL AGE MAGAZINE, "but it's fun. C-3PO and R2-D2 are good characters to work with." John plans on bringing his own distinctive touch to the book, and he relishes the challenge. "I'd really love to have a chance to develop DROIDS into something really distinctive," he said.

John will have his chance to do just that. Working with Dave Manak, there is little chance that he will do anything but his best work to date.

Oh, about the bad news—we fibbed. There is no bad news. Just make sure you don't miss the first exciting issue of DROIDS. —*Sandy Hausler*

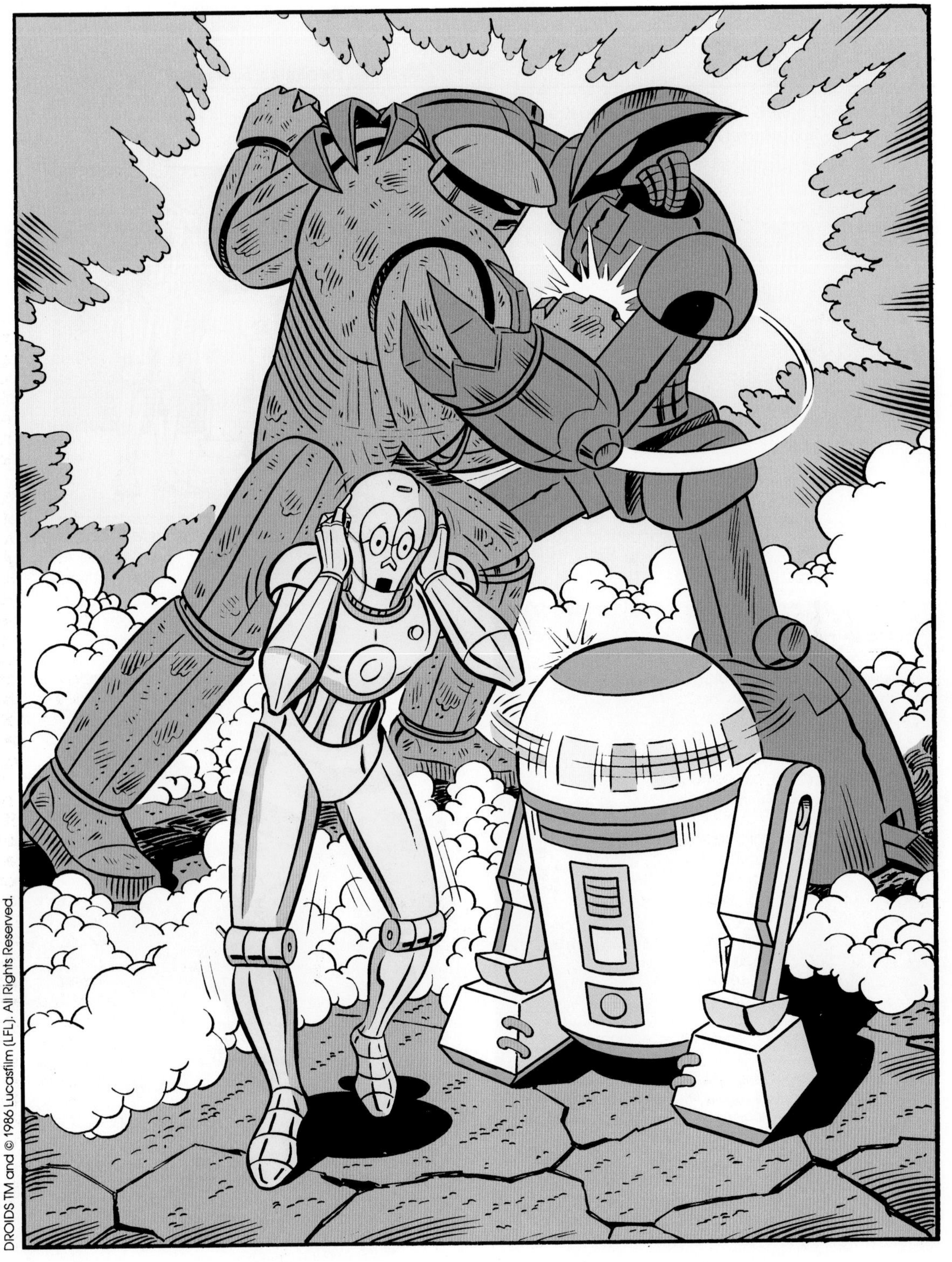